JAPANESE
AMERICAN
HISTORY

JAPANESE AMERICAN HISTORY

An A-to-Z Reference from 1868 to the Present

Brian Niiya, Editor

The Japanese American National Museum

Foreword by
Senator Daniel K. Inouye

Facts On File

Japanese American History: An A-to-Z Reference from 1868 to the Present

Facts On File, Inc.
460 Park Avenue South
New York NY 10016
USA

Library of Congress Cataloging-in-Publication Data
Japanese American history : an A-to-Z reference from 1868 to the
   present / Brian Niiya, editor ; foreword by Daniel K. Inouye.
      p.   cm.
   Includes bibliographical references and index.
   ISBN 0-8160-2680-7
   1. Japanese Americans—History—Encyclopedias.   I. Niiya, Brian.
E184.J3J3355   1993
973′.04956—dc20   92-35753

A British CIP catalogue record for this book is available from the British Library.

Facts On File books are available at special discounts when purchased in bulk quantities for businesses, associations, institutions or sales promotions. Please call our Special Sales Department in New York at 212/683–2244 or 800/322–8755.

Text design by Rob Yaffe
Jacket design by Jane Kobayashi
Composition and manufacturing by the Maple-Vail Book Manufacturing Group
Printed in the United States of America

10 9 8 7 6 5 4 3 2 1

This book is printed on acid-free paper.

CONTENTS

FOREWORD

DANIEL K. INOUYE,

UNITED STATES SENATOR

The United States, it has often been said, is a nation of immigrants. During the decades following the Second World War, America was likened to a melting pot and integration was sought through cultural assimilation of its diverse population. In the years following the bicentennial of the founding of our republic, cultural diversity and the integration of positive contributions from our diverse citizenry have come to be considered the strength of our great nation. As my mother used to say: "I take from the old ways what I think is good and useful. I take from the new ways what is good and useful. Anyone would be foolish not to."

Japanese Americans have played an active part in the development of this country for over 100 years. This history begins during the latter part of the 19th century when the Issei immigrants came in increasing numbers, mainly from prefectures along Japan's Inland Sea. My grandfather was a part of this migration during the latter part of the 19th century as he set out from his Fukuoka village to the cane fields of Hawaii. The Issei worked hard in the fields, factories, forests, cities and on the seas, and made vital contributions to the plantation ecomomy in Hawaii and to the industrial development of western America.

The immigrant Isseis' quick adjustment to the work opportunities and adaptation to life in America were made in spite of hardships. Through a series of laws they were deprived of the most elementary civil rights: citizenship, owning or leasing land and interracial marriage. They found security in ethnic enclaves in both rural and urban settings. They threw all their energies into their new lives, developing unique social, economic and religious institutions as they adapted to America. They came to rely on each other in this new environment and encouraged harmony and mutual aid within the family and community. The Issei promoted a code of ethics involving reciprocal obligations, mutual responsibility, respect for elders and the value of hard work. They taught these values and attitudes to their children, the Nisei. Denied naturalization rights and land ownership, the Issei invested all their dreams, hopes and desires in the Nisei.

Perhaps the single most critical event in this history was the incarceration of the Japanese Americans during World War II. Betrayed by their government, they became the innocent victims of racism and wartime hysteria. Although not a single case of espionage or sabotage was ever attributed to Japanese Americans, they were singled out, uprooted from their homes and exiled to desolate internment centers, under the false premise of military necessity. It is indeed amazing that under these circumstances Nisei men and women volunteered for service in the armed forces to prove their loyalty to the United States of America. They distinguished themselves with uncommon valor.

After the war, Japanese Americans returned to the larger society. In the postwar period of economic opportunities, the Nisei were able to make great strides in fields that had been previously barred such as civil service, education and law. This is a story of the reaffirmation of the strength of diversity in our multicultural society. It is now time for our third and fourth generations to take up the reins.

This history is replete with achievements of the brave Issei pioneers and their decendants: innovative agriculturalists, enterprising businessmen and world renowned physicians and scientists. There are names that are easily recognizable: U.S. Senator Spark Matsunaga, Congressmen Norman Mineta and Robert Matsui, sculptor Isamu Noguchi, *Star Trek* actor George Takei, astronaut Ellison Onizuka and of course Olympic gold medalist Kristi Yamaguchi. These success stories are real, they are exciting and dramatic, and worthy of public recitation. They are the result of the priceless legacy inherited from the immigrant generation who taught the importance of human values. This was the Isseis' legacy, their contribution to the development of this nation.

Japanese American History is the first work of its kind to provide an overview of the Japanese American experience. It is but one product of the Japanese American National Museum, a newly established permanent national institution for preservation of the history and achievements of Americans of Japanese ancestry. The museum promotes mutual understanding and goodwill in our pluralistic society through an appreciation of America's cultural diversity. I commend Facts On File and the Japanese American National Museum for making the history of Japanese Americans available to the general public through this important publication.

INTRODUCTION

This encyclopedia is meant to reflect the current state of knowledge in the field of Japanese American studies. It is intended for a general audience that may or may not know anything about the Japanese American experience. It consists of three major parts: a narrative historical overview, a chronology of Japanese American history and dictionary entries pertaining to the history of Japanese Americans.

Though numerically small, Japanese Americans have played a major role in American history, especially in the history of the American West. Arriving at more or less the same time to the shores of Hawaii and the western United States as the bulk of Eastern, Southern and Central Europeans were arriving at Ellis Island, Japanese Americans have been a vital part of America for well over a century. This book focuses on the history of Japanese immigrants and their American-born descendants, collectively known as Japanese Americans, Americans of Japanese Ancestry or *nikkei,* among other terms.

Despite its long history, relatively little was known about this American ethnic group until relatively recently. Though the subject of much scholarly and popular research and writing, Japanese Americans have remained somewhat mysterious to other Americans, in part because through the years the literature on them has almost done more to obscure than to illuminate. In the 1910s and 1920s, for example, an enormous amount of attention was paid to this relatively small minority group in the mass media. It was the subject of newspaper and magazine stories, academic journal articles, novels, even movies. Unfortunately, nearly all this literature had overtly political overtones, mostly vilifying Japanese Americans and blaming them for real and imagined maladies of the time. As a small and politically powerless group, they were easy targets for opportunistic politicians, farmers, businessmen, editors and plain racists. The anti-Japanese movement of this period culminated in the prohibition of further Japanese immigration after 1924; Japanese immigrants already here were prohibited from purchasing agricultural land in most of the states in which they resided and were prohibited from becoming naturalized American citizens. The literature on Jap-

anese Americans from this period reflects this anti-Japanese climate, presenting a one-sided and often blatantly false portrait of the group. Though there were a few white Americans who held a different opinion, this literature too is of limited value today, being in some ways just as one-dimensional as the anti-Japanese literature. Even the Japanese American voices that spoke out in defense of their community are problematic today, since generally they did not address the concerns and viewpoints of the majority of Japanese immigrants, but the interests of élites that were often not always the same as those of most Japanese immigrants. Thus, though there is a large body of literature about Japanese Americans in this period, it is mostly of interest to scholars studying the anti-Japanese movement, and tells us little about the true nature of the Japanese American community of that time.

The story is much the same for other periods. With the onset of World War II and the Japanese attack on Pearl Harbor, Japanese Americans became associated with the enemy. The popular literature of the time made no distinction between the Japanese and the American of Japanese ancestry. In the immortal words of General John L. DeWitt, head of the Western Defense Command during World War II, "A Jap's a Jap. . . ." Because of such thinking, some 120,000 Japanese Americans from the mainland United States were forcibly removed from the West Coast and incarcerated in American concentration camps. The literature on Japanese Americans from this period reflects such thinking and thus tells us little about the true nature of Japanese American communities of the time.

In the 1950s and 1960s, the literature on Japanese Americans changed dramatically. As the country grappled with race problems and the civil rights movement, Japanese Americans suddenly became the "model minority." In books, magazine and newspaper articles, and television shows, Japanese Americans were portrayed as a uniformly hard-working, quiet, law-abiding people who managed to achieve economic success without governmental help despite being subjected to deplorable racism. When not producing "success story" narratives of their own, liberal social scientists and historians in this period began to reexamine the history of racism against Japanese Americans, producing many studies of the anti-Japanese movement and the concentration camps focusing on what was done to "these poor people." Ultimately, the literature on Japanese Americans from this period, though certainly of greater value than the earlier material, still presents a one-sided view of Japanese Americans that tells us little about the Japanese Americans themselves.

Only in the last 20 years or so has the real story of the Japanese American experience begun to emerge. Spurred by the rise of ethnic studies, and especially Asian American studies, in our nation's colleges and universities, a new generation of scholars has finally delved into the Japanese American experience from an inside perspective. This new work has focused on the thoughts and actions of the Japanese Americans themselves rather than on external images of them or on what was done to them. Utilizing Japanese-language sources, oral histories and other previously neglected source materials, these new scholars (as well as some older ones) have illuminated a new world of *issei* labor militants, *nisei* draft resisters, and *nikkei* women writers, among other subjects. New and innovative interpretations of earlier topics of research such as the World War II concentration camps have also been put forward.

This book is a child of Asian American studies and the research of the last 20 years. It would not have been possible to do a work such as this 20, or even 10, years ago. I have tried to use the best of the new scholarship to put together a work that represents the extent of our knowledge on Japanese Americans today. The strengths and weaknesses of this book represent the strengths and weaknesses in the field today. As such, it was beyond the scope of this work to do much original research, with the exception of some preliminary explorations of very recent history. As the first reference work of its kind, there is undoubtedly much that has been left out; it is my hope that future editions will address some of the gaps in our knowledge. Wherever possible, I have tried to encourage users of this book to read more about the topic at hand by providing sources and suggestions for further reading. I hope readers will be inspired to tap into some of the exciting recent literature on Japanese Americans to learn more about this American ethnic group and about American history as a whole.

A few conventions were followed in the preparation of this book:

- Throughout the text, small capitals are used to indicate terms that have an entry in the dictionary portion of the book. Thus a reference to the REDRESS MOVEMENT means that there is a corresponding entry in the dictionary section.
- For the sake of simplicity, names are presented in Western name order; that is, given name first, family name last, such as Kyutaro Abiko, Sen Katayama and Kristi Yamaguchi.
- Though some Japanese words have long vowel sounds, long vowel symbols, or macrons, are not used in this book.
- Japanese-language terms or expressions not found in the dictionary entries are, however, defined or translated parenthetically.

A pronunciation guide for Japanese-language words appears on page xii. Separate introductions preface the chronology and dictionary sections.

Any work of this kind could not be accomplished without the help of many people. Special thanks are owed the staff members of the Japanese American National Museum, especially exhibit curator Akemi Kikumura and former program coordinator Dean Toji, both of whom initiated this project along with chief curator James Hirabayashi (who provided support and sound advice despite his disappointment at not being included in the encyclopedia), director Irene Hirano, Karen Ishizuka, Alison Kochiyama, Sara Iwahashi and Jennifer Mikami. I also owe a debt to the staff of the UCLA Asian American Studies Center, especially director Don Nakanishi, reading room coordinator Marjorie Lee and *Amerasia Journal* associate editor Glenn Omatsu. The editorial board for this project—Lloyd Inui, Harry H. L. Kitano, Gail Nomura, Don Nakanishi, Franklin Odo, Gary Okihiro and Stephen Sumida—provided helpful input and constant encouragement. The following people contributed helpful critiques or ideas: Roger Daniels, Chris Friday, Stephen Fugita, Evelyn Nakano Glenn, Brian Hayashi, Jack Herzig, Lane Hirabayashi, William Hohri, Bruce Iwasaki, Masakazu Iwata, Tetsuden Kashima, Kats Kunitsugu, Valerie Matsumoto, Mei Nakano, Raymond Okamura, Glenn Omatsu, Larry Rosensweig, Mitziko Sawada, Ed Suguro, Clifford Uyeda, Michi Weglyn, Charles Wong, K. Stanley Yamashita and Evelyn Yoshimura. Alice Niiya also read through a near complete version of the manuscript.

This book would not have been possible without the direct contributions of Eiichiro Azuma, Donald Collins, Tracy Endo, Donald Estes, Suzanne Hee, Stacey Hirose, Alice Hom, Ronald Inouye, Edith Kaneshiro, Scott Kurashige, Emily Lawsin, Marjorie Lee, Dennis Yamamoto, Stan Yogi, David Yoo and especially Glen Kitayama. Special thanks are also owed to Kristine Saneto for her able assistance with the photographs. Facts On File project editor Kathy Ishizuka and copy editor Michael Laraque provided expert assistance and ably kept the project on track. I would also like to acknowledge Karen Umemoto, my spouse, for her tangible and intangible contributions to this project.

Lastly, the greatest debt is owed to the literally hundreds of scholars whose original research has found its way into these pages in one form or another. If more people are inspired to read their work, I will have done my job.

Brian Niiya

PRONUNCIATION GUIDE

Though they may seem difficult, most Japanese words are relatively easy to pronounce. This is because vowels are pronounced in only one way and consonants pronounced more or less as in English. Vowel sounds are as follow:

a as in *ma*
e as in *memo*
i as in *me*
o as in *mow*
u as in *moo*

The one consonant that is pronounced somewhat differently in Japanese than in English is "r." There is no "r" sound in Japanese; the sound denoted by "r" is actually pronounced somewhere between an "r," an "l," and a "d."

Japanese words can be broken down easily by syllables containing one vowel with no, one or two consonants. The syllables are unstressed. Every letter is pronounced. Thus *sake* is pronounced sah-keh (not sa-key!) and *kachigumi* is pronounced kah-chee-goo-me. Double consonants are also both pronounced; *Nippon* is pronounced neep-pone. Double vowels are often run together to form one syllable; thus *issei* is pronounced ees-saye rather than ees-say-ee.

ACRONYMS

The following acronyms occur frequently in this volume:

AAPA   Asian American Political Alliance
AFSC   American Friends Service Committee
AJA   Americans of Japanese Ancestry
BCA   Buddhist Churches of America
CANE   Committee Against Nihonmachi Evictions
CWRIC   Commission on Wartime Relocation and Internment of Civilians
ESC   Emergency Service Committee
FPC   Fair Play Committee (Heart Mountain)
HSPA   Hawaii Sugar Planters Association
ILWU   International Longshoremen's and Warehousemen's Union
JACL   Japanese American Citizens League

JARP   Japanese American Resource Project
JMLA   Japanese-Mexican Labor Association (see 1903 OXNARD STRIKE)
LTPRO   Little Tokyo People's Rights Organization
MIS   Military Intelligence Service
MISLS   Military Intelligence Service Language School
NJASRC   National Japanese American Student Relocation Council
NABM   North American Buddhist Mission
SCRPWU   Southern California Retail Produce Workers Union
VVV   Varsity Victory Volunteers
WDC   Western Defense Command
YMBA   Young Men's Buddhist Association (see 1920 PLANTATION STRIKE)

THE JAPANESE IN AMERICA

GARY Y. OKIHIRO

Within the sound of waves stand lonely tombstones nearly obliterated by sand. The weathered stones face the sea from whence came the people. Thousands of miles away from that cemetery near Lahaina, Maui, the wind rustles the dry grass that surrounds a solitary marker near Sacramento, California. Beneath the sun-baked soil rests the remains of a 19-year-old woman.

The quiet of those long forgotten places, broken by only the sound of wave and wind, speaks to us today of a people who came to America mainly as migrant laborers, settled the land and built vibrant communities, were uprooted from their homes and were made outcasts, but returned to rebuild their lives for themselves and their heirs.

This is their story.

Migrants, 1865–1909

The story began in the late 1700s, when the growing industries of New England sought overseas markets. Yankee traders sailed the seas, departing with American manufactures to sell abroad and returning with goods from Europe, South America and the Caribbean, Africa and Asia. American sailors, on their way to and from China, stopped at a refreshment station midway in the Pacific—Hawaii. The arrival of traders in the Hawaiian kingdom, both European and American, was soon followed by American missionaries and settlers, who in 1835 established a sugar plantation system that required large numbers of workers to tend the fields and run the mills.

Another part of the story involved European settlements in the Caribbean and Central and South America. The sugar and other kinds of plantations, mines and public works in those colonies had an insatiable appetite for laborers, and after the end of the African slave trade in the early 1800s, they began looking toward Asia to help satisfy their needs. Thus started the Chinese "coolie" trade that resembled the African slave trade in many ways. American ships participating in that traffic in human cargo transported coolies who had stamped on their chests the letters "C" (California), "P" (Peru), or "S" (Sandwich Islands or Hawaii), indicating their destinations.

A third part of the story's beginning involved America's westward expansion across the continent and the idea of manifest destiny that supplied the reason and justification for America's conquest and removal of American Indians and its seizure of lands in the Southwest and California in 1848 after a war with Mexico. The California gold rush solidified America's destiny as a Pacific power, and, in an exercise of its naval strength for commercial advantage, the U.S. dispatched a fleet under the command of Commodore Matthew C. Perry to "open" Japan to Western trade in 1854. America's manifest destiny in the Pacific reached new heights with the annexation of the Philippines in 1898 and Hawaii in 1900.

Meanwhile, the expansion of Hawaii's sugar industry, aided by America's Civil War (1861–1865), prompted the need for more workers at a time when the native Hawaiian population was rapidly decreasing primarily due to disease. Further, Chinese laborers, imported by the planters beginning in 1852, were leaving the plantations in large numbers for other work. In 1865, Hawaii's foreign minister who was also a plantation owner wrote to an American businessman in Japan:

Could any good agricultural laborers be obtained from Japan or its dependencies to serve like the Chinese, under contract for 6 or 8 years? If so, send me all the information you can and state at what cost per head they could be landed here; and if their wives and children could be induced to come with them.

On May 17, 1868, as a result of that recruitment effort, the *Scioto* set sail from Yokohama for Honolulu carrying 149 Japanese migrants—141 men, six women, and two children. Among the *gannenmono* or "first year people" (so called because they migrated during the first

1

year of Meiji rule) were samurai, cooks, *sake* brewers, potters, printers, tailors, wood workers, a hairdresser and a 13-year-old heavy drinker nicknamed "Ichi the Viper." The journey took 33 days, during which the travelers encountered a storm so fierce that after it ended, many men, it was reported, cut off their topknots and threw them into the sea in thanks.

A stowaway, Yonekichi Sakuma, kept a diary of the voyage, providing a glimpse of conditions on board the ship. He counted 500 bags of unpolished rice, 20 bags of polished rice, and plenty of *shoyu* (soy sauce), *miso* and firewood in the *Scioto*'s hold. Many of the passengers, noted Sakuma, did not eat the first few days because of seasickness. The men spent their time polishing rice and in horseplay. Twelve days before sighting land, Kodzu Wakichi died and was buried at sea. On June 19, 1868, the *Scioto* cast anchor in Honolulu harbor.

On shore, the king greeted the *gannenmono* with gifts of salted fish and clothing. The *Hawaiian Gazette* wrote of this first shipload of Japanese workers: "They are very good natured and lusty looking set of fellows. They are very polite withal, having picked up our salutation of 'aloha' . . . and the impression is prevalent that they will make peaceable and efficient laborers, and give satisfaction." After a two-week recuperation period, the *gannenmono* were sent to plantations mainly on Maui, Oahu and Kauai to work in the fields, although a few served as domestic servants.

Plantation labor was harsh, and the soft hands of potters, cooks and tailors blistered and hardened hoeing the red earth, stripping razor-sharp cane leaves off the stalks, and hauling bundles of cane. Besides the physical rigors of working under the hot tropical sun, the *gannenmono* had to obey strict plantation rules that exacted 10 hours of daily labor, fines for showing up late for work and curfew violations, wage deductions for breaking or losing tools, and a penalty of two days of extra work for every day lost through sickness caused by the "laborer's own imprudence."

Before the end of the first month, both planters and workers lodged complaints with the government. Planters demanded refunds for sickly workers (one man died shortly after first stepping into the field), and workers protested the withholding of half their $4 monthly wage and the slave-like selling of their contracts between planters. Workers even asked for pay for days lost because of foul weather.

Eventually, 40 *gannenmono* returned to Japan before the completion of their three-year contracts, and all but one of them signed a public statement charging Hawaii's planters with cruelty and with not living up to the contract terms. Of those who remained in the islands, one committed suicide, and several of the men married Hawaiian women. The last survivor, Sentaro Ishii, passed away in 1936 at the ripe old age of 102.

Unlike the *gannenmono issei* ("first generation") pioneers who were recruited to Hawaii for their labor, the first *issei* settlers in California were displaced from their homes by the political forces that ended the Tokugawa shogunate and ushered in the Meiji restoration. About a year after the *Scioto*'s crossing, on May 27, 1869, the Pacific Mail Company's *China* steamed into San Francisco Bay, carrying an exploratory party of samurai, farmers and tradesmen, and four women.

The group, followers of feudal lord Matsudaira Katamori of Aizu Wakamatsu, proceeded up the Sacramento river to Placerville and established the Wakamatsu Tea and Silk Farm Colony on 600 acres of land. They brought with them mulberry trees for silk farming, bamboo for food and furniture, tea seeds and other varieties of plants native to Japan in hopes of establishing a prosperous farm colony.

Water, however, was scarce, and the weakened seedlings failed to thrive in the dry California soil. As a result, the colony survived less than two years. A few returned to Japan; others drifted away. Okei Ito, a young woman 19 years old, died in 1871 and was buried near the original colony. Her tombstone bears the simple epitaph: "In memory of Okei, died 1871, age 19 years, a Japanese girl."

The experiences of the *gannenmono* and Wakamatsu colonists reveal much about the Japanese American story. The *gannenmono*, like many others who followed them, were labor recruits and sojourners, while the Wakamatsu pioneers, like others who followed them, were driven from their homes and came with the intention of settling. The first *issei* were a diverse lot, mainly men but also women, mostly adults but also children, and from all walks of life both privileged and lowly. They were individuals, rugged and weak, principled and flawed, ambitious and shiftless. A good number of both original groups returned to Japan, but most, whether out of choice or circumstance, made America their home, married and had children, and were buried in the soil they had laid claim to by making it productive.

Among the *gannenmono* was 19-year-old Tomi Ozawa and her husband Kintaro. Ozawa was eight months pregnant when she boarded the *Scioto*, and her baby, Yotaro, was probably born in Hawaii and if so was the first *nisei* ("second generation"), although Hawaii was not yet an American territory. A girl, Itoko, and a boy, Arthur Kenzaburo, completed the Ozawa family. Yotaro became the first Japanese in the Hawaiian police force, Itoko at the tender age of 12 served as translator for the Hawaiian government in negotiations with Japan, and Arthur received a law degree in Michigan and practiced law in Hawaii.

From those beginnings sprang the Japanese American community, infused with fresh migrations from Japan to these shores. It was not until after the 1886 labor convention signed by Hawaii and Japan, however, that significant numbers of Japanese migrants arrived in Hawaii mainly as contract workers and in California as student laborers. Broadly, the pattern of Japanese migration was as follows: it began after Chinese workers were excluded from the U.S. in 1882; it was a labor migration; it involved return migration to Japan, but also featured remigration from Hawaii to the West Coast; and it was virtually halted by the Gentlemen's Agreement of 1908 and finally by the 1924 Exclusion Act.

The voices of *issei* migrants enliven the pages of statistics and dates. "My parents were farmers," recalled Hashiji Kakazu. "Potatoes were planted for food, and our sugar cane was made into sugar to make money. That's how we lived in Okinawa." Kakazu accompanied his dad to Hawaii as a teenager: "Well, everyone then came to Hawaii to earn some money. I just followed my dad. For the cost of transportation to come to Hawaii our land was placed under a mortgage. And we borrowed some money, about $100, from the moneylender. After we came to Hawaii we sent money back." By boat, they sailed from Okinawa to Kobe and on to Honolulu. "I got quite seasick. I couldn't eat for about four days. And after about four days a person named Takamine from my village came to visit me when I was sick. And even now, I won't forget that person. She was sick, too, and after she came to see me, that night, she died. Sometimes, even now I wonder if she knew she was going to die and came to say farewell to me."

"I was born in Kokura, Fukuoka Ken, on September 11, 1880," began Kane Kozono. "My home was more in the country than in the city." Kozono had six older brothers, and she grew up mainly helping her mother. "I was married in Japan when I was twenty-two and had one child there. My husband was a farmer, as was my father. My husband came here to the States three years earlier than I did. When he didn't come back to Japan, his parents asked me to go and bring him back. They thought that two of us working for a few years would give us enough money to come home." Kozono recalled hearing that quick fortunes could be made in America, but being the only daughter, she felt a deep attachment to her mother. When she finally decided to leave, Kozono told her mother, " 'Although I'm going to America, please don't feel lonely when I leave you, Mama. Don't let loneliness make you ill. Don't die of it.' She then replied, 'Your husband is there waiting for you, so you'd better go. I'd probably worry about you even if you stayed here with us.' Such was my mother."

Poems composed by *issei* expressed the hopes of those who dared leave home and cross the vast ocean:

Day of spacious dreams!
I sailed for America,
Overblown with hope.
(Ichiyo)

Huge dreams of fortune
Go with me to foreign lands,
Across the ocean.
(Rizan)

Family fortunes
Fall into the wicker trunk
I carry abroad.
(Ryokuso)

Despite dreams of the fabled *Tenjiku* or "faraway place," America's streets were not paved with gold, and life and work was made even more difficult by labor recruiters, banks, and migration agents who charged extortionate fees, and by the conditions of labor on the Hawaiian plantations and in the fields and orchards of the West Coast. Coupled with economic exploitation was racial discrimination—in social attitudes and practices, laws and statutes—that limited Japanese American opportunities and excluded them from the full enjoyment of life, liberty and property.

"I was from Miiri-son, Asa-gun, Hiroshima Prefecture, and went to Hawaii as an immigrant worker at the age of 17," recalled Ko Shigeta. "I wanted to save money in Hawaii and go back to Japan as soon as possible." Shigeta worked at Aiea plantation on the island of Oahu for $14 a month, paying a monthly fee of $7 or $8 for sleeping quarters. "Fifty of us, both bachelors and married couples, lived together in a humble shed—a long ten-foot wide hallway made of wattle and lined along the sides with a slightly raised floor covered with a grass rug, and two tatami mats to be shared among us." He reflected on his life: "I often wished I was back in Japan instead of enduring this hardship in Hawaii. The lives of all the Japanese working on the sugar farms were the same as mine, more or less."

In San Francisco, student laborers were the largest group within a growing Japanese American community that numbered about 3,000 in 1890. "The rank and file are of the poor student class, youths who have rashly left their native shores," described a newspaper. "Hundreds of such are landed every year, with miserably scant funds in their pockets. . . . Their object is to earn, with the labour of their hands, a pittance sufficient to enable them to pursue their studies in language, sociology, and politics." These students frequently lived in basement quarters described as "cave-like dwellings" with "sooty curtains," and "the kitchens were filthy and disorderly to the extreme." Without usual stoves, cooking was done on oil stoves that emitted a thick, black smoke that darkened the rooms.

Baishiro Tamashiro remembered his first day of work at Lihue plantation on the island of Kauai. "Since we used knives, our hands were blistered. . . . It sure was hard work. We had no time to rest. We worked like machines. For 200 of us workers, there were seven or eight *lunas* [overseers] and above them was a field boss on a horse. We were watched constantly." Women typically worked by day alongside other women in the cane fields, and at night at home in domestic labor. "At night after having the children go to bed, and having taken my bath close to bedtime," explained Tsuru Yamauchi, "I did the children's ironing, trying not to make much noise. They could hear everything, you know; the walls were so close to each other. It was 10 o'clock when I went to bed." A *hole hole bushi* (*bushi* or "songs" composed mainly by women as they stripped cane leaves called *hole hole* work) captured a mother's lament:

It's starting to pour
There goes my laundry
My baby is crying
And the rice just burned.

In California, Masuo Akizuki remembered: "When I came to San Jose the day after my arrival, everybody was working in the countryside. The boarding houses in San Jose Japantown found jobs for us. They brought us by horse carriage to the place to work, and we each were given one blanket. Our living conditions were miserable at that time. We slept next to a horse stable on our blankets and some straw. . . . When we finished the work, we went back to the boarding house and rested there until the next job came around." Japanese migrant workers followed the seasons and crops in circuits that extended from the Imperial Valley near the Mexican border to the canning and fishing industries of Washington and Alaska.

According to the 1910 U.S. census, Japanese numbered 79,675 in Hawaii and 72,157 on the mainland, women comprising 24,891 or 31.2 percent of Hawaii's total, and 9,087 or 12.6 percent of those on the mainland. That significant gender gap among a population made up almost exclusively of marriage-age people yielded extraordinary results. Women, most of whom were married, were at once deprived of sisterly contact and pursued and tormented by men. Tsuru Yamauchi was so afraid of harassment by men that she insisted on having her husband accompany her in the early morning darkness to the outdoor kitchen where she prepared their lunch. Women were imported by men to work as prostitutes and they were kidnapped and held against their will, but they also fled abusive husbands and found lovers from among the bachelors. A *hole hole bushi* suggested:

Tomorrow is Sunday, right?
Come over and visit.
My husband will be out
    watering cane
And I'll be home alone.

Japanese American migrant workers faced a whole range of barriers to their social mobility and advancement. The first rule of Maui's Waihee plantation was: "Laborers are expected to be industrious and docile and obedient to their overseers." In a 1904 editorial, the planters' newspaper advised its readers on how to control the "plantation coolie": "yield to his demands and he thinks he is the master and makes new demands; use the strong hand and he recognizes the power to which, from immemorial times, he has abjectly bowed. There is one word which holds the lower classes of every nation in check and that is Authority." The courts and plantation *lunas* and police enforced rules and collected fines, meted out corporal punishment, and imprisoned workers deemed incorrigible or idle and thus vagrants.

On the mainland, Japanese Americans heard racial epithets and were the victims of physical attacks. "It was about 3 P.M. one day when I passed this place on my way home," reported an *issei* in Seattle. "I ran across four or five children in their middle teens coming home from school. One of them suddenly yelled 'Goddam Jap!' and hit me on my right eye. It began to bleed. . . . When I was told by the doctor that if the eyeball was damaged it would also affect my sight in the other eye and I might become totally blind, I was terribly sad, thinking that I had come all the way to the States just to be blinded." Japanese faced discrimination in employment, lived in segregated neighborhoods and attended "Oriental schools," had their homes and businesses destroyed in riots and arson, and were physically driven out of towns.

The *issei*, however, were not merely "docile and obedient," but challenged racism and exploitation through the courts, asserting their human dignity and thereby helping to democratize America. As early as 1891, a Japanese worker named Mioshi argued before the Hawaiian Supreme Court that the contract labor system was a form of slavery, and in that same year, Ekiu Nishimura filed a writ of *habeas corpus* against the commissioner of immigration for refusing her entry and detaining her at the port of San Francisco. The commissioner had deemed her excludable under the Chinese Exclusion Act of 1882 that prohibited entry to Chinese workers and to idiots, lunatics, convicts, or "persons likely to become a public charge." Although both cases were denied, they were heard in the highest courts of the kingdom and nation, and revealed a feisty spirit of resistance from among a people frequently depicted as fatalistic and passive.

In February 1903, 500 Japanese and 200 Mexican agricultural workers in Oxnard, California, formed the Japanese-Mexican Labor Association under the leadership of Kozaburo Baba. Employed as field hands in the sugar beet industry, the workers attacked the system of contracting and subcontracting, the commissions they were charged, and the policy requiring them to buy only from designated stores. The newly formed union struck, and by March it had grown to 1,200 members or about 90 percent of the entire work force. On March 23, in a bloody confrontation, a striking Mexican worker was shot and killed and two other Mexicans and two Japanese were wounded. The union, in negotiations, broke the monopoly of the contractors and reached a settlement by the end of the month. Despite the fact that the union was denied an American Federation of Labor (AFL) charter because of the AFL's longstanding opposition to Asians, the Oxnard strike showed the American labor movement that agricultural workers could be organized into an effective union regardless of race or national origin.

Collective action by workers on the plantations of Hawaii included protests against particularly abusive *lunas*, over wages and work conditions, and against unreasonable rules. A government report listed 20 strikes by Japanese plantation laborers during 1900 alone totaling 7,806 field hands, cane cutters and strippers, and mill workers. In 1905, workers joined together in the Japanese Reform Association "to extricate the 70,000 Japanese from the clutches of the Keihin Bank and the immigration companies. . . ." The association demanded and won reforms from Japan's government that closed down Keihin Bank and restricted the activities of emigration company agents.

Clearly the most significant protest of the time took place in 1909 when 7,000 Japanese workers from all major plantations on Oahu joined in a four-month-long strike for higher wages. The movement for higher wages began the previous year when the Higher Wage Association was formed and when its request for a salary increase from $18.00 to $22.50 per month was rejected by the planters. Beginning in May 1909, laborers walked off the job, citing inflation without wage increases for years, families and the growing number of dependents, and a salary scale that paid whites more than Japanese for equal work. "Is it not a matter of simple justice, and moral duty to give [the] same wages and same treatment to laborers of equal efficiency, irrespective of race, color, creed, nationality, or previous condition of servitude?" they asked.

The planters and some members of Hawaii's Japanese community condemned the strike as the work of agitators and as a program designed to create "an irresponsible class of laborers" and "loafers." Managers evicted strikers and their families, in some cases giving them twenty-four hour notices, and by June there were over 5,000 displaced Japanese living in makeshift shelters in downtown Honolulu which was likened by an eyewitness to "a battlefield with everything in extreme confusion." The Higher Wage Association was branded a "criminal organization" and its leaders were arrested and imprisoned on conspiracy charges. About two weeks before the leaders were convicted, the association called an end to the strike on August 5, 1909.

The great strike of 1909 closes this first phase of the Japanese American story—the migrant years. The period from 1865 to 1909 was a time of labor migration, induced by capitalism's need for cheap workers and by America's manifest destiny in the Pacific that involved trade, conquest and the settlement of Hawaii and the West Coast. On March 14, 1907, President Theodore Roosevelt issued an executive order ending Japanese remigration from Hawaii to the mainland, and in 1908 the Gentlemen's Agreement virtually sealed off the U.S. to Japanese migrant laborers. The 1909 plantation strike was, in part, a response to those exclusion acts by Japanese workers who no longer saw themselves as migrants but as settlers.

Settlers, 1909–1941

An Okinawan song titled "My Mother Dear," written as a conversation between mother and migrant-child, recounted the process by which migrants became settlers.

> Let me take my leave, my mother.
> Earn money and come home, my child,
> As I stay home and pray to the gods.
> To this Hawaii from the far away Okinawa
> We have come all the way for the sake of money.
> Thinking it'd only be a few years we came,
> But we have now grown our roots deep
>   and with green leaves.

Crucial to the growing of roots "deep and with green leaves" was the coming of *issei* women that increased, ironically, after the signing of the restrictive Gentlemen's Agreement in 1908. Although the agreement's intention was to stop the flow of Japanese migration, its terms failed to bar entrance to the wives of men already in the U.S. Among Japanese Americans in 1910, for example, there were only 13,970 married women in Hawaii and 5,581 married women on the mainland, but by 1920, that number had nearly doubled to 22,373 in Hawaii and had leaped fourfold to 22,193 on the mainland.

Most of the women who came during this period arrived as "picture brides." The practice conformed to

Japanese culture in that marriage was usually arranged by parents, and was formalized by entering the bride's name in the groom's family registry. The go-between brokered an agreement between families, and with the woman in Japan and man in the U.S., the couple were married and met each other often for the first time at piers in Honolulu, Seattle and San Francisco, using pictures to identify their spouses. Rikae Inouye described one such bride:

> Most of the people on board were picture brides. I came with my husband. When the boat anchored, one girl took out a picture from her kimono sleeve and said to me, "Mrs. Inouye, will you let me know if you see this face?" She was darling. Putting the picture back into her kimono sleeve, she went out to the deck. The men who had come to pick up their brides were there. It was like that. I felt they were bold.

"The picture brides were full of ambition, expectation, and dreams," recalled Ai Miyasaki. "None knew what their husbands were like except by the photos. I wondered how many would be saddened and disillusioned. There were many." Some men sent pictures that were years old; others had their photographs taken wearing borrowed suits. "In reality, the men carried blanket rolls on their backs and were farm laborers." Sometimes couples were incompatible, and women found themselves stuck with abusive husbands. "Many Issei mothers suffered much, but they could not afford to go back to Japan. Their expectations were great, so the disappointment was as great," Miyasaki observed.

> Mother doesn't age!
> Dreamland keeps her just the same
> As when I left her.
> (Dontsuku)

> My pillow a dream;
> Home-town scenes in sleeping head.
> Mother, I miss you!
> (Koyo)

Kame Kakazu remembered how as a teenager she grew bored with school, and how when her parents discussed a marriage offer from a young man in Hawaii, she pondered and dreamed of riches and a quick return to Okinawa. Upon marriage, she sailed with other picture brides on the *Satora Maru*, leaving behind a mother and father she would not see again. Kakazu, having never left home before, immediately missed her mother, and seasickness and the seemingly endless ocean that separated her from her parents made her even more miserable. She felt demeaned at the Honolulu Immigration Station where the women were stripped, inspected, deloused and placed in a holding area until claimed by men. Kakazu accompanied her husband to a small plantation camp set amidst acres of cane fields that she cultivated with her young and tender hands from early morning to late afternoon. In the dark of night next to a man she hardly knew, Kakazu recalled crying quietly for her mother and for her plight.

But *issei* women were also strong. They not only bore the next generation; they built new homes and communities through the sweat of their labor. Sadako Takahara remembered her mother, Ito Isshiki, who worked as a cook for a railroad camp, and later operated a small hotel in Tacoma. Without benefit of a midwife, Isshiki delivered her own baby, and as the family grew, took on all sorts of jobs, picking strawberries, mending gunny sacks and serving as a maid. "Standing by her," described Takahara, "I watched her heavy body heaving over the washboard, and panting, as she laundered big sheets by hand in the bathtub of our house." Mother, she testified, labored "as if work were her hobby. . . . I can never thank her enough, because she was our foundation."

> New Years—and mother
> Today, too, wears her apron.
> No holidays for her.
> (Tamu)

> In America
> Little girl-child born to me.
> Doll Festival today!
> (Seppo)

The exuberance of festival, the conjoining of tradition and innovation in culture, and the birth of future mothers—in America—were the deeds of *issei* women. That "she was our foundation" extended far beyond individual families to all Japanese Americans in this alien land that was becoming theirs by virtue of labor and birth. Women not only made families possible; their labor added income to households, enabling the survival of the Japanese American community. As noted by Tsuru Yamauchi, plantation worker, washerwoman, cannery worker and mother of four children, "We could not have managed without both his (her husband's) wages and mine for a sufficient livelihood. Our small income provided the children's Japanese school tuition and this and that. Even if we didn't spend too much on food, there were times when we had to spend extra money. We could not expect the children to stay healthy on noodles alone."

On the mainland, Japanese American women's productivity facilitated the transition from migrant labor to settlement. Households could purchase and rent land, before the passage of alien land laws, more easily with two incomes, and women made the land more productive by joining men in the fields and orchards. "I never thought of women as being different," explained a farmer. "We all worked side by side all day, did everything together. No, not that different." A farm woman added: "Yes, it was hard work. . . . I helped carry those sweat boxes, full of raisins. We had to load them onto the truck and we didn't have equipment in those days. Those boxes must have weighed over 150 pounds. . . . I'd carry one side, he [her husband] carried the other." Her husband nodded and said simply: "She worked . . . that's a powerful woman there."

Both my hands grimy,
Unable to wipe away
The sweat from my brow,
Using one arm as towel—
That was I . . . working . . . working.

Warm to the sad heart,
The thought of Pacific Sea
Touching Japan shores.
I found some solace
Listening to the sound of waves.

No respite, no rest.
Every moment filled with work.
No time for *tankas* ["short poems" of 31 syllables
   in five lines],
No moment all the day long.
Pitiable way to live!

We could not forget,
Nor yet go back to Japan.
Without our homeland
Most of us Issei were like
Trees that were slowly dying.

In every gray hair,
In every wrinkled feature,
Issei in America
Confide dark, secret hardships
And pains of days gone by.
(Kimiko Ono)

Women held families together frequently under difficult and trying conditions. Wataru Ishisaka described early settler society as filled with "bars, gambling, and prostitution." As a consequence, marriages were fragile. Some wives were kidnapped, others ran away. "Those people who built successful families," noted Ishisaka, "were the ones who had the patience and endurance to stick it out, even though they might have had legitimate

complaints." Oftentimes women exercised "patience and endurance" for the sake of the children.

Takae Washizu recalled working with her husband as a migrant laborer in northern California, and later as a sharecropper. She woke up at 4 A.M. to feed the farm workers and her children, washed the breakfast dishes, and joined the crew in farm labor. She did the same for lunch and dinner, returning early from the fields to cook and feed the workers and children, cleaned up, and washed clothes by lantern light before turning in at midnight. "I had to work as hard as the men," she stated modestly. "I wanted to run away from my husband, for he was too old and too small-minded for me to communicate with, but I couldn't leave my children. I couldn't trust my husband to raise the children; besides I didn't have anyplace to go. I was just patient and dreamed about my children's bright future. . . . The life we had here was sometimes almost unbearable," concluded Washizu.

Mothers can do all
Required to live and endure
In this bitter world.
(Mitsuko)

Women preserved and transmitted culture within the family, especially in the rearing of children. They held the center. "I think Mom was strong, that's what I think," declared a *nisei*. "You know everything went through my mother. . . . We didn't ask Dad directly. Dad was never much of a talker, everything was Mom." Women also organized and influenced the formation of social groups and functions—from church groups to art, music and dance clubs to events such as baby showers and community outings and picnics—that united entire communities, and thereby promoted a sense of ethnic identity and solidified the Japanese presence in America.

Japanese Americans built churches, both Buddhist and Christian. They erected halls to serve as language schools and places for plays and samurai films, bonsai and *ikebana* exhibits, judo lessons and poetry readings, and potlucks and parties. They cleared fields for *sumo* rings and baseball diamonds with bleachers that seated hundreds of cheering fans. They lined streets with shops that sold *miso* and tofu, rice and noodles, fresh fish and medicinal herbs, along with repair shops for bicycles, watches and tools. They operated hotels and bath houses, restaurants and bars, poolhalls, and gambling and dance clubs that were scattered among offices of trading companies, physicians and midwives, and newspapers. From Japan came touring baseball teams, *sumo* wrestlers, movie stars and theatrical companies and musicians, adding elements to a mix that included Fourth of July parades and picnics, barbecues and beauty contests.

Life was celebrated and death commemorated among Japanese Americans who totaled, in 1920, 109,274 in Hawaii and 111,010 on the mainland, in 1930, 139,631 in Hawaii and 126,948 on the mainland. The range of the Japanese American experience varied as widely as the land and people that surrounded the Japanese, and perhaps candid snapshots reveal more about Japanese Americans than do the faces that appear in formal group photographs.

The Japanese American family album might begin with one's name, one's identity: "My real name is Ryuko," explained a *nisei*. "But I got Thelma because when I was going to school, when I first started school the teacher couldn't pronounce my name, Ryuko. So she gave me her mother's name." For *nisei* children, disliking one's Japanese name, taking on Anglicized names, being given English names were commonplace features of growing up in a society that pressed for conformity to the dominant culture—a crippling process given the patriotic label of "Americanization."

Names had other disabilities and benefits. The alien land laws on the mainland prohibited *issei* from owning or leasing land, but *nisei* could own and lease land, having been born in the U.S. and thus being American citizens. "There was so much anti-Japanese feeling in those days! They called us 'Japs' and threw things at us," remembered Choichi Nitta. "When I made a trip to Marysville to look for land, someone threw rocks. . . . By that time, the Alien Land Law was in effect. I was Sunday School superintendent and was teaching the youth class. A young Nisei . . . man came from Hawaii. This young man came into my class, and we became acquainted with each other. I bought the property in his name."

Infants, out of necessity, went to work with their parents, carried on their mother's backs as the women toiled or they were placed on the margins of fields in makeshift shelters built to ward off the sun and biting insects. As they grew older, children learned to play among themselves and take care of their younger sisters and brothers. "During the summer mother took us two little girls and went to a farm in the countryside to pick strawberries," recalled Sadako Takahara. "Early in the morning we went to the fields, taking lunch boxes along. While my mother was picking, we little ones became bored and so we played by throwing dirt on the berries she had already picked. 'That's the reason why we don't want to hire women with children,' the managers complained."

That inability to play with and rear their children weighed heavily on *issei* parents. Kimiko Ono took care of tomatoes in the spring: "I watered the plants in the greenhouses, taking the three children along with me,"

she remembered. "Even when the children were tired of playing and fussed, I couldn't quit and go to them. Meanwhile the crying voices would stop, and many times I found my youngsters sleeping on the ground. Telling myself, 'Poor little things! When you grow up I will let you do whatever you want to do . . . only please forgive your mama now . . .' I worked continually." Sometimes neglect led to serious injury to and even the death of children.

A strong sense of community and of supporting one another helped to counter isolation and nurtured many children. Tsuru Yamauchi lived next door to a childless couple from Hiroshima named Kamikawa. "They loved my children as though they were their own," recalled Yamauchi. "They took them everywhere to play and were like real parents. I cannot forget them." Others shared in the rearing and socialization of her children: "My children were taken care of by everyone. We lived in that manner," Yamauchi explained. Neighbors and friends served as surrogate extended families for Japanese in America who lacked Japan's kin-based social system.

Group membership was affirmed in community picnics that were held in settings where people could relax and be themselves. A *nisei* recalled the Del Rey, California, annual picnic: "We'd go all the way over near Shaver Lake. The family would take the old model T and oh, we had a big time. All day Sunday. We wanted to get away from all the people because the first generation wanted to get drunk. . . . The men sang and clapped . . . they were rowdy ones. The women watched and took care of the kids." Organizers planned games for children and adults alike, with prizes such as pencils, erasers, tablets and books for the winners. "The parents all ran too," added another *nisei*, "the old ladies did spoon races where they run and carry something in a spoon and try not to drop it."

At first, individual families packed their own lunches, but later they organized potlucks and eventually barbecues. Menus included *musubi* (rice balls) and sushi, *nishime* (mixed vegetable pot), *somen* (cold noodles), pickled vegetables, and teriyaki beef and chicken. Charcoal fires filled the air with white smoke and the unmistakable smell of teriyaki drew the revelers to the laden table. As Japanese Americans acculturated, the menu diversified to include *kim chee* (Korean spicy, pickled vegetables), *lomi* salmon (Hawaiian salted salmon with tomatoes and onions), sushi hotdogs (hotdogs wrapped with rice and seaweed), and taco and potato salads. The food was washed down with soda water and beer, and watermelon was a summertime favorite for dessert.

Obon (summer festival for the dead) connected the people to their ancestral past, in the beating *taiko* drums and circles of dancers and in the lanterns that showed

the spirits the way back home. Obon was also a time for reestablishing ties among the living, from the elderly to the young, in the dance, but also in the food and game booths that lined the cordoned off streets and church grounds. Oshogatsu (New Year's celebration) was clearly the most important community event in the annual calendar. "Shogatsu," remembered a *nisei*, "it was a biiiggg deal, open house deal." Families and groups worked together at *mochitsuki* or rice pounding to make *mochi*, and parents cooked throughout New Year's eve in preparation for the day-long feast. Special foods with meaning—for good health, long life, prosperity—were served to guests who made the rounds, from miles around, visiting the homes of their kinfolk and friends.

Americanization, an education of English-only, compelled *issei* parents to build Japanese schools for their children with whom they could not communicate, both linguistically and culturally. Besides promoting intergenerational understanding, Japanese-language schools helped to define a people and equip them with tools to resist cultural extinction. Miyoko Tsujikawa asked of the younger generations: "I want them to study Japanese language and understand Japanese culture and history. . . . I also want them to respect their parents and their seniors. Further, I want them to always feel pride in being Japanese-Americans, who have inherited blood inferior to none." Children attended Japanese school after the close of public schools and on Saturdays, making Japanese schools unpopular among many Japanese American youth.

At the same time, not knowing English crippled the *issei* in their dealings with whites. "Not being able to speak English," remarked an *issei* woman, "was equivalent to becoming an idiot." Freedom of movement was curtailed, jobs and advancement were restricted, and *issei* were embarrassed and made the butt of jokes, even when they tried to learn English. In the absence of adult schools, *issei* were placed with children who spoke English from birth and who tormented their older classmates. Raisuke Tamura was 16 years old when placed with seven- and eight-year-olds, and moved from school to school in Seattle. The children, Tamura recalled, "called me 'Jap!' and pushed my head or pulled my hair."

The Great Depression of the 1920s and '30s was a difficult time for most Americans. For some Japanese Americans, these years simply perpetuated their poverty, and were a kind of leveler in that whites "came down to our level and began to know hunger," as put by a *nisei* farmer. For other Japanese Americans, the depression hit hard, especially those who were displaced by the abundant, cheap labor. "In Sacramento many people were picking things out of garbage cans," described Wataru Ishisaka. "Well, so many Japanese were suffering

that the Japanese Association organized an emergency relief program and brought food to the needy during the night so that they, who needed relief, wouldn't be embarrassed by it."

> Living through those years,
> Bearing up, tolerating
> That we were despised,
> That we were called "immigrants,"
> We built our present status.
> (Suteko Ujimoto)

Building that "present status," that claim to Americanness, involved both creating a community and situating it on American soil. Demanding one's rights was a constant struggle for Japanese in the contested terrain that was America. "People know Hawaii as the paradise of the Pacific and as a sugar-producing country, but do they know that there are thousands of laborers who are suffering under the heat of the equatorial sun, in field and in factory, and who are weeping under 10 hours of hard labor and with the scanty pay of 77 cents a day?" declared the Japanese Federation of Labor. "Look at the silent tombstones in every locality. Few are the people who visit these graves of our departed friends, but are they not emblems of Hawaii's pioneers in labor?"

With that ringing declaration, Filipino and Japanese workers began the great plantation strike of 1920 that paralyzed Hawaii's sugar industry on Oahu, lasted for nearly six months, and cost the planters an estimated $11.5 million. Like a wind-whipped cane fire, the strike spread from plantation to plantation as workers demanded higher wages, better working conditions and an end to salaries that discriminated among laborers based on their race and ethnicity. The workers saw their cause as just and as a part of the American way, "as laborers living under the great flag of freedom and justice," but Hawaii's rulers described the strike as "an anti-American movement designed to obtain control of the sugar business of the Hawaiian Islands."

Strikers carried the portrait of Abraham Lincoln—liberator of black plantation workers—and marched under banners bearing the inscriptions, "We Want To Live Like Americans" and "God Has Created Us Equal." The *Honolulu Star-Bulletin* countered: "Americans do not take kindly to the spectacle of several thousand alien Asiatics parading through the streets with banners flaunting their hatred of Americanism and American institutions and insulting the memory of the greatest American president since Washington." The planters evicted over 12,000 strikers and their families from plantation homes, contributing to almost a hundred deaths due to exposure and unhealthy conditions in the crowded, makeshift tent cities that sprang up all over the island. "Lives went out like candle flames in a gust of wind," testified an eyewitness.

The planters conceded nothing to the workers when they ended their strike and returned to the plantation. Despite that veneer of restored normalcy, relationships and perceptions had forever changed, and things would never be the same after the strike of 1920. One of the most significant outcomes was the belief within America's government and military that the strike was engineered by Japan for the takeover of Hawaii. "Never lose sight of the real issue," editorialized the *Honolulu Star-Bulletin,* "is Hawaii to remain American or become Japanese?" In contrast to the West Coast, that question seemed all the more urgent and pertinent in Hawaii where Japanese Americans totaled 42.7 percent of the population in 1920 and 37.9 percent in 1930.

A 1923 federal commission report described the "menace of alien domination" as the principal danger posed by Hawaii's Japanese: *"we believe that the question of National Defense and the necessity to curtail the domination of the alien Japanese in every phase of the Hawaiian life is more important that all the other problems combined. . . ."* Army intelligence labeled the Japanese American presence "our military problem," and kept a close watch over Japanese American leaders, organizations and their activities in Hawaii throughout the 1920s and '30s. As the prospect of war with Japan loomed ever larger, military and civilian intelligence drew up increasingly detailed plans to contain the perceived danger.

An early army plan in 1923, for example, called for martial law, registration of all enemy aliens, internment of those deemed security risks, and controls over labor. Then Colonel John L. De Witt—later general and commander of the Western Defense Command during World War II—headed the army's War Plans Division that recommended those precautions for the territory's civilian population. De Witt's proposal contained the two major features of all subsequent plans for Hawaii's defense: internal security achieved through neutralizing the "Japanese menace" and economic vigor maintained by controlling Japanese American labor. According to that view, Japanese Americans were both a curse and a blessing largely because of their numbers and their importance to Hawaii's sugar industry.

The Japanese American family album became the object of close and intense scrutiny. The numbers of men and women, child-bearing rates and child-rearing practices, religious beliefs and Buddhist churches, Japanese language schools and teachers, social and cultural organizations and clubs, and places of residence and work all became suspect in the name of national security. Wrote President Franklin D. Roosevelt in 1936, "One obvious thought occurs to me—that every Japanese citizen or

non-citizen on the Island of Oahu who meets these Japanese ships or has any connection with their officers or men should be secretly but definitely identified and his or her name placed on a special list of those who would be the first to be placed in a concentration camp in the event of trouble."

Roosevelt's "obvious thought" was not limited to Japanese Americans who met visiting Japanese naval vessels, but extended to all who were identified as "dangerous or undesirable." As recorded by the nation's chief naval officer in 1936, "The President also asked the Acting Secretary of the Navy what arrangements and plans have been made relative to concentration camps in the Hawaiian Islands for dangerous or undesirable aliens or citizens in the event of national emergency." The military was far ahead of the President in regards to the "Japanese menace," and assured him that it was "a routine matter for those responsible for military intelligence to maintain lists of suspects, who will normally be the first to be interned . . . in the event of war."

While the Army compiled "lists of suspects" in Hawaii, military and civilian intelligence on the mainland drew up lists of West Coast Japanese American community leaders who were similarly marked for internment in the event of war with Japan. Surveillance of West Coast Japanese American communities began at least as early as World War I, rose in importance after the 1920 sugar plantation strike in Hawaii, and became urgent after Japan's invasion of Manchuria in 1931. By mid-1941, the Justice Department had a list of over 2,000 mainland Japanese Americans whom they considered to be dangerous or potentially dangerous. In reality, those names simply represented the leadership of the West Coast Japanese American community and those whose jobs were deemed vital to the national security, such as fishermen, farmers and produce distributors. Those on the "ABC" list were targeted, without benefit of trial or proof of wrongdoing, for summary arrest and detention.

I bid farewell
To the faces of my sleeping children
As I am taken prisoner
Into the cold night rain.
(Muin Ozaki)

Outcasts, 1941–1945

As smoke still rose from the wreckage that was America's Pacific fleet the Sunday morning of December 7, 1941, the plans for Hawaii's defense, decades in the making, became operational. At the suggestion of the military commander, Hawaii's governor telephoned the president at 12:40 P.M., and had the following conversation: "Gov. said Short [army commander] had asked for martial law and he thought he should invoke it. President replied he approved. Gov. said main danger from local Japs." Martial law, suspension of *habeas corpus* and restrictions on civil liberties—all quite extraordinary measures on U.S. soil—were proclaimed in Hawaii the afternoon of that "day of infamy."

An icy wind swept through Japanese American households with the dawning of December 7th. Japanese Americans feared being questioned, feared being suspected of disloyalty, feared being accused of being Japanese. "An extreme degree of fear was present," wrote an observer of the Japanese community in Hawaii, "their state of mind was comparable to that of a criminal expecting a severe punishment for a major offense." The difference, however, was that Japanese Americans, both as a group and as individuals, were not convicted of any criminal or civil offense, and although Hawaii's people did not know this at the time, even military and civilian intelligence knew that those on their suspect list had not committed any act of espionage or sabotage but were there simply because they were leaders of the Japanese American community.

Despite the military governor's public assurance that everyone would be treated equally, it was apparent to all that Japanese Americans had been singled out for special treatment. Thirteen arresting squads fanned out throughout Honolulu and Oahu's rural districts in the early afternoon of December 7th, and within a three-hour period, forcibly removed Japanese American aliens and citizens alike from their families and homes. By December 8th, 391 Japanese Americans had been apprehended, and by the day after, 93 German and 13 Italian aliens had been similarly arrested. The scene at the Military Intelligence Division office was described by an army officer as "a constant stream of Japanese going through the MID office in those first days, and many were cleared upon first questioning." In other instances, entire groups of Japanese Americans were rounded up and detained for no particular reason, and "nobody even knew who they were, where they came from, or under whose authority they were apprehended. They even went without food for a while."

For Yasutaro Soga, esteemed community leader and newspaper editor, the events of Sunday morning filled him with a feeling of expectation, and instead of his usual kimono, Soga put on his suit and shoes. "My family looked at me with [a] queer expression on their faces, but I read books as if nothing would happen," he recalled. The anticipated knock at the door came later that evening. "Shigeo [his eldest son] answered the door bell. There were three, taller than six feet and young, military policemen. . . . They told me to come to the immigration office. Without hesitation, I replied, 'surely' and went to my bedroom to wear my vest. They followed me around the house. My wife helped me wear my vest and coat." As he was being escorted past the gate, his wife, who had come out with him, whispered to him in a low voice, " 'Don't catch a cold.' I wanted to say something," he remembered, "but the voice couldn't come out."

Soga was taken by car through the deserted, darkened streets of Honolulu, stopping at designated homes to pick up other Japanese American "subversives." In the blackout, he lost his sense of direction and had no idea of who his fellow "prisoners" were. From time to time at roadblocks, armed sentries stopped and searched the car. Finally, they arrived at the immigration station, and the men were led into a room on the first floor of the building. Military police conducted body searches under a dim light and confiscated many of the men's personal belongings. Soga was then marched upstairs in the dark, his arm grasped firmly by a military policeman. "Suddenly he threw me in one of the rooms," recalled Soga. "What astounded me was that first I felt the stuffiness in the dark room and then I didn't know how many people were kept in the room, but I couldn't find an inch [of] space for myself to sit down." He stumbled about in the dark feeling his way around until someone helped him to the top of a bunk bed near a window.

In the light of daybreak, Soga discovered that the room was packed with 64 "brothers," nearly all of whom he knew. Rows of triple-decked beds and bed mats spread over the floor were the sole furnishings in the room, and the crowded and unsanitary conditions created a revolting stench in the single bathroom next door. He described the general atmosphere in the immigration station as "bloodthirsty." "The M.P.'s attitudes were rough. Things could have burst into bloodshed once a false step was taken." Soga remembered his first morning in detention when a young military policeman ordered the men around, pointing his bayonet directly at them. "I was so furious," he recalled, "as if my blood started flowing backward. I almost threw my mess kit at him." On reflection, however, "if we had expressed our feelings," Soga explained, "we would have died . . . a dog's death from the thrust of his bayonet."

Various techniques were employed to strip the internees of their dignity. The men lined up for their meals under the watchful eyes of soldiers with pointed bayonets, and were forced to sit on the ground in the courtyard to eat. Despite a large, covered room adjacent to the courtyard, recalled Soga, "we had to eat in the yard no matter how wet the ground was, or even when the rain started pouring during our meal." Japanese Americans used the mess kits and lone bucket of wash water dirtied by the white internees who always ate before them. "I couldn't stand that because even these prisoners looked down on us," declared Soga. After their meal, the men were allowed to walk and stretch in the court-yard for only 10 to 20 minutes before they were led back to their "filthy small room."

On the third day, about one-half of the 200 internees held at the immigration station were taken to Pier 5 by soldiers with bayonets and machine guns, and put on a barge typically used to haul pineapple. As the vessel transported the men to Sand Island at the mouth of the harbor, looking back, the internees could see the city of Honolulu, the verdant Nuuanu Valley leading to the Pali, and the cloud-covered Koolau mountain range. Ahead of them was the flat, barren, coral-covered Sand Island, and beyond that, the Pacific. Life for them in an American concentration camp was about to begin.

For mainland Japanese Americans, Pearl Harbor brought a descending chill similar to that experienced in Hawaii. Agents of the Federal Bureau of Investigation (FBI) arrested and detained several thousand Japanese, German and Italian aliens even before Roosevelt signed the presidential proclamation that allowed the apprehension of any alien Japanese "deemed dangerous to the public peace or safety of the United States." By the morning of December 8th, FBI agents and military police had picked up 736 Japanese and a smaller number of Germans and Italians, and before the end of the week, the Japanese American total had grown to 1,370. Those who were selected for permanent internment were sent to Army and Immigration and Naturalization Service internment camps such as Fort Lincoln (North Dakota), Fort Missoula (Montana), Santa Fe (New Mexico) and Crystal City (Texas).

Kiyo Hirano of Sausalito, California, remembered how the night before Pearl Harbor she and her children had gone to bed looking forward to Sunday and a peace agreement between the U.S. and Japan. Instead, the morning brought the shocking news of war. "That whole day I spent speechless, seated in front of the radio," noted Hirano. "I will never forget that morning of December 7th, 1941." Choichi Nitta recalled: "It was on a Sunday, and on the way to church I heard about it over the radio in my car but couldn't believe it. When I got home, I turned on the radio, and the Pearl Harbor attack was broadcast extensively. I was shocked!"

"They arrested my wife and myself, but later on the same day she was allowed to go home," recalled Masao Itano. "We were quite worried about leaving our children. The FBI went through our house and even picked up a toy pistol. I was taken to the County Courthouse and stayed in jail overnight before I was sent to San Francisco." Yoshito Fujii remembered December 7th: "Later at night I heard that the FBI had taken away some Japanese people for interrogation. I couldn't understand why. . . . One Japanese after another was arrested, and they never returned home. They weren't

criminals; so I was confused." Mary Tsukamoto was in church that Sunday when her husband burst into the service to announce that Pearl Harbor had been attacked. "I remember how stunned we were. And suddenly the whole world turned dark." She recounted how in the days that followed, Mr. Tanigawa and Mr. Tsuji were taken away by the FBI, and "we had no idea what they were going through. We should have been more aware. One Issei, Mr. Iwasa, committed suicide. So all of these reports and the anguish and the sorrow made the whole world very dark."

"After the Pearl Harbor attack, the FBI men from San Francisco came to Salinas every day, and every day I went around to check on our church members to see if anyone had been taken in," remembered Kiyoshi Noji. "In those days, we didn't know who would be taken in, so most of the Issei men had a couple of small suitcases packed and ready." Masao Itano described his detention in San Francisco while awaiting his fate: "Our meals were black coffee and bread. On an empty stomach, they tasted good. People who were there before us used to hoard the bread for a night snack, but we newcomers didn't know that the evening meal was omitted." Yoshito Fujii was held at the immigration office for three weeks pending his hearing. "My children visited me once in a while," he said. "We had no privacy, though. A guard was with us. My children, being small, couldn't understand why I was kept there. The bigger one was six or seven years old. The smaller one was about a year old." Fujii was sent to Fort Lincoln.

Twelve-year-old Donald Nakahata remembered his father who was a part-time newspaperman and community leader in San Francisco. Probably on the day after Pearl Harbor, his father left for San Jose, believing that the Japanese American community there needed his help. "I walked him to the bus stop," said Nakahata. "We went down Pine Street down to Fillmore to the number 22 streetcar, and he took the 22 streetcar and went to the SP [Southern Pacific] and took the train to San Jose. And that was the last time I saw him." Nakahata later learned that his father had been picked up by the FBI, held in detention somewhere in San Francisco, and taken to several concentration camps. "Dad was gone," recalled Nakahata, "and we just heard from him a little. . . . He apparently suffered several more strokes in various camps. But I know he was in Fort Sill, Oklahoma, and Camp Livingston, Louisiana, and I think he died in Bismarck, North Dakota. It's really kind of sad if you think about it, that I don't know where he died."

Sadakusu Enomoto recalled the confusion of those days. "Rumors started that we would be put in camps, but I didn't think we would be killed. When we were traveling by train to North Dakota," he continued, "the shades were always down; and whenever we stopped, there were machine guns. But there were so many of us together that I wasn't scared. I thought they did those things because of the war." Masao Hirata returned home from work one day to find FBI agents waiting for him. "They took me to jail in Indio," he remembered. "Then that same night around midnight I was moved to a jail in Riverside. The next morning I was taken to Pasadena and stayed there until they took me and others who were arrested to Sante Fe, New Mexico, for a hearing." After the hearing, guards put a number on Hirata's clothes, took his picture and conducted body searches on Hirata and others like him, who were then placed on a train and taken to Roseburg in the middle of the desert. "Everyone on the train and those left in the camp cried because we didn't know where they would take us," recalled Hirata. At Roseburg, "there was a high watchtower and machine guns were set. They took away all of our possessions including money and locked us in a room. They told us that they would shoot us if we got closer than three feet of the fence."

Sand Island, Hawaii, was not only a place of confinement, but also a powerful object lesson to a subject people. Men and women—leaders of their community— were reduced to mere wards of Hawaii's rulers. The first group on the island, upon their arrival, were straightaway directed into a room where they were stripped naked and subjected to body searches. They were then led outside where, in the rain and gathering darkness, were ordered to erect 20 tents. Priests, newspaper editors, businessmen and physicians toiled at an unfamiliar task. "We were soaking wet from rain and perspiration, and finally we finished building tents about 9 o'clock at night," Soga wrote in his diary. "We all lay ourselves in makeshift beds in wet clothes that night."

Men and women internees were kept separate, and Japanese American men were segregated from the Germans and Italians. Living conditions were spare and the environment on this desolate coral island made life even more difficult, particularly for the sick and infirm. The island was hot by day, with a glaring heat that reflected off the white surface, and cold by night, with an ocean wind that blew unobstructed across the flat landscape. "A dust wind kept blowing almost every day in December," recorded Soga, "and the night air was shivering cold." In addition, when it rained, the area flooded leaving a dampness that penetrated everywhere. The tents leaked and they had no floor covering, consequently, the cots that served as beds for the internees sat in pools of water whenever it flooded and, even after the pools had dried, the cots and bed covers were soaked by the rising humidity from the saturated ground.

Life on Sand Island was both monotonous and stressful. Each day was regimented around roll calls in the morning and at night. "In the beginning we were restless

because we were incarcerated without any investigations," remembered Suikei Furuya. "But, as the days went by, our nervousness was gone . . . and we began to desire to have investigations as soon as possible, for we were certain that we could go home as soon as the authority investigated our records. We had never done anything wrong in our lives." The stress of waiting, of not knowing, of separation from family and home worked on the minds of the internees, and "some of them became neurotic and others became insane," wrote Furuya.

"I suspected that unless we were mentally strong," observed Soga, "some of us would begin to have nervous breakdowns and act in unusual behaviors. We were insecure and impatient." He told of an internee who slashed his wrists with a razor blade in an attempted suicide after repeated questioning by the FBI. The man survived but was held in isolation and his tent mates were all subjected to strip searches. Another internee, a slightly effeminate priest, insisted he was pregnant, went insane, and had to be watched and restrained for three days by his fellows. "We grew desolated more and more," chronicled Soga. "Our joyless days continued day after day. In order to divert our feelings, smutty stories (sexual and obscene) were popular in every tent."

Terror and punishment were as prominent as the occasional kiawe bushes that grew on the island's featureless surface. The whistle, calling internees to roll calls and inspections, blew on the slightest whim, reported Soga, sometimes seven to eight times a day. Guards were wanton in their display of firepower, and if internees challenged or failed to follow orders, guards were instructed to shoot to kill. One day and for no apparent reason, guards lined up Japanese Americans against the wall and threatened to shoot them if they refused to do as they were told, and in another instance, gathered them in a warehouse, locked the door, and with machine guns pointed toward the men, announced that they would all be shot. When a handmade knife was found on priest Ryoshin Okano, several guards quickly surrounded him with pointed pistols and stripped him naked. They then turned to his companions and, despite nightfall, "we were gathered in the open space and we took off our clothes," recalled Soga. "We had to remain standing for a long time until they finished searching our clothes. Other guards searched our tents and took away our fountainpens and pencils. We were frozen to death in the cold, windy, and barren field."

A central mission of Sand Island, it seems, was to break the spirit of the internees. The process began with the swift, forcible removal of individuals from their families and homes. They were given no reason for their arrest or explanation of where they were being taken or for how long. At the immigration station and on Sand Island, their powerlessness was prominently underscored by excessive displays of arms, omnipresent guards, frequent roll calls and punishment meted out for "insolence" and a host of offenses. Being forced to eat in the rain, use dirty utensils and wash water, sleep in flooded tents, and void in cans and buckets were unnecessary and contemptuous of the flower of the *issei* generation. Solitary confinement, a diet of only water and hard crackers, insistent interrogations, useless labor such as fly-swatting, and cruel punishment such as digging unexploded shells worked on the body as well as the mind.

Strip searches, as common as the mosquitoes that bred in the island's stagnant pools, revealed the utter vulnerability of the internees whose outer defenses were breached both physically and psychologically. "They stripped us down and even checked the anus," exclaimed an internee with indignation. "We were completely naked. Not even undershorts. They even checked our assholes." Having wrestled through the night, the internees despaired of seeing the dawn. "None of us could see a light in our future," wrote Soga. Sand Island was a terminus for some, a place where dreams died and lives ended.

Men scrounged for cigarette butts discarded by guards, rolled the tobacco in toilet paper and passed the numbing narcotic from man to man around the tent. A *nisei* attorney visited Sand Island on Christmas Eve, 1941, and "he was appalled at the unshaven faces, dishevelled hair, and grimy appearance of the detainees, many of whom were his former friends." While Sand Island might have symbolized degeneration, it also exemplified the courage and strength of a people. Soga recalled, in a story that showed the tenacity of the human spirit amidst conditions of unmitigated oppression: "Almost all of us slept in the clothes that we wore in the daytime, for we didn't know when a sudden disturbance might occur, and also we didn't want to die disgracefully."

In California, fisherman Minejiro Shibata was sent to Fort Lincoln in North Dakota. "Being around the tenth of February," he remembered, "it was severely cold. The unprepared ones had only a shirt. I was cold and hungry all the time in the camp. I was afraid I might not be able to get out of there alive." The food was meager and poorly prepared. "We were given only a few spoonfuls of rice with a trace of meat in it. I was too hungry to sleep at night, but it didn't sound graceful to complain about our hunger all the time, so everybody clenched his teeth and bore the hunger like a warrior's son. Later on, a Japanese cook came, and the food improved."

Masao Hirata, held captive in the New Mexico desert, found separation from his wife and children the most difficult aspect of his detention. "I worried about my wife and my six little children whom I had left behind," he recollected. "I also worried about the land already planted with seedlings. You can't imagine how I felt at that time. I would have been happier if they had put my

family together in a camp. Being separated from them made it unbearable."

My wife and children
Live in a far away land.
How lonely are the nights
Behind these barbed wire fences.
(Sojin Takei)

Outside those barbed wire fences, the Office of the Military Governor ruled over Hawaii's people from Iolani Palace, the last seat of an independent Hawaiian monarchy. Martial law involved "control of the civilian population" through general orders and military tribunals. Everyone was subjected to blackouts and curfews, controls over wages, rents and prices, and rationing, but enemy aliens and citizens of enemy ancestry were the targets of special restrictions. Hawaii's *issei* were required to carry their alien registration cards at all times, had to observe curfew provisions that applied only to them, were excluded from certain places and jobs, were forbidden to write or publish any "attack or threats" against the government, and *nisei* who worked in restricted areas had to wear special badges with black borders that clearly marked them as Japanese.

Japanese culture, *issei* leadership and community structures were the casualties of a domestic war waged in the territory against Japanese Americans. "Immediately after the outbreak of war," wrote two students, "rumors circulated that any objects which were 'Japanese' were incriminating and that many Issei were being interned because of possession of them. During the days that followed, almost every Japanese family had a thorough housecleaning, and all objects which were kept for sentimental reasons were pulled out of trunks and destroyed." Letters, photographs, books, magazines, records, and flags and emblems were buried or burned. Japanese language schools and newspapers were closed by military order, Shintoism was banned, and although Buddhism was officially permitted, nearly all of its priests were interned and its adherents threatened with similar treatment. The army, in fact, desecrated Buddhist temples such as the Jodo-shu temple in Honolulu which was converted into an infantry battalion headquarters, and soldiers plundered the Hilo temple, taking the great brass lamps and costly ceremonial vestments.

Family and community festivals such as Obon, Mochitsuki and New Year's Day, Girl's and Boy's Day, and Japanese-style weddings went unobserved or fell into disuse. The *issei* bore the stigma of enemy alien, while the *nisei* were tainted by their Japanese cultural heritage, but were also wooed toward Anglo conformity. The *issei* represented an obsolete mentality, an old world flavor that had become distasteful; the *nisei* symbolized the future—a new direction and style—in full pursuit of the elusive American dream. "We are afraid. We don't know what to do," testified an *issei* of that period. "Even our own children don't let us go out. If we go out, we will be the focus of hate and revenge. So we stay in the house." Within that atmosphere of fear created by and nurtured under martial law, thus, Japanese American homes served as prisons for the *issei*, but also for the *nisei* who were constantly reminded by the military that they were "on the spot" and had to prove their "Americanness."

The Army's Counter Intelligence Corps, created on January 1, 1942, in Hawaii to detect and prevent espionage and sabotage and to uncover "treason, sedition, subversive activity and disaffection," helped to ensure that demonstration of Americanness. The work of the corps' agents soon filled a room with about 75 file cabinets containing at least 60,000 files and more than 148 index card drawers holding 20,000 names. Japanese Americans were encouraged, as part of their patriotic duty, to supply names to Army and FBI agents for investigation and possible internment. The "ceaseless investigation of suspected subversive elements" and apprehension of those deemed dangerous to the internal security were the tactics of the corps to put Japanese Americans on the defensive and thereby hold them in check.

"Evacuation" and "relocation," terms generally associated only with the West Coast, were a reality for a sizable number of Japanese Americans in Hawaii. Less than two weeks after the attack, farmers in the West Loch area of Pearl Harbor were given two days to pack up and leave their farms, although they were permitted to return during daylight hours to move their livestock and harvest their crops. Many, who had recently borrowed substantial amounts and had invested "practically all of their life's savings" to farm the land, suffered "heavy losses." The next week, military police ordered 1,500 Japanese American residents of the Iwilei district near Honolulu harbor to move out by morning or be shot. The displaced people worried over "disposal of furniture and other belongings, care of the aged and ill, and the handling of pets," and those with nowhere to go found temporary shelter at Kaiulani School. Some eventually settled in a low-cost housing project, but a year later others were still homeless.

What ultimately saved Hawaii's Japanese Americans from mass removal and confinement was not the "aloha spirit" or widely believed notion of a racial paradise, but the cold recognition by the military of the importance, indeed necessity, of Japanese American labor to produce the food and products required for the territory's economic survival. Work was also seen as a way of social control. "An idle Jap with a family to feed is more dangerous than one under supervision and working with other races," declared the military governor. Thus, he resisted as much as he could the persistent demands by the president and secretary of the navy for the internment of greater numbers of Japanese Americans in the islands. "Both the President and the Secretary of the Navy," wrote the assistant secretary of war, "continuously refer to the desirability of moving Japanese from the Island of Oahu to some other Island rather than to bring any numbers of them to the United States." As a compromise, the army sent to mainland concentration camps 1,875 Japanese Americans, while holding, from 1941 to 1945, 1,466 Japanese Americans in Hawaii's concentration camps.

In California, Kiyo Hirano recalled: "Among those whites who had been our friends just a day before [Pearl Harbor] were those who now turned into enemies, who fired us from our jobs, who yelled, 'Get out Japs,' in front of our doors." But Hirano also remembered whites who treated Japanese Americans with kindness and others who merely tolerated them, asking them to remain on the job. At first, California newspapers urged restraint, like the December 9, 1941, editorial of the *San Francisco Chronicle:* "The roundup of Japanese citizens in various parts of the country . . . is not a call for volunteer spy hunters to go into action. Neither is it a reason to lift an eyebrow at a Japanese, whether American-born or not. . . . There is no excuse to wound the sensibilities of any persons in America by showing suspicion or prejudice. That, if anything, is a help to fifth column spirit. An American-born Nazi would like nothing better than to set the dogs of prejudice on a first-class American Japanese."

Toward the end of January 1942, however, there was a dramatic shift in newspaper sentiment from advocating tolerance for Japanese Americans to favoring their internment. The *Los Angeles Times,* for example, editorialized on January 23, 1942: "Many of our Japanese, whether born here or not, are fully loyal and deserve sympathy rather than suspicion." Just five days later, the *Times* asserted that "the rigors of war demand proper detention of Japanese and their immediate removal from the most acute danger spots." Clearly the most significant event that influenced that change in newspaper attitude (and in popular opinion) was the January 25, 1942, release of the Roberts Committee Report, which alleged, without proof, that the Pearl Harbor attack was greatly abetted by spies centered around Japan's consulate in Honolulu.

On January 27, 1942, Lieutenant General John L. DeWitt, commander of the Western Defense Command, reported to Washington: "There's a tremendous volume of public opinion now developing against the Japanese of all classes, that is aliens and non-aliens, to get them off the land. . . . Since the publication of the Roberts Report they feel that they are living in the midst of a lot of enemies. They don't trust the Japanese, none of them." In conversation with his subordinate, DeWitt confided that German and Italian aliens and all Japanese—aliens *and* citizens—should be "put . . . to work in internment camps. . . . We've waited too long as it is. Get them all out."

California governor Culbert Olson, in a radio broadcast speech a few days after the release of the Roberts Report, alleged that "it is known that there are Japanese residents of California who have sought to aid the Japanese enemy" and that Japanese Americans "have shown indications of preparation for fifth column activities." In response to that threat, the governor announced, "general plans [have been] agreed upon for the movement and placement of the entire adult Japanese population in California at productive and useful employment within the borders of our state, and under such surveillance and protection . . . as shall be deemed necessary."

On February 11, 1942, according to the assistant secretary of war, Franklin D. Roosevelt authorized the army to prepare for the removal and detention of large numbers of West Coast Japanese Americans. The assistant secretary of war reported: "we talked to the President and the President, in substance, says go ahead and do anything you think necessary . . . if it involves citizens, we will take care of them too. He says there will probably be some repercussions, but it has got to be dictated by military necessity. . . ."

Attorney General Francis Biddle wrote to Roosevelt on February 17, 1942. Instead of arguing for the civil liberties of Japanese Americans, Biddle warned that their mass removal would disrupt West Coast agriculture and tie up transportation and thousands of much needed troops, and thus urged that "so large a job must be done after careful planning." His was the strongest voice in the president's cabinet for restraint. On Thursday, February 19, 1942, Roosevelt signed Executive Order 9066 that authorized the army to designate military areas from which "any or all persons may be excluded" and to provide for the "transportation, food, shelter, and other accommodations as may be necessary" for those excluded persons.

"We read about President Roosevelt's Executive Order 9066," remembered Mary Tsukamoto. "We realized that we needed to be able to rise to the occasion to help in whatever way we could in our community. We had many meetings at night and the FBI was always lurking around. We were told we couldn't stay out after eight o'clock in the evening." Riyo Orite recalled that spring and summer of 1942: "Hearing a lot of rumors from my customers every day, I felt uneasy. They tried to encourage me, but

I felt helpless about the boarding house and procrastinated about closing this business. My husband had died the year before, and it was a difficult time. Then the evacuation came along. It was awful. Because of racial prejudice, people threw rocks at us, and I was scared and worried."

"A lot of things just nagged at us and harassed us, and we were frightened, but even in that atmosphere I remember we frantically wanted to do what was American," said Mary Tsukamoto. "We started to buy war bonds, and we took first aid classes with the rest of the Hakujin [white] people in the community. We went out at night to go to these classes, but we worried about being out after eight o'clock. It was a frightening time. Every little rule and regulation was imposed only on the Japanese people."

On February 25, 1942, the navy served eviction notices to about 500 Japanese American families on Terminal Island in San Pedro, California, giving them 48 hours to leave. "Near panic swept the community, particularly where the family head was in custody. Word spread quickly and human vultures in the guise of used-furniture dealers descended on the island. They drove up and down the streets in trucks offering $5 for a nearly new washing machine, $10 for refrigerators. . . . And the Japanese, angry but helpless, sold their dearly purchased possessions because they didn't know what to do. . . ." The few hundred Japanese families on Bainbridge Island, near Seattle, were similarly forcibly evicted from their island homes in March 1942. Meanwhile, DeWitt issued proclamations that divided Washington, Oregon, California and Arizona into military areas from which enemy aliens and all Japanese Americans would eventually be excluded, and instituted an 8 P.M. to 6 A.M. curfew for enemy aliens and Japanese, both aliens and citizens.

"Several weeks before May," reported Takae Washizu, "Soldiers came around and posted notices on telephone poles. It was sad for me to leave the place where I had been living for such a long time. Staring at the ceiling in bed at night, I wondered who would take care of my cherry tree and my house after we moved out. I also thought about my mother in Japan." The soldiers, Washizu remembered, "were mean" and "whenever I did something wrong, they put the muzzle of their rifle on my long hair" as they rounded up the Sacramento Japanese Americans. "We were given sandwiches, oranges, and milk for lunch. Each family was given a number. The bill for the evacuation camp had been passed, so that the camp was legal."

Yuri Tateishi, her husband, and their four children lived in West Los Angeles when the war began. They, like many other Japanese Americans, had to sell their household goods for a pittance, and slept in an empty house the night before they were taken away. On April 26, 1942, the family wakened early, walked to the designated spot with many others, and boarded the bus that took them to Manzanar. But before getting on the bus, a nurse discovered that Tateishi's youngest son had broken out with measles that morning. "He was almost three, but I was carrying him, and she said, 'I'm sorry but I'm going to have to take him away.'" Despite the reassurances of a kind white neighbor who promised to check on her son, Tateishi worried about having to leave him behind especially when she did not know where they were going. "When I thought about how he might wake up and be in a strange place, with strange people," recalled Tateishi, "I just really broke down and cried. I cried all morning over it, but there was nothing we could do but leave him." The child, fortunately, rejoined his family after three weeks.

Separations sometimes were permanent. Mary Tsukamoto told about Mrs. Kuima who had cared for her retarded son for 32 years. When Kuima was about to be taken away, the welfare office ruled that her son could not go with her, but had to be institutionalized. "It was a very tragic thing for me to have to tell her," said Tsukamoto, "and I remember going out to the field— she was hoeing strawberries—and I told her what they told us, that you can't take your son with you. And so she cried, and I cried with her." A few days before Kuima was evicted from her farm, her son was taken away to the institution. About a month later, in Fresno "Assembly Center" where the family was being held, Mrs. Kuima received word that her son had died. "All these years she loved him and took care of him, he only knew Japanese and ate Japanese food," commented Tsukamoto. "I was thinking of the family; they got over it quietly; they endured it."

But enduring oppression did not necessarily mean accepting it, and resignation to the inevitability of confinement did not necessarily imply agreement with its legitimacy. In quiet and dramatic ways, Japanese Americans resisted the range of instruments employed to subjugate them. Some destroyed their possessions, rather than sell them at much reduced prices to avaricious buyers, and others privately arranged the transfer of their farms to friends and neighbors, instead of submitting to a takeover by the Farm Security Administration.

The mass removal and confinement of Japanese Americans was a profoundly racist act not only because the criterion for internment was based on a racial designation, but also because the program was a stark feature of the prevailing power relations of white over yellow. Identification numbers instead of names, horse stalls instead of rooms, transportation in truck beds, and seem-ingly endless lines all worked to erase one's identity and dignity. Sadae Takizawa, through her poems, recorded the thoughts and feelings of internees at Tanforan, an "assembly center" in northern California:

I recall
Noah's flood
In ancient times.
Angry waves
were surging in these days.

People are crowded
In a long line
Like a snake.
The crowd is waiting
For a meal in the dust and wind.

Standing
At the edge of an abyss,
My soul
Is deeply agitated,
Running in fright.

Despite her fear, Takizawa could also say:

Because I am
A Japanese woman,
I should
Stand firmly
At all times.

And stand firmly they did. On March 28, 1942, Minoru Yasui challenged the military imposed curfew to stop, through the courts, the impending mass removal of Japanese Americans. "It was my feeling and belief, then and now," explained Yasui, "that no military authority has the right to subject any United States citizen to any requirement that does not equally apply to all other U.S. citizens." Yasui consequently walked the streets of Portland, Oregon, that Saturday evening with the intention of getting arrested for violating DeWitt's curfew order. At about 11 P.M., and getting tired of walking, Yasui spotted a policeman and asked him to arrest him; instead, the officer refused and told Yasui, "'Run along home, sonny boy, or you'll get in trouble.' So I had to go on down to the Second Avenue police station and argue myself into jail."

Yasui's constitutional challenge was soon joined, in Seattle, by Gordon Hirabayashi who refused to report to the Civil Control Station on May 11 or 12, 1942. Hirabayashi contended that by reporting for removal, he would be waiving his rights as an American citizen. In California, Fred Korematsu hid in Oakland and San

Francisco and refused to leave with the rest of the Japanese Americans who were being sent to concentration camps. Korematsu was discovered on May 30, 1942, in San Leandro and charged with violating the army's exclusion order. According to the FBI, local police had arrested nine other Japanese Americans hiding in San Francisco and six in Sacramento, including Koji Kurokawa who had hidden for three weeks in the basement of the house in which he had worked as a "houseboy."

The cases of Yasui, Hirabayashi and Korematsu eventually reached the U.S. Supreme Court and their disposition in 1944 formed the constitutional justification for the entire wartime policy of Japanese American removal and detention. Their rehearing during the 1980s finally affirmed the correctness of the men's cause—their protestations of civil rights as American citizens—and the falsity of and racism in the government's claim of "military necessity" in the program that placed over 110,000 people into concentration camps.

In Hawaii, young *nisei* men sought to extend the protections of the Constitution to all Japanese Americans by serving in their country's armed forces to repel the Fascist and racist threat on foreign battlefields and on the homefront. At the time of Japan's attack, there were about 1,500 *nisei* recruits serving in the 298th and 299th Infantry. On December 10, three days after Pearl Harbor, the army disarmed all Japanese American soldiers, confined them to their quarters, and hemmed them in with military guards and machine guns. Two days later, they were rearmed without explanation and placed on beach patrols, although the 317 *nisei* in the Territorial Guard were dismissed by Hawaii's military governor in January 1942. Despite their arbitrary indictment and rejection, *nisei* urged the formation of, and about 170 joined, the Varsity Victory Volunteers (VVV), a cheap labor battalion, "to fight," in the words of a VVV member, "a twofold fight for tolerance and justice."

From December 1941 to April 1942, the army worried over the *nisei* soldiers serving in the 298th and 299th, who might become, according to Hawaii's military, "a potential force in our midst completely armed and equipped for organized resistance." Individuals whom they suspected of disloyalty, accordingly, were summarily dismissed by the army, and at the end of March, the War Department ordered an end to *nisei* recruitment. In May, the army's chief of staff authorized the formation and removal from the territory of a segregated unit of Japanese Americans on the suggestion of Hawaii's commander.

Without notice, the army gathered Hawaii's *nisei* soldiers at Schofield Barracks, took away their rifles, encamped them away from the regular troops, and ringed their tents with barbed wire. On June 5, the army organized the 1,432 men as the Hawaiian Provisional Battalion and shipped them to the mainland. "Before we had any chance to bid goodbye to our loved ones," recalled Spark M. Matsunaga, "we found ourselves on board a troopship sailing for God-knew-where. Speculation was rife that we were headed for a concentration camp." After five days, the men reached San Francisco Bay and traveled by train to Camp McCoy, Wisconsin.

Referring to their seven months of training at Camp McCoy, Matsunaga said: "We pictured ourselves as a battalion of forced laborers." The army subjected the *nisei* to further indignities, such as marching and training with wooden guns because they could not be trusted with real arms, and playing the part of Japanese soldiers—the enemy—in mock combat with white troops—the Americans. The Army sent a *nisei* contingent on a secret project to Mississippi to hide in the dense forests from tracking dogs, because military strategists believed the "Japanese race" exuded a distinctive odor.

Hawaii's Japanese American soldiers were later joined by mainland volunteers and draftees, most of whom had come from concentration camps, and were organized into the segregated 100th Infantry Battalion and 442nd Regimental Combat Team. *Nisei* soldiers—among the most decorated and decimated of World War II—and their heroic deeds must be set against their racist treatment by America's military and against the wider context of martial law and selective detention in Hawaii and of mass removal and confinement on the mainland. They indeed battled on two fronts and against two foes—fascism and racism.

Just as heroic were the deeds of Japanese Americans who resisted the draft on the principle of "fair play." About 200 *nisei* at Heart Mountain concentration camp in Wyoming organized themselves as the Fair Play Committee (FPC) in 1943 and declared: "We, the Nisei have been complacent and too inarticulate to the unconstitutional acts that we were subjected to. If ever there was a time or cause for decisive action, IT IS NOW!" The resisters explained that their protest was not motivated by a fear "to risk our lives for our country," but by the government's denial of their rights—"without due process of law as guaranteed by the Constitution and Bill of Rights, without any charges filed against us, without any evidence of wrongdoing on our part. . . ." Further, the government had not restored their civil rights or even acknowledged wrongdoing, and, under those conditions, had ordered them to serve in that government's army and in a segregated unit. "The FPC believes that unless such actions are opposed *NOW*, and steps taken to remedy such injustices and discriminations *IMMEDIATELY*, the future of all minorities and the future of this democratic nation is in danger."

Under the leadership of Kiyoshi Okamoto, a soil test engineer from Hawaii, the Fair Play Committee actively contested the government's arbitrary application of *nisei* rights and responsibilities, and ultimately challenged the legality of America's concentration camps. At the end of the largest draft resistance trial in U.S. history, in June 1944, 63 *nisei* resisters were found guilty and sentenced to three years in prison. Separate charges were filed against the committee's leaders and James Omura, an editor for the *Rocky Shimpo* and supporter of the resisters, accusing them of engaging in a conspiracy to subvert the selective service system. Although Omura was found innocent, all seven of the committee's leaders, including Okamoto, were found guilty and sentenced to terms of two and four years in prison.

After having served time at McNeil Island and Leavenworth federal penitentiaries, the Japanese American draft resisters received a pardon on Christmas Eve 1947 from President Harry Truman. That act vindicated the principle upon which the dissident patriots stood; in the words of federal district judge Louis Goodman in his dismissal of indictments against 26 draft resisters at Tule Lake concentration camp, "it is shocking to the conscience that an American citizen be confined on the ground of disloyalty, and then, while so under duress and restraint, be compelled to serve in the armed forces, or be prosecuted for not yielding to such compulsion." As they sat in their Leavenworth cell, Guntaro Kubota, an *issei* leader of the Fair Play Committee, told his fellow *nisei* leader Frank Emi: "Emi, I'm really proud to be here with you fellows. If I don't ever do anything else in my life, this will be the proudest thing I ever did because I had a part in your fight for a principle."

Mitsuye Endo resolved early in her life to "fight for a principle." In 1942 Endo agreed to serve as the test case against the government's internment program. "I was very young, and I was very shy, so it was awfully hard to have this thing happen to me," remembered Endo. "In fact, when they came and asked me about it, I said, well, can't you have someone else do it first. It was awfully hard for me." But she decided to go ahead with the challenge, "because they said it's for the good of everybody. . . ."

As her case, *Ex parte Endo,* wound its way up toward the U.S. Supreme Court, Endo remained in Topaz concentration camp, despite her ability to leave, because she did not want to jeopardize the suit. On December 18, 1944, the Supreme Court unanimously declared invalid the detention of Japanese Americans and ordered Endo's "unconditional release." "An admittedly loyal citizen," a justice wrote, "has been deprived of her liberty for a period of years. Under the Constitution she should be free to come and go as she pleases. Instead, her liberty of motion and other innocent activities have been prohibited and conditioned. She should be discharged."

The effect of Endo's challenge was immediate. One day before the Supreme Court's ruling on the matter and in anticipation of its decision, the Army's Western Defense Command announced that its exclusion of loyal Japanese Americans from the West Coast was terminated, effective January 2, 1945. Endo's defiant claim exposed the racist nature of the detention program and finally opened the gates of America's concentration camps. "Do I have any regrets at all about the test case?" Endo reflected. "No, not now, because of the way it turned out."

Heirs, 1945–Present

"People were allowed to leave the camp after January, 1945," recalled Nisuke Mitsumori. "They gave us identification cards and told us that the government would give us official permission to return if we brought these identification cards to them. It was the government's decision, but we were still called 'Japs' by others. When the first Japanese family went back to Pasadena, the people who received this Japanese family were harassed. Somebody wrote some unpleasant things on their garage door. . . ." Shoichi Fukuda likewise remembered the hostile reception in California. "I came back to California in May," he said. "Everybody was afraid of being attacked by the white people. The war was still going on at that time, and prejudice and oppression were very severe."

Sumio Doi and his family returned to their California farm in January 1945. Hearing cars one night, Doi went out to investigate and found his barn in flames. He and his father managed to put out the fire, but two days later, again hearing noises, Doi opened the door and shots were fired into the house. Sticks of dynamite and burnt fuses and matches were later found under a corner of the packing shed. Sheriff Charles Silva posted a guard at the Doi ranch and vowed to protect the family from further violence. After an investigation, several men and women confessed to the crime, but despite the evidence against the three brought to trial, the jury acquitted them.

Besides racism and "No Japs Wanted" signs, Japanese Americans faced the formidable task of rebuilding their lives, typically with only their labor and the $25 given to them by the War Relocation Authority when they left the concentration camps. "When we got out of the camp," recalled Masao Hirata, "they gave each of us only twenty-five dollars per person. I experienced unspeakable hardships to support all my family. I will never forget it." Hirata and his family had no place to stay, no car, and no tools to cut the tall weeds that had taken over his farm. "But I had to work to support my family; so I borrowed old tools and worked on my farm. Every Japanese person had to start again from the beginning."

An *issei* farmer testified shortly after his return to California: "Before war I had 20 acres in Berryessa. Good land, two good houses, one big. 1942 in camp everybody say sell, sell, sell. Maybe lose all. Lawyer write, he say sell. I sell $650 acre. Now the same land $1500 acre. I lose, I cannot help. All gone. Now I live in hostel. Work like when first come to this country. Pick cherries, pick pears, pick apricots, pick tomatoes. Just like when first come. Pretty soon, maybe one year, maybe two years, find place. Pretty hard now. No use look back. Go crazy think about all lost. Have to start all over again like when come from Japan, but faster this time."

In San Jose, Japanese Americans and supportive whites, most prominently women, worked as the Council for Civic Unity to ease the resettlement of nearly 2,000 Japanese Americans in the Santa Clara Valley. In her final report dated June 12, 1946, Evelyn Settles, chair of the hostel committee of the Council for Civic Unity, summed up the effort to rehabilitate "thousands of worthy citizens who were so rudely displaced": "Many problems were met and solved that had not been dreamed of. . . . There are many things that I am sure every member wished could have been done better, but each did the best he or she could under the circumstances. It has been a good year, for the friendships made have been real and are the kind that will endure."

One of the most significant consequences of the war for mainland Japanese Americans was the government's policy of "relocation." Commenting on that program of relocation, Secretary of the Interior Harold Ickes stated: "Its [War Relocation Authority] long-range objective will be to bring about a better economic adjustment and a more satisfactory Nation-wide distribution of a minority group which was doubtless too heavily concentrated before the war in one particular section of the country." As a result, whereas before the war an estimated 88.5 percent of the mainland Japanese Americans lived on the West Coast, only about 55 percent lived on the West Coast in 1947. Although the West Coast numbers would grow, the effects of relocation were a new population distribution and the demise of some communities.

The lifting of martial law in Hawaii on October 24, 1944 and the closing of America's concentration camps the following year enabled the return of Japanese American exiles—internees confined in mainland camps and *nisei* soldiers—to the islands. *Issei* poet Sojin Takei, returning home from mainland concentration camps, looked toward the shore and hoped for the dawning of a new era:

Koko Head nears,
And now Diamond Head!

How bright the sea is
Shining in morning sunlight!

But Hawaii's Japanese Americans realized that full equality would only be gained through struggle. "We who by God's will were permitted to return," declared Katsumi Kometani, veteran of the 100th Battalion, "and you who are fortunate to be here have a challenge—an obligation to those who now peacefully sleep under the white crosses in Italy and France—to build a better Hawaii." Kometani reminded Hawaii's rulers that full equality for Japanese Americans was an irrefutable claim: "By the blood and tears of our people we have earned a place for ourselves in this community. . . . We have helped win the war on the battlefront but we have not yet won the war on the homefront. We shall have won only when we attain those things for which our country is dedicated, namely, equality of opportunity and the dignity of man."

The postwar beginnings of that struggle for "equality of opportunity and the dignity of man" were situated in multiracial politics and labor unions in which Japanese Americans played a key role. Prominent in that civil rights movement was the International Longshoremen's and Warehousemen's Union (ILWU) and its leaders, including Yasu Arakaki, Jack Kawano, Jack Hall and Hideo "Major" Okada, who helped organize stevedores and plantation workers. "We haven't been satisfied with our wages and living conditions on this plantation for a long time," explained a laborer in 1945. "We tried to organize, but we couldn't get ahead because we had no protection or backing from any group. The boss fired anyone who tried to organize the men." In 1946, sugar plantation workers won a wage increase after a 79-day strike, and in 1949, dockworkers crippled island shipping and won a wage increase after a bitter 177-day strike. Of those achievements, Hawaii's delegate to Congress John A. Burns would later say: "The foundations of democracy in Hawaii were laid by the ILWU, because they freed the working man of the plantations . . . from the economic and political control of management."

Recovering from their war wounds in a Jersey City hospital, Sakae Takahashi and Daniel K. Inouye talked about thwarted opportunities in the past and about hopes for a brighter future. Takahashi recalled the harsh realities that had stifled his father's dreams for an education, he spoke of police brutality during the 1924 Hanapepe strike, and he asked Inouye, "Most of all I want to know why there has to be a limit to our hopes." Takahashi attacked the territory's elite and promised that he would work to create a new, more democratic Hawaii. Inouye concurred: "What I'm interested in is tomorrow," he said. "I want my kids to have an even break. I demand it."

In 1948, while an undergraduate at the University of Hawaii, Inouye talked to John Burns about the future of the territory's Democratic party. Together they forged an alliance of Japanese Americans, workers, Asians, Hawaiians, and whites—groups exploited and excluded by the white elite—with a new generation of leaders, including many former veterans who had taken advantage of the G.I. Bill of Rights to obtain college degrees. "We had played a small but vital part in the great war, and now that it was won we were not about to go back to the plantation," remembered Inouye of his fellow *nisei* political leaders. "We wanted our place in the sun, the right to participate in decisions that affected us. Day after day, at rally after rally, we hammered home the point that there must be no more second-class citizens in the Hawaii of tomorrow."

The coalition ushered in the "revolution of 1954" that ended over 50 years of Republican party—the party of the elite—rule in Hawaii. For the first time, after the ballots had been counted in the 1954 territorial elections, Democrats captured both the House and Senate of the legislature, and Japanese Americans filled nearly half of those seats. Japanese American politicians who won seats in the 1954 "revolution" and who helped reshape Hawaii included Daniel Inouye, Sakae Takahashi and Spark Matsunaga. Hawaii achieved statehood in 1959, Inouye became the first Asian American congressman in 1959 and first *nisei* senator in 1962, and Patsy Takemoto Mink became the first Asian American woman elected to the Congress in 1964.

In 1973, George R. Ariyoshi became the first Asian American governor, and in 1978 Jean Sadako King became Hawaii's first woman lieutenant governor. "As far as the Japanese were concerned," said Dan Aoki, a Democratic party leader, "it was very seldom that even when they were trained and educated that they came out on top. . . . The election of George Ariyoshi was the climax of it all. . . . It's not that we wanted to elect a Japanese governor. No, it's not that idea. We just wanted a non-white person to prove to the people that one doesn't have to be a white person to be a leader." Ariyoshi attributed his success to his parents—embodied in the phrase, *okage sama de* (I am what I am because of you)—and their stress on education. "Early on, my father encouraged me to attain a good education," remembered Ariyoshi. "That guidance and my parents' generous support have been very much responsible for my educational advancement and whatever measure of success I have been able to attain. Okage sama de."

Japanese Americans helped to transform Hawaii, apart from politics, by entering professions such as law and education, becoming attorneys and justices of the state supreme court, and teachers, principals, professors and the president of the University of Hawaii. Many more helped to build a new Hawaii by continuing to work on the sugar and pineapple plantations, in carpentry and skilled crafts, and in contracting and business. Women found opportunities outside the plantation by going to Honolulu to work as maids, barbers and cannery workers, and by pursuing education to become teachers, secretaries and bookkeepers, and nurses.

Dorothy Ochiai Hazama recalled learning to sew her own dresses when she was nine years old, helping in her parents' store when she was 11, and working in the fields when she was 12. "I donned thick working clothes and got into open trucks at dawn," she said. "I did hoe-hana work in sugar and pineapple fields." When she reached 16 "that magical age when I could finally get out of the hot sun and field work and earn some decent wages at the pineapple cannery," Hazama worked every summer at the cannery to support her high school and university education. "In retrospect," she reflected, "I can see that the tradition of work had become an important value. . . . I received a lot of advice and encouragement from my mother and my mother-in-law who said: 'You have worked hard for an education so use it. Go to work; we will help you to take care of your children while you teach.' I have no regrets—I feel very fortunate to have had a very fulfilling life."

Cross-cultural coalitions and the struggle to maintain an ethnic identity took different forms on the mainland as compared with those in Hawaii. Japanese Americans comprised a miniscule percentage of the total population and, even among Asian groups, would be exceeded by Filipinos as the second largest group behind the Chinese in the 1980 census. In 1990, Japanese Americans totaled about 600,000 on the mainland and 247,000 in Hawaii. Assimilation, cultural erasure and historical amnesia were values advocated by the government in its relocation program and by wider society in its push for conformity and consensus. "Never before have I seriously attempted to dissect my feelings and attitudes about myself as a Japanese-American," wrote a *sansei* (third generation). "I suspect because certain truths about oneself are unbearably painful, I preferred to postpone my confrontation with reality until I was able to cope with the consequences of such a confrontation."

But confront that reality they did, in their effort to rebuild their war-ravaged communities. Churches and community halls, stores and restaurants, offices and homes became theirs, scattered about in suburbia but also clustered together in Japantowns. They organized clubs and celebrations, and promoted Japanese American culture for the wider community and for their children. Like the *issei* pioneers, their children and grandchildren combined elements from Japan with those found in America and made them uniquely Japanese American. In San Jose, Japanese Americans celebrate the seasonal cycles in the summer Obon led by the Buddhist temple, the fall Aki Matsuri led by the Methodist church, and the spring Nikkei Matsuri led by a coalition of community organizations. An appropriate metaphor for that creative cultural process is the hot dog sushi, written about by *sansei* author and farmer David Mas Masumoto, a hot dog wrapped in rice and seaweed. The result is a harmonious and delectable creation.

Japanese Americans confronted America's social reality through political action such as in the 1960s campaign to repeal Title II of the Internal Security Act of 1950 and the massive 1980s movement for redress and reparations. The 1950 act authorized the attorney general to apprehend and detain any person suspected of engaging in acts of espionage or sabotage, ignoring due process, and Title II of the act provided for detention camps for those deemed subversive. In 1971, after four years of effort, Title II was repealed. Edison Uno, a leader in the campaign, pointed out that in working openly to repeal Title II, Japanese Americans freed themselves from the internalized doubt and self-blame that they had borne since their detention. "Once we realized that we should no longer suffer the pain and agony of false guilt," wrote Uno, "we accepted our experience as part of our Japanese American heritage, that part of our history which involved a struggle for survival against tremendous odds which would test the character and spirit of each of us."

Having passed that test, "the thrill of victory must be used to energize the next struggle," concluded Uno, who was among the first to push for an organized drive for redress and reparations for the victim's of America's concentration camps. Through the work of many individuals and groups, most notably the National Coalition for Redress and Reparations, Japanese American Citizens League and National Council for Japanese American Redress, Congress established in 1980 the Commission on Wartime Relocation and Internment of Civilians to ascertain the impact of the removal and detention program and to recommend appropriate remedies. The commission recommended, in 1983, that the government offer a formal apology to the victims and pay $20,000 to each of the 62,500 survivors. The legislation was enacted in 1988, and the first payments began in 1990.

The movement for redress and reparations, like other earlier civil rights efforts, linked young and old in their struggle for self and collective definition. Glen Kitayama recalled how the redress movement and his grandfather's stories about life in the concentration camps helped him to understand himself and his community. "I looked around the room," remembered Kitayama, "and I saw about 70 isseis and niseis fighting not only for monetary compensation, but also for justice and dignity. I started to think about my grandfather and my parents—and for

the first time, I felt like I was beginning to understand them as human beings." Yasuko Sakamoto described an elderly *issei* woman, whose "rounded shoulders seemed to express her own long history in the U.S.," at the news conference following President George Bush's signing of the bill authorizing reparations payments. "Thank you very much for your effort," the woman said to Sakamoto. "This happened because of your hard work."

That gratitude flows in both directions. A youthful poet, identified only as Jason, a student at Hawaii's Kalakaua Intermediate School, wrote the following poem titled "Baban, My Greatgrandma":

> My great grandma's skin
> is wrinkled very much.
> Like when you stay in the water
> for a great long time.
> When you get out of the water
> it clears up. But I know that
> hers will never fade.
> Sometimes she calls me in her
> room, she says pretty soon Baban
> die. I feel sad and I'm silent.
> She is so brave. She is the
> great sweet apple waiting to be
> eaten.

Reflecting on her life, Sadae Takizawa observed: "It is a joy to live for eighty-eight years. However, you can't help feeling lonely after all of your friends have died." But the *issei* pioneers left behind children, who in turn had children, and the stories told by the first migrants were passed on from generation to generation. "I believe children and grandchildren must know the way their grandparents walked," declared Osuke Takizawa. "You are a homeless dog without your identity," he noted. "Losing identity is the same as losing money: you lose your way of life."

In his evocative open letter to the *issei*, David Masumoto lamented the decline of the Del Rey, California, Japanese American farming community. "Even those born here," he wrote, "have grown distant and foreign," having forsaken "the dust and sweat and natural forces" for the enchantment of the cities. "How will I remember the scenes of your youth?" asked Masumoto of the first generation. "Time and death have thinned your ranks, you no longer occupy whole rows of tables at picnics or potlucks." Del Rey Hall, built by "skilled hands and strong backs" and the scene of community potlucks, *samurai* movies, and plays, stood for 60 years "like a monument to your belief in community." What will become of Del Rey? wondered Masumoto. "You, the *Issei,* will soon die and we shall follow. Yet perhaps even in your death you teach us all that change is part of our life and of Japanese culture? You, the *Issei,* have left us a history, a spirit that lives within our memories so long as we continue to ask and wonder."

"I am 91 years old. My own life! When I think about it, I can't believe that I'm all that age," exclaimed Tsuru Yamauchi. "Old-time people were really admirable beyond words. . . . They had to take their young children out to the fields in the dirt and lay them down on the blankets while they continued to work. . . . We never did think that women who came to Hawaii had to work that hard." Still, Yamauchi determined, "After 70 years I feel there's no better place than Hawaii. When we first came, we didn't think we could stay very long. But after all, the place one stays is the best. . . . Life is good here."

And indeed, life has been good for Japanese Americans. But life has also been harsh and unremitting, and the perils of absorption and exclusion, assimilation and segregation, model citizen and unfair competitor are persistent themes in the Japanese American story. Just as tenacious, however, is the theme of resistance, by which people who "didn't think we could stay very long" put down roots and through their effort made the alien and hostile land yield fruit. And Japanese Americans can say with Yamauchi that "life is good here," because we helped to make it so.

Sources

The poetry and *hole hole bushi* on the previous pages were published in: pp. 3, 6, 7, 9—Kazuo Ito, *Issei: A History of Japanese Immigrants in North America* (Seattle: Japanese Community Service, 1973), trans. Shinichiro Nakamura and Jean S. Gerard; p. 4—Franklin Odo, unpublished *hole hole bushi* to be included in a forthcoming book on *issei* literature; p. 4—Franklin S. Odo and Harry Minoru Urata, "Hole Hole Bushi: Songs of Hawaii's Japanese Immigrants," *Mana* (Hawaii ed.) 6, no. 1 (1981); p. 5—Ethnic Studies Oral History Project and United Okinawan Association of Hawaii, *Uchinanchu: A History of Okinawans in Hawaii* (Honolulu: University of Hawaii, Ethnic Studies Program, 1981); pp. 10, 14, 20—Jiro Nakano and Kay Nakano, eds., *Poets Behind Barbed Wire* (Honolulu: Bamboo Ridge Press, 1984); p. 17—Eileen Sunada Sarasohn, ed., *The Issei: Portrait of a Pioneer* (Palo Alto: Pacific Books, 1983); and p. 22—Eric Chock, ed., *small kid time hawaii* (Honolulu: Bamboo Ridge Press, 1981).

Bibliography

The following books, selected from among a wider selection of sources, contain the oral histories and reminiscences quoted in this essay.

Ethnic Studies Oral History Project and United Okinawan Association of Hawaii. *Uchinanchu: A History of Okinawans in Hawaii* (Honolulu: University of Hawaii, Ethnic Studies Program, 1981).

Dorothy Ochiai Hazama and Jane Okamoto Komeiji. *Okage Sama De: The Japanese in Hawai'i, 1885–1985* (Honolulu: Bess Press, 1986).

Kazuo Ito. *Issei: A History of Japanese Immigrants in North America* (Seattle: Japanese Community Service, 1973), trans. Shinichiro Nakamura and Jean S. Gerard.

Timothy J. Lukes and Gary Y. Okihiro. *Japanese Legacy: Farming and Community Life in California's Santa Clara Valley* (Cupertino: California History Center, 1985).

David Mas Masumoto. *Country Voices: The Oral History of a Japanese American Family Farm Community* (Del Rey, Calif.: Inaka Countryside Publications, 1987).

Gary Y. Okihiro. *Cane Fires: The Anti-Japanese Movement in Hawaii, 1865–1945* (Philadelphia: Temple University Press, 1991).

Eileen Sunada Sarasohn, ed. *The Issei: Portrait of a Pioneer* (Palo Alto, Calif.: Pacific Books, 1983).

John Tateishi, ed. *And Justice For All: An Oral History of the Japanese American Detention Camps* (New York: Random House, 1984).

INTRODUCTION TO THE CHRONOLOGY

The following is a detailed chronology of Japanese American history. Its purpose is twofold. First of all, it provides basic names, dates and synopses of major events in Japanese American history. If, for example, one wants to know the exact date the 442nd Regimental Combat Team was activated or the names of the Hawaii Seven, these details can be found here. Secondly, the chronology provides a glimpse of the major issues affecting the Japanese American community during a given period, at least for those that can be pegged to specific dates.

The chronology includes important events in the history of Japanese Americans as a whole and of Japanese Americans in a specific community. Important events that did not directly involve Japanese Americans but affected the Japanese American community are also included. For example, Japan's invasion of China in 1937 did not directly involve Japanese Americans, but did affect the actions of *issei* and *nisei*. Major events in American and world history are included in italics to provide a context for the Japanese American entries. Other entries in the chronology are included because they are interesting, even though they may be of limited importance to the community as a whole. No dates of birth or death for individuals mentioned in chronology entries are included unless the birth or death constitutes a major event in and of itself. Short citations below each entry give the source of the entry. "Daniels 77 (102)" means that the entry was taken from page 102 of Daniels's 1977 work. Complete citations for all works mentioned in the chronology are included at the end of this section. Short citations without a page number refer to a work devoted entirely to the event under discussion. Items in small capitals have entries in the dictionary section.

CHRONOLOGY OF JAPANESE AMERICAN HISTORY

1258 The first "recorded" shipwrecked Japanese sailors land at Makapuu Point on Oahu, Hawaii. Two such drifters land in 1258 and five more land in 1270 on Maui; they were said to be carrying sugar cane and to have introduced it to the islands. Although such early drifts are certainly possible, this particular date (cited in United 71 (5))—and the supposed introduction of sugar cane by the Japanese—can be traced to 1930s Japanese propaganda—the invention of such early contact serving to justify later Japanese claims to the islands. United 71 (5); Braden 76

1610–1613 A Japanese diplomatic party sails to America. According to Hata 78 (16–17), they merely sailed down the California coast and landed in Mexico in 1610, one decade before the Pilgrims landed at Plymouth rock. According to Hosokawa 69 (9), they landed at Acapulco in 1613 and a dozen stayed on there, becoming the first Japanese immigrants to North America.

1778 Captain James Cook "discovers" the Sandwich Islands—i.e., Hawaii. This first European contact would be followed by a dramatic shrinking of the native Hawaiian population due largely to the introduction of Western diseases. Estimated to be 300,000 at the time of European settlement, the native population stood at 71,019 when the first official census was taken in 1853. Lind 67 (16–17)

March 26, 1790 The U.S. Congress, through the act of 1790, decrees that "any alien, being a free white person who shall have resided within the limits and under the jurisdiction of the United States for a term of two years, may be admitted to become a citizen thereof." The phrase "free white person" remained intact until 1873 when "persons of African nativity or descent" was added. This act would be used to deny citizenship to Japanese and other Asian immigrants until the mid-20th century. (See CITIZENSHIP.) Chuman 76 (6)

September 1835 Twenty-six-year-old William Hooper of Ladd and Co., an American mercantile firm, establishes Hawaii's first successful sugar PLANTATION in Koloa, Kauai. This introduction of a market economy with wage labor would dramatically change Hawaii's history, serving as the "pull" for hundreds of thousands of immigrant laborers who would arrive in the next century. It would also further the destruction of native Hawaiian society and culture. Liu 85 (84–89); Takaki 83 (3–15)

November 11, 1841 Five shipwrecked Japanese sailors land in Hawaii. One of them is MANJIRO NAKAHAMA who goes on to the mainland; the other four stay on in Hawaii. One of them, Denzo Kuke, marries a Hawaiian woman and becomes a Hawaiian citizen. "Timeline of the Japanese in Hawaii." *Hawaii Herald,* 5 July 1985: A12–13

1848 Enacted under pressure from foreign interests, the Great Mahele ("Great Division") changes the system of land ownership in Hawaii. Where previously all lands were owned by the king, the Great Mahele distributed land to other sectors of the native population as well. In 1850, a new land law extended land ownership privileges to include foreigners. The next 40 years would see a massive transfer of land ownership to the HAOLES who were able to purchase land cheaply from chiefs eager to "get rich quick" and who used the courts to fleece land from many commoners. By 1890, three out of four privately held acres were owned by *haoles.* The Great Mahele was the step which led directly to the rise of the sugar PLANTATIONS in Hawaii. Liu 85 (89–91); Takaki 83 (17–18)

1850 The Masters and Servants Act of 1850, enacted under pressure from sugar growers, was an attempt to regulate native Hawaiian laborers. It allowed growers to commit a worker to their plantation for a fixed period (usually two years) and provided stiff penalties for desertion. Such regulations would also be applied to future plantation workers brought in from abroad in years to come.   Liu 85 (96–97); Okihiro 91 (15); United 71 (70)

July 8, 1853   Commodore Matthew Perry sails into Tokyo Bay with four heavily armed warships carrying a letter from President Fillmore of the United States demanding the opening of Japan to Western trade. He withdraws to Okinawa for the winter, promising to return for a reply the following spring.   Reischauer 74 (114–15); Sansom 49 (277); Walworth 66 (3)

February 1854   Commodore Perry returns to Japan with 10 armed ships. Having no real choice, the Japanese sign a treaty on March 31, 1854, opening the ports of Shimoda and Hakodate to American ships and allowing a limited amount of trade. Once open, there would be no stopping further incursion by the West—Japan would sign similar agreements with Great Britain, Russia and Holland within two years.   Reischauer 74 (115–16); Sansom 49 (278)

July 29, 1858   Japan signs a treaty with the United States on board the American warship *Powhatan* that grants the U.S. consular jurisdiction, low fixed tariffs and access to more ports, among other concessions. The treaty also has no fixed duration. This was the first of several unequal agreements Japan was forced to sign with Western nations. The renegotiation of these agreements was to be a Japanese preoccupation in the years to come.   Sansom 49 (290–91)

March 17, 1860   The *Kanrin Maru,* a small Japanese ship carrying the first Japanese diplomatic mission to the U.S., arrives in San Francisco. It would be followed 12 days later by the *Powhatan,* an American warship carrying a Japanese diplomatic mission that would continue on to Washington, D.C. where the party would meet with President James Buchanan. The *Kanrin Maru* served as a vanguard for the *Powhatan* expedition and left for Japan (via Hawaii) on May 8.   Hinkle 44; Miyoshi 79; Young 83

late 1860   A Sunday school for Japanese is established at Howard Presbyterian Church in San Francisco. The students study Christianity using a Chinese translation of the New Testament.   Yoshida 89 (160)

March 10, 1865   A letter from Robert Crichton Wyllie, Hawaii's foreign minister, to Japan-based American businessman Eugene M. Van Reed inquires about the possibility of Japanese laborers being brought to Hawaii to work on the sugar PLANTATIONS. "I myself could take 500 for my own estates," he writes. The

process leading to Japanese labor migration to Hawaii begins. (See GANNENMONO.)   Okihiro 91 (19)

August 1867   An interim amity agreement between Hawaii and Japan is signed. It contains no concrete provisions but provides for friendship and trade between the two countries.   United 71 (38)

January 3, 1868   A coup d'état in Kyoto results in the "restoration" of imperial rule in Japan. This will become known as the MEIJI RESTORATION.   Reischauer 74 (121)

May 17, 1868   The *Scioto* sets sail out of Yokohama for Hawaii, carrying 153 Japanese bound for employment on the sugar PLANTATIONS. These adventurers constitute the first mass emigration of Japanese overseas. They become known as the GANNENMONO.   United 71 (40)

May 27, 1869   The S.S. *China* arrives in San Francisco carrying the first emigrant party to the U.S. Led by John Henry Schnell, it would go on to establish the short-lived WAKAMATSU COLONY.   Hosokawa 69 (31–32)

August 17, 1869   Kagenori Uyeno is invested with the office of Japan's special envoy to Hawaii; he is specifically designated by the Japanese government to investigate the fate of the GANNENMONO amid allegations of mistreatment. (See UYENO EMBASSY.)   United 71 (54)

July 8, 1870   The first large anti-Oriental gathering in the United States takes place in San Francisco. A torchlight vigil through the city is followed by an evening of anti-Chinese speeches. A resolution calling for an end to Chinese immigration is adopted. Anti-Chinese sentiment would run high in California throughout the decade of the 1870s. Daniels 77 (16)

August 19, 1871   "A Treaty of Friendship and Commerce Between the Kingdom of Hawaii and the Empire of Japan" is signed. It offers hope to Hawaii that Japan will soon allow labor migration of its subjects to Hawaii. United 71 (71)

August 29, 1871   Feudal domains in Japan are completely abolished and replaced by PREFECTURES controlled by the Tokyo government.   Reischauer 74 (127)

January 15, 1872   The Iwakura Mission arrives in San Francisco. It is dispatched by the emperor in an attempt to renegotiate the unequal treaties Japan had been forced to sign with Western powers. Unfortunately for them, the time is not yet right for such a venture. Kim 86 (324–25)

1874   Doshisha University, the first Christian university in Japan, is founded in Kyoto. Many future Japanese Christian ministers in the United States would be trained at this institution.   United 71 (227)

1875   The United States and Hawaii conclude the Reciprocity Treaty, granting Hawaii the right to export sugar to the U.S. duty free. This results in huge profits for sugar growers in Hawaii and a great expansion of the sugar industry there, which in turn, leads to the need for more labor.   Takaki 83 (18–19)

February 18, 1875   Section 2169, Title XXX of the Act of February 18, 1875 states that the right of naturalization can be granted only to "free white persons and to aliens of African nativity and to persons of African descent." These words would be used over and over again to prevent ISSEI from gaining American citizenship. (See CITIZENSHIP.)   Naka 39 (30–31)

March 1876   The six Japanese businessmen known as the "Oceanic group" (from the name of the ship they sailed on) arrive by train in New York. Three of them—RYOICHIRO ARAI, TOYO MORIMURA and Momotaro Sato—settle in New York to become the first known New York *issei*.   Miyakawa 72 (157)

1877   The first two Japanese graduate from the U.S. Naval Academy at Annapolis. Japanese had been allowed admission at Annapolis since 1868 and at West Point since 1872. Annapolis graduate Sotokichi Uriu (class of 1881) would became a Japanese national hero for launching the raid on Russian warships in Chemulpo during the Russo-Japanese War.   Hata 78 (47)

October 6, 1877   The GOSPEL SOCIETY (Fukuin Kai) is formed by Methodist and Congregationalist student converts in San Francisco's Chinatown. KANICHI MIYAMA is the advocate of the 10-member group that meets every Saturday for Bible study and public speaking while Keizo Koyano is the first president. It is not only the first Japanese Christian group in the U.S., but perhaps the first Japanese American group of any kind.   Suzuki 79 (14–15); Ichioka 88 (16)

1879   TADAATSU MATSUDAIRA arrives in Colorado to work for the Union Pacific Railroad. He had recently graduated from Rutgers with an engineering degree and would go on to be named assistant to Colorado's chief inspector of mines in 1886. Matsudaira may have been the first Japanese to arrive in Colorado.   Endo 85 (101)

1880   Captain Andrew McKinnon settles in Gresham and opens the Orient (saw) Mill; his wife, Miyo Iwakoshi, is the first Japanese to settle in Oregon.   Pursinger 66 (252)

February 1880   The Yokohama Specie Bank is established in Yokohama as a foreign exchange bank. One-third of its initial capitalization is provided by the Meiji government. It would go on to play a major role in the lives of the emigrant Japanese.   Yagasaki 82 (244)

March 4, 1881   Hawaiian king Kalakaua arrives in Japan for a visit to secure improved relations between the countries. (See KING KALAKAUA'S VISIT.)   United 71 (74)

May 6, 1882   U.S. Congress passes the CHINESE EXCLUSION ACT OF *1882 over the veto of President Garfield. Chinese immigration would be essentially shut off for the next 60 years.*   Schlesinger 83 (349)

November 10, 1882   John Makini Kapena is sent by the Hawaiian government to Japan to press for the allowing of labor migration to Hawaii.   United 71 (84)

October 18, 1883   Thirty-seven Japanese divers leave Japan for Thursday Island in Australia under three-year labor contracts. This case marks the first time that permission is granted to overseas requests for Japanese labor.   Moriyama 85 (9); United 71 (84)

early 1884   Hawaiian special envoy Curtis P. Iaukea arrives in Japan with a new emigration proposal for the importation of Japanese workers to Hawaii on a regular basis. Japan begins to indicate that it may accept the concept of labor migration if strictly regulated. Moriyama 85 (9–10); United 71 (86–87)

September 1884   Hawaiian consul ROBERT W. IRWIN returns to Japan with a labor contract proposal that will be approved by the Japanese government. Recruitment for laborers can begin.   United 71 (89)

December 1884   Recruitment begins; "Information Regarding Emigration" is distributed throughout Japan. Twenty-eight thousand applications are received to fill 600 emigrant slots. The Japanese government ends up selecting a total of 945 to make up the first contingent to Hawaii, of which 420 are from Yamaguchi PREFECTURE. In addition to 676 males, 150 females and 110 children are included in the selected group.   Takaki 83 (43); United 71 (90)

February 8, 1885   The *City of Tokio* arrives in Honolulu carrying the first 944 official migrants from Japan to Hawaii. [The number of passengers varies in different accounts depending on whether government officials are included in the count.] (See KANYAKU IMIN.)   Kotani 85 (9–11); Odo/Sinoto 85 (39); Takaki 83 (43–44); United 71 (94)

March 1885   Two small strikes occur one month after arrival—at Paia on Maui and at Papaikou on Hawaii. The Paia strike is spurred by the plantation's refusal to punish a brutish Hawaiian ox-tender. The workers are each fined $5 plus court costs of $1. The Papaikou strike centered around the lack of overtime pay.   Odo/Sinoto 85 (195–96); United 71 (99–100)

May 16, 1885   The First Japanese Presbyterian Church of San Francisco (Dai-ichi Nihonjin Choro Kyokai) is organized by 33 members of the Golden Gate Gospel Society. This latter group had been formed by Congregationalists who split off from the GOSPEL SOCIETY in 1881 and 1883. The Golden Gate Gospel Society was dissolved in Aug. 1886 and a Japanese YMCA was organized in its place under the guidance of Dr. ERNEST A. STURGE.   Ichioka 88 (17); Yoshida 89 (171–72)

June 17, 1885   The second group of Japanese labor migrants arrives in Hawaii on the *Yamashiro Maru* along with Japanese Special Commissioner Katsunosuke Inouye. Inouye comes for the purpose of checking on the numerous complaints of Japanese laborers. He threatens to take back the 988 would-be immigrants if their rights can't be protected. On July 21, a protocol is signed by Special Commissioner Inouye and Hawaii's Foreign Minister Gibson ostensibly to protect the rights of Japanese immigrant workers. (See IMMIGRATION CONVENTION OF 1886.)   United 71 (100)

August 22, 1885   The Japanese newspaper *Bocho Shimbun* reports that the *Yamashiro Maru* returned to Japan with 8,000 yen in remittances sent back by the first group of laborers to relatives in Japan after only a few months of work. Despite the meager wages they receive, the laborers would continue to remit large sums of money back to Japan. (See REMITTANCES TO JAPAN.)   United 71 (211)

September 2, 1885   Rioters attack and set fire to the Chinatown in Rock Springs, Wyoming, killing 28 Chinese miners and wounding 15. Several hundred others are driven out of town and an estimated $148,000 worth of goods are destroyed. The "Rock Springs Massacre" resulted from anti-Chinese sentiment over their role as cheap labor and as strikebreakers. Although 16 white suspects were arrested and tried, all were acquitted. (See ANTI-CHINESE MOVEMENT.)   Tsurutani 89 (23–24)

1886   Aikawa Shiga publishes the *Shinonome Zasshi*, believed to be the first Japanese American newspaper, in San Francisco. Six copies of the paper were found in 1984. Aikawa returned to Japan in 1914. (See NEWSPAPERS.)   "Copies of First Nikkei Newspaper Found." *Rafu Shimpo,* 28 Aug. 1984: 1.

1886   HIROSHI YOSHIIKE begins growing chrysanthemums commercially in Oakland. He is the first Japanese flower grower in northern California.   Yagasaki 82 (39)

January 28, 1886   After suspending emigration for a time, Japan reaches an agreement with Hawaii, and the IMMIGRATION CONVENTION OF 1886 is signed. This agreement was to protect laborers from abuse and even granted them the right to vote. However, its provisions were abrogated by the Bayonet Convention of 1887. Odo/Sinoto 85 (22–26); United 71 (131)

February 14, 1886   The third immigration vessel from Japan, the *City of Peking,* arrives in Honolulu with 927 people, including new consul general Taro Ando. United 71 (104)

1886   Fifty Japanese laborers at Koloa Plantation refuse to work, citing a myriad of complaints including bad working conditions, irregular pay and being forced to work when sick. They are swiftly jailed. Taro Ando, Japanese consul general, and JOJI NAKAYAMA, the immigration bureau's chief inspector of Japanese immigrants, scold the laborers and implore them to return to work.   Kotani 85 (34)

June 1886   A San Francisco agency of the Yokohama Specie Bank is established in the Phelan Building on Market Street.   Yagasaki 82 (244–46)

September 1886   The Japanese Methodist Episcopal Mission on the Pacific Coast is organized under superintendent Reverend M. C. Harris. Spectacular growth follows: from 90 members in 1887 to 200 in 1891, to 733—with 650 petitioners, 21 Japanese pastors and a network of four other churches and a Women's Home—by 1894.   Ichioka 88 (18–19)

1887   Kohei Tanaka arrives in San Diego to work at the Hotel del Coronado manufacturing Japanese-style

Contract laborers landing from the S.S. *Miike Maru*, May 1893. The years 1885–1894 marked the period of official government-sponsored labor migration from Japan to Hawaii, resulting in some 29,000 *issei* arriving in the Islands.   *Hawaii State Archives*

charcoal. He is said to be the first ISSEI to settle in San Diego. Later that year, the first Japanese business, the Go Ban at 1065 5th, is opened by proprietor Azumagasaki Kikumatsu.   Estes 78 (426)

Summer 1887   A party of 30 people organized by Kakugoro Inoue arrives in San Francisco with hopes of starting an agricultural colony in California. Financed by YUKICHI FUKUZAWA, the group buys 20 acres of land in Calaveras County. The venture is short lived. Ichioka 88 (10)

July 6, 1887   The Bayonet Constitution is forced on King Kalakaua of Hawaii by HAOLE rebels. Among the results of this action is the abolition of citizenship for Asian immigrants, abrogating one of the key provisions of the IMMIGRATION CONVENTION OF 1886.   "Timeline of the Japanese in Hawaii." *Hawaii Herald,* 5 July 1985: A12–13

September 1887   The IMMIGRATION CONVENTION OF 1886 is further revised so that laborers now have to pay for both their own passage and their own inspectors. United 71 (106)

October 10, 1887   In Hawaii, Reverend KANICHI MIYAMA organizes the Mutual Assistance Society—later to become the Japanese Benevolent Society. Miyama begins a campaign to bring Christianity to the Japanese plantation workers. Though he succeeds in converting

Japanese consul general Taro Ando among others, he is not successful with the vast majority of plantation workers.   Ogawa 78 (46–47); United 71 (228, 236)

January 7, 1888   Exiles from the Japanese People's Rights Movement form the PATRIOTIC LEAGUE in San Francisco. Escaping from political persecution in Japan, the group seeks to continue their movement here and keeps in touch with compatriots in Japan. They publish a weekly from 1888–93 under various titles, starting with *Dai-Jukyu Seiki* (19th century); it is repeatedly banned by the Meiji government.   Ichioka 88 (16, 19)

1889   Shintaro Takaki opens the first Japanese business in Oregon, a restaurant in Portland.   Pursinger 66 (252)

February 11, 1889   *The Japanese Constitution is promulgated as a gift from the emperor to the people.*   Reischauer 74 (142)

March 2, 1889   Jodo-Shinshu priest Soryu Kagai arrives in Honolulu to survey the situation on the islands. Though he reports back to Japan that a Hawaiian mission is needed, the first Buddhist temple would not be built there until 1894.   Odo/Sinoto 85 (77); Ogawa 78 (50); "Timeline of the Japanese in Hawaii." *Hawaii Herald,* 5 July 1985: A12–13

October 29, 1889   KATSU GOTO is lynched in Hawaii. A prominent merchant and interpreter, Goto is killed by those who do not like the advocacy work he performs on behalf of Japanese plantation workers. Kotani 85 (33–34); Odo 85 (164)

1890 The McKinley Tariff nullifies the two-cent-per-pound benefit to Hawaii sugar planters granted underthe Reciprocity Act. The planters' increased costs lead to attempts to lower wages for plantation workers. United 71 (107)

1890 One hundred seventy workers strike for better conditions at Heeia on Oahu. Three representatives walk to Honolulu to take matters up with the consulate and the Immigration Bureau. When Immigration Bureau director JOJI NAKAYAMA meets them, he reportedly throws their petition on the floor and berates them for complaining. When all the men threaten to go back to Japan, however, their demands are met. United 71 (125–26); Kotani 85 (34)

January 1890 The San Francisco consul reports the first "official" Japanese prostitutes in America. Japanese prostitutes may have been in San Francisco as early as the 1860s. (See PROSTITUTES.) Ichioka 77a (2–3)

February 1890 A shoemaking operation started by Tsunetaro Jo and Tadayoshi Sekine is forced out of business by the Boot and Shoemakers' White Labor League. They organize the *Nihonjin Kutsuko Domeikai* (Japanese Shoemakers' League) in response and turn to shoe repairing to avoid competing with the white shoemakers. Ichioka 88 (94)

October 30, 1890 In Japan, the Imperial Rescript of Education is promulgated. The document sets forth ethical principles governing education and represents a rejection of Western values in favor of traditional values. The principles of the imperial rescript would be adopted by many JAPANESE-LANGUAGE SCHOOLS in the United States, to the alarm of anti-Japanese activists and to the chagrin of many NISEI. Taylor 84 (31)

1891 Shokko Giyukai (Friends of Labor) is formed in San Francisco by FUSATARO TAKANO, Hannosuke Sawada, Tsunetaro Jo and others, under the influence of the American Federation of Labor. Takano would correspond with AFL president Samuel Gompers from 1894 to 1898, probably with the goal of organizing workers in Japan. The existence of such a group belies claims by the exclusionists that Japanese workers were ignorant about matters of labor organization. Ichioka 88 (92–93)

1891 The Greater Japanese Association, the first such organization, is formed in San Francisco by SUTEMI

CHINDA, the Japanese consul from 1890–94. (See JAPANESE ASSOCIATIONS.) Ichioka 77c (411)

May 1891 Fearful of any activity that might precipitate exclusion like that imposed on Chinese, the Greater Japanese Association asks the Japanese foreign ministry to stop the emigration of prostitutes. (See PROSTITUTES.) Ichioka 77a (16)

October 1891 Chushichi Tanaka uses his "influence" as a pimp to become the first Japanese railroad LABOR CONTRACTOR in the United States in Nampa, ID. The first labor contractor in California and Nevada is Genji Hasegawa, also a noted pimp. (See PROSTITUTES.) Ichioka 77a (11–12)

December 1891 Wages paid to Japanese laborers in Hawaii are reduced to $12.50 per month. Under increasing financial pressure, planters attempt to lower wages further to $10 in 1892, but have the notion rejected by the Japanese government. United 71 (107)

December 1891 The Nihon Yoshisha Emigration Company is formed as a partnership between prominent businessmen Yasujiro Yoshikawa and Teiichi Sakuma. It is the first of many such companies that ship labor abroad for profit. (See EMIGRATION COMPANIES.) Ichioka 88 (47)

1892 PATRIOTIC LEAGUE members Masao Yamato, Tokuji Watari, Tsutao Sugawara and others publish the first daily Japanese American newspaper. Initially titled *Soko Shimbun* (San Francisco News), it becomes *Soko Shimpo* (San Francisco Daily) in 1893 and *Soko Jiji* (San Francisco Times) in 1895 before bowing out in 1897. A second daily, the *Kimmon Nippo* (Golden Gate Daily), is published 1893–95. (See NEWSPAPERS.) Ichioka 88 (20)

January 1, 1892 Ellis Island opens. The "Gateway to America" for European immigrants would see the entry of over 20 million people in the next 50 years. Schlesinger 83 (373)

early 1892 Sotaro Endo pioneers floriculture in Southern California when he begins growing garden plants, carnations and violets on a leased lot at the corner of South Main and West Jefferson in Los Angeles. Yagasaki 82 (106)

January 1892 A Caucasian field boss in Hawaii shoots Ihei Higashi in the leg for no apparent reason. His coworkers take the case to court where the offender is given six months in jail. He appeals to a superior court and is acquitted amidst charges of bribery. An out-of-court settlement is eventually reached.   United 71 (125)

January 18, 1892 In the first case involving a Japanese person decided by the United States Supreme Court, the Court upholds the decision of the California immigration commissioner to deny Ekiu Nishimura entry to the U.S. on the basis of a Congressional Act of March 3, 1891. This act allowed officials to deny entry to "a person without visible means of support, without relatives or friends in the United States, and a person unable to care for herself, and liable to become a public charge." In upholding Nishimura's exclusion, the Court upholds the right of an immigration inspector to arbitrarily deny entry to immigrants under the provisions of this act. (See NISHIMURA V. UNITED STATES.)   Chuman 76 (12–14)

May 1892 Led by the *Morning Call,* the *San Francisco Examiner* and the *San Francisco Bulletin,* the first ANTI-JAPANESE MOVEMENT begins. It culminates in the San Francisco Board of Education resolution of June 10, 1893, relegating Japanese students to the segregated Chinese school. After intervention by the Japanese consul, the resolution is soon rescinded, ending this early chapter of anti-Japanese agitation.   Hata 78 (132–45)

May 1892 San Francisco brothel owner Genji Hasegawa supplies 70 to 80 laborers to the Southern Pacific to become the first known LABOR CONTRACTOR in California. It is said that Consul CHINDA SUTEMI persuaded him to abandon prostitution for legitimate business. Ichioka 88 (59, 62)

June 3, 1892 The *Nippon Shuho* becomes the first Japanese newspaper in Hawaii. It was started by ex-immigration inspector Bunichiro Onome as a vehicle to criticize the U.S. Bureau of Immigration for its treatment of the Japanese. (See NEWSPAPERS.)   Odo/Sinoto 85 (145); United 71 (231)

August 1892 The Yokohama Specie Bank opens a branch in Hawaii. This branch handles remittances to Japan from ISSEI in Hawaii. By 1941, it had $3,124,000 in savings.   United 71 (211, 213)

1893 The first permanent Japanese settlement in Chicago is said to have been established at around the time of the Columbian Exposition of 1893.   Albert 80 (110)

January 17, 1893 The Hawaiian monarchy falls. To protect the interests of the 25,000 Japanese laborers in Hawaii, the Japanese warship *Naniwa* is dispatched to

the islands, arriving on February 23. It returned to Japan in May, satisfied that all was in order.   United 71 (130)

June 1893 Two hundred fifty Japanese workers leave their plantation at Kukuihaele to protest an incident in which a LUNA shot and wounded a Japanese field hand. Fuchs 61 (113)

1894 The labor convention of January 28, 1886, comes to an end. From this point on, the Japanese government stops sponsoring immigration to Hawaii and private EMIGRATION COMPANIES take over.   Moriyama 85 (30)

1894 Gakuo Okabe of the Jodoshu establishes the first Buddhist temple in Hawaii in the plantation town of Hamakua on the island of Hawaii. The Jodo-shinshu sect, destined to become the most important to Japanese immigrants, would establish its first mission in 1897. Odo/Sinoto 85 (77–78); United 71 (229)

1894 Japanese workers at H. P. Faye's plantation at Mana, Kauai, strike after an assault by a LUNA on a laborer. Eighty-nine strikers are arrested and sentenced to hard labor.   Kotani 85 (33)

1894 The *Hawaii Shimpo* begins publication as a weekly under the management of Chusaburo Shiozawa. It will last to 1922, undergoing several changes of name and ideology in the interim.   United 71 (232)

1894 The Wilson Gormann Tariff restores Hawaii's preferential treatment in the supply of sugar to the U.S. This preferential treatment had been terminated by the McKinley Tariff of 1890.   United 71 (138)

January 1894 A LUNA named Schimmelpfennig beats a Japanese laborer at Koloa in Hawaii; a mob of Japanese workers chase him through the streets and refuse to work until the case is laid before the Japanese consul. Fuchs 61 (113)

March 1894 In an effort to restrict further immigration from Japan, the Hawaiian government passes a law requiring all free Japanese (i.e., non contract) immigrants to possess $50 and "visible means of support" before being allowed to land. Many get around this law by borrowing the $50 from EMIGRATION COMPANIES. United 71 (138)

April 12, 1894 The Japanese government issues the Imin hogokisoku or the Emigrant Protection Ordinance. It becomes law on April 29, 1896, and takes effect on June 1 in more detailed form. This law regulates the EMIGRATION COMPANIES and allows the government to maintain control of essential parts of the emigration process.   Moriyama 85 (33); Ichioka 88 (47–48)

May 25, 1894   The SHIN SEKAI (New World) appears. Destined to become one of the two major ISSEI papers along with the NICHIBEI SHIMBUN, it is launched as a San Francisco Japanese YMCA house organ. Chief editor Hachiro Soejima ends the paper's association with the YMCA in 1897.   Ichioka 88 (20)

June 27, 1894   In the first ISSEI naturalization case to reach the U.S. district court level, it is decided that an *issei* named Saito not be allowed citizenship because he is literally not a "free white person" as the naturalization act of 1790 requires. (See CITIZENSHIP.) Chuman 76 (6–7)

November 22, 1894   A Treaty of Commerce and Navigation between Japan and the U.S. is signed and later proclaimed on March 21, 1895. It does not go into effect until July 17, 1899. The language of the treaty guarantees Japanese in the United States "full and perfect protection for their persons and property." The spirit of the agreement is soon undetermined. (See TREATY OF COMMERCE AND NAVIGATION OF 1894 BETWEEN JAPAN AND THE UNITED STATES.)   Chuman 76 (14, 16, 25)

November 23, 1894   Over 200 laborers march from Kahuku to Honolulu to protest the beating of a worker by a ruthless LUNA. The 38-mile march takes all day, the workers reaching Honolulu around midnight. Upon presenting their grievances to Goro Narita, the Japanese chargé d'affaires to Hawaii, they are arrested, fined and forced to walk back to the plantation.   Takaki 83 (148); Kotani 85 (33)

April 17, 1895   The Treaty of Shimonoseki ends the Sino-Japanese War. The war had begun on August 1, 1894 in Korea. China cedes Taiwan, the Pescadores Islands, the Liaotung Peninsula in Manchuria and, in effect, Korea to Japan.   Reischauer 74 (373)

May 1895   The Kula Japanese School is founded in Maui by merchant Seiji Fukuda with teacher Tamaki Gomi. It is the first language school on the islands. (See JAPANESE LANGUAGE SCHOOLS.)   Odo/Sinoto 85 (127–28)

October 15, 1895   *The Yamato* debuts in Hawaii as a mimeographed, semiweekly newspaper, begun by Shintaro Anno and Hamon Mizuno. It became the *Yamato-Shimbun* in 1896 and the NIPPU JIJI in 1906. Odo/Sinoto 85 (146)

1896   A branch of the KEIHIN BANK is opened in Honolulu. The bank is said to be ruthless in its collection of loans advanced to the emigrants and of insurance premiums and that legal action against the defaulter's Japanese guarantors takes place often. Resentment against the Keihin Bank eventually leads to the formation of the JAPANESE REFORM ASSOCIATION in 1905.   United 71 (142–43)

1896   Two hundred railroad workers strike against contractors W. H. Remington and Hifumi Kumamoto in the Pacific Northwest. A 10-cent wage hike results, but the strike leaders are dismissed.   Ichioka 80b (344)

April 6, 1896   Rev. TAKIE OKUMURA opens a small language school in Honolulu with Hido Kuwahara as the teacher. It is the second language school on the islands.   B. Smith 48 (108); Odo/Sinoto 85 (128)

May 6, 1896   The U.S. Supreme Court upholds the "separate but equal" concept in its decision on Plessy v. Ferguson. *The decision would effectively legalize restrictive "Jim Crow" laws for nearly 60 years.*   Schlesinger 83 (382)

June 1896   The Republic of Hawaii legislature approves the SAKE BILL (officially, "An Act to Increase the Duty on Liquors, Still Wines and Other Beverages Made from Materials Other Than Grape Juice") over President Dole's veto. This law applies an almost prohibitive duty on sake (Japanese rice wine) imports. Eventually, immigrants would brew sake locally.   Conroy 78 (121–23)

August 1896   Japanese field hands in Hawaii rough up LUNA Charles K. Fardin after he attempts to unjustly dock a worker's wages at Paia. Four are arrested as a result of this incident.   Fuchs 61 (114)

September 1, 1896   Rev. TAKIE OKUMURA opens a Japanese vocational school in Honolulu to teach men how to cook and women how to sew. Sixty students enroll.   Odo/Sinoto 85 (154)

March 10, 1897   A shipload of would-be immigrants on the *Shinshu Maru* are denied permission to enter Hawaii. Two other ships from Japan receive the same reception. Along with the SAKE BILL, this "immigrant rejection" was a manifestation of anti-Japanese fears in Hawaii and a gentle push towards annexation of Hawaii by the United States. (See IMMIGRANT REJECTION OF 1897.)   Conroy 78 (125–30); United 71 (139)

July 14, 1897   The first news of the great Klondike strike reaches San Francisco with the arrival there of $750,000 in *gold. In the next three years, some 100,000 persons—including many* ISSEI *—would head to Alaska.*   Kanazawa 89; Schlesinger 83 (387)

November 1897 After a LUNA breaks the arm of a Japanese worker at Ewa plantation, Japanese workers strike. They march through the night to Honolulu where they are turned back. Their leaders are arrested and fined $3 each.   Fuchs 61 (114)

December 1897 *Rodo Sekai* (Labor World), Japan's first labor journal, begins publication with SEN KATAYAMA as its editor.   Ichioka 71 (2)

1898 Tetsuo Takahashi and Ototaka Yamaoka form the ORIENTAL TRADING COMPANY of Seattle (Matajiro Tsukuno becomes the third partner in 1899). The contracting company supplies laborers for the Great Northern and the Northern Pacific railroads (1904, 1906–07). It becomes the largest of all LABOR CONTRACTORS on the mainland, with some 2,500 to 3,000 workers at its peak.   Ichioka 80b (330); Ichioka 88 (58)

1898 The first Shinto shrine in Hawaii is erected in Hilo to honor Amaterasu Omi Kami (the Sun Goddess). A similar shrine is built in Honolulu in 1905.   United 71 (229)

1898 *In its decision on the case* U.S. V. WONG KIM ARK, *the United States Supreme Court affirms the citizenship of an American-born Chinese American under the Fourteenth Amendment. This case would serve as a precedent to future attempts to strip* NISEI *of their citizenship.*   Chuman 76 (183–84)

March 3, 1898 The Rose Hotel, the first Japanese boardinghouse in Los Angeles, is opened by Sanjuro Mizuno to accommodate Japanese railroad workers. Hosokawa 69 (120)

April 1898 W. H. Remington and Hifumi Kumamoto found the Tacoma Construction and Maintenance Company. This contracting firm would supply laborers to the Northern Pacific (1898–1903, 1905) and the Oregon Short Line railroads and eventually become one of the three major contractors in the Pacific Northwest. Ichioka 80b (329); Ichioka 88 (58)

April 24, 1898 *Spain declares war on the United States. The Spanish American War would end on December 10, 1898, with the signing of the Treaty of Paris, which, among other things, ceded the Philippines, Puerto Rico and Guam to the U.S.*   Schlesinger 83 (389, 393)

July 1898 Led by Honpa Hongwanji ministers Eryu Honda and Ejun Miyamoto, the Bukkyo Seinenkai (Young Men's Buddhist Association) is founded in San Francisco.   Yoshida 89 (123)

July 7, 1898 The annexation of Hawaii by the United States is completed with the signing of the Newlands Resolution. The official transfer of sovereignty takes place on August 12 at an "Annexation Day" ceremony in Honolulu.   Conroy 78 (138); Odo/Sinoto 85 (206); United 71 (135)

July 26, 1898 The first group of approximately 100 emigrants from Fukushima PREFECTURE arrive in Hawaii accompanied by Dr. Tomizo Katsunuma, a veterinarian who had played a key role in recruiting them. Eventually, some 10,000 Fukushimans would come to Hawaii, though a third went on to the mainland and another third would return to Japan.   Kimura 88 (33)

October 1898 The Shakaishugi Kenkyu Kai (Society for the Study of Socialism) is formed. Five of the original 12 members would go on to play a role among ISSEI socialists in America: KIYOSHI KAWAKAMI, SEN KATAYAMA, Isao Abe, Kiichi Kaneko and Shusui Kotoku. Ichioka 71 (2)

1899 The Nichibei Kinyusha (Japanese-American Financial Company) is the first financial institution to be established by local Japanese in San Francisco. It goes on to become the Nichibei Ginko (Japanese-American Bank) in 1903.   Yagasaki 82 (253)

1899 Gorokichi Nakasuji builds a new fishing boat specially designed to catch tuna in Hawaiian waters. The 32-foot-long boat is only 5.8 feet wide and allows Japanese fishermen to greatly expand their range of operations. As a result of this innovation, the tuna market sees prices drop from around $2.00 per fish to 25¢ to 50¢ per fish. Nakasuji is later credited with the installation of gasoline engines in his boats.   United 71 (207–08)

April 3, 1899 Two existing dailies, the *Soko Nihon Shimbun* (San Francisco Japan News) and the *Hokubei Nippo* (North American Daily) merge to form the NICHIBEI SHIMBUN (Japanese American News). Under the leadership of founder KYUTARO ABIKO, it would become the most influential and widely read ISSEI paper. Matsumoto 85 (14); Ichioka 88 (20–21)

September 1, 1899 Nishi Hongwanji leaders in Japan send two Buddhist missionaries—Shuyei Sonoda and Kukuryo Nishijima—to San Francisco. Their arrival on this date marks the founding of the Hokubei Bukkyo

Women were a vital part of the plantation labor force in Hawaii from the beginning, performing both agricultural and domestic tasks. *Hawaii State Archives*

Dan or North American Buddhist Mission (NABM). The NABM would become the BUDDHIST CHURCHES OF AMERICA (BCA) in 1944.   Hosokawa 69 (130); Kashima 77 (6–7, 15)

January 8, 1900   The first 27 men from Okinawa PREFECTURE arrive in Hawaii on the S.S. *City of China*. They left Naha on Dec. 5, arrived in Osaka on Dec. 13, and set sail from Yokohama on Dec. 30. Their emigration was arranged by KYUZO TOYAMA, known as the "Father of Okinawan Overseas Emigration." They are taken to the Ewa Plantation where they encounter prejudice from the NAICHI in addition to the usual plantation rigors.   Ishikawa 81 (81); Kimura 88 (49–50)

January 20, 1900   The Great Chinatown Fire razes downtown Honolulu, rendering 6,000 homeless. Of these, 3,500 are Japanese. One hundred seventy-six Japanese establishments are destroyed. The fire starts when the government-sponsored burning of a dwelling of a bubonic plague victim (apparently a standard practice at the time) gets out of control. The Japanese community eventually files claims with the territorial government for over $600,000 in damages and receives about half that amount.   Odo/Sinoto 85 (156); United 71 (156–57)

March 12, 1900   The Honolulu Nipponjin Shoin Doshikai (Honolulu Japanese Merchants Association) is formed by 37 ISSEI merchants to aid victims of the Great Chinatown Fire. The organization is the forerunner of the Honolulu Japanese Chamber of Commerce. "Timeline of the Japanese in Hawaii." *Hawaii Herald,* 5 July 1985: A12–13

April 4, 1900   Japanese workers at the Pioneer Mill in Lahaina, Maui strike over the deaths of three mill hands, virtually seizing control of the plantation and the town. The strike results in major concessions. Other successful strikes on Maui take place at about the same time at Olowalu Plantation and Spreckelsville Plantation. Takaki 83 (148–49)

April 30, 1900   The Organic Act is signed by President William McKinley. This act incorporates Hawaii as a territory of the United States. As a territory, contract labor was no longer legal in Hawaii once the act went into effect on June 14. As a result, over 20 major strikes took place within a month. Over 8,000 laborers participated in these strikes, which called for, among other things, higher wages, reduced work hours and the hiring of Japanese overseers.   Odo/Sinoto 85 (196); Takaki 83 (149)

May 7, 1900   In San Francisco, the first large-scale anti-Japanese protest in California takes place. Organized by various local labor groups, it may have been instigated by the Sailor's Union. The major political speaker at the gathering is JAMES D. PHELAN, mayor of San Francisco. This burst of anti-Japanese activity is brought about by forces seeking a renewal of the CHINESE EXCLUSION ACT OF 1882. Daniels 77 (21)

May 19, 1900   Upon discovery of a bubonic plague victim in Chinatown, a compulsory inoculation order is issued to all Japanese and Chinese in San Francisco. Ichioka 77c (412)

May 31, 1900   Spurred by the inoculation order of May 19 and the first public anti-Japanese meeting of May 7, the Japanese Deliberative Council of America is formed in San Francisco. This is the immediate precursor of the JAPANESE ASSOCIATION of America.   Ichioka 77c (412)

July 15, 1900   The main facilities of the Japanese Benevolent Society's Japanese Charity Hospital are completed in the Kapalama district in Honolulu. This hospital later merges with the Japanese Hospital in Liliha and eventually becomes Kuakini Hospital. (See JAPANESE HOSPITALS.)   Odo/Sinoto 85 (100); United 71 (236–38)

August 2, 1900   In response to the growing anti-Japanese feeling, the Japanese Foreign Ministry stops issuing passports to male or female laborers headed for the U.S. or Canada.   Ichioka 80a (343)

November 23, 1900   Forty-three Japanese and Portuguese women field hands at the Kilauea Plantation strike for higher wages. The strike ends on December 3 and results in a wage increase from $8 to $10 per month. This is one of two 1900 strikes in Hawaii to involve inter-ethnic cooperation.   Takaki 83 (149–50); Odo/Sinoto 85 (196)

1901   The first Japanese baseball team in Hawaii is organized by Reverend TAKIE OKUMURA; many others soon follow. Okumura's team is made up of students from his boarding school and is called "JBS"; the team becomes "Excelsior" in 1904.   Odo/Sinoto 85 (78–79)

1901   Reverend TAKIE OKUMURA starts the newspaper *Honolulu Shimbun*. It becomes the daily *Hawaii Nichi Nichi Shimbun* in 1903 and lasts until 1914.   United 71 (233)

November 25, 1901   In a petition signed by every major Japanese contractor in the United States, an appeal is made to the Japanese Foreign Ministry to lift the ban on laborers.   Ichioka 80b (332)

1902   In San Francisco, the Japanese Boardinghouse Keepers Association is formed. This group works to recruit laborers from Hawaii for local labor contractors. Ichioka 80b (333)

April 8, 1902   The new three-story Fresno Buddhist Church building is dedicated. The church was founded on Jan. 28, 1900, the day ISSEI in Fresno, California, organized a Young Buddhist Association branch. This building burned down in 1919 and was replaced by a concrete structure.   Hata, Akira. "Church Observes 62nd Anniversary." *Rafu Shimpo*, 20 Dec. 1961: II, 19–20.

May 19, 1902   Queen Liliuokalani of Hawaii attends a Buddhist service commemorating the birthday of Saint Shinran, the founder of the Hongwanji sect. Orchestrated by Reverend YEMYO IMAMURA, the queen's visit receives wide press coverage in Japan and serves to increase the self-respect of Buddhist believers.   Kimura 88 (155)

June 1902   The Japanese Government relaxes its August 1900 restrictions to allow former laborers in the United States to return. Wives and family members of U.S. residents are also allowed passage.   Ichioka 80b (327)

1903   Reverend Shozui Wakabayashi opens the first Japanese Buddhist church in Portland. He later starts the area's first Japanese-language school.   Yasui 75 (233)

Feb. 11, 1903   Five hundred Japanese and 200 Mexican workers form the Japanese-Mexican Labor Association, with Kozaburo Baba as president. In addition to serving as an example of inter-ethnic unity, this organization tests organized labor's Asian exclusion stance. (See 1903 OXNARD STRIKE.)   Almaguer 84; Ichioka 88 (96–97)

March 1903   The Executive Committee of the Republican Territorial Central Committee passes a resolution stating that Asians should not be employed on public works in Hawaii since they are so badly needed on the plantations. Fears caused by the influx of Japanese plantation workers to the city lead to the resolution. Fuchs 61 (209)

April 1903   The first issue of the RAFU SHIMPO is published in Los Angeles. The paper eventually grows to become the largest Japanese American daily newspaper.   K. Hayashi 87; "Story of Rafu Shimpo: Road to an Achievement." *Rafu Shimpo*, 14 Mar. 1970: B1+.

April 4, 1903   KYUZO TOYAMA accompanies 35 men from Okinawa who land in Honolulu aboard the *S.S. Hong Kong Maru*. Along with five others who arrive within three months, this group becomes known as the "Shijunin-gumi" (Forty men company). This second group would trigger a large increase in Okinawan immigrants in the next few years.   Ishikawa 81 (81); Kimura 88 (52)

April 6, 1903   The U.S. Supreme Court rules that Kaoru Yamataya, a Japanese woman who had arrived in Seattle on July 11, 1901, was lawfully excluded by immigration officials as a person "likely to become a public charge." This decision differs from that of Ekiu NISHIMURA V. U.S. only in that the person seeking entry is at least entitled to "due process of law." (See YAMATAYA V. FISHER.)   Chuman 76 (16–17)

November 1903   Hawaii-based consul Miki Saito organizes the Central Japanese League. It initially gains "wide acceptance" by the Japanese in Hawaii but loses it by supporting the planters in the 1904 Waipahu Strike. Many of its directors were also associated with the KEIHIN BANK.   Okihiro 91 (28); United 71 (147)

November 1903   Joseph Sakai arrives in Jacksonville, Florida, with the idea of forming a Japanese farming colony. This venture eventually becomes the YAMATO COLONY.   Pozzetta/Kersey 76 (66)

December 17, 1903   Orville and Wilbur Wright execute the first four flights of a heavier-than-air vehicle in Kitty Hawk, North Carolina.   Schlesinger 83 (410)

1904　Nobuyuki Yamashiro is the first to begin a *shoyu* (soy sauce) brewing venture in Hawaii. Until this time, the immigrants had relied on imports from Japan. His company becomes the Hawaii Shoyu Co. in 1906. Odo/Sinoto 85 (166)

April 1904　The San Francisco-based Nichibei Ginko (Japanese-American Bank) opens a Los Angeles branch. This bank operates until October 1909.　Yagasaki 82 (254)

May 1904　One thousand four hundred of 2,400 Japanese laborers strike the Oahu Sugar Co. in Waipahu over the issue of compulsory lotteries. Although 27 armed police are sent in, the strike is won after a week when the field overseer resigns and the LUNA responsible for the lotteries is fired. Although they were involved in many strikes over the years, the Japanese workers displayed a new level of organizational skill in winning this one.　United 71 (170–71); Odo/Sinoto 85 (196–97)

November 18, 1904　HAWAII SUGAR PLANTERS ASSOCIATION trustees adopt a resolution stating that all skilled positions on the plantation will be filled by "American citizens, or those eligible for citizenship." Though not mentioned explicitly, Japanese and other Asian workers are effectively barred from such positions through this resolution.　Takaki 83 (75–76)

December 1904　A sizable demonstration involving 2,000 men takes place at Waialua. Workers are unhappy about not receiving higher wages despite a three cent per pound increase in the price of sugar from 1903 to 1904.　Fuchs 61 (117)

1905　The Hawaii Territorial Legislature passes a law requiring emigrant agents (i.e., mainland recruiters) to pay a $500 licensing fee annually. Such legislation is passed in a futile attempt to stem the tide of workers leaving the PLANTATIONS for higher wages on the mainland.　Takaki 83 (144)

February 23, 1905　The *San Francisco Chronicle* front-page headline reads: "The Japanese Invasion: The Problem of the Hour." This launches an unrelenting string of editorials against the Japanese that serve to shift the ANTI-JAPANESE MOVEMENT into high gear.　Daniels 77 (24–26); Ichioka 77c (413)

Laborers' quarters at the Hilo Plantation, Hawaii. Conditions both in the fields and in the plantation villages fueled the workers' discontent.　*Hawaii State Archives*

May 14, 1905 The ASIATIC EXCLUSION LEAGUE is formed in San Francisco, marking the official beginning of the ANTI-JAPANESE MOVEMENT. Among those attending the first meeting are labor leaders (and European immigrants) Patrick Henry McCarthy and Olaf Tveitmoe of the Building Trades Council of San Francisco and Andrew Furuseth and Walter McCarthy of the Sailor's Union. Tveitmoe is named the first president of the organization.   Daniels 77 (27–28)

May 19, 1905 Three Japanese newspapers—*Shin Nippon, Hawaii Nichi Nichi* and HAWAII SHIMPO—sponsor a public mass meeting to organize the JAPANESE REFORM ASSOCIATION and to petition the Japanese government to investigate the immigration companies and the KEIHIN BANK.   United 71 (147)

May 22, 1905 After a LUNA beats a Japanese laborer so severely that the worker loses an eye, outraged workers call for the luna's dismissal at the Kaanapali Camp on Maui. Other workers from nearby camps in Lahaina join in and by May 24, 1,400 Japanese workers demonstrate in protest. A riot results and police and national guardsmen arrive. One striker is killed and two are wounded. The strike is settled on May 29 with a number of the demands met, including the firing of the luna. Takaki 83 (150)

May 27, 1905 Admiral Heihachiro Togo leads Japan's navy in its destruction of the Russian Baltic Squadron in the Tsushima Straits. Togo becomes a hugely popular figure among Hawaii ISSEI at this time, due largely to his two visits there as captain of the *Naniwa* in 1893 and 1897.   Stephan 84 (15–16)

September 5, 1905 *The Treaty of Portsmouth ends the Russo-Japanese War. It had begun on February 9, 1904, with a surprise attack on the Russian navy. Russia gives up any claims to Korea and Manchuria and cedes the southern half of Sakhalin Island to Japan.*   Reischauer 74 (148–45)

December 1905 California Congressmen Duncan E. McKinlay of Santa Rosa and Everis A. Hayes of San Jose introduce bills into Congress calling for an end to further Japanese immigration. Though the bills receive support from influential Alabama Congressman Oscar W. Underwood, who likens the "Japanese problem" to race issues in the South, no further action is taken on them.   Daniels 77 (29)

1906 Demanding higher wages, 1,700 Japanese workers strike at the Waipahu Plantation on Oahu. Despite plantation manager E. K. Bull's calling in of the police,

the strikers stand firm and gain some concessions. Takaki 83 (151)

1906 KYUTARO ABIKO purchases land in Livingston, California, which eventually becomes the YAMATO COLONY, an attempted utopian farming community. Matsumoto 85 (19)

April 18, 1906 *The San Francisco earthquake and the resultant fires level much of the city. Five hundred thousand people are rendered homeless and 500 are killed.*   Schlesinger 83 (413)

May 1906 In the aftermath of the earthquake, the California Flower Growers Association (Kashu Kaki Saibai Kumiai) is formed in San Francisco, consisting only of ISSEI growers. A house leased by the Domoto brothers called Lick Place becomes the first flower market in the city.   Yagasaki 82 (49)

June 1906 Temporarily quieted by the earthquake, anti-Japanese agitation begins again with renewed vigor. Many physical attacks against Japanese residents are reported. Four scientists from Tokyo Imperial University who had arrived in San Francisco to inspect the earthquake damage are attacked more than a dozen times in various parts of the city.   Daniels 77 (33)

June 1, 1906 Shusui Kotoku forms the Shakai Kakumeito (Social Revolutionary Party) in Oakland as an organization linking Japanese Socialist groups located around the Bay Area. One of their first actions is to support the International Seamen's Union of the Pacific strike. Ironically, the California and American Socialist Parties adopted resolutions to restrict Asian laborers within a year.   Ichioka 71 (4–5)

September 1906 The JAPANESE REFORM ASSOCIATION disbands, having succeeded in getting the Japanese foreign ministry to issue an order restraining the KEIHIN BANK from further harsh treatment of immigrants to Hawaii.   Okihiro 91 (28–29); United 71 (147)

October 1906 With the encouragement of the ASIATIC EXCLUSION LEAGUE, the Cooks and Waiters Union (San Francisco) initiates a boycott against the many Japanese owned "American food" restaurants that had sprung up since the earthquake. The number of such restaurants declines from 30 to 17 by the end of 1908.   Thomas 52 (30)

October 11, 1906 The San Francisco Board of Education passes a resolution to segregate Chinese, Japanese and Korean children from the rest. Though little noticed at first in San Francisco (it would actually affect only a handful of children), it would soon escalate into an international incident. (See GENTLEMEN'S AGREEMENT and SAN FRANCISCO SCHOOL BOARD SEGREGATION ORDER OF 1906.   Daniels 77 (34)

December 20, 1906 The first issue of *Kakumei* (Revolution), the official journal of the Shakai Kakumeito, is published in Berkeley, California. The following English passage is picked up by the local American press and causes a furor: "Our policy is toward the overthrow of Mikado, King, President as representing the Capitalist Class as soon as possible, and we do not hesitate as to means."   Ichioka 71 (6)

1907 Reverend Misaki Shimazu founds the first Japanese organization in Chicago, the Japanese YMCA. It closes for lack of interest in 1936.   Albert 80 (112)

February 18, 1907 Congress approves amending existing immigration legislation, thus allowing President Roosevelt to issue an executive order stopping the migration of Japanese laborers from Hawaii and Mexico on March 14, 1907. In concert with the GENTLEMEN'S AGREEMENT, this action ends labor immigration to the U.S. and puts LABOR CONTRACTORS out of business. (See IMMIGRATION ACT OF 1907.)   Daniels 77 (43–44); Ichioka 80b (347)

February 20, 1907 Under the leadership of the LABOR CONTRACTORS, a mass meeting is held in Los Angeles to protest the amending of immigration statutes cutting off immigration from Hawaii or Mexico. A similar meeting takes place in Portland on February 23. Petitions and telegrams arising from these meetings beseech the Japanese foreign ministry to fight the amendment and to push for direct immigration to the U.S. Later meetings of a similar nature take place in San Francisco and Seattle as well.   Ichioka 88 (70)

June 28, 1907 In a period marked by the exclusion of all Asian laborers from established labor unions, the United Mine Workers of America international executive board allows Asian miners to join in southern Wyoming. The peculiar set of circumstances around the labor dispute there made this perhaps the only example of Asian labor being allowed to join an established union during this period. (See ROCK SPRINGS STRIKE.)   Ichioka 88 (113–25)

September 1907 KICHIMATSU KISHI purchases 3,500 acres of land for $72,000 in Terry, Texas, to start a rice farming project. His becomes the largest of several Japanese-owned rice farms in the state.   Walls 87 (86)

November 3, 1907 (the birthday of the Meiji emperor) Shakai Kakumeito (Social Revolutionary Party) members write an "Open Letter to Mutsuhito Emperor of Japan" threatening assassination and pin it to the entrance of the Japanese Consulate General in San Francisco. The resulting furor results in the disbanding of the group.   Ichioka 71 (7–8)

1908 The Salinas Valley Japanese Agricultural Contractors' Association (Nihonjin Nogyo Keiyakusha Kumiai) and the Delta Agricultural Association (Kawashimo Nogyo Domei Kai) are formed. They become two of the earliest Japanese agricultural cooperative groups in California.   Yagasaki 82 (175–76)

1908 NAOICHI HOKOSANO founds the *Denver Shimpo*, Colorado's first Japanese newspaper. It became the *Santo Jiji* in 1915, and in 1918 it merges with the *Colorado Shimbun* to become the *Colorado Times (Kakushu Jiji)*. It continues publication until the late 1950s.   Endo 85 (103–04)

February 4, 1908 At the behest of new San Francisco consul general Chozo Koike, the JAPANESE ASSOCIATION of America is organized as the new central body of local groups. It replaces the disbanded United Japanese Deliberative Council of America, which had been plagued by financial and other problems.   Ichioka 77c (415–16)

June 7, 1908 Given the large concentration of Japanese laborers and LABOR CONTRACTORS working in the vineyards of the Fresno area (Japanese make up some 60 percent of the labor force), a group of 53 Japanese contractors meet to discuss ways to ensure maximum profits for all. They form the Central California Contractor's Association, whose members agree to seek a uniform rate of $1.65 per pound from farmers for the coming season.   Ichioka 71 (8)

August 20, 1908 The FRESNO RODO DOMEI KAI (Fresno Labor League) is organized with Tetsugoro Takeuchi as the central figure. It becomes a labor union of about 2,000 members.   Ichioka 71 (8)

September 1908 Tajiro Sumida founds the HONOLULU JAPANESE SAKE BREWING CO., LTD. Since sake is normally brewed during Japanese winters, the company had to invent a new method for brewing sake since Hawaii lacks a cold season. Through a long process of trial and error, such a process was pioneered in Hawaii. Odo/Sinoto 85 (158); United 71 (208)

December 1, 1908 The Higher Wage Association (Zokyu Kisei Kai) is formed at a meeting in Honolulu

Plantation worker, Puunene, Maui, 1908. Women constituted some 20 percent of *issei* plantation workers from the beginning of Japanese labor migration to the Islands. *R. J. Baker photograph, Hawaii State Archives*

around the issues of higher wages for PLANTATION workers and an end to the wage scale that paid different wages to workers of different nationalities for the same work. It submits specific requests to the Planters Association in January 1909. (See 1909 PLANTATION STRIKE.) Odo/Sinoto 85 (197)

January 1, 1909 JAPANESE ASSOCIATION of America affiliated locals are given the right to issue (and share in the fees collected from) certificates of registration by the Japanese consul in San Francisco. These certificates resulted from the GENTLEMEN'S AGREEMENT and were legally required for Japanese laborers to live in the United States. Later in the month, the Japanese Association holds their first official conference in San Francisco to decide the administrative procedures for registration. Ichioka 77c (417, 419–20)

February 1909 California's Alien Land Bill is defeated in the State Assembly. The bill stipulated that any alien purchasing land had to become a citizen within five years or else lose the land. As "ALIENS INELIGIBLE TO CITIZENSHIP," Japanese immigrants would thus not be able to purchase land. A similar but harsher measure would pass four years later. (See 1913 (CALIFORNIA) ALIEN LAND LAW.) Chuman 76 (41–42)

March 29, 1909 Kinmon Ginko branches in San Francisco and Los Angeles close their doors with a note

reading "closed for three days for arrangements" pinned to the door. They would never reopen. Despite the efforts of the JAPANESE ASSOCIATION, all attempts to save the Japanese American owned bank (established in 1905–06) failed. This was the first of seven Japanese American banks to fail in 1909. Yagasaki 82 (258)

May 1909 The Japanese foreign ministry announces that all overseas Japanese must register with the embassy or consular office in the country in which they reside. The foreign ministry delegates the local JAPANESE ASSOCIATIONS with the responsibility to carry out this registration. Ichioka 77c (420)

May 9, 1909 Japanese workers at Aiea Plantation walk out, beginning the 1909 PLANTATION STRIKE. By June, 7,000 workers and their families are on strike on Oahu and remain out until August. Kotani 85 (42–45)

June 1, 1909 *The National Association for the Advancement of Colored People (NAACP) is formed by W. E. B. Du Bois.* Schlesinger 83 (417)

June 1909 The Los Angeles City Market is established by a private corporation on the corner of San Pedro and Ninth. It would soon become known as the NINTH STREET MARKET. An ethnically diverse enterprise, Japanese owned 18 percent of the stock and occupied 120 of the 180 produce stalls in the market yard. Iwata 62 (34); Yagasaki 82 (192)

August 5, 1909 Higher Wage Association delegate Tamekichi Mori stabs SOMETARO SHIBA outside the U.S. District Court. Shiba was the unpopular editor of the HAWAII SHIMPO and an informer to the HAWAII SUGAR PLANTERS ASSOCIATION. This incident effectively ends the 1909 PLANTATION STRIKE. Kotani 85 (45)

August 25, 1909 The FRESNO RODO DOMEI KAI organizes a convention of Japanese laborers in Fresno, drawing 300 workers. Ichioka 71 (11)

September 19, 1909 The FRESNO RODO DOMEI KAI holds a joint rally with the Fresno International Workers of the World (IWW) local which draws Mexican and Italian IWW speakers. Ichioka 71 (11)

October 18, 1909 Both Nichibei Ginko branches close their doors on the order of the Superintendent of Banks of California. This effectively marks the end of ISSEI-run banking enterprises in California. The liquidation of this bank would not be completed until August 1922. Yagasaki 82 (258)

March 1910   The Territorial Supreme Court rejects the appeal of four leaders of the 1909 PLANTATION STRIKE for obstructing the operations of the sugar plantations (third degree conspiracy). Yokichi Tasaka, YASUTARO SOGA, Motoyuki Negoro and FRED KINZABURO MAKINO begin jail terms. They are pardoned by the governor four months later and receive a hero's welcome from a crowd of 1,000 upon release.   Kotani 85 (45)

April 1, 1910   Registration of Japanese in the United States begins through JAPANESE ASSOCIATION of America locals. Registration continues until September 30. Ichioka 77c (420)

May 1910   The so-called "Daigyaku Jiken," a crackdown on Socialists by the Japanese government, begins, prompted by a supposed plot to assassinate the emperor. By its conclusion, 26 were found guilty and 12 were executed.   Ichioka 71 (2–3)

February 21, 1911   A new Treaty of Commerce and Navigation between the United States and Japan, effective on July 17, 1911 is signed. It is later ratified by Congress and proclaimed by President William Howard Taft on April 5. (See TREATY OF COMMERCE AND NAVIGATION OF 1911 BETWEEN JAPAN AND THE UNITED STATES.)   Chuman 76 (44–45)

November 3, 1911   In Bakersfield, Shojiro Takeda's "disrespect" of the Meiji Emperor's picture touches off an affair of lèse-majesté.   Ichioka 71 (12–14)

1912   Yoshin Sakurai makes his debut on Broadway in the George M. Cohan play *Get Rich Quick Wallingford*. A former valet of Cohan's, he plays a valet in the play. He is believed to be the first Japanese actor to appear on Broadway.   Kanazawa, Tooru. "Issei on Broadway." *Scene* 5.10 (Feb. 1954): 15–17

early 1912   Mitsusaburo Yamamoto and Fukutaro Muraoka introduce winter celery to Chula Vista, California. In later years, Chula Vista becomes the "Celery Capital of the World."   Estes 78 (429)

January 1912   ISSEI flower growers in San Francisco establish the California Flower Market Inc. as a marketing cooperative. The market would move several times before settling on Fifth Street, adjacent to other ethnic markets, in 1924. This Japanese market was the largest, with 17,000 square feet of space. It remained at this location until 1956.   Yagasaki 82 (49–52)

March 20, 1912   Four hundred OKINAWAN workers go on strike in Pa'ia, Maui to demand the firing of a

The labor of *issei* women was vital to both Hawaii sugar plantations and to mainland agriculture. However, this often put the burden of childcare onto siblings who were only slightly older.   *R. J. Baker photograph, Hawaii State Archives*

LUNA and some plantation policemen who had tried to disperse a wedding party.   Odo/Sinoto 85 (200)

April 1912   At a meeting in a Japanese restaurant, the Southern California Flower Growers Association (Nanka Kaengyo Kumiai) is born. A flower market is proposed even though two earlier attempts had failed. This would become the SOUTHERN CALIFORNIA FLOWER MARKET, INC.   Yagasaki 82 (110)

August 1912   TETSUO TOYAMA begins publishing *Jitsugyo no Hawaii*, a monthly magazine that would become one of Hawaii's most successful.   Wakukawa 81 (242)

December 7, 1912 Disturbed by rumors that the NIPPU JIJI had begun to receive subsidies from the HAWAII SUGAR PLANTERS ASSOCIATION, FRED KINZABURO MAKINO begins to publish the HAWAII HOCHI. Kotani 85 (57)

1913 Roy Fukuda of the Lake Labish, Oregon, area develops the famous "Golden Plume" celery, "forerunner of all choice varieties of today." Pursinger 66 (257)

January 1913 The first SOUTHERN CALIFORNIA FLOWER MARKET is opened on South Los Angeles Street by Japanese growers. The formal incorporation takes place a year later. Yagasaki 82 (111)

February 1913 An agency of the San Francisco branch of the Japan-based Yokohama Specie Bank opens in downtown Los Angeles to handle remittances of Southern California Japanese. Another agency opens in Seattle four years later. Yagasaki 82 (247)

May 19, 1913 California Governor HIRAM JOHNSON signs the 1913 (CALIFORNIA) ALIEN LAND LAW, effective on August 10. Ichioka 84 (159)

1914 The Rafu Jindokai (Japanese Humane Society of Los Angeles), with sponsorship from the JAPANESE ASSOCIATION, opens a home for orphan children of Japanese descent. Better known as the Shonien, the home was directed by Rokuichi "Joy" Kusumoto. It has been called "the Japanese community's finest achievement in social welfare." Kuramoto 76 (12–13)

April 1914 The first group of 47 SUMO wrestlers arrive from Japan for a week-long exhibition tournament at the Civic Auditorium in Honolulu and tour of the islands. Three of the wrestlers apparently "defected" to Hawaii. United 71 (166)

June 28, 1914 *Archduke Francis Ferdinand, Crown Prince of Austria, is assassinated in Sarajevo, Yugoslavia, kicking off a series of events leading to the start of World War I.* Schlesinger 83 (425)

October 1914 The Japanese Congregational Church of San Francisco, established in 1905, merges with the Japanese Presbyterian Church to become the Soko Nihonjin Kiristo Kyokai (Japanese Church of Christ of San Francisco), the first Japanese American denominationally federated church. Yoshida 89 (204–05, 234)

October 1914 A movement in California to enact legislation that would totally prohibit Japanese immi-grants from leasing agricultural land meets opposition from Japan, Washington, D.C., and many Californians due to World War I and Japan's participation on the side of the Allies. Anti-Japanese forces would remain relatively quiet until after the war. Abrams 87 (169–72)

February 1915 The Hawaiian territory-wide Japanese Educational Association is formed in an attempt to unify the JAPANESE LANGUAGE SCHOOLS against attacks from both inside and outside the community. One of their first goals is to produce new textbooks reflecting the Japanese experience in Hawaii and encouraging Americanization. Odo/Sinoto 85 (128–29)

October 1915 In the midst of the Japanese exclusion movement, BUNJI SUZUKI attends the conventions of the California State Federation of Labor and the AFL as a "fraternal delegate" from Japan. He would return for the 1916 conventions as well. Despite forming fledgling labor organizations in both years, his appearances had little or no effect on the status of Japanese workers in the U.S. Ichioka 83 (1)

Summer 1916 Professor Yaichi Haga of Tokyo Imperial University arrives in Honolulu to rewrite the textbooks used in JAPANESE LANGUAGE SCHOOLS. His new edition pleases neither Hawaiian authorities nor the Japanese community. Odo/Sinoto 85 (129)

August 1916 In response to the KAKEOCHI crisis, the JAPANESE ASSOCIATION of America issues a guide to be distributed at points of embarkation in Japan to PICTURE BRIDES concerning "proper" conduct. Ichioka 80a (353)

September 1916 The Sumitomo Bank becomes the second Japanese bank to expand to the U.S. with the opening of its San Francisco Agency in downtown San Francisco on California Street. Other branches would follow: Seattle and New York in 1918, Los Angeles in 1924, Sacramento in 1925 and Hawaii in 1916. Yagasaki 82 (247–48)

September 18, 1916 Longshoremen of various nationalities strike in Hawaii for higher wages and recognition of their union. The strike ends on October 10 with a pay increase but no union recognition. In an attempt to break the coalition, the stevedoring firm rehires all but the Japanese strikers. Three hundred others go back on strike for two weeks in support. The company relents a little by agreeing to rehire the Japanese when the strikebreakers leave. Odo/Sinoto 85 (200)

October 1916 The JAPANESE ASSOCIATION of America asks the T.K.K. Line (a Japanese steamship company) to assign matrons to its ships to supervise young, America-bound women in reaction to stories of indiscretions on past journeys.   Ichioka 80a (353)

October 1916 BUNJI SUZUKI returns to America and again attends the AFL and California Federation conferences; he also creates the JAPANESE FEDERATION OF LABOR in America as a successor to his 1915 JAPANESE LABOR LEAGUE OF AMERICA.   Ichioka 83a (13)

1917 The U.S. State Department grants legal recognition to the photo-marriage, allowing PICTURE BRIDES and their spouses to dispense with a second wedding ceremony in the United States.   Ichioka 80a (347)

February 5, 1917 Overriding President Woodrow Wilson's veto, Congress votes an Immigration Bill into law that includes a literacy test requirement. The law also creates an "Asiatic Barred Zone," which has the effect of excluding from the U.S. all Asians except those from Japan or the Philippines.   Abrams 87 (206–07); Kim 86 (306–07)

March 1917 The anti-Japanese film *Patria* appears on American movie screens. The Hearst-distributed film depicts Japanese soldier/farmers attacking the United States through Mexico and with the aid of Mexicans. Abrams 87 (208–09)

April 2, 1917 *President Wilson asks Congress to declare war on Germany. The U.S. soon formally enters World War I.*   Schlesinger 83 (432)

August 1917 Japanese labor leaders in Hawaii form the Plantation Laborers Wage Increase Investigation Association, a union of plantation workers. Its petition is turned down by the HAWAII SUGAR PLANTERS ASSOCIATION.   Fuchs 61 (214)

August 17, 1917 An all-Japanese company of the U.S. Army is organized in Hawaii. At about the same time, an Officer's Training Camp opens there with several Japanese officers commissioned upon graduation. Orders to the 838 soldiers of "Company D" of the First Regiment of the National Guard of Hawaii are given in Japanese and the group marches to a Japanese cadence. (See WORLD WAR I VETERANS.)   Naka 38 (44); United 71 (168)

August 20, 1917 A committee to study the need for higher wages on the PLANTATIONS is formed in Hono-

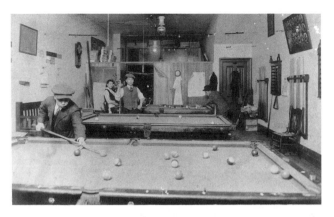

Pool hall, Los Angeles, California, 1918. Pool halls and other enterprises serving the needs of a migrant labor population were among those commonly started by *issei*. *John Nishimura Collection, Japanese American National Museum Photographic & Moving Image Archive*

lulu. It recommends that wages be raised, but does not press the issue due to World War I.   United 71 (186)

November 21, 1917 Nellie Grace Oliver, a middle-aged, Caucasian schoolteacher, organizes the Japanese Boys Club and the Japanese Girls Club. They will eventually become known as the Olivers, Southern California's first NISEI social club.   Waugh 78 (136)

1918 KYUTARO ABIKO starts the Cressey Colony near Livingston, CA, the second of his three utopian Christian farming colonies.   Matsumoto 85 (19)

1918 In a relatively rare example of intraethnic labor activity, Japanese fishermen in Hawaii walk off their jobs on 83 boats to protest perceived excessive profits by Japanese boat owners.   Odo/Sinoto 85 (200)

November 11, 1918 *The armistice treaty formally ending the "Great War" is signed.*   Schlesinger 83 (436)

December 19, 1918 Judge Horace W. Vaughn of the U.S. District Court for Hawaii states that Japanese, Chinese and Korean veterans of World War I are eligible for naturalization under the Act of May 9, 1918. As a result, 398 Japanese, 99 Koreans and four Chinese are granted citizenship by November 14, 1919. Unfortunately for these men, their citizenship would be revoked by the TOYOTA V. UNITED STATES decision of May 25, 1925. (See CITIZENSHIP and WORLD WAR I VETERANS.) Naka 39 (48, 64–70)

1919 KYUTARO ABIKO establishes CORTEZ COLONY, the third of his three utopian farming communities, seven miles northwest of Livingston, California, and seven miles south of Turlock.   Matsumoto 85 (19)

January 4, 1919   The Judd proposal appears in the *Honolulu Advertiser*. A forerunner of laws restricting the activities of JAPANESE-LANGUAGE SCHOOLS, it advocates licensing for all teachers in Japanese schools and their placement under the supervision of the Department of Public Instruction.   United 71 (217)

January 29, 1919   The 18th Amendment—Prohibition—is ratified and goes into effect on Jan. 16, 1920. Schlesinger 83 (436)

March 16, 1919   To commemorate the Taisho emperor, the Phoenix fountain in Kapi'olani Park is completed. It is financed by the local Japanese community and designed by the Tokyo Art School and features a bronze phoenix topping two tiered basins over a granite pedestal. It would become known to some as "the chicken in Waikiki." It was destroyed during World War II. Odo/Sinoto 85 (193)

March 31, 1919   After five years of relative dormancy due primarily to World War I, California senator JAMES D. PHELAN launches the next phase of the ANTI-JAPANESE MOVEMENT with an address before the state legislature. Citing the Japanese as not only an economic threat but a military one, he advocates a more stringent ALIEN LAND LAW, an end to Japanese immigration and stronger coastal defenses. The address also serves as the beginning of his campaign for reelection.   Daniels 77 (81–82)

October 1919   Alarmed white residents of Hood River, Oregon, form the Anti-Asiatic Association. The association supports exclusion and the prohibition of land ownership by the Japanese and its members vow not to sell or lease to ISSEI.   Yasui 75 (242–43)

October 1919   The JAPANESE ASSOCIATION of America passes a resolution recommending the end of picture marriages to the Japanese government. This resolution is in response to anti-Japanese forces that viewed such marriages as an example of Japanese immorality. Consul Tamekichi Ota and the executive board of the central body issue a press release announcing this resolution on October 31. The Japanese Association rank and file were not happy with this development.   Fujita 29 (225); Ichioka 77c (431); Tsurutani 89 (184)

November 29, 1919   Irate over the decision made by Consul Ota and the central body of the JAPANESE ASSOCIATION over abolishing the PICTURE BRIDES, the locals meet to voice their disapproval. On December 1,

Railroad workers, ca. 1920s.   *Etsuo Hirose Collection, Japanese American National Museum Photographic & Moving Image Archive*

every officer and staffer of the central body formally resigns.   Ichioka 77c (433)

December 1, 1919   The first meeting of the Japanese Federation of Labor in Hawaii is held in Honolulu and attended by 58 representatives from four islands. All wage requests would be channeled through this body. The organization's name is changed to the Hawaii Laborer's Association in April 1920.   Kotani 85 (46–47); United 71 (187)

1920   The U.S. Commissioner of Education surveys education in Hawaii, and in its report to the governor, recommends: "Abolish all foreign language schools at the next session of the legislature. . . ." (See JAPANESE LANGUAGE SCHOOLS.)   United 71 (217)

January 19, 1920   Three thousand members of the Filipino Labor Union walk off their jobs in Hawaii; Japanese workers soon join them. By early February, 8,300 PLANTATION laborers are on strike, representing 77 percent of the work force. (See 1920 PLANTATION STRIKE.)   Kotani 85 (48–49)

March 1, 1920   The Japanese Foreign Ministry begins to issue passports only to women who accompany their husbands to the United States, effectively ending the PICTURE BRIDE era.   Ichioka 80a (357)

April 3, 1920   Strike leaders organize the "77 cent parade." Three thousand Japanese and Filipino strikers and their families march through Honolulu carrying banners asking "Can You Live on 77¢ Per Day?" (See 1920 PLANTATION STRIKE.)   United 71 (191)

May 5, 1920   Niccola Sacco and Bartolomeo Vanzetti are arrested for the robbery and murder of the paymaster at a shoe factory in Braintree, Massachusetts. Convicted the following year, they would be executed on August 23, 1927. Their trial and execution would come to symbolize the anti-Communist, anti-immigrant tenor of the times.   Schlesinger 83 (438)

June 1920   Faced with mass discontent in the association, Consul Ota withdraws the endorsement right, ending the special relationship between the JAPANESE ASSOCIATIONS and the Japanese government.   Ichioka 77c (433)

July 3, 1920   A protest rally drawing almost 1,000 people is organized by the NICHIBEI SHIMBUN to condemn the consul's decisions to withdraw the endorsement right and to outlaw PICTURE BRIDES.   Ichioka 77c (433)

August 26, 1920   The 19th Amendment—Women's Suffrage—is enacted.   Schlesinger 83 (439)

September 2, 1920   The JAPANESE EXCLUSION LEAGUE OF CALIFORNIA is organized at Native Sons Hall in San Francisco. Though State Senator J. M. Inman is named president, former newspaper publisher V. S. MCCLATCHY becomes the main force behind the league.   Daniels 77 (91)

November 1920   The new 1920 (CALIFORNIA) ALIEN LAND LAW, a more stringent measure intended to close loopholes in the 1913 (CALIFORNIA) ALIEN LAND LAW, passes as a ballot initiative. It becomes effective on December 9.   Ichioka 84 (163)

November 24, 1920   At a special session of the Hawaii Legislature, Act 30 is signed into law. It is the most serious attempt to date to regulate the JAPANESE-LANGUAGE SCHOOLS in Hawaii. (See ACT 30 OF THE SPECIAL SESSION LAWS OF 1920.)   United 71 (218–19)

1921   Angered by the 1920 PLANTATION STRIKE, the sugar planters send a delegation to Washington, D.C., to request from Congress special permission to bring in 30,000 Chinese to replace Japanese labor. Hearings before the Committee on Immigration and Naturalization fail to convince Congress, however.   United 71 (195–97)

January 5, 1921   A hostile crowd greets several Japanese families from California when they attempt to get off the train at the Harlingen, Texas, station. Agitated by the Harlingen American Legion Post, the crowd makes it known that the families are unwelcome and forces them to move on. With the passage of the 1920 (CALIFORNIA) ALIEN LAND LAW, pressure mounts in many other places to enact similar legislation so as to prevent resettlement of California ISSEI. Three weeks after the Harlingen incident, an ALIEN LAND LAW is introduced into the Texas legislature by Senator R. M. Dudley of El Paso.   Walls 87 (119–20)

February 26, 1921   The Arizona legislature enacts its first Alien Land Act, modeled after the one in California. (See ALIEN LAND LAWS.)   Sato 73 (320)

March 1921   The Washington legislature passes its ALIEN LAND LAW. The law does not apply to any alien "who in good faith declared his intention to become a citizen"; however, since Japanese could not do this, the law does apply to them.   Ichioka 84 (167–note 39)

March–April 1921   Several TANOMOSHI go bankrupt in the Los Angeles area, causing a good deal of panic and chaos in the ISSEI community. Total losses amount to around $200,000 and have a greater impact than even the bank failures of 1909. In response, the Japanese Chamber of Commerce of Southern California forms the Rafu Tanomoshi-ko Ippan Kinyu Hogo Kyokai (Los Angeles Protective Association of Tanomoshi-ko and General Finance) in June as a protective organization for *tanomoshi* in the wake of the many recent failures.   Yagasaki 82 (268)

April 1921   The ALIEN LAND LAW is passed in Texas. However, after the introduction of the bill in January, Japanese residents form a JAPANESE ASSOCIATION in Texas. Led by Saburo Arai, this group organizes meetings and collects money to finance lobbying efforts in Austin. In the state house, Representative W. E. Pope of Corpus Christi offers an amendment exempting all Japanese already in the state from the bill. Thus, the Texas Alien Land Law affected only Japanese moving to Texas after passage of the bill.   Walls 87 (120–22)

July 8, 1921   California state attorney U. S. Webb announces that CROPPING CONTRACTS are illegal. They had been used as a means to get around the 1920 (CALIFORNIA) ALIEN LAND LAW. This announcement would soon be challenged in court.   Ichioka 84 (164)

July 19, 1921   Armed white raiders deport 58 Japanese laborers from Turlock, California, by truck and warn them not to return. (See TURLOCK INCIDENT.)   Ichioka 76 (196)

Issei worked hard but also took time out to have fun. Los Angeles, California, ca. 1920s. *Kenneth Yamamoto Collection, Japanese American National Museum Photographic & Moving Image Archive*

October 11, 1921 The Northern California-based JAPANESE ASSOCIATION of America convenes a special session of their delegate assembly. Having been approached by the Japanese Agricultural Association, the delegates pass a $25,000 litigation budget to fight the 1920 (CALIFORNIA) ALIEN LAND LAW. They initiate the WEBB V. O'BRIEN case to test the ban on CROPPING CONTRACTS on October 13. In the meantime, another group, the Central Japanese Association of Southern California, initiates the PORTERFIELD V. WEBB case on October 18 to test the ban on leasing. These two groups soon joined forces.   Ichioka 84 (165)

November 5, 1921 Members of the two land litigation committees challenging the 1920 (CALIFORNIA) ALIEN LAND LAW—the JAPANESE ASSOCIATION of America and the Central Japanese Association of Southern

California—meet and form a joint committee. They agree to share litigation costs in anticipation of going to the Supreme Court. They go on to initiate the FRICK V. WEBB case on February 7, 1922, testing the prohibition on the buying and selling of stock in land companies. Ichioka 84 (165–66)

December 20, 1921 A Santa Clara County, California, court rules that CROPPING CONTRACTS do not violate the 1920 (CALIFORNIA) ALIEN LAND LAW in its decision on WEBB V. O'BRIEN. Although this decision will be reversed by the U.S. Supreme Court later, it does allow the practice of cropping contracts to continue for two more years.   Ichioka 84 (166)

1922 Los Angeles area Japanese florists form the Southern California Florist Association. By 1932, it

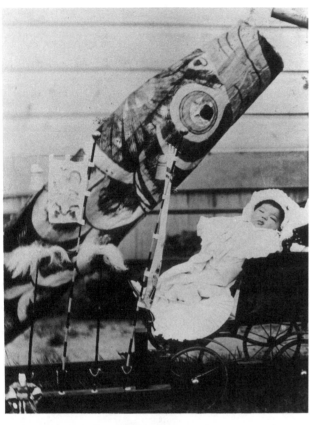

The 1920s saw the dawning of the *nisei* (second generation). *Kathleen Yamazaki Collection, Japanese American National Museum Photographic & Moving Image Archive*

numbers 73 members, plus 278 family members and 170 unrelated employees.   Yagasaki 82 (143–44)

May 1, 1922 The California Supreme Court upholds the right of Hayao Yano to serve as the guardian for his daughter Tetsubumi, nullifying a key provision of the 1920 (CALIFORNIA) ALIEN LAND LAW. (See YANO, ESTATE OF TETSUBUMI.)   Consulate 78 (Vol. II: 500–50); Chuman 76 (80–81)

September 22, 1922 The CABLE ACT is passed by Congress. Under this law, Asian female citizens marrying ALIENS INELIGIBLE TO CITIZENSHIP (i.e., Asian immigrant males) would lose their own citizenship. The act was amended in 1931.   Chuman 76 (165)

November 13, 1922 The U.S. Supreme Court rules on the Ozawa case, definitely prohibiting Japanese from becoming naturalized U.S. citizens on the basis of race. This ban is in effect until 1952. A similar case involving the denial of naturalization is also ruled upon. (See CITIZENSHIP, OZAWA V. UNITED STATES, and YAMASHITA V. HINKLE.)   Chuman 76 (70–71)

November 22, 1922 The Territorial School Commission issues further restrictive regulations on the JAPANESE-LANGUAGE SCHOOLS in Hawaii. Kindergarten, first and second grades are to be gradually eliminated in these schools.   United 71 (221)

December 28, 1922 The Palama JAPANESE-LANGUAGE SCHOOL files an injunction to test the constitutionality of the November 22, 1922, (and future) regulations on the language schools. The case proves to be a controversial and divisive issue in the Japanese American community. By 1923, only 87 out of 143 Japanese schools had joined the test case.   Kotani 85 (64); United 71 (221)

1923 The Showa Gakuyukai, an association of OKINAWAN students, is formed with the aid of numerous community leaders. The group promotes the idea of Hawaii as a permanent home and urges Okinawans on PLANTATIONS to seek an education.   Sakihara 81a (113)

February 1923 Oregon passes an ALIEN LAND LAW on the California model after failed attempts to pass a similar measure in 1917, 1919 and 1921.   Yasui 75 (247)

March 1923 The California legislature strengthens the 1920 (CALIFORNIA) ALIEN LAND LAW: it broadens the restrictions to include "the usage cultivation, and occupancy of agricultural land for beneficial purposes," essentially banning CROPPING CONTRACTS. It also attempts to get around the ruling on the Yano case. (See YANO, ESTATE OF TETSUBUMI.)   Ichioka 84 (167)

April 27, 1923 Yet more restrictions on Japanese language schools are approved by the Hawaiian Territorial Legislature. Act 171 incorporates the School Commission regulations of November 22, 1922, and grants greater regulatory powers to the Department of Public Instruction. Worst of all, Act 171 levies a licensing fee on the schools of $1 per pupil. The test case plaintiffs are able to get an injunction preventing Act 171 from being applied pending the outcome of the case.   Kotani 85 (64); United 71 (222)

May 1923 At a meeting in San Francisco of NISEI delegates from various parts of California, the American Loyalty League is formed, led by Fresno dentist THOMAS YATABE. The group promoted good relations between *nisei* and Caucasians and emphasized *nisei* loyalty and patriotism. They were an important precurser of the JAPANESE AMERICAN CITIZENS LEAGUE.   Hosokawa

September 1, 1923 The Kanto area is hit by a major earthquake. The resulting fires raze Yokohama and Tokyo; 225,000 are killed and 400,000 injured.   United 71 (198)

November 12, 1923   The U.S. Supreme Court rules on ALIEN LAND LAW cases, upholding the ban on leasing in Washington and California. (See PORTERFIELD V. WEBB and TERRACE V. THOMPSON.)   Consulate 78 (Vol. II: 1–110, 213–359); Ichioka 84 (167–68)

November 19, 1923   The U.S. Supreme Court overturns the O'Brien decision and upholds the Frick decision, reaffirming bans on CROPPING CONTRACTS and on the purchasing of stock in land companies by "ALIENS INELEGIBLE TO CITIZENSHIP." These decisions, along with the ones upholding the ban on leasing made just one week before, result in a total defeat for the ISSEI court challengers of the ALIEN LAND LAWS. (See FRICK V. WEBB and WEBB V. O'BRIEN.)   Consulate 78 (Vol. II: 111–79, 360–499); Ichioka 84 (168)

May 26, 1924   The U.S. Supreme Court decides ASAKURA V. CITY OF SEATTLE ET AL. The city had tried to pass an ordinance preventing aliens from being pawnbrokers; the U.S. Supreme Court strikes it down as being in violation of the TREATY OF COMMERCE AND NAVAGATION OF 1911 BETWEEN JAPAN AND THE UNITED STATES.   Consulate 78 (Vol. I: 280–343)

May 26, 1924   President Calvin Coolidge signs the 1924 immigration bill into law, effectively ending Japanese immigration to the U.S. (See IMMIGRATION ACT OF 1924.)   Ichihashi 69 (309)

November 1924   The JAPANESE ASSOCIATION of America publishes the report of Manroku Matsumoto. An agricultural expert, Matsumoto was sent to the South to survey the area for possible resettlement in the wake of the disastrous 1923 Supreme Court decisions. He concludes that several areas in the South, especially Georgia and Florida, look promising.   Ichioka 88 (241)

December 20, 1924   The Yokohama Specie Bank head office instructs the San Francisco branch that it might now consider loans to local Japanese. JAPANESE ASSOCIATION of America general secretary Takimoto Tamezo had been sent to Japan in October to request such loans to help farmers pay off their land purchases, made more urgent by the upholding of the 1920 (CALIFORNIA) ALIEN LAND LAW in the courts. The bank goes on to loan $101,800 to farmers in the Fresno area. Though much more than they had ever loaned before, it is far less than the $646,000 the farmers had requested. Ichioka 84 (171–72)

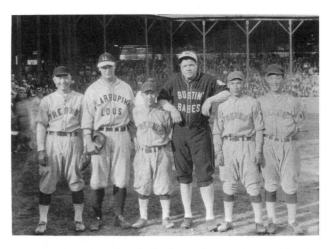

Japanese American baseball players in Fowler, California, ca. 1920s. From left to right: Johnny Nakagawa, Lou Gehrig, Kenichi Zenimura, Babe Ruth, Fred Yoshikawa and Harvey Iwata. *Ayako Okamura Collection, Japanese American National Museum Photographic & Moving Image Archive*

April 1925   Yet more restrictions on JAPANESE-LANGUAGE SCHOOLS are enacted by the Hawaii Territorial Legislature. Act 152 imposes civil and criminal penalties for non-payment of the $1.00 per student assessment and prohibits the schools from seeking injunctions against future regulations. The test case plaintiffs file for and receive an injunction against Act 152 in the U.S. District Court.   United 71 (222)

May 11, 1925   The U.S. Supreme Court upholds the 1920 (CALIFORNIA) ALIEN LAND LAW in deciding *Cockrill et al. v. People of State of California.* W. A. Cockrill had tried to buy land in his name for the children of S. Ikada.   Chuman 76 (207); Consulate 78 (Vol. II: 551–624)

May 25, 1925   The U.S. Supreme Court strips Toyota Hidemitsu of his U.S. citizenship, granted in 1921 after his service in World War I. (See TOYOTA V. UNITED STATES and CITIZENSHIP.)

July 12, 1925   An armed and drunken mob attacks and expels ISSEI laborers from the town of Toledo, Oregon. The workers had been brought in just two days earlier to work in a lumber mill. I. is one of several similar incidents involving the expulsion of Japanese Americans from small West Coast towns. (See TOLEDO INCIDENT.)   S. Tanaka 78 (116)

February 21, 1926   The RAFU SHIMPO begins its English edition, published once a week, with this "announcement": "This is the resume of the news among those who live in Southern California. Our long-hoped-

Takayoshi Store, Bainbridge Island, Washington. As the Japanese American population became more settled, more Japanese American families turned to farming and small businesses as means of support. *Bainbridge Island Japanese American Community Collection, Japanese American National Museum Photographic & Moving Image Archive*

for wishes are materialized, and so here we have a medium to publish news of the second generation, for the second generation, and by the second generation. Therefore, you people of Southern California, get busy and send in some news of general interest to everybody. . . ." *Rafu Shimpo*, 21 Feb. 1926: 2.

April 1, 1926   The Japanese Foreign Ministry officially ends its relationship with the JAPANESE ASSOCIATION of America. With the IMMIGRATION ACT OF 1924 effectively nullifying the GENTLEMEN'S AGREEMENT, there is no longer a need for the endorsement right system that had been the basis of their relationship.   Ichioka 77c (435)

May 5, 1926   Reverend SEIKAN HIGA purchases and begins to put out the *Yoen Jiho* of Koloa, Kauai. Espousing a strong pro-labor philosophy, the paper goes on to become one of the leading voices of the Hawaii OKINAWAN community.   Ethnic 81 (564)

May 19, 1926   San Diego's first Buddhist church is founded. It consists of a rented room on 6th and Market streets. A permanent site is dedicated in 1931.   Estes 78 (446–48)

February 1927   The East Bay Flower Growers Association is organized and a market begun in downtown Oakland. This association is made up of both Japanese and white (mainly Italian) florists.   Yagasaki 82 (81–83)

February 21, 1927   The U.S. Supreme Court unanimously rules that the laws passed by the Hawaii legis-

lature to control the JAPANESE-LANGUAGE SCHOOLS—Act 152 (April 1925), Act 171 (April 27, 1923) and Act 30 (November 24, 1920)—are all unconstitutional. In addition to removing the laws from the books, the territorial government had to refund $20,000 in fees collected from the schools. Japanese school enrollment and popularity would reach new highs in the early 1930s. Kotani 85 (65)

May 21, 1927   Charles Lindbergh pilots the Spirit of St. Louis *from New York to Paris, completing the first solo crossing of the Atlantic.*   Schlesinger 83 (449)

August 1927   The New Americans, a group for young NISEI led by TAKIE OKUMURA and his son Umetaro, hold their initial conference. They would go on to meet once a year until 1941, increasing in membership each year. Nine hundred delegates would attend the 15 conferences. (See NEW AMERICANS CONFERENCE.)   United 71 (245); Nomura 87

August 1927   The OKINAWAN community in Hawaii flocks to the docks to meet Admiral Kenwa Kanna of the flagship *Katori*. As a fellow Okinawan in the Imperial Navy, Kanna is a source of pride.   Sakihara 81a (110)

1928   Oregon asparagus growers organize the Mid-Columbia Vegetable Growers' Association. Before long the association would ship 50,000 crates of asparagus a year to points east.   Yasui 75 (249)

1928   The Nippon Orchestra, led by bandleader Dan Nishikawa, is formed. It is the first of what would be many Japanese American bands in Hawaii. Their repertoire included standard Western and Japanese songs, current dance music and original compositions.   Hirayama, Laura. "The Heyday of Japanese Music: Pre- and Post-War Period." *Hawaii Herald*, 21 Aug. 1981: 6–7.

January 1, 1928   JAMES YOSHINORI SAKAMOTO publishes the first issue of the *Japanese American Courier* in Seattle. The weekly was the first mainland paper to be exclusively geared to the NISEI.   Ichioka 86–87 (49)

1929   The Japanese American Savings Association is organized in Los Angeles by 25 NISEI. It would serve as both a savings and loan and a social activities center. Yagasaki 82 (278)

September 1, 1929   Three Los Angeles ISSEI reach the peak of Mt. Whitney (14,500 ft)—Tadashi Kinoshita, an insurance agent; Yoneo Sakai, Los Angeles correspondent for the *San Francisco Nichibei;* and Shuki Nakamura of the *Rafu Nichibei.* Kinoshita authored a book about the adventure, *Beikoku Arupusu Tohaki* (A Diary of Climbing the North American Alps). Honda, Harry. "Little Tokyo Life (No. 6): No. American 'Alps.'" *Pacific Citizen*, 24 Feb. 1984: 3.

October 29, 1929 The Stock Market crash of "Black Tuesday" proves to be the forerunner of the Great Depression. Schlesinger 83 (454)

November 19, 1929 After a quick trial and failed appeal, NISEI Myles Fukunaga is hanged in Hawaii for the murder of George Gill Jamieson. (See FUKUNAGA CASE.) Kotani 85 (77)

December 27, 1929 Ichiro Nakaima arrives in Hawaii to campaign for a candidate in the OKINAWAN elections, unwittingly setting off a divisive battle within the Okinawan community in Hawaii. (See the NAKAIMA INCIDENT.) Ethnic 81 (565)

August 29, 1930 The first convention of the JAPANESE AMERICAN CITIZENS LEAGUE (JACL) opens in Seattle. One hundred two registered delegates attend. The JACL would grow to become the largest Japanese American political organization during and after World War II. Hosokawa 82 (36)

November 1930 The first Japanese Americans are elected to public office in Hawaii. NISEI Republicans Tasaku Oka and Masayoshi Yamashiro are elected to the Territorial House, while Noboru Miyake is elected to the Kauai County Board of Supervisors. "Timeline of the Japanese in Hawaii." *Hawaii Herald*, 5 July 1985: A12–13

1931 Japanese growers in the San Francisco Bay Area establish the California Chrysanthemum Growers Association, at the time one of many ethnic cooperative groups in the floriculture industry. With the changes in the flower business in the post-war period encouraging greater individualism, this group retained its ethnic cooperativism into the '80s. In 1981, it celebrated its 50th anniversary and continues to function as a cooperative, with all 51 members being Japanese. Yagasaki 82 (385–86)

July 1931 The Chuo Sangyo Kumiai (Co-operative Farm Industry of Southern California) is formed in Los Angeles, destined to become one of the most successful marketing cooperatives in Southern California. It would be part of an ISSEI network that would control the supply—and hence the price—of produce shipped to Los Angeles. Yagasaki 82 (205–07)

September 12, 1931 Thalia Massie, a Caucasian woman, is allegedly beaten and assaulted by a group of Hawaiian and Japanese men. The incident leads to controversial court decisions and vigilante action. (See MASSIE CASE.) Kotani 85 (77–84); United 71 (252)

September 18, 1931 The "Manchurian Incident" begins. Middle-level Japanese army officers autonomously blow up a strip of railroad and blame it on the Chinese, justifying a quick attack on Manchuria. This leads to the formation of the puppet state of Manchukuo, in September 1932. Reischauer 74 (190–91)

1932 A group of Japanese on Kauai form a cooperative that starts its own pineapple cannery at Kauai Homestead near Kapoa. This company would later become Hawaiian Fruit Packers. United 71 (206)

1932 Opponents of Idaho Governor C. Ben Ross place an ad in the newspaper attacking Ross for leasing his farm to an ISSEI. Despite the racist appeal and the anti-Japanese climate exacerbated by Japan's invasion of Manchuria, Ross wins reelection. Sims 78 (4)

April 1932 The California Chrysanthemum Growers Association is established in Redwood City as a non-profit cooperative. By 1939 it had 56 members. The association moved to Palo Alto in 1941 and is active to this day. It is made up of Japanese growers on the Northern California peninsula. Yagasaki 81 (86–87)

May 16, 1932 The Community Employment Agency of Beverly Hills, with the endorsement of the Chamber of Commerce, begins a campaign to exclude non-citizens in domestic and gardening jobs—a thinly veiled means of excluding Japanese gardeners. This event spurs the Japanese gardeners to organize. Tsuchida 84 (448–49)

June 1932 The Japanese Athletic Union (JAU) is formed in Los Angeles to coordinate the burgeoning NISEI club athletic teams in L.A. Waugh 78 (140)

1933 The San Diego Celery Growers Association emerges from an agreement stemming from the Chula Vista anti-Japanese movement. Anti-Japanese spokesman Fred Stafford is president and local grower Tsuneji Chino is vice-president. Estes 78 (448)

April 1933 To counter American criticism of Germany's anti-Semitic laws, Adolf Hitler cites America's anti-Asian discriminatory laws. Abrams 87 (4)

June 5, 1933 Mexican berry pickers in the San Gabriel Valley, California, strike against the largely Japanese

Sumo tournaments were major events in many pre–World War II Japanese American communities. *K. Sakamoto Collection, Japanese American National Museum Photographic & Moving Image Archive*

growers for higher wages. Within a week, up to 7,000 Mexican workers walk off Japanese farms along the coast as well. The strike is "won" by the Japanese on July 6 with substantial help from the white community. (See EL MONTE BERRY STRIKE.)   Spaulding 34; Wollenberg 72 (155–64)

July 1933 SHOJI NOGUMO begins the racially mixed Japanese Gardeners' Association in Hollywood. By the late '30s, it would become all Japanese American. Similar groups were also formed in uptown Los Angeles and West Los Angeles. The three associations merged as the

Boy Scouts in Hawaii during the "Makahiki Ho," 1933. *Hawaii State Archives*

SOUTHERN CALIFORNIA GARDENERS FEDERATION in 1937. By 1940, the federation had 900 members, representing about one-third of all gardeners in those areas. Tsuchida 84 (450)

September 1933 A farmer's conference is held in Los Angeles sponsored by the Central JAPANESE ASSOCIATION of Southern California, Nanka Nogyo Kumiai (Japanese Farmers Association of Southern California) and Nikka Nogyo Kumiai (Japan-California Farmers Association). Thirty-six Japanese agricultural associations are represented and an umbrella organization, the Nanka Chuo Nokai (Central Agricultural Association of Southern California), is formed. It would go on to become the NANKA NOKAI RENMEI (Southern California Farm Federation).   Yagasaki 82 (211–12)

1934 The JAPANESE AMERICAN CITIZENS LEAGUE (JACL) adopts a resolution endorsing the deportation of "undesirable alien communists who are found guilty of subversive acts. . . ."   Ichioka 86–87 (54)

Spring 1934 The Union Flower Market (formed in 1930 by Japanese and Caucasian growers excluded from the SOUTHERN CALIFORNIA FLOWER MARKET) sues the Southern California Flower Market for $300,000 damages, the largest lawsuit in the history of the Southern California Japanese American community. The suit dragged on for three years before being decided in favor of the defendant.   Yagasaki 82 (156–57)

June 13, 1934 The RAFU SHIMPO prints an article in which the JACL suggests the institution of NISEI WEEK by LITTLE TOKYO stores to encourage NISEI patronage. The first Nisei Week takes place later that summer. Waugh 78 (123)

August 17, 1934 White farmers in Arizona's Salt River Valley stage a 150-car parade and set the date of August 25 for all Japanese to leave the area. This sets off an international incident that would last until the following spring. (See SALT RIVER VALLEY INCIDENT.) August 79

1935 The Japanese Mutual Aid Society of Chicago is formed. This becomes the major prewar organization of Chicago providing social services for the ISSEI. It maintained close ties with the consulate and began a language school shortly before the war.   Albert 80 (112–13)

January 22, 1935 The California State Legislature considers SB 231, a bill that would provide segregated schools for Japanese Americans. It did not pass.   James 87b (21)

May 1935 The first Hawaiian statehood bill is introduced into the U.S. House of Representatives. In hearings before Congress on the issue throughout the 1930s, the fear of a Japanese electoral majority is most often cited as a reason not to grant Hawaii statehood. Ogawa 78 (234)

June 1935 The NANKA NOKAI RENMEI (Southern California Farm Federation) emerges out of the Nanka Chuo Nokai at a Japanese farmers' meeting. This federation would play a large role in the Southern California Japanese farming community's "unprecedented vigor" at this time. Yagasaki 82 (212)

June 1935 Japanese farm laborers in Los Angeles form the California Farm Laborers Association. It is headed by Tokijiro Saisho, a Socialist from Saga. This organization would play a key role in the Venice celery workers' strike of 1936. (See VENICE CELERY STRIKE.) Tsuchida 84 (458)

June 24, 1935 President Franklin D. Roosevelt signs the NYE-LEA BILL into law. It grants U.S. citizenship to 500 World War I veterans of Asian descent, most of them Japanese. It had been introduced into Congress on April 2, 1935, by Clarence F. Lea of California who at one time was an ardent exclusionist. Gerald P. Nye of North Dakota introduced the Senate version on April 4. Naka 39 (140)

August 14, 1935 President Roosevelt signs the Social Security Act into law. Schlesinger 83 (469)

September 27, 1935 In the California District Court ruling of T. ABE V. FISH AND GAME COMMISSION, Section 990 of the Fish and Game Code—which had prevented those who hadn't resided in the state for one year from selling fish—is struck down. The State Supreme Court upholds this decision on November 25. Chuman 76 (228–29)

October 1935 A six-member U.S. congressional committee arrives in Hawaii to conduct statehood hearings. Ninety out of 105 delegates testify in favor of statehood. United 71 (254)

April 17, 1936 Led by the California Farm Laborers Association and the Federation of Farm Workers of America, 1,000 Mexican, Japanese and Filipino celery pickers strike against Japanese growers in Venice. After the farmers reject their demands, the strike spreads. It would eventually end on June 8 when 1,500 Mexican workers accept a small raise. (See VENICE CELERY STRIKE.) Tsuchida 84 (458–59)

Many *issei* worked in the commercial fishing industry. *Hideo Shimazu Collection, Japanese American National Museum Photographic & Moving Image Archive*

1937 Sometime between 1935 and 1937, while he is Chief of U.S. Army Intelligence in Hawaii, George S. Patton authors a plan to take 126 prominent Hawaiian Japanese Americans (and two Caucasians) hostage in the event of a war with Japan. Of the 126, 31 are NISEI. The plan would be declared obsolete in May 1940 and never implemented. Slackman 84

May 1937 The SOUTHERN CALIFORNIA RETAIL PRODUCE WORKERS UNION (SCRPWU), an all-NISEI organization, is formed in Los Angeles. The SCRPWU came about as a direct result of the efforts by the AFL–affiliated Local 770, Retail Food Clerks to organize retail produce workers. In one week, the SCRPWU had signed up over 1,000 members. Modell 77 (142–43)

August 1937 The INTERNATIONAL LONGSHOREMAN'S AND WAREHOUSEMAN'S UNION (ILWU) is established. H. Kim 86 (319–20)

1937 JACK KAWANO's Honolulu Longshoremen's Association joins the ILWU. This organization had been formed because American Federation of Labor–affiliated unions would not accept "Oriental" members. Kotani 85 (126)

October 1937 On October 6–22, extensive hearings are held by a U.S. Congress–appointed committee on Hawaii. Forty-one of 67 witnesses favor statehood. United 71 (255)

February 1938 Japanese "ultranationalist" Seigo Nakano visits Honolulu en route home from Germany. He notes the rising Axis powers and stresses the need

"I am a fruitstand worker. It is not a very attractive nor distinguished occupation, and most certainly unappealing in print. I would much rather it were a doctor or lawyer . . . but my aspirations of developing into such (were) frustrated long ago by circumstances . . . (and) I am only what I am, a professional carrot washer." Taishi Matsumoto, "The Protest of a Professional Carrot Washer," *Kashu Mainichi,* April 4, 1937. *Jane Ota Collection, Japanese American National Museum Photographic & Moving Image Archive*

to drive whites out of Asia. His visit and the content of his speeches is covered widely in the Hawaii vernacular newspapers.   Stephan 84 (30)

August 1, 1938   Striking Hilo dock workers face an Inter-Island Steamship Company vessel run by armed strikebreakers. Picketers are attacked with tear gas, fire hoses and, finally, buck shot and bird shot. At least 50 strikers are wounded. Although the strike is broken, the "HILO MASSACRE" helps build labor solidarity in Hawaii. Fuchs 61 (238); Puette 88

September 6, 1938   The RAFU SHIMPO reports a "riot and fist fight" at the conclusion of NISEI WEEK and singles out the Cougars club of Boyle Heights as the instigators.   Waugh 78 (134)

November 1938   A group of Hilo residents organize a drive for "Japanese Patriotic Bonds" to support the Japanese war effort. By the end of the year, over a million yen are raised.   United 71 (257)

February 20, 1939   Twenty thousand people fill Madison Square Garden in New York to attend a Deutschamerikanische Volksbund–sponsored rally to celebrate Hitler and the success of the Nazis in Europe.   Commission 82 (288)

September 1, 1939   Nazi Germany invades Poland. Great Britain and France declare war on Germany two days later. Los Angeles Times, 1 Sept. 1939: 1; Schlesinger 83 (477)

April 1940   At a general meeting of Japanese farmers held in Los Angeles and attended by over 200 ISSEI and NISEI from all parts of the state, the Kashu Nisei Nogyo Renmi (sic) (Nisei Farmers' Federation of California) is formed. It was essentially a vehicle to encourage and instruct *nisei* to become farmers and to maintain their parents' farms. This organization was necessitated by the deteriorating relations between the United States and Japan and the tenuous status of the *issei.*   Yagasaki 82 (217–18)

April 1940   The SOUTHERN CALIFORNIA GARDENERS FEDERATION begins its journal *Gadena no Tomo* (The Gardener's Friend) out of its old newsletter *Gadena Shimbun.*   Tsuchida 84 (450)

June 1940   The Far Eastern Olympics is held in Tokyo. Joining the teams from Japan, Manchukuo, the Philippines, etc. is a Japanese American team from Hawaii.   Duus 87 (30)

June 5, 1940   Germany invades France. Paris would fall just nine days later.   Schlesinger 83 (480)

July 1940   Longshore-plantation workers at Ahukini landing in Kauai go out on strike. The 298-day strike would be the longest in Hawaiian labor history. Though it ended with only minor gains for the workers, the strike was significant for its multiracial (mainly Filipino and Japanese American) character and for the important role played by the ILWU.   Beechert 85 (277–79)

August 1940   The Los Angeles City Council considers a proposal by developers to build a housing tract that would allow whites and Asians but would exclude all others. The Jefferson Park development was to be in the Baldwin Hills section of the city and was vigorously supported by the NISEI. Though the council would reject the project, a *nisei*-organized committee successfully sued to get development approved. After all that, few Japanese Americans bought lots and the project was dead within a year.   Modell 77 (14–15)

October 14, 1940   The U.S. Nationality Act of 1940, effective January 13, 1941, is passed into law. It stipulates that American citizens of foreign parents can lose their citizenship if they reside abroad for over six months and do such things as serve in a foreign military service, vote in a foreign election or work for a foreign government. The law is clearly aimed at NISEI going to school or working in Japan.   Chuman 76 (280–81); United 71 (259); Stephan 84 (26)

October 16, 1940 *The United States imposes an embargo on scrap metal exports to Japan.*   Stephan 84 (78)

November 4–11, 1940 The "GRAND CONGRESS OF OVERSEAS COMPATRIOTS" is held in Tokyo, ostensibly to celebrate the Japanese empire's 2,600th birthday. One thousand nine hundred *doho* (compatriot) delegates from 27 countries attend, including 188 from Hawaii. Stephan 84 (49)

May 9, 1941 MIKE MASAOKA's ultra-patriotic "JAPANESE AMERICAN CREED" is read into the *Congressional Record* by Senator Elbert D. Thomas of Utah.   Masaoka/Hosokawa 87 (49–51); Tsukano 85 (89)

June 1941 Itaru Tachibana, an Imperial Japanese Navy language officer, is arrested in a sting operation in Hollywood, California, and held on spy charges. The case had a major impact on public opinion, but also revealed the nature and primitive state of the Japanese espionage network. Rather than go through a politically charged spy trial, U.S. authorities deported Tachibana.   Kumamoto 79 (55–56)

July 1941 *The U.S. Pacific fleet moves its headquarters from San Diego to Pearl Harbor, Hawaii.*   Stephan 84 (81)

July 18, 1941 A delineation of authority is agreed to between the Department of Justice (DOJ) and the War Department over enemy internment policy. The DOJ would be responsible for the arrests and loyalty hearings of aliens listed as potentially dangerous. Those aliens would be arrested by the FBI and placed under the custody of the Immigration and Naturalization Service. After their hearings, those to be interned would go to camps administered by the War Department.   Clark 80 (7)

July 25, 1941 A Presidential Order freezes Japanese assets in the United States and causes a run on Japanese banks.   United 71 (260)

August 1941 Castle and Cooke terminals sign an agreement with the ILWU covering longshoremen in Honolulu Harbor. This is the first major inroad by the ILWU (or any other union) in Hawaii.   Ogawa 78 (357)

August 18, 1941 In a letter to President Roosevelt, Representative John Dingell of Michigan suggests incarcerating 10,000 Hawaiian Japanese Americans as hostages to ensure "good behavior" on the part of Japan. Smith 91 (81)

October–November 1941 Curtis B. Munson, special representative of the State Department, gathers information on Japanese American loyalty in Hawaii and the West Coast, as commissioned by the president. (See MUNSON REPORT.)   Weglyn 76 (14)

November 1, 1941 The MILITARY INTELLIGENCE SERVICE LANGUAGE SCHOOL opens at the Presidio, San Francisco, with four NISEI instructors and 60 students, 58 of whom are Japanese American. The school is later forced to move to Minnesota after the exclusion order. Commission 82 (254)

November 7, 1941 John Franklin Carter forwards the MUNSON REPORT to the president. The report largely affirms that Japanese Americans are by and large loyal to the U.S. and would pose little threat as a group. Apparently, the president did not read the entire report and may have read only Carter's brief summary. Commission 82 (51–52)

November 12, 1941 Fifteen Japanese American businessmen and community leaders in Los Angeles's LITTLE TOKYO are picked up in an FBI raid. Records and membership lists for such organizations as the Japanese Chamber of Commerce and the Central JAPANESE ASSOCIATION are seized. The 15 would cooperate with authorites, while a spokesman for the Central Japanese Association stated: "We teach the fundamental principles of America and the high ideals of American democracy. We want to live here in peace and harmony. Our people are 100% loyal to America."   Kumamoto 79 (68–69)

December 6, 1941 The NIPPU JIJI headline: "Far East Crises Somewhat Eased, No War Will Occur in the Pacific."   Stephan 84 (39)

December 7, 1941 The U.S. Navy base at Pearl Harbor is attacked. Martial law is immediately declared in Hawaii.

December 7, 1941 Local authorities and the FBI begin to round up the ISSEI leadership of the Japanese American communities in Hawaii and on the mainland. By 6:30 A.M. the following morning 736 *issei* are in custody; within 48 hours, the number would be 1,291. Caught by surprise for the most part, these men are held under no formal charges and family members are forbidden from seeing them. Most would spend the war years in enemy alien INTERNMENT CAMPS run by the Justice Department.   Kumamtoto 79 (69–70)

December 8, 1941   The SAND ISLAND detention camp in Honolulu Harbor is activated to house "potentially dangerous" people picked up in Hawaii. Sand Island, with a capacity of 565, is used for 15 months, and would close on March 1, 1943. Internees begin to be transferred to INTERNMENT CAMPS on the mainland in early 1942. Ogawa 91 (136)

December 11, 1941   The Western Defense Command is established, with Lt. Gen. JOHN L. DEWITT as commander. The West Coast is declared a theater of war.   Wilson/Hosokawa 80 (191)

December 15, 1941   After a brief visit to Hawaii, Secretary of the Navy Frank Knox tells the press, "I think the most effective Fifth Column work of the entire war was done in Hawaii with the possible exception of Norway" despite a complete lack of evidence to support such a charge of sabotage.   Commission 82 (55)

December 19, 1941   At a Cabinet meeting, Secretary of the Navy Frank Knox recommends that all Japanese aliens on the Hawaiian Islands be interned on an island other than Oahu.   Commission 82 (264)

December 22, 1941   *Life* magazine publishes the article "How to tell Japs from the Chinese."   Girdner/Loftis 69 (11)

December 27, 1941   All civilians (over age six) on Oahu are ordered to be fingerprinted and registered. Commission 82 (267)

January 8, 1942   The HAWAII HOCHI and the NIPPU JIJI resume publication under order from the military governor of Hawaii to keep the Japanese community informed. The military maintained strict control over the papers' contents.   United 71 (264)

January 12, 1942   "Wholesale internment, without hearing and irrespective of the merits of individual cases, is the long and costly way around, as the British discovered by painful experience; for by that method not only are guiltless aliens themselves demoralized, but the nation is deprived of a valuable source of labor supply at a time when every available man must be at work."—Attorney General FRANCIS BIDDLE, before a conference of mayors, Washington, D.C.   Leighton 45 (17)

January 19, 1942   The Hawaii Territorial Guard is given orders from Washington to release all men of

Japanese ancestry. The Territorial Guard had been formed immediately after Pearl Harbor to replace the Japanese National Guardsmen who had been inducted into the military in prior months.   Ogawa 78 (321)

January 23, 1942   It is decided that all Japanese American soldiers on the mainland will be assembled in camps in Arkansas and Alabama. Most end up at Camp Robinson, Arkansas, where they would perform non-battle related tasks for nearly two years before being allowed to go into battle with the 442ND REGIMENTAL COMBAT TEAM.   Duus 87 (19, 54)

January 25, 1942   The ROBERTS COMMISSION, appointed by the president and chaired by Supreme Court Justice Owen J. Roberts, issues its report, the first official inquiry into Pearl Harbor. Though stopping short of implicating Japanese Americans in espionage activity, it doesn't go out of its way to exonerate them either. Daniels 71 (49–50)

January 28, 1942   The *Royal T. Frank*, a small transport vessel, is sunk by Japanese torpedos between Maui and Hawaii. Almost all of the 29 killed are Japanese Americans—the first Japanese American soldiers to be killed in World War II.   Duus 87 (94)

January 30, 1942   After his dismissal from the Hawaii Teritorial Guard, Shigeo Yoshida drafts a petition on behalf of the 169 former NISEI members. The petition is sent to General DELOS EMMONS on this date; one month later, the VARSITY VICTORY VOLUNTEERS, an all *nisei* non-combat labor unit, is formed.   Kotani 85 (95)

February 2, 1942   "A viper is nonetheless a viper wherever the egg is hatched. . . . So, a Japanese American born of Japanese parents, nurtured upon Japanese traditions, living in a transplanted Japanese atmosphere and thoroughly inoculated with Japanese . . . ideals, notwithstanding his nominal brand of accidental citizenship almost inevitably and with the rarest exceptions grows up to be a Japanese, and not an American in his . . . ideas, and is . . . menacing . . . unless . . . hamstrung. Thus, while it might cause injustice to a few to treat them all as potential enemies, . . . I cannot escape the conclusion . . . that such treatment . . . should be accorded to each and all of them while we are at war with their race."—from a *Los Angeles Times* editorial. Leighton 45 (17–18)

February 8, 1942   The EMERGENCY SERVICE COMMITTEE (ESC), consisting of NISEI businessmen and professionals, is established on Oahu. Its purpose is to mobilize Japanese American support for the war effort to try to minimize tensions with the non-Japanese American population. Within eight months, the ESC held 170 meetings encouraging Japanese Americans to donate blood, buy war bonds, join volunteer labor battalions, etc.   Kotani 85 (102–03)

February 12, 1942 Seventy-five Japanese employees of the Union Pacific Railroad in Wyoming are dismissed under suspicion of sabotage on a railroad line between Cheyenne and Laramie on which they worked.   Nelson 76 (3)

February 19, 1942 A mass meeting in which NISEI leaders proclaim Japanese American loyalty to the United States draws 1,500 people to the Maryknoll Catholic Mission in Los Angeles. It is sponsored by the JACL, the Japanese American Legion Post, the California Young Buddhists League and other groups.   Girdner/Loftis 69 (102)

February 19, 1942 President Roosevelt signs EXECUTIVE ORDER 9066, which allows military authorities to exclude anyone from anywhere without trial or hearings. Though the subject of only limited interest at the time, this order in effect set the stage for the entire mass removal and detention.   Commission 82 (2); Masaoka/Hosokawa 87 (86)

February 21, 1942 The TOLAN COMMITTEE hearings open in San Francisco. Testimony at these hearings on "National Defense Migration" reveals the depth of anti-Japanese feelings on the West Coast as well as divergent opinions springing from the Japanese American community. Unfortunately for Japanese Americans, the decision to forcibly remove all Japanese Americans was made prior to the hearings.   Daniels 71 (74–81); Hosokawa 69 (286)

February 23, 1942 A lone Japanese submarine surfaces off the coast at Goleta (near Santa Barbara) and begins a 15-minute "attack" of an oil refinery. Although no injuries and little damage resulted, the incident creates a sensation in the press.   Girdner/Loftis 69 (109)

February 23, 1942 The military governor of Hawaii, Lt. Gen. DELOS C. EMMONS, activates the Corps of Engineers Auxilary—i.e., the VARSITY VICTORY VOLUNTEERS (VVV)—as part of the 34th Combat Engineers Regiment. Made up of 150 NISEI, many of whom had been dismissed from the territorial guard, the VVV did non-combat labor such as digging ditches or breaking rocks. The VVV lasted 11 months and many of its

Jerome "Relocation Center" High School, Jerome, Arkansas. *Tora Renge Collection, Japanese American National Museum Photographic & Moving Image Archive*

members subsequently joined the 100TH INFANTRY BATTALION.   Ogawa 78 (321); Kotani 85 (95)

February 24, 1942 In Los Angeles, reports of enemy aircraft result in air-raid sirens and massive anti-aircraft fire. Two people die of heart attacks and three are killed in auto accidents in the massive traffic tie-up that results. The cause of the commotion is later determined to be a lost U.S. weather balloon. (See BATTLE OF LOS ANGELES.)   Girdner/Loftis 69 (109–10)

February 25, 1942 The navy informs Japanese American residents of TERMINAL ISLAND near Los Angeles Harbor that they must leave in 48 hours. They are the first group to be removed en masse and suffer especially heavy losses as a result.   Commission 82 (108)

February 27, 1942 Idaho Governor Chase Clark tells a congressional committee in Seattle that Japanese would be welcome in Idaho only if they were in "concentration camps under military guard." Some credit Clark with the idea for CONCENTRATION CAMPS.   Sims 78 (5)

March 2, 1942 JOHN L. DEWITT issues Public Proclamation No. 1, which creates Military Areas Nos. 1 and 2. Military Area No. 1 included the western portion of California, Oregon and Washington, and part of Arizona, while Military Area No. 2 included the rest of these states. The proclamation also hinted that people might be excluded from Military Area No. 1.   Commission 82 (100)

March 18, 1942 The president signs Executive Order 9102 establishing the WAR RELOCATION AUTHORITY with MILTON EISENHOWER as director. It is allocated $5.5 million.   Commission 82 (107)

March 21, 1942 The first advance groups of Japanese American "volunteers" arrive at MANZANAR. The WRA would take over on June 1 and transform it into a "RELOCATION CENTER."   Cates 80 (45)

March 21, 1942 Public Law 503 is signed into law by President Roosevelt. This law provides criminal sanctions for violations of EXECUTIVE ORDER 9066. Commission 82 (99)

March 23, 1942 During the "VOLUNTARY RESETTLEMENT" period, a JAPANESE AMERICAN CITIZENS LEAGUE chapter in Utah writes a letter discouraging Japanese Americans from the West Coast from moving there. Since the local Japanese Americans "have established a reputation through industry and good behavior. . . . It appears exceedingly unwise to disturb and disrupt this status. . . . Strangers from other localities might be undesireable in adjustment to these settled conditions."   Arrington 91 (95)

March 24, 1942 The first Civilian Exclusion Order by the army is issued for the Bainbridge Island area near Seattle. The 45 resident Japanese American families there are given one week to prepare. By the end of October, 108 exclusion orders would be issued, and all Japanese Americans in Military Area No. 1 and the California portion of No. 2 would be incarcerated in American CONCENTRATION CAMPS.   Commission 82 (109–12); U.S. Department of War 78 (362–66)

March 24, 1942 Public Proclamation No. 3 is issued, establishing a curfew from 8:00 P.M. to 6:00 A.M. for Japanese Americans in Military Area No. 1 and requiring them to stay within a five-mile radius of their homes.   Hohri 88 (29)

March 26, 1942 Led by Fred Isamu Wada, 21 people leave Oakland en route to Keetley, Utah, to form KEETLEY FARMS, the largest community of "voluntary resettlers" outside the West Coast.   Taylor 86 (333, 337)

March 27, 1942 The army issues Public Proclamation No. 4 prohibiting the changing of residence for all Japanese Americans in Military Area No. 1, effectively ending the "voluntary evacuation." (See VOLUNTARY RESETTLEMENT.)   Commission 82 (103)

March 28, 1942 In order to test the curfew regulations in court, Minoru Yasui enters a Portland police station at 11:20 P.M. to present himself for arrest. (See YASUI V. UNITED STATES.)   Girdner/Loftis 69 (203)

March 30, 1942 A War Department order discontinues the induction of NISEI into the armed services on the West Coast.   Commission 87 (187)

Spring 1942 Eight NISEI students arrive at the University of Idaho in Moscow only to be told that their admission was canceled. Amidst rumors of lynch mobs, two women are placed in jail for their own protection. This incident becomes known as "The RETREAT FROM MOSCOW."   Girdner/Loftis 69 (337)

April 6, 1942 MIKE MASAOKA presents an 18-page list of JACL recommendations to WRA director MILTON EISENHOWER, pledging the organization's support: "By having Japanese Americans laud the work of the War Relocation Authority, we may be able to create a favorable public sentiment which will permit your office to do that which you desire in the relocation of our group." Drinnon 87 (67–68)

April 7, 1942 Ten Western governors meet with WRA officials at the Intermountain Conference. The attitude towards resettlement in these states is "antagonistic and hostile."   Myer 71 (281)

April 18, 1942 *Sixteen U.S. B-25 bombers launched from the carrier* Hornet *fly over Tokyo, Yokohama, Nagoya and Kobe. Although little in the way of damage results, psychological implications are great.*   Stephan 84 (113)

April 20, 1942 G. A. Momberg's operation opens for business in Livingston, California. It is a management/custodial corporation begun for the benefit of residents of the three Japanese American farming communities begun by KYUTARO ABIKO—CORTEZ, Yamato and Cressey—in anticipation of being removed. It is believed to be the only organization of its kind for preserving Japanese American farms during the internment. (See YAMATO COLONY (CALIFORNIA).)   Matsumoto 85 (111)

May 1942 Police captain JOHN BURNS announces an Americanization program for Japanese Americans in Hawaii advocating that "a definite break" be made "from those things and institutions which are or represent Japan itself."   Ogawa 78 (316)

May 1, 1942 Having "voluntarily resettled" in Denver, NISEI journalist JAMES OMURA writes a letter to a Washington law firm inquiring about retaining their services to seek legal action against the government for violations of civil and constitutional rights and seeking restitution for economic losses. He was unable to afford the $3,500 fee required to begin proceedings.   Hohri 88 (30)

May 8, 1942 The first "volunteers" (from Imperial Valley, California) arrive at the Colorado River "Relocation Center," or POSTON. Seven thousand four hundred fifty Japanese Americans would arrive in the next three weeks.   Leighton 45 (61)

May 13, 1942 Forty-five-year-old Ichiro Shimoda, a Los Angeles gardener, is shot to death by guards while trying to escape from Fort Sill (Oklahoma) Enemy Alien Internment Camp. The victim was seriously mentally ill, having attempted suicide twice since being picked up on December 7. He is shot despite the guards' knowledge of his mental state.   Kashima 91 (53–54)

May 16, 1942 Hikoji Takeuchi, a NISEI, is shot by a guard at MANZANAR. The guard claimed that he shouted at Takeuchi and that Takeuchi began to run away from him. Takeuchi claimed he was collecting scrap lumber and didn't hear the guard shout. His wounds indicated that he was shot in the front. Though seriously injured, he eventually recovers.   Weglyn 76 (91, 295—note 33)

May 16, 1942 Accompanied by his lawyer, 24-year-old NISEI University of Washington student Gordon Hirabayashi walks into the local FBI office to challenge the constitutionality of the exclusion and curfew orders. (See HIRABAYASHI V. U.S.)   Irons 83

May 21, 1942 The agricultural leave program begins when 15 inmates are released from the Portland "assembly center" to help thin beets in eastern Oregon. Commission 82 (182)

May 25, 1942 The War Department reestablishes the MILITARY INTELLIGENCE SERVICE LANGUAGE SCHOOL at Camp Savage in Minnesota. It had been forced to move from its original location at the Presidio in San Francisco as a result of the exclusion order.   Nyberg, John. "3,500 Minnesota-Trained Nisei Act as 'Eyes, Ears.'" *Minneapolis Star-Journal*, 22 Oct. 1945. Rpt. in Ichinokuchi 88 (43)

May 26, 1942 General George C. Marshall suddenly issues orders establishing the Hawaiian Provisional Infantry Battalion to be made up of Japanese Americans in the Hawaii National Guard. The vast majority of these men were drafted in late 1940. After Japanese plans for an attack on nearby Midway Island were intercepted, many in Hawaii feared an attack of Hawaii by

Japanese in American uniforms. General DELOS EMMONS petitioned Washington for permission to remove the Japanese American guardsmen to the mainland. On June 5, 1,432 members of the Hawaii Provisional Infantry Battalion left Honolulu for San Francisco without getting the chance to say goodbye to loved ones. Ironically, the American victory at Midway was announced on the following day. (See 100TH INFANTRY BATTALION.) Duus 87 (20–21)

May 29, 1942 Largely organized by Quaker leader Clarence E. Pickett, the NATIONAL JAPANESE-AMERICAN STUDENT RELOCATION COUNCIL is formed in Philadelphia with University of Washington dean Robert W. O'Brien as director. By war's end, 4,300 NISEI would be in college.   Girdner/Loftis 69 (336); Weglyn 76 (106)

May 30, 1942 Administrators at the Santa Anita "Assembly Center" receive orders from the army to put 800 to 900 workers on a camouflage net project. It would prove to be either a great success or a burden, depending on one's point of view. (See SANTA ANITA CAMOUFLAGE NET PROJECT AND STRIKE.)   Girdner/Loftis 69 (181)

June 1942 The movie *Little Tokyo, U.S.A.* is released by Twentieth Century-Fox. In it, the Japanese American community is portrayed as a "vast army of volunteer spies" and "blind worshippers of their Emperor," as described in the film's voiced-over prologue.   Leonard 90 (465)

June 1942 The first official WRA resettlers from the camps arrive in Chicago, though others are said to have arrived as early as March.   Albert 80 (114)

June 3–6, 1942 *The Battle of Midway results in a tremendous victory for the Allies, turning the tide of the war.* Schlesinger 83 (489)

June 5, 1942 More than 1,700 Japanese Americans in Hawaii present a check to the U.S. government for "bombs on Tokyo."   Commission 82 (280)

June 12, 1942 The Hawaiian Provisional Infantry Battalion is activated as the 100TH INFANTRY BATTALION while in Oakland, California. Three trains taking three different routes take the men to Camp McCoy, Wisconsin. Arriving there on June 16, they train there for the next six months.   Duus 87 (22–23); C. Tanaka 82 (13)

June 17, 1942 The War Department announces that it won't "accept for service with the armed forces Japanese or persons of Japanese extraction, regardless of citizenship status or other factors." Commission 82 (187)

June 17, 1942 MILTON EISENHOWER resigns as WRA director. DILLON MYER is appointed to replace him. Commission 82 (183)

June 18, 1942 A meeting of the "self-governing council" at the Santa Anita "Assembly Center" called to discuss camp conditions and to make recommendations results in 11 arrests. The group is charged with not having a policeman present, speaking in Japanese and conspiring to circulate a petition. Brief jail terms would be served and the AMERICAN CIVIL LIBERTIES UNION would later take up their case. Girdner/Loftis 69 (182–83)

June 23, 1942 The Civic Planning Board, composed of both ISSEI and NISEI, approves a constitution for the municipal government of POSTON and vote to submit it to the director. Three days later, they learn that a WRA plan for self-government had been completed on June 5 and would be implemented. The key difference: only *nisei* could hold elective office in the WRA plan. Leighton 45 (95)

June 26, 1942 The Army Chief of Staff G-2 Section recommends the formation of a Board of Military Utilization of U.S. Citizens of Japanese Ancestry. Made up of five colonels from the Army Chief of Staff office and DILLON S. MYER, the committee begins work on July 1 to determine whether a Japanese American unit ought to be sent to Europe. In its report of September 14, it would oppose the formation of such a unit "because of the universal distrust in which they are held." Duus 87 (54–56)

July 2, 1942 In Federal District Court, the case of REGAN V. KING is decided. John T. Regan, an exclusionist, had sued to remove NISEI from the voter registration roles in San Francisco. Citing the precedent of the 1898 U.S. V. WONG KIM ARK Supreme Court decision involving a second-generation Chinese American, the court ruled that *nisei* cannot be denied their citizenship. Chuman 76 (183–84)

July 17, 1942 President Roosevelt authorizes the resettlement of up to 15,000 persons from Hawaii "considered as potentially dangerous to national security" and their family members. Fewer than 2,000 Japanese Americans from Hawaii would actually ever be interned on the mainland. Commission 82 (273, 277)

July 17, 1942 The first wages—on a $19/$16/$12 scale—are paid to residents at POSTON. In Poston as in the other WAR RELOCATION AUTHORITY camps, the top $19 monthly wage went to doctors and other professionals; the $16 wage to teachers, secretaries, and other support staff; and the $12 wage to laborers. Complaints soon arise over the low scale, the slow pay process and the classification system. Leighton 45 (105–06)

July 20, 1942 The WAR RELOCATION AUTHORITY (WRA) issues a policy statement on RESETTLEMENT from the camps. *Nisei* who had never studied in Japan, who had a verified job waiting on the outside, and who could pass security clearances by the WRA, FBI and other intelligence agencies, are the only ones eligible for resettlement. These restrictions and the long clearance process virtually guaranteed that few would actually be able to resettle. Commission 82 (183)

July 20, 1942 The first groups of internees arrive at the GILA RIVER "Relocation Center." Cates 80 (45)

July 22, 1942 A severe storm at POSTON does $50,000 worth of damage, resulting from blown off roofs, broken windows, etc. Many residents blame the damage on the flimsy construction of the barracks, which they see as another indication of government disregard of their interests. Leighton 45 (106–07)

July 27, 1942 Two ISSEI—Brawley, California farmer Toshiro Kobata and San Pedro fisherman Hirota Isomura—are shot to death by camp guards at the Lordsburg, New Mexico, enemy alien INTERNMENT CAMP. The men had allegedly been trying to escape. It would later be reported, however, that upon their arrival to the camp, the men had been too ill to walk from the train station to the camp gate. Kashima 91 (53)

August 4, 1942 A routine search for contraband at the Santa Anita "Assembly Center" turns into a "riot." Eager military personnel became overzealous and abusive, which, along with the failure of several attempts to reach the camp's internal security chief, triggered mass unrest, crowd formation and harassment of the searchers. Military police with tanks and machine guns quickly ended the incident. The "overzealous" military personnel were later replaced. Commission 82 (147–48)

August 10, 1942 The Spanish consul and a State Department official visit the army-administered camp at Lordsburg, New Mexico, to settle a labor dispute that had been going on since June. The Lordsburg military commander had been ordering internees to work without pay to build military facilities, a violation of the Geneva convention. Protests had been met with threats and barracks arrests. Kashima 91 (55)

August 10, 1942 The first Japanese Americans arrive at MINIDOKA "Relocation Center" in Idaho.   United States 46 (17)

August 12, 1942 The first 292 "volunteers" arrive at HEART MOUNTAIN, Wyoming.   Nelson 76 (21)

August 27, 1942 The first Japanese Americans arrive at GRANADA "Relocation Center," or Amache in Colorado.   United States 46 (17)

September 11, 1942 The first Japanese Americans arrive at the Central Utah "Relocation Center," or TOPAZ in Utah.   United States 46 (17)

September 17, 1942 The first volunteers from HEART MOUNTAIN leave to work in the beet fields in the surrounding area—but only on the condition that they be returned to Heart Mountain by December 1, as demanded by Wyoming governor Nels Smith.   Nelson 76 (39)

September 18, 1942 The first Japanese Americans arrive at ROHWER "Relocation Center" in Arkansas. United States 46 (17)

October 1942 The HAWAII HOCHI changes its name to the HAWAII HERALD in an effort to "Americanize" the paper's name. The name would eventually be changed back some ten years later.   "A Brief History of the Hawaii Herald." *Hawaii Herald* 11.16 (18 May 1990): 3

October 1, 1942 The WRA issues liberalized rules for leaving the camps, allowing for (a) short term leave (30 days), (b) work group leave and (c) indefinite leave (i.e., RESETTLEMENT).   Commission 82 (183)

October 6, 1942 The first Japanese Americans arrive at JEROME "Relocation Center" in Arkansas.   United States 46 (17)

October 12, 1942 Secretary of War HENRY STIMSON designates General DELOS C. EMMONS as military commander of Hawaii under Executive Order 9066. Commission 82 (273)

October 20, 1942 President Roosevelt calls the "RELOCATION CENTERS" "CONCENTRATION CAMPS" at a press conference. The WRA had consistently denied that the term "concentration camps" accurately described the camps.   Girdner/Loftis 69 (237)

October 29, 1942 MARY OYAMA MITTWER's "HEART MOUNTAIN Breezes" column begins to appear in the

Camp inmates performed most of the work that needed to be done. *K. Nagai Collection, Japanese American National Museum Photographic & Moving Image Archive*

Powell Tribune, a weekly paper in a local Wyoming community. The column extolls the American nature of the incarcerated Japanese Americans. She is replaced by John Kitasako in February 1943.   Nelson 76 (41–42)

October 31, 1942 Twenty-six men from the 100TH INFANTRY BATTALION (Company B, Third Platoon) leave Camp McCoy for Ship Island and Cat Island, off the Mississippi gulf coast. They would spend five months there, on special assignment to help train attack dogs to recognize and attack Japanese based on their supposedly unique scent. Predictably, the plan did not work.   Duus 87 (46–49)

early November 1942 Laborers at HEART MOUNTAIN walk off their jobs, demanding higher wages and better working conditions. The administration refuses their demands and breaks the strike by appealing for other volunteers. Given the desperate need for coal at the center and the encouragement by the *Heart Mountain Sentinel* (the camp newspaper) enough people come forward to break the strike.   Nelson 76 (81–82)

November 3, 1942 Representing the national AMERICAN CIVIL LIBERTIES UNION, Chairman of the Board of Directors John Haynes Holmes, General Council Arthur Garfield Hays, and Director Roger Baldwin write a letter to General JOHN DEWITT. An excerpt: "we cannot refrain from expressing to you our congratulations on so difficult a job accomplished with a minimum of hardship, considering its unprecedented character. Never before were American military authorities confronted with an evacuation of this magnitude; and it is testimony to a high order of administrative organization that it was accomplished with so comparatively few complaints of injustice and mismanagement."   Drinnon 87 (118)

November 14, 1942   At Poston, an attack on a man widely perceived to be an informer results in the arrest of two popular inmates. This incident soon escalates into a mass strike. (See POSTON STRIKE.)   Girdner/Loftis 69 (261)

mid-November 1942   Japanese American hospital workers at HEART MOUNTAIN walk out in protest of their pay differential with Caucasian workers and their ill treatment by some hospital administrators. Three leaders of the protest are arrested and eventually removed to LEUPP ISOLATION CENTER. The strike peters out soon after.   Nelson 76 (82–83)

November 30, 1942   Takeo Tada is beaten by a group of men at GILA RIVER frustrated over the lack of clothing allocations and angry at the administration in general. Tada was widely perceived by others to be an "INU." The incident narrowly avoids becoming a riot or uprising as in similar cases at POSTON two weeks earlier and MANZANAR one week later.   Cates 80 (170–73)

December 1942   The Minneapolis Resettlement Committee is formed; the St. Paul Resettlement Committee had been formed a few months earlier. Each is in operation before the WRA opens its Minneapolis office in February 1943.   Albert 80 (141–42)

December 1, 1942   The TOPAZ Public Library opens with 7,000 books. Attendance soon reaches 450 people per day.   Kawakami 91 (29)

December 5, 1942   Fred Tayama is attacked and seriously injured by a group of inmates in Manzanar. The arrest of the popular Harry Ueno for the crime triggers a mass uprising. (See MANZANAR UPRISING.)   Okihiro 73 (24)

December 10, 1942   The WRA establishes a prison at MOAB, Utah, for recalcitrant inmates.   Drinnon 87 (63)

1943   Dr. THOMAS YATABE founds the Chicago JACL chapter. By the early 1950s, it would become the largest JACL chapter in the U.S. Initially, the relationship between the JACL and the CHICAGO RESETTERS COMMITTEE would not be amicable.   Albert 80 (122–24)

January 6, 1943   The 100TH INFANTRY BATTALION leaves Camp McCoy, Wisconsin, by train. It arrives two days later at Camp Shelby, Mississippi.   Duus 87 (39)

January 29, 1943   A War Department press release announces the registration program for both recruitment

Farewell ceremony for *nisei* soldiers, Iolani Palace, Hawaii, March 28, 1943.   *Hawaii State Archives*

for military service and leave clearance. (See LOYALTY QUESTIONS.)   Collins 85 (28)

early February 1943   The HEART MOUNTAIN CONGRESS OF AMERICAN CITIZENS is formed to challenge the JACL policy of cooperation with the camp administration.   Nelson 76 (103–04)

February 1, 1943   The 442ND REGIMENTAL COMBAT TEAM is activated.   C. Tanaka 82 (17)

February 5, 1943   Governor Lester C. Hunt of Wyoming signs a bill denying the right to vote to HEART MOUNTAIN residents.   Nelson 76 (51)

February 21, 1943   Thirty-five men from TULE LAKE "RELOCATION CENTER" who refuse to fill out the LOYALTY QUESTIONS are arrested without warning and imprisoned. All are from Block 42, known for containing many "troublemakers."   Drinnon 87 (86–87)

March 28, 1943   The Honolulu Chamber of Commerce holds a farewell ceremony in front of Iolani Palace for 2,686 NISEI volunteers for the 442ND REGIMENTAL COMBAT TEAM. A crowd of 15,000–17,000 looks on. The soldiers had been selected from the 10,000 *nisei* in Hawaii who had volunteered immediately upon the announcement of the formation of the 442nd.   Duus 87 (58)

April 11, 1943   JAMES HATSUKI WAKASA, a 63-year-old chef, is shot to death by a sentry at TOPAZ while allegedly trying to escape through a fence. It is later determined that Wakasa had been inside the fence and facing the sentry when shot. The sentry would stand a general court marshall on April 28 at Fort Douglas, Utah, and be found not guilty.   Daniels 88 (228–31); Weglyn 76 (312)

April 13, 1943 "A Jap's a Jap. There is no way to determine their loyalty. . . . This coast is too vulnerable. No Jap should come back to this coast except on a permit from my office."—General JOHN L. DEWITT, head, Western Defense Command, before the House Naval Affairs Subcommittee.   Girdner/Loftis 69 (276–77)

April 21, 1943 Army officials in Washington announce the Japanese execution of a number of Doolittle fliers who had bombed Tokyo.   Nelson 76 (59)

April 23, 1943 Jack Carberry begins his imflammatory series of six articles in the *Denver Post* about food surpluses at HEART MOUNTAIN; "Food Is Hoarded for Japs in U.S. While Americans in Nippon Are Tortured" runs the first headline.   Nelson 76 (59)

April 27, 1943 The WRA prison is moved from MOAB, Utah, to Leupp, Arizona. (See LEUPP ISOLATION CENTER.)   Drinnon 87 (63)

late April 1943 Seventy-five Japanese truck drivers at HEART MOUNTAIN walk out following a fist fight between their Japanese foreman and a Caucasian employee. The strike lasts four days.   Nelson 76 (83)

May 1943 The 442ND REGIMENTAL COMBAT TEAM begins training in Mississippi. It would train until March 1944 before sailing for Europe on May 1 and joining the 100TH INFANTRY BATTALION in June.   Kotani 85 (108)

June 1943 A junior college at MANZANAR is formally recognized and accredited by the California State Department of Education.   Girdner/Loftis 69 (311)

June 1, 1943 In a letter written from the LEUPP ISOLATION CENTER in Arizona, JOE KURIHARA calls on the government to "set an approximate damage of $5,000 for each and every evacuee of voting age and start them on in any industry benefitting the country as a whole." Hohri 88 (32)

June 8, 1943 Hearings in front of the so-called Costello Committee, a subcommittee of the DIES COMMITTEE, begin. Made up of reactionary types determined to prove that the WRA was "coddling" the incarcerated Japanese Americans, the hearings begin with sensational anti-Japanese witnesses. The testimony of WRA head

DILLON MYER and others in Washington, D.C., on July 7 would thoroughly discredit the earlier witnesses. Drinnon 87 (38); Commission 82 (226)

June 21, 1943 The United States Supreme Court rules on the *Hirabayshi* and *Yasui* cases, upholding the constitutionality of the curfew order in finding both men guilty of violating the curfew. The constitutionality of the exclusion order is not ruled upon and will not be until the KOREMATSU V. U.S. decision one year later. (See HIRABAYASHI V. U.S. and YASUI V. U.S.)   Irons 83

July 15, 1943 The WRA announces its segregation policy. Segregated are to be persons who "by their acts have indicated that their loyalties lie with Japan during the present hostilities or that their loyalties do not lie with the United States." (See LOYALTY QUESTIONS.) Commission 82 (208)

August 1943 The (California) Assembly Interim Committee on the Japanese Problem, known as the GANNON COMMITTEE, is set up. It would hold an "investigation" on whether the forcibly removed Japanese Americans should be allowed to return to California. Girdner/Loftis 69 (363)

August 21, 1943 The 100TH INFANTRY BATTALION finally leaves for active duty in Europe. It lands at Oran, North Africa, on September 2 after a 13-day journey. Tanaka 82 (24); Duus 87 (77)

September 13, 1943 The separation of internees at TULE LAKE "RELOCATION CENTER" begins. After the LOYALTY QUESTIONS episode, "loyal" internees are transported from Tule Lake to other camps. Five days later, "disloyal" internees from other camps begin to arrive at Tule Lake.   Thomas/Nishimoto 69 (88)

September 22, 1943 The 100TH INFANTRY BATTALION lands on the beach at Salerno, south of Naples. It would truck north for a few days. It suffers its first casualty on September 28 when 1st Lt. Conrad Tsukayama is hit by a fragment from a land mine set off by a passing jeep. The battalion sees its first action on September 29 at Chiusano. Baseball star Shigeo "Joe" Takata is its first member to be killed in action and its first to receive the Distinguished Service Cross.   Tanaka 82 (28–29); Duus 87 (89–97)

October 16, 1943 After two serious truck accidents in three days, the DAIHYO SHA KAI, a camp-wide representative body of internees, forms amidst growing unrest

at TULE LAKE "SEGREGATION CENTER".   Thomas/
Nishimoto 69 (114–19)

November 3, 1943 The 133rd Regiment, with the
100TH INFANTRY BATTALION as its second battalion,
begins its offensive against German positions along the
Volturno, just south of Naples. The Germans were attempting to buy time there, while consolidating the
Gustav Line 15 miles to the north.   Duus 87 (100–
01)

November 4, 1943 The Tule Lake uprising caps a
month of strife. Tension was high since the administration had fired 43 coal workers involved in a labor dispute
on October 7. (See TULE LAKE "SEGREGATION CEN-
TER.")   Commission 82 (209–210)

December 2, 1943 Amidst a myriad of potential
problems, LEUPP ISOLATION CENTER is closed by the
WRA.   Drinnon 87 (107)

*December 17, 1943 The various Chinese Exclusion Acts
are repealed.*   Schlesinger 83 (494)

December 31, 1943 All 199 men in the Tule Lake
STOCKADE begin with a hunger strike brought about by
being put on a bread-and-water diet. The petition reads:
"We the undersigned have voluntarily vowed to undergo
hunger strike until such time as everyone here in the
stockade is released back to the Colony simultaneously
and unconditionally." Getting no official reaction, the
strike ends on January 6, 1944.   Drinnon 87 (112)

January 14, 1944 NISEI eligibility for the draft is
restored. In the camps, reaction to the announcement
would be mixed.   Commission 82 (246)

January 24, 1944 The 100TH INFANTRY BATTALION
moves into action at Cassino, one of the keys to the
Gustav (or Winter) Line protecting Rome. According
to General Mark Clark, "The battle of Cassino was the
most grueling, the most harrowing, and in one aspect
the most tragic, of any phase of the war in Italy." It took
a total of four major assaults and four months to take
Cassino; the 100th participated in the first two assaults.
On January 20, the 100th had 832 men; less than 500
remained when they were ordered back to Alife on
February 22.   C. Tanaka 82 (39–42); Duus 87 (118–
24)

January 26, 1944 Spurred by the announcement of
the draft a few days before, 300 people attend a public
meeting at HEART MOUNTAIN. Here, the Fair Play Committee is formally organized. KIYOSHI OKAMOTO is cho-

sen chairman and PAUL T. NAKADATE vice-president. (See
HEART MOUNTAIN FAIR PLAY COMMITTEE.)   Nelson
76 (121)

February 1944 Merrill's Marauders arrive in North
Burma. For the next seven months, this American ground
combat unit led by Brig. General Frank Merrill would
make a series of daring and extremely dangerous raids
to harass and disrupt the enemy in the China-Burma-
India theater. Among the Marauders were 14 NISEI
linguists/infantrymen—Edward Mitsukado, Thomas K.
Tsubota, Herbert Y. Miyasaki, Robert Y. Honda, Roy
K. Nakada, Roy Matsumoto, Ben S. Sugeta, Grant
Hirabayashi, Jimmy Yamaguchi, Russell K. Kono, Henry
Gosho, Calvin Kobata, Howard Furumoto and Akiji
Yoshimura.   Yoshimura, Akiji. "Fourteen Nisei and the
Marauders." *Pacific Citizen,* 25 Dec. 1959. Rpt. in Ichinokuchi
88 (85–94)

February 16, 1944 President Roosevelt signs Executive Order 9423, which transforms WRA authority to
the Department of the Interior.   Commission 82 (228)

March 1, 1944 Four hundred NISEI attend a HEART
MOUNTAIN FAIR PLAY COMMITTEE public rally. A resolution stating that men drafted into military service
should refuse to report for the physical or for induction
is unanimously passed.   Nelson 76 (125–26)

March 20, 1944 Forty-three Japanese American soldiers are arrested for refusing to participate in combat
training at Ft. McClellan, Alabama. Eventually, 106 are
arrested for their refusal, undertaken to protest the treatment of their families in U.S. CONCENTRATION CAMPS.
Twenty-one are convicted and serve prison time before
being paroled in 1946. The records of 11 are cleared by
the Army Board of Corrections of Military Records in
1983. (The other 10 did not apply for clearance.)
"Army Records of Camp Protesting Nisei Cleared." *Rafu
Shimpo,* 1 Sept. 1983: 1

March 26, 1944 The 100TH INFANTRY BATTALION
lands at Anzio beachhead, a second front between the
Gustav Line and Rome. Little progress would be made
for the next couple of weeks as the two sides faced each
other across a no-man's land. It is during this period
that Colonel Gordon Singles assumed command of the
battalion. After a daring daytime raid by 100th members
Young Oak Kim and Irving Akahoshi to take two German POWs nets the needed information, the Fifth Army
launches its attack at Anzio on April 23. The push to
Rome follows—Rome falls on June 5.   C. Tanaka 82
(44); Duus 87 (129–37)

Many Japanese Americans in the U.S. Army had to venture into American concentration camps to visit friends and family. *Mary Kamimura Collection, Japanese American National Museum Photographic & Moving Image Archive*

late March 1944 KIYOSHI OKAMOTO and Isamu Horino of the HEART MOUNTAIN FAIR PLAY COMMITTEE are "deported" to TULE LAKE "SEGREGATION CENTER," in an attempt by the administration to break up the committee.   Nelson 76 (133)

May 10, 1944 A Federal Grand Jury issues indictments against 63 HEART MOUNTAIN draft resistors. The 63 are found guilty and sentenced to jail terms on June 26. They would be granted a pardon on December 24, 1947. (See U.S. V. FUJII, ET AL.)   Chuman 76 (257–58)

May 24, 1944 Shoichi James Okamoto is shot to death by a guard at TULE LAKE "SEGREGATION CENTER" after stopping a construction truck at the main gate for permission to pass. Private Bernard Goe, the guard, would be acquitted after being fined a dollar for "unauthorized use of government property"—a bullet. Drinnon 87 (43); Weglyn 76 (312)

June 2, 1944 The 442ND REGIMENTAL COMBAT TEAM arrives at Naples harbor after a 28-day Atlantic crossing. It would be met by the 100TH INFANTRY BATTALION on June 10 in Civitavecchia, 40 miles northwest of Rome. C. Tanaka 82 (47); Duus 87 (156)

June 6, 1944 D-Day Operation Overlord takes place, beginning just after midnight. The largest invasion force in history consists of 4,000 invasion ships, 600 warships, 10,000 planes and 176,000 troops. The landing takes place on the beaches of Normandy between Cherbourg and LeHavre. By *the end of the day, 150,000 troops are entrenched on the beach.*   Schlesinger 83 (497)

June 26, 1944 As part of the Thirty-fourth Division, the 442ND REGIMENTAL COMBAT TEAM, with the 100TH INFANTRY BATTALION as its new first battalion, goes into combat for the first time. Its objective is Belvedere, a town south of Florence and the Gothic Line. When the new troops run into immediate trouble, the battle-tested 100th moves in from the rear, surprising the Germans and capturing the town in three hours. The 100th receives the first of its three Presidential Unit Citations for this action and the battle of Sassetta the next day.   C. Tanaka 82 (53); Duus 87 (156–57)

June 30, 1944 JEROME becomes the first camp to close when the last internees are transferred to ROHWER. United States 46 (17)

July 1944 Gyodo Kono founds the Midwest Buddhist Temple in Chicago. It would become the largest and most prosperous Japanese church in the city.   Albert 80 (128)

July 1944 Masao Akiyama, a 27-year-old KIBEI, is charged with violating the Selective Service Act, the first NISEI to be so charged in Hawaii.   Ogawa 78 (324)

July 1944 The first contingent of the Dixie Mission arrives in Yenan in remote northwestern China. The Dixie Mission is a U.S. Observer group stationed in Communist-held northern China to gather information on both Japanese troops and the Communist regime in general. Five NISEI linguists—KOJI ARIYOSHI, Jack Ishii, George I. Nakamura, Sho Nomura and Tosh Uesato—are part of the mission.   Nomura, Sho. "The Dixie Mission: The Story of a Little-Known Group of Nisei GIs." In Ichinokuchi 88 (109–24)

July 1, 1944 President Roosevelt signs Public Law 405, the so-called "denaturalization bill." This bill allows native-born United States citizens to renounce their citizenships in time of war.   Drinnon 87 (129)

July 2, 1944 WRA officials have workers place "large pieces of beaverboard" on the fence separating the STOCKADE at Tule Lake to prevent visual contact between inmates and their families. (See TULE LAKE "SEGREGATION CENTER.")   Drinnon 87 (116, 126)

July 2, 1944 Yaozo Hitomi, the pro-administration manager of the Tule Lake co-op, has his throat slit with a knife, killing him. (See TULE LAKE "SEGREGATION CENTER.")   Drinnon 87 (126)

July 10, 1944 After weeks of effort to secure permission, Northern California ACLU director Ernest Besig finally visits Tule Lake to confer with the numerous inmates with grievances. (See TULE LAKE "SEGREGATION CENTER.") Drinnon 87 (127–28)

July 19, 1944 To protest the "denial of due process of law," Tule Lake STOCKADE inmates begin their second hunger strike. This one lasts until August 13—minus a five-day intermission when the men are hospitalized. (See TULE LAKE "SEGREGATION CENTER.") Drinnon 87 (130)

July 21, 1944 Seven members of the HEART MOUNTAIN FAIR PLAY COMMITTEE are arrested—Robert KIYOSHI OKAMOTO, Isamu Sam Horino, PAUL TAKEO NAKADATE, Frank Seishi Emi, Gentaro Kubota, Minoru Tamesa and Tsutomu Wakaye—along with outside journalist JAMES OMURA. Their trial over "unlawful conspiracy to counsel, aid and abet violators of the draft" begins on October 23. All but Omura would eventually be found guilty. (See U.S. V. OKAMOTO ET AL.) Chuman 76 (258)

Summer 1944 The Minneapolis Church Federation sponsors the formation of the United Christian Ministry to Japanese Americans in the Twin Cities. Its purpose is to educate local people and resettle Japanese Americans "so that Japanese Americans here in the Twin Cities may become fully assimilated." Albert 80 (143)

August 1944 The MILITARY INTELLEGENCE SERVICE LANGUAGE SCHOOL moves to nearby Fort Snelling from Camp Savage to meet the need for expanded facilities. Weckerling, John. "Nisei Language Experts: Japanese Americans Play Vital Roles in U.S. Intelligence Service in WWII." In Ichinokuchi 88 (192)

August 22, 1944 Under pressure from WAYNE COLLINS and Ernest Besig, the Tule Lake STOCKADE is shut down and all prisoners are "released." Drinnon 87 (133–35)

August 31, 1944 The War Department lifts all restrictions on colleges NISEI are allowed to enroll in. Girdner/Loftis 69 (336)

September 1944 Two NISEI soldiers from HEART MOUNTAIN stationed in Mississippi apply to Wyoming secretary of state Mart T. Christensen for absentee ballots—a direct challenge to the anti-Japanese voting law of 1943. Their request is denied. Nelson 76 (154)

September 12, 1944 Three POSTON inmates—Ignatius Elmer Yamamoto, Dr. George Ochikubo and Kiyoshi Shigekawa—file a lawsuit in the Federal Courts seeking an injunction against Major General Charles H. Bonesteel, commanding officer of the Western Defense Command, to restrain him from excluding them from California. On June 1, 1945, Judge Peirson M. Hall decides the case and upholds the exclusion, resorting to the "MILITARY NECESSITY" explanation. "Little-Known WW II Internment Legal Battle Surfaces." *New York Nichibei*, 11 Apr. 1985: 1–2

September 26–27, 1944 The 442ND REGIMENTAL COMBAT TEAM (including the 100TH INFANTRY BATTALION) leaves Naples for France. The 442nd had been at the Arno Line west of Florence monitoring enemy movements. After the Normandy invasion, the Allied armies established a second front in southern France on August 15 to draw the enemy away from Normandy. The 442nd lands at Marseilles on September 30 and is attached to the Thirty-sixth Division, also known as the Texas Division. Kotani 85 (109); Duus 87 (159–60)

October 14, 1944 The 442ND REGIMENTAL COMBAT TEAM arrives in the Vosges Mountains. Located east of Paris near the German border, it is a hilly, heavily forested area. The two main cities of the region are Epinal and St. Die; on the railroad connecting the two is the little town of Bruyeres. Allied forces had been engaged in heavy fighting here since September 30. The 442nd joins the fighting here on October 16; after three days of fighting, the 100TH INFANTRY BATTALION takes Hill A, the key to Bruyeres. The forests, filled with mines and well-hidden enemy soldiers, required tanks to flush out. On the same day (October 18), the second battalion captures Hill B and Japanese American soldiers enter the town. The 100th receives its second Presidential Unit Citation for this action. Duus 87 (161–72)

October 22, 1944 The 100TH INFANTRY BATTALION takes Biffontaine. Although it meets little resistance in taking the town, it is isolated and vulnerable to the inevitable enemy counterattack and suffers many casualties. Help does not arrive until the 24th. Duus 87 (183–87)

October 24, 1944 Presidential Proclamation No. 2627 formally ends martial law in Hawaii. Little changes, however, in the day-to-day way of life on the islands as curfews, restricted areas and censorship remain in place. Commission 82 (268)

October 27–30, 1944 The 442ND REGIMENTAL COMBAT TEAM rescues an American battalion cut off and surrounded by the enemy. Eight hundred casualties are incurred in the rescue of 211 men. After this rescue, the

The 442nd Regimental Combat Team. *U.S. Army Collection*

442nd is ordered to keep advancing in the forest; it would push ahead without relief or rest until November 9. (See "LOST BATTALION.")   C. Tanaka 82 (90–99); Duus 87 (188–212)

November 1944 Colorado voters turn back a measure that would have amended the constitution to prohibit Japanese aliens from owning land. This measure had earlier been passed by the Colorado house, but nixed by the state senate. Colorado has never had an ALIEN LAND LAW.   Endo 85 (105)

November 12, 1944 General John Dahlquist calls an assembly to honor the 442ND REGIMENTAL COMBAT TEAM. Upon receiving the troops, he says to Lt. Colonel Virgil Miller, "I ordered that all the men be assembled." Miller replies, "Yes sir. All the men are what you see." Of the 2,943 men in the 442nd who entered the Vosges, there were 161 dead, 43 missing and 2,000 wounded— 882 of them seriously.   Duus 87 (217)

December 17, 1944 Public Proclamation No. 21 is issued, rescinding the mass exclusion orders.   Commission 82 (235)

December 18, 1944 The United States Supreme Court issues its decisions on the *Korematsu* and *Endo* cases. The former decision upholds the constitutionality of the exclusion order while the latter finds that the government cannot detain "concededly loyal" persons against their will. Though it effectively throws open the doors of the camps, the Endo decision does not address the constitutionality of the mass removal and detention of Japanese Americans. (See KOREMATSU V. U.S. and ENDO, EX PARTE.)   Irons 83

December 27, 1944 Renunciants and ISSEI leaders involved in pro-Japan demonstrations at TULE LAKE "SEGREGATION CENTER" begin to be transferred to Justice Department–administered INTERNMENT CAMPS. Other groups follow on January 26, February 11 and March 4, 1945. They are moved to SANTA FE, New Mexico, and Fort Lincoln, North Dakota.   Clark 80 (35–36)

January 1945 The local American Legion Post has 16 names of NISEI servicemen removed from the Hood River, Oregon, honor role. After the incident receives national publicity, the names are replaced on March 12, 1945. (See HOOD RIVER INCIDENT.)   Girdner/Loftis 69 (396)

January 2, 1945 Restrictions preventing RESETTLEMENT on the West Coast are removed, although many exceptions remain. A few carefully screened Japanese Americans had returned to the coast in late 1944. Girdner/Loftis 69 (380–81)

January 8, 1945 The packing shed of the Doi family is burned and dynamited and shots are fired into their home. The family had been the first to return to California from GRANADA and the first to return to Placer County, having arrived three days earlier. Although several men are arrested and confess to the acts, all would be acquited. Some 30 similar incidents would greet other Japanese Americans returning to the West Coast between January and June.   Girdner/Loftis 69 (389–90); Leonard 90 (468); Myer 71 (xxix)

Garden created by Kuichiro Nishi at Manzanar "Relocation Center," California, 1945. *Mary Ishizuka Collection, Japanese American National Museum Photographic & Moving Image Archive*

March 12, 1945   After the announcement that three apparent resistance leaders were to be removed, the former Tule Lakers at the SANTA FE INTERNMENT CAMP riot. The entire Tule Lake group is segregated a few days later. (See TULE LAKE "SEGREGATION CENTER.")   Clark 80 (37–38)

March 16, 1945   The WRA issues "new regulations sharply curtailing the residual rights of individuals at Tule Lake"; the STOCKADE is reopened. (See TULE LAKE "SEGREGATION CENTER.")   Drinnon 87 (145)

March 28, 1945   The 442ND REGIMENTAL COMBAT TEAM departs the south of France for Italy once again. Their four-month stay in France in relative luxury and comfort would be dubbed the "champagne campaign." One thousand two hundred and fourteen new replacements had joined the unit in France, along with 265 recovered wounded who returned. They would join the 92nd unit, an all-black division, in "mopping up" in Italy. Fighting would end in Italy on May 2.   Duus 87 (226–28)

April 1–June 21, 1945   *The Battle of Okinawa takes place. The Allied victory results in 80,000 American and 120,000 Japanese casualties.*   Schlesinger 83 (499)

April 5–6, 1945   At dawn on the 6th, the 442ND REGIMENTAL COMBAT TEAM launches a surprise attack on Nazi mountainside positions in the Apennines. The 3rd Battalion had climbed 3,000 feet with full battle gear during the night to get in position for the attack. In one day, their attack breaks the Nazi Gothic Line, which had withstood Allied assaults for months. Kotani 85 (121)

April 13, 1945   *President Franklin D. Roosevelt dies of a cerebral hemorrhage.*   *Los Angeles Times*, 13 Apr. 1945: 1

May 1945   ILWU members of the Stockton Unit of Warehouse Union, Local 6 refuse to work with a Japanese American in violation of all established ILWU policy. The ILWU national leadership takes swift action to remedy the situation, especially since the ILWU would soon undertake a massive campaign to unionize Japanese American workers in Hawaii. (See STOCKTON INCIDENT.)   Schwartz 80

May 7, 1945   *The surrender of Germany ends the war in Europe.*   Schlesinger 83 (500)

May 21, 1945   The Hawaii legislature passes the Hawaii Employment Relations Act—the "Little Wagner Act"—which accords agricultural workers the same organizing rights as industrial workers.   Fuchs 61 (357)

August 6, 1945   *The atomic bomb is dropped on Hiroshima. Three days later, a second bomb is dropped on Nagasaki. The war would end on August 14.*   Schlesinger 83 (500)

August 28, 1945   WAYNE COLLINS's visit with Tule Lake Project Director Raymond Best results in the release of five teenagers imprisoned without charge since June 3 and the permanent closing of the STOCKADE. (See TULE LAKE "SEGREGATION CENTER.")   Drinnon 87 (151)

October 24, 1945   All government functions revert to civilian authority in Hawaii.   Ogawa/Fox 91 (135)

October 29, 1945   The 1399th Engineering Construction Battalion, an all-NISEI group that handled many vital construction projects in Hawaii, is awarded a Meritorious Service Plaque for "superior performance and record of accomplishment and exceptional devotion to duty." (See THE "CHOWHOUNDS.")   Kotani 85 (113)

November 13, 1945   WAYNE COLLINS files two mass petitions for 987 renunciants from Tule Lake in the U.S. District Court, San Francisco. Although most succeed in retaining their citizenship, the process would drag out for years. (See RENUNCIATION OF CITIZENSHIP and TULE LAKE "SEGREGATION CENTER.")   Weglyn 76 (255)

November 21, 1945   *The United Auto Workers go on strike in Detroit. This would be the first of many strikes in the immediate postwar period including those by Western Electric telephone mechanics (January 9, 1946), the United Steelworkers (January 21, 1946), and 400,000 members of the United Mine Workers (April 1, 1946).*   Schlesinger 83 (502, 514)

November 29, 1945   The Okinawa Relief Clothing Drive Committee is formally organized, sponsored by the Honolulu Council of Churches. It was the brainchild of Pfc. Taro Higa upon his return from the American invasion of Okinawa. One hundred fifty-one tons of clothing was shipped out by February 5, 1946. This would be just one of many Okinawa relief efforts led by OKINAWANS in Hawaii.   Sakihara 81a (115–16)

Late 1945   The CHICAGO RESETTLERS COMMITTEE, a NISEI group set up to help other *nisei* with the RESETTLEMENT process, is founded with Harry Maeda as chairman.   Albert 80 (120–21)

Late 1945 Former *Rocky Shimpo* columnist Ryoichi Rujii founds the *Chicago Shimpo*.   Albert 80 (125–26)

1946 The Twin Cities (Minnesota) chapter of the JACL is formed. It adopts the name Twin Cities United Citizens League, becoming the only JACL chapter not to use the JACL name.   Albert 80 (152–53)

January 7, 1946 Hearings begin to determine whether renunciants should be deported or released. (See RENUNCIATION OF CITIZENSHIP.)   Weglyn 76 (257)

March 20, 1946 TULE LAKE "SEGREGATION CENTER" closes, culminating "an incredible mass evacuation in reverse." In the month prior to the closing, some 5,000 inmates had to be moved, many of whom were elderly, impoverished, or mentally ill and with no place to go. Of the 554 persons left there at the beginning of the day, 450 are moved to CRYSTAL CITY, 60 are released, and the rest are "relocated."   Weglyn 76 (259)

May 22, 1946 The JACL holds a banquet in honor of WAR RELOCATION AUTHORITY director DILLON S. MYER at the Roosevelt Hotel in New York. He is celebrated for his "courageous and inspired leadership" and as a "champion of human rights and common decency." Drinnon 87 (9)

June 29, 1946 Congress passes Public Law 471, the G.I. Fiancees Act. This act allows the alien fiancée of an American soldier who had served in World War II to enter the United States for three months. After a marriage within that period, the wife could stay in the United States as a permanent resident alien. Under the provisions of this act and the earlier War Brides Act, signed into law by President Truman on Dec. 28, 1945, some 40,000 brides would enter the country.   Chuman 76 (300–01); Kim 86 (542–43)

July 15, 1946 The 442ND REGIMENTAL COMBAT TEAM is received on the White House lawn by President Truman. "You fought not only the enemy but you fought prejudice—and you have won," remarks the president.   Commission 82 (260); Murphy 54 (282)

September 1946 The SOUTHERN CALIFORNIA FLOWER MARKET officially reopens in Los Angeles. An office there had been open since November 1945 to make preparations.   Yagasaki 82 (334)

November 5, 1946 California voters reject Proposition 15 by a vote of 1,143,780 to 797,067. Called "Validation of Legislative Amendments to ALIEN LAND LAW," Prop. 15 would have incorporated the Alien Land Law into California's state constitution. The defeat of Prop. 15 marked the first time in the state's history that an anti-Asian ballot initiative was voted down.   Chuman 76 (204–06); Leonard 90 (478)

November 18, 1946 A settlement is reached on the first territory-wide, industry-wide strike in Hawaii history. Beginning on September 1 and involving 28,000 workers on 33 sugar plantations, the settlement marks a clear-cut victory for the workers.   Kotani 85 (119–20)

1947 Former Kauai ILWU leader Ichiro Izuka writes a pamphlet entitled "The Truth About Communism in Hawaii." Like JACK KAWANO, he became fed up with JACK HALL's leadership of the ILWU and had taken to red-baiting.   Kotani 85 (122)

June 30, 1947 U.S. District Court Judge Louis E. Goodman orders that the petitioners in WAYNE COLLINS's suit of November 13, 1945, be released; native-born American citizens could not be converted to enemy aliens and could not be imprisoned or sent to Japan on the basis of renunciation. Three hundred two persons are finally released from CRYSTAL CITY and SEABROOK FARMS, New Jersey, on September 6, 1947. (See RENUNCIATION OF CITIZENSHIP.)   Weglyn 76 (260)

September 5, 1947 In the federal district court of Los Angeles, the case of Yuichi Inouye, Miye Mae Murakami, Tsutako Sumi, and Mutsu Shimizu v. Clark is decided. The four had renounced their citizenship under duress at TULE LAKE "SEGREGATION CENTER" and were restored U.S. citizenship in this decision. It would be upheld in the Ninth Circuit Court of Appeals on Aug. 26, 1949. (See INOUYE, YUICHI ET AL. V. CLARK.) Chuman 76 (269–72)

December 24, 1947 The HEART MOUNTAIN draft resistors receive a presidential pardon. (See U.S. V. FUJII ET AL.)   Hohri 91 (197)

January 1948 Ten NISEI growers start Golden State Wholesale Florists to wholesale Japanese American grown flowers, primarily to the East Coast.   Yagasaki 82 (333–34)

January 19, 1948 The United States Supreme Court reverses the ruling of the California Supreme Court in the OYAMA V. CALIFORNIA case, ruling a key provision of the ALIEN LAND LAW unconstitutional. NISEI Fred Oyama had lost land he had purchased with funds provided by his father in an escheat action in 1944 that was upheld on appeal in 1946. Oyama had then filed suit claiming that as the son of an "ALIEN INELIGIBLE TO

CITIZENSHIP," he faced a greater burden of proof than other citizens in accepting a gift of money to buy land from his father. With this decision, the practice of *nisei* buying land for their ISSEI parents is essentially ruled beyond the scope of the Alien Land Law.   Chuman 76 (203–14)

June 1948   Two NISEI—Pfc. Fumitake Nagato and Pfc. Saburo Tanamachi—are interred at Arlington National Cemetery. They are the first Japanese Americans to be buried there since 1898.   Masaoka/Hosokawa 87 (205–06)

June 7, 1948   In TAKAHASHI V. FISH AND GAME COMMISSION, the U.S. Supreme Court rules that California could not bar "ALIENS INELIGIBLE TO CITIZENSHIP" from fishing off the coast for a living.   Chuman 76 (231)

July 2, 1948   President Truman signs the JAPANESE AMERICAN EVACUATION CLAIMS ACT, a measure to compensate Japanese Americans for certain economic losses attributable to their forced evacuation. Although some $38 million was to be paid out through provisions of the act, it would be largely ineffective even on the limited scope in which it operated.   Nakasone-Huey 86 (8–9, 218)

August 11, 1948   HAROLD SAKATA wins an Olympic silver medal in weightlifting in the light-heavyweight division, becoming the first Japanese American to win an Olympic medal. He would later go on to greater fame as professional wrestler Tosh Togo and as Oddjob in the James Bond movie *Goldfinger*.   Wallechinsky 84 (479)

December 7, 1948   The "Christmas Cheer" program, which solicits food and gifts for the Japanese American underprivileged in Los Angeles, begins. Two hundred and thirty-eight are aided in 1948; a high of 367 would be reached in 1950. The local JACL and RAFU SHIMPO are key movers of the program.   Joe, Sue Takimoto. "Ten Years of Christmas Cheer." *Rafu Shimpo*, 20 Dec. 1957: II-3, 14

1949   The Japanese American Community Center opens in Minneapolis. It goes on to become the focus of the Twin Cities Japanese American community. It would close for lack of funds in June 1965.   Albert 80 (154, 159)

March 1949   A 178-day longshoreman's strike begins in Hawaii. It would cripple the island economy for

Despite the best efforts of the War Relocation Authority, Japanese American communities such as Los Angeles's Little Tokyo were reestablished soon after displaced Japanese Americans returned to the West Coast. *Sumiko Akashi Collection, Japanese American National Museum Photographic & Moving Image Archive*

months and turn the tide of public opinion against the ILWU. (See 1949 STRIKE.)   Fuchs 61 (359–61)

February 7, 1950   Senator Joseph R. McCarthy tells a Wheeling, West Virginia, crowd that the State Department is harboring Communists. McCarthy's anti-Communist activities would preoccupy the nation for the next four years. Schlesinger 83 (523–24)

April 1950   The House Un-American Activities Committee comes to Hawaii. JACK KAWANO and 38 others refuse to answer questions about Communist activity in the ILWU. The "RELUCTANT 39" are indicted in the U.S. District Court.   Kotani 85 (123)

June 25, 1950   North Korea invades South Korea. The Korean War would drag on for three years before a ceasefire agreement is reached in July 1953.   Schlesinger 83 (522)

August 1950 In order to adjust to changes in the floriculture industry, the SOUTHERN CALIFORNIA FLOWER MARKET, INC. is closed and is replaced by the NISEI-run Southern California Flower Growers, Inc.   Yagasaki 82 (334)

May 9, 1951 The Hollywood premiere of MGM's *Go For Broke* takes place at the Egyptian Theatre. It is attended by, among others, 100 NISEI Purple Heart winners and the mother of Congressional Medal of Honor winner SADAO MUNEMORI. The movie, which details the derring-do of the 442ND REGIMENTAL COMBAT TEAM, stars Van Johnson and is produced by Dore Schary and directed by Robert Pirosh.   Mori, Henry. "First Nighters at 'Go For Broke' Premiere Pay Homage to Battling Nisei Soldiers." *Rafu Shimpo,* 10 May 1951: 1

July 1951 JACK KAWANO heads for Washington where he will testify for five months before the House Un-American Activities Commission about the Communist Party and the ILWU.   Kotani 85 (125)

September 21, 1951 The UNITED OKINAWAN ASSOCIATION OF HAWAII is inaugurated, as an umbrella organization for existing Okinawan organizations. Its original 14 member clubs would increase to 39 by 1980. Controversy over the need for an exclusively Okinawan organization would curtail early membership.   Adaniya 81 (327)

October 12, 1951 The Japanese Casualty Insurance Association of Los Angeles, a predominently NISEI group, is formed. Willie Funakoshi is named the first president. Ten local agencies make up the association.   "Insurancemen Celebrate 20 Years Since Founding." *Rafu Shimpo,* 22 Nov. 1971: 1

January 1952 After ten years as the HAWAII HERALD, the Hawaii Japanese American newspaper reverts to its former name, HAWAII HOCHI. The *Hochi* had changed its name during World War II in an effort to "Americanize."   "A Brief History of the Hawaii Herald." *Hawaii Herald* 11.16 (18 May 1990): 3

January 2, 1952 In OKIMURA V. ACHESON, the U.S. Supreme Court rules that Okimura's forced service in the Japanese army during World War II should not result in his loss of citizenship.   Chuman 76 (317–18)

April 17, 1952 The California State Supreme Court rules the ALIEN LAND LAW unconstitutional by a 4-3 vote. Newspaper publisher Sei Fujii directly challenged the law after it had been weakened by the OYAMA V. CALIFORNIA decision four years previous. (See FUJII SEI V. STATE OF CALIFORNIA.)   "California Supreme Court Rules Alien Land Law Unconstitutional." *Rafu Shimpo,* 18 Apr. 1952: 1

June 2, 1952 In the case of KAWAKITA V. UNITED STATES, the U.S. Supreme Court upholds lower court decisions against Tomoya Kawakita, a U.S. citizen convicted of treason for acts committed in Japan during World War II and sentenced to death. His sentence would be commuted to life imprisonment in 1953 and he would later be granted a pardon by President Kennedy and sent back to Japan.   Chuman 76 (288–90)

June 27, 1952 Successfully overriding President Truman's veto the Senate (57-26) follows the House (278-113) to vote the McCarran Bill into law. Among other things, it grants Japan a token immigration quota and allows ISSEI naturalization. In effect on December 24, Congress had initially passed the bill on June 11 and it had been vetoed on June 25. (See IMMIGRATION ACT OF 1952.)   "Issei Granted Citizenship Rights as Senate Follows House in Approving McCarran Bill." *Rafu Shimpo,* 27 June 1952: 1

July 9, 1952 The California Supreme Court upholds a lower court decision overturning the ALIEN LAND LAW in MASAOKA, ET AL., V. STATE OF CALIFORNIA. This decision comes three months after the FUJII SEI V. STATE OF CALIFORNIA case.   Chuman 76 (220–21)

July 26, 1952 TOMMY KONO becomes the first Japanese American Olympic gold medalist, winning the lightweight weightlifting title with a total lift of 362.5 kg. HAROLD SAKATA was the first JA Olympic medalist, having won a silver in the 1948 light-heavyweight weightlifting competition. By the end of the Helsinki Games, Japanese Americans won four gold, one silver and two bronze medals. The other medalists (all in swimming): July 29—FORD KONNO, gold, 800 meter freestyle relay; July 30—Ford Konno, silver, 400 meter freestyle; Aug. 1—YOSHINOBU OYAKAWA, gold, 100 meter backstroke; Evelyn Kawamoto, bronze, 400 meter freestyle relay; Aug. 2—Ford Konno, gold, 1500 meter freestyle; Evelyn Kawamoto, bronze, 400 meter freestyle.   *Rafu Shimpo,* various

December 1952 The first Japanese television program in Hawaii is broadcast on KGMB. The popular local Japanese American band Shochiku Orchestra is among the featured performers. Japanese television would become a staple of life for many Japanese Americans in both Hawaii and the major communities of the mainland in the years to come.   Hirayama, Laura. "The Heyday of Japanese Music: Pre-and Post-War Period." *Hawaii Herald*, 21 Aug. 1981: 6–7 and "Japanese Language Programming: The Fading Signal." *Hawaii Herald*, 16 Oct. 1981: 1–3.

1953   The Southern California Japanese Credit and Savings Unions Association is established, consisting of eight (soon to be ten) credit unions. The estimated total capital of affiliated credit unions was $2.5 million by 1959.   Yagasaki 82 (280)

February 10, 1953   Reverend Jonathan Machida, pastor of the Seattle Japanese Methodist Church, becomes the first West Coast ISSEI to gain naturalization. Gonkichi Clement Yanagi is the first Californian to be sworn in on February 16.   "Is First to be Naturalized on West Coast." *Rafu Shimpo*, 13 Feb. 1953: 1

June 19, 1953   Julius and Ethel Rosenberg are electrocuted in an Ossining, New York, prison. They are the first Americans to be executed for treason during peacetime. Schlesinger 83 (534)

June 19, 1953   The HAWAII SEVEN—CHARLES FUJIMOTO, Eileen Kee Fujimoto, Dwight James Freeman, Jack D. Kimoto, Dr. John Reinecke, KOJI ARIYOSHI and JACK HALL—are convicted on Smith Act violations of conspiring to teach communism and other related charges. Their convictions come about largely as a result of JACK KAWANO's testimony before the House Un-American Activities Committee. Though the convictions would be overturned five years later, the trial and convictions helped to severely curtail ILWU influence in Hawaii. Kotani 85 (126)

Summer 1953   The first Cherry Blossom Festival takes place in Honolulu, sponsored by the Honolulu Japanese Junior Chamber of Commerce. Violet Niimi is named the first queen.   "Timeline of the Japanese in Hawaii." *Hawaii Herald*, 5 July 1985: A12–13

September 30, 1953   JOHN AISO is sworn in as a municipal court judge in Los Angeles, becoming the first mainland Japanese American to hold a judiciary post. He had been appointed by Governor EARL WARREN on September 18.   "Aiso Takes Oath for Municipal Jurist Post." *Rafu Shimpo*, 1 Oct. 1953: 1

October 27, 1953   Seven men receive the Congressional Medal of Honor from President Eisenhower. Among them is army Sgt. HIROSHI "HERSHEY" MIYAMURA of Gallup, New Mexico, the second NISEI to receive the nation's highest military honor.   "Gallup Nisei Ex-GI Among Seven Korean War Heroes Awarded CMH by President." *Rafu Shimpo*, 27 Oct. 1953: 1

January 1954   The Central Pacific Bank is granted its charter from the State of Hawaii. The brainchild of NISEI veterans DAN AOKI, DANIEL INOUYE, Shigeto Kanemoto and Mike Tokunaga, it is the first Japanese American owned bank in postwar Hawaii. ISSEI leader Koichi Iida serves as chairman of the board until his death. By 1984 the Central Pacific Bank would be the fourth largest in the state and would have 16 branches.   Hazama/Komeiji 86 (211)

April 14, 1954   At SACRAMENTO City Hall, a plan to tear down and rebuild a 15 block area including most of the city's Japanese town is announced. Opposition to the plan among Japanese American residents is quickly voiced. The plan was implemented in 1958, leveling most of the city's Japan Town.   Cole 75 (74); "Redevelopment Project in Sac'to to Oust Japanese." *Rafu Shimpo*, 17 Apr. 1954: 1

April 14, 1954   The Japanese American Optimist Club of Los Angeles is formed at a lunch meeting at the new Ginza Restaurant by "leading Japanese American businessmen in Li'l Tokio." It is the first all-NISEI Optimist Club. Eiji Tanabe is named charter president. "Nisei Form 1st Optimist Group Here." *Rafu Shimpo*, 15 Apr. 1954: 1

May 17, 1954   The U.S. Supreme Court rules on Brown v. Board of Education, striking down the doctrine of "separate but equal."   Wilson/Hosokawa 80 (287)

June 7, 1954   Attorney Theodore Tamba files a petition for executive clemency on behalf of NISEI convicted war criminal IVA TOGURI D'AQUINO with the president of the United States. There is no response from President Eisenhower. Tamba, a Swiss American, had been part of the defense council during her 1949 trial. Fourteen years later, on November 4, 1968, a second petition would be filed by WAYNE COLLINS; it would be denied.   Uyeda 80 (12,21)

August 31, 1954   Public Law 751 is passed, making JAPANESE PERUVIANS forcibly removed from Peru and placed in United States Justice Department camps during World War II eligible for naturalization.   Weglyn 76 (289)

November 11, 1954   To celebrate Veterans Day, 50,000 new citizens are naturalized. At the Hollywood Bowl, a mass naturalization ceremony for 7,568 includes 1,024 ISSEI.   "Mass Hollywood Bowl Rite Joins 7600 as New Americans; Issei Number Over 1000." *Rafu Shimpo*, 12 Nov. 1954: 1

February 16, 1955 The opening ceremonies of Hawaii's 28th Legislature mark the first time in Hawaii's history that both houses are controlled by the Democrats. Japanese Americans played a key role in this outcome. (See "REVOLUTION OF 1954.")   Ogawa 78 (377)

March 1955 In California, Assembly Bill 1671, authored by Thomas Maloney of San Francisco, is introduced. It would require the licensing of all maintenance gardeners in the state. A fee of $25 would be required to get a license. Japanese American gardeners united in opposition to this bill in a flurry of activity before an April 6 hearing, attended by 100 JA gardeners. The bill may have had the unintended effect of spurring effective organization of JA gardeners.   "Gardeners May Be Licensed Under Proposed State Bill." *Rafu Shimpo,* 18 Mar. 1955: 1

April 1955 "California's Amazing Japanese" by Demaree Bess appears in the *Saturday Evening Post.* It reads in part: "The Japanese residents of California have lifted themselves higher in a few postwar years than they did in the preceeding half century, and the agitation against them has been almost silenced." (See "MODEL MINORITY.")   "Postwar Nisei Success Story Told in Satevepost." *Rafu Shimpo,* 26 Apr. 1955: 1

July 28, 1955 The SOUTHERN CALIFORNIA GARDENERS FEDERATION is formed. The following Gardeners' Associations make up the Federation: Gardena, Pasadena, East San Gabriel Valley, Hollywood, Riverside, Los Angeles Uptown, East Los Angeles, San Fernando, Sierra Madre, L.A. Southwest, San Gabriel and West Los Angeles. Oxnard and Whittier would join in 1959, Bakersfield in 1960, and Long Beach in 1971.

October 17, 1955 After winning the world's light-heavyweight lifting championship on October 15, TOMMY KONO wins the Mr. Universe title in Munich. It is one of three Mr. Universe or Mr. World titles Kono would win.   "Tommy Kono Wins 1955 Title as Mr. Universe." *Rafu Shimpo,* 18 Oct. 1955: 1

December 1, 1955 Rosa Parks is arrested in Montgomery, Alabama, for refusing to give up her seat on a bus to a white man. This incident sparks the beginning of the civil rights movement.   Schlesinger 83 (545)

December 3, 1955 At the Northern California CINO (California Inter-collegiate NISEI Organization) convention in San Jose, a letter by S. I. HAYAKAWA is read stating: "I believe Nisei social organizations should cease to exist. . . . These are social crutches that are not needed anymore—but so long as we use them we shall

imagine they are needed." These remarks are rebutted in part by convention general chair Bob Fuchigami in his closing address in which he defends the value of *nisei* organizations and gatherings such as this one.   "Social, Athletic Clubs Used as Crutch Charges Professor to Collegians." *Rafu Shimpo,* 7 Dec. 1955: 1

January 1956 A *Reader's Digest* article extolls the "amazing turnabout" in Japanese American fortunes since the war. (See "MODEL MINORITY.")   "Japanese American Story Reported in Reader's Digest." *Rafu Shimpo,* 19 Dec. 1955: 1

June 26, 1956 Gang war between the Dominators and the Koshakus send two to the hospital in Los Angeles. One of the injured, Donald Morishita, had been the victim of a knife attack the previous year. (See NISEI CLUBS/GANGS.)   "Teenage Gang War Breaks Out in Eastside; Two Koshakus Injured." *Rafu Shimpo,* 27 June 1956: 1

September 12, 1956 The new San Francisco Flower Terminal opens at Brannon and 6th Street. The major markets of the Flower Terminal are the San Francisco Flower Growers Association and the Japanese American-owned California Flower Market.   Yagasaki 82 (381)

November 6, 1956 California's Proposition 13 passes by a 2-1 margin, removing the ALIEN LAND LAW from the books. It had already been rendered inoperative by the IMMIGRATION AND NATIONALITY ACT OF 1952 and various court decisions.   "Last of State's Racist Measures Gone as Voters Repeal Alien Land Law." *Rafu Shimpo,* 7 Nov. 1956: 1

January 2, 1957 MIKE MASAOKA is featured on NBC's "This Is Your Life." The JACL headquarters obtains two copies of the kinescope and makes them available for local showings.   "Your Life's Film Available by CL." *Rafu Shimpo,* 14 Mar. 1957: 1

March 1957 The JACL national headquarters sends out letters to 480 TV stations asking that certain wartime propaganda films not be shown. The letter specifically names *Air Force, Across the Pacific, Little Tokyo, USA, Betrayal from the East, Black Dragons* and *Behind the Rising Sun.*   "Ask Video Officials to Curb Wartime Anti-Nisei Pictures." *Rafu Shimpo,* 28 Mar. 1957: 1

March 7, 1957 The California State Board of Education votes for a new investigation of state textbooks. This investigation is prompted by Delano elementary school pupil Gene Nakagama's refusal to attend school because he would have to read a story repeatedly containing the word "Jap." "Sansei Shuns Textbook with Bias Race Identity." *Rafu Shimpo,* 8 Mar. 1957: 1

June 3, 1957 NISEI/SANSEI gang wars in Los Angeles involving the Dominators and Black Juans send three to the hospital and seven to juvenile authorities. Chains, knives, baseball bats and guns are used. (See NISEI CLUBS/GANGS.) "Juvenile Gang Warfare Perils Seinan Residents." *Rafu Shimpo,* 5 June 1957: 1

September 25, 1957 President Eisenhower orders U.S. troops into Little Rock, Arkansas, to enforce a federal court order requiring Central High to admit black students. Schlesinger 83 (549–50); Wilson/Hosokawa 80 (287)

March 26, 1958 MIYOSHI UMEKI becomes the first person of Japanese descent to win an Academy Award, as Best Supporting Actress for her performance in *Sayonara.* McNulty, Patrick. "Sleepless Miyoshi Still Can't Get Over Winning Film Oscar." *Rafu Shimpo,* 28 Mar. 1958: 1

March 31, 1958 In the NISHIKAWA V. DULLES decision, the U.S. Supreme Court rules that an American citizen who had served in the Japanese army cannot be denied citizenship unless it can be shown that he served voluntarily. Chuman 76 (284, 370)

April 18, 1958 Richard Shuji Sumii is killed by stray gunfire at a fight between two SANSEI gangs (the Black Juans and the Junior Cogents) at a Los Angeles Chinatown dance. The 16-year-old honor student's death sets off a chain reaction of parental and community response to the gang problem. (See NISEI CLUBS/GANGS.) "Gang Bullet Murders Honor Student at Dance." *Rafu Shimpo,* 19 Apr. 1958: 1; Ikeda 59

July 23, 1958 At a meeting of the Los Angeles Japanese Chamber of Commerce, a nonprofit organization called The Japanese American Youth, Inc. (JAY, Inc.) is formed to combat juvenile delinquency, largely through promoting alternative youth activities put on by new and existing groups. The organization would be incorporated on September 25. At a meeting on October 7, Kenji Ito is named as head of JAY, Inc. Ikeda 59; "Juvenile Study Group to File for Incorporation." *Rafu Shimpo,* 24 July 1958: 1; "Youth Probe Members Elect Officers, Set Prog." *Rafu Shimpo,* 8 Oct. 1958: 1

November 1958 The California Gardeners' Coordinating Council is formed, consisting of the Northern California Gardeners' Association, the Southern California Gardeners' Council and the Southern California Gardeners' Federation, Inc.

February 1959 After a meeting between Southern California farmers and the Immigration and Naturalization Service, temporary visas are granted to 390 Japanese laborers. They join the 1,165 Japanese contract farm workers already in the U.S. "US Resumes Farm Labor Importation Program." *Rafu Shimpo,* 28 Feb. 1959: 1

March 11–12, 1959 The U.S. Senate and House pass the Hawaii Statehood Bill. Hawaii's official admission to the Union as the 50 state occurs five months later, on August 21. Hazama/Komeiji 86 (194)

May 20, 1959 In a public ceremony, citizenship is restored to 4,978 NISEI who had renounced their citizenship under duress during and after World War II. However, a general amnesty is not granted—350 other renunciants are denied restoration at this time and individual hearings on these cases would stretch out for nearly another decade. (See RENUNCIATION OF CITIZENSHIP.) Weglyn 76 (263–64)

August 21, 1959 Hawaii becomes the 50 state. Wilson/Hosokawa 80 (283)

September 22, 1959 President Eisenhower signs a bill amending the IMMIGRATION AND NATIONALITY ACT OF 1952, allowing some 57,000 aliens to join their families in the United States. About 1,000 Japanese become immediately eligible for entry. "1000 Japanese Can Join Families as Ike Signs I&N Amendments." *Rafu Shimpo,* 24 Sept. 1959: 1

1961 A group of NISEI found the Japanese American Community Services of Southern California (JACS). This social service organization and the many other organizations spun off from it would play a key role in the Los Angeles Japanese American community of the late 1960s and 1970s. Chin, Rocky. "The House That JACS Built." *Bridge* 2.6 (Aug. 1973): 5–10

October 19, 1961 The premiere of MGM's *Bridge to the Sun* at the Beverly Theatre is attended by co-stars JAMES SHIGETA and Carroll Baker. Shigeta is presented with an honorary scroll by the JACL. The movie is based on the memoirs of a Caucasian woman married to a Japanese diplomat before, during and after World War II. " 'Bridge' Cinema Wins Applause, Scroll from JACL." *Rafu Shimpo,* 20 Oct. 1961: 1

1962 Seiji Horiuchi becomes the first Japanese American on the mainland to be elected to a state legislature when he is elected to the Colorado House of Representatives. He would serve only until 1964. Endo 85 (106)

October 22–28, 1962 The Cuban Missile Crisis takes place. Schlesinger 83 (562)

October 26, 1962 The JACL begins a letter drive to ABC protesting the use of the word "Japs" in the October 11 (debut episode) and October 25 broadcasts of "McHale's Navy." Later shows do not use the term. "CL Continues Flow of Protest Letters to ABC on TV Series." *Rafu Shimpo,* 15 Nov. 1962: 1

November 6, 1962 DANIEL K. INOUYE of Hawaii becomes the first Japanese American to be elected to the United States Senate, with a resounding victory over Republican challenger Ben Dillingham. Inouye had been the first Japanese American elected to the House of Representatives in 1959. Hazama/Komeiji 86 (194); Inouye/Elliott 67 (292–93)

November 6, 1962 By a vote of 123,542 to 41,206, Idaho voters approve a constitutional amendment extending basic American rights to naturalized ASIAN AMERICANS. They had been excluded from voting, holding civil office and serving as jurors. Idaho had been the last state to hold such restrictions. However in Washington, voters reject a measure to repeal the state's ALIEN LAND LAW 392,000 to 372,000. In 1960, they had rejected repeal 564,000 to 467,000. U.S. Supreme Court decisions have effectively nullified the law. "Defeat Ban on Oriental Rights." *Rafu Shimpo,* 7 Nov. 1962: 1; "Washington Bias State Law Still Haunts Aliens." *Rafu Shimpo,* 10 Nov. 1962: 1

November 20, 1962 President John F. Kennedy signs an order banning racial discrimination in federally owned or aided housing, affecting around 50 percent of future suburban homes. "JFK Signs Bill to Erase Bias in US-Loan Homes." *Rafu Shimpo,* 21 Nov. 1962: 1, 3

November 21, 1962 Merit Savings and Loan Association, the first financial institution in Los Angeles's LITTLE TOKYO to be locally owned, officially opens. It opens with savings account pledges of over $1 million. Bruce T. Kaji is the president. "Merit Savings Opens for Business Tomorrow." *Rafu Shimpo,* 20 Nov. 1962: 1

1963 The Shibata brothers, along with eight recent immigrants from Kagoshima PREFECTURE, begin the Salinas Greenhouse. By 1964, it has 120,000 square feet of greenhouses on 100 acres of land. The Salinas Greenhouse spurs a flurry of Kagoshima-KENJINKAI activity in the area; within 10 years, over 40 families from Kagoshima would operate greenhouses in the Salinas Valley. Yagasaki 82 (394–95)

February 27, 1963 Hawaii State Senator Kazuhisa Abe introduces a bill that would eliminate Christmas and Good Friday as legal holidays in favor of a one-day observance called "Holiday for Religious Worship." He also introduces another bill which would make Wesak Day (the birthday of the Buddha) a legal holiday. The bills are attacked by Japanese Americans and non-Japanese Americans alike and are roundly defeated, obscuring the intriguing legal questions they raise. "Bussei Leaders Miffed Over Bills to Abolish Yule Holiday." *Rafu Shimpo,* 6 Mar. 1963: 1

April 1963 Kyu Sakamoto's "Sukiyaki" hits #1 on the American pop music charts, a first for a person of Japanese descent and for a record sung in Japanese.

August 28, 1963 Dr. Martin Luther King, Jr., delivers the "I Have a Dream" speech in Washington, D.C., culminating a civil rights march of 200,000 persons. Wilson/Hosokawa 80 (287)

November 22, 1963 President Kennedy is assassinated while riding in a motorcade in Dallas. Vice President Lyndon B. Johnson takes the presidential oath of office later in the day. Los Angeles Times, 23 Nov. 1963: 1

March 1964 The Marina Del Rey National Bank, the first Japanese American controlled commercial bank in the U.S., holds an organizational shareholders meeting in Los Angeles. Taul Watanabe, president of West Bay Financial Corporation, is elected chairman of the board. Total capitalization is expected to be at least $1 million. "Name Marina Del Rey Board of Directors." *Rafu Shimpo,* 27 Mar. 1964: 1

July 2, 1964 President Johnson signs the Civil Rights Act of 1964. The House vote, taken earlier in the day, was 289-126; the Senate vote on June 19 was 72-27. Beckler, John. "Civil Rights Bill Passes; Johnson to Sign Tonight." *Rafu Shimpo,* 2 July 1964: 1

November 3, 1964 In Hawaii, PATSY TAKEMOTO MINK becomes the first ASIAN AMERICAN woman elected to the U.S. Congress. In California, voters approve Proposition 14 by a 2-1 margin. It nullifies fair housing laws by allowing the seller of property to discriminate against potential buyers on any basis. The proposition would later be struck down by the courts. Masaoka, Mike M. "A Christmas Sermon." *Rafu Shimpo,* 19 Dec. 1964: 4; "Timeline of the Japanese in Hawaii." *Hawaii Herald,* 5 July 1985: A12–13

January 1965 The end of the Bracero era on December 31, 1964 precipitates a farm-labor crisis in California. Japanese laborers known as *tanno,* under three-year contracts with the State Department, face early departure. There are 1,200 *tanno* in California; the first leave in late February. "'Tanno' Squeeze-Out Ignites Crisis as Growers Forced to Hire Jobless." *Rafu Shimpo*, 9 Jan. 1965: 1

January 31, 1965 "The Nisei–the Pride and the Shame" is broadcast on CBS as part of the network's "Twentieth Century" series. The half-hour documentary hosted by Walter Cronkite focuses on the Japanese American World War II experience. "Nisei Are Subject of CBS-TV Program Sunday." *Rafu Shimpo*, 28 Jan. 1965: 1

February 21, 1965 Malcolm X is assassinated in New York City. Schlesinger 83 (569)

August 1965 The Watts uprising takes place in Los Angeles. Los Angeles Times, 13 Aug. 1965: 1

October 1965 The family of KEISABURO KODA is awarded $362,500 compensation under the JAPANESE AMERICAN EVACUATION CLAIMS ACT of 1948. Although it is the largest (and last) settlement under the act, it represents a fraction of actual losses sustained by the Kodas as a result of their forced removal. Their attorney, James Purcell, estimates the losses at $1 million in property and $1.4 million in profits. Ironically, Koda had died only months before the decision. "Pre-war Farmers Settle Eviction for $350,000." *Rafu Shimpo*, 8 Oct. 1965: 1

October 3, 1965 President Johnson signs Public Law 89-236, amendments to the Immigration and Nationality Act. This new immigration legislation for the first time considers Asians equal to Europeans in immigration matters. Great numbers of Asians will eventually enter the U.S. under the provisions of this legislation. (See IMMIGRATION ACT OF OCTOBER 3, 1965.) Masaoka, Mike M. "Equality in Immigration." *Rafu Shimpo*, 20 Dec. 1965: ii-b; 10

January 9, 1966 An article titled "Success Story: Japanese American Style" appears in the *New York Times*. "By any criterion of good citizenship that we choose, the Japanese-Americans are better than any group in our society, including native-born whites," writes author William Peterson. (See "MODEL MINORITY.")

June 10, 1966 The California Supreme Court strikes down Proposition 14, passed in November 1964, as unconstitutional. It had nullified fair housing laws and allowed owners the right to sell or not to sell their homes to anyone they wanted. "Blow to Housing Bias as California Supreme Court Rules Against Prop. 14." *New York Nichibei*, 19 May 1966: 1

August 1966 Kazuharu Hamasaki arrives from Hiroshima with photographs of 94 women in an attempt to revive the PICTURE BRIDE phenomenon. The idea had stemmed from the response of local men to a 1965 tour of Hiroshima beauty queens. The new business venture would receive a great deal of publicity, most of it negative, resulting in its quick demise. Ogawa 78 (411–13)

August 20, 1966 MITSUYOSHI FUKUDA becomes the first Japanese American vice president of a BIG FIVE company. Hazama/Komeiji 86 (210)

April 10, 1967 The U.S. Supreme Court rules that Japanese American savings seized at the beginning of World War II can be recovered. A lower court had ruled that a 60-day statute of limitations prevented such recovery. A 1957 ruling had the deposits being repaid at the postwar exchange rate of 361.5 yen to the dollar; the new decision allowed recovery at the prewar rate of 4 yen to the dollar. The decision affected up to $10 million deposited at the Yokohama Specie Bank. "Yen Claimants Will Be Paid at Postwar Rate." *Rafu Shimpo*, 10 Apr. 1967: 1

May 13, 1967 Thirty-four Japanese American janitors put in their last days of work at Seattle University. The school had contracted their maintenance out to the Dependable Maintenance Company, which offered the men their old positions at higher wages providing they joined the union; all of them refused to join and quit. "Seattle Janitors Jobless; Won't Join Union." *Rafu Shimpo*, 13 May 1967: 1

November 15, 1967 The official opening of the Kajima Building takes place. The 16-story structure in Los Angeles's LITTLE TOKYO is occupied primarily by the Sumitomo Bank of California and is the first Japanese constructed skyscraper in the U.S. "Dinner at Yamato Climaxes Debut Celebrating." *Rafu Shimpo*, 28 Nov. 1967: 1

1968 American involvement in the Vietnam War peaks as some 541,000 U.S. soldiers find themselves stationed in Vietnam. Some 57,000 Americans and hundreds of thousands of Vietnamese would eventually be killed in the conflict. Schlesinger 83 (572)

March 6, 1968 The last of WAYNE COLLINS's renunciation cases is finally decided—23 years after the original renunciation of citizenship. (See RENUNCIATION OF CITIZENSHIP.) Weglyn 76 (265)

March 28, 1968 The dedication of San Francisco's $15 million Japanese Cultural and Trade Center takes place. The project had begun in 1960.   "Unwrap $15 Million Center." *Rafu Shimpo*, 28 Mar. 1968: 1

April 1968 "SANSEI Concern" begins to meet at UCLA. Other Asian American student groups also start up at this time such as the ASIAN AMERICAN POLITICAL ALLIANCE (AAPA) at Berkeley (May) and AAPA chapters at USC and San Francisco State (August).   Chin, Rocky. "The House That JACS Built." *Bridge* 2.6 (Aug. 1973): 8; Umemoto 89 (62)

April 4, 1968 *Dr. Martin Luther King, Jr., is shot to death on the balcony of a Memphis motel.*   *Los Angeles Times*, 5 Apr. 1968: 1

June 5, 1968 *Senator Robert F. Kennedy is shot and killed in Los Angeles while delivering a victory speech after winning the California Democratic presidential primary.* *Los Angeles Times*, 5 June 1968: 1

August 26, 1968 Senator DANIEL K. INOUYE of Hawaii delivers the keynote address at the Democratic National Convention in Chicago.   "Nisei Senator Keynotes Demo Convention." *Rafu Shimpo*, 27 Aug. 1968: 1

September 1968 "Oriental Concern" (previously "SANSEI Concern") calls an ASIAN AMERICAN conference at Lake Arrowhead, California, entitled "I am Yellow, Curious." Over 200 Asian Americans attend.   Chin, Rocky. "The House That JACS Built." *Bridge* 2.6 (Aug. 1973): 8

November 6, 1968 The San Francisco State College student strike begins. Destined to be the longest student strike in American history, it would end with the college starting the first School of Ethnic Studies in the country. (See SAN FRANCISCO STATE STRIKE.)   Umemoto 89 (1)

November 26, 1968 Robert R. Smith resigns as president of strife-torn San Francisco State College. He is replaced by Professor S. I. HAYAKAWA, "internationally known semanticist." (See SAN FRANCISCO STATE STRIKE.) Bow, James. "Hayakawa Handed S.F. State Situation." *Rafu Shimpo*, 27 Nov. 1968: 1

January 7, 1969 "The Evolution of the Asian in America," the University of California at Berkeley's first ASIAN AMERICAN studies course, begins. Over 100 students pre-enroll for a class limited to 80 students. Paul Takagi oversees the course.   "Asian American Course Popular at UC Berkeley." *Rafu Shimpo*, 8 Jan. 1969: 1

February 21, 1969 One hundred twenty-five Japanese Americans picket a Community Interest Committee

of NIHONMACHI (San Francisco) dinner featuring S. I. HAYAKAWA as a speaker. A similar protest of over 100 people takes place when Hayakawa speaks to the JACL Pacific Southwest convention at the Disneyland Hotel in Anaheim on April 26, 1969. This event is possibly the first ASIAN AMERICAN MOVEMENT demonstration in Southern California. Both protests are organized by the members of the ASIAN AMERICAN POLITICAL ALLIANCE. Chin, Rocky. "The House That JACS Built." *Bridge* 2.6 (Aug. 1973): 8; Umemoto 89 (70)

March 1969 The HAWAII HERALD, an English-language Japanese American weekly tabloid begins publication. Published by the HAWAII HOCHI, the *Herald* is edited by Ronald Maruyama. This version of the *Herald* would last until 1973.   "A Brief History of the Hawaii Herald." *Hawaii Herald* 11.16 (18 May 1990): 3

March 18, 1969 Dr. THOMAS NOGUCHI is fired as Los Angeles County coroner. His resignation had been asked for on February 21 by county chief administrative officer L. S. Hollinger. Noguchi's dismissal and later charges of racism result in a community-wide battle to win his reinstatement. After six weeks of hearings (May 12 to June 24), Noguchi is reinstated as coroner on July 31, 1969.   *Gidra*, various

March 21, 1969 The SAN FRANCISCO STATE STRIKE is settled. The conflict had begun on November 6, 1968, and revolved around the issue of community/student control of the university. ASIAN AMERICAN students had been among those involved in the strike.   Church, Jim. "SF State Strike Appears Ended." *Rafu Shimpo*, 22 Mar. 1969: 1

April 1969 GIRDA 1.1 appears. Published originally by UCLA students, it would come to be known as "the voice of the ASIAN AMERICAN MOVEMENT."

April 1969 Asian Americans for Action—the first ASIAN AMERICAN political organization in New York— is co-founded by Kazu Iijima and Minn Matsuda.   Omatsu 86 (84)

April 3, 1969 "Orientals in America," the first ASIAN AMERICAN Studies course at UCLA, begins. Yuji Ichioka is the principal instructor.   *Gidra* 1.2 (1969): 6

April 15, 1969 HARRY KITANO's book *Japanese Americans: The Evolution of a Subculture* is published. "Kitano's 'Evolution of Subculture' Arrives from Publishers April 15." *Rafu Shimpo*, 8 Apr. 1969: 1

July 20, 1969 *Neil A. Armstrong becomes the first person to walk on the moon.*   *Los Angeles Times*, 21 July 1969: 1

September 20–21, 1969 The first nationwide ASIAN AMERICAN Studies conference is held at Berkeley. Sponsored by the University of California's Davis, Berkeley and Los Angeles branches, it is attended by 60 people representing 16 campuses. Fourteen of those 16 campuses offered Asian American Studies courses the following year. Watanabe, Colin. "Asian American Studies Conference." *Gidra* 1.7 (Oct. 1969): 2, 11

September 22, 1969 San Francisco State College becomes the first university to offer an ASIAN AMERICAN Studies program within the first school of ethnic studies in the nation. Eighteen courses are initially offered, including "The Japanese Americans in the United States" taught by EDISON UNO. "S.F. State First to Have Asian American Dept." *Rafu Shimpo,* 24 Sept. 1969: 1; Umemoto 89 (122)

September 28, 1969 A One Hundred Year Celebration of the ISSEI is held in Griffith Park in Los Angeles. Sponsored by the Pioneer Project and the Pioneer Community Center, the event features a keynote address by recently reinstated coroner THOMAS NOGUCHI, an *issei* talent show, and a plea for ASIAN AMERICAN Studies both in Japanese and in English. Matsuoka, Jim. "Issei Centennial." *Gidra* (Oct. 1969): 2

October 18, 1969 The Japanese Community Pioneer Center opens its doors in Los Angeles. It is a senior citizen center initiated primarily by young people. Similar institutions would soon begin in many other Japanese American communities. (See PIONEER CENTERS.) Komai, Michael M. "Japanese Community Pioneer Center: The Story of an Institution." *Rafu Shimpo,* 21 Dec. 1978: II-20-21; Matsuoka, Jim. "Pioneer Center Opens in Little Tokyo." *Gidra* 1.8 (Nov. 1969): 3

November 15, 1969 The Anti-Vietnam Peace March takes place in San Francisco with 100,000 to 275,000 marchers. The Ad Hoc Japanese Americans for Peace, led by Ray Okamura, Kathy Reyes and EDISON UNO organize an Asian American delegation of over 300. Uno, Edison. "Peace March Participant Relates Nisei Experience." *Rafu Shimpo,* 19 Nov. 1969: 1+

December 27, 1969 The first annual MANZANAR PILGRIMAGE takes place. These trips back to Manzanar would inspire pilgrimages to other CONCENTRATION CAMPS in the years to come. Yoneda 83 (200)

January 17, 1970 Two hundred Asian Americans participate in an "Asian Americans for Peace" march in Los Angeles LITTLE TOKYO. A rally follows on Weller Street. *Gidra* 2.2 (1970): 5; "Little Tokyo Site of Asian American March . . ." *Rafu Shimpo,* 19 Jan. 1970: 1

"Asian Americans for Peace" march and rally, Los Angeles, January 17, 1970. By the early 1970s, many young Asian Americans were determined to prove that they were anything but "quiet Americans." *UCLA Asian American Studies Collection, Japanese American National Museum Photographic & Moving Image Archive*

April 18, 1970 Said to be the first "all-Asian" academic conference, "Asians in America" is held at Yale University. It is attended by 300 persons, mostly students from New York, New Haven, Boston and Cambridge. It is sponsored by the Asian American Students Association at Yale. "Nearly 300 Attend Asian Conference." *New York Nichibei,* 23 Apr. 1970: 1–2

May 4, 1970 Four students are killed at Kent State (Ohio) University when national guardsmen open fire into a crowd of anti-war protesters. Los Angeles Times, 5 May 1970: 1

June 29, 1970 The Department of Housing and Urban Development officially approves the LITTLE TOKYO Neighborhood Development Program; the project had been voted in by the Los Angeles City Council on January 29, 1970. (See REDEVELOPMENT.) "HUD Okays Implementation of LT Project." *Rafu Shimpo,* 29 June 1970: 1.

July 10, 1970 A resolution by the JACL's Northern California-Western Nevada District Council calling for reparations for the World War II removal and incarceration of Japanese Americans is announced. Titled "A Requital Supplication" and championed by EDISON UNO, this resolution would have the JACL seek a bill in Congress awarding individual compensation on a per diem basis, tax-free. (See REDRESS MOVEMENT.) "League Council Asks Reparations from Government for Evacuation." *Rafu Shimpo,* 10 July 1970: 1

July 29–30 1970 The first Southland Inter-Collegiate Conference of ASIAN AMERICAN Studies is held at Long Beach State University, co-chaired by Allan Nishio and Alan Nitake.   "CSULB-based Conclave Proposes Uniting Asian American Studies." *Rafu Shimpo,* 10 Aug. 1970: 1

29 August 1970 An antiwar demonstration organized by the Chicano Moratorium Committee takes place. Said to be the largest antiwar demonstration ever held in Los Angeles, some 20,000 participate in the march and rally. Police break up the protest with clubs and tear gas. Journalist Ruben Salazar is killed by police later in a related incident. "Chicano Moratorium." *Gidra* 2.9 (October 1970): 10–11.

December 1970 The Bay Area Community Chapter (BACC) of the JACL is founded. Similar "activist" chapters such as the Chicago Liberation chapter, are also being formed at this time.   Yoneda 83 (197); Albert 80 (228)

March 9, 1971 After an earlier protest on February 9 fails to budge the Seattle Central Community College administration, 50-70 Oriental Student Union members occupy administration offices for 100 minutes to protest the lack of Asian administrators. Of the school's 90 administrators, 87 are white and three are black. The administration agrees to freeze the next vacancy in their ranks for an Asian.   "Students Protest in Seattle." *Rafu Shimpo,* 18 Feb. 1971: 1; "Seattle Youths Occupy School, Get Concession." *Rafu Shimpo,* 10 Mar. 1971: 1

March 20, 1971 The SOUTHERN CALIFORNIA GARDENERS FEDERATION celebrates its 16th anniversary and dedicates its new building at 333 E. 2nd Street near Los Angeles's LITTLE TOKYO. The program is attended by 600. The $75,000 building on a $55,000 property is mortgage-free.   Mori, Henry. "Over 600 Share in SCGF Structure Opening." *Rafu Shimpo,* 22 Mar. 1971: 1

April 13, 1971 NORMAN Y. MINETA becomes the first Japanese American mayor of a "major American metropolis." He had been elected to the San Jose City Council in 1966 and became vice mayor in 1969. He receives 30,496 votes of 49,777 cast; his closest challenger receives 6,902.   Riley, Brendon. "San Jose Becomes First Major City to Elect Nisei Mayor in California." *Rafu Shimpo,* 14 Apr. 1971: 1

April 16–18, 1971 The first National Asian American studies conference takes place in Los Angeles. PATSY TAKEMOTO MINK is the guest speaker at the opening banquet; HARRY KITANO does the summary and evaluation. Among the workshop leaders are ROGER DANIELS,

Yuji Ichioka, Yasuo Sakata, Stanford Lyman, Ruban Alcantara, Gerald Sue, Stanley Sue, Franklin Odo, Isao Fujimoto, and Dennis Ogawa.   *Bridge* 1.1 (1971): 35; "Patsy Mink Addresses Fete Tonight." *Rafu Shimpo,* 16 Apr. 1971: 1

May 16, 1971 "Peace Sunday" is held at the Biltmore Bowl in downtown Los Angeles. Organized by ASIAN AMERICANS for Peace, 2,000 attend to hear such speakers as SPARK MATSUNAGA and Jane Fonda.   *Gidra* (June 1971): 10–11

June 18, 1971 Native Hawaiian activists and concerned citizens gather at the Kawaiahao Church in Honolulu to protest the appointment the previous day of Matsuo Takabuki, a prominent NISEI lawyer well connected to the Democratic Party, as trustee of the Bishop Estate. Many Hawaiians feel that the position ought to have gone to a native Hawaiian; others object to Takabuki's connections to developers.   Ogawa 78 (489–91)

June 1971 The NISEI FARMERS LEAGUE (NFL) is organized in Reedley, California. The group of 125 includes area farmers of all races and is formed as a reaction to Cesar Chavez's United Farm Workers Organizing Committee and out of a perception that Chavez's group had been consciously selecting Japanese American farms to picket. The NFL's membership would swell to 1,400 by 1975.   Fugita 78 (52–53); Fugita/O'Brien 77 (146); "UFWOC Irks Reedley Nisei." *Rafu Shimpo,* 14 July 1971: 1

August 15, 1971 The AMERASIA BOOKSTORE opens in Los Angeles LITTLE TOKYO.   *Gidra* (Aug. 1971):24

Demonstration, Los Angeles, August 1970. The demonstration centers on the Los Angeles production of the play *Lovely Ladies, Kind Gentlemen,* **a musical version of the movie** *Teahouse of the August Moon,* **in which all the Asian roles are played by white actors in "yellowface."** *UCLA Asian American Studies Collection, Japanese American National Museum Photographic & Moving Image Archive*

September 25, 1971 President Nixon signs a bill repealing Title II of the Internal Security Act of 1950, culminating a long fight by Asian American activists. (See EMERGENCY DETENTION ACT OF 1950, REPEAL OF.) Yoneda 83 (196)

October 20, 1971 ABC agrees to change the title of an upcoming TV movie to "If Tomorrow Comes" from "My Husband, the Enemy" under pressure resulting from a letter-writing campaign initiated by GEORGE TAKEI. The movie, about a white woman who marries a NISEI man during World War II, was scheduled to be aired on December 7. Kayano, Ellen Endo. "ABC-TV Changes Movie Title; JACL Succeeds." *Rafu Shimpo,* 21 Oct. 1971: 1.

January 9, 1972 Mike Wallace narrates a "Sixty Minutes" segment on Japanese Americans. The piece is called "100% Americans." *Rafu Shimpo,* 7 Jan. 1972: 1

January 12, 1972 Congresswoman PATSY TAKE-MOTO MINK announces her candidacy for the Democratic presidential nomination. She announces in Oregon, while putting her name on the primary ballot there. She is believed to be the first Japanese American to run for president. "Her Presidential Bid No Joke." *Rafu Shimpo,* 19 Jan. 1972: 1

March 25, 1972 ASIAN AMERICAN students at the City College of New York take over the building housing the Asian studies office for three days; the protest ends with most of the students' demands adopted. Yanagida, R. Takashi. "Asian Students vs. the Administration: The Confrontation at CCNY." *Bridge* 1.5 (1972): 11–12

May 15, 1972 Okinawa reverts to Japan. A "Celebration Commemorating the Reversion of Okinawa to Japan" is held in Hawaii on the same day and is attended by 1,200 people. Ethnic Studies 81 (37)

August 20, 1972 The annual Los Angeles NISEI WEEK Parade is disrupted by antiwar protesters. The Van Troi Anti-Imperialist Youth Brigade, made up of 150 ASIAN AMERICAN students, march in the parade and set fire to a Japanese "rising sun" flag. In the meantime, the Thai Binh Brigade pass out leaflets and chant slogans from an adjacent building. The protest action sparks both condemnation and approval from various segments of the community. Murase, Mike. "Nisei Week." *Gidra* 4.9 (Sept. 1972): 2–3

September 19, 1972 NBC broadcasts "Guilty by Reason of Race," a documentary on the World War II mass removal and incarceration of Japanese Americans.

Reaction to the show is mixed in the Japanese American community. In the general community, 300 people call NBC to protest the broadcast, while 40 call to praise it. Sharbutt, Jay. "AP Writer Analyzes NBC Program." *Rafu Shimpo,* 2 Oct. 1972: 1

September 24, 1972 The first annual Los Angeles LITTLE TOKYO Health Fair is held. Staffed by medical volunteers from the community and targeted at ISSEI and older NISEI, the Health Fair provides a chance for the needy to receive free health services. *Rafu Shimpo,* 23 Sept. 1972: 1

October 25, 1972 New York Asian American groups organize a protest outside the International Ladies Garment Workers Union headquarters to protest a racist poster. The poster in question contains the words "Don't Buy Made in Japan." Herman 74 (49)

December 20, 1972 The Los Angeles Community Redevelopment Agency's Board of Directors selects a group headed by the large Japanese corporation Kajima International to be the developer for the Little Tokyo hotel complex. This decision is met by protest from the local community. (See REDEVELOPMENT.) "Asiamerica Inc. Challenges CRA Kajima Hotel Decision." *Rafu Shimpo,* 28 Dec. 1972: 1

February 1973 The Committee Against Nihonmachi Eviction (CANE) forms in San Francisco over "a common predicament—eviction from our homes and places of business at the hands of the San Francisco Redevelopment Agency (RDA) and giant corporate interests." (See REDEVELOPMENT.) "What Is CANE?" *CANE Publication,* Apr. 1975: n.pag.

May 1973 Sakura Square, a one-block complex of shops, housing and a remodeled Buddhist church, opens in downtown Denver. The housing complex in the center of Sakura Square is Tamai Towers, a 204-unit low/moderate income high rise. Endo 85 (107)

August 1, 1973 H. R. Haldeman's lawyer John J. Wilson calls Senator DANIEL K. INOUYE "that little Jap" at the Watergate committee hearings, resulting in a great uproar. Wilson later writes a letter to the *Nichi Bei Times* explaining that he was unaware that "Jap" was an insult. Herman 74 (52); "Racial Slur by Haldeman Attorney Criticized." *Rafu Shimpo,* 2 Aug. 1973: 1

September 18, 1973 David Cunningham wins the Los Angeles City Council seat vacated by Mayor Tom Bradley. Actor GEORGE TAKEI places a close second, far ahead of the other 32 candidates.   "Cunningham & Takei Finish 1,2 on Tuesday." *Rafu Shimpo,* 19 Sept. 1973: 1

October 1973 With the resignation of the ailing JOHN A. BURNS, GEORGE R. ARIYOSHI becomes the first Asian American governor of Hawaii. With fellow NISEI NELSON DOI as lieutenant governor, Ariyoshi is reelected in 1974 to the first of his three terms as governor. Hazama/Komeiji 86 (195)

May 16, 1974 Three hundred members of the ASIAN AMERICAN community in New York begin picketing at the Confucius Plaza construction site where the De-Matteis Corporation refused to hire Asian workers. Asian Americans for Equal Employment demand the hire of at least 40 workers. In the first four days of picketing, 48 people were arrested.   "NY Asians Demonstrate for Jobs; 48 Arrested." *Rafu Shimpo,* 29 May 1974: 1.

July 1974 Four hundred attend a community forum in San Francisco titled "Concentration Camps USA—A Tribute to the Past and Present." Organized by various local groups, it attempts to link history with present realities.   "S.F. J-Town Forum Concentration Camps." *New York Nichibei,* 11 July 1974: 1

August 8, 1974 President Richard Nixon resigns from office, effective the following day. Vice President Gerald Ford assumes the presidency.   Los Angeles Times, 8 Aug. 1974: 1

August 17, 1974 Elisa Akemi Cuthbert becomes the first multiracial person to win NISEI WEEK queen honors. The string of multiracial queens to follow will eventually become a source of controversy.   "Elisa Cuthbert New NW Queen." *Rafu Shimpo,* 19 Aug. 1974: 1

September 1974 The Housing Committee of the International District Youth Council forms to combat redevelopment in Seattle's International District. The catalyst of this new redevelopment is the planned construction of the Seattle Kingdome stadium nearby. Out of this group comes the Committee for the Corrective Action Program, dealing "specifically with the impact of the stadium on the community." (See SEATTLE NIHON-MACHI/INTERNATIONAL DISTRICT.)   "International District: Seattle's Housing Struggle." *One Year of Struggle: CANE,* 1974: n.pag.

September 1974 Fujio Matsuda becomes president of the University of Hawaii. He remains in this post until May 1984. Matsuda had previously been director of transportation for the State of Hawaii.   Hazama/Komeiji 86 (253)

September 27, 1974 About 100 demonstrators picket the groundbreaking of the New Otani Hotel in Los Angeles, protesting the lack of low-cost housing promised by the Community Redevelopment Agency. The protest was sponsored by the Little Tokyo Anti-Eviction Task Force. (See REDEVELOPMENT.)   Chuman, Dwight. "100 Picket Hotel Groundbreaking." *Rafu Shimpo,* 27 Sept. 1974: 1

November 5, 1974 NORMAN MINETA of San Jose, California, becomes the first mainland Japanese American to be elected to Congress.   "Mineta First Mainland JA in Congress." *Rafu Shimpo,* 6 Nov. 1974: 1

February 13, 1975 Nine Committee Against Nihonmachi Eviction members chain themselves together in the Western Addition Redevelopment headquarters in a protest of REDEVELOPMENT in San Francisco's NI-HONMACHI (Japan Town). One hundred supporters look on.   "What Is CANE?" *CANE Publication,* Apr. 1975: n.pag.

April 26, 1975 The San Fernando Valley JACL hosts a public forum on reparations for the World War II removal and incarceration victims. The six-person panel is hosted by Paul Tsuneishi and includes Edwin C. Hiroto, Masamune Kojima, EDISON UNO, Gail Chew Nishioka and Bob Ronka. Two hundred persons attend. Endo, Ellen. "Interest in Evacuee Reparations Rekindled." *Rafu Shimpo,* 30 Apr. 1975: 1

September 18, 1975 WENDY YOSHIMURA is arrested with Patty Hearst in San Francisco. Her resultant trial (beginning on October 18, 1976) and conviction for illegal possesion of weapons (on Jan. 20, 1977) becomes the locus of Asian American community support and protest over the seemingly severe treatment given her.   *Bridge* 5.2 (1977): 37–38

December 13, 1975 The LITTLE TOKYO Towers senior citizens housing complex opens in Los Angeles and is officially dedicated. It features 300 subsidized units.   "Mineta Keynotes LT Towers Dedication Rites." *Rafu Shimpo,* 15 Dec. 1975: 1

February 19, 1976 President Ford issues "An American Promise," a presidential proclamation terminating EXECUTIVE ORDER 9066. The proclamation does not contain an apology.   Hohri 91 (197)

March 11, 1976 "Farewell to MANZANAR" airs on NBC. The movie version of the James Houston/Jeanne Wakatsuki Houston book is directed by John Korty. Critical response is generally favorable, though many

ASIAN AMERICANS (notably Chinese American writer Frank Chin in a February *Rafu Shimpo* article) criticize it. Endo, Ellen. " 'Farewell to Manzanar' Places Second in TV Ratings." *Rafu Shimpo*, 12 Mar. 1976: 1

May 3, 1976 MICHI WEGLYN's *Years of Infamy* is published. It would soon become one of the most widely read and influential works on the wartime forced removal and incarceration of Japanese Americans.

September 16, 1976 In the so-called Bakke case, the California Supreme Court upholds lower court rulings that special admissions programs for minorities at public schools are unconstitutional. "Court Hits Minority Admissions." *Rafu Shimpo*, 17 Sept. 1976: 1

December 5, 1976 The Little Tokyo People's Rights Organization (LTPRO) stages a march and rally in LITTLE TOKYO to protest the scheduled eviction of Sun Hotel residents, set for February 28, 1977. (See REDEVELOPMENT.) Tatsukawa, Steve. "Sunday Rally Brings Attention to Evictions." *Rafu Shimpo*, 6 Dec. 1976: 1.

January 19, 1977 President Ford grants a pardon to IVA IKUKO TOGURI D'AQUINO, culminating a long battle by the Japanese American community. She had served 6.5 years in prison for her activities in Japan during World War II as one of several women making English-language propaganda broadcasts. She was the only one prosecuted. "Toguri Pardoned." *Rafu Shimpo*, 19 Jan. 1977: 1

February 28, 1977 After "a spirited discussion" by LITTLE TOKYO community members, the Los Angeles City Council votes to support the Community Redevelopment Agency's handling of the Sun Hotel situation and vote down the Little Tokyo People's Rights Organization's demands for a moratorium on evictions. The Sun Hotel is emptied as scheduled. Simross, Lynn. "Little Tokyo Image Slowly Changing." *Los Angeles Times*, 6 Mar. 1977: 2+

June 13, 1977 The LITTLE TOKYO People's Rights Organization (LTPRO) blocks a moving firm's attempt to clear the Sun Building, set to be vacated by June 17. The LTPRO sets up a 24-hour guard over their offices there to protest the evictions. The group also organizes a rally in front of the building on June 18; on that same day, Little Tokyo small businessmen and the Community Redevelopment Agency hold a "community ceremony" on the site of the Japanese Village Plaza, set to open July 1978. After holding off the evictions for over three weeks, L.A. County marshalls conduct a pre-dawn raid on July 6 to capture the last of the LTPRO members in the Sun Building. Demolition of the building begins immediately thereafter. (See REDEVELOPMENT.) "LTPRO Occupies Sun Bldg. to Defy Eviction." *Rafu Shimpo*, 13 June 1977: 1; "Japanese Village Plaza, LTPRO Stage Events." *Rafu Shimpo*, 18 June 1977: 1; "Marshalls Evict Activists in Pre-Dawn LT Raid." *Rafu Shimpo*, 6 July 1977: 1

October 5–9, 1977 Representatives of over 100 churches congregate in San Francisco to celebrate the centennial of the Japanese Christian Mission in North America. A community banquet in Los Angeles takes place on October 16. "Large Local Contingent to Attend Christian Centennial Rites." *Rafu Shimpo*, 3 Oct. 1977: 1

October 17, 1977 From a *Los Angeles Times* article: "Despite great odds, Japanese Americans have become the most successful racial minority in U.S. history." (See "MODEL MINORITY.") Waugh 78 (16)

November 17, 1977 The Hawaii *hisshokai* (Hawaii Victory Society)—a group made up of Japanese Americans who believe that Japan actually won World War II—formally disbands some 32 years, 3 months and 2 days after the end of the war. (See KACHIGUMI.) Stephan 84 (174)

March 31, 1978 Congressional hearings before the House Judiciary Subcommittee on Administrative Law and Governmental Relations are held in Los Angeles to discuss legislation (H.R. 5150) that would provide medical assistance to American victims of the atomic bombings of Hiroshima and Nagasaki. Three hundred attend the hearings. No such legislation has yet been approved. (See HIBAKUSHA.) Chuman, Dwight. "U.S. A-Bomb Survivors' Legislation Supported at Hearing." *Rafu Shimpo*, 3 Apr. 1978: 1

April 29–30, 1978 At meetings held in San Francisco by the JAPANESE AMERICAN CITIZENS LEAGUE's NATIONAL COMMITTEE FOR REDRESS (NCR), the body's official plan is announced. This plan consists of seeking a lump-sum redress appropriation from Congress. Individual payments to camp survivors would be made from this lump sum, with the remainder to be administered by a NIKKEI commission. Before the plan can be formally announced at the JACL convention of July 17–22 in Salt Lake City, however, several groups take exception to it. One of the prime dissenters would be the Evacuation Redress Committee of the Seattle JACL chapter. Based on five years of research, this group criticizes the NCR proposal on several fronts in arguing for direct individual reparations. (See REDRESS MOVEMENT.) Seattle Group Disputes Redress Plan." *New York Nichibei*, 6 July 1978: 1–2

May 13, 1978 Two thousand people march in San Francisco during the West Coast Anti-Bakke Mobilization, climaxing in a "national week of struggle" against the Bakke decision. The Bakke decision had struck down affirmative action racial quotas as unconstitutional. Among the participants: Asian Pacific Student Union, CANE, LTPRO and several JACL chapters. "Anti-Bakke Decision Mobilization." *Rafu Shimpo,* 16 May 1978: 1

June 20, 1978 "Talk Story: Our Voices in Literature and Song; Hawaii's Ethnic American Writers' Conference" begins in Honolulu. The conference, the first of its kind, was organized by Talk Story, Inc., a organization dedicated to the recognition and development of local Hawaiian literature begun two years earlier by Stephen Sumida, Arnold Hiura and Marie Hara. Sumida 91 (239)

June 28, 1978 The U.S. Supreme Court rules that racial quotas at the University of California at Davis medical school are unconstitutional and that Allan Bakke must be admitted. On the other hand, the Court rules that granting special consideration to underrepresented groups would be allowed. Los Angeles Times, 29 June 1978: A1

July 25–27, 1978 At the JACL biennial convention in Salt Lake City, a resolution is adopted calling for redress in the form of individual payments of at least $25,000 per person. (See REDRESS MOVEMENT.) "Ad Opposes Redress Commission Plan." *New York Nichibei,* 7 June 1979: 1–2.

October 1978 Five students at Washington State University (WSU) and from the Spokane JACL chapter file a class-action suit against the school in the U.S. district court in Spokane claiming that the lack of an Asian American studies program violates the 1964 Civil Rights Act. WSU had ethnic studies programs for Black, Chicano and Native American students. "Spokane JACL, Students File Suit Against WSU for Discrimination." *Rafu Shimpo,* 12 Oct. 1978: 1

October 5, 1978 President Carter signs House Joint Resolution 1007, establishing the first ten days of May as "Asian Pacific American Heritage Week." "President Signs Resolution Calling for Asian-Pacific Wk." *Rafu Shimpo,* 21 Oct. 1978: 1

November 7, 1978 JEAN SADAKO KING becomes the first woman to be elected Hawaii's lieutenant governor. "Timeline of the Japanese in Hawaii." *Hawaii Herald,* 5 July 1985: A12-13

January 1979 A JACL delegation meets with the four sympathetic Japanese American members of Congress (INOUYE, MATSUNAGA, MATSUI and MINETA) in Washington on the redress issue. The legislators suggest that the group's first priority ought not be monetary reparations, but rather a public acknowledgment of the fact that a wrong had been committed. This advice is taken by the JACL NATIONAL COMMITTEE FOR REDRESS; they decide to request a congressional commission to "establish an official determination of the injustice" at their March 3–4 national meeting in San Francisco. (See REDRESS MOVEMENT.) Tateishi 91 (192)

May 1979 The NATIONAL COUNCIL FOR JAPANESE AMERICAN REDRESS is formed in Seattle by a group of people unhappy with the JACL decision to seek from Congress a study commission rather than direct compensation. (See REDRESS MOVEMENT.) Hohri 91 (196)

August 7, 1979 Senator DANIEL INOUYE introduces legislation to form what would become the COMMISSION ON WARTIME RELOCATION AND INTERNMENT OF CIVILIANS; the House version is introduced on September 28. It would be approved by the Senate on May 22, 1980, and by the House on July 21, 1980. It was signed into law by President Carter on July 31. Tateishi 91 (193)

November 5, 1979 The United States Embassy in Iran is seized by angry Iranian students who vow to keep the 60 Americans there hostage until the Shah of Iran is sent back to stand trial in Iran. The hostage crisis would last until January 1981. Los Angeles Times, 5 Nov. 1979: A1; Los Angeles Times, 21 Jan. 1981: A1

November 28, 1979 Representative Mike Lowry (D-WA) introduces the World War II Japanese-American Human Rights Violations Act (H.R. 5977) into Congress. This NCJAR–sponsored bill is largely based on research done by ex-members of the Seattle JACL chapter. It proposes direct payments of $15,000 per victim plus an additional $15 per day interned. Given the choice between this bill and the JACL–supported study commission bill introduced two months earlier, Congress opts for the latter. Chin, Rockwell. "The Long Road: Japanese Americans Move on Redress." *Bridge* 7.4 (Winter 1981–82): 14; Hohri 91 (198)

December 1979 The Japanese American Fair Play Committee is formed in the San Francisco Bay Area to protest anti-Iranian actions by individuals and the government with the advent of the hostage crisis. " 'Fair Play' Unit Critical of Anti-Iranian Hysteria." *Rafu Shimpo,* 23 Jan. 1980: 1

January 19, 1980 The first public conference on the redress issue is sponsored by the NCJAR. Called "Japanese

America: Contemporary Perspectives on the Internment," it is held before an SRO crowd of 400 at the Seattle Central Community College Auditorium. The conference director is Karen Seriguchi; Mike Lowry is the main speaker. Predictably, the direct payments approach is supported over the study commission approach.

February 16, 1980 The Los Angeles Coalition on Redress/Reparations (the precursor of the NATIONAL COALITION FOR REDRESS/REPARATIONS [NCRR]) sponsors a conference/workshop at the Little Tokyo Towers where the various redress strategies are presented and discussed. Representatives from the JACL-NCR (study commission approach), NCJAR (Lowry bill), and LTPRO (direct payments and community fund) are present. More than twenty-five representatives attend and seem to generally favor individual payments of some sort. (See REDRESS MOVEMENT.) Suzuki, Cecil. "Monetary Compensation Favored as Redress." *Rafu Shimpo,* 20 Feb. 1980: 1

March 11, 1980 Senator S. I. HAYAKAWA states that all Iranians in this country should be put in camps "the way we did with the Japanese in World War II." He also announces plans to introduce a bill—The American Sovereignty Protection Act—which would set up the mechanism for such an action. The other Japanese American members of Congress and many others denounce the idea. Chuman, Dwight. "JAs Blast Sen. Hayakawa." *Rafu Shimpo,* 12 Mar. 1980: 1

May 9, 1980 Three buildings at the Defense Language Institute, Presidio of Monterey, California, are named for NISEI MILITARY INTELLIGENCE SERVICE soldiers killed in action during World War II. The three are Frank Hachiya of Hood River Valley, Oregon; Terry Mizutari of Hilo, Hawaii; and George Nakamura of Watsonville, California. Ichinokuchi 88 (202)

May 16, 1980 The first issue of the new HAWAII HERALD appears. The *Herald* becomes an important and widely read English language tabloid for Hawaii's Japanese American community. "A Brief History of the Hawaii Herald." *Hawaii Herald,* 11.16 (18 May 1990): 3

July 12, 1980 The NATIONAL COALITION FOR REDRESS/REPARATIONS (NCRR) is formed at a Los Angeles meeting. It had been initiated by the LTPRO and includes the Asian Pacific Student Union, JACL-San Jose, NCJAR, New England Nisei, Nihonmachi (San Jose) Outreach Committee and the Tule Lake Committee, among others. "Nat'l Coalition on Redress/Reparations." *New York Nichibei,* 7 Aug. 1980: 1

July 31, 1980 President Carter signs Public Law 96-317 calling for a congressional commission to study the World War II internment of Japanese Americans for the purpose of establishing that a wrong had been committed. This commission is called the COMMISSION ON WARTIME RELOCATION AND EVACUATION OF CIVILIANS (CWRIC). *Bridge* 7.3 (1980): 45

November 15–16, 1980 The NCRR holds its first nationwide conference on the campus of California State University, Los Angeles. A cultural night featuring a wealth of Japanese American performers and artists takes place on the 15th. "Cultural Presentations Set for Redress Conf." *Rafu Shimpo,* 12 Nov. 1980: 1

January 21, 1981 *Ronald Reagan is sworn in as the 40th president of the United States.* *Los Angeles Times,* 21 Jan. 1981: A1

March 7, 1981 Opening ceremonies of an exhibit honoring the 442ND REGIMENTAL COMBAT TEAM at the Army Museum at the Presidio of San Francisco take place. Over 2,000 NISEI veterans attend, including MIKE MASAOKA, Senator DANIEL INOUYE and Senator SPARK MATSUNAGA. "Presidio 442nd Exhibit Dedicated." *Rafu Shimpo,* 9 Mar. 1981: 1

July 14, 1981 The CWRIC holds a public hearing in Washington, D.C., as part of its investigation into the internment of Japanese Americans during World War II. Similar hearings would be held in many other cities throughout the rest of 1981. The emotional testimony by Japanese American witnesses about their wartime experiences would prove cathartic for the community and might be considered a turning point in the REDRESS MOVEMENT. In all, some 750 witnesses testify. The last hearing takes place at Harvard University on December 9, 1981. Chuman, Dwight. "Wartime Relocation Hearings Open." *Rafu Shimpo,* 15 July 1981: 1; Irons 89 (8)

Fall 1981 The Los Angeles Wholesale Flower Terminal is constructed by the Japanese American–owned Southern California Flower Growers, Inc. The new building has 103,000 square feet of business space. (See SOUTHERN CALIFORNIA FLOWER MARKET, INC.) Yagasaki 82 (414–16)

March 5, 1982 Los Angeles County Chief Medical Examiner-Coroner THOMAS NOGUCHI is again asked to resign, this time by county chief administrative officer Harry L. Hufford. This request is apparently triggered by a critical *Los Angeles Times* story in December alledging lax administration. After refusing to resign, he is suspended without pay by the County Board of Supervisors on March 25 before being demoted to "physician specialist" on April 15. He had earlier been fired in 1969, but was reinstated due largely to successful community pressure.   Chuman, Dwight. "Noguchi Asked to Resign." *Rafu Shimpo*, 8 Mar. 1982: 1; ———. "Noguchi Suspended Without Pay." *Rafu Shimpo*, 26 Mar. 1982: 1; ———. "Noguchi to Fight Demotion by Supervisors." *Rafu Shimpo*, 16 Apr. 1982: 1.

June 19, 1982 Vincent Chin, a 27-year-old Chinese American engineer, is beaten to death in Highland Park, Michigan. The lenient sentences meted out to his killers spark an uproar in ASIAN AMERICAN communities across the country. (See VINCENT CHIN CASE.)   Suzuki, Cecil. "Detroit's Asian Americans Outraged by Lenient Sentencing of Chinese American Man's Killer." *Rafu Shimpo*, 5 May 1983: 1

June 25–27, 1982 Representatives from 20 Asian Pacific women's organizations meet in La Jolla, California, for the first National Network of Asian/Pacific Women convention. Irene Hirano and Pat Luce are elected co-chairs of the organization.   "Asian Pacific Women to Form Nat'l Network." *Rafu Shimpo*, 28 July 1982: 1

August 17, 1982 Governor Edmund G. Brown of California signs into law Assembly Bill 2710, providing a $5,000 payment to Japanese American state employees fired in 1942.   "Seek Whereabouts of More Than 150 Former Nikkei State Employees Eligible for Reparations." *Rafu Shimpo*, 10 Sept. 1982: 1

December 8, 1982 Representative Mervyn M. Dymally (D-Gardena) of California introduces two redress bills into Congress. One would provide for $25,000 individual payments to internment survivors or their spouses or children; the other would create a $3 billion community restoration fund. (See REDRESS MOVEMENT.)   "Dymally Says He Hopes Redress Bills Will Spark Discussion About Gov't's WWII Actions." *Rafu Shimpo*, 9 Dec. 1982: 1

January 19, 1983 A legal team led by Dale Minami and Peter Irons files a petition of *error coram nobis* on behalf of Fred Korematsu in the San Francisco federal district court. Judge Marilyn Patel, regarded as the most sympathetic of the 15 possible judges, is assigned to the case. Identical petitions on behalf of Gordon Hirabayashi and Min Yasui are filed in Seattle and Portland, respectively, by the end of the month. Judge Robert C. Belloni is assigned the Yasui petition and Judge Donald S. Voorhees the Hirabayashi case. (See CORAM NOBIS CASES.) Irons 89 (17–18)

February 22, 1983 After 18 months of research, the CWRIC issues its report, entitled *Personal Justice Denied*. Tateishi 91 (195)

March 16, 1983 The NCJAR files a class-action suit against the government in federal district court, Washington, D.C. The suit seeks $24 billion in damages for the "unlawful" segregation, arrest, exclusion and imprisonment of Japanese Americans during World War II. Suzuki, Cecil. "Japanese Americans File Massive Class Action Lawsuit Asking $24 Billion Redress From Gov't." *Rafu Shimpo*, 16 Mar. 1983: 1

March 21, 1983 The headline " 'No Nuke' Japs Protest Visit by U.S. Carrier" appears on page 5 of the *New York Post*. A "Concerned Japanese Americans" group protests and receives an apology.   "Post Apologizes for Racial Slur." *New York Nichibei*, 14 Apr. 1983: 1

May 9, 1983 More than 500 people march through downtown Detroit to support the American Citizens for Justice protesting the fine and probation sentences of Vincent Chin's killers. Chin had been killed by two laid-off autoworkers one year earlier. (See VINCENT CHIN CASE.)   "More Than 500 Take to the Streets in Detroit to Protest Lenient Sentencing of Chin Killers." *Rafu Shimpo*, 10 May 1983: 1

May 22, 1983 In a *New York Times* article titled "1941 Cables Boasted of Japanese-American Spying" by Charles Mohr, retired government official David Lowman cites the so-called "MAGIC" CABLES as a means to discredit the recent findings of the CWRIC. The cables are subsequently shown to be of little consequence to the "MILITARY NECESSITY" debate.   Kanazawa, Teru. "Investigation Reveals No Basis for Fear by US Govt of 1941 JA Espionage." *New York Nichibei*, 16 June 1983: 1–2

June 16, 1983 The CWRIC issues its formal recommendations to Congress concerning redress for Japanese Americans interned during World War II. They include the call for $20,000 individual payments to those still alive who spent time in the CONCENTRATION CAMPS. (See REDRESS MOVEMENT.)   *Bridge* 8.3 (1983): 5

June 22, 1983 Redress bills are introduced to implement the recent CWRIC findings. Senator Alan Cranston (D-CA) sponsors the Senate version (S 1520), which does not specify an amount for individual compensation; Rep. Mike Lowry (D-WA) sponsors the House version (HR 3387), which supports the CWRIC's $20,000 figure. (See REDRESS MOVEMENT.)   Suzuki, Cecil. "Cranston Introduces Redress Bill." *Rafu Shimpo*, 22 June 1983: 1

October 6, 1983   House Majority Leader Jim Wright (D-TX) introduces a bill in Congress (HR 4110) to implement the full CWRIC recommendations of $20,000 individual payments, a $5 million trust fund and a formal apology. (See REDRESS MOVEMENT.)   "Reparations Bill Introduced into Congress." *Rafu Shimpo,* 12 Oct. 1983: 1

November 10, 1983   San Francisco Federal District Court Judge Marilyn Hall Patel rules that the 1942 conviction of Fred Korematsu should be vacated, granting the petition for a writ of *error coram nobis.* (See KOREMATSU V. UNITED STATES and CORAM NOBIS CASES.) Irons 89 (23–26); Nash, Philip Tajitsu. "Korematsu's Wartime Conviction Vacated: Judge Rules No Military Necessity for Wartime Incarceration of Japanese-Americans." *New York Nichibei,* 17 Nov. 1983: 1–2

November 17, 1983   Senator SPARK MATSUNAGA (D-HI) introduces S 2116, a companion bill to HR 4110, calling for the implementation of CWRIC recommendations. (See REDRESS MOVEMENT.)   "Matsunaga Introduces Redress Legislation, S. 2116 in Senate." *Rafu Shimpo,* 21 Nov. 1983: 1

January 15, 1984   "Sanga Moyu" begins its year long television run on NHK in Japan. It is a series based on the book(s) *Futatsu no Sokoku* by Toyoko Yamazaki about one Japanese American family's World War II experience.   "NHK Serial on Japanese Americans Draws Large Japan TV Audience." *Rafu Shimpo,* 30 Jan. 1984: 1

January 26, 1984   Portland Judge Robert C. Belloni grants the government's motion to vacate Min Yasui's conviction and dismiss the *coram nobis* petition. Yasui's hearing had taken place just 10 days earlier. This refusal to consider the petition is a disappointment to the community, especially in the wake of an earlier finding in San Francisco on November 10, 1983, granting the petition. Yasui went on to appeal this decision, but died in November 1986 before a decision could be reached. (See CORAM NOBIS CASES.)   Irons 89 (29)

March 1984   The debut on American television of the NHK drama "Sanga Moyu" is "postponed." This story of a NIKKEI family's experience during World War II, was controversial for its depiction of the divided loyalties of the KIBEI. The JACL had objected to showing the program, claiming it might hurt the REDRESS MOVEMENT. It has yet to be seen in the U.S.   "NHK Postpones U.S. Showing." *New York Nichibei,* 8 Mar. 1984: 1

May 17, 1984   District of Columbia District Court Judge Louis Oberdorfer dismisses the NCJAR's class action suit, stating that too much time had passed since the creation of the CONCENTRATION CAMPS. This decision is later appealed.   "Federal Judge Grants Government Motion to Dismiss Redress Lawsuit." *Rafu Shimpo,* 17 May 1984: 1

June 18–20, 1984   *The Washington Times* runs a three-part article by Gene Goltz alledging that opponents of redress were ignored by the CWRIC and the press; he quotes S. I. HAYAKAWA, Lillian Baker, Daniel Lundgren and others.   Kanazawa, Teru. "Washington Times Continues Scathing Attack on Redress Drive." *New York Nichibei,* 5 July 1984: 1–2

January 7, 1985   HR 442 is reintroduced to the House by Representative Jim Wright; it is virtually identical to HR 4110, introduced in 1983. (Legislation must be reintroduced with each session of Congress.) Senator SPARK MATSUNAGA reintroduces S 1053 into the Senate. (See REDRESS MOVEMENT.)   "Redress Legislation Reintroduced." *Rafu Shimpo,* 7 Jan. 1985: 1

January 24, 1985   Mission specialist ELLISON ONIZUKA becomes the first Japanese American in space on the Space Shuttle *Discovery.* It returns to Earth on January 27.   "Space Shuttle Releases Spy Satellite." *Rafu Shimpo,* 26 Jan. 1985: 1

January 29, 1985   Fumiko Kimura is rescued after walking off a pier in a suicide attempt involving her two children who had both drowned. She is eventually tried for first degree murder and child endangerment, raising questions about the law and cultural customs of immigrants. She pleads no contest on October 18 to a reduced charge of voluntary manslaughter and is sentenced to probation with psychiatric supervision.   "Kimura Sentenced to 5-Years Probation in Drowning Deaths of Children." *New York Nichibei,* 12 Dec. 1985: 1–2

March 26, 1985   Over 700 people attend a Redress Forum at New York University sponsored by the Asian/Pacific American Law Students Association and co-sponsored by black, Latino and Jewish student groups. STEVEN OKAZAKI's "Unfinished Business" is shown and Min Yasui and Fred Korematsu speak. Two hundred fifty attend a similar event two weeks later at Yale, featuring Peter Irons and legal scholar (and assistant attorney general during WW II) Herbert Wechsler.   Nash, Philip Tajitsu. "700 Attend Redress Forum at NYU; Yasui and Korematsu Speak." *New York Nichibei,* 4 Apr. 1985: 1–2; ———. "250 Attend Redress Forum at Yale; Wechsler-Irons Dialog Featured." *New York Nichibei,* 25 Apr. 1985: 1–2

July 1985   City View Hospital in East Los Angeles closes. It is the last of the Japanese ethnic hospitals in Los Angeles. (See JAPANESE HOSPITALS.)   Garvey,

Kathryn. "The Rise & Fall of Japanese Ethnic Hospitals." *Tozai Times* 3.26 (Nov. 1986): 1

July 13, 1985 The first ever "summit" of redress groups takes place at the San Francisco headquarters of the JACL. JACL president Frank Sato had called the meeting, attended by representatives from *NCRR*, *NCJAR* and the Washington Coalition for Redress (WCR). Good will is promoted; little else is agreed upon. (See REDRESS MOVEMENT.)   Hohri, William. "Redress Groups Attend 'Summit' Meet Called by JACL Pres Frank Sato." *New York Nichibei*, 25 July 1985: 1–2; "Redress Groups Present Proposals For Joint Activity at 'Summit.'" *New York Nichibei*, 1 Aug. 1985: 1–2

September 12, 1985 California state assemblyman Gil Ferguson denounces a proposal to give $750,000 to the Japanese American National Museum in Los Angeles's LITTLE TOKYO. Ferguson cites World War II in blasting the bill and several Republican legislators gather around him and begin cheering and chanting, "Rambo, Rambo, Rambo." The bill passes anyway. It had been introduced by Sen. Art Torres and had already passed the state senate. It is soon signed by Governor George Deukmejian. Later, on April 28, 1986, the Los Angeles Community Redevelopment Agency gives the museum $1 million. On May 6, 1986, the Los Angeles City Council gives the museum a 50-year lease on the historic Nishi Hongwanji building on First Street for $1 per year.   "Legislators Cheer and Chant 'Rambo' as Ferguson Opposes Funding." *New York Nichibei*, 26 Sept. 1985: 1–2; "Gov. Deukmejian Approves Funding." *New York Nichibei*, 10 Oct. 1985: 1–2; "Japanese American National Museum Gets $1 Million; Also Permanent Site." *New York Nichibei*, 22 May 1986: 1

September 14–15, 1985 "Coming of Age: The NISEI and the Japanese Immigrant Press," an academic conference focusing on the 1930s, is held at UCLA. Yuji Ichioka is the conference director.   Rassouli, Patricia Tahara. "Coming of Age: The Nisei and the Japanese Immigrant Press." *Tozai Times* 1 (Sept. 1985): 1, 20

January 21, 1986 The U.S. Court of Appeals for the District of Columbia overturns the U.S. District Court dismissal of the NCJAR suit, allowing the suit to go to trial pending further appeals. In the 2-1 vote, Judges James Kelly Wright and Ruth Bader Ginsburg rule that the statute of limitations has not run out. The appeal was heard on September 24, 1985, before Judges Ginburg, Wright and Howard Thomas Markey. The government would petition to rehear the case in front of an *en-banc* panel, but this would be denied on May 30 by the 12 judges of the Court of Appeals in D.C. by a 6-6 vote, upholding the January 21 decision in favor of the plaintiffs.   Hohri, William. "Appeal Heard in Washington Court; Decision Awaited." *New York Nichibei*, 3 Oct. 1985: 1–2; "Federal Appeals Court Orders Redress Suit to Go to Trial; 'Tremendous Victory' Says Hohri." *New York Nichibei*, 30 Jan. 1986: 1–2; Willgerodt, Penny Fujiko. "Jan 21 Decision in Hohri v. U.S.A. 'Hotly-Debated' But Upheld." *New York Nichibei*, 12 June 1986: 1–2

January 28, 1986 The Space Shuttle *Challenger* explodes soon after lift-off killing the seven astronauts aboard. One of the seven is ELLISON S. ONIZUKA, the first Japanese American in space.   Ogawa 86 (13)

February 10, 1986 U.S. District Court Judge Donald Voorhees overturns Gordon Hirabayashi's evacuation conviction, citing governmental misconduct. Strangely, his conviction for violating curfew is upheld. Although similar to the recent judicial victories of Fred Korematsu and Minoru Yasui, Hirabayashi's was the result of a full judicial review of government conduct. The two-week evidentiary hearing began on June 17, 1985. Since neither side was pleased by the outcome, the case would be appealed. (See HIRABAYASHI V. U.S. and CORAM NOBIS CASES.)   "Judge Overturns Hirabayashi's 1942 Evacuation Conviction Citing Government Misconduct." *New York Nichibei*, 27 Feb. 1986: 1–2; Irons 89 (36–43)

November 4, 1986 PATRICIA SAIKI becomes the first Japanese American Republican woman to be elected to the House of Representatives, winning in Hawaii. In California, proponents of Proposition 63, the initiative naming English the official language of California, account for 70% of the vote.   "Inouye, Saiki Winners in Hawaiian Elections." *Rafu Shimpo*, 5 Nov. 1986: 1; Quan, Martie. "English Becomes Official Language by a Landslide." *Rafu Shimpo*, 5 Nov. 1986: 1.

April 14, 1987 NIKKEI community activist Warren Furutani is elected to the board of the Los Angeles Unified School District. He becomes the first Japanese American to serve on this board.   "Potpourri." *Rafu Shimpo*, 19 Dec. 1987: Magazine II-18–22

April 20, 1987 The U.S. Supreme Court hears the government's appeal on the *NCJAR* lawsuit. The court had agreed to hear the case on November 17, 1986. Soliciter General Charles Fried argues the government's case by claiming that (1) the appeal was filed in the wrong court, and (2) the statute of limitations should have begun in 1976, when President Ford declared the forced removal a "national mistake." Only eight justices hear the case; Justice Scalia had recused himself since he had heard it earlier at the court of appeals level.   Willgerodt, Penny Fujiko. "Supreme Court Agrees to Hear Gov't

Petition." *New York Nichibei,* 27 Nov. 1986: 1–2; ———.
"NCJAR's Day at Supreme Court." *New York Nichibei,* 30 Apr.
1987: 1–3

June 1, 1987   The Supreme Court delivers its decision on the NCJAR suit, declaring it was indeed heard in
the wrong court. The decision of the U.S. Court of
Appeals for the District of Columbia Circuit is vacated
and the case is remanded to the U.S. Court of Appeals
for the Federal Circuit.   "Supreme Court Sides with
Gov't: Decides NCJAR Case Was Heard in Wrong Court."
New York Nichibei, 4 June 1987: 1

July 25–29, 1987   The NCRR sponsors a delegation
of about 120 to Washington, D.C., in order to lobby
for HR 442.   Ota, John. "NCRR & Delegation Lobbies
for Redress." *New York Nichibei,* 13 Aug. 1987: 1

September 17, 1987   HR 442 passes the U.S. House
of Representatives. The bill would have the U.S. government officially apologize for its World War II internment of Japanese Americans and award $20,000 to each
camp survivor. It must pass the Senate and be signed by
the president to become law. (See REDRESS MOVEMENT.)
"Potpourri." *Rafu Shimpo,* 19 Dec. 1987: Magazine II-18–22

October 1, 1987   "A More Perfect Union: Japanese
Americans and the United States Constitution" opens at
the Smithsonian Institution's National Museum of
American History. The exhibit examines the constitu-
tional process through the internment experience.
"Japanese Americans and the United States Constitution."
Tozai Times 4 (Oct. 1987): 1, 8–9

January 12, 1988   Judge Donald S. Voorhees vacates
Gordon Hirabayashi's curfew violation conviction after
an appeals court ruling issued in September 1987. This
unanimous ruling by a three-member appeals panel (Alfred
T. Goodwin, Mary M. Schroeder and Joseph J. Farris),
stemming from a March 2, 1987 hearing, strongly upholds allegations of governmental misconduct, upholds
Voorhees's vacating of Hirabayashi's evacuation order
conviction and reverses Voorhees's upholding of Hirabayshi's curfew violation conviction. A final Justice Department appeal had been denied on December 24,
1987. (See HIRABAYASHI V. U.S. and CORAM NOBIS
CASES.)   Irons 89 (43–46)

August 10, 1988   HR 442 is signed into law by
President Ronald Reagan. It provides for individual
payments of $20,000 to each surviving internee and a
$1.25 billion education fund, among other provisions.
(See REDRESS MOVEMENT.)   "It's V-R Day!" *New York
Nichibei,* 18 Aug. 1988: 1

October 31, 1988   The U.S. Supreme Court disal-
lows the class action suit *Hohri et al. v. U.S.,* 88-215.
First filed by the NCJAR on March 16, 1983, the suit
asked for some $27 billion from the government for the
wrongful imprisonment of Japanese Americans during
World War II. This decision effectively ends the efforts
of the NCJAR.   "Supreme Court Crushes NCJAR Lawsuit." *Pacific Citizen,* 4 Nov. 1988: 1, 9

January 11, 1989   Loni Ding's "The Color of Honor"
is shown nationwide on PBS. The feature-length docu-
mentary focuses on the NISEI who joined the MILITARY
INTELLIGENCE SERVICE during World War II.   Chester,
Jeff. "PBS Special Will Tell Nikkei Veterans' Tales." *New York
Nichibei,* 29 Dec. 1988: 1–2

November 21, 1989   President Bush signs the 1990
Appropriations bill for Commerce, State, Justice and the
Judiciary that converts redress payments into an entitle-
ment program starting in October 1990. Though redress
legislation had been approved for over a year, no money
had been appropriated to make payments. As an entitle-
ment program, redress payments will automatically be
funded and all payments will be made by the end of
1993. (See REDRESS MOVEMENT.)   "Bush Signs Commerce, State, Justice and Judiciary Appropriations Bill." *Pacific
Citizen,* 1 Dec. 1989: 1

May 20, 1990   Rick Noji of the University of Washington wins the Pac-10 high jump title with a jump of
7'2-1/2". Noji stands 5'8" tall.   Kumasaka, Ryo. "Noji
Soars to Victory." *Northwest Nikkei* 2.6 (June 1990): 6

June 16, 1990   The grand opening of the Hawaii
Okinawa Center takes place, culminating a year of events
commemorating the 90th anniversary of Okinawan immigration to Hawaii. The $9 million structure features
a 1,500-seat auditorium and banquet complex and an
office/library/display building. (See UNITED OKINAWAN
ASSOCIATION OF HAWAII.)   Chinen, Karleen. "Hawaii
Okinawa Center: A Dream Come True." *Hawaii Herald* 11.13
(6 July 1990): 1, 8–9

October 9, 1990   The first nine redress payments are
made at a Washington, D.C., ceremony. One hundred
seven-year-old Reverend Mamoru Eto of Los Angeles is
the first to receive his check. (See REDRESS MOVEMENT.)
"First Redress Checks, Apology Presented to Nine at WDC
Event." *Pacific Citizen,* 12 Oct. 1990: 1

December 22, 1990   Alan Parker's *Come See the
Paradise* opens. A feature film in which the World War
II removal and internment of Japanese Americans serves
as a backdrop to an interracial love story, *Paradise* opens

to mixed reviews from both Japanese American and mainstream media.   "Alan Parker's Film on WWII Japanese American Internment Draws Different Comments." *Pacific Citizen,* 25 Jan. 1991: 5

February 21, 1992   KRISTI YAMAGUCHI, a YONSEI from Fremont, California, wins the gold medal in figure skating at the Winter Olympics in Albertville, France. World and American champion Yamaguchi becomes the first American woman to win the Olympic title in figure skating since Dorothy Hamill in 1976 and the first Japanese American to win a Winter Olympics gold medal. "Kristi Yamaguchi Wins Gold." *Rafu Shimpo,* 22 Feb. 1992: 1

COMPLETE CITATIONS FOR CHRONOLOGY

Abrams, Bruce A. "A Muted Cry: White Opposition to the Japanese Exclusion Movement, 1911–1924." Diss., City University of New York, 1987.

Adaniya, Ruth. "United Okinawan Association of Hawaii." In Ethnic Studies Oral History Project/United Okinawan Association of Hawaii. *Uchinanchu: A History of Okinawans in Hawaii.* Honolulu: Ethnic Studies Program, University of Hawaii at Manoa, 1981. 324–36.

Albert, Michael Daniel. "Japanese American Communities in Chicago and the Twin Cities." Diss., University of Minnesota, 1980.

Almaguer, Tomas. "Racial Domination and Class Conflict in Capitalist Agriculture: The Oxnard Sugar Beet Workers' Strike of 1903." *Labor History* 25.3 (1984): 325–50.

Arrington, Leonard J. "Utah's Ambiguous Reception: The Relocated Japanese Americans." In Daniels, Roger, Sandra C. Taylor, and Harry H. L. Kitano, eds. *Japanese Americans: From Relocation to Redress.* Salt Lake City: University of Utah Press, 1986. Revised edition. Seattle: University of Washington Press, 1991. 92–98.

August, Jack. "The Anti-Japanese Crusade in Arizona's Salt River Valley, 1934–35." *Arizona and the West* 21.2 (Summer 1979): 113–36.

Beechert, Edward D. *Working in Hawaii: A Labor History.* Honolulu: University of Hawaii Press, 1985.

Braden, Wythe E. "On the Probability of Pre-1778 Drifts to Hawaii." *Hawaiian Journal of History* 10 (1976): 75–89.

Cates, Rita Takahashi. "Comparative Administration and Management of Five War Relocation Authority Camps: America's Incarceration of Persons of Japanese Descent during World War II." Diss., University of Pittsburgh, 1980.

Chuman, Frank F. *The Bamboo People: The Law and Japanese-Americans.* Del Mar, Calif.: Publisher's Inc., 1976.

Clark, Paul Frederick. "Those Other Camps: An Oral History Analysis of Japanese Alien Enemy Internment during World War II." Thesis, California State University, Fullerton, 1980.

Cole, Cheryl L. *A History of the Japanese Community in Sacramento, 1883–1972: Organizations, Businesses and Generational Response to Majority Domination and Stereotypes.* San Francisco: R & E Research Associates, 1975.

Collins, Donald E. *Native American Aliens: Disloyalty and the Renunciation of Citizenship by Japanese Americans During World War II.* Westport, Conn.: Greenwood Press, 1985.

Commission on Wartime Relocation and Internment of Civilians. *Personal Justice Denied: Report of the Commission on Wartime Relocation and Internment of Civilians.* Washington, D.C.: Government Printing Office, 1982.

Conroy, Hilary. *The Japanese Frontier in Hawaii, 1868–1898.* Berkeley: University of California Press, 1953. New York: Arno Press, 1978.

Consulate-General of Japan. *Documental History of Law Cases Affecting Japanese in the United States, 1916–1924. 2 Vols.* San Francisco: Consulate-General of Japan, 1925. New York: Arno Press, 1978.

Daniels, Roger. *Asian America: Chinese and Japanese in the United States since 1850.* Seattle: University of Washington Press, 1988.

———. *Concentration Camps, U.S.A.: Japanese Americans and World War II.* New York: Holt, Rinehart and Winston, 1971.

Daniels, Roger. *The Politics of Prejudice: The Anti-Japanese Movement in California and the Struggle for Japanese Exclusion.* 1962. 2nd edition. Berkeley: University of California Press, 1977.

Drinnon, Richard. *Keeper of Concentration Camps: Dillon S. Myer and American Racism.* Berkeley: University of California Press, 1987.

Duus, Masayo. *Unlikely Liberators: The Men of the 100th and the 442nd.* Honolulu: University of Hawaii Press, 1987.

Endo, Russell. "Japanese of Colorado: A Sociohistorical Portrait." *Journal of Social and Behavioral Sciences* 31 (Fall 1985): 100–10.

Estes, Donald H. "Before the War: The Japanese in San Diego." *Journal of San Diego History* 24.4 (1978): 425–55.

Ethnic Studies Oral History Project/United Okinawan Association of Hawaii. *Uchinanchu: A History of Okinawans in Hawaii*. Honolulu: Ethnic Studies Program, University of Hawaii at Manoa, 1981.

Fuchs, Lawrence H. *Hawaii Pono: A Social History*. New York: Harcourt, Brace and World, 1961.

Fugita, Stephen S. "A Perceived Ethnic Factor in California's Farm Labor Conflict: The Nisei Farmer's League." *Explorations in Ethnic Studies* 1.1 (1978): 50–72.

Fugita, Stephen S., and David J. O'Brien. "Economics, Ideology, and Ethnicity: The Struggle between the United Farm Workers Union and the Nisei Farmers League." *Social Problems* 25.2 (Dec. 1977): 146–56. Reprinted in *Asian-Americans: Social and Psychological Perspectives, Vol. II*. Russell Endo, Stanley Sue, and Nathaniel N. Wagner, eds. Palo Alto, Calif.: Science and Behavior Books, Inc., 1980. 260–71.

Fujita, Michinari. "The Japanese Associations in America." *Sociology and Social Research* 13.3 (Jan.–Feb. 1929): 211–28.

Girdner, Audrie, and Anne Loftis. *The Great Betrayal: The Evacuation of the Japanese-Americans during World War II*. Toronto: Macmillan, 1969.

Hata, Donald Teruo. *'Undesirables': Early Immigrants and the Anti-Japanese Movement in San Francisco, 1892–1893: Prelude to Exclusion*. New York: Arno Press, 1978.

Hayashi, Katie Kaoru. "History of the Rafu Shimpo: Evolution of a Japanese-American Newspaper, 1903–1942." Thesis, California State University, Northridge, 1987.

Hazama, Dorothy Ochiai, and Jane Okamoto Komeiji. *Okage Sama De: The Japanese in Hawai'i*. Foreword by Daniel Inouye. Honolulu: Bess Press, 1986.

Herman, Masako, comp. and ed. *The Japanese in America 1843–1973: A Chronology and Fact Book*. Dobbs Ferry, NY: Oceana Publications, 1974.

Higa, Saburo. "The Okinawans on the Big Island." In Ethnic Studies Oral History Project/United Okinawan Association of Hawaii. *Uchinanchu: A History of Okinawans in Hawaii*. Honolulu: Ethnic Studies Program, University of Hawaii at Manoa, 1981. 260–66.

Hinkle, George. "Samurai in San Francisco, the Japanese Embassy of 1860." *California Historical Society Quarterly* 23.4 (Dec. 1944): 335–47.

Hohri, William. "Redress as a Movement Towards Enfranchisement." In Daniels, Roger, Sandra C. Taylor, and Harry H. L. Kitano, eds. *Japanese Americans: From Relocation to Redress*. Salt Lake City: University of Utah Press, 1986. Revised edition. Seattle: University of Washington Press, 1991. 196–99.

———. *Repairing America: An Account of the Movement for Japanese American Redress*. Pullman: Washington State University Press, 1988.

Hosokawa, Bill. *JACL: In Quest of Justice*. New York: William Morrow and Co., 1982.

———. *Nisei: The Quiet Americans*. New York: William Morrow & Co., 1969.

Ichihashi, Yamato. *Japanese in the United States: A Critical Study of the Problems of the Japanese Immigrants and Their Children*. Stanford: Stanford University Press, 1932. New York: Arno Press, 1969.

Ichinokuchi, Tad, ed. *John Aiso and the M.I.S.: Japanese-American Soldiers in the Military Intelligence Service, World War II*. Los Angeles: Military Intelligence Service Club of Southern California, 1988.

Ichioka, Yuji. "The 1921 Turlock Incident: Forceful Expulsion of Japanese Laborers." In Gee, Emma, ed. *Counterpoint: Perspectives on Asian America*. Los Angeles: Asian American Studies Center, University of California, 1976. 195–99.

———. "*Amerika Nadeshiko*: Japanese Immigrant Women in the United States, 1900–1924." *Pacific Historical Review* 48.2 (May 1980): 339–57. [80a]

———. "Ameyuki-san: Japanese Prostitutes in Nineteenth-Century America." *Amerasia Journal* 4.1 (1977): 1–21. [77a]

———. "A Buried Past: Early Issei Socialists and the Japanese Community." *Amerasia Journal* 1.2 (July 1971): 1–25.

———. "The Early Japanese Immigrant Quest for Citizenship: The Background of the 1922 Ozawa Case." *Amerasia Journal* 4.2 (1977): 1–22. [77b]

———. "An Instance of Private Japanese Diplomacy: Suzuki Bunji, Organized American Labor, and Japanese Immigrant Workers, 1915–1916." *Amerasia Journal* 10.1 (Spring/Summer 1983): 1–22.

———. *The Issei: The World of the First Generation Japanese Immigrants, 1885–1924*. New York: The Free Press, 1988.

———. "Japanese Associations and the Japanese Government: A Special Relationship, 1909–1926." *Pacific Historical Review* 46.3 (Aug. 1977): 409–38. [77c]

———. "Japanese Immigrant Labor Contractors and the Northern Pacific and the Great Northern Railroad Companies, 1898–1907." *Labor History* 21.3 (1980): 325–50. [80b]

———. "Japanese Immigrant Response to the 1920 California Alien Land Law." *Agricultural History* 58.2 (Apr. 1984): 157–78.

Ikeda, Gerald H. "Japanese-Americans Fight Delinquency." *California Youth Authority Quarterly* 12.2 (Summer 1959): 3–6.

Inouye, Daniel K, with Lawrence Elliot. *Journey to Washington*. Englewood Cliffs, NJ: Prentice-Hall, 1967.

Irons, Peter, ed. *Justice Delayed: The Record of the Japanese American Internment Cases*. Middletown, Conn.: Wesleyan University Press, 1989.

———. *Justice at War: The Story of the Japanese American Internment Cases*. New York: Oxford University Press, 1983.

Ishikawa, Tomonori. "A Study of the Historical Geography of Early Okinawan Immigrants to the Hawaiian Islands." In Ethnic Studies Oral History Project/United Okinawan Association of Hawaii. *Uchinanchu: A History of Okinawans in Hawaii*. Honolulu: Ethnic Studies Program, University of Hawaii at Manoa, 1981. 80–104.

Iwata, Masakazu. "The Japanese Immigrants in California Agriculture." *Agricultural History* 36.1 (Jan. 1962): 25–37.

James, Thomas. "The Education of Japanese Americans at Tule Lake, 1942–1946." *Pacific Historical Review* 41.1 (Feb. 1987): 25–58. [87a]

———. *Exile Within: The Schooling of Japanese Americans, 1942–1945*. Cambridge: Harvard University Press, 1987. [87b]

Kanazawa, Tooru J. *Sushi and Sourdough: A Novel*. Seattle: University of Washington Press, 1989.

Kashima, Tetsuden. "American Mistreatment of Internees During World War II: Enemy Alien Japanese." In Daniels, Roger, Sandra C. Taylor and Harry H. L. Kitano, eds. *Japanese Americans: From Relocation to Redress*. Salt Lake City: University of Utah Press, 1986. Revised edition. Seattle: University of Washington Press, 1991. 52–56.

———. *Buddhism in America: The Social Organization of an Ethnic Religious Institution*. Westport, CT: Greenwood Press, 1977.

Kawakami, Toyo Suyemoto. "Camp Memories: Rough and Broken Shards." In Daniels, Roger, Sandra C. Taylor, and Harry H. L. Kitano, eds. *Japanese Americans: From Relocation to Redress*. Salt Lake City: University of Utah Press, 1986. Revised edition. Seattle: University of Washington Press, 1991. 27–30.

Kim, Hyung-Chan, ed. *Dictionary of Asian American History*. Westport, CN: Greenwood Press, 1986.

Kimura, Yukiko. *Issei: Japanese Immigrants in Hawaii*. Honolulu: University of Hawaii Press, 1988.

Kotani, Roland. *The Japanese in Hawaii: A Century of Struggle*. Honolulu: Hochi, Ltd., 1985.

Kumamoto, Bob. "The Search for Spies: American Counterintelligence and the Japanese American Community." *Amerasia Journal* 6.2 (1979): 45–75.

Kuramoto, Ford H. *A History of the Shonien, 1914–1972: An Account of a Program of Institutional Care of Japanese Children in Los Angeles*. San Francisco: R & E Research Associates, 1976.

Leighton, Alexander H. *The Governing of Men: General Principles and Recommendations Based on Experience at a Japanese Relocation Camp*. New Jersey: Princeton University Press, 1945.

Leonard, Kevin Allen. " 'Is That What We Fought For'? Japanese Americans and Racism in California, the Impact of World War II." *Western Historical Quarterly* 21.4 (Nov. 1990): 463–82.

Lind, Andrew W. *Hawaii's People*. 1955. Second Edition. 1961. Third Edition. Honolulu: University of Hawaii Press, 1967.

Liu, John M. "Cultivating Cane: Asian Labor and the Hawaiian Sugar Plantation System within the Capitalist World Economy, 1835–1920." Diss., University of California, Los Angeles, 1985.

Masaoka, Mike, and Bill Hosokawa. *They Call Me Moses Masaoka*. New York: William Morrow, 1987.

Matsumoto, Valerie J. *Farming the Home Place: A Japanese American Community in California, 1919–1982*. Ithaca, New York: Cornell University Press, 1993.

Miyakawa, T. Scott. "Early New York Issei: Founders of Japanese-American Trade." In Conroy, Hilary, and T. Scott Miyakawa, eds. *East Across the Pacific: Historical and Sociological Studies of Japanese Immigration and Assimilation*. Santa Barbara, Calif.: American Bibliographical Center-Clio Press, 1972. 156–86.

Miyoshi, Masao. *As We Saw Them: The First Japanese Embassy to the United States (1860)*. Berkeley: University of California Press, 1979.

Modell, John. *The Economics and Politics of Racial Accommodation: The Japanese of Los Angeles 1900–1942*. Chicago: University of Illinois Press, 1977.

Moriyama, Alan T. *Imingaishi: Japanese Emigration Companies and Hawaii, 1894–1908*. Honolulu: University of Hawaii Press, 1985.

Murphy, Thomas D. *Ambassadors in Arms: The Story of Hawaii's 100th Battalion*. Honolulu: University of Hawaii Press, 1954.

Myer, Dillon S. *Uprooted Americans: The Japanese Americans and the War Relocation Authority during World War II*. Tucson: University of Arizona Press, 1971.

Naka, Harry Maxwell. "The Naturalization of Japanese War Veterans of the World War Forces." Thesis, University of California, Berkeley, 1939.

Nakasone-Huey, Nancy N. "In Simple Justice: The Japanese-American Evacuation Claims Act of 1948." Dissertation, University of Southern California, 1986.

Nelson, Douglas W. *Heart Mountain: The History of an American Concentration Camp*. Madison, Wisconsin: The State Historical Society of Wisconsin, 1976.

Nomura, Gail M. "The Debate Over the Role of Nisei in Prewar Hawaii: The New Americans Conference,

1927–1941." *Journal of Ethnic Studies* 15.1 (Spring 1987): 95–115.

Odo, Franklin S., and Kazuko Sinoto. *A Pictorial History of the Japanese in Hawaii, 1885–1924.* Honolulu: Bishop Museum Press, 1985.

Ogawa, Dennis M. *Ellison S. Onizuka: A Remembrance.* Honolulu: Onizuka Memorial Committee, 1986.

———. *Kodomo No Tame Ni, For the Sake of the Children: The Japanese American Experience in Hawaii.* Honolulu: University Press of Hawaii, 1978.

Ogawa, Dennis M.,and Evarts C. Fox. "Japanese Internment and Relocation: The Hawaii Experience." In Daniels, Roger, Sandra C. Taylor, and Harry H. L. Kitano, eds. *Japanese Americans: From Relocation to Redress.* Salt Lake City: University of Utah Press, 1986. Revised edition. Seattle: University of Washington Press, 1991. 135–38.

Okihiro, Gary Y. *Cane Fires: The Anti-Japanese Movement in Hawaii, 1865–1945.* Philadelphia: Temple University Press, 1991.

———. "Japanese Resistance in America's Concentration Camps: A Reevaluation." *Amerasia Journal* 2.1 (1973): 20–34.

Omatsu, Glenn. "Always a Rebel: An Interview with Kazu Iijima." *Amerasia Journal* 13.2 (1986–87): 83–98.

Pozzetta, George E., and Harry A. Kersey. "Yamato Colony: A Japanese Presence in South Florida." *Tequesta* 36 (1976): 66–77.

Puette, Bill. *The Hilo Massacre: Hawaii's Bloody Monday August 1st, 1938.* Honolulu: Center for Labor Education and Research, University of Hawaii, 1988.

Pursinger, Marvin G. "The Japanese Settle in Oregon: 1880–1920." *Journal of the West* 5.2 (Apr. 1966): 251–63.

Reischauer, Edwin O. *Japan: The Story of a Nation.* Revised edition. New York: Knopf, 1974.

Sakihara, Mitsugu. "Okinawans and Religion in Hawaii." In Ethnic Studies Oral History Project/United Okinawan Association of Hawaii. *Uchinanchu: A History of Okinawans in Hawaii.* Honolulu: Ethnic Studies Program, University of Hawaii, 1981. 180–87. [81b]

———. "Okinawans in Hawaii: An Overview of the Past 80 Years." In Ethnic Studies Oral History Project/United Okinawan Association of Hawaii. *Uchinanchu: A History of Okinawans in Hawaii.* Honolulu: Ethnic Studies Program, University of Hawaii at Manoa, 1981. 105–23. [81a]

Sansom, G. B. *The Western World and Japan: A Study in the Interaction of European and Asiatic Cultures.* New York: Knopf, 1949.

Sato, Susie. "Before Pearl Harbor: Early Japanese Settlers in Arizona." *Journal of Arizona History* 14.4 (Winter 1973): 317–34.

Schlesinger, Arthur M, Jr., general editor. *The Almanac of American History.* New York: G. P. Putnam's Sons, 1983.

Schwartz, Harvey. "A Union Combats Racism: The ILWU's Japanese-American 'Stockton Incident' of 1945." *Southern California Quarterly* 42.2 (1980): 161–76.

Sims, Robert C. "The Japanese American Experience in Idaho." *Idaho Yesterdays* 22 (Spring 1978): 2–10.

Slackman, Michael. "The Orange Race: George S. Patton, Jr.'s Japanese-American Hostage Plan." *Biography* 7.1 (1984): 1–49

Smith, Bradford. *Americans from Japan.* Philadelphia: J. B. Lippincott Co., 1948.

Smith, Geoffrey S. "Racial Nativism and Origins of Japanese American Relocation." In Daniels, Roger, Sandra C. Taylor, and Harry H. L. Kitano, eds. *Japanese Americans: From Relocation to Redress.* Salt Lake City: University of Utah Press, 1986. Revised edition. Seattle: University of Washington Press, 1991. 79–87.

Spaulding, Charles B. "The Mexican Strike at El Monte, California." *Sociology and Social Research* 18 (Aug. 1934): 571–80.

Stephan, John. *Hawaii under the Rising Sun: Japan's Plans for Conquest after Pearl Harbor.* Honolulu: University of Hawaii Press, 1984.

Sumida, Stephen H. *And the View from the Shore: Literary Traditions of Hawai'i.* Seattle: University of Washington Press, 1991.

Suzuki, Lester E. *Ministry in the Assembly and Relocation Camps of World War II.* Berkeley: Yardbird Publishing Co., Inc., 1979.

Takaki, Ronald. *Pau Hana: Plantation Life and Labor in Hawaii, 1835–1920.* Honolulu: University of Hawaii Press, 1983.

Tanaka, Chester. *Go for Broke: A Pictorial History of the Japanese American 100th Infantry Battalion and the 442nd Regimental Combat Team.* Richmond, Calif.: Go for Broke, Inc., 1981.

Tanaka, Stefan. "The Toledo Incident: The Deportation of the Nikkei from an Oregon Mill Town." *Pacific Northwest Quarterly* 69.3 (July 1978): 116–26.

Tateishi, John. "The Japanese American Citizens League and the Struggle for Redress." In Daniels, Roger, Sandra C. Taylor, and Harry H. L. Kitano, eds. *Japanese Americans: From Relocation to Redress.* Salt Lake City: University of Utah Press, 1986. Revised edition. Seattle: University of Washington Press, 1991. 191–95.

Taylor, Sandra C. "The Ineffectual Voice: Japan Missionaries and American Foreign Policy, 1870–1914." *Pacific Historical Review* 53.1 (Winter 1984): 20–38.

———. "Japanese Americans and Keetley Farms: Utah's

Relocation Colony." *Utah Historical Quarterly* 54.4 (Fall 1986): 328–44.

Thomas, Dorothy S. *The Salvage*. Berkeley: University of California Press, 1952.

Thomas, Dorothy S., and Richard Nishimoto. *The Spoilage*. Berkeley: University of California Press, 1946, 1969.

Tsuchida, Nobuya. "Japanese Gardeners in Southern California, 1900–1941." In Cheng, Lucie, and Edna Bonacich, eds. *Labor Immigration Under Capitalism: Asian Workers in the United States Before World War II*. Berkeley: University of California Press, 1984. 435–69.

Tsukano, John. *Bridge of Love*. Honolulu: Hawaii Hosts, Inc., 1985.

Tsurutani, Hisashi. *America Bound: The Japanese and Opening of the American West*. Betsey Scheiner, trans. Tokyo: Japan Times, Inc., 1989.

Umemoto, Karen Nora. "Asian American Students in the San Francisco State College Strike, 1964–1968." Thesis, University of California, Los Angeles, 1989.

United Japanese Society of Hawaii. *History of Japanese in Hawaii*. James H. Okahata, ed. Honolulu: United Japanese Society of Hawaii, 1971.

United States Department of the Interior. *The Evacuated People: A Quantitative Description*. Washington, D.C.: U.S. Government Printing Office, 1946.

United States Department of War. *Final Report: Japanese Evacuation from the West Coast 1942*. 1943. New York: Arno Press, 1978.

Uyeda, Clifford I. *A Final Report and Review: The Japanese American Citizens League, National Committee for Iva Toguri*. Seattle: Asian American Studies Program, University of Washington, 1980.

Wakukawa, Seiyei. "A Brief History of Thought Activities of Okinawans in Hawaii." In Ethnic Studies Oral History Project/United Okinawan Association of Hawaii. *Uchinanchu: A History of Okinawans in Hawaii*. Honolulu: Ethnic Studies Program, University of Hawaii at Manoa, 1981. 233–42.

Wallechinsky, David. *The Complete Book of the Olympics*. New York: Viking Press, 1984.

Walls, Thomas K. *The Japanese Texans*. San Antonio: Institute of Texan Cultures, 1987.

Walworth, Arthur. *Black Ships Off Japan: The Story of Commodore Perry's Expedition*. Introd. Sir George Sansom. Hamden, Conn.: Archon Books, 1966.

Waugh, Isami Arifuku. "Hidden Crime and Deviance in the Japanese-American Community, 1920–1946." Diss., University of California, Berkeley, 1978.

Weglyn, Michi. *Years of Infamy: The Untold Story of America's Concentration Camps*. New York: William Morrow & Co., 1976.

Wilson, Robert A., and Bill Hosokawa. *East to America: A History of the Japanese in the United States*. New York: Morrow, 1980.

Wollenberg, Charles M. "Race and Class in Rural California: The El Monte Berry Strike of 1933." *California Historical Quarterly* 51.2 (Summer 1972): 155–64.

Yagasaki, Noritaka. "Ethnic Cooperativism and Immigrant Agriculture: A Study of Japanese Floriculture and Truck Farming in California." Diss., University of California, Berkeley, 1982.

Yasui, Barbara. "The Nikkei in Oregon, 1834–1940." *Oregon Historical Quarterly* 76.3 (Sept. 1975): 225–57.

Yoneda, Karl G. *Ganbatte: Sixty-Year Struggle of a Kibei Worker*. Los Angeles: Asian American Studies Center, University of California, Los Angeles, 1983.

Yoshida, Ryo. "A Socio-Historical Study of Racial/Ethnic Identity in the Inculcated Religious Expression of Japanese Christianity in San Francisco, 1877–1924." Diss., Graduate Theological Union (Berkeley, Calif.), 1989.

Young, Dana B. "The Voyage of the *Kanrin Maru* to San Francisco, 1860." *California History* 61 (Winter 1983): 264–75.

INTRODUCTION TO THE ENCYCLOPEDIA

The encyclopedia section consists of brief entries describing events, people, organizations, communities and terms important to understanding the Japanese American experience. Each entry is followed by a list of one or more works "for further reading"; for the most part, the work or works mentioned here is/are also the source(s) for the entry. In cases where additional primary material was used to compile the entry, this fact will be noted below the entry. The name of the person who wrote the entry is at the very bottom of each entry; where no name appears, the entry was written by Brian Niiya.

Since the encyclopedia is built on existing research, the principal criterion for inclusion is the existence of reliable secondary sources on a given topic. Beyond this, the criteria for inclusion differs for the various types of entries.

Events important to the Japanese American experience that are the primary topic of a book, academic journal article or graduate thesis are included. Additionally, events listed in the chronology that seemed to deserve more space than alotted there are described in greater detail here. Also included are multi-event phenomena such as the ANTI-JAPANESE MOVEMENT or the REDRESS MOVEMENT.

Similarly, *organizations* important to the Japanese American experience are included if they are the primary topic of a book, academic journal article or graduate thesis, or are prominently featured in the course of such writings. Organizations that are Japanese American in character such as the JAPANESE AMERICAN CITIZENS LEAGUE are included as are organizations which are not but which had a major impact on Japanese American history, such as the AMERICAN CIVIL LIBERTIES UNION.

Communities that are the subject of a book-length academic study covering both the pre– and post–World War II eras are included as are communities that are the subject of two or more article-length academic studies covering the pre- and postwar periods. Though they are both historically important Japanese American communities, TERMINAL ISLAND is included because it is the subject of doctoral dissertations by Kanichi Kawasaki

(1931) and Kanshi Stanley Yamashita (1985); Fresno, which is not the subject of any academic research, is not.

Terms that have a unique meaning in a Japanese American context, whether Japanese or English language derived, are included if they are defined and play a significant part in an academic study or studies. Other basic Japanese American terms are included and defined if they are used in the course of other entries or in the chronology.

People present by far the most difficult cases for inclusion or exclusion. There are at least two groups of people to consider: (a) those who played an important role in the history of Japanese Americans and (b) Japanese Americans who are famous or have achieved great deeds in their fields but who have little direct connection to Japanese American communities or history. Given the approach this book favors, people in the first category are the most important to include. However, since the most famous Japanese Americans—actors, artists and athletes among them—tend to come out of the second category, it seemed important to include a selection of them as well. Thus the following criteria, partly objective and partly subjective, were arrived at: Any Japanese American (defined as a person of at least 50 percent Japanese ancestry for whom the United States—including pre-annexation Hawaii—is or was his or her permanent home) who falls into any of the following categories is automatically included.

(1) The subject of (a) a non self-published, book-length biography (not an autobiography); (b) a biographical profile of article length in an academic journal or anthology book; or (c) a profile of significant length in the course of a book-length acadmic work

(2) The subject of an entry in any of the following reference works:
(a) *The Celebrity Who's Who: By the Editors of Who's Who in America* (New York: World Almanac, 1986)
(b) *The Dictionary of American Biography* (New York: Charles Scribner's Sons) through Supple-

ment 8 (1988) covering people who died before 1970

(c) *The Dictionary of Asian American History,* Hyung-chan Kim, editor (Westport, Conn.: Greenwood Press, 1986)

(d) *Dictionary of Literary Biography* (Detroit: Gale Research Co.); up to 1984

(e) *Notable American Women* (Cambridge, Mass.: Harvard University Press); includes the 1980 supplement covering those who died before 1975

(f) *Who's Who in American Art* (New York: Bowker)

(3) Any recipient of the Nobel or Pulitzer Prizes, an Academy (of Motion Picture Arts and Sciences) Award, an Olympic gold medal (Summer or Winter; individual sports only) or Congressional Medal of Honor

Additionally, the following categories of people were considered:

(1) Non–Japanese Americans who played a key role in the history of the Japanese American community. Key figures in the anti-Japanese movement and the World War II mass incarceration are among those included. However, since the focus is on the Japanese Americans themselves and not what was done to or for them, only the most important non–Japanese Americans are included

(2) Japanese Americans who have achieved national prominence in various fields, including art, literature, business, education, law, sports, science, medicine and entertainment

(3) Japanese Americans who hold positions of prominence within regional Japanese American communities. These people might be religious leaders, heads of community organizations, journalists, businessmen, or others who played a key role in shaping the history of a particular Japanese American community

Of course the existence of reliable information remains a key factor in who was and was not included. Additionally, people who are deceased or who are identified most strongly with a historic moment now past (such as TOMMY KONO or THOMAS NOGUCHI) are more likely to be included as are those who fall into an "underrepresented category" such as women, SANSEI, YONSEI and SHIN-ISSEI. Also, people who are prominent mostly for their role in a particular organization or event are often described in the course of the entry for that organization or event and are not given an entry of their own. One who is interested in them can find their name and references to them in the chronology or dictionary in the name index. Finally, it is important to remember that the focus of this work is historical, and therefore many who are prominent in the Japanese American community today are not included here but may well be in future editions.

JAPANESE AMERICAN HISTORY: ENTRIES A TO Z

A

"ABC" list The "ABC" list was a government file created before World War II that classified potential "enemy aliens" into three groups:

Group A: The so-called "known dangerous" who required intense scrutiny. "Considered the front line of Fifth Column force . . . ."
Group B: Persons presumed to be "potentially dangerous"
Group C: Those "believed to be operating at the very periphery of the enemy intelligence network but were watched because of their . . . propagandist activities"

For people of Japanese ancestry, "those deemed sinister enough to warrant top billing [Group A] included fishermen, produce distributors, Shinto and Buddhist priests, farmers, influential businessmen, and members of the Japanese Consulate. . . . Japanese language teachers KIBEIS, martial arts instructors, community servants, travel agents, social directors, and newspaper editors were among the suspects with B or C categorization."

By early 1941, over 2,000 people of Japanese ancestry were under surveillance by the government and were classified under these groups. In the weeks that followed the bombing of Pearl Harbor, 2,192 Japanese aliens were arrested by the FBI on the West Coast—about 10 percent of the adult Japanese immigrant population. During the first year of the war, 12,071 aliens of German, Italian and Japanese ancestry were arrested and put into Justice Department administered INTERNMENT CAMPS. Approximately 10,000 of those arrested were Germans and Italians who belonged to either pro-Nazi or Fascist organizations—over half of whom were released after receiving a government hearing. In contrast, of the Japanese who were arrested, over two-thirds remained in internment camps for the duration of the war.

For further reading, see Peter Irons. *Justice at War: The Story of the Japanese American Internment Cases.* New York: Oxford University Press, 1983. GLEN KITAYAMA

Abe, Kentaro (1888–1940) Labor organizer. Kentaro Abe was one of the core ISSEI Communist Party members in the Los Angeles area in the 1930s. His main work was organizing restaurant workers, and he served as president of the Los Angeles Japanese Restaurant Employees Union from its inception in 1933. As head of this organization, he led the 1934 strike against the U.S. Cafe chain, a strike that ended successfully for the workers. The union got an AFL charter in 1935, but remained a segregated union. The local disbanded in September 1938. Abe was also involved with farm labor as well as a part of the Rodo Kyoyukai (Laborers Cooperative and Friendly Society) and chaired a public forum to support the Venice celery strikers on May 26, 1936. In later years, Abe also worked with the Los Angeles Friends of Japanese Labor, which served as an employment agency for Japanese workers. (See VENICE CELERY STRIKE.)
For further reading, see Nobuya Tsuchida. "Japanese Gardeners in Southern California, 1900–1941." In Cheng, Lucie, and Edna Bonacich, eds. *Labor Immigration Under Capitalism: Asian Workers in the United States Before World War II.* Berkeley: University of California Press, 1984. 435–69. See also Karl G. Yoneda. *Ganbatte: Sixty-Year Struggle of a Kibei Worker.* Los Angeles: Asian American Studies Center, University of California, Los Angeles, 1983.

Abe, Tokunosuke (1885–1941) Fisheries entrepreneur and political activist. Descended from an old samurai family, Abe was born in Iwate PREFECTURE in 1885. After completing high school and marrying, he immigrated to the United States in 1900. Arriving in Seattle, he worked for three years at a variety of jobs before moving to Los Angeles. There he attended Woodbury College, graduating with a degree in business administration and accounting.
In 1916, Abe accepted employment as the secretary of the San Diego Vegetable Growers Association and

moved his family south. Three years later, he left the position to join the MK Fishing Company owned by MASAHARU KONDO as office manager and accountant.

With the collapse of Kondo's company in 1931, Abe reorganized what was left of the operation, and in 1931 incorporated the Southern Commercial Company. Beginning with three employees and a small 10-ton boat he was able within five years to increase the company's size to over 200 employees with 25 boats, making the enterprise the largest fishing fleet under private management in Southern California at the time.

Abe's personal success was counterbalanced by anti-Japanese legislation increasingly directed against Japanese American fishermen (see ANTI-JAPANESE MOVEMENT). The first such legislation was Assembly Bill 135 in 1919; between that date and 1933, the California legislature considered seven separate bills to deny commercial fishing licenses to Japanese Americans. All the legislation cited United States citizenship as the criterion for obtaining a commercial fishing license. Since the ISSEI were classified as "ALIENS INELIGIBLE TO CITIZENSHIP," the legislation's target was all too apparent. Tokunosuke Abe played a major role in defeating each of these pieces of legislation.

Through the selective application of Section 990 of the State Fish and Game Code, which also had a citizenship requirement, California's Attorney General Ulysses S. Webb, the author of the 1913 (CALIFORNIA) ALIEN LAND LAW, initiated legal action against Abe and his boat the *Osprey*. Abe immediately sued the State Fish and Game Commission to test the validity of the code. In the case *T. Abe v. Fish and Game Commission*, the superior court found that Section 990 of the code violated the equal protection of the law clause of the Fourteenth Amendment of the United States Constitution. Webb immediately appealed, but the lower court ruling was upheld by the state court of appeals and affirmed by the state supreme court in 1935.

Abe's last major legislative battle was fought in 1938 when Democratic assemblyman Samuel W. Yorty of Los Angeles introduced Assembly Bill 335, which would have eliminated three out of every four Japanese Americans in California's commercial fishery. Lawyer Walter T. Tsukamoto, national president of the JAPANESE AMERICAN CITIZENS LEAGUE, and Abe wrote at the time that the Yorty bill would have the practical effect of removing all Issei from ever being employed in commercial fishing. Abe and his allies ultimately defeated the bill, but not without a long and intense battle that saw the state's Japanese American fishermen pitted against Naval Intelligence, the Congress of Industrial Organizations, the U.S. Attorney for Southern California, the American Legion and the NATIVE SONS OF THE GOLDEN WEST, to name only a few.

Abe died in San Diego of a massive stroke on January 3, 1941.

For further reading, see Frank F. Chuman *The Bamboo People: The Law and Japanese-Americans*. Del Mar, CA: Publisher's Inc., 1976 and Donald H. Estes. " 'Offensive Stupidity,' and the Struggle of Abe Tokunosuke." *Journal of San Diego History* 28.4 (1982): 249–68. DONALD H. ESTES

Abe v. Fish and Game Commission. See ABE, TOKUNOSUKE.

Abiko, Kyutaro (1865–1936) Newspaper publisher, banker, farm colony pioneer. A highly respected ISSEI leader, Kyutaro Abiko is known for beginning what would become the most influential Japanese newspaper in America and for starting three utopian farming communities in California. Abiko was born in 1865 in Niigata PREFECTURE in western Honshu. Because his mother died soon after his birth, he was raised by his maternal grandparents. As finances were tight, he helped with the family business by selling candles and paper in nearby villages. At the age of 17, he set out for Yokohama with the intention of going to America to make his fortune. Being unable to do this at first, he spent several years in Tokyo where he took English classes and converted to Christianity, being baptized at the Sakanamachi Church of Christ in 1883. At age 20, he journeyed to San Francisco, reportedly with only a dollar in his pocket. He became involved with the San Francisco Fukuinkai (GOSPEL SOCIETY), serving as one of its presidents. He also worked as a SCHOOLBOY while attending grade school to learn English, then operated a laundry and a restaurant before purchasing two Japanese-language newspapers with four friends and merging them to form the NICHIBEI SHIMBUN in 1899.

Based in San Francisco, the *Nichibei Shimbun* went on to become the most widely read Japanese-language daily in the U.S. At its peak in the 1920s, it came out in two editions and had a combined press run of 25,000 copies. Through the *Nichibei*, Abiko influenced many with his ideas about race relations in America. He was an early advocate of permanent settlement, feeling that many of the problems the ISSEI faced could be attributed to their migrant labor orientation. In fighting against the exclusion movement, Abiko advocated a campaign of education, believing that the most important source of the problems experienced by the *issei* stemmed from ignorance. While acknowledging that economics and racism played major roles, he believed that if white Americans could understand all that Japanese Americans had contributed and would contribute to their adopted country, many of the misunderstandings could be ironed out. The *Nichibei* shifted its emphasis to the NISEI in January 1924, seeing them as the future of the Japanese in

Kyutaro Abiko.   *Lily Abiko Collection, Japanese American National Museum Photographic & Moving Image Archive*

America once the EXCLUSION ACT passed. He advocated a role for the *nisei* as cultural ambassadors between Japan and America. From 1925, he began sponsoring *nisei* excursions to Japan.

Abiko had also long dreamt of beginning a permanent Japanese utopian community. Soon after launching the *Nichibei,* he began several other ventures aimed towards attaining his goal. In 1902, he founded the Nichibei Kangyosha (Japanese American Industrial Company), which handled contract labor and the acquisition of farmland. Through this company, he became a major labor contractor, supplying laborers to the railroad, agricultural and mining industries in several states. Prior to 1907, Abiko successfully used agents in Hawaii to attract workers to the mainland. He also began the Nichibei Kinyusha, a savings and loan company. Through these concerns, he bought land in Merced County and began the YAMATO COLONY. *Issei* families began settling on this land in 1906 and by 1920, the Yamato Colony comprised 2,450 acres. In 1907, he started the Beikoku Shokusan Kaisha (American Land and Produce Company) to acquire more land. Abiko would begin two

other colonies, Cressey in 1918 and CORTEZ in 1919, all located in the same general area near Livingston and Turlock, California. Because of his liberal financing, many *issei* were able to buy land in one of his colonies. However with the 1913 depression, the Nichibei Kinyusha went under. Although they faced numerous difficult times, his colonies went on to flourish and they remain more or less in operation to the present day.

Abiko died in 1936. His wife, Yonako, served as the publisher of the *Nichibei Shimbun* until the paper ceased publication in 1942 with the forced removal of all West Coast Japanese Americans imminent.

For further reading, see Bill Hosokawa. *Nisei: The Quiet Americans.* New York: William Morrow & Co., 1969; Yuji Ichioka. "A Study in Dualism: James Yoshinori Sakamoto and the Japanese American Courier, 1928–1942." *Amerasia Journal* 13.2 (1986–87): 49–81 and *The Issei: The World of the First Generation Japanese Immigrants, 1885–1924.* New York: The Free Press, 1988; Valerie J. Matsumoto. "The Cortez Colony: Family, Farm and Community among Japanese Americans, 1919–1982." Diss., Stanford University, 1985; Hisashi Tsurutani. *America Bound: The Japanese and Opening of the American West.* Betsey Scheiner, trans. Tokyo: Japan Times, Inc., 1989; Ryo Yoshida. "A Socio-Historical Study of Racial/ Ethnic Identity in the Inculcated Religious Expression of Japanese Christianity in San Francisco, 1877–1924." Diss., Graduate Theological Union (Berkeley, Calif.), 1989.

Abiko, Yasuo (1910–1988)   Newspaper editor. Son of the *Nichibei Times* editor KYUTARO ABIKO, Yasuo Abiko began his career in news as a subscription collector. He gradually worked his way up to editorial work and was editor of the English section of the *Nichibei Times* at the outbreak of World War II. After the war, Abiko gathered enough typesetting materials to reestablish the newspaper. Under Yas Abiko, the English section was a four-page tabloid featuring general interest and news from Japan on page one; club and church news on page two; sports on page three; and classified ads on page four. He demonstrated his diligence by frequently putting out the paper singlehandedly for up to three months at a time. In addition, Yasuo Abiko was an active member of the JACL and the Japanese American Optimists.

For further reading, see Dorothy Anne Stroup. "The Role of the Japanese-American Press in its Community." Thesis, University of California, Berkeley, 1960.   SCOTT KURASHIGE

Act 30 of the Special Session Laws of 1920   Anti–JAPANESE-LANGUAGE SCHOOL legislation. In the Hawaii of the early 1920s, the key issue of the Japanese American community was the fate of the Japanese-language schools. Faced with growing opposition to the schools, mainly because they were seen as hindering Americanization, the Japanese community decided to act to regulate the schools before such regulation could be thrust upon them. A committee of 18 was appointed and drew up a proposal which was eventually signed into law by the Hawaii legislature as Act 30 on November 24, 1920, to go into effect on July 21, 1921. Act 30 required all foreign-language schools to get a permit from the Department of Public Education and all its teachers to pass a test on American history, democracy and English. Additionally, the schools were limited to hours after the public schools got out and students could attend them no more than one hour a day, six hours a week, or 38 weeks a year. As stated in its text, the purpose of Act 30 was "to regulate and not to prohibit the conducting of foreign language schools and the teaching of foreign languages, but to regulate them so that the Americanization of the students may be promoted and the Department is hereby directed to carry the Act into effect in accordance with the spirit of this declaration." It would not be enough—within two years, still more restrictive legislation targeting Japanese schools would be passed.

For further reading, see Ann Leilani Halsted. "Sharpened Tongues: The Controversy over the 'Americanization' of Japanese Language Schools in Hawaii, 1919–1927." Dissertation, Stanford University, 1989; John N. Hawkins. "Politics, Education and Language Policy: The Case of Japanese Language Schools in Hawaii." *Amerasia Journal* 5.1 (1978): 39–56; and United Japanese Society of Hawaii. *History of Japanese in Hawaii.* James H. Okahata, ed. Honolulu: United Japanese Society of Hawaii, 1971.

Aiso, John Fujio (1909–1987)   Director of the MILITARY INTELLIGENCE SERVICE LANGUAGE SCHOOL, judge. From the time he won an oratorical contest at Hollywood High School in 1925, John Aiso had been one of the most famous mainland NISEI. He was best known as the stern head of the Military Intelligence Service Language School during World War II and the first mainland Japanese American judge.

Born in Burbank, California, on December 14, 1909, Aiso's early years were marked by achievement and prejudice. As a ninth grader, he was elected president of his junior high school but due to pressure from unhappy parents, the student government was dissolved for that year. At Hollywood High School, he was named valedictorian and became the first Japanese American to be elected an Ephebian (a high school honor society). After winning the oratorical contest for the right to represent his school in regional competition—the winner of which would receive $500, a trip to Europe and the right to travel to Washington, D.C., for the national finals—Aiso was approached by the principal and reportedly told to either give up the contest or the valedictory honor. Despite the obvious prejudice behind this request and

despite wide and sympathetic coverage of the incident in the vernacular press and the *Los Angeles Times,* Aiso withdrew from the contest. His runner-up at Hollywood High eventually won the national finals, accompanied by Aiso as a traveling companion and coach. After graduation from Hollywood High, Aiso studied Japanese at Seijo Gakuen in Tokyo for a year and then returned to the States to attend Brown University where he graduated cum laude in 1931. He graduated from Harvard Law School in 1934 and studied Japanese law at Chuo University in 1936–37.

In 1937, he took a position with a subsidiary of the British-American Tobacco Company in Manchukuo, the Japanese puppet state in Manchuria. Despite increasing repression, Aiso spent nearly three years there. Returning to the United States due to hepatitis, he was drafted in December 1940 and reported for duty in April 1941 as a 31-year-old private second class. He soon found himself assigned to a company that repaired trucks, an occupation which he knew nothing about. At the time, plans were being formulated for a Japanese-language school under the intelligence section of the Fourth Army and a search was conducted for those with a command of Japanese. After passing the test with flying colors, Aiso was assigned to this school first as a student, then as an assistant instructor, then as the head instructor. The Military Intelligence Service Language School (MISLS) opened on November 1, 1941, in San Francisco; it moved to Minnesota in May of 1942. Eventually, some 6,000 students were to graduate from this school, many of whom performed vital intelligence work in the Pacific war. In October 1945, Aiso left the MISLS for a post in the occupation forces. When he left active duty in 1947, he held the rank of lieutenant colonel.

After a period of general legal practice, Aiso was appointed a commissioner of the Los Angeles Superior Court in September 1952 and became a judge of the municipal court a year later. In November 1953, he was named a judge in the Superior Court of Los Angeles County. In 1968, he was appointed by Governor Ronald Reagan as an associate justice of Division Five of the California Court of Appeals for the Second Appellate District. Aiso retired in 1972, joining the law firm of O'Melveny & Myers as a special counsel, a position he held until suffering a mild stroke in February 1984. Aiso was killed by a mugger in December 1987. (See MILITARY INTELLIGENCE SERVICE.)

For further reading, see Kiyoshi Yano. "Participating in the Main Stream of American Life Amidst Drawback of Racial Prejudice and Discrimination: John F. Aiso, A Leader of the Niseis." In Ichinokuchi, Tad, ed. *John Aiso and the M.I.S.: Japanese-American Soldiers in the Military Intelligence Service, World War II.* Los Angeles: Military Intelligence Service Club of Southern California, 1988. 4–35. Translated into English by Haruo Kugizaki and edited by John Aiso.

[Also used to compile this entry was "Famed Nisei Judge Dies." *Pacific Citizen*, 1–8 Jan. 1988: 1–2.]

Ala Moana Case   See MASSIE CASE.

Alien Land Laws

Laws enacted by various western states that prevented Japanese (and other Asian) immigrants from purchasing agricultural land. Although the laws were aimed at ISSEI farmers, they made no specific reference to "Japanese" or "Orientals." Often the phrase "ALIENS INELIGIBLE TO CITIZENSHIP" was used instead. First enacted in the 1910s, the laws generally remained in effect until well after World War II.

As the principal site of the ANTI-JAPANESE MOVEMENT, California was the first state to enact an Alien Land Law in 1913 that prevented ownership of land by "aliens ineligible to citizenship" and restricted leases by such people to three years. Since Japanese and other Asian immigrants were prohibited from becoming naturalized citizens, the law applied to them and, by and large, only to them. Signed by Governor Hiram Johnson on May 19, 1913, the law culminated a long effort by anti-Japanese forces in the state. Though *issei* farmers were largely able to get around this law through various means, it did affect the scope of *issei* farming and the types of crops they attempted to grow. It also sent a clear message to the *issei* about how their adopted country viewed them.

With the rise of anti-foreign sentiment in the post–World War I years, a revived anti-Japanese movement emerged in California whose goal was to stop all immigration from Japan and to make life as difficult as possible for Japanese immigrants already in the U.S. Viewing the 1913 Alien Land Law as ineffective, these exclusionist forces pushed for another much more stringent measure. This new law appeared as a ballot initiative and was passed by a three-to-one margin in November 1920. The 1920 law was much more restrictive, forbidding even leasing and sharecropping by Japanese immigrants in an attempt to limit their role in agriculture to that of laborer. Japanese community response to the new law took the form of a series of test cases instigated by the JAPANESE ASSOCIATION of America to test its constitutionality in a variety of ways. The Japanese community was stunned when the U.S. Supreme Court handed down its decisions in four of these test cases in a one-week span of November 1923—each decision resulting in defeat for the *issei*. Along with the OZAWA V. U.S. decision of the previous year and the EXCLUSION ACT of the next year, these decisions cemented the status of Japanese immigrants in America.

After the passage of the 1920 law in California, other western states began to enact similar laws, largely out of fear that "hordes" of California Japanese would invade their states. For the most part, these laws were similar to the California model, though details differed. For example, in the state of Washington, laws passed in 1921 and 1923 prohibited ownership of land "by aliens other than those who in good faith have declared their intention to become citizens of the United States." It was another way of singling out Japanese and other Asian immigrants who, being prohibited from naturalization, could not "in good faith" declare their intent to naturalize. In the state of Texas, an alien land law passed in 1921 allowed Japanese immigrants already present in the state to own land, but prevented *issei* arriving after the passage of the law from purchasing land.

Despite the Alien Land Laws and despite the failure of the various legal challenges they instigated, Japanese Americans still played a major role in farming in California and the West. The laws were extremely difficult to enforce and some *issei* were able to maintain ownership of farm land because local authorities tacitly allowed it. Others made verbal agreements to lease land from sympathetic non-Japanese landowners. Perhaps the most common method of getting around the laws was to register the land in the name of NISEI children, who were citizens by birth. Though not totally successful in limiting *issei* to migrant farm work, the Alien Land Laws did make life infinitely more difficult for *issei* farmers, dramatically affecting the nature and volume of *issei* farming, and drove many Japanese immigrants to look elsewhere—South America, Mexico, Manchuria and many other areas—for places to live and raise their families.

Various legal decisions after World War II—especially OYAMA V. CALIFORNIA in 1948 and FUJII SEI V. STATE OF CALIFORNIA in 1952—invalidated key aspects of the Alien Land Law, making it unenforceable. However, the laws often stayed on the books in the various states for many more years. The State of Washington did not repeal its Alien Land Law until 1966. (See 1913 CALIFORNIA) ALIEN LAND LAW, 1920 (CALIFORNIA) ALIEN LAND LAW, CROPPING CONTRACTS, FRICK V. WEBB, PORTERFIELD V. WEBB, TERRACE V. THOMPSON, and WEBB V. O'BRIEN.)

For further reading, see Frank F. Chuman. *The Bamboo People: The Law and Japanese-Americans*. Del Mar, CA: Publisher's Inc., 1976; Yuji Ichioka. "Japanese Immigrant Response to the 1920 California Alien Land Law." *Agricultural History* 58.2 (Apr. 1984): 157–78 and *The Issei: The World of the First Generation Japanese Immigrants, 1885–1924*. New York: The Free Press, 1988; Dudley O. McGovney, "The Anti-Japanese Land Laws of California and Ten Other States." *California Law Review* 35 (1947): 7–54. For the specifics of the land laws in Washington State and Texas, see Gail M. Nomura. "Washington's Asian/Pacific American Communities." In White, Sid, and S. E. Solberg, eds. *Peoples of Washington: Perspectives on Cultural Diversity*. Pullman: Washington State University

Press, 1989. 113–55; and Thomas K. Walls. *The Japanese Texans*. San Antonio: Institute of Texan Cultures, 1987.

"Aliens ineligible to citizenship" Phrase used in the wording of ALIEN LAND LAW legislation. Because existing federal naturalization laws allowed the right of naturalization only to "free white persons and to aliens of African nativity and to persons of African descent," use of the phrase "aliens ineligible to citizenship" in discriminatory legislation aimed at Chinese or Japanese immigrants was a way to make sure the legislation applied to Asians without specifically mentioning the targeted groups. It was also a way for California and other western states to put the onus of discrimination on the federal government rather than on themselves—it was after all the federal government which did not allow Japanese immigrants to become citizens, not the states. Their status as "aliens ineligible to citizenship," a status cemented by the Supreme Court's OZAWA V. UNITED STATES decision in 1922, represented to the ISSEI a hurtful and definitive rejection by their adopted country and established that they could not become truly American no matter how much they may have wanted to. (See 1913 (CALIFORNIA) ALIEN LAND LAW.)

For further reading, see Frank F. Chuman. *The Bamboo People: The Law and Japanese-Americans*. Del Mar, CA: Publisher's Inc., 1976; Roger Daniels. *The Politics of Prejudice: The Anti-Japanese Movement in California and the Struggle for Japanese Exclusion*. 1962. 2nd edition. Berkeley: University of California Press, 1977; and Harry Maxwell Naka. "The Naturalization of Japanese War Veterans of the World War Forces." Thesis, University of California, Berkeley, 1939.

Amache See Another name for GRANADA.

amegoro Colloquial term for the pimps who lived off prostitutes' earnings in the early Japanese American community. The term literally means "American thug."

For further reading, see Yuji Ichioka. "Ameyuki-san: Japanese Prostitutes in Nineteenth-Century America." *Amerasia Journal* 4.1 (1977): 1–21 and *The Issei: The World of the First Generation Japanese Immigrants, 1885–1924*. New York: The Free Press, 1988.

Amerasia Bookstore Los Angeles ASIAN AMERICAN bookstore and community institution. Founded in 1971 at the height of the ASIAN AMERICAN MOVEMENT, the store has been a center of activity and a source for hard-to-find materials on and by Asian Americans despite ongoing financial difficulties and three moves.

The store was founded by a group of young SANSEI activists and college students who felt that an Asian American bookstore was needed given the growing number of Asian American studies courses being taught at the time. The bookstore opened in a cramped second-floor space on 1st Street in Los Angeles's LITTLE TOKYO in August 1971. Originally run as a collective and with no paid staff, Amerasia gradually evolved into a nonprofit corporation, then to a more or less traditional small business as the years went by. Despite these changes, the people running the store have always been almost entirely Japanese American.

In addition to being a source for books, Amerasia Bookstore also once sold clothing and arts and crafts, and today also sells videotapes and compact discs. At different times in its history, the store has also put on concerts, workshops, readings and other programs, and once featured a little café area. The type of books carried at the store has also changed over the years. Where the store once carried mainly materials on Japanese and Chinese Americans, the changing demographics of the community has demanded that the stock change with it, so that materials on Filipino, Korean, Southeast Asian, and Pacific Islander Americans today command much of the floor space.

The store has been on the verge of closing several times due to lack of funds, but has always managed to adapt to the changes in the community and stay alive. Though it no longer has a storefront, the store continues as a mail order operation, and plans and fundraising continue for the return of Amerasia Bookstore in the future.

For further reading, see Brian T. Niiya "Our Place: Twenty Years of Amerasia Bookstore . . . and More to Come." *Tozai Times* 7.77 (Feb. 1991): 1, 12–13.

Amerasia Journal Academic journal dedicated to the study of Asian Americans. Throughout its history, *Amerasia Journal* has been the only academic journal focusing exclusively on Asian American Studies. Begun in 1971 as a quarterly published by the Yale Asian American Students Association, the journal became a semi-annual published by the UCLA Asian American Studies Center by Volume 2 in 1973. Though the journal primarily publishes academic studies, it has published short stories, poetry, essays, reviews and many other types of work over the years. Since 1977, it has published annual selected bibliographies of works on Asian Americans that are heavily relied upon by Asian American studies scholars. The journal has had four editors; current editor Russell Leong has served in that capacity since 1977. The journal has published many works concerning Japanese Americans; of special interest is Vol. 13, No. 2 (1986–87), a special issue titled "The Coming of Age of the *Nisei*" with Yuji Ichioka as consulting guest editor. It continues to be published at UCLA and, since Vol

17 (1991), the journal has published three issues per year.

Amerasian Term for an American with one Asian or part-Asian parent and one non-Asian parent. With the high rate of intermarriage by Japanese Americans, many YONSEI and succeeding generations of Japanese Americans are Amerasian. Many Amerasians are the offspring of American soldiers and Asian-born women they met while on duty in Asia. The term HAPPA (or *hapa*) is also sometimes used for Amerasians whose Asian parent is of Japanese ancestry. Literally meaning "half" in Japanese, the term is used with pride by some, but considered somewhat pejorative by others. The term "Afroasian" is sometimes used for Amerasians whose non-Asian parent is African or African American, while "Euroasian" or "Eurasian" is sometimes used for Amerasians whose non-Asian parent is of European ancestry. There doesn't seem to be a consensus as to which of these terms—including "mixed race," "multiracial," "racially mixed" and others—is the one that ought to be standard.

In the early 1970s, the term Amerasian had a completely different meaning in some circles. As a by-product of the movement by young Asian Americans—mostly SANSEI and American-born Chinese Americans—to forge a positive identity as neither Asian nor mainstream American (which would latter become known as the ASIAN AMERICAN MOVEMENT), "Amerasian" was briefly used to refer to Americans of Asian ancestry between the discrediting of the term "Oriental" and the adoption of the term "ASIAN AMERICAN." The young activists referred to themselves for a time as the "Amerasian Generation." The name of the AMERASIA BOOKSTORE, among other community organizations and events from the period, stems from this definition of Amerasian.

For further reading on Amerasian identity, see Christine Catherine Iijima Hall. "The Ethnic Identity of Racially Mixed People: A Study of Black Japanese." Diss., University of California, Los Angeles, 1980; George Kitahara Kich. "Eurasians: Ethnic/Racial Identity Development of Biracial Japanese/White Adults." Diss., Wright Institute Graduate School (Berkeley), 1982; Stephen L. H. Murphy-Shigematsu. "The Voices of Amerasians: Ethnicity, Identity, and Empowerment in Interracial Japanese Americans." Diss., Harvard University, 1986; Maria P. P. Root, ed. *Racially Mixed People in America*. Newbury Park, Calif.: Sage Publications, 1992; Michael Charles Thornton. "A Social History of a Multiethnic Identity: The Case of Black Japanese Americans." Diss., University of Michigan, 1983. See also the 1985 holiday edition of the *Pacific Citizen* (20–27 Dec. 1985) for several articles on Amerasian identity, including pieces by Lane Ryo Hirabayashi, VELINA HASU HOUSTON, and other prominent mixed-race Japanese Americans.

American Civil Liberties Union (ACLU) Private organization dedicated to defending Americans whose civil rights have been violated. The ACLU was officially formed in 1920 and clams over 270,000 members, maintaining a national office in New York, a legislative office in Washington, D.C., and branch offices in 46 states. The ACLU has often found itself defending the civil rights of unpopular groups or individuals—those who need the protection of the Bill of Rights the most.

Given its purpose of defending civil liberties, it is not surprising that the ACLU was one of the only organizations to come to the defense of Japanese Americans forcibly removed and detained during World War II. Lawyers from the ACLU played key roles in the various legal challenges to the curfew and evacuation orders—the KOREMATSU V. U.S., YASUI V. U.S. and EX PARTE ENDO cases. Individual ACLU members were among the few vocal critics of America's CONCENTRATION CAMPS. However, due to a split within the organization, the ACLU as a whole did not play as aggressive a role as it could have in defending Japanese Americans during the war.

All agree that the essential problem was a split between the national board and the California affiliates over the plan of action concerning the camps. An unusual coalition of conservatives, liberals and leftists on the national board all opposed a resolution condemning EXECUTIVE ORDER 9066 for different reasons—the conservatives saw the need to defer to presidential authority in wartime, the liberals shared a special loyalty to FRANKLIN D. ROOSEVELT, and the leftists wanted to ensure American support for the Soviet's war effort and were unwilling to take action that might undermine such support. This coalition forced a referendum out of which a resolution supporting the essential points of EO 9066 was adopted as the official ACLU position. Ernest Besig of the Northern California affiliate and others reacted with anger to this stance; the Northern California affiliate nearly severed its relationship with the ACLU in the months to come. The close political ties between many ACLU officials and various figures in the Roosevelt administration may have made the organization reluctant to launch a concerted assault on the executive order. ACLU director Roger Baldwin also formed a close relationship with WAR RELOCATION AUTHORITY director DILLON MYER, leading to charges that he had sold out the organization's principles.

Contemporary historians differ in their assessment of ACLU actions during the war. In his history of the ACLU, Walker acknowledges some mistakes, but views the organizational response as "a shining moment." He writes, "[a]lmost alone it challenged this wholesale violation of individual rights." He notes that even the weak resolution the organization did pass provided the basis for challenging the evacuation order in the courts. However, Weglyn and Drinnon, among others, view the actions of the ACLU as having aided and abetted the violation of civil rights by doing nothing about it and doing everything it could to stop Besig and others from pursuing the test cases. Individual ACLU members Besig, A. L. WIRIN, and WAYNE COLLINS all played important roles in defending the rights of Japanese Americans with or without the blessing of the national organization. See Samuel Walker. *In Defense of American Liberties: A History of the ACLU.* New York: Oxford University Press, 1990 for a defense of ACLU actions; Richard Drinnon. *Keeper of Concentration Camps: Dillon S. Myer and American Racism.* Berkeley: University of California Press, 1987; and Michi Weglyn. *Years of Infamy: The Untold Story of America's Concentration Camps.* New York: William Morrow & Co., 1976 for condemnations.

American Committee of Justice Anti-exclusionist group of the early 1920s. (See IRISH, JOHN POWELL.)

American Friends Service Committee Best known for its relief and peace efforts around the world since its founding in 1917, the American Friends Service Committee (AFSC) is recognized in the Japanese American community for the help it provided the community during World War II. The committee donated educational materials to the CONCENTRATION CAMPS and were extremely influential in lobbying for a program that allowed "loyal" NISEI to leave the camps for colleges in the interior parts of the country. Many of the *nisei* students were also the recipients of much needed funding from the AFSC and probably could not have attended college were it not for their efforts (see NATIONAL JAPANESE AMERICAN STUDENT RELOCATION COUNCIL). The AFSC was also helpful in funding fellow Quaker Gordon Hirabayashi in his historic test case on the curfew and exclusion orders imposed on Japanese Americans (see HIRABAYASHI V. UNITED STATES.)
For further reading, see Hugh Barbour and William J. Frost. *The Quakers.* New York: Greenwood Press, 1988; Commission on Wartime Relocation and Internment of Civilians. *Personal Justice Denied: Report of the Commission on Wartime Relocation and Internment of Civilians.* Washington, D.C.: Government Printing Office, 1982; and Peter Irons. *Justice at War: The Story of the Japanese American Internment Cases.* New York: Oxford University Press, 1983.   GLEN KITAYAMA

Americans of Japanese ancestry Term adopted by Hawaii NISEI soldiers during World War II that was extensively used by Japanese Americans in Hawaii. In the charged atmosphere of World War II Hawaii, there were those who felt that the Japanese language-based term *nisei* was somehow un-American while "Japanese American" seemed to place too much emphasis on the "Japanese," and "Japanese-American" seemed to imply

that they were less than fully "American." "Americans of Japanese Ancestry" or "AJA" became the term of choice for many at this time. It was even used by Hawaii Japanese American soldiers of the 100TH INFANTRY BATTALION or 442ND REGIMENTAL COMBAT TEAM as a way to differentiate themselves from mainland *nisei*. The term is still used by some in Hawaii, though "Japanese American" and, in recent years, "Nikkei" have become more commonly used.
For further reading, see Andrew W. Lind. *Hawaii's Japanese: An Experiment in Democracy.* Princeton: Princeton University Press, 1946.

Amerika mura Term for Japanese villages populated mainly by people who had lived and worked in America for a time. In many cases, REMITTANCES TO JAPAN by village sons living in the United States financed the modernization of the village and made it relatively wealthier than neighboring villages.
For further reading, see Takeshi Fukutake, et al. *Amerika mura—Imin soshutsu mura no jittai* [An American Village: The Impact of Emigration upon the Village]. Tokyo: University of Tokyo Press, 1953; though this volume is in Japanese, it contains a summary of its findings in English.

anti-Chinese movement Organized movement of the late 19th century that had as its goal the ending of Chinese immigration. The anti-Chinese movement was a precursor to the later ANTI-JAPANESE MOVEMENT.
    Overt racial discrimination against Chinese immigrants first occurred during the gold rush of the 1850s, when they began to arrive in the U.S. in large numbers. Anti-Chinese attitudes spread as America's economic and industrial development demanded the skills of many Chinese immigrant laborers. They soon became a scapegoat for the economic and labor crisis in California and were the target of mounting frustration. Fueled by railroad and large industrial monopolies that applied heavy political pressure in Washington, angry racist labor union leaders, frustrated by unemployment and depressed wages, also blamed the Chinese, whom they considered economic threats. The completion of the transcontinental railroad in 1869 exacerbated the unemployment problem and led to intensified anti-Chinese activities.
    As anti-Chinese sentiment and outbreaks of racial violence intensified, the cry to cease and prohibit further Chinese immigration became louder. The political platforms during the presidential elections of 1876 and 1880 centered around the mounting social and economic crises of the nation, which found Chinese laborers to be their cause. The culmination of this anti-Chinese movement came with the congressional endorsement and enactment of the CHINESE EXCLUSION ACT OF 1882 and its subse-

quent supplements and revisions intended to suspend and prohibit the immigration of Chinese to America.

For further reading, see Mary Roberts Coolidge. *Chinese Immigration*. New York: H. Holt & Co., 1909; Roger Daniels. *The Politics of Prejudice: The Anti-Japanese Movement in California and the Struggle for Japanese Exclusion*, 1962. 2nd edition. Berkeley: University of California Press, 1977; Stuart Creighton Miller. *The Unwelcome Immigrant: the American Image of the Chinese, 1785–1882*. Berkeley: University of California Press, 1969; Clarence Elmer Sandmeyer. *The Anti-Chinese Movement in California*. Urbana: University of Illinois Press, 1973; and Alexander Saxton. *The Indispensable Enemy: Labor and the Anti-Chinese Movement in California*. Berkeley: University of California Press, 1971.   MARJORIE LEE

anti-Japanese movement   Organized movement to end further emigration from Japan. Beginning as a local California phenomenon promulgated mostly by organized labor in 1905, the anti-Japanese movement ultimately succeeded in getting national immigration legislation passed and swaying national public opinion encompassing all social classes against Japanese immigrants by 1924.

The movement might be divided into two main periods separated by World War I. The first period, beginning in 1905, was preceded by two brief bursts of anti-Japanese activity in 1892 and 1900. Both of these episodes were tied to anti-Chinese sentiment, which had been rampant in the West since the 1870s and had resulted in the exclusion of all Chinese immigration in 1882 (See ANTI-CHINESE MOVEMENT and CHINESE EXCLUSION ACT OF 1882). In May 1892, a series of anti-Japanese articles in the *Morning Call*, the *San Francisco Examiner* and the *San Francisco Bulletin* appeared, leading to a San Francisco School Board resolution on June 10, 1893, requiring Japanese students to attend the segregated Chinese school. After intervention by the Japanese consul, the resolution was rescinded and the furor soon died down. Then, in 1900, when the renewal of Chinese exclusion was being discussed, there were some calls for Japanese to be included, but a lack of popular support prevented any such action being taken. At the time, Japanese immigration was just beginning its period of highest concentration, though the actual number of Japanese immigrants was very small.

The real beginning of the anti-Japanese movement came in February 1905 with a series of articles in the *San Francisco Chronicle* citing Japanese immigration as the "problem of the day." This was followed by the formation of the ASIATIC EXCLUSION LEAGUE in May 1905. This organization was made up almost entirely of members of labor organizations in the San Francisco area. This early stage of the movement was characterized by the intense participation of organized labor, which decried the "unfair competition" allegedly posed by Jap-

anese immigrants, their "low standard of living," their inability or unwillingness to become American (the coined term "unassimilable" was often used to describe them), their lack of hygiene and other similar traits they were supposed to have. In October 1906, the SAN FRANCISCO SCHOOL BOARD SEGREGATION ORDER OF 1906 was issued, relegating pupils of Japanese descent to segregated schools. This mostly symbolic order—there were few Japanese children actually in the schools since the ISSEI population at the time consisted almost entirely of single men—angered a Japan anxious to prove itself a first-class economic and military power, and an international incident ensued. After delicate diplomatic negotiations, the GENTLEMEN'S AGREEMENT OF 1907–08 was negotiated between the United States and Japan, whereby Japan agreed to stop issuing passports to laborers headed for the United States. Meanwhile, back in California, concern over *issei* farming led to the passage of the 1913 (CALIFORNIA) ALIEN LAND LAW, which prohibited "ALIENS INELIGIBLE TO CITIZENSHIP"—i.e., Japanese immigrants—from purchasing agricultural land. With Japanese immigration apparently slowed to a trickle and farmland safely in the hands of white farmers, explicit anti-Japanese activity slowed for a time.

The second major phase of the anti-Japanese movement was played out in the years following World War I. In the context of an intense anti-foreign sentiment prevalent in the United States, anti-Japanese activity took place on an entirely different level. The image of *issei* as unfair and undesirable labor competition had been replaced by one of "YELLOW PERIL," the first wave of a Japanese invasion of ambitious and ruthless agents of Tokyo out for economic domination, of "little brown men" out to abduct white women and claim California for their own. Through this sort of imagery, anti-Japanese sentiment moved out of the realm of organized labor and was adopted by a powerful coalition of opportunistic politicians such as United States senators JAMES PHELAN and HIRAM JOHNSON, nativist groups such as the NATIVE SONS AND DAUGHTERS OF THE GOLDEN WEST, the anti-foreign American Legion and farmers groups. There was also the widespread perception that both the 1913 Alien Land Law and the Gentlemen's Agreement had failed since *issei* farm holdings had increased since their adoption and since seemingly large numbers of *issei* women, including many PICTURE BRIDES, had arrived in the 1910s, bringing with them the beginnings of families and communities. In addition to savage anti-Japanese rhetoric in the mass media, this revival of the anti-Japanese movement also included a series of wholesale removals of Japanese immigrants in a number of small towns in California and Oregon. (See the TURLOCK INCIDENT, the TOLEDO INCIDENT, and the SALT RIVER VALLEY INCIDENT, for example.) In reaction, an organized non-Japanese opposition to the movement began, led by Protestant missionaries such as SIDNEY GULICK as well as some international businessmen and peace activists. The Japanese immigrants themselves fought the various restrictions in the courts through the JAPANESE ASSOCIATIONS. It was to no avail. The 1920 (CALIFORNIA) ALIEN LAND LAW was passed, closing off loopholes in the 1913 law. Led by former newspaper publisher V. S. MCCLATCHY and Senator Johnson, the anti-Japanese movement culminated in the IMMIGRATION ACT OF 1924, which ended all further emigration from Japan. The other major goal of the movement—the stripping of citizenship from the NISEI—would not be accomplished.

Though the active anti-Japanese movement died down after exclusion, its legacy no doubt influenced the mass removal and incarceration of all West Coast Japanese Americans just 18 years later. Echos of the same old—and still groundless—charges of being "unassimilable" and loyal to Japan would ring out again in the winter of 1942, bringing needless hardship and tragedy to a whole new generation of Japanese Americans. Many Japanese observers also cite the anti-Japanese movement as one of many factors eventually leading to war between Japan and United States.

For further reading: Roger Daniels. *The Politics of Prejudice: The Anti-Japanese Movement in California and the Struggle for Japanese Exclusion*. 1962. 2nd edition. Berkeley: University of California Press, 1977; Carey McWilliams. *Prejudice: Japanese-Americans; Symbol of Racial Intolerance*. Boston: Little, Brown, & Co., 1944; and Eldon R. Penrose *California Nativism: Organized Opposition to the Japanese, 1890–1913*. San Francisco: R & E Research Associates, 1973. These, among many others provide overviews of the anti-Japanese movement, while Yuji Ichioka. "Japanese Immigrant Response to the 1920 California Alien Land Law." *Agricultural History* 58.2 (Apr. 1984): 157–78 and *The Issei: The World of the First Generation Japanese Immigrants, 1885–1924*. New York: The Free Press, 1988 deal in part with Japanese immigrant response to the movement. Bruce A. Abrams. "A Muted Cry: White Opposition to the Japanese Exclusion Movement, 1911–1924." Diss., City University of New York, 1987 discusses white opposition to the movement, while pieces in Akira Iriye, ed. *Mutual Images: Essays in American-Japanese Relations*. Cambridge: Harvard University Press, 1975 note the impact of the movement on American-Japanese relations. See the other related entries for further references.

Aoki, Dan (1916–1986)

Hawaii Democratic Party leader, key aide to ex-governor JOHN BURNS. Dan Aoki played a key role in the rise of the Democratic Party in Hawaii and served as Governor John Burns's aide for 30 years.

Born in Kona, Hawaii, Aoki attended local public schools on the island of Maui. For a young Aoki, attending the University of Hawaii as a sociology major where, ironically, future Congressman SPARKY MATSUNAGA was his college roommate, politics was furthest from his mind. It was not until the Second World War that Aoki reached a turning point when he joined the 442ND REGIMENTAL COMBAT TEAM. Aoki returned from action in Europe with a Bronze Star for his heroic efforts and a new attitude about fighting for social change.

After the war, Aoki was one of the founding members of the 442nd Veteran's Club. It was through this organization that he first became acquainted with John Burns, then a Democratic candidate for Congress. Aoki actively campaigned for various Democratic candidates while playing a vital role in the party during its rise to power in Hawaii (see REVOLUTION OF 1954).

When John Burns was elected Hawaii's congressional delegate in a landslide victory over the incumbent in 1956, Aoki accompanied him to Washington, D.C., as administrative assistant. With Aoki's assistance, Burns lobbied heavily for statehood, which was granted to Hawaii in 1959. For nearly three decades, Aoki served as Governor John Burns's right-hand before retiring in 1978. He died on June 12, 1986.

TRACY ENDO

Aoki v. Deane

Test case challenging the segregation of Japanese pupils from San Francisco public schools in 1906. The segregation order precipitated an international incident. (See SAN FRANCISCO SCHOOL BOARD SEGREGATION ORDER and GENTLEMEN'S AGREEMENT.)

Arai, Clarence Takeya (1901–1964)

Lawyer and JAPANESE AMERICAN CITIZENS LEAGUE leader. Clarence Arai was a key figure in the founding of the Japanese American Citizens League. Arai received his law degree from the University of Washington in 1924 and was an early member of the Seattle Progressive Citizens League. He became a leading proponent for the formation of a West Coast–wide NISEI federation of citizens leagues. After being elected Seattle Progressive Citizens League president in 1928, Arai and League vice president George Ishihara toured the West Coast to push for a federation. While in Los Angeles, he met Yone Utsunomiya, whom he would marry in 1930. At a meeting in San Francisco, Arai proposed a National Council of Japanese-American Citizens Leagues and called a meeting for Seattle in 1930. He was elected president of the National Council. The meeting in Seattle, held in August 1930, became the founding convention of the Japanese American Citizens League.

Arai also practiced law in Seattle and became active in local politics, serving as a Republican precinct committeeman, vice president of the Thirty-seventh Legislative District Republican Club and delegate to the state Republican convention. In 1934, he launched a bid for a seat in the state legislature, finishing fifth in a field of five. With the advent of World War II, Arai and his family were sent to Puyallup "ASSEMBLY CENTER" and to the CONCENTRATION CAMP in Minidoka, Idaho. Suffering from hypertension, he had a mild stroke while in camp. After returning to Seattle in 1945, the Arai's only son died of cancer at the age of nine. Arai's own deteriorating health led to his giving up law and taking up photography. Yone supported the family and took care of Clarence until his death in 1964.

For further reading, see Bill Hosokawa. *JACL in Quest of Justice: The History of the Japanese American Citizens League.* New York: William Morrow, 1982.

Arai, Ryoichiro (1855–1939) Silk importer. Longtime New York resident Ryoichiro Arai was a leading figure in building the direct silk trade between Japan and America. He was born Ryosuke Hoshino in Gumma PREFECTURE, the fifth son of the Hoshino family of silk producers. His elder brother Chotaro Hoshino was a leading silk producer in the region. He was adopted by the Arai family and his name was changed to Ryoichiro. Arai studied in Tokyo, learning English and accounting in addition to traditional Japanese subjects. He was encouraged to go to America by Chotaro and others to promote the direct silk trade for the benefit of his country. On the advice of YUKICHI FUKUZAWA, Arai and five other young Japanese men interested in promoting trade journeyed to America, arriving in New York in March 1876. Along with fellow traveler Momotaro Sato, Arai formed the Sato Arai Company, which traded in raw silk, in the spring of 1878. The company eventually dissolved in 1881 after Sato's return to Japan.

While living frugally and studying English, Arai worked to counteract the prevailing low opinions about both Japanese silk (nearly all silk imported to America at the time came from China) and Japanese people. Arai was finally successful in obtaining a large order from the New York silk importer B. Richardson & Son; however, because of the lack of direct communications with Japan, the price quoted turned out to be far below the prevailing price in Japan, thereby nearly bankrupting the family business. Called on to renegotiate the price, Arai insisted on meeting the contract, thereby impressing Richardson, who voluntarily paid an extra dollar per pound. This, the first direct transaction between a Japanese producer and an American importer, proved to be a landmark in the Japanese silk trade. Japan eventually became the largest source of raw silk for American industry.

In 1880, Arai became the New York representative of the Doshin Company, a much larger and better capitalized Japanese firm. In 1893, he resigned from this company and returned to Japan. He started two new companies: with three partners, the Yokohama Kiito Gomei Kaisha, a new silk export company, and with Ichizaemon Morimura, the Morimura Arai Company to represent Yokohama Kiito Kaisha in the United States. Morimura Arai handled one-third of direct silk exports from Japan to the U.S. by 1908 and was one of the first to import American cotton to Japan in significant quantities. In 1901, Arai was elected to the board of governors of the Silk Association of America.

Arai was a pioneering member of the New York Japanese community and helped to establish The Nippon Club in 1905 and the Japan Society of New York in 1907.

For further reading, see T. Scott Miyakawa. "Early New York Issei: Founders of Japanese American Trade." In Conroy, Hilary and T. Scott Miyakawa, eds. *East Across the Pacific.* Santa Barbara, Calif.: American Bibliographic Center-Clio Press, 1972. 156–86 and Haru Matsukata Reischauer. *Samurai and Silk*: A *Japanese and American Heritage.* Cambridge, Mass.: Belknap Press of Harvard University Press, 1986.

Ariyoshi, George Ryoichi (1926–   ) Lawyer, politician, governor of Hawaii. George Ariyoshi had the distinction of being the first Japanese American lieutenant governor and governor in the nation. In his long political career, he has never lost an election.

A NISEI, Ariyoshi's father Ryozo arrived in Hawaii in 1918. A SUMO wrestler from Fukuoka PREFECTURE, Ryozo eventually ran several small businesses, including a tofu shop and R & M Dry Cleaning in Kalihi. He met his future wife Mitsue Yoshikawa, a native of Kumamoto Prefecture, during a sumo exhibition on the island of Hawaii. George was the eldest of four Ariyoshi children and graduated from McKinley High School in 1944. After a stint at the University of Hawaii, he graduated from Michigan State University in 1949 with a degree in history and political science. He went on to the University of Michigan Law School, earning his J.D. in 1952, at which time he opened a law practice after returning to Hawaii.

Along with several other Japanese American Democrats, Ariyoshi was first elected to office in 1954, winning a seat in the Territorial House of Representatives (see REVOLUTION OF 1954). He won a seat in the Territorial Senate in 1958, eventually becoming majority leader. In 1970, he became the lieutenant governor of Hawaii and became acting governor in 1973 when his close friend and colleague JOHN BURNS stepped down for health reasons. Ariyoshi went on to serve three full terms as governor, retiring in 1986. His tenure as governor is the longest in Hawaii's territorial and state history.

In 1955 Ariyoshi married Jean Miya Hayashi and the couple had three children. Ariyoshi lives in Hawaii and is a consultant and businessman.

For further reading, see Allicyn Chiyeko Levi. "George R. Ariyoshi: His Politics and Family." *Hawaii Herald* 21 Feb.

1986; 1, 13.; and Paul C. Phillips. *Hawaii's Democrats Chasing the American Dream.* Washington, D.C.: University Press of America, 1982.

Ariyoshi, Koji (1914–1976) Longshoreman, journalist. Ariyoshi was born in Kona, Hawaii, where he grew up observing the inequalities of the PLANTATION labor system. As a young man, he journeyed to the mainland, where he attended the University of Georgia on a scholarship, majoring in journalism. Working as a longshoreman in San Francisco when World War II began, he was incarcerated along with all other West Coast Japanese Americans, ending up at MANZANAR. While in Manzanar, he co-founded the Manzanar Citizens Federation, a seemingly unlikely coalition of radicals and JAPANESE AMERICAN CITIZENS LEAGUE members. He was married in camp (to Taeko Ito) and entered the military, where he graduated from the MILITARY INTELLIGENCE SERVICE LANGUAGE SCHOOL in June 1943. He went on to serve in Yenan in northern China for two years as part of the Dixie Mission. The Dixie Mission—so named because it was set in "rebel" territory—was charged with coordinating Chinese Communist rebels in the war effort against the common Japanese enemy. During his tour of duty, Ariyoshi formed close relations with leaders of the Communist forces and was dismayed to see U.S. policy turn increasingly towards the Chinese Nationalists and Chiang Kai-shek once the war with Japan was over.

When his military service ended in July 1946, Ariyoshi and family settled in New York City, then returned to Hawaii in 1948. There, he founded the *The Honolulu Record,* where, as editor, he lent staunch support to the labor movement and the ILWU. Prompted by the testimony of former ILWU member JACK KAWANO, seven Hawaiians (the "HAWAII SEVEN") including Ariyoshi, were arrested and convicted on Smith Act charges during the Red Scare in 1953. Though the convictions were eventually overturned, the *Record* was suspended. Ariyoshi started a retail flower business to make a living. In 1972–73 he returned to China for a triumphant visit and reunion with Chou En-lai, among others. He was later appointed by Governor JOHN BURNS as president of the Hawaii Foundation for History and the Humanities. In April 1976, six months before his death, he was honored in a resolution adopted by the Hawaii House of Representatives.

For further reading, see Dennis M. Ogawa. *Kodomo No Tame Ni, For the Sake of the Children: The Japanese American Experience in Hawaii.* Honolulu: University Press of Hawaii, 1978; Clifford Uyeda. "Profiles in History: Koji Ariyoshi." *Nikkei Heritage* 3.1 (Winter 1991): 7–8; and Karl G. Yoneda. *Ganbatte: Sixty-Year Struggle of a Kibei Worker.* Los Angeles: Asian American Studies Center, University of California, Los Angeles, 1983.

Asahis Formed in 1905, the Asahis became the most famous Japanese American baseball team in Hawaii during its glory days in the 1920s and '30s. From a group of teenagers who played in a sandlot in Iwilei, the team entered league play in 1907. Though it struggled initially, the team soon became dominant in both Japanese American leagues and in the multi-ethnic Oahu Junior League. Led by manager, captain and star pitcher STEERE NODA, the team won Junior League championships from 1911 to 1914. The team toured Japan in 1915.

Having dominated the Juniors, the team was moved up to the Senior level in 1920 and won the Honolulu Baseball League championship in 1924. In 1925, the Asahis and other top teams formed the Hawaii Baseball League (HBL), made up of teams representing various ethnic groups. In addition to the Asahis, there were the All-Chinese, the Braves (made up of Portuguese players) and the Wanderers (made up of HAOLE), among others. Winning HBL titles in 1925 and 1926, the Asahis battled the Braves for dominance in the pre–World War II years.

With the onset of World War II, the team recruited several haole players in 1942 and changed its name to the Athletics in 1943 to placate anti-Japanese sentiment. Ironically, team owner Katsumi Kometani and several former players were fighting with the 100TH INFANTRY BATTALION in Europe at this time. Switch-hitting center fielder and former Asahi Joe Takata was the first 100th member to be killed in action. The team was kept together in part through the efforts of JOHN BURNS, who became the team's acting owner. Though the team became all–Japanese American again after the war and took back its old name in 1947, it was forced to integrate again for good in 1956. The team of Japanese Americans and non–Japanese Americans won five more championships in the 1960s.

Among those who played for the Asahis over the years were Pacific Coast League players Kensu Nishida and Jimmy Horio; Japanese professional league stars Bozo Wakabayashi and Ted Kameda; two-sport legend Wally Yonemine, a San Francisco 49er football player and one of the greatest Japanese major league stars of all time; legendary power hitter Larry Kamishima; strong armed catcher Yoshio "Kaiser" Tanaka; speedy Lawrence "Peanuts" Kunihisa; and former Major League infielder and current Minor League manager Lenn Sakata.

For further reading, see Roland Kotani. "Asahis: the 75-Year Legacy." *Hawaii Herald* 15 May 1981: 8–9 and Gaylord C. Kubota. "Roots of AJA Baseball." *Hawaii Herald* 20 Mar. 1981: 7, 12.

Asakura v. City of Seattle Case brought before the U.S. Supreme Court that involved a Seattle city ordinance (No. 42323) passed in July 1921 that limited the issuing of pawnbroking licenses to citizens. Asakura, an ISSEI and a pawnbroker in Seattle since 1915, contended that the ordinance violated the TREATY OF COMMERCE AND NAVIGATION OF 1911 BETWEEN THE U.S. AND JAPAN, the Washington state constitution, and the equal protection and due process clauses of the Fourteenth Amendment of the U.S. Constitution. The trial court found in favor of Asakura, but the Washington State Supreme Court reversed the decision in 1922. The U.S. Supreme Court in turn reversed the Washington Supreme Court, stating that the ordinance violated the 1911 treaty between the U.S. and Japan, which allowed citizens of both countries to "carry on trade" in the other. Underlying the decision was the question as to what extent the treaty-making powers of the federal government could nullify the power of the states to pass laws in their interest.

For further reading, see Moritoshi Fukuda. *Legal Problems of Japanese Americans.* Tokyo: Keio Tsushin, 1980. The case transcript is included in Consulate-General of Japan. *Documental History of Law Cases Affecting Japanese in the United States, 1916–1924. 2 Vols.* New York: Arno Press, 1978. 280–343.

DENNIS YAMAMOTO

Asawa, Ruth (1926–   )   Nisei artist known for her wire mesh sculptures and bronzed "baker's clay" sculptures.

Ruth Asawa was born on January 27, 1926, in Norwalk, California, where she remained with her parents, Umakichi and Haru Asawa, until World War II. After the bombing of Pearl Harbor by the Japanese, her father was taken to an INTERNMENT CAMP in New Mexico. In 1942, Asawa, her mother and her siblings were sent to Santa Anita "ASSEMBLY CENTER," in Pasadena, California. Six months later Asawa and her family were sent to the CONCENTRATION CAMP at ROHWER, Arkansas.

In 1943, while she was incarcerated at Rohwer, Asawa applied and was accepted to Milwaukee State Teachers College in Wisconsin. After completing three years there, Asawa gave up pursuing her degree and transferred to Black Mountain College, North Carolina, in 1946. While at Black Mountain College, Asawa studied under artist Joseph Albers. She completed her degree in art in 1949. In that same year, Asawa and a fellow Black Mountain College student and architect, Albert Lanier, married. The couple moved to San Francisco, California.

Asawa is a highly successful artist. She has had numerous one-woman exhibitions of her artwork and is represented in many museums, including the DeYoung Museum (1960), the San Francisco Museum of Art (1973) and the Fresno Arts Center and Museum (1978). She has had her work shown at the Oakland Museum of Art (1959) and the Whitney Museum of American Art (1958). Asawa has also been commissioned to create a number of public works of art, including a fountain of a mermaid and child in Ghiradelli Square, San Francisco (1966), a bronze plaque in San Francisco's Golden Gate Park's Japanese tea garden (1974) and a cast bronze fountain at the Beringer Winery in St. Helena, California.

In addition to being a successful artist, Asawa has also been active in her community. Asawa is the co-founder of the School of the Arts Foundation and served as president of its board from 1968–1984. She also worked on the NEA Task Force on the Education and Training of Artists from 1977–1978 and worked on the President's Commission of Mental Health "Role of the Arts" program in the same year.

Asawa has also received awards from the Contra Costa chapter of the Japanese American Citizens League, the San Francisco Big Sisters (1980) and the Japanese Cultural and Community Center of Northern California (1989). February 12, 1982, was proclaimed "Ruth Asawa Day" in San Francisco. STACEY HIROSE

Asian American   The preferred term for Americans of Asian ancestry, whether native or foreign born. As with the terms "African American" and "Chicano," the roots of the term "Asian American" are political. For years, the term "Oriental" was used to refer to Asians and Americans of Asian ancestry alike. Starting in the late 1960s, Asian American activists began rejecting the term "Oriental" on two grounds. One was that the term "Oriental" was not a term chosen by Asians but one applied to them by outsiders. The term was also felt to have a connotation of otherness vis-à-vis the term "Occidental." Secondly, "Oriental" failed to distinguish between Asians and Americans of Asian ancestry. By the early to mid-seventies, the term "Asian American" prevailed over a number of contenders to become the preferred term, which it remains today.

Asian American movement   Catch-all term for the flurry of political and social activity undertaken by Asian American young people in the 1960s and 1970s. Inspired by the anti-war, women's, civil rights and Black Power movements of the 1960s, young ASIAN AMERICANS—mostly American-born Chinese Americans and SANSEI—organized to focus attention on political causes in the Asian American community and to delve into their own history and identity as Asian Americans. Although the movement was derided by many older Asian Americans, it has left a lasting legacy that includes a host of social-service, political and cultural organizations in the various Asian American communities, Asian American studies in colleges and universities, a wealth of popular and academic literature on the Asian American experi-

The Asian American Movement brought a new activism to Asian American communities as typified by this January 1972 demonstration against the proposed U.S.–Japan Security Pact or Ampo. *UCLA Asian American Studies Collection, Japanese American National Museum Photographic & Moving Image Archive*

War movement, a participation that was often accompanied by a realization of the racial nature of the war and an identification with its Asian victims.

Whatever its starting point, there was clearly something going on by the end of the 1960s. The pages of GIDRA, the unofficial journal of the movement, was filled with accounts of new organizations and the ongoing struggles of the times. The early 1970s saw the beginning of many enduring activities. There were the PIONEER CENTERS, health fairs and other social-service organizations for the ISSEI and other elderly. There was a renewed interest in Asian and Asian American art and culture, reflected in the return of community MOCHI-TSUKIS, the discovery of TAIKO drumming, the founding of ASIAN AMERICAN THEATER companies and the explosion of individual creative expression found in the works of such artists as JANICE MIRIKITANI, HIROSHIMA and LAWSON FUSAO INADA. There was the fight for ethnic studies, manifested in the beginning of Asian American studies programs in several West Coast universities. There was a renewed interest in history, especially in the mass removal and detention of Japanese Americans during World War II as manifested in the first camp pilgrimages (see MANZANAR PILGRIMAGE) and formation of Japanese American historical organizations. There was the start of community legal services and community-oriented businesses such as AMERASIA BOOKSTORE. There was the continued political organizing and militant action around such issues as discrimination, racist media portrayals and the REDEVELOPMENT of Asian American communities around the country. Most importantly, there was a new sense of pride in being Asian American.

There were undoubtedly aspects of the movement that did not endure—communal living and hallucinogenic drug use are two which come to mind. The political ideology of many of the movement organizations and activities faded in time as the realities of survival in a decidedly capitalist world loomed. By the mid-'70s, many movement people had moved on to the "real" world of family life and job hunting. It is unclear when—or even if—the movement came to an end.

The legacies of the movement are also difficult to quantify. In addition to the various organizations and activities that trace their origins to the movement, and the art, literature and scholarly research that came out of it, it effected something more. It changed the lives of many people active in the movement who now pursue socially meaningful work in their post-movement lives. It profoundly influenced the course of events in the Asian American community since then, setting the groundwork for the redress movement, among other things. It has also permanently changed the Asian American community and what it means to grow up Asian American. Though not of comparable impact, the Asian

ence, the adoption of the term "Asian American" and, arguably, the success of the REDRESS MOVEMENT.

The starting point of the movement is difficult to gauge with any precision. There was the movement among Japanese Americans that sprang up around the repeal of Title II of the Internal Security Act of 1950 (see EMERGENCY DETENTION ACT OF 1950, REPEAL OF), which was the first time many young Japanese Americans learned in detail about the mass incarceration of World War II. There was the formation of organizations on college campuses such as the ASIAN AMERICAN POLITICAL ALLIANCE and Oriental Concern. There was the participation of Asian American students in the SAN FRANCISCO STATE STRIKE of 1968. There was the community mobilization around the apparently racially motivated firing of Los Angeles County coroner THOMAS NOGUCHI in 1969. There was also the individual participation of many Asian Americans in the anti–Vietnam

American movement was to the *sansei* what the anti-Japanese movement was to the *issei* and the CONCENTRATION CAMPS to the *nisei*—the measuring stick for their identity as Japanese Americans.

For further reading, see Susie H. Ling "The Mountain Movers: Asian American Women's Movement, Los Angeles, 1968–1976." Thesis, University of California, Los Angeles, 1984 and "The Mountain Movers: Asian American Women's Movement in Los Angeles." *Amerasia Journal* 15.1 (1989): 51–67; Lon Y. Kurashige. "The Asian American Movement, 1968–1972: The Politics of Meanings." Thesis, University of Wisconsin, 1989; Minako K. Maykovich. "Political Activation of Japanese American Youth." *Journal of Social Issues* 29.2 (Spring 1973): 167–85; Ronald Tanaka. "Culture, Communications and the Asian Movement in Perspective." *Journal of Ethnic Studies* 4.1 (Spring 1976): 37–52; Karen Nora Umemoto. "Asian American Students in the San Francisco State College Strike, 1964–1968." Thesis, University of California, Los Angeles, 1989; and " 'On Strike!' " San Francisco State College Strike, 1968–69: The Role of Asian American Students." *Amerasia Journal* 15.1 (1989): 3–41. *Amerasia Journal,* itself a product of the movement, devoted an issue—15.1 (1989)—to the legacy of the San Francisco State strike and the movement.

Asian American Political Alliance

Early ASIAN AMERICAN student organization. The Asian American Political Alliance (AAPA) was one of many organizations formed on college campuses by Japanese Americans and other Asian American students during the late 1960s. AAPA chapters formed as primarily political organizations for the stated purpose of social and political change.

AAPA strove to incorporate Asian Americans of various ethnic groups—at the time, this meant mostly Chinese and Japanese Americans with a few Filipino Americans—based upon a platform of anti-imperialism internationally and self-determination over the political, economic, educational and social institutions within ethnic communities domestically. AAPA chapters criticized the racism in educational and other institutions in the United States.

AAPA chapters at various campuses, including the University of California at Berkeley, San Francisco State College and San Jose State University, formed a loose network for the purposes of communication and mutual support. Informal relations were also established with other student organizations in the ASIAN AMERICAN MOVEMENT throughout the state and country such as Oriental Concern. A newspaper published by the Berkeley AAPA reported activities of AAPA members such as Free Huey (Newton) rallies, educational forums on issues in San Francisco's Chinatown, lobbying for the repeal of TITLE II, consumer boycotts, the SAN FRANCISCO STATE STRIKE, the development of Asian American studies courses and programs, support work to save the International Hotel against commercial redevelopment, high school student organizing, draft and youth counseling and various community events.

For further reading, see Paul Jacobs and Saul Landau, with Eve Pell. *To Serve the Devil, Volume II: Colonials and Sojourners.* New York: Random House, 1971 and Karen Umemoto. " 'On Strike!' " San Francisco State College Strike, 1968–69: The Role of Asian American Students." *Amerasia Journal* 15.1 (1989): 3–41.   KAREN UMEMOTO

Asian American theater

Inspired by the rise in ASIAN AMERICAN ethnic identity in the 1960s and 1970s, Asian American theater companies were formed as a part of the ASIAN AMERICAN MOVEMENT. In 1965, eight young and dedicated Asian American actors created the world's first Asian American theater, East West Players (EWP), in Los Angeles. Under the guidance of Mako (MAKOTO IWAMATSU), the first artistic director, East West Players not only became a major force in the Asian American theater community, but also in the expanding American drama scene. This was an arena that offered Asian American actors an opportunity to express themselves and develop their crafts as members of the performing arts. Other Asian American playhouses followed, opening up in other parts of the nation, such as San Francisco, New York and Seattle.

Since its founding in 1965, East West Players has dedicated itself to providing an arena for Asian American actors, writers and directors. The theater, which still exists today in Los Angeles, provides training, exposure and the opportunity to learn skills for Asian American actors in a positive and encouraging atmosphere. In addition, EWP has developed multicultural projects and has continued to serve as a bridge between the East and West. As a major part of the community, EWP also provides audiences with productions and workshops that are diverse, socially relevant, provocative and inspiring. EWP has been recognized by 49 Drama-logue Awards and seven Los Angeles Drama Critics and Los Angeles Weekly Theatre Awards. The productions include classics as well as new plays, with four to six mainstage productions per year including many world premieres.

The Asian American Theatre Workshop, later known as the Asian American Theatre Company (AATC), was co-founded in 1973 by playwright Frank Chin and Janice Chan. The goal of this San Francisco–based theater is "to produce high quality Asian American theatre in order to promote positive role models for the Asian American community as well as the community at large." In addition, the AATC provides training classes and workshops to further its goals. AATC is also an award-winning theater that has earned positive recognition from other theaters, the press and the Asian American community.

New York and Seattle have also developed Asian American theater companies, the Pan Asian Repertory

Theatre and Northwest Asian American Theatre, respectively. Both of these theaters have followed in the footsteps of the East West Players in providing Asian American actors, writers and directors with the opportunity to learn and refine their craft in an inspiring and supportive environment. These theaters are also interested in breaking stereotypes by producing plays that tell stories from the unique perspective of Asian Americans. As evident from Asian American theaters springing up in places such as San Diego, Toronto and Chicago, Asian American theater is starting to have an impact on communities all over America.   SUZANNE HEE

[Quote from "The Life and Times of AACT." *Bridge Magazine* 10.1 (1985).]

Asiatic Exclusion League   The first organization created to promote the exclusion of Japanese immigrants to the United States. Formed in San Francisco in 1905 as a virtual coalition of labor unions, the Asiatic Exclusion League played an important role in the first stages of the ANTI-JAPANESE MOVEMENT.

The league was formed by delegates from 67 organizations at a meeting in San Francisco on May 14, 1905. Prominent local labor leaders took up positions of leadership in the league; the first president was Olaf Tveitmoe of the Sailor's Union. The league's exclusionist principles were based on objection to Japanese immigrants primarily on economic grounds. Japanese immigrant laborers were said to maintain a low standard of living, allowing them to work for less money than white laborers. It was also felt that Japanese immigrants were unwilling and incapable of assimilating. Racial considerations, including the ever-present fear of miscegenation, were also part of the league's platform. Though never particularly large or wealthy, the league's mostly European immigrant leaders churned out anti-Japanese propaganda, instigated boycotts against Japanese businesses and worked with sympathetic politicians to try and pass anti-Japanese legislation. Pressure from the league helped bring about the SAN FRANCISCO SCHOOL BOARD SEGREGATION ORDER OF 1906 and the league also supported anti-Japanese land legislation as well.

Though Asiatic Exclusion League influence waned by 1911 and disappeared altogether soon thereafter, other non-labor-dominated organizations would emerge to continue its work. (See JAPANESE EXCLUSION LEAGUE OF CALIFORNIA.)

For further reading, see Roger Daniels. *The Politics of Prejudice: The Anti-Japanese Movement in California and the Struggle for Japanese Exclusion.* 1962. 2nd edition. Berkeley: University of California Press, 1977.

"assembly centers"   Temporary detention centers that housed Japanese Americans who had been forcibly re-moved from the West Coast in the early months of World War II. After the issuing of EXECUTIVE ORDER 9066 on February 19, 1942, and the designation of Military Areas 1 and 2 in early March, Japanese Americans were removed from their homes on the West Coast, neighborhood by neighborhood, in a series of 108 "Civilian Evacuation Orders" starting in late March. Prior to settling in WAR RELOCATION AUTHORITY (WRA)—administered CONCENTRATION CAMPS (euphemistically called "relocation centers"), detainees spent much of the spring and summer of 1942 in so-called "assembly centers." The chart on page 111 lists the 16 facilities, giving their peak populations and opening and closing dates.

Administered by the Wartime Civil Control Administration (WCCA), the "assembly centers" were hastily erected quarters located throughout California and the West at fairgrounds, racetracks and other similar facilities. While conditions varied from center to center, they were generally as poor as might be expected given the haste with which they were put up. Residents complained of overcrowding, shoddy construction, communal showers and outhouses, and many other similar problems. Perhaps the worst indignity of all was being housed in odious horse stables, as detainees at the former racetracks Tanforan and Santa Anita were. Security was tight as military police patrolled the perimeters and regulated visitors while internal police held rollcalls and enforced curfews. Overzealous policing led to a small riot at the Santa Anita center on August 4, 1942.

By the middle of the summer, the "assembly centers" were being emptied and the inmates transferred to more permanent "relocation centers." By the end of October, the transfer was complete and all were safely ensconced in concentration camps administered by the WRA.

For further reading, see Commission on Wartime Relocation and Internment of Civilians. *Personal Justice Denied: Report of the Commission on Wartime Relocation and Internment of Civilians.* Washington, D.C.: Government Printing Office, 1982 and Audrie Girdner and Anne Loftis. *The Great Betrayal: The Evacuation of the Japanese-Americans during World War II.* Toronto: Macmillan, 1969 for a general overview. See Janet Cormack, ed. "Portland Assembly Center: Diary of Saku Tomita." Trans. Zuigaku Kodachi and Jan Heikkala. *Oregon Historical Quarterly* 81.2 (1980): 149–71; Charles Kikuchi. *The Kikuchi Diary: Chronicle from an American Concentration Camp.* John Modell, ed. and introd. Urbana: University of Illinois Press, 1973; Mine Okubo. *Citizen 13660.* New York: Columbia University Press, 1946. New York: Arno Press 1978. Seattle: University of Washington Press, 1983 for first-person accounts of life in an "assembly center." Anthony L. Lehman *Birthright of Barbed Wire.* Los Angeles: Westernlore Press, 1970 is a history of the Santa Anita "Assembly Center."

Association for the America-Bound   Japanese organization promoting travel to the United States. Founded by Socialist leader SEN KATAYAMA in 1902 in Tokyo, the

| | | Maximum Population | | Dates Occupied | |
| | | Date | Opened | Closed |
Assembly Center	Number	1942	1942	1942
Puyallup	7390	25 July	28 Apr.	12 Sept.
Portland	3676	6 June	2 May	10 Sept.
Marysville	2451	2 June	8 May	29 June
Sacramento	4739	30 May	6 May	26 June
Tanforan	7816	25 July	28 Apr.	13 Oct.
Stockton	4271	21 May	10 May	17 Oct.
Turlock	3661	2 June	30 Apr.	12 Aug.
Salinas	3586	23 June	27 Apr.	4 July
Merced	4508	3 June	6 May	15 Sept.
Pinedale	4792	29 June	7 May	23 July
Fresno	5120	4 Sept.	6 May	30 Oct.
Tulare	4978	11 Aug.	20 Apr.	4 Sept.
Santa Anita	18719	23 Aug.	27 Mar.	27 Oct.
Pomona	5434	20 July	7 May	24 Aug.
Mayer	245	25 May	7 May	2 June
Manzanar	9837		21 Mar.	2 June

(Manzanar was transferred to the WRA and became a "relocation center" after June 2, 1942.)

Association for the America-Bound (Tobei Kyokai) was immediately successful in helping to generate further interest in travel to America. At its peak, the association put out several travel GUIDEBOOKS in addition to the widely read *America-Bound Magazine (Tobei Zasshi)*.

One of the more interesting ventures undertaken by the association was the attempt to start a rice farming colony in Texas in 1906. Having encouraged emigrants to adopt farming as a profitable livelihood, Katayama bought 160 acres of land in Colorado County. For various reasons, the venture failed, although other similar ventures did achieve a measure of success later (see for example the various YAMATO COLONY ventures).

The association became a big financial success through the sales of guidebooks and its magazine and through various membership fees. This success led some of the association's more ardent Socialist members to criticize Katayama for being merely an "American travel agent." However, there is no question that the association played a large role in encouraging immigration to America through Katayama's speaking engagements, the publications and such services as letters of introduction and employment aid.

For further reading, see Hisashi Tsurutani. *America Bound: The Japanese and Opening of the American West*. Betsey Scheiner, trans. Tokyo: Japan Times, Inc., 1989.

B

bakapyo One of two popular games in which Japanese laborers gambled away their wages, *bakapyo* is the Japanese variation of the Chinese term *baahk gap piu* meaning "white pigeon card." Similar to the game of keno, it consists of cards containing 80 Chinese characters from which a player tries to select the one that will come up in a lottery. Since the term *baka* means "fool" in Japanese, the name *bakapyo* has the double meaning of "fool's card" as well as "white pigeon card." (See SHIIGO.)

For further reading, see Yuji Ichioka. *The Issei: The World of the First Generation Japanese Immigrants, 1885–1924*. New York: The Free Press, 1988.

Ban, Shinzaburo (1854–1926) Railroad contractor, retail entrepreneur. Shinzaburo Ban was born and raised in Tokyo and studied English under missionary James Hepburn. Upon graduating from college, he entered the foreign ministry in 1885 and traveled to Hawaii with Consul-General Taro Ando. After being reassigned to Tokyo briefly three years later, he was sent to the U.S. and toured much of the country, investigating prostitutes, pimps and gamblers. He then resigned from the foreign ministry and began an emigration company in Kobe, later returning to the U.S. and in March 1891 establishing himself as a LABOR CONTRACTOR. The S. Ban Company of Portland was one of the three largest labor-contracting firms in the Pacific Northwest. Working primarily with the Oregon Short Line in the 1890s, Ban brought in large numbers of Japanese to work in Oregon. He also began a large mercantile shop in Portland that had branches in Denver; Sheridan, Wyoming; and Tokyo as well as a shingle company and a lumber mill. By 1900, Ban had the largest Japanese business in

The S. Ban store, Pocatello, Idaho. *Yosaburo Kaneko Collection, Japanese American National Museum Photographic & Moving Image Archive*

Oregon and employed as many as 3,000 workers at his peak. A devout Christian, Ban was a founding member of the Portland Japanese Methodist Church in 1893. In 1924, his company went bankrupt, apparently as a result of a run on immigrant savings held by the company. He died on January 18, 1926.

For further reading, see Yuji Ichioka. *The Issei: The World of the First Generation Japanese Immigrants, 1885–1924.* New York: The Free Press, 1988; Kazuo Ito. *Issei: A History of Japanese Immigrants in North America.* Shinichiro Nakamura and Jean S. Gerard, trans. Seattle: Executive Committee for the Publication of *Issei,* 1973; Hisashi Tsurutani. *America Bound: The Japanese and Opening of the American West.* Betsey Scheiner, trans. Tokyo: Japan Times, Inc., 1989; and Barbara Yasui. "The Nikkei in Oregon, 1834–1940." *Oregon Historical Quarterly* 76.3 (Sept. 1975): 225–57.

bango   Worker identification disk used on Hawaii's sugar PLANTATIONS. To keep track of the workers on Hawaii's sugar plantations, plantation owners devised the *bango* system. Workers were assigned numbers, which were stamped onto a small brass or aluminum tag that they were required to carry with them at all times. Their identity on the plantation was tied to these numbers, which were used to keep track of their pay status, including the advances they may have received from the plantation store. Adopted by management in part to rectify the problems they had with the workers' "foreign" names, *bango* were viewed by workers as a dehumanizing facet of plantation life. "They never call a man by his name. Always by the *bango,*" recalled one plantation laborer.

[Quote from R. Takaki 83 (89).]

For further reading, see Franklin S. Odo and Kazuko Sinoto. *A Pictorial History of the Japanese in Hawaii, 1885–1924.* Honolulu: Bishop Museum Press, 1985; and Ronald Takaki. *Pau Hana: Plantation Life and Labor in Hawaii, 1835–1920.* Honolulu: University of Hawaii Press, 1983.

"Battle of Los Angeles"   On the night of February 24, 1942, the city of Los Angeles reacted in panic to what was believed to be an attack by enemy aircraft. A population that was already on edge was even more jittery as a result of a lone Japanese submarine attack near Santa Barbara the night before. Apparently, an unidentified aircraft (later determined to be a lost weather balloon) set off the military defense system over the city, resulting in sirens, antiaircraft fire and panic in the streets. Antiaircraft fire damaged houses and cars, and two people died of heart attacks and three in auto accidents. Predictably, there were reports that Japanese Americans were seen signaling the supposed enemy planes and 20 were arrested. For those so inclined, the "Battle of Los Angeles," fictitious as it might have been, was yet another reason to increase pressure on officials to do something with local Japanese Americans. It was also an indication of how nervous the local population was and how that nervousness could breed irrationality. The next day (February 25), Japanese Americans living on TERMINAL ISLAND near the Los Angeles Harbor were informed they had 48 hours to leave their homes.

For further reading, see Audrie Girdner and Anne Loftis. *The Great Betrayal: The Evacuation of the Japanese-Americans during World War II.* Toronto: Macmillan, 1969.

Bendetsen, Karl R (1907–1989)   World War II U.S. government official. Karl Bendetsen was one of the prime architects of the plan to "relocate" West Coast Japanese Americans during World War II. Born in Aberdeen, Washington, he attended Stanford, receiving an A.B. in 1929 and an LL.B. in 1932. He joined the Officers Reserve Corps about 1932 and opened a law office in 1934 in Aberdeen. He continued to practice law until he was appointed to the office of judge advocate general for the army with the rank of captain. He was promoted to major in 1941 and to colonel the year after.

While serving as head of the Aliens Division of the Provost Marshal General, he played a key role in planning the mass removal of Japanese Americans. He was in effect a liaison between the War Department and the Western Defense Command (WDC) and later served as General JOHN L. DEWITT's chief aide for the mass removal. As the lone westerner involved in the decision-making process in Washington D.C., Bendetsen stated his belief that "a substantial majority of the NISEI bear allegiance to Japan, are well controlled and disciplined by the enemy, and at the proper time will engage in organized sabotage." He went on to help design the mass removal from the coast and later fought the WAR RELOCATION AUTHORITY plan to segregate the "loyal" from the "disloyal" Japanese Americans since part of the WDC's rationale for mass incarceration was that one could not tell the "loyal" from the "disloyal." He received the Distinguished Service Medal from the government for his service. Later, he was appointed assistant secretary of the army by President Truman over the protests of the Japanese American community in 1950. In the 1980s, he was a vocal critic of the REDRESS MOVEMENT. He died on June 28, 1989, at the age of 81.

For further reading, see Commission on Wartime Relocation and Internment of Civilians. *Personal Justice Denied: Report of the Commission on Wartime Relocation and Internment of Civilians.* Washington, D.C.: Government Printing Office, 1982; Roger Daniels. *The Decision to Relocate the Japanese Americans.* Philadelphia: Lippincott, 1975; and Michi Weglyn. *Years of Infamy: The Untold Story of America's Concentration Camps.* New York: William Morrow & Co., 1976.

GLEN KITAYAMA

[Also used to compile this entry: Alfonso A. Narvaez. "Karl Bendetsen, 81, Executive and High Ranking Official." *New York Times,* 30 June 1989: 1–16.]

benshi   Until the outbreak of World War II, *benshi* were men who provided a voice-over narrative to Japanese silent movies. At their peak in the '20s, they often became celebrities in the community. There were as many as 15 *benshi* in Honolulu alone at one time. The *benshi* were often tied to a specific theater which was in turn affiliated with a specific Japanese studio. *Benshi* often traveled with the film when it moved to outlying areas. *Benshi* were often so popular with ISSEI patrons that they and not the movie became the main attraction of going to the theater. They also often had female helpers, called *bansho,* who did sound effects and played instruments during the film. Although World War II ended the careers of *benshi,* many remained well known in their communities. At least one of them, Kamesuke Nakahama, performed into the 1980s at special functions.

For further reading, see Junko Ogihara. "The Exhibition of Films for Japanese Americans in Los Angeles During the Silent Film Era." *Film History* 4 (1990): 81–87; and Grady Timmons. "The Benshi: On Making People Weep." *Kanyaku Imin: A Hundred Years of Japanese Life in Hawaii.* Ed. Leonard Lueras. Honolulu: International Savings and Loan Association Ltd., 1985. 40–41.

Biddle, Francis (1886–1968)   U.S. attorney general during World War II. Francis Biddle, one of the so-called "good guys" in the debate on the mass removal and detention of Japanese Americans during World War II, was a complex character whose job challenged his beliefs and often pitted his moral convictions against his professional judgment. To Japanese Americans, he was the highest ranking government official who attempted to forestall their forced removal. Unfortunately, he was also the man who deferred against his better judgment to those with more clout in FRANKLIN D. ROOSEVELT's Cabinet—specifically Secretary of War HENRY STIMSON. " 'I was new to the Cabinet,' he wrote in 1962, 'and disinclined to insist on my view to a man whose wisdom and integrity I greatly respected.' "

Francis Biddle was born on May 9, 1886, in Paris, France, while his parents were in Europe. A Pennsylvania aristocrat with family ties to both the Republican Party and the Pennsylvania Railroad, he attended Harvard College and Harvard Law School—graduating cum laude from both. In 1911, Biddle won a prestigious clerkship with Oliver Wendell Holmes and then proceeded to serve 23 years in corporate law practice in Philadelphia. After a mid-life conversion to the Democratic Party, Biddle worked 12 years in public life from 1934 to 1946 as chairman of National Labor Board, United States Circuit court judge, solicitor general, attorney general and a judge at the Nuremberg trials of accused Nazi war criminals.

In his role as attorney general from 1941 to 1945, Biddle recognized the racism and economic opportunism directed toward the Japanese Americans and tried to obstruct their mass removal. His efforts, however, were not strong enough. Though he was one of the senior members in Roosevelt's Cabinet, he was outranked in both age and respect by his counterpart in the War Department, Henry Stimson. Later, Biddle regretted the treatment of Japanese Americans: "We should never have moved the Japanese from their homes and their word. It was un-American, unconstitutional and un-Christian." Later in life, Biddle served as chairman of Americans for Democratic Action and as an advisor to the AMERICAN CIVIL LIBERTIES UNION. He died on October 4, 1968.

For further reading, see Peter Irons. *Justice at War: The Story of the Japanese American Internment Cases.* New York: Oxford University Press, 1983; and Michi Weglyn. *Years of Infamy: The Untold Story of America's Concentration Camps.* New York: William Morrow & Co., 1976.

GLEN KITAYAMA

[Also used to compile this entry was Biddle's *New York Times* obituary, October 5, 1968, from which the 1962 quote comes; the second quote comes from Weglyn.]

Big Five   The five largest mercantile firms in Hawaii that controlled much of Hawaii's financial resources. The firms of Alexander & Baldwin, American Factors, C. Brewer and Company, Castle and Cooke and Theo. H. Davies & Company comprised the Big Five. By the

1930s, the Big Five served as agents for 36 of Hawaii's 38 sugar PLANTATIONS. This meant that they controlled the financial operation of the plantations, paying their bills and taxes, keeping their books, recruiting their labor, etc. The Big Five also created the HAWAII SUGAR PLANTERS ASSOCIATION. Thus the plantations for the most part didn't have to worry about competitors luring workers away with higher wages or undercutting them. The Big Five also controlled the industries that supported the plantations, including transportation, banking, insurance and wholesale and retail merchandising. The concentration of such a high percentage of control over the plantations in so few hands had the effect of reducing competition and contributed to the financial success of all. The leaders of the Big Five were members of the HAOLE elite, an interconnected web of Caucasian families whose roots in Hawaii went back several generations.

For further reading, see Lawrence H. Fuchs. *Hawaii Pono: A Social History.* New York: Harcourt, Brace and World, 1961; and Gary Y. Okihiro. *Cane Fires: The Anti-Japanese Movement in Hawaii, 1865–1945.* Philadelphia: Temple University Press, 1991.

bobora (also bobura) A derogatory word used in Hawaii for Japanese nationals and KIBEI. Taken from the Portuguese word for pumpkin, it supposedly came into use after a Japanese contract laborer sprinkled pumpkin seeds onto his thatched roof, causing fruit to grow. The term is still used in a derisive fashion in Hawaii to refer to tourists from Japan.

Bon See OBON.

boss system See LABOR CONTRACTORS.

buddhahead Term for Japanese Americans from Hawaii, especially vis-à-vis "KOTONKS", a term for Japanese Americans from the mainland. The terms were popularized during World War II when NISEI from Hawaii and the mainland met—and mostly clashed—for the first time in large numbers while in military training as members of the 442ND REGIMENTAL COMBAT TEAM. It was said that the Hawaii *nisei* looked more Japanese and that *Buddha* also sounded like *buta,* Japanese for "pig," thus "pigheads." "Buddhahead" later became a term Hawaiian Japanese Americans used with pride to identify themselves. The term is still used occasionally today by both Hawaiian and mainland Japanese Americans to refer to themselves. It should be noted, however, that the BUDDHIST CHURCHES OF AMERICA frowns on the use of the term.

The Los Angeles Hompa Hongwanji Buddhist Temple was a major branch *(betsuin)* of the North American Buddhist Mission and its successor, the Buddhist Churches of America. The building was recently restored and currently houses the Japanese American National Museum. *Buddhist Churches of America Collection, Japanese American National Museum Photographic & Moving Image Archive*

Buddhist Churches of America National organization of the Nishi Hongwanji (Jodo Shinshu) sect in the continental United States. Headquartered in San Francisco, the Buddhist Churches of America (BCA), formerly known as the North American Buddhist Mission (NABM), is the largest Japanese American Buddhist organization. It encompasses 59 independent churches, 39 branches (affiliated with independent churches), and two gatherings (non-church Buddhist organizations).

The history of Nishi Hongwanji mission began in 1899 with the arrival of two reverends sent by the Kyoto headquarters. Before long, many other missionaries entered the western states to serve the social and religious needs of the immigrant population, and by 1914, there were already 25 churches and branches. Facing the need for an organizational structure and the development of programs for the NISEI, the ministers and lay representatives held the first national meeting in 1914 and established the NABM in San Francisco. It was officially incorporated in 1924. The NABM was largely, if not completely, controlled by the ministers. The bishop *(so-cho)* headed the organization of all the ministers (Renraku Bukkyo Dan) in dealing with various issues. Nonpriests were given little power within the NABM, although they were involved in the management of each individual church they belonged to, serving on the board of directors. Individual member churches thus remained relatively autonomous from the NABM. Also, other lay organizations such as the Young Men's Buddhist Association were not placed under direct authority of the bishop.

In 1944, a meeting of the ministers and lay representatives at TOPAZ resulted in the birth of the Buddhist Churches of America (BCA). As an attempt to reorganize and Americanize the "Sangha" (brotherhood/sisterhood of Buddhists) and to shift emphasis from the Japanese to the English language, the newly organized BCA incorporated the leadership of *nisei* ministers and lay men in its National Council and Board of Directors, while establishing its educational bureau, Sunday school department, youth department and institute of Buddhist studies for the growing American-born generation. As did the NABM, the BCA met the changing social situations and needs of its adherents without losing its religious purpose. To date, the BCA is still an ethnic institution that consists almost entirely of Japanese and Japanese Americans members.

For further reading, see Tetsuden Kashima. *Buddhism in America: The Social Organization of an Ethnic Religious Institution.* Westport, Conn.: Greenwood Press, 1977 and Donald R. Tuck. *Buddhist Churches of America: Jodo Shinshu.* Queenston, Ontario: The Edwin Mellen Press, 1987. Ryo Munekata ed., *Buddhist Churches of America: Vol. 1, 75 Year History.* Chicago: Nobart, Inc., 1974 is an organizational history of the BCA.

EIICHIRO AZUMA

burakumin   Japanese term for outcasts. In Japan, as in many other Asian countries, there have long been people designated as outcasts who have been shunned by the rest of society. Known by various terms including *eta* (once widely used, but now considered derogatory) and *burakumin* (literally "people of special communities"), a whole mythology evolved concerning the supposed physical inferiority of such people and their "polluted" status. *Burakumin* in Japan have traditionally been persons practicing such "defiling" trades as butchering, leathermaking and other occupations involving the slaughter of animals, a taboo in the Buddhist religion.

Burakumin were certainly represented among those who immigrated to the United States, though their numbers might be small. *Burakumin* in the Japanese American population were known to associate closely only with other *burakumin* and to engage in occupations that required little contact with other Japanese Americans. Few marriages between NISEI and ISSEI *burakumin* and non-*burakumin* took place prior to World War II and those that did usually resulted in strained familial relations. Much of the reluctance of *burakumin* to mix with other Japanese Americans seemed to stem less from overt discrimination as from fear of exposure or embarrassment which might result from such mixing.

Because *burakumin* status was a closely guarded secret, little data about the *burakumin* experience among Japanese Americans is known today. The secrecy seems to have had the desired effect, however: among Japanese Americans today, the term has almost disappeared from usage. It is likely that most SANSEI and YONSEI have only the vaguest notion of what the term means.

For further reading, see Hiroshi Ito [pseud]. "Japan's Outcastes in the United States." In DeVos, George, and Hiroshi Wagatsuma, eds. *Japan's Invisible Race: Caste in Culture and Personality.* Berkeley: University of California Press, 1966. 200–21. Other essays in the preceding anthology give background on *burakumin* in Japan.

buranke-katsugi   A Japanese term for a migratory agricultural laborer, especially before the turn of the 20th century. The literal meaning of the term is a person who shoulders a blanket, implying that these laborers had to carry their bedding on their backs.

For further reading, see Yuji Ichioka. *The Issei: The World of the First Generation Japanese Immigrants, 1885–1924.* New York: The Free Press, 1988.

Burns, John Anthony (1909–1975)   Governor of Hawaii. Throughout his career as a politician, John Burns worked closely with NISEI politicians and the Japanese American community in Hawaii for their mutual benefit.

Born in Fort Assinneboine, Montana, Burns became a permanent resident of Hawaii from the age of four. He attended public schools in both Hawaii and Kansas, and graduated from the University of Hawaii in 1930 and 1931. For the next decade, Burns, described as a "stubborn, stone-faced Irishman" served as a police officer and captain for the city and county of Honolulu where he steadfastly defended the Japanese Americans from accusations of disloyalty during World War II. He served as chairman of the Traffic Safety Commission from 1950 to 1954 and as Honolulu civil defense administrator from 1951 to 1955.

During the same time period, from 1948 to 1952, Burns chaired the Honolulu County Democratic Committee and from 1952 to 1956, the Territorial Democratic Central Committee. He served as delegate to the Democratic National Conventions in 1952, 1956, 1960, 1964 and 1968. Throughout his life, Burns upheld the ideals of the Democratic Party of Hawaii and played a vital role in the Democratic political revolution of the 1950s as the leader of that movement (see REVOLUTION OF 1954).

In the 1956 elections, Burns won a landslide victory over Republican incumbent Elizabeth Farrington and became elected as the Democratic delegate to the Eighty-fifth and Eighty-sixth Congresses. During his term, Burns went to the nation's capital to seek statehood for Hawaii, which was finally granted in 1959. Burns lost in his bid to be the first governor of the State of Hawaii. However, Burns won overwhelmingly in the campaign for the governorship in 1962, and presided as the first elected governor of the state of Hawaii for three terms until 1973.

Near the end of his third term, in October 1973, Burns was diagnosed with cancer and stepped down soon thereafter. Lieutenant Governor GEORGE ARIYOSHI became the acting governor and carried the support of the "Burns machine" to victory in the subsequent 1974 election, going on to serve three full terms as governor. Burns died in Honolulu on April 5, 1975. He is buried at Punchbowl National Cemetery.

For further reading, see Lawrence H. Fuchs. *Hawaii Pono: A Social History.* New York: Harcourt, Brace and World, 1961 and Paul C. Phillips. *Hawaii's Democrats: Chasing the American Dream.* Washington, D.C.: University Press of America, 1982. Tom Coffman. *Catch a Wave: A Case Study of Hawaii's New Politics.* Honolulu: University Press of Hawaii, 1973 is a study of the contentious 1970 Hawaii gubernatorial race.

TRACY ENDO

C

Cable Act   Legislation that deprived citizenship to female citizens who married aliens. The legislation, which repealed Section 47 of the Immigration Act of 1917, was sponsored by Congressman John L. Cable of Ohio and passed Congress on September 22, 1922. The law obviously discriminated against women since male citizens who married alien women would not lose their citizenship. The law also had a particularly severe effect on NISEI women who married ISSEI men. While the act allowed women who had lost their citizenship through marriage to an alien to regain it through naturalization upon the ending of that marriage through death or divorce, *nisei* women who had lost their citizenship were ineligible for naturalization on account of their race (see "ALIENS INELIGIBLE TO CITIZENSHIP"). Thus a *nisei* woman who married an *issei* man would lose her citizenship and have no hope for regaining it under the provisions of the Cable Act.

A movement to repeal the Cable Act was spearheaded by the League of Women Voters and other women's groups. SUMA SUGI, a lobbyist for the fledgling JAPANESE AMERICAN CITIZENS LEAGUE, also worked for repeal of the act. An amended act was signed into law on March 4, 1931, which allowed women citizens to keep their citizenship upon their marriage to an alien. Later, on June 25, 1936, a bill repealing the Cable Act was signed by President Franklin D. Roosevelt.

For further reading, see Bill Hosokawa. *JACL in Quest of Justice: The History of the Japanese American Citizens League.* New York: William Morrow, 1982 and Yamato Ichihashi. *Japanese in the United States: A Critical Study of the Problems of the Japanese Immigrants and their Children.* Stanford: Stanford University Press, 1932. New York: Arno Press, 1969.

California Joint Immigration Committee   See JAPANESE EXCLUSION LEAGUE OF CALIFORNIA.

camp reunions   Latter-day reunions of mostly NISEI who were incarcerated in American CONCENTRATION CAMPS during World War II. Contrary to popular belief, reunions among concentration camp survivors have been a fairly recent phenomena. Unlike the camp pilgrimages (see MANZANAR PILGRIMAGE) that date back to the 1960s and have distinct political overtones, the reunions for the most part were a product of the late 1970s and 1980s and served primarily a social function. The first MANZANAR reunion, for example, was organized in 1984 and included dinner, dancing and other social activities. One reason for the popularity of camp reunions (outside of the opportunity to see old friends) could be attributed to the growth of the REDRESS MOVEMENT, which encouraged discussion of the camps and the experiences of those forced to live in them.

cash-leasing (also cash-tenantry)   Cash-leasing was the third of four stages the typical Japanese farmer went through on his way to owning land. After CONTRACT FARMING and SHARE TENANCY, the next step was to rent land for a set rate for anywhere from one to 10 years. Typically, rent was paid in two installments, one upon agreement and one after harvest. This form of farming required a considerable outlay of capital, but allowed the farmer to enjoy in entirety the fruits of his labor. Cash-leasing was often followed by the outright purchase of farmland.

For further reading, see Yuji Ichioka. *The Issei: The World of the First Generation Japanese Immigrants, 1885–1924.* New York: The Free Press, 1988 and Masakazu Iwata. "The Japanese Immigrants in California Agriculture." *Agricultural History* 36.1 (Jan. 1962): 25–37.

Central Utah Relocation Center   See TOPAZ

Chicago Resettlers Committee   Chicago area social-service organization. As more and more people left the CONCENTRATION CAMPS for RESETTLEMENT inland, Chicago emerged as the city of choice for many ISSEI and NISEI. To help the resettlers adjust to their new homes, the Chicago Resettlers Committee (CRC) was formed in 1945 with Harry Maeda as chairman. Initially, the CRC served as a social-welfare organization, helping newcomers obtain jobs and housing. With the growing stabilization of the community, the CRC switched its emphasis to recreational programs and gradually towards programs geared to the aging *issei* generation. In recognition of these changing priorities, its name changed to the Japanese American Service Committee (JASC) in 1954. As the services became more *issei* oriented, the leadership of the JASC became younger as more and more *nisei* were represented to the board of directors. Into the 1980s, the JASC continued to have the largest network of supporters of any Japanese American organization in Chicago. It continues to sponsor fund-raising events and benefit performances and to provide service to the *issei*. The annual JASC community picnic, once a community-wide event, was held for the last time in 1977.

For further reading, see Michael Daniel Albert. "Japanese American Communities in Chicago and the Twin Cities." Diss., University of Minnesota, 1980.

Chin, Vincent case The racially motivated murder of Chinese American Vincent Chin has come to symbolize the increase in anti-Asian violence in the 1980s and '90s. On June 19, 1982, an argument broke out between Chin, a 27-year-old engineer, and two white males in a suburban Detroit strip joint. The two assailants, Ronald Ebens and Michael Nitz, were laid-off autoworkers who, according to witnesses, shouted numerous racial epithets at Chin, including the line "it's because of you [expletive] we're out of work." After being ejected from the theater, one of the men retrieved a baseball bat from the car and chased Chin around the parking lot. When Chin ran away, the two men got in their car and cruised around the neighborhood searching for him. Finding him in front of a nearby fast-food restaurant, Ebens struck Chin numerous times with the bat in the head, chest and knees while Nitz held him. Chin died four days later.

The two assailants were charged with second degree murder, but were allowed to plead guilty to manslaughter. Wayne County Circuit Court Judge Charles Kaufman sentenced both men to three years' probation and fined them $3,780 each. Asian Americans around the country fearful that one could be killed simply for being Asian American expressed outrage at the lenient sentences, which they felt showed a disregard for the life of an Asian American. Shortly after the sentencing, on May 9, 1983, 500 marched and rallied through the streets of Detroit protesting the decision. Asian American organizations banded together and successfully demanded an investigation into possible civil rights violations by the U.S. Department of Justice. On November 2, 1983, a federal grand jury handed down indictments against the two assailants charging them with violating Chin's civil rights. On June 28, 1984, a U.S. district court jury found Ebens guilty while acquitting Nitz. Ebens was eventually sentenced to 25 years in prison. However, on May 1, 1987, a federal appeals court ordered a new trial for Ebens, citing procedural errors in the first trial. A Cincinnati jury acquitted Ebens, ending the legal process. Ebens ended up serving no time in jail. An acclaimed documentary film, *Who Killed Vincent Chin?*, by Renee Tajima and Christine Choy, was based on this case.

Fueled by the decline in American manufacturing jobs, the perception of Japan as a menacing economic power, racism and scapegoating, cases like Vincent Chin's are becoming distressingly common. Stemming the rise of anti-Asian and anti-Japanese feelings and the violence that often results is one of the main problems facing the Japanese American community today.

[Entry compiled from the following: U.S. Commission on Civil Rights. *Recent Activities Against Citizens and Residents of Asian Descent.* Washington, D.C.: U.S. Commission of Civil Rights, n.d. (1985?). 43–44; numerous articles from Asian American newspapers.]

Chinda, Sutemi (1856–1929) Japanese consul and ambassador to the United States. Chinda, who worked as a senior Japanese diplomat since 1885, held two important appointments in the United States during his career. In 1891, when Chinda first arrived in San Francisco, California, to serve as the Japanese consul, Japanese exclusion agitation in the city had not yet gained momentum. However, Chinda foresaw racist anti-Chinese exclusionists targeting Japanese immigrants as the next group to be excluded from immigrating to the United States. Consequently, he urged Tokyo to carefully select Japanese immigrants and to take precautionary measures to ensure that "undesirables" such as prostitutes and gamblers were prohibited from entering the United States. Chinda believed that preventing such "undesirable" immigrants from entering the United States would keep exclusionists, politicians and the general American public from associating Japanese immigrants with Chinese immigrants, thus hindering Japanese exclusion.

In 1913, as the Japanese ambassador to the United States, Chinda asked President Woodrow Wilson and Secretary of State William Jennings Bryan to pressure the California state government to block the passage of the 1913 (CALIFORNIA) ALIEN LAND LAW. Despite Wilson's efforts to satisfy Chinda's request, the law was passed.

For further reading, see Donald Teruo Hata. *'Undesirables': Early Immigrants and the Anti-Japanese Movement in San Francisco, 1892–1893: Prelude to Exclusion.* New York: Arno Press, 1978 and Roger Daniels. *The Politics of Prejudice: The Anti-Japanese Movement in California and the Struggle for Japanese*

Exclusion. 1962. 2nd edition. Berkeley: University of California Press, 1977.   EIICHIRO AZUMA

[Also used to compile this entry: Hyung-Chan Kim, ed. *Dictionary of Asian American History.* Westport, Conn.: Greenwood Press, 1986.]

Chinese Exclusion Act of 1882   Legislation that banned immigration to the United States from China. Officially entitled "An Act to Execute Certain Treaty Stipulations Relating to Chinese," the Chinese Exclusion Act prohibited the immigration of skilled and unskilled Chinese laborers for 10 years. Under the provisions of this law, Chinese immigrants were denied the right to become naturalized citizens or to have their wives join them in America, and all Chinese residents in America were required to obtain certificates of identity in order to leave and re-enter the country. Enacted on May 6, 1882 (22 U.S. Stat 58), the act became the first congressional law to restrict immigration on the basis of race.

Though the passage of the Exclusion Act represented a high point of America's anti-Chinese movement, racial animosity between white labor leaders and politicians against Chinese immigrants turned to acts of violent and overt discrimination in the decades to come. Chinese Americans were accused of creating unhealthy moral influences and competition for jobs within the social and economic fabric of American society.

Over 14 amendments and laws supplemented the Exclusion Act in the succeeding decades, reflecting the escalation of anti-Chinese sentiment stirring across the nation. Their sole intent was to ensure a comprehensive immigration restriction of Chinese to America. Among those laws pivotal in the anti-Chinese movement were the Scott Act of 1888, which further prohibited immigration by denying the re-entry of Chinese laborers who had returned to China; their certificates of identity ensuring re-entry were also to be nullified. The Geary Act of 1892 was passed to renew the 1882 act for another 10 years, in addition to requiring all Chinese laborers in the United States to secure certificates of residence within one year from the passage of this new act. Finally, "An Act to Prohibit the Coming Into and to Regulate the Residence within the United States, its Territories and All Territory under its Jurisdiction, and the District of Columbia, of Chinese and Persons of Chinese Descent," passed on April 29, 1902, extended indefinitely the provisions of the earlier bills and further established regulatory restrictions on the geographical residency of laborers of Chinese origin.

The Chinese Exclusion Act of 1882 led in part to a greater demand for subsequent Japanese labor migration. The legacy of the anti-Chinese movement also led the Japanese government and Japanese immigrant leaders to emphasize that Japanese Americans were different from the Chinese immigrants who preceded them in an unsuccessful attempt to avert similar agitation against them. In a broader sense, the Chinese Exclusion Act was America's first step towards mounting a national movement leading to the controversial quota legislation of the 1920s. For further reading, see Jack Chen. *The Chinese of America.* San Francisco: Harper & Row, 1980; Roger Daniels. *The Politics of Prejudice: The Anti-Japanese Movement in California and the Struggle for Japanese Exclusion.* 1962. 2nd edition. Berkeley: University of California Press, 1977; Him Mark Lai, Joe Huang, and Don Wong. *The Chinese of America, 1785–1980.* San Francisco: Chinese Culture Foundation, 1980; and William L. Tung. *The Chinese in America, 1820–1973: A Chronology & Fact Book.* Dobbs Ferry, N.Y.: Oceana Publications, 1974.   MARJORIE LEE

"chowhounds"   Nickname given to the 1399th Engineering Construction Battalion during World War II. At the outbreak of the war, many Japanese Americans from Hawaii were already in the armed forces and poised to do their part in the war effort. However, due to the anti-Japanese sentiment of the time, many distrusted the NISEI soldiers and, for the most part, they were not allowed to perform combat duties until well into the war. One such group of *nisei* soldiers was the 370th Engineering Battalion. Made up of both drafted and enlisted men, members of the battalion were anxious to take up arms for their country. However, the army brass saw things differently and assigned them to perform non-combat construction and maintenance tasks at home. Members of the battalion complained of poor treatment by superior officers but persevered in doing their duties. In April 1944, the 370th was combined with recent draftees and two other companies to form the 1399th Engineering Construction Battalion. This group was nicknamed the "chowhounds" for its members' allegedly prodigious appetites. It also became known for its exploits in the boxing ring and the softball field. Several *nisei* men from this battalion later served as replacement members of the 442ND REGIMENTAL COMBAT TEAM. The 1399th was responsible for completing 50 major construction projects on the Hawaiian islands. On October 29, 1945, it was awarded a Meritorious Service plaque for "superior performance and record of accomplishment and exceptional devotion to duty."
For further reading, see Roland Kotani. *The Japanese in Hawaii: A Century of Struggle.* Honolulu: Hochi, Ltd., 1985.

citizenship   Unlike other immigrants to the United States, Japanese and other Asians were not permitted to become naturalized American citizens in the first half of the 20th century. Under existing laws, naturalization was then limited to "free white person(s)" (by the Act of March 26, 1790) and "persons of African nativity or descent" (by the 1870 revision of that act). Dating back to the earliest Japanese immigration, there were many attempts by ISSEI to become naturalized U.S. citizens. Though some were successful in this quest, most were rejected on the grounds that since they were neither "white" nor "African," they were not eligible to become citizens.

Perhaps the earliest attempt at naturalization by an *issei* was made by JOSEPH HECO, who is believed to be the first *issei* to have become a naturalized citizen, in 1858. In 1894, a Japanese immigrant named Saito had his application for citizenship denied at the U.S. district court level on the basis of his being "Mongolian" and hence, neither white nor black. *Issei* veterans of the U.S. military Buntaro Kumagai (1908) and Namiyo Bessho (1910) applied for citizenship, but were rejected on account of their race. However, a group of around 400 *issei* WORLD WAR I VETERANS in Hawaii, along with a few on the mainland, were granted citizenship on the basis of the Act of May 9, 1918, which decreed that "any alien" who had served in World War I was eligible for naturalization. Their citizenship was short lived; the TOYOTA HIDEMITSU V. U.S. decision by the Supreme Court in 1925 determined that even war veterans would be ineligible for citizenship. Many similar attempts to gain citizenship were undertaken by other *issei* all over the country.

Their status as "ALIENS INELIGIBLE TO CITIZENSHIP" provided the pretext for the various anti-Japanese laws, and finding a way around that status became a preoccupation of the Japanese immigrant community. That quest ended with the Supreme Court decision in the OZAWA V. U.S. case of 1922, which cemented the status of *issei* once and for all: they could not be citizens, period. With few exceptions (some *issei* World War I veterans were made eligible for citizenship by the NYE-LEA BILL of 1935), *issei* would not be allowed to become naturalized American citizens until 1952.
See Frank F. Chuman. *The Bamboo People: The Law and Japanese-Americans.* Del Mar, CA: Publisher's Inc., 1976 for an overview of the various naturalization related cases. See the various other entries referred to above for references specific to that topic.

Civil Liberties Act of 1988

Enacted on August 10, 1988, to redress the wrongs committed by the United States government toward Japanese Americans during World War II, the Civil Liberties Act of 1988 called for a formal apology written by the president and $20,000 in compensation to each survivor of America's CONCENTRATION CAMPS. The bill was based on recom-

mendations made by the government-appointed COMMISSION ON WARTIME RELOCATION AND INTERNMENT OF CIVILIANS. (See REDRESS MOVEMENT.)

GLEN KITAYAMA

Collins, Wayne Mortimer (1900–1974)

Attorney. Born in 1900 in Sacramento and educated in San Francisco, Collins is best remembered as an ardent fighter for Japanese American civil rights. Described by those who knew him with adjectives like "fiery," "angry," and "volatile," Collins pursued justice for those he felt had been wronged with great passion. In addition to representing Fred Korematsu in a landmark case that tested the constitutionality of the mass removal and detention of Japanese Americans (see KOREMATSU V. UNITED STATES), Collins also represented such unpopular defendants as accused "Tokyo Rose" IVA IKUKO TOGURI D'AQUINO, those who renounced their citizenship at strife-torn TULE LAKE "SEGREGATION CENTER" and JAPANESE PERUVIANS kidnapped from their country for internment in the U.S. and prohibited from returning to Peru.

Though best known for his work in the Korematsu and Toguri cases, perhaps more personally satisfying to Collins was his work with the internees at Tule Lake "Segregation Center." In 1944, Collins was instrumental in closing the STOCKADE at the camp, which was not only used to house the so-called "troublemakers," but was also a tool of suppression for those interned at Tule Lake. The stockade served as a constant reminder of the consequences to be paid if orders were not obeyed.

Collins also worked with the renunciants in the camp (see RENUNCIATION OF CITIZENSHIP). After hearing their case in July of 1945, he decided to represent them to prevent their deportation to Japan. Although the National ACLU objected and disagreed with Collins's stand, he was convinced that these NISEI were coerced into renouncing their citizenship for several reasons: 1) a small clique of Japanese nationalists were terrorizing those who did not renounce their citizenship; 2) the government knew of these terrorists and not only did nothing about it, but actually aided them; and 3) the government, through its "inhuman" treatment of the internees, brought about extreme duress which was responsible for such behavior. Collins fought this case for 14 years until the rights of citizenship were restored to 4,978 *nisei*.

After the war, Collins intervened on behalf of 365 JAPANESE PERUVIANS who were scheduled to be deported to war-torn Japan. These Peruvian citizens, all ot whom were extradited to the United States for incarceration in Justice Department–administered INTERNMENT CAMPS, were denied re-entry into their own country and were not allowed to stay in the U.S. since they were not American citizens. On June 25, 1946, Collins obtained a court order to halt their departure. Eventually, 300 ended up staying in the United States, many of them becoming naturalized citizens following the passage of the MACCARRAN-WALTER ACT OF 1952. Though Peru allowed their re-entry in the mid-1950s, fewer than 100 decided to go back.

To the very end, Wayne Collins never gave up fighting for what he believed in. He won many battles but did not live to see the final vindication of two of his most famous clients: Fred Korematsu (see CORAM NOBIS CASES) and Iva Ikuko Toguri D'Aquino. Historian Richard Drinnon writes that Collins "a wiry, tense Irish-American, . . . made the courtroom his arena for battle after battle to make the Bill of Rights apply to everybody—communists, Nazis, nonwhites, everybody—and apply in wartime as well as in peacetime." Wayne Collins died at the age of 74 on July 16, 1974, aboard an airplane en route to Honolulu.

See Peter Irons. *Justice at War: The Story of the Japanese American Internment Cases.* New York: Oxford University Press, 1983 for Collins's role in the Korematsu case; Clifford I. Uyeda. *A Final Report and Review: The Japanese American Citizens League, National Committee for Iva Toguri.* Seattle: Asian American Studies Program, University of Washington, 1980 for his role in the Toguri case; Donald E. Collins. *Native American Aliens: Disloyalty and the Renunciation of Citizenship by Japanese Americans During World War II.* Westport, Conn.: Greenwood Press, 1985 and Richard Drinnon. *Keeper of Concentration Camps: Dillon S. Myer and American Racism.* Berkeley: University of California Press, 1987 for his role in the various Tule Lake actions; and C. Harvey Gardiner. *Pawns in a Triangle of Hate: The Peruvian Japanese and the United States.* Seattle: University of Washington Press, 1981 for his role in the Japanese Peruvian cases. See also Michi Weglyn. *Years of Infamy: The Untold Story of America's Concentration Camps.* New York: William Morrow & Co., 1976.

GLEN KITAYAMA

[Also used to compile this entry: "JACL director eulogizes defender of Japanese Americans during WW2." *Pacific Citizen* 9 Aug. 1974.]

Colorado River Relocation Center   See POSTON.

Commission on Wartime Relocation and Internment of Civilians

A congressional commission charged with studying the mass removal and incarceration of Japanese Americans during World War II and recommending an appropriate remedy. The Commission on Wartime Relocation and Internment of Civilians (CWRIC) was born on July 31, 1980, with President Jimmy Carter's signing of Public Law 96-317. The CWRIC actually had its beginnings in 1979 when the

JAPANESE AMERICAN CITIZENS LEAGUE decided to act on its goal of seeking redress and pushed for the formation of the committee. This strategy angered some members of the JACL's NATIONAL COMMITTEE FOR REDRESS; in May 1979, some of them split from the JACL to form the NATIONAL COUNCIL FOR JAPANESE AMERICAN REDRESS, a group that tried to get through Congress a bill seeking direct reparations rather than one seeking a study commission.

The commission was chaired by Washington, D.C., lawyer Joan Z. Bernstein and included among its members Long Beach, California, congressman Daniel E. Lungren, former U.S. senator Edward Brooke, Massachusetts congressman Robert Drinan, Arthur S. Flemming, former Supreme Court justice Arthur J. Goldberg, Ishmael V. Gromoff, Philadelphia judge William Marutani and Hugh B. Mitchell.

As part of its research, the CWRIC held hearings beginning in 1981 in several cities across the country. In each city, Japanese Americans testified about their experiences in the CONCENTRATION CAMPS; many talked about these experiences for the first time. After 18 months of research, the CWRIC issued its report on February 22, 1983, published under the title *Personal Justice Denied.* In its final recommendations to Congress on June 16, 1983, the CWRIC issued a formal recommendation calling for individual payments to victims of the camps of $20,000. Five years later, a bill implementing these recommendations for the most part was signed by President Reagan. (See REDRESS MOVEMENT.)

For further reading, see "The Commission." *Bridge* 7.4 (1980): 28; Peter Irons, ed. *Justice Delayed: The Record of the Japanese American Internment Cases.* Middletown, Conn.: Wesleyan University Press, 1989; and John Tateishi. "The Japanese American Citizens League and the Struggle for Redress." In Daniels, Roger, Sandra C. Taylor, and Harry H. L. Kitano, eds. *Japanese Americans: From Relocation to Redress.* Salt Lake City: University of Utah Press, 1986. Revised edition. Seattle: University of Washington Press, 1991. 191–95.

GLEN KITAYAMA

Committee Against Nihonmachi Evictions
1970s organization formed to protest the evictions of elderly Japanese Americans in San Francisco NIHONMACHI (Japan Town) taking place in the name of REDEVELOPMENT.

concentration camps
Euphemistically called "relocation centers" by the WAR RELOCATION AUTHORITY (WRA), the concentration camps were hastily constructed facilities for housing Japanese Americans forcibly removed from their homes and businesses on the West Coast during World War II. Located in isolated areas of the United States on either desert or swampland,

the camps were usually surrounded by barbed wire and guarded by armed sentries. Although the sentries were presumably in place to protect the inmates from hostile outsiders, their guns usually pointed into the camps instead of out of them. Most inmates were transported to their camp by train from an "ASSEMBLY CENTER" between April and September 1942. In all, over 120,000 Japanese Americans served time in these camps.

Conditions in the camps and the experiences of the Japanese American inmates varied greatly. The WRA attempted to create camp communities that resembled normal communities to the greatest extent possible. Thus, each of the 10 camps had schools and hospitals, a newspaper, some degree of democratic self-government and such leisure activities as baseball leagues and movie showings. At the same time, however, life was anything but normal. Japanese American family dynamics were dramatically altered as ISSEI parents saw their authority ebb away with the newfound freedom granted the NISEI. There were several incidents involving guards shooting inmates, including the killing of an elderly *issei* (see JAMES HATSUKI WAKASA). There was also the exacerbation of existing conflicts within the Japanese American community brought about by the forced confinement. Such tensions, coupled with the choices made by WRA officials administering the camps, led to a great deal of conflict within the camps and to explosions such as the MANZANAR INCIDENT and the POSTON STRIKE. In part because of these violent incidents, WRA officials decided to remove the "troublemakers" from each camp, segregating them at one camp. The segregation process, involving a questionnaire with poorly phrased LOYALTY QUESTIONS, led to yet more turmoil.

Once the "loyal" and "disloyal" had been identified, the WRA began to encourage the RESETTLEMENT of the "loyal" outside the barbed wire in inland cities like Chicago or Denver and many *nisei* students were attending college by the end of 1943. However, many of the *issei* were unwilling to leave, fearing the uncertainty of the outside; many stayed in the camps until well after the war was over and had to be evicted as the camps closed. Worse was the treatment of the "disloyal" isolated at TULE LAKE "SEGREGATION CENTER" or at the WRA prisons (see LEUPP). Conditions at Tule Lake led to the tragic RENUNCIATION OF CITIZENSHIP by 5,589 native-born American citizens.

Allowed to return to the West Coast beginning in 1945, Japanese Americans began the long process of rebuilding their lives and communities. Arguably, that process would not be complete for another 45 years, with the culmination of the REDRESS MOVEMENT, a 1970s and '80s drive for reparations and an apology from the U.S. government for the treatment accorded Japanese Americans during World War II.

Each of the ten concentration camps has its own entry in this book. They are: TOPAZ (central Utah), POSTON (Colorado River) and GILA RIVER (Rivers) in Arizona, GRANADA (Amache) in Colorado, HEART MOUNTAIN in Wyoming, JEROME (Denson) and ROHWER in Arkansas, MANZANAR and TULE LAKE (Newell) in California, and MINIDOKA (Hunt) in Idaho.

The literature on the Japanese American concentration camp experience is extensive; the works mentioned below are a representative sample that includes the most widely read works. There are many, many other works available on this topic, however.

Among those works which give a general overview of the concentration camp experience are Allan R. Bosworth. *America's Concentration Camps.* New York: W. W. Norton, 1967; Commission on Wartime Relocation and Internment of Civilians. *Personal Justice Denied: Report of the Commission on Wartime Relocation and Internment of Civilians.* Washington, D.C.: Government Printing Office, 1982; Roger Daniels. *Concentration Camps, U.S.A.: Japanese Americans and World War II.* New York: Holt, Rinehart and Winston, 1971; Roger Daniels, Sandra C. Taylor, and Harry H. L. Kitano, eds. *Japanese Americans: From Relocation to Redress.* Salt Lake City: University of Utah Press, 1986. Revised edition. Seattle: University of Washington Press, 1991; Audrie Girdner, and Anne Loftis. *The Great Betrayal: The Evacuation of the Japanese-Americans during World War II.* Toronto: Macmillan, 1969; and Michi Weglyn. *Years of Infamy: The Untold Story of America's Concentration Camps.* New York: William Morrow & Co., 1976.

Several broader works also contain substantial and valuable overviews of the camp experience. These include Sucheng Chan. *Asian Americans: An Interpretive History.* Boston: Twayne Publishers, 1991; Roger Daniels. *Asian America: Chinese and Japanese in the United States since 1850.* Seattle: University of Washington Press, 1988; Bill Hosokawa. *Nisei: The Quiet Americans.* New York: William Morrow & Co., 1969; and Ronald Takaki. *Strangers from a Different Shore: A History of Asian Americans.* Boston: Little, Brown and Company, 1989.

Many works on the camps focus what was done to the Japanese Americans, typically falling into one of two categories. The first includes works which look at how the decision was made to first remove the Japanese Americans en masse, then to house them in concentration camps. These works include Stetson Conn, Rose C. Engleman, and Byron Fairchild. *Guarding the United States and Its Outposts.* Washington, D.C.: U.S. Department of the Army, Office of the Chief of Military History, 1964; Roger Daniels. *The Decision to Relocate the Japanese Americans.* Philadelphia: Lippincott, 1975; Morton Grodzins. *Americans Betrayed: Politics and the Japanese Evacuation.* Chicago: University of Chicago Press, 1949; Gary Y. Okihiro, and Julie Sly. "The Press, Japanese Americans, and the Concentration Camps." *Phylon* 44.1 (Mar. 1983): 66–83; and Jacobus tenBroek, Edward N. Barnhart, and Floyd Matson. *Prejudice, War, and the Constitution.* Berkeley: University of California Press, 1954. The second category includes works which analyze how the camps were administered. These include Rita Takahashi Cates. "Comparative Administration and Management of Five War Relocation Authority Camps: America's

Incarceration of Persons of Japanese Descent during World War II." Diss., University of Pittsburgh, 1980; Richard Drinnon. *Keeper of Concentration Camps: Dillon S. Myer and American Racism.* Berkeley: University of California Press, 1987; Robert Alan Mossman. "Japanese-American War Relocation Centers as Total Institutions with Emphasis on the Educational Programs." Diss., Rutgers University, 1978; Michael John Wallinger. "Dispersal of the Japanese Americans: Rhetorical Strategies of the War Relocation Authority, 1942–1945." Diss., University of Oregon, 1975; and Toshio Yatsushiro. *Politics and Cultural Values: The World War II Japanese Relocation Centers and the United States Government.* New York: Arno Press, 1978.

Many works look at various aspects of camp life. Among those which look at educational programs in camp are Lane Ryo Hirabayashi. "The Impact of Incarceration on the Education of Nisei Schoolchildren." In Daniels, Roger, Sandra C. Taylor, and Harry H. L. Kitano, ed. *Japanese Americans: From Relocation to Redress.* Salt Lake City: University of Utah Press, 1986. Revised edition. Seattle: University of Washington Press, 1991. 44–51 and Thomas James. *Exile Within: The Schooling of Japanese Americans, 1942–1945.* Cambridge: Harvard University Press, 1987. Works on camp journalism include Lauren Kessler. "Fettered Freedoms: The Journalism of World War II Japanese Internment Camps." *Journalism History* 15.2–3 (1988): 60–69 and John D. Stevens. "From Behind Barbed Wire: Freedom of the Press in WWII Japanese Centers." *Journalism Quarterly* 48 (1971): 279–87. Studies of family life in camp include Leonard Broom [Leonard Bloom], and John I. Kitsuse. *The Managed Casualty: The Japanese-American Family in World War II.* Berkeley: University of California Press, 1956; James K. Morishima "The Evacuation: Impact on the Family." In Sue, Stanley, and Nathaniel N. Wagner, eds. *Asian-Americans: Psychological Perspectives.* Palo Alto, CA: Science and Behavior Books, Inc., 1973. 13–19. Works which focus on women in the camps include Valerie J. Matsumoto "Japanese American Women during World War II." *Frontiers* 8.1 (1984): 6–14 and Mei Nakano. *Japanese American Women: Three Generations, 1890–1990.* Berkeley and Sebastopol, CA: National Japanese American Historical Society and Mina Press, 1990. Among the works documenting the camp experience in photographs are John Armor and Peter Wright. *Manzanar.* Commentary by John Hersey. New York: Times Books, 1988 and Maisie Conrat, and Richard Conrat. *Executive Order 9066: The Internment of 110,000 Japanese Americans.* Cambridge, Mass.: Massachusetts Institute of Technology Press, 1972. Los Angeles: UCLA Asian American Studies Center, 1992.

Many works focus on what might broadly be called resistance in the camps. Such works include studies of uprisings and strikes, draft resistance, "No-No Boys" and renunciation of citizenship. These works include Donald E. Collins. *Native American Aliens: Disloyalty and the Renunciation of Citizenship by Japanese Americans During World War II.* Westport, Conn.: Greenwood Press, 1985; Frank Seishi Emi. "Draft Resistance at the Heart Mountain Concentration Camp and the Fair Play Committee." In Nomura, Gail M., Russell Endo, Stephen H. Sumida, and Russell C. Leong, eds. *Frontiers of Asian American Studies: Writing, Research, and Commentary.* Pullman: Wash-

ington State University Press, 1989. 41–69; Morton Grodzins. "Making Un-Americans." *American Journal of Sociology* 60.6 (May 1955): 570–82; Arthur A. Hansen. "James Matsumoto Omura: An Interview." *Amerasia Journal* 13.2 (1986–87): 99–113; Arthur A. Hansen, and David A. Hacker. "The Manzanar Riot: An Ethnic Perspective." *Amerasia Journal* 2.2 (1974): 112–57; Norman Richard Jackman. "Collective Protest in Relocation Centers." Diss., University of California, Berkeley, 1955; Gary Y. Okihiro "Japanese Resistance in America's Concentration Camps: A Re-evaluation." *Amerasia Journal* 2.1 (1973): 20–34; "Tule Lake under Martial Law: A Study of Japanese Resistance." *Journal of Ethnic Studies* 5.3 (Fall 1977): 71–86; and "Religion and Resistance in America's Concentration Camps." *Phylon* 45 (September 1985): 220–33; James Omura. "Japanese American Journalism During World War II." In Nomura, Gail M., Russell Endo, Stephen H. Sumida, and Russell C. Leong, eds. *Frontiers of Asian American Studies: Writing, Research, and Commentary.* Pullman: Washington State University Press, 1989. 71–80; and Dorothy S. Thomas and Richard Nishimoto. *The Spoilage.* Berkeley: University of California Press, 1946, 1969.

Literary and/or artistic works set in or about the camps include Allen Hendershott Eaton. *Beauty Behind Barbed Wire: The Arts of the Japanese in Our War Relocation Camps.* New York: Harper, 1952; Deborah Gesensway and Mindy Roseman. *Beyond Words: Images from America's Concentration Camps.* Ithaca, N.Y.: Cornell University Press, 1987; Estelle Peck Ishigo. *Lone Heart Mountain.* Los Angeles: Anderson, Ritchie & Simon, 1972; Edward Miyakawa. *Tule Lake.* Waldport, Oreg.: House By the Sea Publishing Company, 1979; John Okada. *No-No Boy.* Rutland, Vt.: Charles E. Tuttle, 1957. San Francisco: Combined Asian American Resources Project, Inc., 1976. Introd. Lawson Fusao Inada. Afterword by Frank Chin. Seattle: University of Washington Press, 1979; Mine Okubo. *Citizen 13660.* New York: Columbia University Press, 1946. New York: Arno Press 1978. Seattle: University of Washington Press, 1983; Georgia Day Robertson. *The Harvest of Hate.* 1946. Introd. Arthur A. Hansen. Forewords by Moto Asakawa and Hiroshi Kamei. Fullerton: Oral History Program, California State University, Fullerton, 1986; Vincent Tajiri, ed. *Through Innocent Eyes: Writings and Art from the Japanese American Internment by Poston I Schoolchildren.* Los Angeles: Keiro Services Press and the Generation Fund, 1990; and *The View from Within: Japanese American Art from the Internment Camps 1942–1945.* Los Angeles: Japanese American National Museum, UCLA Wight Art Gallery and UCLA Asian American Studies Center, 1992.

Finally, there are the many first person recollections of life in camp. These include Roger W. Axford *Too Long Silent: Japanese Americans Speak Out.* New York: Media Publishing and Marketing, Inc., 1986; "The Commission on Wartime Relocation and Internment of Civilians—Selected Testimonies from the Los Angeles and San Francisco Hearings." *Amerasia Journal* 8.2 (1981): 53–105; Eileen Sunada Sarasohn. *The Issei: Portrait of a Pioneer: An Oral History.* Palo Alto, Calif.: Pacific Books, 1983; John Tateishi. *And Justice For All: An Oral History of the Japanese American Detention Camps.* New York: Random House, 1984; and Yoshiko Uchida. *Desert*

Exile: The Uprooting of a Japanese American Family. Seattle: University of Washington Press, 1982.

Citations for many other works that focus on a specific camp or a specific camp-related topic can be found with the entry for that camp or topic.

contract farming   Immigrant Japanese laborers usually passed four stages on their way to acquiring land. The first step from migrant labor was contract farming—the cultivation of land under contract for a set wage. For crops that required large-scale, short-term labor, such as sugar beets, beans or potatoes, contract farming was common. Often, the contract farmer would act as a small-scale labor contractor, hiring and supervising other Japanese laborers. Because it required no capital and was a way out of the ranks of labor, it was popular with Japanese seeking to become farmers. Contract farming often led to SHARE-TENANCY, CASH-LEASING and, finally, outright ownership.

For further reading, see Yuji Ichioka. *The Issei: The World of the First Generation Japanese Immigrants, 1885–1924.* New York: The Free Press, 1988.

coram nobis cases   Popular term used to refer to the reopening of the cases Fred KOREMATSU V. UNITED STATES, Gordon HIRABAYASHI V. UNITED STATES and Min YASUI V. UNITED STATES. *Coram nobis* or ("error before us") refers to the "writ of error coram nobis" that was filed on behalf of Korematsu, Hirabayashi and Yasui. (See following entry.)

In 1981, law historian Peter Irons was doing research for a book on the lawyers who participated in the four famous wartime cases (*Endo v. United States* being the fourth; see ENDO, EX PARTE). While examining archival documents "in dusty cardboard boxes," he discovered complaints from government lawyers dated in 1943 and 1944 that evidence had been suppressed by their superiors in the cases of Korematsu, Hirabayashi and Yasui. In addition, the lawyers charged their superiors had "lied" to the Supreme Court in all three cases. The complaints were ignored. With this newfound evidence, Irons felt that Korematsu et al. had a chance to have their convictions overturned using the obscure writ of error *coram nobis*. Irons contacted them and all three enthusiastically agreed to take up the fight. Fred Korematsu summed it up for Irons perfectly: "They did me a great wrong."

During this time, unknown to Irons, the CWRIC hearings were taking place across the country. The necessary groundswell of support for redress for the wartime mass removal and detention among Japanese Americans was just the push that was needed to start the *coram nobis* cases. On the advice of Min Yasui, Irons proceeded to contact San Francisco attorney Dale Minami, a SANSEI

who was an active member of the Bay Area Attorneys for Redress (BAAR). Since Irons felt that it was necessary to file the petitions in the same cities in which they were originally tried (Korematsu in San Francisco, Hirabayashi in Seattle and Yasui in Portland), Minami was a smart choice to head up the legal team in the Bay Area. Peggy Nagae and Katherine Bannai were chosen for the same duties in Portland and Seattle respectively.

In January of 1983, Korematsu's, Hirabayashi's and Yasui's petitions for writ of error *coram nobis* were filed in the respective U.S. district courts. Phase one was finished. Now the *coram nobis* lawyers needed to hear the government response. Knowing that hardliners such as JOHN J. MCCLOY and KARL BENDETSEN, architect of the mass removal, were still influential in government, it was logical to assume that the response would be to defend the decisions that were made during the war. This was not the case, however. On June 16, 1983, the CWRIC issued its recommendations for REDRESS AND REPARATIONS and proposed that the president issue a pardon to the three petitioners. Following the CWRIC's lead, the lawyers representing the government attempted to negotiate a pardon as an out of court settlement. It was met with a firm rejection. Korematsu emphatically told Dale Minami: "We should be the one pardoning the government."

Fred Korematsu's case was the first to be heard. On October 4, 1983, the government filed its official response. Among other things, they asked Judge Patel to vacate Korematsu's conviction and dismiss the petition. Their argument was that "it would not be appropriate to defend this forty year old misdemeanor conviction." Patel denied the government's motion and later issued her opinion. She cited the CWRIC report and documents presented to her as justification for her reasoning. She also labeled the government response as "tantamount to a confession of error." The judge reminded listeners that she could not reverse the opinions of the Supreme Court and could not correct any errors of law made by the justices. With that in mind, she granted the petition for writ of error *coram nobis,* thus effectively vacating Korematsu's 1944 conviction.

On January 16, 1984, Min Yasui became the second of the three to receive his day in court. Once again, the government asked the court to vacate Yasui's conviction and dismiss the petition. Peggy Nagae and Don Willner, attorneys for Yasui, responded by informing the judge of the damage done to the Japanese American community by the internment and of the need for a judicial response. Ten days later, on January 26, 1984, the judge granted the government's motion to vacate the conviction and dismiss the petition. According to the judge, "the only difference [in the two requests] is that the petitioner asks me to make findings of governmental acts of misconduct that deprived him of his Fifth Amendment rights . . . I decline to make such findings forty years after the events took place. . . . Courts should not engage in that kind of activity." Min Yasui appealed, but passed away before a decision could be made on his request. Once he died, his case died with him.

On May 18, 1984, Gordon Hirabayashi became the last of the three to receive a hearing on his case. One month prior to the hearing, Judge Patel had issued her written opinion on the *Korematsu* case—giving Judge Voorhees, the judge in Hirabayashi's case, just enough time to examine its contents. The government, knowing that Judge Patel's opinion could sway Judge Voorhees, argued that Judge Belloni's verdict in dismissing Yasui's petition was the proper decision. In a twist of strategy, however, the government lawyers insisted that Hirabayashi filed his petition too late because most of the information disputing the "military necessity" claim had been available since the late 1940s. The government lawyers also noted to the judge that the exact same arguments that were heard by the Supreme Court in 1943 were being repeated in 1984. Thus, they argued, the petition should be denied. Judge Voorhees denied the government motion to dismiss the petition and scheduled a full-scale evidentiary hearing for June 17, 1985. Before that date was to arrive, however, the government lawyers attempted several postponements in order to delay the case (the same tactic used in the Yasui case). In addition, they made it clear that they were going to introduce "expert" testimony regarding the "MAGIC" CABLES—intelligence codes that supposedly exposed "massive espionage nets in the West Coast." With pending redress legislation in Congress and the NCJAR class action lawsuit in the courts, the government showed that they were committed to winning this case to slow the momentum of the REDRESS MOVEMENT.

After the hearing, which lasted two weeks, the judge decided to delay his opinion until both sides presented their post-trial briefs, which included summaries of evidence, testimony and legal issues. On February 10, 1986, the judge issued his written opinion. He decided that John J. McCloy's act of withholding JOHN L. DEWITT's original report on the mass removal constituted "an error of the most fundamental character" and required that Hirabayashi's *evacuation* conviction be vacated. Judge Voorhees declined to vacate Hirabayashi's curfew order conviction on the basis that misconduct on the part of the government did not influence that decision. Both sides were unhappy with his opinion and appeals were filed.

On September 24, 1987, Judge Schroeder of the Ninth Circuit Court of Appeals issued her opinion. She ruled that "racial bias was the cornerstone of the internment orders" and that the government "argued a single theory of military necessity" to support both the evacuation and curfew order convictions. Judge Voorhees's ruling on the curfew order conviction was reversed and the case was sent back to him with orders to vacate both convictions. The government showed its dedication to winning the case by petitioning the Ninth Circuit panel to rehear the case. It was rejected on December 24, 1987. On January 12, 1988, Hirabayashi's wartime curfew order conviction was vacated.

For further reading, see Peter Irons. *Justice at War: The Story of the Japanese American Internment Cases*. New York: Oxford University Press, 1983; Peter Irons, ed. *Justice Delayed: The Record of the Japanese American Internment Cases*. Middletown, Conn.: Wesleyan University Press, 1989; and Dale Minami. "Coram Nobis and Redress." In Daniels, Roger, Sandra C. Taylor, and Harry H. L. Kitano, eds. *Japanese Americans: From Relocation to Redress*. Salt Lake City: University of Utah Press, 1986. Revised edition. Seattle: University of Washington Press, 1991. 200–02.   GLEN KITAYAMA

[All quotes are from the introductory essay to *Justice Delayed*.]

coram nobis, writ of error   Little known and seldom used legal procedure used by attorneys for Fred Korematsu, Min Yasui and Gordon Hirabayashi to overturn their wartime convictions. From the Latin words meaning "error before us," the writ of error *coram nobis* can be invoked only after a defendant has been convicted and released from custody and only to raise errors of fact that were knowingly withheld by the prosecution from the judge and the defense.

For further reading, see Peter Irons, ed. *Justice Delayed: The Record of the Japanese American Internment Cases*. Middletown, Conn.: Wesleyan University Press, 1989 and Dale Minami. "Coram Nobis and Redress." In Daniels, Roger, Sandra C. Taylor, and Harry H. L. Kitano, eds. *Japanese Americans: From Relocation to Redress*. Salt Lake City: University of Utah Press, 1986. Revised edition. Seattle: University of Washington Press, 1991. 200–02.   GLEN KITAYAMA

Cortez colony   Japanese American farming colony. Cortez Colony began in 1919 as the third of KYUTARO ABIKO's Japanese Christian farming colonies, located near Livingston, California. Initially, Cortez faced the difficulty of establishing a farming community on largely inhospitable land and amidst inhospitable people. Upon successfully farming the area and establishing cordial relations with the surrounding community, the Great Depression hit. To attain financial solvency, the Cortez Growers Association was formed, which enabled Cortez farmers to cooperatively purchase supplies and market their produce. The cohesion of the Cortez community was also bulwarked by a network of social and cultural organizations based on churches and schools. With the coming of World War II and in anticipation of mass removal, Cortez farmers, in cooperation with farmers from the other Abiko colonies, formed a corporation and hired a white manager to run their farms for them. Because of this arrangement, perhaps the only one of its kind, the community was largely able to return to its original site after the war. The postwar era has seen the usual changes in the community, with the rise of NISEI influence, the aging of the ISSEI and the exodus of the SANSEI to the cities. Additionally, changes in the farming business led to such changes in Cortez as larger farms and more non-Japanese American partners in the Growers Association.

For further reading, see Valerie J. Matsumoto. *Farming the Home Place: A Japanese American Community in California, 1919–1982*. Ithaca, New York: Cornell University Press, 1993.

cropping contracts Legal means that ISSEI farmers used to get around the ban on leasing agricultural land brought on by the 1920 (CALIFORNIA) ALIEN LAND LAW. In an attempt to drive Japanese American farmers completely out of agriculture except in the role of laborers, the 1920 Alien Land Law included a ban on Japanese leasing agricultural land as well as purchasing it. One way for *issei* to lease farmland was to obtain a cropping contract. After finding a white landowner willing to cooperate, the *issei* farmer would sign an agreement whereby he would be "hired" by the landowner to "manage" a farm. The landowner would receive the profits from the crops and would pay the *issei* farmer either a fixed rate or some percentage of that profit. The cropping contract approximated the conditions of a lease in a way the law allowed. Cropping contracts were suddenly declared illegal in July 1921. The legality of cropping contracts was eventually tested in court in the WEBB V. O'BRIEN case. After a lower court ruled that cropping contracts were legal, the Supreme Court overturned that decision in November 1923, definitively ruling them in violation of the 1920 Alien Land Law.

For further reading, see Yuji Ichioka. "Japanese Immigrant Response to the 1920 California Alien Land Law." *Agricultural History* 58.2 (Apr. 1984): 157–78 and *The Issei: The World of the First Generation Japanese Immigrants, 1885–1924*. New York: The Free Press, 1988.

Crystal City Justice Department–administered INTERNMENT CAMP in Texas. Crystal City became known as the "family camp" where ISSEI "enemy aliens" and their families were interned during World War II. With a peak population of over 4,000—including German and Italian internees as well as Japanese Americans—Crystal City was one of the largest of the internment camps.

Within days of the attack on Pearl Harbor, the FBI and other authorities rounded up some 3,000 *issei* in both Hawaii and on the mainland who were judged to be security risks. For the most part, those picked up were the men who were the leaders of the Japanese American community—Buddhist priests, JAPANESE-LANGUAGE SCHOOL teachers, JAPANESE ASSOCIATION officials, etc.— whose only crime was their perceived influence in the community. They were eventually taken to mainland camps administered by the Justice Department where most spent the duration of the war. In November 1942, the Justice Department decided to build a "family camp" to house the men whose families opted to join them in their internment. This camp became Crystal City, built on what had been a housing camp for migrant agricultural laborers in Zavala County in southern Texas.

At its peak, the camp housed nearly 3,000 Japanese Americans, along with 1,000 German Americans and a few Italian Americans. In general, conditions were better here than in the WAR RELOCATION AUTHORITY camps. Unlike the WRA camps, Crystal City residents had individual family units with private kitchen and bathroom facilities. The schools were good and included an "American"-style high school along with "Japanese" and "German" schools for children whose parents planned to return to their native countries. There were newspapers published in English, Japanese and Spanish (the latter by and for the JAPANESE PERUVIANS detained here) and active sports and recreation programs. There was also a swimming pool from which internees could escape the 100-plus degree heat.

For the most part Crystal City residents left the camps after the conclusion of the war to go to Japan or to return to their prewar homes in Hawaii or on the West Coast. Many of those left in the camp after 1945 were the cruelly treated Japanese Peruvians who did not want to return to Japan, were not allowed to stay in America and not allowed to return to Peru. Stuck in limbo, some remained in Crystal City until late 1947. Many who were allowed to leave went to SEABROOK FARMS in New Jersey to take the place of earlier Japanese American workers who were leaving to return to the West Coast. The camp closed in December 1947.

For further reading, see Paul Frederick Clark. "Those Other Camps: An Oral History Analysis of Japanese Alien Enemy Internment during World War II." Thesis, California State University, Fullerton, 1980 and Thomas K. Walls. *The Japanese Texans*. San Antonio: Institute of Texan Cultures, 1987.

D

Daihyo Sha Kai TULE LAKE "SEGREGATION CENTER" internee organization. Literally meaning "representative body," the Daihyo Sha Kai were a group of leaders at Tule Lake who organized around the camp's terrible living conditions. The organization was made up of one representative from each of the 64 residential blocks, seven of whom were chosen to be part of the negotiating committee. Later the negotiating committee was informally augmented to include as many as 10 others at some meetings. The refusal of camp administrators to work with this group led to a good deal of the unrest that plagued the camp later. (See STOCKADE.)

Daniels, Roger (1927–) Pioneering scholar on the history of Japanese Americans. Born in New York City, Daniels served in the merchant marine during World War II and in the army during the Korean War. After doing undergraduate work at the University of Houston, he received M.A. (1958) and Ph.D. (1961) degrees in history from UCLA. He has taught at many universities and has been a professor of history at the University of Cincinnati since 1976.

He has written extensively on Japanese Americans, beginning with his doctoral dissertation, *The Politics of Prejudice,* which focused on the ANTI-JAPANESE MOVEMENT. He has also written on various aspects of the Japanese American World War II experience, along with studies of Japanese Canadian history, Chinese American history and American immigration history.

Daniels's major works on Japanese Americans include the following: *The Politics of Prejudice: The Anti-Japanese Movement in California and the Struggle for Japanese Exclusion.* 1962. 2nd edition. Berkeley: University of California Press, 1977; *Concentration Camps, U.S.A.: Japanese Americans and World War II.* New York: Holt, Rinehart and Winston, 1971; *The Decision to Relocate the Japanese Americans.* Philadelphia: Lippincott, 1975; *Concentration Camps, North America: Japanese in the United States and Canada during World War II.* Malabar, Fla.: Robert E. Krieger Publishing Co., 1981; and *Asian America: Chinese and Japanese in the United States since 1850.* Seattle: University of Washington Press, 1988. He served as co-editor with Sandra C. Taylor and Harry H. L. Kitano of the anthology *Japanese Americans: From Relocation to Redress.* Salt Lake City: University of Utah Press, 1986. Revised edition. Seattle: University of Washington Press, 1991. He also compiled and edited a nine-volume collection of documents on the World War II experience titled *American Concentration Camps: A Documentary History of the Relocation and Incarceration of Japanese Americans, 1942–1945.* Nine Volumes. New York: Garland Publishing, 1989 and edited the 47-volume series of reprints of works on Chinese and Japanese Americans titled "The Asian Experience in North America: Chinese and Japanese" for the Arno Press in 1978. Daniels also co-authored two works with Harry H. L. Kitano which deal in part with Japanese Americans, *American Racism: Exploration of the Nature of Prejudice.* Englewood Cliffs, N.J.: Prentice-Hall, 1970 and *Asian Americans: Emerging Minorities.* Englewood Cliffs, N.J.: Prentice Hall, 1988. He has also published numerous academic journal articles on Japanese Americans.

d'Aquino, Iva Ikuko Toguri (1916–) NISEI accused of being the legendary "Tokyo Rose." Like many

Japanese Americans caught in Japan during World War II and unable to return, Iva Toguri was forced to serve the Japanese government. Upon her return to America, she was tried and convicted of treason and imprisoned. A movement started on her behalf many years later resulted in her being pardoned by President Gerald Ford.

Iva Toguri was born in Los Angeles on July 4, 1916. In June 1941, Toguri's mother learned that her sister in Japan was ill. When her mother was unable to go to Japan, Toguri was sent in her mother's place, leaving the United States on July 5, 1941, with a "Certificate of Identification to Facilitate Return to The United States of America" rather than a United States passport. The certificate allowed her a temporary six-month stay in Japan, during which time Toguri went to the U.S. consulate in Tokyo to apply for a passport. Toguri attempted to return to the United States in October 1941, before the war between the United States and Japan began. However, she could not get clearance to leave Japan because she did not have an American passport. Her application had been denied because, according to the United States consulate in Tokyo, her United States citizenship could not be proven. Without a passport Toguri was refused passage back to the United States on the first repatriation ship after the outbreak of the war. She was unable to leave on the second repatriation ship in September 1942 because she was unable to pay the passage after being hospitalized earlier for malnutrition. As a result, Toguri remained in Japan for the duration of the war.

Although she was harassed by Japanese Security Police officers and advised to change her American citizenship to Japanese citizenship to ensure better treatment while she resided in Japan, Toguri refused to give up her citizenship. In August 1943 Toguri began working as a part-time typist for the Overseas Bureau at NHK (Japan Broadcasting Corporation). In November 1943 she was ordered by the Japanese government to broadcast over Radio Tokyo. Allied prisoners of war who had also been forced to work at Radio Tokyo assured Toguri that she could actually help the United States war effort by taking part in an American music program and by softening anti-American propaganda. In 1945 while working for the Domei News Agency, Toguri met Filipe J. d'Aquino; the two wed on April 19, 1945.

Despite the fact that Toguri was one of 14 English-speaking radio announcers at Radio Tokyo, she alone was arrested and tried as the only "Tokyo Rose." "Tokyo Rose" was a term coined by American soldiers to refer to any female radio broadcaster heard on Japanese-controlled radio stations. Toguri's arrest came as the result of Hearst organization reporters Clark Lee and Harry Brundidge's interview with Toguri on September 1, 1945. The interview was published in *Cosmopolitan,* with the understanding that the magazine would pay Toguri $2,000 for her story. Toguri never received the $2,000, but instead was arrested on October 16, 1945, for trying to demoralize American troops in the Pacific during the war. A month later, on November 17, 1945, she was moved to Sugamo Prison, where Japanese war criminals were incarcerated. Although the Justice Department said on April 27, 1946, that it had no interest in Toguri's case, she was not released from Sugamo due to bureaucracy and problems with journalists.

Walter Winchell of the NATIVE SONS OF THE GOLDEN WEST, began to pressure the Justice Department and Congress to prosecute Toguri for treason. As a result, on August 26, 1948, Toguri was rearrested and incarcerated once again in Sugamo Prison. She returned to San Francisco in September 1948 to stand trial on eight counts of "Overt Acts" for broadcasts she had made on Radio Tokyo from November 1, 1943, to August 13, 1945. On September 29, 1949, Toguri was found guilty of one of the eight counts. The "Overt Act" of which she was accused was: "That on a day during October 1944, the exact date being to the Grand Jurors unknown, defendant in the offices of the Broadcasting Corporation of Japan did speak into the microphone concerning the loss of ships." Toguri was sentenced to 10 years in prison and fined $10,000. Along with the prison term and the fine, Toguri also lost her citizenship, which was automatically taken from her on her conviction of treason. Toguri was released from prison on January 18, 1956, after serving roughly seven years of her sentence. However, the Immigration Service ordered her to leave the United States by April 13, 1956. If not for Toguri's will to fight deportation and the assistance of WAYNE M. COLLINS, her lawyer for the deportation trial, she would have been deported to Japan.

In 1975, Dr. CLIFFORD UYEDA, along with the JAPANESE AMERICAN CITIZEN'S LEAGUE (JACL) and Senator S.I. HAYAKAWA, began a massive campaign for a presidential pardon for Toguri. This was not the first time that Toguri attempted to receive a presidential pardon. In June 1954 attorney Theodore Tamba filed a petition for executive clemency, but received no answer from then-President Dwight D. Eisenhower. Wayne M. Collins filed for a pardon on November 4, 1968, during President Lyndon B. Johnson's administration. However, Richard Nixon was elected the following day. Ultimately the second petition was denied by President Nixon. Since a petition for a presidential pardon can be filed once in a two-year period, Toguri was forced to wait again for a pardon. After two years of campaigning by her supporters, who succeeded in transforming public opinion to her side, Iva Ikuko Toguri d'Aquino was pardoned by President Gerald Ford on his last day of office, January 19, 1977.

For further reading, see Masayo Duus. *Tokyo Rose: Orphan of the Pacific*. Peter Duus, trans. New York: Kodansha International, 1979; Clifford I. Uyeda. "The Pardoning of 'Tokyo Rose': A Report on the Restoration of American Citizenship to Iva Ikuko Toguri." *Amerasia Journal* 5.2 (Fall 1978): 69–93; and *A Final Report and Review: The Japanese American Citizens League, National Committee for Iva Toguri*. Seattle: Asian American Studies Program, University of Washington, 1980. See also John Juji Hada. "The Indictment and Trial of Iva Ikuko Toguri d'Aquino." Thesis, University of San Francisco, 1973, the work which inspired the successful drive for a pardon, and Russell Warren Howe. *The Hunt for "Tokyo Rose"*. Lanham, Md.: Madison Books, 1990. STACEY HIROSE

Day of Remembrance The Day of Remembrance is an annual ceremony held around February 19 in most major cities with a significant Japanese American population to commemorate the signing of EXECUTIVE ORDER 9066. The first Day of Remembrance was held during Thanksgiving weekend in Seattle in 1978 with over 2,000 participants who reenacted the "evacuation" by caravaning to the Puyallup Fairgrounds (a former "ASSEMBLY CENTER") in army trucks and cars. Speeches were given, press conferences were held and, in general, the need for REDRESS AND REPARATIONS was stressed by the organizers. Through the 1980s to the present, the Day of Remembrance has helped to keep the memory of the CONCENTRATION CAMPS alive. (See REDRESS MOVEMENT.)

For further reading, see William Hohri. "Redress as a Movement Towards Enfranchisement." In Daniels, Roger, Sandra C. Taylor, and Harry H. L. Kitano, eds. *Japanese Americans: From Relocation to Redress*. Salt Lake City: University of Utah Press, 1986. Revised edition. Seattle: University of Washington Press, 1991. 196–99. GLEN KITAYAMA

dekasegi-shosei Literally meaning "student-laborer," the *dekasegi-shosei* were those indigent Japanese students who came to America with high ambitions of learning English or other useful skills. Faced with the reality of life in America, education often went by the wayside in the continuing struggle to make a living. The *dekasegi-shosei* began the first Japanese American community institutions such as the GOSPEL SOCIETY as well as the first newspapers. A good number of the earliest *dekasegi-shosei*, some of whom had arrived in the United States a decade or more before large numbers of labor migrants from Japan would arrive in the 1890s, used their greater knowledge of America and the English language to become LABOR CONTRACTORS and attain positions of prominence in the ISSEI community. Many of the future leaders of the *issei* came from the ranks of the *dekasegi-shosei*.

For further reading, see Donald Teruo Hata. *'Undesirables': Early Immigrants and the Anti-Japanese Movement in San Fran-*

cisco, 1892–1893: Prelude to Exclusion. New York: Arno Press, 1978 and Yuji Ichioka. *The Issei: The World of the First Generation Japanese Immigrants, 1885–1924.* New York: The Free Press, 1988.

Denson   Another name for JEROME.

DeWitt, John Lesesne (1880–1962)

Commander of the Fourth Army during World War II. John L. DeWitt is best remembered for his influential role in excluding more than 120,000 Japanese Americans from the West Coast during World War II. Although he is the one who is primarily blamed for the exclusion, it is clear that he was one of many figures responsible for the treatment Japanese Americans received during the war. As lieutenant general in command of the Fourth Army on the West Coast, he was the only government bureaucrat involved in the exclusion debate not to have a law degree. As such, he played the role of middle man while government lawyers argued over the legality of the mass internment.

Born in Fort Sidney, Nebraska, DeWitt was a career military man. Leaving Princeton University at the end of his sophomore year in 1898 to fight in the Spanish-American War, he remained in the army, rising through the ranks. He saw no more combat duty, serving as a supply officer and in other bureaucratic posts.

In the days following Pearl Harbor, DeWitt's reaction was one of a 61-year-old general who was desperately trying to save his job. In his desire not to be caught unprepared like his colleagues in Hawaii, DeWitt overreacted to rumors of invasion and added fuel to an already tense situation. Major General Joseph Stillwell believed that DeWitt acted irresponsibly when he issued public warnings of Japanese attack when there was no substantial evidence that this was true. DeWitt also favored a mass purging of Japanese, German and Italian nationals for security reasons. This, along with his unfounded reports of espionage and sabotage, prompted FBI director J. Edgar Hoover to comment that "the army was getting a bit hysterical." DeWitt, however, stopped short of recommending the imprisonment of American-born Japanese: "An American citizen, after all, is an American citizen," he told Army Provost Marshall ALLEN W. GULLION.

DeWitt, however, was no civil libertarian. Before Pearl Harbor, he managed "to have it happen naturally that Japs are sent to Infantry units" rather than headquarters under his command. His views and actions toward African Americans were similar: when the army assigned more soldiers to the West Coast after December 7th, DeWitt complained that there were "too many colored troops" put under his command. Of course, his later comments to a congressional committee justifying the

mass incarceration of Japanese Americans are legendary: "A Jap's a Jap . . . There is no way to determine their loyalty . . . It makes no difference whether he is an American citizen; theoretically he is still a Japanese and you can't change him."

Whatever doubts DeWitt had concerning mass incarceration gradually dissipated as weeks passed. After receiving intense outside pressure from West Coast politicians and the press and inside pressure from KARL BENDETSEN (the eventual architect of the mass removal and detention hired by Gullion) and the War Department, DeWitt joined his bureaucratic colleagues and became one of the most ardent supporters of the internment. In his report *Final Recommendation,* which was authored by Bendetsen and dated February 13, 1942, DeWitt agreed with the assessment that Japanese Americans had to be removed from all military areas soon to be designated by reason of "MILITARY NECESSITY." This was to be the basis for EXECUTIVE ORDER 9066 signed by President FRANKLIN D. ROOSEVELT on February 19, 1942.

In 1943, DeWitt's *Final Report: Japanese Evacuation from the West Coast* was released, reiterating and expanding on arguments used in *Final Recommendation* to justify the internment. Authored once again by Bendetsen, *Final Report* turned out to be not so "final" after all. The original version, which was ordered destroyed by Assistant Secretary of War JOHN J. MCCLOY, contained a statement by DeWitt that contradicted an earlier statement he made regarding the army's ability to determine "loyalty" among Japanese Americans. The second version, altered by McCloy, corrected the statement to make it consistent so that it could be used as evidence in the government briefs against Gordon Hirabayashi, Min Yasui and Fred Korematsu (see HIRABAYASHI V. U.S., YASUI V. U.S., and KOREMATSU V. U.S.). With the "doctored" version of *Final Report,* the government won its case against the three Japanese American defendants. Forty years later, however, this government cover-up became part of the basis for reopening the wartime convictions of Hirabayashi, Yasui and Korematsu (see CORAM NOBIS CASES).

In September of 1943, DeWitt accepted a less demanding job as commandant of the Army and Navy Staff College in Washington. He retired four years later. In 1954, he was appointed to the grade of full general through an act of Congress. He died on June 20, 1962, at the age of 82.

For further reading, see Commission on Wartime Relocation and Internment of Civilians. *Personal Justice Denied: Report of the Commission on Wartime Relocation and Internment of Civilians.* Washington, D.C.: Government Printing Office, 1982; Roger Daniels. *The Decision to Relocate the Japanese Americans.* Philadelphia: Lippincott, 1975; Peter Irons. *Justice at War:*

The Story of the Japanese American Internment Cases. New York: Oxford University Press, 1983; and Mike Masaoka and Bill Hosokawa. *They Call Me Moses Masaoka.* New York: William Morrow, 1987. DeWitt's *Final Report* was reprinted in 1978: U.S. Department of War. *Final Report: Japanese Evacuation from the West Coast 1942.* 1943. New York: Arno Press, 1978.
                                                    GLEN KITAYAMA

[Also used to compile this entry: "Gen. DeWitt of Army, 82, Dies." *New York Times* 21 June 1962: 31.]

Dies Committee Also known as the Special Committee on Un-American Activities (SCUA), a precursor to the infamous House Un-American Activities Committee (HUAC), it was the brainchild of Martin Dies, a conservative Republican congressman from Texas. In 1938, SCUA was given its first task, to investigate groups and individuals whom they considered to be "un-American." Originally, it was to be a temporary committee, but its alleged "success" in flushing out so-called "subversive elements" earned it yearly renewal until 1945—the year it became a permanent standing committee (HUAC).

As early as July 5, 1941, SCUA, under the leadership of Dies, alleged that Japanese Americans on the West Coast were involved in a conspiracy to aid Japan through espionage, sabotage and fifth column activity. Dies's list of "conspirators" included groups such as the Sakura baseball team, JAPANESE-LANGUAGE SCHOOLS and the Buddhist church that shared the same post office box with a Japanese veterans group. Though Dies could not offer any substantial evidence to back up his allegations, his charges of Japanese conspiracy became the basis for California Attorney General EARL WARREN's testimony to the TOLAN COMMITTEE, Lt. General JOHN DEWITT's *Final Report,* and the West Coast amicus brief in HIRABAYASHI V. UNITED STATES.
For further reading, see David Caute. *The Great Fear.* New York: Simon and Schuster, 1978 and Peter Irons. *Justice at War: The Story of the Japanese American Internment Cases.* New York: Oxford University Press, 1983.   GLEN KITAYAMA

Doi, Isami (1903–1965) Artist and painter. Born in Ewa, Oahu, Doi grew up in Kalaheo, Kauai. He began art studies at the University of Hawaii, then moved to New York, where he received a B.A. from Columbia University. Doi continued his art studies in Paris from 1930–31 and worked on paintings, watercolors, prints and jewelry. Many Japanese American artists in Hawaii after World War II looked on him as their spiritual and aesthetic father because he befriended many of them while in New York, where he advised and encouraged their work. Doi returned to Kauai in 1958 and continued to paint there until his death. His works range from the rich landscape forms of his early years to surrealistic images from Greek and Roman mythology to serene scenes of Kauai transformed into abstractions in rich hues during his later period. Doi has exhibited in Downtown Gallery (New York), the Museum of Modern Art and the California Palace Legion of Honor (San Francisco) among other places.   ALICE HOM

Doi, Nelson K. (1922--) Politician. Nelson K. Doi was the second Japanese American to hold the position of state lieutenant governor. He was born in Pahoa, Hawaii, and attended the University of Hawaii. He graduated from the University of Minnesota Law School in 1948 and married Eiko Oshima in 1949. After serving as an attorney in Hilo, Doi was elected to the Hawaii state senate, serving from 1959 to 1969, and was elected president of the senate in 1962. After leaving the senate, he served as judge for the Third Circuit Court.

Though a Democrat, Doi was not affiliated with the political machine presided over by Governor JOHN BURNS. However, he played a key role in the closely contested gubernatorial race in 1974, when he split from the camp of Burns's rival Tom Gill, a move which many political observers feel reversed the momentum of the race in favor of Burns protégé GEORGE ARIYOSHI. Doi ended up defeating future U.S. Senator Daniel Akaka in the primary and winning the general election to become lieutenant governor while Ariyoshi was elected to the first of his three full terms as governor. Doi served one term and was succeeded by JEAN SADAKO KING in 1978. For further reading, see Paul C. Phillips. *Hawaii's Democrats: Chasing the American Dream.* Washington, D.C.: University Press of America, 1982.   STACEY HIROSE

dual citizenship Citizenship status of many NISEI born before 1925. Though having little effect on the daily life of *nisei,* their dual citizenship status was cited as a reason for suspicion by the ANTI-JAPANESE MOVEMENT and by those who questioned their loyalty during World War II. Dual citizenship came about because Japan considered all children of its citizens to be Japanese citizens, regardless of where they were born. Since all *nisei* were also American citizens by virtue of their being born in the United States, and since virtually all ISSEI maintained their Japanese citizenship since they were not allowed to be American citizens, virtually all *nisei* held both American and Japanese citizenship for a time. On December 1, 1924, the Japanese law was changed so that *nisei* would only hold Japanese citizenship if their parents declared it within 14 days of their birth. *Nisei* holding dual citizenship could also renounce their Japanese citizenship through notification; prior to this law, it had been very difficult for *nisei* to drop their Japanese citizenship. Even after the passage of the law, a good percentage of the *nisei* population kept their dual citizenship, many of them just never getting around to rid themselves of their Japanese citizenship. For a few, this oversight had tragic consequences: some *nisei* visiting Japan just prior to World War II were forced to stay and serve in the Japanese army because of their Japanese citizenship.

For further reading, see Yamato Ichihashi. *Japanese in the United States: A Critical Study of the Problems of the Japanese Immigrants and their Children*. Stanford: Stanford University Press, 1932. New York: Arno Press, 1969; Edward K. Strong. *The Second-Generation Japanese Problem*. Stanford: Stanford University Press, 1934. New York: Arno Press, 1970; Robert A. Wilson and Bill Hosokawa. *East to America: A History of the Japanese in the United States*. New York: Morrow, 1980.

E

Eisenhower, Milton Stover (1899–1985) First director of the WAR RELOCATION AUTHORITY (WRA). Eisenhower is significant in Japanese American history as the first director of the WRA. On the job for only three months, he came to hate his duties as head of the WRA. Much later, he wrote in his memoirs of his regrets on taking the job: "I have brooded about this whole episode on and off for the past three decades, for it is illustrative of how an entire society can somehow plunge off course."

When Eisenhower first accepted the job with the WRA, he was politically unaware of the controversy surrounding Japanese Americans on the West Coast and knew even less of the infighting between the Justice and War Departments. Eisenhower had no military experience to prepare him to work with the officials in the War Department and army. He was trained as a journalist and had worked in the Agriculture Department since 1926. The fact that his brother Dwight was a rising star in the army convinced officials that he was right for the WRA assignment.

Only days after accepting his new post, KARL BENDETSEN made clear to Eisenhower his opposition to "voluntary migration" for Japanese Americans—a plan that most WRA officials thought would be the means for "evacuation" from the West Coast. Soon Public Proclamation Number 4 on March 27, 1942, ending the "VOLUNTARY RESETTLEMENT" period was ordered by General JOHN L. DEWITT, commander of the Western Defense Command. Although Eisenhower came up with the idea for freezing "voluntary resettlement," he did so out of concern that an unsupervised flow of Japanese Americans into the interior states would be dangerous. Instead, he envisioned an organized move of Japanese Americans to rural areas outside of Military Area Number 1 (established by DeWitt) to work on sugar-beet farms.

On April 7, 1942, with the mass removal and detention of Japanese Americans already in progress, Eisenhower appealed to the governors, attorneys general and other officials of the western states (except California) to cooperate with his resettlement plan. This gathering, which was organized by Bendetsen, was not sympathetic to Eisenhower's idea and did not believe his assertion that Japanese Americans could be trusted. After his plea for tolerance toward those of Japanese decent, Eisenhower was stunned at the racist response to his program. The officials made it clear that they wanted CONCENTRATION CAMPS where Japanese Americans could be properly supervised. Under Eisenhower's successor DILLON S. MYER, such camps would be forthcoming.

For further reading, see Richard Drinnon. *Keeper of Concentration Camps: Dillon S. Myer and American Racism*. Berkeley: University of California Press, 1987; Milton S. Eisenhower. *The President Is Calling*. Garden City, New York: Doubleday, 1974; and Peter Irons. *Justice at War: The Story of the Japanese American Internment Cases*. New York: Oxford University Press, 1983.
                                                    GLEN KITAYAMA

El Monte Berry Strike A 1933 labor dispute between Mexican farm workers and Japanese farmers. Involving some 7,000 workers, Mexican government officials and California's agricultural power structure, the El Monte strike was a pivotal one in California history. The strike also brought to the forefront the highly organized nature of the Japanese American community of the time, a key factor in the farmers' eventual "victory" in the conflict.

The strike was rooted in the difficult economic times of the Great Depression, the presence of nearly twice as many farm workers as there were jobs, and the low wages and harsh conditions faced by the farm workers. When organizers from the Cannery and Agricultural Workers Industrial Union (CAWIU) arrived in the San Gabriel Valley, east of Los Angeles, they found a receptive audience. Demands for wages of at least 25¢ per hour were forwarded to Japanese American berry farmers in the area and were rejected. By June 5, 1933, the strike had begun and some 800 workers had walked off their jobs. In much the same manner as Japanese laborers had once struck several decades earlier, the strikers hit when the growers were most vulnerable, when the fruit was ripening on the vines.

The strike spread very quickly to areas outside the San Gabriel Valley, becoming something of a general strike of Mexican workers against Japanese growers. Within a week after it began, some 7,000 workers were on strike. The Comite Pro-Huelga (Pro-Strike Committee) was formed by June 10 to coordinate the various strike actions in Southern California. Led by Los Angeles printer Armando Flores, the Chicano-dominated Comite wrested control of the strike from the CAWIU. The strikers received support from the larger Chicano community and from the highest levels of the Mexican government. Even Japanese immigrants in Baja, California, issued a statement of support for the strikers.

The Japanese American farmers offered a compromise settlement of 20¢ per hour, but this was rejected. With the support of nearly all major organizations within the Japanese American community, including the JAPANESE ASSOCIATIONS, local JAPANESE AMERICAN CITIZENS LEAGUE chapters and the Little Tokyo Businessmen's Association, the farmers called on the community for support. NISEI children were pulled out of school to pick berries, and friends and relatives came from around Southern California to help. Just as important as the internal support of the community was the help the farmers received from the white power structure of the state. With a vested interest in keeping the Mexican farm workers non-unionized, groups such as the El Monte Chamber of Commerce and the Los Angeles County Chamber of Commerce helped to turn public opinion against the strikers through red-baiting and assailing the motives of the Mexican leaders. With the help of the State Bureau of Industrial Relations and the Federal Department of Labor, the strike was settled on July 6, 1933.

Though the terms of the settlement were such that the workers celebrated a "victory," such was not the case. Though the terms of the agreement were adhered to by vegetable farmers on the coast, with the berry season coming to an end, the berry farmers saw no reason to comply. Workers in the San Gabriel Valley ended up no better off than they had been before the strike. Japanese American farmers had "won," but only because their interests coincided with those of the white power structure. The defeat of the El Monte strikers was also part of a larger campaign to crush attempts at farm labor organization, resulting in the virtual destruction of the CAWIU by the end of 1934. Japanese American farmers were to play a similar middleman role in the VENICE CELERY STRIKE of 1936 and in the rise of the NISEI FARMERS LEAGUE in the 1970s.

For further reading, see Abraham Hoffman. "The El Monte Berry Picker's Strike, 1933." *Journal of the West* 12.1 (Jan. 1973): 71–84; Ronald W. Lopez. "The El Monte Berry Strike of 1933." *Atzlan* 1.1 (Spring 1970): 101–15; Charles B. Spaulding. "The Mexican Strike at El Monte, California." *Sociology and Social Research* 18 (Aug. 1934): 571–80; and Charles M. Wollenberg. "Race and Class in Rural California: The El Monte Berry Strike of 1933." *California Historical Quarterly* 51.2 (Summer 1972): 155–64. The strike is also discussed in John Modell. *The Economics and Politics of Racial Accommodation: The Japanese of Los Angeles 1900–1942.* Chicago: University of Illinois Press, 1977 and David J. O'Brien

and Stephen S. Fugita. "Middleman Minority Concept: Its Explanatory Value in the Case of the Japanese in California Agriculture." *Pacific Sociological Review* 25.2 (Apr. 1982): 185–204.

Emergency Detention Act of 1950   (Also known as Title II of the Internal Security Act of 1950.) Passed during the height of the cold war over a presidential veto on September 23, 1950, this act provided the attorney general with the power to "apprehend and . . . detain . . . each person as to whom there is reasonable ground to believe that such person probably will engage in, or probably will conspire with others to engage in, acts of espionage or sabotage." Coming just five years after the release of Japanese Americans from CONCENTRATION CAMPS, many Chinese Americans feared that a similar fate (internment) awaited them due to the new Communist regime in mainland China.

In 1952, the Justice Department, with financial appropriations from Congress, set up six detention camps to be used in case of "emergency"—one of the camps being the infamous TULE LAKE. Funding for the upkeep of the camps continued until 1957. By that time, the Korean War had ended and the McCarthy period had passed. The law, however, remained on the books until repeal in 1971. (See EMERGENCY DETENTION ACT OF 1950, REPEAL OF.)

For further reading, see Roger Daniels. *Asian America: Chinese and Japanese in the United States since 1850.* Seattle: University of Washington Press, 1988 and Raymond Okamura. "Background and History of the Repeal Campaign." *Amerasia Journal* 2.2 (Fall 1974): 73–94.   GLEN KITAYAMA

Emergency Detention Act of 1950, Repeal of   In 1967, the Emergency Detention Act of 1950 gained new notoriety. With the Civil Rights and anti-Vietnam War movements gaining momentum, rumors started to spread that protesters could be put in CONCENTRATION CAMPS just like the Japanese Americans had been during World War II. Charles Allen, Jr., wrote a booklet titled *Concentration Camps USA* that outlined the Emergency Detention Act of 1950 and became the foundation for future articles. Stokely Charmichael and H. Rap Brown, leaders in the Black Power movement, followed with speeches and articles on the subject. The possibility of concentration camps being activated again seemed very real in light of police and government repression aimed at those who dared to protest.

On July 19, 1967, a concerned Japanese American, Raymond Okamura of Berkeley, California, telephoned the JAPANESE AMERICAN CITIZENS LEAGUE (JACL) headquarters to ask what they were doing about the issue. MAS SATOW, national director at that time, replied that there was nothing much the league could do since the Justice Department denied the existence of the camps. Unsatisfied, Satow wrote to the JACL the next day and told them that this was an issue that they and all Japanese Americans should be concerned with.

The campaign to repeal the Emergency Detention Act of 1950 began in late May of 1968 with the founding of the ASIAN AMERICAN POLITICAL ALLIANCE (AAPA) in Berkeley, California. As the first group to promote the use of the term "Asian" rather than "Oriental," AAPA was known for its militancy and its advocacy of Asian pride and unity. This was the beginning of what many have referred to as the "ASIAN AMERICAN MOVEMENT." One of its first acts as an organization was to print up an information leaflet titled "Concentration Camps, USA" which discussed the dangers of Title II. The AAPA spoke about the EDA at rallies organized by the Black Panther Party and also at various other public gatherings—including before the Oakland City Council. Most importantly, however, it started the petition drive to repeal Title II.

On June 2, 1968, a group of Japanese Americans led by Raymond Okamura (now a JACL member) and Mary Anna Takagi of the JACL formed an ad hoc committee to get the JACL involved in the repeal campaign. Starting with a group of seven people, they spoke of how it was important for Japanese Americans to take the lead on this issue. Asians, they felt, were passive beneficiaries of the Civil Rights movement led by African Americans and needed to take a stand for Third World unity. The committee thought that the best means of accomplishing their goals was through the JACL because of its national legislative capability.

From the June meeting, they were able to secure statements of support from different JACL chapters in the Bay area. Unknown to them, the San Francisco and Seattle chapters of the JACL also asked the National JACL to work on the repeal of Title II. They coordinated their efforts through correspondence and kept applying pressure to the national league to take a stand. As expected, President Jerry Enomoto and MIKE MASAOKA responded negatively—stating that such a campaign would cost too much money, create a backlash effect and distract from "higher priority projects and programs."

Determined, the group continued to gather support for their cause among different chapters and eventually had a resolution of support passed at the 1968 JACL national convention. The committee working on the campaign became the official arm of the JACL campaign to repeal Title II. Sensing opportunity, Masaoka insisted that all activities pertaining to the repeal campaign be cleared through him and that no publicity be given. The committee balked at the suggestion and disagreed with the strategy. Eventually, Masaoka acquiesced and agreed to work with the group.

In the meantime, support for the repeal of Title II was gathering around the country. AAPA, now in San Francisco and Los Angeles as well as Berkeley, worked tirelessly in mobilizing the campaign. Organizations in New York and student groups also helped keep the momentum going. Eventually, according to Okamura, "over 150 civic, religious, labor, and ethnic organizations . . . supported the campaign." On September 25, 1971, the campaign to repeal Title II came to a successful conclusion when President Nixon signed H.R. 234. In an ironic twist, Nixon gained his notoriety by spearheading the anti-Communist House Un-American Activities Committee (HUAC) that led to the passage of the Emergency Detention Act of 1950.

For further reading, see Raymond Okamura. "Background and History of the Repeal Campaign." *Amerasia Journal* 2.2 (Fall 1974): 73–94.
GLEN KITAYAMA

Emergency Service Committee NISEI organized group that encouraged Japanese Americans in Hawaii to participate in the war effort to improve morale and to alleviate suspicion directed at the Japanese American community. Groups such as the Emergency Service Committee (ESC) and the Japanese Morale Committees were determined to show that Japanese Americans in Hawaii could be as patriotic as any other group of Americans, much like the JAPANESE AMERICAN CITIZENS LEAGUE on the mainland.

The 1944 "Report of the Emergency Service Committee" stated that the *nisei* were anxious "to prove that they are loyal Americans, ready and willing to . . . do their . . . share to fight the enemy." The group held hundreds of meetings with ISSEI and *nisei* in various parts of Oahu to educate and raise morale. They served as liaisons between the army and the Japanese American community and recruited volunteers for the 442ND REGIMENTAL COMBAT TEAM. They served as volunteers for other service organizations such as the Red Cross. They were also the sponsors of a "Bombs on Tokyo" campaign, which raised over $10,000 for the cause from the Japanese American community. The ESC also played a key role in the "Speak-American" campaign to encourage the *issei* to adopt "American" ways. Some ESC members also advocated the permanent closing of Japanese-language schools, Buddhist and Shinto temples, and other community institutions closed down at the start of the war. Even the term *nisei* was deemed too Japanese; ESC members pushed for the term "AMERICANS OF JAPANESE ANCESTRY" or "AJAs" as an alternative.

Though applauded by many, the activities of the ESC and the Morale Committees were viewed by some to be too extreme. The "Bombs on Tokyo" drive offended many ISSEI and the "Speak-American" campaign was also criticized. It was one thing to support the war effort;

it was another thing entirely to denigrate Japanese cultural institutions and exacerbate tensions between *issei* and *nisei*. Rumors circulated about *nisei* teenagers calling their parents "Japs" who shouldn't tell "Americans" what to do. A situation developed in Hawaii similar to that found in the mainland CONCENTRATION CAMPS (though not nearly as intense) where ESC members were accused of being "INU" (dogs or stoolpigeons, the implication being that they were turning their back on their people) while many *issei* feared being turned in to the FBI or military authorities. As on the mainland, ESC members were also accused of self-serving behavior, since they were granted significant power by the military authorities.

Though some of their members may have gone overboard, there can be little doubt that groups like the ESC performed a valuable function during the war. Like their opponents, they did what they felt was the proper thing under the circumstances and their actions must be understood in the context of the times.

For further reading, see Roland Kotani. *The Japanese in Hawaii: A Century of Struggle*. Honolulu: Hochi, Ltd., 1985 and Andrew W. Lind. *Hawaii's Japanese: An Experiment in Democracy*. Princeton: Princeton University Press, 1946. New York: Arno Press, 1978.

emigration companies   Japanese private businesses that recruited and shipped laborers abroad for profit. Although the first emigration company, the Nihon Yoshisa Emigration Company, was established in December 1891, their rise can be traced to the ending of Japanese government-sponsored immigration from 1894. After the Japanese government established the "Regulations to Protect Emigrants" in that year to govern the emigration companies, they began to grow rapidly in number. By 1898, nine companies shipped 12,393 laborers abroad; in 1899, 21,515 emigrants were shipped by 12 companies. At their peak between 1902 and 1907, some 30 companies sent 98,429 emigrants abroad. The five biggest companies were the Morioka Emigration Company, HIROSHIMA KAIGAI TOKO COMPANY, Nihon Emigration Company, Tokyo Emigration Company and Kumamoto Emigration Company. These companies made use of ties with local officials to recruit laborers and to facilitate passport issuance. They also reinforced existing patterns of migration by recruiting largely in the same PREFECTURES from which the bulk of immigrants had already come.

Although emigration companies played a large role in Japanese immigration to Hawaii and other places, they had only a minor role in direct immigration to the United States. Since the U.S. did not allow contract immigration, the companies were limited to transporting free emigrants until 1898. In that year, the Japanese foreign ministry briefly prohibited the companies from shipping any emigrant to the United States and later enforced the existing laws excluding certain classes rigidly. When the emigration companies began to ship emigrants to Canada, the foreign ministry instituted a quota of 30 per month for Canada in August 1898. Between 1891 and 1897, an average of only 1,400 Japanese were admitted into the U.S. per year, a figure including students and other NON-EMIGRANTS. Japanese statistics indicate that emigration companies brought only 165 emigrants to the U.S. between 1894 and 1898. The later rise in Japanese migration to the U.S. can be attributed to the rise of LABOR CONTRACTORS.

For further reading, see Yuji Ichioka. *The Issei: The World of the First Generation Japanese Immigrants, 1885–1924*. New York: The Free Press, 1988 and Alan T. Moriyama. *Imingaishi: Japanese Emigration Companies and Hawaii, 1894–1908*. Honolulu: University of Hawaii Press, 1985.

Emmons, Delos Carleton   (1888–1965)

Commanding general in Hawaii during World War II and head of the Western Defense Command. As head of the U.S. Army in Hawaii, Delos C. Emmons is often credited with the being the key individual in preventing a mass removal of Japanese Americans in Hawaii during World War II. He later succeeded JOHN L. DEWITT as the head of the Western Defense Command and took actions to end the detention of Japanese Americans in CONCENTRATION CAMPS.

Emmons was born in Huntington, West Virginia, on January 17, 1888. A 1909 graduate of the U.S. Military Academy, he initially was assigned to an infantry unit, but later transferred to aviation. He rose through the ranks, being promoted to colonel in 1938 and major general in 1939. In October 1940, he was given the rank of lieutenant general and became chief of the Air Force Combat Command, becoming the highest ranking officer in the Army Air Forces. He replaced the disgraced Major General Walter C. Short as commander of the Hawaiian Department of the United States Army in December 1941, shortly after the attack on Pearl Harbor.

Emmons played a key role in the fate of Japanese Americans in Hawaii. He countered the wild charges of sabotage by Navy Secretary Frank Knox by stating in mid-December that no evidence of sabotage by Japanese Americans at Pearl Harbor had been found. Throughout 1942, he countered plans hatched in Washington, D.C., to forcibly remove some 20,000 Japanese Americans in Hawaii to either the island of Molokai or to the mainland, citing the logistical problems it would cause, the valuable resources it would eat up and the labor shortages it would cause. Although many other factors came into play, Emmons's efforts contributed to the decision not to remove large numbers of Japanese Americans in Hawaii; ultimately, only 1,875 were removed to the

mainland. Emmons also played a key role in the formation of the 100TH INFANTRY BATTALION and pushed for
allowing NISEI to be inducted into the military. In
September 1943, he was named the commander of the
Western Defense Command, replacing John L. DeWitt,
and immediately began taking steps to end the incarceration of removed Japanese Americans. Emmons later
took over as commanding general in Alaska in June
1944. He retired in 1948 and died on October 3, 1965.
For further reading, see Andrew W. Lind. *Hawaii's Japanese:
An Experiment in Democracy.* Princeton: Princeton University
Press, 1946; Commission on Wartime Relocation and Internment of Civilians. *Personal Justice Denied: Report of the Commission on Wartime Relocation and Internment of Civilians.*
Washington, D.C.: Government Printing Office, 1982; and
John H. Culley. "Relocation of Japanese Americans: The Hawaiian Experience." *Air Force Law Review* 24 (Spring 1984):
176–83.

[Also used to compile this entry was the article on Emmons by Maxine
Block in *Current Biography 1942: Who's News and Why* (New York:
H. W. Wilson Company, 1942. 246–48).]

Endo, Ex Parte Legal case testing the mass detention
of Japanese Americans during World War II. Mitsuye
Endo did not challenge the curfew or "evacuation" orders and never appeared in court, yet her name will
always be remembered alongside those of Gordon Hirabayashi, Fred Korematsu and Min Yasui as one who
dared challenge the government over the legality of
detaining people solely on the basis of race.

The origins of the *Endo* case started about a month
before EXECUTIVE ORDER 9066 was signed into law. In
January of 1942, SABURO KIDO of the JAPANESE AMER-
ICAN CITIZENS LEAGUE (JACL) was informed that Japanese American state employees in California were being
questioned on the assumption that they were Japanese
citizens under Japan's dual nationality act. They were
asked details about past trips to Japan, knowledge of the
Japanese language and ties to any Japanese organization.
Eventually, all were fired from their jobs for "failure of
good behavior, fraud in securing employment, incom-
petency, inefficiency, and acts incompatible with and
inimical to the public service." All were charged with
being citizens of Japan, attending "a Japanese school
conducted by the officials of the Buddhist Church," and
being members of Japanese organizations "violently opposed to the Democratic form of government of the
United States. . ."

Kido recruited attorney James Purcell to work on the
case. Originally, they were just going to work on fighting
those charges, but the rapid pace of the government's
removal and detention program forced them to change
their plans. Instead, they sought out the *ideal* plaintiff

to file a habeas corpus petition, one who was denied the
right to work because of unlawful detention by the army.
Mitsuye Endo was that person.

Endo was considered perfect for this case for a variety
of reasons. She was a state employee at the California
Department of Motor Vehicles; she was a NISEI, thus a
United States citizen; she had never visited Japan; she
could not speak nor read the Japanese language; she was
raised a Methodist by her family and she even had a
brother serving in the army. On July 12, 1942, her
habeas corpus petition was filed in the federal district
court in San Francisco against MILTON EISENHOWER,
then the director of the WAR RELOCATION AUTHORITY
(WRA). In the petition, Eisenhower was asked to show
why Mitsuye Endo was being detained. The hearing was
set for July 20, 1942, by Judge Roche.

Purcell based Endo's petition on the 1866 majority
opinion in *Ex Parte Milligan,* which said that "only by
act of Congress could the writ of habeas corpus be
suspended, and that no military action could be taken
except under martial law conditions." It was clear that
Endo was being detained without trial while martial law
was not declared and the courts were still open. Purcell
also argued that even though General JOHN L. DEWITT
feared Japanese invasion, the West Coast was still not
the victim of attack.

The government lawyer, Alfonso J. Zirpoli, countered
with DeWitt's charge that it was not possible to tell the
"loyal" from the "disloyal" and also that there were a
number of possible fifth columnists among the Japanese
American population. At the end of his presentation, he
urged Judge Roche to dismiss the petition on the grounds
that it exhausted all of the legal remedies demanded by
a writ of habeas corpus. Zirpoli pointed to the furlough
program that was just implemented that day. He did
not, however, mention how Endo could have taken
advantage of such a program when her petition was filed
before the furlough program became effective.

Months passed before Judge Roche issued his verdict.
Under normal circumstances, habeas corpus petitions are
supposed to be handled quickly to avoid further possible
undue detention of the petitioner. In this case, however,
Roche was not in any hurry to make a decision on Endo
in that it affected the status of some 70,000 other
Japanese American citizens. His ruling would not be
heard until July 3, 1943—ten days shy of one year since
the petition had been filed. Roche granted Zirpoli's
dismissal motion and did not give any explanation for
his ruling. An appeal was filed.

In October 1944, the Supreme Court heard the arguments for both the *Endo* and *Korematsu* cases (see
KOREMATSU V. U.S.). In the *Endo* case, the government
argued that since she did not comply with the WRA-
authorized leave program (see "LOYALTY QUESTIONS"),

she had no case to challenge her detention. In their brief, they conceded that "the detention or internment of civilians of the United States against whom no charges of disloyalty or subversiveness have been made, or can be made, for longer than the minimum period necessary to screen the loyal from the disloyal, and to provide the necessary guidance for relocation, is beyond the power of the War Relocation Authority." In short, the government handed the case over to Endo's lawyers on a silver platter. By framing the argument of detention over Endo's non-compliance with WRA leave regulations, they practically conceded defeat—a small price to pay if the overall constitutional question of detention could be avoided.

On November 8, 1944, Justice Douglas circulated his views in the *Endo* case to the other members of the Court. "We are of the view," he stated in a carefully worded opinion, "that Mitsuye Endo should be given her liberty. In reaching that conclusion, we do not come to the underlying constitutional issues which have been argued. For we conclude that, whatever power the War Relocation Authority may have to detain other classes of citizens, it has no authority to subject citizens who are concededly loyal to its leave regulations."

On December 18, 1944, the Supreme Court released its unanimous decision on the *Endo* case. One day earlier, however, aware of the Court's soon-to-be-announced decision on *Endo* and *Korematsu*, the War Department issued a press release stating that "persons of Japanese ancestry whose record have stood the test of Army scrutiny during the past two years" would be "permitted the same freedom of movement throughout the United States as other loyal citizens and law-abiding aliens." With the exception of those falsely presumed to be "disloyal," release from the CONCENTRATION CAMPS would begin on January 2, 1945.

Although Endo's case resulted in victory, it *did not* address the fundamental question of constitutional rights. It did, however, affirm that the Constitution was not a barrier in the military's desire to detain American citizens on the basis of race.

For further reading, see Peter Irons. *Justice at War: The Story of the Japanese American Internment Cases*. New York: Oxford University Press, 1983.   GLEN KITAYAMA

Ennis, Edward (1907–1990)

Ennis, Edward (1907–1990) Government official, attorney. As a Justice Department lawyer during World War II, Ennis played what might be considered a dual role in the incarceration of Japanese Americans. Like his superior, U.S. Attorney General FRANCIS BIDDLE, Ennis was opposed to the CONCENTRATION CAMPS on the grounds that he thought they were unconstitutional. He fought an inside battle with other government lawyers, chiefly HENRY STIMSON and JOHN J. MCCLOY of the War Department, over the legality of the camps and lost bitterly with the signing of EXECUTIVE ORDER 9066. He had neither the political clout nor the seniority in Roosevelt's Cabinet to stop the mass removal and detention.

On the flip side, however, Ennis was also the consummate government bureaucrat: when given orders to perform an assignment, he did so despite his own misgivings. As head of the newly created Alien Enemy Control Unit (AECL), he was in charge of detaining the so-called "enemy alien" Japanese, Germans and Italians that were rounded up after Pearl Harbor, despite the lack of any evidence of wrongdoing. All eventually were granted hearings, where over half of the Germans and Italians were let free. Detainees of Japanese descent were not as fortunate, however—approximately two-thirds of them stayed in Justice Department–administered INTERNMENT CAMPS for the remainder of the war.

Ennis's dual role in World War II can also be seen in his handling of the government cases against Fred Korematsu, Gordon Hirabayashi and Min Yasui. Though he was opposed to the mass detention of Japanese Americans, he was appointed to lead the Justice Department's cases against the three Japanese American defendants. In one famous episode involving the *Korematsu* case (see KOREMATSU V. U.S.), Ennis, along with fellow Justice Department attorney John Burling, read through evidence supplied by the War Department and Lt. General JOHN L. DEWITT that supported the government's claim of "MILITARY NECESSITY" only to discover that it contradicted reports made by the Federal Bureau of Investigation (FBI) and the Federal Communications Commission (FCC). Ennis and McCloy fought over this issue and eventually a compromise was reached: reference to the reports by the FBI and FCC were omitted and replaced with a footnote that barely hinted at other evidence. Both Ennis and Burling signed on to the brief—thus giving their reluctant approval and also exposing the contradictions inherent in their jobs.

After a 14-year stint at the Justice Department, Ennis worked for the AMERICAN CIVIL LIBERTIES UNION from 1955 until 1969 as general council and from 1969 to 1977 as president. He later testified at the COMMISSION ON WARTIME RELOCATION AND INTERNMENT OF CIVILIANS hearings on behalf of Japanese Americans. He died at the age of 82 in 1990 due to complications associated with diabetes. (See also CORAM NOBIS CASES and KARL BENDETSEN.)

For further reading, see Roger Daniels. *The Decision to Relocate the Japanese Americans*. Philadelphia: Lippincott, 1975; Peter Irons. *Justice at War: The Story of the Japanese American Internment Cases*. New York: Oxford University Press, 1983; and Michi Weglyn. *Years of Infamy: The Untold Story of America's*

Concentration Camps. New York: William Morrow & Co., 1976.   GLEN KITAYAMA

[Also used to compile this entry: "Edward J. Ennis, 82; ACLU Official Fought Interning Japanese-Americans." *Los Angeles Times,* 12 Jan. 1990: A-30.]

enryo   Japanese term meaning polite restraint, polite refusal or modesty. The term, which came out of the Confucian ethic of proper behavior towards one's superiors, was originally used to denote thoughtful consideration, but is now more commonly used by Japanese Americans to describe restraint or holding back. *Enryo* is a form of social control that keeps one from imposing, expecting or demanding too much of another.

Some examples of *enryo* given by UCLA sociologist HARRY H. L. KITANO include: one's refusal of a second serving of food; one's initial refusal of a present; one's acceptance of a less desired object although one is given a free choice; and one's hesitancy to ask questions or speak out in a group setting. According to Kitano and Betty S. Furuta, even the SANSEI generation still use the term *enryo* and employ it frequently.

For further reading, see Betty S. Furuta. "Ethnic Identities of Japanese-American Families: Implications for Counseling." In Getty, Cathleen, and Winnifred Humphreys, eds. *Understanding the Family: Stress and Change in American Family Life.* New York: Appleton-Century-Crofts, 1981; Harry H. L. Kitano. *Japanese Americans: The Evolution of a Subculture.* 1969. 2nd Edition. Englewood Cliffs, N.J.: Prentice-Hall, Inc., 1976; *Kodansha Encyclopedia of Japan.* Tokyo: Kodansha, 1983; Amy Iwasaki Mass. *"Amae:* Indulgence and Nurturance in Japanese American Families." Diss., University of California, Los Angeles, 1986.   STACEY HIROSE

Esaki, Leo (1925–)   Physicist. Leo Esaki is a Nobel Prize–winning physicist who rose to prominence while working for IBM. Esaki was born in Osaka and received his Ph.D. at the University of Tokyo in 1959. He spent five years (1956–1960) with the Sony Corporation in Japan, during which time he invented the tunnel diode. In 1960, Esaki emigrated to the United States to work at IBM's Watson Research Center in Yorktown Heights, N.Y. He also served as the device research manager and the director of IBM-Japan. Esaki was awarded the Nobel Prize for physics in 1973. He is married to Masako Araki and has three children.

                                 SCOTT KURASHIGE

[Used to compile this entry: *The Celebrity Who's Who: By the Editors of Who's Who in America.* New York: World Almanac, 1986. 113.]

Exclusion Act   See IMMIGRATION ACT OF 1924.

exclusionists   Those who advocated and worked towards the banning of further emigration from Japan between 1905 and 1924. (See ANTI-JAPANESE MOVEMENT.)

Executive Order 9066   Signed by President FRANKLIN D. ROOSEVELT on February 19, 1942, Executive Order 9066 authorized the War Department to "prescribe military areas . . . from which any or all persons may be excluded . . . The right of any person to enter, remain in, or leave" those areas was at the discretion of the "military authorities." This order, which on the surface made no reference to Japanese Americans or native-born Japanese, served as the basis for the future curfew and "exclusion orders" issued by Lt. General JOHN L. DEWITT and the mass incarceration of all West Coast Japanese American in CONCENTRATION CAMPS. It was rescinded by President Gerald Ford exactly 34 years later. (See DAY OF REMEMBRANCE.)   GLEN KITAYAMA

F

Farrington v. Tokushige   Case decided by the U.S. Supreme Court involving the constitutionality of regulations imposed by the Territory of Hawaii on JAPANESE-LANGUAGE SCHOOLS. On December 28, 1922, the Palama Japanese language school filed a petition for injunction in the territorial circuit court in response to a succession of restrictive laws passed to inhibit the language schools in Hawaii (see for instance ACT 30 OF THE SPECIAL SESSION LAWS OF 1920). Initiated by newspaper publisher KINZABURO MAKINO, the suit also called on other language schools to become co-petitioners. A vicious battle ensued between Makino's HAWAII HOCHI and the more moderate NIPPU JIJI in arguing the merits of taking up the case vs. not resorting to legal means. According to Rev. TAKIE OKUMURA, a lawsuit was not the way to go. "Even if we win on legal points," noted Okumura, "we would only increase their suspicion, and would endanger the future of our children in Hawaii." "It behooves us, who make our homes in this nation, to understand the Americans," said Makino. "And we must never forget that we have to stand up for our rights as guaranteed under the Constitution." Eventually, 88 out of Hawaii's 146 Japanese schools joined the lawsuit.

On February 6, 1923, the circuit court upheld part of Act 30 and struck down other parts of it. The legislature responded with yet more restrictive regulations, including assessing a fee of $1.00 per year per student on the schools. The test case group filed suit in the U.S. district court on June 13, 1925. Many months of legal wrangling saw the case sent to the Ninth Circuit Court of Appeals where a decision declaring the regulations unconstitutional was handed down on March 22, 1926. Ultimate victory came in the U.S. Supreme Court, which upheld the appellate court decision on February 21, 1927. A crowd of 5,000 celebrated the victory on March 27, 1927.

For further reading, see United Japanese Society of Hawaii. *History of Japanese in Hawaii.* James H. Okahata, ed. Honolulu: United Japanese Society of Hawaii, 1971 and Ernest K. Wakukawa. *A History of the Japanese People in Hawaii.* Honolulu: Toyo Shoin, 1938.

[Okumura quote from Kotani, p. 63; Makino's from United Japanese, p. 224.]

522nd Field Artillery Battalion

As part of the 442ND REGIMENTAL COMBAT TEAM, the 522nd Field Artillery Battalion's main claim to fame was liberating survivors of the Dachau concentration camp from the Nazis on April 29, 1945. According to Chester Tanaka, two scouts from the 522nd shot off the locks to one of the gates at the camp. No Nazi officers nor guards were found at Dachau—all had fled prior to the 522nd's arrival.

As of this writing, official army records do not acknowledge the existence of the 522nd at Dachau. The 42nd Infantry Division is given the distinction of rescuing the camp survivors. However, some army historians, NISEI soldiers and camp survivors are now making a case for acknowledgment of the 522nd. Photographs, oral testimony and records in the National Archives are helping to uncover what has been a neglected chapter in Japanese American military history.

For further reading, see Chester Tanaka. *Go for Broke: A Pictorial History of the Japanese American 100th Infantry Battalion and the 442nd Regimental Combat Team.* Richmond, Calif.: Go for Broke, Inc., 1981.　　　　GLEN KITAYAMA

[Also used to compile this entry: Effron, Sonni. "Japanese-American GIs Are Focus of Dachau Memories." *Los Angeles Times,* 1 Dec. 1991: A1.]

442nd Regimental Combat Team

U.S. Army regiment made up of NISEI that saw heavy action during World War II. The exploits of the 442nd and the 100TH INFANTRY BATTALION in the European theater have become legendary and served as an important factor in the postwar world of the Japanese American community.

In July of 1942, a committee formed by the Army Chief of Staff G-2 Section began to meet to consider the question of whether a small Japanese American military unit should be formed. This proposal stemmed from the existence of around 4,000 *nisei* soldiers who had already been inducted by this time, but who were

The 442nd Regimental Combat Team was among the most highly decorated American World War II units of its size. *Hawaii State Archives*

being kept out of active duty out of fear and distrust. While some were in training as the 100th Infantry Battalion, many others had been assembled at Camp Robinson in Arkansas where they performed noncombat related tasks. There was also the matter of the VARSITY VICTORY VOLUNTEERS in Hawaii, a volunteer group made up mostly of *nisei* students who had been booted out the Hawaii Territorial Guard on account of their race. Though engaged in important construction and maintenance work, they and many other *nisei* were anxious to be allowed to "prove their loyalty" through combat duty. After three months of consideration, the committee issued its recommendation opposing the formation of a *nisei* combat unit "because of the universal distrust in which they are held."

However, other factors intervened. Largely through the efforts of Assistant Secretary of War JOHN J. MCCLOY, the War Department decided to form a new Japanese American unit by the end of 1942. The primary factor leading to this decision had to do with issues of image and propaganda. The War Department recognized that the formation of an all-*nisei* unit would be a good way to counter Japanese propaganda emphasizing the discrimination Japanese Americans faced because of their race. There was also the matter of the image the United States presented to its allies as a leader in democracy and freedom. An all-*nisei* combat unit seemed an ideal way to bolster that image. On February 1, 1943, President Roosevelt announced the formation of the 442nd Regimental Combat Team, with the famous words, "Americanism is not, and never was, a matter of race or ancestry."

Early in 1943, the call went out for volunteers for the 442nd. The original plan called for a quota of 3,000 volunteers from the mainland and 1,500 from Hawaii.

Immediately upon the announcement of the 442nd, nearly 10,000 Hawaii *nisei* volunteered and over 2,600 were accepted for induction. Fifteen to seventeen thousand Japanese Americans gathered in Honolulu on March 28, 1943, to send off 2,686 *nisei* volunteers to basic training on the mainland in a gala celebration. By contrast the call for volunteers on the mainland went out mostly to Japanese Americans incarcerated in CONCENTRATION CAMPS who had just been administered a poorly prepared and, to some, an insulting questionnaire (see LOYALTY QUESTIONS). Only 1,256 mainland *nisei* volunteered (out of 23,606 *nisei* of draft age) from the camps and around 800 were accepted for induction.

The volunteers from Hawaii and the mainland began to arrive in Camp Shelby, Mississippi, in March of 1943 and basic training was begun in May. Lasting for 10 months—far longer than the four to six months of training most troops received—training went well, despite the friction that soon developed between the Hawaiian "BUDDHAHEADS" and the mainland "KOTONKS." Given the dramatically different settings from which they came, such friction was not surprising. Hawaiians thought the mainlanders reserved, distrustful and arrogant; mainlanders thought the Hawaiians loud, uncouth and bullying. By the end of training, the antagonisms had largely evaporated—they would disappear entirely after Hawaiians and mainlanders fought side by side—and the unit had taken a new motto, the Hawaiian crap shooter's cry "GO FOR BROKE!"

In March of 1944, the 442nd finally received orders to prepare for overseas shipment. The 442nd left for Europe in May, without their 1st Battalion which had been left behind as a source of replacement troops. They arrived in Naples on June 2 and left for the Anzio beachhead. At a rest area near Civitavecchia, they hooked up with the battle-tested 100th Battalion, which became the new 1st Battalion of the 442nd. Starting on June 26, the 442nd saw their first action in the Rome-Arno campaign at Belvedere and Sassetta. For the next few months, they would battle entrenched German positions in the Italian countryside, helping to clear the approaches to Leghorn, Pisa and Florence. To gain 40 miles, they had suffered 1,272 casualties, roughly one-fourth of their total troop strength. The worst was yet to come.

The 442nd saw their roughest duty in the Rhineland campaign in France in September and October of 1944. Facing heavy and often desperate Nazi opposition, the 442nd liberated the towns of Bruyères, Belmont and Biffontaine. In late October, they were ordered to rescue members of the 141st Regiment's 1st Battalion, which was caught behind enemy lines. The successful and harrowing rescue of the "LOST BATTALION" resulted in 800 *nisei* casualties to rescue 211 men.

After a break of sorts guarding a portion of the Franco-Italian border near Nice, the 442nd returned to Italy in March 1945. There, they participated in the assault that cracked the Gothic Line, attacking Nazi strongholds in the mountains of the Apennines. By mid-May, the war in Europe was over. In 225 days of combat, the 442nd Regimental Combat Team had compiled an impressive battle record. It has been written that the 442nd suffered the highest casualty rate and was the most decorated unit for its size and length of service in American military history. More than 700 had been killed and the number of wounded was three times the strength of the regiment. On July 15, 1946, the 442nd was received on the White House lawn by President Truman, who stated, "You fought not only the enemy but you fought prejudice—and you have won."

The postwar legacy of the 442nd proved to be as impressive as their achievements on the battlefield. In the cold war world, their achievements served as great propaganda for an America still torn by racial inequality. Their deeds would be repeatedly cited in mainland campaigns to overturn the ALIEN LAND LAWS and other discriminatory legislation. In Hawaii, 442nd veterans played crucial roles in the rise of the ILWU and the Democratic Party "REVOLUTION OF 1954." Their story would be featured in countless magazine articles, several books and even a Hollywood movie (starring Van Johnson) titled *Go For Broke*. They were also an important factor in the REDRESS MOVEMENT in the 1980s; the redress bill which passed the house was H.R. 442, named in their honor. Though it should not have been needed, the achievements of the 442nd Regimental Combat Team helped to prove that Japanese Americans were as American as anyone else.

For further reading, see Masayo Duus. *Unlikely Liberators: The Men of the 100th and the 442nd*. Honolulu: University of Hawaii Press, 1987; Roland Kotani. *The Japanese in Hawaii: A Century of Struggle*. Honolulu: Hochi, Ltd., 1985; Thomas D. Murphy. *Ambassadors in Arms: The Story of Hawaii's 100th Battalion*. Honolulu: University of Hawaii Press, 1954; Chester Tanaka. *Go for Broke: A Pictorial History of the Japanese American 100th Infantry Battalion and the 442nd Regimental Combat Team*. Richmond, Calif.: Go for Broke, Inc., 1981; and John Tsukano. *Bridge of Love*. Honolulu: Hawaii Hosts, Inc., 1985.

Fresno Rodo Domei Kai   Early Japanese immigrant labor union. The Fresno Rodo Domei Kai (Fresno Labor League) was organized on August 20, 1908 by Tetsugoro Takeuchi and had a membership of about 2,000 workers. Its aims were strictly to serve the interests of Japanese agricultural workers against both growers and LABOR CONTRACTORS. The official organ of the Labor League, the *Rodo,* was published from November

1908 to September 1909. *Rodo* articles encouraged workers to unite while attacking the emperor system, capitalism and militarism.

In 1909, the Labor League held two major activities. On August 25, 1909, it held a labor convention in Fresno which drew an audience of 300 from throughout the state. On September 19, it held a joint rally with the Fresno branch of the International Workers of the World in which speakers of Mexican and Italian nationalities also spoke. Despite these activities, the league did not really expand, neither opening new branches nor broadening its journal. The decline of the organization was exacerbated by the expenses of a court case resulting from a knife fight between Takeuchi and a critic of the league, Zenjiro Otsuka. The group also faced a hostile Japanese-language press, the opposition of the local JAPANESE ASSOCIATION, and the news of the Daigyaku Jiken (a wholesale crackdown of Socialists by the Japanese government) in 1910. But perhaps the biggest problem the group faced was that of trying to organize migrant laborers who remained in Fresno no more than 2½ months at a time and whose composition was constantly changing. The organization died when Takeuchi left the Fresno area in 1910.

For further reading, see Yuji Ichioka. "Early Issei Socialists and the Japanese Community." In Gee, Emma, ed. *Counterpoint: Perspectives on Asian America.* Los Angeles: Asian American Studies Center, University of California, 1976. 47–62 and Yuji Ichioka. *The Issei: The World of the First Generation Japanese Immigrants, 1885–1924.* New York: The Free Press, 1988.

Frick v. Webb   Test case concerning the prohibition of ISSEI participation in agricultural land companies mandated by the 1920 (CALIFORNIA) ALIEN LAND LAW. The case of *Frick v. Webb* was part of the JAPANESE ASSOCIATION strategy to test the legality of various provisions of the 1920 Alien Land Law in the courts. Raymond L. Frick owned 28 shares of stock in the Merced Farm Co. that he wished to sell to Nobutada Satow; this action violated the provision of the Alien Land Law that prohibited "ALIENS INELIGIBLE TO CITIZENSHIP" from owning stock in agricultural land companies. Frick and Satow filed a Bill of Complaint in the United States district court in San Francisco alleging that the prohibition of this transaction was unconstitutional. The brief for the plaintiffs, presented by land law specialist lawyers Albert H. Elliot and Guy E. Calden, ended by quoting the following lines from Shakespeare's *Merchant of Venice:*

> You take my house, when you do take the prop
> That doth sustain my house;

> You take my life, when you do take the means
> Whereby I live.

On May 23, 1922, the court ruled that the ban on *issei* owning stock in land companies was constitutional and did not violate any treaties between Japan and the U.S.

As with several other land law test cases, the *Frick v. Webb* decision was appealed to the Supreme Court through the sponsorship of the Japanese Associations. On November 19, 1923, the Court upheld the lower court decision, ruling conclusively that *issei* were indeed banned from owing stock in land companies. On the same day, the Court ruled in the WEBB V. O'BRIEN case that CROPPING CONTRACTS would be illegal, while one week earlier, it had upheld the land law's prohibition on leasing in the PORTERFIELD V. WEBB and TERRACE V. THOMPSON decisions. In the space of one week, Japanese immigrant challenges to the Alien Land Law had all been decided and had all resulted in defeat for the *issei*. (See ALIEN LAND LAWS.)

For further reading, see Yuji Ichioka. "Japanese Immigrant Response to the 1920 California Alien Land Law." *Agricultural History* 58:2 (Apr. 1984): 157–78 and *The Issei: The World of the First Generation Japanese Immigrants, 1885–1924.* New York: The Free Press, 1988 for background on the legal test cases; see Consulate-General of Japan. *Documental History of Law Cases Affecting Japanese in the United States, 1916–1924.* 2 Vols. San Francisco: Consulate-General of Japan, 1925. New York: Arno Press, 1978 for transcripts of the legal cases themselves.

Fujii Sei v. State of California   1952 California Supreme Court decision which helped to overturn the 1920 (CALIFORNIA) ALIEN LAND LAW. In 1948, Fujii, owner and publisher of the *Kashu Mainichi*, bought property in the eastern section of Los Angeles and took title to the land in his own name. Fujii was a Japanese alien, and his action was barred by the provisions of the ALIEN LAND LAW that prohibited "ALIENS INELIGIBLE TO CITIZENSHIP" from owning land in California. There was also no treaty existing at the time between the U.S. and Japan that would have allowed Fujii to own the land. The State of California instituted an action to confiscate the land, and the superior court ruled that the property escheated to the state. Fujii appealed to the California Supreme Court, forcing it to directly rule on the right of an ISSEI to purchase land in California, contrary to the provisions of the Alien Land Law. The California Supreme Court ruled on April 17, 1952, that the provisions of the Alien Land Law denying the right to own land to aliens ineligible to citizenship violated the equal protection clauses of both the constitution of California and the Constitution of the United States.

The decision of this case, along with that of MASAOKA HARUYE V. STATE OF CALIFORNIA, elucidated the racially discriminatory nature of the Alien Land Law, which had been in force for over three decades.
For further reading see Frank F. Chuman. *The Bamboo People: The Law and Japanese-Americans.* Del Mar, Calif.: Publisher's Inc., 1976.   DENNIS YAMAMOTO

Fujimoto, Charles K.   Research soil chemist at the Agricultural Experimentation Station at the University of Hawaii and one of the HAWAII SEVEN. In September 1947 Fujimoto and his wife, Eileen Kee Fujimoto, who had been a member of the Communist Party Executive Board from as early as 1946, attended the Communist Party leadership school in San Francisco. A year later, in 1948, Fujimoto proclaimed that he was the chairman of the Communist Party in Hawaii.

Fujimoto is best known as one of the Hawaii Seven who were arrested August 28, 1951, under the Smith Act for conspiring to teach the overthrow of the U.S. government by force and violence. Eileen Kee Fujimoto, the former secretary of the ILWU, was arrested the same day as Fujimoto as one of the Hawaii Seven. Both Fujimoto and his wife were found guilty in 1953 of the charges of conspiracy against the U.S. government. As a result Fujimoto was sentenced to five years in prison and fined $5,000, while Eileen Kee Fujimoto was sentenced to three years and fined $2,000.

Although the Hawaii Seven were successful in their appeal of their charges in January 1958, Fujimoto was removed from positions of influence and was never again employed as a chemist due to his arrest and conviction. According to historian Roland Kotani, despite being blacklisted Fujimoto continued to advocate left-wing views.
For further reading, see Gavan Daws. *Shoal of Time: A History of the Hawaiian Islands.* New York: Macmillan, 1968. Honolulu: University of Hawaii Press, 1974; Lawrence H. Fuchs. *Hawaii Pono: A Social History.* New York: Harcourt, Brace and World, 1961; Dorothy Ochiai Hazama, and Jane Okamoto Komeiji. *Okage Sama De: The Japanese in Hawai'i.* Foreword by Daniel Inouye. Honolulu: Bess Press, 1986; and Roland Kotani. *The Japanese in Hawaii: A Century of Struggle.* Honolulu: Hochi, Ltd., 1985.   STACEY HIROSE

fujinkai   Women's clubs. Before World War II, very few ISSEI women were given the opportunity to serve as board members or presidents of KENJINKAI groups or church groups. Despite this limitation, women did take part in club and church activities. In many cases, wives of club and church leaders formed *fujinkai* to support the activities of the larger organization. As members of the *fujinkai,* women acted as food servers, fund raisers and bazaar organizers. Although the *issei* woman's sphere was severely limited to traditional women's activities such as cooking, serving and entertaining, it was within the realm of the *fujinkai* that an *issei* woman could demonstrate her skill as a leader and an organizer.
For further reading, see Mei Nakano. *Japanese American Women: Three Generations, 1890–1990.* Berkeley and Sebastopol, CA: National Japanese American Historical Society and Mina Press, 1990.   EDITH KANESHIRO

Fujita Yoshiro   Secretary in the Japanese consulate in San Francisco whose journey to the Pacific Northwest in 1891 exposed widespread illegal activity in the Japanese community. Worried about the image of Japan that Japanese immigrants in the United States were promulgating, the Japanese Foreign Ministry sought the help of its consulates to ascertain the condition of the immigrant enclaves. Vancouver consul Shun Sugimura sent reports of gambling and prostitution along with vivid local newspaper accounts of same to an increasingly worried Japanese foreign ministry. The consul in San Francisco, SUTEMI CHINDA, dispatched Yoshiro Fujita on a journey to Washington and Oregon to investigate conditions.

The 11-day journey was eye opening. When he arrived in Seattle, Fujita found about 250 Japanese immigrants, about 40 of whom had legitimate jobs. As for the rest, he wrote "the remaining two hundred Japanese residents are, if not PROSTITUTES or proprietors of houses of pleasure, either gamblers or pimps." With few exceptions, the rest of his trip yielded similar results. At nearly every stop, he found a community of Japanese pimps and prostitutes. (It should be noted that in the "Wild West" of this time where men vastly outnumbered women, illicit activity of this kind was common among all races.) Fujita's reports provide a vivid snapshot of the state of the Japanese community of the time. Within a decade, large-scale labor migration of Japanese workers from Japan and Hawaii would dramatically change the nature and composition of the Japanese American community.
For further reading, see Donald Teruo Hata. *'Undesirables': Early Immigrants and the Anti-Japanese Movement in San Francisco, 1892–1893: Prelude to Exclusion.* New York: Arno Press, 1978, which devotes a chapter to Fujita's trip. See Yuji Ichioka. "Ameyuki-san: Japanese Prostitutes in Nineteenth-Century America." *Amerasia Journal* 4.1 (1977): 1–21 and *The Issei: The World of the First Generation Japanese Immigrants, 1885–1924.* New York: The Free Press, 1988 for more on the characteristics of the early Japanese settlements in the United States.

Fukuda, Mitsuyoshi   War hero, businessman. Fukuda holds the distinction of being the first Japanese American vice president of a BIG FIVE company. He became vice president of industrial relations for Castle & Cooke on August 20, 1966. He joined the company in 1946 after serving in the 100TH INFANTRY BATTALION and attaining the rank of army infantry major, the highest rank awarded any NISEI combat officer.

For further reading, see Dorothy Ochiai Hazama, and Jane Okamoto Komeiji. *Okage Sama De: The Japanese in Hawai'i*. Foreword by Daniel Inouye. Honolulu: Bess Press, 1986.

Fukunaga case Controversial murder case involving a young NISEI man. The kidnapping and murder of a rich HAOLE child by *nisei* teenager Myles Fukunaga was a sensational and famous case in the racially and economically stratified Hawaii of the 1920s. The crime, trial and public reaction to both exposed the toll of poverty and racial discrimination both on the psyches of the Japanese Americans themselves and on equality and justice in the territory's institutions. On Tuesday morning, September 18, 1928, Myles Fukunaga, dressed as a hospital orderly, picked up ten-year-old Gill Jamieson at Punahou School. Earlier, school officials had received a call indicating that Jamieson's mother had been injured in an auto accident and that an orderly was being sent to pick him up at school. About one hour after picking him up, Fukunaga killed the boy, choking him to death after hitting him three times with a steel chisel. His body was left in a clearing of kiawe trees near the Ala Wai canal.

A few hours later, Frederick Jamieson, the vice president of the Hawaiian Trust Company, received a note demanding $10,000 for the safe return of his son. "The world is a mere stage in which we humans are the humble actors or players. We are about to play our part in our secret drama . . . ," read the note, which was signed "We 3 'Kings.'" After receiving a call at around 9:00 P.M., the elder Jamieson followed the instructions in the note and brought the ransom money to the indicated contact point. After turning over $4,000, Jamieson demanded to see his son before paying the rest of the money. The kidnapper agreed, but disappeared into the bushes and didn't return. After this episode, Jamieson sounded the general alarm; the *Honolulu Star-Bulletin* broke the story in its 11:00 P.M. edition.

News of the crime sent shock waves through both the *haole* and Japanese American communities. Numerous groups offered their help in the search for the boy and vigilante groups formed to scour the Japanese sections of the island for suspects. Twenty-eight thousand dollars in reward money was raised in two days. A lynch mob atmosphere prevailed, as several young Japanese American men were arrested on the flimsiest evidence. On Thursday morning, the 20th, the *Star-Bulletin* received a letter from the "Three Kings," verified with a bill from the ransom money, announcing the boy's death and that the writer would "plead guilty" and accept "the death penalty." Later in the day, the boy's body was recovered. His funeral took place on Friday and was attended by hundreds. Then on Sunday, Fukunaga was arrested after

attempting to spend part of the ransom money. Mobs lined the streets to catch a glimpse of the suspect after the arrest was announced; firemen had to clear the mob with fire hoses.

Fukunaga immediately confessed to the crime, telling a sad life story in the process. He was the eldest of six children of a former plantation worker who had graduated Waialua Grammar School at the head of his class. He was an aspiring intellectual who loved Shakespeare and American movies and who embraced *haole* culture while shunning that of his parents. However his dreams were tempered by the reality of his Japanese racial background and his family's dire poverty. He was forced to postpone his education to work to support his family. "That was my biggest disappointment," he wrote in his confession, "I wanted to study." He worked 12-hour days at the Queen's Hospital, giving $35 of his $40 a month wages to his family. He quit after being denied a $5 raise after two years on the job, and took employment at the Seaside Hotel, working 80 hours a week in the pantry. He became increasingly unstable, attempting suicide, and retreating more and more to a world of magazines and books. While he was recovering from appendicitis and unable to work, his family was unable to pay its rent on the small house they occupied near the corner of Beretania and Alapai Streets. A rent collector from the Hawaiian Trust Company visited the family in May 1928 demanding the immediate payment of $20 the family did not have and threatened to evict them. Feeling somewhat responsible for the family's plight, Fukunaga developed a scheme to kidnap Jamieson, partly in revenge against the Hawaiian Trust Company, basing it on the famous 1924 Leopold and Loeb kidnapping and murder case. "I had hard feelings against [the] company . . . A rich company like that could not wait for just a mere $20 sum," he wrote. The plan involved using the ransom money to send his parents back to Japan and to confess to the killing, expecting to be sentenced to death.

His expectations proved correct. The editor of the *Star-Bulletin* undoubtedly spoke for many when he wrote that Fukunaga "must go straight to a legal, fair and honest trial, and straight from the formality of that trial to the gallows which the law provides." His trial lasted one week. Though some segments of the Japanese American community (notably KINZABURO MAKINO) protested on the grounds of Fukunaga's obvious insanity and the differential treatment *haole* perpetrators of similar crimes received (a blatant example of this can be found in the MASSIE CASE that took place two years later), it was to no avail. Myles Yutaka Fukunaga was hanged on November 19, 1929.

For further reading, see Roland Kotani. *The Japanese in Hawaii: A Century of Struggle*. Honolulu: Hochi, Ltd., 1985 and

Dennis M. Ogawa. *Jan Ken Po: The World of Hawaii's Japanese Americans.* Honolulu: Japanese American Research Center, 1973.

[Account and interpretation based on Kotani; all quotes taken from there also.]

Fukuzawa, Yukichi (1835–1901)

Educator. "The greatest popularizer of Western lore" according to historian and former U.S. ambassador to Japan Edwin O. Reischauer, Yukichi Fukuzawa was a leading shaper of opinion in emerging modern Japan. He traveled to the West on several occasions and wrote enormously popular books in Japan—between 1860 and 1893, an estimated 3.5 million copies of his books were in circulation. Beginning his writing prior to the fall of the feudal Tokugawa military regime, his work became progressively more vociferous in its advocation of Western liberalism. Yet he also was a staunch nationalist who believed in adopting the ways of the West in order to make Japan stronger. He went on to found a school which became Keio University, one of Japan's two most prestigious private schools.

Fukuzawa also directly and indirectly encouraged travel and immigration to the U.S. in such books as *Seiyo Jijo* (Western Conditions) in 1866 and *Seiyo Tabi Annai* (A Travel Guide to the West) in 1867, as well as in his Tokyo newspaper *Jiji Shimpo* starting in 1882. He also financed a short-lived attempt to form a Japanese agricultural colony in California in 1887.

For further reading, see Mikiso Hane. *Peasants, Rebels and Outcastes: The Underside of Modern Japan.* New York: Pantheon Books, 1982; Yuji Ichioka. *The Issei: The World of the First Generation Japanese Immigrants, 1885–1924.* New York: The Free Press, 1988; and Edwin O. Reischauer. *Japan: The Story of a Nation.* Revised Edition. New York: Alfred A. Knopf, 1974.

furo

Japanese-style bathtub, or the act of bathing. ISSEI and some NISEI adapted the *furo* to conditions they found in America.

Characteristic of the Japanese-style bath are a deep tub in which bathers are able to immerse themselves up to the neck while seated and the practice of washing outside the tub before entering it to soak and relax. In this way, the bath water stays clean for succeeding bathers. Water is either heated externally or by building a fire under the tub. In Japan, public baths in which many people soaked together in larger tubs were common. Offering to scrub the backs of elders and superiors was a common courtesy.

Accounts of early *issei* life indicate that the *furo* was a highlight in the arduous day of both the Hawaii plantation laborer and the mainland migrant laborer. The hot soak at the end of the day seemed to ease some of the hardship of 10 or 12 or more hours of labor. *Issei* plantation worker Tokusuke Oshiro recalled running back to the plantation camp to be first in the *furo* so the water would still be clean. Portland bathhouse owner Tsuneki Kagawa recalled serving around fifteen men and 10 women on weekdays and 30 men and 20 women with numerous *nisei* children on weekends. Japanese-style baths cost 15¢; the men's tub could hold seven or eight, while the women's held four or five. Kagawa also offered Western (i.e., private) baths for 25¢.

As in Japan, many Japanese American households had their own *furo,* typically located outside or in a separate room without a toilet. (Most of the time, there would be a separate Western-style bathroom with toilet and shower/bathtub elsewhere in the house.) Adapting the basic design to available materials, Japanese American *furo* might be made of metal horse troughs or California redwood and heated by fire, gas burner or hot running water. Though largely abandoned by the SANSEI generation (though like many other Americans, *sansei* or YONSEI might well have a not dissimilar hot tub or jacuzzi in their back yards), many Japanese American households—especially those in rural areas—still have *furo,* though many are seldom used. Bathhouses, also known as *furo-ya* or *sento,* could be found in many pre–World War II Japanese American communities. These public baths served as a center for relaxation and socializing among community members.

Oshiro quote from Ethnic Studies Oral History Project/United Okinawan Association of Hawaii. *Uchinanchu: A History of Okinawans in Hawaii.* Honolulu: Ethnic Studies Program, University of Hawaii at Manoa, 1981. 382; Kagawa's from Kazuo Ito. *Issei: A History of Japanese Immigrants in North America.* Shinichiro Nakamura, Jean S. Gerard, trans. Seattle: Executive Committee for the Publication of *Issei: A History of Japanese Immigrants in North America,* 1973. 861–62. Also used to compile this entry: "Memories of the Old 'Furoya'" *Hawaii Herald* 6 Nov. 1981: 6–7.

Furuya, Masajiro (1862–1938)

Banker, merchant and manufacturer. Born in 1862 in Yamanashi PREFECTURE, Masajiro Furuya became fascinated with the idea of going to the U.S. while serving in the military. Not wanting to go over as a laborer, he spent two years learning the tailoring trade in Tokyo before coming to America at the age of 27. In 1890, he landed in Vancouver and eventually opened a tailor shop in Seattle specializing in women's suits. Two years later he started a grocery store in Seattle while continuing his tailoring on the side. With the great increase of the Japanese immigrant population in the 1890s and early 1900s and the discovery of gold in Alaska, his business grew rapidly. Before long, his mercantile business occupied a six-story building in downtown Seattle that had wholesale and retail import and export divisions. Furuya's store provided a large percentage of the Japanese provisions consumed in the Northwest, and soon branches were opened in Portland, Yokohama, Tacoma, Kobe and Vancouver.

In 1907 Furuya organized the Japanese Commercial Bank, later purchasing control of the faltering Oriental American Bank in 1914 and the Seattle Specie Bank in 1923. By 1928, the three banks had been consolidated as the Pacific Commercial Bank. During World War I Furuya organized the Gudewere Manufacturing Company to produce women's suits and coats.

Known as a frugal and conservative man, Furuya built his financial empire with the help of an able and loyal core of employees. A devout Christian and Seattle First Methodist Church member, he surrounded himself with Christians and encouraged his workers to adopt his faith.

In the midst of the Great Depression, on October 23, 1931, he went bankrupt. Though there were rumors of impropriety in the community, it appears the bank was simply overextended in good times and went under when the economy turned sour. Furuya went to Los Angeles and eventually returned to Japan, dying in Yokohama in February 1938. His name remained so well known that some of his former employees reopened stores bearing his name in Seattle, Yokohama and Vancouver soon after the bankruptcy.

For further reading, see Bill Hosokawa. *Nisei: The Quiet Americans*. New York: William Morrow & Co., 1969; Kazuo Ito. *Issei: A History of Japanese Immigrants in North America*. Shinichiro Nakamura, Jean S. Gerard, trans. Seattle: Executive Committee for the Publication of *Issei: A History of Japanese Immigrants in North America*, 1973; and Hisashi Tsurutani. *America Bound: The Japanese and Opening of the American West*. Betsey Scheiner, trans. Tokyo: Japan Times, Inc., 1989.

G

gaman   Japanese term meaning to endure, persist, persevere, or to do one's best in times of frustration and adversity.

According to UCLA sociologist HARRY H. L. KITANO, *gaman* is a concept that refers to "internalization of, and suppression of, anger and emotion." Thus, Kitano maintains that "to *gaman*" is to take no aggressive retaliatory action against one's misfortunes. Betty S. Furuta asserts that the employment of *gaman* by, for example, the ISSEI during World War II in order to endure the humiliation and hardships of incarceration, is mistaken by many non-Japanese to indicate a lack of assertiveness or initiative rather than strength in the face of difficulty and suffering.

For further reading, see Betty S. Furuta. "Ethnic Identities of Japanese-American Families: Implications for Counseling." In Getty, Cathleen, and Winnifred Humphreys, eds. *Understanding the Family: Stress and Change in American Family Life*. New York: Appleton-Century-Crofts, 1981; Harry H. L. Kitano. *Japanese Americans: The Evolution of a Subculture*. 1969. 2nd Edition. Englewood Cliffs, NJ: Prentice-Hall, Inc., 1976; *Kodansha Encyclopedia of Japan*. Tokyo: Kodansha, 1983.

STACEY HIROSE

gannen-mono   First group of Japanese immigrants to Hawaii. The *gannen-mono* (literally "first year people," so named because they came in the first year after the MEIJI RESTORATION) of 1868 were the first Japanese immigrants to Hawaii and the only Japanese immigrants to Hawaii until 1885.

In a letter dated March 10, 1865, Hawaii foreign minister Robert Crichton Wyllie asked Japan-based American businessman Eugene M. Van Reed to look into the possibility of Japanese laborers being recruited for work on Hawaii's sugar PLANTATIONS. With the rapidly expanding market for sugar on the mainland and the lack of an adequate labor supply to meet this demand, Hawaii's sugar planters looked hopefully to Japan for the solution. Van Reed reported that the possibilities looked good and agreed to seek such labor migration. He was allocated the nominal sum of $1,925 by Hawaii's Bureau of Immigration toward his task. He received permission from the Japanese government to recruit workers for Hawaii, with the stipulation that they be returned to Japan at the completion of their three-year contract. With monthly wages of $4.00 per month and food, lodging and passage paid by the employers, he recruited laborers from the streets of Yokohama. One hundred forty-nine people—141 men, 6 women and 2 children—set sail on the *Scioto* on May 17, 1868.

The group ranged in age from 13 to 46 and was clearly not prepared for the rigors of sugar plantation labor. The Yokohama group consisted largely of adventurers and unemployed city dwellers. They included a hairdresser, cooks, potters and other urban types. Among them was Yonekichi Sakuma, a stowaway who kept a diary of the voyage to Hawaii and TOMI OZAWA, for a time, the only Japanese woman in Hawaii. After a stormy, 33-day voyage which saw the death of one passenger, the *Scioto* landed in Honolulu harbor on June 19, 1868.

After an apparently pleasant welcome to Hawaii, the *gannen-mono* were assigned to plantations on various islands and became virtual slaves. Not only were the former city dwellers not used to the physical demands of laboring under a tropical sun, but they were also dismayed by the authoritarian treatment they received from their employers. Within a month, both planters and laborers had lodged complaints with the Bureau of Immigration. The Meiji government was alarmed at this turn of events and sent the UYENO EMBASSY to Hawaii to investigate charges of mistreatment. The return of 40 *gannen-mono* was secured; the others stayed on. Thirteen laborers completed their three-year contracts before returning to Japan. The rest stayed on as the true pioneers of Hawaii's Japanese American community. Three attended a *gannen-mono* reunion in 1922. The last of the *gannen-mono,* Sentaro Ishii, died on September 18, 1936, at the age of 102.

For further reading, see Hilary Conroy. *The Japanese Frontier in Hawaii, 1868–1898.* Berkeley: University of California Press, 1953. New York: Arno Press, 1978; Masaji Marumoto. " 'First Year' Immigrants to Hawaii & Eugene Van Reed." In Conroy, Hilary, and T. Scott Miyakawa, eds. *East Across the Pacific: Historical and Sociological Studies of Japanese Immigration and Assimilation.* Santa Barbara, CA: America Bibliographical Center—Clio Press, 1972. 5–39; Gary Y. Okihiro. *Cane Fires: The Anti-Japanese Movement in Hawaii, 1865–1945.* Philadelphia: Temple University Press, 1991; and United Japanese Society of Hawaii. *History of Japanese in Hawaii.* James H. Okahata, ed. Honolulu: United Japanese Society of Hawaii, 1971. O. A. Bushnell's *The Stone of Kannon* (Honolulu: University of Hawaii Press, 1979) and The *Water of Kane* (Honolulu: University of Hawaii Press, 1980) are both novels based on the *gannen-mono* story.

Gannon Committee   The Gannon Committee, under the leadership of conservative Chester Gannon (R-Sacramento), was formed in the California state assembly in August of 1943 to deal specifically with the so-called "Japanese problem." Its counterpart in the state senate was chaired by Senator Jack Tenney of Los Angeles where together they formed the Joint Fact Finding Committee on Un-American Activities, also known as the "little DIES COMMITTEE" for their similar scope and tactics.

The first act by the Gannon Committee was to adopt a resolution to keep all Japanese Americans in CONCENTRATION CAMPS until the end of the war. They conducted investigations and hearings on the potential ramifications of letting the Japanese American population back into the state. Witnesses sympathetic to Japanese Americans were heard, but were badgered by the committee. At one point, Gannon told ACLU attorney A. L. WIREN, "I've had all I want of the Civil Liberties Union. Now you get out of here or I'll have an officer put you out." Other sympathetic organizations also testified, but were questioned in such a manner that the hearings resembled an inquisition. Later, individuals such as CAREY MCWILLIAMS and other liberals were targeted for investigation by the committee. A second hearing was held, according to Gannon, "to smoke out pressure groups behind the move to return Japs to the West Coast . . ."

Gannon was fierce in his determination to keep Japanese Americans from returning to California. He and his committee, along with Senator Tenney and his cohorts, were responsible for dozens of bills aimed at Japanese Americans during World War II. His campaign to exclude Japanese Americans did have limits, however: he did not advocate the barring of NISEI from state-supported universities—that, he felt, was unconstitutional.

For further reading, see David Caute. *The Great Fear.* New York: Simon and Schuster, 1978.   GLEN KITAYAMA

Gardena   Suburban city about 10 miles south of downtown Los Angeles known for its large Japanese American community. A pre–World War II farming area populated by many ISSEI strawberry growers and nurseries, Gardena became one of the most important Japanese American residential communities of the postwar era.

The roots of the Gardena Japanese American community go back to the 1900s. In line with the general southern migration of Japanese immigrants from the San Francisco area to the Los Angeles area after the 1906 earthquake, the Japanese population in Gardena grew rapidly. There were 253 Japanese Americans in the Gardena area by 1907 who farmed almost 1,000 acres. An unusual number of these *issei* were family farmers seeking permanent settlement; indeed Gardena had the most balanced sex ratio among *issei* of any area in 1906. The reasons for the rapid growth had to do with Gardena's climate and soil and the access to transportation systems that eased the marketing of crops. Given the settlement orientation of these early ISSEI, a community quickly developed with small businesses and economic and cultural organizations. By 1907, there were among other features, a strawberry growers association, a Japanese hall and a Japanese-language school. The 1910s saw the prewar population peak and begin to decline as the *issei* began to spread to other nearby areas and the farmers began to diversify their crops and move away from strawberries. By 1940, Gardena's Japanese American population stood at 320 out of a total population of 5,509, just 6%.

With the mass removal and detention of Japanese Americans on the West Coast during World War II, the Japanese American community in Gardena ceased to exist. Though a few returned to Gardena when Japanese Americans were allowed back in California in 1945, a dramatic rise in population occurred in the 1950s when the non-white population of Gardena nearly tripled between 1950 and 1957. Growth continued at a slower pace through the 1960s and '70s. By 1970, Japanese Americans numbered 8,412 and made up 20% of the total Gardena population, the highest such percentage for any mainland United States city. Unlike the prewar farming community, the postwar community was a suburban one in which residents lived in tract homes and commuted to nearby jobs or ran local business enterprises. Gardena became a magnet for resettling NISEI, especially for those from Hawaii, and for SHIN-ISSEI, or new immigrants from Japan. The '70s and '80s saw the large-scale influx of major Japanese business enterprises and a plethora of support businesses that followed in their wake. The Gardena of today continues to have a large Japanese American community, with increasing numbers of other Asian Americans also moving in. The 1990 Census shows the population to be 33 percent Asian, 23 percent African American, 22 percent Latino and 22 percent white.

Gardena has been one of the most studied Japanese American communities. For a history of pre–World War II Gardena, see Lane Ryo Hirabayashi and George Tanaka. *The Early Gardena Valley and the Issei*. Gardena, Calif.: Gardena Pioneer Project, 1987 and "The Issei Community in Moneta and the Gardena Valley, 1900–1920." *Southern California Quarterly* 70.2 (Summer 1988): 127–58. For differing perspectives on postwar Gardena, see Kaoru Oguri Kendis. *A Matter of Comfort: Ethnic Maintenance and Ethnic Style among Third-Generation Japanese Americans*. New York: AMS Press, 1989; Philip Motoo Okamoto. "Evolution of a Japanese American Enclave: Gardena, California. A Case Study of Ethnic Community Change and Continuity." Thesis, University of California, Los Angeles, 1991; Joan M. Takaki. "An Ethnographic Study of Occupational Changes of the Japanese in Gardena." Thesis, California State University, Dominguez Hills, 1985; Cathy Lynn Tanimoto. "Changing Japanese Ethnicity: A Case Study of Gardena, California." Thesis, Louisiana State University, 1975; and Steve Tatsukawa. "Gardena: Part One: A Saga of Youth, Drugs and Middle Class Misery." *Gidra* 5.7 (July 1973): 6–8 and "Gardena, Part Two: 'Everybody Needs a Helping Hand.'" *Gidra* 5.9 (Sept. 1973): 1, 5–8.

Gentlemen's Agreement

Gentlemen's Agreement 1908 agreement between Japan and the United States that halted Japanese labor migration to the United States. Negotiated at the highest levels of their respective governments, the Gentlemen's Agreement between Japan and the United States was result of a series of events stemming from the SAN FRANCISCO SCHOOL BOARD SEGREGATION ORDER OF 1906.

The segregation order of October 11, 1906 and the ANTI-JAPANESE MOVEMENT in California that had inspired it were affronts to the pride of Japan and created a delicate diplomatic problem for President Theodore Roosevelt and the United States. Roosevelt dispatched Secretary of Commerce and Labor Victor H. Metcalf, a native Californian, to the West Coast to investigate the situation. Meanwhile, he met with Japanese ambassador Viscount Suizo Aoki on October 29 and read him relevant passages from his forthcoming address to Congress in which he strongly denounced the agitation against the Japanese immigrants. After a trip to Panama, Roosevelt delivered his address to Congress in early December in which he also denounced the segregation order and advocated a congressional act allowing ISSEI to become naturalized citizens. (There is much evidence to suggest that Roosevelt's strong words were primarily for the benefit of the Japanese government as no naturalization bill was ever introduced into Congress at Roosevelt's behest; such a bill could probably have passed over the objections of western and southern congressmen.) Two weeks later, Metcalf's report arrived. He found that a grand total of 93 students of Japanese descent had been affected by the segregation order and, with the exception of a couple of overage students, saw no rationale for segregation.

Both Roosevelt and Metcalf were excoriated in California newspapers and the exclusionist political leaders hardened their stances. Roosevelt and Secretary of State Elihu Root decided to seek negotiations with Japan to restrict further immigration as a way to placate the Californians. Meanwhile, the federal government prepared to challenge the segregation order in the courts. (At a time when segregated schools for American citizens such as the NISEI were legal under the "separate but equal" doctrine, the legal case would claim that the segregation order violated the TREATY OF COMMERCE AND NAVIGATION OF 1894 BETWEEN JAPAN AND THE UNITED STATES in its treatment of Japanese subjects.)

At the opening of the California state legislature in January 1907, a host of anti-Japanese bills were introduced and some of them seemed certain to pass. Before that could happen, Roosevelt and Root met the California congressional delegation and then called San Francisco school officials and California legislative leaders to Washington for a meeting. A week of negotiations followed the groups' arrival on February 8. The California officials agreed to allow Japanese children to attend regular public schools with the exception of the overage or those with limited English and to broaden all further restrictions to apply to all aliens and not just the Japanese. The federal government would withdraw its lawsuits and Roosevelt and Root promised to limit Japanese labor immigration. The legislature was also prevailed upon to hold off on further anti-Japanese legislation pending negotiations with Japan on the labor immigration question. With the adjournment of the state legislature on March 12, the immediate crisis had been averted.

Immediately thereafter, on March 14, Roosevelt signed the IMMIGRATION ACT OF FEBRUARY 20, 1907 into law. It included a provision for ending further Japanese migration from Hawaii, Mexico and Canada. Negotiations with Japan over limiting direct labor migration could now begin in earnest. The core of the Gentlemen's Agreement was the correspondence between the two governments in late 1907 and early 1908 in which Japan agreed to stop issuing passports to the United States to

Gila River "Relocation Center," camp #2, Gila River, Arizona, 1944. *Takeo Fujikawa Collection, Japanese American National Museum Photographic & Moving Image Archive*

laborers. Those who had already been to America and were returning and immediate family members of Japanese laborers already in the U.S. would still be allowed to go.

Roosevelt and Root had appeared to have pulled off a deft diplomatic maneuver, forging a compromise between the rabidly anti-Japanese Californians and a proud Japanese government. It would, however, be short lived. The loopholes in the Gentlemen's Agreement allowed a good number of Japanese to continue to immigrate. Many of them were women who came with husbands who had returned to Japan to marry and many were PICTURE BRIDES who met their husbands for the first time upon their arrival on U.S. shores. The arrival of these women changed the nature of the Japanese American community from one of male migrant laborers to one of families seeking permanent settlement. The growing numbers of *nisei* children and the increasing acreage of agricultural land purchased by *issei* family farmers were the cause of the next round of anti-Japanese agitation.

For further reading, see Roger Daniels. *The Politics of Prejudice: The Anti-Japanese Movement in California and the Struggle for Japanese Exclusion.* 2nd edition. Berkeley: University of California Press, 1977; Raymond A. Esthus. *Theodore Roosevelt and Japan.* Seattle: University of Washington Press, 1966; and Rodman W. Paul. "The Abrogation of the Gentlemen's Agreement: Being the Harvard Phi Beta Kappa Prize Essay for 1936." In Daniels, Roger, ed. *Three Short Works on Japanese Americans.* New York: Arno Press, 1978.

Gidra Los Angeles–based renegade monthly newspaper financed and operated by young ASIAN AMERICAN political activists from 1969 to 1974. Known as the "voice of the ASIAN AMERICAN MOVEMENT," *Gidra* spoke to a whole new generation of SANSEI and other young Asian Americans in their own language. Begun by a group of five UCLA students in 1969, the paper gradually moved off the campus and into the community,

covering such issues as the alleged racially motivated firing of then Los Angeles County Chief Coroner THOMAS NOGUCHI, drug abuse in the Asian American community, and the Vietnam War. The paper was distinguished by its irreverence—humor, cartoons and exuberant creative writing were mixed in with earnest political commentary and news coverage. Though locally oriented, *Gidra* had a national impact both through its effect on youth across the country and by inspiring similar—and mostly very short-lived—publications in other Asian American communities across the country. It also had the distinction of being labeled by future senator S. I. HAYAKAWA as "the silliest damn thing I ever saw." Eventually, the lack of finances, time and energy ended the newspaper. Recently, the old staff reunited along with younger activists for a 20th anniversary edition of the newspaper.

For further reading, see Mike Murase. "Toward Barefoot Journalism." In Gee, Emma, ed. *Counterpoint: Perspectives on Asian America.* Los Angeles: Asian American Studies Center, University of California, 1976. 307–19, a personal reflection on *Gidra* by one of its founders that appeared in its last issue.

GLEN KITAYAMA

Gila River The site of one of 10 CONCENTRATION CAMPS that housed Japanese Americans forcibly removed from the West Coast states during World War II. Some basic data on Gila River is presented below in tabular form:

Official name: Gila River Relocation Center

Location: 45 miles southeast of Phoenix, in Pinal County, Arizona, near Sacaton; the Superstition Mountains loomed in the distance

Land: Leased from the Pima Indian Reservation

Size: 17,000 acres; the center was divided into two camps: Canal (209.5 acres) and Butte (789.25 acres)

Climate: Desert; summer temperatures reached 125 degrees. The *average* daily high temperatures for July, August and September 1942 were 109.6, 104.0, and 99.7 degrees, respectively. Though not as bad as some other camps, duststorms were also a problem here

Origin of camp population: Mostly from Los Angeles (4,952), Fresno (1,972), Santa Barbara (1,797), San Joaquin (815), Solano (695), Contra Costa and Ventura Counties (583)

Via "assembly centers": Most came via Turlock (3,566), Tulare (4,951) and Santa Anita (1,294) "Assembly Centers"; nearly 3,000 came directly to Gila and another 2,000 came from Jerome upon its closing

Rural/Urban: Roughly equal split

Peak population: 13,348

Date of peak: December 30, 1942

Opening date: July 20, 1942

Closing date: Canal Camp: September 28, 1945
Butte Camp: November 10, 1945

Project director(s): Lewis J. Korn, Eastburn Smith, Robert B. Cozzens, L. H. Bennett and Douglas M. Todd

Community analysts: James H. Barnett and G. Gordon Brown

JERS fieldworkers: Shotaro Hikida, Inoue (first name not listed), Charles Kikuchi, Y. Okuno, Joe Omachi, and Earle T. Yusa

Newspaper(s): *Gila News-Courier* (September 12, 1942– September 5, 1945); *Gila Bulletin* (September 8–28, 1945)

Percent who answered question 28 of the loyalty questionnaire positively: 90.5

Number and percentage of eligible male citizens inducted directly into armed forces: 487 (5.0%)

Industry: A camouflage net factory operated from fall 1942 to May 1943; a model warship factory produced 800 models for the navy

Miscellaneous characteristics: Like Poston, Gila was on Indian Reservation land. Unlike Poston, however, WRA director Milton Eisenhower refused to relinquish administrative control of the camp to the Office of Indian Affairs, probably because of the potential for profitable agricultural enterprise here. Much of the administrative staff at Gila came from Office of Indian Affairs personnel.

Gila did in fact have the most extensive agricultural program of all the camps. At its peak, Gila farmed approximately 7,000 acres, 3,000 in vegetable crops, some of which was shipped to other camps. Gila had 2,000 head of cattle, 2,500–3,000 head of hogs, 25,000 chickens and 110 dairy cows. Fields of stock and marigolds were also grown here for center consumption.

Gila saw four project directors in its first eight months; the fourth, L. H. Bennett, remained in that position from December 12, 1942, to July 31, 1945.

The camp was initially marred by inadequate housing as people poured into a center that was not yet complete. This necessitated housing people in every conceivable space—in the midst of near constant 100-degree temperatures—until construction could be completed. Schools opened in October 1942 despite the almost total lack of supplies and furniture.

On November 30, 1942, Takeo Tada was beaten by a group of men. He had been employed by both the Turlock "Assembly Center" and Gila administrations and was targeted as an "INU" by those angry over a delay in clothing allocations and at the administration in general. Hearings resulted in a 30-day jail sentence for the admitted perpetrator, amid a tense atmosphere where much of the camp population supported the attacker, as in the

POSTON STRIKE of two weeks earlier and the MANZANAR INCIDENT of two weeks later. Unlike those two events, this disturbance did not evolve into a campwide "riot" or uprising.

Inadequate sanitation and sewage facilities coupled with the wind, dust and heat, led to outbreaks of diarrhea, tuberculosis, "Valley Fever" and other less serious disorders.

When Eleanor Roosevelt was to visit one of the camps in the spring of 1943, Gila was the one chosen, undoubtedly because it had the best appearance.

Key to categories:

"Size"—includes the total acreage allotted to the camp; often only a fraction of that was used for the camp itself, with the rest used for agriculture or other purposes.

"Origin of camp population"—lists the major counties of origin of the population at this camp; all are California counties unless indicated. The figures in parenthesis are the numbers of individuals from that county in that camp. Taken from Table 19, pp. 61–66 of *The Evacuated People: A Quantitative Description* by the War Relocation Authority (Washington, D.C.: United States Department of the Interior, 1946)

"Via 'assembly centers' "—prior to incarceration at this camp, most Japanese Americans spent time in an "ASSEMBLY CENTER" while the camps were being constructed. This item lists the main "assembly centers" from which the population at this camp arrived. Upon segregation, all camps received "loyals" from Tule Lake and sent "disloyals" to Tule Lake; these transfers are not noted here. Taken from Table 3, page 11 of *The Evacuated People: A Quantitative Description* by the War Relocation Authority (Washington, D.C.: United States Department of the Interior, 1946).

"Rural/Urban"—estimates the rural/urban mix at each camp; based on figures from Table 19, page 61 of *The Evacuated People: A Quantitative Description* by the War Relocation Authority (Washington, D.C.: United States Department of the Interior, 1946).

"Peak population," "Date of peak," "Opening date," and "Closing date"—all are taken from Table 1, page 197 of *WRA: A Story of Human Conservation* by the War Relocation Authority (Washington, D.C.: United States Department of the Interior, 1946).

"Community analyst(s)"—staff of the WRA Community Analysis Section at each camp; consultants are also listed. Taken from, Peter T. Suzuki. "Anthropologists in the Wartime Camps for Japanese Americans: A Documentary Study." *Dialectical Anthropology* 6.1 (Aug. 1981): 23–60.

JERS fieldworkers—Japanese American fieldworkers for the JAPANESE AMERICAN EVACUATION AND RESETTLEMENT STUDY, a massive University of California social scientific research project of the camp experience. Taken from, Peter T. Suzuki. "Anthropologists in the Wartime Camps for Japanese Americans: A Documentary Study." *Dialectical Anthropology* 6.1 (Aug. 1981): 23–60.

"Percent who answered question 28 of the loyalty questionnaire positively"—The final percentage of all eligible inmates—ie, those over the age of 17—who answered Question 28 of the loyalty questionnaire with an unqualified "yes" answer. Calculated from Table 3, pp. 199–200 of *WRA: A Story of Human Conservation* by the War Relocation Authority (Washington, D.C.: United States Department of the Interior, 1946).

"Number and percentage of eligible male citizens inducted directly into armed forces"—Number of Japanese Americans inducted directly into the armed forces from that camp. Does not include those who were inducted after leaving that camp. Numbers were taken from Table 5, page 202 and percentages were calculated from Table 3, pp. 199–200 of *WRA: A Story of Human Conservation* by the War Relocation Authority (Washington, D.C.: United States Department of the Interior, 1946).

The literature on the Japanese American World War II experience is extensive; see the bibliography and the bibliographic entries after the various entries pertaining to this experience for titles of general interest. For works specifically on Gila River, see G. Gordon Brown. "WRA, Gila River Project, Rivers Arizona; Community Analysis Section, May 12 to July 7, 1945—Final Report." *Applied Anthropology* 4 (1945): 1–49; Arthur A. Hansen. "Cultural Politics in the Gila River Relocation Center, 1942–1943." *Arizona and the West* 27 (Winter 1985): 327–62; Rita Takahashi Cates. "Comparative Administration and Management of Five War Relocation Authority Camps: America's Incarceration of Persons of Japanese Descent during World War II." Diss., University of Pittsburgh, 1980; and Robert F. Spencer. "Gila in Retrospect." In Ichioka, Yuji, ed. *Views from Within: The Japanese American Evacuation and Resettlement Study*. Los Angeles: Asian American Studies Center, University of California, Los Angeles, 1989. 157–75.

giri   Japanese term referring to the contractual or moral obligations one incurs as a direct result of the acceptance of favors, gifts, goods or services from another. *Giri,* however, is not contracted between parents and children (see ON), but rather between relative equals.

The recipient has the obligation to compensate one who has provided him or her with a gift or service with of an appropriate gesture of proper value. Consequently, returning a debt "with interest" is not uncommon, because one may deem it appropriate to do so. However, repayment must be carefully considered, because too generous a settlement may engender indebtedness on the

part of one who is accepting the repayment, and another round of obligation may be initiated.

According to Betty S. Furuta, many Japanese Americans are more guided by and imbued with *giri* than they are fully aware.

For further reading, see Betty S. Furuta. "Ethnic Identities of Japanese-American Families: Implications for Counseling." In Getty, Cathleen, and Winnifred Humphreys, eds. *Understanding the Family: Stress and Change in American Family Life.* New York: Appleton-Century-Crofts, 1981 and *Kodansha Encyclopedia of Japan.* Tokyo: Kodansha, 1983.   STACEY HIROSE

"Go For Broke"   The motto of the 442ND REGIMENTAL COMBAT TEAM. The motto comes from a Hawaii crap shooter's expression meaning to shoot the works or to put everything on the line. The expression was also the title of one of the several books about the NISEI soldiers as well as the title of a 1952 Hollywood movie about the 442nd.

For further reading, see Masayo Duus. *Unlikely Liberators: The Men of the 100th and the 442nd.* Honolulu: University of Hawaii Press, 1987; Bill Hosokawa. *Nisei: The Quiet Americans.* New York: William Morrow & Co., 1969; and Roland Kotani. *The Japanese in Hawaii: A Century of Struggle.* Honolulu: Hochi, Ltd., 1985.

Gospel Society (Fukuinkai)   First Japanese immigrant group in America. Organized by early student converts to Christianity, the Gospel Society was the first Japanese immigrant group in San Francisco and perhaps the first in the United States and went on to play an important role in indoctrinating many Japanese in America. The society was officially formed on October 6, 1877, with the goals of providing an environment to study Christianity and helping to spread the word about Christ—and about Christian morality—among Japanese immigrants. The society was nondenominational, being made up of both Methodists and Congregationalists—the former led by KANICHI MIYAMA and Kumataro Nonaka and the latter by Keizo Koyano and Toyosaku Nishimaki. The initial group of 35 met every Saturday for Bible study with Reverend Otis Gibson at the Chinese Methodist Episcopal Mission on 916 Washington Street. The adjoining room became a bunkhouse for society members—conditions were such that this room became known as *ana kura* (literally, "storage hole"). In addition to the weekly Bible meetings, the group did such things as host a reception for the Japanese warship *Chikuba* when it visited San Francisco on July 17, 1880, and help to establish a Japanese cemetery in San Francisco.

In 1882–83, two Congregationalist groups split from the Gospel Society because of Gibson's paternalistic attitude, a desire—perhaps influenced by the ANTI-CHINESE MOVEMENT—to escape the Chinese Mission, and denominational conflict with the Methodists. Many members of both groups switched denominations, forming close ties with the Howard Presbyterian Church. The two groups merged in 1884 and later established the First Japanese Presbyterian Church of San Francisco on May 16, 1885. The group later established the Japanese YMCA on August 27, 1886 under the guidance of E. A. STURGE.

After the split, the Gospel Society officially became a Methodist Mission at the 1886 California Conference and gradually expanded its activities. A FUJINKAI (Women's Association) was formed in 1883 and a branch in Oakland was opened on March 15. 1884. Later, members were involved in forming the Japanese Methodist Episcopal Mission on the Pacific Coast.

With plans to build a church building in 1890, a debate emerged as to whether the Gospel Society ought to merge with the church or whether it should continue as a separate organization. M. C. Harris, superintendent of the Methodist Japanese Mission, pushed for the merger on the grounds that the organizations had similar goals which might be pursued in unison. On the other hand, many Gospel Society members felt that their organization had a significant and separate role in the community, since it included non-Christians as well. A vote was taken and the membership decided against a merger. On January 29, 1891, the still independent Gospel Society moved from their quarters in the Methodist Church at the insistence of Harris. After the move, KYUTARO ABIKO was elected president of the organization. Gradually, the organization's relationship with the Methodist church deteriorated and the group formed an alliance with the Japanese Episcopal Mission of San Francisco in 1896. Eventually, the Gospel Society lost its association with Christianity entirely and became more of a Japanese community self-help organization, playing an important role for many Japanese immigrants, providing cheap room and board, serving as a job clearinghouse and giving English lessons. White leaders who worked with these institutions would also be among the few non-Asians to defend the Japanese from the charges of the ANTI-JAPANESE MOVEMENT. The Gospel Society would last at least until the 1906 earthquake and perhaps a few years beyond it.

For further reading, see Yuji Ichioka. *The Issei: The World of the First Generation Japanese Immigrants, 1885–1924.* New York: The Free Press, 1988 and Ryo Yoshida. "A Socio-Historical Study of Racial/Ethnic Identity in the Inculcated Religious Expression of Japanese Christianity in San Francisco, 1877–1924." Diss., Graduate Theological Union (Berkeley, Calif.), 1989.

Gotanda, Philip Kan (1949–)

Playwright, musician, director. Philip Kan Gotanda is best known for

Philip Gotanda.   *Mark Taper Forum Collection, Japanese American National Museum Photographic & Moving Image Archive*

his musicals and plays about the Japanese American experience and family dynamics. He has been the recipient of numerous grants for playwriting, including Guggenheim, Rockefeller, National Endowment for the Arts and Ruby Schaar-Yoshino fellowships.

A SANSEI, Gotanda was born on December 17, 1949, and raised in Stockton, California. He abandoned a career in law to write music and plays. While at Hastings College of Law in San Francisco, he wrote his first play, a musical entitled *The Avocado Kid, or Zen in the Art of Guacamole.* First produced at East West Players theater in Los Angeles, *The Avocado Kid* is loosely based on the Japanese legend of Momotaro; the main character pops out of an avocado and goes on to defeat a band of outlaws in a musical contest. In 1980, after its production at the Asian American Theatre Company in San Francisco, *The Avocado Kid* received a Cable Car Award nomination for best musical.

Gotanda's other plays include *The Wash, A Song for a Nisei Fisherman, Bullet Headed Birds, The Dream of Kitamura, Yohen, Yankee Dawg You Die, American Tatoo* and, with Rick Shiomi and David Henry Hwang, *Jan Ken Po.* In 1989, *The Wash* was produced as a feature film, starring NOBU MCCARTHY and MAKO as a NISEI couple separating after many years of marriage.

A former TCG/NEA Directing Fellow, Gotanda recently completed directing a short film from his own script entitled *The Kiss.* He serves on the national board of the Theatre Communications Group, is dramaturge at the Asian American Theatre Company and an associate artist with East West Players, the Mark Taper Forum and the Berkeley Repertory Theatre. Gotanda also taught in the Asian American Studies department at San Francisco State University.

For further reading, see *The Wash*. Portsmouth, New Hampshire: Heinemann, 1992. The *Wash* is also included in Misha Berson, ed. *Between Worlds: Contemporary Asian-American Plays*. New York: Theatre Communications Group, 1990.

EMILY LAWSIN

[Also used to compile this entry: Program, AATC production of *The Avocado Kid*, 1980; Program, Sansei Theater Company production of *Life in the Fast Lane*, 1982; Program, East West Players production of *Uncle Tadao*, 1992; Richard Oyama. "'Twist of Fate' Launches Nikkei Playwright's Career." *Rafu Shimpo* 9 April 1986: 1–2; and Janice Arkatow. "For Gotanda, A Destiny in America." *Los Angeles Times* 7 June 1986: V-2+.]

Goto, Katsu (1862?–1889) Merchant, interpreter, lynching victim. Part of the first official group of contract laborers to come to Hawaii from Japan on the *City of Tokio* in 1885, Katsu Goto became a leader among his peers because of his knowledge of the English language and his willingness to help his compatriots. Because of this, he was disliked by local HAOLES and was lynched by a group of them.

Goto was born in around 1862 in the village of Kokufu in Kanagawa PREFECTURE, the eldest of three boys and two girls. He was apparently a good student and came to Hawaii having already picked up some skill in English while in Yokohama. Upon arriving in Hawaii with the first group of contract laborers on February 8, 1885, he was assigned to the Soper Wright and Co. PLANTATION in Ookala where he fulfilled his three-year contractual commitment in 1888. Having become acquainted with Bunichiro Onome who had come to Hawaii as an official interpreter, Goto took over a store previously owned by Onome in the plantation village of Honokaa on the island of Hawaii soon after escaping the plantation. As a storekeeper, he quickly became a success, drawing not only Japanese customers but also native Hawaiian and *haole* ones as well. His ability to speak English and his willingness to help the plantation laborers made him a disliked figure among local plantation owners. Local shopkeepers also resented the competition he created.

The roots of his lynching stemmed from a fire on the Overend Camp in Honokaa on October 19, 1889. Plantation officials blamed the fire on disgruntled Japanese laborers and on Goto, who, it was felt, had been an instigator of discontent among the workers. When a local investigation of the fire netted only one suspect,

plantation owner Robert McLain Overend and his head overseer, Thomas C. Steele, decided to take matters into their own hands by suing seven other Japanese workers whom they suspected in the fire for breach of contract connected to their allegedly feigning illness to get out of work. On the evening of October 28, six of these men went to see Goto about their options. After going to meet with them at the plantation camp, Goto was ambushed as he rode back to his store. The following morning, his body was found swinging from a telephone pole.

The investigation that followed focused on the various people known to have something against Goto. Four men were arrested for the crime in December and went on trial beginning on May 9, 1890 in Hilo. The four included Steele, two other plantation employees and Joseph R. Mills, a storeowner and competitor of Goto's. A jury found all guilty. Judge Francis Albert Judd sentenced all to between four and nine years of hard labor. Two of the men would eventually escape from prison and slip out of Hawaii, while a third was pardoned. Goto's grave at the Hamakua Jodo cemetery in Paauhau was restored in the 1960s.

For further reading, see Allan Beekman. "The Strange Case of Katsu Goto." Honolulu: Heritage Press, 1989 and Franklin S. Odo and Kazuko Sinoto. *A Pictorial History of the Japanese in Hawaii, 1885–1924*. Honolulu: Bishop Museum Press, 1985.

Granada Granada was the site of one of 10 CONCENTRATION CAMPS that housed Japanese Americans forcibly removed from the West Coast states during World War II. Some basic data on Granada is presented below in tabular form:

Official name: Granada Relocation Center
Location: Prowers County, Colorado; located 14 miles east of Lamar and 20 miles west of the Kansas border in the Arkansas River Valley
Land: Purchased from a private party
Size: 10,500 acres
Climate: Located on a hilltop at 3,500 foot elevation; arid and dusty, though not as severe as the Arizona camps
Origin of camp population: Mostly from Los Angeles (3,181), Sonoma (696), Yolo (666), Stanislaus (661), Sacramento (632), and Merced (449) Counties
Via "assembly centers": Most came from Merced (4,500) and Santa Anita (3,063) "Assembly Centers"
Rural/Urban: Roughly equal split
Peak population: 7,318; Granada was the least populous of the camps
Date of peak: February 1, 1943
Opening date: August 27, 1942
Closing date: October 15, 1945

Project director(s): James G. Lindley
Community analysts: E. Adamson Hoebel, John Ralph McFarling, John A. Rademaker
JERS fieldworkers: None
Newspaper(s): *Granada Bulletin* (October 14–24, 1942); *Granada Pioneer* (October 28, 1942–September 15, 1945)
Percent who answered question 28 of the loyalty questionnaire positively: 99.8; Granada had the highest "Yes" percentage of all camps
Number and percentage of eligible citizen males inducted directly into armed forces: 494 (9.9%); Granada had the highest percentage of eligible males inducted into the armed forces
Industry: Granada had a silk-screen poster shop that produced a quarter of a million posters for naval training
Miscellaneous characteristics: Though located in a farming area, the agricultural development of the camp was unimpressive. Granada was at one point plagued by a polio problem that caused the administration to cancel some activities and to stop issuing passes to the outside.

(For the key to the categories, see GILA RIVER).
For further reading: The literature on the Japanese American World War II experience is extensive; see the bibliography and the bibliographic entries after the various entries pertaining to this experience for titles of general interest. Haruo Hayashi. "Self-Identity of the Japanese Americans during the Internment Period: An Archival Research." Diss., University of California, Los Angeles, 1983 is a study of self-identity based on a content analysis of the *Granada Pioneer*.

Grand Congress of Overseas Compatriots 1940 gathering in Tokyo of overseas Japanese. On November 4–11, 1940, a unique event took place in Tokyo. The Grand Congress of Overseas Compatriots—ostensibly held to celebrate Japan's 2,600th birthday—brought together 1,900 overseas Japanese from 27 countries. The congress was sponsored by the Foreign Ministry of Colonization and managed by a committee of both civilian and military officials. SOEN YAMASHITA headed the Hawaii section of this committee.

As the first destination of Japanese emigration, Hawaii sent one of the largest delegations to the congress. Since most of the rest of the delegations came from lands colonized by Japan, the implications of Hawaii's participation suggest that Japanese officials looked upon Japanese Americans in Hawaii as colonists of a sort as well.

The opening ceremony of the congress began with a grand procession of the delegations from the Imperial Palace to Hibiya Hall. Schoolchildren waving flags and shouting *banzai* lined the route. Upon reaching Hibiya, the procession was received by the highest Japanese officials, including Prime Minister Konoe Fumimaro and Army Minister Hideki Tojo. After patriotic ceremonies including the singing of a special song marking the occasion, various speeches were heard. At the end of the ceremony, the following resolution was unanimously adopted:

> On the occasion of the Tokyo Congress of Overseas Compatriots celebrating the 2,600th anniversary of Japan's foundation, we reverently express sincere gratitude to the honorable labor of Imperial soldiers, heroically struggling in a holy war for the establishment of the Greater East Asia Co-Prosperity Sphere, for the construction of a New Order in East Asia.

In the days to come, the delegates heard lectures by military officials and toured an army and a naval base. Some members of the Hawaii delegation even stayed on and went on a three-week tour of Manchuria and North China. In short, the militaristic character of the event became clearer and clearer. The congress certainly succeeded in gaining the confidence of many overseas Japanese in the Greater East Asia Co-Prosperity Sphere concept.
For further reading, see John Stephan. *Hawaii under the Rising Sun: Japan's Plans for Conquest after Pearl Harbor.* Honolulu: University of Hawaii Press, 1984.

guidebooks During the peak period of Japanese overseas migration, many guides appeared on the Japanese market that told would-be migrants to the United States what they might expect on such a trip. Peaking in number between the years 1902 and 1906, these books contained information on such things as obtaining passports, what to expect on the journey and upon arrival, and how to deal with EMIGRATION COMPANIES. There were even magazines devoted to this general topic. One of them, *America-Bound Magazine (Tobei Zasshi)*, was put out by the ASSOCIATION FOR THE AMERICA-BOUND (Tobei Kyokai) and combined information about American life with appeals for socialism. Another, *America-Bound News (Tobei Shinpo)*, was put out by the Christian NIHON RIKKOKAI group. The guidebooks may have influenced many an ISSEI to come to America with the generally rosy picture of life in the U.S. they painted.
For further reading, see Hisashi Tsurutani. *America Bound: The Japanese and Opening of the American West.* Betsey Scheiner, trans. Tokyo: Japan Times, Inc., 1989.

Gulick, Sidney (1860–1945) Congregationalist missionary, Japan expert, peace activist and the leading white American voice opposing the ANTI-JAPANESE

MOVEMENT. In a long and distinguished career, Sidney Lewis Gulick worked for the inextricably linked causes of world peace, Christianity, American-Japanese relations and the welfare of Japanese immigrants in America. In his role as the leading opponent of the anti-Japanese movement, he became a notorious and hated figure to those who supported the cause of Japanese exclusion.

Gulick was born in Micronesia to a family of missionaries and grew up in Hawaii, Spain, Italy, Switzerland and New Haven, Connecticut. While his father worked for the American Bible Society in Japan, Sidney and a sister stayed in Oakland, California, where he graduated from Oakland High School and attended the University of California at Berkeley. Dissatisfied with the relatively cavalier attitude of his peers, he headed east and enrolled at Dartmouth College. After graduating from Dartmouth, he attended Union Theological Seminary in New York, graduating in 1886. Following a long courtship, he married Cara Fisher, a family friend from Oakland, and committed himself to the life of a missionary. He was assigned to a post in Kumamoto, Japan, arriving in January 1888. The first stage of his career, lasting until 1913, saw him in the role of missionary in Japan and Japanese expert to the West. During his early years in Japan he struggled successfully to learn written and spoken Japanese and started a family that would eventually include five children. Reassigned to Matsuyama in 1897, he later took a position in theology at Doshisha University, a renowned Christian school in Kyoto. He also authored, among other books, *The Evolution of the Japanese* (New York: Fleming H. Revell Co., 1903), an influential and widely praised history of modern Japan and analysis of the Japanese "character." Through this and other writings, Gulick gained an international reputation as a scholar and Japan expert. While at Doshisha, Gulick became involved in the Japanese peace movement in the wake of the Russo-Japanese War of 1904–05. With the SAN FRANCISCO SCHOOL BOARD SEGREGATION ORDER OF 1906, he became cognizant of the role of the ISSEI in U.S.–Japan relations. Returning to America for health reasons in June 1913, he would spend most of the next 20 years working for the causes of world peace and just treatment for Japanese Americans.

His concern for Japanese Americans was influenced by several factors. First, California's rude treatment of Japanese immigrants caused resentment against America and thus hindered Gulick's missionary work in Japan. He also saw the effect the anti-Japanese movement could have on U.S.–Japan relations and saw himself as uniquely qualified—which he certainly was given his years of residence in Japan and command of the Japanese language—to interpret the Japanese perspective to Americans. Finally, he saw the discriminatory treatment of the *issei* as un-Christian and morally wrong. Upon his arrival in California in 1913, a campaign to pass what would become the 1913 (CALIFORNIA) ALIEN LAND LAW was in full swing and Gulick delivered lectures opposing it, outlining a new policy that would ensure just treatment of the *issei*. In his 1914 book *The American Japanese Problem,* he didn't argue against the need to regulate immigration, but took issue with the racist methods used to do so. He outlined a plan for restricting immigration from all nations, setting an entry quota based on how many naturalized American citizens had hailed from a particular nation. He also argued that naturalization should be attainable on a non-discriminatory basis and that education towards "Americanization" be encouraged for all immigrants. This moderate and fair-minded plan was generally well received at the time. Gulick's advocacy of these basic principles would eventually make him a hated figure in California and the subject of federal surveillance as a suspected Japanese agent. He also believed that the *issei* themselves should be quiet and dignified in the face of discrimination, believing that protest on their part would hurt their cause. He wrote to a fellow missionary that he hoped Takao Ozawa would drop his appeal in the OZAWA VS. UNITED STATES naturalization case, feeling that it would exacerbate anti-Japanese feelings. In working to oppose the exclusionists, he seldom made contact with the *issei* themselves or worked with them to coordinate activities.

In late 1913, Gulick began his work with the Federal Council of Churches of Christ in America (FCCCA), an association that would last for the next 20 years. Through this and many other organizations, Gulick became a leading figure in the peace movement during and after World War I. After the war, he resumed activity on the "Japanese problem." He published two more books on Japanese-American relations and the *issei,* defending the *issei* against charges of their being "unassimilable" and reiterating his support for a quota immigration system that would include the Japanese. He began an organization called the National Committee for Constructive Immigration Legislation in 1917 to lobby for a quota immigration bill. However, his opponents, notably V. S. MCCLATCHY, succeeded in discrediting him by constantly charging that he was a Japanese agent and that his many years in Japan had blinded him to that country's aggression. Such charges were difficult to refute, given his known friendships with prominent Japanese figures and the difficulty in figuring out where his financial support came from because of the many organizations he worked for. (There is today no particular evidence that he was paid by the Japanese government for his activities.) Through his own writings, Gulick painstakingly outlined a middle ground to the immigration controversy. It would be to no avail: with the passage of the IMMIGRATION ACT OF 1924, the exclusionists prevailed, successfully ending Japanese immigration.

Gulick continued his anti-war activities during the 1920s and early '30s, campaigning for U.S. participation in the World Court and the Kellogg-Briand Peace Pact of 1928, organizing a successful "friendship dolls" exchange program between the U.S. and Japan, and authoring almost a hundred pamphlets for the Council for International Justice and Goodwill. He retired in 1934, living out his life in Hawaii and continuing to write on Japan and deteriorating U.S.–Japan relations. Though World War II made his worst fear of war between the United States and Japan a reality, he recognized that it might be better in the long run for Japan for the militarists to go down in defeat. When there was talk in Hawaii after the Pearl Harbor attack of removing Japanese Americans there to the mainland, he drafted an article deploring the idea and defending the citizenship of Japanese Americans in Hawaii. Gulick died at his daughter's home in Boise, Idaho on December 24, 1945, at the age of 85.

For further reading, see Sandra C. Taylor. *Advocate of Understanding: Sidney Gulick and the Search for Peace with Japan.* Kent, Ohio: Kent State University Press, 1985, a biography of Gulick. See also Bruce A. Abrams. "A Muted Cry: White Opposition to the Japanese Exclusion Movement, 1911–1924." Diss., City University of New York, 1987 and Roger Daniels. *The Politics of Prejudice: The Anti-Japanese Movement in California and the Struggle for Japanese Exclusion.* 1962. 2nd edition. Berkeley: University of California Press, 1977.

Gullion, Allen Wyant (1880–1946)

As provost marshall general for the army, Gullion was the strongest supporter of the mass incarceration of Japanese Americans during World War II. In his role in the debate over whether to forcibly remove all Japanese Americans from the West Coast, he applied constant pressure on General JOHN L. DEWITT to support him in his cause. Well versed in military bureaucracy, perhaps his best move in the debate was recruiting KARL BENDETSEN as DeWitt's liaison with the government. Bendetsen, often referred to as the "architect" of the mass removal and detention, achieved that distinction partly because of the single-minded determination of Gullion to implement mass removal. Gullion served as provost marshall general until 1944 and then joined General Dwight Eisenhower's staff in Europe. He retired the following year on January 1 and died in Washington, D.C., on June 19, 1946.

For further reading, see Peter Irons. *Justice at War: The Story of the Japanese American Internment Cases.* New York: Oxford University Press, 1983.   GLEN KITAYAMA

[Also used to compile this entry was Gullion's *New York Times* obituary, 20 June 1946: 25.]

H

haiku   Seventeen syllable Japanese poetic form. Composing haiku was an important form of recreation, self-expression and camaraderie for many ISSEI. Though its roots go back many centuries in Japan, the development of haiku as a modern art form is fairly recent, dating back to the 1890s. The key elements of haiku include a seventeen-syllable structure consisting of three lines of five, seven and five syllables. The subject matter of haiku usually consists of observations of natural or everyday phenomena, often with a seasonal component. Haiku written by *issei* often included elements unique to their American experience, whether expressing a longing for their homeland, recounting the difficulties of their voyage to America, or lamenting their incarceration in American CONCENTRATION CAMPS during World War II. Despite the importance of haiku clubs and haiku sections in Japanese American newspapers to the *issei,* no English-language study of either the artistic or sociological aspects of Japanese American haiku exists.

Examples of haiku by Japanese Americans can be found in Kazue Matsuda de Christoforo. *Poetic Reflections of the Tule Lake Internment Camp, 1944.* Santa Clara, Calif.: Privately printed, 1988 and Kazuo Ito. *Issei: A History of Japanese Immigrants in North America.* Shinichiro Nakamura, Jean S. Gerard, trans. Seattle: Executive Committee for the Publication of *Issei: A History of Japanese Immigrants in North America,* 1973. The short story "Seventeen Syllables" in Hisaye Yamamoto. *Seventeen Syllables and Other Stories.* Latham, N.Y.: Kitchen Table Women of Color Press, 1988 deals in part with an *issei* woman who writes haiku. See also Stephen H. Sumida. "Hawaii, the Northwest, and Asia: Localism and Local Literary Developments in the Creation of an Asian Immigrants' Sensibility." *The Seattle Review* 11.1 (Spring/Summer 1988): 9–18 and Peter T. Suzuki. "Jinji (The Human Condition) in the Wartime Camp Poetry of the Japanese Americans." *Asian Profile* 15.5 (Oct. 1987): 407–15.

haji   Japanese term meaning shame. According to Betty S. Furuta, *haji* encompasses "feelings of painful embarrassment or a sense of mortification and humiliation so profound that the [one] wishes simply to disappear."

Haji was used primarily by the ISSEI and the NISEI as a means of social control over themselves as well as their children. The notion of *haji* essentially influences one to succeed and achieve in order to bring honor to the family, knowing that to fail will bring disgrace.

For further reading, see Betty S. Furuta. "Ethnic Identities of Japanese-American Families: Implications for Counseling." In

Getty, Cathleen, and Winnifred Humphreys, eds. *Understanding the Family: Stress and Change in American Family Life*. New York: Appleton-Century-Crofts, 1981 and *Kodansha Encyclopedia of Japan*. Tokyo: Kodansha, 1983. STACEY HIROSE

Hall, Jack Wayne (1915–1971)

Labor organizer and ILWU representative for the Hawaii region. Jack Hall played an important role in unionizing Hawaii's plantations and docks and making organized labor a major part of Hawaii's political power structure.

Hall was born on February 28, 1915, in Ashland, Wisconsin. His mother killed herself when he was four and a half, and he was raised in Los Angeles by a grandmother and his father's second family. By age 17, he was a seaman and world traveler. On trips to Asia, he observed the negative impact of colonialism and became drawn to leftist literature. He was a participant in the 1934 San Francisco dock strike and joined the Sailor's Union of the Pacific. In 1935, he arrived in Hawaii, becoming a labor recruiter and organizer and working on the labor newspaper *The Voice of Labor*.

In 1937, a Kauai local of the United Cannery, Agricultural, Packing, and Allied Workers of America (UCAPAWA) was granted a charter. Hall spent the next few years organizing workers for the UCAPAWA in Kauai. He also played a major role in the successful 1937 territorial senate campaign of J. B. Fernandes, ousting a wealthy sugar PLANTATION owner. Fernandes repaid Hall by introducing the Hawaii Employment Relations Act—Hawaii's version of the Wagner Act—in 1939, a measure authored by Hall which would grant all workers, including agricultural laborers, the right to organize and bargain collectively. Though initially rejected, its passage in 1945 was a key factor in the unionization drive. This was also the first of many times Hall would use the political process, working to elect politicians who would be sympathetic to his cause and to defeat those who weren't.

In June 1944, Hall was appointed regional representative for the ILWU. Working together with Frank Thompson, former head of Sacramento local 17, Hall led a drive that would succeed in organizing a high percentage of Hawaii's mostly Japanese and Filipino American plantation and dock workers. By the end of 1945, the ILWU had won 132 out of 138 union elections and had contracts with 33 out of the 34 working plantations in Hawaii. With this newfound power, the workers won major victories in a 1946 plantation workers strike and a 1949 STRIKE of dock workers.

Allegations of Communist influence in the ILWU and Hall's own pro-Communist views surfaced in the late 1940s and resulted in a House Un-American Activities investigation in 1950. Eventually, the testimony of embittered former Hall colleague JACK KAWANO led to the trial and conviction of the HAWAII SEVEN—of which Hall was one—in 1953. Despite this blow, Hall retained his basic popularity with workers unconcerned about ideology ("Most of the boys did not know Communism from rheumatism, but they did hate the bosses, and they believed Jack Hall would help them," recalled one ILWU member) and, as a result, from planters and pro-statehood forces eager for labor peace. His support was an important factor in the rise of JACK BURNS and the Democratic Party (see REVOLUTION OF 1954). Though the ILWU's influence declined in the '60s, Hall continued to be a major player in Hawaii politics until his death on January 2, 1971, at the age of 55.

For further reading, see Edward D. Beechert. *Working in Hawaii: A Labor History*. Honolulu: University of Hawaii Press, 1985; Lawrence H. Fuchs. *Hawaii Pono: A Social History*. New York: Harcourt, Brace and World, 1961; Roland Kotani. *The Japanese in Hawaii: A Century of Struggle*. Honolulu: Hochi, Ltd., 1985; and Sanford Zalburg. *A Spark Is Struck!: Jack Hall and the ILWU in Hawaii*. University Press of Hawaii, 1979.

[Quote from Fuchs, p. 361.]

hakujin Japanese and Japanese American term for a person of European descent. Literally meaning "white person," *hakujin* is a relatively value-neutral term that is still widely used by Japanese Americans, especially NISEI.

Hamada Hikozo [Joseph Heco] (1837–1897)

Interpreter, diplomat, businessman. Shipwrecked sailor Joseph Heco was one of the first Japanese/English bilingual people and probably the first person of Japanese descent to become a naturalized American citizen. Born in Harima, he came to America at the age of 13 when he and several others were rescued by the American ship *Auckland* after the fishing vessel they had been on was wrecked in a storm. Spending nearly a year in limbo in San Francisco, the group was deported and sent back to Japan in 1852. Making it as far as Hong Kong, Heco and two others were "rescued" by a friendly sailor who took them back to San Francisco. He attended school in San Francisco and made arrangements to send the others back to Japan. Living with the family of the collector of customs, he was sent to a Baltimore Catholic school, where he was baptized a Roman Catholic. He became a U.S. citizen on July 7, 1858. In 1859, he went back to Japan as an interpreter for the American consul in Kanagawa E. M. Dorr. He later opened an import-export business in Yokohama, published a newspaper and worked for the Japanese Ministry of Finance. Since 1956, a Japanese organization known as the Josefu Hiko Kinen-kai (Joseph Heco Society) has held an annual memorial service at Aoyama Cemetary in Tokyo in Heco's memory.

For further reading, see Joseph Heco [Hikozo Hamada]. *The Narrative of a Japanese; What He Has Seen and the People He Has Met in the Course of the Last Forty Years*. 2 vols. 1895. Ed. James Murdoch. Yokohama: Yokohama Printing & Publishing Co., Ltd., 1950, an autobiography consisting of journal entries covering his post-shipwreck life. See also Yamato Ichihashi. *Japanese in the United States: A Critical Study of the Problems of the Japanese Immigrants and their Children*. Stanford: Stanford University Press, 1932. New York: Arno Press, 1969. Andrew Y. Kuroda. "Joseph Heco and the Joseph Heco Society." *Pacific Citizen* 2–9 Jan. 1987: 18, 20–21; and Katherine Plummer. *The Shogun's Reluctant Ambassadors: Sea Drifters*. 2nd ed. Tokyo: Lotus Press, 1985. 3rd ed., rev. Portland, OR: Oregon Historical Society, 1991.

Hanihara, Masanao (1876–1932) Japanese ambassador to the United States. Born to a prominent family in Yamanashi PREFECTURE, Hanihara was a career diplomat who served with the Japanese embassy between 1902 and 1911. In 1922, he was appointed as the ambassador to the United States and resided in Washington, D.C., until 1924.

Hanihara unintentionally played a key role in the passing of the IMMIGRATION ACT OF 1924, which excluded Japanese immigrants. Since 1920, exclusionists from California, such as VALENTINE STUART MCCLATCHY, JAMES D. PHELAN and HIRAM JOHNSON, were urging Congress to prohibit the entry of Japanese into the United States. In 1924, when Congress examined immigration bills that attempted to exclude those who were "ALIENS INELIGIBLE TO CITIZENSHIP," Hanihara placed pressure on the American government to stop their passage. In the process, he warned the Secretary of State Charles Evans Hughes that if Japanese exclusion became reality, it would cause "grave consequences" between Japan and the United States. Senator Henry Cabot Lodge interpreted these words to be a "veiled threat" to the United States. Lodge's interpretation influenced many senators' attitudes against Japan and abruptly changed their ambivalent attitude towards Japanese exclusion to one of pro-Japanese exclusion.

For further reading, see Hyung-Chan Kim, ed. *Dictionary of Asian American History*. Westport, CN: Greenwood Press, 1986 and Roger Daniels. *The Politics of Prejudice: The Anti-Japanese Movement in California and the Struggle for Japanese Exclusion*. 2nd ed. Berkeley: University of California Press, 1977.   EIICIRO AZUMA

haole Term used in Hawaii to refer to all Caucasians other than those of Portuguese descent, especially those from the mainland United States. However, according to Morrison, even Caucasians who go back several generations in Hawaii are said to have a mainland "background." The term has a pejorative sense when applied to non-Caucasians in Hawaii; one who is called "haolefied" is one who is perceived to be too subservient to Caucasians, ignorant of his or her own ethnic identity, or simply too proper in manner of speech or dress. Historically, KOTONKS have been perceived by locals to be "haolefied" by local standards.

For further reading, see John Wesley Morrison. "Social Polity and Ethnic Classification in Hawaii." Diss., University of Illinois (Urbana), 1978.

hapa (or happa) Term for a person with one Japanese or Japanese American parent and one non-Asian parent. Evolving from the Hawaii pidgin term *hapa-haole* (literally "half white"), the term had a mildly pejorative connotation at one time. The term has since become widely used, especially in Hawaii, and increasingly on the mainland. (See AMERASIAN.)

For further reading, see Lane Ryo Hirabayashi. "On Being Hapa." *Pacific Citizen* 20–27 Dec. 1985; and Lorraine Oda. "Hapa Identity." *Hawaii Herald* 18 Nov. 1983: 1+.

Hartmann, Sadakichi (1867–1944) Critic, playwright, poet. An important figure in American arts and letters, Sadakichi Hartmann had a wide-ranging career and a colorful life. Opinion of him has varied wildly both over the course of his life and in the years since his death.

Hartmann was born in 1867 on the island of Deshima in Japan to a German trader named Oscar Hartmann and a Japanese mother named Osada. His mother died during his birth, and he and his older brother were sent to Germany where they were raised by wealthy relatives in a luxurious and cultured setting. Rebelling from the discipline of a naval academy he had been enrolled in, Sadakichi ran away to Paris, was disowned by his father, and sent to live with an uncle in Philadelphia in 1882. Here he worked in print shops while devouring art and literature in the evenings. He paid a visit to the elderly poet Walt Whitman, eventually befriending him and translating his German correspondence. He later published a book, *Conversations with Walt Whitman* (1895), recalling those years. In the late 1880s and early 1890s Hartmann made several trips to Europe where he became caught up in the symbolist movement. As one its leading proponents in America, in the late 1880s he began to write essays on art for various papers, gave readings and lectures, and hobnobbed in literary circles in Boston and New York. In 1893, he wrote the symbolist play *Christ;* the New England Watch and Ward Society burned nearly all copies of the play and Hartmann was arrested and jailed. This was followed by the symbolist plays *Buddha* (1897), *Confucius, Mohammed* and *Moses,* and

Sadakichi Hartmann. *University of Riverside, Special Collections*

publications established him as a pioneering critic on photographic technique and on photography as an art form. He was nearly as influential as an art critic, recognizing and promoting the work of many young American artists. In 1901, he published the two-volume *History of American Art,* destined to become a standard textbook and recognized as the first modern history of American art. Beginning around this time, he also began to lecture extensively on art, photography and other topics, an activity he would continue for the rest of his life.

The serious and respected critic was also the flamboyant "King of Greenwich Village," in the late teens and early '20s. Declining health and alcoholism led to professional decline and a growing dependence on friends and admirers for financial support. In the 1920s, he tried his hand unsuccessfully at writing Hollywood movie scripts, though he did appear in the classic silent film *The Thief of Bagdad* with Douglas Fairbanks and Anna May Wong in 1924. He also became a drinking buddy of John Barrymore's and a member of his circle of friends. He spent the last years of his life living with his daughter in Riverside County (California) and successfully avoided the mass incarceration of Japanese Americans during World War II. He died in Florida while visiting another daughter in November 1944.

The last twenty years have seen a great resurgence of interest in Hartmann. Starting in 1970, the *Sadakichi Hartmann Newsletter* was begun to track writing on him and enjoyed a run of about a decade. There was also an important Hartmann exhibit in 1970 at the University of California, Riverside, whose catalog was published as "The Life and Times of Sadakichi Hartmann, 1867–1944." Introd. George Knox. Riverside, Calif.: N.p., 1970. Additional biographical information on Hartmann can be found in the editors' introduction to Harry Lawton and George Knox, ed. *Buddha, Confucius, Christ: Three Prophetic Plays.* New York: Herder and Herder, 1971. Gene Fowler. *Minutes of the Last Meeting.* New York: Viking Press, 1954 centers on Hartmann in Hollywood as part of the John Barrymore crowd.

Hartmann's own writings are numerous. Among the recent reissues are *Japanese Art.* 1904. New York: Horizon Press, 1971; *Sadakichi Hartmann: Critical Modernist: Collected Art Writings.* Ed. Jane Calhoun Weaver. Berkeley: University of California Press, 1991; *The Valiant Knights of Daguerre: Selected Critical Essays on Photography and Profiles of Photographic Pioneers.* Ed. Harry Lawton and George Knox. Berkeley: University of California Press, 1978; *The Whitman-Hartmann Controversy: Including* Conversations with Walt Whitman *and Other Essays.* Ed. George Knox and Harry Lawton. Introd. George Knox. Bern: Herbert Lang, 1976; and the previously mentioned *Buddha, Confucius, Christ.* Additionally, original copies of many of his early works can be found in many academic libraries.

the collection of short stories *Schopenhauer in the Air* in 1899. Hartmann also painted and his pastels were first exhibited in 1894. Artists and photographers found his appearance striking and exotic and featured him in countless works of art throughout his life. From 1898 to 1902, he wrote 350 sketches on New York life for *New York Staats-Zeitung.* He was a dance critic and apparently had unique abilities as a dancer. In 1906, he began to experiment with the Japanese poetry forms of TANKA and HAIKU and published a volume of his work.

At the same time, he began to develop his skills and gain some notoriety as a critic of avant garde art and especially photography. He began the short-lived but influential magazines *Art Critic* in 1893 and *Art News* in 1896. Beginning in that year, Hartmann also became a regular contributor to Alfred Steiglitz's *Camera Notes* and later *Camera Work;* Hartmann's work for these

Hashimoto, Daigoro (1875–1936) Labor contractor. Daigoro Hashimoto was a large Utah-based ISSEI LABOR CONTRACTOR. Originally from Wakayama

PREFECTURE, he arrived in the United States in 1892 at age 17 and first worked for the ORIENTAL TRADING COMPANY in Seattle, becoming a labor contractor there. In 1899, he supplied the San Pedro-Los Angeles-Salt Lake City Railroad with several hundred workers before moving his headquarters to Salt Lake City. There, he set up the Hashimoto Company, and supplied both Japanese and Mexican workers to the Western Pacific Railroad.

For further reading, see Hisashi Tsurutani. *America Bound: The Japanese and Opening of the American West.* Betsey Scheiner, trans. Tokyo: Japan Times, Inc., 1989.

Hawaii Herald   Hawaii Japanese American newspaper. The *Hawaii Herald* has had several incarnations as an English-language Japanese American newspaper serving Hawaii. The name was first applied to the former HAWAII HOCHI in 1942 when the original name was felt to be too "Japanese" in the midst of World War II. The *Hochi* reverted to its original name in 1952. Then in 1969, the *Hawaii Herald* was created by the publisher of the *Hochi* as a separate eight-page weekly tabloid written entirely in English and aimed at a NISEI, SANSEI and YONSEI audience. This version of the *Herald* ceased publication in 1973 in the midst of a national shortage of newsprint.

The current version of the *Herald* dates from 1980. Blending news, features, scholarship and humor told from a Hawaii Japanese American perspective, the *Herald* has built a large and loyal audience that reaches well beyond the boundaries of Hawaii. Original editor Ken Toguchi was succeeded by Arnold T. Hiura. The current editor is Karleen Chinen. The *Herald* continues to publish twice a month.

For further reading, see the *Herald*'s 10th Anniversary Issue, Vol 11, No. 10 (May 18, 1990).

Hawaii Hochi   Hawaii Japanese American newspaper. The *Hawaii Hochi* was started by FRED KINZABURO MAKINO in 1912. After some difficult years, the *Hochi* attained great popularity in the 1920s after championing the strikers' cause in the 1920 PLANTATION STRIKE and the rights of the JAPANESE-LANGUAGE SCHOOLS in the legal controversy of the early 1920s.

In 1928, the *Hochi* surpassed the NIPPU JIJI in circulation. Its editorial policy attacked the oligarchy and urged the NISEI to break ties with Japan. It also dealt forcefully with problems brought on by the caste system in Hawaii and argued for full citizenship for the Japanese Americans. Makino's concept of Americanism was one which emphasized freedom, independence and protest if necessary. The *Hochi* changed its name to the HAWAII HERALD in 1942, but in 1952 reverted to its original name, under which it continues to be published to this day. The paper was purchased in 1962 by Japanese

newspaperman Konosuke Oishi. The *Hochi* began to put out an all-English edition under the name *Hawaii Herald* in 1969.

Hawaii Seven   Seven defendants accused of violating the Smith Act and tried in Hawaii in 1951–53. The trial and conviction of the Hawaii Seven for conspiring to organize the Communist Party and advocating the overthrow of the government by force ended an era in Hawaii's labor history that saw unprecedented gains made by labor against the PLANTATIONS and associated industries.

In the late 1940s, the ILWU had succeeded where all others had failed in organizing Hawaii's laborers across color lines and executing successful actions to improve wages and working conditions. However, conservative forces counterattacked by claiming that the ILWU was under Communist influence and thus a danger to national security. These efforts to undermine the union were aided when key members broke off with the union and denounced it. In 1947, former ILWU leader Ichiro Izuka authored a pamphlet titled *The Truth About Communism in Hawaii,* which was published and distributed by conservative interests and translated into the Ilocano language for Filipino workers by the HAWAII SUGAR PLANTERS ASSOCIATION. The anti-Communist activity turned public opinion against the union, though it may also have strengthened solidarity within the union.

By 1951, JACK KAWANO, one of the key figures in the ILWU's rise, had lost a power struggle within the union to JACK HALL and had quit the union and the Communist Party. In July 1951, he left for Washington, D.C., his trip paid for by businessman Ben Dillingham, and told all he knew about the Communist Party and ILWU to the House Un-American Activities Committee. He would return to start a liquor store with over $8,000 in loans provided by other business and political figures. On the strength of his testimony, seven Hawaiians—Jack Hall, John Reinecke, Dwight James Freeman, CHARLES FUJIMOTO, Eileen Kee Fujimoto, Jack Kimoto and KOJI ARIYOSHI—were arrested in August on Smith Act violations charges. In an atmosphere of anti-Communist hysteria, there was little doubt about the outcome of the trial. On June 19, 1953, the Hawaii Seven were found guilty. The six men were sentenced to five-year prison terms and a $5,000 fine while Eileen Fujimoto received a three-year term and a $2,000 fine. The convictions were overturned on appeal five years later.

Although the ILWU would survive, it would gradually shift its direction to become more mainstream and political. Hall would once again become a key player and a kingmaker in the Democratic Party. Other members of the Hawaii Seven would face blacklists, making it difficult for them to make a living. Ironically, Kawano may have emerged from this episode in worse shape, suffering two business failures before moving to California to start over.

For further reading, see Lawrence H. Fuchs. *Hawaii Pono: A Social History.* New York: Harcourt, Brace and World, 1961 and Roland Kotani. *The Japanese in Hawaii: A Century of Struggle.* Honolulu: Hochi, Ltd., 1985.

Hawaii Shimpo Hawaii Japanese American newspaper. The *Hawaii Shimpo* was begun in 1894 as a weekly under the management of Chusaburo Shiozawa. Although it originally supported the Central Japanese Association upon its formation in 1903, it became bitterly opposed in 1904 and, along with the *Hawaii Nichi Nichi Shimbun* and the *Shin Nippon,* sponsored the JAPANESE REFORM ASSOCIATION, which successfully fought the EMIGRATION COMPANIES and the KEIHIN BANK in Hawaii. In 1908, the *Shimpo* was bought by SOMETARO SHIBA who merged it with the *Hawaii Jiyu Shimbun.* Shiba led the paper down an arch-conservative path, and he was paid by the planters to espouse their cause in the 1909 PLANTATION STRIKE. Shiba became the key figure in the resolution of this strike when he was stabbed by one of the strike supporters. The *Hawaii Shimpo* ceased publication in 1922.

For further reading, see Roland Kotani. *The Japanese in Hawaii: A Century of Struggle.* Honolulu: Hochi, Ltd., 1985.

Hawaii Sugar Planters Association Organization of Hawaiian PLANTATION owners. The Hawaii Sugar Planters Association (HSPA), a body representing the interests of the sugar plantations organized by the BIG FIVE, allowed the planters to speak and act with a unified voice. Founded in 1894, the HSPA allowed planters to centralize information and to conduct agricultural research cooperatively. The main function of the HSPA, however, was to control the cost of labor. With the ending of contract labor in 1900, the HSPA used several different methods to keep labor costs down. Wage fixing kept wages uniformly low and minimized the chances that laborers could get better wages at one plantation than another. In 1901, the Board of Trustees of the HSPA established detailed maximum wage rates to help ensure industry-wide uniformity. To keep workers from leaving the plantations, the HSPA kept information on wages and workers. If a group of workers left one plantation after being denied a raise to a certain wage, all other plantation managers were instructed to offer these workers only the wage they had been paid at the plantation they left. The HSPA also encouraged the use of long-term contracts and the bonus system, both of which deferred part of a workers' payment until the end of a one- or two-year period; workers who left the plantation early would forfeit their bonus. The HSPA also allowed planters to act in a concerted and forceful

manner in the face of labor unrest such as the 1909 PLANTATION STRIKE and the 1920 PLANTATION STRIKE.

For further reading, see Edward D. Beechert. *Working in Hawaii: A Labor History.* Honolulu: University of Hawaii Press, 1985; Gary Y. Okihiro. *Cane Fires: The Anti-Japanese Movement in Hawaii, 1865–1945.* Philadelphia: Temple University Press, 1991; and Ronald Takaki. *Pau Hana: Plantation Life and Labor in Hawaii, 1835–1920.* Honolulu: University of Hawaii Press, 1983.

Hayakawa, Samuel Ichiye (1906–1992) Semanticist, college president, United States senator. An internationally famous semanticist since the 1940s, S. I. Hayakawa became a heroic figure to some because of the way he handled the SAN FRANCISCO STATE STRIKE of 1968. He rode a wave of popularity resulting from his handling of the strike to become the first mainland Japanese American senator in 1976.

S. I. Hayakawa was born on July 18, 1906, in Vancouver, British Columbia, to ISSEI parents. His father had come to the United States in about 1901, and, after returning to Japan to marry, settled in Canada. After trying many different occupations, the elder Hayakawa eventually started a successful import/export business and returned to Japan in 1929. Young S. I. veered away from the family business, excelling in school and deciding to pursue a career in academia. He received his bachelor's degree in 1927 from the University of Manitoba, his master's in 1928 from McGill University in Montreal, and his doctorate from the University of Wisconsin in 1935. He married Margedant Peters, a former student of his, in 1937. He taught in the English department at Wisconsin and authored the book *Language in Action* in 1941, which became a standard text and best-seller, establishing his reputation as a semanticist. He also taught at the Armour Institute of Technology, the Illinois Institute of Technology and the University of Chicago. While in Chicago, he wrote a column for the African American newspaper the *Chicago Daily Defender* and hosted a radio program on the history of jazz. He moved to San Francisco in 1955, becoming the first Japanese American faculty member at San Francisco State College.

In the wake of the growing student unrest of the 1960s and the call for a curriculum that acknowledged America's multicultural origins, Hayakawa became a leader of the conservative segment of the faculty that saw the activists' calls as an "infringement on academic freedom." He became the spokesman of the "Faculty Renaissance Committee" and was selected to become the new president of the school in the midst of the strike of 1968. The image of Hayakawa ripping out the wires from campus protesters' loudspeakers came to symbolize his approach to the conflict. Regarded as a swaggering, heroic tough guy to some, he was considered a repressive, insensitive sell-out by others. He retired as college president in 1972. After changing his party affiliation from Democrat to Republican in 1973, he ran for the U.S. Senate in 1976 as a political newcomer. He emerged from a crowded field to win the Republican nomination and defeated incumbent Democrat John Tunney in the general election.

His Senate tenure was colored by two mostly negative traits. One was his habit of falling asleep on the job, a characteristic which became fodder for journalists and Johnny Carson jokes. The other was his penchant for abruptly and undiplomatically speaking his mind. Among his more famous—and damaging—remarks was his 1979 quip that higher gasoline prices wouldn't hurt the poor since "if they are not working, they do not need gasoline." On issues related to the Japanese American community, he was an active opponent of the REDRESS MOVEMENT and advocated putting Iranians in concentration camps during the hostage crisis "the way we did with the Japanese in World War II." The combination of his substantial achievements and his antipathy to many Japanese American causes made him a controversial figure in the Japanese American community. Since leaving office in 1982, he has been active with the movement to make English the official language of California, serving as honorary chairman of U.S. English.

For further reading, see Amy Tachiki et al., eds. *Roots: An Asian American Reader.* Los Angeles: Asian American Studies Center, University of California, 1971. 30–36 for an interview of Hayakawa by Asian American activists; Paul Jacobs, and Saul Landau. *To Serve the Devil, Volume II: Colonials and Sojourners.* New York: Random House, 1971 for a statement by the Asian American Political Alliance denouncing Hayakawa; and S. I. Hayakawa. "'*Giri* to One's Name': Notes on the Wartime Relocation and the Japanese Character" and "The Japanese-American Generation Gap." In S. I. Hayakawa. *Through the Communication Barrier: On Speaking, Listening, and Understanding.* Ed. Arthur Chandler. New York: Harper & Row, 1979. 131–41 for his own takes on redress and the "success" of Japanese Americans.

[The following were also used to compile this entry: Stall, Bill. "Hayakawa Puts Accent on Action in GOP Senate Bid." *Los Angeles Times* 2 Apr. 1976: II-1, 5; Goff, Tom. "Hayakawa: Samurai or Gentle Sage?" *Los Angeles Times* 14 Oct. 1976: I-1, 3, 24–25; Chuman, Dwight. "JAs Blast Sen. Hayakawa." *Rafu Shimpo* 12 Mar. 1980: 1; Endicott, William. "Hayakawa Slips Out of Capitol Without Fanfare." *Los Angeles Times* 19 Jan. 1983: 1, 21; Green, Blake. "Hayakawa Is Still Politicking: The Ex-Senator's Pet Target Now Is Bilingual Education." *San Francisco Chronicle* 16 Apr. 1984: 19, 21; *Who's Who in America* 46th Edition. Wilmette, IL: Macmillan Directory Division, 1990–91: I-1433.]

Hayakawa, Sessue (1890–1973)

Actor. Sessue Hayakawa was once one of Hollywood's leading figures

Sessue Hayakawa.   *Kaihatsu Collection, Japanese American National Museum Photographic & Moving Image Archive*

during the heyday of the silent film in the 1910s and early '20s. After dropping out of the limelight in the 1930s and '40s, he returned to Hollywood in the 1950s, winning an Academy Award for his performance as Colonel Saito in *The Bridge on the River Kwai.*

Kintaro Hayakawa was born on June 10, 1890, in Chiba PREFECTURE, of which his father was governor. He was sent to the University of Chicago in 1909 to learn banking and graduated in 1913 with a degree in political science. As the story goes, he was passing through Los Angeles on his way back to Japan when he took up acting. Within a year he had his first starring role, in a movie titled *Typhoon,* co-starring Bessie Barriscale, and had married fellow actor Tsuru Aoki. His vivid performance in Cecil B. deMille's *The Cheat* opposite Fannie Ward established him as a major star. In 1918, he founded his own production company, Haworth Pictures Corporation, which was making $2 million a year by 1920. Hayakawa became part of the Hollywood nouveau riche, hosting parties in his lavish 32-room castle, tooling around town in a gold-plated Pierce-Arrow and hobnobbing with colleagues such as Rudolph Valentino and Mary Pickford. He met Presidents Harding and Coolidge, performed for the king of England and claimed to have lost $965,000 in one night of gambling in Monte Carlo.

With the coming of the sound era, Hayakawa's career faded. In the 1930s, he moved to Europe, to paint and make an occasional movie. He spent the World War II years in German-occupied France where he eked out a living as a painter. In 1949, he returned to Hollywood to appear opposite Humphrey Bogart in *Tokyo Joe,* which led a string of similar roles, culminating in *The Bridge on the River Kwai* in 1956. When the second phase of his Hollywood career wound down, he returned to Japan where he pursued an interest in Zen, played golf, taught acting and played the part of the family man. He later became an ordained Zen priest after his wife's death.

For further reading, see Sessue Hayakawa. *Zen Showed Me the Way . . . to Peace, Happiness, and Tranquility.* Ed. Croswell Bowen. Indianapolis: Bobbs-Merrill, 1960, his autobiography.

[Montgomery, Paul L. "Silent Lover and Villain." *New York Times* 25 Nov. 1973: 85 was also used to compile this entry.]

Hayashi, Harvey Saburo (1866–1943)

Physician, community leader, newspaper editor. Pioneering ISSEI Harvey Saburo Hayashi was both physician and newspaper editor for a rural Japanese American community in Kona, Hawaii. Hayashi was born in Fukushima PREFECTURE in Aizu-Wakamatsu City, but grew up in Tonami in northernmost Honshu after his father, a loyal samurai under Lord Matsudaira, fought in an unsuccessful revolt against the Meiji emperor and was exiled there. He attended high school in Aomori and the Aomori Prefectural Medical School, graduating in 1884. Against his father's wishes, he went to Tokyo in April 1885, then to the United States, hoping to continue his education.

He joined members of the GOSPEL SOCIETY in San Francisco, and worked as a SCHOOLBOY and migrant agricultural laborer to earn tuition for further education. He enrolled at Hahnemann Hospital and College in San Francisco, graduating in just four years in 1892 despite the handicaps of language and poverty. It was here he acquired his English name Harvey, after English physiologist and anatomist William Harvey, from a professor who had trouble with Saburo. He traveled in California, and eventually opened a practice in Sacramento. Unhappy there, he considered going back to Japan, but instead joined his friend Rev. Jiro Okabe in Hilo, Hawaii, in 1893. He opened a practice in Honomu and found his calling caring for ISSEI plantation laborers. In 1895, he moved to Holualoa, Kona, where he would remain for the rest of his life.

In August 1895, he returned to Japan for four months to marry Matsu Kawarada, 10 years his junior and from another Aizu samurai family. Upon her arrival in January 1896, she was shocked at the poor conditions in Holualoa, but persevered (see GAMAN); she would live there for over 70 years and bear 12 children.

Life as a rural doctor meant long hours and meager material rewards for Hayashi. Often, his patients were unable to pay him, or could pay only in kind. In addition to being a doctor and father of many children, Hayashi was determined to bring a newspaper to his community.

The *Kona Hankyo* (Kona Echo) was begun by him as a virtual one-man operation in February 1897. The paper would be published for over 40 years, reaching a peak circulation of 500. Hayashi also led the community in successful ventures to establish a Japanese cemetery in 1896, the North Kona JAPANESE LANGUAGE SCHOOL in 1898 (with Matsu as its first teacher) and the Kona Japanese Benevolent Association. Harvey Saburo Hayashi died at his home surrounded by his family on June 1, 1943.

For further reading, see Jiro Nakano. "Harvey Saburo Hayashi: Pioneer Physician." *Hawaii Herald* 5 July 1985: A14+ and *Kona Echo: A Biography of Dr. Harvey Saburo Hayashi.* Kona, HI: Kona Historical Society, 1990.

Heart Mountain

Heart Mountain was the site of one of 10 CONCENTRATION CAMPS that housed Japanese Americans forcibly removed from the West Coast states during World War II. Some basic data on Heart Mountain is presented below in tabular form.

Official name: Heart Mountain Relocation Center

Location: Northwestern Wyoming, in Park County, 13 miles northeast of Cody

Land: Federal reclamation project land

Size: 46,000 acres

Climate: Severe, even by WRA standards, with winter lows dipping to −30 degrees. Elevation: 4,600 feet.

Origin of camp population: Mostly from Los Angeles (6,448), Santa Clara (2,572), San Francisco (678) and Yakima, Washington (843) Counties

Via "assembly centers": Most came from Pomona (5,270) and Santa Anita (4,700) "Assembly Centers"

Rural/Urban: Mostly urban

Peak population: 10,767

Date of peak: January 1, 1943

Opening date: August 12, 1942

Closing date: November 10, 1945

Project director(s): Christopher E. Rachford and Guy Robertson

Community analysts: Asael T. Hansen and Forrest La Violette

JERS fieldworkers: None

Newspaper: *Heart Mountain Sentinel* (October 24, 1942– July 28, 1945)

Percent who answered question 28 of the loyalty questionnaire positively: 95.9

Number and percentage of eligible male citizens inducted directly into armed forces: 385 (4.8%)

Industry: Heart Mountain had a garment factory, a cabinet shop and a sawmill that produced goods for internal consumption. A silk-screen shop produced posters for the other camps and for the navy

Heart Mountain "Relocation Center," Wyoming. *K. Nagai Collection, Japanese American National Museum Photographic & Moving Image Archive*

Miscellaneous characteristics: The weather, along with the shoddy construction of the barracks and a population mostly from Southern California unaccustomed to the cold, contributed to a great many illnesses that resulted in hospital overcrowding in the winter of 1942–43. In addition to the severe climate, Heart Mountain, like many other camps, was also plagued by duststorms and rattlesnakes.

Despite the inhospitability of the area, Heart Mountain was to become one of the most successful camps in terms of agriculture; many crops that had never been grown in the area before were introduced.

Heart Mountain residents were stung by a series of muckraking articles about the camp by *Denver Post* reporter Jack Carberry, alleging, among many other things, that the inmate population was being "coddled."

Heart Mountain was also the site of the only organized resistance to the military draft; see HEART MOUNTAIN FAIR PLAY COMMITTEE.

(For the key to the categories, see the entry for GILA RIVER).

The literature on the Japanese American World War II experience is extensive; see the bibliography and the bibliographic entries after the various entries pertaining to this experience for titles of general interest. There are number of works specifically on Heart Mountain. For a general history of the camp, see Douglas W. Nelson. *Heart Mountain: The History of an American Concentration Camp*. Madison, Wis.: The State Historical Society of Wisconsin, 1976. Rita Takahashi Cates. "Comparative Administration and Management of Five War Relocation Authority Camps: America's Incarceration of Persons of Japanese Descent during World War II." Diss., University of Pittsburgh, 1980 studies the administrative strategies of Heart Mountain and four other camps. Asael T. Hansen. "My Two Years at Heart Mountain: The Difficult Role of an Applied Anthropologist." In Daniels, Roger, Sandra C. Taylor, and Harry H. L. Kitano, eds. *Japanese Americans: From Relocation to Redress*. Revised Edition. Seattle: University of Washington Press, 1991. 33–37 is a reminiscence by the former "community analyst" at Heart Mountain. Lauren Kessler. "Fettered Freedoms: The Journalism of World War II Japanese Internment Camps." *Journalism History* 15.2-3 (Summer/Autumn 1988): 60–69 is a study of journalism in the camps which focuses much attention on the *Heart Mountain Sentinel*. Estelle Peck Ishigo. *Lone Heart Mountain*. Los Angeles: Anderson, Ritchie & Simon, 1972 and Gretel Ehrlich. *Heart Mountain*. New York: Viking, 1988 are creative works set in Heart Mountain, the former a memoir with drawings by a former inmate, the latter a novel.

Heart Mountain Congress of American Citizens   Established at the HEART MOUNTAIN, Wyoming, CONCENTRATION CAMP in early February 1943, the Heart Mountain Congress of American Citizens was organized to protest the registration of NISEI for the Selective Service when their rights as American citizens were being denied. Leaders of the group, believed to be part of a supposed anti-WRA faction in the camp, objected to the "LOYALTY QUESTIONS" on the grounds that they had done nothing to cause anyone to question their loyalty. They openly challenged the leadership of the JAPANESE AMERICAN CITIZENS LEAGUE (JACL) and their policy of cooperation and also objected to the idea of using *nisei* to fight in a "Jim Crow" segregated unit while their families remained behind barbed wire. "The JACL is not truly representative of the citizens," the group proclaimed "[and] should be willing to step aside . . . if Niseidom (sic) cannot get together under its banner." When the registration program was over, approximately one-seventh of the *nisei* refused to cooperate by either not answering QUESTIONS 27 AND 28, giving qualified answers or answering "no." This was not the end to the resistance.

Those who answered the questionnaire in the affirmative immediately started a campaign to urge eligible *nisei* not to volunteer for the army for the reasons stated earlier. Despite heavy pressure from the WRA, the army and the camp newspaper, the *Heart Mountain Sentinel,* to cooperate, a surprisingly high number of *nisei* and other eligible Japanese Americans refused to volunteer. Of the close to 2,300 eligible to join the army, only 38 signed up—half of whom were later declared ineligible because they failed their physicals. (See HEART MOUNTAIN and HEART MOUNTAIN FAIR PLAY COMMITTEE.)
For further reading, see Douglas W. Nelson. *Heart Mountain: The History of an American Concentration Camp.* Madison, Wis.: The State Historical Society of Wisconsin, 1976.
GLEN KITAYAMA

Heart Mountain Fair Play Committee   Group behind the only organized draft resistance in the World War II CONCENTRATION CAMPS. Originally called the "Fair Play Committee of One" when KIYOSHI OKAMOTO was its only member, it later became known as the "Fair Play Committee" (FPC) when he was joined by PAUL NAKADATE, Frank Seishi Emi, Isamu Sam Horino, Minoru Tamesa, Tsutomu Ben Wakaye and Guntaro Kubota. Beginning in February 1944, the FPC organized in HEART MOUNTAIN around the issue of drafting NISEI from the concentration camps for military service. Citing the Constitution, the members of the FPC stated that they would not report to the draft board if called upon until their rights as citizens were restored. They issued three newsletters, held several meetings and attracted a few hundred *nisei* members (only citizens were allowed to join since only citizens were being drafted). When draft notices were issued, 63 men decided not to report for their pre-induction physicals. For this, they were sentenced to three years in prison (See U.S. V. FUJII, ET AL.). As for the seven leaders of the FPC, they were tried for sedition and sentenced to Leavenworth Federal Penitentiary (See U.S. V. OKAMOTO, ET AL.). By August 1944, these men were joined by another 22 resisters of conscience. They too were tried and sentenced to two-year prison terms. In 1946, after the end of the war, the seven leaders of the FPC had their convictions overturned on appeal. Later, on December 24, 1947, President Truman issued a pardon to all the draft resisters.
For further reading, see Douglas W. Nelson. *Heart Mountain: The History of an American Concentration Camp.* Madison, Wis.: The State Historical Society of Wisconsin, 1976. Frank Chin. "Come All Ye Asian American Writers of the Real and the Fake." In Chan, Jeffery Paul, Frank Chin, Lawson Fusao Inada and Shawn Wong, eds. *The Big Aiiieeeee!: An Anthology of Chinese American and Japanese American Literature.* New York: Meridian, 1991. 1–92 includes information on the FPC. FPC

leader Frank Emi has written two accounts of the group's actions: "Draft Resistance at the Heart Mountain Concentration Camp and the Fair Play Committee." In Nomura, Gail M., Russell Endo, Stephen H. Sumida, and Russell C. Leong, eds. *Frontiers of Asian American Studies: Writing, Research, and Commentary.* Pullman: Washington State University Press, 1989. 41–69 and "Resistance: The Heart Mountain Fair Play Committee's Fight for Justice." *Amerasia Journal* 17.1 (1991): 47–51.
GLEN KITAYAMA

Heco, Joseph   See HAMADA HIKOZO.

hibakusha   The term *hibakusha* refers to those who survived the atomic bombings of Hiroshima and Nakasaki in August 1945. Many *hibakusha* suffered grave injuries and have had recurring health problems.

Among the *hibakusha* are perhaps 1,000 Japanese Americans. Several thousand Japanese Americans were in Japan during World War II; many were visiting, working or studying there prior to the outbreak of war and had been unable to get out. Since Hiroshima was one of the main PREFECTURES of origin of Japanese immigrants, a good number of Japanese Americans in Japan were in Hiroshima at the time of the atomic bombing. Many other *hibakusha* came to the United States after the war, often as spouses of Americans.

In the 1970s and '80s, a movement was begun to recognize and aid surviving *hibakusha* in the United States. The locus of activity is the Committee of Atomic Bomb Survivors (CABS), founded in 1971. As a result, various bills that would provide medical assistance to the *hibakusha* were introduced into Congress. To date, none of these bills has been adopted.
For further reading, see Dean Toji. "Japanese American Atomic Bomb Survivors." *East Wind* 1.2 (1982): 3–5. The documentary film *Survivors* by Steven Okazaki also centers on the *hibakusha.*

Higa, Seikan (1887–?)   Methodist minister and OKINAWAN community leader in Hawaii. Rev. Seikan Higa was regarded by many as the most outstanding Christian leader among Okinawans in Hawaii. After graduating from Tokyo Baptist Seminary and becoming an ordained minister, Rev. Higa founded a laborer's church in Tokyo before coming to Hawaii in 1921. Here, he opened a church in the middle of the Japanese American community. His Palama Methodist Church encouraged the coexistence of Buddhism and Christianity and championed such social welfare causes as birth control and the labor movement. These activities resulted in a large and enthusiastic following, which clamored for a church independent of the Methodist Mission. The Dokuritsu Reimei Kyokai (Independent Church of the Dawn) was formed in Palama and continued the work of the old church, starting an employment agency and getting more involved with labor conflicts.

In 1926, Higa went to Koloa, Kauai, and purchased the *Yoen Jiho* newspaper on May 5. This was the first paper published for an Okinawan migrant audience to espouse a strong pro-labor philosophy. Higa used it to keep Okinawan workers informed about the activities of the Hawaii Laborers Association. He turned the paper over to Chinyei Kinjo and returned to Honolulu in 1924. In an interview late in his life, he told about the time in 1924 when he and the Japanese consul general addressed a Japanese workers' rally in Honolulu. The consul general spoke first and warned the workers not to strike. Higa followed with a call for a strike in concert with the Filipino Laborers' Association and told the consul general to "go home."

In 1928, Higa wrote an open letter to the *Hawaii Hochi* in which he expressed disappointment with religion as a means for social change (calling Christianity a "philosophy of resignation"), deciding to pursue social science as an alternative. He also became increasingly Marxist oriented in this period, forming a monthly Socialist study group. Higa left for the Big Island in 1930 to become principal of the Piihanua Japanese School; he assumed a similar position at Honokaa Chu-Jo-Gakko in 1936. After the war, he returned to Honolulu and the ministry at the Wesley United Methodist Church where he remained an active and influential community leader. He received the Fifth Order of the Sacred Treasure from the Japanese government on June 14, 1968—ironically, the same day that his frequent nemesis TETSUO TOYAMA received the same award. He retired in 1972. For further reading, see Arnold T. Hiura, and Vinnie K. Terada. "Okinawan Involvement in Hawaii's Labor Movement"; Mitsugu Sakihara. "Okinawans and Religion in Hawaii"; and Seiyei Wakukawa. "A Brief History of Thought Activities of Okinawans in Hawaii." All in Ethnic Studies Oral History Project/United Okinawan Association of Hawaii. *Uchinanchu: A History of Okinawans in Hawaii.* Honolulu: Ethnic Studies Program, University of Hawaii at Manoa, 1981. 223–32, 180–87 and 233–43.

Higher Wage Association   SEE 1909 PLANTATION STRIKE.

Hilo Massacre   A confrontation between several Hawaiian labor unions and the Inter-Island Steamship Company in Hilo, Hawaii, on August 1, 1938. The Hilo Massacre was rooted in a strike that began on February 4, 1938, nearly five months prior to the confrontation. The strike was not exclusive to one ethnic group or union. Rather, it had multi-ethnic participation and included Chinese, Japanese, Native Hawaiian, Portuguese and Filipino Americans. The strike also involved a num-

ber of unions, including the Honolulu Waterfront Workers' Association, the Inland Boatmen's Union (IBU), the INTERNATIONAL LONGSHOREMEN'S AND WAREHOUSEMEN'S UNION (ILWU), Metal Trades Council (MTC), the Quarryworkers International Union of North America and the Women's Auxiliary of the ILWU. The unions overlooked their political and ethnic differences and combined resources to challenge the Inter-Island Steamship Company, which was backed by "BIG FIVE" company Castle and Cooke and the Matson Navigation Company. The unions, led in part by Hilo longshoreman Harry Kamoku, demanded equal wages with workers on the West Coast of the mainland and closed shop, union shop or preferential hiring practices. However, by July 1938 the strike accomplished little and the Inter-Island Steamship Company refused to meet the unions' demands.

The strike culminated on August 1, 1938, when approximately 170 to 180 union laborers gathered to protest the arrival of the SS *Waialeale,* a ship operated by Inter-Island Steamship Company strikebreakers. The police cautioned the union demonstrators against interference and attempted to disband the otherwise peaceful protest. Despite their orders, the protestors refused to comply and the police began firing their shotguns on the unarmed crowd. Fifty demonstrators, or roughly a third of the group, were injured during the confrontation. Two of the injured were women and another two were children. In total, almost half of those injured during the shooting required hospitalization, though none was killed.

In spite of the injuries incurred from the Hilo Massacre, the strike of 1938 did not achieve any major gains for the unions. Even a lawsuit filed in October 1938 by injured protestor Kai Uratani against the officers responsible for his shooting was lost; Uratani was instead made to pay for the officers' defense costs. The Inter-Island Steamship Company, Castle and Cooke and Matson Navigation refused to concede to any of the unions' demands. Ultimately, however, gains were made by the unions in 1941 when Hawaiian waterfront employers were forced to recognize the ILWU, leading to the large scale unionization of Hawaii's work force in the 1940s. For further reading, see Bill Puette. *The Hilo Massacre: Hawaii's Bloody Monday August 1st, 1938.* Honolulu: Center for Labor Education and Research, University of Hawaii, 1988.

STACEY HIROSE

Hirabayashi v. United States   On May 16, 1942, Gordon Kiyoshi Hirabayashi, a 24-year-old University of Washington student, went to the local FBI office to challenge the "exclusion order" that applied to both immigrant and citizen Japanese living on the West Coast. Accompanied by his lawyer, Arthur Barnett, Hirabayashi handed the FBI a copy of a four-page typewritten statement titled "Why I Refused to Register for Evacuation." Citing "Christian principles" and "a duty to maintain the democratic standards for which this nation lives," Hirabayashi became the second to challenge the removal or curfew orders applying to Japanese on the West Coast—Min Yasui was the first (see YASUI V. U.S.).

After Hirabayashi presented his statement, he was taken to the Maryknoll Mission House where the army gave him the chance to register for the exclusion order. Hirabayashi refused. He was then taken back to the FBI office and charged with violating the exclusion order. When the papers were complete, Hirabayashi was taken to King County Jail. Four days later, on May 20, 1942, he appeared for a preliminary hearing on his case and was granted bail of $5,000—provided that he join the other Japanese Americans who were held at the Puyallup "ASSEMBLY CENTER" near Tacoma. On principle, Hirabayashi chose to remain in jail.

On May 28, 1942, the charges against Hirabayashi were amended to include violation of the curfew order. Unknown to the FBI when the original charge was made, Hirabayashi kept a diary in his briefcase that documented three curfew violations from May 4, 1942, to May 10, 1942. When the briefcase was confiscated, the FBI read through the diary and added the charges.

Hirabayashi finally received his day in court on October 20, 1942. Frank Walters, the attorney handling the case, argued that Hirabayashi's Fifth Amendment right of due process was violated by the exclusion order. Judge Black, in his written opinion, dismissed Walters's version of the Fifth Amendment as a "technical interpretation." "Since Pearl Harbor," Black stated, ". . . we have been engaged in a total war with enemies unbelievably treacherous and wholly ruthless . . . Walters' interpretation [of the due process clause] should not be permitted to endanger all of the constitutional rights of the whole citizenry." Black instructed the jury to find Hirabayashi guilty on both counts. Black also told the jury that Public Law 503 (which provided criminal penalties for violations of the exclusion orders) and Lt. General JOHN L. DEWITT's exclusion order were "valid and enforceable." Within 10 minutes, the jury returned with the instructed verdict: guilty on both counts. On the next day, Hirabayashi received his sentence from Judge Black: 30 days for count one of violating the curfew order and 30 days for count two for violating the exclusion order. On the advice of fellow inmates, Hirabayashi asked for a minimum 90-day sentence so that he could serve his time outside of cellblocks. The judge agreed to his request and sentenced him to 90 days each for both counts to be served concurrently.

Hirabayashi appealed the verdict and, along with Fred Korematsu and Min Yasui, appeared before the court of

Gordon Hirabayashi.   *Gordon Hirabayashi Collection, Japanese American National Museum Photographic & Moving Image Archive*

appeals on February 19, 1943—ironically, the one year anniversary of EXECUTIVE ORDER 9066. Justice Department lawyers, eager to rush the test cases to the Supreme Court, urged the court of appeals to use a somewhat obscure procedure called certification. In essence, they asked the Supreme Court to answer constitutional questions raised by the appeals. In Hirabayashi's case, the Supreme Court was asked to rule on the legality of the exclusion order, the curfew order and Public Law 503.

On June 21, 1943, the Supreme Court issued its opinions on both Hirabayashi's and Yasui's cases. Chief Justice Stone wrote in his opinion: "the danger of espionage and sabotage to our military resources was imminent, and that the curfew order was an appropriate measure to meet it." Stone upheld the curfew order conviction, but declined to rule on the exclusion order violation. Officially, the reasoning was that since the sentences ran concurrently, there was no reason to rule on the second count. However, seeing that the exclusion was a hotly debated topic around the country, it is reasonable to conclude that Stone wanted to avoid the issue. (See also CORAM NOBIS CASES; JOHN J. MCCLOY; and KARL R. BENDETSEN.)

For further reading, see Peter Irons. *Justice at War: The Story of the Japanese American Internment Cases*. New York: Oxford

University Press, 1983. A transcript of the various cases appears in Peter Irons, ed. *Justice Delayed: The Record of the Japanese American Internment Cases.* Middletown, CT: Wesleyan University Press, 1989.   GLEN KITAYAMA

Hirasaki, Kiyoshi (1900–1963) Farmer, community leader. Kiyoshi "Jimmy" Hirasaki became known as the "Garlic King" due to his success with this crop in the Gilroy, California, area. Hirasaki was born in Kumamoto PREFECTURE in 1900 and came to California at the age of 14 to join his father and older brother in Milpitas, California. After attending school for a few years, he went to work for a farmer in Gilroy and learned to produce onion and carrot seeds. When he was 21, he had saved enough money to return to Japan and marry Haruye Yonemitsu; he returned to settle in Gilroy and raise three sons and five daughters. In the early 1920s, he was approached by George Clausen, Sr. and encouraged to grow garlic. Reluctant at first, he eventually tried it and met with great success. By 1941, he was growing 1,500 acres of garlic and was considered the biggest garlic producer in the state.

After the closing of the 1938–39 World's Fair on Treasure Island in San Francisco Bay, Hirasaki bought the remains of the Japanese pavilion there and had parts of it refashioned into a Japanese house and garden, which was connected to his family home in Gilroy. This home was completed in October 1941. Two months later, he was removed by the FBI and interned in South Dakota. His family "voluntarily" resettled and spent the war in Grand Junction, Colorado. After the war, Hirasaki and family returned to Gilroy and put the business back together again. He built a shipping warehouse in 1948 for midwestern and eastern markets. He also moved part of his house to land near this warehouse and turned it into a Japanese community hall in the early 1950s. He also was one of the original financiers of the *Hokubei Mainichi* newspaper and from 1948 served as the first president of its board of directors. His Japanese house still stands and is occupied by his eldest daughter.
For further reading, see Japanese American Curriculum Project. *Japanese American Journey: The Story of a People.* San Mateo, CA: Japanese American Curriculum Project, 1985.

Hiroshima SANSEI pop music group. Hiroshima was formed in the early 1970s in Los Angeles and has come to represent the sound of Asian America to many. Notable for its attempts to blend traditional Japanese instruments such as *koto, shakuhachi* and TAIKO drums into jazz forms, the group has succeeded in building a good sized audience. Hiroshima as recorded seven albums to date: *Hiroshima* (1979) and *Odori* (1981) on Arista and *Third Generation* (1983), *Another Place* (1985), *Go* (1987), *East* (1989) and *Providence* (1992) on Epic. At the time

of its first album, its lineup included bandleader Dan Kuramoto, *koto* player June Okida Kuramoto, drummer Danny Yamamoto, guitarist Peter Hata, *taiko* drummer Johnny Mori, vocalist Teri Kusumoto, keyboardist Richard "Arms" Matthews, Dane Matsumura on bass and Jess Acuna on percussion. The group attracted a fair amount of attention with the release of *Hiroshima,* being named Breakout Artist of the Year by *Performance* magazine in 1980 and garnering a Grammy Award nomination.

By the release of *Odori,* however, things had soured. Artistic differences with Arista and the suicide of Matthews led to the group's asking to be released from their Arista contract; this was granted at a price. After the release of their first Epic album, the group also changed its personnel, with Michael Sasaki replacing Hata on guitar and Barbara Long taking over as vocalist. The resultant album, *Go,* had the distinction of reaching the #1 slot on *Billboard* magazine's jazz album charts in late 1987. In 1989, coinciding with the release of *East,* the group developed and performed a dramatic/musical play titled *Sansei* at the Mark Taper Forum in Los Angeles. Its most recent lineup included the Kuramotos, Yamamoto, Mori and singer Machun.
For further reading, see Ken Mochizuki. " 'We stick together and we do this; that's the story nobody understands.' " *The International Examiner* 19 Nov. 1986: 8–9 and Brian Niiya. " 'Sansei' and the Search for Japanese American Music." *Tozai Times* 5.55 (Apr. 1989): 1, 12.

[This entry was also compiled using Shiki, Joe. " 'Hiroshima': A 'Third Generation' Statement." *Rufu Shimpo,* 14 July 1983: 1; Chang, Heidi. "New Personnel for Hiroshima, but Musical Elements Remain the Same." *East/West* 14 Nov. 1984: 13–14; and Saito, John, Jr. "Hiroshima Hits No. 1 on Billboard Magazine." *Rafu Shimpo* 3 Dec. 1987: 1–2.]

Hokosano, Naoichi (1873–1923) Labor contractor, community leader. Naoichi Hokosano was one of the most prominent members of the small prewar Colorado Japanese community. Born in Ota PREFECTURE, he arrived in the United States in 1893 at the age of 20. Upon arriving in Denver, Colorado, in 1898, he opened a restaurant, but became a LABOR CONTRACTOR in 1903, supplying Japanese labor to various types of industries. Through the Hokosano Office, he became the major "boss" in the Colorado and Wyoming regions.

He later became the president of the Japanese Business Men's Association; helped start the local Buddhist Church in 1916; and founded the state's first Japanese newspaper, the *Denver Shimpo,* in 1908. A stained glass window in the State Capitol building depicting Hokosano was dedicated in 1977.
For further reading, see Russell Endo. "Japanese of Colorado: A Sociohistorical Portrait." *Journal of Social and Behavioral*

Sciences 31 (Fall 1985): 100–10 and Hisashi Tsurutani. *America Bound: The Japanese and Opening of the American West.* Betsey Scheiner, trans. Tokyo: Japan Times, Inc., 1989.

hole-hole bushi Plantation work songs sung by ISSEI laborers. *Hole-hole* is a Hawaiian term for dried sugar cane leaves and *bushi* is the word for song or melody. *Hole-hole bushi* were songs composed by the early *issei* sugar cane workers to express their feelings about work and life in Hawaii. *Hole-hole* work, which involved stripping dried sugar cane leaves from the stalks, was routinely assigned to women who were probably the composers of most of these early songs. The tune for these songs was always the same and was rumored to be taken either from a Hiroshima PREFECTURE harvest song, Kyushu folk songs or the boat songs of Japanese seamen. The words were usually made up spontaneously to express the moods of the workers. Not surprisingly, they were usually downbeat, though they were also sometimes humorous and bawdy. Some translated typical lyrics include: "Two contract periods have gone by. We are still here. Destined to become fertilizer for sugar cane," "Let me sleep if it rains. Let me rest if it shines. Let me get drunk if it is cloudy," "My term will expire. But my heart remains with the woman down below," "Woe is me. The wife I sent for with my savings has gone to another man," "Tomorrow is Sunday. Come and visit me. My husband will be out watering the fields. I'll be alone," and "Don't come now—I see my husband coming. Come later when we can be alone."

For further reading, see Roland Kotani. *The Japanese in Hawaii: A Century of Struggle.* Honolulu: Hochi, Ltd., 1985; Franklin S. Odo and Kazuko Sinoto. *A Pictorial History of the Japanese in Hawaii, 1885–1924.* Honolulu: Bishop Museum Press, 1985; Gary Y. Okihiro. *Cane Fires: The Anti-Japanese Movement in Hawaii, 1865–1945.* Philadelphia: Temple University Press, 1991; Ronald Takaki. *Pau Hana: Plantation Life and Labor in Hawaii, 1835–1920.* Honolulu: University of Hawaii Press, 1983; and United Japanese Society of Hawaii. *History of Japanese in Hawaii.* James H. Okahata, ed. Honolulu: United Japanese Society of Hawaii, 1971.

Honda, Harry Journalist. Harry Honda is best known for his long association with the PACIFIC CITIZEN newspaper. Honda was editor of the *PC* for 30 years, from 1952 to 1982. Since stepping down as editor in October of 1982, he has remained actively involved in the paper, first as general manager/operations, most recently as editor emeritus. Prior to his association with *PC,* he wrote for various Japanese American newspapers in both Los Angeles and San Francisco.

Hongo, Garrett Kaoru (1951–) Poet. Winner of the Lamont Poetry Prize. A YONSEI, Garrett Hongo was born on the Big Island of Hawaii and grew up in Oahu and Los Angeles. After attending Pomona College, he received a Thomas J. Watson fellowship to study in Japan, where he did his first serious poetry writing in 1974. Hongo received his M.F.A. in creative writing from the University of California, Irvine, in 1980. His poems have appeared in numerous publications, such as *The New Yorker, Antaeus, The Missouri Review,* and *Poetry Northwest.* He is the author of two poetry collections, *Yellow Light* and *The River of Heaven;* the latter was the 1987 Lamont Poetry Selection of the Academy of American Poets. He has also written a play entitled *Nisei Bar and Grill,* and co-authored *The Buddha Bandits Down Highway 99* with Alan Chong Lao and LAWSON FUSAO INADA. Hongo has taught Asian American studies at the University of Washington and currently teaches English at the University of Oregon. He is the editor of a forthcoming anthology of Asian American poetry.

For further reading, see *The River of Heaven.* New York: Alfred A. Knopf, 1988 and *Yellow Light.* Middletown: Wesleyan University Press, 1982. Stephen H. Sumida cites Hongo's poetry in *And the View from the Shore: Literary Traditions of Hawai'i.* Seattle: University of Washington Press, 1991. See also Alice Evans. "A Vicious Kind of Tenderness: An Interview with Garrett Hongo." *Poets and Writer Magazine* (Sept.–Oct. 1992): 36–46.

EMILY LAWSIN

[Also used to compile this entry: M. Matsushita. "Garrett Hongo." *Tozai Times* (January 1987): 10–11.]

Honolulu Japanese Sake Brewing Co. Ltd. Although sake had been available in Hawaii since the late 1880s, the stiff prices demanded ($3 per gallon vs. $12–$15 per month wages on the plantation) for the imported variety led to much illegal home brewing. Tajiro Sumida came to Hawaii from Hiroshima in 1899 at age 16. He opened the Sumida store in 1904. In September 1908, he set up the Honolulu Japanese Sake Brewing Co. Ltd., the first sake brewery in Hawaii and also the first outside Japan. Despite fermentation problems caused by the warm weather, the first product, called "Takarajima," was sold in December 1908. Sumida later invented a refrigeration process to solve the fermentation problem and by 1914, he was manufacturing 300,000 gallons of sake. His refrigeration process was adopted by many Japanese breweries so that they could brew year round. During the Prohibition era of 1920–34, the company survived by making ice. With the repeal of Prohibition, the brewery went back to making sake, expanding its operations and introducing new varieties, including Takara Masamune. The beginning of World War II brought a new problem—due to a serious shortage, rice was to be used only as a food. This time, the brewery survived by making *shoyu* (soy sauce). The company was purchased by Takara Shuzo in 1986.

For further reading, see Franklin S. Odo and Kazuko Sinoto. *A Pictorial History of the Japanese in Hawaii, 1885–1924.* Honolulu: Bishop Museum Press, 1985 and Leonard Lueras. "Isle Sake Brewery Is One of a Kind." *Honolulu Star-Bulletin and Advertiser* 17 Jan. 1971: A-10.

Honouliuli

United States Army–run detention camp that was located on the island of Oahu, Hawaii, near the town of Ewa. Honouliuli received its internees from SAND ISLAND detention camp after its closure on March 1, 1943.

Under the supervision of Captain Siegfried Spillner, the camp held predominantly ISSEI, and a significantly smaller number of German Americans and prisoners of war. In September 1945 Honouliuli was the last concentration camp to close in the Territory of Hawaii.

For further reading, see Dennis M. Ogawa and Evarts C. Fox. "Japanese Internment and Relocation: The Hawaii Experience." In Daniels, Roger, Sandra C. Taylor, and Harry H. L. Kitano, eds. *Japanese Americans: From Relocation to Redress.* Salt Lake City: University of Utah Press, 1986. Revised edition. Seattle: University of Washington Press, 1991. 135–38; Gary Y. Okihiro. *Cane Fires: The Anti-Japanese Movement in Hawaii, 1865–1945.* Philadelphia: Temple University Press, 1991; and Patsy Sumie Saiki. *Ganbarre! An Example of Japanese Spirit.* Honolulu: Kisaku, Inc., 1982.   STACEY HIROSE

Honpa Hongwanji of Hawaii

Jodo Shinshu organization of Hawaii. Honpa Hongwanji of Hawaii was the Hawaiian equivalent of the North American Buddhist Mission, or later the BUDDHIST CHURCHES OF AMERICA in the continental United States.

In Hawaii, the missionary activities of the Nishi Hongwanji started in late 1897. In the summer, Japanese Buddhists requested the Kyoto headquarters of the Nishi Hongwanji to dispatch missionaries. Soon two priests were sent to Hawaii; one was assigned to Honolulu, the other to Hilo. Before long, more and more priests entered the Hawaiian Islands, which resulted in the emergence of the Honpa Hongwanji of Hawaii.

In 1899, YEMYO IMAMURA became the second bishop of the Honpa Hongwanji of Hawaii, a position he was to hold until his death in 1932. In 1900, he organized the Young Men's Buddhist Association, which soon offered not only religious education but also English-language classes to Japanese immigrants. Two years later, Imamura also founded the first Buddhist JAPANESE-LANGUAGE SCHOOL in Honolulu after he heard that an already existing Christian school mocked and debased Buddhism. In his rivalry with Christian leader TAKIE OKUMURA, Imamura also was involved in non-religious matters pertaining to the Japanese community in Hawaii. His successful intervention in strikes by Japanese laborers

were especially significant, for it made white leaders of Hawaii recognize the influence that Honpa Hongwanji Buddhism exerted over Japanese immigrants. In 1904, for example, Japanese strikers of Waipahu Plantation did not listen to anyone but Imamura, not even the consul general of Japan. After this incident, white planters cooperated in missionary activities of Imamura's priests on their properties, so that many temples were built near or within PLANTATIONS. Around 1920, there were 60 temples with a total membership of 75,000. Also, some 4,000 children attended 33 Sunday schools.

After the internment of the priests during World War II, the Honpa Hongwanji of Hawaii revived rapidly. The leadership had already been transferred to the NISEI, and lay officials, along with priests, were given the right to elect their own bishop who had been appointed by the chief abbot of the home temple in Kyoto. In 1967, the mission elected its first English-speaking bishop, marking the NISEI era in Hawaiian Buddhism.

For further reading, see Louise H. Hunter. *Buddhism in Hawaii: Its Impact on a Yankee Community.* Honolulu: University of Hawaii Press, 1971.   EIICHIRO AZUMA

Hood River Incident

In January 1945, the names of 16 NISEI servicemen were removed from the Hood River, Oregon, honor roll in front of the city hall by the local American Legion post. One of those whose names was removed was Frank Hachiya, who had been killed while a member of the MILITARY INTELLIGENCE SERVICE in the Philippines. The removal of the names was part of a larger campaign of threats and boycotts intended to keep Japanese Americans who had been removed from Hood River three years earlier from returning. Although the campaign was promoted under the guise of patriotism, economic factors may have been the paramount cause, given that the Japanese American farmers had been responsible for 25 percent of the total fruit production in the area prior to the war. The removal of the names garnered widespread public attention in national magazines. The intense spotlight on Hood River and the American Legion led to the reinstatement of the names six weeks later. The hysteria gradually began to die down. Though this incident was widely publicized, it was certainly not isolated; Japanese Americans returning to many West Coast communities faced similarly chilly receptions.

For further reading, see Audrie Girdner, and Anne Loftis. *The Great Betrayal: The Evacuation of the Japanese-Americans during World War II.* Toronto: Macmillan, 1969.

Hoover, J. Edgar (1895–1972)

Director, Federal Bureau of Investigation (FBI). To many, J. Edgar Hoover *was* the FBI. From the day he took office on May

14, 1924, to the day he died in 1972, Hoover ran the organization with an iron fist. He guided the FBI from a small operation to one of great stature through his demand for meticulous intelligence work.

From 1931 through World War II, Hoover conducted intelligence operations on Japanese Americans living on the West Coast and in Hawaii. His findings, for the most part, confirmed the loyalty of the majority but damaged the reputation of others. On the night Pearl Harbor was bombed, Hoover's FBI began a round up of 1,291 Japanese Americans on the grounds that they were on their "A" list of "known dangerous" individuals (see "ABC" LIST). (The criteria for getting on a list was easy: one only had to be a leader in the Japanese American community.) Because of this successful intelligence sweep, Hoover was confident in vouching for the loyalty of the rest of the community. When the idea for mass removal of all Japanese Americans from the West Coast was raised, Hoover objected on the grounds that all of the potential "disloyals" had already been arrested and detained by his agents.

Later during his tenure, Hoover became famous for his zeal in wiping out the so-called threat of communism in the United States. His files on Dr. Martin Luther King, Jr. and other civil rights leaders have become legendary, both for their volume and unabashed bias.
For further reading, see Bob Kumamoto. "The Search for Spies: American Counterintelligence and the Japanese American Community." *Amerasia Journal* 6.2 (1979): 45–75. There are also many general biographical works on Hoover. Two of the most recent are Curt Gentry. *J. Edgar Hoover: The Man and His Secrets.* New York: Norton, 1991 and Richard Gid Powers. *Secrecy and Power: The Life of J. Edgar Hoover.* New York: The Free Press, 1987.   GLEN KITAYAMA

[Also used to compile this entry: Frank F. Graham. "J. Edgar Hoover, 77, Dies; Will Lie in State in Capitol." *New York Times* 3 May 1972: 1.]

Hosokawa, William K. (1915–   )   Journalist Bill Hosokawa has served as the principal historian for the JAPANESE AMERICAN CITIZENS LEAGUE (JACL) while serving as a respected writer and editor for the *Denver Post*. A native of Seattle and a graduate of the University of Washington, Hosokawa began his career abroad working for the *Singapore Herald* in 1938 and the *Shanghai Times* and *Far Eastern Review* until 1941. He returned to the United States just a few weeks before the attack on Pearl Harbor. Forcibly removed along with all other Japanese Americans on the West Coast, he spent the war years in a CONCENTRATION CAMP at HEART MOUNTAIN, Wyoming, where he served as editor of the *Heart Mountain Sentinel*. He left camp in 1943 to take a position with the *Des Moines Register,* moving on to the *Denver*

Post in 1946. He eventually became the editorial page editor for the *Post*. In addition to writing a weekly column for the PACIFIC CITIZEN continuously since 1942, he has written several books on Japanese Americans, most on matters relating to the JACL. He received an honorary doctorate from the University of Denver in 1990.
For further reading, see Bill Hosokawa. "The Uprooting of Seattle." In Daniels, Roger, Sandra C. Taylor, and Harry H. L. Kitano, eds. *Japanese Americans: From Relocation to Redress.* Salt Lake City: University of Utah Press, 1986. Revised edition. Seattle: University of Washington Press, 1991. 18–20, which consists of autobiographical reflections on the World War II years. Hosokawa's other writings on Japanese Americans include the following: *Nisei: The Quiet Americans.* New York: William Morrow & Co., 1969; "The Cherishing of Liberty: The American Nisei." In Tachiki, Amy et al., eds. *Roots: An Asian American Reader.* Los Angeles: Asian American Studies Center, University of California, 1971. 215–20; *JACL in Quest of Justice: The History of the Japanese American Citizens League.* New York: William Morrow, 1982. He is also the co-author of the autobiographies *They Call Me Moses Masaoka.* New York: William Morrow, 1987 and *The Two Worlds of Jim Yoshida.* New York: Morrow, 1972 with Mike Masaoka and Jim Yoshida, respectively, and of the historical work *East to America: A History of the Japanese in the United States.* New York: Morrow, 1980 with Robert A. Wilson.

Houston, Velina Hasu (1957–   )   Award-winning playwright and poet Velina Hasu Houston is best known for her reflections on her experience as a multiracial Asian as well those on the experiences of other Japanese American women.

Born in Japan to a Japanese mother and an African American–American Indian father, Houston wrote her first poem at the age of eight and became interested in playwriting at the age of 15. In 1959, her family was relocated to Junction City, Kansas, near the large Fort Riley army base. Her childhood experiences as the daughter of a Japanese war bride and a U.S. serviceman formed the basis of many of her plays, including the award-winning *Asa Ga Kimashita* (Morning Has Broken), *American Dreams* and *Tea*. The three plays trace the life of a Japanese woman who marries an African American–American Indian soldier. The first play tells of the shame that the marriage brings upon her mother's family in post-war Japan. The second play focuses on the soldier who brings his Japanese bride home to New York. The third play, set in Junction City, is the story of five Japanese war brides and their struggle to survive in a midwestern environment. For the latter piece, Houston interviewed 50 Japanese war brides residing in Kansas.

A recipient of two Rockefeller fellowships for writing, Houston's other works include *Thirst,* a play about three

Japanese American sisters who explore their existence in contemporary America after the death of their mother, *Albatross* and *Kokoro Kara* (From the Heart). Houston's poems also center around the Japanese American experience and her own identity as a woman, a multiracial Asian and an artist. Excerpts from her collection of poetry entitled *Green Tea Girl in Orange Pekoe Country* have been published in various periodicals. Houston currently teaches at the University of Southern California's School of Theatre.

For further reading, see Velina Hasu Houston. "Tea." *Plays in Progress* 9.5 New York: Theatre Communication Group, 1985; "On Being Mixed Japanese in Modern Times." *Pacific Citizen* 20–27 Dec. 1985: B1–B3; and "Amerasian Girl." *Gidra: The Twentieth Anniversary Edition* (1990): 111.

EMILY LAWSIN

[Also used to compile this entry: Nanette Asimov. "Neither Black nor White: Multiracial people just want to be themselves." *San Francisco Chronicle* 4 July 1986: 26.]

Hunt Another name for MINIDOKA.

I

Ichihashi, Yamato (1878–1965) Stanford University instructor Yamato Ichihashi, himself a Japanese immigrant, wrote about Japanese immigration and the Japanese immigrant community in the U.S. prior to World War II. He is best known for his landmark 1932 work, *Japanese in the United States,* the standard text on the subject until well after the war. As a writer, teacher and lecturer, he defended Japanese immigrants against the charges of the ANTI-JAPANESE MOVEMENT and promoted good relations between Japan and the United States.

Born in Aichi PREFECTURE, the third of nine children of a former samurai family, Ichihashi attended public school in Nagoya. He opted to go to the United States to further his education, arriving in San Francisco in 1894. Attending school in San Francisco, he graduated from Lowell High in 1902 and entered Stanford University, graduating with an A.B. in 1907 and an A.M. in 1908, both in economics. He was an assistant in the economics department at Stanford from 1908 to 1910 and worked under Harry A. Millis on a United States Immigration Commission project studying Japanese immigration. Ichihashi went on to Harvard University, receiving a Ph.D. and authoring a dissertation on Japanese immigration and the immigrant community in the U.S., in 1913.

For a number of years, talks had taken place between the Japanese consul and Stanford officials about a Japanese government–sponsored position at the university in Japanese studies. With much attention focused on what would become the 1913 (CALIFORNIA) ALIEN LAND LAW, the Japanese Foreign Ministry launched a campaign to educate the American public about Japanese immigration. In line with the goals of this campaign, the proposal for the Stanford position was revived. Funding of $3,000 was granted by the Japanese government through a pair of dummy private donors for a one-year appointment. Ichihashi was appointed to fill this position to teach courses in Japanese history and government and to promote good relations between the U.S. and Japan. The position was renewed for three years in 1914 and again in 1917. Finally, in 1920, as the anti-Japanese movement intensified and what would become the 1920 (CALIFORNIA) ALIEN LAND LAW appeared on the ballot, the Foreign Ministry established a $37,500 endowment (again through a dummy private donor) to make the position permanent. After 15 years, Ichihashi was finally granted tenure in 1928.

Ichihashi's situation was a difficult one. On the one hand, he was employed by Stanford, which expected him to teach and write in an objective and scholarly fashion. On the other hand, his salary was paid by the Japanese government, which expected him to defend them and represent their interests to the American public. The situation was exacerbated by critics who accused Ichihashi of being a Japanese propagandist and surveillance by U.S. intelligence agencies. Beginning with the 1913 JAPANESE ASSOCIATION of America–sponsored pamphlet *Japanese Immigration: Its Status in California,* his writings used objective facts and statistics to put the best possible face on Japanese immigration and the immigrant community—this despite the fact that he privately held little regard for ISSEI leaders and "common" folk alike.

Along with all other West Coast Japanese Americans, Ichihashi and his family spent the World War II years in American CONCENTRATION CAMPS. He went from the Santa Anita "ASSEMBLY CENTER" to MANZANAR, TULE LAKE "RELOCATION CENTER" and GRANADA. He eventually returned to Stanford where he remained until his death in 1965.

For further reading, see Yuji Ichioka. " 'Attorney for the Defense': Yamato Ichihashi and Japanese Immigration." *Pacific Historical Review* 55.2 (May 1986): 192–225 and *The Issei: The World of the First Generation Japanese Immigrants, 1885–1924.* New York: The Free Press, 1988. Ichihashi's own books—especially *Japanese in the United States: A Critical Study of the Problems of the Japanese Immigrants and their Children.* Stanford: Stanford University Press, 1932. New York: Arno Press, 1969—remain widely available.

ie Japanese term designating the basic household unit. A key concept in Japanese society, *ie* literally means "house" or "household." The term has evolved in Japan to include both kinship-based and non-kinship-based groupings within Japanese society. In a Japanese American context, *ie* also describes the ethnic solidarity felt among Japanese Americans, which is strengthened in the face of prejudice and discrimination experienced in the United States. The ISSEI increasingly began to overlook prefectural and class distinctions among themselves. Thus, the boundaries of *ie* were extended to include the larger Japanese American community rather than solely the immediate household.

On the one hand, ie, like HAJI, was used as a form of social control over the NISEI. According to HARRY H. L. KITANO, this modified concept of the *ie* put more pressure on the *nisei* to succeed and sacrifice, for the failures and deviant acts of the *nisei* not only reflected poorly on immediate family and kin, but the entire Japanese American community as well. On the other hand, *ie* served as the basis of the social support and solidarity so prevalent in the world of the *issei* and *nisei*.

For further reading, see Betty S. Furuta. "Ethnic Identities of Japanese-American Families: Implications for Counseling." In Getty, Cathleen, and Winnifred Humphreys, eds. *Understanding the Family: Stress and Change in American Family Life*. New York: Appleton-Century-Crofts, 1981; Harry H. L. Kitano *Japanese Americans: The Evolution of a Subculture*. 1969. 2nd Edition. Englewood Cliffs, NJ: Prentice-Hall, Inc., 1976; *Kodansha Encyclopedia of Japan*. Tokyo: Kodansha, 1983; and Sylvia Junko Yanagisako. *Transforming the Past: Tradition and Kinship among Japanese Americans*. Stanford: Stanford University Press, 1985. STACEY HIROSE

Imamura, Yemyo (1867–1932) Buddhist priest. Born in Fukui, Japan, Rev. Imamura arrived in Hawaii in 1899 to administer to adherents of the Jodo Shinshu sect, Hawaii's largest. His career was marked by efforts to reconcile the differences between Buddhism and Christianity while also attending to the needs of the Japanese immigrant community. He became bishop of the HONPA HONGWANJI and worked out of the Fort Street Temple after its construction in 1900. One of his first activities was to establish a Young Men's Buddhist Association (YMBA), which helped immigrants learn English and adjust to Hawaiian society, on the model of the YMCA. The YMBA would go on to start a magazine called *Dobo,* open a night school and sponsor everything from religious lectures to sporting events. Rev. Imamura continually reiterated his mission of Americanization through Buddhism and also succeeding in convincing many non-Japanese that helping to build a stable community through preserving certain aspects of Japanese belief was a part of this Americanization process.

For further reading, see Louise H. Hunter. *Buddhism in Hawaii: Its Impact on a Yankee Community*. Honolulu: University of Hawaii Press, 1971; Franklin S. Odo and Kazuko Sinoto.

A Pictorial History of the Japanese in Hawaii, 1885–1924. Honolulu: Bishop Museum Press, 1985 and Dennis M. Ogawa. *Kodomo No Tame Ni, For the Sake of the Children: The Japanese American Experience in Hawaii*. Honolulu: University Press of Hawaii, 1978.

Imazeki, Howard (1907–) Howard Imazeki is best known in the Japanese American community as the longtime editor of the *Hokubei Mainichi* English section.

Born in Japan, Imazeki immigrated to the United States with his family in 1918 to be with his father. He joined the staff of the San Francisco–based NICHIBEI SHIMBUN right out of Sacramento Junior College; soon thereafter he became embroiled in a 1931 strike of *Nichibei* employees. After the strike, he joined the staff of the *Hokubei Asahi,* which soon merged with the SHIN SEKAI. Just prior to the merger, he left to continue his education. Wanting to attend a top-notch journalism school and to get out of California, he ended up at the University of Missouri, graduating in 1934. He returned to San Francisco to become the English section editor of the *Shin Sekai Asahi Shimbun*.

After getting married in 1937 and having a baby in 1938, he was forced to leave journalism in order to better support his family. He entered the poultry business with his father, becoming a partner in the American Poultry Company in Sacramento. In 1942, he, his wife and their three children, along with all other Japanese Americans on the West Coast, were forcibly removed from their home and incarcerated in a CONCENTRATION CAMP. The Imazekis ended up at TULE LAKE "RELOCATION CENTER" where Howard served as editor of the camp newspaper, the *Tulean Dispatch*. In February 1943, he left camp for Boulder, Colorado, where he taught Japanese for the Navy Language School. He also did overseas propaganda broadcasts for the Office of War Information in Denver and San Francisco. In 1946, he went to Japan as a civilian interpreter/translator. He was joined by his family two years later. He remained in Japan until 1954. Having become a naturalized citizen in 1953, he and his family returned to the United States in 1954. At that point, he became the English section editor for the *Hokubei Mainichi,* a post he held into the 1970s. As the *Hokubei* editor, Imazeki introduced many new features, including yearly *zadankai,* or community forums, on topics of interest to the community, in the yearly holiday editions.

For further reading, see Dorothy Anne Stroup. "The Role of the Japanese-American Press in Its Community." Thesis, University of California, Berkeley, 1960.

Immigrant Rejection of 1897 Action by the Hawaiian government involving the return to Japan of over 1,000 would-be Japanese immigrants attempting to enter the islands. The Hawaiian government feared that the Japanese population was getting too large and was a threat to its authority. Consequently, attempts were made to diversify the plantation work force by bringing in workers from Europe or the United States but these failed. The Hawaiian government had also levied a discriminatory tax on Japanese rice wine (see SAKE BILL) and, starting in 1894, required laborers arriving from Japan to possess either a labor contract or 100 yen "show money" to be allowed entrance to Hawaii. The rejection of 463 would-be Japanese immigrants aboard the *Shinshu Maru* on March 10, 1897, underscored the anti-Japanese activity and would be followed by more rejections on the next two shipments of Japanese laborers. All told, over 1,000 would-be Japanese laborers were sent home by the Hawaiian government. The rejections were of questionable legality under Hawaii laws and under previous agreements between Hawaii and Japan. Predictably, a Japanese government not inclined to take perceived slights from anyone reacted quickly and angrily. In the exchange of correspondence that followed, Japan demanded a 250,000 yen indemnity for treaty violations brought about by the rejection.

If the Hawaiian government had precipitated a conflict with Japan to force the United States to move quickly in annexing it, the plan worked. With the election of William McKinley as president of the United States in November 1896, Hawaiian officials recognized that many proponents of annexation would also be brought to power. Hawaiian officials worked with renewed vigor with the State Department, and the annexation resolution was eventually signed by McKinley on July 7, 1898. As part of the agreement, Hawaii was persuaded to settle with Japan over the immigrant rejection and a 150,000 yen compromise settlement was reached. Though Japan had no designs on Hawaii itself, the fear of Japanese influence in Hawaii was a factor—though not the most significant factor—in America's annexation of Hawaii.

For further reading, see Hilary Conroy. *The Japanese Frontier in Hawaii, 1868–1898.* Berkeley: University of California Press, 1953. New York: Arno Press, 1978; Gavan Daws. *Shoal of Time: A History of the Hawaiian Islands.* New York: Macmillan, 1968; Thomas J. Osborne. "Trade or War? America's Annexation of Hawaii Reconsidered." *Pacific Historical Review* 50.3 (Aug. 1981): 285–307; and United Japanese Society of Hawaii. *History of Japanese in Hawaii.* James H. Okahata, ed. Honolulu: United Japanese Society of Hawaii, 1971.

Immigration Act of February 20, 1907   An act whose provisions were born of the negotiations between the U.S., Japan and the city authorities of San Francisco following the San Francisco Board of Education's resolution to segregate children of Japanese ancestry attending public grammar schools. Section 1 of this act effectively prohibited Japanese laborers who held passports for Hawaii, Mexico or Canada from entering the continental United States. The act was enacted on February 20, 1907, and took effect on July 1, 1907. (See GENTLEMEN'S AGREEMENT and SAN FRANCISCO SCHOOL BOARD SEGREGATION ORDER.)

Immigration Act of 1924   Immigration legislation which, among other things, ended all further Japanese immigration to the United States. The enactment of this act, with its provision of Japanese exclusion, represented a final victory after nearly two decades of agitation by the ANTI-JAPANESE MOVEMENT. The act infuriated Japan and adversely affected U.S.–Japan relations. Japanese immigration would be curtailed until 1952 (with the exception of post–World War II war brides of American servicemen).

By the early 1920s, there was a general sentiment across the nation that immigration needed to be restricted somehow. Given this sentiment, there were two differing approaches as to how this might be accomplished. California and the West, represented by Senator HIRAM JOHNSON and ex-newspaper publisher V. S. MCCLATCHY, wanted immigration legislation that would include a provision banning all immigration from Japan. Their reasons for wanting exclusion had to do with economic and political opportunism, fear of the "YELLOW PERIL" and racism. On the other hand, much of the rest of the country wanted a quota immigration bill primarily aimed at restricting European immigration that would not overtly discriminate against Japan or any other country. Such a bill was forcefully lobbied for by SIDNEY GULICK, a former missionary in Japan and leading opponent of the anti-Japanese movement. A bill of the first type was introduced into the House by Congressman Albert Johnson of Washington, passing easily in April 1924. However, it was felt that getting the bill passed in the Senate would be very difficult since Senate members would be less inclined to anger Japan by voting down even a token immigration quota for Japan. The turning point of the Senate campaign for the bill came when Secretary of State Charles Evans Hughes asked Japanese Ambassador Masanao Hanihara to write a letter summarizing the GENTLEMEN'S AGREEMENT of 1907–08 since the provisions of the agreement were not widely known, having resulting from "secret" correspondence between the president and the Japanese government. Hanihara's letter outlined the agreement and appealed to the senators to reject any bill that would end all Japanese immigration. His letter concluded with the following passage:

Relying on the confidence you have been good enough to show me at all times, I have stated or rather repeated all this to you very candidly and in a most friendly spirit, for I realize, as I believe you do, the grave consequences which the enactment of the measure retaining that particular provision [that is, ending Japanese immigration] would inevitably bring upon the otherwise happy and mutually advantageous relations between our two countries.

Out of this seemingly innocuous diplomatic-speak, Henry Cabot Lodge, senior senator from Massachusetts and the chairman of the Senate Foreign Relations Committee, seized upon the phrase "grave consequences" with outrage, calling it a "veiled threat." Lodge's interpretation turned the tide in favor of exclusion, and the bill passed the Senate. After his request to delay the implementation of exclusion was rejected by Congress, President Coolidge signed the bill into law on May 24, 1924. The more or less national support for limiting European immigration and Coolidge's vulnerability in the West and South in an election year no doubt influenced him to not veto the bill.

Reaction to the law in Japan was bitter and angry, while reaction in the United States was mixed, varying by region. Upon passage of the law, both Hanihara and American ambassador to Japan Cyrus E. Woods resigned in protest. Since the passing of the bill meant the rejection of even a token quota amounting to no more than a couple of hundred persons, Japan viewed the legislation as a serious affront. Militarists in Japan could and would use the exclusion act as evidence of America's feelings about Japan and as ammunition in arguing for a more aggressive military build-up. In California, the reaction of the exclusionists was one of jubilation. Among the Japanese immigrants, the act represented the final indignity, after ALIEN LAND LAWS, the OZAWA VS. UNITED STATES naturalization decision and the upholding of the discriminatory land laws in the courts.

For further reading, see Roger Daniels. *The Politics of Prejudice: The Anti-Japanese Movement in California and the Struggle for Japanese Exclusion*. 1962. 2nd edition. Berkeley: University of California Press, 1977; Rodman W. Paul. "The Abrogation of the Gentlemen's Agreement: Being the Harvard Phi Beta Kappa Prize Essay for 1936." In Daniels, Roger, ed. *Three Short Works on Japanese Americans*. New York: Arno Press, 1978; and Peter Heywood Wang. *Legislating 'Normalcy': The Immigration Act of 1924*. San Francisco: R & E Research Associates, 1975 for discussions of how the law came to be passed. See Yuji Ichioka. *The Issei: The World of the First Generation Japanese Immigrants, 1885–1924*. New York: The Free Press, 1988 for Japanese immigrant reaction to its passage, Lee Arne Makela. "Japanese Attitudes towards the United States Immigration Act of 1924." Diss., Stanford University, 1973 for Japanese reaction, and Bruce A. Abrams. "A Muted Cry: White Opposition to the Japanese Exclusion Movement, 1911–1924." Diss., City University of New York, 1987 and Sandra C. Taylor. *Advocate of Understanding: Sidney Gulick and the Search for Peace with Japan*. Kent, Ohio: Kent State University Press, 1985 for white American efforts to stop the legislation.

Immigration Act of October 3, 1965   Immigration act abolishing the discriminatory national origins quota system that had heavily favored immigration by northern and western Europeans and that effectively terminated racial discrimination against Japanese and other Asian peoples who wished to immigrate to the United States. The act banned discrimination against an alien because of race, religion or national origin, and immigrants were allowed to become citizens after only five years. The 1965 Immigration Act was based on a system of preferences, with priority given to the reuniting of families and the admission of needed workers.

The act and its amendments have resulted in a dramatic change in the nature of immigration to the United States and in the composition of the Asian American community. Where most immigrants had come from Europe throughout American history, most of those who have come since 1965 have been from Asia, Mexico or South and Central America. Where Japanese Americans once made up the largest Asian American national group, Japanese Americans today rank behind Chinese and Filipino Americans and just ahead of Asian Indian and Korean Americans in population. The 1965 act permanently changed the Asian American population and, like the IMMIGRATION ACT OF 1924, its effects will be felt for generations to come.

For further reading, see Moritoshi Fukuda. *Legal Problems of Japanese Americans*. Tokyo: Keio Tsushin, 1980. Ronald Takaki. *Strangers from a Different Shore: A History of Asian Americans*. Boston: Little, Brown and Company, 1989 and Sucheng Chan. *Asian Americans: An Interpretive History*. Boston: Twayne Publishers, 1991 are both historical studies of Asian Americans that contain accounts of the 1965 act and its effects.

Immigration and Nationality Act of 1952   Omnibus immigration and nationality legislation sponsored by Congressman Francis E. Walter of Pennsylvania and Senator Pat McCarran of Nevada that is also known as the Walter-McCarran Act. The act made all races eligible for naturalization and eliminated race as a bar to immigration. ISSEI who were previously ineligible for citizenship could finally become naturalized. This is not to say, however, that the act was not discriminatory. The act established a national origins quota system, and racial ancestry determined the quota area to which a person was chargeable for the purposes of immigration. The act delineated the continent of Asia and almost the entire area encompassed by the Pacific

Ocean as the Asia-Pacific Triangle. A Caucasian born outside of this area could be allotted to the quota assigned to a nation of the Asia-Pacific Triangle, but an Asian born outside of the Asia-Pacific Triangle would still have to enter the United States for permanent residence under the Asian nation of his or her ancestry. Japan was only allotted 185 immigrants a year. On June 25, 1952, President Truman vetoed the bill, but both the House and the Senate overrode the veto and the bill became law. In the years to come, many *issei* did take advantage of the new law to officially become American citizens after decades of being "ALIENS INELIGIBLE TO CITIZENSHIP."

For further reading, see Frank F. Chuman. *The Bamboo People: The Law and Japanese-Americans.* Del Mar, CA: Publisher's Inc., 1976. See Bill Hosokawa. *JACL in Quest of Justice: The History of the Japanese American Citizens League.* New York: William Morrow, 1982 and Mike Masaoka and Bill Hosokawa. *They Call Me Moses Masaoka.* New York: William Morrow, 1987 for accounts of Japanese American Citizens League lobbying on behalf of the bill.　　　　DENNIS YAMAMOTO

Immigration Convention of 1886　Agreement between Hawaii and Japan regarding the immigration of Japanese laborers and the treatment of those laborers in Hawaii. The roots of the agreement stemmed from allegations of mistreatment of the first group of Japanese laborers in Hawaii which filtered back to Japan. Special Commissioner Katsunosuke Inouye (son of Japanese foreign minister Kaoru Inouye) was sent to Hawaii with the second group of laborers in June 1885 to investigate. After threatening to take the 988 would-be workers back with him if their rights could not be protected, Inouye was able to negotiate a protocol with Hawaii officials which was signed on July 21. Further negotiation led to the Immigration Convention, signed on January 28, 1886, in Tokyo.

The convention's provisions were sweeping. All migrants were to be subject to the approval of the Kanagawa prefectural governor and free steerage passage was to be guaranteed. ROBERT W. IRWIN was designated as Special Agent of the Hawaii Bureau of Immigration. The Hawaiian government was to provide inspectors, interpreters and doctors for the welfare of the laborers. The convention even provided the Japanese immigrants the rights of suffrage and naturalization. These provisions were to retroactively apply to all earlier shipments of Japanese laborers as well.

Unfortunately for the migrants, the provisions of the convention were effectively voided just one year later when foreign planters forced the king of Hawaii to change the constitution, abrogating much of his authority. Later that year, the convention was revised to put

Making comfort packages *(imonbukuro)* for a visiting Japanese training ship, 1922.　*Buddhist Churches of America Collection, Japanese American National Museum Photographic & Moving Image Archive*

the burden of paying for the passage to Hawaii and of paying for the inspectors, interpreters and doctors onto the laborers.

For further reading, see Franklin S. Odo and Kazuko Sinoto. *A Pictorial History of the Japanese in Hawaii, 1885–1924.* Honolulu: Bishop Museum Press, 1985 and United Japanese Society of Hawaii. *History of Japanese in Hawaii.* James H. Okahata, ed. Honolulu: United Japanese Society of Hawaii, 1971; the former includes the full text of the convention.

imonbukuro　Gift packets prepared by civilians to be sent to military personnel at war. Filled with nonperishable food and toiletry articles, *imonbukuro* were a way for Japanese civilians to support the nation's war effort. In a Japanese American context, *imonbukuro* were assembled and sent by the thousands by ISSEI to Japanese soldiers in the Sino-Japanese war, starting with the Marco Polo Bridge Incident of 1937. Throughout the 1930s, support for Japanese military activity ran high among the *issei* (and many NISEI as well) and *imonbukuro* represented only one of several ways *issei* showed that support. *Imonbukuro* were no doubt also sent to the many Japanese American soldiers in the United States Army during World War II and all wars since.

For further reading see Yuji Ichioka. "Japanese Immigrant Nationalism: The Issei and the Sino-Japanese War, 1937–1941." *California History* 69.3 (Fall 1990): 260–75, 310–11 and Brian Masaru Hayashi. "'For the Sake of Our Japanese Brethren': Assimilation, Nationalism, and Protestantism among the Japanese of Los Angeles, 1895–1942." Diss., University of California, Los Angeles, 1990 for accounts of Issei nationalism in the 1930s. Yuji Ichioka. "A Study in Dualism: James Yoshinori Sakamoto and the Japanese American Courier, 1928–1942." *Amerasia Journal* 13.2 (1986–87): 49–81 and Hiroshi

Yoneyama. "The Forging of Japanese American Patriotism, 1931–1941." Thesis, University of Tsukuba, 1984 discuss Nisei attitudes toward Japan in the '30s.

Inada, Lawson Fusao (1938–) Poet, writer. Award-winning poet Lawson Inada is best known for his poetry about the Japanese and Asian American experience.

A SANSEI, Inada was born on the west side of Fresno, California, in a multiethnic neighborhood where the roots of his jazz-influenced poetry sprouted. During World War II, he was detained in CONCENTRATION CAMPS in Arkansas and Colorado. His first book, *Before the War, Poems as They Happened,* includes poems around this theme and is believed to be the first book of poetry by an Asian American published by a major publishing company (William Morrow). Beginning in 1969, Inada was active in the Combined Asian American Resources Project in San Francisco, a group that advocated the publication of Asian American literature. Since then, he has served as co-editor of *Aiiieeeee! An Anthology of Asian-American Writers,* and its sequel, *The Big Aiiieeeee! An Anthology of Chinese American and Japanese American Literature* with Frank Chin, Jeffery Paul Chan, and Shawn Wong. Inada also collaborated on *The Buddha Bandits Down Highway 99* with GARRETT HONGO and Alan Chong Lau. His latest book of poetry is titled *Legends from Camp.*

Inada's poems have been published in numerous periodicals, anthologies and newspapers and have been the basis of two writing fellowships from the National Endowment for the Arts. *Rolling Stone* magazine named him one of America's "Heavy 100." His life was the basis for a film entitled *I Told You So,* produced by the Los Angeles public schools and VISUAL COMMUNICATIONS. Inada currently lives in Ashland, Oregon, where he is professor of English at Southern Oregon College. For further reading, see *Before the War, Poems as They Happened.* New York: Morrow, 1971 and *Legends from Camp.* Minneapolis: Coffee House Press, 1992. Inada's work can also be found in *New Directions in Prose and Poetry 23.* J. Laughlin, ed. New York: New Directions, 1971; *Asian-American Authors.* Hsu, Kai-yu and Helen Palubinskas, eds. Boston: Houghton Mifflin Company, 1972; *Aiiieeeee! An Anthology of Asian-American Writers.* Frank Chin, Jeffery Paul Chan, Lawson Fusao Inada, Shawn Hsu Wong, eds. Washington, D.C.: Howard University Press, 1974; and *The Big Aiiieeeee! An Anthology of Chinese American and Japanese American Literature.* Jeffery Paul Chan, Frank Chin, Lawson Inada, Shawn Wong, eds. New York: Meridian, 1991. **EMILY LAWSIN**

Inouye, Daniel Ken (1924–) United States senator from Hawaii, lawyer. Six-term senator Daniel K.

Daniel Inouye. *Daniel Inouye Collection, Japanese American National Museum Photographic & Moving Image Archive*

Inouye of Hawaii has been one of the most visible and influential of all Japanese Americans.

Born in Honolulu, Inouye attended public schools in Hawaii. During World War II, he volunteered for the highly decorated 442ND REGIMENTAL COMBAT TEAM. He compiled a sterling record of military service and was awarded the Distinguished Service Cross, America's second highest military honor. His dreams of going to medical school and becoming a surgeon were dashed when he lost his right arm in action in 1945. While recuperating from his injuries, he decided to study law in order to effect social change in Hawaii.

Inouye graduated from the University of Hawaii in 1950. While a student there, he volunteered his help to JOHN BURNS in his campaign for Congress and began his long association with the Democratic Party during its rise to power in Hawaii (see REVOLUTION OF 1954). Inouye graduated from George Washington University Law School in Washington, D.C., in 1952, and after passing the bar the following year, commenced practice in Honolulu as an assistant public prosecutor. From 1954, Inouye served as majority leader in the territorial house of representatives and from 1958 to 1959 as a member of the territorial senate.

In 1959, Inouye, a Democrat, was elected to the Eighty-sixth Congress as the first representative from the newly recognized state of Hawaii, and was reelected in 1961. At the end of this term, Inouye was elected to the United States Senate. He was reelected in 1968, 1974, 1980, 1986 and 1992. While in Congress, he sat on the Select Committee on Intelligence, Select Committee on Indian Affairs and the Select Committee on Secret Military Assistance to Iran and the Nicaraguan Opposition. He is perhaps best known as having been part of congressional committees investigating both the Watergate and Iran/Contra scandals.

In 1962, Inouye was selected as "One of the 100 Most Important Men & Women in the United States" by *Life* magazine. Inouye's autobiography, entitled *Journey to Washington,* was published in 1967.

For further reading, see Daniel K. Inouye, with Lawrence Elliot. *Journey to Washington.* Englewood Cliffs, N.J.: Prentice-Hall, 1967.   TRACEY ENDO

Inouye, Yuichi et al. v. Clark   Case involving four former internees (Yuichi Inouye, Miye Mae Murakami, Tsutako Sumi and Mutsu Shimizu) who renounced their American citizenship during the Second World War. Inouye was 17 years old at the time he renounced his citizenship, and he had done so because he wished to stay with his parents, who had applied for repatriation to Japan. Murakami, Sumi and Shimizu were all American citizens married to Japanese aliens, and all three were interned at the TULE LAKE "SEGREGATION CENTER." There, they were all pressured to renounce their citizenship by relatives and pro-Japanese elements in the camp. In court, all four contended that their renunciations were the result of undue influence, duress and coercion, and were not free and voluntary acts. Federal district court judge Charles Cavanah agreed, and ordered that their citizenship be restored to them in his decision of September 5, 1947. The federal government appealed the decision to the Ninth Circuit Court of Appeals, but the decision of the federal district court was affirmed on August 29, 1949.

For further reading, see Frank F. Chuman. *The Bamboo People: The Law and Japanese-Americans.* Del Mar, Calif.: Publisher's Inc., 1976.

Internal Security Act of 1950   See EMERGENCY DETENTION ACT OF 1950.

International District   See SEATTLE NIHONMACHI/ INTERNATIONAL DISTRICT.

International Longshoremen's and Warehousemen's Union (ILWU)   West-Coast–based labor union that played a key role in the history of Japanese Americans in Hawaii. Through the efforts of ILWU organizers, Hawaii's sugar plantation and dock workers were organized along pan-ethnic lines, helping to change the balance of power in post–World War II Hawaii. The bulk of the workers involved were Japanese or Filipino American.

The origins of the ILWU can be traced to a rift between the Pacific Coast District of the International Longshoremen's Association (ILA) and the national leadership. Pacific Coast District president Harry Bridges, who had come to power during the San Francisco general strike of 1934, led the break from the ILA when the Congress of Industrial Organizations (CIO) was formed. The ILWU received a CIO charter in August 1937 and was certified by the National Labor Relations Board as the collective bargaining agent for West Coast longshoremen in June 1938.

Led by organizers such as JACK KAWANO, and future Hawaii regional representative JACK HALL, the ILWU succeeded in organizing Hawaii sugar plantation and dock workers by 1945. (This despite the exclusion by a Stockton, California, local of Japanese American workers returning from incarceration in American CONCENTRATION CAMPS; see STOCKTON INCIDENT.) Though there was a long history of labor activism in Hawaii, the rise of the ILWU marked the first time that labor organization took place across ethnic lines on a large scale. Successful strikes of plantation workers in 1946 and dock workers in 1949 (see 1949 STRIKE) followed. With a long history of alleged Communist links, the union came under attack by the House Un-American Activities Committee in the 1950s (see RELUCTANT THIRTY-NINE and HAWAII SEVEN). Though weakened, the union continued to play a major role in Hawaii's politics through the Democratic Party "REVOLUTION OF 1954," which saw many NISEI politicians begin their careers. The ILWU (as well as the ILA) continues to exist to this day.

For further reading, see Edward D. Beechert. *Working in Hawaii: A Labor History.* Honolulu: University of Hawaii Press, 1985; Lawrence H. Fuchs. *Hawaii Pono: A Social History.* New York: Harcourt, Brace and World, 1961; and Roland Kotani. *The Japanese in Hawaii: A Century of Struggle.* Honolulu: Hochi, Ltd., 1985 for accounts of the ILWU in Hawaii and the Nisei.

internment camps   Camps administered by the Justice Department for the detention of enemy aliens deemed dangerous during World War II. While the majority of the approximately 120,000 Japanese Americans who were incarcerated during World War II were in one of the 10 camps administered by the WAR RELOCATION AUTHORITY (WRA), several thousand others came under the jurisdiction of the Justice Department in a separate and parallel internment. The Justice Department program and the existence of the Justice Department administered internment camps remains relatively unknown compared to the WRA camps. (Reflecting the usage of the terms in most recent historical literature, the WRA camps are referred to in this book as "CONCENTRATION CAMPS" while the Justice Department camps are called "internment camps.")

The roots of the Justice Department program can be found in the surveillance of the Japanese American community that had been carried out by various government agencies for a decade prior to World War II. By the time of the attack on Pearl Harbor, lists had been compiled of people within the community who were thought to be "dangerous." (See "ABC" LIST.) By 6:30 A.M. on December 8, 1942, 736 such people had been arrested. By February 16, the number had grown to 2,192 from the mainland United States with another 879 from Hawaii. The people on these lists represented the leadership of the ISSEI community; "dangerous" seemed to translate to any *issei* or KIBEI in a position of power, regardless of action or ideology. Church leaders, JAPANESE ASSOCIATION officials, JAPANESE-LANGUAGE SCHOOL principals and newspaper editors were among those picked up. Initially imprisoned in local jails for the most part, some were questioned and released, while others remained locked up for weeks in camps administered by the army (see, for instance, SAND ISLAND, where many Hawaii *issei* were imprisoned), often without being allowed communication with their families. The removal of these community leaders not only led to severe hardships for their families but effectively transferred the leadership of the community into the hands of the NISEI.

Most of the people who were picked up were eventually transferred to one of the internment camps run by the Justice Department for enemy aliens. These camps varied greatly in size and population type. Among the largest was the CRYSTAL CITY, Texas, camp, which housed those men whose families had opted to join them in internment. Crystal City also housed some German and Italian enemy aliens, as well as a particularly unfortunate group of JAPANESE PERUVIANS. The camp in SANTA FE, New Mexico, housed as many as 2,100 internees, all of whom were *issei* men, while the camp at Seagoville, Texas, housed only women. Other major camps included Fort Stanton, New Mexico; Fort Missoula, Montana; Fort Lincoln, North Dakota; Kenedy, Texas; and Kooskia, Idaho. According to Justice Department records, there were 5,264 Japanese Americans in custody in August 1945, while 153 Japanese diplomats and 1,573 others had been sent "back" to Japan, adding up to a total of just under 7,000 Japanese Americans who had been under the jurisdiction of this program.

Life in these camps was not characterized by the kind of conflicts seen in many of the WRA camps. This might have been due to the more homogeneous population in these camps and in the less ambiguous nature of the relationship between inmates and administrators—it wasn't a case of one group of American citizens guarding another group. This is not to say, however, that life was pleasant in these camps. Three internees were shot to death in the camps and many others reported individual beatings, unlawful threats, questionable rules, solitary confinement and other forms of mistreatment by camp guards. The camps were gradually emptied at the end of the war, with most inmates being released. Crystal City, the last of the camps to close, didn't shut its gates until February 27, 1948.

There is still relatively little written about these camps. Paul Frederick Clark. "Those Other Camps: An Oral History Analysis of Japanese Alien Enemy Internment during World War II." Thesis, California State University, Fullerton, 1980 gives an overview of the program and includes interviews with camp inmates and administrators. Tetsuden Kashima. "American Mistreatment of Internees During World War II: Enemy Alien Japanese." In Daniels, Roger, Sandra C. Taylor, and Harry H. L. Kitano, eds. *Japanese Americans: From Relocation to Redress.* Salt Lake City: University of Utah Press, 1986. Revised edition. Seattle: University of Washington Press, 1991. 52–56 also provides some background and describes several shootings and other mistreatment in detail. Though its focus is on Santa Fe, John J. Culley. "The Santa Fe Internment Camp and the Justice Department Program for Enemy Aliens." In Daniels, Roger, Sandra C. Taylor, and Harry H. L. Kitano, eds. *Japanese Americans: From Relocation to Redress.* Salt Lake City: University of Utah Press, 1986. Revised edition. Seattle: University of Washington Press, 1991. 57–71 includes much of general interest. Among the first person accounts of internment in these camps are Bunya Fujimura. *Though I Be Crushed: The Wartime Experiences of a Buddhist Priest.* Los Angeles: Nembutsu Press, 1985; Rev Yoshiaki Fukuda. *My Six Years of Internment: An Issei's Struggle for Justice.* Commentary by Stanford M. Lyman. San Francisco: Konko Church of San Francisco, 1990; and Take Uchida. "An Issei Interne's Experiences." In Daniels, Roger, Sandra C. Taylor, and Harry H. L. Kitano, eds. *Japanese Americans: From Relocation to Redress.* Salt Lake City: University of Utah Press, 1986. Revised edition. Seattle: University of Washington Press, 1991. 31–32.

interracial marriage   Marriage between partners of different racial or ethnic backgrounds. More precisely, marriages between partners of different racial backgrounds are "interracial marriages," while marriages between partners of different ethnic groups—but possibly of the same race—are "intermarriages." A marriage between a Chinese American and a Japanese American is considered an "intermarriage" but not an "interracial marriage." All interracial marriages are intermarriages but the opposite is not true. Intermarriages are also known as "outmarriages." The rate of intermarriage for a given group is often cited as a measure of that group's assimilation to and acceptance by mainstream American culture, though other interpretations exist.

Compared to other racial groups and other Asian American groups, Japanese Americans intermarry at the highest rate at least on the U.S. mainland. A 1984 study by HARRY H. L. KITANO and others found that Japanese Americans in both Los Angeles County and in Hawaii outmarried at about a 60 percent rate in 1979 and 1980. (It is important to note that this study uses marriages as the unit of measure, not individuals. In this case, they are saying that 60 percent of marriages involve one non-Japanese American partner, which is the same as saying 43 percent of Japanese American individuals are marrying non-Japanese Americans. Most other studies use the individual as the unit of measure.) Such a high rate did not always exist. Anti-miscegenation laws in California and many other states prohibited marriages between Caucasians and people of other races. Thus, most ISSEI and NISEI could not and did not marry outside their group. For Los Angeles County, a 1973 study by Kitano and Akemi Kikumura found the intermarriage rate for Japanese Americans to be 2 percent in 1924–33, 12 percent in 1948–51, 23 percent in 1959 and 49 percent in 1972 (again marriages are used here as the unit of measure). More women than men were found to be outmarrying.

Other studies tend to verify the findings above. In their 1990 study of Asian American intermarriage in California based on 1980 census data, Larry Hajime Shinagawa and Gin Yong Pang found that 83.8 percent of Japanese American men and 64.2 percent of Japanese American women were married to other Japanese Americans. When controlled for population, Japanese Americans were found to be most likely to marry other Japanese Americans, then other Asian Americans, then Caucasians, then African Americans or Latinos. While Japanese American women were much more likely than Japanese American men to outmarry, they found that a good deal of the difference was due to the large number of Japanese war brides who were married to non-Japanese Americans; 27.5 percent of Japanese American women were married to Caucasians, which broke down to 42.1 percent of the foreign-born versus only 14.4 percent of the American-born. With the exception of war brides, the American-born and the young were found to outmarry at much higher rates than others.

In their 1991 book, Stephen S. Fugita and David J. O'Brien found that intermarriage rates also varied by region. In their study of Japanese American men in GARDENA, SACRAMENTO and Fresno, they found a much lower outmarriage rate in Gardena, where the population density of Japanese Americans is much greater. This result suggests that outmarriage rates for SANSEI in places outside of California and Hawaii might be even higher than the studies above indicate. They also found that while those who outmarried participated less in ethnic voluntary associations, they still participated in such organizations at a rate much higher than that found for other ethnic groups, suggesting that the notion of Japanese American ethnicity is not in immediate danger of disappearing.

Though they outmarry at a higher rate than other groups, it seems clear that most Japanese Americans still marry other Japanese Americans. The high outmarriage rate will result in a high percentage of YONSEI and succeeding generations of Japanese Americans being of mixed-race background, which will undoubtedly change the character of the future Japanese American community in ways which are difficult to predict. Any conclusion of intermarriage leading to the end of the Japanese American community seems quite premature.

For further reading, see Russell Endo, and Dale Hirokawa. "Japanese American Intermarriage." *Free Inquiry in Creative Sociology* 11.2 (Nov. 1983): 159–66; Stephen S. Fugita, and David J. O'Brien. *Japanese American Ethnicity: The Persistence of Community*. Seattle: University of Washington Press, 1991; Akemi Kikumura, and Harry H. L. Kitano. "Interracial Marriage: A Picture of the Japanese Americans." *Journal of Social Issues* 29.2 (1973): 67–81; Harry H. L. Kitano, et al. "Asian-American Interracial Marriage." *Journal of Marriage and the Family* 46.1 (Feb. 1984): 179–90; Larry Hajime Shinagawa and Gin Yong Pang. "Marriage Patterns of Asian Americans in California, 1980." In Chan, Sucheng, ed. *Income and Status Differences between White and Minority Americans*. Lewiston, N.Y.: The Edwin Mellen Press, 1990. 225–82; and John N. Tinker. "Intermarriage and Ethnic Boundaries: The Japanese American Case." *Journal of Social Issues* 29.2 (Spring 1973): 49–66 and "Intermarriage and Assimilation in a Plural Society: Japanese-Americans in the United States." *Marriage & Family Review* 5.1 (Spring 1982): 61–74.

inu   Popular term for those perceived as being informants in the World War II CONCENTRATION CAMPS. In the polarized Japanese American communities that inhabited the concentration camps, to be labeled an *inu* was quite literally to have one's life threatened. Meaning "dog" in Japanese, *inu* was the label given to those who were thought to have informed authorities about supposedly suspicious individuals in the Japanese American community. The term later was applied to those perceived to be cooperating too enthusiastically with the Caucasian administrators of the camps. In the particularly charged atmosphere of TULE LAKE "SEGREGATION CENTER," any detainee not behaving in an appropriately anti-American fashion might have been labeled an *inu*. *Inu* were also perceived as having gained some personal advantage such as preferential treatment by authorities for having informed or cooperated with them. Most of the accused *inu* were NISEI; many of the accusers were ISSEI or KIBEI. Members of the JAPANESE AMERICAN CITIZENS LEAGUE (JACL) were sometimes perceived as *inu* by members of the camp community. The aftermath of a beating of a suspected *inu* and JACL member at MANZANAR triggered a mass uprising there in December 1942. Many suspected *inu* were removed from the camps for their own safety in the aftermath of events such as this. The *inu* phenomenon reflected long-standing divisions in the Japanese American community by generation, educational background and ideology that were exacerbated by the close confines of the camps and by the natural tendency for Caucasian military and camp administrative personnel to favor American-born or more overtly "patriotic" or "cooperative" individuals. The term *inu* was also used in much the same way in World War II Hawaii to refer to those who embraced the drive to destroy Japanese cultural institutions and the "Speak American" campaign too enthusiastically. During the World War II period, the term *inu* had much the same type of meaning in the Japanese American community that the term "Uncle Tom" did in the African American community. The term *inu* is no longer used in this fashion today.

For further reading, see Roland Kotani. *The Japanese in Hawaii: A Century of Struggle*. Honolulu: Hochi, Ltd., 1985 for Hawaii; Dorothy S. Thomas, and Richard Nishimoto. *The Spoilage*. Berkeley: University of California Press, 1946, 1969 for Tule Lake, and Michi Weglyn. *Years of Infamy: The Untold Story of America's Concentration Camps*. New York: William Morrow & Co., 1976.

Irish, John Powell (1843–1923) Anti-exclusionist leader. John Powell Irish and his American Committee of Justice waged a lonely campaign against the ANTI-JAPANESE MOVEMENT and the 1920 (CALIFORNIA) ALIEN LAND LAW.

Iowa-born Irish had been a politician and journalist, serving in the Iowa state legislature before becoming editor of the *Oakland Times* and *Alta Californian* from 1882 to 1891. He had also waged an unsuccessful congressional campaign in 1890 and was a rancher in California's Delta County. It was perhaps his experience as a farmer that led to his initial opposition to the proposed land law, since it would prohibit his selling land to ISSEI purchasers. He described his committee's purpose as "to defend the rights of white landowners." He also saw Chinese and Japanese immigrants as having contributed to the economic development of the West and thus deserving of equal treatment. While not arguing against efforts to restrict or ban further immigration, he and his colleagues pressed for just treatment for all aliens

already in the U.S. Unlike SIDNEY L. GULICK, who opposed anti-Japanese agitation primarily because of its negative effect on American-Japanese relations, Irish defended Japanese immigrants on the strength of their accomplishments and by citing the Constitution and the TREATY OF COMMERCE AND NAVIGATION OF 1911 BETWEEN JAPAN AND THE UNITED STATES. Also unlike Gulick, Irish waged personal attacks on such anti-Japanese leaders as V. S. MCCLATCHY and supported efforts by the Japanese immigrants themselves to challenge the land laws. Though ultimately unsuccessful in defeating the 1920 land law, the efforts of Irish were significant in representing the only organized California-based Caucasian effort to defeat the initiative.

For further reading, see Bruce A. Abrams. "A Muted Cry: White Opposition to the Japanese Exclusion Movement, 1911–1924." Diss., City University of New York, 1987.

[Quote is from Abrams 87 (258-note 64).]

Irwin, Robert Walker (1844–?) Hawaiian consul general, special agent for immigration in Japan, 1885–1894. Robert W. Irwin was the single most important figure in starting the official labor migration from Japan to Hawaii in 1885. Under the system of government-sponsored migration developed by Irwin, 28,691 migrants made their way to Hawaii from Japan.

Robert Irwin was born in Denmark in 1844. His father was an American diplomat and politician who had been the mayor of Pittsburgh and a member of the House of Representatives; his mother was a direct descendant of Benjamin Franklin. His four siblings included Agnes Irwin, founder of the Agnes Irwin School of Girls in Philadelphia and the first dean of Radcliffe College. Through his brother Richard, an official with the Pacific Mail Steamship Company in San Francisco, Robert became the Pacific Mail steamship agent in Yokohama in 1866. By 1872, he had secured a position with the firm Walsh, Hall, and Company in Yokohama, through which he became acquainted with many prominent Japanese businessmen and politicians. The most important of these was Kaoru Inouye, later Japan's foreign minister. With Irwin's help, Inouye and some associates began a successful foreign trading firm that eventually became Mitsui Bussan Kaisha (Mitsui Trading Company) in 1876. When Inouye traveled to America and Europe in 1876, Irwin accompanied him. Inouye even arranged for Irwin to marry a Japanese woman, Iki Takechi, in 1882. The couple had six children.

In 1880, the Hawaiian consul general to Japan, Harlan P. Lillibridge, took a leave of absence and Irwin was appointed to replace him; the appointment soon became a permanent one. With Hawaii expressing a growing

Robert Irwin and his wife, Iki, February 11, 1889. *John T. Irwin & Family Collection, Japanese American National Museum Photographic & Moving Image Archive*

interest in securing Japanese labor migration for its sugar PLANTATIONS and anxious to avoid the mistakes of the GANNEN-MONO episode of 1868, Irwin seemed the ideal choice to serve as their representative in Japan, given his connections and reputation there. His close friendship with Foreign Minister Inouye smoothed the negotiations and led to the resumption of labor migration in 1885. Irwin became Hawaii's commissioner of immigration. Given how badly Hawaii needed Irwin and his Japanese contacts, he was able to secure terms ensuring a huge profit for himself, collecting $5.00 for each male immigrant delivered, along with shares of the various other fees involved.

With considerable help from Mitsui Bussan, potential migrants were recruited mostly from Yamaguchi and Hiroshima PREFECTURES, farming areas whose inhabi-

tants were felt to be well suited for plantation work. The first group of 944 migrants arrived in Hawaii on the *City of Tokio* on February 8, 1885, accompanied by Irwin. For the next nine years, Irwin continued to oversee the passage of increasing numbers of Japanese to Hawaii, balancing the needs of a Japanese government intent on maintaining its prestige, Hawaiian planters desiring a docile and hard-working labor force, laborers who wanted fair wages and non-abusive treatment, and his own interests. Irwin's system came to an end with the fall of the Hawaiian monarchy in 1893 and the resulting rise of the EMIGRATION COMPANIES the following year.

For further reading, see Yuriko Irwin, and Hilary Conroy. "Robert Walker Irwin & Systematic Immigration to Hawaii." In Conroy, Hilary, and T. Scott Miyakawa, eds. *East Across the Pacific: Historical and Sociological Studies of Japanese Immigration and Assimilation.* Santa Barbara, Calif.: American Bibliographical Center—Clio Press, 1972. 40–55; Roland Kotani. *The Japanese in Hawaii: A Century of Struggle.* Honolulu: Hochi, Ltd., 1985; and Franklin S. Odo, and Kazuko Sinoto. *A Pictorial History of the Japanese in Hawaii, 1885–1924.* Honolulu: Bishop Museum Press, 1985.

Irwin, Wallace (1876–1959)   Journalist, humorist, novelist. Wallace Irwin created one of the best-known Japanese Americans of his time, the fictional SCHOOLBOY Hashimura Togo. Irwin also wrote the landmark anti-Japanese novel *Seed of the Sun* in 1921.

Born in Oneida, New York, Irwin was reared mostly in Colorado, along with his more famous older brother, novelist Will Irwin. After attending Stanford from 1896 to 1899, he joined the staff of the *San Francisco Examiner* and later edited the *Overland Monthly.* Known for his humorous poetry, he first attained a measure of fame with a book titled *Love Sonnets of a Hoodlum,* a parody of the Petrarchan sonnet cycle written in slang. Moving to New York in 1904, he began to write a series of letters for *Collier's Weekly* under the name Hashimura Togo. Written in fractured English, the Togo character was ridiculously stereotypical, but vaguely sympathetic in a pathetic sort of way. Togo also proved to be enormously popular. The first Hashimura Togo book, *Letters of a Japanese Schoolboy,* appeared in 1909 and was followed by two sequels. At the time, it was said that many people believed the author really to be Japanese. In 1921, Irwin's "serious" novel *Seed of Sun* proved an apt propaganda piece for the ANTI-JAPANESE MOVEMENT, as it depicted Japanese immigrants determined to colonize California on orders from Japan.

He moved on to other subjects after *Seed,* authoring many other books, including a 1941 biography of Dr. Sylvester Lambert, a Western doctor working in the South Pacific, titled *Yankee Doctor in Paradise.* Irwin died on February 14, 1959.

For further reading, see Elaine H. Kim. *Asian American Literature: An Introduction to the Writings and their Social Context*. Philadelphia: Temple University Press, 1982 and John Modell. *The Economics and Politics of Racial Accommodation: The Japanese of Los Angeles 1900–1942*. Chicago: University of Illinois Press, 1977 for discussions of Irwin's work in the context of Asian American images in American literature and the anti-Japanese movement, respectively.

Ishigo, Estelle (1899–1990) Best known as the chronicler in art of the Wyoming HEART MOUNTAIN CONCENTRATION CAMP experience. Of English, Dutch and French ancestry, Ishigo was married to a NISEI and spent most of her life among Japanese Americans. Estelle Peck was born in Oakland in 1899 and moved with her family to Los Angeles at the age of twelve. Apparently unwanted by her parents, she lived with a succession of relatives and at times on the streets and got in trouble with the law. A sympathetic teacher noted her interest in art and directed her to Otis Art Institute, where she found her calling and turned her life around. While at school, she met Arthur Ishigo (1902–57), a San Francisco–born *nisei* who was working as a chauffeur for California Lieutenant Governor Robert Kenny. Antimiscegenation laws at the time prohibited interracial couples from getting married; in 1928, Peck and Ishigo took a trip across the border to Tijuana to be wed. Hoping for a career as an actor, Arthur worked as a janitor at Paramount Studios while Estelle worked as an art teacher. Shunned by her family and by other Caucasians, the couple lived among the Japanese American community.

With the coming of World War II and the removal of all West Coast Japanese Americans to inland concentration camps, the couple faced a dilemma. As a *nisei,* Arthur was required to go while his wife was not. Though he wanted her to stay behind, she accompanied her husband first to the Pomona "ASSEMBLY CENTER," then to Heart Mountain. Throughout the war years, Estelle drew, sketched and painted what she saw, providing a valuable document of life in the American concentration camps. "Strange as it may sound, in this desolate, lonely place I felt accepted for the first time in my life," she later wrote of her time at Heart Mountain. She and her husband remained there until the camp closed in order to record the last days of the camp. They and the others who were left were given $25 and put on a train to the West Coast. "I felt as if I were part of a defeated Indian tribe," she remembered. They lived for several years in poverty in a succession of trailer parks until Arthur got a job as a baggage handler at an airport. After Arthur died of cancer in 1957, Estelle took a job as a mimeograph operator to make ends meet. In 1984,

fellow Heart Mountain inmate Bacon Sakatani found Ishigo living in dire poverty in a squalid apartment, both her legs lost to gangrene. Former Heart Mountain residents made her last years pleasant ones and oversaw the republication of her 1972 book of drawings, *Lone Heart Mountain*. In 1990, filmmaker STEVEN OKAZAKI made a documentary of her life titled *Days of Waiting*. She passed away before seeing the film, which went on to win an Academy Award for Best Documentary Short.

For further reading, see Mas Dobashi. "Estelle Ishigo: Internee 14744." *Tozai Times* 6.71 (Aug. 1990): 8–9; Estelle Ishigo. *Lone Heart Mountain*. Los Angeles: N.p., 1972 and "Nowhere to Go: Views from Inside an American Concentration Camp by Internee No. 14744" *California* 15.5 (May 1990): 72–77.

issei The first generation of immigrant Japanese Americans. The *issei* are the parents of the NISEI, the grandparents of the SANSEI, and the great-grandparents of the YONSEI. As is true for the other generations, the word *issei* comes from the Japanese character for the generation number, in this case, one. The first wave of *issei* came to the United States between 1885 and 1924. Due to restrictive immigration laws, virtually no Japanese immigrants came to this country between 1924 and the end of World War II. Postwar Japanese immigrants are usually referred to as *shin-issei,* the prefix *shin* meaning "new."

The first wave of *issei* immigration had three distinct phases. The first *issei* were mostly young men who came to this country as laborers, many of whom intended to return to Japan after saving money from wages earned in the United States. Later, as more of these men decided to make America their home over a longer period, a higher proportion of women began to immigrate, especially after the GENTLEMEN'S AGREEMENT of 1907–08. These women, many of whom came as PICTURE BRIDES, became the wives of the *issei* men and were generally 10 to 20 years younger than their husbands. Towards the end of the *issei* immigration period, many children came over to join their parents, older siblings or other relatives. These *issei* who were born in Japan but at least partially raised in America became known as YOBIYOSE. Today, very few pre-1924 *issei* remain; most who are still alive are either women or *yobiyose*.

For further reading: Yuji Ichioka is generally regarded as the foremost historian of the *issei*. His book, *The Issei: The World of the First Generation Japanese Immigrants, 1885–1924*. New York: The Free Press, 1988, delves into the economic and political world of the *issei*, from the perspective of the *issei*. Roger Daniels. *The Politics of Prejudice: The Anti-Japanese Movement in California and the Struggle for Japanese Exclusion*. 2nd edition. Berkeley: University of California Press, 1977 is a history of the ANTI-JAPANESE MOVEMENT against the *issei*. Kazuo Ito. *Issei: A History of Japanese Immigrants in North*

America. Shinichiro Nakamura, Jean S. Gerard, trans. Seattle: Executive Committee for the Publication of *Issei: A History of Japanese Immigrants in North America,* 1973 is an invaluable source of oral history accounts by *issei*; because Ito did his interviewing in the 1960s, he was able to talk to many of the earlier *issei* laborers who would die by the time many of the other oral history projects got off the ground 10 to 20 years later. Akemi Kikumura. *Through Harsh Winters: The Life of a Japanese Immigrant Woman.* Novato, Calif.: Chandler and Sharp Publishers, 1981 is a detailed life history of an *issei* woman. Other collections of *issei* oral or written histories include East Bay Japanese for Action. *Our Recollections.* Berkeley: East Bay Japanese for Action, 1986 and Ethnic Studies Oral History Project/United Okinawan Association of Hawaii. *Uchinanchu: A History of Okinawans in Hawaii.* Honolulu: Ethnic Studies Program, University of Hawaii at Manoa, 1981; there are many others. Neither a good anthology of *issei* literature translated into English nor a scholarly analysis of such writings exists.

Iwamatsu, Jun Atsushi [Taro Yashima] (1908–)

Best known as an author and illustrator of children's books, Iwamatsu was born on September 21, 1908, in Kagoshima PREFECTURE in Japan. His father was a doctor and art connoisseur. His mother died of cancer when he was 13; his father died four years later. He enrolled at the Imperial Art Academy in Tokyo in 1927, and though he graduated in 1930, he was disillusioned with the rigid nature of the teaching at the academy. Politically active in leftist circles, he became a member of the Japan Proletarian Artists League. Fearing imprisonment and increasing repression in Japan, Iwamatsu and his wife Mitsu immigrated to the United States in 1939. He continued his studies at the Art Students League in New York City over the next two years. Iwamatsu served in the U.S. Army in the Office of War Information and in the Office of Strategic Services. Because of his involvement with the latter, he could not use his real name, and thus changed it to Taro Yashima.

During and just after World War II, he published two autobiographical volumes of ink drawings with captions, describing his experiences as an artist and leftist in the increasingly militaristic Japan of the 1930s. These books, *The New Sun* (1943) and *Horizon Is Calling* (1947), received critical acclaim.

Since publishing his first children's book *Crow Boy,* in 1955, he has become prominent in the field of children's literature. He has three times been the runner-up for the Caldecott Medal: for *Crow Boy* in 1956, for *Umbrella* in 1959 and for *Seashore Story* in 1968. He also received the Child Study Association of America/Wel-Met Children's Book Award in 1955 for *Crow Boy;* the New York Times Choice of Best Illustrated Children's Books of the Year in 1967 for *Seashore Story;* and the Southern California Council on Literature of Children and Young People Award for significant contribution in the field of illustration in 1968.

Iwamatsu also has held several one-man shows of his works in New York, Los Angeles and Pasadena, among other cities. His paintings have also been purchased for permanent collections in various museums, including the Philips Memorial Museum in Washington, D.C. He also directed the Yashima Art Institute where he taught fundamental techniques and methods of art instruction and founded the Japanese American Artists Society. His wife Mitsu Yashima is also a well-known artist. Daughter Momo and son Mako (MAKOTO IWAMATSU) have both made their mark in the arts as well.

SUZANNE J. HEE/BRIAN NIIYA

[Sources include Anne Commire. *Something About the Author: Facts and Pictures about Contemporary Authors and Illustrators of Books for Young People.* Vol. 14. Detroit: Gale Research, 1978 and Jon Matsumoto. "Taro Yashima: 'My Goal Is in the Art.'" *Tozai Times* 1.6 (March 1985): 8–9, 15.]

Iwamatsu, Makoto [Mako] (1933–)

An acclaimed actor, Mako was also the founding artistic director of the nation's first ASIAN AMERICAN THEATER company, East West Players in Los Angeles. Immigrating from Kobe, Japan, in the late 1940s to join his parents, artists Taro and Mitsu Yashima (see ATSUSHI IWAMATSU), Mako was set to earn a degree in architecture from New York's Pratt Institute. During college, however, he joined some classmates who were involved in scene design for an off-Broadway production. Later, when Mako was a soldier during the Korean War, he decided to give up architecture for a career in acting. Subsequently, he enrolled in the famed Southern California Pasadena Playhouse. At this institution, he studied drama from Greek tragedy to Shakespeare.

Mako's first film role was a one-liner in *Never So Few* (1959), a movie about World War II in which he played a Cambodian soldier in a field hospital. The actor found other roles on the small screen in programs such as "77 Sunset Strip" and "Hawaiian Eye." These shows provided Mako with an income, but he was typecast in roles limited to Asian nationals, soldiers, sailors and gardeners. Mako received his major break in 1966 when he landed the role of a Chinese coolie in *The Sand Pebbles* with Steve McQueen. Mako's outstanding performance earned him an Oscar nomination for Best Supporting Actor. He was later nominated for a Tony Award for Best Actor (Musical) for *Pacific Overtures* in 1976.

As an Asian American actor, Mako was extremely concerned with the portrayal of and opportunities for

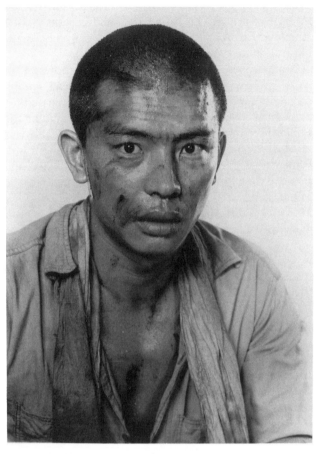

Mako. *Terrance Tam Soon Collection, Japanese American National Museum Photographic & Moving Image Archive*

Asian American actors, writers and directors. Along with Asian American peers Rae Creevey, James Hong, June Kim, Guy Lee, Pat Li and Beulah Quo, Mako created the world's first Asian American theater company: the East West Players. It was not an easy task, yet these individuals persevered. Under Mako's guidance as the first artistic director, East West Players not only became a major force in the Asian American theater community, but also in the larger American drama scene as well. Mako founded this theater because he felt that Asian American performers and writers were not given the chance to play their true selves in mainstream films. As Mako expressed it, "Personally, I am tired of living under an assumed falsehood and an imposed stereotype!" He was able to create an environment at East West Players that recognized the talents of aspiring Asian American artists. In Mako's words, the goal of East West Players was "to preserve and express a language and literature and sound of our own by developing an Asian Pacific American theatre that is vital, truthful and alive. We

should open wide the door to reveal a tapestry of East and West, rich in sensitivity and creativity."

Mako has also continued his acting career, starring in the film version of PHILIP KAN GOTANDA's *The Wash,* and, since leaving East West Players in 1989, in the Broadway production *Shimada* and in the 1993 feature film *Rising Sun.*   SUZANNE HEE

[First quote from "East West Players." *Jade* 1.14 (1975): 26; second quote from "East West's Mako & Shizuko Blend Artistry and Marriage." *Drama-Logue* 8–14 Apr. 1982.]

Iwasaki, Jiro   Businessman, sugar cane grower. Jiro Iwasaki came to Hawaii in March 1893 to try to arrange sugar imports to Japan. He had managed to convince friends in Japan that the increasing population there made a sugar shortage imminent and that they could make a lot of money if they could strike a deal with Hawaiian producers to import sugar to Japan. Convinced of the profitability of his idea, friends and investors financed his trip to Hawaii. Upon arrival, Iwasaki spent six months trying to implement his plan before finally realizing that the Hawaiian PLANTATIONS were under the monopoly of the Americans and that their market was exclusively North American. Unwilling to face his friends in Japan, he remained in Hawaii. In 1894, he became a labor contractor and succeeded in clearing some virgin land in Olaa for a plantation. He later began a coffee business on 500 acres and continued to contract laborers. After brokering a big contracting job in 1900 in Olaa in which he hired 800 workers to open up more raw land, Iwasaki settled in Olaa One Mile and began a general merchandise store. The cluster of houses around the store became known as "Iwasaki Camp." He became one of the largest contract cane growers in the area and reportedly earned over $150,000 a year.

For further reading, see United Japanese Society of Hawaii. *History of Japanese in Hawaii.* James H. Okahata, ed. Honolulu: United Japanese Society of Hawaii, 1971.

J

Japanese American Citizens League   Japanese American civil rights organization. Though indisputably the largest and most influential Japanese American political organization, the Japanese American Citizens League (JACL) has always been controversial within the Japanese American community, having both avid supporters and ardent detractors. Throughout its history, it has maintained a philosophy emphasizing assimilation and Americanization.

The roots of the citizens league movement began in the summer of 1918 with an informal study group consisting of six college educated NISEI in San Francisco calling itself the American Loyalty League. A few years later, a similar group formed in Seattle, under the leadership of CLARENCE ARAI. In May 1923, led by Fresno dentist THOMAS T. YATABE, a statewide American Loyalty League was formed with the help and support of the ISSEI-run JAPANESE ASSOCIATIONS. After an initial burst of activity, this organization began to fade in the late 1920s, with the only the Fresno chapter retaining its initial vigor. Arai's trip to California in 1928 reinvigorated the movement, leading to a series of meetings out of which the JACL emerged. The first National JACL convention took place in Seattle in 1930. Organized by older *nisei* to emphasize loyalty, patriotism and citizenship, the JACL emerged largely as a response to xenophobia expressed by white Americans. With the passage of the IMMIGRATION ACT OF 1924, Japanese immigration was cut off and those *issei* living in the U.S. had no chance of becoming naturalized citizens (see CITIZENSHIP). Thus, the *issei* looked to their American-born children, the *nisei*, as U.S. citizens, to secure the future of Japanese America.

Although its members were regarded as the future leaders of Japanese Americans, the JACL was seen by some ". . . as part of an elite network in the Japanese community." Many of the founders of the organization, like SABURO KIDO, Clarence Arai and Thomas Yatabe, for example, held professional degrees and therefore attracted *nisei* of similar status. Not surprisingly, since the group drew members of higher social position, the politics of the JACL was very conservative and staunchly Republican. The conservatism may also have stemmed from a realistic assessment of its power—given the organization's small size and the distinctly dependent position *nisei* found themselves in to both their parents and the larger community, a strategy of conciliation made more sense than one of angry protest. An example of this strategy came in the successful campaigns the JACL funded in the 1930s to repeal the CABLE ACT and to press for citizenship for *issei* WORLD WAR I VETERANS. In the second campaign especially, lobbyist TOKUTARO SLOCUM pressed loyalty and patriotism to extremes to secure passage of the NYE-LEA BILL. Many in the organization felt that the only way to gain acceptance in the United States was to become 100 percent American and to discourage anything that might cast doubt upon their loyalty (see "JAPANESE AMERICAN CREED").

This pro-American ideology that the JACL adopted put the organization in a difficult position just before and during World War II. As loyal Americans, JACL members were recruited by government officials to act as informers on their own community. War with Japan was a distinct possibility and the government wanted to ensure that they could effectively contain those Japanese Americans who they thought were "suspicious." From the JACL point of view, to refuse the government's request could be interpreted as a sign that Japanese Americans were disloyal. Cooperation, they felt, was the only way that the *nisei* could show their patriotism and ensure the safety of their community.

Their decision to cooperate with U.S. government officials was, to say the least, controversial. In the eyes of some Japanese Americans, the JACL and particularly its most prominent spokesman, MIKE MASAOKA, became the people who led them from the freedom of civilian life to the barren wastelands of the CONCENTRATION CAMPS. Within several of the camps, JACL leaders were the targets of threats and physical violence and had to be removed from the camps for their own protection (see MANZANAR INCIDENT, for example). Because of the controversy surrounding the JACL, the wartime president of the organization, Saburo Kido, estimated that the membership "dwindled down to only about 10 active chapters and about 1,700 members." According to Kido, "it was no longer a matter of pride to belong to the JACL, but rather a thing to be shunned."

The postwar JACL made a remarkable recovery by capitalizing on its newly found influence in Washington, D.C. It sponsored numerous bills that helped improve the lot of Japanese Americans—including the JAPANESE AMERICAN EVACUATION CLAIMS ACT OF 1948 and the MCCARRAN-WALTER ACT. The latter bill, in particular, was significant in that it represented a relaxation of Japanese immigration restrictions and, more importantly, allowed the *issei* to become naturalized citizens.

By the mid-1960s, the JACL firmly established itself as the only recognized organization representing the political interests of Japanese Americans. No other Japanese American group could equal its national influence or membership. Beginning with this period, however, the organization had to seriously confront the aging of its *nisei* leadership, the changing political climate emerging with the civil rights movement and the coming of age of SANSEI youth. The movement to repeal the EMERGENCY DETENTION ACT OF 1950 (see EMERGENCY DETENTION ACT, REPEAL OF) was a good example of this phenomenon.

In the early 1970s, the JACL received the strongest challenge to its leadership when MAS SATOW stepped down as executive director. Alan Nishio, a young *sansei* activist and administrator at California State University at Long Beach, applied for the job as did David Ushio, who, like Masaoka, was a Mormon from Utah. This heated, and sometimes bitter campaign for the directorship was seen by many as a choice between change (Nishio) and the status quo (Ushio). Ushio eventually won the job by a 4 to 3 vote by the personnel committee.

The Los Angeles office, the support base for Nishio, resigned in protest. Ushio served three turbulent years as executive director and later took a job with Jimmy Carter's presidential campaign. Nishio later gained prominence as a leader of the NATIONAL COALITION FOR REDRESS/REPARATIONS.

Another movement that challenged the JACL was the call for REDRESS AND REPARATIONS in 1970. First advanced by EDISON UNO at the 1970 JACL national convention, the redress movement gained momentum despite its lack of support from many of the older leaders. In many ways, parallels can be drawn with the campaign to repeal the Emergency Detention Act of 1950 (see NATIONAL COMMITTEE FOR REDRESS, JACL and REDRESS MOVEMENT).

The JACL remains alive and healthy today. Its national headquarters is located in San Francisco and the organization maintains chapters nationwide. Its national newspaper, the PACIFIC CITIZEN, continues to be a major source of news for Japanese Americans around the country. It has, for the most part, recovered from its controversial past and has attempted to acknowledge its role in the World War II concentration camps through its commission of the so-called "Lim Report," an independent investigation of JACL wartime actions. Due to the controversial nature of the report, however, publication has been delayed.

Much has been written on the JACL, most of it from the perspective of its supporters and leaders. Bill Hosokawa. *JACL in Quest of Justice: The History of the Japanese American Citizens League*. New York: William Morrow, 1982 is a commissioned history of the JACL, while Mike Masaoka, and Bill Hosokawa. *They Call Me Moses Masaoka*. New York: William Morrow, 1987 is the autobiography of the JACL's most famous leader. Differing viewpoints on the JACL during World War II can be found in Roger Daniels. *Asian America: Chinese and Japanese in the United States since 1850*. Seattle: University of Washington Press, 1988; Richard Drinnon. *Keeper of Concentration Camps: Dillon S. Myer and American Racism*. Berkeley: University of California Press, 1987; Paul R. Spickard. "The Nisei Assume Power: The Japanese-American Citizen's League, 1941–1942." *Pacific Historical Review* 52 (May 1983): 147–74; and Michi Weglyn. *Years of Infamy: The Untold Story of America's Concentration Camps*. New York: William Morrow & Co., 1976. The JACL's early history is discussed in Jerrold Haruo Takahashi. "Changing Responses to Racial Subordination: An Exploratory Study of Japanese American Political Styles." Diss., University of California, Berkeley, 1980 and "Japanese American Responses to Race Relations: The Formation of Nisei Perspectives." *Amerasia Journal* 9.1 (1982): 29–57 while its role in postwar legislation is discussed in Frank F. Chuman. *The Bamboo People: The Law and Japanese-Americans*. Del Mar, Calif.: Publisher's Inc., 1976. For an account of the Nishio/Ushio episode, see Lon Y. Kurashige. "The Asian American Movement, 1968–1972: The Politics of Meanings." Thesis, University of Wisconsin, 1989.   GLEN KITAYAMA

[Also used to compile this entry was Jana Monji. "Lim Awaits Publication of Report." *Rafu Shimpo* 12 Sept. 1991. First quote from Takahashi article, p. 48; second quote (Kido) is from Hosokawa, p. 275.]

"Japanese-American Creed"   With war with Japan a distinct possibility and Japanese American loyalty in question, MIKE MASAOKA felt that a statement on how he felt about America needed to be made. The Japanese-American Creed, written by Masaoka in 1940 for the JAPANESE AMERICAN CITIZENS LEAGUE (JACL) national convention was his solution. It symbolized all that the JACL stood for: patriotism, pride and trust in America. Over the years, it has been widely reprinted and has been given out to those that the organization has wished to honor. Here it is in its complete form:

The Japanese-American Creed

I am proud that I am an American citizen of Japanese ancestry, for my very background makes me appreciate more fully the wonderful advantages of this nation. I believe in her institutions, ideals, and traditions; I glory in her heritage; I boast of her history; I trust in her future. She has granted me liberties and opportunities such as no individual enjoys in this world today. She has given me an education befitting kings. She has entrusted me with the responsibilities of the franchise. She has permitted me to build a home, to earn a livelihood, to worship, think, speak, and act as I please—as a free man equal to every other man.

Although some individuals may discriminate against me, I shall never become bitter or lose faith, for I know that such persons are not representative of the majority of the American people. True, I shall do all in my power to discourage such practices, but I shall do it in the American way: above board, in the open, through courts of law, by education, by proving myself to be worthy of equal treatment and consideration. I am firm in my belief that American sportsmanship and attitude of fair play will judge citizenship and patriotism on the basis of action and achievement, and not on the basis of physical characteristics.

Because I believe in America, and I trust she believes in me, and because I have received innumerable benefits from her, I pledge myself to do honor to her at all times and in all places; to support her Constitution; to obey her laws; to respect her flag; to defend her against all enemies, foreign or domestic; to actively assume my duties and obligations as a citizen, cheerfully and without reservations whatsoever, in the hope that I may become a better American in a greater America.

For further reading, see Mike Masaoka, and Bill Hosokawa. *They Call Me Moses Masaoka*. New York: William Morrow, 1987. GLEN KITAYAMA

Japanese American Evacuation and Resettlement Study (JERS)

Large, multidisciplinary research project on Japanese Americans carried out in the World War II CONCENTRATION CAMPS. An independent academic project conducted with the cooperation of the WAR RELOCATION AUTHORITY (WRA), the Japanese American Evacuation and Resettlement Study resulted in a wealth of social scientific data on the concentration camp experience and three early and influential books on the subject. However, JERS has come under criticism for exploiting the experience of the internees without actually doing anything to benefit them and for alleged ethical improprieties committed by its research staff.

The driving force behind the project was Dorothy Swaine Thomas, a sociologist at the University of California, Berkeley. Specializing in social demography, Thomas saw the forced removal of all West Coast Japanese Americans as an ideal opportunity to study a mass migration devoid of the usual selective elements present in voluntary migrations. With the help of other Berkeley professors in other disciplines, an ambitious project was proposed which would study acculturation, psychological adjustment, the economic effect of the removal on California agriculture and the political factors behind the mass removal. The project was funded with over $100,000 by the Rockefeller Foundation, the Columbia Foundation, the Giannini Foundation and the University of California. A staff consisting of graduate and undergraduate students at Berkeley, most of whom were Japanese American, was put together to do participant observation research in the "ASSEMBLY CENTERS" and concentration camps housing the incarcerated Japanese Americans. The focus of the study eventually became TULE LAKE "SEGREGATION CENTER," with GILA RIVER as a secondary focus. JERS personnel also reported from POSTON and MANZANAR. A Chicago office was opened in 1943 to study the RESETTLEMENT of Japanese Americans from the camps to cities in the midwestern and eastern United States.

JERS researchers faced two major problems in collecting data in the camps. One was the perceived lack of direction from Thomas as to what exactly they should be taking note of. "The research difficulty that bothered me most was the persistent feeling that JERS lacked focus. I frequently wished that Dorothy Thomas would specify our research problems more sharply," remem-

bered S. FRANK MIYAMOTO, a JERS staff member. The second was the difficulty of gathering data in a concentration camp setting where group tensions ran so high. To be labeled an INU was to be put in physical danger, and going around asking questions of people was a good way to be so labeled. Thomas also faced the problem of WRA cooperation. In order to have any chance of successfully completing the project, she needed the full cooperation of the WRA. The WRA, on the other hand, lacked good sociological data of the sort JERS was collecting and badly wanted access to it. Thomas succeeded in securing an agreement in which WRA cooperation would be continued and her staff reports kept out of their hands, though she agreed to share some information on administrative matters with them. This collaboration with the WRA, along with the sharing of information by one or more of the participant observers with the FBI, has come under intense criticism by some contemporary observers.

Nonetheless, a great deal of data was gathered by the staff, not only on life in the camps, but on resettlement and on the political factors leading up to the mass removal. In 1946, *The Spoilage,* focusing on Tule Lake and the segment of the population who renounced their citizenship and went to Japan after the war, was published under the authorship of Thomas and RICHARD S. NISHIMOTO. In 1952, *The Salvage* by Thomas appeared, focusing on those who resettled from the camps in the Midwest and East. Finally, in 1954, *Prejudice, War and the Constitution* by Jacobus tenBroek, Edward N. Barnhart and Floyd W. Matson was published, focusing on the political factors behind the mass removal. In 1949, the University of Chicago published former JERS staff member Morton Grodzins' book *Americans Betrayed* over the objections of Thomas. This book focused on the impact of various California pressure groups on the decision to remove all Japanese Americans from the coast. In 1987, an academic conference titled "Views from Within: The Japanese-American Wartime Internment Experience" was organized by Yuji Ichioka at the University of California, Berkeley; a collection of papers presented at that conference was published two years later. Anthropologist Peter Suzuki has been the most vocal critic of JERS.

For further reading, see Yuji Ichioka, ed. "Views from Within: The Japanese American Evacuation and Resettlement Study." Los Angeles: UCLA Asian American Studies Center, 1989. See also Peter T. Suzuki. "The University of California Japanese Evacuation and Resettlement Study: A Prolegomenon." *Dialectical Anthropology* 10 (1986): 189–213 for an extremely critical look at JERS.

[Based on Yuji Ichioka. "JERS Revisited: Introduction." In Ichioka, Yuji, ed. *Views from Within: The Japanese American Evacuation and*

Resettlement Study. Los Angeles: Asian American Studies Center, University of California, Los Angeles, 1989. 3–27 and other papers in this anthology; the quote is from "Reminiscences of JERS" by S. Frank Miyamoto from the same volume.]

Japanese American Evacuation Claims Act

Passed on July 2, 1948, with the assistance of the JAPANESE AMERICAN CITIZENS LEAGUE (JACL), this well-intentioned act attempted to compensate Japanese Americans for material losses incurred as a result of their mass removal and detention during World War II. Numerous restrictions, however, prevented the act from becoming a truly effective measure. To start, claims filed by Japanese Americans were given a ceiling of $2,500. Those that exceeded that amount—approximately 40 percent of the claims—had to wait for special appropriations from Congress; this was unacceptable since many of the applicants were elderly ISSEI or were in immediate need of money. Another problem was that claims had to be supported by documentation and the testimony of a witness to swear he/she owned the property. Considering the haste in which people were removed, this proved to be too much, as many documents were lost, destroyed or thrown away during the war.

In 1950, the first year the government studied the claims, a total of only 211 out of 22,903 claims were processed. At that rate it would have taken the government over 100 years to finish its task. Of the 211, only 137 passed the requirements for compensation; the other 74 were rejected for lack of evidence. Of the 137 who received compensation, only 40% of the amount documented, averaging approximately $450.00, was awarded. Most appalling of all though, was the inefficiency of government bureaucracy: it cost the government about $1,400.00 per case in salaries and operational and investigation expenses to pay an average of $450.00.

The final claim was not paid until 1965, 17 years after the Evacuation Claims Act was passed (see KEISABURO KODA). In total, approximately $38 million was paid out to Japanese Americans—about one-tenth of the value of their estimated losses. Because of the delay in paying the former internees, the total worth of the payments declined, as the value of the dollar depreciated significantly since 1942, the first year of incarceration. Also, the former internees were not compensated for the potential earnings they lost during the war—a time when the rest of America prospered. The inadequacy of the Evacuation Claims Act was a factor in the rise of the REDRESS MOVEMENT in the 1970s and '80s.

For further reading, see Frank F. Chuman. *The Bamboo People: The Law and Japanese-Americans.* Del Mar, Calif.: Publisher's Inc., 1976 and Nancy N. Nakasone-Huey. "In Simple Justice: The Japanese-American Evacuation Claims Act of 1948." Dissertation, University of Southern California, 1986.

Japanese American Industrial Corporation

The Japanese American Industrial Corporation of San Francisco was the largest labor contracting firm in California. It was founded in 1902 by KYUTARO ABIKO and others and supplied labor to the sugar beet, mining and railroad industries. At its peak in 1906, it had some 3,000 laborers under it. Unlike other labor contractors, Abiko didn't pocket the large profits he earned, but reinvested them towards his goal of forming Christian Japanese farming colonies. (See YAMATO COLONY (CALIF.))

For further reading, see Yuji Ichioka. *The Issei: The World of the First Generation Japanese Immigrants, 1885–1924.* New York: The Free Press, 1988.

Japanese American Resource Project

Project to collect documents and other material relevant to Japanese American history. The Japanese American Resource Project Collection housed at UCLA is the largest collection of Japanese American papers in the country. Also included in the collection are oral history tapes, survey data, photographs and art objects.

The idea for the Japanese American Resource Project (JARP) was conceived and approved at the 1960 JAPANESE AMERICAN CITIZENS LEAGUE (JACL) national convention under its original name: "Issei History Project." Each chapter was to appoint a chairperson to raise money to go towards a fund to start the project. By 1962, over $200,000 was raised, but no one in the organization had a clear idea of what the scope of the project should be. T. SCOTT MIYAKAWA from Boston University came up with three objectives: both sociological and historical studies should be written on Japanese Americans and a oral history project should be done as part of the Issei History Project. UCLA, through alumnus and JACL member Frank Chuman, was asked to house the project and was given $100,000 to start it up. Miyakawa was appointed the project chair.

Controversy over the project erupted in 1969 with the proposed publication of *Nisei: The Quiet Americans; A Story of a People* written by JACL member BILL HOSOKAWA. Dr. David Miura and others within the JACL protested the use of the adjective "quiet" in the title to describe the NISEI because it did not reflect the personalities and actions of all *nisei.* Furthermore, they were upset that a project originally called the "Issei History Project" (now called JARP) was planning on publishing a book that focused on the *nisei.* A boycott of the book was planned, but, according to Shig Wakamatsu of the JACL and JARP, failed miserably. The book was a success and the profits helped replenish the JARP fund. Critical reviews, however, were mixed.

Other books that have been published through JARP are *The Japanese American Community: A Three-Genera-*

tion Study, co-authored by Gene N. Levine and Robert C. Rhodes; *The Economic Basis of Ethnic Solidarity: A Study of the Japanese Americans,* by John Modell and Edna Bonacich; *The Economics and Politics of Racial Accommodation: The Japanese in Los Angeles, 1900–1942,* by John Modell; *The Japanese American Community: A Study of Generational Changes in Ethnic Affiliation,* by Darrel M. Montero; *East Across the Pacific: Historical and Sociological Studies of Japanese Immigration and Assimilation,* edited by Hilary Conroy and T. Scott Miyakawa; *The Bamboo People: The Law and Japanese Americans,* by Frank Chuman; and *Planted in Good Soil: A History of the Issei in United States Agriculture,* by Masakazu Iwata. The JARP collection has also been the basis for numerous scholarly articles, masters' theses, Ph.D. dissertations and books throughout the years.

For further reading, see Bill Hosokawa. *JACL in Quest of Justice: The History of the Japanese American Citizens League.* New York: William Morrow, 1982. Guides to the collection include Yuji Ichioka, Yasuo Sakata, Nobuya Tsuchida and Eri Yasuhara, comp. *A Buried Past: An Annotated Bibliography of the Japanese American Research Project Collection.* Berkeley: University of California Press, 1974 and Yasuo Sakata, comp. *Fading Footsteps of the Issei: An Annotated Check List of the Manuscript Holdings of the Japanese American Research Project Collection.* Los Angeles: Asian American Studies Center and Center for Japanese Studies, University of California at Los Angeles and the Japanese American National Museum, 1992.

GLEN KITAYAMA

[Also used to compile this entry: *Gidra* (Oct. 1969): 6; (Nov. 1969): 10, and (Jan. 1970): 17.]

Japanese and Korean Exclusion League See ASIATIC EXCLUSION LEAGUE.

Japanese Association

Pre–World War II ISSEI group. The Japanese Association (Nihonjinkai) was the leading *issei* economic and political organization, offering various services to local residents and serving a bureaucratic function in place of Japanese consulates. Its history began in 1900 with the establishment in San Francisco of the Japanese Deliberative Council of America. Facing the sudden rise of the ANTI-JAPANESE MOVEMENT, the founders sought to "expand the rights of Imperial subjects in America and to maintain the Japanese national image." As the exclusionists launched a harsher anti-Japanese crusade in 1905, key immigrant leaders saw the need to expand the council into a statewide organization to unify Japanese immigrants to fight the exclusion movement. After a mass meeting, which drew representatives from many local Japanese communities, the local councils affiliated with the San Francisco council, which became the central body, the United Japanese Deliberative Council of America. In 1908, based on this network of councils, the Japanese Association of America was formed.

The Japanese Association of America originally embraced all locals in California, Nevada, Utah, Colorado and Arizona. But in 1915, the Central Japanese Association of Southern California was established in Los Angeles to which locals in Southern California, Arizona and New Mexico became affiliated. The Japanese Association of Oregon founded in Portland in 1911 included locals in Oregon, Idaho and Wyoming. Locals in Washington and Montana were affiliated with the Northwest American Japanese Association established in Seattle in 1913. Combined with the Japanese Association of Canada, these four central bodies formed the Pacific Coast Japanese Association Deliberative Council. In 1923, the San Francisco central body had 40 affiliated locals, Los Angeles 21, Seattle 15 and Oregon 10. The Japanese Associations ceased to exist with the advent of World War II.

The four central bodies of the Japanese Association not only fought the exclusion movement but also undertook important bureaucratic functions in place of local Japanese consulates. Under the GENTLEMEN'S AGREEMENT of 1907–1908 with the United States government, the Japanese government had the difficult task of determining who was in fact a bona fide resident in America. Given the fact that many immigrants were dispersed so widely, it was almost impossible for the local consulates to do so. The Japanese government decided to delegate certain bureaucratic functions to the central bodies of the Japanese Association, which then redelegated them to local associations. This three-tiered structure marked the special relationship between the government and the associations.

The most significant role that the Japanese associations undertook was that of processing various certificate applications. The certificates were necessary for Japanese immigrants to return to America after going to Japan or other countries to summon their family members (including "PICTURE BRIDES") or to defer their Japanese military service annually as required by Japanese law. Each immigrant had to apply at the association under whose jurisdiction he or she lived. Then the association endorsed a certificate application after checking the applicant's residency in the jurisdiction and other socioeconomic data. After receiving the endorsed application, the consulate examined it and, if there was no problem, issued the appropriate certificate.

Local Japanese associations also exercised social control over the residents. Acting as semi-governmental offices, the associations had the authority to effectively blacklist persons they considered detrimental to the community. Since the network of the locals was very tight, such information was distributed to Japanese American communities throughout the country and even to Japan. When local Japanese associations launched moral reform campaigns to rid the immigrant communities of gambling and other vices, this social pressure served as an effective weapon.

The Japanese Association also led Japanese immigrants in the fight against legal oppression. Between 1917 and 1923, it was involved in a number of significant lawsuits testing naturalization and ALIEN LAND LAWS (see, for example OZAWA V. U.S. and the various test cases of the 1920 (CALIFORNIA) ALIEN LAND LAW). The central bodies usually formed joint committees to coordinate policies and hire appropriate lawyers. Local associations were assigned to raise the designated amount of money for the court expenses.

For further reading, see Yuji Ichioka. "Japanese Associations and the Japanese Government: A Special Relationship, 1909–1926." *Pacific Historical Review* 46.3 (Aug. 1977): 409–38 and *The Issei: The World of the First Generation Japanese Immigrants, 1885–1924.* New York: Free Press, 1988 and Zaibei Nihonjinkai. *Zaibei Nihonjinshi.* San Francisco: Zaibei Nihonjinkai, 1940.   EIICHIRO AZUMA

Japanese Community Progressive Alliance   See REDRESS MOVEMENT.

Japanese Exclusion League of California
Organization formed just prior to the passage of the 1920 (CALIFORNIA) ALIEN LAND LAW to continue and coordinate ANTI-JAPANESE MOVEMENT activity. The organization was formed on September 2, 1920, at a meeting at Native Sons Hall in San Francisco, where J. M. Inman was named president. Among the vice presidents were representatives of the NATIVE SONS OF THE GOLDEN WEST, the American Federation of Labor, the American Legion, the Moose and the California Federation of Women's Clubs. As a real membership entity, the league was short lived. Financial difficulties led to its becoming a platform for chief exclusionist agitator V. S. MCCLATCHY by 1922. By the spring of that year, McClatchy and HIRAM JOHNSON were virtually subsidizing the whole movement. After the passage of the IMMIGRATION ACT OF 1924, which ended immigration from Japan, the league dissolved and was replaced by the California Joint Immigration Committee, an organization which continued to support nativist causes.

For further reading, see Roger Daniels. *The Politics of Prejudice: The Anti-Japanese Movement in California and the Struggle for Japanese Exclusion.* 1962. 2nd edition. Berkeley: University of California Press, 1977.

Japanese Federation of Labor   The Japanese Federation of Labor was formed by BUNJI SUZUKI during his second trip to the U.S. in 1916. Like its predecessor

the JAPANESE LABOR LEAGUE OF AMERICA, the federation had the essentially conservative goal of gaining acceptance by organized white labor. The federation attempted to do this by unifying existing Japanese labor groups to demonstrate that Japanese did in fact understand the principles of organized labor. There is, however, no evidence to suggest that this aim was ever achieved, and organized labor continued to exclude Asians for many years.

For further reading, see Yuji Ichioka. *The Issei: The World of the First Generation Japanese Immigrants, 1885–1924.* New York: The Free Press, 1988.

Japanese hospitals   As was true for many other ethnic groups, Japanese immigrants saw the need to start their own community institutions, partly because of prejudice from mainstream institutions and partly because these mainstream institutions were not able to meet the particular needs of the immigrant community. The Japanese American hospital, which had its heyday in the 1920s, is one example of such a community institution. The rise of these hospitals can be traced to several factors. For one thing, the Japanese American population was changing due to the high birthrate resulting from the large-scale immigration of ISSEI women after the GENTLEMEN'S AGREEMENT of 1907–08. By the 1920s, many of the oldest *issei* were reaching the age where they needed special health care. Mainstream hospitals often discriminated against Japanese Americans, both in the area of hiring Japanese American doctors and in accepting Japanese Americans as patients. Finally, even those hospitals that did admit Japanese Americans were not able to meet their special dietary, language and general cultural needs.

In Hawaii, the hospitals may have had their roots in the early importation of Japanese medicine to the plantation camps. Despite the free medical care provided by the plantations, familiar Japanese medicines were imported as early as 1892. Agents would distribute the medicines to each family in a paper bag and would return in a few weeks to replenish the supply and collect money for the medicine that was used.

After his arrival in Hawaii in 1893, Dr. Sanzaburo Kobayashi started the first Japanese hospital in Hawaii in 1896. Consisting of 12 rooms, it soon grew to serve some 400 patients a year and a new facility with 25 rooms and more modern equipment was opened on Liliha Street on November 3, 1899. This hospital eventually merged with another in 1901 and moved to new facilities on Kuakini Street in 1918 where it eventually become Kuakini Hospital, the largest of the Japanese hospitals in Hawaii.

Japanese American hospitals in California began as early as 1913. The main catalyst for the Japanese hospital

Opening of a Japanese hospital in Los Angeles, California, December 12, 1929. *Kikuo Tashiro Family Collection, Japanese American National Museum Photographic & Moving Image Archives*

boom on the mainland was the 1918 influenza epidemic. One hospital formed in the wake of this epidemic was the Japanese Hospital of Los Angeles.

Led by Dr. Kikuo Tashiro, five resident Japanese attempted to incorporate the Japanese Hospital on November 23, 1926, but were denied by the California secretary of state because they were "ALIENS INELIGIBLE TO CITIZENSHIP." On May 27, 1927, the California Supreme Court defended the Japanese American physicians' right to incorporate. On appeal, the United States Supreme Court upheld their decision on November 19, 1928, in the JORDAN V. TASHIRO case. The incorporation was finally approved on February 2, 1929. As a commercial venture, the hospital had a corporate president (Dr. Tashiro) rather than a director.

Although these two hospitals were the most famous and durable, many other Japanese hospitals in both Hawaii and the mainland existed in the 1910s and '20s. As mainstream institutions gradually began to accept more Japanese patients and doctors, and as these patients and doctors became American-born to a greater extent, the need for the Japanese hospital declined and they gradually began to shut their doors. Today, the Kuakini Medical Center in Honolulu, Hawaii, which serves a multiethnic clientele, is the last vestige of the Japanese hospitals.

For further reading: Eriko Yamamoto. "The Evolution of an Ethnic Hospital in Hawaii: An Analysis of Ethnic Processes of Japanese Americans in Honolulu through the Development of the Kuakini Medical Center." Dissertation, University of Hawaii, 1988.

Japanese Labor League of America

The Japanese Labor League of America was a group organized by BUNJI SUZUKI during his first trip to America in 1915. It was formed by merging two existing groups, one consisting of day laborers in San Francisco and the other consisting of laundry workers in Oakland. Suzuki had already agreed that exclusion on the basis of the economic argument was acceptable so he focused this organization on raising the standards of living of Japanese workers. By so doing, he reasoned that the American workers could no longer accuse the Japanese of lowering the American standard of living and would eventually accept the Japanese workers into their unions. Such was not to happen anytime soon.

For further reading, see Yuji Ichioka. *The Issei: The World of the First Generation Japanese Immigrants, 1885–1924.* New York: The Free Press, 1988.

Japanese-language schools

Nearly from their inception, Japanese American communities across the country have included Japanese-language schools. Originally set up to emulate schools in Japan so as to prepare young people here for schooling when their families went back to Japan, the schools gradually took on a uniquely American flavor. Attacked as promoting "emperor worship" in the anti-foreign climate of post–World War I America, the schools adapted and survived to reach a peak of popularity prior to World War II. Japanese schools continue to this day to teach the rudiments of Japanese language and culture to YONSEI children whose own parents probably have nearly no facility in the language of their grandparents.

The desire of immigrants to educate their children in the language and culture of their native country is a natural one. For many immigrant groups, this desire was manifest in the form of special schools supplementing American public schools. In addition to preparing the children for life in the native country should the immigrant family decide to return, such language schools, it was said, helped to close the inevitable generation and culture gap between immigrant parents and American-educated children. The first Japanese schools in Hawaii were begun in the 1890s, with their number reaching 11 schools serving over 1,500 students by the turn of the century and 120 schools serving 4,966 pupils by 1907. These schools were often encouraged and even supported financially by the sugar PLANTATIONS to help maintain peace and unity with and among their Japanese work force. On the mainland, the first schools appeared about a decade later, with the number growing to 80 schools with 2,442 pupils by 1918.

From early on, the schools were controversial. To some, it seemed inappropriate for American-born children to be spending so much time learning a "foreign" language and customs. Within the Japanese American community, there was also competition between schools begun by Christian organizations, those run by Buddhists, and independent schools. As a result of these external and internal problems, Japanese schools in Hawaii formed the territory-wide Japanese Educational Association in 1915. One of their first activities was to bring in a Tokyo University professor to rewrite the imported Japanese textbooks to make them more suitable for use in Hawaii, an effort that was destined to please neither critics who still saw the schools as promoting Japan's divine origins nor many in the Japanese American community. During and immediately following World War I, a high level of anti-foreign sentiment pervaded the United States and Hawaii, where the slogan "One Language Under One Flag" was adopted by those who wanted to see language schools severely restricted or eliminated altogether. In 1918, 21 Hawaii legislators introduced bills aimed at controlling these schools. For the next several years, increasingly severe restrictions were placed on the schools by the legislature and the Department of Public Instruction, including who could teach in the schools, the number of hours NISEI could attend the schools and special taxes on the schools, among other things (see ACT 30 OF THE SPECIAL SESSION LAWS OF 1920 for example). On the mainland, a 1921 California State Law required the schools to have a permit from the Superintendent of Public Instruction, limited the hours of instruction to one a day and six per week and required Japanese school teachers to pass a examination in American history and the English language. Given the underlying goal of gradual elimination of Japanese schools that seemed to underlie these laws, something needed to be done.

The early 1920s saw the Hawaii Japanese American community split over what course of action to follow. On one side was KINZABURO MAKINO and his paper the HAWAII HOCHI. Makino led an effort to test the restrictions in the courts. On December 28, 1922, attorney Joseph Lightfoot filed suit on behalf of 16 Japanese schools in the territorial circuit court. The other side was led by Rev. TAKIE OKUMURA and the NIPPU JIJI and its publisher YASUTARO SOGA. This group did not support the lawsuit, arguing that it would only inflame feelings between Japanese Americans and the majority group. Eventually, 88 out of 146 Japanese schools in Hawaii joined the suit. The case wound its way through appeals and finally, in February of 1927, the United States Supreme Court ruled in favor of the Japanese schools, striking down as unconstitutional all attempts to regulate the schools (see FARRINGTON V. TOKUSHIGE). After this victory, Japanese school attendance continued to rise—by 1933, there were 190 Japanese schools in Hawaii serving 43,606 pupils. On the eve of World War II, over 80 percent of *nisei* children in Hawaii attended Japanese schools.

World War II brought about a temporary end to Japanese-language schools both in Hawaii and on the mainland. The schools eventually reopened, though they would never be as influential as they had been prior to the war. Today, Japanese schools whose roots go back to before the war exist in most Japanese American communities to serve the SANSEI and *yonsei* descendants of early Japanese immigrants. In recent years, a second type of Japanese school has emerged to serve the children of Japanese businessmen stationed for a few years in America so that they will not fall behind their peers in Japan and will be able to attend schools in Japan when they return.

The controversy over the language schools and their supposed hindering of "Americanization" is ironic in light of how ineffective they have always been in actually teaching the Japanese language. Though numerous studies exist documenting this ineffectiveness, the most damning evidence might be the result of a 1941 survey of *nisei* soldier Japanese-language ability undertaken for the purpose of choosing candidates for intelligence service: of the 3,700 enlisted *nisei* surveyed, only 3 percent were found to have reached "plenary level," another 4 percent were "proficient," and another 3 percent were deemed usable "only after a prolonged period of training." The other 90 percent did not know enough Japanese even to be considered trainable. Though many *nisei* prior to the war and *sansei* and *yonsei* after the war actively disliked being forced to go to Japanese-language schools, many others did enjoy the experience, not so much for the curriculum, but for the chance to see friends and interact with other Japanese American youth. In light of their limited ability to teach Japanese language and culture, the persistence of Japanese-language schools might be partially explained by the desire of parents to see their children interact with other Japanese Americans.

The literature on Japanese language schools is extensive. There are many pre–World War II studies of the Japanese schools in Hawaii. These include Koichi Glenn Harada. "A Survey of the Japanese Language Schools in Hawaii." Thesis, University of Hawaii, 1934; Shichiro Miyamoto. "A Study of the Japanese Language Ability of Second and Third Generation Japanese Children in a Honolulu Language School." Thesis, University of Hawaii, 1937; Katsumi Onishi. "A Study of the Attitudes of the Japanese in Hawaii Towards the Japanese Language Schools." Thesis, University of Hawaii, 1943; Henry B. Schwartz. "The Foreign Language Schools of Hawaii." *School and Society* 23 (1926): 98–104; Ernest K. Wakukawa. *A History of the Japanese People in Hawaii.* Honolulu: Toyo Shoin, 1938; and Benjamin O. Wist. *A Century of Public Education in Hawaii, 1840–1940.* Honolulu: Hawaii Educational Review, 1940.

Among the more recent studies of the prewar Japanese-language school in Hawaii are Ann Leilani Halsted. "Sharpened Tongues: The Controversy over the 'Americanization' of Japanese Language Schools in Hawaii, 1919–1927." Dissertation, Stanford University, 1989; John N. Hawkins. "Politics, Education and Language Policy: The Case of Japanese Language Schools in Hawaii." *Amerasia Journal* 5.1 (1978): 39–56; and Mariko Takagi. "Moral Education in Pre-war Japanese Language Schools in Hawaii." Thesis, University of Hawaii at Manoa, 1987. See also Roland Kotani. *The Japanese in Hawaii: A Century of Struggle.* Honolulu: Hochi, Ltd., 1985; Franklin S. Odo, and Kazuko Sinoto. *A Pictorial History of the Japanese in Hawaii, 1885–1924.* Honolulu: Bishop Museum Press, 1985; and United Japanese Society of Hawaii. *History of Japanese in Hawaii.* James H. Okahata, ed. Honolulu: United Japanese Society of Hawaii, 1971. Two works which look at the reestablishment of Hawaii Japanese schools after World War II are Yukiko Kimura. "Sociological Significance of Japanese Language School Campaign in Hawaii." *Social Process in Hawaii* 20 (1956): 47–51 and Andrew W. Lind. "Japanese Language School, 1948." Honolulu: University of Hawaii, 1948. 15 pages. Hawaii Social Research Laboratory Report 15.

Prewar works that include information on Japanese schools on the mainland include Reginald Bell. *Public School Education of Second-Generation Japanese in California.* Stanford: Stanford University Press, 1935. New York: Arno Press, 1978; Yamato Ichihashi. *Japanese in the United States: A Critical Study of the Problems of the Japanese Immigrants and their Children.* Stanford: Stanford University Press, 1932. New York: Arno Press, 1969; Edward K. Strong. *The Second-Generation Japanese Problem.* Stanford: Stanford University Press, 1934. New York: Arno Press, 1970; Marian Svensrud. "Attitudes of the Japanese toward Their Language Schools." *Sociology and Social Research* 17.3 (Jan.–Feb. 1933): 259–64; Tamiko Tanaka. "The Japanese Language School in Relation to Assimilation." Thesis, University of Southern California, 1933; and Sakae Tsuboi. "The Japanese Language School Teacher." *Sociology and Social Research* 11.2 (Nov.–Dec. 1926): 160–65. Two contemporary

studies on the prewar Japanese school are Toyotomi Morimoto. "Language and Heritage Maintenance of Immigrants: Japanese Language Schools in California, 1903–1941." Dissertation, University of California, Los Angeles, 1989 and Yoshihide Matsubayashi. "The Japanese Language Schools in Hawaii and California from 1892 to 1941." Diss., University of San Francisco, 1984.

Japanese Mexican Labor Association Organization of Japanese and Mexican agricultural workers formed in Oxnard, California, in 1903. (See 1903 OXNARD STRIKE.)

Japanese Peruvians During World War II, some 2,264 Japanese Latin Americans were deported from their countries of residence and taken to the United States where they were detained with a view to being exchanged for Americans held in Japan. Some 80 percent of these detainees were Japanese Peruvians; the rest came from various Pacific-facing nations from Mexico to Chile. Though ostensibly removed for reasons of continental security, economic factors and racism played a large part. None of the removed was guilty of any crime.

Large-scale immigration from Japan to Peru began in 1899. In much the same way as the West Coast Japanese Americans, Japanese Peruvians were resented as economic competitors and faced anti-Japanese agitation that resulted in the passage of laws stripping second-generation Japanese Peruvians who possessed dual citizenship of Peruvian citizenship and ending Japanese immigration in 1936. With the United States pressuring Latin American nations to round up potentially dangerous Japanese for security reasons even in the months before the Pearl Harbor attack, the Peruvian government seized the opportunity to divest itself of the unwanted Japanese. Early in 1942, the messy process of picking up and jailing influential Japanese Peruvians began; many were able to avoid arrest through bribes. By June, 500 Japanese Peruvians had been shipped to the U.S. along with a smaller number of Japanese Central Americans. All Latin American Japanese were put in one of the Texas INTERNMENT CAMPS: Kenedy, Seagoville or CRYSTAL CITY. Plans were being formulated by both American and Peruvian authorities to remove all 25,000 Japanese Peruvians. However, after the second voyage of the exchange ship *Gripsholm* sent 476 Japanese Peruvians "back" to Japan, exchange negotiations broke off and no further exchanges took place. The questionable "danger" posed by the Japanese Peruvians who had been shipped to the U.S. led to the end of the deportations.

At the conclusion of the war, attempts were made to return the interned to Peru. However, Peru was unwilling to accept them. To dispose of them, the United States government began to send them "back" to Japan.

Between November 1945 and February 1946, about 750 former internees were sent to Japan; 100 managed to gain reentry into Peru through special circumstances such as marriage to a non-Japanese Peruvian. For 365 others about to be sent to Japan, attorney WAYNE COLLINS came to the rescue. Various legal actions by Collins put off their deportation and they were sent to SEABROOK FARMS, New Jersey, in August 1946. Eventually, they were allowed to stay in the United States and 300 did so. Finally in 1952, they were made eligible for U.S. citizenship. Many of these former Japanese Peruvians and their descendants remain in the U.S. to this day.

For further reading, see C. Harvey Gardiner. *Pawns in a Triangle of Hate: The Peruvian Japanese and the United States.* Seattle: University of Washington Press, 1981 and "The Latin-American Japanese and World War II." In Daniels, Roger, Sandra C. Taylor and Harry H. L. Kitano, eds. *Japanese Americans: From Relocation to Redress.* Salt Lake City: University of Utah Press, 1986. Revised edition. Seattle: University of Washington Press, 1991. 142–45 and Michi Weglyn. *Years of Infamy: The Untold Story of America's Concentration Camps.* New York: William Morrow & Co., 1976.

Japanese Reform Association (Kakushin Doshikai)

Organization formed by Japanese PLANTATION workers in Hawaii to represent their interests to Japanese business groups and the sugar plantation owners. In addition to the harsh working conditions Japanese immigrants faced on Hawaii's sugar plantations, they also faced exploitation from their own countrymen in the form of banks and boardinghouses run by the EMIGRATION COMPANIES that charged exorbitant fees. In November 1903, the Central Japanese League was formed by Japan's consul general in Hawaii, Miki Saito. Though supposedly representing all Japanese in Hawaii, the league represented the interests of the consulate, emigration companies, banks and other business groups in its efforts to discourage plantation strikes and outmigration of Japanese workers to the mainland. Largely in response to the league, the Japanese Reform Association was formed in May 1905 to represent the workers' point of view to the government. As a result of the Reform Association, the Japanese government closed down the unpopular KEIHIN BANK and placed restrictions on the actions of the emigration companies. In September 1906, the Reform Association voluntarily disbanded having fulfilled its mission. The Reform Association and the Central Japanese League represented an early division in the Japanese community down class lines, with the league taking positions that coincided with those held by the planters.

For further reading, see Alan T. Moriyama. *Imingaisha: Japanese Emigration Companies and Hawaii, 1894–1908.* Honolulu: University of Hawaii Press, 1985 and Gary Y. Okihiro. *Cane Fires: The Anti-Japanese Movement in Hawaii, 1865–1945.* Philadelphia: Temple University Press, 1991.

Japanese Tea Garden

The Japanese Tea Garden of San Antonio, Texas, was a landmark and tourist attraction as well as a source of controversy during World War II. Located in Brackenridge Park, it was built in 1917–18, largely the creation of San Antonio resident Kimi Jingu. In addition to a pond and garden, it also featured a two-story stone tea pavilion. Given the permanent nature of this structure, a deal was struck with the city allowing Jingu's family to live in the pavilion to provide an atmosphere of authenticity in exchange for the right to sell tea and refreshments to visitors. For the next 24 years, Jingu and his wife Alice Miyoshi Jingu raised six daughters and two sons at the garden. But the attack on Pearl Harbor changed all that. City officials voted to evict the now widowed Alice Jingu and her children. Because she had no other place to go, she refused to leave until the city twice cut off the family's water supply. The Jingus were callously replaced by a Chinese couple and the garden was renamed the "Chinese Tea Garden." After the war, it became known as the "Sunken Gardens," before a final name change took place in October 1984. It was then rededicated as the "Japanese Tea Garden" at a ceremony attended by members of the Jingu family.

The family was resettled with the help of the local Methodist church and many of the Jingu children later moved to Los Angeles. Alice Jingu also moved there and became a film actress, appearing in such movies as *Teahouse of the August Moon* and *Walk Don't Run* before her death in 1969.

For further reading, see Thomas K. Walls. *The Japanese Texans.* San Antonio: Institute of Texan Cultures, 1987.

Jerome

Jerome was the site of one of 10 CONCENTRATION CAMPS that housed Japanese Americans forcibly removed from the West Coast states during World War II. Some basic data on Jerome is presented below in tabular form:

Official name: Jerome Relocation Center
Location: Drew and Chicot Counties, southeastern Arkansas
Land: Farm Security Administration land
Size: 10,000 acres
Climate: Swamp land; green and tropical; humid
Origin of camp population: Mostly from Los Angeles (3,147), Fresno (2,013), Sacramento (993), and Honolulu (445) counties
Via "assembly centers": Most came from Fresno (4,743) and Santa Anita (2,931) "assembly centers"; another 811 came from Hawaii

Jerome "Relocation Center," Arkansas, 1943. *Takeo Fujikawa Collection, Japanese American National Museum Photographic & Moving Image Archive*

Rural/Urban: Roughly equal split

Peak population: 8,497

Date of peak: February 11, 1943

Opening date: October 6, 1942

Closing date: June 30, 1944; Jerome was in operation only 634 days, the shortest of any camp

Project director(s): Paul Taylor and W. O. "Doc" Melton

Community analysts: Edgar C. McVoy and Rachel R. Sady

JERS fieldworkers: None

Newspaper(s): *Communique* (October 23, 1942–February 26, 1943); *Denson Tribune* (March 2, 1943–June 6, 1944)

Percent who answered question 28 of the loyalty questionnaire positively: 75.0; Jerome had the highest percentage of persons answering negatively, giving a qualified answer or refusing to answer

Number and percentage of eligible male citizens inducted directly into armed forces: 52 (0.9%); Jerome had the lowest percentage of eligible male citizens inducted into the armed forces besides Tule Lake

Industry: Jerome had a sawmill that produced goods for internal consumption

Miscellaneous characteristics: There were no guard towers at Jerome and the fences were low; this was because the camp was surrounded by swamps inhabited by four species of the most deadly snakes in America. Farming here was difficult, but the completion in November 1942 of a canal that drained off excess water resulted in some agricultural success.

(For the key to the categories, see the entry for GILA RIVER.)

For further reading: The literature on the Japanese American World War II experience is extensive; see the bibliography and the bibliographic entries after the various entries pertaining to this experience for titles of general interest. General histories of Jerome include Russell Bearden. "The False Rumor of Tuesday: Arkansas's Internment of Japanese-Americans." *Arkansas Historical Quarterly* 41.4 (1982): 327–39 and "Life Inside Arkansas's Japanese-American Relocation Centers." *Arkansas Historical Quarterly* 68 (Summer 1989): 169–96. Carole Katsuko Yumiba. "An Educational History of the War Relocation Centers at Jerome and Rohwer, Arkansas, 1942–1945" Diss., University of Southern California, 1979 and E. J. Friedlander. "Freedom of the Press behind Barbed Wire: Paul Yokota and the Jerome Relocation Center Newspaper." *Arkansas Historical Quarterly* 14.4 (1985): 3–13 are studies of education and journalism, respectively. Edgar C. McVoy. "Social Process in the War Relocation Center." *Social Forces* 22 (Dec. 1943): 188–90 is an account of life at Jerome by a community analyst. Mary Tsukamoto and Elizabeth Pinkerton. *We the People: A Story of Internment in America.* San Jose: Laguna Publishers, 1987 is an autobiography set in part in Jerome.

jiyu imin   Immigrants from Japan who came to Hawaii between the years 1894 and 1908 as "free" migrants. The earlier Japanese immigrants to Hawaii, known as the KANYAKU IMIN, came between the years 1885 and 1894 under the sponsorship of the Japanese government. The *jiyu imin* came under the sponsorship of private EMIGRATION COMPANIES until the GENTLEMEN'S AGREEMENT of 1907–08 ended labor migration to Hawaii and the mainland United States. About 125,000 immigrants from Japan sailed to Hawaii as *jiyu imin,* most of them to work on Hawaii's sugar plantations.

For further reading, see Gary Y. Okihiro. *Cane Fires: The Anti-Japanese Movement in Hawaii, 1865–1945.* Philadelphia: Temple University Press, 1991.

Johnson, Hiram Warren (1866–1945)   Attorney, governor of California, United States senator. Hiram Johnson was a leading figure in the ANTI-JAPANESE MOVEMENT. Born in Sacramento, Johnson practiced law in California until his election as governor in 1910. He was Theodore Roosevelt's vice presidential running mate in 1912 on the Bull Moose Progressive party ticket. Reelected governor in 1914, he resigned in 1917 to assume a Senate seat. Johnson served 28 years in the Senate, during which time he became a leading isolationist.

Governor Johnson was active in getting the 1913 (CALIFORNIA) ALIEN LAND LAW approved by the California legislature, although he had been opposed to a similar measure two years earlier due to pressure from the federal government. When the United States government asked him to refrain from enacting an anti-Japanese land law again in 1913, Johnson protested that California was not discriminating against the Japanese, since the United States already had declared the ISSEI "ALIENS INELIGIBLE TO CITIZENSHIP." Then, in cooperation with Attorney General Ulysses S. Webb, he wrote the so-called Webb land bill, which used "aliens eligible for citizenship" in place of "aliens ineligible to citizenship." This bill was pushed through the state legislature within a few days, and Johnson signed it into law.

After 1920, as a United States Senator, Johnson helped V. S. MCCLATCHY and played a significant role in federal legislation prohibiting Japanese from immigrating to the United States (see IMMIGRATION ACT OF 1924). He died on August 6, 1945.

For further reading, see Roger Daniels. *The Politics of Prejudice: The Anti-Japanese Movement in California and the Struggle for Japanese Exclusion.* 1962. 2nd edition. Berkeley: University of California Press, 1977 and H. Brett Melendy, and Benjamin F. Gilbert. *The Governors of California.* Georgetown, California: The Talisman Press, 1965. EIICHIRO AZUMA

Jordan v. Tashiro   Court case resulting from an attempt by a group of ISSEI doctors to file articles of incorporation for a Japanese hospital in Los Angeles. The office of the California secretary of state refused to file the articles on the ground that Japanese aliens were forbidden to incorporate and lease land in order to establish hospitals. The state court ruled in favor of the *issei* and ordered the office to file the articles. The U.S. Supreme Court agreed to review the decision and affirmed the judgment of the state court, declaring that the language of the TREATY OF COMMERCE AND NAVIGATION OF 1911 BETWEEN THE U.S. AND JAPAN allowing Japanese aliens to lease and occupy land for the purposes of carrying on trade was broad enough to secure Japanese aliens the privilege of maintaining hospitals in the United States. Cases involving the use of land by *issei* for nonagricultural purposes were granted a more liberal interpretation by the courts during this period than cases where they attempted to use and own agricultural land. The Japanese Hospital of Los Angeles was incorporated on February 2, 1929, and went on to become one of the most important of the Japanese hospitals. (See JAPANESE HOSPITALS.)

For further reading, see Moritoshi Fukuda. *Legal Problems of Japanese Americans.* Tokyo: Keio Tsushin, 1980. DENNIS YAMAMOTO

judo   Literally meaning the "Way of Softness," judo is a Japanese martial art that stresses agility and mental judgment. Judo also emphasizes self-defense without the use of a weapon.

Judo had its origins in jujitsu, an older martial art that also followed the method of subduing opponents without the use of arms. Judo was developed as a sport in Japan during the 19th century by Jigoro Kano (1860–1938). Kano established the first school of judo in Tokyo in 1882.

Judo is not only a form of recreation, exercise and physical training for self-defense, but also a method of spiritual training to develop one's character and discipline. Prior to World War II, judo competitions and exhibitions were a vital part of many Japanese American community celebrations. Though not as widely practiced today, judo remains a significant aspect of many Japanese American lives.

For further reading, see John DeFrancis, and V. R. Lincoln. *Things Japanese in Hawaii.* Honolulu: University Press of Hawaii, 1973 and *Kodansha Encyclopedia of Japan.* Tokyo: Kodansha, 1983. STACEY HIROSE

Justice Department camps   Camps administered by the Justice Department for holding enemy aliens during World War II. (See INTERNMENT CAMPS.)

K

kachigumi   Groups of ISSEI who believed Japan would win World War II. Unable to psychologically accept that Japan could be defeated in the war, a small number of *issei* formed underground "victory groups," or *kachigumi.* These groups attempted to challenge American "rumors" of Japan's military losses in the Pacific and aspired to preserve the *issei's* confidence and ethnic pride in Japan.

These *issei* refused to accept Japan's unconditional surrender to Allied forces in August 1945. Instead they chose to believe that Japan had won the war and that the United States was trying to conceal this fact from the general public. After Japan's surrender, the *kachigumi* were renamed *kattagumi* because, according to historian John J. Stephan, *katta,* the past tense, implied that Japan had *won* the war.

By 1949 Japan's defeat was widely accepted by *issei* involved in *kachigumi/kattagumi* groups. Many began to believe that Japan had lost the war when the emperor publicly denied his divinity in 1945. For others, trips back to Japan revealed tremendous devastation, convincing them of Japan's defeat. Despite these events, a handful of people still clung to the belief that Japan had won the war. Stephan notes that some of these people were isolated Japanese soldiers who remained in hiding in the Philippines and Guam decades after World War II had ended. *Kachigumi* also were formed in other Japanese immigrant settlements, most notably in Brazil. The last *kattagumi* group in Hawaii—the Hawaii Victory Society—disbanded in 1977.

For further reading, see John Stephan. *Hawaii under the Rising Sun: Japan's Plans for Conquest after Pearl Harbor.* Honolulu: University of Hawaii Press, 1984. STACEY HIROSE

Kagawa, Lawrence (1904–1973)   The leader of an insurance revolution in Hawaii, Kagawa began his

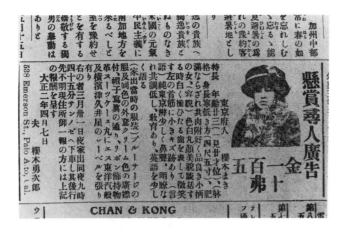

Kakeochi announcement in the *Shin Sekai*, San Francisco, September 1924. *Japanese American Reading Room Collection, Japanese American National Museum Photographic & Moving Image Archive*

career in 1923 with the International Trust Co. in Honolulu and later convinced A. P. Giannini, owner of Occidental Life, to open a Hawaii branch. Occidental Underwriters of Hawaii was founded on February 1, 1933, by Kagawa as an agency of Occidental Life Insurance Company of California. Immediately after the war, "Oxy" became the first insurance company not to charge Asians higher premiums (based on outdated Asian mortality statistics) and also became the first company to use NISEI and American-born Chinese and Filipino agents. As a result, Oxy became the largest insurance company in Hawaii from 1948–58. It was also the first Hawaii firm to invest its money in Hawaiian concerns. Kagawa remained president of Oxy until 1963, when he became chairman and chief executive; he retired in 1970.

For further reading, see Lawrence H. Fuchs. *Hawaii Pono: A Social History.* New York: Harcourt, Brace and World, 1961.

[Also used to compile this entry was "Pioneer Hawaii Insurance Man Larry Kagawa Dead at Age 69." *Rafu Shimpo* 9 Aug. 1973: 1.]

kakeochi   Desertion of husbands by wives. Although there are no statistics to verify it, there is good reason to believe that *kakeochi* was a fairly common occurrence in the PICTURE BRIDE era. The Japanese-language press of the time contains numerous references to *kakeochi*, both in the form of announcements and as feature stories. Although most newspaper accounts emphasize the tragic elements, some also have a comic side. The press also served as a deterrent to *kakeochi* since both the deserting wife and any man that took her in were subject to ostracism by the community. The network of JAPANESE ASSOCIATIONS in the various Japanese communities made resettlement in the communities difficult for such couples.

For further reading, see Yuji Ichioka. *"Amerika Nadeshiko:* Japanese Immigrant Women in the United States, 1900–1924." *Pacific Historical Review* 48.2 (May 1980): 339–57 and *The Issei: The World of the First Generation Japanese Immigrants, 1885–1924.* New York: The Free Press, 1988.

Kanazawa, Tooru J. (1906–   )   A journalist and decorated World War II veteran, Tooru Kanazawa had his first novel published at the age of 83.

A NISEI, Kanazawa was born on November 12, 1906, in Spokane, Washington. His family moved north to Douglas and then to Juneau, Alaska, where his father worked as a barber. His novel, *Sushi and Sourdough,* is based on his youth in the frontier gold-mining town of Juneau and his observations and interactions with the ISSEI salmon-cannery workers there. He relates the family saga of Matajiro Fuse, an *issei* who leaves Seattle with his wife and children to find a better life in Alaska. The novel also gives an historical account of *issei* pioneers in Alaska, through the eyes of Alaskan sourdoughs, or prospectors, Wada Ju (JUJIRO WADA) and FRANK YASUDA.

In 1931, Kanazawa graduated from the University of Washington with a B.A. in journalism. The following year, he wrote for Los Angeles's RAFU SHIMPO newspaper. He moved to New York in 1940 to work as a journalist and, therefore, escaped the mass removal and detention of all West Coast Japanese Americans, including his mother and siblings. In 1943, Kanazawa volunteered for the U.S. military's 442ND REGIMENTAL COMBAT TEAM, an all–Japanese American unit. He was awarded a Bronze Star for meritorious service as a citations writer and as a radio operator assigned to rifle companies. A retired journalist and travel agent, Kanazawa currently resides in New York.

For further reading, see *Sushi and Sourdough: A Novel.* Seattle: University of Washington Press, 1989. See also Clifford Uyeda's review of the book in *National Japanese American Historical Society Newsletter* 3.1 (Winter 1991): 10–11.

EMILY LAWSIN

Kanda, Shigefusa   World War I Red Cross volunteer. Though a good number of ISSEI and NISEI served in the United States armed forces during World War I (see WORLD WAR I VETERANS), most did not get to the front lines in Europe. One of the few who did was Shigefusa Kanda. An *issei*, Kanda had come to Hawaii from Japan 14 years earlier after graduating from Doshisha University. He had been a Christian minister and was then operating a girls' school on Maui. He was also the father of four children. Feeling an obligation to his adopted country, he volunteered to join the Red Cross, but was rejected by the Honolulu chapter. Undeterred by this setback, he set out for Washington, D.C., on

Japanese immigrants landing in Honolulu, 1893. *Hadley Collection, Hawaii State Archives*

May 7, 1918, to offer his services there. Rejected again, he sailed for London (after being rejected for a visa six times). In London, he was finally allowed to join the Red Cross and ended up serving from July 1918 to July 1919. His enthusiastic performance of his duties earned him a service ribbon with two stars, which he wore upon his return to Hawaii via Japan.

For further reading, see United Japanese Society of Hawaii. *History of Japanese in Hawaii.* James H. Okahata, ed. Honolulu: United Japanese Society of Hawaii, 1971 and Ernest K. Wakukawa. *A History of the Japanese People in Hawaii.* Honolulu: Toyo Shoin, 1938.

kanreki   A Japanese celebration observed on one's 60th birthday. According to the Chinese zodiac system, a life cycle on the earth comprises 60 years. After one reaches the age of 60, one is "reborn" and taken back to infancy. As a result, *kanreki* observes one's having reached the midpoint of two eras in one's life.

A *kanreki* celebration is an auspicious event. It includes a large party with family and friends. At a *kanreki* party, the celebrant wears a red *chanchanko* (a sleeveless jacket generally worn by infants) and a red hat. The *chanchanko* symbolizes one's return to infancy, and the color red, or *aka* in Japanese, symbolizes that one has become a baby, or *aka-chan*, once again.

For further reading, see Patsy Y. Nakayama. "Culture and Tradition." *Hawaii Herald* 18 May 1990: 90–98.

STACEY HIROSE

kanyaku imin   Japanese immigrants who came to Hawaii under government contracts. Beginning in 1885 and lasting until 1894, the period of immigration sponsored by the Japanese government, approximately 29,000 Japanese subjects traveled to Hawaii to labor on the sugar PLANTATIONS. In 1894, the Japanese government turned the business of emigration over to private EMIGRATION COMPANIES under government license. Those who migrated between 1894 and the GENTLEMEN'S AGREEMENT of 1907–08 were known as the JIYU IMIN, or free migrants.

For further reading, see Alan T. Moriyama. *Imingaisha: Japanese Emigration Companies and Hawaii, 1894–1908.* Honolulu: University of Hawaii Press, 1985 and Gary Y. Okihiro. *Cane Fires: The Anti-Japanese Movement in Hawaii, 1865–1945.* Philadelphia: Temple University Press, 1991.

kao   Literally meaning "face," it is a concept that deals with the maintenance of one's honor and reputation by presenting oneself properly to the public. As with the concept of IE, *kao* has remained important to the Japanese Americans both on an individual and community level. Not only must one maintain the proper decorum so as to preserve one's reputation within one's family's, but one must also be careful to give the right impression and to avoid hostility and resentment in the larger society.

For further reading, see *Kodansha Encyclopedia of Japan.* Tokyo: Kodansha, 1983.

STACEY HIROSE

Katayama Sen (1859–1933)   Sen Katayama was an internationally known labor leader and a founding member of the Communist Party of America. He was born and raised on a farm in Okayama PREFECTURE and moved to Tokyo to further his education in 1881. While working as a printer and a Chinese literature lecturer, he also became interested in Christianity. When he came to the U.S. in 1884, it was to study theology. However, poverty intervened. While working at a series of menial jobs Japanese immigrants typically engaged in he made contacts among some political refugees from Japan. Still wanting to further his education, he attended the Hopkind Academy of Oakland for one year before going to Maryville College in Tennessee and Iowa College, where he received B.A. and M.A. degrees. He went on to get a B.D. from Yale in 1895. After a 12-year stay in the U.S. as a student and worker, he returned to Japan.

In Japan in 1897, he helped to organize the country's first trade union and established a college settlement called Kingsley Hall. In 1904, he attended the Amsterdam Congress of the Second International as the delegate from the Japanese Socialist Association. On his way, he stopped in San Francisco and Los Angeles and organized Japanese Socialist Association branches. Upon returning to Japan, he continued his work as an organizer, writer for Socialist publications and lecturer. He was sent to prison after the 1912 Tokyo street car strike and, unable to cope with the constant police harassment, returned to the U.S. in 1914. Despite continuous surveillance by consulate officials, Katayama continued his political activities. In 1915, he organized the Japanese Labor Federation of America and in 1916, he began to publish the *Heimin* (Commoner), a Japanese/English-language monthly magazine. He also wrote articles for various Socialist publications and made many speeches endorsing the Russian Revolution of 1917. On September 1, 1919, he became a founding member of the Communist Party of America. After surviving the "Palmer Raids," a roundup of 3,000 suspected "subversive" aliens initiated by Attorney General Alexander Mitchell Palmer, he moved on to New York, Mexico and Canada, before entering the Soviet Union in 1921. He remained there until his death in 1933. His funeral was attended by 150,000 people and he was buried in the Kremlin.

For further reading, see Hyman Kublin. *Asian Revolutionary: The Life of Sen Katayama.* Princeton: Princeton University Press, 1964 and Karl Yoneda. "Sen Katayama: 1859–1933." *Gidra* (Oct. 1973): 11. Kazuhiko Orii, and Hilary Conroy. "Japanese Socialist in Texas: Sen Katayama." *Amerasia Journal* 8.2 (1981): 163–70 is a brief exploration into Katayama's attempt to start a rice colony in Texas.

kattagumi See KACHIGUMI.

Kawabe, Harry Sotaro (1890–1969) Businessman in Alaska and Seattle, Washington. Harry Sotaro Kawabe played a key role in the prewar development of Alaska. Born in Maibara near Osaka, Japan, Kawabe fulfilled his youthful dream of going to America, arriving in Seattle in 1905. There he learned English and began the first of his many commercial ventures by purchasing and operating a hotel and café.

Lured northward in 1909, Kawabe first went to the Kenai Peninsula to cook for the Alaska Trading Company, then to booming Cordova where the Kennecott Copper Company was building a railroad to its mines in the Alaskan interior, and on to Chisana gold country. In 1915 Kawabe settled in Seward where the newly completed Alaska Railroad linked steamship traffic to the territory's interior. He entered the steam laundry business, which prospered with contracts from the railroads, steamship companies and the U.S. military. Within 10 years, Kawabe had significant business holdings.

Alaska's proximity to the Far East and the strategic importance of its Aleutian Islands as stepping stones across the North Pacific Ocean resulted in apprehension towards resident Alaskan Japanese aliens and Japanese Americans during World War II. EXECUTIVE ORDER 9066 removed and interned Japanese from the West Coast, including over 200 Alaskans, of whom Harry Kawabe was one. At war's end, Kawabe decided not to resettle permanently in Alaska, attracted by bustling Seattle where he spent the next several decades prospering in real estate and a Japanese import/export business.

Motivated by a strong desire to improve U.S.-Japan relations, he promoted cultural and civic cooperation and was recognized by awards from the Japanese em- peror as well as local and national U.S. organizations like the JAPANESE AMERICAN CITIZENS LEAGUE. Uniting his continued Alaskan interests with an understanding of the Japanese need for natural resources, he returned to Seward to form the Japanese and American Development Company of Alaska in 1965 which, unfortunately, was in advance of world economic realities. Even after his death in 1969, the Kawabe presence continues in Seattle and Seward through charitable legacies.

For further reading, see Ronald K. Inouye. "Harry Sotaro Kawabe: Issei Businessman of Seward and Seattle." *Alaska History* 5 (Spring 1990): 35–43 and Chas Russell. "Alaska— His Labor of Love." *Rafu Shimpo* 18 Dec. 1967: II-13, 22. Kawabe is also mentioned in Bill Hosokawa. *Nisei: The Quiet Americans.* New York: William Morrow & Co., 1969 and Kazuo Ito. *Issei: A History of Japanese Immigrants in North America.* Shinichiro Nakamura, Jean S. Gerard, trans. Seattle: Executive Committee for the Publication of *Issei: A History of Japanese Immigrants in North America,* 1973.

RONALD K. INOUYE

Kawakami, Karl Kiyoshi (1879–1949) Journalist K. K. Kawakami was a leading defender of Japan and Japanese immigrants in the United States. Born in Yamagata PREFECTURE, Kawakami was a Socialist in his youth and was one of the founders of Japan's Social Democratic Party in 1901. He took his English name after that of Karl Marx. When the party was forced to disband by the Japanese government, Kawakami came to the U.S. as a student, studying political science at the University of Iowa. Upon receiving an M.A., he began to write on Japan and East Asian affairs in English for American magazines and newspapers. His previous antigovernment stance became one of advocacy, representing the Japanese government's interests and trying to convince American readers of the rightness of Japan's international actions. At the same time, he wrote in Japanese for a Japanese audience on American affairs. From 1914 to 1920, he was the director of the Pacific Press Bureau, a news agency established by the Japanese government. His English-language books include *American-Japanese Relations: An Inside View of Japan's Policies and Purposes* (1912), *Asia at the Door: A Study of the Japanese Question in Continental United States, Hawaii, and Canada* (1914), and *The Real Japanese Question* (1921), along with a biography of chemist JOKICHI TAKAMINE published in 1928. As a suspected Japanese agent, he was under surveillance by the FBI and was picked up soon after the Pearl Harbor attack.

For further reading, see Yuji Ichioka. *The Issei: The World of the First Generation Japanese Immigrants, 1885–1924.* New York: The Free Press, 1988. Kawakami's own writings in English which pertain to Japanese immigrants include the following: "The Naturalization of Japanese: What It Would Mean to the United States." *North American Review* 185.617

(June 1907): 394–402; *American-Japanese Relations: An Inside View of Japan's Policies and Purposes*. New York: Fleming H. Revell, 1912; *Asia at the Door: A Study of the Japanese Question in Continental United States, Hawaii, and Canada*. New York: Fleming H. Revell Company, 1914; "The Japanese Question." *The Pacific Review* 1.3 (Dec. 1920): 365–78; "The Japanese Question." *American Association of Political and Social Science, Annals* 93.1 (Jan. 1921): 81–88; *The Real Japanese Question*. New York: Macmillan Co., 1921. New York: Arno Press, 1978; "Japan in a Quandary." *North American Review* 219.821 (Apr. 1924): 474–85; and *Jokichi Takamine: A Record of His American Achievements*. New York: William Edwin Rudge, 1928.

Kawakita v. United States Case brought before the U.S. Supreme Court that involved the alleged treason of an American-born man of Japanese ancestry who served as an English-language interpreter for a Japanese industrial company during World War II. Tomoya Kawakita was born in California in 1921 to Japanese parents and was in Japan from 1939 to 1946. While in Japan, he enrolled at a Japanese university, entered his name in the family register (a legal record of a household) and served as an interpreter for the Oeyama Nickel Industry Co., Ltd., which used the labor of American prisoners of war in its mines and factories. He worked as an interpreter for approximately a year. Kawakita returned to the United States in 1946 after securing a passport from the American consulate at Yokohama, where he declared that he was an American citizen. In 1947, a former prisoner of war recognized Kawakita in Los Angeles and notified the FBI. Kawakita was later charged with 15 counts of treason relating to his alleged mistreatment of prisoners of war. On September 2, 1948, a federal grand jury found Kawakita guilty of eight counts of treason and also found that he had not expatriated himself of his American citizenship, as he had contended. Kawakita was given the death sentence by the presiding federal judge. The U.S. Supreme Court affirmed both the conviction and the death sentence. President Dwight D. Eisenhower commuted Kawakita's sentence to one of life imprisonment on November 2, 1953, and President John F. Kennedy later granted him a presidential pardon on the condition that he return to Japan and never seek entry into the United States. Kawakita spent almost 16 years at the Alcatraz penitentiary. For further reading, see Frank F. Chuman. *The Bamboo People: The Law and Japanese-Americans*. Del Mar, Calif.: Publisher's Inc., 1976. DENNIS YAMAMOTO

Kawamura, Terry Teruo (1949–1969) Recipient, Congressional Medal of Honor. Terry T. Kawamura is one of four Japanese Americans to receive America's highest military honor.

Born in Oahu, Hawaii, Kawamura entered military service in Oahu during the Vietnam War. Corporal Kawamura distinguished himself by heroic action while serving as a member of the 173rd Engineer Company at Camp Radcliffe, Republic of Vietnam, when an enemy demolition team infiltrated the unit quarters area and opened fire with automatic weapons. During the battle, Kawamura threw himself on an explosive charge, in complete disregard to his own safety, and saved the lives of several members of his unit. He was killed as a result of this action. For his courage, he was awarded the Congressional Medal of Honor by the president in the name of the Congress, one of 155 recipients of the award during the Vietnam War. The medal is reserved for those who "distinguish [themselves] conspicuously by gallantry and intrepidity at the risk of [their] life above and beyond the call of duty."
For further reading, see *Congressional Medal of Honor; The Names the Deeds*. Chico, Calif.: Sharp & Dunnigan Publications, 1988. TRACY ENDO

Kawano, Jack (d. 1984) Perhaps no one was as important in Hawaii's labor movement as Jack Kawano. He was from Pahoa on the Big Island. The son of a Japanese contract laborer, he quit school after the seventh grade to work at Hakalau Plantation at age 14. Unhappy with the exploitation inherent in this sort of work, he drove trucks, dug cesspools and built stone walls, each for short periods. While working as a longshoreman on the Honolulu docks, Kawano and others formed the Honolulu Longshoremen's Association since established unions would not take "Oriental" members. At first ineffective, his group joined the West Coast–based INTERNATIONAL LONGSHOREMEN'S AND WAREHOUSEMEN'S UNION in October 1937 and Kawano quickly became the key organizer for the ILWU in Hawaii. By 1941, the ILWU had largely succeeded in unionizing the docks; Castle & Cooke Terminals signed a contract with the ILWU in that year, becoming the first big company to do so.

In 1944, Kawano and the ILWU began to organize plantation workers. Despite harassment from the plantation owners and the wartime government, the unionization drive was a success. Dues-paying ILWU members jumped from 970 in January 1944 to 6,610 in January 1945. With the election of many labor-endorsed candidates in 1945, the "Little Wagner Act," a measure guaranteeing all workers the right to organize and collectively bargain, was passed and ILWU membership reached 30,000 by 1947. A successful strike in September–November 1946 involving 28,000 plantation workers cemented the union's power. But this success was to be short lived.

For a long time, a conflict within the ILWU had been brewing between mainlander JACK HALL and Kawano. In 1944, Hall was named the ILWU regional director for Hawaii by International Secretary Matthew J. Meehan despite the local leadership's preference for Kawano. Under Hall's leadership and with the ILWU headquarter's support, Kawano's influence in the union gradually began to wane. When the 177-day 1949 dock STRIKE was being discussed and negotiated, Kawano had pretty much been removed from any decision-making capacity and dropped out of the Communist Party (CP), feeling that this body was taking mainland orders over the wishes of local party committees. The falling out between Hall and Kawano was complete by 1951, exacerbated by Hall's drinking and his alleged disrespect towards Japanese American members. When the territorial government began to fight the ILWU through "red scare" tactics, it soon found itself a new ally: Jack Kawano. In July 1951, Kawano testified in Washington before the House Un-American Activities Committee, providing great detail about the organization of the Hawaii CP and ILWU. As a result, the HAWAII SEVEN were arrested in August 1951. They were convicted of violating the Smith Act on June 19, 1953, though the convictions were overturned five years later.

Kawano's testimony severely crippled the ILWU's influence and virtually destroyed Hawaii's Communist Party, along with Kawano himself. Ironically, Jack Hall and his union emerged intact and later gained popular acceptance with the ascension of the Democratic Party in Hawaii in the statehood era. Kawano tried unsuccessfully to run a liquor store and a butcher shop. After moving to California, he worked for Lockheed for 17 years in their fiberglass shop, retiring on a small pension. He died in virtual exile in California in 1984.

For further reading, see Edward D. Beechert. *Working in Hawaii: A Labor History.* Honolulu: University of Hawaii Press, 1985; Lawrence H. Fuchs. *Hawaii Pono: A Social History.* New York: Harcourt, Brace and World, 1961; and Roland Kotani. *The Japanese in Hawaii: A Century of Struggle.* Honolulu: Hochi, Ltd., 1985.

Kayamori, Fhoki (1877–1941)

Amateur photographer, cannery watchman and store clerk in Yakutat, Alaska. Born in Tokyo, Kayamori arrived in Yakutat in 1912 as a seasonal worker for the Libby McNeil cannery. A quiet, confirmed bachelor, his photography documented the southeast Alaska community for approximately 30 years. His subjects included people, festivities, buildings, businesses, funerals and parties. A number of his images appear in a 1972 Smithsonian Press publication "Under Mount St. Elias: The History and Culture of the Yakutat Tlingits," the standard reference on these Native Alaskans by anthropologist Federica de Laguna.

When news of the World War II forced removal of Alaskan Japanese and Japanese aliens reached Yakutat, Kayamori expressed his defiance in the ultimate manner—by committing suicide. His 700 photographs remained in Yakutat until 1976, when they were donated to the Alaska State Library in Juneau. His images constitute a unique long-term record of a particular Alaskan community; Yakutat's past is recorded like that of no other Alaskan community.

For further reading, see India Spartz and Ronald K. Inouye. "Fhoki Kayamori: Amateur Photographer of Yakutat, 1912–41." *Alaska History* 6.2 (Fall 1991).   RONALD K. INOUYE

Keetley Farms

Utah "VOLUNTARY" RESETTLEMENT colony. In the days immediately following EXECUTIVE ORDER 9066, Japanese Americans were encouraged to "voluntarily" migrate to areas away from the West Coast. For various reasons, this endeavor was largely unsuccessful. All told, only 4,889 actually did "voluntarily" move inland. The tiny town of Keetley, Utah, was one of the few successful communities resulting from this program. Here, the largest single group of "voluntary" resettlers outside the coast made their home during the war years. They were led by Fred Isamu Wada, a relatively wealthy produce dealer from Oakland, California. Seeking a place to settle his family to avoid internment, Wada took a trip to Utah. He first visited Duchesne County and was received hospitably since the town badly needed farm laborers; however, he opted against this area because of its remoteness. He also visited Keetley on the way back and ended up striking a deal with founder/mayor George A. Fisher to lease 3,500 acres. Upon hearing of this deal, surrounding communities were not happy and tried their best to stop it. Nonetheless, the deal was consummated and Wada began to recruit colonists. He left Oakland with a group of 21; families from San Francisco, Oakland, Los Angeles and Santa Barbara made up the colony, which numbered about 130 by the end of March 1942.

The group was determined to make the colony a success despite formidable obstacles. The land proved to be bad, requiring leveling and the removal of many rocks. The planting season was also short, with the first snow coming as early as September. Additionally, the group was greeted by a pair of dynamite blasts intended to scare them off. But gradually, the group found acceptance, if not prosperity. Before long, Keetley Farms was enlisted in the wartime propaganda efforts of the local press, what with its motto, "Food for Victory" and its illustration of the idea that even Japanese Americans could be accepted if they worked hard enough. Keetley Farms' operations realized only a partial success. In addition to the already mentioned problems, the high cost of transportation to Salt Lake City meant that the colony could do little more than provide for its own needs. It was perhaps most effective as a place where people relocating from the coast or later from the WRA camps could stop en route to other destinations. When the war ended, about two-thirds of the colonists moved back to California; many of the others remained in Utah. For further reading, see Sandra C. Taylor. "Japanese Americans and Keetley Farms: Utah's Relocation Colony." *Utah Historical Quarterly* 54.4 (Fall 1986): 328–44.

Keihin Bank   The principal bank of many Japanese immigrants to Hawaii, the Keihin Bank became notorious among Hawaii ISSEI for its unscrupulous handling of their hard-earned money. Officially called Kabushiki-gaisha Keihin Chokinginko, Keihin Bank was formed by three of the five largest EMIGRATION COMPANIES as a way to squeeze more money out of laborers immigrating to Hawaii's sugar plantations. Capitalized initially at 100,000 yen, the bank opened its main office in Tokyo in 1898 with four branch offices, including one in Honolulu. It profited from immigrants to Hawaii in several ways. Starting from 1894, new arrivals to Hawaii were required to show possession of 100 yen before being allowed into the country. For the many would-be immigrants to Hawaii, a loan would be required to get that 100 yen "show money" *(misegane)*, and for those who came with one of the three emigration companies that founded Keihin Bank, the loan invariably came from Keihin Bank. Borrowing 100 yen in Yokohama, the travelers would be required to repay 112.5 yen upon their arrival in Honolulu just two weeks later. The emigration companies also required contract laborers to deposit 90 to 100 yen at the Keihin Bank as collateral should they fail to fulfill their three-year labor contracts for some reason. If the laborer did fulfill his labor contract, he could get his money back; however, he could get back the full amount only if he went in person to the main branch office in Tokyo, having to settle for receiving small monthly installments otherwise. This system allowed Keihin Bank to collect the maximum interest on workers' money. The bank was also often accused of various dirty tricks to collect unpaid loans, sometimes more than once. The Keihin Bank was so disliked by plantation workers, that the demand to close it down became one of the primary reasons for the formation of the JAPANESE REFORM ASSOCIATION in 1905. Through the efforts of the Reform Association and several Japanese newspapers in Hawaii, Keihin Bank was closed down in Hawaii, effective on October 6, 1907.

For further reading, see Alan T. Moriyama. *Imingaishi: Japanese Emigration Companies and Hawaii, 1894–1908.* Honolulu: University of Hawaii Press, 1985.

James Kai in kendo uniform.   *Fred Kishi Collection, Japanese American National Museum Photographic & Moving Image Archive*

kendo   Literally meaning "the Way of the Sword," *kendo* is the Japanese sport of fencing.

Kendo originated in the Japanese feudal ages as training for the samurai class and is based on the techniques of the two-handed sword of the samurai. Before the Showa period (beginning in 1926) in Japan, *kendo* was customarily referred to as *kenjutsu* or *gekken.*

In the modern practice of *kendo,* steel swords are wielded only occasionally by *kendo* experts in Japan. Instead, the steel swords have been replaced by bamboo swords. Based on the age of the fencer, the length of the bamboo swords varies between roughly three-and-a-half to four feet.

Before World War II, *kendo* was a popular recreational sport with the ISSEI and NISEI.

For further reading, see John DeFrancis and V. R. Lincoln. *Things Japanese in Hawaii.* Honolulu: University Press of Hawaii, 1973 and *Kodansha Encyclopedia of Japan.* Tokyo: Kodansha, 1983.   STACEY HIROSE

kenjinkai   Organizations made up of Japanese Americans descending from the same PREFECTURE in Japan. In the pre–World War II Japanese American community, the *kenjinkai* was an important social and sometimes economic grouping.

The basis of the *kenjinkai* are the prefectures, or *ken*. Bureaucratic units in Meiji Japan, the prefectures are roughly equivalent to states in the U.S. In Japan as in the U.S., conditions, customs and speech patterns differ from region to region. Thus, in the Japanese American immigrant community, there was a natural camaraderie between people from the same prefectures. Additionally, among the ISSEI stereotypes were held concerning persons from particular prefectures. *Kenjinkai*, where *kenjin*, or people hailing from common prefectural backgrounds, met to share friendship and a sense of community through annual picnics, dinner meetings and other such events were a natural result of a shared regional identity. Though largely social in function, *kenjinkai* also served as mutual aid societies of sorts, where one who was down on his luck could seek aid from *kenjin*. *Kenjinkai* also served as a way to encourage children to mingle with and hopefully marry *kenjin*.

With the NISEI and SANSEI, the significance of prefectural background faded, and *kenjinkai* declined in importance after World War II though exceptions exist. The outstanding exception to this trend is the OKINAWAN community, which retains a strong regional identity to this day.

For further reading, see S. Frank Miyamoto. *Social Solidarity among the Japanese in Seattle*. University of Washington Publications in the Social Sciences 11.2 (Dec. 1939): 57–130. Seattle: Asian American Studies Program, University of Washington, 1981. Seattle: University of Washington Press, 1984 and Bradford Smith. *Americans from Japan*. Philadelphia: J. B. Lippincott Co., 1948. Yukiko Kimura. *Issei: Japanese Immigrants in Hawaii*. Honolulu: University of Hawaii Press, 1988 describes in detail the characteristics ascribed by *issei* to people from various prefectures. See also Janice E. Noguchi. "Kenjinkai: Overlooked in Nikkei History." *Hokubei Mainichi* 22–25 Oct. 1985 for an historical account of one *kenjinkai* and its continuing vitality into the 1980s.

Kenmotsu, Sadaichi

Labor leader. Sadaichi Kenmotsu was one of the founders of Rafu Nihonjin Rodo Kyokai (Los Angeles Japanese Workers' Association) in 1925. This group attained a membership of 100 by 1930. Beginning in 1926 Kenmotsu published *Kaikyu Sen* (Class War) in San Francisco. The newspaper became the *Zaibei Rodo Shimbun* (The Japanese Workers in America) in 1928, the official organ of the Japanese Workers' Association of America. On July 27, 1929, Kenmotsu was arrested at a Communist Party anti-war demonstration in San Francisco and turned over to immigration authorities. Although he survived this episode, he was less fortunate on April 14, 1930, when he was caught in a mass arrest of 108 at a strike meeting

in El Centro, California. Two months later, he was tried, convicted, sentenced and set to be deported. He left for the Soviet Union on December 16, 1931, from San Francisco aboard a German ship. He studied at Moscow Lenin School in 1933 and headed the Japanese Seamen's Club in Vladivostok; his activities after this are unknown.

For further reading, see Karl G. Yoneda. *Ganbatte: Sixty-Year Struggle of a Kibei Worker*. Los Angeles: Asian American Studies Center, University of California, Los Angeles, 1983.

kibei

Term for the generation of NISEI who were born in the United States but educated in Japan. For reasons ranging from economic hardship to a desire to retain Japanese culture, many thousands of *nisei* were sent to Japan by their ISSEI parents to be raised by grandparents or other relatives in Japan. After a few or many years of schooling in Japan, they returned to the U.S. to find themselves out of step with their *nisei* peers. *Kibei* remain a subgroup of the *nisei*, distinct in their degree of Japanese- and English-language ability, their socialization as Japanese or Americans, and their identity. Believed most likely to be "disloyal" during World War II, ironically *kibei* were overrepresented in number both in the TULE LAKE "SEGREGATION CENTER" and in the MILITARY INTELLIGENCE SERVICE.

For further reading, see East Bay Japanese for Action. *Our Recollections*. Berkeley: East Bay Japanese for Action, 1986; James Oda. *Heroic Struggles of Japanese Americans: Partisan Fighters from America's Concentration Camps*. Los Angeles: Privately printed, 1980; and Karl G. Yoneda. *Ganbatte: Sixty-Year Struggle of a Kibei Worker*. Los Angeles: Asian American Studies Center, University of California, Los Angeles, 1983 for autobiographical accounts by *kibei*.

Kido, Saburo (1902–1977)

JAPANESE AMERICAN CITIZENS LEAGUE (JACL) leader. Kido was a founding member of the JACL and served as its president at the critical time of the Japanese attack on Pearl Harbor. Born in Hilo, Hawaii, Kido possessed a pidgin accent which would stay with him for the duration of his life. At the age of 19, Kido came to the mainland to attend Hastings Law College in San Francisco and earned his degree in 1926. Concerned about the problems facing Japanese Americans, Kido set up his law practice in San Francisco's Japan Town. In 1926, he met TOM YATABE and the two found that they shared concern over the plight of the NISEI. Kido became a co-founder and the first president of the San Francisco New American Citizens League in 1928. In that same year, he married Mine Harada. Kido remained active in organizing *nisei*, drawing many from all over the West Coast for a conference in April 1929.

At a convention in Seattle in 1930, Kido's New American Citizens merged with Yatabe's American Loyalty League and other organizations to form the Japanese American Citizens League. Within the JACL, Kido assisted TOKIE SLOCUM as he lobbied for citizenship for ISSEI WORLD WAR I VETERANS. By the late 1930s, Kido became executive secretary and was elected president at the JACL convention in 1940. In what would prove a momentous decision, Kido hired young MIKE MASAOKA to be the JACL's first full-time staff member in 1941. Later that year when the Pacific war broke out with the attack on Pearl Harbor, Kido sent a telegram to President Franklin D. Roosevelt pledging the "fullest cooperation" of the JACL to the American war effort. For the duration of the war, Kido (along with Masaoka) remained instrumental in the *nisei* quest to prove their loyalty to the United States. This brand of patriotism in the face of civil rights violations did not rest well with all sectors of the Japanese American community. While incarcerated at POSTON, Kido was attacked by a group of KIBEI and hospitalized for nearly a month. After the war, Kido stayed active with the JACL, advocating immigration and naturalization rights for ISSEI.

For further reading, see Bill Hosokawa. *Nisei: The Quiet Americans.* New York: William Morrow & Co., 1969 and *JACL in Quest of Justice: The History of the Japanese American Citizens League.* New York: William Morrow, 1982.

SCOTT KURASHIGE

Kikuchi, Charles (1917–1988) Diarist, JAPANESE AMERICAN EVACUATION AND RESETTLEMENT STUDY (JERS) researcher, social worker. NISEI Charles Kikuchi played an important role as a researcher in the JERS project. Additionally, his own writings about his life as a young *nisei* and his diary of life in a World War II CONCENTRATION CAMP have been widely read.

His father had come to the U.S. in 1900 and worked in a succession of typical ISSEI migrant worker occupations. After a stint in the U.S. Navy, he opened a barbershop on the east coast of San Francisco Bay and returned to Japan to take a bride in 1913. Charles was the second of eight children. For various reasons, his father took an intense dislike to him, and from the age of eight, he spent the rest of his childhood and adolescence in an orphanage in which he was the only Japanese American. Upon graduating from high school in 1934, he set out for San Francisco to attend college. He graduated from San Francisco State College in 1939. Like many other college-educated *nisei* of the time, he was unable to get a job after graduation and spent two years performing a myriad of menial jobs up and down the coast, never earning more than 25¢ per hour. He finally got a job with the California State Employment Service (at 40¢ an hour) to do a survey on *nisei* occupations in San Francisco. He entered the social welfare program at the University of California at Berkeley in the fall of 1941.

In the confusion surrounding the Japanese American community and the students in the weeks after the Pearl Harbor attack, Kikuchi got involved with the Japanese American Evacuation and Resettlement Project led by sociologist Dorothy Swaine Thomas. Hired as a JERS researcher, he did field work at Tanforan "ASSEMBLY CENTER" and at GILA RIVER. He also kept a detailed diary from the time of Pearl Harbor, a practice he would continue for nearly all his life. His greatest contribution to the JERS project was the series of 64 life history interviews he conducted with *nisei* resettling from the concentration camps in Chicago starting in March 1943. He was inducted into the military and later spent 23 years as a clinical social worker for the Veterans Administration in New York. He was married to world-famous dancer Yuriko and fathered two children. Upon his retirement in 1973, he became a world traveler. He became ill while on an International March for Peace in the USSR in 1988 and died shortly after returning to the U.S., on September 25, 1988.

Kikuchi's written contributions to Japanese American history are threefold. His autobiographical narrative titled "A Young American with a Japanese Face," published anonymously in Louis Adamic's book *From Many Lands,* is a classic exposition of the dilemma of identity prevalent among so many *nisei* of the time. His diaries from Tanforan were later published and provide a rare look at life in an "assembly center." Finally, edited versions of 15 of his life histories are included in the book *The Salvage,* providing a glimpse at the varying attitudes held by *nisei* leaving camp for the Midwest and East. Kikuchi's other life histories, personal papers and diaries remain valuable and largely unexplored by scholars.

For further reading, see "A Young American with a Japanese Face." In Louis Adamic. *From Many Lands.* New York: Harper & Brothers, 1939. 183–234; Charles Kikuchi. *The Kikuchi Diary: Chronicle from an American Concentration Camp.* John Modell, ed. and introd. Urbana: University of Illinois Press, 1973 and "Through the JERS Looking Glass: A Personal View From Within." In Ichioka, Yuji, ed. *Views from Within: The Japanese American Evacuation and Resettlement Study.* Los Angeles: Asian American Studies Center, University of California, Los Angeles, 1989. 179–95; and Dorothy S. Thomas. *The Salvage.* Berkeley: University of California Press, 1952.

King, Jean Sadako (1925–) Politician, lieutenant governor of Hawaii. Jean Sadako King was the first woman to serve in Hawaii's second highest political office.

Born in Honolulu, Hawaii, King attended local public schools before graduating from Sacred Hearts High School, where she was editor of the school annual and class valedictorian. She received master's degrees from both the University of Hawaii and from New York University.

King began her career in politics working as a researcher and speech writer for the Speaker of the House and as a Senate staff member before serving as campaign coordinator for PATSY MINK in her bid for the Democratic Party's presidential nomination in 1972. From 1972, King served a two-year term as state representative for the state of Hawaii, and then a four-year term as state senator from 1974 to 1978. In 1978, she was appointed lieutenant governor under Governor GEORGE ARIYOSHI, an office she held until 1982.

For further reading, see Patsy Sumie Saiki. *Japanese Women in Hawaii: The First 100 Years*. Honolulu: Kisaku, Inc., 1985.

TRACY ENDO

King Kalakaua's visit   In an effort to promote friendship between the two countries and to try to get the Japanese to permit labor emigration, Hawaii's King Kalakaua paid a visit to Japan in 1881. Although the King didn't tell the Japanese of his trip, they learned of his imminent arrival in February 1881 and prepared a grand welcome for him when his ship arrived in Japan on March 4. After meeting with Japanese officials through official channels, the king secretly visited the emperor on March 10 to propose a marriage between his niece Princess Kaiulani and Prince Sadamaro Yamashina. He left Japan on May 15 and eventually received word the following year that the emperor turned down his marriage proposal. He was also unsuccessful in securing labor immigration to Hawaii at that time. His visit did, however, further good relations between the two countries. Japan eventually agreed to allow labor migration to Hawaii beginning in 1885.

For further reading, see United Japanese Society of Hawaii. *History of Japanese in Hawaii*. James H. Okahata, ed. Honolulu: United Japanese Society of Hawaii, 1971.

Kishi Kichimatsu (1880s–1956)   Farmer, founder of Kishi colony in Terry, Texas. In the early years of the 20th century, Texas became the home of several fairly large rice-farming ventures run by Japanese immigrants. One of the largest of these ventures was that of Kichimatsu Kishi in Terry, halfway between Beaumont and Orange. His father was a businessman/banker and Kichimatsu attended Hitotsubashi University with the idea of following in his father's footsteps. With the advent of the Russo-Japanese War in 1904, he enlisted in the quartermaster corps and served in Manchuria in 1904–05. After the war, he thought about remaining in Manchuria to farm, but was dissuaded by the lawlessness of the land. He returned to Japan and worked restively for a sewer pipe firm.

In 1906, he decided to go to the United States to grow rice. Quickly gaining the backing of some of his father's business contacts, he and a friend traveled to the U.S. to scout locations. They found California too hilly and went on to visit south Louisiana, the Carolinas and Mississippi before settling on the flat land of Orange County, Texas, just across the Louisiana border. He signed an agreement to purchase 3,500 acres in Terry for $72,000 in September 1907, becoming the largest Japanese rice farmer in the state. Sixteen Japanese men arrived later in the year to work as tenant farmers or laborers; there were about 40 colonists within a year. The first harvest of 1908 netted a $47,000 gross from 1,600 cultivated acres. The colony did well for the next eight or nine years, growing all the while. In 1916, the dredging of a nearby ship channel brought salt water into the irrigation system of the Kishi colony, destroying two rice crops during the boom years of World War I. However, this event turned out to be a blessing in disguise since the resultant diversification of the colony into TRUCK FARMING, ranching and oil production sustained the colony when the bottom fell out of the rice market in 1924. Thus, when many other large rice farming operations were going under, the Kishi venture continued to prosper and grow. Kishi also became involved in local affairs, building a church and a school and working with various youth groups.

This modern, bustling farm community's demise was sudden and unexpected. The combination of disease, freezes and the Great Depression found Kishi overextended. Unable to pay his debts, he lost all of his land to creditors in September 1931. He and his wife Fuji became dependent on son Taro. A frail and sickly youth, Taro had grown up to attend Texas A & M, becoming a star halfback there. Taro's job with a Japanese shipping company allowed the Kishis to start up again on a much smaller scale a few years later. They worked through World War II and lived out their life as farmers. Fuji died in 1951 and Kichimatsu in 1956. Although the town of Terry no longer exists, a state historical marker dedicated on October 3, 1982, marks the site of the Kishi colony.

For further reading, see Thomas K. Walls. *The Japanese Texans*. San Antonio: Institute of Texan Cultures, 1987.

Kitabayashi Tomo (1887–1945)   Community activist, spy. Born in Osaka, Tomo Kitabayashi arrived in Los Angeles in 1919 as a PICTURE BRIDE. She married a gardener named Yoshisaburo Kitabayashi and worked as a seamstress. She soon began community involvement with the Women's Christian Temperance Union and the Seventh-Day Adventist church as well as with the Japanese International Labor Defense branch, the Japanese Proletarian Artists' League and, under the influence of

Okinawan Marxist artist Yotoku Miyagi, the Communist Party. Miyagi returned to Japan in 1933 and began working for Richard Sorge, a Russian-born German Communist operating a pro-Soviet intelligence network in Tokyo. Kitabayashi returned to Japan in 1937 at the request of Miyagi. She was arrested in 1941 in connection with Sorge and sentenced to five years in prison. She died soon after her parole in February 1945.

For further reading, see Karl G. Yoneda. *Ganbatte: Sixty-Year Struggle of a Kibei Worker.* Los Angeles: Asian American Studies Center, University of California, Los Angeles, 1983.

Kitagawa, Daisuke (d. 1970) Episcopal clergyman, author. Best known as the author of such books as *Issei and Nisei: The Internment Years* (1967) and *Race Relations and the Christian Mission*, Daisuke Kitagawa was also a well-known religious leader. Born in Taihoku, he came to the U.S. to attend Chicago Divinity School and to get a degree from the General Theological Seminary in New York. He went on to work in the state of Washington prior to the war. He continued his work through the forced removal and incarceration and eventually ended up at TULE LAKE "RELOCATION CENTER." Considered to be part of the "pro-American" faction there, he resettled in Minnesota soon after the "disloyals" were moved to Tule Lake. He became the field secretary for the Federated Council of Churches Commission of Japanese American RESETTLEMENT there in 1943. Later, he worked for the Council of Churches from 1956, serving in its Secretariat of Racial and Ethnic Relations from 1960–62. He was working for the World Council of Churches in Geneva at the time of his death in 1970 at age 59.

For further reading: Daisuke Kitagawa. *Issei and Nisei: The Internment Years.* New York: Seabury Press, 1967 is an autobiographical account of his experience during World War II.

[Also used to compile this entry was "Episcopal Clergyman, Author Dies in Geneva." *New York Nichibei* 9 Apr. 1970: 1.]

Kitano, Harry H. L. (1926–) Scholar. Harry H. L. Kitano is a pioneering scholar in Japanese American studies. A native of San Francisco, he grew up there and in the CONCENTRATION CAMP at TOPAZ, Utah. The senior class president and co-captain of the Topaz High School football team, Kitano returned to California after the war and attended the University of California, Berkeley, getting his B.A. (1948), M.S.W. (1951) and Ph.D. (1958) degrees there. He is a professor of social welfare and sociology at UCLA and was named to an endowed chair in Japanese American studies there in 1990. He has also twice served as the director of the UCLA Asian American Studies Center.

Kitano has written many major works on Asian Americans, focusing on housing patterns, race relations, INTERRACIAL MARRIAGE, alcoholism and many other topics. His book *Japanese Americans: Evolution of a Sub-Culture* remains a standard work on Japanese Americans and is soon to see its third edition.

For further reading: Kitano's major works having to do with Japanese Americans or Asian Americans include "Housing of Japanese-Americans in the San Francisco Bay Area." In Glazer, Nathan, and Davis McEntire, eds. *Studies in Housing and Minority Groups.* Berkeley: University of California Press, 1960. 178–97; "Japanese-American Crime and Delinquency." *Journal of Psychology* 66.2 (1967): 253–63; *Japanese Americans: The Evolution of a Subculture.* 1969. 2nd edition. Englewood Cliffs, N.J.: Prentice-Hall, Inc., 1976; "Japanese-American Mental Illness." In *Changing Perspectives in Mental Illness.* Stanley Plog and Robert Edgerton, eds. New York: Holt, Rinehart, and Winston, Inc., 1969; "Interracial Marriage: A Picture of the Japanese Americans." *Journal of Social Issues* 29.2 (Spring 1973): 67–81 (with Akemi Kikumura); "The Model Minorities." *Journal of Social Issues* 29.2 (Spring 1973): 1–9 (with Stanley Sue); "Stereotypes as a Measure of Success." *Journal of Social Issues* 29.2 (Spring 1973): 83–98 (with Stanley Sue); *Race Relations.* Englewood Cliffs, N.J.: Prentice Hall, Inc., 1974; "Japanese Americans: The Development of a Middleman Minority." *Pacific Historical Review* 43.4 (Nov. 1974): 500–19; "The Japanese American Family." In Mindel, Charles H., and Robert W. Habenstein, eds. *Ethnic Families in America: Patterns and Variations.* New York: Elsevier Scientific Publishing Co., Inc., 1976. 41–60 (with Akemi Kikumura); "Asian Americans and the Media." In Berry, Gordon L., and Claudia Mitchell-Kernan, eds. *Television and the Socialization of the Minority Child.* New York: Academic Press, 1982. 151–86 (with Patti Iiyama); "Asian-American Interracial Marriage." *Journal of Marriage and the Family* 46.1 (Feb. 1984): 179–90 (with others); "Japanese-American Drinking Patterns." In Bennett, Linda A., and Genevieve M. Ames. *The American Experience with Alcohol: Contrasting Cultural Perspectives.* New York: Plenum Publishing Corporation, 1985. 335–57 (with others); and *Asian Americans: Emerging Minorities.* Englewood Cliffs, N.J.: Prentice Hall, 1988 (with Roger Daniels). He also served as co-editor (with Roger Daniels and Sandra C. Taylor) of the anthology *Japanese Americans: From Relocation to Redress.* Salt Lake City: University of Utah Press, 1986. Revised edition. Seattle: University of Washington Press, 1991, which he also contributed to. See also "An Interview with Harry Kitano." In Tachiki, Amy et al., eds. *Roots: An Asian American Reader.* Los Angeles: Asian American Studies Center, University of California, Los Angeles, 1971. 83–88.

Kochi, Shinsei Paul (1889–1980) Gardener, writer, OKINAWAN community leader. Shinsei Paul Kochi was born on February 27, 1889, in Nakijin, Kunigashiragun, Okinawa PREFECTURE. He was an only son, and his father died when he was five. He graduated from the prefectural agricultural school in March 1912 and worked as a primary school teacher and village clerk. He became involved in left-wing political activity and left the country for South America with a comrade to learn and study and to escape the increasing political repression. He left Japan on September 2, 1917, and landed in Mexico. Having decided to head to the United States, he underwent tremendous hardships in crossing the Mexican desert before reaching the border, then worked on a Japanese cotton farm prior to crossing at Calexico in March 1918. For the next few years, he was a migrant laborer and "buranketto-boi" ("blanket boy"; see BUR-ANKE KATSUGI) in California. He eventually settled in Los Angeles and became a gardener; he was active in the SOUTHERN CALIFORNIA GARDENERS FEDERATION, writing for its bulletin until the outbreak of World War II. He also wrote for other publications, including *Ryukyu,* the journal of the Okinawan KENJINKAI in the 1930s.

With the coming of the war, he and all other Japanese Americans living on the West Coast were removed to inland CONCENTRATION CAMPS. He was sent to HEART MOUNTAIN. Like many other leftists in camp, he believed in aiding the United States in the fight against facism despite the wrong of the mass incarceration. He left camp at the first opportunity for work on the outside; in May 1943, he took a job with the Omaha Sheep Company in Nebraska. His written accounts of life on the outside were published in the New York newspaper the *Hokubei Jiji* and encouraged other ISSEI to leave camp. He moved to New York in October 1943 and began to work as a civilian employee with the Office of Strategic Services in April 1944, eventually serving on the Indian and Chinese fronts doing translation and propaganda work. While in Asia, he saw the devastation of the war firsthand and became active in organizing relief activities upon his return to the states. He wrote of conditions in Okinawa for newspapers and printed a pamphlet coauthored by Shingi Nakamura upon his return in January 1946. Kochi was among those who started the Committee for the Mobilization of Okinawan Relief in April 1946 in New York and the Okinawan Relief League in Los Angeles in June 1946. For the next five years, he published the newsletter *Kyuen News (Relief News)* while serving as head of the Information Bureau of the Relief League. He made his living as a gardener.

In his later life, he became a consultant and advisor in the formation of the PIONEER CENTER in Los Angeles and was an organizer of the Japanese Welfare Rights Organization and served as its first president. He also served as coeditor of the book *Hokubei Okinawajin Shi (History of the Okinawans in North America;* it was later translated and published in English in 1988) but passed away on December 20, 1980, just prior to its publication.

For further reading: Paul S. Kochi. *Imin No Aiwa (An Immigrant's Sorrowful Tale).* Ben Kobashigawa, trans. Los Angeles: Privately printed, 1978 is a reprinting of a 1937–38 article in which he describes his tortuous journey to America. Kochi is also profiled in Okinawa Club of America, comp. *History of the Okinawans in North America.* Ben Kobashigawa, trans. Los Angeles: UCLA Asian American Studies Center and The Okinawa Club of America, 1988, the work whose Japanese version he coedited.

Kochiyama, Yuri (1921–   )   Human rights advocate and political activist. On an episode of the "Phil Donohue" talk show, a gray-haired Asian American woman boldly stood up from the audience, looked into the camera, and called upon the show's millions of viewers to fight racism wherever it exists in the world. That person was Yuri Kochiyama, a lifelong political activist and internationally recognized human rights advocate. Born in San Pedro, California, where her father operated a fish market, she was incarcerated during World War II at Santa Anita "ASSEMBLY CENTER" and JEROME, Arkansas. It was the CONCENTRATION CAMP experience that forced her to begin to examine racism and injustice in society. After the war, Kochiyama moved to New York City with her husband, Bill Kochiyama, a veteran of the 442ND REGIMENTAL COMBAT TEAM. In the 1950s, she became involved in the Civil Rights movement alongside leaders of the National Association for the Advancement of Colored People (NAACP) and was also inspired by the successful Cuban Revolution.

A turning point in Kochiyama's activist career came in 1960 when she, Bill and her six children moved to Harlem, the predominantly African American neighborhood of New York City. To the politically-minded Kochiyama, moving to Harlem in the midst of the Civil Rights movement was a dream come true. She became active in educational struggles through the Harlem Parents Committee and sent three of her children to the Harlem Freedom School. Kochiyama also worked on community campaigns for better living and working conditions. In 1963, she was arrested along with her oldest son Billy and 600 others while demonstrating for construction jobs for African Americans and Puerto Ricans. While in court, she had the opportunity to meet Malcolm X. This was the beginning of a close and ongoing relationship Kochiyama would have with the revolutionary African American leader. She joined Malcolm's Organization for Afro American Unity in March of 1964 and attended his liberation school. No longer content with Martin Luther King's vision of civil rights, Kochiyama became an adherent to Malcolm's internationalist concept of human rights and his brand of black revolutionary nationalism based on the principles of self-determination, self-reliance and self-defense. In June 1964, she organized a meeting between Malcolm X and the

HIBAKUSHA (atomic bomb survivors). Kochiyama was with Malcolm X at the time of his assassination.

After Malcolm's death, Kochiyama carried on his vision by demonstrating against the Vietnam War, supporting the fight for ethnic studies and seeking solidarity with African Americans, Chicanos and Native Americans. In December 1990, she was selected to be a keynote speaker at a conference in New York City celebrating the life and legacy of Malcolm X. Yuri and Bill still reside in Harlem, where she remains active in movements to achieve Puerto Rican independence, free political prisoners and stop anti-Asian violence. Adding to over five decades of struggle for justice, Yuri Kochiyama remains an inspiration to future generations of activists.

For further reading, see Yuri Kochiyama (as told to Sasha Hohri), "Because Movement Work Is Contagious," *Gidra 1990:* 6, 10 and *Fishmerchant's Daughter: An Oral History.* New York: Community Documentation Workshops, St. Mark's Church in the Bowery, 1981. See also Joann Faung Jean Lee. *Asian American Experiences in the United States: Oral Histories of First to Fourth Generation Americans from China, the Philippines, Japan, India, the Pacific Islands, Vietnam and Cambodia.* Jefferson, N.C.: McFarland & Company, 1991, which contains autobiographical reflections by Kochiyama.

SCOTT KURASHIGE

Koda Keisaburo (1882–1964) Rice farmer. Known as the "rice king," Keisaburo Koda was also the recipient of the largest settlement resulting from the JAPANESE AMERICAN EVACUATION CLAIMS ACT. He was born in Fukushima, the son of a samurai turned rice miller. After serving as a guide for a man from Tokyo who told him about America, he jumped at the opportunity to come to the U.S. in 1906 to join his brother. He moved up and down the West Coast as a migrant farm worker, a laundry worker, an oil driller and a hotel worker. After saving some money, he opened three laundries but soon recognized the limitations of this sort of venture. He then moved to Southern California and began a wholesale fish distribution company with the Tajima brothers and amassed a fortune during the World War I years. With the end of the war, harder times came and he gladly accepted an offer of $250,000 for his business. He then moved to Sacramento to try growing rice and share-cropped 1,400 acres and rented 1,800 more. When the initial crop was destroyed by geese and bad weather, he lost $140,000. After working as a laborer for a time, he tried again and, with the backing of a Jewish friend, grew 2,000 acres of rice in Woodland. From 1924–27, he made $20,000–$30,000 a year in various rice-growing ventures. By 1932, he was growing over 10,000 acres of crops. He pioneered the method of using airplanes to plant rice, built his own mill and established the Kokuho brand. By the eve of World War II, he was worth several million dollars.

Keisaburo Koda. *Tama & Edward Koda Collection, Japanese American National Museum Photographic & Moving Image Archive*

Unfortunately for Koda, money couldn't ensure his freedom after 1942. He spent the war years in the GRANADA, Colorado, CONCENTRATION CAMP. Upon returning to his farm, he found that two-thirds of his land and his mill had been sold off by "friends" without his knowledge. His farming equipment was gone and his hogs had "died." He placed his faith in the legal system to get his land back and, with the help of his sons, he began farming again. The Koda farm began to market a new rice; Kokuho Rose became an instant success and restored his wealth. Upon retirement, Koda helped form a Japanese American insurance company, persuaded the Bank of Tokyo to open a branch in California, and worked on the campaign to gain naturalization rights for the ISSEI. Seventeen years after the passage of the Evacuation Claims Act and over 20 years after being forcibly removed from their land, the Koda family was awarded $362,500 in 1965, a sum hardly sufficient to cover the litigation costs. Ironically, Keisaburo Koda died while visiting Japan in 1964 and didn't live to see a dime of the settlement.

For further reading, see Japanese American Curriculum Project. *Japanese American Journey: The Story of a People.* San Mateo, CA: Japanese American Curriculum Project, 1985.

koden Money offered to the family of the deceased by mourners at a Japanese American funeral. The custom of bringing *koden* ("incense money") to funerals originated in Japan and has been adapted by Japanese immigrants. The money is generally used by the family of the deceased to help defray funeral expenses and acts as a form of death insurance within the community. Though originally a Buddhist or Shinto custom, the practice of bringing *koden* has been adopted by Christian and Buddhist Japanese Americans alike. Money in the form of a check or cash is generally brought to the funeral in a plain envelope with the donor's name and address on the outside. The amount of the *koden* is determined by the donor's relationship to the deceased; if the deceased or members of his/her family have given *koden* at previous funerals for persons in the donor's family, that amount provides a guide as to how much ought to be given. In the weeks after the funeral, it is customary for the family of the deceased to send a thank you card and a small gift (such as a book of stamps) to all who have given *koden*.

Koike, Kyo (1878–1947) Photographer, poet, physician. Dr. Kyo Koike was a pioneering photographer in Seattle and one of the founders of the SEATTLE CAMERA CLUB. A medical doctor by training, he came from Shimane PREFECTURE and arrived in Seattle in around 1916. Though he opened a medical practice in the Empire Hotel Building on Main Street, he soon became known for his interest in literature, translating some 30 volumes of Japanese works into English and also helping to establish the Rainier Ginsha, a HAIKU society. It is said that Koike also collected wildflowers and stamps and was an avid hiker.

He is best known today, however, for his art photography. Specializing in natural landscapes, he was a pictorialist in the sense that he expressed a personal artistic vision through his photos, but did not concern himself much with the darkroom manipulations that pictorialists of the time usually indulged in. In much the same way that Japanese American *haiku* poets and other artists adapted Japanese art forms to American subjects, Koike's work shows the influence of Japanese elements in their composition and lighting. He viewed his photography in much the same way as his poetry, writing that "my . . . idea is based on Oriental tendency much influenced by Japanese literature and pictures to which I am accustomed. I understand Japanese poems, and I think pictorial photography should not be an imitation of paintings, but it should contain a feeling similar to that of poems." He was first exhibited publicly in 1920 at the Frederick & Nelson department store's Pictorial Salon and won his first award with an honorable mention in a *Photo-Era Magazine* contest for March 1922.

In 1923, he joined with a group of around 40 other Japanese amateur photographers to form the Seattle Camera Club. Though it lasted only six years, club members submitted hundreds of prints to photography competitions and attained worldwide recognition. Koike edited the club's twice-monthly newsletter, titled *Notan* (Light and Shade). After the demise of the club in 1929, he wrote extensively on photography in English throughout the 1930s, continuing to advance the notion that photographic art was enhanced by the infusion of other cultural perspectives and decrying the prejudice that ISSEI photographers and artists faced. Forcibly removed with all other Japanese Americans on the West Coast in 1942, he served as a camp doctor at MINIDOKA and returned to Seattle after the war. He passed away soon thereafter on March 31, 1947.

For further reading, see Robert D. Monroe. "Light and Shade: Pictorial Photography in Seattle, 1920–1940, and the Seattle Camera Club." In Tsutakawa, Mayumi, and Alan Chong Lau, eds. *Turning Shadows into Light: Art and Culture of the Northwest's Early Asian/Pacific Community*. Seattle: Young Pine Press, 1982. 8–32 and Carol Zabilski. "Dr. Kyo Koike, 1878–1947: Physician, Poet, Photographer." *Pacific Northwest Quarterly* 68.2 (Apr. 1977): 72–79.

Kondo Masaharu (1877–1948) Fisheries expert and entrepreneur. Born in Kyoto, Japan, in 1877, Kondo attended Tokyo Teikoku Daigaku (Tokyo Imperial University) where he majored in agricultural sciences. That curriculum included fisheries and oceanography, which was Kondo's area of specialty. After graduation he taught at the Imperial Fisheries Institute where he was eventually appointed to the school's board of commissioners. While serving in that capacity he was selected to undertake a tour of the world to study fishery technologies.

Arriving in Los Angeles in 1908, Kondo visited both San Pedro and San Diego and quickly realized the relatively untapped potential of the Southern California fisheries. Completing his tour, he returned to Japan in 1910 where he resumed his teaching position. At the same time he sought and obtained the financial backing necessary to establish a fishing company in San Diego that was eventually expanded to Baja, California.

Returning to the United States in 1912, Kondo organized the MK Fishing Company. He then applied for and received an exclusive fishing concession from the government of Mexico for Turtle Bay (Bahia Tortugas), Baja California. Through the operation at Turtle Bay, Kondo was responsible for bringing the first contract Japanese fishermen to Mexico. With them came fishing technologies that were unknown to the region and that would eventually become the basis for the fisheries of the west coast of Mexico.

In November 1916, Kondo was awarded the Sixth Order of Merit of the Order of the Sacred Treasure for his efforts on behalf of the personnel of the cruiser *Asama*, which was grounded at Turtle Bay in January 1915. He thus became the first Japanese American to receive a decoration from the Japanese government.

In 1920, Kondo expanded his operation to include tuna fishing and brought 70 Japanese contract tuna fishermen to San Diego. These Japanese fishermen introduced native techniques that facilitated the development of what was to become a major regional industry. Among the innovations introduced by Kondo's men and later adopted by the Italians, Portuguese and others was the long, flexible and amazingly strong bamboo pole. Other contributions that came to the fleet as a direct result of Kondo's operation were: fishing two and later three men to a single line to allow the taking of larger fish; the development of specialized tuna lures known as "squids" or feathered "jigs"; chumming bait to create feeding frenzies in the schools of tuna; the use of the first fully refrigerated tuna boats on the Pacific coast; and the use of long-range radio to track the fish.

In 1931, beset by the great depression and the expropriation of his canning operation by the Mexican government, Kondo returned to Japan to seek new funding. Unable to raise the necessary capital, he remained in Japan. He died in Tokyo in 1948.

For further reading, see Manchester E. Boddy. *Japanese in America*. Los Angeles: Privately printed, 1921 and Donald H. Estes. "Kondo Masaharu and the Best of All Fishermen." *Journal of San Diego History* 23.3 (1977): 1–19.

DONALD H. ESTES

Tommy Kono. *Tommy Kono Collection, Japanese American National Museum Photographic & Moving Image Archive*

Konno, Ford (1933–) Before 1952, no Japanese American had ever won an Olympic gold medal. However, at the 1952 Summer Games in Helsinki, three Japanese Americans brought home golds. Along with champions Tommy Kono and Yoshinobu Oyakawa, Ford Konno won gold medals in both 1,500-meter freestyle swimming and the 800-meter freestyle relay. Born in Hawaii and coached by Yoshito Sagawa at the Nuuanu YMCA in Honolulu, Konno became an NCAA champion swimmer while attending Ohio State University. Konno's Olympic achievements came despite the fact that he suffered from a sinus ailment that severely curtailed his training for most of the year. In the 1,500-meter race, Konno shattered the Olympic record by 42 seconds. Ironically, the top three finishers in the race were of Japanese descent—Shiro Hashizume of Japan and Tetsuo Okamoto of Brazil finished second and third respectively. Konno just missed winning a third gold medal in the 400-meter freestyle, falling one stroke behind Jean Boiteux of France.

Konno went on to compete in the 1956 Olympics, winning a silver medal in the 4 × 200 meter freestyle relay. In that same year, he married fellow Olympic swimmer Evelyn Kawamoto. The couple divorced in 1988. Konno still lives in Honolulu where he works in the insurance business and is semi-retired.

SCOTT KURASHIGE

[Used to compile this entry: "Ford Konno Wins 1500-Meter Race at Olympics; Nisei Win Four Gold Medals at Helsinki." *Pacific Citizen* 9 Aug. 1952: 6 and Ken Misumi. "Watch This 'Ford' Go By!" *Pacific Citizen* 19 Dec. 1952: 32 and Takeshi Nakayama. "Swimmer Konno Led Historic Sweep in 1952." *Rafu Shimpo*, 28 July 1992: 1–2.]

Kono, Tamio "Tommy" (1930–) Olympic champion Tommy Kono is probably the greatest Japanese American athlete ever and served as a hero and role model for NISEI and SANSEI youth growing up in the '50s and early '60s. The youngest of four sons born to

SACRAMENTO ISSEI cannery worker parents, his childhood was distinguished by severe asthma, which caused him to miss a third of his school days. Incarcerated in TULE LAKE "RELOCATION CENTER" with the rest of his family, the clean air of the area reportedly helped to clear up his asthma. It was in camp that he first took up weight lifting, something which he quickly recognized he had an aptitude for. After the war, he returned to Sacramento where he entered Sacramento Junior College and began to compete as a serious lifter. By 1950 he was one of the country's top lifters.

In 1951, he was drafted into the U.S. Army. He continued to compete while in the army and served as a cook. His athletic prowess kept him from having to see active duty in the Korean War. He hooked up with a Honolulu-based Korean American physician named Dr. Richard W. You who had just coached a team of young Hawaiian weight lifters to a national team championship. Under You's guidance, Kono reduced to 148 pounds to compete in the lightweight division and won his first national title in 1952. He went on to win Olympic gold medals in 1952 and 1956 and a silver in 1960, each medal coming in a different weight class. His ability to vary his weight by 40 or 50 pounds without losing strength allowed his coaches to utilize him in the division he was most needed in, usually against the toughest opponents. Competing in divisions ranging from lightweight (148 pounds) to middle heavyweight (198 pounds), the 5′6″ Kono set 26 world records and won six world championships. Kono also won the Mr. World title in 1954 and Mr. Universe titles in 1955 and 1957. In 1982, Kono was named the greatest weight lifter of all time by the official publication of the International Weightlifting Federation.

Throughout his reign as America's best weight lifter, Kono was portrayed as a quiet, humble, mild mannered sort who had overcome adversity through sheer determination and hard work to rise to the top. This image was very much in line with the way the entire *nisei* generation was portrayed in the mass media during this period and Kono was in some ways a symbol for the "MODEL MINORITY" Japanese Americans had seemed to become by this time. To Japanese Americans, especially those in Hawaii where he has made his home since 1955, Kono was a hero and role model who symbolized the unlimited possibilities that seemed to be opening up to Japanese Americans at the time.

After his retirement from active competition in 1965, he became a coach and adviser, holding the distinction of coaching Olympic teams for three different countries (Mexico, 1968; West Germany, 1972; United States, 1976). He currently works for the Honolulu Department of Parks and Recreation and coaches young weight lifters on a voluntary basis.

For further reading, see Chris Baker. "Tommy Kono: He Won Gold Medals in 1952 and 1956 for the Country That Put Him in Internment Camp During World War II." *Los Angeles Times* 25 July 1984: VIII–12 and Steve Lum. "Tommy Kono: The Greatest of All Time." *The Hawaii Herald* 15 Nov. 1985: 7.

[The following were used to compile this entry: "Atlas Comes to Life." *Time* 75 (27 June 1960): 69–70; Day, A. Grove. "America's Mightiest Little Man." *Coronet* 48.3 (July 1960): 106–10; and Saito, John, Jr. "Olympic Legend." *Rafu Shimpo* 25 July 1991: 1–2.]

Korematsu v. United States   Landmark Supreme Court case concerning the mass "evacuation" of Japanese Americans during World War II. Fred Toyosaburo Korematsu was an unlikely candidate to become the subject of a test case to challenge the mass forced removal of Japanese Americans from the West Coast in 1942. Employed as a welder in Oakland, he had lost his job when the Boiler Makers Union expelled all of its Japanese American members after the attack on Pearl Harbor.

On March 18, 1942, and March 24, 1942, Korematsu had plastic surgery on his nose and eyes in an attempt to disguise his racial identity. His plan was to marry his Italian American fiancée, Ida Boitano, in Arizona and then move to the Midwest. By having plastic surgery, Korematsu hoped to blend in with European Americans and be allowed to live peacefully with Boitano. According to an FBI agent who questioned him, Korematsu "feared violence should anyone discover that he, a Japanese, was married to an American girl."

On March 27, 1942, the army issued Public Proclamation Number 4, which terminated the "VOLUNTARY" RESETTLEMENT program. Those of Japanese ancestry living in Military Area Number 1 (established with Public Proclamation Number 1 on March 2, 1942) were no longer permitted to change residence without permission from the army. At the time, Korematsu was still trying to earn enough money to marry his fiancée and move east.

On May 9, 1942, Korematsu's parents and three brothers reported to the Tanforan "ASSEMBLY CENTER"; he did not join them. Three weeks later, on May 30, 1942, Korematsu was arrested in San Leandro, California, for violating the "exclusion order." When questioned about his identity, Korematsu gave the police a draft registration card with the name "Clyde Sarah" on it and attempted to claim he was of Spanish-Hawaiian origin. His story quickly disintegrated when the poorly altered draft card proved to be fake.

A few days later, while in the San Francisco County Jail, Northern California AMERICAN CIVIL LIBERTIES UNION (ACLU) lawyer Earnest Besig visited Korematsu and two other NISEI looking for a test case volunteer (Korematsu was one of nine Japanese Americans picked up in the San Francisco area). While the other two opted to plead guilty for violating Public Law 503 (the ordinance that provided for criminal penalties for violations of the military "exclusion order"), Korematsu remained firm in his conviction that what the government did was wrong. In fact, he revealed to the FBI that he intended to fight his case even before he was approached by the ACLU. "I figured I'd lived here all my life and I was going to stay here," he stated later.

Korematsu's case was assigned by Besig to ACLU attorney WAYNE COLLINS. On June 20, 1942, Collins along with Clarence Rust, filed a demurrer (a plea that says even if the opponent's facts are correct, they still do not support his case) that charged the government with 69 violations of Korematsu's rights. On August 31, 1942, the opening round of the case was held before Judge Martin I. Welsh, a member of the infamous NATIVE SONS OF THE GOLDEN WEST. Judge Welsh denied Collins's demurrer and did not acknowledge any of the charges that were filed. On September 8, 1942, Korematsu's case went to trial, absent the vacationing Welsh. Judge Adolphus F. St. Sure replaced him and heard testimony from both sides. St. Sure was impressed with Korematsu, but found him guilty as charged and sentenced him to five years' probation. Collins announced that he was going to appeal and then covered the $2,500 bail that the judge set. Technically, Korematsu was free to go pending his appeal. A military police officer, however, drew a gun on him and insisted that he had orders to take Korematsu into custody. After a few tense moments of legal haggling, the M.P. eventually escorted Korematsu to Tanforan where he rejoined his family.

On February 19, 1943, the one year anniversary of EXECUTIVE ORDER 9066, Korematsu, along with fellow resistors Min Yasui (see YASUI V. U.S.) and Gordon Hirabayashi (see HIRABAYASHI V. U.S.), appeared before the court of appeals. Wayne Collins repeated the charges that were dismissed in the lower court and even added a few more. An appeal to the Supreme Court was filed.

In the meantime, Justice Department lawyers, confident of victory, became eager to rush the three cases to the Supreme Court. Motivating them was the fear that the Mitsuye Endo (see ENDO, EX PARTE) case could reach the Supreme Court at the same time. The strength of the Endo case, they feared, had the possibility of hampering almost sure victory in the other three cases. To speed up the process of getting the case to the Supreme Court, the Justice Department lawyers asked the court of appeals to use a procedure called "certification," a somewhat obscure procedure whereby the Supreme Court would answer constitutional questions raised by the appellate. In Korematsu's case, they were questioned on whether the sentence of probation was an appealable judgment—a technicality at best.

Korematsu appeared before the Supreme Court with Hirabayashi and Yasui on May 10, 1943. Since Korematsu's case could only deal with the question of his sentence, it was clear that his case would be delayed in the long run. On June 1, 1943, it was judged "final and acceptable" and sent back to the court of appeals for ruling on the "exclusion order." His case would not reach the Supreme Court again for another year. The Hirabayashi and Yasui cases were decided at this time in favor of the government.

Before Korematsu's case reached the Supreme Court, a historic debate occurred between the Justice and War Departments over the validity of JOHN L. DEWITT's *Final Report*, the crucial document that was used to uphold the curfew order convictions of Hirabayashi and Yasui. EDWARD ENNIS and John Burling of the Justice Department found that DeWitt's argument of "MILITARY NECESSITY" in justifying the mass removal was false. Specifically, DeWitt's claims of ship-to-shore signaling and espionage activity among Japanese Americans were contradicted by both J. EDGAR HOOVER of the FBI and the Federal Communications Commission (FCC). With this information, Burling attempted to amend the government's brief to the Supreme Court by adding a footnote at the end of it stating the Justice Department's disagreement with DeWitt's *Final Report*. After intense debate with the War Department, an extremely diluted version of the footnote appeared on the government's brief. Instead of condemning DeWitt's *Final Report,* it stated that military judgment was based on "attitudes, opinions, and slight experience, rather than a conclusion based upon objectively ascertainable facts." The statement was compromised and along with it, Ennis and Burling: both signed the government brief despite their objections to the suppression of evidence.

On October 11, 1944, with Allied victory in the war almost assured and with the defeat of Hirabayashi and Yasui over a year old, Korematsu's case returned to the Supreme Court along with Endo's. At issue was Korematsu's violation of "Exclusion Order" Number 34, which prohibited those of Japanese descent from being inside of Military Zone Number 1, which was established with DeWitt's Public Proclamation Number 1. Even though Hirabayashi was convicted of the same offense, the Supreme Court did not rule in his case on the "exclusion order," choosing to rule only on his violation of the curfew law. Korematsu's case was to be the landmark decision on exclusion.

On December 18, 1944, the Supreme Court issued its opinion on the Korematsu case. By a 6 to 3 margin, the justices upheld Korematsu's conviction and with it, DeWitt's allegations in his *Final Report*. In his dissent, Justice Murphy stated: "This exclusion of 'all persons of

Japanese ancestry, both alien and NON-ALIEN,' from the Pacific Coast area on a plea of military necessity in the absence of martial law ought not to be approved. Such exclusions goes over 'the very brink of constitutional power' and falls into the ugly abyss of racism." (See CORAM NOBIS CASES.)

For further reading, see Peter Irons. *Justice at War: The Story of the Japanese American Internment Cases.* New York: Oxford University Press, 1983. Transcripts of the various cases can be found in Peter Irons, ed. *Justice Delayed: The Record of the Japanese American Internment Cases.* Middletown, Conn.: Wesleyan University Press, 1989.   GLEN KITAYAMA

kotonk   Derogatory term for Japanese Americans from the mainland, especially vis-à-vis "BUDDHAHEADS," a term for Japanese Americans from Hawaii. The terms were popularized during World War II when NISEI from Hawaii and the mainland met—and mostly clashed—for the first time in large numbers while in military training as members of the 442ND REGIMENTAL COMBAT TEAM. The term reportedly is derived from the sound coconuts with no meat inside make when they hit the ground, the same sound Hawaiian Japanese Americans jokingly alleged mainlanders made when knocked on their heads. The term is still used today to refer to mainland Japanese Americans and still has a slight pejorative connotation.

For further reading, see Harry H. L. Kitano. *Japanese Americans: The Evolution of a Subculture.* 1969. 2nd Edition. Englewood Cliffs, N.J.: Prentice-Hall, Inc., 1976 and Mary Wakayama and Arnold Hiura. "Two Camps with One Heart: Mainland-Hawaii." *Hawaii Herald,* 2 Dec. 1983.

Kunihisa, Masutaro   Merchant. Masutaro Kunihisa was one of the few ISSEI in Hawaii who became moderately wealthy entrepreneurs. While working as a plantation carpenter for $12.50 a month, he opened a store for plantation laborers in Wahiawa, Oahu, in 1919. He named the store Castner's, after an American army officer who had been involved in building the army's Schofield Barracks. With the help of his wife and 10 children, Castner's flourished, growing to become a large five-and-dime store and eventually, a chain of low-priced department stores.

For further reading, see Lawrence H. Fuchs. *Hawaii Pono: A Social History.* New York: Harcourt, Brace and World, 1961.

Kunitomo, George Tadao (1893–1967)   Scholar. One of the prominent ISSEI in Japan at the outbreak of World War II, George Tadao Kunitomo was born in Fukuoka PREFECTURE in 1893 and studied at Waseda University and Aoyama Gakuin. After a stint in the Japanese army in Siberia from 1918 to 1920, he came to the U.S. He graduated from Oberlin College in 1923 and moved to Hawaii where he became the first Japanese-language instructor at Honolulu's McKinley High.

In 1929, Kunitomo joined the University of Hawaii faculty. He took a leave of absence in 1935 to return to Japan and went back for good in 1937 after receiving a grant to do research at Tokyo Imperial University. He formally resigned from the University of Hawaii in 1939 to become director of a group sponsored by the Foreign Ministry assisting foreign students in Japan.

Kunitomo's wartime writings are not entirely sympathetic to the land in which he spent 14 years. In the preface to a 1943 history of Hawaii which he translated, he notes that "(i)t is only a matter of time before the Hawaiian Islands, a part of the Greater East Asia Co-Prosperity Sphere, make a new start under the Japanese flag." He goes on to say that this new rule will benefit the native Hawaiians: "As Hawaiians are of the Asian race, the Hawaiian Islands will soon, with Japan's victory in the Greater East Asian War, shed America's immoral rule of money and return to East Asia." He also saw this happening with the aid of Japanese Americans: "Over 150,000 compatriots are now scattered throughout the Hawaiian Islands, detained under the enemy's fierce vigilance. But the sufferings of our compatriots will dissolve the moment that the Rising Sun flag unfurls high over the Hawaiian archipelago."

With the end of the war, Kunitomo got a job with the American occupation and went on to teach American literature at Aoyama University in Tokyo. He even returned to Hawaii on a visit in 1966.

For further reading, see John Stephan. *Hawaii under the Rising Sun: Japan's Plans for Conquest after Pearl Harbor.* Honolulu: University of Hawaii Press, 1984.

[Quotes are from Stephan 84.]

Kuniyoshi, Yasuo (1889–1953)   ISSEI artist Yasuo Kuniyoshi became a highly respected and beloved figure in the New York art world from the 1920s until his death. His paintings have been regularly exhibited since 1922 and are of continually escalating value to art collectors in the United States and Japan. He was also a photographer and art teacher in New York for many years.

Born in Okayama PREFECTURE on September 1, 1889, Kuniyoshi, an only child, decided early on that he either wanted to enter military school or come to America. Beguiled by romantic notions of America and discouraged from the military by his father, he journeyed to America at the age of 16 in 1906. Arriving in Seattle knowing little English and having no money or friends, his romantic notions of America were quickly disabused. Like many an *issei* before and after him, he took on odd jobs to support himself. In the spring of 1907, he moved to the sunnier climate of Los Angeles, and attended, at the suggestion of a public school teacher, the Los Angeles School of Art and Design for three years while working as a hotel bellboy and picking fruit during the summers. After briefly considering going into the aviation field ("I soon gave that up too, because I was scared," he wrote in a 1940 autobiographical account), he decided to go to New York to pursue a career in art. Arriving in the fall of 1910, he was initially supported by a friend of his father's who provided him with room and board in exchange for cleaning a studio. For the next few years, he studied and absorbed the happenings in the art world—cubism and 19th-century impressionism were then the rage—while battling loneliness. Enrolling at the Art Students League in September 1916 was the key event of his early life. Here he found friendship and a direction in art and life. He studied there until 1920, the last three years on scholarship. At the Art Students League, he met and befriended fellow young artists including Katherine Schmidt, whom he would marry in 1919. He also gained the sponsorship of Hamilton Easter Field, an arts patron and champion of modern painting who provided him with living and working space in Brooklyn and use of a studio in Ogunquit, Maine, in the summers.

By 1922, he had had his first one-man exhibition at the prestigious Daniel Gallery in New York City and had been featured in a "Younger Artists Series" monograph published by William M. Fisher. He would exhibit almost yearly at the Daniel Gallery in addition to being featured in many other exhibitions. Though selling many paintings by this time, he supported himself until 1925 as a photographer, gaining a reputation as one of the best at photographing works of art. Trips to Europe followed in 1925 and 1928, and he moved to Woodstock, New York, in 1929. In 1931, he returned to Japan for the first time to visit his ailing father and for a one-man exhibit organized by the National Museum of Modern Art. He and Katherine Schmidt were divorced in 1932; in 1935 he married Sara Mazo and toured Mexico and the American Southwest that summer. Beginning in 1933, he took a teaching post at the Art Students League, a post he would occupy until his death. He continued to exhibit and teach throughout the '30s and '40s, and was active in artists' organizations such as the Artists Equity Association and the Artists Congress. He was also vocal and active in denouncing Japanese military aggression during the war years, producing a series of striking war posters for the Office of War Intelligence. In 1944, he took first prize in the prestigious annual exhibition of American painting at the Carnegie Institute of Art in Pittsburgh. A major retrospective exhibition of his work was mounted at the Whitney Museum of American Art in 1948—the first one-man exhibition of a living American artist ever presented there. He died of stomach cancer on May 14, 1953, in New York City while still at an artistic peak.

Though he came to America at a very young age with no previous artistic training in Japan, and though his paintings do not depict identifiably Japanese or Japanese American experiences, many critics have cited his work as having a blend of Japanese and Western stylistic elements. His 1920s work, often featuring images of cows or babies or other images of Americana, was regarded by many as humorous. In the '30s, he became known for his paintings of women and began to explore American landscapes. His later work became increasingly complex and abstract, often featuring images of clowns and masks. Posthumous exhibitions of his work continue, including another major retrospective put together by the University of Texas in 1975 that toured the United States and Japan and a 1989–90 retrospective in Japan. Recently, Japanese collectors have begun to take a great interest in Kuniyoshi's work, dramatically driving up prices. One of his oils, *Mr. Ace,* recently sold for $3 million.

[Basic biographical data for this entry came from the chronology in the exhibit catalog *Yasuo Kuniyoshi 1889–1953: A Retrospective Exhibition* published by the University of Texas at Austin in 1975. Two essays from that volume, "Introduction" by Donald Goodall (pp. 17–45) and "Yasuo Kuniyoshi: A Tribute" by Alexander Brook (pp. 51–55) provided additional information. Also useful was the monograph *Yasuo Kuniyoshi* (New York: American Artists Group, 1945) and the Whitney Museum of Art exhibit catalog *Yasuo Kuniyoshi* (New York: Macmillan, 1948). The former contains a reprint of an autobiographical essay by Kuniyoshi from 1940 from which the quote was taken while the second contains a useful essay by Lloyd Goodrich. Former Kuniyoshi student Josephine Sakurai's moving tribute "Kuniyoshi: artist, American" appeared in *Scene* 5.5 (Sept. 1953): 13–16. The recent information on the value of his work is taken from a newspaper article (Lewis, Jo Ann. "The Disappearing Art of Yasuo Kuniyoshi." *Washington Post* 19 June 1990: C1, 3).]

Kurihara, Joseph Yoshisuke (b. 1895)

Businessman, CONCENTRATION CAMP protestor. A successful businessman and World War I veteran, Joe Kurihara renounced his American citizenship in anger at the country which he felt had betrayed him. Born on the island of Kauai in 1895, he moved with his family to Honolulu at the age of two. He attended a Catholic high school there before coming to California at the age of 20. He moved to Michigan in 1917 to escape the racism of California. While in Michigan, he enlisted in the U.S. Army and served abroad during World War I before being honorably discharged. He returned to California to go to college, graduating with a degree in accounting. He went on to become a successful businessman and fishing boat navigator. While on a fishing expedition, the Japanese invaded Pearl Harbor and his life was changed dramatically.

Joe Kurihara. *William Hohri Collection, Japanese American National Museum Photographic & Moving Image Archive*

He quit his job and tried to offer his services to the war effort only to be repeatedly rebuffed because of his ancestry. Upon hearing news of the plans for the mass removal of all West Coast Japanese Americans, Kurihara went to the JAPANESE AMERICAN CITIZENS LEAGUE expecting to join in protest activity. When he saw that the group planned to cooperate with the government, he broke all ties with the league. While incarcerated at MANZANAR, he decided that if the government was going to treat him like the enemy, he was going to behave like one and be a "Jap 100 percent." He led a pro-Japanese group called the Black Dragons at Manzanar. In the wake of the Fred Tayama beating and the MANZANAR INCIDENT, he was one of those removed from the camp and taken to a prison camp in MOAB, Utah. After being transferred to TULE LAKE "SEGREGATION CENTER," he renounced his citizenship and sailed for Japan, an embittered man, but one determined to "help rebuild Japan politically and economically." "The American Democracy with which I was infused in my childhood is still unshaken," he wrote. "My life is dedicated to Japan with Democracy my goal."

According to NATIONAL COUNCIL FOR JAPANESE AMERICAN REDRESS leader William Hohri, Kurihara should be considered a hero for leading the resistance in camp and for being "the father of the REDRESS MOVEMENT." According to Hohri, Kurihara wrote a letter dated June 1, 1943, from a prison camp in LEUPP, Arizona proposing that the U.S. government pay internees the token sum of $5,000 damages. However, according to labor leader KARL YONEDA, Kurihara threatened to kill Yoneda and others perceived to be "pro-American" at Manzanar. Yoneda further alleges that Kurihara meant that the U.S. would be made to redress internees after Japan had won the war. Regardless of one's view of Kurihara, his actions must be viewed in the context of the betrayal he felt when the country he had gone to war for put him in a concentration camp on account of his ancestry.

For further reading, see Dorothy S. Thomas, and Richard Nishimoto. *The Spoilage.* Berkeley: University of California Press, 1946, 1969, which includes an appendix devoted to Kurihara's words. See also William Hohri "Joe Kurihara: Pioneer for Redress." *New York Nichibei* 14 Aug. 1980: 1 and Karl G. Yoneda. *Ganbatte: Sixty-Year Struggle of a Kibei Worker.* Los Angeles: Asian American Studies Center, University of California, Los Angeles, 1983.

[The following were also used to compile this entry: Hohri, William. "Joe Kurihara: Pioneer for Redress." *New York Nichibei* 14 Aug. 1980: 1; "Letters to the Editor [William Hohri]." *New York Nichibei* 23 Oct. 1980: 1.]

Kurokawa, Colbert Naoya (1890–1978) Public servant. Among the many ISSEI who played a role in the Japanese war effort, few have had a more interesting odyssey than Colbert Kurokawa. He was born in Chiba PREFECTURE in 1890 and, rebelling from his prearranged future as a Buddhist priest, hopped on a ship at age 15 and arrived in Hawaii with 50 cents in his pocket. In his 30 years in Hawaii, Kurokawa enjoyed a high-profile career in community service. He attended Honolulu's Mid-Pacific Institute on scholarship and went on to graduate from Dickenson College in Pennsylvania in 1922. Having converted to Christianity, he was a preacher for a time and a local YMCA official. He was also one of the first members of Honolulu's Lions Club. Additionally, he acted as an interpreter for the local Japanese consul general and later for visiting Japanese naval officials. He returned to Japan in 1935 with his family to become a lecturer in English at Doshisha University until 1939.

At this point, his life assumes an air of mystery. According to his obituary in the *Honolulu Star-Bulletin* (July 19, 1978), he was picked up two days after Pearl Harbor and "given the choice of internment or surrendering his passport." It goes on to say that after two years, Kurokawa found work in a "pharmaceutical research bureau in Tokyo." A biographical sketch printed by the Japan Christian Association and the Kyoto Revival Church for Kurokawa's funeral notes that he was arrested for being "pro-American" and "interned until the end of the war." In a speech delivered at Doshisha on May 27, 1966, he stated "The day after the Pearl Harbor Incident, my American Passport was taken away, and I became interned; most of my publications were confiscated and burnt . . ." He went on to say: "It is not for me to enumerate the persecution, agony, and difficulties of the following three years. They horrify me even now to recall."

In 1942–43, an advisory group called the South Seas Economic Research Center put out in-house reports to the Japanese Imperial Navy on the so-called Greater East Asia Co-Prosperity Sphere. In April 1943, a report from this body called "What Should Be Done with Hawaii?" appeared. Of course the author of the piece, under the name of Kurokawa Naoya, was none other than Colbert Kurokawa. In this report, Kurokawa calls Hawaii under American rule "a cancer to international peace" and suggests that Japan ought to restore the Hawaiian monarchy and turn Hawaii into the "Switzerland of the Pacific." What were the circumstances under which Kurokawa came to write this report? What really happened to him in Japan? The answers are unclear.

Kurokawa returned to Hawaii in 1951 and resumed his interest in community service, working in the insurance business and dabbling in journalism, civic organizations and religion. He returned to Japan in 1958, devoting himself to a religious sect. He died there in 1978. His *Star-Bulletin* obituary bore the headline: "Colbert Kurokawa, Fighter for Global Peace, Dies at 87."
For further reading, see John Stephan. *Hawaii under the Rising Sun: Japan's Plans for Conquest after Pearl Harbor*. Honolulu: University of Hawaii Press, 1984.

Kuroki, Ben (1918–   )   War hero. During and immediately after World War II, NISEI Ben Kuroki's story was often told alongside that of the 442ND REGIMENTAL COMBAT TEAM as an example of *nisei* loyalty and patriotism. Born in Nebraska, the son of a potato farmer, Kuroki was a truck driver at the time Pearl Harbor was attacked. He immediately tried to enlist in the armed forces but was repeatedly turned down until he was accepted by the Army Air Corps. In time, he became a gunner on a Liberator bomber operating out of England and North Africa. After taking part in 25 missions, including the Ploesti attack (a famous attack on the Ploesti oilfields of Rumania), he was eligible to go home. He stayed on for another five missions. After returning to Nebraska and a hero's welcome, he asked for duty in the Pacific. At first he was refused, but he was eventually accepted and flew 28 more B-29 missions over Japan. He emerged from the war a famous man. His biography,

Boy from Nebraska: The Story of Ben Kuroki by Ralph G. Martin, was published in 1946.
For further reading, see Ralph G. Martin. *Boy from Nebraska*. New York: Harper & Row Brothers, 1946, Kuroki's biography. See also Bill Hosokawa. *Nisei: The Quiet Americans*. New York: William Morrow & Co., 1969; Bradford Smith. *Americans from Japan*. Philadelphia: J. B. Lippincott Co., 1948; and Robert A. Wilson, and Bill Hosokawa. *East to America: A History of the Japanese in the United States*. New York: Morrow, 1980.

L

labor contractors   The labor contracting system (also known as the "boss system") flourished among the ISSEI in the United States from around 1891 to 1907. Most laborers arriving on these shores did so without much knowledge of either the English language or how to get a job. Labor contractors or bosses stepped in as middlemen who often housed and fed the workers and assigned them work in exchange for an often hefty portion of their wages. This arrangement also suited employers who were spared the trouble of hiring and firing and could deal only with the contractors. The contractors most often worked with the railroad, agricultural, mining, lumber and fishing industries. During its peak period, the labor contracting system extended throughout the western United States and Alaska.

Railroad labor contracting took place on the largest scale with some companies, such as the ORIENTAL TRADING COMPANY, employing upwards of 3,000 workers. At its peak in 1906, some 13,000 to 14,000 workers labored under railroad contractors. Labor contractors also played large roles in agriculture, canning and mining, among other fields. Labor contractors often came from the ranks of the DEKASEGI-SHOSEI or student laborers and were men who knew more English and had more knowledge of the American labor system than their average countrymen. They parleyed these skills into sometimes considerable fortunes through the labor of their workers. The big railroad contractors made money by taking a commission off the top of their laborers' wages (ranging from 5 to 10 percent) and by assessing numerous other fees for dubious services. These ranged from "office fees" to "hospital fees" to exorbitant room-and-board charges. They often made additional money through such schemes as selling expensive consumer goods, operating gambling halls or bringing in prostitutes on paydays. Although no doubt resentful of the money made by contractors, the typical laborer was so dependent on the contractors that little dissent broke out—the main manner in which protest was expressed was by workers simply quitting to join another contractor offering higher wages. Agricultural contractors operated on a much smaller scale and made much less money, but employed similar methods. The ending of labor immigration to the U.S. in 1907 effectively ended the era of the labor contractor. (See KYUTARO ABIKO, SHINZABURO BAN and MASAJIRO FURUYA.)

For further reading, see Yuji Ichioka. *The Issei: The World of the First Generation Japanese Immigrants, 1885–1924.* New York: The Free Press, 1988 and Hisashi Tsurutani. *America Bound: The Japanese and Opening of the American West.* Betsey Scheiner, trans. Tokyo: Japan Times, Inc., 1989.

land companies Corporate entities formed for the purpose of purchasing land. Such companies were often utilized as a way for ISSEI farmers to get around the provisions of the ALIEN LAND LAWS, especially in the northern and central areas of California. Typically, the company stock was issued to white friends or to citizen NISEI so as to meet the requirement of the land law, but the land was farmed by an *issei*. In 1926, there were over 400 land companies with *issei* roots; 142 of them had ties to the San Francisco–based legal firm Calden and Eliot, the legal counsel of the JAPANESE ASSOCIATION of America.

For further reading, see Yuji Ichioka. *The Issei: The World of the First Generation Japanese Immigrants, 1885–1924.* New York: The Free Press, 1988.

Lazo, Ralph (1924–1992) CONCENTRATION CAMP protestor. Ralph Lazo's symbolic act of accompanying Japanese American friends to America's World War II concentration camps was a powerful expression of solidarity with oppressed people everywhere.

Born in 1924 in Los Angeles, California, to parents of Spanish and Irish ancestry, Ralph Lazo grew up and attended grammar school, junior high and a few years of high school in the heart of Los Angeles. However, Lazo graduated from MANZANAR High School in the middle of the Owens Valley high desert of eastern California amidst friends, but surrounded by barbed wire.

Lazo entered Manzanar at the age of 17 by "passing" as Japanese American in May of 1942, and remained there as did 110,000 other Japanese American prisoners of the United States government until 1944, at which time he was drafted into the army. He is believed to be the only non-NIKKEI without a Japanese American spouse to voluntarily enter camp during World War II. He served in the military until 1946 in the Philippines and was awarded the Bronze Star for his heroic efforts in battle.

After the war, Lazo graduated from UCLA and received his master's degree from California State University, Northridge, before pursuing a career in teaching.

Throughout his life, Lazo remained a loyal friend and supporter of those Japanese Americans he was interned with, and continued to spread word of the injustices of the Second World War through speeches at schools and before other groups. Lazo was a staunch supporter of the REDRESS MOVEMENT and an early monetary contributor in the early stages of the fight.

Lazo passed away on New Year's Day, 1992, almost 50 years after his voluntary internment. When asked "Why did you go? You didn't have to go," Lazo would simply reply: "None of us should have had to go."

TRACY ENDO

Leupp Isolation Center WAR RELOCATION AUTHORITY (WRA) prison camp. In addition to administering 10 "relocation centers" for Japanese Americans forcibly removed from the West Coast during World War II, the WRA also administered a pair of prison camps for citizen "troublemakers" from the other 10 camps. The first was established at Moab, Utah, on a former Civilian Conservation Corps camp in the Utah desert on December 10, 1942. The WRA prison was later moved from Moab to a former boarding school on the Navaho reservation in Arizona called Leupp (pronounced "Loop") on April 27, 1943.

Prisoners at Moab and Leupp were often dispatched there on the flimsiest of evidence—uncorroborated testimony by informants that the accused were not allowed to respond to, supposed participation in actions such as the MANZANAR INCIDENT, or the whim of the project director or other camp administrators. Often prisoners were not granted hearings and not even allowed to say goodbye to their families before being taken away. The prisoners in these camps were separated from their families, provided with nothing to do, and burdened with sentences of indefinite and perhaps infinite length. Surrounded by barbed wire and guard towers, 150 military police guarded 80 prisoners. There were other abuses as well—Harry Ueno, the accused in the MANZANAR beating of Fred Tayama which triggered the above cited incident, reported being transferred from Moab to Leupp (an 11-hour drive) prone in a five-by-six-foot box, with only a single small hole to provide air, with four others. Francis S. Frederick, chief of internal security at Moab and Leupp, commented "how in hell can you Americanize the Japs when Gestapo methods are used in sending them to Leupp . . ." Partly because of the careful documentation of abuses of the prison system kept by Frederick and reported by Leupp director Paul G. Robertson, WRA officials made plans to close down the prison for fear of adverse publicity on October 12, 1943; this action was delayed for two months because of the unrest at TULE LAKE "SEGREGATION CENTER", and Leupp was closed on December 2. Plans were made to reopen Leupp in order to transfer 175 Tule Lake STOCKADE inmates there in April 1944, but canceled three months later.

For further reading, see Richard Drinnon. *Keeper of Concentration Camps: Dillon S. Myer and American Racism.* Berkeley: University of California Press, 1987; Michi Weglyn. *Years of Infamy: The Untold Story of America's Concentration Camps.* New York: William Morrow & Co., 1976.

[Frederick quote cited by Drinnon, p. 102.]

Little Tokyo One of several terms used to refer to the Japanese American area in large cities across the United States. In recent years, the term has come to be used mostly to refer to the Japanese American section of Los Angeles. Among the other terms used generically to refer to urban areas inhabited principally by Japanese Americans are Japanese Town, J-Town and Nihonmachi (literally "Japanese Town").

Since the 1910s, Los Angeles has been the home of more Japanese Americans than any other city in the mainland United States. It was at around this time that Little Tokyo came into existence as a cluster of homes and businesses in the downtown area just south of Chinatown, around the corner of First and San Pedro Streets. By the 1920s, Little Tokyo was the residential, business and cultural hub of the larger Southern California Japanese American community. By 1930, there were 35,000 Japanese Americans in Los Angeles, the majority of whom lived within a three-mile radius of First and San Pedro. The residential community extended as far south as Tenth Street and east into the Boyle Heights area. Produce and flower markets either started by ISSEI or in which *issei* played a major role were located in and around Little Tokyo and served the many Japanese American farmers in the greater Southern California area. Many other businesses between Jackson and Third Streets—restaurants, shops, gambling and entertainment establishments, etc.—served the farmers and local residents as well. Little Tokyo also housed the major churches/temples, newspapers and other cultural institutions that bound the larger Japanese American community together.

This bustling community was reduced to a ghost town by EXECUTIVE ORDER 9066 and the mass removal of all Japanese Americans during World War II. As the Japanese Americans went out, African Americans, lured from the South by the promise of jobs in the defense industry, came in, and the Little Tokyo area took on an African American flavor during the war. Once Japanese Americans were allowed to return to the coast in 1945, Little Tokyo began to slowly rebuild. Though Little Tokyo did revive after the war, there would be major differ-

ences. For one thing, the community now was much smaller, bound by First and Third Streets on the north and south and Los Angeles and Alameda Streets on the west and east. Secondly, although Little Tokyo remained the cultural hub of the larger community, other suburban residential communities (see GARDENA, for example) drew away nearly all the residential population, except the poor and the elderly, and much of the business as well. By the 1960s, the community was a shell of its former self.

The 1970s saw the dramatic REDEVELOPMENT of Little Tokyo, spurred by city planners and the influx of business and money from Japan. In a pattern repeated in J-Towns all over the country, the influx of Japanese businesses proved a mixed blessing at best. On the one hand, they improved the physical appearance and infrastructure of the community; on the other, they were often insensitive to the Japanese American history of the community, sometimes callously evicting and displacing long-time residents and small businesspeople. In many places, anti-redevelopment groups emerged to challenge the nature of development in the J-Towns. Little Tokyo today has almost no residential population except for tenants of subsidized senior citizen housing. Shopping areas, hotels and restaurants are largely geared towards Japanese tourists and businessmen, though a community center and a new Japanese American museum have brought many suburban Japanese Americans back to Little Tokyo.

Though most people today refer to it as "Little Tokyo" or "J-Town," the Los Angeles Japanese American area has had many names over the years. The *issei* used the term "Rafu," the Japanese reading of the Chinese characters for Los Angeles by the earlier Chinese immigrants. Many Japanese American institutions in Los Angeles—such as the RAFU SHIMPO newspaper—still carry the *issei* term. For NISEI coming of age in the 1930s, "Li'l Tokio" was used in most English-language print accounts; this term continued to be used until the 1950s when it was gradually replaced by "Little Tokyo." The term Sho Tokyo—literally "Little Tokyo"—is used by many Japanese speakers today.

There is no existing book length academic or popular history of Los Angeles's Little Tokyo. There are, however, many works which deal with some aspect of Japanese life in Los Angeles. Among the early general studies of Japanese Americans in Los Angeles are Fumiko Fukuoka. "Mutual Life and Aid among the Japanese in Southern California with Special Reference to Los Angeles." Thesis, University of Southern California, 1937; Young Il Kim. "A Study of Some Changes in the Los Angeles Japanese Settlement since 1950 with an Analysis of Selected Communities." Thesis, California State University, Los Angeles, 1963; William M. Mason, and John A. McKinstry. *The Japanese of Los Angeles.* Los Angeles: Los Angeles County

Museum, 1969; Chotoku Toyama. "The Japanese Community in Los Angeles." Thesis, Columbia University, 1926; Gretchen Long Tuthill. "A Study of the Japanese in the City of Los Angeles." Thesis, University of Southern California, 1924; and Kiyoshi Uono. "The Factors Affecting the Geographical Aggregation and Dispersion of the Japanese Residents in the City of Los Angeles." Thesis, University of Southern California, 1927.

Recent studies which focus on a particular aspect of Japanese American life in Los Angeles include Brian Masaru Hayashi. "'For the Sake of Our Japanese Brethren': Assimilation, Nationalism, and Protestantism among the Japanese of Los Angeles, 1895–1942." Diss., University of California, Los Angeles, 1990; Ford H. Kuramoto. *A History of the Shonien, 1914–1972: An Account of a Program of Institutional Care of Japanese Children in Los Angeles.* San Francisco: R & E Research Associates, 1976; John Modell. *The Economics and Politics of Racial Accommodation: The Japanese of Los Angeles 1900–1942.* Chicago: University of Illinois Press, 1977; Nobuya Tsuchida. "Japanese Gardeners in Southern California, 1900–1941." In Cheng, Lucie, and Edna Bonacich, eds. *Labor Immigration Under Capitalism: Asian Workers in the United States Before World War II.* Berkeley: University of California Press, 1984. 435–69; and Noritaka Yagasaki. "Ethnic Cooperativism and Immigrant Agriculture: A Study of Japanese Floriculture and Truck Farming in California." Diss., University of California, Berkeley, 1982.

Works which look at Japanese Americans in Los Angeles through an Asian American movement lens include Susie H. Ling. "The Mountain Movers: Asian American Women's Movement, Los Angeles, 1968–1976." Thesis, University of California, Los Angeles, 1984 and "The Mountain Movers: Asian American Women's Movement in Los Angeles." *Amerasia Journal* 15.1 (1989): 51–67; Little Tokyo Anti-Eviction Task Force. "Redevelopment in Los Angeles' Little Tokyo." In Gee, Emma, ed. *Counterpoint: Perspectives on Asian America.* Los Angeles: Asian American Studies Center, University of California, 1976. 327–33; Jim H. Matsuoka. "Little Tokyo, Searching the Past and Analyzing the Future." In Tachiki, Amy et al., eds. *Roots: An Asian American Reader.* Los Angeles: Asian American Studies Center, University of California, 1971. 322–34.

Hisaye Yamamoto. "A Day in Little Tokyo." *Amerasia Journal* 13.2 (1986–87): 21–28 is a short story that follows a Japanese American farm family as they take a day trip into Little Tokyo in the 1930s. Jon H. Shirota. *Pineapple White.* Los Angeles: Ohara Publications, Inc., 1972 is a novel set in the Little Tokyo of 1949, providing a rare look at life in resettlement era L.A. Lastly, Ichiro Mike Murase. *Little Tokyo: One Hundred Years in Pictures.* Art direction and design by Michael Nakayama. Los Angeles: Visual Communications/Asian American Studies Central, Inc., 1983 is a book of photographs with introductory text that gives an overview of the history of Los Angeles's Little Tokyo.

Little Tokyo Anti-Eviction Task Force   See RE-DEVELOPMENT.

Livingston   See YAMATO COLONY (CALIF.).

Lost Battalion   Texas Battalion rescued by the 442ND REGIMENTAL COMBAT TEAM. In October 1944, 275 members of the 141st Infantry Regiment from Texas were trapped. The members of the so-called "Lost Battalion" had overextended themselves and were surrounded by German troops in eastern France; after three days they had used up their food, water and medical supplies, and looked to be in a hopeless situation. The 442nd Regimental Combat Team had just liberated Bruyères, Belmont and Biffontaine and, after just two days of rest, were ordered to rescue the trapped battalion. Two other battalions from the same regiment had tried to rescue them earlier, but had been driven back. Fighting the mountain and forest terrain, shells bursting from trees and the enemy, progress was slow. After two days, less than a mile had been gained. Getting word that the "Lost Battalion" was in dire straits, the NISEI troops covered the rest of the distance on the third day, encountering furious opposition. The first advance patrol reached the Texans on the fourth day (October 30); the "Lost Battalion" had been saved.

But at what cost? In order to rescue the 211 men of the "Lost Battalion," the 442nd had suffered 800 casualties. There were grumblings that *nisei* lives had been sacrificed in order to save those of white Americans. Senator DANIEL KEN INOUYE, a participant in the rescue, has said, "I am absolutely certain that all of us were well aware that we were being used for the rescue because we were expendable."

For further reading, see Masayo Duus. *Unlikely Liberators: The Men of the 100th and the 442nd.* Honolulu: University of Hawaii Press, 1987; Bradford Smith. *Americans from Japan.* Philadelphia: J. B. Lippincott Co., 1948; and Roland Kotani. *The Japanese in Hawaii: A Century of Struggle.* Honolulu: Hochi, Ltd., 1985.

[Quote from Kotani]

loyalty questions   Two questions designed to test the loyalty of alien and citizen Japanese Americans in the World War II CONCENTRATION CAMPS. Positive answers to the questions numbered 27 and 28 on each of two questionnaires prepared by the War Department and WAR RELOCATION AUTHORITY (WRA), made male NISEI of draft age eligible for service in the army. "Yes" replies on the WRA form made aliens and citizens of Japanese descent who were held in the camps eligible for release and RESETTLEMENT in areas outside of the West Coast exclusion zones.

The mood of the American public, particularly during the early years of World War II, was hostile to all things

Japanese, including Japanese Americans held in the camps. By early 1943, the War Department came to realize that many of these were loyal Americans, and that they would like to have an opportunity to prove it. This belief was encouraged by the JAPANESE AMERICAN CITIZENS LEAGUE (JACL), which petitioned President Franklin D. Roosevelt, in November, 1942, for a reinstatement of the draft for citizens of Japanese descent. On January 28, 1943, Secretary of War HENRY L. STIMSON announced the formation of a special all-Nisei, 5,000-man combat unit (see 442ND REGIMENTAL COMBAT TEAM). Army teams were scheduled to visit the 10 WRA-administered camps beginning on February 6, to register all male *nisei* of draft age. Each had to complete a special questionnaire, designed to test their "loyalty" and willingness to serve in the armed forces.

About the same time, DILLON MYER, national director of the WRA, became convinced that life in the camps was bad, and that all "loyal" internees should have complete freedom restored. He saw as the solution a program which would segregate the internees by loyalty, with those acknowledged as "loyal" to the United States allowed to leave the centers for resettlement. Those designated as "disloyal" would remain confined in a camp set aside for this purpose.

Myer was quick to realize how a mass registration of the type proposed by the War Department would benefit his own agency's resettlement policy. His suggestion for a joint operation was readily accepted by the army. Unfortunately, the registration program was poorly planned and executed. As a result, a plan that was intended to be humanitarian brought continued incarceration and worse to many otherwise "loyal" Japanese Americans in the camps.

The two government agencies believed that the planned registration would be approved as an important step toward ending discrimination against persons of Japanese descent. Acceptance of military service would prove their essential loyalty to the country at large. Every male citizen of military service age was to fill out a questionnaire which, in addition to calling for basic personal information, would contain two loyalty questions. Number 27 on the army form stated: "Are you willing to serve in the armed forces of the United States on combat duty, wherever ordered?" and Number 28 asked: "Will you swear unqualified allegiance to the United States of America and faithfully defend the United States from any and all attack by foreign or domestic forces, and foreswear any form of allegiance to the Japanese Emperor, or any other foreign government, power, or organization?"

The War Department form for male *nisei* bore the Selective Service System seal and was entitled "Statement of United States Citizens of Japanese Ancestry." The WRA form was entitled "Application for Leave Clearance." The form titles, wording of questions, and the fact that the army questionnaire was voluntary while the WRA's was compulsory led to misunderstanding and trouble.

Question 28 proved offensive to the *nisei,* who considered themselves loyal American citizens. A "yes" answer implied that they once had an allegiance to Japan and its emperor. The War Department realized that there might also be resentment in asking *nisei* to volunteer for an army that had only recently rejected them on suspicion of disloyalty. Consequently, army teams made serious efforts to prepare for *nisei* questions and to calm their fears.

Since the WRA's purpose was the eventual release of all "loyal" internees, it required that all adults in the centers comply with its registration program. The agency formulated questionnaires similar to those prepared by the War Department for draft-age male *nisei,* all ISSEI and female *nisei.* Male *nisei* were required to answer an abbreviated version of the WRA form. The loyalty questions, Numbers 27 and 28, were altered to read, respectively:

If the opportunity presents itself and you are found qualified, would you be willing to volunteer for the Army Nurse Corps or the WAAC [Women's Army Auxiliary Corp]?

Will you swear unqualified allegiance to the United States of America and forswear any form of allegiance or obedience to the Japanese Emperor, or any other foreign government, power, or organization?

Unlike the Army, the WRA failed to prepare camp residents by educating them about the coming registration. In its optimism, the agency failed to see the problems that would arise. It did not even bother to change a question that asked alien males if they would serve in women's army organizations. Both *issei* and *nisei* residents were seriously disturbed by the program. For the alien group, denied American citizenship by law, a "yes" to Question 28 would make them stateless, while a "no" could lead to deportation. They had also come to think of the centers as safe havens from the hostile Caucasian population. Consequently, compulsory "leave clearance" forms indicated they would be forced into what they believed to be dangerous outside communities. Many *nisei,* in turn, bowed to parental will, and gave negative responses to the loyalty questions. Numerous other *nisei* chose to give "no" answers as a means to protest the mass removal and detention and all that had happened since then.

The reaction against registration reached its greatest intensity at the TULE LAKE "RELOCATION CENTER." The failure of the camp administration to prepare residents, combined with its use of deception, force, arrests and threats of fines and long prison terms, led to massive resistance, refusal to register and a large number of requests for repatriation or expatriation. Of 10,843 *issei* and *nisei* in Tule Lake that were eligible to register, 4,491 either refused to register, refused to answer the loyalty questions or gave "no-no" answers to Questions 27 and 28. Of 77,842 eligible in all 10 centers, 74,588 registered. Of these, 65,312 answered Number 28 in the affirmative.

Although the mass registration was described by the WRA as one of the most turbulent periods in its history, the agency accomplished its objective of speeding resettlement from the centers. Army recruitment was also a moderate success, with over 1,200 volunteering for service from the 10 centers. Those who had answered one or both loyalty questions in the negative, or who had refused to answer, were designated as "disloyal" to the United States. During the months of September and October 1943, they were sent to the newly established TULE LAKE "SEGREGATION CENTER." For many of these, the registration program was another injustice suffered at the hands of the government.

For further reading, see Donald E. Collins. *Native American Aliens: Disloyalty and the Renunciation of Citizenship by Japanese Americans During World War II.* Westport, Conn.: Greenwood Press, 1985; Audrie Girdner, and Anne Loftis. *The Great Betrayal: The Evacuation of the Japanese-Americans during World War II.* Toronto: Macmillan, 1969; Dorothy S. Thomas, and Richard Nishimoto. *The Spoilage.* Berkeley: University of California Press, 1946, 1969; and Michi Weglyn. *Years of Infamy: The Untold Story of America's Concentration Camps.* New York: William Morrow & Co., 1976.   DONALD E. COLLINS

Ludlow Massacre The Ludlow Massacre occurred on April 20, 1914, when state militia brought in to crush striking miners in the southern Colorado coalfields opened fire on a strikers' camp, killing 21 persons, including two women and 11 children. The strike had erupted in September 1913 when the multiethnic labor force—mainly Mexican, Italian, Slavic and Greek—sought to remedy the semi-feudal conditions in these mines. As a result of the Ludlow Massacre, striking miners seeking revenge went after company property and strikebreakers. The resulting war with federal troops ended in 45 additional deaths. Eight days after the Ludlow Massacre, the nearby Forbes mining camp was attacked by 300 armed strikers who were seeking revenge for two earlier razings of the camp when occupied by strikers. Of the nine strikebreakers who were killed, four were Japanese—Kotaro Ito, Masukichi Niwa, Tetsuji Hino and

Luna, 1908. Assigned to ensure the productivity of laborers by any means necessary, the luna came to symbolize the oppressive conditions of Hawaii's sugar plantations. *R. J. Baker photograph, Hawaii State Archives*

Jobei Murakami. The strike was settled at the end of 1914.

For further reading, see Yuji Ichioka. *The Issei: The World of the First Generation Japanese Immigrants, 1885–1924.* New York: The Free Press, 1988.

luna Field supervisors on the Hawaiian sugar plantations, the *luna* were charged with exacting the most work possible from plantation laborers through any means possible, including verbal abuse or corporal punishment if necessary. As such, they acted as the intermediary between plantation management and the workers. They were responsible for getting the workers to the fields on time, making sure they worked at a satisfactory pace, recording the time they worked and maintaining control over the workers. The *luna* were usually HAOLE, though they were sometimes Portuguese or Hawaiians.

For further reading, see Roland Kotani. *The Japanese in Hawaii: A Century of Struggle.* Honolulu: Hochi, Ltd., 1985; Franklin S. Odo, and Kazuko Sinoto. *A Pictorial History of the Japanese in Hawaii, 1885–1924.* Honolulu: Bishop Museum Press, 1985; and Ronald Takaki. *Pau Hana: Plantation Life and Labor in Hawaii, 1835–1920.* Honolulu: University of Hawaii Press, 1983 for general descriptions of working conditions on the plantations.

M

McCarran-Walter Immigration and Naturalization Act Immigration statute which, among other things, granted ISSEI the right to naturalization. (See IMMIGRATION AND NATIONALITY ACT OF 1952.)

Nobu McCarthy. *Terrance Tam Soon Collection, Japanese American National Museum Photographic & Moving Image Archive*

McCarthy, Nobu (1938–) Actress Nobu McCarthy was a Hollywood star of the 1950s and a key figure in the Asian American cultural scene in the 1990s. "Discovered" by a Hollywood agent in LITTLE TOKYO, she went to audition for an extra part even though she could not speak English. While walking across the Paramount lot, she was spotted by the director and cast as the leading lady in *The Geisha Boy*, opposite Jerry Lewis and SESSUE HAYAKAWA. A string of roles followed in such movies as *Tokyo After Dark, Five Gates to Hell, Wake Me When Its Over,* and *Walk Like a Dragon*. For the most part, these were stereotypical roles as geisha girls and docile "lotus blossoms." In the 1970s and '80s, she appeared in such highly regarded films as *Farewell to Manzanar, The Karate Kid, Part II* and *The Wash* in more well-rounded roles.

Since 1989 she has been the Artistic Director of East West Players, an ASIAN AMERICAN THEATER group in Los Angeles. SUZANNE HEE/BRIAN NIIYA

McClatchy, Valentine Stuart (1857–1936) Newspaper publisher. V. S. McClatchy was one of the major figures in the ANTI-JAPANESE MOVEMENT. The son of James McClatchy, founder of the liberal *Sacramento Bee* newspaper, V. S. McClatchy served as the publisher of the newspaper until just before 1920. A prominent advocate of Japanese exclusion and on good terms with all the leaders of the various exclusionist groups, he used the *Bee* as a vehicle for anti-Japanese propaganda. After his retirement, he devoted himself to what he believed was a holy cause.

Between 1920 and 1924, he was the real leader of the JAPANESE EXCLUSION LEAGUE OF CALIFORNIA organized in September 1920, as historian ROGER DANIELS sees it. With HIRAM JOHNSON, the senior senator from California, he continuously lobbied Congress to exclude Japanese immigrants, while writing many anti-Japanese commentaries. He made JAPANESE-LANGUAGE SCHOOLS targets, arguing that their presence testified to the fact that all Japanese Americans were loyal to Japan. In March 1924, McClatchy described the Japanese before the Senate Committee on Immigration as "less assimilable and more dangerous as residents in this country than any other of the peoples ineligible under our laws . . ." He warned, "they come here specifically and professedly for the purpose of colonizing and establishing here permanently the proud Yamato race" (see "YELLOW PERIL"). Within a month, Congress passed the Immigration Act of 1924, which prohibited the entry of Japanese immigrants into America. Until his death in 1936, McClatchy remained the leader of the California Joint Immigration Committee, successor of the Exclusion League.

For further reading, see Roger Daniels. *The Politics of Prejudice: The Anti-Japanese Movement in California and the Struggle for Japanese Exclusion.* 1962. 2nd edition. Berkeley: University of California Press, 1977; and Justine B. Detwiler, ed. *Who's Who in California, 1928–1929.* San Francisco: Who's Who Publishing Company, 1929. EIICHIRO AZUMA

McCloy, John J. (1895–1989) Attorney, bureaucrat, diplomat, banker. John J. McCloy led a varied life, but to Japanese Americans, he will best be remembered as one of the government officials most responsible for their incarceration in American CONCENTRATION CAMPS during World War II. As assistant secretary of war in FRANKLIN D. ROOSEVELT's Cabinet, McCloy enjoyed great influence in decisions concerning the fate of Japanese Americans. His skill as a lawyer was a primary asset in justifying the incarceration of over 120,000 Japanese Americans.

McCloy was born in Philadelphia on March 31, 1895. He entered Amherst College in 1912 and graduated four years later with honors. After college, he entered Harvard Law School, receiving his degree in 1921. By 1929, McCloy was a partner in the Wall Street firm of Carvath, de Gersdoff, Swaine and Wood. It was his work there that attracted the attention of HENRY STIMSON, the secretary of war in Roosevelt's Cabinet, in 1940.

As assistant secretary of war, McCloy was instrumental in carrying out the government's policy of forcibly removing Japanese Americans from the West Coast. One prime example of his zeal was his role in altering JOHN L. DEWITT's *Final Report* on the removal of Japanese Americans. In the original version of the *Final Report,* DeWitt wrote that it was "impossible" to identify the "loyal" Japanese Americans from the "disloyal." Noticing that the report smacked of racism, McCloy sent the report back to be revised so that it would support the government's assertion that the mass removal and detention was based on "military necessity." In addition, all copies of the original *Final Report* were ordered to be burned, to destroy any evidence of its existence. The only record of the original report was left in KARL BENDETSON's confidential file at the Presidio in San Francisco. Clearly McCloy's skill in handling this affair was a prime reason for the Supreme Court's upholding of the wartime convictions of Fred Korematsu (see KO-REMATSU V. U.S.), Min Yasui (see YASUI V. U.S.) and Gordon Hirabayashi (see HIRABAYASHI V. U.S.).

Later in life, McCloy gained fame as president of the World Bank and as high commissioner for post-war Germany. He was an advisor to many presidents, both Republican and Democrat, from Roosevelt in 1940 to Ronald Reagan in the 1980s. McCloy was also part of the much-criticized Warren Commission that investigated the assassination of President John Kennedy. To the end, he was a staunch defender of the mass incarceration of Japanese Americans. The internment program, he would later say, was "reasonably undertaken and thoughtfully and humanely conducted." He died at the age of 93 on March 11, 1989.

For further reading, see Roger Daniels. *The Decision to Relocate the Japanese Americans.* Philadelphia: Lippincott, 1975; Peter Irons. *Justice at War: The Story of the Japanese American Internment Cases.* New York: Oxford University Press, 1983; and Michi Weglyn. *Years of Infamy: The Untold Story of America's Concentration Camps.* New York: William Morrow & Co., 1976. GLEN KITAYAMA

[Also used to compile this entry was McCloy's *New York Times* obituary, 12 Mar. 1989.]

McWilliams, Carey (1905–1980) Writer, activist, attorney, government official. Born in 1905, Carey McWilliams is remembered for many things by many people. To farm laborers, particularly Filipinos, he was the author of *Factories in the Field* (1939), a damning account of the systematic oppression of the fieldworkers. To intellectuals, he was the editor of *The Nation,* a progressive weekly magazine that covered current polit-

ical issues. But to Japanese Americans, McWilliams is best remembered as a friend and foe for his role during their World War II internment.

While a California government official in 1942, McWilliams was supportive of the internment program and even wrote an article titled "Goodbye Mr. Moto" which "explained" why, in a soon to be widely circulated phrase, all Japanese Americans looked alike: the NISEI, he said, were "Americans with Japanese faces." Of the CONCENTRATION CAMPS, he commented that they were an "accomplishment": "this may not be as exciting as bombing Japanese warships in the Coral Sea," he told *Harper's* magazine, "but it must be credited as a major feat for the Army."

To McWilliams's credit, he began to change his views after visiting the "ASSEMBLY CENTERS" at Pomona and Santa Anita—noticing the barbed wire, armed soldiers and nighttime searchlights. Still, McWilliams insisted that the centers were not concentration camps. Two years later, however, he expressed a decidedly different opinion. In his 1944 book *Prejudice: Japanese-Americans; Symbol of Racial Intolerance,* he gave the first in-depth account of how and why the mass removal and incarceration was allowed to happen.

To the very end, McWilliams was (in his own words) "an unreconstructed, unapologetic radical." His political stand in *Prejudice* was but one example of a man who oftentimes was outside of the liberal mainstream. He died in 1980.

For further reading, see Richard Drinnon. *Keeper of Concentration Camps: Dillon S. Myer and American Racism.* Berkeley: University of California Press, 1987; Alexander Saxton. "Goodbye to a Colleague: Carey McWilliams, 1905–1980." *Amerasia Journal* 7.2 (1980): v–vii; and Michi Weglyn. *Years of Infamy: The Untold Story of America's Concentration Camps.* New York: William Morrow & Co., 1976. See also Carey McWilliams. *Prejudice: Japanese-Americans; Symbol of Racial Intolerance.* Boston: Little, Brown, & Co., 1944; McWilliams also wrote *Brothers Under the Skin.* 1943. Revised edition. 1951. Boston: Little, Brown & Company, 1964, a work about various racial minority groups in the United States that has one chapter on Japanese Americans. GLEN KITAYAMA

[Also used to compile this entry: William Overand. " 'Exiled' Author Looks Back to L.A." *Los Angeles Times,* 5 July 1978: IV-1.]

"Magic" cables Declassified in 1977, the "Magic" cables were decoded communications from the Japanese government to their consular offices in the United States from December 1940 to December 1941. Their existence and contents were brought out in a May 22, 1983, *New York Times* article by Charles Mohr and in subsequent articles in the *San Francisco Chronicle* and the *Los Angeles Herald-Examiner.* The instigator of all the pub-

licity was David Lowman, an ex-government employee who used them to criticize the findings of the COMMISSION ON WARTIME RELOCATION AND INTERNMENT OF CIVILIANS (CWRIC). In the *Times* article, he stated, "Anyone reading this flow of messages during 1941 could easily conclude that thousands of resident Japanese were being organized into subversive organizations."

Further investigations by the CWRIC and by interested individuals revealed the innocuous nature of the cables and their distortion in the press accounts. The cables reveal Japanese attempts to find Japanese Americans to engage in espionage but serve only as a monument to their failure in that endeavor. As *New York Nichibei* editor Teru Kanazawa pointed out, "not one cable links direct intelligence data to a Japanese American or resident Japanese who is not a consular employee." About the press attention, she wrote, "The wartime atmosphere of secrecy, insinuation and innuendo . . . with which all three newspaper articles are imbued . . . has no rationale in this time of 'peace,' unless a quasi-war is being fought against Nikkei redress activity." Lowman also put an article in the "Opinion" section of the *Baltimore Sun* rehashing his accusations. Despite the rather obvious intent of the "Magic" cables' disclosure to discredit the REDRESS MOVEMENT, and the inconclusive nature of their contents, opponents of redress continue to cite them to this day.

For further reading, see John A. Herzig "Japanese Americans and MAGIC." *Amerasia Journal* 11.2 (Fall/Winter 1984): 47–65.

Kinzaburo Makino.   *Hawaii Hochi Collection*

[The following were also used to compile this entry: Kanazawa, Teru. "Investigation Reveals No Basis for Fear by US Govt of 1941 JA Espionage." *New York Nichibei* 16 June 1983: 1–2; ———. "More Reports Say Alleged Wartime JA Spy Activity Casts New Light on FDR's Internment Order." *New York Nichibei* 23 June 1983: 1–2; ———. "CWRIC Takes Stand on 'Magic' Cable Traffic." *New York Nichibei* 7 July 1983: 1–2; ———. "Lowman Continues Attack on Commission's Findings." *New York Nichibei* 14 July 1983: 1–2.]

Makino, Fred Kinzaburo (1877–1953)

Newspaper publisher, community leader. Fred Kinzaburo Makino was one of the leaders of the pre-war Japanese American community in Hawaii. He strove to ensure that Japanese Americans had the same rights as anybody else, through confrontation if necessary. He was born in Yokohama in 1877, the son of an English silk merchant and a Japanese woman. After working briefly as a clerk, he was sent to Hawaii by his family in an effort to reform his happy-go-lucky ways. He arrived in Hawaii in 1899 and joined his eldest brother Jo in a successful retail business venture. Fred Makino opened his own drug store in Honolulu in 1901. His store quickly became a hangout, not so much because of the merchandise he sold but because of his knowledge of the law and his fluency in the English language. His aggressive attitude made him a good spokesman for his people.

His initial claim to fame was the key role he played in the Higher Wage Association and the subsequent 1909 PLANTATION STRIKE. Disturbed by the megalomania displayed by strike leaders in the NIPPU JIJI, and disturbed by rumors that this paper was receiving a subsidy from the HAWAII SUGAR PLANTERS ASSOCIATION, Makino started the HAWAII HOCHI in 1912. His paper went on to play a key role at the start of the 1920 PLANTATION STRIKE. However, his severe criticism of Japanese Federation of Labor conduct in this strike drove his paper to the edge of bankruptcy and made him almost as unpopular among strikers as his nemesis TAKIE OKUMURA. In the '20s, Makino was the leader of the campaign to fight the restrictions levied on JAPANESE-LANGUAGE SCHOOLS in Hawaii. The *Hochi* spearheaded the drive to test these restrictions in court and to gain support for the test case among the language schools. Despite the opposition of the moderate *Nippu Jiji* and the conservative Takie Okumura, the drive was successful. When the U.S. Supreme Court decided in favor of the language schools in 1927, the *Hawaii Hochi* saw its circulation increase dramatically and became the most widely read of the Japanese papers in Hawaii. In later years, the *Hochi* defended the rights of Myles Fukunaga (see FUKUNAGA CASE) and the vigilante victims in the MASSIE CASE. Makino also rose to the defense of the language schools when Okumura called for a ban on them in 1940. He died on February 17, 1953, at the age of 75, just one year before NISEI war veterans initiated the Democratic Party takeover of Hawaii politics (see REVOLUTION OF 1954), continuing the fight for full rights that Makino had started.

For further reading, see Compilation Committee for the Publication of Kinzaburo Makino's Biography, ed. *Life of Kinzaburo Makino*. Honolulu: Hawaii Hochi, 1965, a biography of Makino in both Japanese and English with photographs. See also Roland Kotani. *The Japanese in Hawaii: A Century of Struggle*. Honolulu: Hochi, Ltd., 1985; Harry H. L. Kitano *Japanese Americans: The Evolution of a Subculture*. 1969. 2nd Edition. Englewood Cliffs, N.J.: Prentice-Hall, Inc., 1976 and Dennis M. Ogawa. *Kodomo No Tame Ni, For the Sake of the Children: The Japanese American Experience in Hawaii*. Honolulu: University Press of Hawaii, 1978.

Mako See IWAMATSU, MAKOTO.

Manjiro See NAKAHAMA, MANJIRO.

Manzanar Manzanar was the site of one of 10 CONCENTRATION CAMPS that housed Japanese Americans forcibly removed from the West Coast states during World War II. Some basic data on Manzanar is presented below in tabular form:

Official name: Manzanar Relocation Center
Location: Inyo County, California, in the Owens Valley, 225 miles north of Los Angeles
Land: Land controlled by the City of Los Angeles for its municipal water supply
Size: 6,000 acres
Climate: Desert, extreme winters and summers. Mt. Whitney and Mt. Williamson could be seen in the distance, making Manzanar one of the most scenic of camp sites
Origin of camp population: Mostly from Los Angeles County (8,828)
Via "assembly centers": Manzanar began as an "assembly center"; see below
Rural/Urban: Overwhelmingly urban
Peak population: 10,046
Date of peak: September 22, 1942
Opening date: June 1, 1942; Manzanar began as a Wartime Civil Control Administration "assembly cen-

ter" and opened on March 22, 1942; it came under War Relocation Authority jurisdiction on June 1.
Closing date: November 21, 1945
Project director(s): Roy Nash, Harvey N. Coverley, Solon T. Kimball and Ralph P. Merritt
Community analysts: John de Young and Morris E. Opler
JERS fieldworkers: Mari Okazaki and Togo Tanaka
Newspaper: *Manzanar Free Press* (April 11, 1942–September 8, 1945); the paper started while Manzanar was an "assembly center" and continued to publish through the camp's transfer to WRA jurisdiction
Percent who answered question 28 of the loyalty questionnaire positively: 86.9
Number and percentage of eligible male citizens inducted directly into armed forces: 174 (2.5%)
Industry: Manzanar had a camouflage net factory that operated from June to December 1942; also a garment factory, a cabinet shop and a mattress factory that produced goods for internal consumption
Miscellaneous characteristics: Manzanar was probably the most closely guarded of all the camps, due in part to its origin as a WCCA camp, its location within the Western Defense Command's restricted zone, and the extreme hostility of the local population.

Counting its WCCA director (Clayton Triggs), Manzanar had five directors/managers in its first eight months. Merritt took over as director on November 19, 1942, and remained in this position until the camp's closing. Manzanar was a relatively turbulent center; the MANZANAR INCIDENT of December 1942 exposed deep rifts in the population.

(For the key to the categories, see the entry for GILA RIVER.)

For further reading: The literature on the Japanese American World War II experience is extensive; see the bibliography and the bibliographic entries after the various entries pertaining to this experience for titles of general interest. Academic studies of Manzanar include Rita Takahashi Cates. "Comparative Administration and Management of Five War Relocation Authority Camps: America's Incarceration of Persons of Japanese Descent during World War II." Diss., University of Pittsburgh, 1980; Rollin Clay Fox. "The Secondary School Program at the Manzanar War Relocation Center." Diss., University of California, Los Angeles, 1946; and Toshio Yatsushiro. *Politics and Cultural Values: The World War II Japanese Relocation Centers and the United States Government*. New York: Arno Press, 1978. Photographic studies of Manzanar include Ansel Easton Adams. *Born Free and Equal: Photographs of the Loyal Japanese-Americans of Manzanar Relocation Center, Inyo County, California*. New York: U.S. Camera, 1944; Ansel Easton Adams and Toyo Miyatake. *Two Views of Manzanar: An Exhibition of Photographs*. Los Angeles: Frederick S. Wight Art Gallery, University of California, Los Angeles, 1978; and John Armor and Peter Wright. *Manzanar*. Photographs by Ansel Adams.

Manzanar "Relocation Center," California. *Robert A. Nakamura Collection, Japanese American National Museum Photographic & Moving Image Archive*

Commentary by John Hersey. New York: Times Books, 1988. Jeanne Wakatsuki Houston and James D. Houston. *Farewell to Manzanar.* Boston: Houghton Mifflin Co., 1973 is a memoir by a former inmate set in Manzanar. For works dealing specifically with the Manzanar incident, see the bibliographic essay after that entry.

Manzanar Incident Mass uprising of MANZANAR residents in protest of camp conditions. On the night of December 5, 1942, JAPANESE AMERICAN CITIZENS LEAGUE (JACL) leader Fred Tayama was severely beaten by six men. At the hospital, he identified one of the attackers as Harry Ueno, a cook who had been active in trying to organize kitchen workers in the camp and a vocal critic of the JACL. By the morning of December 6, three suspects were taken into custody at the center. One of them, Ueno, was taken to the nearby Inyo County Jail. Later that morning, a mass meeting took place in protest of Ueno's imprisonment. A committee

of five was appointed to negotiate with the project director, who eventually agreed to return Ueno to the camp for trial in exchange for cooperation on various matters. Later that day, crowds reassembled and demanded Ueno's outright release; a list of other "INU" was also read aloud and plans were made to get them. Another group decided to go after Tayama to finish him off; he was hidden under a hospital bed and was not found. The project director called in the military police to quiet the mob. They sprayed tear gas, but it was ineffective in the wind. Either before or after an empty car was started and aimed at the police (it missed), they began to fire live ammunition into the crowd. One person was killed immediately and 10 were injured; a second person later died (according to official statistics; the actual number of injured was probably much higher). A group of suspected *inu* including TOKUTARO SLOCUM, TOGO TANAKA and Tayama was spirited out of the camp for its own safety. A number of suspected agitators including JOE KURIHARA were also removed. Whether viewed as a "riot" or as an "uprising," this incident exposed the underlying tensions present in the camp and spurred the WAR RELOCATION AUTHORITY to quicken its plans to segregate the "loyal" from the "disloyal"—plans which would prove to be disastrous. (See LOYALTY QUESTIONS.)

For further reading, see Arthur A. Hansen and David A. Hacker. "The Manzanar Riot: An Ethnic Perspective." *Amerasia Journal* 2.2 (1974): 112–57 and Gary Y. Okihiro. "Japanese Resistance in America's Concentration Camps: A Reevaluation." *Amerasia Journal* 2.1 (1973): 20–34. For other accounts of this event, see Commission on Wartime Relocation and Internment of Civilians. *Personal Justice Denied: Report of the Commission on Wartime Relocation and Internment of Civilians.* Washington, D.C.: Government Printing Office, 1982; Audrie Girdner, and Anne Loftis. *The Great Betrayal: The Evacuation of the Japanese-Americans during World War II.* Toronto: Macmillan, 1969; and Dorothy S. Thomas, and Richard Nishimoto. *The Spoilage.* Berkeley: University of California Press, 1946, 1969. Sue Kunitomi Embrey, Arthur A. Hansen, and Betty Kulberg Mitson. *Manzanar Martyr: An Interview with Harry Y. Ueno.* Fullerton: Oral History Program, California State University, Fullerton, 1986 gives Ueno's account of the incident.

Manzanar Pilgrimage

Journeys back to the World War II CONCENTRATION CAMP by former internees and others. The MANZANAR Pilgrimage has become an important annual event for Japanese Americans in Southern California and has became a catalyst for other camp pilgrimages as well.

The first Manzanar Pilgrimage was held on December 28 and 29, 1969. It was organized by the Organization of Southland Asian American Organizations—a coalition group of activists working on civil rights and educational activities. Leaders of the group included Warren Furutani, Jim Matsuoka, Mori Nishida, EDISON UNO and other activists in the community. (Soon after, the group was renamed the Manzanar Committee with Furutani and Sue Embrey acting as co-chairs.) The main purpose of the event was to clean and restore the cemetery grounds at Manzanar and also to highlight the campaign to repeal TITLE II OF THE INTERNAL SECURITY ACT.

Over the years, the Manzanar Pilgrimage has become an annual event allowing both older and younger generations to come together and experience the physical environment of the camp. Highlights have always included updates on political events affecting the Japanese American community and efforts to get Manzanar preserved as a historic landmark and later as a national historic site. In the late 1970s and throughout the 1980s, the Manzanar Pilgrimage was a major catalyst of the REDRESS MOVEMENT. The 1992 Pilgrimage marking the 50th anniversary of EXECUTIVE ORDER 9066 was the largest ever.   GLEN KITAYAMA

Manzanar Pilgrimage, 1973. *Ed Ikuta photo, UCLA Asian American Studies Collection, Japanese American National Museum Photographic & Moving Image Archive*

[Used to compile this entry: Edison Uno. "Manzanar—More Than a Memory." *Rafu Shimpo* 12 Jan. 1970.]

Masaoka v. State of California

California court case challenging the 1920 (CALIFORNIA) ALIEN LAND LAW. Haruye Masaoka was an elderly ISSEI widow whose sons built a home for her after the Second World War so that she could live out her life in comfort. Five of her six sons, all born in the United States, served with distinction in the 442ND REGIMENTAL COMBAT TEAM, and one of them was killed in action. Mrs. Masaoka was a Japanese alien, and under the provisions of the Alien Land Law, her sons were not allowed to make a gift of land to her. The family brought an action in the Los Angeles Superior Court to quiet title to the property and to determine whether the property escheated to the state under the provisions of the Alien Land Law. Judge Thurmond Clarke quieted title in the mother and sons on March 16, 1950, and also held that the Alien Land Law was unconstitutional since it violated the Fourteenth Amendment of the U.S. Constitution. The State of California appealed the decision to the California Supreme Court, which affirmed the judgment of the Superior Court on July 9, 1952, citing its decision in FUJII V. STATE OF CALIFORNIA. Though the Alien Land Law would remain on the books, the Masaoka and Fujii decisions effectively made the law unenforceable.

For further reading, see Frank F. Chuman. *The Bamboo People: The Law and Japanese-Americans.* Del Mar, CA: Publisher's Inc., 1976.   DENNIS YAMAMOTO

Masaoka, Mike Masaru (1915–1991) JAPANESE AMERICAN CITIZENS LEAGUE (JACL) official, lobbyist, community leader.

Arguably the most famous and most influential Japanese American of his time, Mike Masaoka played a decisive role in shaping the history of the Japanese American community during the World War II and RESETTLEMENT years. As such, he is a figure of some controversy with both ardent admirers and detractors within and outside the community.

Masaoka was born in 1915 in California, but grew up in Utah, far from the heart of the Japanese American community and became a Mormon. Since his father was killed in an accident when Mike was nine, the large family was brought up and supported by a determined mother. Masaoka became a champion debater in high school and found a job with the fledgling JACL soon after graduation. His role in the organization grew quickly and he was hired as the organization's first executive secretary in August 1941, being sent to Washington, D.C. With the attack on Pearl Harbor, Masaoka and the JACL pledged their support to the government and opted for a strategy of cooperation with what soon became a mass removal of all West Coast Japanese Americans. Despite disagreeing with the need for such drastic measures, Masaoka felt that there was no choice but to go along with it, and he advised the WAR RELOCATION AUTHORITY on how best to administer the CONCENTRATION CAMPS that were constructed to house the removed Japanese Americans. Masaoka was also one of the prime supporters of allowing NISEI into the American armed forces, viewing military service as the best way for Japanese Americans to "prove" their loyalty. When the all-*nisei* 442ND REGIMENTAL COMBAT TEAM was formed, Masaoka became the first *nisei* to volunteer for it.

Serving as a public relations agent during the war, he became the JACL Washington, D.C., lobbyist in the postwar years. As such, he played a key role in the various legislative actions that benefited Japanese Americans, such as the JAPANESE AMERICAN EVACUATION CLAIMS ACT of 1948 and the MCCARRAN-WALTER IMMIGRATION AND NATURALIZATION ACT of 1952. He later began his own lobbying firm and worked in Washington, representing Japanese business concerns for 20 years before sustaining three heart attacks. In ill health for a number of years, he died on June 26, 1991. His autobiography, *They Call Me Moses Masaoka*, was published four years earlier. He was married—to Etsu Mineta, sister of congressman NORMAN MINETA—for nearly 50 years and the couple had adopted two children.

Masaoka's philosophy was to get access to and work within the existing political system to effect change. As he stated in his autobiography, "[w]hat we accomplished was achieved through 'the system.'" He believed it was important for *nisei* to demonstrate "loyalty" to their country in order to gain such access, and thus he staunchly advocated military service and authored the super patriotic "JAPANESE AMERICAN CREED." In his quest for assimilation and access to the decision makers, however, many of his detractors feel he went too far. He once proposed the formation of a "suicide battalion" of *nisei* whose actions would be guaranteed by ISSEI being held as hostages by the U.S. government. He and the JACL also advocated the turning in of those Japanese Americans deemed "disloyal" or dangerous to the FBI and other authorities. He also believed that such actions as challenging EXECUTIVE ORDER 9066 in the courts in 1942 were inappropriate, and he initially opposed pursuing what became the landmark YASUI V. U.S. case. Whatever one thinks of his wartime actions, his life was undeniably one of achievement. Upon his death, Norman Mineta called Masaoka "one of the greatest Americans of the 20th Century."

For further reading, see Mike Masaoka, and Bill Hosokawa. *They Call Me Moses Masaoka*. New York: William Morrow, 1987, his autobiography. For laudatory descriptions of Masaoka's actions in the context of the JACL, see Bill Hosokawa. *Nisei: The Quiet Americans*. New York: William Morrow & Co., 1969 and *JACL in Quest of Justice: The History of the Japanese American Citizens League*. New York: William Morrow, 1982. For less sanguine portrayals of Masaoka, see Richard Drinnon. *Keeper of Concentration Camps: Dillon S. Myer and American Racism*. Berkeley: University of California Press, 1987 and Michi Weglyn. *Years of Infamy: The Untold Story of America's Concentration Camps*. New York: William Morrow & Co., 1976. Masaoka was also the subject of the popular television program "This Is Your Life" on January 2, 1957.

[Quote #1 from *Moses*, p. 23–24; #2 from *Rafu Shimpo* 28 June 1991.]

Massie case

Court case concerning a white woman's accusation of rape by five non-white men in pre-war Hawaii. The alleged rape of Thalia Massie, wife of a navy officer, and the subsequent murder of one of the accused revealed the blatant racism that permeated all levels of 1930s Hawaiian society and the difficulties non-white persons faced there.

On the evening of September 12, 1931, 20-year-old Thalia Fortescue Massie, the wife of navy Lieutenant Thomas Massie, angrily left the Ala Wai Inn nightclub after an argument with another man. A tipsy Massie went for a walk down John Ena Road for some fresh air around midnight. About one hour later, she flagged down a passing car, asking the driver, "Are you white?"

Her face was bruised, her lips swollen and her jaw broken. She stated that she had been abducted and beaten up by five or six "Hawaiian boys," but because of the darkness neither got a good look at the assailants nor at their car's license plates. When she got home, she related the episode to her husband, who called the police. Up to this point, no mention of the word "rape" had taken place. Soon thereafter, five young men were arrested. Horace Ida, David Takai, Ben Akakuelo, Joseph Kahahawai and Henry Chang—two Japanese Americans, two Hawaiian Americans and one Hawaiian-Chinese American—had gotten into a fight over a traffic incident while returning home from a dance and luau. Matching the general description of Massie's assailants, they were picked up and brought before her. Despite her earlier statements, she positively identified three of the men as her assailants. When it was revealed that three of the defendants had previous criminal records, two having been convicted for attempted rape, the case against them seemed strong.

The five men went on trial in November. There was no physical evidence of rape reported by the doctor who examined Massie in the emergency room nor by those who had examined the defendants. Massie's own doctor reported that she suffered from a medical condition that reduced the sharpness of her vision and that she had been under the influence of opiates at the time she identified her attackers. Evidence of tire tracks, beads in the defendants' car and a reported abortion all proved to be falsified. The defendants presented numerous witnesses testifying to their whereabouts when the crime was allegedly committed. A racially mixed jury deliberated for four days and failed to come to a verdict. A mistrial was declared and the five defendants were released on bail.

Hawaii's HAOLE and naval communities reacted with anger and calls for vigilante action. Admiral William Pratt, chief of naval operations, wrote "American men will not stand for the violation of their women under any circumstances. For this crime, they have taken the matter into their own hands when they have felt that the law has failed to do justice." Six days after the declaration of mistrial, a group of vigilantes kidnapped Ida and beat him unconscious. Then Massie's mother, Grace H. B. Fortescue, and Thomas Massie abducted Kahahawai on January 8, 1932, with the aid of two enlisted men, and killed him. The murderers were caught trying to dispose of the body by dropping it off a cliff. The legendary lawyer Clarence Darrow was hired to defend the accused for a $25,000 fee. Meanwhile, lurid accounts in the nation's press made the case a national issue of white supremacy. Despite Darrow's efforts to convince the jury of the group's temporary insanity—his dramatic summation took four-and-a-half hours—the four

defendants were found guilty of manslaughter. Judge Charles Davis sentenced them to 10 years of hard labor on May 4. Military and business leaders applied pressure on the governor to pardon the group. Governor Lawrence Judd commuted their sentences from 10 years to one hour, the one hour to be served in his office. The four convicted murderers had cocktails and met with the governor for an hour and walked away free. Efforts to retry the four remaining men accused of Massie's rape were eventually dropped. Hawaii's Japanese American and other ethnic communities wondered about the justice of a legal system that could mete out such dramatically different treatment to convicted murderers who were wealthy and *haole* and those who were poor and non-white (see the FUKUNAGA CASE, for example).
For further reading, see Gavan Daws. *Shoal of Time: A History of the Hawaiian Islands.* New York: Macmillan, 1968.; Lawrence H. Fuchs. *Hawaii Pono: A Social History.* New York: Harcourt, Brace and World, 1961; Roland Kotani. *The Japanese in Hawaii: A Century of Struggle.* Honolulu: Hochi, Ltd., 1985; and Theon Wright. *Rape in Paradise.* 1966. Introd. Glen Grant. Honolulu: Mutual Publishing, 1990. The case also served as the basis of a best-selling novel, Norman Katkov. *Blood and Orchids.* New York: St. Martin's Press, 1983, and a 1986 network television miniseries of the same name.

Masumizu Kuninosuke (1849–1915) Wakamatsu colonist. Kuninosuke "Kuni" Masumizu was the only known member of the WAKAMATSU COLONY to settle in the United States and raise a family. He settled in Sacramento where he operated a fish store. His wife, Carrie, was the daughter of a Blackfoot Indian woman and an African American former slave. The couple had three children. In 1969, Masumizu's descendants were "discovered" when a story on the 100th anniversary of the colony ran in a local paper. The Elebeck family included Masumizu's grandchildren and great-grandchildren, all of whom considered themselves to be "Negro." Thus, the only known descendants of the first mainland Japanese American settlement are in fact African American.
For further reading, see Bill Hosokawa. *Nisei: The Quiet Americans.* New York: William Morrow & Co., 1969 and Stanley Williford. "Descendents in U.S. Negro." *Pacific Citizen* 10 April 1970: 1.

Matsudaira, Tadaatsu (1855–1888) Engineer. Tadaatsu Matsudaira was an important mining engineer in early Colorado. He arrived in the United States at the age of 17 and earned a degree from Rutgers University in civil engineering. He worked as an engineer for the Union Pacific in Wyoming in 1879, then went to the Colorado School of Mines in Golden. He later became an assistant to Colorado's inspector of mines. He married

Robert Matsui.   *Robert Matsui Collection, Japanese American National Museum Photographic & Moving Image Archive*

the daughter of General Archibald Sampson, a retired Army officer.

For further reading, see Bill Hosokawa. *Nisei: The Quiet Americans*. New York: William Morrow & Co., 1969.

Matsui, Robert Takeo (1941–)   Politician, U.S. representative from California. Congressman Robert Matsui has been a staunch supporter of the Japanese American community throughout his political career. Born in SACRAMENTO, California, Matsui attended the local Sacramento public schools before going on to receive a B.A. from the University of California, Berkeley, in 1963. Upon his graduation, he attended the University of California, Hastings College of Law, where he received his J.D. in 1966. Matsui passed the California bar in 1967 and began to practice law in Sacramento.

Matsui served as president of the JAPANESE AMERICAN CITIZENS LEAGUE in 1969, before serving two terms on the Sacramento City Council, District 8, from 1971 to 1977. As city councilman, he served on the Sacramento

Regional Advisory Board of Justice Planning, Sacramento Area Civil Defense and Disaster Council and Sacramento-Yolo Port District Board of Elections. He was vice mayor in 1977.

In 1978, Matsui, a Democrat, was elected to the Ninety-sixth congress. While in Congress, he served on the Ways and Means Committee, as well as the Select Committee on Narcotics Use and Control. He has won reelection seven times.

As one of few Japanese American politicians in the 1980s, Congressman Matsui played an important role in congressional action and debate over the forced removal and incarceration of Japanese Americans during World War II and in the passage of the CIVIL LIBERTIES ACT OF 1988. He campaigned briefly for the Senate in the 1992 elections, but called off his bid due to the illness and subsequent death of his father.   TRACY ENDO

Matsumoto, Kisaburo   Developer. Kisaburo Matsumoto came to Hawaii in 1891 and initially worked as a laborer at the Pacific Guano Fertilizer Factory. In 1894, he sent his emotionally disturbed wife back to Japan and changed his name to Kikutaro. His first venture in developing came in 1897 when he leased land in Moiliili and built a boardinghouse for workers of the Moiliili Quarry. He soon began building houses for rich HAOLES and built himself a seven-bedroom house with leftover materials. He married a local girl, Kia Mahiai, when she was 14 and had four children by her before her death at age 23. He came to prominence in 1914 when the ship S. C. *Allen*, filled with lumber, became stranded on coral off Waikiki. Unable to get the lumber off the ship, the owners sold it to Matsumoto, who mortgaged all his properties to do so. In pondering how to get the lumber off the ship, he dropped a few pieces overboard—and found that all of them drifted ashore at the same place. Upon renting this shore property, he successfully collected the lumber. Due to the shortage of lumber brought on by the First World War, he had a virtual monopoly on home building. Many small houses and big profits followed. Matsumoto went on to build the Yokohama Specie Bank building and the Japanese Consulate on Nuuanu Street.

For further reading, see Patsy Sumie Saiki. *Japanese Women in Hawaii: The First 100 Years*. Honolulu: Kisaku, Inc., 1985.

Matsunaga, Masayuki "Spark" (1916–1990)   Three-term United States senator from Hawaii and a leading advocate for peace.

Born on the island of Kauai to a poor family of Japanese immigrants, Matsunaga worked his way through both high school and college, graduating from the University of Hawaii with honors in 1948 and from Harvard

Law School in 1951. During World War II, Matsunaga was a highly decorated member of the 100TH INFANTRY BATTALION of the 442ND REGIMENTAL COMBAT TEAM and was wounded twice during combat in Italy.

Matsunaga served as a public prosecutor for Honolulu before being elected to Hawaii's territorial house in 1954. Elected to the House of Representatives in 1962, he went on to serve seven consecutive terms, during which time he sponsored legislation to repeal TITLE II OF THE EMERGENCY DETENTION ACT.

Matsunaga defeated colleague and friend PATSY TAKEMOTO MINK in a 1976 Senate race and went on to fill important posts on the Finance Committee and was chairman of the International Trade and Aging subcommittees. A longtime advocate of peace and the goodwill ambassador for Hawaii, Matsunaga lobbied for 22 years before finally, in 1984, persuading Congress to establish a U.S. Peace Institute.

Always a proponent of Asian American causes, Matsunaga engineered passage of the CIVIL LIBERTIES ACT OF 1988 as the act's main Senate sponsor. During debate, the senator was forced to take a deep breath and halt mid-sentence when recounting to the Senate the story of an elderly CONCENTRATION CAMP internee who was shot while retrieving a ball for his grandson. (See JAMES HATSUKI WAKASA).

More recently, Matsunaga supported a joint U.S.-Soviet exploration of Mars as a symbol of the end of the Cold War; he authored *The Mars Project* in 1986. One result of his efforts was for 1992 to be declared an International Space Year and to have Hawaii become the site of a center for space exploration. Senator Matsunaga cast his last votes supporting an extension of the Clean Air Act from a wheelchair 10 days before his death on Easter Sunday, 1990, at age 73.   TRACY ENDO

Matsura, Frank (1874?–1913) Photographer

Frank Matsura left behind a legacy of valuable photographs documenting life in the Okanogan area of central Washington (state) in the early years of the 20th century. He was one of the first non-native American settlers in the region and the only Japanese American in the county throughout his life there. His outgoing nature and fluency in English made him a prominent and well-liked member of the community.

His life before his sudden appearance in Okanogan is something of a mystery. Passport records indicate that he was 29 years old when he arrived in Conconully, a faded mining town in Okanogan county, in 1903. It was rumored that he was a newspaperman or a pantomime artist for the Japanese army; his demeanor and social skills indicated an educated and cultured background. In Conconully, he took a job as a cook's helper and laun-

Frank Matsura with one of his photographic subjects, Chelsea Woodward. *Historical Photograph Collections, Washington State University Libraries*

dryman at a local hotel. From the beginning he took pictures of local events, developing them in the laundry-room sinks after hours. He quickly made many friends and became known for his photographs of the surrounding scenery. As a way to produce some income from his photography, he introduced picture postcards to the region that became quite popular. In 1907, he moved to Okanogan upon the incorporation of the town and devoted himself full time to photography, opening up a small two-room shop. His photographs of local events and the local cowboys and Indians began to appear in the local newspaper, the *Okanogan Independent*. After receiving some money from an unknown benefactor in 1908, he purchased equipment enabling him to take indoor portraits. From this point, his business became very profitable. Local residents and people from the surrounding frontier flocked to his studio for portraits. Matsura also began to sell "Oriental curios" at the front of his store as well. In 1909, he was able to build a separate house on two lots, on which he planted flowers and erected a swing and parallel bars for local children. He collapsed and died suddenly of tuberculosis on June

16, 1913. His funeral—held at the town auditorium because the church was too small—was the largest held in the town up to that time. He never married, though there were reports of an apparently unsuccessful trip to Japan in search of a bride.

Matsura's photographs are a valuable record of one of the last western frontiers. Largely through the efforts of Matsura's friend and later superior court judge William Compton Brown and some fortuitous accidents, many of his glass negatives and prints have been preserved. Many of his photos are on display at the Okanogan County Historical Society; the Washington State University library houses a Frank Matsura archive.

For further reading, see JoAnne Roe. *Frank Matsura: Frontier Photographer*. Murray Morgan, introd. Seattle: Madrona Publishers, 1981 and "Frank S. Matsura: Photographer on the Northwest Frontier." *American West* 19.2 (Mar./Apr. 1982): 20–29.

Meiji Restoration The "restoration" of the Meiji emperor to the throne, ending the feudal Tokugawa era. The resulting Meiji era saw Japan's transformation, politically, socially and economically, to a Western-style modern state.

The Meiji Restoration began on January 3, 1868, with a coup d'état against the Tokugawa Shogunate, or military regime, by anti-shogunate forces led by the southern provinces of Satsuma and Choshu. The years following the coup, which reinstated the political authority of the emperor, saw numerous political, social and economic changes in Japan and a movement towards unity and centralization. The city of Edo was renamed Tokyo and replaced Kyoto as the national capital of Japan. The following year, four major *daimyo* (feudal lords) acquiesced their control of their *han* (feudal domains) to the imperial government of Japan. Two years later, in 1871, the *han* were replaced by PREFECTURES; *damiyo* were replaced by appointed governors; and class distinctions were eliminated. It was also during this year that farmers were allowed last names; were given title to their lands; were given freedom of movement and occupation; and were assigned monetarily payable tax. Another important reform was that elementary education was made universal and compulsory for all children. In 1873, the lunar calendar was converted to the Gregorian calendar and universal conscription and a new land tax were instituted. Five years later, the Privy Council was established, and the following year, in 1889 the Japanese constitution was officially accepted. The first Japanese Imperial Diet (Parliament) convened in 1890, and that same year, the Imperial Rescript on Education was issued.

It was during the Meiji era that the Japanese began emigrating in large numbers to foreign countries, in-

cluding the Territory of Hawaii and the United States. It was the Meiji government that sponsored the first stage of ISSEI contract labor migration to the Territory of Hawaii (1885–1894). Because most of the *issei* who came to Hawaii and the United States were raised during this period, they brought with them and passed on to their NISEI children Meiji ideologies, values, manners and patterns of speech.

The Meiji era and its associated period of reforms came to a close with the death of the Meiji emperor, Mutsuhito, in 1912.

For further reading, see Mikiso Hane. *Peasants, Rebels and Outcasts: The Underside of Modern Japan*. New York: Pantheon Books, 1982; Yuji Ichioka. *The Issei: The World of the First Generation Japanese Immigrants, 1885–1924*. New York: The Free Press, 1988; and *Kodansha Encyclopedia of Japan*. Tokyo: Kodansha, 1983.   STACEY HIROSE

Military Intelligence Service United States Army branch in which many Japanese Americans served during World War II, utilizing their language skills in the Pacific Theater. Though much less well known than the NISEI who served in the 100TH INFANTRY BATTALION and 442ND REGIMENTAL COMBAT TEAM, the Japanese Americans who served in the Military Intelligence Service (MIS) played a key role in the Allied victory over Japan.

After receiving their training at the MILITARY INTELLIGENCE SERVICE LANGUAGE SCHOOL, Japanese American soldiers proficient in both Japanese and English were shipped overseas and attached to different units needing their services in the Pacific. With these units, the *nisei* served in many different capacities. Their translation skills were used to decipher captured enemy documents such as maps, battle plans, orders etc., which helped the Allies know what the enemy was planning and when. The capture and translation of such documents played an important role in many battles in the Pacific, including the invasions of the Philippines and Okinawa. Interpreters' skills were used to interrogate captured prisoners of war and to persuade cornered enemy units to surrender. One often-told story involves a *nisei* in the MIS named Kenji Yasui who persuaded a Japanese unit to surrender by successfully impersonating their Japanese commanding officer. Their writing skills were used to generate propaganda designed to undermine enemy morale and to convince them to surrender. Other *nisei* served with the famed Merrill's Marauders in Burma while others played a role in the Dixie Mission, an army observer group in China's Yenan province that rubbed elbows with such future leaders of China as Mao Tse-tung and Chou En-lai.

At the war's conclusion, many *nisei* served in similar capacities in occupied Japan. *Nisei* served as interpreters and translators at the war crimes trials and with the occupation government in Japan. All told, nearly 6,000 Japanese Americans served in the Military Intelligence Service during and after World War II. Maj. General Charles Willoughby, General MacArthur's intelligence chief stated "The Nisei saved a million lives and shortened the war by two years." Whether true or not, it seems clear that the *nisei* in the Military Intelligence Service played a key role in the Allied war effort in the Pacific.

For further reading, see Roland Kotani. *The Japanese in Hawaii: A Century of Struggle.* Honolulu: Hochi, Ltd., 1985; Joseph D. Harrington. *Yankee Samurai: The Secret Role of Nisei in America's Pacific Victory.* Detroit: Pettigrew Enterprises, Inc., 1979; and Tad Ichinokuchi, ed. *John Aiso and the M.I.S.: Japanese-American Soldiers in the Military Intelligence Service, World War II.* Los Angeles: Military Intelligence Service Club of Southern California, 1988. The acclaimed film *The Color of Honor* by Loni Ding deals in large part with the *nisei* of the Military Intelligence Service.

Military Intelligence Service Language School

Language school that trained some 6,000, mostly NISEI, soldiers in the Japanese language, in preparation for duty in the Pacific Theater during World War II. In addition to the highly publicized exploits of the *nisei* soldiers of the 100TH INFANTRY BATTALION and the 442ND REGIMENTAL COMBAT TEAM, a third group of *nisei* soldiers expert in the Japanese language were performing vital intelligence tasks in the Pacific war, serving as translators, interpreters and interrogators as part of the MILITARY INTELLIGENCE SERVICE (MIS). Nicknamed the "YANKEE SAMURAI," they received their training at the Military Intelligence Service Language School (MISLS) at Camp Savage and later at Fort Snelling, Minnesota.

As tensions between the United States and Japan increased prior to the attack on Pearl Harbor, the need for trained linguists to do intelligence work became acute. Given the difficulty of the written Japanese language, few Americans had enough ability in the language to do military work. A small school was set up in San Francisco as part of the Fourth Army under the command of Captain (later Colonel) Kai E. Rasmussen, a West Point graduate who had spent four years with the United States Army in Tokyo. Given that extremely few Caucasians had any knowledge of Japanese at all, it soon became apparent that Japanese Americans would have to play a major part in the new school. It was hoped that a sufficient number of *nisei* could be found who knew Japanese well enough to be able to do intelligence work with only minimal training in military terminology. A survey conducted under Rasmussen's direction in the summer of 1941, however, indicated otherwise—of the 3,700 enlisted *nisei* surveyed, only 3 percent were found to have reached "plenary level," another 4 percent were "proficient," and another 3 percent were deemed usable

"only after a prolonged period of training." The other 90 percent did not know enough Japanese even to be considered trainable.

On November 1, 1941, the Fourth Army Intelligence School opened at the Presidio in San Francisco with 60 enlisted students and eight civilian instructors. The students and instructors had been selected primarily on the basis of language ability and had to pass background security investigations as well. Fifty-eight of the 60 students were *nisei*. The chief instructor, JOHN F. AISO, later to be the director of academic training of the MISLS, was discovered by Rasmussen as a buck private working in a truck repair outfit. After six months of intense study, 45 of the 60 students graduated, with 35 being sent on active duty to the Pacific Theater and the other 10 being retained to join the teaching staff. These first graduates would soon prove to be invaluable assets to the Allied divisions they joined in the Pacific.

While the first graduates of the language school were exiting in May 1942, Japanese American residents of the Pacific coast states were in the process of being rounded up for eventual mass removal and incarceration in inland CONCENTRATION CAMPS. The combination of growing anti-Japanese sentiment on the coast and the need for a larger facility led to the moving of the school to Camp Savage, a 132-acre former Civilian Conservation Corps facility on the outskirts of Minneapolis. On June 1, 1942, the newly named Military Intelligence Service Language School opened with 200 students and 15 instructors. The rigorous training began at 8:00 A.M. and lasted to 4:30 P.M. and continued after a break from 7:00 to 9:00 P.M. Even after "lights out" at 11 P.M., many students could be found in the barracks latrine cramming for the regular Saturday tests. Only Saturday afternoons and Sundays were free for sports, dances or trips into Minneapolis or St. Paul. Each class was larger than the one before it, and the curriculum grew more focused and more specialized. By the time the fourth Camp Savage class was started in January 1944, the MISLS consisted of 1,100 students and 100 instructors. By the time the school moved to nearby Fort Snelling in August 1944, the MISLS had turned out 1,600 enlisted graduates, 142 officer candidates and 53 officers.

The facilities as Fort Snelling represented a quantum leap forward for the students, with well-insulated buildings and complete recreational facilities. An ever-increasing student body continued to enter the school, drawn more and more from the ranks of volunteers and draftees. After the end of the war in the Pacific, still more interpreters were needed for duty in Allied-occupied Japan. MISLS enrollment peaked at the beginning of 1946 when 3,000 students and 160 instructors occupied 125 classrooms. Among the students were members of the Women's Army Corps (WACS), 51 of whom graduated from Fort Snelling, 47 of whom were *nisei*. When the MISLS closed in June 1946 in preparation for a move back to the West Coast, some 6,000 linguists had graduated, about 85 percent of whom were *nisei*. These graduates, known as MISer's or "Yankee Samurai," served with distinction in the Pacific during and after World War II.

For further reading, see Masaharu Ano. "Loyal Linguists: Nisei of World War II Learned Japanese in Minnesota." *Minnesota History* 45 (1977): 273–87; Joseph D. Harrington. *Yankee Samurai: The Secret Role of Nisei in America's Pacific Victory.* Detroit: Pettigrew Enterprises, Inc., 1979; Tad Ichinokuchi, ed. *John Aiso and the M.I.S.: Japanese-American Soldiers in the Military Intelligence Service, World War II.* Los Angeles: Military Intelligence Service Club of Southern California, 1988.

"military necessity"   Oft-cited rationale for the mass removal and detention of West Coast Japanese Americans during World War II. Though intelligence work by the FBI and the various military intelligence agencies agreed that the Japanese American community posed little threat in the event of war (see for instance MUNSON REPORT), the citing of "military necessity" continued well into the war. In its decision on the landmark KO-REMATSU V. U.S. case in 1944, the Supreme Court accepted the rationale of "military necessity" in upholding Korematsu's conviction even though a substantial body of evidence was then available that might have disputed that position. Later research disclosed that evidence casting doubt on the "military necessity" rationale was consciously withheld by government attorneys prosecuting Korematsu and the other defendants (see HIRABAYASHI V. U.S. and YASUI V. U.S.), leading to the CORAM NOBIS CASES of the 1980s. The other planks on which the "military necessity" case rested—Japanese American fifth column activity in the Pearl Harbor attack, isolated Japanese submarine attacks on the West Coast, the pattern of Japanese American land holdings etc.—proved to be either false or irrelevant. The specious and difficult-to-disprove claim of "military necessity" hid the real political nature of the decision to remove and detain Japanese Americans.

For further reading, see Commission on Wartime Relocation and Internment of Civilians. *Personal Justice Denied: Report of the Commission on Wartime Relocation and Internment of Civilians.* Washington, D.C.: Government Printing Office, 1982; Roger Daniels. *Asian America: Chinese and Japanese in the United States since 1850.* Seattle: University of Washington Press, 1988; and Michi Weglyn. *Years of Infamy: The Untold Story of America's Concentration Camps.* New York: William Morrow & Co., 1976.

Mineta, Norman Yoshio (1931–)   Politician, U.S. congressman from California. Norman Mineta was the first Japanese American to serve as mayor of a major

Norman Mineta.   *Norman Mineta Collection, Japanese American National Museum Photographic & Moving Image Archive*

American city and the first from the mainland to be elected to Congress.

Born in San Jose, California, Mineta attended local public schools in San Jose as well as in HEART MOUNTAIN, Wyoming, and Evanston, Illinois, during World War II, before graduating from San Jose High in 1949 and the University of California, Berkeley, in 1953. From 1953–56, Mineta served in the United States Army.

Mineta began his career in politics in 1962 as a member of the San Jose Human Relations Commission and served on the Board of Directors for the San Jose Housing Authority in 1966. From 1967, Mineta, as a representative of the city of San Jose, served as councilman, from 1968 to 1971 as vice mayor, and from 1971 to 1974, as mayor of his hometown. In 1974, Mineta was elected to the Ninety-fourth congress. In the 97th Congress, Mineta was appointed to the position of Democratic deputy whip and became a member of the Democratic Steering and Policy Committee. He has been reelected nine times.

As one of few Japanese American politicians in the 1980s, Representative Mineta played a leading role in congressional action and debate over the mass removal and incarceration of Japanese Americans during World

War II and the passage of the CIVIL LIBERTIES ACT OF 1988. TRACY ENDO

Minidoka Minidoka was the site of one of 10 CONCENTRATION CAMPS that housed Japanese Americans forcibly removed from the West Coast states during World War II. Some basic data on Minidoka is presented below in tabular form:

Official name: Minidoka Relocation Center
Location: Jerome County, south-central Idaho, six miles north of Eden
Land: Federal reclamation project land, part of the Gooding Reclamation District
Size: 33,500 acres
Climate: Severe; plagued by dust storms
Origin of camp population: King, Washington (6,098), Multnomah, Oregon (1,927), Pierce, Washington (1,051) counties
Via "assembly centers": Most came from Puyallup (7,150) and Portland (2,318) "assembly centers"
Rural/Urban: Mostly urban
Peak population: 9,397
Date of peak: March 1, 1943
Opening date: August 10, 1942
Closing date: October 28, 1945
Project director(s): Harry Stafford
Community analysts: Gordon Armbruster, John de Young, and Elmer R. Smith
JERS fieldworkers: James Sakoda
Newspaper: *Minidoka Irrigator* (September 10, 1942– July 28, 1945)
Percent who answered question 28 of the loyalty questionnaire positively: 98.7
Number and percentage of eligible male citizens inducted directly into armed forces: 594 (8.8 percent)
Industry: Minidoka had a garment factory which produced goods for internal consumption
Miscellaneous characteristics: Minidoka was regarded by many as the "best" of the camps. Its positive atmosphere stemmed from its relatively homogeneous population and its relatively benevolent administration. Additionally, as a camp not in the Western Defense Command restricted area, security was lighter there than at other camps.

(For the key to the categories, see the entry for GILA RIVER.)

The literature on the Japanese American World War II experience is extensive; see the bibliography and the bibliographic entries after the various entries pertaining to this experience for titles of general interest. Works specifically on Minidoka include Jerome T. Light. "The Development of a Junior-Senior High School Program in a Relocation Center for People of Japanese Ancestry during the War with Japan." Diss., Stanford University, 1947; James M. Sakoda. "Minidoka: An Analysis of Changing Patterns of Social Interaction." Diss., University of California, Berkeley, 1949 and "The 'Residue': The Unresettled Minidokans, 1943–1945." In Ichioka, Yuji, ed. *Views from Within: The Japanese American Evacuation and Resettlement Study.* Los Angeles: Asian American Studies Center, University of California, Los Angeles, 1989. 247–84; and Robert C. Sims. "Japanese Americans in Idaho." In Daniels, Roger, Sandra C. Taylor, and Harry H. L. Kitano, ed. *Japanese Americans: From Relocation to Redress.* Salt Lake City: University of Utah Press, 1986. Revised edition. Seattle: University of Washington Press, 1991. 103–11. Reminiscences of life in Minidoka include Frances E. Haglund. "Behind Barbed Wire." *Integrated Education* 16.2 (Mar.–Apr. 1978): 3–8; Laura Maeda. "Life at Minidoka: A Personal History of the Japanese-American Relocation." *Pacific Historian* 20.4 (1976): 379–87; and Monica Sone. *Nisei Daughter.* Boston: Little, Brown and Company, 1953. Introduction by S. Frank Miyamoto. Seattle: University of Washington Press, 1979.

Mink, Patsy Takemoto (1927–) Congresswoman, educator. The first Asian American woman elected to the U.S. Congress, Representative Mink has had a long history of public service. Throughout her public service career, she has worked to improve the quality of education in Hawaii and the rest of the United States. She has also been an advocate of women's rights.

Born in Maui, Mink attended local public schools in Hawaii and eventually went on to the University of Hawaii to earn a bachelor's degree in zoology and chemistry. Eager to extend her education beyond the field of science, she enrolled in law school at the University of Chicago, eventually earning her degree in 1951. Returning to Hawaii as the first Japanese American woman lawyer, no firm was willing to hire her. She responded by opening her own law office. During this time, while a young wife and working mother, she began her long association with the Democratic Party during its rise to power in Hawaii (see REVOLUTION OF 1954). Her 35-year career in politics began in 1956 when she served in the Territory of Hawaii's House of Representatives. Since then, she has devoted most of her adult life to public service.

In 1964, Mink was elected to Congress. During her 12 years in Congress, she served on the Education and Labor Committee, the Interior and Insular Affairs Committee and the Budget Committee. She even made a bid for the Democratic presidential nomination in 1972, running on a platform emphasizing women's rights and opposition to the Vietnam War. After an unsuccessful run for the Senate in 1976 (she lost to friend and fellow Democrat SPARK MATSUNAGA), she served a final year in the House. After her term ended, she remained active in politics in Washington, D.C., and Hawaii, serving on the Honolulu City Council from 1983–87.

Patsy Mink. *Patsy Mink Collection, Japanese American National Museum Photographic & Moving Image Archive*

Then in 1990, Mink returned to Congress. After the death of Senator Matsunaga, Congressman Daniel Akaka was appointed to succeed him. On September 27, 1990, Mink won a special election for Akaka's vacated seat in the House and began a new two-year term in November of 1990. She was reelected in 1992.

In addition to serving as an elected representative, Mink has written numerous articles about law and has taught law at the University of Hawaii.

For further reading, see Patsy Sumie Saiki. *Japanese Women in Hawaii: The First 100 Years.* Honolulu: Kisaku, Inc., 1985.

EDITH KANESHIRO

[Also used to compile this entry was Jon Matsumoto. "No Fluke." *Rafu Shimpo* 6 Sept. 1991: 1.]

Mirikitani, Janice (1942–)

SANSEI poet, choreographer, community activist, feminist. Born in Stockton, California, Mirikitani spent the early years of her life in ROHWER Relocation Center. Although she has few personal memories of her life in camp, she has written poetry about its effect on the Japanese American community. Using her mother's testimony before the COMMISSION ON WARTIME RELOCATION AND INTERN-MENT OF CIVILIANS as the basis for a poem titled "Breaking Silence," Mirikitani wrote about the unvocalized feelings of the Japanese American community, feelings that rarely emerged during the community's 40 years of silence regarding the removal and incarceration. This work became the central poem of her most recent anthology, *Shedding Silence,* published in 1987. Her first anthology of prose and poetry, *Awake in the River,* first published in 1978, was well-received and has gone into its third printing. In addition to her two books of poetry and prose, she has also served as an editor for other anthologies, most notably *Making Waves,* a collection of writings by Asian American women. Through her work, Mirikitani challenges her readers to think about racism, sexism and injustice. In addition to Asian American themes, she has written about battered women, abused children, nuclear disaster and numerous other social issues.

Mirikitani's activities are varied. In addition to writing, she has been a full-time community activist. In 1969, she became program director of Glide Memorial Church of San Francisco, an organization dedicated to providing services for the people of the Tenderloin district, an area

Janice Mirikitani. *Janice Mirikitani Collection, Japanese American National Museum Photographic & Moving Image Archive*

rife with crime, drugs, poverty and homelessness. In 1982, she became the president of the Glide Foundation, assuming the responsibilities of fund-raising and overseeing a budget of over $2 million. She and her husband, Rev. Cecil Williams, a prominent leader in San Francisco's African American community, have worked to create a more humane environment for the poor, the homeless and the abused of San Francisco by promoting community services through dance, theatre, writing and music. Because of her achievements and her commitment to the community, the California State Assembly named Mirikitani "Woman of the Year" in the 17th Assembly District.

For further reading, see Mirikitani's books *Awake in the River.* San Francisco: Isthmus Press, 1978 and *Shedding Silence.* Berkeley: Celestial Arts, 1987.   EDITH KANESHIRO

Mittwer, Mary Oyama (1907–) NISEI writer and advice columnist. Born in Fairfield, California, Mary Oyama exhibited a talent for writing at a young age. As a young woman, she briefly studied journalism. During the 1930s, she began writing for various Japanese American newspapers. Along with other *nisei* women writers of the 1930s, she explored issues such as interracial dating, marriage, ethnicity and Japanese American women's roles in American society.

From 1935 to 1941, she wrote an advice column for a San Francisco Japanese American newspaper using the pen name "Deirdre." As Deirdre, she advised her readers about proper etiquette in the white world. She addressed *nisei* concerns about love, marriage and proper behavior at a time when young *nisei* were growing into adulthood. For further reading, see Valerie J. Matsumoto. "Desperately Seeking 'Deirdre': Gender Roles, Multicultural Relations, and Nisei Women Writers of the 1930s." *Frontiers* 12.1 (1991): 19–32.   EDITH KANESHIRO

Miyakawa, T. Scott (1906–1981) T. Scott Miyakawa was one of the first scholars to document the Japanese American experience. He was one of the few mainland NISEI born at around the turn of the century and who grew up on the West Coast. Despite earning a degree from Cornell in 1929, he was unable to land a job with an American company and ended up working for the Southern Manchurian Railroad Company as the manager of their New York office. Since this company came into being as a result of Japanese militaristic activity, his working there put him on an FBI blacklist. When World War II came, he was thus kept from working with the MILITARY INTELLIGENCE SERVICE LANGUAGE SCHOOL despite his exceptional proficiency in the Japanese language. After the war, he earned a Ph.D. from Columbia University and became professor emeritus at Boston University and at the University of Massachusetts

in Boston. From the early 1950s, he had been collecting information on Japanese American history and his interest in the subject sold the JAPANESE AMERICAN CITIZENS LEAGUE on the JAPANESE AMERICAN RESOURCE PROJECT (JARP) in the early 60s. He became the first director of the Japanese American Resource Project, serving from 1962–1965.

For further reading, see Yasuo Sakata. "T. Scott Miyakawa (1906–1981) and Japanese American History." *Amerasia Journal* 8.2 (1981): v–viii. Miyakawa's own work includes T. Scott Miyakawa. "Early New York Issei: Founders of Japanese-American Trade." In Conroy, Hilary, and T. Scott Miyakawa, eds. *East Across the Pacific: Historical and Sociological Studies of Japanese Immigration and Assimilation.* Santa Barbara, Calif.: American Bibliographical Center-Clio Press, 1972, in the pioneering Japanese American historical anthology he co-edited with Hilary Conroy.

Miyama, Kanichi (1847–1936) Methodist minister. More than any other individual, the Reverend Kanichi Miyama is given credit for spreading Christianity among the Japanese laborers in Hawaii. Born to a samurai family in Yamaguchi PREFECTURE, he studied English and navigation and came to San Francisco after failing in business in Tokyo. He converted to Christianity under the influence of the Reverend Otis Gibson, the superintendent of the Chinese Mission of the Methodist Episcopal Church in San Francisco, being baptized on February 22, 1877. After serving as a pastor in San Francisco, he arrived in Honolulu in 1887 from the San Francisco Methodist Conference and made an immediate impact as the first Japanese-speaking Christian evangelist.

He toured Oahu and the neighbor islands to talk to the workers about the evils of gambling and drinking. His most important convert was Japanese consul general Taro Ando, who had been deeply moved by one of Miyama's sermons. Ando eventually converted his wife and his consular staff and organized the first ISSEI temperance society. Naturally, the efforts of Miyama and Ando to Christianize the masses received much favorable publicity in the American religious press. An 1889 article in a Church of Christ magazine praised Miyama profusely. Miyama also formed the Mutual Assistance Society in 1887, later known as the Japanese Benevolent Society. Miyama received much help in his efforts with the subsequent arrival of the Reverend Jiro Okabe in 1888 and the Reverend TAKIE OKUMURA in 1897.

For further reading, see Franklin S. Odo, and Kazuko Sinoto. *A Pictorial History of the Japanese in Hawaii, 1885–1924.* Honolulu: Bishop Museum Press, 1985; Dennis M. Ogawa. *Kodomo No Tame Ni, For the Sake of the Children: The Japanese American Experience in Hawaii.* Honolulu: University Press of Hawaii, 1978; United Japanese Society of Hawaii. *History of Japanese in Hawaii.* James H. Okahata, ed. Honolulu: United Japanese Society of Hawaii, 1971; and Ryo Yoshida. "A Socio-

Historical Study of Racial/Ethnic Identity in the Inculcated Religious Expression of Japanese Christianity in San Francisco, 1877–1924." Diss., Graduate Theological Union (Berkeley, Calif.), 1989.

Miyamoto, Kazuo (1897–1988)   Writer, physician. Kazuo Miyamoto is best known for his landmark novel *Hawaii: End of the Rainbow.*

A NISEI, Miyamoto was born on the island of Kauai, Hawaii, in 1897. He attended Stanford University and studied medicine at Washington University Medical School in St. Louis, Missouri.

A U.S. Army WORLD WAR I VETERAN, Miyamoto was later arrested on December 7, 1941, imprisoned without trial for 11 months, then freed. The U.S. authorities did this allegedly because of public health research that Miyamoto performed during the 1930s that was published in Japan. Following these incidents, he volunteered for three years as a physician in the TULE LAKE hospital during World War II. While there, he continued to keep a journal of his observations for the purpose of writing a novel. The end result was his historical novel, *Hawaii: End of the Rainbow,* which was based on 17 years of Miyamoto's journals. Comprised of five "books," the novel tells the epic history of Hawaii's Japanese immigrants and their families. The first three "books" tell of the lives of two pioneering Japanese immigrant laborers and the children they raised in Hawaii. Books 4 and 5 detail their wartime internment experience, focusing on the ISSEI leaders who were arrested and imprisoned in Honolulu after the bombing of Pearl Harbor. The latter portion of the novel tells of their subsequent return to the islands. Following World War II, Miyamoto practiced medicine again in Honolulu and continued writing. For further reading: Miyamoto's published works include *Hawaii: End of the Rainbow.* Rutland, Vt.: Charles E. Tuttle, 1964. First Tut Book ed., 1968; *A Nisei Discovers Japan.* Tokyo: Japan Times Press, 1957; and *Vikings of the Far East.* New York: Vantage Press, 1975. See also Stephen H. Sumida. *And the View from the Shore: Literary Traditions of Hawai'i.* Seattle: University of Washington Press, 1991 and Ken Toguchi. "The Book that Led to Internment." *Hawaii Herald* 5 Dec. 1980: 4–5.

EMILY LAWSIN

Miyamoto, Shotaro Frank (1912–)   Sociologist S. Frank Miyamoto was a pioneering scholar in the study of Japanese American communities and was a key researcher on the JAPANESE AMERICAN EVACUATION AND RESETTLEMENT STUDY project during World War II. A native of Washington, he grew up largely outside the Seattle Japanese American community in a mostly white suburb. He entered the University of Washington in 1930 intending to major in engineering. After briefly dropping out of school for financial reasons in 1932, he reentered determined to study sociology and psychology.

Upon finishing his B.A., he went on to obtain an M.A. in sociology. His master's thesis became a study of the Japanese American community in Seattle. Published under the title "Social Solidarity among the Japanese in Seattle," the work has become a classic and has been republished twice. He went on to pursue a doctorate at the University of Chicago beginning in 1939 and completed his exams by the spring of 1941. Returning to Seattle to write his dissertation, he received an entry-level teaching appointment at the University of Washington.

As with all other West Coast Japanese Americans, the outbreak of World War II changed everything. He and his family (he had married soon after Pearl Harbor) were sent to Puyallup "ASSEMBLY CENTER." Prior to this, he had hooked up with Dorothy Thomas through personal contacts and was hired as a researcher on the Japanese Evacuation and Resettlement Study (JERS) project. As a JERS researcher, he conducted fieldwork while incarcerated at TULE LAKE "RELOCATION CENTER" and as a resettler in Chicago. He went on to complete his doctoral dissertation at the University of Chicago, utilizing the research conducted at Tule Lake. He rejoined the Department of Sociology at the University of Washington, where he has remained throughout his academic career, retiring in 1980.

For further reading: S. Frank Miyamoto. *Social Solidarity among the Japanese in Seattle.* University of Washington Publications in the Social Sciences 11.2 (Dec. 1939): 57–130. Seattle: Asian American Studies Program, University of Washington, 1981. Seattle: University of Washington Press, 1984 is still available and widely read today. Miyamoto contributed three essays to Yuji Ichioka, ed. *Views from Within: The Japanese American Evacuation and Resettlement Study.* Los Angeles: Asian American Studies Center, University of California, Los Angeles, 1989: "Dorothy Swaine Thomas as Director of JERS: Some Personal Observations" (31–63); "Reminiscences of JERS" (141–55); and "Resentment, Distrust, and Insecurity at Tule Lake" (127–40). His doctoral dissertation is "The Career of Intergroup Tensions: A Study of the Collective Adjustments of Evacuees to Crises at the Tule Lake Relocation Center." Diss., University of Chicago, 1950.

Among his many other writings on Japanese Americans are "Immigrants and Citizens of Japanese Origins." *American Association of Political and Social Science, Annals* 233 (Sept. 1942): 107–13; "The Japanese Minority in the Pacific Northwest." *Pacific Northwest Quarterly* 54.4 (Oct. 1963): 143–49; "A Survey of Some Changes in the Seattle Japanese Community Since Evacuation." *Research Studies of the State College of Washington* 15 (1947): 147–54 (with Robert W. O'Brien); "An Immigrant Community in America." In Conroy, Hilary, and T. Scott Miyakawa, eds. *East Across the Pacific: Historical and Sociological Studies of Japanese Immigration and Assimilation.* Santa Barbara, Calif.: American Bibliographical Center-Clio Press, 1972. 217–43; "The Forced Evacuation of the Japanese Minority during World War II." *Journal of Social Issues* 29.2

(Spring 1973): 11–31; and "Problems of Interpersonal Style among the Nisei." *Amerasia Journal* 13.2 (1986–87): 29–45.

Miyamura, Hiroshi "Hershey" (1926–)

Congressional Medal of Honor recipient. Hershey Miyamura was a machine gun squad leader and member of Company H, 7th Infantry Regiment, 3rd Infantry Division during the Korean War. On April 24, 1951, his squad was in a defensive position near Taejon-Ni, Korea, where the enemy attacked and threatened their position. Courageously, Miyamura jumped from behind the shelter and fought off the enemy with his bayonet, killing approximately 10 of the enemy line men. Then, he returned to his position and administered first aid to his wounded soldiers and at the same time took charge of the evacuation. Yet, another enemy squad soon attacked their shelter, and Miyamura defended his troops by firing machine guns into the enemy's charge.

He then ordered his men to withdraw as he continued to fire his weapon. He killed more than 50 of the enemy before he depleted his ammunition. Although he was severely injured, he was determined to repel the attack until his position was overrun. He fought intensely against an overwhelming number of enemy soldiers.

Miyamura was then captured and spent 28 months as a prisoner of war. He was awarded the Congressional Medal of Honor for his valor, but this remained a secret for his protection because he was still a prisoner. Miyamura was finally released on August 21, 1953, and was subsequently presented the Medal of Honor from President Dwight D. Eisenhower at the White House.

Presently, Miyamura (nicknamed "Hershey" because one of his teachers could not pronounce "Hiroshi") runs a gas station in Gallup, New Mexico. He has been living there ever since he returned from the Korean War in 1953.　　　　　　　　　　　　　Suzanne J. Hee

[Used to compile this entry: National AJA Veterans Reunion, Kailua-Kona, Hawaii, Program. June 27–July 1, 1990.]

Miyatake, Toyo (1895–1979)

Photographer. Known as a leading figure in the Los Angeles LITTLE TOKYO community, Miyatake also was a noted photographic artist. He was born in Kagawa PREFECTURE, the youngest of three sons. Along with his brothers and mother, he came to the United States in 1909 to rejoin his father who had come to the U.S. earlier to look for work. The family initially lived behind the confectionary shop run by the father, then later on a house in Jackson Street in Little Tokyo.

Having earlier dreamed of being an artist, he began to seriously take up the study of photography against the will of his parents at the age of 21. His first teacher

Toyo Miyatake. *Miyatake Family Collection, Japanese American National Museum Photographic & Moving Image Archive*

was Harry Shigeta, later a successful commercial photographer in Chicago. In September 1923, Miyatake purchased the Toyo Photo Studio, which coincidentally bore his own name. Becoming established as a photographer, he won prizes in many exhibitions, including one at the 1926 London International Photography Exhibition. At this time, he also studied with world famous photographer Edward Weston. Having married in 1922 and with a son born in 1924, he struggled to make ends meet despite his many awards. After photographing the 1932 Olympics in Los Angeles for the *Asahi Shimbun*, he and his family returned to Japan due to his father's illness and eventual death. Efforts at starting a studio in Japan failed and he returned to the U.S. after a year. Starting up the Toyo Miyatake Studio on Central Avenue, Los Angeles, he prospered this time.

With the coming of World War II, he and his family were sent to the CONCENTRATION CAMP at MANZANAR, California. During the war, all his cameras were in storage; however, he took with him a lens for which he had a carpenter in camp build a camera out of wood. With that camera and the tacit approval of the administration—even though photography was officially banned at the camps—Miyatake took many photographs documenting life at Manzanar.

He returned to Little Tokyo and reopened his studio after the war, becoming a fixture in the community. He was named Grand Marshall of the NISEI WEEK festival in 1978. The Miyatake studio still exists and is run by his son Archie.

For further reading, see Atsufumi Miyatake, Taisuke Fujishima, and Eikoh Hosoe, eds. *Toyo Miyatake Behind the Camera 1923–1979*. Special English edition. Trans. Paul Petite. Tokyo: Bungeishunju Co., Ltd., 1984 for a sampling of photographs from throughout Miyatake's career. See also Ansel E. Adams, and Toyo Miyatake. *Two Views of Manzanar: An Exhibition of Photographs*. Los Angeles: Frederick S. Wight Art Gallery, University of California, Los Angeles, 1978 for more Manzanar photographs.

[Also used to compile this entry: "650 Attend Toyo Miyatake Fete." *Rafu Shimpo* 26 Aug. 1978: 1; "Noted Photographer, Toyo Miyatake, Dead." *Rafu Shimpo* 22 Feb. 1979: 1].

Moab WAR RELOCATION AUTHORITY prison camp; see LEUPP ISOLATION CENTER.

mochinige *Mochinige* is the ISSEI term for instances of labor contractors' running off with workers' salaries. One of the many perils agricultural laborers faced was the prospect of *mochinige*. Growers paid LABOR CONTRACTORS a negotiated sum to handle all aspects of laborer management, including paying them. Apparently fairly common before the turn of the century, *mochinige* declined as as workers became more savvy and as the level of cooperation between contractors and workers increased, improving their livelihood and making such tactics less necessary.

For further reading, see Yuji Ichioka. *The Issei: The World of the First Generation Japanese Immigrants, 1885–1924*. New York: The Free Press, 1988.

mochitsuki New Years (OSHOOGATSU) ritual involving the pounding of rice to make soft *mochi* cakes. Traditionally a family or community activity, the women would soak and cook the special *mochi* rice after which the men would take turns pounding the *mochi* rice with a large wooden mallet in a stone or wood mortar until it was soft and smooth. Another man would kneel next to the *mochi*, moistening and turning it between the pounding; sometimes a second person would pound alternately from the other side. It was imperative that a consistent rhythm be kept up lest the *mochi* "turner" get his hands squashed. The pounded *mochi* would then be divided into small portions, covered with starch or flour, and made into small cakes; some of the cakes would be

Mochitsuki in the White River Valley, Washington. *White River Valley Japanese American Community Collection, Japanese American National Museum Photographic & Moving Image Archive*

filled with a sweet bean paste. The finished *mochi* is one of the traditional New Year foods.

As with many other such rituals, many changes have occurred over the years. While many Japanese Americans still eat *mochi* on New Years Day, the *mochi* is usually purchased today. When it is not purchased, it is often produced with new machines specially made to ease the process. The resurgence of ethnic pride brought about by the ASIAN AMERICAN MOVEMENT of the 1960s and '70s has seen a renewed interest in the community *mochitsuki* in many Japanese American communities. There is at least one major difference: today women take their turns pounding the *mochi* alongside the men.

For further reading, see John DeFrancis with the assistance of V. R. Lincoln. *Things Japanese in Hawaii*. Honolulu: University Press of Hawaii, 1973 for a description of the process in a Japanese American context.

"model minority" Stereotypical image of ASIAN AMERICANS and especially Japanese Americans. The origin of the "model minority" thesis dates back to the early 1950s when films such as *Go For Broke* and various newspaper and magazine articles chronicled the apparent success of the NISEI in overcoming racism and discrimination (see the chronology section for examples of such articles). In the 1960s, the theme gained popularity, with Chinese Americans as well Japanese Americans being included in the accounts. *U.S. News and World Report,* for example, wrote in 1966 that the Chinese American community was "winning wealth and respect by dint of its own hard work." In the same year, sociologist William Peterson gave a glowing review of Japanese Americans in his story for the *New York Times,* "Success Story, Japanese-American Style." Peterson stated: "Even in a country whose patron saint is the Horatio

Alger hero [the fictitious slave in Alger's books who turned misfortune into success through hard work], there is no parallel to this success story." Soon, other publications followed.

The main crux of the model minority argument stemmed from outside observations of the "Oriental" community. Articles often cited low crime rates in Japantowns and Chinatowns, high educational achievements, high median family incomes and high outmarriage rates to whites as proof of their success and acceptance. "Visit any Chinatown, U.S.A.," stated *U.S. News and World Report,* "and you find an important racial minority pulling itself up from hardship and discrimination to become a model of self-respect and achievement in today's America."

Critics argued that the data used to "prove" the model minority thesis were misleading. Higher median family incomes, for example, were due to a higher number of workers living in the same household. Educational achievements, though higher than average, were not proportionate to level of income. Also, critics thought, many of the social services needed in the communities were being denied because of the assumption that everything was fine.

Though some Asians welcomed the model minority label as a compliment to hard work, others clearly saw it as a detriment. Writer Frank Chin, for one, viewed such a concept as an example of "racist love": "a white supremacist stereotype . . . expressed in the form of praise." "The assumption," Chin asserted, "is that white racism is a thing of the past." Other critics have also pointed out the divisive nature of the praise given to Asian minorities. Oftentimes, it was used in a way to portray other minorities, particularly African Americans, as lazy complainers. *U.S. News and World Report,* for example, criticized the channeling of money towards "Negroes and other minorities" when "Chinese-Americans were moving ahead on their own—without help from anyone else."

Today, the model minority tag continues to be applied to new Asian immigrant groups. Asian American scholars have been quick, however, to point out the fallacies of the label.

For further reading, see Frank Chin. "Backtalk." In Gee, Emma, ed. *Counterpoint: Perspectives on Asian America.* Los Angeles: Asian American Studies Center, University of California, 1976. 556–57 and Bob H. Suzuki. "Education and Socialization of Asian Americans: A Revisionist Analysis of the 'Model Minority' Thesis." *Amerasia Journal* 4.2 (1977): 23–52 for respectively irreverent and scholarly debunking of the model minority myth. The *U.S. News* article can be found reprinted in *Roots: An Asian American Reader.* Los Angeles: Asian American Studies Center, University of California, 1971. 6–8. Among the host of other recent articles which debunk the model minority myth are Curtis Chang. "Streets of Gold: The Myth of the 'Model Minority'." *Harvard Political Review* 14.4 (Oct. 1987): 6–9; David Crystal. "Asian Americans and the Myth of the Model Minority." *Social Casework* 70.7 (Sept. 1989): 405–13; Russell Endo. "Japanese Americans: The 'Model Minority' in Perspective." In Gomez, Rudolph, Clement Cottingham, Russell Endo, and Kathleen Jackson, eds., and introd. *The Social Reality of Ethnic America.* Lexington, Mass.: D.C. Heath and Company, 1974. 189–213; Masako Iino. "Japanese Americans in Contemporary American Society: A 'Success Story'?" *Japanese Journal of American Studies* 3 (1989): 115–40; and Harry H. L. Kitano, and Stanley Sue. "The Model Minorities." *Journal of Social Issues* 29.2 (Spring 1973): 1–9.

GLEN KITAYAMA

Mori, Ishiko Shibuya (1899–1972) Physician, journalist, poet. Born an only child to a prominent family of physicians in Chiba, Japan, Mori became a doctor to avoid an arranged marriage. As a youth, Mori was independent and outspoken. Her parents found these characteristics "unladylike," so they sent her to live with a strict aunt hoping to change their daughter's ways. In spite of her parents' wishes, Mori did not change. Fearing an end to the Shibuya family line of physicians since they had no male heir, Mori's parents arranged to have their then 13-year-old daughter marry a 50-year-old physician. Refusing to marry the doctor, she decided to become a physician herself, hoping to continue the Shibuya family profession.

Discouraged by limited opportunities for female doctors in Japan, Mori decided to leave for Hawaii. In 1927, she began working at the Japanese Hospital in Honolulu where she met her husband Motokazu Mori, also a doctor. Soon after her marriage, she decided to devote her time to raising her husband's children by a former marriage. However, after having two children of her own, she returned to work in 1934 as a journalist. The Yomiuri Newspaper Company of Japan hired her as a special correspondent from Hawaii. She wrote about life in Hawaii for a Japanese audience.

One of her assignments was to cause her great hardship. On December 5, 1941, Ishiko Mori was asked to write a report on life and military activity in Hawaii. As requested, she complied. On December 7, she and her husband were arrested without charge along with many other prominent ISSEI. Although they were never convicted of a crime, they were sent to a Justice Department INTERNMENT CAMP in CRYSTAL CITY, Texas. They were interned for four years. While interned, Mori and her husband served as camp doctors.

In 1946, they were allowed to return to Hawaii to be with their children and relatives. Forced to work due to her husband's declining health, Ishiko Mori became a research assistant at the American Cancer Society. After the death of her husband, she transferred to the University of Hawaii where as an assistant in epidemiology she contributed to a research article titled "Stomach Cancer Among Japanese in Hawaii."

In spite of her unfortunate experience with journalism in 1941, she continued writing. In addition to writing articles for various Japanese newspapers, she also wrote poetry. In 1968, she was honored by Japan's minister of foreign affairs for her efforts to promote understanding between Japan and America.

For further reading, see Barbara Bennett Peterson, ed. *Notable Women of Hawaii*. Honolulu: University of Hawaii Press, 1984.　　　　　　　　　　　　　　　EDITH KANESHIRO

Mori, Toshio (1910–1980)　Prolific writer Toshio Mori chronicled the lives of Japanese Americans in hundreds of short stories and six novels. He was born in Oakland, California, the youngest of three boys in a family that ran a bathhouse (see FURO). Upon selling the bathhouse in 1913, his father started a floristry and nursery with two relatives, then moved to San Leandro in 1915 to start his own nursery. Toshio remained in San Leandro for almost his entire life.

He became interested in art as a youth and also became an avid reader of dime novels and short stories. In addition to aspiring to be a writer, he also dreamed of playing major league baseball—his high school coach apparently thought highly enough of him to arrange a tryout with the Chicago Cubs. While working in the family nursery, he took up writing seriously in 1932. Despite working long hours at the nursery, he steadfastly wrote four hours each night. Intent on publishing in mainstream publications, he did not contribute to the NISEI vernacular press like many of his *nisei* writer colleagues. He persisted despite receiving piles of rejection slips, until getting his first publication in a magazine called *Coast* in 1938. "Discovered" by William Saroyan as a result, Mori, published in several magazines over the next three years, including JAMES OMURA's *Current Life*. His collection of short stories based on Japanese American community life in Oakland, *Yokohama, California,* was set to be published in 1942.

With the attack on Pearl Harbor and the onset of World War II, publication was put off. With all other West Coast Japanese Americans, Mori was forcibly removed and sent to Tanforan "ASSEMBLY CENTER" and the CONCENTRATION CAMP at TOPAZ, Utah. He continued to write in camp, contributing to the literary journal *Trek* at Topaz. After the war, *Yokohama, California* was finally published in 1949. Mori continued to write steadily until 1965, penning short stories and six novels, and was published regularly in the PACIFIC CITIZEN and *Hokubei Mainichi*. Mori's work, like that of several other *nisei* writers, was rediscovered in the 1970s by a new generation of SANSEI students, writers and critics. A

second collection of his short stories was published in 1979, along with one of his novels. Despite the recent critical acclaim he has received, the vast majority of his output remains unpublished.

For further reading, see Peter Horikoshi. "Interview with Toshio Mori." In Gee, Emma, ed. *Counterpoint: Perspectives on Asian America.* Los Angeles: Asian American Studies Center, University of California, 1976. 472–79; Lawson Fusao Inada. "Tribute to Toshio." In Janice Mirikitani, et al., eds. *Ayumi: A Japanese American Anthology.* San Francisco: Japanese American Anthology Committee, 1980. 179–80 and "Of Place and Displacement: The Range of Japanese American Literature." In Houston Baker, Jr., ed. *Three American Literatures: Essays in Chicano, Native American, and Asian American Literature for Teachers of American Literature.* Introd. Walter J. Ong. New York: Modern Language Association, 1982. 254–65; Russell Leong. "Toshio Mori: An Interview." *Amerasia Journal* 7.1 (1980): 89–108; David R. Mayer. "Akegarasu and Emerson: Kindred Spirits of Toshio Mori's 'The Seventh Street Philosopher'." *Amerasia Journal* 16.2 (1990): 1–10; and David Palumbo-Liu. "Toshio Mori and the Attachments of Spirit: A Response to David R. Mayer." *Amerasia Journal* 17.3 (1991): 41–47. Mori's own published writings include *Yokohama, California.* Introd. William Saroyan. Caldwell, Idaho: Caxton Printers, Ltd., 1949. Introd. Lawson Fusao Inada. Seattle: University of Washington Press, 1985; *The Chauvinist and Other Stories.* Los Angeles: Asian American Studies Center, University of California, Los Angeles, 1979; and *Woman from Hiroshima.* San Francisco: Isthmus Press, 1979. For a more or less complete listing of his published short stories, see King-Kok Cheung, and Stan Yogi, eds. *Asian American Literature: An Annotated Bibliography.* New York: The Modern Language Association of America, 1988.

Morimura, Toyo (1854–1899)　Toyo Morimura was a pioneer in the area of Japanese-American trade. He was born in Tokyo to a merchant family in 1854. Toyo attended Keio Gijuku (later Keio University) and, after graduating, joined his merchant brother Ichizaemon in business. On the advice of YUKICHI FUKUZAWA, Toyo and five other young Japanese men interested in promoting trade journeyed to America, arriving in New York in March 1876. With fellow traveler Momotaro Sato, Morimura established the Hinode Company in November 1876, selling Japanese merchandise both wholesale and retail. After Sato's return to Japan in 1878, the business was reorganized as Morimura Brothers and Company in 1879. The firm prospered, grossing over $100,000 by 1880. Overcoming difficulties with transferring funds and finding marketable products, the firm was successfully importing and wholesaling items such as china and ceramics by 1882.

For further reading, see T. Scott Miyakawa. "Early New York Issei: Founders of Japanese American Trade." In Conroy, Hilary and T. Scott Miyakawa, eds. *East Across the Pacific.* Santa Barbara, Calif.: American Bibliographic Center-Clio Press, 1972. 156–86.

Morita, Noriyuki "Pat" (1932–) Actor. Once a controversial stand-up comedian (he once had the nickname "The Hip Nip"), Pat Morita became a major television & film actor in the 1980s. He was born in Isleton, California, in the SACRAMENTO area. His parents were farm laborers who later started a Chinese restaurant. Morita spent much of his childhood in the hospital with spinal tuberculosis and was crippled until he was 11. Along with all other West Coast Japanese Americans, he spent the World War II years in an American CONCENTRATION CAMP. After the war, he worked for a time in the family restaurant before landing a job with Aerojet General. He eventually became a department head and was making a good living. Unhappy nonetheless, he decided to quit his job and go into show business. He became a nightclub comedian for eight years in Hawaii and Southern California, and was often criticized by members of the Japanese American community for perpetuating stereotypes in his material.

Since the mid-1960s, he has worked regularly in film and television. He has appeared in supporting roles in the movies *Thoroughly Modern Millie* (1967), *The Shakiest Gun in the West* (1968), *Cancel My Reservation* (1972), *Midway* (1976), *Full Moon High* (1982), *Savannah Smiles* (1983) and many others. In 1984, he received the starring role of Miyagi, a kind-hearted karate instructor, in *The Karate Kid,* a film that became a critical and commercial success. For his performance in this movie, Morita was nominated for an Academy Award for Best Supporting Actor. He has since starred in two *Kid* sequels (1986 and 1989) and in *Captive Hearts.* He has also appeared in *Lena's Holiday* (1991) and *Honeymoon in Las Vegas* (1992).

Morita has also appeared in dozens of television shows. He had regular roles in the situation comedies "The Queen and I" (1969), "Sanford and Son" (1974–75), "Happy Days" (1975–76 and 1982–83), and "Blansky's Beauties" (1977). He left his role as drive-in owner Arnold on "Happy Days" to star in the short-lived series "Mr. T and Tina" (1976) as Taro "Mr. T" Takahashi, a Japanese inventor living in Chicago. The show revolved around the culture clashes between Mr. T and his young midwestern-born housekeeper Tina. After his emergence in the *Karate Kid* movies, he starred as the title character in the police/private eye dramatic series "Ohara" (1987–88).

[The following were used to compile this entry: "Pat Morita Get (sic) 1st 'Real' Role." *Rafu Shimpo,* 18 June 1984: 1; White, Ken. "In More Ways than One, this Kid Is a Winner." *Tozai Times,* 1 (Oct 1984): 8–9.]

Munemori, Sadao War hero, sole NISEI recipient of the Congressional Medal of Honor for service during World War II. The Congressional Medal of Honor, the highest decoration that can be bestowed on an American soldier, has been awarded to four Japanese Americans. The first and only member of the famed 100TH INFANTRY BATTALION or 442ND REGIMENTAL COMBAT TEAM to receive the honor was Sadao Munemori. Born in Los Angeles, Munemori attended Lincoln High and enlisted in the army shortly after Pearl Harbor. Initially assigned to the MILITARY INTELLIGENCE SERVICE LANGUAGE SCHOOL, he requested a transfer to a combat unit, and was inducted into the 442nd. He received the Medal of Honor posthumously for diving on a German grenade to save the lives of two other American soldiers on April 5, 1945, near Seravezza, Italy. He was 22 years old. A troop transport—the U.S.S. *Sadao S. Munemori*—was later named after him.

According to MIKE MASAOKA, many other *nisei* had been recommended for the Congressional Medal of Honor but all were denied and awarded Distinguished Service Crosses or other awards instead. After he spoke to Utah Senator Elbert D. Thomas about this, Munemori's recommendation for the award was the only one involving a *nisei* that hadn't been acted on, and the award was subsequently made to him. Many other *nisei* who fought in World War II—including those who served in the MILITARY INTELLIGENCE SERVICE—may well have been equally deserving of this honor. Four Japanese Americans have won the award—Munemori and HIROSHI H. "HERSHEY" MIYAMURA, for action in the Korean War, and RODNEY J. T. YANO and TERRY T. KAWAMURA, both for action in the Vietnam War.

For further reading, see Bill Hosokawa. *Nisei: The Quiet Americans.* New York: William Morrow & Co., 1969 and Mike Masaoka, and Bill Hosokawa. *They Call Me Moses Masaoka.* New York: William Morrow, 1987.

[Also used to compile this entry was the "National AJA Veterans Reunion" program, Kona, Hawaii, 1990.]

Mung, John See NAKAHAMA, MANJIRO.

Munson Report Secret government intelligence report on the loyalty of the pre–Pearl Harbor Japanese American community. With relations between Japan and the United States deteriorating rapidly in the fall of 1941, war with Japan seemed an ever greater possibility. As part of the preparation for such a war, State Department special representative Curtis B. Munson was dispatched to the West Coast and to Hawaii to investigate the loyalty of the Japanese American community in the event of a war. He spent October and part of November 1941 investigating, and produced a 25-page report that was delivered to President Roosevelt and the Departments of State, War, and the Navy in early November.

The report found that, for the most part, the Japanese American community posed little threat to the security of the United States. Based largely on existing intelligence work by the FBI and army and navy intelligence—intelligence work which had been ongoing for over a decade—the report concluded that "only 50 or 60 [mostly KIBEI] in each [naval] district can be classed as really dangerous" and these people had already been identified and were being closely watched by the various intelligence services. He dismissed the NISEI as showing "a pathetic eagerness to be Americans" and thus no threat. While the ISSEI may be "loyal romantically to Japan," the combination of their old age and their decision to make America their home and their children's home led Munson to conclude that the "traditional Japanese ethic, when faithfully adhered to, would not only justify, but more positively demand, his [the *issei*] taking the side of the United States." Munson's conclusion: "For the most part the local Japanese are loyal to the United States or, at worst, hope that by remaining quiet they can avoid concentration camps or irresponsible mobs. We do not believe that they would be at the least any more disloyal that any other racial group in the United States with whom we went to war. Those being here are on a spot and they *know it*." While acknowledging the differing personalities and positions of Japanese Americans in Hawaii, Munson reached the same general conclusion on the matter of loyalty.

In the days immediately following the Pearl Harbor attack, Munson reiterated the conclusions of his report and further suggested to the president that (1) a strong statement of support be issued for the *nisei* "from high government authority"; (2) *nisei* offers of assistance should be encouraged and accepted; and (3) *nisei* should be encouraged to assume positions of leadership in the community. Despite the clearheadedness of Munson's report and post–Pearl Harbor recommendations, both were virtually ignored. On February 19, EXECUTIVE ORDER 9066 authorized military authorities to designate areas from which civilians might be excluded. In the weeks to come, Japanese Americans would be excluded from the West Coast for reasons of "MILITARY NECESSITY," setting the stage for the mass removal and incarceration of all West Coast Japanese Americans in the months and years to come.

For further reading, see Michi Weglyn. *Years of Infamy: The Untold Story of America's Concentration Camps*. New York: William Morrow & Co., 1976. For further information on prewar surveillance of the Japanese American community, see Bob Kumamoto. "The Search for Spies: American Counterintelligence and the Japanese American Community." *Amerasia Journal* 6.2 (1979): 45–75.

Murayama, Makio (1912–   ) Biochemist, medical researcher. Makio Murayama is best known for his pioneering research on sickle cell anemia.

A KIBEI, Murayama was born August 10, 1912, in San Francisco, one of seven children of Hakuyo and Namiye Murayama. The four-year-old Murayama was sent to Japan to live with a great-aunt after the death of his father. He lived in Japan for 10 years, returning to San Francisco at the age of 14. While attending Lowell High, he became engrossed with chemistry, going on to attend the University of California, Berkeley, while working as a hotel janitor at night to support himself. After receiving his B.A. in 1938, he continued his graduate study at Berkeley in biochemistry and physics, working for a time with J. Robert Oppenheimer and receiving his M.A. in 1940. With the attack on Pearl Harbor, his family was sent to the MINIDOKA, Idaho CONCENTRATION CAMP; Murayama, however, was ordered to report to Chicago to work as a physicist on the Manhattan Project. Turned away when they found out he was Japanese, he managed to find a job as a chemist at the Children's Hospital of Michigan. Even while in Michigan, he was tailed by an FBI agent whom he came to recognize. "What a waste of taxpayer's money," he recalled telling the agent.

While working with Dr. James L. Wilson at the Children's Hospital, he first became acquainted with sickle cell anemia through the suffering of child victims. He moved to Bellevue Hospital in New York with Wilson in July 1943 to become director of the pediatric laboratory, moving with Wilson to the University of Michigan in April 1945. In October 1945 he married Sonoko Soga. He received his Ph.D. in immunochemistry in 1953. Upon receiving his degree, he did postgraduate work for two years at the California Institute of Technology with Linus Pauling, the foremost authority on sickle cell diseases, continuing his studies at the University of Pennsylvania from 1956–58. In 1958, he was hired by the National Institutes of Health in Bethesda, Maryland, as a biochemist. After a trip to England, he became the only scientist in the facility to concentrate on the disease. He spent six years building a three-foot-high model of a hemoglobin molecule at home in the evenings out of plastic, aluminum and steel, held together by 70,000 screws, each representing an atom. With the aid of his model, he came to a new understanding of the sickling process, publishing a landmark paper in 1966 in the medical journal *Science*. His discovery led to a controversial and highly publicized treatment for the disease involving urea discovered by Robert Nalbandian in 1970. The work by Murayama and Nalbandian led to great increases in funding for research on the disease, though Murayama continued to work alone at the NIH. For his work in sickle cell anemia, he received the 1969 Association for Sickle Cell Anemia award and the 1972 Martin Luther King, Jr. medical achievement award.

For further reading, see *Current Biography 1974*. New York: H. W. Wilson Co., 1974. Murayama and Nalbandian coauthored the book *Sickle Cell Hemoglobin: Molecule to Man*. Boston, Little, Brown, 1973.

Myer, Dillon S. (1891–1982)

Bureaucrat, WAR RELOCATION AUTHORITY (WRA) director. Dillon S. Myer's significance in Japanese American history comes from his role as director of the War Relocation Authority, the governmental department charged with administering the World War II CONCENTRATION CAMPS for Japanese Americans. Myer was born and raised in Hebron, Ohio, and experienced a typical midwestern childhood. He went on to attend Ohio State University, majoring in agronomy, and graduated in 1914. In 1916, he began his career as a bureaucrat in the government's agricultural complex. Because of his rapid rise in the bureaucracy, he was exempted from the draft in World War I. He attained the position of assistant chief of the Soil Conservation Service in 1938. When MILTON EISENHOWER resigned as director of the WRA on June 17, 1942, he recommended Myer as his successor. Myer would remain in charge for the duration of the WRA's existence.

Up until recently, history had been kind to Myer. On May 22, 1946, the JAPANESE AMERICAN CITIZENS LEAGUE (JACL) honored him with a citation commending him for his "courageous and inspired leadership" and as a "champion of human rights and common decency." He was generally perceived to have performed a difficult job at least adequately. However, recent scholars have disputed this perception. Such works as MICHI WEGLYN's *Years of Infamy* question Myer's treatment of those he considered "troublemakers." Richard Drinnon's 1987 biography of Myer titled *Keeper of Concentration Camps: Dillon S. Myer and American Racism* paints a picture of a man determined to assimilate the Japanese Americans whether they wanted to be or not. Thus, he courted those who shared his vision—such as the JACL—and rewarded them with special privileges. Those who didn't share his vision—the draft resistors or other "troublemakers"—were shown little mercy (see STOCKADE). Drinnon also points out that Myer believed the mass incarceration was justified. He employed a similar strategy towards Native Americans in his stint as director of the Bureau of Indian Affairs. Prior to his death, he opposed the REDRESS MOVEMENT.

For further reading, see Richard Drinnon. *Keeper of Concentration Camps: Dillon S. Myer and American Racism*. Berkeley: University of California Press, 1987 and Michi Weglyn. *Years of Infamy: The Untold Story of America's Concentration Camps*. New York: William Morrow & Co., 1976. Dillon S. Myer.

Uprooted Americans: The Japanese Americans and the War Relocation Authority during World War II. Tucson: University of Arizona Press, 1971 is Myer's own account of his World War II actions.

N

Nagasawa, Kanaye (1852–1934)

Vintner. In the late 1800s and early 1900s, Kanaye Nagasawa was one of California's most prominent wine makers. Nagasawa was born Hikosuke Isonaga in Kagoshima in 1852. His father was a part of the Satsuma clan of southern Japan. When Shimazu, lord of Satsuma, decided to send a number of young samurai to Europe to learn Western ways, the 13-old Isonaga was one of 15 young men chosen. In order to conceal the secret nature of this mission (overseas travel at that time still being prohibited), each person took assumed a new name. From this point on, Hikosuke became Kanaye Nagasawa. The group left Japan in April 1865 and arrived in England two months later. After studying English in Scotland, he and one other member of the group visited the United States. While in the States, they met Thomas Lake Harris, the founder of the "Brotherhood of the New Life" religious cult. Due to financial difficulties, all but six of the students had been called back to Japan; upon hearing this, Harris offered to support the six and to pay for their education in exchange for their labor. In August 1867, Nagasawa and the others left London for Harris's colony in New York.

Thomas Harris owned a 2,000-acre vineyard in Salem-on-Erie where he cultivated wine grapes. The work involved in the fields was difficult for the samurai youth and shortly all but Nagasawa returned to Japan, their quests for Western knowledge fulfilled. Nagasawa, meanwhile, decided to stay on in the States and learned about wine making from noted vintner Dr. John Hyde. A few years later, Harris decided to move his colony to the warmer climate of California and Nagasawa followed, arriving by transcontinental railroad in 1875. They set up shop in the hills surrounding Santa Rosa, originally on 400 acres which would grow to 2,000 acres. The colony was called "Fountain Grove." Nagasawa managed the 500-acre vineyard and was brewmaster. When Harris returned to New York in 1892, Nagasawa took over management of the entire wine operation. Upon the death of Harris in 1906, Nagasawa became master of Fountain Grove. He became a recognized wine maker in California, and Fountain Grove became one of the top 10 labels in the country. Nagasawa was a wine judge at the 1915 Panama-Pacific Exposition in San Francisco. He never married. With the passage of the prohibition amendment in 1920, wine making came to an end at

Fountain Grove. Nagasawa lived out his life here and died 11 days before his 83rd birthday in 1934. Because of the 1913 (CALIFORNIA) ALIEN LAND LAW, he was unable to leave his property to his heirs. A bronze plaque in his honor stands at the site of the old winery.

For further reading, see Japanese American Curriculum Project. *Japanese American Journey: The Story of a People.* San Mateo, Calif.: Japanese American Curriculum Project, 1985 and "Mystery Man of Japan." *Kashu Mainichi* 19–22 Jan. 1988.

Nagumo Shoji (1890–1976) Gardener. Shoji Nagumo was a leader in early efforts to form a gardeners' association and his autobiography became widely read among other gardeners. He was unusually well-educated for an immigrant, having received 16 years of formal education in Japan. He became a gardener in typical fashion when he was hired as a helper by an old friend for $5 a day. He was also hired by other gardeners before picking up their excess customers and beginning his own business. In the '20s, he formed an association with a housing contractor to build gardens for new houses; he continued to care for these gardens when the houses were sold, illustrating how the boom in gardening was tied to the housing construction boom. In 1933, he became a leader in the formation of the Japanese Gardeners' Association of Hollywood. This group was one of three which comprised the first SOUTHERN CALIFORNIA GARDENERS FEDERATION in 1937. He worked as a gardener for 35 years. In his autobiography, *Gadena Goroku* (A Gardener's Essays) published in 1960, he cited the reasons why he considered gardening the ideal urban job: (1) it provided a high steady income; (2) it took place outdoors with nature, contributing to good health, and it was a challenging job that provided an outlet for creativity; and (3) it allowed him to be his own boss and keep stress at a minimum. He received the 5th Order of the Sacred Treasure from the Japanese government in 1970.

For further reading, see Nobuya Tsuchida. "Japanese Gardeners in Southern California, 1900–1941." In Cheng, Lucie, and Edna Bonacich, eds. *Labor Immigration Under Capitalism: Asian Workers in the United States Before World War II.* Berkeley: University of California Press, 1984. 435–69.

[Also used to compile this entry was the 1980 annual of the Southern California Gardeners Federation.]

naichi Term used to refer to non-Okinawan Japanese Americans by members of the Okinawan community. Meaning "internal" or "inside," the term originally was used prior to World War II to refer to the four major Japanese islands and all smaller islands, including Okinawa, vis-à-vis *gaichi* ("outside" or "external"), used to refer to former territorial lands such as Korea and Taiwan. In popular usage in both Japan and the Japanese immigrant community, the term has been used by those who descended from OKINAWA PREFECTURE to differentiate themselves as UCHINANCHU from those hailing from prefectures on the four main islands. People from the other prefectures did not use the term to refer to themselves.

For further reading, see Yukiko Kimura. "Social-Historical Background of the Okinawans in Hawaii" and Mitsugu Sakihara. "Okinawans in Hawaii: An Overview of the Past 80 Years." Both in Ethnic Studies Oral History Project/United Okinawan Association of Hawaii. *Uchinanchu: A History of the Okinawans in Hawaii.* Honolulu: Ethnic Studies Program, University of Hawaii at Manoa, 1981. 51–71, 105–23.

Nakadate, Paul Takeo (1915–1964?) Member of the HEART MOUNTAIN FAIR PLAY COMMITTEE. Born in Montebello, California, in 1915, Paul Nakadate found himself in the CONCENTRATION CAMP at HEART MOUNTAIN, Wyoming, after being forcibly removed from the West Coast along with all other Japanese Americans. While at Heart Mountain, Nakadate, along with six other men, formed the Fair Play Committee. He was elected vice-chair of the Fair Play Committee in January 1944. Nakadate later assumed the role as acting chair of the Fair Play Committee when its elected chair, KIYOSHI OKAMOTO, was taken from Heart Mountain to TULE LAKE "SEGREGATION CENTER" on March 29, 1944.

For further reading, see Douglas W. Nelson. *Heart Mountain: The History of an American Concentration Camp.* Madison, Wis.: The State Historical Society of Wisconsin, 1976.

STACEY HIROSE

Nakahama, Manjiro (also known as Manjiro or John Mung; 1827–1898) Shipwrecked sailor, diplomat. In the years prior to the MEIJI RESTORATION of 1868 when contact between Japan and the West was virtually nonexistent, a number of shipwrecked Japanese sailors who were rescued by Americans and educated in the United States gained a measure of fame as go-betweens between the two nations. Along with JOSEPH HECO, Manjiro Nakahama was the most famous of them and is generally considered to be the first Japanese to speak English effectively. He was born in 1827 in Tosa PREFECTURE. In 1841, he was shipwrecked and marooned on a Pacific islet with four fellow fishermen for six months before being rescued by an American ship captained by William H. Whitfield. After dropping off his companions in Hawaii, Whitfield took Manjiro to his home in New Bedford, Mass., arriving on May 7, 1843. He lived with the Whitfields and attended school there before leaving to spend three years on a whaling ship in Asia. He then set out to visit Japan, arriving home on October 5, 1852. Although he might have been executed for leaving Japan, he was instead welcomed by the authorities and served his country by assuming various diplomatic posts there. One of these was as the interpreter on the *Kanrin Maru* expedition in 1860, the first modern Japanese voyage to America. He became a professor of English in 1869 in the Kaisei Gakko, the forerunner of Tokyo University and went on to visit the U.S. again in 1870. He died in Tokyo in 1898.

For further reading, see Hisakazu Kaneko. *Manjiro: The Man Who Discovered America*. Boston: Houghton Mifflin, 1956 and Emily V. Warriner. *Voyager to Destiny*. New York: Bobbs-Merrill, 1956 and "The Ordeal of the *Kanrin Maru*." *American Heritage* 14.5 (Aug. 1963): 95–97 for biographies of Manjiro and Masuji Ibuse. *John Manjiro, the Castaway: His Life and Adventures*. Trans. H. Kaneko. Tokyo: Nichei-ei Bunka Kyosha, 1947 for a fictionalized account of his life. For works on Japanese shipwrecked sailors, see Wythe E. Braden. "On the Probability of Pre-1778 Drifts to Hawaii." *Hawaiian Journal of History* 10 (1976): 75–89 and Katherine Plummer. *The Shogun's Reluctant Ambassadors: Sea Drifters*. 2nd ed. Tokyo: Lotus Press, 1985. 3rd ed., rev. Portland, Or.: Oregon Historical Society, 1991.

Nakaima incident The Nakaima incident of 1929–30 dramatically split the Okinawan community in Hawaii and may have influenced Hawaii Okinawan political activity in the years to follow. The controversy centered around an election in Okinawa between extreme right-wing and left-wing candidates. In 1928, conservative retired Japanese navy admiral Kenwa Kanna asked prominent Okinawan Hawaiian publisher TETSUO TOYAMA for help in raising campaign funds in Hawaii. While Toyama was helping Kanna, he received a request from Okinawan journalist Shuncho Higa for help in supporting an extreme left-wing candidate in the same election. Higa had helped Toyama while the latter was getting started by introducing him to leading figures in Okinawan politics and business. Assuming that Toyama shared his ideology, Higa also asked Toyama to take care of a visiting lecturer who would soon arrive in Hawaii to speak on behalf of his candidate.

On December 27, 1929, Ichiro Nakaima, a Tokyo University graduate and Okinawan bureaucrat, arrived in Hawaii. Faced with a sensitive situation, Toyama used his influence to paint Nakaima as a Communist, which had the effect of turning some away from Nakaima and others away from Toyama. He escalated the attacks by printing a private letter from Higa and informing the U.S. Immigration Service of Nakaima's activities, seeking to have Nakaima deported. Factionalism divided the Okinawan community for a time.

Nakaima's case was heard by a territorial court and dismissed for lack of evidence on March 12, 1930.

Meanwhile, UCHINANCHU social awareness seemed to rise because of this controversy, while Toyama's reputation suffered great harm because of his actions.

For further reading, see Seiyei Wakukawa. "A Brief History of Thought Activities of Okinawans in Hawaii." In Ethnic Studies Oral History Project/United Okinawan Association of Hawaii. *Uchinanchu: A History of Okinawans in Hawaii*. Honolulu: Ethnic Studies Program, University of Hawaii at Manoa, 1981. 233–42.

Nakamura Gongoro (1890–1965) Nakamura was a legal advisor and community leader among the ISSEI within both the OKINAWAN community and the Japanese American community as a whole both before and after World War II. He was born in 1890 in Hanechi district in Okinawa and sailed for the U.S. in 1906, ending up in Los Angeles. He attended Los Angeles High School and eventually graduated from the University of Southern California Law School. As an *issei* "ALIEN INELIGIBLE TO CITIZENSHIP," he was unable to practice law. In 1923, he became secretary of the Imperial Valley Nihonjin Sangyo Kumiai (Japanese Producers Association) and became active in the JAPANESE ASSOCIATIONS during the time the litigation strategy to challenge the 1920 (CALIFORNIA) ALIEN LAND LAW was being discussed. He also opened a legal office in Los Angeles in 1924 to advise fellow *issei;* he moved the office briefly to the Salt River Valley in Arizona in the wake of the SALT RIVER VALLEY INCIDENT of 1934. In the 1930s, Nakamura served as president of the Los Angeles Japanese Association and of the Southern California Central Japanese Association, one of the four main Japanese Association central bodies on the West Coast. In the days prior to World War II, he accompanied NISEI journalist TOGO TANAKA to Washington, D.C., and met with the attorney general and with First Lady Eleanor Roosevelt to discuss concerns about the Japanese American community.

With the outbreak of World War II, he was arrested and sent to a series of INTERNMENT CAMPS administered by the army or by the Justice Department. He ended up spending most of the war years at CRYSTAL CITY, Texas. In April 1946, he returned to Los Angeles to reopen his legal service. In addition to working with resettlers to help them reopen businesses, he also worked for the benefit of JAPANESE PERUVIANS who were being forcibly returned to Japan and was active in Okinawan relief efforts. In the 1950s, he served as president of the Japanese Chamber of Commerce and became one of the first *issei* in Southern California to become a naturalized citizen with the passage of the MCCARRAN-WALTER ACT OF 1952. He also became active in the JAPANESE AMERICAN CITIZENS LEAGUE and the Republican Party. He died in 1965; his funeral was attended by over 3,000 people.

For further reading, see Okinawa Club of America, comp. *History of the Okinawans in North America*. Ben Kobashigawa, trans. Los Angeles: UCLA Asian American Studies Center and The Okinawa Club of America, 1988.

Nakano, Yosuke W. (1887–1961)

Engineer. A native of Yamaguchi PREFECTURE, engineer Yosuke Nakano became known as an authority on the use of structural cement in construction. Nakano came to the United States at age 19, first to California, then attended the school of architecture at the University of Pennsylvania. He joined the architectural firm Wark and Company in Philadelphia and became chief engineer for the firm in 1918. Over the next 40 years, he took part in the construction of over 200 buildings, mostly in New York and Philadelphia. He became a U.S. citizen in 1953 after the passage of the MCCARRAN-WALTER IMMIGRATION AND NATURALIZATION ACT, one of the first ISSEI on the East Coast to do so. He died while on vacation in Kobe, Japan, at the age of 73.

SUZANNE J. HEE

[Used to compile this entry: Hyung-Chan Kim, ed. *Dictionary of Asian American History*. Westport, Conn.: Greenwood Press, 1986.]

Nakashima, George (1905–1990)

Woodworker, craftsman. George Nakashima became world renowned for his painstakingly hand-crafted wooden furniture. Working primarily with black walnut or redwood, his pieces often have an unfinished look, displaying cracks and holes as well as the natural grain, shape or even bark of the trees used.

Nakashima was born in Spokane, Washington, in 1905. His was educated at the University of Washington where he studied forestry and architecture. He continued his education at Ecole Americaine des Beaux Arts at Fontainebleau in France. After completing his studies there in 1928, he then went on to earn a master's degree in architecture at the Massachusetts Institute of Technology in 1929. His love of wood was so great that he traveled abroad to France, India and Japan to study with other architects, woodworkers and carpenters to learn their craft and methods. He also worked in the Tokyo office of American architect Antonin Raymond beginning in 1937.

Nakashima returned to the United States in 1939 and married Marion Okajima. Comparing architectural practices in America with what he had learned in Asia about craft methods, he came to the conclusion that architecture could not be his lifelong work and decided to concentrate on making furniture. However, not long after he made this decision, World War II broke out and Nakashima, his wife and their infant daughter were forcibly removed, from their home along with all other West Coast Japanese Americans. They spent the war years at the MINIDOKA, Idaho, CONCENTRATION CAMP. Able to practice his trade in camp, Nakashima resettled in New Hope, Pennsylvania, with the help of Raymond, in 1943. He began his furniture business in 1945.

Nakashima's mostly handmade furniture was primarily made to order. As his client list grew, his business expanded to include 12 other craftsmen. His work appeared at the Museum of Modern Art in New York and the Renwick Gallery in Washington; he was also the subject of a retrospective at the American Craft Museum in Manhattan in 1989. Nakashima's awards and honors include the 1952 gold medal for craftsmanship from the American Institute of Architecture; the Local Chapter American Institute of Architects Award for Craftsmanship, Miami, Florida, 1959; National Gold Medal, Exhibition of the Building Arts, New York City, 1962; and the Catholic Art Association Medal, 32nd Annual Convention, 1969. He became a fellow of the American Craft Council in 1979.

In 1989 a fire in a Princeton, N.J., home destroyed 111 of his pieces. Nakashima passed away one year later at his home in New Hope.

For further reading, see George Nakashima. *The Soul of a Tree: A Woodworker's Reflections*. Tokyo: Kodansha International, 1981 and Derek E. Ostergard. *George Nakashima: Full Circle*. New York: Weidenfeld & Nicolson, 1989.

SUZANNE J. HEE/BRIAN NIIYA

[Also used to compile this entry: Renwick Gallery. *Woodenworks: Furniture Objects by Five Contemporary Craftsmen: George Nakashima, Sam Maloof, Wharton Esherick, Arthur Espenet Carpenter, Wendell Castle*. St. Paul: Minnesota Museum of Art, 1972 and Wolfgang Saxon. "George Nakashima Is Dead at 85: Designer and Master Woodworker." *New York Times* 17 June 1990: A30.]

Nakayama, Joji

Chief of the Hawaiian Bureau of Immigration's Japanese section, 1886–95. Japanese immigrant plantation workers in Hawaii faced many hardships. In addition to the back-breaking labor, low wages and brutal treatment by LUNA that they experienced on a daily basis, they were also exploited by their own countrymen, who were sometimes willing to exploit workers while ostensibly helping them. ISSEI laborers faced EMIGRATION COMPANIES that tried to squeeze every penny they could from them, the notorious KEIHIN BANK, indifferent Japanese consular officials, as well as Joji Nakayama, the so-called "scoundrel inspector." Nakayama had been brought to Hawaii by ROBERT IRWIN on the first shipload of migrant workers from Japan in 1885 as the chief inspector of the workers. He and his staff were to monitor the medical condition of the workers and to facilitate communication between them and the plantation management. Later, under the terms of the IMMIGRATION CONVENTION OF 1886, Nakayama became the head of the Hawaiian Bureau of Immigration's Japanese section. In this position, he was essentially being paid by the planters to protect the rights of the Japanese workers. Given such an arrangement, it is not surprising that he ended up protecting the rights of the planters more than those of the workers. He consistently sided with the planters in any labor dispute, actively berating the laborers for striking. He endeavored to keep workers on the job, once instructing his staff to "act firmly with the laborers who are generally ignorant men." In 1891, Nakayama helped Irwin secure a wage cut for Japanese contract immigrants from the Japanese government. Irwin later recommended that Nakayama be given a bonus of $2,000 from the immigrants' protection fund, plus $200 a month, retroactive for one year. Additionally, he received $50 from each man who came to Hawaii with a wife but left without one, supposedly to pay for her passage. By the end of his term, he was making approximately $6,000 per year, about 40 times the personal income of the plantation workers he purportedly represented. A HOLE-HOLE BUSHI lamented,

The laborers keep on coming
Overflowing these Islands
But it's only Inspector Nakayama
Who rakes in the profits.

For further reading, see Roland Kotani. *The Japanese in Hawaii: A Century of Struggle*. Honolulu: Hochi, Ltd., 1985 and Gary Y. Okihiro. *Cane Fires: The Anti-Japanese Movement in Hawaii, 1865–1945*. Philadelphia: Temple University Press, 1991.

[Quote from Kotani 85 (35); *hole-hole bushi* from Odo, Franklin S., and Urata, Harry Minoru. "Hole Hole Bushi: Songs of Hawaii's Japanese Immigrants." *Mana* (Hawaii ed.) 6.1 (1981): 72 quoted in Okihiro 91 (26–27).]

Nakazawa, Ken (1883–1953)

Educator, writer. Dr. Ken Nakazawa is known primarily for his role as a prewar instructor of Japanese language and culture at the University of Southern California (USC). He was born in Fukushima PREFECTURE on December 18, 1883, and moved to the U.S. in 1908. He attended the University of Oregon as an English major and began to write articles on Japanese culture while a student there. These articles were published in such magazines as *McCalls*, *Atlantic Monthly* and *Asia*. His collection of short stories *Weaver of the Frost* was published in 1927 by Harper & Brothers. In 1926, Nakazawa took on a position at USC as a lecturer in Japanese and Chinese literature, Japanese language and Japanese art appreciation. He was the first person of Japanese descent to teach at a major university in the United States. He remained at USC until the outbreak of the war. He also worked as the Japanese vice-consul in Los Angeles, serving as a sort of English-language ambassador, giving lectures on Japanese art, literature and culture before various civic organizations. Because of this association with the consulate, he was interned in Justice Department–administered INTERNMENT CAMPS in Arizona and Idaho and then deported to Japan on the exchange ship *Gripsholm* in June 1942. He reentered the U.S. in Feb. 1952.

For further reading, see Ken Nakazawa. *Writings of Professor Ken Nakazawa*. Foreword by Albert O. Nakazawa and Warren M. Nakazawa. Illustrated by Tomiko Nakazawa. N.p.: Privately printed, 1982.

[Also used to compile this entry was "Noted Lecturer Succumbs After Brief Illness." *Rafu Shimpo* 29 Sept. 1953: 1.]

Nanka Nogyo Kumiai See NINTH STREET MARKET.

Nanka Nokai Renmei

The Nanka Nokai Renmei (Southern California Farm Federation) was born out of the old Nanka Chuo Nokai at a meeting of Japanese farmers in June 1935. This federation linked 24 of the numerous Japanese agricultural cooperatives in Southern California and had a total membership of 1,560. It encouraged cooperative purchasing and marketing, negotiated with labor and merchants' associations, dealt with the ALIEN LAND LAWS and put out radio broadcasts of market conditions. (The radio broadcasts were aired in Japanese every morning for 30 minutes.) The federation also began publishing the *Kashu Nosan Shuho* (California Produce Weekly) in November 1935; it became the *Kashu Sangyo Nippo* (California Industrial News) in April 1936. Although this federation of cooperatives went far beyond any organization of Japanese farmers in the decades prior, it still left much to be desired. Many criticized the federation for its disunity and the lack of cooperation between its small-scale farmers.

For further reading, see Noritaka Yagasaki. "Ethnic Cooperativism and Immigrant Agriculture: A Study of Japanese Floriculture and Truck Farming in California." Diss., University of California, Berkeley, 1982.

National Coalition for Redress/Reparations (NCRR)

One of three major national organizations seeking redress for Japanese Americans incarcerated in government CONCENTRATION CAMPS during World War II. The organization was formed out of the Los Angeles Community Coalition on Redress/Reparations, which in turn came out of L.A.'s Little Tokyo People's Rights Organization's Redress Committee. Charter members of the NCRR felt the need to organize a grass roots organization that would be the voice of the Japanese American community. The JAPANESE AMERICAN CITIZENS LEAGUE (JACL), they felt, was not accountable and in fact had backed off of their redress proposal to pursue the formation of a government commission on the camps. The kickoff conference for the NCRR took place on November 15, 1980, at California State University, L.A., with about 400 participants. Members of the JACL and the newly formed NATIONAL COUNCIL FOR JAPANESE AMERICAN REDRESS attended and formed a somewhat shaky united front for redress at the conference—a prelude to the civil hostilities that would simmer between the three groups in the years to come.

Initially, the NCRR favored redress in the form of direct individual payments of at least $25,000 per person plus the formation of a community fund. A bill that provided for these demands was introduced into Congress by Rep. Mervyn M. Dymally (D-Calif.) on December 8, 1982. In the meantime, the NCRR organized community testimony for the COMMISSION ON WARTIME RELOCATION AND INTERNMENT OF CIVILIANS (CWRIC) hearings in 1981 and ensured that the demand for monetary reparations was heard. In 1983, the commission recommended to Congress that the government pay $20,000 in damages to those interned in U.S. concentration camps during World War II.

From 1983, the NCRR threw its support primarily behind the direct payment bills introduced immediately after the CWRIC recommendations—H.R. 4110, introduced into the House by Jim Wright on October 6, 1983, and S. 2116, introduced into the Senate by SPARK MATSUNAGA on November 17, 1983. Both were defeated in committee, as were other bills submitted in the next Congress.

In 1987, redress bills H.R. 442 and S. 1009 were introduced in the House and Senate and quickly generated momentum in Congress. The NCRR, continuing in its grass roots tradition, mobilized an Asian American delegation 120 strong to lobby for the redress bill in Washington, D.C., from July 25, 1987, to July 29, 1987. The NCRR delegation made over 100 congressional visits, solidifying support among some members while gaining endorsements from others. On September 17, 1987, H.R. 442 was passed by the House of Representatives. The Senate version, S. 1009, was passed the following year on April 20, 1988. After threatening to veto the legislation, President Ronald Reagan eventually signed the redress bill on August 10, 1988.

Since the passage of the redress bill, the NCRR has been very active in the appropriations process and was quick to protest the delay in funding the legislation. They, along with the JACL, were instrumental in assisting the OFFICE OF REDRESS ADMINISTRATION in locating eligible individuals for redress. Over the years, the NCRR has published the *NCRR Banner* and has been willing to speak out on other issues not necessarily limited to the Japanese American community. In 1990, the group celebrated its 10th anniversary with a conference at California State University, Long Beach, and changed its name to Nikkei for Civil Rights and Redress. (See REDRESS MOVEMENT.)   GLEN KITAYAMA

National Committee for Redress, JACL   Redress subgroup of the major Japanese American civil rights organization. The formation of the National Committee for Redress (NCR) at the 1976 JAPANESE AMERICAN CITIZENS LEAGUE (JACL) National Convention represented the first serious action toward redress taken by the organization. Previous attempts to gather support for redress stalled after passing resolutions in 1970, 1972 and 1974. Under the leadership of EDISON TOMIMARO UNO, the architect of the previous proposals, the group was charged with researching the issue and adopting legislation to be considered at the next convention in 1978. At first, they started with the proposal of a community fund ("block grants") and immediately encountered resistance from the Seattle chapter. By the time the 1978 convention came around, they adopted a proposal calling for $25,000 reparations payments for each person forcibly removed and detained in CONCENTRATION CAMPS during World War II.

Surprisingly, the latter proposal was also met with resistance from the Seattle group. To start with, the plan did not make any provisions for those who were forced from their West Coast homes but not incarcerated in the camps (i.e., the "VOLUNTARY" RESETTLERS). Also, it did not include reparations to those who were affected outside the domain of the Western Defense Command, namely those in Hawaii, Alaska and other parts of the country. Still, the plan passed despite these objections and despite the opposition of older leaders like MIKE MASAOKA. (At the time, Masaoka thought "the whole idea of seeking monetary recompense for a sacrifice we accepted in a time of war was disturbing.")

On the weekend of March 3–4, 1979, the NCR of the JACL, on the advice of the four Democratic NIKKEI congressmen, switched its support for legislation calling for direct individual payments and instead proposed the creation of a government commission to study the matter and recommend solutions. The main reasons given for the change were fiscal conservatism and the vociferous attacks on redress by Senator S. I. HAYAKAWA of California. Some in the organization questioned the authority of the NCR to change the official position mandated by the delegates at the 1978 National Convention. Many others felt that the JACL was "waffling" on the issue and was putting too much trust in the government. John

Tateishi, leader of the NCR since the 1978 convention, explained: "The majority of the committee members expressed the view that if the circumstances allowed, they would vote in favor of legislation directly aimed at compensation. But given the political realities and the mood of the Congress and the public . . . , we voted in favor of legislation seeking the creation of a federal commission."

On July 30, 1980, the CWRIC was created by an act of Congress. Formed mainly to investigate matters surrounding the camps and to recommend appropriate remedies, the CWRIC had no power to act on specific grievances—only to hear them. Still, hearings were set to be conducted in 20 cities across the nation beginning the next year. In hindsight, the commission hearings were the turning point of the REDRESS MOVEMENT. With community involvement, the demand for individual monetary reparations was heard in almost every statement. Whether or not that was the intention of the NCR is debatable. One thing is certain, however: the CWRIC hearings united the Japanese American community and the JACL behind the cause. Even previous opponents of redress like Masaoka were won over to the movement after the hearings.

The NCR and its later incarnation, the Legislative and Education Committee (LEC) of the JACL, went on to play a crucial role in the redress movement. With its political contacts in Washington, D.C., they were able to help form a national strategy for the redress movement. Always controversial among some grass roots activists, they nonetheless were a force to be reckoned with.

For further reading, see William Hohri. *Repairing America: An Account of the Movement for Japanese American Redress*. Pullman: Washington State University Press, 1988; Mike Masaoka, and Bill Hosokawa. *They Call Me Moses Masaoka*. New York: William Morrow, 1987; and John Tateishi. "The Japanese American Citizens League and the Struggle for Redress." In Daniels, Roger, Sandra C. Taylor, and Harry H. L. Kitano, eds. *Japanese Americans: From Relocation to Redress*. Salt Lake City: University of Utah Press, 1986. Revised edition. Seattle: University of Washington Press, 1991. 191–95. The most complete account of the NCR's activities in the legislative arena can be found in Esther Scott and Calvin Naito. "Against All Odds: The Japanese American's Campaign for Redress." *Pacific Citizen* 20–27 Dec. 1990: A-3+, a paper by two students at Harvard's Kennedy School of Government.

GLEN KITAYAMA

National Council for Japanese American Redress

(NCJAR) One of three major national organizations that worked for some sort of redress for Japanese Americans incarcerated in government CONCENTRATION CAMPS during World War II. Although the NCJAR was formed in Seattle in May 1979, its origins can be traced to the

NATIONAL COMMITTEE FOR REDRESS—JACL meeting in San Francisco of March 3 and 4, 1979. At this meeting, the JAPANESE AMERICAN CITIZEN'S LEAGUE (JACL) group opted against pursuing a direct payments REDRESS/REPARATIONS bill and decided instead to lobby for the formation of a congressional commission to study the concentration camps. Angered by this strategy, a group of primarily Seattle JACL members led by William Hohri of Chicago dropped out and formed the NCJAR in order to seek redress in the form of direct individual payments. Through their lobbying, Rep. Mike Lowry (D-Wash.) introduced the World War II Japanese-American Human Rights Violations Redress Act (H.R. 5977), a bill based on a proposal made by the Seattle chapter of the JACL four years earlier that called for a direct payment of $15,000 per victim plus $15 for each day interned. This bill, which had no support from any of the NIKKEI congressmen, was killed in favor of the commission bill, which established the COMMISSION ON WARTIME RELOCATION AND INTERNMENT OF CIVILIANS.

After this defeat, the NCJAR switched its redress efforts from the legislative branch to the judicial branch. On March 16, 1983, the NCJAR filed a class action suit against the government seeking $24 billion in damages. Initially dismissed because too much time had elapsed since the camp episode, it was resurrected when an appeals court overturned the decision on January 21, 1986, thereby clearing the way for a trial. The government appealed to the U.S. Supreme Court in 1987, resulting in a ruling on June 1 that NCJAR's appeal had been heard in the wrong court. The case was sent to the U.S. Court of Appeals for the Federal Circuit for a ruling on the original dismissal.

In the meantime, the redress legislation in Congress was moving at an accelerated pace. Included in the bill was the "extinguishment of claims" clause, which said that any person who accepted redress payments through legislation could not bring suit against the government for the same claim. Though the clause did not mention the NCJAR by name, it was clear that the language referred to the lawsuit. The redress bill eventually passed both houses of Congress and was signed by the president on August 10, 1988. Many observers feel that the presence of the NCJAR suit in the courts, which had the potential for costing the government a huge amount of money, made Congress more amenable to passage of the legislation awarding the token sum of $20,000 to camp survivors. The NCJAR lawsuit was disallowed by the Supreme Court on October 31, 1988, effectively ending the efforts of the group. The NCJAR disbanded shortly thereafter. (See REDRESS MOVEMENT.)

For further reading, see William Hohri. "Redress as a Movement Towards Enfranchisement." In Daniels, Roger, Sandra

C. Taylor and Harry H. L. Kitano, eds. *Japanese Americans: From Relocation to Redress.* Salt Lake City: University of Utah Press, 1986. Revised edition. Seattle: University of Washington Press, 1991. 196–99 and *Repairing America: An Account of the Movement for Japanese American Redress.* Pullman: Washington State University Press, 1988. GLEN KITAYAMA

National Japanese American Student Relocation Council

Private organization set up to help NISEI students in America's World War II CONCENTRATION CAMPS attend college. Through the efforts of the National Japanese American Student Relocation Council, some 4,000 *nisei* were able to escape incarceration to attend some 600 colleges and universities outside the restricted area.

At the time of the mass removal and detention of Japanese Americans, the *nisei* were a generation on the brink of adulthood. The median age of the *nisei* was 17 and about 3,000 *nisei* were attending college, with an additional 4,000 in the 12th grade in the 1941–42 school year. Since the vast majority of *nisei* attended college on the West Coast, their mass removal meant the end of college for them.

From the beginning, there were many efforts set up to help these students to continue their education. Various West Coast–based groups worked to help students in their area; many of these groups met in March 1942 at the University of California to centralize their efforts. The National Student Relocation Council was formed at a meeting on May 29, 1942, in Chicago set up by Clarence Pickett, executive secretary of the AMERICAN FRIENDS SERVICE COMMITTEE and attended by representatives of major universities along with YMCA/YWCA, church, government and *nisei* leaders. Robbin W. Barstow, president of Hartford Seminary, was named national director, while Joseph Conrad headed the West Coast office in San Francisco; temporary offices operated in Seattle, Portland and Berkeley. In March of 1943, the organization centralized its activities in Philadelphia and changed its name to the National Japanese American Student Relocation Council (NJASRC).

The scope of the NJASRC included various activities connected to getting *nisei* college students out of camp and into schools. It worked with the WAR RELOCATION AUTHORITY and other government agencies to help *nisei* navigate the tortuous maze of red tape involved in getting the appropriate security clearances to leave camp. It worked with colleges and universities to persuade them to accept *nisei* students, often against vehement protests by the surrounding communities. It worked within the camps themselves, recruiting potential students and encouraging their participation in the program. It also raised money (Japanese Americans themselves also raised large sums of money) for scholarships and other financial aid for the departing students. After 1944, when some of the security red tape was cut and opposition to the *nisei* eased in college communities, the NJASRC concentrated on raising morale among college-age *nisei* in the camps, largely by sending *nisei* attending colleges back to the camps to speak and answer questions about life on the "outside." The NJASRC disbanded in the spring of 1946, its work completed.

The experience of the college *nisei* was a difficult one. They found themselves part of a select group leaving the confining but relatively secure life of the camps for the uncertainty of life in other parts of the country. Whether they liked it or not, they were seen both inside and outside the Japanese American community as the vanguard and as representatives of their people. In many cases, *nisei* students were followed by extended families and friends who joined them in their new homes after the war. The pressure to perform well was intense. They received receptions running the gamut from heartfelt welcomes to outright rejections (see the "RETREAT FROM MOSCOW," for example). In all, the NJASRC and the college *nisei* helped to reestablish Japanese Americans in the postwar world and provided a ray of hope in the bleakest of times. As a means of paying tribute to their benefactors, a group of *nisei* in New England, many of whom were helped by the NJASRC, formed the Nisei Student Relocation Commemoration Fund in 1980, a scholarship fund that helps Southeast Asian refugee students attend college.

For further reading, see Thomas James. "Life Begins with Freedom: The College Nisei, 1942–1945." *History of Education Quarterly* 25 (Spring/Summer 1985): 155–74 and Robert W. O'Brien. *The College Nisei.* Palo Alto, Calif.: Pacific Books, 1949. New York: Arno Press, 1978. For more on the Nisei Student Relocation Commemoration Fund, see Jeanie Hibino. "New England Nisei—Recalling the Past & Working for the Future." *Asian Week* 7 Feb. 1992: 2, 27.

"Native American aliens"

New classification given to those NISEI who renounced their U.S. citizenship during World War II. In effect, by renouncing the only citizenship that they possessed, they became stateless people. Many of these people expatriated to Japan, but many others fought to have their citizenship restored. (See WAYNE COLLINS and RENUNCIATION OF CITIZENSHIP.)

For further reading, see Donald E. Collins. *Native American Aliens: Disloyalty and the Renunciation of Citizenship by Japanese Americans During World War II.* Westport, Conn.: Greenwood Press, 1985 and Michi Weglyn. *Years of Infamy: The Untold Story of America's Concentration Camps.* New York: William Morrow & Co., 1976. GLEN KITAYAMA

Native Sons of the Golden West

California nativist organization. The Native Sons of the Golden West and its sister group, the Native Daughters of the Golden West, were among the loudest and most blatantly racist groups involved in the ANTI-JAPANESE MOVEMENT. Formed in 1875 (by Virginia-born Albert Maver Winn, a former mayor of Sacramento), the organization was made up of the sons of those who had migrated to California in the gold rush of 1849. Membership in the organization was limited to white males born in California on or after July 7, 1846, and officially stood for "the preservation of California's historical past, the honoring of the pioneers and a steadfast adherence to their lofty principles." The Native Daughters was formed 10 years later.

In the early years of the 20th century, the group played an influential role in California politics. One of its major preoccupations was with Japanese immigrants. Throughout the peak period of the anti-Japanese movement, the Native Sons and Daughters' monthly called the *Grizzly Bear* was perhaps the most reactionary of all publications in its depiction of Japanese Americans. League members played key roles in the various anti-Japanese organizations, including the JAPANESE EXCLUSION LEAGUE OF CALIFORNIA, and its members included such leading anti-Japanese movement figures as HIRAM W. JOHNSON, JAMES D. PHELAN and William Randolph Hearst. The Native Sons and Daughters advocated the ending of the GENTLEMEN'S AGREEMENT, the ending of the PICTURE BRIDE practice and the banning of further Japanese immigration. Later members of the Native Sons included California governors EARL WARREN and Edmund G. Brown, and President Richard M. Nixon.

For further reading on the Native Sons and the anti-Japanese movement, see Roger Daniels. *The Politics of Prejudice: The Anti-Japanese Movement in California and the Struggle for Japanese Exclusion*. 1962. 2nd edition. Berkeley: University of California Press, 1977. See Peter Thomas Conmy. "The Origin and Purposes of the Native Sons and Native Daughters of the Golden West." N.p.: Native Sons of the Golden West, 1956 for an organizational history.

New Americans Conferences   Conferences held to discuss the role of Hawaii NISEI in the future of Hawaii. Held from 1927 to 1941 at the YWCA building in Honolulu, the New Americans Conferences were forums organized by Hawaii's Japanese and HAOLE elites for the benefit of *nisei* leaders. The conferences provided a forum for the *nisei* to hear advice from the leaders of Hawaii and to ponder their own future.

The roots of the conferences lay in TAKIE OKUMURA's Americanization campaigns of the 1920s. After the 1920 PLANTATION STRIKE and the growing controversy over JAPANESE-LANGUAGE SCHOOLS, Okumura saw the need for a campaign to encourage ISSEI to adopt American values and customs. The first such campaign was held in January 1921 and continued annually for the next six years. In the course of these campaigns, Okumura saw the large numbers of young adult NISEI who were growing up with inferiority complexes, who were not taking part in the political process and who were being encouraged to leave the plantations by their parents despite the lack of other options. Additionally, *nisei* were coming of age at a time when their loyalty to the United States was being questioned and when there was widespread fear about what would happen when their votes constituted a majority in Hawaii.

The New Americans Conferences were a response that could be applauded by all. Okumura formed an executive committee of prominent *haole* and Japanese American leaders along with an associate committee of prominent *nisei* to plan the conferences. First held in August 1927, the conferences brought *nisei* leaders from all over the Islands together. They were led in discussions of topics of interest by various prominent (and mostly *haole*) discussion leaders and listened to talks by other prominent citizens. They also got the chance to meet each other and members of the *haole* elite at afternoon and evening social functions. Among the most frequent topics of discussion were questions of employment and plantation work, questions of assimilation and social problems, and questions of voting and the "responsibilities of citizenship." A total of 900 delegates attended the 15 conferences.

The conferences provided members of the *haole* elite an opportunity to try to convince the *nisei* of the viability of the status quo. Speakers warned them that there were few options outside the plantations and that despite their college degrees they shouldn't look down on plantation work. Other speakers gave them tips on how to become better citizens and reminded them of the need to demonstrate their loyalty. The delegates themselves expressed a variety of views, with some addressing the discrimination and lack of opportunity *nisei* still faced in Hawaii, especially on the plantations. The conferences underscored the fact that the *nisei* were not passively accepting the role thrust upon them, but struggling with various issues in order to forge their own future. The New Americans Conferences came to an end after 1941.

For further reading, see Gail M. Nomura. "The Debate Over the Role of Nisei in Prewar Hawaii: The New Americans Conference, 1927–1941." *Journal of Ethnic Studies* 15.1 (Spring 1987): 95–115 and Jisoo Sanjume. "An Analysis of the New Americans Conference from 1927 to 1938." Thesis, University of Hawaii, 1939.

newspapers   Japanese American newspapers have played an important role in the Japanese American community from its beginnings to the present. The first papers put out by Japanese immigrants probably began to appear in the 1880s—the *Shinonome Zasshi* published in San Francisco in 1886 may have been the first. In 1892, PATRIOTIC LEAGUE members published the *Soko Shimbun,* the first of several papers produced by that group. In that same year, the *Nippon Shuho* became the first Japanese immigrant paper in Hawaii. In the next two decades, newspapers started by ISSEI proliferated and were published throughout Hawaii and much of the continental United States.

The major newspapers of the *issei* period were the NICHIBEI SHIMBUN on the mainland and the NIPPU JIJI and HAWAII HOCHI in Hawaii. Begun by labor contractor, banker and farm colony pioneer KYUTARO ABIKO in 1899, the *Nichibei Shimbun* became the most widely read of all Japanese American newspapers on the mainland. Based in San Francisco, the paper also published several other editions for consumption in other major California Japanese American communities. At its peak in the 1920s, its combined circulation reportedly topped 25,000. Through the 1910s and 1920s, publisher YASUTARO SOGA's *Nippu Jiji* was the most widely read paper in Hawaii. After spearheading the successful legal challenge of the Hawaii territorial restrictions on the JAPANESE-LANGUAGE SCHOOLS in the 1920s, publisher KINZABURO MAKINO's *Hawaii Hochi* became the most widely read Japanese American paper in Hawaii. Other important pre–World War II papers included the RAFU SHIMPO and *Kashu Mainichi* (Los Angeles), the *Ofu Nippo* (Sacramento), the SHIN SEKAI (San Francisco) and the HAWAII SHIMPO.

With the maturation of the NISEI generation, many of the above-mentioned papers began to come out with English-language supplements in the 1920s. The 1930s saw the full development of daily English sections in the major papers and the arrival of exclusively English-language papers such as JAMES SAKAMOTO's *Japanese American Courier* and the JAPANESE AMERICAN CITIZENS LEAGUE paper the PACIFIC CITIZEN. The identity dilemmas of the *nisei* were worked out in the pages of these papers.

The advent of World War II saw the temporary shutting down of Japanese American papers. In Hawaii, the major papers were soon encouraged to start again—under the "Americanized" names *Hawaii Times (Nippu Jiji)* and HAWAII HERALD *(Hawaii Hochi)*—to keep the Japanese American community of Hawaii informed. On the mainland, the mass removal and detention of all West Coast Japanese Americans put a halt on the major Japanese American papers—for a few, the halt would be permanent. Several papers that published inland kept going through the war—the *Pacific Citizen*, JAMES OMURA's *Rocky Shimpo,* the UTAH NIPPO, and the *Colorado Times*. Japanese Americans in the "ASSEMBLY CENTERS" and CONCENTRATION CAMPS produced a myriad of newspapers to keep the various camp communities informed. (See the entries for the various WAR RELOCATION AUTHORITY camps for the names and dates of the various camp newspapers.)

Japanese American newspapers continued publication into the postwar era for an increasingly English-speaking population. Reflecting the demographic shift in the population, the Los Angeles–based *Rafu Shimpo* became the most widely read mainland Japanese American paper. In the 1960s, '70s and '80s, a number of exclusively English-language papers appeared to serve *nisei*, SANSEI, YONSEI and non–Japanese American audiences. Some of these include the *Hawaii Herald* (Honolulu), *Crossroads* (1950s–60s; defunct) and the *Tozai Times* (Los Angeles), and the *Northwest Nikkei* (Seattle). There have also been many ASIAN AMERICAN papers that were produced in part by Japanese Americans and which reported on the Japanese American community; these papers include GIDRA (Los Angeles, 1969–74), *Asian Week* and *Rodan* (San Francisco, 1970s; defunct) and the *International Examiner* (Seattle). Among the other major Japanese American papers that still publish Japanese sections are the *Chicago Shimpo, New York Nichibei, Hokubei Mainichi* and *Nichibei Times* (the former *Nichibei Shimbun*) (San Francisco). Though there are few *issei* alive today, the increasing number of post-1965 immigrants from Japan has kept up the demand for Japanese-language papers. A new group of exclusively Japanese-language papers has also appeared in recent years to serve new immigrants and the increasing number of Japanese visitors and business people in America. Though not nearly as influential nor as expansive as they once were, Japanese American newspapers are poised to continue into the 21st century.

Though there is no complete history of Japanese American newspapers in either Hawaii or on the mainland, there is a substantial literature on various aspects of the papers. Among the works examining some aspect of the Japanese American press are Katie Kaoru Hayashi. "History of the Rafu Shimpo: Evolution of a Japanese-American Newspaper, 1903–1942." Thesis, California State University, Northridge, 1987; Haruo Higashimoto. "Assimilation Factors Related to the Functioning of the Immigrant Press in Selected Japanese Communities." Diss., Brigham Young University, 1984; Robert E. Park *The Immigrant Press and its Control.* New York: Harper & Brothers, 1922; Jin-Ok Son. "Japanese-American Newspapers: A Content Analysis." Thesis, University of Texas, Austin, 1984; Franklin S. Odo, and Kazuko Sinoto. *A Pictorial History of the Japanese in Hawaii, 1885–1924.* Honolulu: Bishop Museum Press, 1985 (contains a chapter devoted to Japanese immigrant newspapers in Hawaii); Shunzo Sakamaki. "A History of the Japanese Press in Hawaii." Thesis, University of Hawaii, 1928; and Dorothy Anne Stroup. "The Role of the Japanese-American Press in its Community." Thesis, University of California, Berkeley, 1960. See also Seizo Oka's privately published "A

Chronological History of the Japanese Newspapers in America (1880s–1941)."

Among the studies of journalism in America's World War II concentration camps are E. J. Friedlander. "Freedom of the Press behind Barbed Wire: Paul Yokota and the Jerome Relocation Center Newspaper." *Arkansas Historical Quarterly* 14.4 (Winter 1985): 3–13; Jay Friedlander. "Journalism Behind Barbed Wire, 1942–1944: An Arkansas Relocation Center Newspaper." *Journalism Quarterly* 62.2 (Summer 1985): 243–46; Haruo Hayashi. "Self-Identity of the Japanese Americans during the Internment Period: An Archival Research." Diss., University of California, Los Angeles, 1983 (based on the Granada camp paper); Lauren Kessler. "Fettered Freedoms: The Journalism of World War II Japanese Internment Camps." *Journalism History* 15.2–3 (Summer/Autumn 1988): 60–69; James Omura. "Japanese American Journalism During World War II." In Nomura, Gail M., Russell Endo, Stephen H. Sumida, and Russell C. Leong, eds. *Frontiers of Asian American Studies: Writing, Research, and Commentary.* Pullman: Washington State University Press, 1989. 71–80; and John D. Stevens "From Behind Barbed Wire: Freedom of the Press in WWII Japanese Centers." *Journalism Quarterly* 48 (1971): 279–87.

See the entries for the various newspapers and newspaper people noted above for references specific to those topics.

Nichibei Nenkan   The *Nichibei Nenkan* (Japanese American Yearbook) was published by the NICHIBEI SHIMBUN from 1905 to 1918. Among other things, the yearbook carried a listing of all Japanese farmers in California, giving their form of ownership and acreage. The yearbook also carried useful information on purchasing land and operating farms for those interested in agriculture.
For further reading, see Yuji Ichioka. *The Issei: The World of the First Generation Japanese Immigrants, 1885–1924.* New York: The Free Press, 1988.

Nichibei Shimbun   At its peak, the *Nichibei Shimbun* (Japanese American News) was the most widely read ISSEI newspaper. Founded by KYUTARO ABIKO and others, it was formed on April 3, 1899, out of the merger of two existing dailies, *Soko Nihon Shimbun* (San Francisco Japan News) and *Hokubei Nippo* (North American Daily). By 1910, the *Nichibei* had become the leading *issei* paper, with subscribers throughout California, the Pacific Northwest and the Rockies. During this period, the paper reflected Abiko's belief in the need for Japanese to establish roots in America; the slogan *dochaku eiju* (settlement on the land and permanent residency) was adopted. To promote settling, the paper put out the NICHIBEI NENKAN (Japanese American Yearbook) from 1905–1918 as a reference guide to Japanese farming and farmers. Consistent with this editorial slant, the paper decried the California ALIEN LAND LAWS of 1913 and 1920, championed the fight for naturalization, and

was one of the first papers to appeal to the NISEI. When the terms for *issei* life in America had been set in the mid-'20s with the Ozawa naturalization case (see OZAWA V. U.S.), the various Supreme Court rulings upholding the Alien Land Laws and the IMMIGRATION ACT OF 1924, the *Nichibei Shimbun* switched its emphasis to the *nisei.* The paper continues to this day on a much smaller scale as the *Nichibei Times,* covering events in the San Francisco Bay area Japanese American community in both English and Japanese sections. It was published for years by YASUO ABIKO, son of Kyutaro Abiko.
For further reading, see Yuji Ichioka. *The Issei: The World of the First Generation Japanese Immigrants, 1885–1924.* New York: The Free Press, 1988 and Dorothy Anne Stroup. "The Role of the Japanese-American Press in its Community." Thesis, University of California, Berkeley, 1960.

night blindness   An affliction that affected many IS-SEI railroad workers, night blindness was caused by the malnutrition brought about by a diet consisting almost entirely of a thin bacon soup with flour dumplings. Night blinded men could literally not see at night. Chicken soup, made from chickens purchased from local farmers out of their meager wages, served as a cure of sorts.
For further reading, see Kazuo Ito. *Issei: A History of Japanese Immigrants in North America.* Shinichiro Nakamura, Jean S. Gerard, trans. Seattle: Executive Committee for the Publication of *Issei: A History of Japanese Immigrants in North America,* 1973 and Hisashi Tsurutani. *America Bound: The Japanese and Opening of the American West.* Betsey Scheiner, trans. Tokyo: Japan Times, Inc., 1989.

Nihon Rikkokai   The Nihon Rikkokai was a Japanese Christian organization that encouraged emigration to the United States and other countries as a way for the poor to improve their lives. Founded as the Tokyo Worker's Society by Hyodayu Shimanuki, pastor of the Church of Christ in Kanda, in January 1903, the organization originally set out to aid poor students. After a six-month trip to the United States, Shimanuki began to urge the students to go to America, and reformed his organization into the Nihon Rikkokai (Japan Endeavor Society). The organization instructed its charges in the ways of American life, teaching such things as business skills and cooking. The organization also put out GUIDE-BOOKS for travel to the United States as well as the *America-Bound News* starting in 1906. A San Francisco chapter began to meet monthly in 1908; its members played a key role in organizing the Japanese Reformed Church in 1910. When labor migration to the United States was essentially ended by the GENTLEMEN'S AGREE-MENT of 1907–08, the Nihon Rikkokai continued to encourage such migration—even if it meant doing so illegally. It became known as a "stowaway society" for actively teaching those who were willing how to go

Staff of the *Nichibei Shimbun*. *Lily Abiko Collection, Japanese American National Museum Photographic & Moving Image Archive*

about gaining illegal entry to the U.S. Shigeshi Nagata, Shimanuki's successor as chairman of the Nihon Rikkokai, even started a "stowaway training school" in Misaki-cho, Kanagawa, in 1924. It is said that students there would practice swimming four kilometers to shore with packages of clothing wrapped in oilskin on their heads. It is estimated that the Nihon Rikkokai helped some 7,000 people immigrate to the United States.

For further reading, see Hisashi Tsurutani. *America Bound: The Japanese and Opening of the American West*. Betsey Scheiner, trans. Tokyo: Japan Times, Inc., 1989 and Ryo Yoshida. "A Socio-Historical Study of Racial/Ethnic Identity in the Inculcated Religious Expression of Japanese Christianity in San Francisco, 1877–1924." Diss., Graduate Theological Union (Berkeley, Calif.), 1989.

Nihonjinkai   See JAPANESE ASSOCIATION.

Nihonjin Kutsuko Domeikai   The Nihonjin Kutsuko Domeikai (Japanese Shoemakers' League) was an organization formed by Japanese shoemakers in San Francisco in reaction to pressure from white shoemakers. The roots of this group began in 1889 when Tsunetaro Jo and Tadayoshi Sekine opened a small shoe shop on Mission Street. When they successfully negotiated a secret contract with an American manufacturer and recruited another 15 shoemakers from Japan, the Boot and Shoemakers' White Labor League learned about this arrangement and pressured the manufacturer to end the relationship. Jo and Sekine were forced to close their shop in February 1890 due to union pressure.

Realizing that white labor was not about to let them enter the manufacturing field, they reopened their business in May 1890 as a shoe repair shop. In 1892, Jo and others formed the Nihonjin Kutsuko Domeikai to oversee the burgeoning number of Japanese starting shoe repair businesses. The original membership of 20 increased to 167 by 1904 and peaked at 327 in 1909. The organization controlled membership, regulated the placement of new shops, established repair prices, set standards of training and work quality, and engaged in cooperative buying. Working like a guild, the Nihonjin Kutsuko Domeikai served to reinforce the niche into which Japanese shoemakers were pushed by white labor antagonism.

For further reading, see Yuji Ichioka. *The Issei: The World of the First Generation Japanese Immigrants, 1885–1924.* New York: The Free Press, 1988.

Nihonmachi   Literally, "Japan Town," Nihonmachi is a generic term used to refer to the Japanese residential or business section within a larger urban area. Many other terms—J-Town, LITTLE TOKYO, Japantown etc.—are also used. "Nihonmachi" is often used to refer to the Japanese area of San Francisco.

Niihau incident   The Niihau incident occurred in the immediate aftermath of the Pearl Harbor attack when a lone Japanese pilot crash landed on the tiny Hawaiian island of Niihau. Owned by Aylmer Robinson, the 48-square mile island was essentially one large ranch. Aside from Robinson, only two Japanese families and about 180 Hawaiians lived there. Niihau had no telephones or radios and was not served by any daily inter-island transportation. On December 7, 1941, a Japanese plane piloted by Shigenori Nishikaichi crashed on the island. Yoshio Harada, a NISEI caretaker, was lunching at the Robinson ranch when, at around 2 P.M., a Hawaiian worker fetched him. Upon talking to Nishikaichi, Harada learned about the Pearl Harbor attack. In Robinson's absence, Harada decided to guard the pilot until a boat scheduled to arrive the next day came in.

Unfortunately, all boats were grounded after Pearl Harbor and when the scheduled boat failed to arrive, Harada had Nishikaichi taken to the house and guarded. Meanwhile, one of the Hawaiians took a map and some documents from the pilot. After sleeping for a long time, Nishikaichi discovered the missing map and documents and demanded their return. Ishimatsu Shintani, a 60-year-old ISSEI who headed the other Japanese American family, conveyed this message to those who held the missing items; when they refused to surrender them, Shintani went into hiding, realizing the danger of the situation.

As days went by, Harada and Nishikaichi talked and the latter became more and more agitated. He finally decided to go after his stuff; for whatever reason, Harada decided to try and help him. Both men were armed.

While searching for the missing items, Nishikaichi began to set fire to the village. However, one native—Benjamin Kanahele—was hiding in the village and attacked Nishikaichi. Although the pilot fired three shots, hitting Kanahele, the Hawaiian managed to kill him by crushing his head on the rocks. Harada shot himself. Previously, two men had snuck off the island to get help. When Lt. Jack Mizuha of the 299th Infantry arrived with 13 men and Aylmer Robinson, the episode was over. Robinson gave Umeno Harada, Yoshio Harada's wife, an hour to pack and get off the island. She was jailed for two months at Wailua Jail before being interned for the war's duration in Justice Department run INTERNMENT CAMPS at SAND ISLAND and HONOULIULI. Despite his actions, Ishimatsu Shintani was questioned by the FBI and interned for four years at various places.

This incident raises questions about possible Japanese American cooperation with the Japanese in the event of an invasion, though it provides little insight because of the unusual conditions on Niihau and the unclear reasons behind Harada's actions.

For further reading, see Allan Beekman. *The Niihau Incident: The True Story of the Japanese Fighter Pilot Who, After the Pearl Harbor Attack, Crashlanded on the Hawaiian Island of Niihau and Terrorized the Residents.* Honolulu: Heritage Press of the Pacific, 1982; Harry H. L. Kitano. *Japanese Americans: The Evolution of a Subculture.* 1969. 2nd Edition. Englewood Cliffs, N.J.: Prentice-Hall, Inc., 1976 and Patsy Sumie Saiki. *Ganbarre! An Example of Japanese Spirit.* Honolulu: Kisaku, Inc., 1982.

Nikka Nogyo Kumiai   See THIRD STREET MARKET.

nikkei   *Nikkei* is the term many Japanese Americans use to refer to themselves today. It is generally used in the same way as the term "Japanese American" both as a noun and an adjective. Its increasing usage might have something to do with the breaking down of the generational terms—ISSEI, NISEI, SANSEI, YONSEI—beyond the fourth generation (*gosei,* would be the next one). (How would one designate the child of one immigrant and one *sansei* parent? *Sansei* and non-Japanese American parents? *Nisei* and *yonsei* parents?)

Nikkei has at least two additional meanings in a Japanese context. It is a term used by Japanese to indicate any person of Japanese descent who immigrated abroad or is the descendant of such immigrants. Thus to someone from Japan, Japanese Americans, Japanese Brazilians and other nationals of Japanese descent would all be *nikkei. Nikkei* also has separate and unrelated meanings in a Japanese business context, as in, for example, the Nikkei Stock Index.

1949 Strike Long and grueling labor dispute that tested the limits of the INTERNATIONAL LONGSHORE-MEN'S AND WAREHOUSEMEN'S UNION (ILWU)'s power. By 1949, the ILWU had pretty much succeeded in organizing Hawaii's sugar plantation workers and dock workers. In 1948, negotiations for the sugar workers had proceeded quietly, with the union accepting a cut in some places to help struggling plantations. But when the time for negotiation came up for dock workers in 1949, both sides took a hard line. The union pointed out the 32-cent gap between Hawaii and mainland long-shoremen's wages; management offered a strict 8-cent raise and refused to accept arbitration. The strike, which saw 2,000 workers walk out for 178 days, began in March. Because of its dependence on shipping, Hawaii was devastated by the strike. Although some cargo continued to be unloaded in Hawaii, shipping to and from the West Coast was almost completely cut off because of ILWU control of these ports. Old divisions manifested themselves again; the mainstream press resorted to red scare tactics, and the U.S. Congress and President Truman were asked to intervene. By June, 20,000 were unemployed and the number was increasing by 1,000 a week. Many small businesses were going under and many others were in jeopardy. Food shortages also occurred. With the union's rejection of a 14-cent increase recommended by a board appointed by the governor, public opinion began to turn against the union.

On July 20, 2,000 strikers clashed with non-striking dock workers at Hawaii Stevedores, Ltd., a non-union company, resulting in 29 injuries. Other clashes followed. On August 6, the territorial legislature passed a dock-seizure law that allowed the governor to proclaim a state of emergency and to seize seven companies. Feeling the effects of the strike, the stevedoring companies agreed to resume negotiations. After off-the-record negotiations in Honolulu, a settlement was reached on October 7 for a 14-cent raise, eight cents of which would be retroactive from March 1 to June 29, plus an additional 7-cent increase beginning on March 1, 1950. Although the union won this battle, it cost the workers much in lost wages; additionally, the public disapproval of the strike may have had something to do with the ILWU's downfall, soon thereafter.

For further reading, see Lawrence H. Fuchs. *Hawaii Pono: A Social History.* New York: Harcourt, Brace and World, 1961.

1909 Plantation Strike Four-month-long strike of Japanese sugar PLANTATION workers that was the first major labor dispute in the history of Hawaii's sugar industry.

By 1908, Hawaii's sugar planters were doing well. Their $22 million profit in that year came largely at the expense of their Japanese laborers, who continued to be paid $18 per month despite the rising cost of living. Portuguese and Puerto Ricans doing the same work received $22.50 per month. Motoyuki Negoro, a Honolulu law clerk, began a series of essays in the NIPPU JIJI newspaper in 1908 calling attention to these conditions and calling for higher wages. In November 1908, the *Nippu Jiji* sponsored a meeting of community leaders in which editor YASUTARO SOGA and Honolulu drugstore owner FRED KINZABURO MAKINO called for a public campaign for higher wages. HAWAII SHIMPO newspaper president SOMETARO SHIBA called for patience and further discussion; he and Makino reportedly almost came to blows. On December 1, a meeting of 40 higher wage supporters resulted in the formation of the Higher Wage Association (Zokyo Kisei Kai) led by Makino and Negoro. A mass meeting attended by 1,700 in mid-December resulted in demands including at least $22.50 per month in wages, and these demands were forwarded to the HAWAII SUGAR PLANTERS ASSOCIATION. In the weeks that followed, Makino and Negoro rounded up support for the Higher Wage Association among the workers while the *Nippu Jiji* represented their line. The *Hawaii Shimpo* continued to oppose labor militancy.

After five months and no discernable reaction by the planters, a call for stronger action arose. On May 9, 1909, the first workers walked out. By June, 7,000 workers were on strike. The Higher Wage Association strategy was for the Oahu laborers to strike while the laborers on other islands continued to work and to support the strikers. Japanese consul general Senichi Uyeno called on the strikers to go back to work. The planters took a hard line and began evicting strikers and their families from the plantations. By mid-July, 5,000 Japanese refugees were in Honolulu. They were largely supported by the association and the larger community. Rice was also supplied by Chinese merchants. The planters reacted by offering strikebreakers $1.50 per day. The government also began to clamp down on the strike leaders, resulting in a string of arrests for many of them. Soga alone was arrested 10 times (the first as early as February 26) on a variety of charges. The planters' cause continued to be trumpeted in the Japanese community by the *Hawaii Shimpo,* which, unbeknownst to the public, was receiving a monthly subsidy from the planters. Faced with these obstacles, the strike began to lose steam. On August 3, a Higher Wage Association member stabbed Shiba; the strike officially ended two days later. The strike leaders (Soga, Makino, Negoro and Yokichi Tasaka) were convicted of third-degree conspiracy and sentenced to 10 months in prison and a $300 fine. Although the Higher Wage Association was eventually crushed, the planters lost more than $2 million. Three months later, wages were raised to $22 per month and other improvements resulted. However, these gains ostensibly came as the result of a request by a coalition of conservative Japanese leaders including Shiba that also condemned the Higher Wage Association, an obvious attempt by the planters to discredit the strike leaders and to promote Shiba and the conservatives as the "true" leaders of the ISSEI. Meanwhile, the strike leaders were pardoned by the government after serving four months and left prison to a hero's welcome by several hundred supporters.

For further reading, see Edward D. Beechert. *Working in Hawaii: A Labor History*. Honolulu: University of Hawaii Press, 1985; Lawrence H. Fuchs. *Hawaii Pono: A Social History*. New York: Harcourt, Brace and World, 1961; Roland Kotani. *The Japanese in Hawaii: A Century of Struggle*. Honolulu: Hochi, Ltd., 1985; Franklin S. Odo, and Kazuko Sinoto. *A Pictorial History of the Japanese in Hawaii, 1885–1924*. Honolulu: Bishop Museum Press, 1985; Gary Y. Okihiro. *Cane Fires: The Anti-Japanese Movement in Hawaii, 1865–1945*. Philadelphia: Temple University Press, 1991; and Ronald Takaki. *Pau Hana: Plantation Life and Labor in Hawaii, 1835–1920*. Honolulu: University of Hawaii Press, 1983.

1913 (California) Alien Land Law California law prohibiting the purchase of agricultural land by Japanese immigrants and restricting the leasing of such land by them to three years. The law came about after many years of political infighting among the various factions in California politics after the perceived failure of the GENTLEMEN'S AGREEMENT among anti-Japanese circles. Though the provisions of the law were relatively easy for the ISSEI farmers to circumvent, it still had a major impact both on the type of farming they would undertake in the years to come and in their perception of their status in their adopted country.

Starting in 1908, the Democratic Party began to use anti-Japanese issues to their advantage, and in the 1910 gubernatorial elections, made dramatic gains in the legislature, though the Progressive Republicans and governor HIRAM JOHNSON still held the majority. The growing anti-Japanese sentiment in the state led to the introduction of 27 anti-Japanese measures in the 1911 legislature. One of the measures, a law which would ban the purchase of land by "ALIENS INELIGIBLE TO CITIZENSHIP," passed the state senate, but was squelched in the assembly due to pressure from the Taft administration and from organizers of the Panama-Pacific International Exposition of 1915 in San Francisco, both of whom wanted to avoid offending Japan.

The 1912 presidential election saw Democrat Woodrow Wilson emerge victorious. Though he narrowly lost California, his California campaign benefited from his support of Japanese exclusion and his opponent Theodore Roosevelt's supposed support for naturalization rights for Japanese immigrants. When the 1913 California legislature met, some 40 anti-Japanese measures were

introduced, including a number concerned with land ownership. Essentially, there were two types of bills: those that restricted land ownership by all aliens and those that would only apply to "aliens ineligible to citizenship." Largely through the efforts of Governor Johnson, a bill of the second type became the most favored. This time there would be no stopping it. Efforts by the Pan-Pacific Exposition people were to no avail as their presentation before the legislature on April 2 was torpedoed by emotional testimony from farmers opposing *issei* land ownership. Word of the California bill reached Japan and segments of the population there called for war with the United States. On April 22, President Wilson sent telegrams to Governor Johnson and the legislature calling for a nondiscriminatory land bill that did not single out Japanese immigrants. Despite an eleventh-hour trip to California by Secretary of State William Jennings Bryan, the Alien Land Law was overwhelmingly passed by both halves of the legislature and signed by Johnson on May 17, 1913, to become effective on August 10.

The law prohibited *issei* and companies in which *issei* held the majority of stock from purchasing agricultural land and limited the leasing of such land to three years. Land already owned by *issei* could not be given or sold to another *issei*. Although it was fairly easy to get around the law by setting up land companies with citizens holding the majority of stock, purchasing the land in the name of NISEI children or other means, the law had a significant impact on *issei* life.

Given the three-year leasing limit, for instance, *issei* farmers opted to grow only crops that could return a profit quickly rather than invest in orchards or vineyards, which would take longer to mature. The law no doubt encouraged other *issei* to leave America altogether for Japan or for other parts of the New World. Despite the sting of the law, the perception of many Californians was that the law was ineffective and, in the repressive days after World War I, the ANTI-JAPANESE MOVEMENT would return with a vengeance to remedy this. (See 1920 (CALIFORNIA) ALIEN LAND LAW, ALIEN LAND LAWS.)

For further reading, see Roger Daniels. *The Politics of Prejudice: The Anti-Japanese Movement in California and the Struggle for Japanese Exclusion*. 1962. 2nd edition. Berkeley: University of California Press, 1977; Yuji Ichioka. "Japanese Immigrant Response to the 1920 California Alien Land Law." *Agricultural History* 58.2 (Apr. 1984): 157–78 and *The Issei: The World of the First Generation Japanese Immigrants, 1885–1924*. New York: The Free Press, 1988; Herbert P. LePore. "Prelude to Prejudice: Hiram Johnson, Woodrow Wilson and the California Land Law Controversy of 1913." *Southern California Quarterly* 61.1 (Spring 1979): 99–110; and Spencer C. Olin. "European Immigrant and Oriental Alien: Acceptance and Rejection by the California Legislature of 1913." *Pacific Historical Review* 35.3 (Aug. 1966): 303–15.

1903 Oxnard Strike   Strike involving Japanese and Mexican farm laborers in Oxnard, California. The 1903 strike of farm laborers in Oxnard, a coastal community about 50 miles north of Los Angeles, showed both the power of inter-ethnic cooperation and the adamancy of organized labor's anti-Japanese stance. With the building of the American Sugar Beet Company factory in 1898 came a tremendous expansion of sugar beet growers in the area. The Western Agricultural Contracting Company (WACC) was the major LABOR CONTRACTOR and supplied mainly Japanese and Mexican labor to the growers. WACC labor harvested 75 percent of the sugar beet crop in 1902. Early in 1903, the WACC recruited 120 Japanese workers and assigned them to a subcontractor. These new workers protested this arrangement on the grounds that it broke promises made to them by the WACC and quickly organized their fellow workers. On February 11, 1903, 500 Japanese and 200 Mexican workers formed the Japanese-Mexican Labor Association (JMLA) with Kozaburo Baba as president. Among other things, the JMLA was the first farm workers union in California. The JMLA protested receiving lower wages than promised by the WACC, having to pay an additional commission to the subcontractor and being forced to patronize the company store. These complaints must have struck a chord; by the end of March, 1,200 workers representing 90 percent of the labor force were out on strike. After a shooting incident resulted in the death of one striker and injured four others on March 23, negotiations between the growers, the WACC and the JMLA commenced. On March 30, an agreement was reached wherein the WACC canceled all its contracts but one, breaking the WACC monopoly.

Local labor councils looked favorably upon the JMLA but not the national bodies. JMLA secretary J. M. Lizarras applied for an American Federation of Labor (AFL) charter under the name of the Sugar Beet and Farm Laborers' Union of Oxnard. Because the AFL would only accept them if they booted out their Asian members, the union refused to accept the charter. This was consistent with established AFL policy of not accepting Asians. This policy remained unchanged until the 1930s.

For further reading, see Tomas Almaguer. "Racial Domination and Class Conflict in Capitalist Agriculture: The Oxnard Sugar Beet Workers' Strike of 1903." *Labor History* 25.3 (1984): 325–50; Stephen S. Fugita. "A Perceived Ethnic Factor in California's Farm Labor Conflict: The Nisei Farmer's League." *Explorations in Ethnic Studies* 1.1 (1978): 50–72; and Yuji Ichioka. *The Issei: The World of the First Generation Japanese Immigrants, 1885–1924.* New York: The Free Press, 1988.

1920 (California) Alien Land Law   California ballot initiative that tightened the loopholes in the 1913 (CALIFORNIA) ALIEN LAND LAW and reinvigorated the ANTI-JAPANESE MOVEMENT, setting it on the road to exclusion. The law banned "ALIENS INELIGIBLE TO CITIZENSHIP" from purchasing and leasing agricultural land, purchasing stock in land companies that owned or leased agricultural land and appointing themselves guardians of minors who owned such land. Stunned by the potential impact of the laws, the Japanese immigrant community mounted a drive to test the various provisions of the law in the courts. The court decisions resulted in a total defeat for the ISSEI. Although the law did not succeed in relegating the *issei* to migrant labor status, it did have a devastating impact on the Japanese community, leading to a decline in *issei* land holdings and a reaffirmation of their unequal status in their adopted country.

Led by white farmers, opportunistic politicians such as United States Senator JAMES PHELAN and nativist groups such as the NATIVE SONS OF THE GOLDEN WEST, anti-Japanese agitation began anew in 1919 after the relative quiet of the World War I years. These groups seized upon the perceived failures in the GENTLEMEN'S AGREEMENT and the 1913 Alien Land Law, citing the greatly increased numbers of NISEI due to the influx of *issei* women and the increase in *issei*-owned farmland since 1913. Using YELLOW PERIL rhetoric to fan fears of a Japanese invasion, miscegenation and agricultural economic domination, anti-Japanese forces from all levels of California society formed a powerful coalition. One of the first orders of business was the drafting of a revised land law that would close off the loopholes of the 1913 law. Drafted by March 1920, enough signatures were quickly obtained to put it on the November 1920 ballot. An intense campaign for its passage ensued, led by politicians such as Phelan, the American Legion, the Native Sons and Daughters, farmers and most California newspapers. A campaign against the laws was launched by the JAPANESE ASSOCIATION of America and by a small number of non-Japanese groups opposed to the anti-Japanese movement led by Protestant missionaries such as SIDNEY GULICK. The measure passed by a three-to-one margin and became effective on December 9, 1920.

Recognizing the dire threat the new law represented to the economic heart of the Japanese community, *issei* leaders fought the law on two fronts. On the one hand, farmers devised various means to get around the law. Until they were ruled illegal, CROPPING CONTRACTS—whereby *issei* became "employees" or "managers" rather than tenants—were a popular way of retaining control of farmland. Utilizing citizen middlemen to lease land, relying on oral agreements or forming land companies owned by citizens that "hired" *issei* to "manage" the farm were other means of circumventing the law. On the other hand, the Japanese Associations mounted an intense legal campaign to test various aspects of the law in the courts. PORTERFIELD V. WEBB, FRICK V. WEBB, WEBB V. O'BRIEN and the YANO GUARDIANSHIP CASE challenged the constitutionality of the ban on leasing, the ban on ownership of stock in land companies, the ban on cropping contracts, and the ban on guardianship, respectively. While the *Yano* decision did invalidate the ban on guardianship, allowing *issei* to serve as guardians of *nisei* children who owned farmland, all the other cases ended in defeat for the *issei*. In a one-week period in November 1923, decisions on the other three cases upheld the legality of the other provisions of the 1920 Alien Land Law. The line in the sand had been drawn.

There is some disagreement among scholars as to the effectiveness of the law. Some claim it was ineffective, citing lax enforcement, the ability of the *issei* to use guardianship and other means to get around it, and the fact that *issei* land ownership was already nearly as high as it would have gotten anyway. Others see the law as having had a major economic and psychological impact on the immigrant community. After years of steady increase, for instance, *issei* land ownership began to decline after 1920. As yet another sign that they were not wanted in their adopted country and could never be true Americans, the law had a demoralizing effect on many *issei,* prompting some to leave the country for Japan or other parts of the New World. In the context of the OZAWA V. U.S. decision of 1922 definitively banning *issei* from becoming naturalized citizen and the IMMIGRA-TION ACT OF 1924, which ended all further immigration from Japan, the 1920 Alien Land Law and its upholding by the courts did certainly set the limits for just how much Japanese immigrants would be allowed to achieve in their adopted country.

For further reading see Roger Daniels. *The Politics of Prejudice: The Anti-Japanese Movement in California and the Struggle for Japanese Exclusion.* 1962. 2nd edition. Berkeley: University of California Press, 1977; Robert Higgs. "Landless by Law—Japanese Immigrants in California Agriculture to 1941." *Journal of Economic History* 38.1 (Mar. 1978): 205–26; Yuji Ichioka. "Japanese Immigrant Response to the 1920 California Alien Land Law." *Agricultural History* 58.2 (Apr. 1984): 157–78 and *The Issei: The World of the First Generation Japanese Immigrants, 1885–1924.* New York: The Free Press, 1988.

1920 Plantation Strike

The 1920 PLANTATION strike was significant for its length, size and scope, multiethnic character, and for the long-term effects it had on planter-worker relations and on Hawaii's Japanese American community. At its peak, the six-month-long strike saw 8,300 Japanese and Filipino American workers representing 77 percent of the work force on Oahu participate.

In the years since the 1909 PLANTATION STRIKE, the cost of living in Hawaii had risen dramatically while

1920 sugar plantation strike in Hawaii. *Toraki Kurashima Collection, Japanese American National Museum Photographic & Moving Image Archive*

wages failed to keep pace. The work force had became more settled and families had continued to grow. In November of 1917, an Association for Higher Wages formed and petitioned the planters for wage increases, bonus system reform and day care. Though the HAWAII SUGAR PLANTERS ASSOCIATION (HSPA) refused their request, no further action was taken by the plantation workers because of World War I and the possible misrepresentation of their motives during a war. However, soon after the war ended, continued unsatisfactory conditions led to intense labor organization. Through Young Men's Buddhist Association (YMBA) chapters on the various islands, various higher wage groups began to organize starting in October 1919. A five-day meeting of these groups in December 1919 led to the formation of the Federation of Japanese Labor, a group organized along the lines of the American Federation of Labor. The new group announced a set of demands that included an increase of the minimum wage (from 77¢ to $1.25 a day for men and from 58¢ to 95¢ a day for women), reform of the bonus system, an eight hour work day, eight weeks of paid maternity leave for women workers, and improved health care and recreational facilities, among other things. The plans were summarily rejected by the planters by January 1920.

As the federation was mulling over its options, including a possible strike later in the year, 2,600 Filipino American and 300 Spanish and Puerto Rican plantation workers walked off their jobs on six plantations on Oahu on January 20, 1920. Caught by surprise and their hand somewhat forced by members who refused to cross picket lines, the federation joined the strike on January 23. As in the 1909 strike, the planters were ruthless in opposing the strikers. Some 2,000 strikebreakers were brought in, lured by wages two to three times what the strikers were asking for. Pablo Manlapit, leader of the Filipino Labor Union, was offered a $25,000 bribe by the planters and called off the strike on February 8. (Many Filipino American workers continued to strike, however; Manlapit reversed himself and revealed the attempted bribe on February 10.) Strikers were evicted from plantation housing starting on February 18; some 12,020 people were displaced, one-third of whom were children. Thousands of refugees streamed into Honolulu in the midst of an influenza epidemic—some believed the planters deliberately sped up the evictions to coincide with the epidemic. According to Federation of Japanese Labor estimates, 95 Filipino Americans and 55 Japanese Americans died in the epidemic. Perhaps most damaging were accounts in the press that portrayed the strike not as an American labor conflict but as an "invasion" or an attempt by Japanese "agitators" to take over the sugar industry, thus threatening national security. In short, it was the fear of the YELLOW PERIL being invoked again. "The strike is an attempt on the part of the Japanese to obtain control of the sugar industry. It is in line with Japanese policy wherever they colonize. It is a part of the Japanization of Korea, Manchuria, Eastern Inner Mongolia, Shantung, and Formosa," warned the *Pacific Commercial Advertiser* on February 2, despite the renunciation of the strike by the Japanese consuls in Honolulu. "Is control of this industrialism of Hawaii to remain in the hands of Anglo-Saxons or is it to pass into those of alien Japanese agitators?" asked the *Honolulu Star-Bulletin* on February 13. Japanese businessmen, the Japanese Chamber of Commerce and the Japanese Association of Hawaii along with prominent HAOLE led by the Reverend Albert W. Palmer drafted a plan calling for the end of the strike by the federation and the arrangement of elections of an "employee's committee" on each plantation by the planters. Though the federation agreed to accept the proposal on February 27 if the planters would do the same, such an agreement by the HSPA was not forthcoming.

Faced with such opposition along with money and morale problems, solidarity began to wane and internal conflicts over tactics arose. To raise morale, theatrical performances were held and the "77¢ Parade" of 3,000 Japanese and Filipino American strikers was organized. "How can we live like Americans on 77¢?" read their signs. The strike ended quietly on July 1 in a near total victory for the planters. However, the six plantations struck on Oahu lost an estimated $11.5 million. Three months later, wages rose by 50 percent and in the next few years, housing conditions and recreational facilities improved. Although many Japanese Americans had sought to leave the plantations before, the aftermath of the strike saw a flood of ISSEI and especially NISEI leave the plantations for good. Japanese American workers would never again make up a majority of the plantation labor force. Meanwhile, hoping to rid themselves of the troublesome Japanese American workers, the planters began an ultimately unsuccessful campaign to replace them with Chinese migrant labor.

For further reading, see Lawrence H. Fuchs. *Hawaii Pono: A Social History*. New York: Harcourt, Brace and World, 1961; Roland Kotani. *The Japanese in Hawaii: A Century of Struggle*. Honolulu: Hochi, Ltd., 1985; Franklin S. Odo and Kazuko Sinoto. *A Pictorial History of the Japanese in Hawaii, 1885–1924*. Honolulu: Bishop Museum Press, 1985; Gary Y. Okihiro. *Cane Fires: The Anti-Japanese Movement in Hawaii, 1865–1945*. Philadelphia: Temple University Press, 1991; and Ronald Takaki. *Pau Hana: Plantation Life and Labor in Hawaii, 1835–1920*. Honolulu: University of Hawaii Press, 1983. For an account of the attempt to bring in Chinese laborers, see John E. Reinecke. *Feigned Necessity: Hawaii's Attempt to Obtain Chinese Contract Labor, 1921–23*. San Francisco: Chinese Materials Center, 1979.

[Quotes from Okihiro.]

Ninth Street (Produce) Market   Los Angeles produce market. With the growth in Japanese agriculture in the early 1900s, the cramped facilities at the so-called THIRD STREET MARKET in Los Angeles were found to be lacking. A group of Japanese immigrants who used this market formed the Nanka Nogyo Kumiai (Japanese Farmers' Association of Southern California) in November 1907 to propose the establishment of a new market. This proposal was discussed at an October 1908 meeting attended by 70 members. The new Los Angeles City Market opened in June 1909 at San Pedro and Ninth Streets and became known as the Ninth Street market. The initial executive board consisted of a Caucasian president, Chinese and Italian vice-presidents, a Japanese secretary and a Russian accountant. Japanese owned 18 percent of the shares in this market at the time it opened. One hundred twenty of the 180 stalls were occupied by Japanese initially, but only four out of 44 commission merchants were Japanese. The Japanese presence at the Ninth Street Market continued to be high in the decades to follow; for instance, some 50 percent of all transactions in the early 1930s involved Japanese.

In the early days of the Ninth Street Market, relations between tenants there and tenants at the old Third Street Market became strained. In support of the Ninth Street Market, the Nanka Nogyo Kumiai started the *Shinichiba Joho* (New Market News) and later the *Rafu Asahi Shinbun*. By the 1910s, the two groups had reconciled and a group called the Shinwa Club (Friendship Club) was even formed to promote good relations between the two groups. Other groups affiliated with the Ninth Street Market included the Ninth Street Market Wholesalers

Directors in front of Nippon Kan Theatre advertising screen, ca. 1910. *Nippon Kan Heritage Association Collection, Japanese American National Museum Photographic & Moving Image Archive*

Association, established in 1929, the Ninth Street Yardmen's Association, also begun in 1929, and the Ninth Street Young Men's Association, begun in 1927.

For further reading, see Noritaka Yagasaki. "Ethnic Cooperativism and Immigrant Agriculture: A Study of Japanese Floriculture and Truck Farming in California." Diss., University of California, Berkeley, 1982.

Nippon Kan Theatre Built in 1909, in the heart of Seattle's old Japantown, the Nippon Kan Theatre served as a focal point for Japanese American community affairs. The building was the venue for many cultural and political events from the early 1900s to 1942. After numerous changes in ownership and financial struggles, it was finally restored in 1981, and opened its doors again to community use. The Nippon Kan is included on the National Register of Historic Places and is now part of the refurbished Kobe Park Building.

Located at Yesler and Seventh Avenue, the Nippon Kan was built by the Cascade Investment Company, formed by Takahashi, Hirade and Tsukuno. From 1909 to 1942, numerous political debates, musicals, concerts, puppet shows, plays, operas and symphonies were performed at the theater. JUDO, KENDO, SUMO wrestling and other Japanese martial arts competitions were also held there. In addition, the Japanese community sponsored church fund-raisers and sports team banquets there. The theater was also home to *koto, shakuhachi, biwa, shamisen* (all stringed musical instruments) and Kabuki performing groups.

During this time, MASAJIRO FURUYA, a prominent banker, acquired the building and sold stock to community members to raise capital. In 1932, Furuya went bankrupt and the property reverted to his creditors. The Tanaka family managed the hall until the forced removal of Japanese Americans to CONCENTRATION CAMPS at the beginning of World War II, at which time Caucasian friends took over. The theatre then lost revenue due to mismanagement and rent restrictions and was again seized by the bank. In 1946, Saiji Nakamura purchased the property and lived in and managed the apartments upstairs. However, the theater remained vacant as Nakamura's hopes to refurbish the building went unfulfilled and community interest in the theater waned. He sold the building in 1967 to Abie Label.

In 1969, Betty and Edward Burke, then president of the Seattle Chapter of the American Institute of Architects, purchased the building. The building had a leaky roof, broken windows and suffered from minor fire damage. Their original intent was to convert the building to office space, until the new owners discovered the theater inside. Because of economic difficulties, the building plans were delayed. As the Burkes learned more about the theater and the history of Seattle's Japanese American community, they became committed to preserving the Nippon Kan and placed it on the National Register of Historic Places. They obtained a silent partner and a grant to redevelop the building.

In February 1981, the restored theater re-opened to a lecture/demonstration of Kabuki. The Nippon Kan Heritage Association, a nonprofit organization independent of the hall, produced the Japanese Performing Arts series initiated by the Burkes. Since then, the theater has become a well-known venue not only for performing arts groups from Japan but for theater groups, conventions, lecture series, community socials, new music series, jazz and rock troupes, and chamber music groups. All have benefited from the theatre's flexible hall space and good acoustics.

Edward and Betty Burke left the theater and the Kobe Park Building in a business dispute in 1990. The building is now owned by Samuel Strom and managed by Martin Smith, Inc. Spectra Communications, an Asian American public relations and consulting firm, took over management of the theater in February 1991. It now houses the theater, Spectra Communications, the *International Examiner* newspaper and other private offices.

For further reading, see Ed Burke and Betty Burke. "In a Chorus of Shadows: The Story of the Nippon Kan and its Restoration." In Tsutakawa, Mayumi, and Alan Chong Lau, ed. *Turning Shadows into Light: Art and Culture of the Northwest's Early Asian/Pacific Community*. Seattle: Young Pine Press, 1982. 46–53 and David Takami. *Executive Order 9066: 50 Years Before and 50 Years After; A History of Japanese Americans in Seattle*. Seattle, Wash.: Wing Luke Asian Museum, 1992.

EMILY LAWSIN

The *Nippu Jiji* building, ca. 1930s. *Kinichi Asami Collection, Japanese American National Museum Photographic & Moving Image Archive*

[Also used to compile this entry: Mary Akamine. "Resignations at Nippon Kan triggered by business dispute." *International Examiner* 5 Sept. 1990: 4; Midori Kono Thiel. "Burkes leave Nippon Kan: Twenty years of 'heartaches, much happiness.' " *International Examiner* 5 Sept. 1990: 5; and Doug Chin, and Peter Bacho. "The origins of the International District." *International Examiner* 21 Nov. 1984: 5–6.]

Nippu Jiji   The *Nippu Jiji* was the most popular Japanese newspaper in Hawaii in the 1910s and early 1920s and remained highly influential until World War II. It's convoluted history began with the formation of the *Nippon Shuho,* Hawaii's first Japanese newspaper, on June 3, 1892. Its founder was Bunichiro Onome, an ex-immigrant inspector who founded it in order to criticize the Bureau of Immigration for its treatment of Japanese immigrants. After only a few months, it became the *Honolulu Hochi.* In 1893, it changed ownership and became the *Nijjiseiki,* then the *Honolulu Hochi* and the *Hawaii Shimbun* in 1894. On October 15, 1895, it debuted as *The Yamato,* a mimeographed semi-weekly paper put out by Shintaro Anno and Hamon Mizuno, and served as the mouthpiece of the Japanese private immigration companies. It became the *Yamato Shimbun* in 1896.

In the meantime, a young editor named YASUTARO SOGA began to work for the HAWAII SHIMPO in 1899. In 1905, he was urged to take over the *Yamato Shimbun* by a friend, but balked since he had consistently taken a stance against the immigration companies and didn't want to join enemy ranks. However, the immigration companies were on their way out of Hawaii by this time and were looking to liquidate their possessions. Assured of this fact, Soga took over the paper in May 1905,

changed the name to the *Nippu Jiji,* and completely changed the editorial policy in 1906. Soga soon became a key figure in the 1909 PLANTATION STRIKE and the *Nippu Jiji* became the mouthpiece of the strikers. In the years following the strike, it became the most popular Japanese paper in Hawaii but also adopted a more cautious editorial policy. Although it was more conservative than KINZABURO MAKINO's HAWAII HOCHI, the *Nippu Jiji* consistently pushed for the Americanization of the second-generation immigrants and supported the Japanese-language schools. When the *Hochi* spearheaded the successful court fight on behalf of the language schools, it passed up the *Nippu* in circulation. The *Nippu Jiji* became the *Hawaii Times* in 1942 and continues to publish to this day.

For further reading, see Lawrence H. Fuchs. *Hawaii Pono: A Social History.* New York: Harcourt, Brace and World, 1961; Franklin S. Odo, and Kazuko Sinoto. *A Pictorial History of the Japanese in Hawaii, 1885–1924.* Honolulu: Bishop Museum Press, 1985; United Japanese Society of Hawaii. *History of Japanese in Hawaii.* James H. Okahata, ed. Honolulu: United Japanese Society of Hawaii, 1971; and Robert A. Wilson, and Bill Hosokawa. *East to America: A History of the Japanese in the United States.* New York: Morrow, 1980.

nisei   Second-generation Japanese Americans. The *nisei* are the children of the ISSEI, the parents of the SANSEI and the grandparents of the YONSEI. As is true of the other generations, the word *nisei* comes from the Japanese character for the generation number, in this case, "two." The *nisei* are the first American-born generation. Most mainland *nisei* were born between the years 1915 and 1935; in Hawaii large numbers were born about a decade earlier. The word *Nisei* was once used to refer to all Japanese Americans, but is not commonly used in that regard today.

Nearly all *nisei* share a common background. Many grew up in a rural setting, whether on Hawaii sugar plantations or mainland family farms, were part of a large family, had a different first language than their parents, had a father who started his family fairly late in life, attended both a regular school and private JAPANESE-LANGUAGE SCHOOLS and had their lives dramatically changed by events stemming from World War II. One major division among the *nisei* is between those who were educated in the United States and the KIBEI who were sent to Japan for a part of their education as children and who tended to be more Japanese in outlook than the other *nisei.* Nearly all *nisei* see the World War II years as a key turning point in their lives whether it meant "VOLUNTARY" RESETTLEMENT, life in an American CONCENTRATION CAMP; military service in the 442ND REGIMENTAL COMBAT TEAM, the 100TH INFANTRY BATTALION or the MILITARY INTELLIGENCE SERVICE; RESETTLEMENT out of the camps to midwestern or eastern cities; being branded "disloyal" NO-NO BOYS sent to TULE LAKE "SEGREGATION CENTER"; or renunciation of their American citizenship and a journey "back" to a Japan they had never been to. Many *nisei* were in a position to benefit from the expanding postwar economy and became part of what was known as the "MODEL MINORITY;" others never recovered from the war and died in poverty. Today, the *nisei* are in their later years, intent on leaving behind a legacy of their achievements for the generations to come through the many local and national Japanese American historical organizations that have sprung up over the last few years.

Much of the existing literature on the Japanese Americans focuses on the *nisei* experience. What follows are some major works dealing with specific aspects of the *nisei* experience.

There is a relatively small body of literature dealing with *nisei* prior to World War II, focusing on identity and politics. These works include Yuji Ichioka. "A Study in Dualism: James Yoshinori Sakamoto and the Japanese American Courier, 1928–1942." *Amerasia Journal* 13.2 (1986–87): 49–81; Valerie J. Matsumoto. "Desperately Seeking 'Deirdre': Gender Roles, Multicultural Relations, and Nisei Women Writers of the 1930s." *Frontiers* 12.1 (1991): 19–32; Gail M. Nomura. "The Debate Over the Role of Nisei in Prewar Hawaii: The New Americans Conference, 1927–1951." *Journal of Ethnic Studies* 15.1 (Spring 1987): 95–115; Jerrold Haruo Takahashi. "Changing Responses to Racial Subordination: An Exploratory Study of Japanese American Political Styles." Diss., University of California, Berkeley, 1980 and "Japanese American Responses to Race Relations: The Formation of Nisei Perspectives." *Amerasia Journal* 9.1 (1982): 29–57; Eileen Hisayo Tamura. "The Americanization Campaign and the Assimilation of the Nisei in Hawaii, 1920 to 1940." Diss., University of Hawaii, 1990; and Hiroshi Yoneyama. "The Forging of Japanese American Patriotism, 1931–1941." Thesis, University of Tsukuba, 1984.

Works dealing with *nisei* during World War II and its immediate aftermath are numerous; references to them can be found under the various headings listed above. Works dealing with the *nisei* after World War II are also numerous. Many deal with *nisei* "success" and achievement while many others debunk the so-called "model minority" characterization; see the "MODEL MINORITY" entry for references to such works. There are also many studies of *nisei* assimilation or identity; see for example Stephen S. Fugita, and David J. O'Brien. *Japanese American Ethnicity: The Persistence of Community.* Seattle: University of Washington Press, 1991 and Harry H. L. Kitano. *Japanese Americans: The Evolution of a Subculture.* 1969. 2nd edition. Englewood Cliffs, N.J.: Prentice-Hall, Inc., 1976. See also the various multi-generational studies found in the SANSEI entry.

Autobiographical and/or literary works by *nisei* are also numerous. Among them are Tom Ige. *Boy from Kahaluu: An Autobiography.* Honolulu: University of Hawaii Press, 1989; Daniel K. Inouye, with Lawrence Elliot. *Journey to Washington.* Englewood Cliffs, N.J.: Prentice-Hall, 1967; Mike Masaoka, and Bill Hosokawa. *They Call Me Moses Masaoka.* New York:

William Morrow, 1987; Toshio Mori. *Yokohama, California.* Introd. William Saroyan. Caldwell, Idaho: Caxton Printers, Ltd., 1949. Introd. Lawson Fusao Inada. Seattle: University of Washington Press, 1985; Milton Murayama. *All I Asking for Is My Body.* 1959. San Francisco: Supa Press, 1975. Afterword by Franklin Odo Honolulu: University of Hawaii Press, 1988; John Okada. *No-No Boy.* Rutland, Vt.: Charles E. Tuttle, 1957. San Francisco: Combined Asian American Resources Project, Inc., 1976. Introd. Lawson Fusao Inada. Afterword by Frank Chin. Seattle: University of Washington Press, 1979; Monica Sone. *Nisei Daughter.* Boston: Little, Brown and Company, 1953. S. Frank Miyamoto, introd. Seattle: University of Washington Press, 1979; Mary Tsukamoto, and Elizabeth Pinkerton. *We the People: A Story of Internment in America.* San Jose: Laguna Publishers, 1987; Hisaye Yamamoto. *Seventeen Syllables and Other Stories.* Latham, N.Y.: Kitchen Table Women of Color Press, 1988; and Karl G. Yoneda. *Ganbatte: Sixty-Year Struggle of a Kibei Worker.* Los Angeles: Asian American Studies Center, University of California, Los Angeles, 1983.

nisei clubs/gangs As is true of many other immigrant and minority communities, youth clubs/gangs were a part of the Japanese American community. When the coming of age of the NISEI generation in the 1930s was combined with lack of opportunity and discrimination, gang activity was one result. Ironically, many *nisei* gangs were rooted in legitimate clubs that were formed to keep youth off the streets. Rivalries between the clubs from various areas became manifest at events that brought them together—dances, house parties and NISEI WEEK, for example—in the form of gang fights. Though they occasionally fought gangs of other ethnicities, most conflicts seemed to be with other *nisei* clubs/gangs.

Gang-type activity continued in the World War II CONCENTRATION CAMPS and into the postwar era. Many SANSEI growing up in the 1950s and '60s in urban areas were also involved in such activity. The 1958 shooting of a *sansei* honor student caught in the crossfire of two *sansei* gangs at a Los Angeles Chinatown dance brought much attention to the juvenile delinquency problem in the Japanese American community. Though Japanese American gangs are virtually nonexistent today, there are undoubtedly many Japanese American youths who are involved in illegal activity.

As is probably true of people of all ethnic groups who join gangs, Japanese American youth gang members sought a sense of community and self-esteem they otherwise lacked. Many *nisei* coming of age in the '30s grew up in households where both parents worked long hours in family farms or businesses and faced a future that seemed to hold distinctly limited possibilities. Many *nisei* in the '30s and *sansei* in the '50s and '60s grew up without a positive sense of ethnic identity and gained a sense of belonging only from clubs/gangs. Given the importance of clubs/gangs to the self-image of their members, conflict was inevitable, as small perceived slights often evolved into gang warfare. Additionally, Japanese cultural values encouraging group behavior and problem solving may have added to the problem. Indeed, *nisei* and *sansei* who grew up in tight-knit Japanese American communities often were involved in gang type activity. The desire to keep problems inside the community has also resulted in an almost total lack of research and writing on this topic, perhaps contributing to the stereotype of Japanese Americans as a "MODEL MINORITY." For further reading, see Isami Arifuku Waugh. "Hidden Crime and Deviance in the Japanese-American Community, 1920–1946." Diss., University of California, Berkeley, 1978. For an account of the aftermath to the 1958 incident, see Gerald H. Ikeda "Japanese-Americans Fight Delinquency." *California Youth Authority Quarterly* 12.2 (Summer 1959): 3–6. For a series of interviews with *sansei* gang members, see Roy Nakano. "Them Bad Cats: Past Images of Asian American Street Gangs." *Gidra* 5.1 (Jan. 1973): 4–7; Jeff Furumura, Tom Okabe and Roy Nakano. "Them Bad Cats, Part II." *Gidra* 5.6 (June 1973): 1, 5–7; Jeff Furumura. "Them Bad Cats, Part III: Past Images of Asian American Street Gangs." *Gidra* 5.7 (July 1973): 9–11; and Jeff Furumura. "Them Bad Cats: A Follow-Up." *Gidra* 5.8 (Aug. 1973): 14.

Nisei Farmers League   Organization of mostly small California farmers formed in June 1971 by NISEI tree fruit and grape growers in Fresno and Tulare Counties in central California. The Nisei Farmers League (NFL) grew into a large and influential organization within a few years. It was begun as a response by *nisei* farmers to Cesar Chavez's United Farm Workers (UFW) and the perception that the UFW was targeting *nisei* farms for unionization drives and picketing. Several *nisei* farms were also vandalized. The 100 or so members of the NFL at the end of 1971 were nearly all Japanese American; by 1976, the organization had 1,500 members, only 40 percent of whom were Japanese American. The group was led by Parlier fruit grower Harry Kubo.

Initially, the NFL formed "picket patrols," which would engage in counterpicketing demonstrations at farms targeted by the UFW. Typically, the NFL would occupy one side of a street and the UFW the other, with sheriffs separating them. Reportedly, UFW leaders would bait the *nisei,* with references to the forced incarceration of World War II, such as "Why do you support the white growers when they put you into the CONCENTRATION CAMPS?" Many growers viewed Chavez and his organization as "Communist fronts" intent on taking over the food industry. In October 1974, the UFW tried to sue the NFL for inhibiting its strike efforts; a 1975 injunction was subsequently issued that set guidelines for picketing and counterpicketing. In August 1972, the organization intervened in the White Rivers Farm strike in Delano-Poplar, 100 miles south of Fresno & Tulare

Nisei Farmers League founder Harry Kubo.   *Harry Kubo Collection, Japanese American National Museum Photographic & Moving Image Archive*

counties. The dispute involved a large grape operation that had signed a UFW contract, but which under new ownership refused to renew the contract. Despite the apparent support of the UFW by the majority of White Rivers workers, the NFL agreed to help by supplying and protecting Fresno area workers and playing a key role in breaking the strike.

With its growing clout, the NFL also entered the legislative realm with its 1976 drive to defeat California Proposition 14, a referendum that would have provided additional funding for the Agricultural Labor Relations Act of 1975, thereby strengthening the UFW's ability to organize. NFL leader Kubo led a coalition of agricultural interests in opposing the measure. Advertisements for the farmers' position featured Kubo's picture and equated the measure with the loss of freedom brought on by the forced removal and incarceration of Japanese Americans in concentration camps during World War II. The measure was defeated by a 2-1 margin.

The NFL enjoyed a great deal of support from mainstream agricultural powers. In 1975, Secretary of Agriculture Earl L. Butz attended their banquet, praising them for their ". . . reputation of being fiercely loyal to the ideals and the concepts that make America great."

In the Japanese American community, the NFL ellicited strong reactions, both pro and con. Many *nisei,* especially those in rural areas, supported the group, while many SANSEI, especially those in urban areas, actively identified with and supported the UFW. The debate in the press found its way to the JAPANESE AMERICAN CITIZENS LEAGUE (JACL) during the Proposition 14 campaign; facing pressure from different segments of its membership, it finally took the view that as a labor-management dispute, it was outside the realm of JACL action.

For further reading, see Stephen S. Fugita "A Perceived Ethnic Factor in California's Farm Labor Conflict: The Nisei Farmer's League." *Explorations in Ethnic Studies* 1.1 (1978): 50–72; Stephen S. Fugita, and David J. O'Brien. "Economics, Ideology, and Ethnicity: The Struggle between the United Farm Workers Union and the Nisei Farmers League." *Social Problems* 25.2 (Dec. 1977): 146–56 and *Japanese American Ethnicity: The Persistence of Community.* Seattle: University of Washington Press, 1991.

[Butz quote cited in Fugita 78, p. 68.]

nisei sports leagues Begun in the 1930s for idle NISEI youth, all-*nisei* (and later SANSEI and YONSEI) sports leagues have been a major part of the mainland Japanese American community. The most popular and organized leagues were in the sport of basketball, both because of its relatively low cost of equipment and because Japanese Americans preferred to play amongst themselves rather than with non-Japanese because of the differential in physical size. The leagues were highly organized by age, skill and sex, and included regional, state and even national championships at one time. They also had all-star teams and awards banquets. The leagues reached peaks of popularity just prior to World War II and in the late 1940s and 1950s. There were also leagues for baseball, volleyball and other sports. They continue to exist as segregated leagues to this day, though a limited number of other ASIAN AMERICANS are allowed to play in most leagues. Then as now, most Japanese American newspapers feature extensive coverage of the leagues.

In Hawaii, by contrast, the dominant sport was baseball. Because most of Hawaii's population was Asian American and because baseball skill was not so directly related to physical size, Japanese American teams competed in leagues with those of other ethnic groups on an equal level. One such Japanese American team, the ASAHIS, was highly successful in Hawaii baseball leagues. For further reading, see Dexter Fong. "A Socio-Historical Study of the California Nisei Athletic Union 'AA' North-South Basketball." Thesis, California State University, Sacramento, 1973; Harry H. L. Kitano. *Japanese Americans: The Evolution of a Subculture.* 1969. 2nd edition. Englewood Cliffs, N.J.: Prentice-Hall, Inc., 1976; Haruo Nogawa. "A Study of a Japanese-American Basketball League and the Assimilation of its Members into the Mainstream of United States Society (California)." Diss., Oregon State University, 1984; Haruo Nogawa, and S. J. Suttie. "A Japanese-American Basketball League and the Assimilation of its Members into Mainstream of United States Society." *International Review for the Sociology of Sport* 19.3–4 (1984): 259–71; and Isami Arifuku Waugh. "Hidden Crime and Deviance in the Japanese-American Community, 1920–1946." Diss., University of California, Berkeley, 1978.

Nisei Week Annual celebration of Japanese American heritage held in Los Angeles's LITTLE TOKYO. The week-long summer celebration features various cultural events, including a carnival, a beauty contest and a parade. Similar events are held in the San Francisco and Honolulu Japanese American communities.

The first Nisei Week festival took place in 1934 out of a partnership between Los Angeles ISSEI and NISEI leaders who were concerned about the decline of the Little Tokyo area, which was due in part to the *nisei's* preferring to shop outside the community. The stated purpose of the festival was to help the businesses of Little Tokyo by encouraging *nisei* to shop there. Though the initial event lost money, succeeding Nisei Weeks became more and more popular, drawing interest from those outside the Japanese American community curious about the "exotic" foods and culture of the Japanese. Tens of thousands of people attended the parade and "street ondo," (a communal dance held as a part of the parade) which concluded the event in the late 1930s. These events were sometimes marred by significant *nisei* gang activity. With the mass removal and incarceration of all West Coast Japanese Americans during World War II, Nisei Week was stopped temporarily, resuming again in 1949. In the 1970s, the Nisei Weeks were marked by Vietnam War protests and controversies over the beauty contest. Recent Nisei Weeks have seen an increasing Japanese corporate presence. In 1990, the 50th Nisei Week was held.

For further reading, see the annual Nisei Week commemorative programs, especially the 1990 issue, which includes text and photos of all of the 50 prior Nisei Weeks.

Nishikawa v. Dulles Case brought before the U.S. Supreme Court in 1958 involving the loss of citizenship by a Japanese American who was conscripted into and served in the Japanese army during World War II. Mitsugi Nishikawa was born in California in 1916 and resided in the United States until 1939, at which time he went to Japan for further studies after graduating from the University of California. His name was entered into the family register, and he also submitted to a physical examination, as required by the Military Service Law of Japan. He was inducted into the Japanese army on March 1, 1941, and served in China, Indochina, the Philippines and Manchuria before he was finally discharged in September 1945. The U.S. government contended that Nishikawa had forfeited his citizenship by serving in the armed forces of a foreign state, but the United States Supreme Court held on March 31, 1958, that Nishikawa could not be denied his U.S. citizenship since the government failed to prove convincingly that Nishikawa served voluntarily.

For further reading, see Frank F. Chuman. *The Bamboo People: The Law and Japanese-Americans.* Del Mar, Calif.: Publisher's Inc., 1976. For other accounts of *nisei* who were forced to serve in the Japanese military during World War II, see the memoir Jim Yoshida, and Bill Hosokawa. *The Two Worlds of Jim Yoshida.* New York: Morrow, 1972, the novel George Nakagawa. *Seki-Nin (Duty Bound).* Arthur Hansen, ed. Fullerton: California State University, Fullerton, Oral History Program, 1989, and the article Floyd C. Watkins. "Even His

Name Will Die: The Last Days of Paul Nobuo Tatsuguchi." *Journal of Ethnic Studies* 3.4 (Winter 1976): 37–48.

DENNIS YAMAMOTO

Nishimoto, Richard S. (1904–1950s)   Richard S. Nishimoto was a key staff member of the JAPANESE AMERICAN EVACUATION AND RESETTLEMENT STUDY (JERS), providing detailed accounts of activities at POSTON and serving as coauthor of *The Spoilage,* one of the three official JERS publications.

Nishimoto's background was an unusual one. Born in Tokyo on August 23, 1904, he attended a Japanese elementary school until age 12 and an American Episcopal missionary intermediate school from the ages of 13 to 16. At the age of 17, he came to California to rejoin his parents. While helping out with his father's export business, he attended Lowell High school, graduating in 1925. From there, he went on to Stanford and earned an engineering degree in four years, graduating

Nisei Week Parade in Little Tokyo, Los Angeles, California, 1937.   *Karen L. Ishizuka Collection, Japanese American National Museum Photographic & Moving Image Archives*

Richard Nishimoto.   *Yae Nishimoto Collection, Japanese American National Museum Photographic & Moving Image Archive*

in 1929. While all of his Caucasian classmates received job offers upon graduation, Nishimoto did not. In the 1930s, he worked at various jobs, including running an insurance brokerage firm and preparing income tax forms on the side. In the mid-1930s, he began to operate a fruit and vegetable market in GARDENA, California. With the coming of World War II, Nishimoto, his NISEI wife and two daughters were removed along with all other Japanese Americans on the West Coast to inland CON-CENTRATION CAMPS, in their case, the camp at Poston, Arizona.

He quickly became a leader among the internee population at Poston. Given his relatively high level of education in both Japan and the United States, his fluency in both the Japanese and English languages, and his ISSEI generational status, he commanded immediate respect among all segments of the camp population. He also proved himself to be a capable administrator and problem solver with a great deal of personal ambition. He became a block manager in 1943 and eventually the supervisor of block managers and adviser to both internees and WAR RELOCATION AUTHORITY (WRA) leader-

ship in Poston. At the same time he was directly involved in the politics of the camp, he also reported on those activities as a member of the JERS research staff. Drawn to JERS through his relationship with JERS staff member Tamie Tsuchiyama, Nishimoto was hired as an assistant to Tsuchiyama in early 1943. As a fieldworker, he contributed voluminous data on conditions at Poston, including a personal journal. Throughout the next two years, Nishimoto played the dangerous dual role of camp leader and researcher, keeping his JERS activities secret.

Upon leaving Poston in 1945, he continued to work with JERS, joining project leader DOROTHY SWAINE THOMAS at the University of California, Berkeley. Though the exact nature of his contribution is unknown, he coauthored *The Spoilage* (University of California Press, 1946) with Thomas and as a consultant played an indirect role in the publication of the other two JERS books. Despite the leadership qualities he displayed in camp and the key role he played in the JERS project, the postwar years were destined to be sad ones for him. Outside the artificial world of the concentration camp, his influence and importance to the community ebbed. Unable to find any sort of academic position, he searched for any kind of employment. Before his death in the mid-1950s, his last job was as a night watchman at a San Francisco hotel.

For further reading, see Lane Ryo Hirabayashi, and James Hirabayashi. "The 'Credible' Witness: The Central Role of Richard S. Nishimoto in JERS." In Ichioka, Yuji, ed. *Views from Within: The Japanese American Evacuation and Resettlement Study*. Los Angeles: Asian American Studies Center, University of California, Los Angeles, 1989. 65–94.

Nishimura v. United States   Case brought before the U.S. Supreme Court in 1892 involving congressional acts that authorized immigration officials to deny entry to immigrants who, in their judgment, were likely to become public charges. Ekiu Nishimura, a 25-year-old Japanese woman, was deemed to be such an immigrant by immigration officials when she arrived in San Francisco from Yokohama on May 7, 1891. This was in spite of the fact that Mrs. Nishimura had been married for two years to a man who had been a resident of the United States for a year and who was to meet her in San Francisco. Mrs. Nishimura also managed to produce $21 in U.S. currency, the average amount of money brought by newly arrived foreign immigrants. She managed to take her case to the U.S. Supreme Court, where she contended that she was deprived of her liberty without due process of law since an administrative official was given the exclusive power to determine her right to land in the United States. The U.S. Supreme Court ruled against her on January 18, 1892. This case was the first involving a person of Japanese ancestry to be decided by the United States Supreme Court.

For further reading, see Frank F. Chuman. *The Bamboo People: The Law and Japanese-Americans*. Del Mar, Calif.: Publisher's Inc., 1976.   DENNIS YAMAMOTO

Nitobe, Inazo (1862–1933)   Scholar, author and professor. Born the son of a high-ranking samurai family in northern Japan, Nitobe attended the prestigious Sapporo Agricultural College (later Hokkaido University). Influenced by American missionaries who were also his teachers, Nitobe soon became a devout Christian. After graduating from the school, he entered Tokyo Imperial University, majoring in English literature and economics. In 1884, he went to the United States and attended Johns Hopkins University, after which he spent four years in a university in Germany. In 1891, he married Mary Patterson Elkinton, a Philadelphia Quaker, and the couple returned to Japan.

Nitobe was a leading author and scholar of United States-Japan relations and Japanese society. His most noted work is *Bushido: the Soul of Japan,* which advocates peace and understanding between the Japan and the United States. Yet, the 1924 Immigration Act, which excluded the Japanese from immigrating to the United States, enraged him to such an extent that he declared that he "would not step upon the shores of the United States until [the] law was repealed." However, nine years later Nitobe returned to the United States for a lecture tour in which he explained Japan's political positions in East Asia to an American public that was rapidly becoming anti-Japanese in the face of Japan's invasion of China. In the following year, Nitobe died after attending a conference in Canada.

For further reading, see Sharlie C. Ushioda. "Man of Two Worlds: An Inquiry into the Value System of Inazo Nitobe (1862–1933)." In Hilary Conroy and T. Scott Miyakawa, eds. *East Across the Pacific*. Santa Barbara, Calif.: American Bibliographical Center-Clio Press, 1972.   EIICHIRO AZUMA

Noda, Alice Sae Teshima (1894–1964)   The wife of STEERE NODA, Alice Noda was a pioneer in two fields in Hawaii: dental hygiene and cosmetology. Her first professional achievement was in the field of dental hygiene. In 1922, she graduated from the Honolulu Dental Hygiene School. Soon after graduation, she began to work for the Department of Public Instruction. Then in 1924, she was asked to head her former school.

As her career was advancing, her interest in health was also expanding. To her, personal hygiene also played an important role in health. Interested in diet and appearance, Alice Noda studied cosmetology in Los Angeles. In 1923, she opened a salon in Honolulu, the first in a chain of salons. In 1936, she went to Japan and opened a salon in the Ginza where she introduced permanent waves and Western hairstyles to Japanese women. By the late 1930s, Noda had become a prominent businesswoman, dividing her time between Tokyo and Honolulu.

In addition to her business, she was an active member of various women's groups. She gave talks, was an active fund-raiser, and was recognized as a leader by her peers. For further reading, see Barbara Bennett Peterson, ed. *Notable Women of Hawaii.* Honolulu: University of Hawaii Press, 1984.   EDITH KANESHIRO

Noda, Steere Gikaku (1892–1986)   Lawyer, politician, sportsman. Steere Noda was one of the first NISEI in Hawaii to gain prominence, becoming a lawyer and successful politician on the Islands. The son of an Ewa plantation worker, Noda first achieved fame as a baseball player. "Banzai" Noda was a pitcher and founding member of the ASAHIS in 1905 and was later one of the top amateur players on the Islands. The first graduate of Japanese High School in Honolulu in 1911, he was also a star baseball player at Mid Pacific Institute and began his career as a deputy collector for the Internal Revenue Service upon graduation. He later became a district court clerk and interpreter while he studied law, becoming the first *nisei* to work in Hawaii's court system in 1917. He became an attorney at law licenced to practice in the District Court of Honolulu on September 6, 1924. His clients were almost entirely ISSEI and *nisei*.

Noda and his wife, ALICE TESHIMA NODA, and their four children led a high-profile life. While Alice headed a dental hygiene school and wrote a syndicated beauty column, Steere practiced law and promoted many sports events featuring visiting and local athletes. He ran for the Board of Supervisors in Honolulu and lost immediately before the war; before he could run again, World War II began. After the war, in 1948, he was elected to the territorial house of representatives and later, in 1959, to the state senate. He was also a delegate to the statehood hearings in Washington D.C. Among his many awards are the Fifth Order of Rising Sun, bestowed by the Japanese government for his post–World War II relief efforts on behalf of Japan, and the Gold Cross, the highest award of the International Amateur Wrestling Foundation, for his support of amateur wrestling.

For further reading, see Lawrence H. Fuchs. *Hawaii Pono: A Social History*. New York: Harcourt, Brace and World, 1961; Gaylord K. Kubota. "Roots of AJA Baseball." *Hawaii Herald* 20 Mar. 1981: 7, 12; Patsy Sumie Saiki. *Japanese Women in Hawaii: The First 100 Years*. Honolulu: Kisaku, Inc., 1985; and Mary Wakayama. "Banzai Noda: Japanese American Pioneer." *Hawaii Herald* 3 Aug. 1984: 1.

Noguchi, Hideyo (1876–1928)   Bacteriologist, parasitologist and immunologist, Hideyo Noguchi literally devoted his life to medicine, helping to find cures for several diseases. Born at Inawashiro in northern Japan, Noguchi lived in poverty and had his hand severely burned as an infant. Nevertheless, he was inspired to pursue a medical career by Dr. K. Watanabe, the doctor who restored his hand. After graduating from Tokyo Medical College in 1897, Noguchi worked as a lecturer, a journal editor and an author of textbooks. He also served as a chief advisor to the International Sanitary Board in its fight against an outbreak of bubonic plague in China. After meeting American pathologist Simon Flexner, Noguchi decided to move to the United States to work under Flexner at the University of Pennsylvania. In 1904, he published important research on the study of snake venom in a volume titled *The Action of Snake Venom upon Cold-blooded Animals*. While at the Rockefeller Institute of Medical Research, Noguchi invented an innovative method for diagnosing syphilis. This pathbreaking research led him to also study Rocky Mountain spotted fever and later yellow fever. Noguchi became a global crusader in the treatment of yellow fever, conducting a comparative study of the disease on American Indians, Latin Americans and Africans. Unfortunately, from his exposure to the disease, Noguchi himself contracted yellow fever and died in Africa in 1928. He has been called "the outstanding figure in microbiology since Pasteur and Koch" by the *Concise Dictionary of American Biography*.

For further reading, see Gustav Eckstein. *Noguchi*. New York: Harper, 1931 and Isabell Rosanoff Plesset. *Noguchi and His Patrons*. Rutherford, N.J.: Fairleigh Dickinson University Press, 1980. See also *The Dictionary of American Biography*. New York: Charles Scribner's Sons.   SCOTT KURASHIGE

Noguchi, Isamu (1904–88)   One of the most important and celebrated sculptors of the 20th century, Noguchi is best known for his stone and stainless steel sculptures and his gardens. He also painted, worked with clay and designed stage sets, lighting equipment and furniture.

Noguchi was born on November 17, 1904, in Los Angeles, California. His father was ISSEI poet Yone Noguchi, and his mother was European American writer Leonie Gilmour. Although born in California, he was brought up in Japan from the age of two. For the next 12 years, he studied in Japanese and Jesuit schools. In 1918, at the age of 14, he was sent by his mother to Rolling Prairie, Indiana, where he attended the Interlaken School. However, the school was soon converted to a truck training camp for the U.S. Army, leaving Noguchi stranded. The school director eventually arranged an apprenticeship for him with Gutzon Borglum, the sculptor of Mt. Rushmore, in Stamford, Connecticut. Here, Noguchi discovered the world of sculpture, but was discouraged by Borglum from becoming a sculp-

tor. Consequently, Noguchi decided to study medicine at Columbia University. For two years, 1923 and 1924, he worked hard in a restaurant to pay for his tuition, but he soon realized that becoming a sculptor was his ultimate goal in life. With the support of his mother, he attended the Leonardo da Vinci School in Greenwich Village. Though trained classically, he was influenced principally by abstraction.

In 1927, he went to Paris on a Guggenheim Fellowship, working as an assistant to Constantin Brancusi for six months. Returning to New York in 1929, he supported himself by doing portrait busts in bronze and terra cotta. In 1930, he traveled to Paris, then took the Trans-Siberian Railroad through Asia, spending eight months in Beijing, where he studied brush painting, and six months in Japan. Among his works of the 1930s is a 72-foot long mural in Mexico City depicting scenes from Mexican history and his first large commission, a 10-ton stainless steel sculpture for the Associated Press Building in New York. In 1935, he began what would be a lifelong collaboration with choreographer Martha Graham, designing sets and props for her productions. In addition to Graham, he later worked with George Balanchine and Merce Cunningham.

During World War II he voluntarily spent six months at POSTON, Arizona, with incarcerated West Coast Japanese Americans. In 1951, he married Japanese actress Yoshiko Yamaguchi; the couple divorced in 1955.

Among his many major works of the post–World War II period are the gardens for the UNESCO building in Paris (1956–58), the Sunken Garden for the Beinicke Rare Book and Manuscript Library at Yale (1960–64), the Billy Rose Sculpture Garden for the Israeli Museum in Jerusalem and "Bolt of Lightning," a 102 foot tall stainless steel tribute to Benjamin Franklin in Philadelphia (1984). In 1985, the Isamu Noguchi Garden Museum was opened in Long Island City, Queens.

In 1968 Noguchi was the subject of a major retrospective at the Whitney Museum of American Art. A 1980 Whitney exhibit featured his landscapes and theater sets. Another major Noguchi retrospective took place in 1978 at the Walker Art Center. In 1982, he received the Edward MacDowell Medal for outstanding lifetime contribution to the arts and in 1987, he was awarded the National Medal of Arts by President Ronald Reagan.

Isamu Noguchi died of heart failure on December 30, 1988.

For further reading, see Dore Ashton. *Noguchi: East and West*. New York: Knopf, 1991; John Gordon. *Isamu Noguchi*. New York: Frederick A. Praeger, 1968; Nancy Grove and Diane Botnick. *The Sculpture of Isamu Noguchi, 1924–1979: A Catalogue*. New York: Garland Press, 1980; Sam Hunter. *Isamu Noguchi*. New York: Abbeville Press, 1978; *Isamu Noguchi*.

Zurich, Switzerland: City-Druck AG, 1972; and Isamu Noguchi. *A Sculptor's World*. New York: Harper & Row, 1968.

[Also used to compile this entry: Michael Brenson. "Isamu Noguchi, the Sculptor, Dies at 84." *New York Times* 31 Dec. 1988: 1, 9 and Hyung-Chan Kim, ed. *Dictionary of Asian American History*. Westport, Conn.: Greenwood Press, 1986.]

Noguchi, Thomas (1927–)   A world renowned forensic pathologist and a former chief coroner for Los Angeles County, Thomas Noguchi is perhaps most widely known as a result of his having been fired from his coroner's position in 1969. The curious nature of his firing and its occurrence at a period of increasing social activism by Asian Americans led to his dismissal's becoming a *cause célèbre* in the Asian American community and a key event in the development of the ASIAN AMERICAN MOVEMENT in Southern California.

Noguchi was born and raised in Japan. He graduated from Nippon Medical School and was an intern at Tokyo Imperial Hospital. He also received a degree in law. At age 25, he came to the U.S. to study pathology in 1952. He went on to study at Loma Linda University and to intern at Orange County General Hospital. He joined the L.A. County Coroner's Office in 1961. After a good deal of heated discussion, he was elected chief coroner by the L.A. County Board of Supervisors by a 3-2 vote on December 19, 1967.

On February 21, 1969, he was suddenly asked to resign by county chief administrative officer L. S. Hollinger over budget conflicts and his priorities in running the office. He handed in his resignation on February 25, effective on March 4. On March 4, he withdrew his resignation and was suspended by the Board of Supervisors for 30 days. His wife alleged racial discrimination in the episode. Noguchi was then fired by the Board by a 5-0 vote on March 18 after Hollinger's statement that he was "in need of psychiatric care, stemming from apparent use of drugs." Noguchi's lawyer vowed to appeal the decision. He was granted a full hearing before the Board, which lasted from May 12 to June 24. Finally on July 31, 1969, Thomas Noguchi was reinstated as chief coroner. Throughout his hearing, the case drew intense interest and support from the community. Much money was raised for Noguchi's defense and a group called Japanese United in the Search for Truth (J.U.S.T.) was formed. The core of supporters assembled for Noguchi's case would go on to play a key role in many other political battles in the years to come.

During his tenure as chief coroner, Noguchi presided over many notable investigations, including the cases of Robert Kennedy, Sharon Tate and the other victims of the Manson "family," and John Belushi. After 13 eventful years, Noguchi was demoted in 1982. Among the charges leveled against him was that he was too eager to seek publicity. Although he also fought this action, it was to no avail—he currently serves as deputy coroner at the Los Angeles County Medical Center. Ironically, he had just been elected president of the National Association of Medical Examiners at the time of his demotion. Since that time, he has written four books: *Coroner* (1983), his autobiography and a best-seller, *Coroner at Large* (1985), *Unnatural Causes* (1988) and *Physical Evidence* (1990).

For further reading, see Thomas T. Noguchi, with Joseph DiMona. *Coroner*. New York: Simon and Schuster, 1983.

[Also used to compile this entry: "Noguchi Leaving Post After Sirhan Trial." *Rafu Shimpo* 26 Feb. 1969:1; "Mrs. Noguchi Charges Racial Bias." *Rafu Shimpo* 5 Mar. 1969:1; "Noguchi Fired; Lawyer Will Appeal Decision." *Rafu Shimpo* 19 Mar. 1969: 1; *Gidra* 1.2 (1969): 1; *Gidra* 1.5 (1969): 16; Endo, Ellen. "Noguchi Wins Reinstatement as Coroner." *Rafu Shimpo* 31 July 1969: 1; *Gidra* 1.6 (1969): 2; Humphrey, Mark. "What Drives Asian-Americans?" *AsiAm* 1.1 (Dec. 1986): 9, 60–63; Ong, Henry. "The Rebels." *AsiAm* 2.10 (Oct. 1987): 22.]

"non-alien"   WAR RELOCATION AUTHORITY (WRA) euphemism meaning "American citizen." A number of euphemisms were used by the WRA with regard to the mass incarceration of Japanese Americans during World War II. Other terms included "evacuation" (forced removal or exclusion) and "relocation camp" (concentration, detention or prison camp). The use of the euphemism "non-alien" is a typical example of how far the government and WRA went to underplay the forced removal and detention both to the general public and to the Japanese American population.

For further reading, see Raymond Y. Okamura. "The American Concentration Camps: A Cover-Up through Euphemistic Terminology." *Journal of Ethnic Studies* 10.3 (Fall 1982):95–108.

GLEN KITAYAMA

no-no boy   A misnomer that refers to individuals, both male and female, who either refused to answer the "LOYALTY QUESTIONS" or answered in the negative. No-no boys were stigmatized as being "disloyal" to the United States and labeled "troublemakers" by the WAR RELOCATION AUTHORITY, the administrators in charge of the CONCENTRATION CAMPS. Once identified, they were segregated to the TULE LAKE "SEGREGATION CENTER" so that all of the so-called "bad apples" would not corrupt the "loyal" internees. Out of frustration with the way that their human rights were violated, many eventually renounced their American citizenship and expatriated to Japan (see RENUNCIATION OF CITIZENSHIP). Many others, after renouncing their citizenship, attempted to regain it after the war with the help of attorney WAYNE COLLINS.

No-No Boy is also the title of a novel written by JOHN OKADA that was originally published in 1957. It tells the story of a reluctant no-no boy trying to find his place in a post-war America hostile to Japanese Americans and a community that has rejected him as a "troublemaker" for the stand he took during the war. Ignored upon its initial publication, it was rediscovered in the 1970s and is now considered a classic.

For further reading, see Donald E. Collins. *Native American Aliens: Disloyalty and the Renunciation of Citizenship by Japanese Americans During World War II*. Westport, Conn.: Greenwood Press, 1985; John Okada. *No-No Boy*. Rutland, Vt.: Charles E. Tuttle, 1957. San Francisco: Combined Asian American Resources Project, Inc., 1976. Introd. Lawson Fusao Inada. Afterword by Frank Chin. Seattle: University of Washington Press, 1979; and Michi Weglyn. *Years of Infamy: The Untold Story of America's Concentration Camps*. New York: William Morrow & Co., 1976.   GLEN KITAYAMA

North American Buddhist Mission The pre-war incarnation of the BUDDHIST CHURCHES OF AMERICA.

Nye-Lea Bill Bill that allowed approximately 500 Asian veterans of World War I to become American citizens. TOKUTARO SLOCUM, a wounded army veteran who was born in Japan but adopted as a youth by an American family, played an integral role as a lobbyist for the bill. The bill was sponsored by Congressman Clarence F. Lea of California in the House of Representatives and by Senator Gerald Nye of North Dakota in the Senate, and was passed by Congress despite opposition from groups such as the California Joint Immigration Committee.

President Franklin D. Roosevelt signed the bill on June 24, 1935. The passage of this bill and the repeal of the CABLE ACT in 1936 were the first significant steps toward eroding the racial requirements in the naturalization laws of the United States applied against Asians. (See WORLD WAR I VETERANS.)

For further reading, see Frank F. Chuman. *The Bamboo People: The Law and Japanese-Americans*. Del Mar, Calif.: Publisher's Inc., 1976 and Harry Maxwell Naka. "The Naturalization of Japanese War Veterans of the World War Forces." Thesis, University of California, Berkeley, 1939. Bill Hosokawa. *JACL in Quest of Justice: The History of the Japanese American Citizens League*. New York: William Morrow, 1982 describes the Japanese American Citizens League's role in lobbying for the bill's passage.   DENNIS YAMAMOTO

O

Obata, Chiura (1885–1975) Artist, painter, designer and teacher. Born in Sendai, Japan, Obata began

training in freehand painting under the tutelage of Moniwa Chikusen at the age of eight. Trained and educated at Kogyo Terasaki in the Shijyo school of painting and by Gaho Hashimoto of the Kano school, he studied painting, sculpture, architecture, landscape design and handicrafts. In 1903 Obata arrived in San Francisco, where he accepted many commissions to decorate and paint murals in display rooms for various department stores and hotels. Soon Obata had numerous one-man shows and exhibitions of his paintings, watercolors and wood block prints throughout the United States. In 1932 he became an instructor at the University of California art department, while continuing his art shows and lectures around the country. In 1942 he had an exhibition of 120 of his paintings at International House, Berkeley, which was donated to the University of California for a scholarship to help a student, regardless of race, who "has suffered the most from" World War II. Along with all other West Coast Japanese Americans, Obata was forcibly removed and detained. He went first to Tanforan "ASSEMBLY CENTER" in San Bruno, California, where he organized an art school. Works from the Tanforan art school were exhibited at Mills College and Berkeley. Obata left Tanforan for TOPAZ, Utah, where he began another art school. During the 11 months he spent in American CONCENTRATION CAMPS, he created more than 500 paintings. After retiring from active teaching at the University of California, Obata was awarded emeritus status. He continued to lecture, exhibit and paint in his senior years.

For further reading, see Deborah Gesensway, and Mindy Roseman. *Beyond Words: Images from America's Concentration Camps*. Ithaca, N.Y.: Cornell University Press, 1987 and *The View from Within: Japanese American Art from the Internment Camps, 1942–1945*. Los Angeles: Japanese American National Museum, UCLA Wight Art Gallery and UCLA Asian American Studies Center, 1992.   ALICE HOM

Obon Annual Buddhist summer festival commemorating the spirits of the dead. Traditionally, Obon is observed in private religious rituals over a period of three days, from July 13 to July 15. On the first day, the spirits of dead are said to return to earth to visit their relatives' homes. On that day, families pay their respects to their ancestors by tending their graves. In the evening, families burn incense and suspend paper lanterns in front of their homes to greet the returning spirits. On the second day, a mat is placed in front of the families' shrines, the memorial tablets of the deceased are placed on them, food offerings are made, and families summon a Buddhist priest to chant sutras for the dead. During the evening of the third day, the spirits depart for the realm of the dead. In a ceremony called the *toro nagashi*, the spirits are guided on their return journey by candle-lighted paper lanterns set afloat on a river by their relatives.

Japanese Americans today place little emphasis on the private Buddhist rituals surrounding Obon; they are rituals that most NIKKEI no longer believe in or observe. Rather, for the *Nikkei,* Obon has generally evolved into a secular social community festival held in various Japanese American communities from the mid-afternoons through the evenings on weekends in July and August. The proceeds from the festival benefit the Buddhist churches that organize them.

The Japanese American Obon festival encompasses traditional Obon folk dances *(Obon odori)* that commemorate the spirits of the dead, live traditional Obon music that accompanies Obon dances, food, carnival games and fund-raising raffles. The festivals are an occasion for Japanese Americans (and increasing numbers of non-Japanese Americans) to watch Japanese Obon folk dancing, to meet and socialize with family and friends in the Japanese American community, to eat Japanese American and American food, and, especially for the children, to play the carnival-style games.
For further reading, see John DeFrancis, and V. R. Lincoln. *Things Japanese in Hawaii.* Honolulu: University Press of Hawaii, 1973; Judy Van Zile. "Japanese Bon Dance and Hawaii: Mutual Influences." *Social Processes in Hawaii* 30 (1983): 49–58; and Christine Reiko Yano. "Japanese Bon Dance Music in Hawaii: Continuity, Change and Variability." Thesis, University of Hawaii at Manoa, 1984. [The "o" in *obon* is an honorific form added to the base word *bon;* the terms *obon* and *bon* can be used more or less interchangeably in an English-language context.]   STACEY HIROSE

Office of Redress Administration   As part of the Justice Department's duty to administer the payments mandated by the CIVIL LIBERTIES ACT OF 1988, the Office of Redress Administration (ORA) was established to find eligible redress recipients and to address questions about the process. Soon after it was organized, the ORA held workshops around the country in communities having a significant Japanese American population, enlisted the help of community organizations like the JAPANESE AMERICAN CITIZENS LEAGUE and the NATIONAL COALITION FOR REDRESS/REPARATIONS, and set up a hotline people could call to ask questions about their eligibility. In total, the ORA located approximately 75,000 eligible recipients—about 15,000 over the original estimate when the redress bill was first passed. On October 9, 1990, much of the hard work they put into finding former camp inmates paid off as the first redress checks were presented in a ceremony at the White House. According to most community activists who were involved in the appropriations process, the ORA did an excellent job in administering the program.

GLEN KITAYAMA

Okada, John (1923–1971)   Novelist. Rejected by the Japanese American community when it first appeared in 1957, John Okada's landmark novel *No-No Boy* has since been recognized as a classic of ASIAN AMERICAN literature.

A native of Seattle, Okada attended Broadway High before World War II and was removed with all other Japanese Americans on the West Coast, spending the war years in the MINIDOKA, Idaho, CONCENTRATION CAMP. After leaving camp to attend college, he volunteered for the army, being discharged in 1946 as a sergeant. He graduated from the University of Washington with a degree in English and received an M.A. from Columbia in 1949. He returned to Washington to get a degree in library science and got a job working at the Seattle Public Library. He later moved to Detroit, working at the public library there and as a technical writer, all the while pursuing his interest in creative writing. After the publication of *No-No Boy* by Charles E. Tuttle in 1957—it flopped in its initial release, virtually ignored by the Japanese American community—Okada worked on a second novel, focusing on an ISSEI protagonist. Reputed to be nearly complete at the time of his death, that novel and all his other papers were destroyed by his family shortly after his death. (See also NO-NO BOY.)
For further reading, see the introduction and afterword in the University of Washington reprinting of *No-No Boy,* first published in 1976, the former by Lawson Inada, the latter by Frank Chin; see also Jeffery Paul Chan, Frank Chin, Lawson Fusao Inada, and Shawn Wong, eds. *The Big Aiiieeeee!: An Anthology of Chinese American and Japanese American Literature.* New York: Meridian, 1991. Literary criticism on Okada includes Jesse Hiraoka. "A Sense of Place." *Journal of Ethnic Studies* 4.4 (Winter 1977):72–75; Lawson Fusao Inada. "The Vision of America in John Okada's *No-No Boy.*" In Wolodymyr T. Zyla, and Wendell M. Aycock, eds. *Ethnic Literature since 1776: The Many Voices of America.* Lubbock: Texas Tech Press, 1978. 275–87 and "Of Place and Displacement: The Range of Japanese American Literature." In Houston Baker, Jr., ed. *Three American Literatures: Essays in Chicano, Native American, and Asian American Literature for Teachers of American Literature.* Introd. Walter J. Ong. New York: Modern Language Association, 1982. 254–65; Dorothy Ritsuko McDonald. "After Imprisonment: Ichiro's Search for Redemption in *No-No Boy.*" *Melus* 6.3 (1979): 19–26; and Stephen H. Sumida. "Japanese American Moral Dilemmas in John Okada's *No-No Boy* and Milton Murayama's *All I Asking for Is My Body.*" In Nomura, Gail M., Russell Endo, Stephen H. Sumida, and Russell C. Leong, eds. *Frontiers of Asian American Studies: Writing, Research, and Commentary.* Pullman: Washington State University Press, 1989. 222–33.

Okamoto, Kiyoshi Robert   Chairman of the HEART MOUNTAIN FAIR PLAY COMMITTEE. Okamoto was a Hawaii-born NISEI who once worked as a sugar mill superintendent. He resided in Los Angeles, California, and worked as a construction engineer before being forcibly removed from his home along with all other West Coast Japanese Americans during World War II. He ended up in the HEART MOUNTAIN camp in Wyoming.

While interned, Okamoto made speeches that advocated, among other things, the reform of camp living conditions, the freedom of speech in camp, and the constitutional rights of the imprisoned Japanese Americans. He protested the United States government's abridgement of the internees' constitutional rights and their forced removal and incarceration without due process. Okamoto was allegedly speaking of redress for the internees while he was in camp. He referred to himself as the Fair Play Committee of One.

After one of his speeches, Okamoto was approached by several members of what would be the Fair Play Committee of Seven. After the Fair Play Committee's formation, Okamoto was elected as its chair. He continued making speeches, along with PAUL TAKEO NAKADATE about the *nisei's* constitutional rights, due process, and the unfairness of the institution of the draft in the CONCENTRATION CAMPS. It was Okamoto's speeches that were used as the basis of the educational bulletins the Fair Play Committee distributed at Heart Mountain concentration camp in 1944. He and the other leaders of the FPC were arrested and convicted of conspiracy and sentenced to prison. (See U.S. V. OKIMOTO, ET AL.)

In 1946, after his 18-month imprisonment at Fort Leavenworth Penitentiary for his involvement in the Fair Play Committee, Okamoto changed the organization's name to the Fair Rights Committee. He incorporated in California in order to seek restitution for former Japanese American internees. Little is known about Okamoto's life after 1946.

For further reading, see Frank Seishi Emi. "Draft Resistance at the Heart Mountain Concentration Camp and the Fair Play Committee." In Nomura, Gail M., Russell Endo, Stephen H. Sumida, and Russell C. Leong, eds. *Frontiers of Asian American Studies: Writing, Research, and Commentary.* Pullman: Washington State University Press, 1989. 41–69; William Hohri. *Repairing America: An Account of the Movement for Japanese American Redress.* Pullman: Washington State University Press, 1988; and Douglas W. Nelson. *Heart Mountain: The History of an American Concentration Camp.* Madison, Wis.: The State Historical Society of Wisconsin, 1976.   STACEY HIROSE

Okazaki, Steven (1951–)

Academy Award–winning filmmaker Steven Okazaki is one of America's leading young cineasts. He is best known for his films dealing with the Japanese American experience.

Originally from Venice, California, Okazaki attended film school at San Francisco State University. After graduating, he immediately began making movies for children in a 10–15 minute format for Churchill Films.

He has since made five major films. The first, *Survivors,* is a full-length documentary about American HIBAKU-SHA, or atomic bomb survivors. His second documentary, *Unfinished Business,* was nominated for an Academy Award in 1986. The film focuses on three men who challenged the legality of the World War II removal and detention of Japanese Americans in test court cases. Next came *Living on Tokyo Time,* a melodrama about a Japanese woman (played by Minako Ohashi) who marries a Japanese American man (played by Ken Nakagawa) in order to stay in the United States. Okazaki wrote the script with longtime collaborator John McCormick. In *Days of Waiting,* Okazaki documents the life of artist ESTELLE PECK ISHIGO, a Caucasian woman who was incarcerated with her NISEI husband in an American CONCENTRATION CAMP during World War II. The film won an Oscar for Best Documentary Short Subject and a George Peabody Award in 1991. Okazaki wrote, produced and directed *Troubled Paradise,* his latest film, which explores Hawaii's Big Island and the social and political problems that face its native population. The film features performances by noted native dancers and musicians.   EMILY LAWSIN

[Used to compile this entry were Nancy Matsumoto. "Steve Okazaki." *AsiAm* 2.8 (Aug. 1987): 26–33; "Steven Okazaki wins 1991 Media Award from ACV." *New York Nichibei* 6 June 1991: 1; "Days of Waiting Meets Oscar & Peabody . . ." *Asian American Network* (National Asian American Telecommunications Association Newsletter) 8.2 (Summer 1991): 1, 9.]

Okei (?–1871)

The first Japanese woman to die in America, the legendary Okei was a member of the ill-fated WAKAMATSU COLONY of 1869. Little is known about her except that she remained in the U.S. after the colony disbanded, and died in 1871. A grave marker on Gold Hill north of Sacramento, California, commemorates her death with the words:

In Memory of Okei.
Died in 1871.
Age 19 years.
A Japanese girl.

Despite the paucity of information about her, she has become something of a romantic figure to modern writers drawn by the poignancy of this lone young woman who died in a strange land.

For further reading, see Bill Hosokawa. *Nisei: The Quiet Americans.* New York: William Morrow & Co., 1969; Harry H. L. Kitano. *Japanese Americans: The Evolution of a Subculture.* 1969. 2nd Edition. Englewood Cliffs, N.J.: Prentice-Hall, Inc., 1976; and Henry Taketa. "1969, the Centennial Year." *Pacific Historian* 13.1 (Winter 1969): 1–16.

Okimura v. Acheson Case heard before the U.S. Supreme Court in 1952 involving the citizenship status of a NISEI who had served in the Japanese Army and voted in a Japanese election. Kiyokura Okimura was a *nisei* born in Hawaii in 1921 who had spent much of his childhood being educated in Japan (see KIBEI). After returning to Hawaii for two years, he went back to Japan to continue his education with the intent of teaching in a JAPANESE-LANGUAGE SCHOOL in Hawaii. After graduating from high school in Japan, he was ordered by the Japanese government to take a teaching job there. In June 1942, he was ordered to serve in the Japanese Army under threat of imprisonment. He served with the Japanese Army in China until he was captured in August 1945. After the war ended, he took up the study of Buddhism with the intention of becoming a Buddhist priest in Hawaii. In the interim, he voted in a 1947 Japanese election. His application for a U.S. passport in 1949 was denied on the grounds that he had forfeited his citizenship by virtue of his foreign military service and of his having voted in the election. A federal district court ruled that Okimura's citizenship could not be revoked unless he had become a naturalized citizen of another country. The United States Supreme Court upheld the decision on appeal, ruling that foreign military service under the threat of physical beating was not sufficient grounds for withdrawing citizenship. The Okimura case set a precedent for many similar cases involving *nisei* who had been forced to serve in the Japanese military.

For further reading, see Frank F. Chuman. *The Bamboo People: The Law and Japanese-Americans.* Del Mar, Calif.: Publisher's Inc., 1976.

Okinawans Prefectural subgroup within the Japanese American community. (See UCHINANCHU.)

Okubo, Mine (1912–) NISEI artist Mine Okubo is known in the Japanese American community primarily for her depictions of life in the World War II CONCENTRATION CAMPS. One of seven children, she was born in Riverside, California. Okubo's mother was an artist and graduate of the Tokyo Art Institute; her father was a merchant and gardener. She attended the University of California at Berkeley, graduating in 1936 with a master's degree in art. In 1938 she received the Bertha Taussig Traveling Scholarship, which allowed her to travel in Europe. Upon returning to the United States in 1939, she painted murals at several Bay Area sites as part of the Federal Arts Program.

Along with all other Japanese Americans on the West Coast, Okubo and her family were forcibly removed from their homes and incarcerated in American concentration camps. While at Tanforan "ASSEMBLY CENTER" and TOPAZ, Utah, she drew and painted scenes of the camps and their people. Some 200 pen-and-ink drawings became the basis of the book *Citizen 13660,* which paired Okuba's spare depictions with sometimes satirical text in an unforgettable portrait of life in camp. The book, the first by a Japanese American internee, was well received both inside and outside the Japanese American community. In addition to these drawings, Okubo also worked in charcoal and watercolors. Working day and night on her art, Okubo remembered that "to discourage visitors, I put a sign up on my door that said 'quarantined.'"

Okubo also contributed drawings to the literary magazine *Trek* at Topaz. These drawings led to an offer from *Fortune Magazine* to resettle in New York and work for them. She left camp in 1944. In the next few years, she became successful in the commercial art field, contributing work to such major publications as *Time, Life* and the *New York Times* and illustrating books for major publishers. She left commercial art and New York briefly from 1950 to 1952 to return to Berkeley to lecture on art. Upon returning to New York, she eschewed commercial concerns in pursuit of her own artistic vision. She had major exhibits at the Mortimer Levitt Gallery in New York in 1951, the Image Gallery in Stockbridge, Massachusetts, in 1964, the Oakland Art Museum in 1972 and, most recently, a 40-year retrospective at the Catherine Gallery and Basement Workshop in New York in 1986. Like many other *nisei* artists and writers, she was rediscovered by a new generation of ASIAN AMERICANS in the 1970s and '80s.

For further reading, see Betty La Duke. "On the Right Road: The Life of Mine Okubo." *Art Education* 40.3 (May 1987): 42–48 and Shirley Sun. *Mine Okubo: An American Experience.* San Francisco: East Wind Printers, 1972.

[Quote from La Duke, p. 45.]

Okumura, Takie (1865–1951) Reverend Takie Okumura was one of the most important leaders of the pre-war Japanese American community in Hawaii. He continually advocated accommodation, believing that to be the best strategy to minimize conflict and maximize assimilation.

Born in 1865 Okumura was the eldest son of a samurai family. After failing at various commercial pursuits, he became a liberal political activist in Tokyo. Hoping to gain the confidence of his Christian friend Kenkichi Kataoka, Okumura visited Ichibano Church. Within a year, Okumura was baptized. After graduating from Doshisha Theological Seminary, he decided to come to Hawaii in 1894 to do missionary work. Shocked by the proliferation of prostitution in the Hawaii Japanese community, he garnered attention by cooperating with au-

Takie Okumura, 1895. *Makiki Christian Church Collection.*

thorities in wiping out this activity after the Chinatown fire of 1900. He soon took over as pastor of Nuuanu Church and successfully solicited contributions from the HAOLE community to improve the building. He undertook a lone evangelical crusade on the plantations in November 1902. Despite the hostility he often experienced, he stuck to it and, with more *haole* assistance, he began his own church in 1904. His Makiki Christian Church began with only 24 members; by 1932 membership numbered over 1,200. In these early years, Okumura also founded the first JAPANESE-LANGUAGE SCHOOL in Hawaii in 1896, the first Japanese library in 1897, the first Japanese baseball team in 1899 and the first Japanese YMCA in 1900.

Given the support he received from planters, it is not surprising that Okumura backed sugar growers in the 1909 PLANTATION STRIKE. After the strike, however, he successfully petitioned for a pardon for the imprisoned strike leaders. Ironically, one of the freed leaders was his future nemesis, FRED KINZABURO MAKINO. Okumura and Makino would bump heads on many issues over the years. In the 1920 PLANTATION STRIKE, Okumura took an anti-labor position and even refused to let his church be used by strikers evicted from the plantations. In the Japanese school controversy of the 1920s, Okumura denounced those who sought to test restrictions on the schools in court: "It is foolhardy to resort blindly to litigation. Even if we win on legal points, we would only increase their [the Americans'] suspicion, and would endanger the future of our children in Hawaii." At the same time, Okumura also spearheaded the "New American" movement, a campaign aimed at exhorting NISEI to adopt Christianity and to remain on the plantations. This campaign was of course enthusiastically endorsed by the planters. (See NEW AMERICANS CONFERENCES.)

In 1932, Okumura erected a new Makiki Church, patterned after a Japanese castle. He continued to preach Christianity, to hold annual New Americans Conferences from 1927 and to rail against the Buddhist priests' ties to Japan's militarist government. He retired from the pastorate in 1937. Okumura's vision of a decreasingly influential Buddhist church and language schools was realized as a result of World War II. He must also have felt vindicated when many *nisei* soldiers took up the "100% American" cry that he had been trumpeting for years. Reverend Takie Okumura died on Feb. 10, 1951, at the age of 87.

For further reading, see Takie Okumura. *Seventy Years of Divine Blessing.* Kyoto: Naigai Publishing Co., 1940, Okumura's autobiography. See also Harry H. L. Kitano. *Japanese Americans: The Evolution of a Subculture.* 1969. 2nd edition. Englewood Cliffs, N.J.: Prentice-Hall, Inc., 1976 and Roland Kotani. *The Japanese in Hawaii: A Century of Struggle.* Honolulu: Hochi, Ltd., 1985 for biographical information on Okumura. Dennis M. Ogawa. *Kodomo No Tame Ni, For the Sake of the Children: The Japanese American Experience in Hawaii.* Honolulu: University Press of Hawaii, 1978 contains excerpts from Okumura's writings while Gail M. Nomura. "The Debate Over the Role of Nisei in Prewar Hawaii: The New Americans Conference, 1927–1951." *Journal of Ethnic Studies* 15.1 (Spring 1987): 95–115 and Jisoo Sanjume. "An Analysis of the New Americans Conference from 1927 to 1938." Thesis, University of Hawaii, 1939 look at his role in the New Americans movement; the latter also contains a brief biographical sketch of Okumura.

[Quote from Kotani 85.]

Omura, James Matsumoto (1912–) NISEI

journalist. Omura was born on November 17, 1912, on Bainbridge Island, Seattle. He was employed in numerous occupations from the time he left junior high school in 1926 until 1940.

By 1940 Omura accumulated enough money from several of his jobs to found a Japanese American literary/public affairs magazine, *Current Life.* Omura's wife, Fumi Okuma, helped him publish and edit the short-lived magazine, which featured radio programming, sports news, women's issues, poems and fiction by emerging Japanese American writers, and social commentaries.

During its 15-month existence, Omura attempted to use *Current Life* to recognize the achievements of the *nisei* and to demonstrate to the Japanese American community and mainstream American society that the *nisei* were an integral part of American society. With the United States' entry into World War II and its resultant anti-Japanese atmosphere, Omura and his wife attempted to relocate *Current Life* during the "VOLUNTARY" RESETTLEMENT period to Colorado, a state in the "free zone." However, their attempt failed and Omura instead founded an employment agency to help Japanese Americans who had relocated to the Denver area.

Omura is also known for his involvement in the TOLAN COMMITTEE hearings. His presence at the hearings was particularly noteworthy in that he was the only Japanese American attending who was not affiliated with the JAPANESE AMERICAN CITIZENS LEAGUE (JACL). In testimony he spoke out against any plan that would forcibly remove all Japanese Americans from the West Coast; he also disputed the assumption that the JACL represented the Japanese American community as a whole. Because Omura and his wife had resettled in Denver, they were not detained in a CONCENTRATION CAMP during World War II.

In Denver, Omura became the editor of the Denver-based Japanese American newspaper *Rocky Shimpo*. In 1944, Omura wrote editorials in public support of the HEART MOUNTAIN FAIR PLAY COMMITTEE, a group that advocated resistance to the military draft by *nisei* until their freedom was restored. He was the only newspaper editor to print the Fair Play Committee's press releases. Omura also engaged in an editorial battle in defense of draft resistance with the editors of the JACL's publication PACIFIC CITIZEN and the Heart Mountain camp newspaper, *The Heart Mountain Sentinel*. For his actions, Omura was tried in 1944 with the seven leaders of the Fair Play Committee for counseling, aiding and abetting the violation of the Selective Service Act (see U.S. V. OKAMOTO, ET AL.). However, unlike the Fair Play Committee members, Omura was found innocent of the charges.

After the war, he became a landscaper in Colorado, serving two terms as president of the Colorado Landscape Body.

All but ignored by the Japanese American community for many years, Omura has been recently recognized by the Japanese American and greater Asian American communities for his courageous actions in support of the Heart Mountain Fair Play Committee and *nisei* draft resistance during World War II.

For further reading, see Arthur A. Hansen. "James Matsumoto Omura: An Interview." *Amerasia Journal* 13.2 (1986–87): 99–113 and James Omura. "Japanese American Journalism During World War II." In Nomura, Gail M., Russell Endo, Stephen H. Sumida, and Russell C. Leong, eds. *Frontiers of Asian American Studies: Writing, Research, and Commentary.* Pullman: Washington State University Press, 1989. 71–80. See the various citations under the Fair Play Committee entry as well.   STACEY HIROSE

on   A Japanese term referring to the social and psychological obligations and debt that one acquires as the result of receiving from another a favor or gift of extraordinary proportions. One is said to receive *on* from one's parents and ancestors who are responsible for giving one life.

Unlike the more contractual mutual obligation inherent in GIRI, *on* is so profound that it can never be completely repaid in one's lifetime. For example, repayment to parents would be expressed in OYAKOKO, which requires caring for parents in their old age, continuing the family line, maintaining an unblemished family name and honoring parents even after their deaths.

As in the case of *giri*, even the more recent generations of Japanese Americans are influenced by *on*, unconsciously, in many cases.

For further reading, see Betty S. Furuta. "Ethnic Identities of Japanese-American Families: Implications for Counseling." In Getty, Cathleen, and Winnifred Humphreys, eds. *Understanding the Family: Stress and Change in American Family Life.* New York: Appleton-Century-Crofts, 1981 and *Kodansha Encyclopedia of Japan.* Tokyo: Kodansha, 1983.   STACEY HIROSE

100th Infantry Battalion   A U.S. Army battalion made up of NISEI from Hawaii that saw heavy action during World War II. The 100th Infantry Battalion and the later 442ND REGIMENTAL COMBAT TEAM were both made up of *nisei* soldiers, who carved out an exemplary military record during their service in the European Theater during World War II.

The 100th Infantry Battalion had its roots in the prewar Japanese American volunteers and draftees in Hawaii. After basic training, most of these recruits were assigned to Hawaii National Guard units, which became the 298th and 299th Infantry Regiments after the attack on Pearl Harbor. For the next six months, these soldiers performed vital local duties such as guarding airfields and beaches and helping to build military installations. In May of 1942, General DELOS EMMONS, provisional military governor of Hawaii, recommended that all Japanese American soldiers in the 298th and 299th be organized into a special battalion and taken to the mainland. Upon receiving reinforcements to alleviate Hawaii's troop shortage, Emmons organized the *nisei* soldiers into a new provisional battalion and assigned Lt. Colonel Farrant L. Turner to command the outfit. Although 16 of the 24 original officers of the battalion were *nisei*, the top two in command and all the company commanders were Caucasian.

On June 5, 1942, the Hawaiian Provisional Infantry Battalion, 1,432 men strong, departed on a trip to the mainland that would be shrouded in secrecy. After arriving in Oakland, they were activated as the 100th Infantry Battalion on June 12. Unaffiliated with any regiment, the 100th was designated a "separate" battalion, and, as a result, was larger than the typical battalion. Still not knowing where they were to be taken, the soldiers traveled east on three trains taking three different routes before arriving at Camp McCoy, Wisconsin. The 100th, or "One Puka Puka" (*puka* is Japanese/Hawaiian slang for "hole" or "zero") as they called themselves, would spend the next six months training in the fields and woods of Camp McCoy. Although there would be tangles with other, non-Japanese American soldiers, the training went smoothly. Many soldiers established close relationships with the generally friendly local community. In January 1943, the 100th was transferred to Camp Shelby in Mississippi, the second largest army training camp in the country, to complete its training. The training in the heat and humidity of the Deep South was difficult, as was grasping the intricacies of local race relations—more than one *nisei* soldier scratched his head in puzzlement when faced with choosing between "White" and "Colored" facilities. The 100th finally shipped out for battle on August 21, 1943.

The 100th Infantry Battalion landed in Oran, North Africa, on September 2, 1943, and was assigned to the 133rd Regiment of the 34th "Red Bull" Division of the Fifth Army. It saw its first frontline action later that month in Salerno, Italy, and suffered its first casualties. The 100th would see heavy action in Italy, including actions at the Battle of Cassino in January 1944, a key to the retaking of Rome, and at Anzio beachhead, a second key front on the road to Rome beginning in March. After the Allied capture of Rome—the 100th Battalion just missed being the first Allied battalion to enter the city—the 100th retreated to a rest area near Civitavecchia where it was joined by fellow *nisei* soldiers in the 442nd Regimental Combat Team. The battle-tested 100th became the first battalion of the 442nd in June 1944 and would see a great deal more front-line action before the end of the war.

By the time the 442nd arrived in Europe, the soldiers of the 100th had already made quite a name for themselves. Their strong performance in battle, their unusually low rate of shell shock, and their many casualties—the 100th, which had originally numbered around 1,300, had suffered 900 casualties by the time it joined the 442nd—led to glowing accounts in the Allied press. A report in *Time* magazine in July 1944 noted that "[a] group of sinewy oriental soldiers only one generation removed from a nation that was fighting fanatically against the U.S. was fighting just as fanatically for it."

The glowing achievements and sacrifices of the 100th Battalion would be continually cited in many different contexts during, immediately after and long after World War II.

For further reading, see Masayo Duus. *Unlikely Liberators: The Men of the 100th and the 442nd.* Honolulu: University of Hawaii Press, 1987; Roland Kotani. *The Japanese in Hawaii: A Century of Struggle.* Honolulu: Hochi, Ltd., 1985; Thomas D. Murphy. *Ambassadors in Arms: The Story of Hawaii's 100th Battalion.* Honolulu: University of Hawaii Press, 1954; Chester Tanaka. *Go for Broke: A Pictorial History of the Japanese American 100th Infantry Battalion and the 442nd Regimental Combat Team.* Richmond, Calif.: Go for Broke, Inc., 1981; and John Tsukano. *Bridge of Love.* Honolulu: Hawaii Hosts, Inc., 1985.

Onizuka, Ellison Shoji (1946–1986)   As the first Japanese American in space, Ellison Onizuka was a bona fide local hero and role model. Born in Keopu, North Kona, Onizuka attended Konawaena High School. From there, he went to the University of Colorado and emerged in December 1969 with an M.S. in aerospace engineering. He joined the air force shortly thereafter as a flight test engineer and did a one year stint at Air Force Test Pilot School at Edwards AFB in 1974–75. In 1977, he was one of 8,000 who applied to be astronauts and was one of the 35 selected in January 1978. In 1982, he was selected to fly on a November 1983 secret space shuttle mission for the Department of Defense. Postponed several times, the flight of the *Discovery* took place on January 24–27, 1985. When the space shuttle *Challenger* exploded soon after takeoff on January 28, 1986, Onizuka was killed along with six others.

Dennis M. Ogawa. *Ellison S. Onizuka: A Remembrance.* Honolulu: Onizuka Memorial Committee, 1986 is a biographical tribute with many photographs. See also Dorothy Ochiai Hazama, and Jane Okamoto Komeiji. *Okage Sama De: The Japanese in Hawai'i.* Foreword by Daniel Inouye. Honolulu: Bess Press, 1986.

Onuki, Hachiro (1849–1921)   Businessman. Hachiro Onuki, born in Japan, arrived in Boston in 1876 with a group of American naval cadets who probably had smuggled him onto their ship. Onuki changed his name to Hutchlon Ohnick and later moved to Phoenix, Arizona, where he received a franchise to supply the city with gas or electric light, or both. In 1888, Ohnick married Catherine Shannon. Because of his business ability and the confidence of his partners, he was asked to work for the Phoenix Illuminating Gas and Electric Company as superintendent. In 1901 he moved to Seattle where he opened the Oriental American bank with two other ISSEI.   ALICE HOM

Oriental Trading Company   The Oriental Trading Company was one of three major LABOR CONTRACTORS in the Pacific Northwest and may have been the largest one in the U.S. at its peak. Based in Seattle, it began as a two-man partnership between Tetsuo Takahashi and Ototaka Yamaoka in 1898; Matajiro Tsukuno became a third partner in 1899. It began as the contractor for the Seattle and International Railway in early 1898 and became the regular contractor for the Great Northern from 1899 and for the Northern Pacific in 1904 and from 1906. At its height, it probably employed 2,500 to 3,000 laborers.

In 1899, Yamaoka returned to Japan to establish a branch office of the company in Yokohama to facilitate recruiting since the contract with the Great Northern required large numbers of workers. Yamaoka had arranged for the Morioka Emigration Company to ship 2,500 laborers, but the Foreign Ministry refused to issue them passports given its institution of a new quota system for the U.S. in April 1900. Yamaoka then used contacts with officials in Shizuoka to forge passports and to smuggle workers recruited elsewhere through there. Although he and his accomplices were eventually caught by the government, the Oriental Trading Company claimed it got 3,000 to 4,000 laborers into the U.S. by this illegal method. The actions of this and other labor contractors was almost entirely responsible for the dramatic increase in Japanese immigration to the U.S. from 1899 on.

For further reading, see Yuji Ichioka. "Japanese Immigrant Labor Contractors and the Northern Pacific and the Great Northern Railroad Companies, 1898–1907." *Labor History* 21.3 (1980): 325–50 and *The Issei: The World of the First Generation Japanese Immigrants, 1885–1924.* New York: The Free Press, 1988; and Hisashi Tsurutani. *America Bound: The Japanese and Opening of the American West.* Betsey Scheiner, trans. Tokyo: Japan Times, Inc., 1989.

Oshoogatsu   Oshoogatsu is a Japanese term used in reference to New Year's celebrations. For many Japanese Americans, Oshoogatsu is the most important holiday of the year.

Traditionally a time of purification and renewal, preparations are made to start off the New Year with a clean slate. Consequently, debts are paid, disputes are settled, new clothes are bought and worn, and homes are cleaned. New Year's cards are traditionally sent to relatives and friends, but Japanese Americans have, for the most part, replaced these with Christmas cards. Special decorations are also displayed in the home. For example, one such decoration, the *kadomatsu* (or gate pine arrangement), is placed in the doorway of a home. It is believed that displaying such decorations as the *kadomatsu* will ward off demons, encourage the New Year deity to visit the home and ensure its residents prosperity, purity and a long and happy life. Also in the tradition of preparing

Sanpans in Kewalo Basin, Oahu, Hawaii, decorated to celebrate the New Year.   *Hawaii State Archives*

for Oshoogatsu is the making or pounding of *mochi* (Japanese rice cakes, generally white in color, made with special rice flour; see MOCHITSUKI). The making of *mochi* is an Oshoogatsu tradition, done either as a community event or privately in the home. It involves pounding the rice flour into a soft, doughy consistency. The *mochi* is then used in various New Year's dishes or presented as an offering along with *sake* or *toso* (rice wine), *kaki* (persimmons), and other traditional Japanese New Year's foods at the home *toshidana* ("year shelf"), or altar.

In the tradition of Oshoogatsu, on New Year's Eve, people visit Buddhist temples to hear temple bells toll 108 times, chasing away the evils of the old year. Additionally, families gather on New Year's Eve to eat a special New Year's dinner consisting of traditional New Year's dishes. However, today Japanese Americans celebrate Oshoogatsu with less emphasis on religious practices and rituals. Rather, they attend secular parties with family and friends, and watch or participate in the display of fireworks to celebrate the incoming of the New Year.

Traditionally, New Year's Day festivities begin with a breakfast of *ozoni* (broth made with *mochi* and vegetables) shared by family members. Japanese Americans who still observe religious traditions associated with Oshoogatsu attend Shinto temples to receive blessings and purification from the priest. The remainder of the day is usually spent visiting with family and friends and eating various New Year foods that are said to ensure happiness, wealth, fertility and luck.

For further reading, see John DeFrancis, and V. R. Lincoln. *Things Japanese in Hawaii.* Honolulu: University Press of Hawaii, 1973 and Dorothy Ochiai Hazama and Jane Okamoto Komeiji. *Okage Sama De: The Japanese in Hawai'i.* Foreword by Daniel Inouye. Honolulu: Bess Press, 1986. [The "o" in *oshoogatsu* is an honorific form added to the base word *shoogatsu;* either term can be used in an English-language context.]

STACEY HIROSE

Ota Kamado (1884–1958) Produce merchant, Okinawan (see OKINAWANS) community leader. Kamado Ota was born in 1884 in the Yonagusuku district of Okinawa and graduated in 1902 from First Middle School. He answered an ad for an EMIGRATION COMPANY and sailed for Mexico, landing in San Francisco along the way in May 1904, before arriving at the coal mines of Coahuila. Conditions there were harsh for contract laborers, but because of his high school education, he was hired as the company clerk. When he discovered legal abnormalities in the labor contracts and gathered the miners together to protest, he was arrested, but escaped and headed north with a group of other Okinawan migrants.

Wanting to study agriculture, he ran a farm starting in 1905, then got a job with the Meyer-Darling Produce Company, eventually overseeing its Japanese section. In 1915, along with Anko Hirashiki and Chodo Okutake, he formed the Star Produce Company in Los Angeles. In 1920, Star Produce moved to the new Seventh Street Produce Market. Star Produce soon became one of the leading produce companies in Southern California.

Ota was active in the Los Angeles area Okinawan community as well, being a founder of the early Los Angeles Okinawan organization Doshikai in 1906. He was later president of the Nanka Okinawa KENJINKAI and the Southern California branch of its successor organization, the Okinawa Kaigai Kyokai (Okinawan Overseas Association). He was also a leader in the formation of the Nanka Chuo Sangyo Kumiai (Southern California Central Producer's Union) in 1930.

Along with all other West Coast Japanese Americans, Ota was interned during World War II and his business was shut down. Burdened by illness and age, he struggled to restart his business after the war. He died on July 7, 1958.

For further reading, see Okinawa Club of America, comp. *History of the Okinawans in North America*. Ben Kobashigawa, trans. Los Angeles: UCLA Asian American Studies Center and The Okinawa Club of America, 1988.

Ota, Shelley (1911–) Shelley Ayame Nishimura Ota wrote the first published novel in English based on the Japanese American immigration experience.

Ota, a NISEI, graduated from the University of Hawaii where she pursued her interests in writing. Her husband, a physician, died in military service during World War II. As the mother of four children, a free-lance writer and substitute teacher in Milwaukee, Ota wrote the acclaimed novel *Upon Their Shoulders* in 1951. The novel,

a family saga about Taro and Haruko Sumida and their daughter Alice, describes their experiences as Japanese Americans in Hawaii. Told in five parts, the story spans six decades, beginning in the late 19th century, when the Sumidas emigrate to Hawaii as part of the first wave of Japanese contract laborers. After their initial experience on Hawaii's Hillstone sugar plantation, the Sumidas move to Honolulu's NIHONMACHI and discover that racism and violence prevail in the city just as much as in the rural setting of the plantation. The saga continues, highlighting the struggles of the Sumidas and that of other families, and concludes shortly after World War II.

For further reading, see Ota's *Upon Their Shoulders*. New York: Exposition Press, 1951. See also Stephen H. Sumida. *And the View from the Shore: Literary Traditions of Hawai'i*. Seattle: University of Washington Press, 1991.   EMILY LAWSIN

Oyakawa, Yoshinobu Yoshinobu Oyakawa was one of three Japanese Americans (along with weightlifter TOMMY KONO and swimmer FORD KONNO) to win a gold medal at the 1952 Summer Olympics at Helsinki, Finland. Oyakawa won the gold by defeating Frenchman Gilbert Bozon in the 100-meter backstroke, establishing a new Olympic record in the process.

Born in Hilo, Hawaii, Oyakawa was the son of Reverend E. K. Oyakawa of the Papaikou Pilgrim Church. He began swimming in 1948 and trained under coach Charles (Sparky) Kawamoto of the Hilo Athletic Club. Oyakawa's aquatic prowess earned him a scholarship to Ohio State University where he joined Konno. His gold medal victory made Oyakawa the first from the Big Island to accomplish such a feat.

After the Olympics, he graduated from Ohio State with a degree in education, served two years in the Air Force and settled in Ohio. He made the Olympic team again in 1956, finishing eighth in the same event. In 1960, he moved to Oak Hills High School in Cincinnati where he taught and coached swimming until retiring in 1985. Married to the former Mariko Yamane, the couple has five children.   SCOTT KURASHIGE

[Entry compiled from "Sports." *Pacific Citizen* 9 Aug. 1952: 6; "Sports." *Pacific Citizen* 16 Aug. 1952: 6 and Takeshi Nakayama. "Oyakawa Swims to Gold in 1957." *Rafu Shimpo* 31 July 1992: 1–7.]

oyakoko The Japanese term for filial piety or duty to one's parents. *Oyakoko* encompasses such things as one's duty to respect one's parents and provide and care for them in sickness and old age.

For further reading, see Dorothy Ochiai Hazama, and Jane Okamoto Komeiji. *Okage Sama De: The Japanese in Hawai'i*. Foreword by Daniel Inouye. Honolulu: Bess Press, 1986;

and *Kodansha Encyclopedia of Japan.* Tokyo: Kodansha, 1983.

STACEY HIROSE

Oyama v. California Case brought before the U.S. Supreme Court in 1948 that successfully challenged the 1920 (CALIFORNIA) ALIEN LAND LAW. Kajiro and Kohide Oyama, both Japanese "ALIENS INELIGIBLE TO CITIZENSHIP," purchased six acres of agricultural land in California and took title to the property in the name of their American-born son Fred. Mr. Oyama petitioned the Superior Court of San Diego County to become the guardian of his son's person and estate in 1935, which the court allowed. In 1937, the Oyamas bought two additional acres of property belonging to the American-born minor child of Japanese alien parents. Title was again taken in the name of Fred Oyama. The Oyama family was forced to leave their home in California in 1942 due to EXECUTIVE ORDER 9066 and spent the war years in an American CONCENTRATION CAMP. In 1944, the State of California filed a petition to declare an escheat of the property on the ground that the land was obtained with the intent to violate and evade the Alien Land Law, with action being brought against both Fred and his father. The California supreme court upheld the action of the state in 1946. In a six to three decision, the United States Supreme Court reversed the California supreme court on January 19, 1948. The U.S. Supreme Court held that provisions of the Alien Land Law violated the equal protection clause of the Fourteenth Amendment of the U.S. Constitution. Specifically, the Supreme Court struck down Section 9(a) of the Alien Land Law, which provided that property would escheat to the state if the purchase of such property was funded by an alien ineligible to citizenship and title to the property was taken in the name of another person, stating that it discriminated against minor citizens whose parents were ineligible to citizenship. This decision paved the way for other successful attacks on the Alien Land Law such as FUJII SEI V. STATE OF CALIFORNIA and MASAOKA V. STATE OF CALIFORNIA.

For further reading, see Frank F. Chuman. *The Bamboo People: The Law and Japanese-Americans.* Del Mar, Calif.: Publisher's Inc., 1976 and Moritoshi Fukuda. *Legal Problems of Japanese Americans.* Tokyo: Keio Tsushin, 1980.

DENNIS YAMAMOTO

Ozawa, Seiji (1935–) Musical director and conductor. Born in Hoten, Manchuria, Ozawa moved to Tokyo in 1944 with his parents. He trained in European and American musical traditions at the Toho School of Music and graduated in 1959. From there he studied with Eugene Bigot in France and Herbert von Karajan in Berlin. While in Europe he won first prize in the International Competition for Young Orchestra Con-

ductors. Ozawa made his debut with the New York Philharmonic Orchestra in 1961 and was named the sole assistant conductor for the 1964–65 season. Then he was appointed permanent conductor for the Toronto Symphony Orchestra, serving in that position from 1965–1969. Ozawa became the music director of the San Francisco Symphony Orchestra in 1970 and of the Boston Symphony Orchestra in 1973, where he remains today. In 1984, Ozawa formed the Saito Kinen Orchestra in honor of Japanese Western classical music pioneer Hideo Saito, with the orchestra made up of Saito's former pupils.

For further reading, see Philip Hart. *Conductors: A New Generation.* New York: Charles Scribner's Sons, 1979 and Helena Matheopoulos. *Maestro: Encounters with Conductors of Today.* New York: Harper & Row, 1982; the former contains a profile of Ozawa, the latter, an interview. ALICE HOM

Ozawa, Tomi Tomi Ozawa was one of only five female GANNEN-MONO and the only one to remain in Hawaii. When she arrived in 1868, she was a 19 year-old student. Her husband was 27-year-old Kintaro. Her son Yotaro may have been born on the 34-day journey from Japan; her daughter Itoko was the first Japanese girl born in Hawaii in 1872. Ozawa was the only Japanese woman in Hawaii from 1871–1885.

For further reading, see Patsy Sumie Saiki. *Japanese Women in Hawaii: The First 100 Years.* Honolulu: Kisaku, Inc., 1985.

Ozawa v. U.S. Landmark Supreme Court case that definitively established that ISSEI could not become American citizens. The *Ozawa* decision of 1922 marked the end of a long quest by Japanese immigrants for American citizenship. Along with the Supreme Court rejection of their challenges to the 1920 (CALIFORNIA) ALIEN LAND LAW the following year and the banning of all further immigration from Japan in 1924, the Ozawa decision helped to underscore the limits of *issei* life in their adopted country. *Issei* would not be allowed to become U.S. citizens until the passage of the IMMIGRATION AND NATIONALITY ACT OF 1952.

The question of naturalization rights had been a topic of discussion in the Japanese American community for years (see CITIZENSHIP). The existing laws limiting naturalization to "free white persons" and "aliens of African nativity or descent" were ambiguous and had been interpreted in varying ways. Prior to 1906, a number of Japanese immigrants had successfully sought naturalized citizenship. The remarks of President Theodore Roosevelt in response to the SAN FRANCISCO SCHOOL BOARD SEGREGATION ORDER OF 1906 apparently supporting naturalization rights for the *issei* brought about a flurry of discussion on that topic within the Japanese American community. However it was the passage of the 1913

(CALIFORNIA) ALIEN LAND LAW that brought the issue to the fore. The Pacific Coast Japanese Association Deliberative Council, a federation of JAPANESE ASSOCIATION central bodies representing all parts of the western United States and Canada, was formed in April 1913 and took up the issue of naturalization as one of its priorities. After examining and rejecting the possibilities of seeking naturalization through diplomatic or legislative means, a strategy of seeking a test case was decided upon.

Takao Ozawa's circumstances proved to be ideal for such a case. Born in Kanagawa PREFECTURE in 1875, he had been a resident of the United States continuously since 1894 and had become for all intents and purposes a perfectly assimilated *issei*. He had graduated from Berkeley High School and had attended the University of California, worked for an American company, spoke only English at home, married an American educated woman, and had no ties to any Japanese organization or community. He had filed a petition of intent for naturalization on August 1, 1902, in Alameda County, California, and filed for naturalization on October 16, 1914. When he was denied, he took his case to the United States district court in Hawaii where it was again denied in March 1916. His appeal was referred by the Ninth Circuit Court of Appeals in San Francisco to the U.S. Supreme Court on May 31, 1917. With the help of a special naturalization committee set up by the Pacific Coast Japanese Association Deliberative Council and headed by Ototaka Yamaoka, the case headed for the Supreme Court. Former U.S. Attorney General George W. Wickersham was hired as Ozawa's chief counsel. A potential problem over the 12-year gap between Ozawa's petition of intent and his petition to naturalize—technically, a maximum of seven years was allowed—opened up a debate in the pages of Japanese American newspapers over whether the case ought to be supported or not. A second case was sought in the event the Ozawa case was thrown out on a technicality; that case turned out to be YAMASHITA V. HINKLE.

The Supreme Court ruling came on November 13, 1922. The lower court rulings were upheld and Ozawa was denied citizenship. For all intents and purposes, the citizenship status of the Issei had been definitively set.

For further reading, see Yuji Ichioka. "The Early Japanese Immigrant Quest for Citizenship: The Background of the 1922 Ozawa Case." *Amerasia Journal* 4.2 (1977): 1–22 and *The Issei: The World of the First Generation Japanese Immigrants, 1885–1924*. New York: The Free Press, 1988. For a transcript of the Ozawa case, see Consulate-General of Japan. *Documental History of Law Cases Affecting Japanese in the United States, 1916–1924. 2 Vols.* San Francisco: Consulate-General of Japan, 1925. New York: Arno Press, 1978, Vol. I.

P–Q

Pacific Citizen Newspaper of the JAPANESE AMERICAN CITIZENS LEAGUE (JACL). The *Pacific Citizen* has been an important part of the JACL since its inception in the 1930s. The roots of the paper go back to the *Nikkei Shimin,* a semimonthly that first appeared on October 13, 1929, published by the New Americans Citizens League of San Francisco, a founding body of the JACL. Its first editor was NISEI writer Iwao Kawakami, and it operated out of SABURO KIDO's home/law office. In 1930, it was renamed the *Pacific Citizen* and it officially became the organ of the JACL in 1932. An all-English language paper by and for the NISEI, the *Citizen* was a four-page monthly that experienced financial difficulties throughout the 1930s. The production of the paper was taken over for six years by JAMES YOSHINORI SAKAMOTO of Seattle in 1933. In 1939, the paper returned to San Francisco and was edited by Evelyn Kirimura. Problems continued to dog the paper; after the May 1940 issue, no paper appeared for four months. In early 1942, the decision was made to move the paper and the national headquarters of the JACL to Salt Lake City in order to avoid the mass removal imposed on all Japanese Americans from the West Coast.

Veteran vernacular newspaper editor LARRY TAJIRI was brought in to edit the *Pacific Citizen*. With his wife Marion Tsuguyo Tajiri, Tajiri made the *Pacific Citizen* into a vital source of news of interest to the Japanese American community during World War II. As the most widely read of four Japanese American newspapers that published during the war, the *Pacific Citizen* reported on news from the CONCENTRATION CAMPS, the exploits of the *nisei* soldiers and the trials of RESETTLEMENT, and provided news of the latest government directives. Larry Tajiri wrote a column titled "Nisei USA," while Marion wrote one titled "Ann Nisei's." There were also columns by Saburo Kido and BILL HOSOKAWA. The paper ran eight dense pages and contained no advertising. Due to wartime paper shortages, circulation was limited to under 9,000.

For various reasons, the paper's circulation dropped dramatically after the war. From the wartime figure of nearly 9,000, circulation stood at 5,400 in 1948. In 1952, it was decided to move the paper to Los Angeles while the national headquarters of the JACL moved to San Francisco. This decision, along with the decision to start an "operating committee" to oversee the editorial content of the paper, led to the resignation of Tajiri. HARRY HONDA became the editor beginning with the October 4, 1952, issue. Circulation and revenue problems continued to plague the paper through the 1950s, until finally in 1961, subscription was made a JACL membership requirement. The *Pacific Citizen* continues to publish as a weekly, reporting on both news on the Japanese American community at large and on the JACL in particular. Following Honda's retirement, the paper has had a succession of mostly SANSEI editors in the 1980s and '90s, though Honda continues to play a vital role in the paper as "editor emeritus."

For further reading, see Bill Hosokawa. *JACL in Quest of Justice: The History of the Japanese American Citizens League.* New York: William Morrow, 1982.

Patriotic League   The Patriotic League was a political club formed by political exiles from the People's Rights Movement in Japan. Formed on January 7, 1888, in San Francisco it put out a weekly paper from 1888–93 initially titled the *Dai-Jukyu Seiki* (Nineteenth Century)—the title changed seven times to counter repeated bannings by the Meiji government. Additionally, the league put on lectures and kept in contact with Japanese compatriots. League members later put out the first daily Japanese paper in the U.S. (the *Soko Shimbun*) and also became early and important labor contractors.

For further reading, see Yuji Ichioka. *The Issei: The World of the First Generation Japanese Immigrants, 1885–1924.* New York: The Free Press, 1988.

Phelan, James Duval (1861–1930)   Banker, San Francisco mayor, U.S. senator. James Duval Phelan was one of the leaders of the ANTI-JAPANESE MOVEMENT. With other exclusionists like Governor HIRAM JOHNSON and VALENTINE STUART MCCLATCHY, he played a central role in enacting oppressive legislation against Japanese immigrants in California.

Born in San Francisco and the son of a wealthy banker, Phelan studied law at the University of California. From the 1880s, he had been engaged in anti-Chinese activities (see ANTI-CHINESE MOVEMENT). Starting in 1897, he served as Democratic mayor of San Francisco for three terms until 1902, during which time he became a leading advocate for the anti-Japanese movement, a growing movement led by labor unions. In 1913, he was active in the passage of the 1913 (CALIFORNIA) ALIEN LAND LAW. As a representative of the California State Federation of Labor, he told the state legislature not to be concerned about Japan's possible boycott of the Panama-Pacific Exposition, because "the exposition will be in California only a year, while the white race . . . will be here forever . . . we cannot sell our birth right for a tea garden. . . ."

In 1919, approaching the end of his term as U.S. senator, Phelan launched a new anti-Japanese campaign. He contended that the Japanese were a menace to America economically, socially and militarily (see "YELLOW PERIL"). Using slogans like "Keep California White," he called for a more stringent alien land law. At the same time, he made the practice of PICTURE BRIDE marriages a target of attack, claiming it was a barbaric custom. His campaign contributed to the termination of picture bride immigration and the enactment of the 1920 (CALIFORNIA) ALIEN LAND LAW, although he was defeated for the Senate. His final effort to exclude Japanese immigrants was made before the Senate Committee on Immigration in March 1924. With the passage of the IMMIGRATION ACT OF 1924, Phelan was said to have gloated, "I [am] repaid for my efforts, the Japs are routed." Phelan died in 1930.

For further reading, see Roger Daniels. *The Politics of Prejudice: The Anti-Japanese Movement in California and the Struggle for Japanese Exclusion.* 1962. 2nd edition. Berkeley: University of California Press, 1977 and Justice B. Detwiler, ed. *Who's Who in California, 1928–1929.* San Francisco: Who's Who Publishing Company, 1929.   EIICHIRO AZUMA

picture brides   ISSEI women who came to the United States to marry husbands they knew only from photographs. The picture marriage was a way for *issei* men to marry and raise families in their adopted land without the expense and trouble of returning to Japan. Though a perfectly acceptable variation of Japanese marriage customs, the picture marriages were attacked by the EXCLUSIONISTS as proof of Japanese immorality and barbarism and were subsequently banned by the Japanese government as a result. Like the immigrant men who preceded them, the picture brides themselves were often shocked by the difficulties they would have to face in their new homes.

In the years between the GENTLEMEN'S AGREEMENT of 1907–08 and 1920, women made up a significant part of Japanese immigration to the United States. While there were only 410 married *issei* women in the United States in 1900, the number reached 22,193 by 1920. The arrival of these women was the key element in the settling of the Japanese American population and the beginning of families and permanent communities. While some women arrived to join husbands who were already in America and others came with husbands who had returned to Japan to marry them, the majority came as picture brides. A man seeking a wife would send a photograph of himself back to Japan where, through a go-between, his family would seek an appropriate wife based on such factors as her family background, health, age and wealth. Such a process was not all that different from a typical Japanese arranged marriage of the time. Though the bride and groom would likely meet before the marriage, they would usually not know each other well and would have little say in the choice of marriage partner. The fact that the groom was entirely absent from the marriage ceremony represented only a slight

Picture brides arriving at Angel Island, California. *Japanese American History Archive Collection, Japanese American National Museum Photographic & Moving Image Archive*

variation of the norm. Once the bride's name was entered into the husband's family registry, the marriage was official from the Japanese point of view.

The road to life in America was a difficult one for the picture brides. After an arduous journey by ship, they faced the often bewildering series of inspections at the immigration station. If their and their husband's paperwork was in order, the couple would meet for the first time. Because the U.S. government did not recognize the picture marriage, there would be a mass wedding ceremony, often right on the docks. (After 1917, picture marriages were recognized and the mass weddings were no longer necessary.) Once married, there was often the trip to the clothing store to acquire Western clothing. If all this wasn't enough, the picture brides often found that the men they had just married bore little resemblance to the photos they had seen. The men often sent photos that were heavily retouched, taken years earlier or even of another man entirely. They also often exaggerated

their success in this country, claiming to be hotel owners, for instance, when they might have been only busboys. The men were usually 10 to 15 years older than their wives and often looked even older due to years of hard physical labor. As might be expected, some women refused to marry their husbands and demanded to be taken back to Japan. Others left their husbands for other men in succeeding years (see KAKEOCHI). The vast majority of brides, however, endured happily or otherwise made the best of the situation they faced.

The large numbers of picture brides that were arriving by the late 1910s became a major point of contention in the revival of the ANTI-JAPANESE MOVEMENT. Mostly dormant since the passage of the 1913 (CALIFORNIA) ALIEN LAND LAW and World War I, the arrival of the picture brides and the resultant arrival of increasing numbers of NISEI children soon caught the attention of the exclusionists. They objected to picture brides not only because of the supposed immorality of the custom, but because they felt the large numbers of immigrant women violated the spirit of the Gentlemen's Agreement that they thought had ended Japanese immigration for all intents and purposes. To placate the exclusionists, the Japanese government stopped issuing passports to picture brides on March 1, 1920, effectively ending the picture bride era. This decision was greeted with indignation on the part of the *issei* themselves. At the time picture marriages were stopped, some 24,000 single *issei* men remained on the mainland alone; for most, the end of picture marriages meant the end of their hope of ever marrying.

For further reading, see Yamato Ichihashi. *Japanese in the United States: A Critical Study of the Problems of the Japanese Immigrants and their Children*. 1932. New York: Arno Press, 1969; Yuji Ichioka. "*Amerika Nadeshiko:* Japanese Immigrant Women in the United States, 1900–1924." *Pacific Historical Review* 48.2 (May 1980): 339–57 and *The Issei: The World of the First Generation Japanese Immigrants, 1885–1924*. New York: The Free Press, 1988; and Mei Nakano. *Japanese American Women: Three Generations, 1890–1990*. Berkeley and Sebastopol, Calif.: National Japanese American Historical Society and Mina Press, 1990 for general descriptions of the picture bride process. See Kazuo Ito. *Issei: A History of Japanese Immigrants in North America*. Shinichiro Nakamura, Jean S. Gerard, trans. Seattle: Executive Committee for the Publication of *Issei: A History of Japanese Immigrants in North America,* 1973; East Bay Japanese for Action. *Our Recollections*. Berkeley: East Bay Japanese for Action, 1986 and the various volumes put out by the University of Hawaii Ethnic Studies Oral History Project for oral or first-person written accounts of picture brides. Yoshiko Uchida. *Picture Bride*. Flagstaff, AZ: Northland Press, 1987 is a novel focusing on the life of a picture bride.

pinpu Japanese pimps who made their living off of Japanese prostitutes, mostly before the turn of the century. (See also AMEGORO, PROSTITUTES.)

For further reading, see Yuji Ichioka. "Ameyuki-san: Japanese Prostitutes in Nineteenth-Century America." *Amerasia Journal* 4.1 (1977): 1–21 and *The Issei: The World of the First Generation Japanese Immigrants, 1885–1924*. New York: The Free Press, 1988 and Hisashi Tsurutani. *America Bound: The Japanese and Opening of the American West*. Betsey Scheiner, trans. Tokyo: Japan Times, Inc., 1989.

Pioneer Centers Formed in the late 1960s by mostly young ASIAN AMERICAN activists, Pioneer Centers were established around the country as a result of the need to provide culturally sensitive senior citizens centers for the aging ISSEI. In Los Angeles, the Japanese Community Pioneer Center (JCPC) was formed out of a club founded by Mori Nishida, Jim Matsuoka and others called Nanka Nikkeijin Pioneer Kai. The JCPC officially opened its doors on Saturday, October 18, 1969, at 125 Weller Street in Little Tokyo. They provided a recreation room

where senior citizens could enjoy games and companionship, sponsored cultural programs and field trips and, in general, became the catalyst for government-sponsored hot meals programs and other programs for the elderly. Many activists point to the formation of the Pioneer Centers as part of the beginning of the ASIAN AMERICAN MOVEMENT. GLEN KITAYAMA

[Used to compile this entry were Henry Mori. "Pioneer Kai sees support unit start." *Rafu Shimpo* 4 Aug. 1969 and "Pioneer Center a reality." *Rafu Shimpo* 15 Oct. 1969.]

plantations From the late 1800s to the mid 1900s, sugar plantations constituted the heart of the Hawaiian economy. The labor needs of the expanding plantation economy in the late 1800s was the primary reason for the beginning of Japanese labor migration to Hawaii starting in 1885. Through the BIG FIVE and the HAWAII SUGAR PLANTERS ASSOCIATION, the planters directly or indirectly controlled nearly all aspects of life in Hawaii. For the majority of Japanese immigrants, the plantation was to dominate their life in Hawaii. The influence of the plantations began to wane by the mid-20th century with the rise of foreign and domestic competition for the mainland sugar market and expansion of the tourist economy.

For further reading, see Edward D. Beechert. *Working in Hawaii: A Labor History*. Honolulu: University of Hawaii Press, 1985; Lawrence H. Fuchs. *Hawaii Pono: A Social History*. New York: Harcourt, Brace and World, 1961; Noel J. Kent. *Hawaii, Islands Under the Influence*. New York: Monthly Review Press, 1983; John M. Liu. "Cultivating Cane: Asian Labor and the Hawaiian Sugar Plantation System within the Capitalist World Economy, 1835–1920." Diss., University of California, Los Angeles, 1985; and Ronald Takaki. *Pau Hana: Plantation Life and Labor in Hawaii, 1835–1920*. Honolulu: University of Hawaii Press, 1983. For works specifically about Japanese Americans in Hawaii and the plantations, see Roland Kotani. *The Japanese in Hawaii: A Century of Struggle*. Honolulu: Hochi, Ltd., 1985; Franklin S. Odo, and Kazuko Sinoto. *A Pictorial History of the Japanese in Hawaii, 1885–1924*. Honolulu: Bishop Museum Press, 1985; and Gary Y. Okihiro. *Cane Fires: The Anti-Japanese Movement in Hawaii, 1865–1945*. Philadelphia: Temple University Press, 1991. Fictional works centering around Japanese Americans and the plantations include Kazuo Miyamoto. *Hawaii: End of the Rainbow*. Tokyo: Charles E. Tuttle, 1964; Milton Murayama. *All I Asking for Is My Body*. 1959. San Francisco: Supa Press, 1975. Afterword by Franklin Odo. Honolulu: University of Hawaii Press, 1988; and Shelley Ayame Nishimura Ota. *Upon Their Shoulders*. New York: Exposition Press, 1951.

Porterfield v. Webb Test case brought before the U.S. Supreme Court in 1923 that challenged the 1920 (CALIFORNIA) ALIEN LAND LAW ban on leasing land to

ISSEI. Porterfield was a U.S. citizen and California resident who wished to lease 80 acres of land located in Los Angeles County to Mizuno, an *issei* farmer. The Alien Land Law of 1920 prohibited the leasing of land to "ALIENS INELIGIBLE TO CITIZENSHIP," and imposed penalties on those who attempted to do so. Porterfield challenged the reasonableness and constitutional validity of the Alien Land Law, which essentially prohibited *issei* from purchasing, leasing, owning and using land, especially agricultural land. On November 12, 1923, the U.S. Supreme Court upheld the ban on leasing by deciding against Porterfield. On the same day, the Supreme Court also upheld the ban on leasing of a similar Alien Land Law in effect in the state of Washington in the case of TERRACE V. THOMPSON. These decisions severely hampered the agricultural efforts of the Japanese for the next three decades.

For further reading, see Frank F. Chuman. *The Bamboo People: The Law and Japanese-Americans*. Del Mar, Calif.: Publisher's Inc., 1976. Yuji Ichioka. *The Issei: The World of the First Generation Japanese Immigrants, 1885–1924*. New York: The Free Press, 1988 describes the backing of this and the other land law test cases by the JAPANESE ASSOCIATIONS. The transcript of the case can be found in Consulate-General of Japan. *Documental History of Law Cases Affecting Japanese in the United States, 1916–1924. 2 Vols*. New York: Arno Press, 1978. 213–359.   DENNIS YAMAMOTO

Poston   Poston was the site of one of 10 CONCENTRATION CAMPS that housed Japanese Americans forcibly removed from the West Coast states during World War II. One of two camps located in the Arizona desert, Poston was located on an Indian reservation and was the only camp to be administered by the Office of Indian Affairs (OIA) (until the end of 1943) rather than the WAR RELOCATION AUTHORITY (WRA). Some basic data on Poston is presented below in tabular form:

Official name: Colorado River Relocation Center
Location: Yuma County, Arizona, 17 miles south of Parker
Land: On the Colorado Indian Reservation
Size: 71,000 acres; Poston was the largest of the camps
Climate: Desert; perhaps the hottest of all camps
Origin of camp population: Mostly from Los Angeles (2,750), Tulare (1,952), San Diego (1,883), Orange (1,636), Fresno (1,590), Imperial (1,512), Monterey (1,506), and Santa Cruz (1,222) Counties
Via "assembly centers": Most either came to Poston directly (11,738) or came from Salinas (3,459) or Santa Anita (1,573) "ASSEMBLY CENTERS"; Poston also received 469 transfers from Justice Department–administered INTERNMENT CAMPS, the highest figure of any WRA camp
Rural/Urban: Mostly rural

Peak population: 17,814, the most populous besides TULE LAKE "SEGREGATION CENTER"
Date of peak: September 2, 1942
Opening date: May 8, 1942
Closing date: Unit I: November 28, 1945
   Unit II: September 29, 1945
   Unit III: September 29, 1945
Project director(s): Wade Head and Duncan Mills
Community analysts: Alexander Leighton, Edward H. Spicer, Elizabeth Colson and David H. French; Conrad Arensberg and Laura Thompson were consultants
JERS fieldworkers: Richard S. Nishimoto and Tamie Tsuchiyama
Newspaper: *Poston Chronicle* (May 13, 1942–October 23, 1945)
Percent who answered question 28 of the loyalty questionnaire positively: 93.7
Number and percentage of eligible male citizens inducted directly into armed forces: 611 (4.8 percent)
Industry: A camouflage net factory operated from fall 1942 to May 1943
Miscellaneous characteristics: The most notable incident at Poston was the POSTON STRIKE, described in detail in the following entry. There was another strike involving 56 adobe workers in August 1942 that was quickly settled. Poston was named after Charles Poston, the "Father of Arizona." One of the most intensively studied of all the camps, Poston housed a social science laboratory under the leadership of Alexander Leighton while under the OIA in addition to having WRA community analysts and JAPANESE AMERICAN EVACUATION AND RESETTLEMENT STUDY fieldworkers.

Tensions between the OIA and the WRA led to the latter taking over administration of Poston at the beginning of 1944. The OIA had ideas of starting large-scale farming ventures with the Japanese Americans on a semi-permanent basis; this conflicted with the WRA's strategy of encouraging "loyal" residents to leave for RESETTLEMENT as soon as possible.

(For the key to the categories, see the entry for GILA RIVER.)

For further reading: The literature on the Japanese American World War II experience is extensive; see the bibliography and the bibliographic entries after the various entries pertaining to this experience for titles of general interest. For a general account of life in Poston, see Paul Bailey. *City in the Sun: The Japanese Concentration Camp at Poston, Arizona*. Los Angeles: Westernlore Press, 1971. Academic works on Poston include Conrad M. Arensberg. "Report on a Developing Community: Poston, Arizona." *Applied Anthropology* 2.1 (Oct.–Dec. 1942): 1–21; Rita Takahashi Cates. "Comparative Administration and Management of Five War Relocation Authority Camps: America's Incarceration of Persons of Japanese Descent during World War II." Diss., University of Pittsburgh, 1980 and Toshio

Yatsushiro. *Politics and Cultural Values: The World War II Japanese Relocation Centers and the United States Government.* New York: Arno Press, 1978. Two published works came out of the Poston Bureau of Sociological Research: Bureau of Sociological Research, Colorado River War Relocation Center. "The Japanese Family in America." *American Association of Political and Social Science, Annals* 229 (Sept. 1943): 150–56 and Alexander H. Leighton. *The Governing of Men: General Principles and Recommendations Based on Experience at a Japanese Relocation Camp.* New Jersey: Princeton University Press, 1945. Creative works coming out of Poston include Vincent Tajiri, ed. *Through Innocent Eyes: Writings and Art from the Japanese American Internment by Poston I Schoolchildren.* Los Angeles: Keiro Services Press and the Generation Fund, 1990 and Georgia Day Robertson. *The Harvest of Hate.* Forewords by Moto Asakawa and Hiroshi Kamei. 1946. Introduction by Arthur A. Hansen. Fullerton: Oral History Program, California State University, Fullerton, 1986. New York: Lynx Books, 1989, the former a collection of work by Poston children, the latter a novel set in Poston. Poston is also recollected in various pieces by short story writer and playwright Wakako Yamauchi and short pieces by Noriko Sawada and Hisaye Yamamoto. For works dealing specifically with the Poston Strike, see the bibliographic essay after that entry.

Poston Strike   The strike at POSTON was one of two major blowups in the CONCENTRATION CAMPS in late 1942. (The other was the MANZANAR INCIDENT.) The strike was the manifestation of long-standing tensions in the community exacerbated by the camp environment. By WAR RELOCATION AUTHORITY decree, only NISEI were allowed to hold elective office, and the Community Council at Poston consisted entirely of young *nisei*. They quickly succeeded in alienating the administration by being too inquisitive and in upsetting the residents who distrusted their JAPANESE AMERICAN CITIZENS LEAGUE orientation and their inexperience. They were seen by many as "administration stooges" or as a "child council." To try to bring ISSEI into the decision-making process, the Issei Advisory Board was formed in August, but the utter lack of power granted this group only increased tensions. Competition between the Community Council and this advisory council ensued and people seen as "INU" were physically attacked.

On November 14, 1942, one such inmate was beaten severely with a piece of pipe. Quickly, 50 suspects were arrested and two were held for further questioning. Both were quite popular among camp residents. When it became known that these men were to be tried in an Arizona court on the outside (it was widely perceived that no Japanese could get a fair trial outside camp), protest erupted. An *issei* delegation visited the project director on November 17 to request the suspects' release. They were refused. After a second unsuccessful meeting the following day, a general strike ensued. The Com-munity Council resigned as a body in support of the strike and in fear, and crowds began to gather around the jail holding the two suspects. In the meantime, the project director had left to attend a meeting, leaving the camp in charge of an assistant. With the beginning of the strike, some in the administration urged him to call in the army and to impose martial law; he choose the negotiation route. Meanwhile, over the next few days, all services except the police, fire department and hospital were closed down. Strike leaders stood around bonfires, played Japanese militaristic music and extolled the emperor. Eventually, the administration made concessions, agreeing on November 23 to release one prisoner outright and to try the other within the center. Meanwhile, after 10 days, the strike began to erode as many *nisei* tired of it. The *issei* leaders were recognized by the administration and agreed to try to help stop the beatings and to establish better rapport between administration and internees.

For further reading, see Alexander H. Leighton. *The Governing of Men: General Principles and Recommendations Based on Experience at a Japanese Relocation Camp.* New Jersey: Princeton University Press, 1945; Gary Y. Okihiro. "Japanese Resistance in America's Concentration Camps: A Re-evaluation." *Amerasia Journal* 2.1 (1973): 20–34; and Edward H. Spicer, Asael T. Hansen, Katharine Luomala, and Marvin K. Opler. *Impounded People: Japanese Americans in the Relocation Centers.* Washington, D.C.: U.S. Department of Interior, U.S. Government Printing Office, 1946. Tucson: University of Arizona Press, 1969.

prefectures   Westernized governmental districts that replaced the feudal system of the *han,* or feudal domains. The closest American counterpart to the Japanese prefecture is the state; however, a prefecture does not wield as much autonomy and power as an American state.

The establishment of prefectures *(ken)* occurred in 1871 during the MEIJI RESTORATION. The establishment of prefectures was one of the many reforms made during the period to consolidate, centralize, and Westernize governmental control of Japan. Initially in 1871, former *han,* regardless of size, were made into prefectures. These former *han* formed 306 prefectures and three *fu* (metropolitan prefectures). From 1871 until the final redistricting in 1888, the 306 prefectures and three *fu* were consolidated into larger prefectures and *fu.* That final tally resulted in today's 43 prefectures (including Okinawa) and three *fu* in Japan.

For further reading, see Mikiso Hane. *Peasants, Rebels and Outcastes: The Underside of Modern Japan.* New York: Pantheon Books, 1982 and *Kodansha Encyclopedia of Japan.* Tokyo: Kodansha, 1983.

STACEY HIROSE

prostitutes   A majority of the first Japanese women to arrive on U.S. shores were undoubtedly prostitutes.

In the same way that poor Japanese women known as Karayuki-san, especially those from the islands off Kumamoto PREFECTURE, were forced into prostitution in China and Southeast Asia through kidnapping or poverty, many women also became prostitutes in the American West. Reports of Japanese prostitutes in the United States, known as Ameyuki-san, date back to the 1860s, and they frequented the same areas that housed migrant ISSEI male laborers in the railroad, mining, and agricultural industries. These prostitutes were often forcefully held by PINPU (pimps) or AMEGORO who reaped the economic benefits of the women's toils. In at least a few cases, men who began as pimps used their earnings to become LABOR CONTRACTORS or other "legitimate" businessmen.

Both the Japanese government and leaders of the *issei* community condemned the prostitution, gambling and liquor that many single *issei* migrant workers indulged in. They were afraid that such vices would tarnish the image of all Japanese, and many campaigns based on morality and religion were launched to rid the community of them. The proliferation of these vices also became a plank in the ANTI-JAPANESE MOVEMENT campaigns to have further Japanese immigration halted. But until the *issei* community began to change in composition from single males to families with children, there was little that could be done to stop prostitution and the other vices.

The lives of the Ameyuki-san were undoubtedly filled with misery. Many were forced into prostitution through abduction; others "chose" to sell themselves as the only option of making a living or to pay off debts. While some may have eventually returned to Japan and others may have married here, the majority of prostitutes probably died alone.

For further reading, see Yuji Ichioka. "Ameyuki-san: Japanese Prostitutes in Nineteenth-Century America." *Amerasia Journal* 4.1 (1977): 1–21 and *The Issei: The World of the First Generation Japanese Immigrants, 1885–1924*. New York: The Free Press, 1988 and Hisashi Tsurutani. *America Bound: The Japanese and Opening of the American West*. Betsey Scheiner, trans. Tokyo: Japan Times, Inc., 1989. Tomoko Yamazaki. *The Story of Yamada Waka: From Prostitute to Feminist Pioneer*. Ann Kostant, Wakako Hironaka, trans. New York: Kodansha International, 1986 is a biography of a former prostitute who became a noted writer and feminist in Japan.

Questions 27 and 28 See LOYALTY QUESTIONS.

R

Rafu Shimpo Los Angeles–based Japanese American daily newspaper. From its modest beginnings in 1903, the *Rafu Shimpo* has become the most popular Japanese American newspaper in the post–World War II era.

The *Rafu* was founded in April 1903, by Rippo Iijima, Masaharu Yamaguchi and Seijiro Shibuya to serve the growing Japanese American community in Los Angeles. Its early days saw many changes of management as the fledgling paper battled the relatively entrenched San Francisco–based dailies NICHIBEI SHIMBUN and SHIN SEKAI, both of which opened up Los Angeles offices at around the same time. The paper came close to shutting down a number of times, most notably when it became embroiled in a controversy over the new NINTH STREET PRODUCE MARKET, which resulted in a boycott of the paper in 1909. A new management team took over the paper in 1914, with Sho Inoue as president and Henry Toyosaku (H. T.) Komai taking over as manager. In 1915, the paper moved from First Street to 104 North Los Angeles Street. Komai took over as president in 1922. That position would remain in the family for the next 70 years.

Weekly English sections first appeared on February 21, 1926. Twenty-year-old UCLA education student Louise Suski was the first English-section editor. The English-section became a daily feature on January 11, 1932. TOGO TANAKA became coeditor of the paper in April 1936; under Tanaka's leadership, the special Holiday and Graduation issues were initiated. Due to World War II and the forced removal of all West Coast Japanese Americans, the *Rafu Shimpo* temporarily ceased publication with the issue of April 4, 1942.

With Japanese Americans beginning to return to the coast in 1945, the paper resumed publication with the January 1, 1946, issue under the leadership of Akira Komai, son of H. T., who was still being held in an INTERNMENT CAMP at SANTA FE, New Mexico. The printing press and type had remained in the Los Angeles St. building through the war. Financially strapped, the paper was kept going by a $1,500 contribution from three employees. The first postwar editors were Teiho Hoshida, Japanese section (a post he would hold for 39 years), and Henry Mori, English section.

The postwar years saw the rapid growth of the paper. The circulation of 500 in 1946 grew to over 20,000 over the next 30 years, making it the most widely read of any Japanese American paper. A large part of that audience read it for the reprints of Japanese news from the *Mainichi Shimbun* or for the coverage of the local Japanese American sports leagues, which Akira Komai played a big part in starting. The paper moved to new quarters two more times due to REDEVELOPMENT in Los Angeles's LITTLE TOKYO, first in 1950 to make room for the police station expansion called Parker Center, then in 1978 to make way for the Japanese American Cultural and Community Center. Akira's son Michael Komai took over as president of the *Rafu Shimpo* in 1983 upon Akira's death. The *Rafu Shimpo* remains one of the most influential of Japanese American papers today.

For further reading, see Katie Kaoru Hayashi. "History of the Rafu Shimpo: Evolution of a Japanese-American Newspaper, 1903–1942." Thesis, California State University, Northridge, 1987; Jon Takasugi. "English Section Evolves from Weekly Feature to Community Daily." *Rafu Shimpo* 7 Oct. 1986: 1+; and Kiyoshi Yano. "The Rafu Shimpo's 83-Year Journey to No. 25,000." *Rafu Shimpo* 7 Oct. 1986: 1+.

redevelopment The 1950s, '60s and '70 was a period of urban renewal in many major cities in the United States. In an attempt to attract businesses and consumers back to downtown areas that had become run down, local city councils in conjunction with the federal government devised master plans to revitalize central cities. In many West Coast cities, Japantowns were located in downtown areas and would be directly affected by redevelopment activity. In the decades from the 1950s to the 1970s, Japanese American communities in several cities were affected by redevelopment. In most cases, the general outline was the same: initial optimism over the prospect of a shiny new physical environment that turned to disappointment and often disapproval at the large-scale evictions and forced relocations that resulted. For a people rebuilding from the forced removal and detention of World War II, the prospect of more forced moves was especially unwelcome.

The early 1950s saw the first hints of what was to come. A healthy bite was taken out of Los Angeles's LITTLE TOKYO in the early 1950s to make way for an expansion of the police station known as Parker Center. Over 1,000 tenants living on the north side of First Street had to be evicted in what became known as the "second relocation." A major redevelopment plan in SACRAMENTO, California, in 1958 resulted in the leveling of a 15 square block area; the heart of Sacramento's historic Japanese American community fell victim. Although business owners and residents were reimbursed at fair prices, residents looked upon the episode and mass exodus as another example of governmental discrimination, though some welcomed the destruction of the "ghetto" and the forced assimilation of Japanese Americans into the larger community which resulted.

In Los Angeles and San Francisco in the 1960s, a new factor was thrown into the equation: the influx of Japanese capital into historically Japanese American neighborhoods. Though welcomed at first by Japanese Americans, the Japanese businesses later drew their ire over their lack of sensitivity to and understanding of the Japanese American community and experience.

The late 1960s and early 1970s saw the maturation of plans for the preservation and redevelopment of J-Towns in Los Angeles and San Francisco. In Los Angeles, when the idea for redevelopment was first proposed for its Little Tokyo area, it was greeted with universal enthusiasm. Plans for a revitalized Little Tokyo included a cultural and community center that would house local community organizations, a theater for the performing arts and a gymnasium; a 1,000-unit low-income apartment complex to house Japanese American senior citizens; a couple of new street malls to serve local businesses; and a new hotel complex to take care of visitors. Everybody seemed to benefit from this arrangement: the city and local merchants would generate more money with added business while the community would get a new center and senior citizens complex. What could go wrong?

Plenty, as people would soon discover. Problems started to arise out of the proposed hotel project. Under the original guidelines, local businesses would sell their property to the Community Redevelopment Agency (CRA) and then have a chance to buy the property back to develop. With the hotel project, allegations of corrupt "behind-the-scenes" deals arose when a major multinational corporation from Japan was granted the right to develop the property at the Second and Weller Street triangle over a Japanese American company formed by local businesspeople. To make matters worse, the Sun Building, which housed most of the local community groups, was located on the proposed hotel site and was scheduled to be demolished. With the community center nowhere near construction, the Japanese American community felt that big business from Japan was being given priority over community concerns.

Perhaps the first lesson learned by local merchants was that they could not compete with the influx of foreign capital. Besides losing the hotel project, they could not raise enough money to bid on the street mall planned for Moline Alley (now the Japanese Village Plaza) and were slow in raising funds for the community center and senior citizens complex. Many openly questioned the reasoning for redevelopment if the community was destroyed in the process. Community groups and local residents were threatened with eviction and given no place to stay. Businesses were forced to relocate—sometimes out of Little Tokyo—and faced an uncertain future of being able to reestablish themselves once redevelopment was finished.

Unlike the 1950s, however, the community fought back. With the rise of the ASIAN AMERICAN MOVEMENT, Japanese American young people formed the Little Tokyo Anti-Eviction Task Force (later the Little Tokyo People's Rights Organization or LTPRO) in the early 1970s as a result of the problems faced by the community. A similar organization, the Committee Against Nihonmachi Evictions (CANE), arose in San Francisco. When the construction of the Kingdome threatened

Seattle's Asian American business district, a protest movement also developed there. These groups called attention to the negative aspects of redevelopment by calling the press, contacting city councils and organizing the Japanese American community around the issue. The organizations also resorted to more militant tactics when cornered—to prevent the demolition of important buildings in their respective communities, members of LTPRO occupied the building for several weeks until removed by police in a pre-dawn raid, while CANE members chained themselves around the building. Debates over what the course of redevelopment should be and what actions should be taken raged within the communities.

The struggle turned out to be a prolonged one. The New Otani Hotel went up as planned in Los Angeles, residents were evicted and many Japanese American businesses were forced to close. On the positive side, however, subsidized low income housing in the form of the 300-unit Little Tokyo Towers and 100-unit Miyako Apartments were completed largely through the pressure of the community. Also, the Japanese American Cultural and Community Center (JACCC), threatening at one point to be like the Japan Trade Center in San Francisco, was eventually completed and more importantly, made accessible to the community groups.

The mobilization against wanton eviction and destruction of historical Japanese American communities had one additional beneficial aspect—it laid much of the groundwork for what would become the REDRESS MOVEMENT. LTPRO became the Los Angeles Community Coalition for Redress/Reparations, which evolved into the NATIONAL COALITION FOR REDRESS/REPARATIONS, one of the three major national redress organizations. More importantly, the complacency of the 1950s had been at least partially broken; in the 1980s, that silence would be forever abandoned.

For further reading, see Ichiro Mike Murase. *Little Tokyo: One Hundred Years in Pictures*. Art direction and design by Michael Nakayama. Los Angeles: Visual Communications/Asian American Studies Central, Inc., 1983 and Cheryl L. Cole. *A History of the Japanese Community in Sacramento, 1883–1972: Organizations, Businesses and Generational Response to Majority Domination and Stereotypes*. San Francisco: R & E Research Associates, 1975 for accounts of redevelopment in Los Angeles and Sacramento, respectively. More on Los Angeles redevelopment can be found in Little Tokyo Anti-Eviction Task Force. "Redevelopment in Los Angeles' Little Tokyo." In Gee, Emma, ed. *Counterpoint: Perspectives on Asian America*. Los Angeles: Asian American Studies Center, University of California, 1976. 327–33. For more on this topic, see the chronology.

GLEN KITAYAMA/BRIAN NIIYA

redress and reparations According to *Webster's New Collegiate Dictionary*, "redress" is "a means or a possibility of seeking a remedy." It also means "to set right" and "to make up for." "Redress" can also mean "compensation for wrong or loss: reparation." "Reparations" refers to the act of making amends, usually in the form of compensation. It is a specific form of redress. In the case of Japanese Americans, a remedy was pursued to compensate them for their wrongful detention in CONCENTRATION CAMPS during World War II.

One Japanese American redress organization, the NATIONAL COALITION FOR REDRESS/REPARATIONS (NCRR), was very careful in choosing its name in order to make the distinction between the two terms. Since "redress" on its own could imply only a remedy or an apology, it was not seen as sufficient to only campaign around that issue. "Reparations," on the other hand, left no doubt that monetary compensation was to be demanded. Eventually, "redress" and "reparations" came to be synonymous, hence the term "REDRESS MOVEMENT."

GLEN KITAYAMA

redress movement Movement organized by the Japanese American community to obtain an apology and compensation from the United States government for its wrongful actions towards them during World War II.

EDISON UNO is often credited as being the "father" of the redress movement. At the 1970 JAPANESE AMERICAN CITIZENS LEAGUE (JACL) National Convention, he, along with some other renegades in the JACL who were working on the repeal of the EMERGENCY DETENTION ACT, introduced a resolution for the JACL to seek compensation through legislation for the wrongs committed by the U.S. government in interning over 120,000 people of Japanese ancestry during World War II. The JACL, which had not yet taken a stand on the Vietnam War and had for the most part stayed away from the Civil Rights movement, did not seem ready to adopt a resolution in favor of redress. The resolution, however, did pass, but went nowhere. Similar resolutions at JACL National Conventions passed in 1972 and 1974 with Uno's perseverance, but they too died after approval.

In the early 1970s, the Seattle Evacuation Redress Committee of the JACL formed to continue the cause taken up by Uno. Clearly, it was another renegade group trying to push the National JACL into action. On November 19, 1975, it unveiled what is now known as the "Seattle Plan," which called for individual reparations of $5,000 to each person who "voluntarily resettled" (see VOLUNTARY RESETTLEMENT) and to those who were forcibly removed from the West Coast and incarcerated in CONCENTRATION CAMPS. In addition, a sum of $10 per day interned would be added to the fixed compensation of $5,000. Payment of the money would come from a special fund set up by the Internal Revenue Service. The Seattle Plan came into conflict with the proposal offered by the National JACL. Instead of individual reparations, the National proposed that "block grants" be paid to individual Japanese American organizations.

In 1976, the NATIONAL COMMITTEE FOR REDRESS (NCR) was established at the JACL National Convention. This represented the group's first serious action taken on the issue. The group was charged with researching the issue and adopting legislation to be considered at the next convention in 1978. At first, it started with the proposal of a community fund ("block grants") and immediately encountered resistance from the Seattle group. By the time the 1978 convention came around, the NCR adopted a proposal demanding $25,000 in reparations for each person forcibly removed.

Surprisingly, the latter proposal was also met with resistance from the Seattle group. To start, the plan did not make any provisions for those who were removed, but not detained in the camps (i.e., the "voluntary resettlers"). Secondly, it did not include reparations to those who were forcibly removed from areas outside of the Western Defense Command, namely those in Hawaii, Alaska and in other parts of the country. Lastly, they disagreed with the idea of putting a Japanese American commission in charge of allocating the money. Nobody, after all, was immune from corruption. Still, the proposal passed despite their objections and the opposition of older leaders like MIKE MASAOKA.

In the meantime, the struggle against the REDEVELOPMENT of Japantowns across the nation was taking place. Major cities, wanting to revitalize their downtown central business districts, attempted to rebuild without the approval of those who were affected most: the tenants who lived and worked there. At first, when the idea was initially proposed, it was greeted with enthusiasm. Japantowns, after all, had become run-down over the years and were in need of a face lift. Controversy started, however, when long-time ISSEI residents were threatened with eviction and given no place else to live. Local businesspeople saw the influx of Japanese yen and wondered if there would be a place for them when redevelopment was finished. Activists in the Japanese American community mobilized around the issue and saw this as another example of American racism. Groups like the Little Tokyo People's Right Organization (LTPRO) in Los Angeles protested redevelopment and eventually won major concessions. Out of this struggle emerged the Los Angeles Community Coalition for Redress/Reparations (LACCRR) and other local redress groups around the country. The idea for redress started to gain momentum in the Japanese American community.

On the weekend of March 3–4, 1979, the NCR of the JACL switched its support for direct individual payments and instead favored the creation of a government commission to study the matter and recommend solutions. The main reasons given for the change were fiscal conservatism and the vociferous attacks on redress by S. I. HAYAKAWA, the conservative U.S. senator from California who was of Japanese descent. Some in the organization questioned the authority of the NCR to change the official position mandated by the delegates at the 1978 National Convention. Many others felt that the JACL was waffling on the issue and was putting too much trust in the government. As a result of this action by the NCR, the NATIONAL COUNCIL FOR JAPANESE AMERICAN REDRESS (NCJAR) was formed consisting of William Hohri of Chicago and members of the JACL in Seattle in May of 1979.

The first action by NCJAR was to find a member of Congress to sponsor a redress bill. Since the four Democratic Japanese American congressmen supported the creation of a government commission, support was not likely to come from them. Instead, Congressman Mike Lowry from Seattle became the first to sponsor redress legislation. Not surprisingly, the proposed legislation was almost a duplicate of the "Seattle Plan" written years earlier. The bill, with no support from the NIKKEI congressmen, was killed in committee.

On July 30, 1980, the COMMISSION ON WARTIME RELOCATION AND INTERNMENT OF CIVILIANS (CWRIC) was created by an act of Congress. Formed mainly to investigate matters surrounding the camps and to recommend appropriate remedies, the CWRIC had no power to correct grievances and was seen by some as a "cop-out" by the JACL. Still, hearings were set to be conducted in 20 cities across the nation beginning the next year.

One group that objected to the formation of the CWRIC was the NATIONAL COALITION FOR REDRESS/REPARATIONS (NCRR). Organized on July 12, 1980, primarily out of LACCRR in Los Angeles, the NCRR also included the Nihonmachi Outreach Committee in San Jose, Concerned Japanese Americans in New York, Japanese Community Progressive Alliance in San Francisco and the Asian Pacific Student Union (APSU) on the West Coast. Like NCJAR, the NCRR saw no need for a commission to investigate the camps and viewed the formation of the CWRIC with suspicion. With the JACL backing off from its demands for monetary compensation, the NCRR felt that it was necessary to organize around the CWRIC hearings to make sure that the voice of the Japanese American community would be heard. The addition of the NCRR to the redress movement added the necessary grass-roots angle in what was to become a long struggle.

In 1981, while the CWRIC conducted it hearings, another important wing of the redress movement was just beginning. Peter Irons, a law historian, was conducting research on the wartime convictions of Fred Korematsu, Gordon Hirabayashi, and Min Yasui for a book he was writing. During this process, he came across evidence that the government purposely suppressed evidence in presenting its cases against the three wartime resisters. After meeting with them, he and a group of SANSEI lawyers worked to get their convictions overturned using a little-known petition procedure called *writ of error coram nobis*. The research uncovered in the CORAM NOBIS CASES was instrumental in the advancement of the redress movement.

The CWRIC hearings were the turning point of the redress movement. With community involvement, the demand for individual monetary reparations was echoed in almost every statement. Previous opponents of redress, like Mike Masaoka and other conservative members of the JACL, were won over to the movement after the hearings. The often emotional testimony was a cathartic for the community, as many former concentration camp inmates spoke of their experiences in public for the first time.

In December 1982, the CWRIC issued its report *Personal Justice Denied*. It was an exhaustive work that combined the testimonies heard at the hearings and research conducted by a team led by Aiko Yoshinaga-Herzig. No recommendations were made at that time, but it was clear that the commission was sympathetic to the issue of redress. By the middle of the next year, there was much rejoicing as the CWRIC recommended, among other things, $20,000 individual compensation to those interned and a formal apology. This recommendation was to be the basis for the many redress bills that were to follow.

In the meantime, the NCJAR was conducting a separate attack on the government for its wartime violation of civil rights. It raised money to retain a law firm, conducted intensive research and, on March 16, 1983, brought a class action law suit against the government on behalf of the over 120,000 victims of the camps. Though the suit was eventually dismissed after a long journey through the court system, it placed the necessary pressure on the government to pay reparations.

In 1987, redress bills H.R. 442 and S. 1009 were introduced in the House and Senate. With the support of the Nikkei congressional delegation, the bill quickly generated momentum in Congress. For the first time, the redress bill was voted out of committee and was scheduled for a vote by the full Congress. The NCRR, continuing in its grass-roots campaign, mobilized an Asian American delegation to lobby for the redress bill in Washington, D.C. Originally, the group anticipated only a few dedicated participants. However, word spread about their efforts and over 120 people made the journey to Washington from July 25, 1987, to July 29, 1987.

Many more supported them through financial donations. The NCRR delegation made over 100 congressional visits, solidifying support among some members and changing the minds of others in Congress about the bill.

On September 19, 1987, the 200th anniversary of the Constitution, H.R. 442 passed by a margin of 243 to 141. Later, the Senate passed its own version of the bill on April 20, 1988, and sent it to President Ronald Reagan for his signature. At first, the president threatened to veto the bill because of fiscal restraints in the federal budget. Several events, however, could have changed his mind in favor of the bill. One was the stunning defeat of fellow conservative Daniel Lungren to the office of California State Treasurer in an election year. Lungren, who was a leader against the movement for redress, was nominated for the office by the California governor and was rejected largely because of the vocal protests led by the Japanese American community. Another could have been the over 20,000 letters and mailgrams sent to the president in support of the bill. There were many reasons why the president eventually signed the redress bill on August 10, 1988, and they will be debated for years to come by scholars and proponents of the three major redress groups. Over two years later, on October 9, 1990, the first redress payments were made to the oldest living survivors of America's concentration camps.

Relatively little has been written on the redress movement at this time. Excerpts from the CWRIC hearings can be found in "Commission on Wartime Relocation and Internment of Civilians: Selected Testimonies From the Los Angeles and San Francisco Hearings." *Amerasia Journal* 8.2 (Fall/Winter 1981): 54–105. For an overview of the redress movement, see Roger Daniels. "The Redress Movement" and "Redress Achieved, 1983–1990." In Daniels, Roger, Sandra C. Taylor, and Harry H. L. Kitano, eds. *Japanese Americans: From Relocation to Redress*. Salt Lake City: University of Utah Press, 1986. Revised edition. Seattle: University of Washington Press, 1991. 188–90; 219–23. William Hohri. *Repairing America: An Account of the Movement for Japanese American Redress*. Pullman: Washington State University Press, 1988 is an autobiographical account by the founder of the NCJAR. Mike Masaoka, and Bill Hosokawa. *They Call Me Moses Masaoka*. New York: William Morrow, 1987 is the autobiography of a major JACL leader which includes information on the JACL's role in the redress movement. See also Yuriko Kaminaga. "Social Change through Legal Means: A Case Study of the Japanese American Legal Movement." Diss., University of California, San Diego, 1987; Margot Beth Kempers. "Contemporary Dimensions of Group Rights: The Maine Indian Land Claims and Japanese-American Redress." Diss., Brandeis University, 1986; Yasuko I. Takezawa. "Children of Inmates: The Effects of the Redress Movement among Third Generation Japanese Americans." *Qualitative Sociology* 14.1 (Spring 1991): 39–56; and Eric K. Yamamoto. "Friend or Foe or Something Else: Social Meanings of Redress and Reparations." *Denver Journal of Interna-*

tional Law and Policy 20: 2 (Winter 1992): 223–42. See the various entries listed above for more information on those topics.   GLEN KITAYAMA

[Also used to compile this entry: Miya Iwataki. "Redress/Reparations Lobby Shows that People are Makers of History." *Rafu Shimpo* August 10, 1988; NCRR video: *Justice Now! Reparations Now!*; "Senate Passes Bill to Compensate Japanese American Internees." *Rafu Shimpo* April 21, 1988.]

Regan v. King   California court case involving an attempt to strip NISEI of their citizenship. John T. Regan, grand secretary of the NATIVE SONS OF THE GOLDEN WEST, brought an action in June 1942 against Cameron King, registrar of voters for the City and County of San Francisco. The action was brought in a federal district court, and Regan wanted King to strike the names of more than 2,600 *nisei* residents of California from the register of voters. King contended that the Japanese Americans were born in the United States and therefore citizens, and were thus entitled to be registered as voters. Federal District Judge Adolphus F. St. Sure was presented with the question of whether those of Japanese ancestry who were born in this country were citizens. Judge St. Sure noted several cases decided by the U.S. Supreme Court on this issue, such as U.S. V. WONG KIM ARK, and followed precedent by ruling that people born in the U.S. were citizens, regardless of their ancestry. The case was dismissed and the decision was affirmed on appeal.

For further reading, see Frank F. Chuman. *The Bamboo People: The Law and Japanese-Americans.* Del Mar, Calif.: Publisher's Inc., 1976.   DENNIS YAMAMOTO

Reimei   NISEI literary journal published in Salt Lake City between 1931 and 1933. Edited by Yasuo Sasaki, a *nisei* who later published two volumes of poetry (*Ascension* and *Village Scene/Village Herd*), *Reimei* was one of a handful of literary journals published by *nisei* in the prewar years. Others included *Leaves* (produced in Los Angeles in the early 1930s), *Gyo-Sho: A Magazine of Nisei Literature* (published circa 1935 by the English Club of Cornell College in Mount Vernon, Iowa) and *Current Life* (a magazine published by JAMES OMURA in San Francisco between October 1940 and December 1941). *Reimei* was an outgrowth of the Reimei Association of the Intermountain States, a *nisei* youth club. The journal first appeared in March 1931 as a mimeographed collection of stories, poems, essays and book reviews by Reimei members. In July 1932, the journal began a new series as a professionally printed quarterly with contributions from the leading *nisei* writers of the era, including Toyo Suyemoto, Chiye Mori, Iwao Kawakami and Carl Kondo.   STAN YOGI

"relocation centers"   Euphemistic term for WAR RELOCATION AUTHORITY–administered camps; see CONCENTRATION CAMPS.

Reluctant 39   Group of 39 witnesses affiliated with the INTERNATIONAL LONGSHOREMEN'S AND WAREHOUSEMEN'S UNION (ILWU) in Hawaii who refused to testify before the House Un-American Activities Committee (HUAC) in April 1950. In the wake of the bitter 1949 STRIKE, a climate of anti-Communist hysteria had been fomented in Hawaii by the anti-union press and pro-plantation management forces to defeat the strikers by claiming they were Communist-dominated. Though these tactics failed in the short term—the strike ended only when the dockworkers had succeeded in securing a 21-cent increase—they had the effect of diminishing public support of the ILWU. In April 1950, 66 residents of Hawaii were called on to testify before HUAC about their knowledge of Communist activity in the Islands. Of those called, 39 refused to testify, a group which became known as the Reluctant 39. They were indicted for contempt of Congress, but were eventually acquitted. Among the Reluctant 39 were many NISEI labor leaders, including JACK KAWANO, who one year later would break off from the Communist Party and the ILWU and blow the whistle on his former comrades. For further reading, see Lawrence H. Fuchs. *Hawaii Pono: A Social History.* New York: Harcourt, Brace and World, 1961 and Roland Kotani. *The Japanese in Hawaii: A Century of Struggle.* Honolulu: Hochi, Ltd., 1985.

remittances to Japan   From the time of the initial arrival of Japanese in Hawaii and on the mainland, a large portion of wages received from their work was sent back to Japan. This was consistent with a DEKASEGI-SHOSEI orientation, of people who intended only to work in the U.S. for a short time before returning home to Japan.

The first record of such remittances came on August 22, 1885, when the *Bocho Shimbun* reported that 8,000 yen had been sent back to Japan by the first group of Japanese laborers in Hawaii who had arrived only six months previously. According to a report by the Finance Ministry, Japanese laborers from abroad sent back 12.2 million yen by 1902, over 80 percent of that total from Hawaii, the mainland United States and Canada. Given that this amount of money came from fewer than 100,000 workers who probably averaged $1.00 per day in wages, this is a significant amount of money. Such remittances to family members and others in Japan provided a large boost to the economies of areas that sent many emigrants abroad; these areas often became known as AMERIKA MURA ("American villages").

For further reading, see Hisashi Tsurutani. *America Bound: The Japanese and Opening of the American West.* Betsey Scheiner, trans. Tokyo: Japan Times, Inc., 1989 and United Japanese Society of Hawaii. *History of Japanese in Hawaii.* James H. Okahata, ed. Honolulu: United Japanese Society of Hawaii, 1971.

renunciation of citizenship During World War II, 5,589 American citizens of Japanese descent, or nearly one of every 14 Japanese Americans eligible to do so, renounced their United States citizenship. The renunciations took place between December 1944 and July 1945, with minor exceptions, in TULE LAKE "SEGREGATION CENTER" in the state of California.

It is now recognized that the vast majority of the renunciations had little to do with "loyalty" or "disloyalty" to the United States, but were instead the result of a series of complex conditions and factors that were beyond the control of those involved. Prior to discarding citizenship, most or all of the renunciants had experienced the following misfortunes: forced removal from homes; loss of jobs; government and public assumption of disloyalty to the land of their birth based on race alone; and incarceration in a "segregation center" for "disloyal" ISSEI and NISEI who had either requested repatriation/expatriation to Japan or had refused to answer or gave negative replies to two "LOYALTY QUESTIONS" on government questionnaires.

Once confined at Tule Lake, the renunciants had experienced even harsher conditions, including: long-term mutual hostility between camp residents and the project administration; martial law; curfew; fear of arrest and imprisonment without hearings or trials in the infamous STOCKADE; and intimidation, threats, violence, and even murder, by radical pro-Japanese organizations that sought to impose their will on the population of the camp.

These were some of the conditions existing in Tule Lake on July 1, 1944, when President FRANKLIN D. ROOSEVELT signed Public Law 405 of the 78th Congress, an amendment to the Nationality Act of 1798, that permitted a citizen of the United States to renounce his or her citizenship during time of war, upon approval of the attorney general.

The Renunciation Law was the product of a combination of forces. (1) Anti-Japanese groups and politicians who had sought to deprive citizens of Japanese descent of their citizenship from as early as 1921. In 1943, the NATIVE SONS OF THE GOLDEN WEST pushed for national legislation to achieve this goal. At least five bills were introduced in Congress from October 1943 through February 1944 aimed at the allegedly disloyal internees. (2) The WAR RELOCATION AUTHORITY (WRA) wanted to free internees in the nine remaining camps to resettle in areas outside the West Coast exclusion zone and feared that problems in Tule Lake would harm this goal. WRA national director DILLON MYER believed there were between one and two thousand "disloyal" *nisei* (mostly Japan-educated KIBEI) in Tule Lake. (3) The U.S. Justice Department, which under Attorney General FRANCIS BIDDLE believed that legislation was needed to keep those believed to be "disloyal" in detention. Biddle felt that if "disloyal" citizens in Tule Lake were given the opportunity to renounce their citizenship, that they would do so. They would thus become alien enemies subject to detention and deportation from the United States. He consequently drafted the bill that was eventually passed as the Renunciation Law. In order to make it constitutional, the legislation was made to apply to all American citizens. It was, however, prepared and passed solely with those at Tule Lake in mind.

For several months after its passage, the Renunciation Law evoked little interest among the citizen *nisei* in Tule Lake. Interest was avid, however, among the alien *issei* leaders of the radical pro-Japanese underground movement, who adopted it as a part of their program. The radicals considered themselves to be the only "true Japanese" in the camp, and sought to force other residents into their organizations through methods that included terror, intimidation, rumor, threats, violence and murder. By the end of the year, the majority of the camp was at least nominally under their control. The acquiescence of Tule Lake administrators to the radicals' activities gave residents the impression that they (the radicals) had government support. Nevertheless, a substantial majority of the camp's citizens remained uninterested in renunciation and did not welcome the law that gave them the opportunity.

The lack of interest in renunciation changed dramatically on December 17, 1944, with two unpopular administrative decisions that threw Tule Lake into a state of mass hysteria. On that day, detainees were told by the WRA that all the camps, including Tule Lake, would close within a year, and by the Western Defense Command that Japanese Americans were free to return to the West Coast. The announcements struck fear into Tuleans, who had come to view the center as a haven from an unfriendly and antagonistic public outside the camps. News reports of violence to Japanese Americans who had returned to their homes were translated by highly anxious residents into a fear of possible shootings and worse in outside communities. The announcements also brought fears of economic impoverishment and family separation due to reinstitution of the draft.

The citizen *nisei* became subjected to pressures from parents, who believed that they would not be forced out of camp if their children renounced; and from the radical pro-Japan organizations that greatly increased their militant activities, violence and threats to secure renunciations. As a result, the flood of applications for renunciation of citizenship sent to the Department of Justice in Washington, D.C. became so great that the Tule Lake post office suffered a temporary breakdown soon after the December 17th announcements.

Department of Justice teams, headed by Assistant Attorney General John L. Burling, were in Tule Lake from January 11 to March 17, 1945, and again briefly in July, to hold individual hearings for those who had applied for renunciation of citizenship. The radical organizations held massive demonstrations and trained their members to answer questions so as to ensure approval of applications. Burling tried in vain to stop the pressure tactics of the radicals. WRA administrators and staff members realized that many citizens were renouncing citizenship to avoid forced resettlement and for reasons other than national allegiance. They attempted to persuade the Department of Justice to postpone the hearings, but without success. Burling rejected claims that the pressures exerted on the renunciants were of a nature sufficient to invalidate the renunciations.

The Department of Justice received over 6,000 applications for renunciation of citizenship. Of this number, 5,589 were approved. All but 128, which were spread over the eight other camps, were from Tule Lake. Seven of every 10 citizens age 18 and above at Tule Lake gave up their citizenship.

Even while the renunciation hearings were being held, many renunciants began to regret their actions and sought ways to undo what they had done. A flood of letters was sent to the Department of Justice and other agencies pleading to allow them to withdraw their renunciations and asking permission to resettle in the United States. While the WRA and other agencies were sympathetic, the Department of Justice took a hard line, which it continued to hold for two decades. The renunciants were told that there was no way to restore citizenship. And rather than permitting resettlement in the U.S., the Department planned to deport all to Japan.

Renunciants interested in restoration of citizenship and avoidance of deportation began to organize during August and September 1945. The Tule Lake Defense Committee, formed to coordinate their efforts, hired WAYNE M. COLLINS, a San Francisco attorney, to represent them. On November 13, 1945, only two days before the ships were to depart, Collins filed suits in U. S. district court in San Francisco, stopping deportation. The suits asked that the renunciants be set at liberty, their applications for renunciation be declared void and that their citizenship be restored.

The main defense used in the mass suits was duress by the U. S. government. Collins argued that even the most radical members of the pro-Japanese groups were entitled to restoration of citizenship because all had suffered forced removal from their homes, incarceration in camps and other hardships at the hands of the federal government. The renunciation cases remained in the courts for 22 years. Collins persisted through periods of victory and defeat, and in the face of opposition from the Department of Justice and the national office of the AMERICAN CIVIL LIBERTIES UNION, particularly through its Los Angeles representative, A. L. WIRIN. His victory for three renunciants in the *Murakami* case forced thousands in Collins's mass suits to resort to individual appeals to obtain restoration of citizenship. Of the 5,589 persons whose applications for renunciation were accepted, 5,409 asked to have their citizenship returned, and 4,978 such requests were granted. Ironically, when the last case was brought up on March 6, 1968, the renunciant changed his mind, and withdrew from the suit.

For further reading, see Donald E. Collins. *Native American Aliens: Disloyalty and the Renunciation of Citizenship by Japanese Americans During World War II*. Westport, Conn.: Greenwood Press, 1985; Audrie Girdner, and Anne Loftis. *The Great Betrayal: The Evacuation of the Japanese-Americans during World War II*. Toronto: Macmillan, 1969; Dorothy S. Thomas, and Richard Nishimoto. *The Spoilage*. Berkeley: University of California Press, 1946, 1969; and Michi Weglyn. *Years of Infamy: The Untold Story of America's Concentration Camps*. New York: William Morrow & Co., 1976.   DONALD E. COLLINS

resettlement   Term used by the WAR RELOCATION AUTHORITY (WRA) to refer to the migration of Japanese Americans from the CONCENTRATION CAMPS in which they were incarcerated during World War II. The term is also used to refer to the movement of Japanese Americans out of restricted areas prior to their forced removal; see "VOLUNTARY" RESETTLEMENT.

As part of the its philosophy in dealing with the 120,000 Japanese Americans under its jurisdiction, the WRA and its director DILLON S. MYER encouraged Japanese Americans who could pass the various security clearances to leave the confines of the "relocation centers" for parts east and north. The underlying reason for this geographical emphasis was that Myer believed it was important for Japanese Americans not to go back to the West Coast and the JAPANTOWNS from which they came; being in such tightly knit ethnic enclaves was part of what got them into trouble in the first place. By this line of thinking, it was important for the NISEI to expand their horizons by going to different parts of the country, the better for them to become more "Americanized" and to blend in with the local population. Additionally, it was felt that there would be greater economic opportunity and less discrimination in eastern and midwestern cities that had seen few Japanese Americans before. Finally, it was felt that Japanese Americans could ease labor shortages in these areas brought on by the war. Indeed, the WRA was besieged by requests for presumably cheap Japanese American labor from around the country.

By July 1942, even as people were still arriving in the 10 WRA concentration camps, the WRA was instituting regulations for "leave" and "permanent resettlement." The WRA hoped to have 75,000 people out of the camps by the end of the year. For various reasons, this was not to be. For one thing, many people did not want to leave the camps once settled there. Especially for the ISSEI who had lost everything by being forcibly removed from their homes, there was little incentive to leave camp for an uncertain existence in a hostile outside world. Even for those *nisei* who were anxious to leave camp for the outside, the convoluted leave clearance process created seemingly endless delays and discouraged others from even trying. Additionally, there was still a good deal of resistance by civic leaders in the communities targeted to receive Japanese Americans. The WRA opened a field office in Chicago in January 1943 to expedite the process and would open 41 others by the end of the year. Still, by the end of 1943, only 17,000 people had left the camps. (Many of these were college students; see NATIONAL JAPANESE AMERICAN STUDENT RELOCATION COUNCIL.) By January 1945, about one-third had left the camps.

Among the most popular initial destinations for those who sought resettlement were Denver and Salt Lake City. They were the closest to the West Coast and already had sizable Japanese American communities prior to the war. They became such popular destinations that the WRA was forced to discourage further resettlement in the intermountain area, fearing a backlash in local public opinion and the rise anew of ethnic communities. (Both occurred anyway.) After this, Chicago became the most popular destination, along with Minneapolis/St. Paul, Cleveland, St. Louis and New York. Communities of resettlers emerged in these and other midwestern and eastern cities as parents and other relatives joined *nisei* who had moved there earlier. However, when Japanese Americans were allowed to return to the West Coast in 1945, many resettlers left to return to the coast. Having reached a peak in 1945–46, the Japanese American populations declined in most of these cities. There are still substantial Japanese American communities today in most of the resettlement cities, however.

There is no definitive study of the resettlement period or process. A general study that focuses on those who resettled in the Midwest and East is Dorothy S. Thomas. *The Salvage.* Berkeley: University of California Press, 1952, a product of the JAPANESE AMERICAN EVACUATION AND RESETTLEMENT STUDY. Tetsuden Kashima. "Japanese American Internees Return—1945 to 1955: Readjustment and Social Amnesia." *Phylon* 41.2 (June 1980): 107–15 provides one interpretation of the resettlement period and its aftermath.

Studies of resettlement to areas outside the West Coast or of Japanese American communities made up primarily of post–World War II resettlers include Michael Daniel Albert. "Japanese American Communities in Chicago and the Twin Cities." Diss., University of Minnesota, 1980; Emory S. Bogardus. "Resettlement Problems of Japanese-Americans." *Sociology and Social Research* 29.3 (Jan.-Feb. 1945): 218–66; Miyako Inoue. "Japanese-Americans in St. Louis: From Internees to Professionals." *City & Society* 3.2 (Dec. 1989): 142–52; Mitziko Sawada. "After the Camps: Seabrook Farms, New Jersey, and the Resettlement of Japanese Americans, 1944–47." *Amerasia Journal* 13.2 (1986–87): 117–36; Koji Shimada. "Education, Assimilation and Acculturation: A Case Study of a Japanese-American Community in New Jersey." Diss., Temple University, 1975; Sandra C. Taylor. "Leaving the Concentration Camps: Japanese American Resettlement in Utah and the Intermountain West." *Pacific Historical Review* 60.2 (May 1991): 169–94; and Eugene S. Uyeki "Process and Patterns of Nisei Adjustment to Chicago." Diss., University of Chicago, 1953.

Studies of resettlement to the West Coast and its aftermath include Leonard Bloom. "A Controlled Attitude-Tension Survey." *University of California Publications in Culture and Society* 2.31 Mar. 1948 (1): 25–48; Leonard Bloom and Ruth Riemer. *Removal and Return.* Berkeley: University of California Press, 1949; and Emory S. Bogardus. "The Japanese Return to the West Coast." *Sociology and Social Research* 31.3 (Jan.–Feb. 1947): 226–33.

"retreat from Moscow"   Incident involving NISEI students in Idaho during World War II. Soon after Japanese Americans removed from the West Coast had been settled in the CONCENTRATION CAMPS, a generally successful program was begun to move *nisei* out of the camps and into colleges and universities where they could continue their education. One of the early setbacks to this program was the so-called "retreat from Moscow." It had been arranged that six *nisei* students would attend the University of Idaho at Moscow in the spring of 1942. However, when the students got there, they found that they were refused admission. Though the college president was in favor of their being there, the governor and a group of locals objected. Vigilante activity ensued and two of the students were placed in jail for protective custody. After a week, the students were transferred to another state. Though this and other incidents involving unfriendly receptions for *nisei* students received wide publicity, such incidents were relatively rare. *Nisei* students later attended the University of Idaho without incident.

For further reading, see Audrie Girdner and Anne Loftis. *The Great Betrayal: The Evacuation of the Japanese-Americans during World War II.* Toronto: Macmillan, 1969 and Robert W. O'Brien. *The College Nisei.* Palo Alto, Calif.: Pacific Books, 1949. New York: Arno Press, 1978.

"revolution of 1954"   Term applied to the dramatic transformation in the composition of the territorial government of Hawaii as a result of the 1954 elections. After years of domination by the Republican Party, the Democrats gained majorities in the territorial house and senate and in many local bodies for the first time. Many of the NISEI who played a key role in this transformation went on to become major figures in Hawaii politics for the next few decades.

For various reasons, it was clear that a change in Hawaii's political leadership was in the offing in the years after World War II. Most important was the demographic shift that resulted from a whole generation of American-born Japanese, Filipino and Chinese Americans coming of age; along with the native Hawaiians, these groups were most likely to favor the Democrats. Secondly, there was the matter of the INTERNATIONAL LONGSHOREMEN'S AND WAREHOUSEMEN'S UNION (ILWU), which by 1946 had attained tremendous power through the organization of dock and plantation workers in Hawaii. Finally, there was the general feeling of returning minority World War II veterans—including those of the all-*nisei* 100TH INFANTRY BATTALION and 442ND REGIMENTAL COMBAT TEAM—that things could not go back to how they were before, that having fought for their country, they were determined to have equal opportunity to participate in all aspects of American society.

Despite public opinion polls that showed a majority of Hawaiians favoring the Democrats by 1948, the Republicans managed to hold on to their advantage until 1954. This was due in large part to conflicts within the Democratic Party, with various factions vying for control. There was also the matter of the "red scare" of the late 1940s and early 1950s that tainted the names of many ILWU members who represented a major faction within the Democratic Party. By 1952, the more moderate faction of the party led by former police captain JOHN BURNS and a core of *nisei* veteran supporters led by 442nd Club president DAN AOKI had gained control.

The 1954 election was indeed a "revolution." Democrats came away with two-thirds of the seats in the territorial house and nine out of 15 seats in the senate. Almost half of these legislators were *nisei*. (There had been no *nisei* in the legislature 10 years earlier.) They included such future stalwarts as DANIEL INOUYE, Sakae Takahashi and SPARK M. MATSUNAGA. The Democrats also emerged with control over local politics on the islands of Oahu, Kauai and Maui.

Ironically, Burns was defeated for the post of territorial representative to Congress by Elizabeth P. Farrington. Burns would win that post in 1956 and later became the first elected governor of the State of Hawaii. Democratic—and *nisei*—control of Hawaii politics reached a peak of sorts in the 1970s, when the governor was Burns

protégé GEORGE ARIYOSHI and the two U.S. senators were Inouye and Matsunaga.

For further reading, see Lawrence H. Fuchs. *Hawaii Pono: A Social History.* New York: Harcourt, Brace and World, 1961 and Roland Kotani. *The Japanese in Hawaii: A Century of Struggle.* Honolulu: Hochi, Ltd., 1985.

Rivers   See GILA RIVER.

Roberts Commission Report   The Roberts Commission, chaired by Supreme Court Justice Owen J. Roberts, issued a report on January 23, 1942, on its findings concerning the bombing of Pearl Harbor. Among other things, the report concluded that Japanese spies, some attached to the consulate, some not, were partially responsible for the bombing. The report did not blame the resident Japanese population, but it also did not go out of its way to exonerate them either. It simply implied what military officers thought to be true at the time, despite the lack of corroborating evidence to back it up. The report was also critical of counterespionage efforts in Hawaii, implying that the disaster there could have been prevented, and suggested that something should be done on the West Coast while there was still time. Within one month, President Roosevelt signed EXECUTIVE ORDER 9066. Other members of the Roberts Commission were Major General Frank McCoy, Brigadier General Joseph McNarney, Admiral William Standley and rear Admiral Joseph Reeves—all military officers.

For further reading, see Commission on Wartime Relocation and Internment of Civilians. *Personal Justice Denied: Report of the Commission on Wartime Relocation and Internment of Civilians.* Washington, D.C.: Government Printing Office, 1982; Roger Daniels. *The Decision to Relocate the Japanese Americans.* Philadelphia: Lippincott, 1975; and Michael Slackman. *Target: Pearl Harbor.* Honolulu: University of Hawaii Press, 1990.

GLEN KITAYAMA

Rock Springs Strike   During the period when organized labor excluded all Asian laborers from its ranks and agitated for Chinese and Japanese exclusion, there was one instance of cooperation between Japanese laborers and an organized union. This occurred in the mines of southern Wyoming in 1907. The Union Pacific Coal Company was the dominant force in mining there, accounting for 64 percent of the total output from the southern field and 47 percent of the state's production in 1907. Although the United Mine Workers of America (UMWA) had been formed in the 1890s, it did not penetrate Wyoming until 1903 and was limited to the northern fields only. Union Pacific was highly anti-union and hired workers of many different nationalities to make organization difficult. Japanese laborers represented the largest single ethnic group at Union Pacific, though they constituted less than 20 percent of the labor force. The center of operations for Union Pacific was in Rock Springs. Isolated and having an economy entirely dominated by the company, Rock Springs itself was also a formidable obstacle for would-be organizers, since being blacklisted by the company precluded making a living in the town.

In May of 1907, UMWA officials from District 22 (covering southern Montana and northern Wyoming) arrived in Rock Springs to start an organizing drive. This drive was an instant success. Arriving in town on May 19, District 22 president Thomas Gibson and international executive board official Michael F. Purcell planned a mass assembly on May 21. Despite threats of firing from the company, a large group attended and 400 miners signed up. When the company locked out these men the following day, many others were driven to take up the cause; by the end of the week, not a single mine was in operation. The only groups still reporting to work were the Chinese and Japanese who were reorganized by the company and put to work so as to at least keep one mine open. A 10 percent raise offered to any miner who would quit the union on June 1 failed to break the ranks.

Just a few weeks before, President Roosevelt's executive order of March 14 had ended Japanese labor immigration. Unable to recruit more Asian workers, the company was forced to negotiate. A conference between the Union Pacific and UMWA leaders on June 8 in Omaha resulted in a temporary settlement in which the union would be recognized and allowed to organize. Exact terms of the settlement were to be decided at a July 15 meeting in Denver. After this victory, it was decided that Japanese and Chinese miners would be allowed into the union. This was made official on June 28 when the UMWA international executive board met and passed a resolution to that effect.

On July 10, Wyoming UMWA locals met in Denver to prepare for the July 15 negotiations. At this meeting were three Japanese labor contractors—Chikai Kondo, Rokuhiko Suzuki and Heitaro Ueda—as official delegates from Rock Springs and Frontier. At the July 15 meeting, the three petitioned UMWA president John Mitchell for special Japanese officers or Japanese Districts within any division where Japanese laborers were employed. This proposal was rejected. At this meeting, the UMWA negotiated a 20 percent wage increase, an eight hour day and many other improvements. The wage differential between Asian and white labor was reduced (from $1.10 to $.30) but not abolished.

Like all other unions at the time, the UMWA and its president Mitchell was actively anti-Asian in orientation and supported Asian exclusion. However, local conditions at Rock Springs dictated that the local body accept Asian laborers, and the international went along with it. As indicated by the retention of the split wage scale, solidarity and equality at the national level had little to do with the admission of Asian labor.

For further reading, see Yuji Ichioka. "Asian Immigrant Coal Miners and the United Mine Workers of America: Race and Class at Rock Springs, Wyoming, 1907." *Amerasia Journal* 6.2 (1979): 1–24 and *The Issei: The World of the First Generation Japanese Immigrants, 1885–1924*. New York: The Free Press, 1988.

Rohwer   Rohwer was the site of one of 10 CONCENTRATION CAMPS that housed Japanese Americans forcibly removed from the West Coast states during World War II. Some basic data on Rohwer is presented below in tabular form:

Official name: Rohwer Relocation Center
Location: Desha County, southeastern Arkansas
Land: Farm Security Administration land
Size: 10,161 acres
Climate: Wooded swamp land; high heat and humidity, with sudden rains
Origin of camp population: Mostly from Los Angeles (4,324) and San Joaquin (3,516) Counties
Via "assembly centers": Most came from Santa Anita (4,415) or Stockton (3,802) "ASSEMBLY CENTERS"; Rohwer also received the highest number of transfers from Jerome (2,734) upon that camp's closing
Rural/Urban: Mostly urban
Peak population: 8,475
Date of peak: March 11, 1943
Opening date: September 18, 1942
Closing date: November 30, 1945
Project director(s): Raymond Johnson
Community Analysts: Margaret Lantis, Katherine Luomala and Charles Wisdom
JERS fieldworkers: None
Newspaper: *Rohwer Outpost* (October 24, 1942–July 21, 1945); *Rohwer Relocator* (August 1–November 9, 1945)
Percent who answered question 28 of the loyalty questionnaire positively: 94.9
Number and percentage of eligible male citizens inducted directly into armed forces: 274 (4.7 percent)
Miscellaneous characteristics: In an early episode, inmate volunteers clearing brush were marched off to jail at gunpoint by locals who thought they were Japanese paratroopers. Because of the irregular weather, farming was difficult here despite relatively fertile soil. The climate also led to problems with mosquitos and chiggers.

(For the key to the categories, see the entry for GILA RIVER.)

The literature on the Japanese American World War II experience is extensive; see the bibliography and the bibliographic entries after the various entries pertaining to this experience for titles of general interest. General histories of Jerome include Russell Bearden. "The False Rumor of Tuesday: Arkansas's Internment of Japanese-Americans." *Arkansas Historical Quarterly* 41.4 (1982): 327–39 and "Life Inside Arkansas's Japanese-American Relocation Centers." *Arkansas Historical Quarterly* 68 (Summer 1989): 169–96. Carole Katsuko Yumiba. "An Educational History of the War Relocation Centers at Jerome and Rohwer, Arkansas, 1942–1945." Diss., University of Southern California, 1979 and Lauren Kessler. "Fettered Freedoms: The Journalism of World War II Japanese Internment Camps." *Journalism History* 15.2–3 (Summer/Autumn 1988): 60–69 are studies of education and journalism, respectively.

Roosevelt, Franklin Delano (1882–1945)

Thirty-first president of the United States. Most of the literature surrounding the forced removal and incarceration of Japanese Americans has focused on the role FDR's subordinates played, while portraying Roosevelt as having his hands full in dealing with World War II. While this may be true to a large degree, it is often overemphasized—almost to the point where history has absolved him of any responsibility. In this way, time has been kind to FDR.

Peter Irons, in his book *Justice at War*, described FDR as a man with "humanitarian impulses," but one who was "no Eleanor Roosevelt" when it came to civil rights. Historian Gary Okihiro confirmed this by documenting FDR's contingency plan, dated August 10, 1936, to intern Japanese Americans in case of war: "One obvious thought occurs to me," Roosevelt wrote, "that every Japanese citizen or non-citizen on the Island of Oahu who meets these Japanese ships or has any communication with their officers or men should be secretly but definitely identified and his or her name placed on a special list of those who would be the first to be placed in a concentration camp in the event of trouble." Roosevelt's plan served as a blueprint of events to come: special intelligence files were drawn up (see "ABC" LIST) and CONCENTRATION CAMPS were used to imprison Japanese Americans. While FDR may not have been the driving force behind the internment, it is clear that he was no casual observer either.

For further reading, see Peter Irons. *Justice at War: The Story of the Japanese American Internment Cases.* New York: Oxford University Press, 1983; Gary Y. Okihiro. *Cane Fires: The Anti-Japanese Movement in Hawaii, 1865–1945.* Philadelphia: Temple University Press, 1991; and Michi Weglyn. *Years of Infamy: The Untold Story of America's Concentration Camps.* New York: William Morrow & Co., 1976.　　GLEN KITAYAMA

S

Sacramento　Sacramento, California, was the site of the fourth-largest Japanese American community in the mainland United States on the eve of World War II. The history of the Japanese Americans in the Sacramento area began in the early 1890s when some LABOR CONTRACTORS brought immigrant laborers to area farms. To serve the increasing numbers of such immigrants, many Japanese businesses were established in Sacramento in the ensuing years. Before long, the city became the hub of a larger Japanese American population consisting mostly of agricultural laborers working in the Sacramento Valley in such areas as the Sacramento River Delta, Placer and Marysville. The downtown Japanese business district in Sacramento consisted of a few blocks centered around M Street on the north and south and Fourth Avenue on the east and west.

In 1900, the immigrant leaders of the city organized the Kyogi-kai (deliberative council), which affiliated with the Japanese Deliberative Council of San Francisco. With the upsurge in the ANTI-JAPANESE MOVEMENT, the Kyogi-kai was dissolved and replaced by the Japanese Deliberative Council in 1905. In order to combat the exclusion movement, this organization cooperated with the San Francisco headquarters. In 1908, the council became the JAPANESE ASSOCIATION of Sacramento, which had affiliated locals in Florin, Courtland, WALNUT GROVE, Isleton, Loomis, Placer and Marysville. Until the outbreak of World War II, the association served as the leading organization in the community.

The Sacramento Japanese American community was among the earliest on the mainland to support both Christian and Buddhist churches. As early as 1893, there was a Japanese Methodist church in the city, soon followed by Presbyterian and Baptist churches. The Buddhist church, on the other hand, was established in 1899. The JAPANESE-LANGUAGE SCHOOL, known as Sakura Gakuen, was the largest of its kind.

On the eve of World War II, the Japanese American population of Sacramento was 2,879, trailing only Los Angeles, San Francisco and Seattle among mainland cities. During the war, all Japanese Americans on the West Coast were forcibly removed and incarcerated in American CONCENTRATION CAMPS. After the war, many returned to the area; by 1952 the total number of Japanese American households was 15 percent greater than it was before the war. In addition to agriculture, state government served as a major employer of Japanese Americans in Sacramento. In 1958, much of the Japanese American downtown business district was lost to REDEVELOPMENT. In recent years, Sacramento has become known as the home and political base of Congressman

ROBERT MATSUI, who has represented Sacramento since 1978 as one of two Japanese Americans in Congress from the mainland United States.

For further reading, see Cheryl L. Cole. *A History of the Japanese Community in Sacramento, 1883–1972: Organizations, Businesses and Generational Response to Majority Domination and Stereotypes.* San Francisco: R & E Research Associates, 1975; Shin-'ichi Kato. *Beikoku Nikkeijin Hyakunenshi.* San Francisco: Shin Nichibei Shimbun-sha, 1961; Nichi Bei Times. *Nichi Bei Jiji Jushoroku, 1951.* San Francisco: Nichi Bei Times, 1951; Ken Suyama. "The Asian American Experience in the Sacramento River Delta." In Tachiki, Amy et al., eds. *Roots: An Asian American Reader.* Los Angeles: Asian American Studies Center, University of California, 1971. 298–301; and Zaibei Nihonjinkai. *Zaibei Nihonjinshi.* San Francisco: Zaibei Nihonjinkai, 1940.   EIICHIRO AZUMA

Saibara, Seito (1861–1939) Lawyer, politician, Texas rice farmer. Seito Saibara abandoned a promising political career in Japan to come to America, where he dreamed of starting a Japanese rice colony. He was born into the Tosa clan, an ally of the Satsuma and Choshu clans which backed the MEIJI RESTORATION, in 1861 in the village of Izuma on Shikoku. When Tosa official Taisuke Itagaki broke with the Satsuma and Choshu élites, he began the Risshisha (Society of Free Thinkers). When Seito Saibara traveled to Kochi to go to school, he attended the Risshisha English School. Soon thereafter, the Satsuma Rebellion broke out. Risshisha members organizing a similar rebellion were discovered and arrested. Saibara was among those arrested, though he was soon released because of his age. By the age of 19, Saibara was a political activist making speeches against the Meiji government. He moved to Tokyo to attend Shigematsu Law School and became one of only 11 people in Japan admitted to the bar in 1886. He returned to Kochi to practice law. He was soon arrested again and accused of conspiring to kill the prefecture's Meiji-appointed governor, a charge which was eventually dropped after a drawn-out legal process. Saibara went on to join Itagaki in the latter's Liberal Party and moved to Osaka to practice law in 1891. In 1898, Saibara was elected to the Japanese House of Representatives. At about this time, he converted to Christianity. Soon after joining the Tamon Congregational Church in Kobe, he was asked to become the president of Doshisha University, a Christian college in Kyoto, in July 1899. Despite the certainty of his reelection to the House in 1902 and his presidency of a prestigious college, Saibara decided to leave the country to study theology in Connecticut.

He left Japan on April 7, 1902. After stopping in London to witness King Edward VII's coronation, he arrived on the East Coast and became friends with Consul General Sadatsuchi Uchida. After a year of study, Saibara began to seriously consider settling in America.

Uchida had long advocated rice-farming operations in Texas, seeing it as a possible cheap source of rice for Japan. In 1903, Saibara began to write letters to friends and relatives urging them to come join him in his venture. He arrived in Texas on August 26, 1903, and began to tour the state searching for a site for his colony. In mid-September, he purchased 304 acres near Webster, a small town between Houston and Galveston, for $5,750. Within a month, he was joined by the cousins Toraichi and Rihei Onishi and Shotaro Nishimura, each of whom bought 300 acres nearby. On January 24, 1904, Saibara was joined by his wife Taiko and his 18-year-old-son Kiyoaki. Friends and relatives of the Onishis also arrived and work on the project commenced in earnest.

The Saibara project was initially profitable and had grown to over 900 acres by 1909. One of his great disappointments, however, was his inability to gain U.S. citizenship. Within three weeks of his arrival in Houston in 1903, he filed his intent to naturalize. When this was declared invalid, he was dissuaded from taking the case to court by a Japanese official. Later decisions (most notably OZAWA V. U.S.) reaffirmed the naturalization law excluding Japanese. Meanwhile, in 1907, Saibara asked his father Masuya to sell out and come to Texas. The 74-year-old Masuya was joined on his journey by many of his former tenants. Content to remain on his farm, Seito Saibara turned down an invitation to become Japan's minister of education. He expanded into cotton and oranges, as well as a nursery, but was virtually wiped out by the post–World War I crash in rice prices. The ending of Japanese immigration in 1924 cut off his labor supply and ended his hopes. He and his wife left Texas in 1924 to settle in Pindamonhangaba, Brazil, where he worked for eight and a half years to establish a similar rice colony. In 1932, after visiting Texas, he went back to Japan to discuss a tomato-growing venture in Taiwan. However, after a serious illness in 1937, he decided to return to Texas to his son's farm to live out his life. Only intervention by Secretary of War HENRY STIMSON enabled him to stay. He died in April of 1939 at the age of 78. His son Kiyoaki continued to farm until his retirement in 1964. The former location of the Saibara farm is in the midst of what is currently one of the richest rice-growing areas in the state.

For further reading, see Kiyoko T. Kurosawa. "Seito Saibara's Diary of Planting a Japanese Colony in Texas." *Hitotsubashi Journal of Social Studies* 2.1 (Aug. 1964): 54–80 and Thomas K. Walls. *The Japanese Texans.* San Antonio: Institute of Texan Cultures, 1987.

Saiki, Patricia Fukuda (1930–) Politician, Republican congresswoman from Hawaii, educator. Patricia Saiki was the first Japanese American Republican woman to be elected to Congress.

Born Patricia Hatsue Fukuda in Hilo, Saiki attended public schools in Hawaii and received her B.S. at the University of Hawaii in 1952. She pursued a career in teaching from 1952 to 1964 at various intermediate and high schools both in Hawaii and Toledo, Ohio.

Saiki first won a seat as delegate to the 1969 Constitutional Convention and from that moment on, became hooked on politics. A member of the Hawaii state house of representatives from 1968 to 1974, Saiki also ran for and won Hawaii state senate seats in 1974 and 1978. She never lost her interest in education, as her campaigns focused on the need to improve the educational system of Hawaii. Saiki led the fight to establish a teacher's union as the first president of the Hawaii Government Employees Association. She presided as commissioner of the Western Interstate Commission on Higher Education and also received a presidential appointment as a member of the Fund for the Improvement of Higher Education.

After serving as secretary and vice-chairman of the Hawaiian Republican Party, Saiki was elected chairman in 1983. From January 1987 she served a two-year term as a Republican to the 100th Congress. While in Congress, Saiki served on the Banking, Finance, and Urban Affairs Committee, Merchant Marine Committee and a Select Committee on Aging.

For further reading, see Patsy Sumie Saiki. *Japanese Women in Hawaii: The First 100 Years.* Honolulu: Kisaku, Inc., 1985.

TRACY ENDO

Sakakida, Richard World War II hero. A NISEI from Hawaii, Richard Sakakida enlisted as a sergeant in the Counter Intelligence Corps (CIC) in March 1941. After taking an intensive course in army intelligence, he was shipped off to the Philippines where he was assigned undercover work. Once there, Sakakida assumed the identity of a draft dodger who jumped ship to avoid conscription. Finding a job with a trading company, Sakakida made contacts with numerous Japanese businessmen and was able to gather a large volume of information for military intelligence.

On December 8, 1941, the day after Pearl Harbor, he encountered the first of his many troubles. He was arrested by the Filipino police and thrown into an internment camp on the suspicion of being a spy for the Japanese. After he was cleared by the authorities, Sakakida was released later in the month and then worked near the front deciphering Japanese signal codes and monitoring communications. As the Japanese Army advanced, Sakakida and another *nisei* in the CIC, Arthur Komori, were ordered to leave the Philippines by General Douglas MacArthur. Instead of boarding, however, Sakakida gave his seat to another *nisei* in the belief that he would have a better chance of survival than his friend. This decision proved to be fateful.

Sakakida was eventually captured along with other Americans as Corregidor fell. While other prisoners were forced to endure a death march similar to the one at Bataan, Sakakida was left behind out of the belief that he had important information to offer. For this, he was forced to endure five months of torture at Bilibid prison. Here, Sakakida stuck to the story that he was a draft dodger and told his captors that he was forced under duress to work for the Americans. Eventually, the Japanese, believing he was a civilian, assigned him work at the 14th Army Headquarters. Here, he was exposed to many classified documents but had nobody to relay them to. As luck would have it, he established contact with the wife of a jailed Filipino resistance leader, Earnest Tupas, and was able to mastermind his and 500 other Filipinos' escape. Sakakida himself led the raid that freed the Tupas and his men and was able to sneak back into his position at Japanese headquarters. With the Tupas free, Sakakida passed on valuable information to the Filipino resistance, which was then able to relay that information to the U.S. military. He continued to do this until General Yamashita was forced to move headquarters to Baguio. By this time Sakakida had come under extreme suspicion, so he used this as an opportunity to escape. He was able to find a guerrilla unit, but was abandoned in the jungle when he was wounded in the stomach by enemy fire. For four months, he struggled to survive on grass and wild fruits. He suffered from malaria, dysentery and beriberi until he was found by some American soldiers weeks after the war had ended. After recovering, Sakakida was assigned to the War Crimes Investigation team and helped to locate and identify Japanese war criminals. In 1947, he transferred to the air force and stayed there until his retirement as a lieutenant colonel in 1975. As of this writing, he is living comfortably in the San Francisco Bay area.

For further reading, see Ian Sayer and Douglas Botting. *America's Secret Army: The Untold Story of the Counter Intelligence Corps.* London: Grafton Books, 1989, which contains a chapter on Sakakida.

GLEN KITAYAMA

Sakamoto, James Yoshinori (1903–1955) Newspaper publisher. One of the leading proponents of the "100% American" philosophy, James Sakamoto began the first NISEI newspaper and was a key figure in the early JAPANESE AMERICAN CITIZENS LEAGUE (JACL). He was born in Seattle in 1903 and attended public school there. His parents were from Yamaguchi PREFECTURE and were small businesspeople. While attending

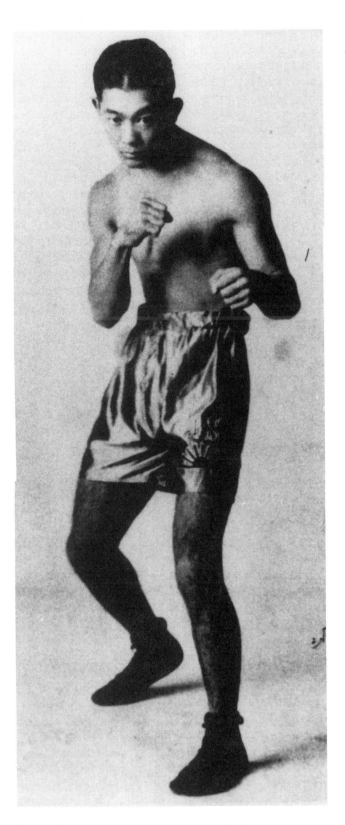

James Sakamoto, Japanese American featherweight contender, ca. 1920. *Nippon Kan Heritage Association Collection, Japanese American National Museum Photographic & Moving Image Archive*

Franklin High, Sakamoto was a star athlete in baseball, judo, boxing, and as a 128-lb. halfback in football. Before graduating, he moved to the east and attended school in Princeton, N.J. He took a job as English editor of the New York based *Japanese American News;* he also pursued a professional boxing career, becoming proficient enough to fight at Madison Square Garden. He suffered detached retinas in both eyes sometime in 1926, and when he returned to Seattle in November 1927, he was well on his way to blindness.

Upon arriving in Seattle, he saw the need for a *nisei* organization that would promote "Americanism" and saw the basis of such an organization in the practically defunct Seattle Progressive Citizens League. With this goal in the back of his head, he started the *Japanese American Courier* on January 1, 1928. It was the first exclusively English newspaper for *nisei* and featured national news, news from Japan, local community news and sports, and editorials urging the adoption of a "100% American" outlook. He also supported the Citizens League movement and became a strong backer of the JACL upon that organization's formation. He served as its national president from 1936–38. Though never a big financial success, the *Courier* lasted until 1942.

After the outbreak of World War II, Sakamoto founded and chaired the JACL Emergency Defense Council, an organization formed to work with governmental authorities, in part to report "subversive" action in the Japanese American community. In February 1942, Sakamoto testified before the TOLAN COMMISSION, opposing forced removal, but, like other JACL figures, pledging to cooperate with whatever the government had in mind. With the forced removal of Japanese American residents of the Seattle area to Tanforan "ASSEMBLY CENTER," he received the chance to implement that pledge. Without elections or inmate consent, Sakamoto was appointed "Chief Supervisor" of the "Japanese Staff" at Tanforan. In this position, he and his staff were to be the liaisons between the inmate population and the Caucasian staff of the center and exercised great power.

With the transfer of the Tanforan population to MINIDOKA, Sakamoto's power waned. Unable to reestablish the *Courier,* he found a job as a telephone solicitor in Seattle. He was killed when hit by a car on his way to work in 1955.

For further reading, see Roger Daniels. *Asian America: Chinese and Japanese in the United States since 1850.* Seattle: University of Washington Press, 1988; Bill Hosokawa. *Nisei: The Quiet Americans.* New York: William Morrow & Co., 1969; and Yuji Ichioka. "A Study in Dualism: James Yoshinori Sakamoto and the Japanese American Courier, 1928–1942." *Amerasia Journal* 13.2 (1986–87): 49–81.

Sakata, Harold (d. 1982) Athlete, actor. Harold Sakata's exploits as an Olympic weightlifter, a professional wrestler and an actor made him a Hawaiian hero. Raised in Kona on the Big Island, Sakata trained to become a weightlifter with makeshift materials. He constructed dumbbells by filling ketchup cans with cement and also utilized broomsticks weighted with rocks. In addition, Sakata worked as a PLANTATION worker, a carpenter's helper, a stevedore and a ditchdigger. Sakata's training enabled him to win the Mr. Hawaii title in bodybuilding and weightlifting in 1946. Two years later, he captured a silver medal in weightlifting at the 1948 London Olympics. In the course of his weightlifting career, Sakata also won several U.S. championships. He was inducted into the International Hall of Fame for weightlifting in 1972.

After the Olympics, Sakata went on to become a professional wrestler under the name of Tosh Togo. This provided good preparation for an acting career. Producer Harry Saltzman and director Guy Hamilton of the James Bond series discovered Sakata while watching him wrestle on television in London. Sakata is best known for playing Odd Job, one of the most gruesome James Bond villains, in the film *Goldfinger* (1964). Odd Job killed his victims by slicing off their heads with a steel-rimmed razor-sharp bowler hat. Sakata was also featured in a cold medicine commercial in which a whole room is engulfed when he sneezes. He appeared in the films *The Poppy Is Also a Flower, The Phynx, Dead of Night, The Wrestler* and *Goin' Coconuts,* and in the television shows "Gilligan's Island," "Hawaii Five-0" and "Police Woman." Sakata died of cancer in 1982 at the age of 56.

SCOTT KURASHIGE

[Entry compiled from his obituaries in the *Hawaii Herald* 6 Aug. 1982 and *New York Times* 31 July 1982. He also has an entry in David Ragan. *Who's Who in Hollywood: The Largest Cast of International Film Personalities Ever Assembled.* New York: Facts On File, Inc., 1992. p. 1489.]

sake bill Discriminatory legislation passed by the Hawaiian government to tax sake. The sake bill of June 1896 was part of a series of actions taken by the Hawaiian government against Japanese immigrants in the 1890s that led eventually to Hawaii's annexation by the United States. These restrictions included an 1894 law that denied naturalization rights to Japanese immigrants and that required would-be immigrants to have either a labor contract or 100 yen "show money" in hand or else be refused admission. "An Act to Increase the Duty on Liquors, Still Wines and Other Beverages Made From Materials Other Than Grape Juice" was passed in June 1896 to take effect on July 1, 1897. The law was worded such that the sizable new tax would apply to sake (Japanese rice wine) and sake only. The law had been supported by leaders of the temperance movement and by

representatives of California's wine industry who saw the large quantities of sake imported from Japan as hurting their business in Hawaii. With some logic, they questioned why Hawaii should be able to export its sugar to California at a favorable rate while California wine did not receive the same consideration from the Hawaiian government. Hawaiian President Sanford Dole argued for a less overtly discriminatory law, but the bill passed over his veto. Since sake played an important role in Japanese cultural life, the $1.00 a gallon tax on sake was met with outrage in the Japanese community. Although the Japanese government eventually complained to Hawaii about the law, its response was fairly subdued compared to that caused by the IMMIGRANT REJECTION OF 1897 a year later. Once Hawaii was annexed by the United States, easing fears of a Japanese invasion for the time being, the sake law was adjusted so that sake no longer fell under the category of alcoholic beverages taxed at the highest rate.

For further reading, see Hilary Conroy. *The Japanese Frontier in Hawaii, 1868–1898.* Berkeley: University of California Press, 1953. New York: Arno Press, 1978 and Alan T. Moriyama. *Imingaisha: Japanese Emigration Companies and Hawaii, 1894–1908.* Honolulu: University of Hawaii Press, 1985.

Salt River Valley incident From 1922 to 1925, a number of incidents involving the harassment or even the expulsion of Japanese Americans from rural communities occurred. Although the incident in the Salt River Valley came a little later, it belongs in the same general category as these incidents. In the summer of 1934, white farmers in Arizona's Salt River Valley formed an Anti-Alien Committee, leveling the usual charges against Japanese farmers (see YELLOW PERIL). On August 17, this committee staged a 150-car parade through Phoenix and set a deadline of August 25 for the Japanese to get out. Before long, the Japanese consul from Los Angeles, the JAPANESE AMERICAN CITIZENS LEAGUE, the Japanese government and the U.S. government were all involved in this matter.

Arizona state officials fanned the flames of this incident since their primary election was set for September 11. Meanwhile a series of bombings hit local Japanese American farmers and their friends beginning in September. As the bombings continued without any arrests being made, the Japanese government became more and more angry. Spurred on by the Anti-Alien Committee, Japanese farmers were also harassed through the "enforcement" of the existing ALIEN LAND LAW and were being called into court. On February 5, 1935, a radical revision of this law was introduced to the Arizona house that would have effectively driven the Japanese out of farming. Responding to the Japanese government and wanting to avoid an international incident, the State

Department effectively killed the bill by threatening to cut off federal money if it passed. The death of the bill on March 21 marked the end of the blatant attempt to drive the Japanese out of the Salt River Valley, though hard feelings lingered for years. (See TOLEDO INCIDENT, TURLOCK INCIDENT.)

For further reading, see Jack August. "The Anti-Japanese Crusade in Arizona's Salt River Valley, 1934–35." *Arizona and the West* 21.2 (Summer 1979): 113–36; Teruko Kachi. "The Arizona Anti-Japanese Movement, 1934." *Tsudajuku Daigaku Kiyo* [Journal of Tsuda College] 11 (1979): 111–23; and Susie Sato. "Before Pearl Harbor: Early Japanese Settlers in Arizona." *Journal of Arizona History* 14.4 (Winter 1973): 317–34.

San Francisco School Board Segregation Order of 1906

ANTI-JAPANESE MOVEMENT–inspired action against Japanese pupils that triggered an international incident and led to the GENTLEMEN'S AGREEMENT. Though it actually affected only a handful of schoolchildren, the action by the San Francisco School Board had monumental consequences for the future of Japanese Americans and transformed the "Japanese problem" from a California issue to a national and international issue.

Starting with the barrage of anti-Japanese articles in the *San Francisco Chronicle* in early 1905 and continuing with the formation of the ASIATIC EXCLUSION LEAGUE in May 1905, antagonism toward Japanese immigrants in the San Francisco area had been on the rise. This agitation continued in the tradition of that directed against Chinese immigrants since the 1870s. California congressmen introduced bills into Congress that would stop further Japanese immigration in December 1905 and ISSEI in San Francisco faced boycotts and physical violence, especially after the great earthquake of April 1906. In this climate of anti-Japanese agitation, the San Francisco School Board, carrying out a campaign promise of Mayor Eugene E. Schmitz, ordered all Japanese and Korean pupils to join the Chinese students at a segregated school. Though little attention was paid to the matter locally—it later turned out that there were only 93 pupils of Japanese ancestry in the entire San Francisco school system—word of the order soon reached Tokyo and the matter took on international significance.

Fresh from a stunning victory over Russia in the Russo-Japanese War, Japan was in the process of asserting its position as a first-class international power. Upset by the nature of the Segregation Order as an affront to its prestige, Japanese authorities soon made their feelings known to President Theodore Roosevelt. Recognizing Japan's status, Roosevelt sought to find some middle ground that would satisfy both Japanese pride and California's anti-Japanese movement. The eventual result, the Gentlemen's Agreement, would end up satisfying neither party.

For further reading, see Roger Daniels. *The Politics of Prejudice: The Anti-Japanese Movement in California and the Struggle for Japanese Exclusion.* 2nd edition. Berkeley: University of California Press, 1977 and Charles M. Wollenberg. *All Deliberate Speed: Segregation and Exclusion in California Schools, 1855–1975.* Berkeley: University of California Press, 1976.

San Francisco State strike

Student strike resulting in the first School of Ethnic Studies in the country. On December 6, 1968, students at San Francisco State College (now known as San Francisco State University) began what was to become the longest student strike in U.S. history. The strike was organized by members of the Third World Liberation Front (TWLF), a coalition of six student organizations, including the Black Students Union, Philippine-American Collegiate Endeavor, Intercollegiate Chinese for Social Action, ASIAN AMERICAN POLITICAL ALLIANCE, Mexican American Students Confederation and the Latin American Students Organization. Students called for changes for a more relevant and accessible education to meet the needs of "Third World" communities in America. Among the 15 TWLF demands was the establishment of the first school of ethnic studies in the country.

Japanese American students played a significant role in the strike as part of the coalition. Penny Nakatsu, Paul Yamazaki, Francis Oka, Miyo Ota, JANICE MIRIKITANI, Richard Wada and others were among the active participants, conducting educational activities, coordinating community outreach organizations, planning strategy, lobbying and organizing other students. Some participated in the many innovative activities leading up to the strike, including the Experimental College, the Community Involvement Program and the Work-Study Program. They founded the campus chapter of the Asian American Political Alliance in the summer of 1968. AAPA members attempted to gather support for the strike within the Japanese American community, sponsoring a community meeting at Christ United Presbyterian Church in San Francisco's Japantown on December 6, 1968, and a protest and press conference with community leaders, including Yori Wada of the YMCA and Lloyd Wake of Glide Memorial Church on February 21, 1969. Japanese American faculty also played an important role. James Hirabayashi, Pearl Sonoda, Dora Tachibana, Taiko Hara and Kenji Murase were among those who put their careers on the line to establish ethnic studies. The strike ended in March 1969 with a compromise settlement that included the establishment of the School of Ethnic Studies. Following the strike, students, faculty and community members developed a Japanese American curriculum of about 10 courses that was integrated into the newly formed Asian American Studies Department within the School of Ethnic Studies.

The strike took place against the backdrop of the civil rights, anti-war, women's and oppressed nationality movements of the sixties. The changes demanded of the university were part of a broader call for "self-determination" and political power to define the future of distinct ethnic groups in America. The demand for ethnic studies was developed to address distorted and Eurocentric interpretations of history and contemporary issues and to assert the voices of the people themselves. Many students participated in the further development of ethnic studies and pursued a wide range of community activities.

For further reading, see Karen Umemoto. " 'On Strike!' San Francisco State College Strike, 1968–69: The Role of Asian American Students." *Amerasia Journal* 15.1 (1989): 3–41. *Amerasia Journal* 15.1 is a special issue devoted to commemorating the 20th anniversary of the strike.

KAREN UMEMOTO

sanba   Japanese for "midwife." During the early part of the century, many NISEI children were delivered by midwives rather than doctors. These midwives often worked in rural areas and charged between $20 and $50 for their services. If families could not afford a doctor's or midwife's fees, women sometimes gave birth alone or were assisted by their husbands.

For further reading, see Mei Nakano. *Japanese American Women: Three Generations, 1890–1990.* Berkeley and Sebastopol, Calif.: National Japanese American Historical Society and Mina Press, 1990. Kazuo Ito. *Issei: A History of Japanese Immigrants in North America.* Shinichiro Nakamura, Jean S. Gerard, trans. Seattle: Executive Committee for the Publication of *Issei: A History of Japanese Immigrants in North America,* 1973 includes first person accounts of Issei childbearing experiences.

EDITH KANESHIRO

Sand Island   Army-run World War II detention camp located near the entrance of Honolulu Harbor on the island of Oahu, Hawaii. Sand Island originally belonged to the Immigration and Naturalization Service and served as one of its branches. In 1941 the U.S. Army decided to use Sand Island as a concentration camp because of its convenient yet isolated location. The island was located near Honolulu and the office of the military governor, but was separated by water, which isolated internees from strategic targets and hindered their escape. In addition, the island's quarantine station was ready for immediate use by the army.

Those Hawaii ISSEI who were arrested on December 7, the day of the Japanese attack on Pearl Harbor, were held temporarily in either the Honolulu immigration station on Oahu, Kilauea Military Camp on Hawaii Island, the Wailua County Jail and Kalaheo Stockade on Kaui or the Haiku internment camp on Maui. The Sand Island camp was activated on December 8, 1941, and

the first group of internees incarcerated at Sand Island arrived on December 9, 1941. For the first six months of their imprisonment at the camp, internees lived in tents, though barracks were eventually built. Sand Island held predominantly Japanese and Japanese American men and a smaller number of Germans, Italians and women of various nationalities. Some internees stayed for the duration of the war in Hawaiian camps while others were transferred from Sand Island to the mainland CONCENTRATION CAMPS or INTERNMENT CAMPS.

When Sand Island closed on March 1, 1943, to become a part of the expanded Honolulu Port of Embarkation, many of the internees were sent to mainland concentration camps or internment camps. Internees who were not transferred remained in Hawaii and were sent to HONOULIULI camp located near Ewa on Oahu. However, the Immigration Station on the island continued to be used for temporary custody for Japanese aliens who were awaiting interrogation and internment proceedings.

For further reading, see Roland Kotani. *The Japanese in Hawaii: A Century of Struggle.* Honolulu: Hochi, Ltd., 1985; Dennis M. Ogawa, and Evarts C. Fox. "Japanese Internment and Relocation: The Hawaii Experience." In Daniels, Roger, Sandra C. Taylor, and Harry H. L. Kitano, eds. *Japanese American: From Relocation to Redress.* Salt Lake City: University of Utah Press, 1986. Revised edition. Seattle: University of Washington Press, 1991. 135–38; and Gary Y. Okihiro. *Cane Fires: The Anti-Japanese Movement in Hawaii, 1865–1945.* Philadelphia: Temple University Press, 1991.   STACEY HIROSE

sansei   Third-generation Japanese Americans. The *sansei* are the children of the NISEI, the grandchildren of the ISSEI and the parents of the YONSEI. As is the case for other generation designations, the word *sansei* comes from the Japanese character for the number of the generation, in this case, three. Most *sansei* were born between the years 1945 and 1965, during the "baby boom" period. Though they may actually be *nisei* or *yonsei*, many Japanese Americans born in the *sansei* period share in the *sansei* identity and consider themselves to be *sansei*. On the mainland, the term also connotes the generation born after "camp" (the forced removal and incarceration of all Japanese Americans on the West Coast) that has no first-hand memory of the internment.

While there is a common experience and culture shared by nearly all *sansei*, the *sansei* generation is characterized by its extreme diversity. While some *sansei* have a strong Japanese American or ASIAN AMERICAN identity, others have little identification with other Japanese Americans. As compared with the *nisei*, fewer *sansei* live in Japanese American communities and fewer still live in rural areas. While some *sansei* were active in political movements of the 1960s and '70s such as the ASIAN AMERICAN MOVEMENT, others have been apolitical. While many *sansei* marry non–Japanese Americans, the majority marry other Japanese Americans. The direction the Japanese American community takes under *sansei* leadership remains to be seen.

There have been many social scientific studies of *sansei* identity or assimilation. These include Jerry R. Egusa. "A Comparative Study of Third-Generation Japanese-American Males and Females in Relation to 'the Motive to Avoid Success'." Diss., University of San Francisco, 1983; Mark Gehrie. "Sansei: An Ethnography of Experience." Diss., Northwestern University, 1973; Fumiko Hosokawa. *The Sansei: Social Interaction and Ethnic Interaction Identification among the Third Generation Japanese*. Palo Alto: R & E Research Associates, Inc., 1978; Hilla Kuttenplan Israely. "An Exploration into Ethnic Identity: The Case of Third Generation Japanese Americans." Diss., University of California, Los Angeles, 1976; Kaoru Oguri Kendis. "Persistence and Maintenance of Ethnicity among Third-Generation Japanese Americans." Diss., University of Pittsburgh, 1979; Patti Shirakawa Magarifuji. "A Comparative Study of Ethnic Identity of Third Generation Japanese Americans in California and Hawaii." Diss., California School of Professional Psychology, 1982; Margaroh Maruyama. "Diversities in the Development of Ethnic Identification among the Third Generation Japanese Americans." *Sociologica Internationalis* 14 (1976): 221–43; Minako K. Maykovich. *Japanese American Identity Dilemma*. Tokyo: Waseda University Press, 1972; Eugene Tashima. "Livingston Sansei: Rural Perspectives on Group Identity and Community." Thesis, University of California, Los Angeles, 1985; and Wayne S. Wooden, Joseph J. Leon, and Michelle T. Toshima. "Ethnic Identity among Sansei and Yonsei Church-Affiliated Youth in Los Angeles and Honolulu." *Psychological Reports* 62.1 (Feb. 1988): 268–70. Additionally, there are many comparative studies of *sansei* vs. *nisei* and/or *issei* identity/assimilation/acculturation, including John W. Connor. *Tradition and Change in Three Generations of Japanese Americans*. Chicago: Nelson-Hall, Inc., 1977; Christie W. Kiefer. *Changing Cultures, Changing Lives*. San Francisco: Jossey-Bass, 1974; Darrel M. Montero. *Japanese Americans: Changing Patterns of Ethnic Affiliation over Three Generations*. Boulder, Colo.: Westview Press, 1980; and Eric M. Woodrum. "Japanese American Social Adaptation over Three Generations." Diss., University of Texas, Austin, 1978.

While there is no history of the *sansei* generation, there are many literary works that document various aspects of the *sansei* experience both in Hawaii and on the mainland. Some representative works include Eric Chock and Darrell H. Y. Lum, eds. *The Best of Bamboo Ridge*. Honolulu: Bamboo Ridge Press, 1986; Lawson F. Inada. *Before the War: Poems as They Happened*. New York: Morrow, 1971; Cynthia Kadohata. *The Floating World*. New York: Viking, 1989; David Mas Masumoto. *Silent Strength*. Tokyo: New Currents International, Co., Ltd., 1985; Janice Mirikitani. *Shedding Silence*. Berkeley: Celestial Arts, 1987; and David Mura. *Turning Japanese: Memoirs of a Sansei*. New York: Atlantic Monthly Press, 1991.

Santa Anita Camouflage Net Project and Strike

At the Santa Anita "ASSEMBLY CENTER," a project involving the manufacture of military camouflage nets was successfully carried out. In the summer of 1942, 800 camp inmates put together 22,000 nets, resulting in a savings to the government that more than offset the entire cost of feeding the camp population. The project employed only citizen volunteers who worked 44-hour weeks in eight-hour shifts, producing 250–260 large nets per day at their peak. The nets varied in size from $22' \times 22'$ to $36' \times 60'$.

On a Tuesday in June, one net worker suddenly stopped what he was doing. When told to resume, he refused, stating that he was hungry and couldn't continue working. Others soon joined him, and before long 800 workers were engaged in a sit-down strike, shutting down the net-making operation. Although dissatisfaction with the food had triggered the strike, the generally poor working conditions were the primary cause. Many workers were allergic to the hemp nets, and thick burlap dust and dye fumes irritated lungs, eyes and throats. Additionally, workers had to labor kneeling on the floor for eight-hour stretches under the hot sun. After their shifts, they then had to wait in long lines for meals. For this, they were paid $8 a month. They also resented the pressure tactics the administration used to make them "volunteer" for the work: high school classes were closed down and all other jobs frozen until the net project quota was reached. Later on the day of the strike, representatives met with the camp administration and reached a quick agreement so that everyone was back to work by the following evening. The main concessions were to allow women to work half days and to improve the food provided.

For further reading, see U.S. Department of War. *Final Report: Japanese Evacuation from the West Coast 1942*. 1943. New York: Arno Press, 1978; Audrie Girdner, and Anne Loftis. *The Great Betrayal: The Evacuation of the Japanese-Americans during World War II*. Toronto: Macmillan, 1969; and Michi Weglyn. *Years of Infamy: The Untold Story of America's Concentration Camps*. New York: William Morrow & Co., 1976.

Santa Fe New Mexico INTERNMENT CAMP that housed mostly ISSEI men during World War II. The camp at Santa Fe was one of the largest of the Justice Department–administered camps housing Japanese American "enemy aliens" during World War II. The camp was located on a hillside within Santa Fe city limits and consisted of 28 acres. The former Civilian Conservation Corps campsite was surrounded by barbed wire with guard towers and searchlights placed at frequent intervals.

The history of the camp consists of two distinct phases. Initially, it was thought of as a temporary station where enemy aliens picked up by the FBI in the days and weeks after the Pearl Harbor attack could be housed and evaluated. The first group of 425 *issei* men arrived at Santa

Fe on March 14, with the 1942 population peaking at 826 in April. The 826 men were all from California and represented the *issei* leadership of the various Japanese American communities in that state. For the next few months, individual hearings were conducted, resulting in the release or parole of 523, with the other 302 being transferred to other prison camps under U.S. Army jurisdiction. (One inmate died in captivity.) The last internee left Santa Fe on September 24 and the camp was left empty. The camp's second phase began in February 1943, when the army transferred all its civilian prisoners to the Justice Department. Santa Fe was reopened in March 1943 to hold these enemy aliens indefinitely. On March 23, the first group of 357 arrived. There were 1,257 by June and 1,783 by August. The maximum population was 2,100 in June 1945. A total of 4,555 people passed through the camp.

As with the other internment camps, internee treatment was governed by the Geneva Convention, resulting in a facility that resembled a prisoner-of-war camp. Geneva Convention regulated the type and amount of food internees received (5.2980 pounds per man), the type of work they could and could not be compelled to do, the type of internee self-government that was required, and many other facets of life. The camp had an extensive recreation program and facilities, including a 19-acre farm, a garden, two softball diamonds, two tennis courts, a fenced 40-acre hiking area and a nine-hole golf course. There were educational classes, organized sports, movies and an active theatrical group. Supervised visiting hours of at least two hours a week were allowed. Visits to WAR RELOCATION AUTHORITY (WRA) camps, usually to a dying relative, were allowed under guard. Surveys by the State Department and the International Red Cross conducted in 1942 reached the same general conclusion that physical conditions at Santa Fe were good and compared favorably with other similar prison camps.

The relatively peaceful nature of the camp probably had to do with the homogeneous nature of the internees as well as the unambiguous Geneva Convention regulations that governed their treatment. The internees were all *issei* men, most of whom were middle-aged or older—the average age of the camp population in 1943 was 52. The primary complaint of these men was that they were being kept separate from their families; though many were transferred to CRYSTAL CITY or to WRA camps where they could be reunited, the process was slow and many grew impatient.

The relative peace was shattered with the arrival of 366 inmates from TULE LAKE "SEGREGATION CENTER" in late 1944 and early 1945. For various reasons, Tule Lake had been torn by unrest and violence in prior months and camp officials decided to treat the problem by transferring "troublemakers" to Santa Fe and to an-

other internment camp at Fort Lincoln, North Dakota. On March 12, 1945, a minor revolt took place at Santa Fe, stemming from the removal of three of the Tule Lake "troublemakers" to a separate prison camp. The incident was put down by Immigration and Naturalization Service Border Patrol officers in about 10 minutes and resulted in four injuries to internees and the short-term segregation of 360 participants in a stockade. In June, 399 others from Tule Lake arrived and were absorbed into the population with no further incident.

With the conclusion of the war, the population was dispersed, with most either being sent back to Japan or released. The last 12 inmates were sent to Crystal City and the camp closed in May 1946.

For further reading, see Paul Frederick Clark. "Those Other Camps: An Oral History Analysis of Japanese Alien Enemy Internment during World War II." Thesis, California State University, Fullerton, 1980 and John J. Culley. "The Santa Fe Internment Camp and the Justice Department Program for Enemy Aliens." In Daniels, Roger, Sandra C. Taylor, and Harry H. L. Kitano, eds. *Japanese Americans: From Relocation to Redress.* Salt Lake City: University of Utah Press, 1986. Revised edition. Seattle: University of Washington Press, 1991. 57–71.

Satow, Masao "Mas" (1908–1977)

JAPANESE AMERICAN CITIZENS LEAGUE (JACL) leader. Mas Satow was a fixture in the JACL from near its inception all the way up to his final days. Born in San Mateo, California, Satow moved with his family to Los Angeles when he was a toddler. Barely able to afford college, Satow nonetheless earned his bachelor's degree from UCLA in 1929. He furthered his studies at Princeton Theological Seminary, where he received a degree in theology in 1932. Satow connected with the JACL in 1932, two years after the organization's founding convention was held. It was not long before Satow became a key figure in the JACL. In 1932, at the JACL convention in Los Angeles, he served as the deputy registrar. By 1936, Satow had been elected assistant executive secretary. In addition, he was appointed by President JAMES SAKAMOTO to head the Second-Generation Development Program, which was designed to integrate NISEI into American society as productive citizens. During World War II, Satow was incarcerated (with his newlywed wife Chizuko) first at Santa Anita "ASSEMBLY CENTER" and then at GRANADA.

After being released from camp in 1944, he resettled (see RESETTLEMENT) in Milwaukee and assumed the position of national board field representative for the Young Men's Christian Association (YMCA). Satow, who prior to the war had been the general secretary of the YMCA in Los Angeles's LITTLE TOKYO, was able to assist internees with YMCA resources and continued serving the JACL as the Eastern-Midwest district representative. After JACL national secretary MIKE MA-

SAOKA left his position in 1946 to become the organization's full-time lobbyist in Washington, D.C., the JACL called upon Satow to take his place. Although Satow, who by this year was now second vice president of the JACL, originally intended to hold the position for no more than a year, he stayed on to serve as national secretary (later renamed national director) for over a quarter of a century. During this time, Chizuko also played an active role in JACL affairs. In addition, Mas was also a committee member for the JAPANESE AMERICAN RESEARCH PROJECT. In 1973, Masao Satow ended a long and distinguished career when he retired from the position of JACL national director. After retirement, he worked as a senior adviser to the president of Sumitomo Bank in California. After Satow passed away in 1977, the National JACL Headquarters in San Francisco was named in memory of him.

For further reading, see Bill Hosokawa. *Nisei: The Quiet Americans.* New York: William Morrow & Co., 1969 and *JACL in Quest of Justice: The History of the Japanese American Citizens League.* New York: William Morrow, 1982.

SCOTT KURASHIGE

schoolboy Term for a male ISSEI student who took on live-in domestic work as a means to earn a livelihood while going to school. Taking a position as a schoolboy was often the only option available for recent arrivals from Japan who wished to stay in the U.S. Though the pay was poor even by the standards of *issei* laborers—about $1.50 per week plus board in 1900—domestic work did provide a roof over one's head and the opportunity to learn English and the ways of America. The learning process also included a crash course in the running of an American household—this education resulted in a great many serio-comic misadventures. In the years immediately prior to the GENTLEMEN'S AGREEMENT, the number of Japanese schoolboys peaked. "Situations wanted" ads placed by *issei* seeking schoolboy positions proliferated in city newspapers. Over 4,000 Japanese domestics could be found in San Francisco alone during this time.

With the ending of labor migration, the number of Japanese schoolboys dropped to virtually none by the end of the 1910s. By and large, the typical *issei* did not stay in domestic work for long, moving on to try farm work or other types of migrant labor in the quest for a farm or business of his own. Despite the brevity of the Japanese schoolboy era, the image of the docile Japanese servant speaking comically broken English lingered for years in the popular imagination, fueled by "literary" works such as the various adventures of the fictional schoolboy Hashimura Togo by WALLACE IRWIN and by portrayals in film and television. (See DEKASEGI-SHOSEI.)

For further reading, see Roger Daniels. *The Politics of Prejudice: The Anti-Japanese Movement in California and the Struggle for Japanese Exclusion.* 1962. 2nd edition. Berkeley: University of California Press, 1977 and Elaine H. Kim. *Asian American Literature: An Introduction to the Writings and their Social Context.* Philadelphia: Temple University Press, 1982.

schoolgirl Term for young ISSEI and NISEI women who did domestic work while ostensibly attending school. Prior to World War II, a great many Japanese American women became schoolgirls. For *issei* women, as for *issei* men before them, live-in domestic service was a popular occupation for new arrivals. However, while SCHOOLBOYS tended to hold their positions for relatively short periods of time before moving on to other things, schoolgirls often remained in domestic service for years. With the coming of children, many *issei* women continued in domestic service as day workers. Many *nisei* women also took schoolgirl positions during or just after their high school years. It was a socially acceptable way for them to make a little money and to learn Western customs and culture prior to marriage. Many also attended sewing school on the side. With the rise of the *nisei* to middle-class status in the postwar years, few *sansei* became schoolgirls.

For further reading, see Evelyn Nakano Glenn. *Issei, Nisei, War Bride: Three Generations of Japanese American Women in Domestic Service.* Philadelphia: Temple University Press, 1986.

Seabrook Farms Large-scale farming operation that recruited many Japanese American workers from American CONCENTRATION CAMPS during World War II. Later, Seabrook Farms, New Jersey, attracted thousands of Japanese Americans resettling (see RESETTLEMENT) from the camps that held them during the war. These Japanese American workers helped Seabrook Farms to become one of the major frozen food producers in the country and established a Japanese American community there that still exists today.

The origin of Seabrook Farms goes back to World War I when Charles F. Seabrook took over his father's 60-acre farm. Utilizing the latest in farming and processing technology, Seabrook Farms became a major producer of frozen and canned vegetables by the 1930s. At its peak in the 1940s, one-fifth of the nation's frozen vegetables bore the Seabrook Farms label. In 1949, it produced 65 million pounds of frozen and 10 million pounds of canned vegetables.

Japanese American labor was a major factor in the success of Seabrook Farms. For years the farm had difficulty in finding a steady source of labor, a situation exacerbated by World War II. Seabrook management had tried various measures to alleviate the problem, from mobilizing locals to bringing in labor from as far away as Jamaica. Having a reputation as good farmers who were quiet and law-abiding, "loyal" Japanese Americans seemed an ideal solution to the labor shortage. Throughout 1944, Seabrook officials brought in trial groups from the camps. They also sent recruiters to the camps and placed favorable stories about the farm in camp papers. They also placed favorable articles about Japanese Americans in local papers to calm area residents who might have objected to the arrival of Japanese American labor.

The measures succeeded beyond expectations. The first Japanese Americans arrived in February 1944 and there were 300 by August, 831 by December and 1,688 by December 1945. By January 1947, the number of Japanese Americans peaked at between 2,300 and 2,700; at this point, they made up just about one-half of the total work force at Seabrook. The large numbers of arrivals caused some housing shortages for a time. Hours were long and work difficult, with wages beginning at about 50¢ per hour, though they varied depending on the type of work performed and with union status. There were complaints by some NISEI that only Caucasians were being promoted to top managerial positions.

Though Japanese Americans continued to come to Seabrook Farms through 1945 and 1946—including 178 JAPANESE PERUVIANS from the CRYSTAL CITY INTERNMENT CAMP—many began to leave as well. For most, Seabrook was an interlude, and many Japanese American workers began to return to the West Coast after 1945. By 1949, the Japanese American population at Seabrook had dwindled to 1,200, less than half what it had been in 1947. After peaking in the 1940s, Seabrook Farms itself began to decline in the 1950s as newer and larger food processing facilities began to be built elsewhere (the plant at Seabrook eventually closed). By 1954, the Japanese American population had fallen to 900, and in 1970, there were just 530 Japanese Americans in Seabrook. There is still a small Japanese American presence in Seabrook today. A group of former and present Seabrook Japanese American community members are currently formulating plans for a Seabrook Japanese American museum.

For further reading, see Mitziko Sawada. "After the Camps: Seabrook Farms, New Jersey, and the Resettlement of Japanese Americans, 1944–47." *Amerasia Journal* 13.2 (1986–87): 117–36 and Koji Shimada. "Education, Assimilation and Acculturation: A Case Study of a Japanese-American Community in New Jersey." Diss., Temple University, 1975.

Seattle Nihonmachi/International District   The origins of Seattle, Washington's Nihonmachi (Japantown) date back to 1891, when a city map shows that Dearborn Street was then called "Mikado Street." Seattle was a main port of entry for Japanese immigrants, with steamships docking at Smith Cove at the north end of Elliott Bay. The Japanese formed communities just south of the downtown district, near the waterfront and Pi-

Yamatoya on Jackson Street, 1917.   *Nippon Kan Heritage Association Collection, Japanese American National Museum Photographic & Moving Image Archive*

oneer Square area, most of which was surrounded by Puget Sound tide flats.

Many of the Northwest's ISSEI came from rural regions in Hiroshima, Yamaguchi and Okayama PREFECTURES in Japan. According to the 1890 U.S. census, there were about 360 Japanese in Washington State, the majority living in Seattle. By 1900, the number increased to 5,617. They came to Seattle, many eventually working on the railroads, or operating hotels, barber shops, bathhouses, gambling establishments, laundries and restaurants. Some traveled outside of the city to work in canneries or nearby farms.

In the following years, more Japanese moved east along Jackson and Yesler Streets, especially after Jackson Street was regraded in 1908. The community prospered and grew. By the mid-1920s, Nihonmachi extended from Second Avenue, along Main Street, to Eighth Avenue, with clusters of businesses along Jackson, King, Weller, Lane and Dearborn Streets. With the move of the JAPANESE-LANGUAGE SCHOOL from Second Avenue to the Buddhist Church, and then to its current location on 15th & Weller, the physical boundaries of the Japanese American community stretched even further. During this period, many Japanese children also attended the old South School, renamed the Main Street School, at Sixth Avenue and Main Street, and later, Bailey Gatzert School. In her autobiography, *Nisei Daughter,* MONICA SONE describes her days at these schools.

Nihonmachi was also home to many Japanese community affairs. Numerous social, cultural and political events were held at the old Atlas Theater, the NIPPON KAN THEATRE and the Seattle Betsuin Buddhist Temple. The *Japanese American Courier,* one of the first English-language Japanese American newspapers in the country, had its office in the heart of Nihonmachi. The newspaper was published by Seattle native JAMES SAKAMOTO, who later helped found the JAPANESE AMERICAN CITIZENS LEAGUE (JACL), and became the organization's second national president.

As the NISEI grew older, they saw the need for a more political community organization. In 1921, the Seattle Progressive Citizen's League was formed, followed by the national Japanese American Citizens League. In August 1930, the JACL held its founding national convention in Seattle.

Japanese Americans prospered in Nihonmachi until April 21, 1942, when World War II evacuation orders were posted in Seattle. Most of the jobs held by the Japanese were taken over by local Filipino and Chinese workers. Within days, businesses were sold or shut down, as Japanese Americans were forcibly removed to the Puyallup "ASSEMBLY CENTER," on the site of the annual Western Washington State Fair. The internees were held there until August and September 1942, when most of the Japanese Americans from Seattle, 7,050 of them, were incarcerated at MINIDOKA, near Hunt, Idaho.

After the war, many of the Japanese American families who moved back to Seattle began living outside the old Nihonmachi. The total Japanese population in Seattle decreased from a peak of 7,000 in 1940 to 5,800 in 1950. The community was still clustered along Yesler and Jackson, from 4th to 23rd Avenues, though many of its former residences were occupied by Seattle's growing African American community.

With the civil rights movement of the 1960s and 1970s, Seattle's Asian communities banded together on political issues, including the preservation of the old neighboring Nihonmachi and Chinatown areas, which Japanese, Chinese and Filipinos had long called home. The area was renamed the International District/Chinatown to be more inclusive and reflective of the diverse Asian groups that live and work there. One of the significant issues that brought the communities together was the protest against the construction of the Kingdome stadium, now located on the west side of the district. In the process, government funding for low-income housing and social services for the neighborhood's elderly non-English-speaking residents was received. Seattle remains one of the largest Japanese American communities on the mainland United States.

The classic study of Seattle's pre–World War II Japanese American community remains S. Frank Miyamoto. *Social Solidarity among the Japanese in Seattle.* University of Washington Publications in the Social Sciences 11.2 (Dec. 1939): 57–130. Seattle: Asian American Studies Program, University of Washington, 1981. Seattle: University of Washington Press, 1984. Two early University of Washington master's theses on the Seattle Japanese American community are Katharine Jane Lentz. "Japanese-American Relations in Seattle." Thesis, University of Washington, 1924 and Katharine Dally Woolston. "Japanese Standard of Living in Seattle." Thesis, University of

Washington, 1927. See also John A. Rademaker. "The Ecological Position of the Japanese Farmers in the State of Washington." Diss., University of Washington, 1939.

Post–World War II studies of the Seattle area Japanese American community include Doug Chin, and Peter Bacho. "The Origins of the International District." *International Examiner.* 17 Oct. 1984, 21 Nov. 1984 and 19 Dec. 1984; S. Frank Miyamoto, and Robert W. O'Brien. "A Survey of Some Changes in the Seattle Japanese Community Since Evacuation." *Research Studies of the State College of Washington* 15 (1947): 147–54; Gail M. Nomura. "Washington's Asian/Pacific American Communities." In White, Sid, and S. E. Solberg, eds. *Peoples of Washington: Perspectives on Cultural Diversity.* Pullman: Washington State University Press, 1989. 113–55; and David Takami. *Shared Dreams: A History of Asian and Pacific Americans in Washington State.* Seattle: Washington State Centennial Commission, 1989 and *Executive Order 9066: 50 Years Before and 50 Years After; A History of Japanese Americans in Seattle.* Seattle, Wash.: Wing Luke Asian Museum, 1992.

Seattle is also the setting of three classic Asian American works: Monica Sone. *Nisei Daughter.* Boston: Little, Brown and Company, 1953. S. Frank Miyamoto, introd. Seattle: University of Washington Press, 1979; John Okada. *No-No Boy.* Rutland, Vt.: Charles E. Tuttle, 1957. San Francisco: Combined Asian American Resources Project, Inc., 1976. Introd. Lawson Fusao Inada. Afterword by Frank Chin. Seattle: University of Washington Press, 1979 and Kazuo Ito. *Issei: A History of Japanese Immigrants in North America.* Shinichiro Nakamura, Jean S. Gerard, trans. Seattle: Executive Committee for the Publication of *Issei: A History of Japanese Immigrants in North America,* 1973. Mayumi Tsutakawa and Alan Chong Lau, eds. *Turning Shadows into Light: Art and Culture of the Northwest's Early Asian/Pacific Community.* Seattle: Young Pine Press, 1982 includes articles on early Japanese American photographers in Seattle and the NIPPON KAN THEATRE.

EMILY LAWSIN

senryu   Seventeen-syllable Japanese poetic form. Along with HAIKU and TANKA, *senryu* was one of the major poetic forms practiced by the ISSEI. Like *haiku, senryu* has a 17-syllable structure grouped in lines of five, seven, and five syllables. Senryu differs from *haiku* in subject matter, with the former focusing on the human condition, often in a satirical manner, and the latter on observations of nature. As with the other poetic forms, Japanese American *senryu* reflected the uniquely American experiences of the Japanese immigrants.

For further reading and examples of Japanese American *senryu,* see Janice Mirikitani, et al., eds. *Ayumi: A Japanese American Anthology.* San Francisco: Japanese American Anthology Committee, 1980; Marvin K. Opler, and F. Obayashi. "Senryu Poetry as Folk and Community Expression." *Journal of American Folklore* 58.227 (Jan.–Mar. 1945): 1–11; Stephen H. Sumida. "Hawaii, the Northwest, and Asia: Localism and Local Literary Developments in the Creation of an Asian Immigrants' Sensibility." *The Seattle Review* 11.1 (Spring/Summer 1988): 9–18; and Peter T. Suzuki. "Jinji (The Human

Condition) in the Wartime Camp Poetry of the Japanese Americans." *Asian Profile* 15.5 (Oct. 1987): 407–15.

shakko bands   ISSEI term for groups of unemployed chronic gamblers who hung around gambling halls seeking handouts from big winners. The term apparently comes from *shi ge,* Chinese for 10 pieces, which corresponds to the 10 cents often begged for. The term broadened in usage to include any group of heavy gamblers. *Shakko* bands were also reputed to take jobs as strikebreakers.
For further reading, see Hisashi Tsurutani. *America Bound: The Japanese and Opening of the American West.* Betsey Scheiner, trans. Tokyo: Japan Times, Inc., 1989.

share-tenancy (also share-tenantry)   Share-tenancy was often the second step (after CONTRACT FARMING) taken by Japanese laborers on their way to becoming independent farmers. This was basically a sharecropping agreement whereby the tenant's share increased or decreased depending on the resources the owner provided. For instance, if a tenant farmer provided his own horses and equipment and the owner provided only land, the tenant's share of the crop would rise. Share tenancy required more capital than contract farming and entailed greater risks, but could be much more lucrative. After being share-tenants, many farmers advanced to CASH-LEASING and outright ownership of land.
For further reading, see Yuji Ichioka. *The Issei: The World of the First Generation Japanese Immigrants, 1885–1924.* New York: The Free Press, 1988 and Masakazu Iwata. "The Japanese Immigrants in California Agriculture." *Agricultural History* 36.1 (Jan. 1962): 25–37.

shashin-kekkon   Japanese term literally meaning "picture marriage." See PICTURE BRIDES.

Shiba Sometaro   ISSEI journalist Sometaro Shiba was a key player in the 1909 PLANTATION STRIKE. Shiba discouraged militant action by Japanese laborers against the sugar planters and generally represented the views of the HAWAII SUGAR PLANTERS ASSOCIATION (HSPA) in the pages of his newspaper, the HAWAII SHIMPO. It was later revealed that his purchase of the paper in 1908 was assisted by an HSPA official and that he received a $100 per month subsidy from the planters. During the strike, he and a group of conservatives tried to take over the rival paper NIPPU JIJI while its leaders were imprisoned, a move that failed. In addition to the financial support he received from the HSPA, Shiba seemed to identify with the HAOLE elite and aspired to be like them. He was proud of his command of the English language and of his contacts with prominent planters. As a result of his actions against the strikers, he was highly unpopular

James Shigeta.   *Terrance Tam Soon Collection, Japanese American National Museum Photographic & Moving Image Archive*

among them. On August 5, 1909, he was attacked and stabbed by a striker; this event eventually led to the resolution of the strike.
For further reading, see Roland Kotani. *The Japanese in Hawaii: A Century of Struggle.* Honolulu: Hochi, Ltd., 1985.

Shigeta, James (1933–   )   Actor and singer. James Shigeta is one of only a handful of Asian American actors to play romantic leads in Hollywood films. Born in Honolulu, Hawaii, he attended New York University, majoring in creative writing, but switching to music after his first year. His entertainment career began after he won the "Ted Mack Amateur Hour" television show as a singer. However, the Korean War intervened and Shigeta served two and half years as a marine, achieving the rank of staff sergeant. After being discharged, he began singing at the Los Angeles Players' Club and was offered a lead in a revue in Japan. There, Shigeta became a popular singer, releasing many hit records and starring in stage productions and four motion picture musicals. His popularity brought him back to Hollywood to co-star with Shirley MacLaine and Louis Jourdan on television's "Chevy Show," which led to a film career and such hits as *The Crimson Kimono, Walk Like a Dragon, Cry for Happy, Bridge to the Sun* and *Flower Drum Song.* He was the only Asian American actor of his generation to play the romantic lead in Hollywood motion pictures. His recent work includes *The Yakuza, Die Hard* and the stage musical *City of Broken Promises.*

ALICE HOM

shiigo *Shiigo* or *shiikoi* is the Japanese term for the game of fantan, one of two principal gambling games engaged in by Japanese laborers. A very simple game, it was particularly susceptible to manipulation by dishonest operators. To play, a large number of coins was piled on a table. Players placed bets on how many coins would remain on the table after the pile was decreased by four coins at a time. Obviously, only zero, one, two or three coins would be left. Since bets were placed openly at the beginning of the game, the house could use sleight of hand to ensure that the least heavily bet on possibility resulted. (See BAKAPYO.)
For further reading, see Yuji Ichioka. *The Issei: The World of the First Generation Japanese Immigrants, 1885–1924.* New York: The Free Press, 1988.

shikata ga nai Phrase meaning "it cannot be helped" or "it must be done." The phrase is an expression of resignation and perseverence in the face of difficult or trying situations that are painful but inevitable. *Shikata ga nai* was the attitude often adopted by the ISSEI as they endured racist citizenship laws, exclusionary laws, ALIEN LAND LAWS and, later, their incarceration in CONCENTRATION CAMPS during World War II. The passive aspect of the expression should not be overstated, however, since Japanese Americans have always been quick to respond to difficulty when there is something that can be done.
For further reading, see Betty S. Furuta. "Ethnic Identities of Japanese-American Families: Implications for Counseling." In Getty, Cathleen, and Winnifred Humphreys, eds. *Understanding the Family: Stress and Change in American Family Life.* New York: Appleton-Century-Crofts, 1981; Jeanne Wakatsuki Houston, and James D. Houston. *Farewell to Manzanar.* Boston: Houghton Mifflin Co., 1973; and Ronald Takaki. *Strangers from a Different Shore: A History of Asian Americans.* Boston: Little, Brown and Company, 1989.

STACEY HIROSE

Shima, George See USHIJIMA KINJI.

Shimoda, Yuki (d. 1981) One of the leading Japanese American actors of his time, best known to many for his performance in the 1976 television movie *Farewell to Manzanar.* Born and raised in SACRAMENTO in the early 1920s, his parents operated a hotel and restaurant business. He spent the war years at TULE LAKE "RELOCATION CENTER," leaving to go to Chicago to teach

Japanese at the University of Chicago, where he also earned a degree in accounting. He began his career in show business as a dancer for the Chicago Opera. He moved to New York and played bit and chorus parts until his big break in *Teahouse of the August Moon.* He went on the appear in the hit plays *South Pacific, The King and I,* and *Auntie Mame.* His success in the latter brought him to Hollywood, where he reprised his role in the film version. He went on to appear in such pictures as *Majority of One, MacArthur,* and *Midway,* as well as many TV shows and commercials. In addition to *Manzanar,* Shimoda also was active in ASIAN AMERICAN THEATER and film, working in East-West Players productions and in films like *Hito Hata: Raise the Banner* (a pioneering independent feature film based on the ISSEI experience). He died in 1981.

[Compiled from Suzuki, Cecil. "Community Pays Final Respects to Yuki Shimoda." *Rafu Shimpo* 26 May 1981: 1.]

shin-issei Term for a post–World War II immigrant from Japan. The prefix *shin* means "new."

Shin Sekai San Francisco ISSEI newspaper. The *Shin Sekai* was one of California's major Japanese-language newspapers prior to World War II. The *Shin Sekai* published its first issue on May 25, 1894. At first, it was the house organ of the Japanese Young Men's Christian Association (YMCA). Half a year before its initial publication, Japanese residents of San Francisco gathered to celebrate the birthday of the Meiji emperor. After the commemoration, a member of the YMCA was overheard to say that the custom of bowing before the emperor's portrait was an act of idolatry. This comment quickly spread throughout the community, and the YMCA came under severe criticism. To defend themselves in print, Hachiro Soejima, the paper's first editor and publisher, launched the *Shin Sekai.* In 1897, Soejima severed ties with the YMCA over a disagreement and turned the *Shin Sekai* into an independent newspaper. Its circulation remained as low as 80 in 1894 and 200 in 1897. In competition with the NICHIBEI SHIMBUN founded in 1899, the *Shin Sekai* increased its readers by establishing local branches in Sacramento, Fresno, Los Angeles and San Jose, among other cities. Its rivalry with the *Nichibei Shimbun* continued until the outbreak of World War II.

In September 1932, the *Shin Sekai* went into bankruptcy. Its staff members then cooperated to re-establish the newspaper as the *Shin Sekai Nichi Nichi Shimbun.* With Toyoji Abe as the chief editor, it then merged with the *Hokubei Asahi* and became the *Shin Sekai Asahi Shimbun* in June 1935. It ceased to exist shortly after Pearl Harbor.

For further reading, see Yuji Ichioka. *The Issei: The World of the First Generation Japanese Immigrants, 1885–1924.* New York: Free Press, 1988 and Zaibei Nihonjinkai. *Zaibei Nihonjinshi.* San Francisco: Zaibei Nihonjinkai, 1940.

EIICHIRO AZUMA

Shogatsu See OSHOOGATSU.

Slocum, Tokutaro "Tokie" Nishimura (1895–?)

World War I veteran and "superpatriot." Born in Japan, Slocum immigrated to the United States with his parents at the age of 10 and was among the first Japanese settlers in the North Dakota plains. While still a youth, Tokie was adopted by the Slocum family of Minot, North Dakota. Slocum attended the University of Minnesota and went on to law school at Columbia University. When World War I broke out, he put his education on hold to fight in the 328th Infantry in France (see WORLD WAR I VETERANS). Gassed while in combat, Slocum experienced medical problems for years due to the noxious inhalation. For his wartime valor, Slocum achieved the rank of sergeant-major and became the highest ranking Asian in the U.S. Army. Although Japanese immigrants were deemed "ALIENS INELIGIBLE TO CITIZENSHIP" by American law, Slocum became a naturalized citizen on the basis of a 1918 congressional act that made "any alien" veteran who served honorably in the war eligible for citizenship.

Slocum was continuing law studies at Columbia when the Supreme Court handed down the TOYOTA V. U.S. decision, which ruled that ISSEI war veterans were excluded from those eligible for naturalization. Tokie reacted to the decision with disbelief and subsequently went on a one-man crusade to establish naturalization rights for *issei* war veterans. Law school became pointless since nearly every state required citizenship for admittance to the bar. Consequently, Slocum traveled all over the country to elicit support for his cause from politicians, Japanese American organizations and veterans' groups. He met up with the JAPANESE AMERICAN CITIZENS LEAGUE (JACL) at its founding conference in 1930 and became an official lobbyist of the organization in 1934. His hard work and dedication were rewarded when Congress passed the NYE-LEA BILL in 1935, at last granting naturalization rights to *issei* war veterans. With his intense lobbying, Slocum even garnered the grudging support of Japanese exclusionist V. S. MCCLATCHY. Just prior to World War II, Slocum continued to demonstrate his patriotism by heading up the special Southern California JACL committee to assist the Federal Bureau of Investigation's investigation of Japanese Americans. He also testified before the TOLAN COMMITTEE, which in the eyes of many branded him as an informant (see

"INU"). Slocum was incarcerated at MANZANAR, where he worked on the camp police force, and was a central target (along with Fred Tayama and others) of the MANZANAR INCIDENT in December 1942.

For further reading, see Bill Hosokawa. *Nisei: The Quiet Americans.* New York: William Morrow & Co., 1969 and *JACL in Quest of Justice: The History of the Japanese American Citizens League.* New York: William Morrow & Co., 1982; Harry Maxwell Naka. "The Naturalization of Japanese War Veterans of the World War Forces." Thesis, University of California, Berkeley, 1939; and Michi Weglyn. *Years of Infamy: The Untold Story of America's Concentration Camps.* New York: William Morrow & Co., 1976.

Soga, Sei

Although she is best known as the wife of NIPPU JIJI publisher YASUTARO SOGA, Sei Soga was a community leader in her own right. After his first wife died leaving him with a young son, Yasutaro Soga returned to Japan and married Sei Tarizawa. She was unusual in that she was a high school graduate who had participated in her father's campaign for a seat in the Diet (Japanese parliament).

Once in Hawaii, she joined the Japanese Women's Society, the Women's Christian Temperance Union, the American Red Cross and the Pan-Pacific Women's Organization. She was known for being a forceful and dynamic leader whose personality countered the stereotype of the ISSEI woman.

Patsy Sumie Saiki. *Japanese Women in Hawaii: The First 100 Years.* Honolulu: Kisaku, Inc., 1985.

Soga, Yasutaro (1873–1957)

For years, Yasutaro Soga was the publisher of the NIPPU JIJI, one of Hawaii's most influential Japanese-language dailies. He came to Hawaii in 1896 after studying at the Tokyo Pharmacy School and the English Law Institute. He began his career in journalism at the HAWAII SHIMPO in 1899 and, along with Masajiro Takahashi and Masako Takahashi, served as reporter, editor, layout man, etc. for that paper. He took over the *Yamato Shimbun* in May 1905 and changed its editorial policy; he also changed the paper's name to the *Nippu Jiji* in 1906. As the *Nippu* emerged as the mouthpiece of the strikers, he became a leading figure in the Higher Wage Association during the 1909 PLANTATION STRIKE. He was arrested over 10 times on various charges at the time of the strike.

In 1919, he introduced an English-language section to the *Nippu*, the first such regular section in any Japanese paper anywhere in the world. He attended the coronation of Emperor Taisho in 1915, the 1921 Washington Conference on the limitation of naval arms and the 1934 Japanese Imperial Chrysanthemum Party in Tokyo. With the outbreak of World War II, Soga was picked up by local authorities and held in various INTERNMENT CAMPS for the duration of the war. He received the Fifth Order of the Sacred Treasure from the Japanese government in 1956.

For further reading, see Roland Kotani. *The Japanese in Hawaii: A Century of Struggle.* Honolulu: Hochi, Ltd., 1985 and United Japanese Society of Hawaii. *History of Japanese in Hawaii.* James H. Okahata, ed. Honolulu: United Japanese Society of Hawaii, 1971.

[Also used to compile this entry was "Yasutaro Soga." *Rafu Shimpo* 5 Mar. 1957: 1.]

Sokabe, Shiro (1865–1949)

The Reverend Shiro Sokabe was pastor of Honomu Church from 1894 to 1942 and the founder of the Honomu Gijuku, a Christian boarding school in Hawaii. He was born in Fukuoka PREFECTURE on June 26, 1865. The eldest son of a samurai, he was raised in strict fashion by his father Michiyue and stepmother Yone. As a teenager, he ran away from home, wandering for years before settling in Imabari in Ehime Prefecture in 1883. Here he became a Christian under the guidance of the Reverend Tokio Ise Yokoi, becoming active in his church and doing missionary work. After two years, he left Imabari for Kumamoto to attend the Oye Gijuku; when that school closed in 1886, he went to Kyoto to attend Doshisha Theological School. Due in part to financial hardship, he left the school without graduating in 1890. In 1891, he went to Kooriyama Congregational Church in Nara Prefecture, which he attended for two years, then to Midorino Congregational Church in Gunma Prefecture in 1893. He was recruited by the Reverend Jiro Okabe of Hawaii and left in March 1894; in the same year, Okabe also recruited Sokabe's former Doshisha colleague the Reverend TAKIE OKUMURA. Sokabe arrived in the small town of Honomu, north of Hilo, on Hawaii Island, later that month and would spend the rest of his life there.

In Honomu he found a group of poorly educated and badly treated plantation laborers and a plantation camp beset by social problems such as gambling, alcoholism, prostitution and adultery. He set out to gather money to build a decent school for the children as a first step. In December 1896, he returned to Japan and married Shika Nagagawa, a young Christian widow with a son, who was head nurse at Doshisha Hospital. The couple returned to Hawaii in March 1897, leaving Shika's son behind to continue his education; he was to join them in 1906. Upon his return, Sokabe started the Honomu Gijuku, a Christian Japanese-language boarding school. The school soon gained a good reputation and grew rapidly with the support of the Honomu Sugar Company and the local Japanese American community, moving into new quarters in 1900 and expanding again in 1908 as its enrollment approached 150. The Sokabes and their teachers taught Japanese language, history and culture in the classroom, along with Christian morality, manners and behavior. The poverty of the surrounding community and its being a haven for orphans, mistreated wives and the elderly caused the *Gijuku* (school) to experience financial difficulties its entire life.

Sokabe was regarded as a stern but kindly taskmaster who maintained a serious demeanor at all times. Known as a man of integrity and loyalty who disliked individual awards or honors, he was dubbed the "Saint of Honomu" by his supporters. He enjoyed singing and the school became known for its Christmas pageants. Like his ideological compatriot Takie Okumura, Sokabe trusted in the good faith of the local sugar planters who had been so helpful to him, and opposed efforts by the plantation workers to strike despite their meager wages and poor working conditions. As a result, he was perceived by some in Honomu as a traitor. In 1908, a rival Buddhist Japanese-language school was erected, capping the growing rivalry between the Buddhists and the Christians in Honomu.

After some 25 years of marriage, Sokabe's wife Shika became ill and died in 1920 while attending to family matters in Japan. Due to his duties at Honomu, Shiro was unable to be with his wife when she died. The couple had been childless and their relationship was apparently a platonic one. In 1921, Sokabe established a separate Japanese-language school next to the *gijuku.* In 1926, the *gijuku* was renovated. A fund-raising drive for a chapel that would bear his wife's name fell short of its goals, however.

After the Pearl Harbor attack, Sokabe was taken in for questioning by the FBI, but was released immediately. He was asked to retire in 1942. He died on July 3, 1949.

For further reading, see Jiro Nakano. *Samurai Missionary: The Reverend Shiro Sokabe.* Honolulu: Hawaii Conference of the United Church of Christ, 1984.

Sone, Monica (1919–)

Writer, psychologist. Monica Itoi Sone is best known for her influential autobiography, *Nisei Daughter.*

A NISEI, Sone was born in 1919 in Seattle, Washington. She lived with her parents in the old Carollton Hotel, an establishment in the Pioneer Square District, just a few blocks from Seattle's NIHONMACHI, that they managed. She attended Bailey Gatzert School and Seattle's Japanese-language school. Sone recounts her childhood experiences in *Nisei Daughter.* Published in 1953,

Southern California Flower Market, Los Angeles, California, ca. 1930s. *Southern California Flower Market Collection, Japanese American National Museum Photographic & Moving Image Archive*

Sone's memoir also details Japanese Americans' reactions to the Japanese attack on Pearl Harbor and her internment at MINIDOKA.

Later, Sone resettled (see RESETTLEMENT) in Chicago and enrolled at Hanover College in Hanover, Indiana. She obtained her master's degree in clinical psychology from Western Reserve University in Cleveland, Ohio. *Nisei Daughter* was reprinted in 1979, when Sone became involved in the REDRESS MOVEMENT. She currently lives with her husband Gary in Canton, Ohio, where she is a semi-retired clinical psychologist.

For further reading, see Sone's *Nisei Daughter*. Boston: Little, Brown and Co., 1953. Seattle: University of Washington Press, 1979. See also Elaine Kim. *Asian American Literature: An Introduction to the Writings and their Social Context*. Philadelphia: Temple University Press, 1982.　　EMILY LAWSIN

Soo, Jack　See SUZUKI, GORO.

Southern California Farm Federation　See NANKA NOKAI RENMEI.

Southern California Flower Market, Inc.　ISSEI-run Los Angeles flower marketing cooperative. By the early 1910s, Japanese floriculture in Los Angeles had been firmly established. At a meeting held in April 1912, the Southern California Flower Growers Association was born, and with it came the proposal of a flower market based on San Francisco's Japanese-run California Flower Market. Although several prior attempts had been made to start flower markets in Los Angeles, each had eventually ended in failure. As a result of the April 1912 meeting, the Southern California Flower Market was opened in January 1913 in a small facility on South Los

Angeles Street. After a year there, the market moved to Wall Street, and in October 1922, the market moved to a permanent location further south on Wall Street. This facility was expanded in 1932 to encompass an area covering 20,000 square feet. Its membership at this time was 159.

Beyond providing an outlet for members' goods, the market also had other functions. In the 1930s, a research department was begun, which helped members keep up to date with the latest in floricultural technology. The department also put out the Japanese-language periodical *Flower Market News*. In 1914, a sales department was organized to promote the shipment of flowers to the eastern U.S. Although this venture was not successful at this time, eastern markets later became significant for Southern California floriculturists with the formation of the Golden Floral Company in 1916 by members of the Southern California Flower Market. The eastern market grew slowly, and by the outbreak of World War II, it accounted for over $1 million in revenue per year. A cooperative purchasing department was founded in 1926 and bought such things as seeds, hardware and fertilizer at bulk rates. A mutual assistance department instigated systematic KODEN payments, which served as a de facto life insurance policy for members.

In 1915, the market dropped its Japanese-only membership policy, though the actual effect of this was minimal since space limitations and the stiff membership fees kept new members to a minimum. Due to space considerations, the market had a membership that was restricted to 159. Although the number of Japanese flower growers in Los Angeles and the scope of the floricultural industry itself increased dramatically, the number of members stayed the same. One result of this was a remarkable increase in the cost of the market's membership fee. In 1914, the fee was $25; by 1930, it was $2,000.

Another result of the restrictions was the formation of rival markets. The American Florists Exchange was formed in 1921 in downtown Los Angeles by flower growers of various ethnicities. A number of Japanese began to join them in the mid-thirties. Though relations were cool at first, the two flower markets began to cooperate in the thirties with the formation of the Southern California Floral Association, Inc., a trade organization, in May 1933. Another competitor was the Union Flower Market, organized by white and Japanese growers in 1930. After a proposed merger with the Southern California Flower Market in 1931, the two sides became entangled in disagreement. After much fruitless negotiation, the Union Market sued the Southern California Market in 1934 for $300,000 in damages. The legal dispute lasted for over three years before the case was decided in favor of the defendant.

With the advent of World War II, leaders of the Southern California Flower Market transferred official power to the NISEI. Anticipating forced removal, the *issei* leaders assumed that the *nisei* would be allowed to continue their businesses, and they formed the Southern California Floral Exchange, a nonprofit corporation owned entirely by *nisei*, on January 26, 1942. Of course this precaution was to prove useless, as all Japanese Americans regardless of citizenship were "relocated" from the West Coast. With the coming of the evacuation orders, the market distributed 40 dollars to each member and attempted to find inland property on which its members might continue their operations. Due largely to resistance from local populations, this search proved to be fruitless. (See "VOLUNATRY" RESETTLEMENT.) With the removal nearing, members of the Southern California Flower Market, Inc. decided to give full management power to its legal advisor, and all accounts were closed on March 31, 1942. During the war, the flower industry boomed and those that took over the *issei* businesses enjoyed great prosperity.

Even while incarcerated, Los Angeles flower growers were meeting to discuss their return to business. Some even obtained temporary releases to meet with colleagues at other camps or to visit Los Angeles and meet with managers of the markets. When Japanese Americans were allowed back on the coast, action was swift. The market opened an office in November 1945 and the market itself officially reopened in September 1946.

Due to changes both in the flower industry and in the Japanese community, the Southern California Flower Market, Inc. was closed in October 1950. In its place, the Southern California Flower Growers, Inc. was formed, consisting largely of *nisei*, who were rapidly taking over their fathers' businesses. This new operation proved to be quite successful and quickly restored the Japanese Americans to prominence in the Los Angeles flower industry. In the years since, this organization has largely lost its ethnic component as non-Japanese have become involved at every level from stockholder to tenant. The social activities so important in the thirties are a thing of the past.

For further reading, see Noritaka Yagasaki. "Ethnic Cooperativism and Immigrant Agriculture: A Study of Japanese Floriculture and Truck Farming in California." Diss., University of California, Berkeley, 1982.

Southern California Gardeners Federation

For various reasons, gardening became a profession many Japanese Americans took up both before and after World War II. Many of these gardeners who worked in the Southern California area became members of the Southern California Gardeners Federation (SCGF), a prewar and postwar organization of Japanese American gardeners.

In 1933, Japanese gardeners' associations were established in Hollywood, uptown Los Angeles and West Los Angeles. In 1937, the three joined forces to form the SCGF.

At its peak, the SCGF had around 900 members, representing about one-third of the Japanese gardeners in Southern California. Although the three associations ran TANOMOSHI and prevented members from competing for routes, they were largely social organizations. The federation attempted to do much more. In an effort to keep members abreast of the latest gardening techniques, the SCGF organized field trips and put out educational articles in its monthly newsletter, *Gadena Shimbun,* and beginning in 1940 in its journal, *Gadena no Tomo.* The SCGF also tried to settle inter-association route disputes and put pressure on non-paying customers. It also tried to raise gardening fees and improve ways of rubbish disposal; in these endeavors, it was less than successful, due largely to rank-and-file apathy. This apathy was brought about by (1) the good money the gardeners were making in spite of difficulties; (2) the belief of many members that trash removal was their responsibility anyway; (3) the general feeling that neither issue was important enough to join forces with the distrusted white gardeners; and (4) the nature of gardening, which caused members to see themselves as small businessmen rather than laborers and thus made them distrustful of anything that appeared to be a union.

After the war, a new organization with the same name (and many of the same members) formed in Los Angeles in 1955. Consisting initially of 14 member associations, this incarnation of the SCGF eventually became far more powerful than its predecessor. In 1958, it became part of the statewide California Gardeners' Coordinating Council along with the Northern California Gardeners' Association and the Southern California Gardeners' Council. The SCGF remains a force in the Japanese American community to this day.

For further reading, see Nobuya Tsuchida. "Japanese Gardeners in Southern California, 1900–1941." In Cheng, Lucie, and Edna Bonacich, eds. *Labor Immigration Under Capitalism: Asian Workers in the United States Before World War II.* Berkeley: University of California Press, 1984. 435–69. For more on Japanese Americans in gardening, see Ronald Tadao Tsukashima. "Cultural Endowment, Disadvantaged Status and Economic Niche: The Development of an Ethnic Trade." *International Migration Review* 25.2 (Summer 1991): 333–54

Southern California Retail Produce Workers Union

All-NISEI organization of retail produce workers in Los Angeles. Formed in reaction to the resurgence of organized labor in Los Angeles, the Southern California Retail Produce Workers Union (SCRPWU) served to represent *nisei* workers' interests to the ISSEI in a way that was non-threatening to the *issei* power structure.

Led by Thomas Hiromu Yamate, the SCRPWU was formed in May 1937 and enrolled 1,000 members in a week. It was recognized by the *issei*-run Retail Market Operators' Association within two weeks. The SCRPWU came about in the wake of the successful organization of wholesale produce workers—including *nisei*—by the Produce Drivers and Employees Union and the attempt by Local 770, Retail Food Clerks to do the same for retail produce workers. Because of the high concentration of *nisei* workers and *issei* operators in this industry, it was imperative for Local 770 to recruit *nisei* members for it to be successful. By challenging SCRPWU members to join up if they were "real Americans," Local 770 was largely unsuccessful. *Nisei* believed that they could work with the *issei* for the benefit of the Japanese American community as a whole and also rejected the white union out of distrust. This was understandable given the long history of anti-Asian agitation such unions had engaged in. Local 770 reacted to rejection by the *nisei* and *issei* by trying to launch racially tinged boycotts against "Japanese" enterprises, appealing to whites to "buy American," further alienating *nisei* workers.

With the wedge between white organized labor and the SCRPWU firmly driven, one *issei*-run business took advantage of the situation. In 1938, the Three Star Produce Company, the largest of the *issei* retail chains, launched a campaign to purge itself of SCRPWU members. The union reacted by filing a civil suit against the chain and appealing to the community for support. Both the union and Three Star claimed they were doing what was good for Japanese Americans and accused the other of self-interest. The dispute was eventually settled internally. In late 1940, Yamate retired, with union members becoming more troubled by the lack of action in the face of wage cuts forced on it by *issei* markets. In March 1941 the Retail Clerks International chartered the Fruit & Vegetable Store Employees (Japanese) Union, Local 510, led by Robert K. Sato, which absorbed most of the SCRPWU membership. World War II put an end to any further developments.

For further reading, see John Modell. *The Economics and Politics of Racial Accommodation: The Japanese of Los Angeles 1900–1942.* Chicago: University of Illinois Press, 1977.

Stimson, Henry Lewis (1867–1950)

Cabinet member in the Taft, Hoover and Roosevelt administrations. In the context of Japanese American history, Henry Stimson is best known for his support of Japanese American "evacuation" during World War II. As secretary of war in FRANKLIN D. ROOSEVELT's Cabinet, he was a leading advocate within the administration for the mass removal of all Japanese Americans from the West Coast and succeeded in applying the necessary pressure to implement the plan.

Stimson was born in New York City on September 21, 1867. A graduate of Harvard Law School, he began his career in government in 1906 as a United States attorney in New York. He served as secretary of war for President Taft from 1911 to 1913 and later became secretary of state under President Hoover from 1929 to 1933. Because of his long experience in government, Roosevelt appointed him secretary of war in 1940. Considered an elder statesman by that time, Stimson, a Republican, enjoyed the respect he received in Roosevelt's New Deal government. He had the ear of the president—something that his counterpart at the Justice Department, FRANCIS BIDDLE, lacked. In pushing for the "evacuation" program, Stimson clearly had the upper hand in the fierce debates that preceded EXECUTIVE ORDER 9066. One of his best political moves was to appoint KARL BENDETSEN—known as the "architect" of the "evacuation" plans—as a liaison between the War Department and Lt. General JOHN L. DEWITT, head of the Western Defense Command. Later in the war, Stimson was the official who made the crucial recommendation to drop the atomic bomb on Hiroshima and Nagasaki—a decision he neither hesitated to make nor regretted later in life. He died on October 20, 1950, at the age of 83.

For further reading, see Roger Daniels. *Concentration Camps, U.S.A.: Japanese Americans and World War II.* New York: Holt, Rinehart and Winston, 1971; Peter Irons. *Justice at War: The Story of the Japanese American Internment Cases.* New York: Oxford University Press, 1983; and Michi Weglyn. *Years of Infamy: The Untold Story of America's Concentration Camps.* New York: William Morrow & Co., 1976 for a discussion of Stimson's role in the decision to "evacuate." Among the broader biographical works on Stimson are Richard Nelson Current. *Secretary Stimson: A Study in Statecraft.* New Brunswick: Rutgers University Press, 1954; Larry G. Gerber. *The Limits of Liberalism: Josephus Daniels, Henry Stimson, Bernard Baruch, Donald Richberg, Felix Frankfurter, and the Development of the Modern American Political Economy.* New York: New York University Press, 1983; Godfrey Hodgson. *The Colonel: The Life and Wars of Henry Stimson, 1867–1950.* New York: Knopf, 1990; Elting Elmore Morison. *Turmoil and Tradition: A Study of the Life and Times of Henry L. Stimson.* Boston: Houghton Mifflin, 1960; Armin Rappaport. *Henry L. Stimson and Japan, 1931–33.* Chicago: University of Chicago Press, 1963; and Henry L. Stimson, and McGeorge Bundy. *On Active Service in Peace and War.* 1947. New York: Octagon Books, 1971.

GLEN KITAYAMA

[Also used to compile this entry: "Henry L. Stimson Dies at 83 In His Home on Long Island." *New York Times* October 21, 1950, p. 1.]

stockade Isolation center located in TULE LAKE "SEG-REGATION CENTER." The stockade was maintained by the army and WAR RELOCATION AUTHORITY (WRA) for the detention of persons believed by those agencies to be threats to the peace and security of the camp. The Japanese American residents of Tule Lake viewed it as a prison in which community leaders and other innocent persons were held without hearings or trials. The stock-ade was a major issue that helped destabilize conditions at the center throughout its nine-month existence.

The stockade came into being as a result of what the army and "segregation center" administration wrongly perceived as a riot. On November 1, 1943, the DAIHYO SHA KAI (a democratically elected community organiza-tion), acting through its 14-member Negotiating Com-mittee, forced a meeting with national WRA director DILLON MYER and project director Raymond Best. The committee was acting in response to community anger over the firing of 800 Tule Lake farm workers and their replacement by strikebreakers from other centers. When a crowd of several thousand internee residents, in a peaceful show of support for their leaders, surrounded the building in which the meeting took place, rumors among Caucasian personnel magnified the demonstra-tion to riot proportions. On November 4, several minor altercations occurred when 150 to 200 internees sur-rounded the motor pool to prevent trucks from leaving to pick up strikebreakers. Calls went out to the army unit outside the camp, which then entered with tanks, armored cars and machine guns. On November 13, martial law was declared, the stockade created and the arrest of Daihyo Sha Kai and farm leaders ordered.

National and local WRA misconceptions about the facts of the November incidents led administrators to conclude that the arrest and incarceration of prominent Daihyo Sha Kai and farm leaders, as well as "trouble-makers" and anti-administration internees, was neces-sary. Fear that further disturbances might hinder the WRA's plans for resettling internees held in the nine remaining camps caused government officials to firmly oppose releasing those in the stockade. On the other hand, fear of arrest permeated the center for months, and the imprisonment of moderate leaders and respected members of the community made the stockade a major issue among Tule Lake residents. Every group aspiring afterwards to community leadership made releases from the stockade a major objective; the administration met every attempt with evasion and rejection. The issue helped turn the administration and internee communities into mutually hostile factions.

On November 26, 1943, the WRA and army joined in a massive search for members of the Daihyo Sha Kai in hiding. Long lines of soldiers swept through the camp searching every man, woman and child, many at bayonet point. Only one leader was found, but 90 other persons were arrested, some merely for lack of army identification cards. The army continued searching the residents' bar-racks for 12 days and nights. By the end of December, approximately 200 people were confined in the stockade. Charges were seldom stated, and all were held without hearings or trials, some for as long as 10 months. The WRA considered charges and trials to be unnecessary, since the incarceration was merely regarded as an "ad-ministrative separation" of persons within the camp. By the end of December, the number of stockade inmates totaled approximately 200. This number eventually rose to an estimated 300 to 450.

The treatment of those arrested was unnecessarily harsh. Those taken on November 26 were herded into army trucks and shoved into a room in the military barracks. There, they were made to sit for hours in crowded conditions on the floor, during which time they were denied even visits to the latrine. Some reported being questioned in a dark room in third-degree style, including beatings with rubber hoses.

The WRA refused to consider the men prisoners, and preferred the term "detainees." Regardless of terminol-ogy, the inmates found conditions within the stockade to be severe. Located in a remote area of the camp, the isolation center consisted of three barracks surrounded by fences and guarded by sentry towers and search lights. All forms of communication with other internees was hindered or prohibited. Virtually their only form of contact was waving between fences located a hundred yards apart. Even this was barred after the administration erected a beaver-board fence to block their view.

Every so often the army conducted raids, often at midnight, that appeared to be harassment. On one night-time raid, the inmates were made to stand in their underwear in the snow for several hours, with a machine gun pointed at them. The inmates carried out three hunger strikes against such conditions, but without suc-cess.

Efforts within the Tule Lake internee community to win freedom for the detainees were continuous. On January 5, 1944, underground activists wrote for help to the Spanish Embassy, which represented Japanese interests in the United States. As a result of a protest by the Japanese government on April 18, and State De-partment probing, 276 inmates were freed by April 29. On May 23, the army withdrew from the stockade, and the WRA took over control.

The closing of the stockade was finally brought about through the intercession of the American Civil Liberties Union (ACLU) of Northern California. Ernest Besig, director of the San Francisco office, spent July 10–11, 1944, at Tule Lake. During this time staff and admin-istrators attempted to obstruct his efforts, even to the point of pouring salt in the gas tank of his automobile. Besig then enlisted the aid of his ACLU colleague WAYNE M. COLLINS, who, in a stormy meeting with National WRA Director Myer, Project Director Best and others, forced the immediate closing of the stockade under threat of a *habeas corpus* suit and a full-scale exposé of the violation of the constitutional rights of U. S. citizens imprisoned without trials. The stockade was closed on August 19, 1944. Within days, all physical evidence of it had been removed. Although a new stockade was built in 1945 because of the crisis involving RENUNCIATION OF CITIZENSHIP, the issue ceased to be a concern among residents of Tule Lake.

For further reading, see Donald E. Collins. *Native American Aliens: Disloyalty and the Renunciation of Citizenship by Japanese Americans During World War II*. Westport, Conn.: Greenwood Press, 1985; Richard Drinnon. *Keeper of Concentration Camps: Dillon S. Myer and American Racism*. Berkeley: University of California Press, 1987; John Tateishi. *And Justice For All: An Oral History of the Japanese American Detention Camps*. New York: Random House, 1984; Dorothy S. Thomas, and Richard Nishimoto. *The Spoilage*. Berkeley: University of California Press, 1946, 1969; and Michi Weglyn. *Years of Infamy: The Untold Story of America's Concentration Camps*. New York: William Morrow & Co., 1976.   DONALD E. COLLINS

Stockton incident   Just before the time the INTERNATIONAL LONGSHOREMEN'S AND WAREHOUSEMEN'S UNION (ILWU) would successfully unionize the multiracial plantation and dock workers in Hawaii, a curious incident was taking place on the mainland. One ILWU unit in Stockton, California, refused to work with a Japanese American in direct contradiction to the ILWU's policy of being "a champion of social justice and an opponent of racial discrimination." Since the union was actively wooing Japanese American workers in Hawaii at that time, their leaders wasted no time in trying to defuse the situation. Both the national president Harry Bridges and Local 6 president Richard Lyndon were annoyed at the Stockton group. After several unsuccessful meetings, the unit was suspended and five of its members were put on trial. All were found guilty on July 21, 1945. With its hand forced, Japanese American workers began entering the Stockton unit within a few weeks. The forceful action by the national organization to uphold the union's principles in defense of Japanese Americans and against public opinion was the type of stand organized labor had seldom taken on behalf of Asian laborers up to that time.

For further reading, see Harvey Schwartz. "A Union Combats Racism: The ILWU's Japanese-American 'Stockton Incident' of 1945." *Southern California Quarterly* 42.2 (1980): 161–76.

Sturge, E. A. (1856–?)   Presbyterian church leader. Minister and medical doctor E. A. Sturge was an influential and beloved figure among ISSEI Christians in the San Francisco Bay area. Born in Cleveland on April 29, 1856, he decided early in life to dedicate himself to helping others through missionary and medical work. He completed an M.D. at the University of Pennsylvania in 1880 and journeyed to Thailand as a medical missionary. In five years in Thailand, he and his wife Annie treated thousands of Thai patients in a hospital they built, until contracting cholera themselves. To recover their health, they came to San Francisco in the summer of 1885. Except for brief visits, they would never leave the city.

Originally intending to work in the Chinese mission, Sturge was assigned to work with the Japanese largely because he did not speak Chinese. In July of 1886, he was officially appointed to work with the Japanese in San Francisco by the Board of Foreign Missions of the Presbyterian Church. He eventually became the superintendent of the Japanese Presbyterian Churches on the Pacific coast, a post he held until 1922.

He became something of a father figure for the Japanese immigrants he worked with, and he and his wife were much beloved by them. Evidence of this can be found in the various anniversary celebrations they staged for him. For instance on the 15th anniversary of their missionary work in 1903, the *issei* collected $1,000, which they gave to the Sturges for a trip to Japan. In 1912, *issei* Presbyterians opened the Sturge Library in San Francisco. Most impressive of all, a group of *issei* who had studied under Sturge but who had returned to Japan organized a society in his honor in 1933. This group, named the Sutojikai [Sturge Society], had 54 members when it began.

For further reading, see Ryo Yoshida. "A Socio-Historical Study of Racial/Ethnic Identity in the Inculcated Religious Expression of Japanese Christianity in San Francisco, 1877–1924." Diss., Graduate Theological Union (Berkeley, Calif.), 1989.

Sugahara, Keiichi "Kay" (1909–1988)   Businessman. The story of Kay (Keiichi) Sugahara is the rags-to-riches story of a self-made millionaire. Born in Seattle, he grew up in Los Angeles and was orphaned at 13. He worked his way through school, employed at a fruit stand and sleeping in a Methodist church dormitory. He graduated from UCLA in 1932. Upon graduation, he founded the Universal Exchange Customs Brokerage House, becoming the first Japanese American customs broker in the continental U.S. He specialized in handling the business of Japanese importers in Southern California. By the age of 29, he had made his first million. He also played a key role in the early JAPANESE AMERICAN CITIZENS LEAGUE chapter in Los Angeles and in the first NISEI WEEK festivals.

Within four years, he had not only lost most of his fortune when his ships were attacked in the Pacific, but, like all other West Coast Japanese Americans, he found himself in a CONCENTRATION CAMP. As one of the older NISEI at GRANADA, Colorado, he advocated cooperation with the U.S. authorities and persuaded many not to renounce their citizenship or "repatriate" to Japan (see RENUNCIATION OF CITIZENSHIP). He volunteered for duty with the Office of Strategic Service and served in India. He also made many contacts in Japan. Due to his influence there, he was involved in shaping U.S. policy towards Japan in the occupation period and helped to organize the American Council for Japan. One of his associates during this period was Yasuhiro Nakasone who later became the prime minister of Japan.

Within a few years, he had rebuilt his fortune as the head of a shipping empire. He became chairman of the board of Fairfield Maxwell Ltd., a privately held oil and shipping operation controlling 40 U.S. corporations. He also chaired the United States-Asia Institute, an independent, nonprofit organization founded in 1979. One of its goals is to raise the image of Asian Americans. In February 1983, Sugahara made headlines by proposing a $10 billion fund called the Partnership in Prosperity Fund to a National Governor's Association Meeting; the idea was for Japanese corporations to invest in America in order to improve its image. Sugahara belonged to no Japanese American or Asian American organizations after the war. He died of liver cancer in 1988 and is interred in Arlington National Cemetery.

For further reading, see Teru Kanazawa. "Kay Sugahara— 'Nisei Onassis.'" *Tozai Times,* 1 (Aug. 1985): 1, 10–11, 20.

Sugi, Suma JAPANESE AMERICAN CITIZENS LEAGUE (JACL) lobbyist. Suma Sugi is best known for successfully lobbying on behalf of the JACL for the amendment of the CABLE ACT. Passed in 1922 and targeted at the ISSEI, the Cable Act was a racist law that stripped citizenship from any American woman who married an "ALIEN INELIGIBLE TO CITIZENSHIP." Sugi was sent from Los Angeles to Washington, D.C., by the JACL and is considered the first NISEI lobbyist. She helped convince Congress to amend the act in early 1931 so that women previously affected by the law were no longer subject to loss of citizenship.

For further reading, see Bill Hosokawa. *Nisei: The Quiet Americans.* New York: William Morrow & Co., 1969.

SCOTT KURASHIGE

Sugimoto, Henry (1900–1990) Artist. Henry Sugimoto was born in 1900 in Gozenmatsu, Wakayama PREFECTURE. After he finished his studies at Wakayama Middle School, he traveled to Hanford, California, to join his parents who had immigrated years earlier. Sugi-

Henry Sugimoto. *Photo by Norman Sugimoto.*

moto graduated from Hanford High School and then went on to continue his studies at the University of California at Berkeley. He eventually transferred to the California College of Arts, where he received his Bachelor of Fine Arts degree in 1928.

After completing his studies, he taught art and Japanese language for a living. He also traveled to France and Mexico to develop and hone his art. With the outbreak of World War II, Sugimoto and his family were forcibly removed from Hanford to the Fresno "ASSEMBLY CENTER" and then transported to the CONCENTRATION CAMPS at JEROME and later ROHWER, Arkansas. After the war, the family resettled in New York City where Sugimoto designed fabric and continued to paint. (See RESETTLEMENT.)

Sugimoto has received numerous awards. His paintings have been exhibited in many public and private galleries in the United States, Europe and Japan. During the 1980s, both the Smithsonian Institution and the Wakayama Modern Art Museum acquired some of Sugimoto's paintings for their permanent collections.

Though his paintings encompass many styles and subjects, Sugimoto is best known for his depictions of the World War II concentration camps. These emotionally charged works reveal many aspects of the Japanese American experience during World War II, conjuring the fear and trauma and other facets of life within the barbed wire fences. Later in his life, Sugimoto also painted a series of canvases depicting the pre–World War II ISSEI experience.

Henry Sugimoto died at the age of 90 on May 8, 1990, at his home in New York.

For further reading, see Deborah Gesensway, and Mindy Roseman. *Beyond Words: Images from America's Concentration Camps.* Ithaca, N.Y.: Cornell University Press, 1987 and *The View from Within: Japanese American Art from the Internment Camps, 1942–1945.* Los Angeles: Japanese American National Museum, UCLA Wight Art Gallery, and UCLA Asian American Studies Center, 1992. SUZANNE J. HEE

sumo Japanese wrestling. Sumo is Japan's national sport and has roots dating back some 2,000 years. Sumo contests involve two men facing each other in a small ring, with each trying to force the other out of the ring. Sumo wrestlers are known as *sumotori*.

In the pre–World War II Japanese American community, sumo was a popular form of recreation and entertainment. The first recorded matches took place in 1885, soon after the arrival of the first KANYAKU IMIN, for the entertainment of King Kalakaua and other Hawaiian officials and royalty. Sumo served as a diversion from harsh PLANTATION working conditions; before long, tournaments were being held to find the best wrestlers at each plantation camp. Sumo tournaments were also held at many community celebrations ranging from church festivals to visits of Japanese naval ships during its peak years of popularity in the 1910s and '20s. Like many other activities associated with Japan, sumo declined in popularity immediately before and during World War II. Though still popular among some Japanese Americans today, it has never come close to recapturing its prewar prominence.

For further reading, see Gaylord Kubota. "Hawaii's Sumo and Kendo Traditions." *Hawaii Herald* 5 Nov. 1982: 8–9; "Sumo Supplement." *Hawaii Herald* 18 May 1984: B.

Suto, Kotaro (c. 1882–1963) Kotaro Suto is credited with being one of the builders of Miami Beach, Florida. He came to Miami from San Francisco at age 32 during World War I to work as a gardener for land developer Carl Fisher. Before long, Suto and Fisher were working together. Suto used his gardening skills to add beauty to Fisher's developments. Suto soon set up his own nursery but continued to volunteer his services to the community, providing plants for various civic projects. At the outbreak of World War II, community testimony on his behalf kept the FBI at bay and allowed him to continue his business. When he and his wife

decided to go back to Japan to retire, a farewell ceremony was held at City Hall. But realizing that he belonged in Miami, he returned there soon after going to Japan. His story was dramatized in an episode of the ABC TV series *Dupont Cavalcade Theater* titled "Call Home the Heart" in 1956.

For further reading, see Bill Hosokawa. *Nisei: The Quiet Americans.* New York: William Morrow & Co., 1969.

[Also used to compile this entry was Larry S. Tajiri. "TV Productions." *Pacific Citizen* 9 Mar. 1956: 3.]

Suzuki, Bob H. Educator, university administrator. When he was appointed to be president of California State Polytechnic University, Pomona, in 1991, Bob Suzuki became the first American-born Japanese American to head a major university in the continental U.S. A NISEI born in Portland, Oregon, Suzuki originally focused his academic career in the scientific arena, earning bachelor's and master's degrees in mechanical engineering from the University of California, Berkeley. After earning his Ph.D. in aeronautics from the California Institute of Technology, Suzuki taught aerospace engineering at the University of Southern California for four and a half years. Subsequently, Suzuki's career took a major shift when he entered the School of Education at the University of Massachusetts at Amherst and also became involved in Asian American Studies. His groundbreaking work "Education and the Socialization of Asian Americans: A Revisionist Analysis of the 'Model Minority' Myth" (first published in 1977) detailed the problems with stereotyping Asian Americans as high achievers. In 1981, Suzuki entered administration, working at California State University campuses at both Los Angeles and Northridge, before accepting the presidency at Pomona.

For further reading, see Bob H. Suzuki "Education and Socialization of Asian Americans: A Revisionist Analysis of the 'Model Minority' Thesis." *Amerasia Journal* 4.2 (1977): 23–52. Reprinted in *Asian-Americans: Social and Psychological Perspectives, Vol. II.* Russell Endo, Stanley Sue, and Nathaniel N. Wagner, eds. Palo Alto, Calif.: Science and Behavior Books, Inc., 1980. 155–75. SCOTT KURASHIGE

[Other sources for this entry include Kariann Yokota, "New President Challenged by Budget Cuts Facing Cal Poly Pomona," *Rafu Shimpo* 23 Oct. 1991 and "Man of Change." *Rafu Shimpo* 24 October 1991.]

Suzuki, Bunji (1885–1946) Japanese labor leader. In the midst of ANTI-JAPANESE MOVEMENT, Bunji Suzuki appeared at the 1915 and 1916 conventions of the California State Federation of Labor and the American

Federation of Labor. In 1915, SIDNEY L. GULICK, a clergyman and the foremost white opponent of the Japanese exclusion movement, met with Paul Scharrenberg, an ardent exclusionist and secretary of the California State Federation of Labor. At this meeting, the suggestion was made for an exchange of fraternal delegates between labor organizations of Japan and the United States. During his subsequent trip to Japan, Gulick searched for a likely candidate and settled on Suzuki. Bunji Suzuki had graduated from Tokyo Imperial University and was a practicing Christian with a working knowledge of English. He also headed a conservative labor group called the Yuaikai, which claimed a membership of about 7,000 at the time. Since the Foreign Ministry looked on radical labor leaders with suspicion, the selection of the social reformer Suzuki met with their approval.

In June of 1915, Suzuki left for the United States. After meeting with various labor groups, labor leaders and Japanese immigrant groups, he attended the California State Federation of Labor convention in Santa Rosa in October. He was greeted warmly as he accepted the convention's call to exclude Asians on economic grounds. He went on to attend the AFL convention in San Francisco the following month and attended a dinner hosted by KINJI USHIJIMA for Samuel Gompers. Before his return, he also organized the JAPANESE LABOR LEAGUE OF AMERICA by merging two existing labor groups in the Bay area for the purpose of raising the standards of Japanese workers in cooperation with white workers. This venture soon faded into obscurity.

He returned the following year to attend the same two conventions. At the State Federation convention held in Eureka, he indirectly raised the issue of allowing Japanese workers to join. When the resolution calling for Asian exclusion was raised (similar to the one that had been passed for the previous six years in a row), another group raised a resolution to organize and accept Asian workers. This group was too small to have much effect, however; the first resolution was passed as usual and the second referred to the Executive Council, where it died. After this convention, Suzuki formed the JAPANESE FEDERATION OF LABOR, a coalition of various fraternal bodies, in the hope of recognition by the AFL. This was not forthcoming. He went on to attend the AFL convention in Baltimore where he raised the issue of accepting Japanese workers, but this question was not even considered at the convention.

Suzuki's visits had no effect on the labor unions and no effect on the Japanese workers—they remained excluded from established organized labor. The two main beneficiaries of the visits were organized labor and Suzuki himself. By according such civil treatment to Suzuki and by his accepting the exclusion of Japanese labor on economic grounds, exclusionists such as Scharrenberg could pass themselves off as reasonable people whose concerns about Asian labor were acceptable to a Japanese labor representative. Suzuki benefited from the increased prestige he received in Japan and was able to build the Yuaikai into a major labor federation. Both sides benefited at the expense of Japanese workers in America.

For further reading, see Yuji Ichioka. *The Issei: The World of the First Generation Japanese Immigrants, 1885–1924.* New York: The Free Press, 1988 and Stephen S. Large. "The Japanese Labor Movement, 1912–1919; Suzuki Bunji and Yuaikai." *Journal of Asian Studies* 29.3 (May 1970): 559–79.

Suzuki, Chiyoko "Pat" (1931–   )   Actress and singer. NISEI Pat Suzuki is best known for her role in the musical *Flower Drum Song*. A native of Cressy, California (one of KYUTARO ABIKO's farming colonies), Suzuki was the youngest of four children. Along with her family, she was incarcerated at the CONCENTRATION CAMP in GRANADA, Colorado, during World War II. After returning to the coast, she entered Mills College in 1948; while attending San Jose State, she began to sing in nightclubs on weekends. Traveling to New York, she joined the road company of the play *Teahouse of the August Moon* and worked for three years at a Seattle-area club called The Colony. In 1957, she received her big break, landing a role in the Rogers and Hammerstein musical *Flower Drum Song*. She later appeared in the film version of the play as well. She shared the December 22, 1958, cover of *Time* magazine with MIYOSHI UMEKI. Since that time, she has continued to sing and has appeared on television and in films, including a major role in the 1970s Burt Reynolds movie *Skullduggery* and a regular role in the short-lived television series "Mr. T and Tina."
SUZANNE J. HEE

Suzuki, Goro [Jack Soo] (1915–1979)   Actor. Jack Soo was best known for his role as the wisecracking detective Nick Yemana in the popular 1970s television series "Barney Miller." He was born in Oakland and began his career as a singer/comic in Watsonville, California in 1941. He spent two years incarcerated at TOPAZ, where he continued to perform. After his release, he restarted his show business career in a Chinese club in Cleveland. He worked as a barkeeper/singer and was advised by the owner to change his name to "Soo"; the other employees were told that he couldn't speak Chinese because he came from Iowa. In 1949, he joined Joey Bishop as a straight man before beginning to work clubs on his own. His break came in the Broadway musical *Flower Drum Song*. He played Sammy Fong in both stage and screen versions. He went on to appear in the

Jack Soo. *Terrance Tam Soon Collection, Japanese American National Museum Photographic & Moving Image Archive*

films *The Green Berets, She Lives,* and *Who's Been Sleeping in My Bed?*

T

taiko Large barrel-shaped drum used in various kinds of Japanese ceremonies and music. Japanese Americans, especially SANSEI, have adopted *taiko* drumming as a gesture of cultural identity and to perform a uniquely Japanese American music. Since the early 1970s, many Japanese American *taiko* drumming groups have formed throughout the country, performing at community events and cultural celebrations.

For further reading, see Johnny Mori. "Taiko." *Gidra 20th Anniversary Edition* (1990): 60, a description of making a *taiko* Japanese American–style.

Tajiri, Larry (1914–1961) Born in Los Angeles, Larry Tajiri held newspaper posts throughout his life and proved to be among the most influential of the NISEI journalists. His career began at Los Angeles Poly-

technic High School; during his tenure as editor in 1931, the school's newspaper, the POLY OPTIMIST, garnered the award for best school paper in Southern California. Tajiri left college during his freshman year to take the post of editor of the English section of the *Kashu Mainichi,* a Los Angeles Japanese American newspaper.

In 1934, Tajiri went to San Francisco to work on the English staff of the NICHIBEI SHIMBUN, a much larger paper and arguably the leading Japanese American daily in the United States. He shared editorial responsibilities with the veteran *nisei* journalist Kay Nishida. Tajiri wrote regularly in his column entitled "Village Vagaries," which he had brought with him from the *Kashu.* "Vagaries" reflected his broad interests, which included international politics, labor/unionization issues, and the Hollywood scene. His writing offered insightful commentary on how various events affected Japanese Americans. Politically progressive, Tajiri often supported labor and unionization efforts among the Japanese, especially among *nisei* workers. His coverage of the 1936 Salinas Lettuce Strike recognized the difficult position of *nisei* employed by ISSEI owners who had been targeted by labor unions. In the late 1930s, Tajiri helped organize Young Democrats groups in San Francisco and Oakland.

Throughout his journalism career, Tajiri maintained an avid interest in the arts and literature. He staunchly supported *nisei* artists, poets and writers, featuring them in a literary section of the *Nichibei.* Tajiri himself dabbled in fiction, and his stories appeared in *nisei* literary journals.

In 1940, Tajiri left the *Nichibei* to take a post in New York City as a staff writer for the Japan-based Tokyo and Osaka *Asahi.* After the Pearl Harbor attack, however, Tajiri found himself out of a job and returned to Los Angeles. Shortly afterwards, the JAPANESE AMERICAN CITIZENS LEAGUE (JACL) approached Tajiri and his wife, Marion Tsuguyo (Okagaki) Tajiri, also a journalist, about editing the JACL paper, the PACIFIC CITIZEN. The Tajiris left for Salt Lake City in early 1942 and edited the paper during the turbulent war years and in the early postwar period (1942–52).

Larry Tajiri devoted his last stint as a journalist attending to his love of the arts. In late 1952, he joined the staff of the *Denver Post* as an art and literary critic. He wrote for the *Post* until his death in 1961.

For further reading, see Jerrold Haruo Takahashi. "Japanese American Responses to Race Relations: The Formation of Nisei Perspectives." *Amerasia Journal* 9.1 (1982): 29–57 for more on Tajiri as an opinion leader in the prewar *nisei* community. See Bill Hosokawa. *JACL in Quest of Justice: The History of the Japanese American Citizens League.* New York: William Morrow, 1982 for one view of Tajiri's tenure as *Pacific Citizen* editor.   DAVID YOO

[Also used to compile this entry: *Nichibei Shimbun* May 20, 1931; October 24, 1934; October 16, 1936; June 19, 1940. Interview with Marion Tajiri, Berkeley, Calif., May 21, 1992.]

Takaezu, Toshiko (1922–   ) Artist, ceramist. Toshiko Takaezu, the sixth child in a family of 11, was born on June 17, 1922, in Pepeeko, Hawaii, to Shinsa and Kama Takaezu. Her father labored in Hawaii's sugar cane fields. Although the family was poor, Takaezu's parents managed to provide for their children, eight of whom were educated and eventually entered a variety of professions.

In 1948, Takaezu enrolled in the Honolulu School of Art with the intention of becoming a sculptor. When she realized the dedication and work that was required, she decided to work with clay and become a ceramist. In 1951, she traveled to Michigan and attended Cranbrook Academy of Art in Bloomfield. She landed her first teaching position at the University of Wisconsin in 1954 and continued to teach there until 1955. In that same year, Takaezu went to Japan to study with master potter Toyo Kaneshige for eight months. In Japan, she was able to explore her own background and come to terms with her identity as an American and as a Japanese. She returned from Japan in 1956 and found a teaching position at the Cleveland Institute of Art, where she remained for eight years. In 1964, she moved to Clinton, New Jersey, where she worked in a large studio on the ground floor of a theater building. Since 1967, she has been teaching at the Visual Arts Program at Princeton University.

Takaezu has had a remarkable career as a ceramist. Her accomplishments include: one-woman shows at the Honolulu Academy of Arts, Indiana State University, Lewis and Clark College, Contemporary Arts Center of Hawaii, University of Wisconsin and the New Jersey State Museum. She was the recipient of the Dickson College Award in 1982, an award that has been presented only 11 other times in the last 25 years. Her work appears in private and public collections including the Boston Museum of Fine Arts, Butler Institute of American Arts, New York Museum of Contemporary Crafts, Baltimore Museum and Dickson College.

Her works employ a wide range of media besides ceramics, including textile weaving, bronze sculpture and painting. However, she is most noted for her outstanding talent in ceramics and has played a vital role in the international interest in ceramic art. As Takaezu comments on her relationship with clay, "One of the best things about clay is that I can be completely free and honest with it. And the clay responds to me. The clay is alive and responsive to every touch and feeling. When I make it into form, it is alive, and even when it is dry, it is still breathing! I can feel the response in my hands, and I don't have to force the clay. The whole process is an interplay between the clay and myself, and often the clay has much to say."

For further reading, see Deborah Dubrovsky. "Toshiko Takaezu." In Burstyn, Joan N., ed. *Past and Promise: Lives of New Jersey Women*. Metuchen, N.J.: Scarecrow Press, 1990 and Tomi Kaizawa Knaefler. "Toshiko Takaezu: Madonna of the Clay." In Lueras, Leonard, ed. *Kanyaku Imin: A Hundred Years of Japanese Life in Hawaii*. Honolulu: International Savings and Loan Association Ltd., 1985. 102–03.

SUZANNE J. HEE

[Quote from Knaefler, p. 102.]

Takahashi v. Fish and Game Commission Court case challenging the World War II–era law banning ISSEI from fishing. In the 1935 case of ABE, T. V. FISH AND GAME COMMISSION, Section 990 of the California Fish and Game Code was declared invalid because it discriminated between residents and nonresidents of the United States. In 1943, while Japanese Americans were incarcerated in American CONCENTRATION CAMPS, the California legislature, in an effort to discourage their return, amended Section 990 to provide that a commercial fishing license can be granted to anyone other than an alien Japanese. Section 990 was amended again in 1945, this time denying licenses to "ALIENS INELIGIBLE TO CITIZENSHIP" rather than specifically denying them to alien Japanese. In 1947, Torao Takahashi, an *issei* who had engaged in commercial fishing from 1915 to 1941, when he was taken away to MANZANAR, brought an action against the Fish and Game Commission to compel it to issue him a license. The Los Angeles County Superior Court ordered the Fish and Game Commission to issue Takahashi a license, holding that Section 990 was unconstitutional since it discriminated against Takahashi solely because of his race. The California Supreme Court reversed the superior court, ruling that the state, in the interests of conservation, could expressly exclude aliens from fishing and hunting. The U.S. Supreme Court reversed the California Supreme Court on June 7, 1948, and ordered the Fish and Game Commission to issue Takahashi a license. This case, along with cases such as OYAMA V. CALIFORNIA, made it clear that statutes that discriminated on the basis of race would be declared invalid by the courts.

For further reading, see Frank F. Chuman. *The Bamboo People: The Law and Japanese-Americans*. Del Mar, Calif.: Publisher's Inc., 1976.

DENNIS YAMAMOTO

Takahashi Shizuko Christian activist Shizuko Takahashi was a pioneer ISSEI woman in San Francisco and the mother of 12. A native of Chiba PREFECTURE, Shizuko Higuchi was sent away at age 10 in 1886 to attend the first class of the Christian girls' school run by missionaries Joseph and Sarah Ann Cosand. One of her classmates was Umeko Tsuda, later the founder of Tsuda College and the sister-in-law of *issei* publisher KYUTARO ABIKO. Graduating at age 17 and having become a Quaker, Shizuko stayed on at the school, working as an interpreter until she was 24. At that time, she met Chiyokichi Takahashi. An *issei,* he had been a migrant laborer and SCHOOLBOY in America prior to opening a tailor shop in Oakland. Though he was not Christian and did not meet with the approval of Shizuko's colleagues, the couple was married and settled in Oakland in 1901.

Like many *issei* women, Shizuko was initially disappointed at the poor living conditions of the Japanese section of the city. She became active in the local church and founded a Japanese mother's club. She and her growing family welcomed new arrivals from Japan as the Japanese American community in Oakland and Berkeley grew rapidly. With the growing family, the Takahashi's moved to Berkeley where Chiyokichi remodeled the old church building. Though Shizuko was plagued by asthma and the family lived in relative poverty, the 1910s were happy years in which the children grew and a Japanese American community emerged around them. In all, the couple had 12 children. Active in the PTA, Shizuko also joined the University of California Mother's Club, becoming its first Japanese member. In 1932, three of her children received degrees from the university, and in 1940, she was named Mother of the Year by the club; by that time, nine of her children had graduated from the University of California. In the meantime, Chiyokichi had turned his hobby of cultivating bonsai into a profitable business.

The family was forcibly removed with all other West Coast Japanese Americans during World War II. They were taken to Tanforan "ASSEMBLY CENTER" and POSTON. The family resettled (see RESETTLEMENT) in Chicago briefly before returning to California. Shizuko passed away in the years following the return home.

For further reading, see Eleanor Hull. *Suddenly the Sun: A Biography of Shizuko Takahashi.* New York: Friendship Press, 1957.

Takamine, Jokichi (1854–1922)   Chemist, industrial leader. Takamine was born to Seichi and Yukiko Takamine in Takaoka, Japan. After graduating from the University of Tokyo in 1879, he was sponsored by the government to study abroad at Glasgow University and Anderson's College. In addition, he studied the manufacturing of soda and fertilizers during summer vacations. Takamine first came to the United States in 1884 when he represented Japan at the international Cotton Centennial Exposition in New Orleans. At this event, he met Caroline Fitch Hield, whom he would marry the next year. Though he returned to Japan to serve in a variety of high positions within the government and later the private sector, Takamine made America his adopted home. He developed a potent starch-digesting enzyme, which he named Takadiastase, from a special type of fungus. The enzyme proved valuable to medicine and was produced by Parke, Davis and Company. But, Takadiastase was not the last of Takamine's important contributions to the medical field. According to the *Concise Dictionary of American Biography,* the "crowning achievement" of Takamine's career came in 1901 when he isolated adrenalin from the suprarenal gland and became the first to discover gland hormones in pure form. Besides his work, Takamine devoted his energy to bridging the cultural gap between the East and West. He studied Western art and civilization while promoting Japanese culture to the American public. Takamine was cofounder and president of both the Japanese Association of New York and the Nippon Club.

For further reading, see Karl Kawakami. *Jokichi Takamine: A Record of his American Achievement by K. K. Kawakami.* New York: W. E. Rudge, 1928. See also *The Dictionary of American Biography.* New York: Charles Scribner's Sons.

SCOTT KURASHIGE

Takano, Fusataro (1868–?)   Labor leader. During the period when organized labor excluded Japanese from its ranks, the actions and writings of Fusataro Takano challenged labor's contention that Japanese lacked the inclination or ability to participate in unionization. Takano was born in Nagasaki and lived in Tokyo and Yokohama before deciding to come to America. Arriving in San Francisco in 1886, he studied English and worked as a SCHOOLBOY before a short-lived attempt to start a small store. He became an itinerant laborer in 1889 and became interested in labor history through reading books. He soon was writing about labor issues for publications both here and in Japan and corresponded with American Federation of Labor president Samuel Gompers from 1894 to 1898. Despite his many articles in *American Federationist* and Gompers's positive response to his letters, Takano did not succeed in changing the anti-Japanese orientation of organized labor. Gompers's continued assertion that Japanese did not have the ability to be good union men despite his knowledge of Takano indicates that the real reason for organized labor's exclusion of Asians was racially motivated. (See ANTI-JAPANESE MOVEMENT.)

For further reading, see Yuji Ichioka. *The Issei: The World of the First Generation Japanese Immigrants, 1885–1924.* New York: The Free Press, 1988 and Hyman Kublin. *Asian Revo-*

lutionary: *The Life of Sen Katayama*. Princeton: Princeton University Press, 1964.

Takei, George Hosako (1939–)   Actor, writer,
politician. Though George Takei will always be known for his role as Mr. Sulu on "Star Trek," he has had a varied career in different fields. He was born in Los Angeles and spent the war years in the CONCENTRATION CAMPS at ROHWER, Arkansas, and at TULE LAKE, California. He moved back to L.A. and went on to attend the University of California, Berkeley, where he majored in architecture. After two years, he switched majors and schools and emerged from the University of California, Los Angeles, with a B.A. and M.A. in theater arts. His big break was a role in the movie *Ice Palace* with Richard Burton in 1960. He went on to appear in *Hell to Eternity* (1960), *Red Line 7,000* (1965) and *The Green Berets* (1968) as well as the TV shows "Hawaiian Eye," "Perry Mason" and "The Twilight Zone" before "Star Trek." In between roles, he studied at the Shakespeare Institute at Stratford-upon-Avon in England in 1962, the Desilu Workshop in 1963–64, and Sophia University in Tokyo in 1970. After "Star Trek" (1966–69), he performed in Frank Chin's play *Year of the Dragon* in New York and on PBS and appeared in the various *Star Trek* motion pictures and numerous television programs. He recently became the first Japanese American to get a star on Hollywood's Walk of Fame and received a Grammy Award in 1988 for Best Spoken Word performance for his reading of the *Star Trek IV* novelization. Most recently, he has appeared in the feature film *Return from the River Kwai*.

George Takei also has had a parallel career in politics. In 1973, he ran for a seat on the Los Angeles City Council, placing second to David Cunningham. In 1975, he ran against Mike Roos for the state assembly, but pulled out when Roos demanded television time equal to Takei's "Star Trek" appearances. Takei also attended the 1972 Democratic Convention in Miami as a delegate for candidate George McGovern and served as an alternate delegate at the 1976 Democratic convention. He has also been an active supporter in Mayor Tom Bradley's campaigns. He served on the Los Angeles Rapid Transit District Board of Directors from 1973–84 and is currently president of the El Pueblo State Historic Park Association. Additionally, he founded the Golden Security Thrift and Loan Association in 1981, a bank catering mostly to Southeast Asian immigrants, and published a science fiction novel titled *Mirror Friend, Mirror Foe* in 1979.

For further reading, see John Nakashima. "George Takei." *Tozai Times* 2 (Apr. 1986): 1, 6–7; Guy Aoki; "George Takei: Steering a Course to Stardom." *AsiAm* 2.2 (Feb. 1987): 12–16, 95–101; and Shi Kagy. "Saga of a Renaissance Man." *Transpacific* 5.3 (May/June 1990): 26+.

Tanaka, Togo W. (1916–)   Journalist, business-
man. Togo Tanaka was a leading NISEI journalist in Los Angeles during the pre–World War II period. Born in Portland, Oregon, Tanaka moved with his family to Los Angeles as an infant. He attended public schools in Hollywood, working at his parents' fruit and vegetable stand after classes. He edited the *Hollywood High School News* in his senior year and graduated with honors in 1931. Tanaka then matriculated at the University of California, Los Angeles, and for a brief period during his freshman year, worked on the staff of the *Daily Bruin*. Tanaka majored in political science, in part out of respect for his father, who envisioned for his son a career in diplomatic service of the Japanese government.

In 1934, during his junior year at UCLA, Tanaka began work as an associate editor of the English staff at the *Kashu Mainichi*. He was hired by the flamboyant publisher of the *Kashu*, Sei Fujii, to help translate editorials from Japanese to English. A year later, he moved from the *Kashu* to the RAFU SHIMPO, the leading Japanese American daily in Southern California. He joined Louise Suski as an editor of the English-language section in 1936. Suski had been editor of the section since its inception in February of 1926.

Tanaka contributed a regular column ("Post Script") during his six-year stay at the paper. He covered the issues of the times, discussing anti-Japanese activity, *nisei* vocation/career issues, and the ramifications of U.S. citizenship. The *nisei*, in his view, needed to stake their claim in America, even though their parents were denied the opportunity to become naturalized citizens. Although he expressed some early criticism of the JAPANESE AMERICAN CITIZENS LEAGUE (JACL), Tanaka, by the outbreak of war between the U.S. and Japan, had become identified with the leadership of the JACL.

In October 1941, Tanaka had been sent to Washington, D.C. by *Rafu* publisher H. T. Komai to try to secure publishing rights in the event of a U.S.-Japan war. During this trip, Tanaka gained a private meeting with First Lady Eleanor Roosevelt and spoke to her regarding the plight of the ISSEI and *nisei*. In the aftermath of Pearl Harbor, the FBI arrested Tanaka along with other community leaders. Released after spending 12 days in jail, Tanaka was never charged nor was he given any explanation as to why he was detained. Tanaka and his wife Jean (Wada) and their child were removed to the Santa Anita "ASSEMBLY CENTER" and then to MANZANAR.

Tanaka accepted a position from the WAR RELOCATION AUTHORITY to become a "documentary historian"—a position that earned him the label of informer (INU) and a place on the "hit list." In December of 1942, in the wake of the MANZANAR UPRISING, Tanaka was moved to another site in Death Valley for his own protection. While there, he wrote reports that became part of the JAPANESE AMERICAN EVACUATION AND RESETTLEMENT STUDY, a University of California research project on the camps.

After Death Valley, the Tanakas moved to Chicago where they remained for 13 years before heading back to Los Angeles. Tanaka has since enjoyed an extremely successful career in business.

For further reading, see Togo W. Tanaka "How to Survive Racism in America's Free Society." In Arthur A. Hansen and Betty E. Mitson, eds. *Voices Long Silent: An Oral Inquiry into the Japanese American Evacuation.* Japanese American Project, California State University, Fullerton, 1974. 83–109. His post–Pearl Harbor experiences are detailed in Bill Hosokawa. *JACL in Quest of Justice: The History of the Japanese American Citizens League.* New York: William Morrow, 1982.

DAVID YOO

[Also used to compile this entry: interview with Togo Tanaka, Los Angeles, Calif., May 18, 1992.]

tanka   Japanese poetic form. Tanka are poems of 31 syllables arranged in lines of five, seven, five, seven, and seven syllables. As with HAIKU and SENRYU, tanka were popular among the ISSEI, who composed *tanka* reflecting their experiences and impressions in America.

For further reading: examples of Japanese American *tanka* can be found in Lucille M. Nixon, and Tomoe Tana, ed. and trans. *Sounds from the Unknown: A Collection of Japanese American Tanka.* Denver: A. Swallow, 1963; Gail M. Nomura. *"Tsugiki, A Grafting: A History of a Japanese Pioneer Woman in Washington State." Women's Studies* 14.1 (1987): 15–37; and Peter T. Suzuki. "Jinji (The Human Condition) in the Wartime Camp Poetry of the Japanese Americans." *Asian Profile* 15.5 (Oct. 1987): 407–15.

tanomoshi   Community-based rotating credit system prevalent among the ISSEI. In the world of the *issei,* credit was difficult to come by. As more and more *issei* began to look to a permanent future in America through the purchase of farm land or the setting up of a small business, credit became a necessity. Neither established American nor Japanese banks would lend money to Japanese immigrants. Though the immigrants established their own banks to try to get around this, the immigrant banks were undercapitalized and prone to failure. One way *issei* got access to the large sums of money needed to set up a farm or business was through the *tanomoshi.* Though there were many variations, the *tanomoshi* essentially worked as follows: a group of Japanese immigrants, often from the same PREFECTURE, would get together and contribute a sum of money to a pot on a periodic basis. The members would then take turns receiving the full pot of money after each period. The *tanomoshi* would continue until each member had his turn at the pot. For example, if the *tanomoshi* consisted of 10 members who each contributed $100 at a time, each member would receive $1,000 in turn. The order of recipients would be determined by lottery or by bidding on interest, with the person willing to pay the highest interest getting to go first. The relatively large sum of money that could be generated by a *tanomoshi* could then be used as the down payment on land or other types of major purchases. Of course the *tanomoshi* system only worked if the members who had already received their money continued to pay into the pot. In order for a *tanomoshi* to be formed, each member of the group had to trust that each other member would uphold his responsibilities. There is some disagreement among scholars about just how important *tanomoshi* were to the overall economic status of the *issei.*

For further reading, see Harry H. L. Kitano. *Japanese Americans: The Evolution of a Subculture.* 2nd edition. Englewood Cliffs, N.J.: Prentice-Hall, Inc., 1976; Ivan H. Light. *Ethnic Enterprise in America: Business and Welfare among Chinese, Japanese and Blacks.* Los Angeles: University of California Press, 1972; and Frank Miyamoto. *Social Solidarity among the Japanese in Seattle.* Seattle: University of Washington Press, 1984. For a discussion of Japanese immigrant banks, see Noritaka Yagasaki. "Ethnic Cooperativism and Immigrant Agriculture: A Study of Japanese Floriculture and Truck Farming in California." Diss., University of California, Berkeley, 1982.

Tenchoosetsu   A Japanese holiday celebrated on November 3 to commemorate the Meiji emperor's birthday on November 3, 1852. Before World War II Tenchoosetsu was celebrated by most Japanese Americans and was considered by the ISSEI to be a holiday of major importance. However, due to the Japanese attack on Pearl Harbor and anti-Japanese militarist sentiment, Tenchoosetsu was no longer observed by the *issei* after World War II and has generally been forgotten by present-day generations of Japanese Americans.

For further reading, see Dorothy Ochiai Hazama, and Jane Okamoto Komeiji. *Okage Sama De: The Japanese in Hawai'i.* Foreword by Daniel Inouye. Honolulu: Bess Press, 1986; *Kodansha Encyclopedia of Japan.* Tokyo: Kodansha, 1983; and Ronald Takaki. *Strangers from a Different Shore: A History of Asian Americans.* Boston: Little, Brown and Company, 1989.

STACEY HIROSE

Teragawachi, Usaku (1889–1964)   Usaku Teragawachi is known as one of Hawaii's best portrait photographers. His photographs provide a revealing look at the Hawaii Japanese community from World War I to the Great Depression. He was born in Yamaguchi PREFECTURE and arrived in Hawaii in 1906 as a contract laborer. After doing his time on the Big Island, he moved to Hilo where he worked as a photographer's apprentice. In 1913, he established his own shop, called the Art Photography Gallery, in Honolulu at 20 Hotel Street. He spent his career as a portrait photographer, but he also photographed such community events as funeral processions or religious ceremonies. He also hand-painted kimonos later in his career. In 1981, 4,000 of his glass negatives were discovered and donated to the Bishop Museum.

For further reading, see Ray Tsuchiyama. "Worlds Rediscovered." In Leonard Lueras, ed. *Kanyaku Imin: A Hundred Years of Japanese Life in Hawaii*. Honolulu: International Savings and Loan Association Ltd., 1985. 45–46.

Terminal Island Located in San Pedro Bay, about 25 miles south of downtown Los Angeles, Terminal Island is about 3½ miles long from east to west and ¾ mile wide. From about the turn of the century, ISSEI fisherman began to settle on the island. Fish canneries and a burgeoning Japanese American community developed shortly thereafter. Known as East San Pedro or Fish Harbor, the Japanese American community on Terminal Island occupied the southeastern portion of the island and was distinct from the mostly white community of Terminal, which occupied the central part of the island. The residents of East San Pedro were almost entirely Japanese, with about two-thirds of them coming from Wakayama PREFECTURE.

Fishing was the economic heart of the community, with nearly all men either working on fishing boats or operating businesses that supported the fish industry workers and nearly all women working in one of the fish canneries in the area. Nearly all lived in company-owned housing. East San Pedro included institutions found in most similarly sized Japanese American communities— Buddhist and Christian churches, a Japanese school, a community center, a baseball team, a Japanese Association, an active Wakayama KENJINKAI, an occupational cooperative (in this case the Japanese Fisherman's Union or Nihonjin Gyogyo Kumiai), a school (Walizer Elementary School was 98 percent Japanese American), etc. At its peak, there were nearly 3,000 Japanese Americans here. Because of the homogeneity of the population and the physical barrier separating it from the mainland, the people of Terminal Island maintained a particularly strong sense of identity.

Within three months of the Pearl Harbor attack, the Japanese American community of Terminal Island was no more. Because of its supposed "strategic" location, military authorities targeted Japanese Americans on Terminal Island. On February 9, all ISSEI with commercial fishing licenses were rounded up and taken to INTERNMENT CAMPS administered by the Justice Department. Then, on February 26, all Japanese Americans on Ter-

minal Island were notified that they would have to leave within 48 hours. The shocked citizenry was housed in churches and community centers on the mainland until moved to the "ASSEMBLY CENTERS" and WAR RELOCATION AUTHORITY camps with the other West Coast Japanese Americans in the months to come. Terminal Island was the first Japanese American community to be removed en masse.

Whereas many other Japanese American communities were able to return and rebuild after the war, such was not possible for the Terminal Islanders. In addition to having no homes to return to and having lost their boats and equipment, *issei* also faced a 1944 law banning them from regaining commercial fishing licenses. Some did return to the general vicinity, while a large number settled in the Japanese American agricultural colony at SEABROOK FARMS, New Jersey; most just dispersed, blending into the general Japanese American population.

Though nearly nothing remains of the East San Pedro community today, Terminal Island lives on in the memory of those who once lived there. A 1970 reunion of former Islanders drew nearly 1,000 people—this from a community that had fewer than 3,000 people some 30 years earlier. Such reunions and other social events continue to this day and serve to continue the tradition and memory of Terminal Island even if it doesn't exist physically.

For further reading, see Kanichi Kawasaki. "The Japanese Community of East San Pedro, Terminal Island, California." Thesis, University of Southern California, 1931 and Kanshi Stanley Yamashita. "Terminal Island: Ethnography of an Ethnic Community: Its Dissolution and Reorganization to a Non-Spatial Community." Diss., University of California, Irvine, 1985. See also Yamashita's "Terminal Island: An Island in Time." *Rafu Shimpo* 14 Dec. 1991: B4+. For another view of the community focusing on the harsh World War II removal, see Jeanne Wakatsuki Houston, and James D. Houston. *Farewell to Manzanar*. Boston: Houghton Mifflin Co., 1973.

Terrace v. Thompson Case brought before the U.S. Supreme Court in 1923 involving a challenge to the ban on leasing imposed by the Alien Land Law of the state of Washington. Terrace, a U.S. citizen and resident of the state of Washington, wished to lease some agricultural land he owned to Nakatsuka, a farmer who was born in Japan. The Alien Land Law of Washington forbade the leasing of land "by aliens other than those who in good faith have declared their intention to become citizens of the United States." Terrace contended that the Washington Alien Land Law was unconstitutional, but the U.S. Supreme Court upheld its validity on November 12, 1923. The Court also upheld the validity of the California Alien Land Law on the same day in its decision on PORTERFIELD V. WEBB. In both cases the Court noted that the states had the authority to regulate who owned, occupied and used farm land located within them, and that the TREATY OF COMMERCE AND NAVIGATION OF 1911 BETWEEN THE U.S. AND JAPAN did not confer the right to own or lease land for agricultural purposes to Japanese aliens in the United States. For further reading, see Frank F. Chuman. *The Bamboo People: The Law and Japanese-Americans.* Del Mar, Calif.: Publisher's Inc., 1976 and Moritoshi Fukuda. *Legal Problems of Japanese Americans.* Tokyo: Keio Tsushin, 1980. The transcript of the case can be found in Consulate-General of Japan. *Documental History of Law Cases Affecting Japanese in the United States, 1916–1924. 2 Vols.* New York: Arno Press, 1978. 1–110.

DENNIS YAMAMOTO

Third Street (Produce) Market Los Angeles wholesale produce market. The first public market in Los Angeles was begun in about 1890 and was originally located near Ninth and Los Angeles streets. When this market moved to Third and Central, it became known as the Third Street Market. With the growth of Southern California agriculture, specifically the Japanese component, the Third Street market gradually became too small to accommodate the many Japanese farmers. Scarcity of space and unfair rents led a group of Japanese farmers to start a new market; this would become known as the NINTH STREET MARKET when it opened in 1909. As a result, the Third Street Market lost many of its tenants. Some of its remaining Japanese merchants as well as some who returned from the new market organized the Nikka Nogyo Kumiai (Nippon-California Farmers Association) in October 1909 to try to bolster its strength. A dispute over penalties imposed for moving from one to the other led to strained relations between tenants of the two markets. The RAFU SHIMPO tended to support the Third Street Market while other papers favored the Ninth Street Market. By 1910, the feud had been resolved and cooperation between the two markets began, lasting until the war.

For further reading, see Noritaka Yagasaki. "Ethnic Cooperativism and Immigrant Agriculture: A Study of Japanese Floriculture and Truck Farming in California." Diss., University of California, Berkeley, 1982.

thousand cranes An offering symbolizing long life and health made at Japanese American ceremonies such as weddings. A symbol of longevity in Japanese culture, the crane is one of the easiest to make and most popular shapes in origami, or Japanese paper folding. In Japan, a thousand cranes (*sembazuru* in Japanese) are folded and strung as an offering to make a wish come true, or as a "get well" token to one who is sick. Perhaps the most famous example of the latter is the case of a little girl injured in the atomic bomb blast at Hiroshima who began to fold a thousand cranes, but died before reaching

her goal. In her honor, schoolchildren and other visitors bring *sembazuru* to Hiroshima's Peace Park to this day.

In a Japanese American context, the thousand cranes are more often found at weddings, something one rarely sees in Japan. In addition to symbolizing long life, the act of making the cranes is significant as well. If made entirely by the bride, they are said to be symbolic of patience. If made by a group of close friends and relatives, the making of the cranes signifies the group's friendship and willingness to work hard for the bride. Recent trends have been towards the aesthetic arrangement and framing of the cranes to facilitate display after the wedding.

For further reading, see Araki/Horii 84 for instructions on how to fold origami cranes and Patsy Y. Nakayama. "Culture and Tradition." *Hawaii Herald,* 18 May 1990: 90–98 for the significance of the thousand cranes in a Japanese American context.

Title II See EMERGENCY DETENTION ACT OF 1950.

Togasaki, George Kiyoshi JAPANESE AMERICAN CITIZENS LEAGUE (JACL) pioneer, Japanese educator and journalist. George Togasaki was born in San Francisco in 1895. He was the son of Kikumatsu and Shige (Kushida) Togasaki. As a child, George went with his parents and siblings to greet shiploads of immigrants and to assist them with their adjustment to life in America. In 1906, Togasaki was one of 93 Japanese American students affected by the discriminatory policies of the San Francisco Board of Education when it set up segregated schools (see SAN FRANCISCO SCHOOL BOARD SEGREGATION ORDER OF 1906). During World War I, he served in Europe with the U.S. Army. Upon his return, Togasaki was one of a small group of NISEI in San Francisco who formed the American Loyalty League in 1918, a precursor of the JACL. Subsequently, Togasaki moved to Tokyo where he became president of the *Japan Times,* an English-language publication. In addition, he was the first chairman of the board of Japan's International Christian University and president of the 600,000-member Rotary International in 1968–69.

For further reading, see Bill Hosokawa. *Nisei: The Quiet Americans.* New York: William Morrow and Company, Inc., 1969.

Tokyo Club As was true of many if not most immigrant communities, organized crime played a major role in the early Japanese American community. In the 1920s and '30s, the Tokyo Club was an important and generally little known part of the Japanese American community. Before 1920, it had been a loose network of gambling clubs. But in the '20s, it matured into a gambling syndicate with links in most major cities in the western United States, headquartered in Los Angeles. Although kidnapping, extortion and murder accompanied its gambling, booze and prostitution enterprises, the club also served the community by providing for the needy, loaning money to businessmen and farmers, and supporting cultural activities and scholarship funds. During the depths of the depression in the '30s, the club fed 60 to 80 people a day. For these reasons, the Tokyo Club had at least the tacit approval of the community, which also saw the club as an alternative to the Chinese gambling establishments in nearby Chinatown. In its heyday in the late '20s and early '30s, the Tokyo Club made over $1 million per year and had local police and civic officials in its pockets. Largely an organization run for and by ISSEI, the Tokyo Club began to decline by the late '30s due to internal conflicts and the changing demographics of the community. Additionally, the election of a reform mayor in Los Angeles in 1938 also hurt the club badly. By the eve of World War II, it was on its last legs, though the internment of Japanese Americans during the war may have prolonged its influence due to an atmosphere in the camps conducive to gambling.

For further reading, see Isami Arifuku Waugh. "Hidden Crime and Deviance in the Japanese-American Community, 1920–1946." Diss., University of California, Berkeley, 1978. See also Kats Kunitsugu. "Yamato Hall in Little Tokyo Had Colorful History." *Pacific Citizen* 11 Oct. 1968: 6 and Larry Tajiri. "Little Tokyo's Underworld." *Pacific Citizen* 10 Sept. 1949: 4.

Tolan Committee Congressional committee formed in the early days of World War II to "investigate" the possibility of removing Japanese Americans and others from strategic areas. Led by Congressman John H. Tolan (D-Oakland) of California, the Tolan Committee—officially the House Select Committee Investigating National Defense Migration—held hearings from February 21 to March 7, 1942, in San Francisco, Los Angeles, Portland and Seattle to address questions of forced migration. The committee has been called "a sham" by contemporary observers MICHI WEGLYN and BILL HOSOKAWA because the decision to forcibly remove all Japanese Americans from the West Coast had already been made in Washington, D.C., before the hearings actually began.

The witnesses at the hearings were mostly antagonistic towards Japanese Americans. Setting the early tone was the testimony of California attorney general and soon-to-be gubernatorial candidate EARL WARREN, who presented a mass of data illustrating Japanese American land use patterns. He claimed that the supposed clustering of ISSEI property around military installations was ominous and beyond coincidence. Warren also repeated the often-heard line that it was impossible to determine the "loyalty" of Japanese Americans. Perhaps more troubling for

Japanese Americans was a letter from Secretary of the Navy Frank Knox that repeated his wild, fabricated stories of Japanese American fifth-column activity in the Pearl Harbor attack (see Chronology for Knox's immediate post–Pearl Harbor remarks). Despite the falsity of his claims, pro-Japanese American witnesses had no basis at the time on which to refute them and could only argue that mainland Japanese Americans were different from those in Hawaii. Representatives of such groups as the California Joint Immigration Committee repeated the usual litany of anti-Japanese charges. By contrast, the first witness called to speak on the question of removing Italian Americans was San Francisco mayor Rossi; much of the discussion centered on the DiMaggios of baseball fame and their undisputed Americanism.

Witnesses who spoke for Japanese Americans included a few academicians, religious figures and labor leaders, as well as Japanese Americans themselves. JAPANESE AMERICAN CITIZENS LEAGUE (JACL) leaders looked upon the hearings as a last chance to forestall mass removal and took the hearings very seriously. MIKE MASAOKA, JAMES SAKAMOTO and other JACL leaders testified before the committee, citing the Americanism of the NISEI and arguing against mass removal of Japanese Americans, but pledging to cooperate with the government if such were to happen. The only Japanese Americans to actively oppose mass removal in the hearings were journalists JAMES OMURA and Caryl Omura.

As expected, the Tolan Committee took no steps to forestall the mass removal of Japanese Americans that was already under way. The Committee believed the wild stories of Knox and endorsed the need for EXECUTIVE ORDER 9066 as proposed by the president. The committee did express some concern for the soon-to-be forcibly removed, reporting on scams to scare Japanese Americans into selling their property for rock bottom prices and recommending the appointment of an Alien Property Custodian to prevent such practices. It also did not advocate mass incarceration, but hearings at the "ASSEMBLY CENTERS" and a program of resettlement with job placement inland for the "loyal." On the mass removal of Germans and Italians, the committee concluded that "any such proposal is out of the question if we intend to win this war."

For further reading, see Commission on Wartime Relocation and Internment of Civilians. *Personal Justice Denied: Report of the Commission on Wartime Relocation and Internment of Civilians.* Washington, D.C.: Government Printing Office, 1982; Roger Daniels. *Asian America: Chinese and Japanese in the United States since 1850.* Seattle: University of Washington Press, 1988; Mike Masaoka, and Bill Hosokawa. *They Call Me Moses Masaoka.* New York: William Morrow, 1987; and Michi Weglyn. *Years of Infamy: The Untold Story of America's Concentration Camps.* New York: William Morrow & Co., 1976. The transcript of the hearings has been republished in part by Arno Press: U.S. House of Representatives, Select Committee Investigating National Defense Migration. *National Defense Migration: Hearings.* 1942. New York: Arno Press, 1978.

["Sham" quotes are from Weglyn, p. 284 and Masaoka/Hosokawa, p. 84; Germans and Italians quote cited in *Personal*, p. 287.]

Toledo Incident   In the 1920s, several incidents involving the eviction of Japanese workers from small towns occurred. One of these took place in Toledo, a small town on the central Oregon coast.

During World War I, construction of a spruce mill was begun in Toledo by the U.S. Army Spruce Division. The war ended before the mill could be completed, however, and the mill was eventually purchased and completed in 1920 by C. D. Johnson, who started the Pacific Spruce Company. By 1923, the mill employed 800 men and was by far the largest employer in the town.

In 1925, Johnson decided he wanted to bring in a few ISSEI laborers to work on the "green chain," a particularly difficult job disdained by white workers that involved the sorting of lumber as it left the mill on a revolving chain. On May 1, 1925, the company held a meeting with local community members explaining that only a few Japanese workers would be brought in, that they would only work the "green chain," and that no white workers would lose jobs because of it. Unconvinced, townspeople at this meeting passed a resolution vowing to protest the importation of foreign labor into the community. Later, on June 30, the Lincoln County Protective League was formed to "use all honorable means to protect our communities from the employment of Japanese or other Oriental labor." Despite these sentiments, Johnson and the company pressured town businesspeople to rescind the earlier resolution against foreign labor and went ahead and made arrangements to bring in the *issei* through a LABOR CONTRACTOR.

On July 10, 25 *issei* arrived in town and a total of about 35 were in place by the next day. Tension mounted in the town. On Sunday, July 12, 300 to 500 people gathered by the mill to hear speeches by agitators and to confront mill officials. Before long, the mob had dispatched the mill officials and deputies and made their way to the *issei's* quarters where the workers were forcibly removed, in some cases beaten, and loaded onto trucks specially hired for the occasion. The *issei* workers were sent back to Portland, never to return to Toledo.

Because no property was damaged and nobody was seriously injured—and because the agitators no doubt had the support of most people in the community—no criminal charges were filed. However, pressure from the

Japanese government on Washington, D.C., officials led to a grand jury investigation of the incident. Not surprisingly, the grand jury failed to indict the Toledo agitators in January 1926.

However, this was not the end of the affair. With the help of the JAPANESE ASSOCIATION of Oregon, civil suits demanding $25,000 each in damages were filed on behalf of five of the removed mill workers. In July of 1926, a Portland judge awarded one of the plaintiffs $2,500 in damages; the other cases were soon settled out of court. In the end, both sides had more or less gotten what they wanted—the removed workers had won at least token compensation, while the town of Toledo remained free of the "YELLOW PERIL." Eventually, Mennonite workers were brought in from outside the community to work the "green chain." No objections were raised. (See also SALT RIVER VALLEY INCIDENT and TURLOCK INCIDENT for instances of similar removals.)

For further reading, see Stefan Tanaka. "The Toledo Incident: The Deportation of the Nikkei from an Oregon Mill Town." *Pacific Northwest Quarterly* 69.3 (July 1978): 116–26. For more on Japanese Americans in Oregon before World War II, see Marvin G. Pursinger. "The Japanese Settle in Oregon: 1880–1920." *Journal of the West* 5.2 (Apr. 1966): 251–63; Marjorie R. Stearns. *The History of the Japanese People in Oregon.* San Francisco: R & E Research Associates, 1974 (a reprint of a 1937 Master's thesis); and Barbara Yasui. "The Nikkei in Oregon, 1834–1940." *Oregon Historical Quarterly* 76.3 (Sept. 1975): 225–57.

Tomita, Teiko (1896–1990)   Poet. Teiko Tomita, a pioneer Japanese women in the Pacific Northwest, is known for the TANKA poems she composed about her life in the United States.

An ISSEI, Tomita was born on December 1, 1896, in Osaka PREFECTURE, Japan. The second of nine children born to the Matsui family, Tomita began writing *tanka* poems when she was a student at a girls' high school in Japan. One of her teachers there gave her the pen name of Yukari, which she also used in America. Similar to HAIKU, *tanka* poems are short traditional Japanese poems that consist of 31 syllables arranged in five lines of five, seven, five, seven and seven syllables successively. The form is used to convey aspects of life, love and deep emotions.

After high school, Tomita took a one-and-a-half-year course at a normal school in Japan, where she earned a certificate to teach at the elementary school level. She was a teacher until her marriage to Masakazu Tomita in late 1920. An *issei* farming near Wapato, Washington, Masakazu Tomita had corresponded with his wife-to-be for two years prior to meeting and marrying her in Japan. The newlyweds traveled in Japan until February 1921, when they left for Wapato to farm on the Yakima Indian Reservation. Tomita thought that they would live

Teiko Tomita. *Kay Hashimoto Collection, Japanese American National Museum Photographic & Moving Image Archive*

only a few years in the U.S.; however, she was never able to return to see her parents again.

As a result of anti-Japanese sentiment and ALIEN LAND LAWS, Tomita and her husband lost the right to lease their farm on the reservation shortly after their arrival in the U.S. Tomita's husband then found work as a foreman at a nursery in Satus. There she worked as a cook for the laborers working under her husband. In 1929, the couple moved to Sunnydale, near Seattle, where the Seattle-Tacoma International Airport now stands, and started their own nursery. Being closer to Seattle enabled Tomita to meet more Japanese Americans and to resume her poetry writing. In 1939, she joined a Seattle *tanka* club and although she was not able to attend its monthly meetings, she submitted poems for criticism. Some were eventually published in Japan. After the bombing of Pearl Harbor, Tomita had to burn all of her poetry

manuscripts for fear that the U.S. military would find them and assume that she had some sort of dubious connection with Japan. In 1942, the Tomitas were interned in TULE LAKE "RELOCATION CENTER," California. A year later, they were moved to HEART MOUNTAIN, Wyoming, where Tomita kept journals and resumed writing poetry. In 1945, the Tomitas lived in Minnesota after securing a work release from camp. They then moved back to Seattle, where Tomita took the only paying job available, as a garment worker. She continued to write and her poetry was published in an *issei* poetry anthology entitled *Renia no yuki* (Snow of Rainier). The Tomitas lived in Sunnydale until 1967, when the Sea-Tac airport expanded, thereby forcing them to relocate to Seattle, where their daughter's family lived.

Tomita wrote *tanka* poems that described the experiences of a pioneer Japanese woman in Washington State. She described her feelings of separation from her family and later, the effects that the war had on her and her coworkers. Reading like diary entries, her poetry is a portrait of the history of *issei* in America.

For further reading, see Gail M. Nomura. "Tsugiki, a Grafting: A History of a Japanese Pioneer Woman in Washington State." *Women's Studies* 14.1 (1987): 15–37 and Mihara Senryu, et al., *Renia no yuki* (Snow of Rainier). Kamakura, Japan: Choonsha, 1956. Tomita's more recent poetry (1983) also appeared monthly in *Hokubei Hochi*, a Seattle newspaper.

EMILY LAWSIN

Topaz Topaz was the site of one of 10 CONCENTRATION CAMPS that housed Japanese Americans forcibly removed from the West Coast states during World War II. Some basic data on Topaz is presented below in tabular form:

Official name: Central Utah Relocation Center

Location: Millard County, Utah, near Abraham, 140 miles south of Salt Lake City

Land: Mix of public domain land, land which had reverted to the county for non-payment of taxes and land purchased from private parties

Size: 19,800 acres

Climate: Temperatures ranged from 106 degrees in summer to −30 degrees in winter; located at an elevation of 4,600 feet, the region was subject to a constant wind that resulted in frequent dust storms

Origin of camp population: Mostly from Alameda (3,679), San Francisco (3,370), and San Mateo (722) Counties

Via "assembly centers": Nearly all (7,676) came from Tanforan "Assembly Center"

Rural/Urban: Overwhelmingly urban

Peak population: 8,130

Date of peak: March 17, 1943

Opening date: September 11, 1942

Closing date: October 31, 1945

Project director(s): Charles F. Ernst (9/42 to 6/44) and Luther T. Hoffman (6/44 to 10/45)

Community analysts: Oscar F. Hoffman and Weston LaBarre

JERS fieldworkers: Doris Hayashi and Frederick Hoshiyama

Newspaper: *Topaz Times* (September 17, 1942–August 31, 1945)

Percent who answered question 28 of the loyalty questionnaire positively: 89.4

Number and percentage of eligible male citizens inducted directly into armed forces: 472 (7.3 percent)

Miscellaneous characteristics: Topaz featured an organized protest against the registration questionnaire, in which a petition was circulated demanding the restoration of rights as a prerequisite for registration. ISSEI chef JAMES HATSUKI WAKASA was shot to death by a guard on April 11, 1943. The literary and arts magazine *Trek* was produced here.

(For the key to the categories, see the entry for GILA RIVER.)

The literature on the Japanese American World War II experience is extensive; see the bibliography and the bibliographic entries after the various entries pertaining to this experience for titles of general interest. For a general history of Topaz, see Leonard J. Arrington. "The Price of Prejudice: The Japanese-American Relocation Center in Utah during World War II." In Daniels, Roger, ed. *Three Short Works on Japanese Americans.* New York: Arno Press, 1978. 46 pages. First-person autobiographical accounts of life in Topaz include Toyo Suyemoto Kawakami. "Camp Memories: Rough and Broken Shards." In Roger Daniels, Sandra C. Taylor, and Harry H. L. Kitano, eds. *Japanese Americans: From Relocation to Redress.* Revised Edition. Seattle: University of Washington Press, 1991. 27–30; Eleanor Gerard Sekerak. "A Teacher at Topaz." In Roger Daniels, Sandra C. Taylor, and Harry H. L. Kitano, eds. *Japanese Americans: From Relocation to Redress.* Salt Lake City: University of Utah Press, 1986. Revised edition. Seattle, University of Washington Press, 1991. 38–43; Yoshiko Uchida. "Topaz, City of Dust." *Utah Historical Quarterly* 48.3 (Summer 1980): 234–43; and *Desert Exile: The Uprooting of a Japanese American Family.* Seattle: University of Washington Press, 1982. Mine Okubo. *Citizen 13660.* New York: Columbia University Press, 1946. New York: Arno Press, 1978. Seattle: University of Washington Press, 1983 is a book of drawings and captions recounting the author's experiences at Tanforan "Assembly Center" and Topaz. Yoshiko Uchida. *Picture Bride.* Flagstaff, Ariz.: Northland Press, 1987 is a novel centering on an *issei* woman which concludes in Topaz.

Toyama Kyuzo (1868–1910) Kyuzo Toyama is regarded by many as the "Father of OKINAWAN overseas emigration." He was originally a schoolteacher and principal in Kin Village in Okinawa, but resigned his job in protest against the corrupt regime of Governor Shigeru Narahara. He joined the Okinawa People's Rights movement led by Noboru Jahana. When this movement was crushed by the government, he devised a plan to send peasants overseas. He learned of immigration programs to Hawaii while studying in Tokyo in 1896–98. After many attempts to gain permission for such a venture were blocked by Narahara, he finally secured permission. He soon began to recruit Okinawans to go to Hawaii and in 1899, led 30 men (aged 21 to 35) as the first contract laborers from Okinawa to Hawaii. They left Naha on December 5, 1899, arriving in Hawaii on January 3, 1900. This group experienced rough conditions in Hawaii, facing not only hard work and violent overseers, but also discrimination from the many non-Okinawan (known as NAICHI) Japanese already in Hawaii. Many blamed their unhappiness on Toyama and vowed to kill him. However, when the members of this group began to trickle back to Okinawa with enough money to buy good land and build houses with tile roofs, many others sought to immigrate to Hawaii. Toyama led a second group of 40 to Hawaii on April 6, 1903. By 1907, 8,500 Okinawans were in Hawaii, comprising about 20 percent of the total Japanese population there.

For further reading, see Y. Scott Matsumoto. "Okinawan Migrants to Hawaii." *Hawaiian Journal of History* 16 (1982): 125–33 and Mitsugu Sakihara. "Okinawans in Hawaii: An Overview of the Past 80 Years." In Ethnic Studies Oral History Project/United Okinawan Association of Hawaii. *Uchinanchu: A History of Okinawans in Hawaii.* Honolulu: Ethnic Studies Program, University of Hawaii at Manoa, 1981. 105–23.

Toyama Tetsuo Journalist, OKINAWAN Hawaiian community leader. Tetsuo Toyama founded and published a monthly periodical titled *Jitsugyo no Hawaii* (Commercial Hawaii) in August 1912 that became one of the leading publications of the Okinawan Hawaiian population.

According to Ryoin Toyohira, he was one of the three leading lights of Japanese American journalists in Hawaii, the others being YASUTARO SOGA and KINZABURO MAKINO. On the other hand, Seiyei Wakukawa wrote that "(e)very issue of his magazine was filled with personal attacks and repulsive flattery without fail." At any rate, *Jitsugyo no Hawaii* continued to do well even after the NAKAIMA INCIDENT in which he played a key part. After the war, it was renamed the *Shimin* (Citizen) and continued publication until 1970. Toyama received the Fifth Order of the Sacred Treasure from the Japanese government on June 14, 1968, the same day as his ideological rival Reverend SEIKAN HIGA received the same award.

For further reading, see Seiyei Wakukawa. "A Brief History of Thought Activities of Okinawans in Hawaii." In Ethnic Studies Oral History Project/United Okinawan Association of Hawaii. *Uchinanchu: A History of Okinawans in Hawaii*. Honolulu: Ethnic Studies Program, University of Hawaii at Manoa, 1981. 233–42. Tetsuo Toyama. *Eighty Years in Hawaii*. Tokyo: Tosho Printing Co., 1971 is Toyama's autobiography; its text is partially in English and partially in Japanese.

Toyota v. United States Case brought before the U.S. Supreme Court in 1925 involving the naturalization of an ISSEI veteran of the U.S. armed forces. Hidemitsu Toyota served in the U.S. Coast Guard from 1913 to 1923, saw action in World War I and received an honorable discharge. He was granted citizenship by a lower court on the basis of a federal law enacted in 1918 that allowed any alien who served in the U.S. armed forces during World War I to become naturalized. A circuit court canceled Toyota's certificate of citizenship, and when Toyota appealed to the U.S. Supreme Court, the Court affirmed the cancellation on May 25, 1925. The Court held that the categories of aliens eligible for naturalization based on distinctions of color and race should not be enlarged, and that radical changes to naturalization policies should not be made. Specifically, the Court noted that recent laws granting naturalization to alien veterans of World War I were intended to benefit Filipinos rather than Japanese.

For further reading, see Frank F. Chuman. *The Bamboo People: The Law and Japanese-Americans*. Del Mar, Calif.: Publisher's Inc., 1976; Jeff H. Lesser. "Always 'Outsiders': Asians, Naturalization, and the Supreme Court." *Amerasia Journal* 12.1 (Spring-Summer 1985–1986): 83–100; and Harry Maxwell Naka. "The Naturalization of Japanese War Veterans of the World War Forces." Thesis, University of California, Berkeley, 1939. DENNIS YAMAMOTO

Toyota, Tricia Newscaster Tricia Toyota is one of several well-known Asian American female anchors in West Coast and Hawaiian cities. She holds a bachelor's degree in communications and home economics from Oregon State University and a master's degree in journalism, with an emphasis in electronic journalism, from the University of California, Los Angeles. Her professional career began in 1970, when she worked at KNX Newsradio as a copyperson before moving to action reporter as well as writer and producer. In 1972 Toyota became a weekend anchor for KNBC-TV, Los Angeles, where she headed the station's coverage of special events and hosted the public affairs series "Sunday" and "News Conference 4 L.A." Since joining KCBS-TV in 1985, she has been the anchor of Action News at Noon and Action News at Six. Toyota cofounded the Asian American Journalists Association and has received many awards, including the Los Angeles Human Relations Commission Achievement Award, the Greater Los Angeles YWCA "Communicator of the Year" award and the Los Angeles City Asian American Association "Person of the Year" award. ALICE HOM

Treaty of Commerce and Navigation of 1894 Between Japan and the United States This treaty provided that the citizens of both countries would have full liberty to enter, travel or reside in any part of the territory of the other and enjoy protection for their property and persons. Both nations also conferred most favored nation status on one another. Only the right of the states to maintain police power for reasons of security limited the rights guaranteed to resident Japanese to travel and reside in the United States. The treaty also contained a provision that specifically allowed the U.S. to exclude Japanese immigrants. It was signed on November 22, 1894, and proclaimed on March 21, 1895, but did not go into effect until July 17, 1899.

For further reading, see Frank F. Chuman. *The Bamboo People: The Law and Japanese-Americans*. Del Mar, Calif.: Publisher's Inc., 1976 and Moritoshi Fukuda. *Legal Problems of Japanese Americans*. Tokyo: Keio Tsushin, 1980. DENNIS YAMAMOTO

Treaty of Commerce and Navigation of 1911 Between Japan and the United States Diplomatic agreement solidifying relations between Japan and the United States. By the 1911 treaty, the two nations agreed on reciprocal relations while reaching a compromise on the volatile issue of Japanese immigration. The compromise, which essentially formalized the restriction of immigration provisions of the GENTLEMEN'S AGREEMENT, served to ensure the treaty's ratification by placating anti-Japanese interests in the West. On the other hand, a passage in the 1894 treaty that Japan found offensive—it denied equal protection to subjects of one country in the other—was removed and the rights of Japanese subjects in the U.S. were guaranteed. The Taft administration also used the awarding of the 1915 Panama-Pacific Exposition to San Francisco (over New Orleans) as a bargaining chip to secure California's approval. The ratification of the treaty marked the last time the federal government would be able to appease ANTI-JAPANESE MOVEMENT forces while maintaining good relations with Japan. The treaty was signed on February 21, 1911, and was in force from July 17, 1911, to January 26, 1940.

For further reading, see Frank F. Chuman. *The Bamboo People: The Law and Japanese-Americans*. Del Mar, Calif.: Publisher's Inc., 1976; Moritoshi Fukuda. *Legal Problems of Japanese Americans*. Tokyo: Keio Tsushin, 1980; and Teruko Okada Kachi. *The Treaty of 1911 and the Immigration and Alien Land Law*

Strawberry farming, Watsonville, California. *Hiroshi Shikuma Collection, Japanese American National Museum Photographic & Moving Image Archive*

Issue Between the United States and Japan 1911–1913. New York: Arno Press, 1978. A copy of the text of the treaty can be found in Consulate-General of Japan. *Documental History of Law Cases Affecting Japanese in the United States, 1916–1924. 2 Vols.* New York: Arno Press, 1978. 396–401.

truck farming Due to technological advances in transportation and cold storage in the late 19th and early 20th centuries, a transformation in farming occurred. Where once farmers grew vegetables on a small scale for local consumption (utilizing greenhouses in cold weather areas), they could now grow them on a large scale for distribution and sale in distant places. Among the most popular truck farming crops are tomatoes, lettuce, celery, cantaloupes and onions.

Japanese American farmers in the western states were among those who were best able to benefit from the truck farming revolution. For ISSEI farmers looking to rise from the ranks of migrant labor to SHARE TENANCY, CASH LEASING and land ownership, truck crops presented a viable option. They could be intensively grown on relatively small parcels of land for a good profit. With the advent of the ALIEN LAND LAWS in 1920s, more *issei* turned to truck crops, which lent themselves to being grown on leased land which might have to be vacated quickly and which required relatively small initial capital outlays. Also, with skill and hard work, these crops could be grown on the less desirable land that the *issei* were often limited to. *Issei* farmers formed cooperative organizations to aid in the growing of truck crops while other *issei* dedicated themselves to building produce markets or retailing these crops. The combination of Japanese American cooperativism, the rise in demand for fresh vegetables, and the racism of the land laws and general anti-Japanese sentiment led to truck farming's becoming an economic mainstay of the Japanese American community. On the eve of World War II, *issei* and NISEI farmers grew truck crops that accounted for 30 to 35 percent of the total dollar value of such crops grown in California and raised 90 percent of all snap beans, spring and summer celery, peppers and strawberries. The prosperity of the Japanese American truck farmers trickled down to the rest of the Japanese American community, providing livelihoods to those who marketed and retailed the produce and to those who ran businesses in the J-Towns that served the needs of the farmers.

For further reading, see Masakazu Iwata. "The Japanese Immigrants in California Agriculture." *Agricultural History* 36.1 (Jan. 1962): 25–37 for an overview of *issei* truck farming. See Noritaka Yagasaki. "Ethnic Cooperativism and Immigrant Agriculture: A Study of Japanese Floriculture and Truck Farming in California." Diss., University of California, Berkeley, 1982 for a discussion of cooperative produce marketing by the *issei*. See also Timothy J. Lukes and Gary Y. Okihiro. *Japanese Legacy: Farming and Community Life in California's Santa Clara Valley*. Cupertino, Calif.: California History Center, 1985; John Modell. *The Economics and Politics of Racial Accommodation: The Japanese of Los Angeles 1900–1942*. Chicago: University of Illinois Press, 1977 and John Adrian Rademaker. "The Ecological Position of the Japanese Farmers in the State of Washington." Diss., University of Washington, 1939 for discussions of truck farming in specific regions.

Tsukiyama, Wilfred Chomatsu (1897–1966)

Lawyer, judge. Best known as the first chief justice of Hawaii's State Supreme Court, Wilfred Tsukiyama was also one of the first Japanese American lawyers in Hawaii. He graduated from McKinley High School in 1918 and, after serving in World War I, attended Coe College in Cedar Rapids, Iowa, until 1921. He received a bachelor of law degree from the University of Chicago Law School and became an active Republican in 1924. In 1929, he was appointed to the post of deputy attorney for the city and county of Honolulu. He became the city and county attorney in 1933. With the coming of hostilities between Japan and the U.S., Tsukiyama stepped down from his post voluntarily to take up private practice. After the war, he was rewarded for his humble stance by being elected to the Hawaii legislature and serving from 1946–59; he was president of the senate for the last six years. He was appointed chief justice two months after statehood in 1959. He has also held many civic posts.

For further reading, see Lawrence H. Fuchs. *Hawaii Pono: A Social History*. New York: Harcourt, Brace and World, 1961 and "Tsukiyama Story." *Rafu Shimpo* 20 Dec. 1963.

Tsutakawa, George (1910–)

George Tsutakawa has enjoyed a long and successful career as an artist and teacher in Seattle. Though known as one of the world's leading designers of water fountains, he has produced prints, oils and watercolors, sculpted in metal and wood, designed furniture, worked in *sumi-e* (ink painting), and designed bronze masks.

Tsutakawa was born in Seattle in 1910, but educated in Japan from 1917–27, making him a KIBEI. Upon returning to the United States, he graduated high school in Seattle and attended the University of Washington School of Art. He was an important member of the Seattle art scene of the 1930s, associating with many other local artists of the time and painting and exhibiting regularly. At the same time, he managed the family produce business until his induction into the army in early 1942. He eventually became an instructor at the MILITARY INTELLIGENCE SERVICE LANGUAGE SCHOOL. In 1946, he returned to Seattle and began a 30-year association with the University of Washington. He be-

came a full time instructor in art there in 1947, received his M.F.A. in sculpture in 1950 and became a full professor in 1955. In 1956, he returned to Japan for the first time since 1927 and discovered the stacked rock structures of the Himalayas known as *obos;* both the trip and the *obos* were to have a profound impact on his future art. His first public water fountain, "Fountain of Wisdom" was erected in 1960 at the Seattle Public Library. Since then, he has designed and executed 60 water fountains around the world. He retired in 1976, devoting himself to travel and art. In 1990, a retrospective exhibition of 60 years of his art was held at the Bellevue (Washington) Art Museum.

For further reading, see Martha Kingsbury. *George Tsutakawa*. Introd. Sumio Kuwabara. Seattle: University of Washington Press, 1990, a profusely illustrated catalog of the 1990 retrospective exhibit. See also Gervais Reed. "George Tsutakawa, An Introduction." *Journal of Ethnic Studies* 4.1 (Spring 1976): 1–3; "George Tsutakawa, A Conversation on Life and Fountains." *Journal of Ethnic Studies* 4.1 (Spring 1976): 4–36; and "Meet One of the World's Best Water Sculptors." *Rafu Shimpo* 21 Dec. 1968: II-9.

Tule Lake "Relocation Center"

Tule Lake was the site of one of 10 CONCENTRATION CAMPS that housed Japanese Americans forcibly removed from the West Coast states during World War II. When the "loyal" and "disloyal" were separated in 1943, Tule Lake was chosen as the "segregation center" for the "disloyal" (see TULE LAKE "SEGREGATION CENTER" below). Some basic data on Tule Lake is presented below in tabular form:

Official name: Tule Lake Relocation Center

Location: Klamath Falls Basin in Northern California, just south of the Oregon border. The closest town was Newell, California. Tule Lake is located just across the road from Lava Beds National Monument and the site of the Modoc War of 1872–73

Land: Federal reclamation project land

Size: 26,000 acres

Climate: Relatively mild, for a WAR RELOCATION AUTHORITY (WRA) camp site; the land was a dry lake bed 4,000 feet above sea level covered with sagebrush

Origin of camp population: Mostly from Sacramento (4,984), King, Wash. (2,703), Placer (1,807), Pierce, Wash. (946), Yuba (476), and Hood River, Or. (425) Counties

Via "assembly centers": Most came via Sacramento (4,671), Pinedale (4,011) or Marysville (2,455) "Assembly Centers"; another 3,166 came directly to Tule Lake

Rural/Urban: Roughly equal split

Peak population: 18,789; peak population occurred after Tule Lake had become a "segregation center"

Date of peak: December 25, 1944
Opening date: May 27, 1942
Closing date: March 20, 1946; Tule Lake closed as a "segregation center"
Project director(s): Elmer Shirrell, Harvey Coverly and Raymond Best
Community analysts: Marvin K. Opler
JERS fieldworkers: Frank S. Miyamoto, James Sakoda, Tamotsu Shibutani, Tetsuo Najima and Chet Yamauchi
Newspaper: *Tulean Dispatch* (June 15, 1942–October 30, 1943)
Percent who answered question 28 of the loyalty questionnaire positively: 84.4
Number and percentage of eligible male citizens inducted directly into armed forces: 57 (0.5 percent); Tule Lake had the lowest percentage of eligible male citizens inducted into the armed forces
Industry: Tule Lake had a cabinet shop and a bakery that produced goods for internal consumption
Miscellaneous Characteristics: Tule Lake was beset by much unrest even prior to segregation. A farm laborers' strike occurred on August 15, 1942, over the lack of promised goods and salaries. Packing shed workers struck in September, while a mess hall workers' protest took place in October 1942. The unrest culminated in large numbers of people refusing to register (see LOYALTY QUESTIONS), leading to Tule Lake's designation as the "segregation center."

With the decision to segregate the "loyal" from the "disloyal" on the basis of the 1943 loyalty questionnaire, Tule Lake was chosen as the the camp where "disloyals" would be isolated. Tule Lake became "Tule Lake Segregation Center" in the fall of 1943. At that time, "loyal" Tuleans were supposed to be moved to another camp while "disloyals" from the other camps came to Tule Lake; however, many such "loyals" declined another move and stayed on at Tule Lake.

(For the key to the categories, see the entry for GILA RIVER.)

The literature on the Japanese American World War II experience is extensive; see the bibliography and the bibliographic entries after the various entries pertaining to this experience for titles of general interest. Most of literature on Tule Lake focuses on the post-segregation period; some of these works are listed with the entry for TULE LAKE "SEGREGATION CENTER." Among the works which deal with pre-segregation Tule Lake, there are Rita Takahashi Cates. "Comparative Administration and Management of Five War Relocation Authority Camps: America's Incarceration of Persons of Japanese Descent during World War II." Diss., University of Pittsburgh, 1980; Thomas James. "The Education of Japanese Americans at Tule Lake, 1942–1946." *Pacific Historical Review* 56.1 (Feb. 1987): 25–58; Lauren Kessler. "Fettered Freedoms: The Journalism

of World War II Japanese Internment Camps." *Journalism History* 15.2-3. (Summer/Autumn 1988): 60–69; and S. Frank Miyamoto. "Resentment, Distrust, and Insecurity at Tule Lake." In Ichioka, Yuji, ed. *Views from Within: The Japanese American Evacuation and Resettlement Study.* Los Angeles: Asian American Studies Center, University of California, Los Angeles, 1989. 127–140. For a memoir of a former inmate at pre-segregation Tule Lake, see Daisuke Kitagawa,. *Issei and Nisei: The Internment Years.* New York: Seabury Press, 1967.

Tule Lake "Segregation Center" Originally one of the 10 "relocation centers" created by the WAR RELOCATION AUTHORITY (WRA) to house persons of Japanese descent forcibly removed from the West Coast during World War II, it was transformed, during the latter half of 1943, into a center for citizens and aliens of Japanese descent that the WRA believed were either loyal to Japan or who had indicated by their actions that their loyalties did not lie with the United States. The "segregation center," because of the nature of its population and the supervision it received, was the most turbulent of all the centers operated by the WRA.

Tule Lake "Segregation Center" was created following disturbances associated with loyalty questionnaires administered by the War Department and WRA during February and March 1943. Although the negative responses by many Japanese Americans to the LOYALTY QUESTIONS were in reality protests against their removal and incarceration, many persons in the public at large viewed those Japanese Americans as disloyal to the U.S. As a result, the WRA received pressure from Congress, the army, the JAPANESE AMERICAN CITIZENS LEAGUE and its own project directors to segregate the "disloyal" in a separate center.

The WRA conceived the "segregation center" as a place in which persons loyal to Japan could pursue a Japanese way of life, with the expectation that most would eventually move to Japan. The agency modified its plans, however, in order to avoid the hardships that separating family members of differing loyalties would engender. In the process, it created a center inhabited by persons possessing varying degrees of "loyalty" and "disloyalty" to the U.S. The antagonism between persons of differing beliefs was a major source of turmoil during much of the "segregation center's" history.

On July 15, 1943, the WRA announced that the following would be sent to the "segregation center": aliens and citizens of Japanese descent who had applied for repatriation or expatriation to Japan (7,222 people); those who had answered the loyalty questions in the negative or had refused to answer (4,785 people); those who had been denied clearance to leave the centers for any reason; and paroled aliens from Department of Justice INTERNMENT CAMPS who were recommended for detention. However, the WRA went beyond this and included all persons in its centers it believed to be anti-administration or "troublemakers," as well as loyal family members who wished to accompany segregants and approximately 6,000 residents of TULE LAKE "RELOCATION CENTER" who chose to remain in the camp rather than undergo another forced move. Except for about 3,500 internees who had to await construction of barracks, the move to Tule Lake took place during September and October 1943.

The camp into which the segregants came was depressing physically and otherwise. A newly erected heavy wire-mesh "man-proof" fence surrounded them, while elevated block houses and watch towers with armed sentries prevented escape. Outside the fence, a battalion of military police with armored cars and tanks stood in full view of the residents. Permission to resettle was denied to all regardless of "loyalty" status. Also, self-government, as established in other centers, was not allowed, although a representative committee could be organized as an advisory council to the administration.

The failure of administrators to understand or trust the internee community resulted in a condition of mutual hostility that endured until the closing days of the center. In October 1943, project director Raymond Best refused to negotiate seriously with the internee community organization (the DAIHYO SHA KAI) and its Negotiating Committee. This was followed by a forced meeting in which WRA director DILLON S. MYER and other administrators were surrounded by thousands of peaceful residents who came to support their representatives, and a few days later by several minor altercations. Fearful staff members misinterpreted this as a riot, resulting in sensationalized stories in the nation's press.

The army entered Tule Lake on November 4, and martial law was declared nine days later. The center was not returned to civilian control until January 15, 1944. During this time, the residents suffered real repression. A curfew kept people indoors and put an end to many recreational activities. The army arrested anyone suspected of being anti-administration, including many innocent people. A STOCKADE was constructed in which several hundred people were held for up to nine months without hearings or trials. The residents carried out a partial strike to protest these conditions. Even moderate individuals came to feel hostility for the army and project administration, and any person or group cooperating with them.

The WRA's failure to carry out its plan to segregate "loyal" from "disloyal" internees resulted in the greatest and most prolonged disturbances at Tule Lake. Of the 18,422 persons segregated in the center, more than one-fourth, including 4,517 citizens, were classed as "loyal." In addition, many of those classified as "disloyal" were segregated as a result of protest rather than actual loyalty

to Japan. It should be noted that WAYNE COLLINS, attorney for those who later renounced their citizenship, argued that even the most fanatically pro-Japanese were once "loyal," but changed allegiance because of injustices suffered during and after the forced removal from their homes in 1942.

The pro-Japanese element consisted primarily of ISSEI, and was an insignificant minority in the early days of the center. Referred to as resegregationists, they operated as underground groups, whose main goal was the resegregation of the true Japanese, i.e., themselves, from those "loyal" to the U.S. and "fencesitters." Through such tactics as intimidation, beatings, rumors and other forms of pressure, including murder in one instance, they pushed for their program of resegregation. During the latter half of 1944, they came out in the open and, at least nominally, came to dominate the entire camp.

With the passage of the Renunciation Law in July 1944, the resegregationists added RENUNCIATION OF CITIZENSHIP as one of their objectives. They were aided by government announcements, both made on December 17, 1944, to the effect that Tule Lake and all other WRA centers would close within a year and that Japanese Americans were once again to be permitted to resettle in the West Coast states. Tule Lake residents had by then developed an almost pathological fear of the violence they believed awaited them in West Coast communities. They saw the "segregation center" as a safe haven from the hostility of Americans on the outside, and renunciation of citizenship as the only means to prevent forced resettlement. NISEI children, faced with pressure from parents on one side, and the militant tactics of the resegregationist on the other, surrendered their citizenship in droves. After repeated failures, the Department of Justice and WRA ended the domination of the resegregationists and brought the camp under control, although not before 5,589 *nisei* had given up their citizenship. The renunciation crisis kept Tule Lake open longer than any of the other WRA centers. In the final days, it was taken over by the Department of Justice, and closed its doors for good on March 28, 1946.

For further reading, see Donald E. Collins. *Native American Aliens: Disloyalty and the Renunciation of Citizenship by Japanese Americans During World War II*. Westport, Conn.: Greenwood Press, 1985; Dorothy S. Thomas, and Richard Nishimoto. *The Spoilage*. Berkeley: University of California Press, 1946, 1969; and Michi Weglyn. *Years of Infamy: The Untold Story of America's Concentration Camps*. New York: William Morrow & Co., 1976.   DONALD E. COLLINS

Turlock incident   Mass expulsion of Japanese laborers from a central California town. As had happened to Chinese laborers in an earlier era, Japanese laborers faced mass expulsions from certain farming communities. In

Turlock, California, such an incident occurred in 1921. On July 20, a carefully coordinated attack on 58 Japanese laborers took place in which armed white men awoke the ISSEI where they slept, loaded them on trucks and took them out of town, warning them not to return. Around 150 people were involved in the deportation that seemed to have the sanction of the surrounding community: the use of trucks and cars and the convenient unavailability of the local police during the raid were evidence of this. A week earlier, armed white men had driven 10 Japanese workers out of nearby Livingston while many Japanese in the area had been robbed in recent months by bandits who had not been caught. In the wake of the Turlock incident, the Japanese consul protested formally, though he could do no more than this. California governor William D. Stephens and the JAPANESE EXCLUSION LEAGUE decried the incident, reasoning (correctly as it turned out) that it would hurt the exclusionist cause. Six participants in the expulsion were arrested and tried. The trial was postponed twice for lack of witnesses. When the trial took place, beginning on April 26, 1922, only eight Japanese witnesses were found and only one of these was able to make a positive identification. The six were acquitted in 10 minutes by the all-white jury. Similar incidents took place in California in Delano (1922), Los Angeles (1922 and 1924), Porterville (1922), Hopland (1924) and Woodlake (1926), and in Toledo, Oregon (1925) and the Salt River Valley in Arizona (1934). (See TOLEDO INCIDENT, SALT RIVER VALLEY INCIDENT.)

For further reading, see Yuji Ichioka. "The 1921 Turlock Incident: Forceful Expulsion of Japanese Laborers." In Gee, Emma, ed. *Counterpoint: Perspectives on Asian America.* Los Angeles: Asian American Studies Center, University of California, 1976. 195–99 and Valerie Matsumoto. "The Cortez Colony: Family, Farm and Community among Japanese Americans, 1919–1982." Diss., Stanford University, 1985.

U

Uchida, Yoshiko (1921–1992)

Yoshiko Uchida is best known as a writer of fiction for children and young adults that focuses on Japanese culture and the Japanese American experience. She has also written fiction and nonfiction for adults.

A NISEI, Uchida was born in Alameda, California, and grew up in Berkeley. She wrote her first stories at the age of 10. She went on to attend the University of California at Berkeley, earning a B.A. in English, history and philosophy. Shortly before graduation, Uchida and all other West Coast Japanese Americans were uprooted from their homes and incarcerated in inland CONCENTRATION CAMPS during World War II. Sent to TOPAZ, Utah, Uchida taught elementary school and first developed her interest in children's literature. Leaving Topaz after a year, she attended Smith College in Massachusetts and earned a masters degree in education. While living in New York, she published her first book, *The Dancing Kettle,* a collection of Japanese folktales. In 1952, she went to Japan for two years, supported by a Ford Foundation fellowship.

In the years since, she has authored numerous books for young people, many focusing on the Japanese American experience. *A Jar of Dreams, The Best Bad Thing,* and *The Happiest Ending* focus on a young *nisei* girl growing up in a Japanese American family not unlike her own. *Journey to Topaz* and *Journey Home* recount the camp experience through the eyes of young people. Later, she authored *Desert Exile: The Uprooting of a Japanese American Family,* an autobiographical account of her own experience during the war. In 1987, the adult novel *Picture Bride* was published to an enthusiastic reception.

For further reading, see Japanese American Curriculum Project. *Japanese American Journey: The Story of a People.* San Mateo, Calif.: Japanese American Curriculum Project, 1985 and Yoshiko Uchida. *The Invisible Thread.* Englewood Cliffs, N.J.: Julian Messner-Silver Burdett Press, 1991, her autobiography. See King-kok Cheung and Stan Yogi. *Asian American Literature: An Annotated Bibliography.* New York: Modern Language Association of America, 1988 for a more or less complete listing of her work.

Uchinanchu

The preferred term for Japanese Americans of Okinawan descent. Within the Japanese American community, the Uchinanchu represent perhaps the largest subgroup. The Uchinanchu are the descendants of Japanese immigrants from Okinawa, a Japanese PREFECTURE located in the Ryukyu Islands to the south of the four main islands of Japan. Uchinanchu speak a unique dialect of Japanese and have a culture that differs from that of Japanese from the four main islands, known as NAICHI to Uchinanchu. Because of this unique culture, and also in part because of discrimination from the Naichi, Japanese Americans of Okinawan origin retain an identity as Uchinanchu even in the SANSEI and YONSEI generations, long after Naichi have lost any prefectural identity.

In broad outline, the history of Uchinanchu immigration and settlement parallels that for Japanese Americans at large. Large-scale Okinawan migration to Hawaii began in 1900, largely through the efforts of KYUZO TOYAMA, known as "the Father of Okinawan overseas migration." The Uchinanchu population swelled in the years prior to the GENTLEMEN'S AGREEMENT and by 1924, there were approximately 17,000 to 20,000 in Hawaii and a like number on the mainland. Stereotyped as being relatively uneducated and "coarse," Uchinanchu bore the brunt of discrimination not only from white

Americans but from Naichi as well. During the period of settlement in the 1920s and '30s, separate Uchinanchu community institutions such as newspapers, churches and cultural organizations were formed. The coming of World War II broke down many of the barriers between Uchinanchu and Naichi. However, because of the differences in culture, Uchinanchu interest in Okinawan relief efforts immediately after World War II and reversion of Okinawa to Japan in the early 1970s, Uchinanchu organizations remained and thrived after the war. The Uchinanchu community remains a strong subgroup within the Japanese American community.

For further reading, see Ethnic Studies Oral History Project/ United Okinawan Association of Hawaii. *Uchinanchu: A History of Okinawans in Hawaii.* Honolulu: Ethnic Studies Program, University of Hawaii at Manoa, 1981 and Okinawa Club of America, comp. *History of the Okinawans in North America.* Ben Kobashigawa, trans. Los Angeles: UCLA Asian American Studies Center and The Okinawa Club of America, 1988 for sizable anthologies documenting the Uchinanchu experience in Hawaii and on the mainland, respectively. Both books feature articles on various aspects of the Uchinanchu and include profiles of community organizations and prominent people in the community. See also Yukiko Kimura. *Issei: Japanese Immigrants in Hawaii.* Honolulu: University of Hawaii Press, 1988 for more on early Okinawan immigrants to Hawaii and Wesley I. Ueunten. "The Maintenance of the Okinawan Ethnic Community in Hawaii." Thesis, University of Hawaii at Manoa, 1989.

Umeki, Miyoshi (1929–   )   Actress. Miyoshi Umeki is one of just three Japanese Americans to receive an Academy Award, winning as Best Supporting Actress in 1957 for her role in *Sayonara.*

Umeki was born in Otaru, Hokkaido, Japan in 1929. She grew up in a crowded household among eight brothers and sisters and seven apprentices who worked at her father's growing iron factory. Having enjoyed singing from a young age, she was "discovered" by three American occupation soldiers brought to the Umeki home as guests of her English-speaking brother. All of them were musically inclined and came to the house almost every night. The soldiers would sing for the family, and one night they asked Umeki to join them in singing a tune. Although shy at first, Umeki became more confident of her voice. By the time she was 16, she began to sing with G.I. bands in their service clubs. At night, Umeki listened to U.S. Army radio and tried to imitate the singing of Dinah Shore, Peggy Lee and Doris Day. Eventually, she got her first break on Japanese radio and television.

In the 1950s, Umeki came to the United States and made a living singing in small nightclubs. Finally, her agent booked her on Tennessee Ernie Ford's TV show and Arthur Godfrey's morning show. It was on the

Miyoshi Umeki.   *Terrance Tam Soon Collection, Japanese American National Museum Photographic & Moving Image Archive*

Godfrey show that Umeki was discovered by a Warner Bros. casting director who hired her for the role of Katsumi in *Sayonara* (1957). Next, she was cast in Rodgers and Hammerstein's *Flower Drum Song,* in which she played the role of Mei Li.

Umeki's career did not stop with the Broadway production of *Flower Drum Song.* Her film performances include *Cry for Happy* (1961); the film version of *Flower Drum Song* (1961); *The Horizontal Lieutenant* (1961); and *A Girl Named Tamiko* (1963). Umeki also appeared in the television series "The Courtship of Eddie's Father" (1969–1972) as housekeeper Mrs. Livingston.

SUZANNE J. HEE

[Sources for this entry include *Time* magazine. December 22, 1958, and Thomas G. Aylesworth and John S. Bowman. *The World Almanac Who's Who of Film.* New York: Bison Books, 1987.]

United Okinawan Association of Hawaii   Congress of OKINAWAN clubs in Hawaii. The United Okinawan Association of Hawaii was formed in 1951 and

was the first successful long-term pan-Okinawan organization in Hawaii. In its early years, its primary concern was with Okinawan-American relations, but its emphasis has shifted in the last two decades towards promoting a positive sense of identity for people of Okinawan descent in Hawaii and preserving Okinawan American culture.

Though there had been earlier efforts to form pan-Okinawan organizations in Hawaii—the earliest of these dating to 1907—all such prewar efforts were short-lived. At the same time, however, many Okinawan organizations based on common Okinawan origin or common interest formed in the prewar era and continued to prosper after the war. In the immediate postwar era, many such organizations were active in relief efforts to aid war-torn Okinawa. As a result of rivalries that developed out of the relief activities, a renewed effort to start a pan-Okinawan organization was launched. After much difficulty, the United Okinawan Association of Hawaii was born on September 21, 1951, as a congress of existing organizations rather than as a new organization with its own membership. Fourteen clubs were charter members of the organization.

In the early years of the United Okinawan Association, the mostly ISSEI membership concentrated on activities involving relations with Okinawa. The U.S. government worked through the association in creating government programs to help bring young Okinawan farmers to Hawaii for training and to bring Okinawan Americans to Okinawa to promote goodwill as part of the Hawaii-Okinawa Friendship Mission. With the reversion of Okinawa to Japan in 1972, the association began to concentrate more on activities aimed at the local Hawaii community. Since 1960, it has been involved in planning anniversary celebrations commemorating the arrival of the first Okinawan immigrants to Hawaii in 1900. Such celebrations occur every five years; the most recent such event in 1990 saw the dedication of the $9 million Hawaii Okinawa Center. The association has also been active in the yearly Okinawan Cultural Jubilees and many other cultural and historical activities. The association remains a vital force within Hawaii's Japanese American community.

For further reading, see Ruth Adaniya. "United Okinawan Association of Hawaii." In Ethnic Studies Oral History Project/United Okinawan Association of Hawaii. *Uchinanchu: A History of Okinawans in Hawaii*. Honolulu: Ethnic Studies Program, University of Hawaii at Manoa, 1981. 324–36.

Uno, Edison Tomimaro (1929–1976) Teacher, writer, activist. Perhaps more than any other individual, Edison Uno was responsible for launching the REDRESS MOVEMENT within the Japanese American community. He was born in Los Angeles on October 19, 1929, the ninth of 10 children born to George and Riki Uno. He

was 12 when the attack on Pearl Harbor dramatically changed his life. In February 1942, two FBI men appeared at the Uno house and took the elder Uno away. As an enemy alien whom someone had decided was dangerous, George Uno was shuttled to a succession of INTERNMENT CAMPS in inhospitable parts of the U.S.: Missoula, Montana; Fort Lincoln, North Dakota; Lordsburg, New Mexico, and SANTA FE, New Mexico. In the meantime, he was not allowed to contact his family for a year. They began their wartime odyssey at Santa Anita Racetrack before moving on to GRANADA, Colorado, and finally reuniting with their father at the family Justice Department–administered INTERNMENT CAMP at CRYSTAL CITY, Texas. When the war ended, the family was allowed to return to Los Angeles, but Edison remained in camp with his father until October 31, 1946. Edison spent 1,647 days in American CONCENTRATION CAMPS.

After the war, Edison returned to Los Angeles and attended Marshall High, serving as senior class president. He also became president of the East Los Angeles chapter of the JAPANESE AMERICAN CITIZENS LEAGUE (JACL) at age 18, becoming the youngest chapter president ever. After marrying Rosalind Kido, he enrolled at Los Angeles State College and, after graduating from there, he attended Hastings College of Law in San Francisco. While at Hastings, he suffered his first heart attack. On the advice of his doctors, he gave up his ambition to be a lawyer and became something of a professional activist for Japanese American concerns. Among the issues he worked on are the repeal of TITLE II in the early '70s, the presidential pardon of IVA TOGURI D'AQUINO, the writing of MICHI WEGLYN's landmark *Years of Infamy*, the children's book *Japanese Americans: The Untold Story* in 1970, and the NBC-produced documentary "Guilty by Reason of Race." Uno also spoke out in favor of the striking San Francisco State students in 1969 (see SAN FRANCISCO STATE STRIKE). One of his most important contributions was his nearly lone call for redress in the early 1970s. This was one struggle he would not live to see through to the end—on December 24, 1976, Edison Uno died at the age of 47 of a heart attack.

For further reading, see Japanese American Curriculum Project. *Japanese American Journey: The Story of a People*. San Mateo, Calif.: Japanese American Curriculum Project, 1985.

Ushijima, Kinji [George Shima] (1864–1926) Under the name George Shima, Kinji Ushijima became in all probability the wealthiest and one of the most famous ISSEI. As the famed "Potato King" of California, his story continues to be cited as an example of the success achieved by hardworking Japanese immigrants in the agricultural arena.

Ushijima was born in Kurume, a small town near Fukuoka on the island of Kyushu, in 1864 to a farming family. In 1885 an early appreciation for classical Chinese literature led the young Ushijima to Tokyo where he hoped to become a scholar. Abandoning his goal of becoming a Chinese scholar, he became interested in learning English and decided to go to the United States for further study. He arrived in San Francisco in 1889, changed his name to George Shima, and began the difficult life of the DEKASEGI-SHOSEI. He first worked as a SCHOOLBOY and polished his English skills. Within a year of his arrival in San Francisco, he became a migrant farm laborer in the Sacramento delta region. Utilizing his knowledge of English and farming, he soon became an agricultural LABOR CONTRACTOR.

The Sacramento delta area of the 1890s was already well established as a productive agricultural region. However, many potentially fertile areas were underutilized due to the unpredictable flooding of the Sacramento and San Joaquin Rivers. In collaboration with some *dekasegi-shosei* friends, Shima began to purchase this inexpensive land in a joint farming venture. After much trial and error, he eventually found moderate success growing potatoes on the swampy land in the late 1890s. By 1900, his holdings were estimated at over 1,000 acres, with another 2,000 acres under joint tenantship. He also began to undertake ever-larger land reclamation ventures, rigging an elaborate system of dikes and pumps to clear fertile land for more farming. By 1913, he had reclaimed more than 28,800 acres of land and was widely known as the "Potato King" of California.

But despite his tremendous financial success, he was, as an *issei,* faced with many of the same difficulties suffered by his compatriots. His attempt to buy a home in a ritzy Berkeley neighborhood in 1909 led to widely publicized attempts to stop him. "Jap Invades Fashionable Quarters" and "Jap Puts On Airs" were some of the headlines of local papers. Only when he erected a high fence (to "keep the other children from playing with mine," he sarcastically quipped) and donated $500 to the YMCA did the furor die down. In part because of this house buying episode, Shima became increasingly active in fighting the ANTI-JAPANESE MOVEMENT, which used exaggerated stories about Shima and others to fan fears among Californians of a "Japanese takeover." Shima served as president of the JAPANESE ASSOCIATION of America from 1909 and tried unsuccessfully to prevent passage of the 1913 (CALIFORNIA) ALIEN LAND LAW through his connections with Governor HIRAM JOHNSON. Like many other *issei,* Shima's optimism that *issei* would find acceptance through acculturation, hard work and good citizenship changed over time as the 1920 (CALIFORNIA) ALIEN LAND LAW, the OZAWA, TAKAO VS. U.S. naturalization decision and the EXCLUSION ACT OF 1924 cemented the status of *issei* as second-class residents. At the time of his death, there was speculation that he

was planning to return to Kurume and that he had built an American-style home there. He had also investigated the feasibility of farming ventures in Korea and Mexico.

When he died in 1926, he left an estate estimated to be between $15 and $17 million. His pallbearers included David Starr Jordan, chancellor emeritus of Stanford University, and James Rolph, Jr., mayor of San Francisco. However, the success of George Shima and other wealthy *issei* farmers and entrepreneurs should not be overstated. For as these men learned, all the money in the world could not buy citizenship and equality in the prewar United States of America.

For further reading, see Donald Teruo Hata and Nadine Hata. "George Shima: 'The Potato King of California'." *Journal of the West* 25.1 (Jan. 1986): 55–63 and Toshio Yoshimura. *George Shima: Potato King and Lover of Chinese Classics.* N.p. [Japan]: N.pub., 1981 for biographical profiles of Shima. Addition information on Shima can be found in Roger Daniels. *The Politics of Prejudice: The Anti-Japanese Movement in California and the Struggle for Japanese Exclusion.* 2nd edition. Berkeley: University of California Press, 1977; Audrie Girdner and Anne Loftis. *The Great Betrayal: The Evacuation of the Japanese-Americans during World War II.* Toronto: Macmillan, 1969; Yuji Ichioka. *The Issei: The World of the First Generation Japanese Immigrants, 1885–1924.* New York: The Free Press, 1988; Paul Jacobs and Saul Landau. *To Serve the Devil, Volume II: Colonials and Sojourners.* New York: Random House, 1971; and Kaizo Naka. "Social and Economic Conditions among Japanese Farmers in California." San Francisco R & E Research Associates, 1974.

U.S. v. Fujii et al. Case involving 63 draft resisters at HEART MOUNTAIN. In the CONCENTRATION CAMP at Heart Mountain, Wyoming, an organized resistance to the military draft emerged led by the HEART MOUNTAIN FAIR PLAY COMMITTEE. This was the only such resistance movement at any of the camps. On March 25, 1944, the first 12 draft resistors were arrested, and by the beginning of May, 63 resistors had been arrested. On May 10, indictments against the 63 were handed down. At the arraignment, all pleaded "not guilty" and the largest mass trial in Wyoming history began on June 12, 1944. U.S. District Attorney Carl Sackett presented the prosecution's case while Denver attorney Samuel D. Menin handled the defense. On June 26, Judge Kennedy found the 63 guilty and sentenced each to three years in a federal penitentiary. They went to jail in early 1944, half to Leavenworth and half to McNeil Island, Washington. The convictions were upheld on an appeal on March 12, 1945. The 63 received a presidential pardon on December 24, 1947. The leaders of the Fair Play Committee were arrested and tried in U.S. V. OKAMOTO ET AL.

For further reading, see Douglas W. Nelson. *Heart Mountain: The History of an American Concentration Camp.* Madison, Wis.: The State Historical Society of Wisconsin, 1976.

U.S. v. Okamoto et al. Due to their successful organization of a draft resistance movement at the HEART MOUNTAIN CONCENTRATION CAMP, seven members of the HEART MOUNTAIN FAIR PLAY COMMITTEE'S executive council along with sympathetic *Rocky Shimpo* (Denver) editor JAMES OMURA were "secretly" indicted in May 1944 for unlawful conspiracy to counsel, aid and abet violation of the Selective Service Act. The Heart Mountain Seven were Robert Kiyoshi Okamoto, Isamu Sam Horino, PAUL TAKEO NAKADATE, Frank Seishi Emi, Guntaro Kubota, Minoru Tamesa and Tsutomu Wakaye. On July 21, 1944, the eight were arrested. At the arraignment, the eight pled "not guilty" and asked for a jury trial. On October 23, 1944, the trial began with ACLU lawyer A. L. WIRIN defending the seven committee members and Sidney Jacobs defending Omura. The jury found Omura not guilty and the others guilty. Judge Eugene Rice sentenced the seven to two- and four-year prison terms. Wirin soon filed an appeal and the verdict was eventually overturned.

For further reading, see Frank F. Chuman. *The Bamboo People: The Law and Japanese-Americans.* Del Mar, Calif.: Publisher's Inc., 1976 and Douglas W. Nelson. *Heart Mountain: The History of an American Concentration Camp.* Madison, Wis.: The State Historical Society of Wisconsin, 1976.

U.S. v. Wong Kim Ark 1898 Supreme Court decision that upheld the citizenship of any person born in the United States regardless of race. The *Wong Kim Ark* case served as the leading legal precedent in the various attempts to strip NISEI of their citizenship, most notably in the REGAN V. KING case during World War II.

Wong Kim Ark was born in San Francisco to Chinese immigrant parents in 1873. He went to visit China in 1894 and was denied readmittance upon his return to the U.S. the following year on the grounds that he was not a citizen and thus barred by the CHINESE EXCLUSION ACT OF 1882. His case was eventually heard by the United States Supreme Court, which affirmed his citizenship under the Fourteenth Amendment of the Constitution.

For further reading, see Frank F. Chuman. *The Bamboo People: The Law and Japanese-Americans.* Del Mar, Calif.: Publisher's Inc., 1976 and William L. Tung. *The Chinese in America, 1820–1973: A Chronology and Fact Book.* Dobbs Ferry, NY: Oceana Publications, Inc., 1974. 104–05.

Utah Nippo Utah-based Japanese American newspaper. Founded in 1914, the *Utah Nippo* was notable for (a) being one of only four Japanese American publications on the mainland that published during World War II; (b) being the only Japanese American newspaper based in Utah for most of its life; and (c) having been published by only two people, husband and wife, since its inception in 1914.

The *Utah Nippo* was begun on November 3, 1914, by Uneo Terasawa, an immigrant farmer originally from Nagano PREFECTURE. He had been a correspondent for the SHIN SEKAI prior to founding his own paper. At the time, there was already one Japanese American paper in Utah, the *Rocky Mountain Times,* published by Shiro Iida. The *Times* was said to have a Christian orientation while the *Nippo* had a Buddhist one. In 1927, the two papers merged when the *Nippo* bought the *Times* and absorbed its employees and physical facilities. In 1939, founder Terasawa passed away and his wife Kuniko took over as publisher. Under her leadership, the paper began to put out an English section beginning on September 1, 1939, and was one of four Japanese American papers on the mainland to publish during the war. (The others were the *Rocky Shimpo, Colorado Times* and PACIFIC CITIZEN.) The paper continued to publish on a triweekly basis (it had been a daily until 1931), going biweekly in 1971 and weekly in 1975. The circulation of the paper peaked at over 8,000 during the World War II years and has declined on a more or less consistent basis since that time, hovering between 1,000 and 2,000 in the 1950s and '60s and declining to less than 1,000 since 1968. The paper continued to publish as a monthly until the death of Kuniko Terasawa in 1991.

For further reading, see Haruo Higashimoto. "Assimilation Factors Related to the Functioning of the Immigrant Press in Selected Japanese Communities." Diss., Brigham Young University, 1984.

Uyeda, Clifford (1917–) NISEI activist and pediatrician. Uyeda was born on January 14, 1917, in Olympia, Washington, and raised in Tacoma, Washington. In 1940 Uyeda graduated *cum laude* from the University of Wisconsin where he received a bachelor of arts degree in English. Just before the United States's entry into World War II, Uyeda began medical school at Tulane University in New Orleans, Louisiana. As a result, he was not incarcerated in an American CONCENTRATION CAMP during the war as were all Japanese Americans then on the West Coast. Uyeda did his internship in Pediatrics at Harvard Medical School and at Massachusetts General Hospital in Boston, Massachusetts. During the Korean War, Uyeda was a captain in the United States Air Force, serving as a medical doctor from 1951–53. Three years later, in 1956, he married Helen Sachie Nakamura.

Uyeda is a notable *nisei* activist in the Japanese American community. In 1975, Uyeda was a key figure in securing the JAPANESE AMERICAN CITIZENS LEAGUE'S (JACL) support for a massive campaign to attain a presidential pardon for accused "Tokyo Rose" IVA TOGURI D'AQUINO. He played a vital role in Toguri D'Aquino's being pardoned in 1977 by mobilizing, organizing and directing the campaign, along with authoring informational pamphlets about the Tokyo Rose case.

From 1977–1980, Uyeda served as the JACL national president, and in 1977–78, he was the JACL's National Redress Chairperson. In addition, Uyeda was one of the founders of the JACL's Golden Gate chapter based in San Francisco, California. As a JACL leader, he has been instrumental in insisting that the organization come to terms with its controversial actions during World War II, introducing a resolution that would have the organization apologize for its vilification of *nisei* draft resisters (see HEART MOUNTAIN FAIR PLAY COMMITTEE, for example) and other dissidents.

In addition to his work with the JACL, Uyeda has also been involved with the National Japanese American Historical Society (NJAHS). He served as NJAHS president from 1988–1992 and has edited its quarterly newsletter, *Nikkei Heritage,* since 1985. Outside of the Japanese American community, Uyeda has been an active member of Greenpeace, the Sierra Club and the World Affairs Council of California.   STACEY HIROSE

Uyeno embassy   Japanese expedition to Hawaii in 1869 launched in an effort to protect the rights of the GANNEN-MONO. On August 17, 1869, Kagenori Uyeno was named special envoy to Hawaii and soon set sail from Yokohama to San Francisco. After a brief stay in San Francisco (during which time he changed from "feudal prince attire" to "smart American attire"), he journeyed to Hawaii, arriving in Honolulu on December 27, 1869. On December 31, he presented his views concerning the disposition of the Gannen-mono to Hawaii officials. After 10 days of sometimes bitter negotiation, an agreement was reached to allow 40 of the Gannen-mono to return home. At one point, it is said that Uyeno became angry enough to threaten to ask his government to send a warship to Hawaii for a showdown if Japan's demands weren't met.

For further reading, see United Japanese Society of Hawaii. *History of Japanese in Hawaii.* James H. Okahata, ed. Honolulu: United Japanese Society of Hawaii, 1971.

V

Varsity Victory Volunteers   All-NISEI labor battalion in World War II Hawaii. The formation of the Varsity Victory Volunteers (also known as the VVV or Triple V) represented one response to anti-Japanese prejudices in Hawaii following the Pearl Harbor attack.

In the anxious days immediately after the Pearl Harbor attack, many Japanese Americans played key roles in keeping order in Hawaii. One such group were the many *nisei* members of the Hawaii Territorial Guard (not to be confused with those who were in National Guard units in Hawaii; these Nisei became the core of the 100TH INFANTRY BATTALION). In the six weeks after Pearl Harbor, the territorial guardsmen patrolled up to 150 posts in the Honolulu area, freeing up regular army units for other duties. However, due to the rising anti-Japanese sentiment during this time, the *nisei* members of the Territorial Guard were kicked out on January 19, 1942, despite their entirely satisfactory service up to that time.

A petition signed by 169 former members of the Guard was sent to DELOS EMMONS, the commanding general on Hawaii, on January 30. It read in part: "Hawaii is our home; the United States our country. We know but one loyalty and that is to the Stars and Stripes. We wish to do our part as loyal Americans in every way possible and we hereby offer ourselves for whatever service you may see fit to use us." As a result of the petition, the Corps of Engineers Auxiliary attached to the 34th Combat Engineers Regiment—the Varsity Victory Volunteers—was formed one month later. The all *nisei* group spent the next year working six days a week doing construction and manual labor of all kinds. VVV members contributed to the blood bank and bought $27,850 worth of war bonds as well. Due in part to the 100th Battalion, the VVV and other Japanese Americans who voluntarily helped in the war effort, the ban on Nisei in the army was lifted. On January 31, 1943, the VVV was disbanded. Many VVV members went on to become members of the 442ND REGIMENTAL COMBAT TEAM.

For further reading, see Roland Kotani. *The Japanese in Hawaii: A Century of Struggle.* Honolulu: Hochi, Ltd., 1985; Andrew W. Lind. *Hawaii's Japanese: An Experiment in Democracy.* Princeton: Princeton University Press, 1946; and Yutaka Nakahata and Ralph Toyota. "Varsity Victory Volunteers: A Social Movement." *Social Process in Hawaii* 8 (1943): 29–35.

Venice Celery Strike   The strike by 1,000 Mexican, Japanese and Filipino celery pickers against Japanese farmers was significant in that it pitted different segments of the Japanese American community against each other. The strike began on April 17, 1936, in Venice, California. Locked out of existing labor unions as they had always been, Japanese farm laborers had organized their own association called the California Farm Laborers Association (CFLA). This group, together with the Federation of Farm Workers of America, called the strike, demanding a significant wage increase and the recognition of the CFLA by the growers as a bargaining body. Their adversaries were the Southern California Farm Federation, a body of 800 Japanese farmers who rejected their demands. (See NANKA NOKAI RENMEI.)

Within a few days, the strike spread to many other areas of Southern California, including Lomita, San Pedro,

Dominguez Hills, Norwalk, Montebello, San Gabriel and Oxnard. Given the potential losses the harvest season strike might have caused, most institutions in the Japanese American community—the JAPANESE ASSOCIATIONS, the Little Tokyo Businessmen's Association, the Los Angeles JAPANESE AMERICAN CITIZENS LEAGUE chapters and the RAFU SHIMPO among them—came down in favor of the growers. The Japanese gardeners associations were about the only ones to support the strikers. With the support of mainstream institutions, the strikers were painted as Communists; NISEI strike-breaking units were organized and protected by the police. The dispute ended on June 8 when 1,500 Mexican workers accepted a smaller wage increase, effectively breaking the coalition. The strike indicated the extent to which the interests of the ISSEI farmers coincided with those of the white power structure and the willingness of the farmers to use any weapons at hand to battle the strikers even if some of them were fellow Japanese.

For further reading, see John Modell. *The Economics and Politics of Racial Accommodation: The Japanese of Los Angeles 1900–1942.* Chicago: University of Illinois Press, 1977; and Nobuya Tsuchida. "Japanese Gardeners in Southern California, 1900–1941." In Lucie Cheng and Edna Bonacich, eds. *Labor Immigration Under Capitalism: Asian Workers in the United States Before World War II.* Berkeley: University of California Press, 1984. 435–69.

"voluntary" resettlement The "voluntary" moving and resettlement of Japanese Americans excluded from the designated military areas along the West Coast. For a three-week period during World War II after Japanese Americans had been excluded from the West Coast but before plans for CONCENTRATION CAMPS had been finalized, a period of "voluntary" resettlement took place. Government officials hoped that the Japanese Americans barred from keeping their homes on the West Coast would make arrangements to move inland on their own, saving valuable Military resources.

After the issuing of EXECUTIVE ORDER 9066 essentially authorized the military to bar anyone anywhere for any reason, General JOHN L. DEWITT issued Public Proclamation 1 on March 2, 1942, creating Military Areas 1 and 2. Military Area 1 consisted of the western portion of Washington, Oregon and California, and the southern portion of Arizona; the rest of these states made up Military Area 2.

The proclamation also noted that people might be excluded from Military Area 1 in the near future. DeWitt indicated that Japanese Americans would be the first to be excluded and that they would be free to move outside the prohibited areas on their own in anticipation of exclusion. Government officials saw such "voluntary" resettlement as a way to save money and resources better applied directly to the war effort. Because Japanese Americans in Hawaii had resettled on their own from areas they were excluded from after the Pearl Harbor attack, there was optimism that "voluntary" resettlement would work on the West Coast.

There was one major difference. While Japanese Americans in Hawaii could move in with friends and relatives in other parts of the islands, the 107,000 Japanese Americans living in Military Area 1 knew few people who lived elsewhere. Additionally, state government officials and residents of neighboring states reacted with outrage that Japanese Americans were being encouraged to move there. If Japanese Americans were not to be trusted on the West Coast, they reasoned quite rationally, why should they be any more trustworthy inland? Most Japanese Americans feared moving into such hostile territory where they would know no one; the few who tried to move inland on their own faced hostile receptions wherever they turned. Sometimes even other Japanese Americans turned their backs on "voluntary" resettlers: a JAPANESE AMERICAN CITIZENS LEAGUE chapter in Utah warned potential resettlers on the coast that their arrival might jeopardize the good relations the Utah Japanese Americans had built up with the surrounding community over the years.

The failure of "voluntary" evacuation was recognized when the army issued Public Proclamation No. 4 on March 27 prohibiting Japanese Americans from leaving the area. A program to supervise the removal of Japanese Americans from the West Coast would have to be instituted instead. All told, 4,889 out of 107,500 Japanese Americans left Military Area No. 1 "voluntarily," most moving to Colorado and Utah. (See KEETLEY FARMS for one group of Japanese Americans who "voluntarily" moved to Utah and started an agricultural colony.) For those who "voluntarily" moved to the eastern parts of the coast states, "voluntary" resettlement hit them doubly hard. They found that when the supervised removal of West Coast Japanese Americans began, they would have to move yet again, this time to the "ASSEMBLY CENTERS" and CONCENTRATION CAMPS administered by the government.

For further reading, see Commission on Wartime Relocation and Internment of Civilians. *Personal Justice Denied: Report of the Commission on Wartime Relocation and Internment of Civilians.* Washington, D.C.: Government Printing Office, 1982; Audrie Girdner and Anne Loftis. *The Great Betrayal: The Evacuation of the Japanese-Americans during World War II.* Toronto: Macmillan, 1969; and Michi Weglyn. *Years of Infamy: The Untold Story of America's Concentration Camps.* New York: William Morrow & Co., 1976 for an overview of "voluntary" resettlement. See Leonard J. Arrington. "Utah's Ambiguous Reception: The Relocated Japanese Americans." In Daniels, Roger, Sandra C. Taylor and Harry H. L. Kitano, eds. *Japanese Americans: From Relocation to Redress.* Revised edition. Seattle: University of Washington Press, 1991. 92–98; Roger Daniels. "Western Reaction to the Relocated Japanese Americans: The Case of Wyoming." In Daniels, Roger, Sandra C. Taylor and Harry H. L. Kitano, eds. *Japanese Americans: From Relocation to Redress.* Revised edition. Seattle: University of Washington Press, 1991. 112–16; and Robert C. Sims. "Japanese Americans in Idaho." In Daniels, Roger, Sandra C. Taylor and Harry H. L. Kitano, eds. *Japanese Americans: From Relocation to Redress.* Revised edition. Seattle: University of Washington Press, 1991. 103–11 for the reactions of Utah, Idaho and Wyoming respectively to the resettling Japanese Americans.

W

WACs Women's Army Corps volunteers. Although not as famous as their male counterparts in the 442ND REGIMENTAL COMBAT TEAM, 100TH INFANTRY BATTALION and MILITARY INTELLIGENCE SERVICE, NISEI women also served their country during World War II.

Although the WAC replaced the Women's Army Auxiliary Corps (WAAC) on July 1, 1943, it was not until three months later that Japanese American women were accepted for service into the WAC. Unlike their male counterparts who were mostly drafted into the service, the *nisei* women volunteered for service in the WAC. The majority of these women volunteered after leaving the CONCENTRATION CAMPS, but a smaller number of them volunteered while still in camp.

Others volunteered from Hawaii and other states that were not subject to mass removal and detention.

Training for the WAC began in Hawaii in 1943 with approximately 60 *nisei* women volunteering from Hawaii. According to historian Mei Nakano, the WACs served at numerous Army bases throughout the country, in medical detachments, in the Public Information Office, and as typists, clerks and researchers in occupied Japan and Germany. For the most part, *nisei* WACs were given clerical, administrative and motor transport assignments. They did not serve in combat overseas.

In 1944 the first contingent of seven *nisei* WACs reported to Fort Snelling, Minnesota, to be trained, as were their male *nisei* counterparts, in the Japanese language to serve in the Military Intelligence Service. The women were not, however, trained as active interrogators, but were trained to be translators of the written Japanese language. According to former WAC Miwako Yanamoto, approximately 50 *nisei* women trained at Fort Snelling.

According to CLIFFORD UYEDA of the National Japanese American Historical Society, during World War II and the immediate postwar period, over 300 *nisei* women served in the WAC.

For further reading, see Dorothy Ochiai Hazama and Jane Okamoto Komeiji. *Okage Sama De: The Japanese in Hawai'i.*

Foreword by Daniel Inouye. Honolulu: Bess Press, 1986; Mei Nakano. *Japanese American Women: Three Generations, 1890–1990.* Berkeley and Sebastopol, Calif.: National Japanese American Historical Society and Mina Press, 1990; and Clifford I. Uyeda, and Barry Saiki, eds. *The Pacific War and Peace: Americans of Japanese Ancestry in Military Intelligence Service 1941 to 1952.* San Francisco, Calif.: Military Intelligence Service Association of Northern California and the National Japanese American Historical Society, 1991. STACEY HIROSE

[An interview with Miwako Yanamoto was also used to compile this entry.]

Wada, Jujiro (1872–1937) Alaskan dog musher, marathon runner, cook, prospector, adventurer. Born in 1872 in Ehime PREFECTURE on Shikoku Island, Japan, Wada was sent to the United States to be educated. Reputedly shanghaied in San Francisco, he worked three years on a whaling ship in Alaska and the Canadian Arctic until 1894. He returned to Alaska upon learning of his exclusion from the family estate when his parents died.

Wada's reputation extended not only to the coastal areas of Alaska, but also to the gold rush areas of Fairbanks and the Canadian Klondike. His role in enticing Klondikers to stampede to Fairbanks is disputed, but his presence in interior Alaska is clear. Wada worked with miners, cooked on steamships, ventured to Herschel Island and traded furs with the Eskimos of the northern Alaska coast. His dealings were sometimes contentious, but his many other activities are legendary.

No one was contentious of Wada's ability as a marathon runner; he won in Nome, Fairbanks and Dawson. He is also credited with initiating the Seward to Iditarod winter dog sled trail.

Later years saw him venture below the northern parts of Alaska and Canada to other provinces and the lower 48 states. It was on one of these trips that he contracted pneumonia and died in San Diego, California, in 1937. For further reading, see R. N. DeArmond. "This Is My Country." *Alaska* 54.3 (1988). Wada is also mentioned in Kazuo Ito. *Issei: A History of Japanese Immigrants in North America.* Shinichiro Nakamura, Jean S. Gerard, trans. Seattle: Executive Committee for the Publication of *Issei: A History of Japanese Immigrants in North America,* 1973 and in Tooru J. Kanazawa. *Sushi and Sourdough: A Novel.* Seattle: University of Washington Press, 1989. RONALD K. INOUYE

Wakamatsu Colony Colony of Japanese immigrants often cited as being the first such settlement on the mainland United States. The Wakamatsu Colony was an ill-fated attempt by a group of Japanese settlers to start a tea and silk farming community in Northern California. The group was led by German merchant John Henry

Schnell, a trader in Wakamatsu during the period of the MEIJI RESTORATION. Being associated with those who had opposed the victorious imperial forces, Schnell and a small group apparently decided to sneak out of the country to start anew in America. (At the time, it was illegal for Japanese subjects to leave the country.) The group arrived at Gold Hill in El Dorado County, California, on June 9, 1869. The venture to grow tea and raise silkworms foundered and the colony fell apart within three years. Of the 22 or so colonists, the subsequent histories of only a few are known. One of them was OKEI, the first Japanese woman to die on American soil. Another was MASUMIZU KUNINOSUKE, who apparently married a black woman and died in 1915. During the fairly elaborate centennial commemoration of the Wakamatsu Colony in 1969, a family descended from Kuninosuke was located—the mixed race family considered themselves black.

For further reading, see Harry H. L. Kitano. *Japanese Americans: The Evolution of a Subculture*. 2nd Edition. Englewood Cliffs, N.J.: Prentice-Hall, Inc., 1976; Henry Taketa. "1969, the Centennial Year." *Pacific Historian* 13.1 (Winter 1969): 1–16; and Robert A. Wilson and Bill Hosokawa. *East to America: A History of the Japanese in the United States*. New York: Morrow, 1980.

Wakasa, James Hatsuki   ISSEI chef killed by a CONCENTRATION CAMP sentry. On April 11, 1943, James Hatsuki Wakasa was shot to death by guard Gerald B. Philpott near the fence at TOPAZ. A 63-year-old, single *issei* man, Wakasa had come to the United States in 1903 and had been an instructor of cooking at Camp Dodge, Iowa, during World War I. Initial press accounts reported that he had been shot while trying to escape; later evidence showed that he was facing the guard when shot. Two weeks later, Philpott was found "not guilty" at a general court martial, concluding the incident. Wakasa was the most famous of the handful of Japanese Americans killed by guards during their wartime incarceration. An emotional account of Wakasa's story was told by Senator SPARK MATSUNAGA during Congressional debate over the issue of monetary redress for Japanese Americans who had been removed and detained during the war.

For further reading, see Roger Daniels. "Relocation, Redress, and the Report: A Historical Appraisal." In Daniels, Roger, Sandra C. Taylor and Harry H. L. Kitano, eds. *Japanese Americans: From Relocation to Redress*. Salt Lake City: University of Utah Press, 1986. Revised edition. Seattle: University of Washington Press, 1991. 3–9 and Michi Weglyn. *Years of Infamy: The Untold Story of America's Concentration Camps*. New York: William Morrow & Co., 1976.

Wakayama, Ernest Kinzo (1895–?)   CONCENTRATION CAMP dissident. A NISEI World War I veteran from Hawaii, Ernest Kinzo Wakayama is notable for having been one of the few who challenged the legality of the mass removal of West Coast Japanese Americans in the courts, filing a writ of *habeas corpus* in August 1942 on behalf of himself and his wife. While the others who challenged the legality of the removal and incarceration—Gordon Hirabayashi, Fred Korematsu, Min Yasui and Mitsuye Endo—all became well-known figures, Wakayama remained relatively obscure. The reason for this obscurity has to do with his notoriety as one of the leaders of the radical, resegregationist, pro-Japan faction at TULE LAKE "SEGREGATION CENTER" in late 1944 and his RENUNCIATION OF CITIZENSHIP and deportation to Japan, where he remained to the end of his life.

Like fellow World War I veteran JOE KURIHARA, Wakayama apparently became embittered over his treatment by his own country and turned against it. He became a central figure in the academic controversy over the JAPANESE AMERICAN EVACUATION AND RESETTLEMENT (JERS) project. Rosalie Wax, the key JERS fieldworker at Tule Lake, portrayed Wakayama as a ruthless gang leader who was not above using intimidation and violence to silence opponents. She admitted to providing information about Wakayama to the FBI that led to his renunciation of citizenship and removal to Japan. JERS critic Peter Suzuki portrays Wakayama as a heroic figure tragically wronged by Wax who renounced his citizenship only under duress. There are clearly elements of truth in both portrayals; how Wakayama is ultimately perceived remains to be determined.

The JERS publication Dorothy S. Thomas and Richard Nishimoto. *The Spoilage*. Berkeley: University of California Press, 1946, 1969 utilizes Wax's work in portraying Wakayama's actions (he is given the pseudonym Stanley Masanobu Kira in this work); Wax discusses her fieldwork in Tule Lake, including that involving "Kira," in Rosalie H. Wax. *Doing Fieldwork: Warnings and Advice*. Chicago: University of Chicago Press, 1971; Peter T. Suzuki. "The University of California Japanese Evacuation and Resettlement Study: A Prolegomenon." *Dialectical Anthropology* 10 (1986): 189–213 includes biographical data on Wakayama while castigating the JERS project. These data are repeated in Peter T. Suzuki. "For the Sake of Inter-University Comity: The Attempted Suppression by the University of California of Morton Grodzins' *Americans Betrayed*." In Ichioka, Yuji, ed. *Views from Within: The Japanese American Evacuation and Resettlement Study*. Los Angeles: Asian American Studies Center, University of California, Los Angeles, 1989. 95–123; S. Frank Miyamoto. "Dorothy Swaine Thomas as Director of JERS: Some Personal Observations." In Ichioka, Yuji, ed. *Views from Within: The Japanese American Evacuation and Resettlement Study*. Los Angeles: Asian American Studies Center, University of California, Los Angeles, 1989. 31–63 responds to Suzuki's allegations about Wax and JERS.

Wakimoto-Nishimura Company   Formed by Tsutomu Wakimoto and Ryuun Nishimura in 1902, the

Wakimoto-Nishimura Company was a large labor contracting (see LABOR CONTRACTORS) firm that supplied workers to railroads in the Rocky Mountain region. Wakimoto was from Hyogo PREFECTURE and came to the United States at the age of 22 in 1888. Like most ISSEI, he held many different jobs in the U.S., working for a time as a SCHOOLBOY. He first became a contractor in 1897, sending 500 men to work on the Santa Fe Railroad. In 1902, he teamed up with Nishimura, a former Buddhist priest from Saga prefecture to supply workers to the Union Pacific Railroad. In the Cheyenne area alone, the Wakimoto-Nishimura Company supplied between 800 and 1,000 laborers and at one time may have employed as many as 2,000. Later, Wakimoto set up offices in Cheyenne and set up a boardinghouse there. He also unsuccessfully tried to contract laborers for work on the Panama Canal.

For further reading, see Hisashi Tsurutani. *America Bound: The Japanese and Opening of the American West.* Betsey Scheiner, trans. Tokyo: Japan Times, Inc., 1989.

Walnut Grove A Japanese American farm community in the Sacramento (California) River Delta. Located some 30 miles south of SACRAMENTO, Walnut Grove is a small community in which a white élite owned all the town's property and surrounding agricultural fields. Under such a unique political economy, Asian immigrants, namely, Chinese, Japanese, East Indians and Filipinos, always competed with each other, while serving the interests of white landowners. The racial hierarchy of Walnut Grove also produced a segregated "Oriental School," which all Asian children were forced to attend.

Many Japanese immigrants entered Walnut Grove in the late 19th century. A man from Aichi PREFECTURE, Toshiro Tsurumi, was responsible for the rapid increase of the Japanese population. After establishing a personal network with white landowners, he assisted his fellow countrymen to find employment as agricultural laborers or tenant farmers, so that the majority of early Japanese immigrants in Walnut Grove were from Aichi prefecture. Japanese immigrants worked under an ethnic labor-contracting system. In a unit called *kumi,* a gang of laborers entered a contract with Japanese tenant farmers through the good offices of the local JAPANESE ASSOCIATION and boardinghouses. With the development of asparagus farming, Walnut Grove attracted thousands of migratory Japanese laborers in the harvest season.

During the first two decades of this century, Japanese tenant farmers dominated the asparagus industry in the area. Although white landowners generally controlled the rights of shipping and marketing the crop, the Walnut Grove ISSEI cultivated more than half of California's total asparagus acreage (12,000 acres) in 1918. Among them, Kamajiro Hotta, known as "the Asparagus King,"

farmed 1,400 acres. However, the 1920 (CALIFORNIA) ALIEN LAND LAW forced the farmers to give up tenancy and work as farm foremen for landowners, which led to the decline of Japanese agriculture.

Japanese businesses in Walnut Grove flourished in the midst of Chinatown, catering to the agricultural laborers and farmers. With the rapid increase of the Japanese population, Japanese businesses almost dominated Walnut Grove Chinatown by 1910. After the devastating fire of 1915, the Japanese residents established their own town. The Japanese town in Walnut Grove had a local Japanese association office, a Japanese Methodist church, a Buddhist church, various prefectural associations and later a JAPANESE AMERICAN CITIZENS LEAGUE chapter. Despite the forced removal and detention of all Japanese Americans during the World War II, many former residents returned to Walnut Grove, and it is still the home of many NISEI today.

For further reading, see Eiichiro Azuma. "Walnut Grove: Japanese Farm Community in the Sacramento River Delta, 1892–1942." Thesis, University of California, Los Angeles, 1992 and Richard K. Beardsley. "Ethnic Solidarity Turned to New Activism in a California Enclave: The Japanese Americans of the 'Delta'." Hirabayashi, Lane Ryo, ed., introd. *California History* 68 (Fall 1989): 100–15.   EIICHIRO AZUMA

Walter-McCarran Act See IMMIGRATION AND NATIONALITY ACT OF 1952.

War Relocation Authority Governmental agency charged with administering America's CONCENTRATION CAMPS. The War Relocation Authority (WRA) was a civilian agency created by Executive Order 9102 on March 18, 1942, to oversee the detention of Japanese Americans during World War II. MILTON S. EISENHOWER was the first director and was succeeded by DILLON S. MYER. The idea for the agency came from a meeting among FRANKLIN D. ROOSEVELT's top advisors on February 27, 1942. Since none of the departments under the president's office wanted to take responsibility for implementing EXECUTIVE ORDER 9066, Attorney General FRANCIS BIDDLE suggested that a single head be appointed to administer the so-called "evacuation." Eisenhower was chosen to be that person.

When Eisenhower first took the post as WRA director, he was unaware of the internal controversies surrounding the mass removal of Japanese Americans. He knew that it was his job to "relocate" them, but did not know of KARL BENDETSEN's and others' plans of making permanent concentration camps. At a meeting Bendetsen concluded with governors of the western states on April 7, Eisenhower asked for cooperation in implementing his five-point plan for resettling Japanese Americans in rural areas to work on sugar-beet farms. He pleaded for tolerance toward the Japanese Americans and in return was greeted with a racist barrage that literally stunned him. The governors wanted nothing short of a concentration camp where Japanese Americans could be watched under armed guard. A few months later, Eisenhower resigned his post—in part because of the insomnia he developed as a result of the job.

Dillon Myer was appointed director by Roosevelt on June 17, 1942 and immediately molded the WRA into his own image. As a matter of policy, he insisted on using terminology that to him more accurately described the job he and others in the WRA were performing: the WRA camps were not "concentration camps," but "relocation centers," "temporary havens," or "wayside stations"; Japanese Americans were not "inmates" or "internees," but "evacuees"; "evacuees" who resisted his authority were "troublemakers" and so on.

The legacy of Myer and the WRA was most keenly felt in the segregation policy that was implemented with the LOYALTY QUESTIONS. Those that answered yes to the litmus test were given passes to leave the camps for work or school, while those who answered no were labeled "disloyal" and sent to TULE LAKE "SEGREGATION CENTER." Myer was an authoritarian leader: those who cooperated with him and the WRA—such as the JAPANESE AMERICAN CITIZENS LEAGUE (JACL)—were rewarded while those that did not were severely punished and blackballed. For example, members of the HEART MOUNTAIN FAIR PLAY COMMITTEE paid the price for disobedience by serving prison terms in Leavenworth Federal Penitentiary. Others, such as the DAIHYO SHA KAI at Tule Lake, bore the brunt of the blame for supplies being cut off to other internees. In all, Myer should be credited for at least one achievement: he operated a very efficient agency until its end on June 30, 1946.

Myer and the WRA have not always had such a notorious reputation. In fact, up until the 1970s, Myer was almost universally admired for being a benevolent father figure to Japanese Americans, an administrator who made a tough situation much more bearable. In 1946, for example, the JACL held a testimonial dinner in his honor, calling Myer a "champion of human rights and common decency." With new scholarly research, however, beginning with MICHI WEGLYN's *Years of Infamy* in 1976, Myer's and the WRA's image has been tarnished almost beyond repair. Even their most loyal Japanese American defender, MIKE MASAOKA of the JACL, later conceded in his autobiography that Myer was a "jail-keeper"—albeit an unwilling one.

For further reading, see Richard Drinnon. *Keeper of Concentration Camps: Dillon S. Myer and American Racism*. Berkeley: University of California Press, 1987; Sue Kunitomi Embrey. *The Lost Years: 1942–46*. Los Angeles: Manzanar Committee, 1972; Peter Irons. *Justice at War: The Story of the Japanese American Internment Cases*. New York: Oxford University Press, 1983; Mike Masaoka, and Bill Hosokawa. *They Call Me Moses Masaoka*. New York: William Morrow, 1987; and Michi Weglyn. *Years of Infamy: The Untold Story of America's Concentration Camps*. New York: William Morrow & Co., 1976.

GLEN KITAYAMA

Warren, Earl (1891–1974) World War II attorney general and governor of California and chief justice of the U.S. Supreme Court. As the attorney general of California in 1942, Earl Warren played a key role in creating the climate in which the forced removal and detention of West Coast Japanese Americans could be carried out. He later presided over a Supreme Court known for its commitment to civil rights.

Earl Warren was born on March 19, 1891, in Los Angeles (ironically, in the section of town which would become LITTLE TOKYO) but grew up in Bakersfield, a semi-rural railroad town 200 miles northeast of Los Angeles. His father worked for the Southern Pacific Railroad and as a young man, Earl Warren worked during summer vacations as a railroad "call boy." Growing up in a place like Bakersfield during the height of the ANTI-JAPANESE MOVEMENT undoubtedly influenced his perceptions of Japanese and other Asian Americans.

Warren attended the University of California at Berkeley and also graduated from the law school there, after which he served in the army during World War I. His first professional job came when he was hired as a deputy on the staff of Ezra Decoto, District Attorney of Alameda County in 1920. He became the chief deputy in 1923 and replaced the retiring Decoto in 1925 as district attorney, a position he would hold for some 13 years. At the time, Alameda was one of the three largest counties in California, and Warren presided over what was in effect one of the state's busiest law practices. He established a reputation as a tough prosecutor with an antipathy to "extreme radicalism" of the sort some New Deal programs represented, but with a relatively strong commitment to basic civil rights for minorities and criminal defendants. At a time when coercion and beating confessions out of suspects was commonplace, Warren was known for not engaging in such tactics.

In 1938, Warren was elected attorney general of the State of California. In that office, he would be remembered most for his role in the removal and detention of Japanese Americans. As the attorney general, Warren was vocal in casting suspicion on Japanese Americans and repeated numerous cliches about them, such as there being no way to determine their loyalty, that their culture could not be comprehended by Americans, and that the Japanese government exerted control over the Japanese American population. At a conference of sheriffs and district attorneys on February 2, 1942, he made the infamous statement that the complete absence of sabotage by Japanese Americans was itself evidence that such sabotage was forthcoming: "It seems to me that it is quite significant that in this great state of ours we have had no fifth column activities and no sabotage reported. It looks very much to me as though it is a studied effort not to have any until the zero hour arrives." In his testimony before the TOLAN COMMITTEE, Warren's comments were accompanied by elaborate maps and charts purporting to show how Japanese American settlement patterns near military and strategic installations "appears to manifest something more than coincidence." While there is some question as to the degree Warren actually influenced the decision to remove all Japanese Americans from the West Coast, there is no question about his anti-Japanese sentiment, his own support for removal, or his influence on leading opinion makers such as columnist Walter Lippman in regard to the removal issue.

Partly on the strength of his pro-removal stance, Warren was elected governor of California in 1942. He ran for vice president in 1948 on the ticket with Thomas E. Dewey that lost to incumbent Harry S Truman. Warren ran for president himself in 1952, losing the Republican nomination to Dwight D. Eisenhower. Eisenhower appointed Warren soliciter general in August 1953, a position Warren accepted with Eisenhower's assurance that he would be appointed to the first available Supreme Court vacancy. When Chief Justice Fred M. Vinson died unexpectedly on September 8, 1953, Warren was named to replace him as chief justice.

According to many observers, Earl Warren was one of the greatest and most influential Supreme Court justices ever. The Warren Court's unanimous decision in the *Brown v. Board of Education* case in 1954 broke down the "separate but equal" doctrine and set the stage for the desegregation of the South. Many other decisions that followed greatly expanded the rights of minorities and criminal defendants in the years to come. Warren retired as chief justice in 1969 and died on July 9, 1974.

Despite his status as a defender of civil rights, Warren never publicly apologized for his role in the World War II removal and detention of Japanese Americans. The closest he came was in his posthumously published memoirs: "I have since deeply regretted the removal order and my own testimony advocating it, because it was not in keeping with our American concept of freedom and the rights of citizens. . . . It was wrong to react so impulsively, without positive evidence of disloyalty, even though we felt we had a good motive in the security of our state." According to former Supreme Court Justice Arthur J. Goldberg (who later served on the COMMISSION ON WARTIME RELOCATION AND INTERNMENT OF CIVILIANS), Warren said about the evacuation, "You

know, in retrospect, that's one of the worst things I ever did." His World War II actions remain a black mark on his legacy.

For further reading, see Commission on Wartime Relocation and Internment of Civilians. *Personal Justice Denied: Report of the Commission on Wartime Relocation and Internment of Civilians*. Washington, D.C.: Government Printing Office, 1982; James J. Rawls. "The Earl Warren Oral History Project: An Appraisal." *Pacific Historical Review* 41.1 (Feb. 1987): 87–97; and Jacobus tenBroek, Edward N. Barnhart and Floyd Matson. *Prejudice, War, and the Constitution*. Berkeley: University of California Press, 1954 for Warren's role in the WW II removal and detention; among the many Warren biographies are Bernard Schwartz. *Super Chief: Earl Warren and His Supreme Court—A Judicial Biography*. New York: New York University Press, 1983; and Earl Warren. *The Memoirs of Earl Warren*. New York: Doubleday, 1977.

Wax, Rosalie Hankey   Anthropologist Rosalie Hankey Wax played a key role in the JAPANESE AMERICAN EVACUATION AND RESETTLEMENT PROJECT as a fieldworker at TULE LAKE "RELOCATION CENTER." She has received lavish praise by some for the quality of her work there and has been castigated by others for ethical lapses. (See ERNEST KINZO WAKAYAMA.)

Webb v. O'Brien   Test case challenging the ban on sharecropping agreements of the 1920 (CALIFORNIA) ALIEN LAND LAW. O'Brien, a U.S. citizen and California resident, and Inouye, an ISSEI farmer, wished to enter into a CROPPING CONTRACT whereby Inouye would plant, cultivate and harvest crops on agricultural land owned by O'Brien. O'Brien filed a suit to enjoin the attorney general from enforcing the Alien Land Law, and the superior court granted an injunction. The attorney general, U.S. Webb, appealed, contending that the state had an interest in preventing such sharecropping agreements since the "ALIEN INELIGIBLE TO CITIZENSHIP" would actually enjoy the possession of the land. The U.S. Supreme Court agreed with Webb and held on November 19, 1923, that the Alien Land Law of 1920 legally prohibited sharecropping agreements between citizens and aliens ineligible to citizenship.

For further reading, see Frank F. Chuman. *The Bamboo People: The Law and Japanese-Americans*. Del Mar, Calif.: Publisher's Inc., 1976 and Moritoshi Fukuda. *Legal Problems of Japanese Americans*. Tokyo: Keio Tsushin, 1980. The case transcript can be found in Consulate-General of Japan. *Documental History of Law Cases Affecting Japanese in the United States, 1916–1924. 2 vols*. New York: Arno Press, 1978. 111–79.

DENNIS YAMAMOTO

Weglyn, Michi Nishiura (1929–)   Historian, activist. One time fashion designer Michi Weglyn is best known for authoring *Years of Infamy,* perhaps the most important book ever written on the mass removal and detention of West Coast Japanese Americans during World War II. Hers was the first major work on this experience to come from the pen of a Japanese American.

Weglyn was born in 1929 in Brentwood, California. During World War II, she and her family were forcibly removed from their home and sent to the GILA RIVER CONCENTRATION CAMP in Arizona. Due to poor health conditions, Weglyn contracted tuberculosis. After the war, she made a living designing costumes, working for "The Perry Como Show" among others.

Years of Infamy was published in 1976. After eight years of collecting data, Weglyn managed to interpret the camp experience of Japanese Americans during World War II without hiding her anger as a NISEI. Though not an autobiography, it has deeply affected the Asian American community and influenced all works on the World War II experience that have followed it.

Weglyn has long been a leader of the Japanese American community in New York City and a friend of many organizations within the community. In June 1990, Weglyn was awarded an Honorary Doctorate from Hunter College for her contributions and dedication to the Asian American community.

For further reading, see Michi Weglyn. *Years of Infamy: The Untold Story of America's Concentration Camps.* New York: William Morrow & Co., 1976. Secondary accounts of this book include Jeffery Paul Chan, Frank Chin, Lawson Fusao Inada and Shawn Wong, eds. *The Big Aiiieeeee!: An Anthology of Chinese American and Japanese American Literature.* New York: Meridian, 1991 (which also contains an excerpt from the book); Raymond Y. Okamura. "The Concentration Camp Experience from a Japanese American Perspective: A Bibliographical Essay and Review of Michi Weglyn's *Years of Infamy.*" In Gee, Emma, ed. *Counterpoint: Perspectives on Asian America.* Los Angeles: Asian American Studies Center, University of California, 1976. 27–30; and "Revisions in Japanese American History: Review of Books Published in 1976." *Journal of Ethnic Studies* 5.3 (Fall 1977): 112–15.

SUZANNE J. HEE

White Point (also known as White's Point) Southern California ISSEI resort. For a brief period in the 1920s, White Point, near San Pedro, California, was a resort run by and for *issei* that drew guests from miles around. White Point, located four miles west of San Pedro, featured a 70-foot wide beach with 300-foot cliffs rising picturesquely behind. The first Japanese arrived here in 1899 and were abalone fishermen. At first, they were quite successful and by 1903 a cannery had been built. Around 20–25 fishermen lived here and caught other shellfish as well. The community was closed down by the state in 1905 after complaints from neighbors and accusations of spying.

A few years later, Tajimi Tagami, a farmer from the West Adams area of Los Angeles, rode his buggy to the cliffs hoping to cure his rheumatism. A soak in the natural mineral springs at White Point did the trick. In 1917, Tagami and investors leased the land and began building a hotel and restaurant that was completed in 1920. During its heyday as a resort, from 1925–35, White Point featured a 50-room, two-story hotel/restaurant with a ballroom dance floor, three salt-water pools (one Olympic size), an enclosed boating area and a bathhouse. The bathhouse was fed by a pump house that heated the mineral water. "Endo's barge" was anchored three miles offshore for fishing. There was a direct bus line to LITTLE TOKYO and a Red Car Line from San Pedro. A 1927 tidal wave destroyed the pool and damaged the hotel; the 1933 earthquake closed the hot springs. As a result of these and other factors, the resort declined in the mid-1930s. It was appropriated by the military during World War II because of its supposedly strategic location.

For further reading, see Jon Takasugi. "White Point." *Rafu Shimpo* 5-6-7 June 1985.

Wirin, Abraham Lincoln (1901–1978) Attorney for the AMERICAN CIVIL LIBERTIES UNION (ACLU) of Southern California and the JAPANESE AMERICAN CITIZENS LEAGUE (JACL). A. L. Wirin had a long career representing the interests of Japanese Americans on the West Coast and other unpopular causes during the World War II and postwar years.

A. L. Wirin was born in 1901 into a poor Jewish family in Russia. In 1909, the Wirins immigrated to America, where A. L. was raised in a Jewish ghetto near Boston. Renamed Abraham Lincoln (a name he detested), he preferred to be called by his initials and was better known as "Al." His concern for civil liberties was apparent from an early age. As a schoolboy during World War I, he was fined five dollars for breach of the peace after he vocally protested an assault on antiwar marchers by a group of sailors. Financial sacrifices by his parents enabled Wirin to attend Harvard University, where he graduated *cum laude* after only three years. He received his law degree in 1925 from the Boston University Law School.

After graduation, Wirin moved to New York, where he went to work in the national office of the American Civil Liberties Union. There he became a close friend of its founder, Roger Baldwin, who later praised him as "probably the most energetic, daring and successfully skillful practitioner we ever had anywhere." In 1931, Wirin moved to Los Angeles, where he established a partnership with J. B. Tietz that combined civil liberties work with bankruptcy law.

As attorney for the Congress of Industrial Organizations (CIO), Wirin fought for the rights of workers and labor unions. In 1933, he was kidnapped, beaten and left in the desert by vigilantes after filing a suit in federal court on behalf of Mexican vegetable workers in Southern California. When World War II began, he was fired by the CIO and evicted from his office after being told to choose between that organization's all-out support for the war effort and the ACLU. He stuck by his principles and chose to continue defending civil liberties.

During World War II, Wirin's revulsion over the mass removal and detention of Japanese Americans caused him to become deeply and sometimes emotionally involved in their defense. He used a number of forums in attempting to inform the public that most of the clamor for exclusion of Japanese Americans from the West Coast came from spokesmen for commercial interests. Wirin also worked for Japanese American interests both as a private attorney seeking clients for pay and as attorney for both the Southern California branch of the ACLU and the JACL. In addition, he worked closely with the ACLU national leadership to secure test cases that would challenge the legality of government activities relating to the removal and detention of Japanese Americans.

The war gave Wirin an opportunity to fulfill one of his admitted ambitions—to take part in oral arguments before the United States Supreme Court. At least partially in pursuit of this goal, he urged the ACLU to become involved in the *Hirabayashi* case in early 1943 (see HIRABAYASHI V. U.S.). Through an aggressive campaign to participate in the Union's test cases, he played an important role in the preparation of briefs. During the week of May 10, 1943, he spoke from the Court's podium in defense of both Yasui and Korematsu (see YASUI V. U.S. and KOREMATSU V. U.S.).

In late 1945, Wirin entered TULE LAKE "SEGREGATION CENTER" in an attempt to secure test cases for the ACLU in an effort to bypass the cases already secured there by WAYNE COLLINS, who refused to be bound by ACLU prohibitions on how to argue cases. Wirin's success in winning restoration of citizenship for three renunciants was seen as a threat to the more than 4,000 clients in Collins's mass suits. Collins remained Wirin's bitter enemy over this until his death.

Wirin continued to represent various Japanese American interests throughout and after World War II. He defended NISEI draft resisters who felt it unjust to be forcibly taken into military service while being confined in CONCENTRATION CAMPS; ISSEI seeking United States citizenship; *nisei* "strandees," who had been unable to return to the U.S. from Japan when World War II began; *nisei* who had renounced their American citizenship and were seeking its restoration; and numerous others. He reached the Supreme Court's podium again in 1948, in the ALIEN LAND LAW–related case of OYAMA V. CALIFORNIA. A short time later, Wirin won another victory before the Supreme Court, overturning a 1943 California law that denied fishing licenses to resident *issei*.

Wirin's activities were sometimes controversial, resulting in occasionally harsh criticism from some who might ordinarily be considered his friends. Ernest Besig, director of the Northern California branch of the ACLU, criticized Wirin's methods, and protested his invasion of the San Francisco branch's territory in pursuit of cases. Even Wirin's friend Roger Baldwin considered him, at least temporarily, to be a liability to the national ACLU for his defense of the Communist Party and its members in the 1950s. The JACL dropped him as attorney for the same reason.

On the whole, however, even Wirin's detractors never doubted his dedication to civil liberties. That he never let his reputation or the lack of popularity of his clients get in the way of defending peoples' rights is demonstrated by those for whom he fought. These included: Nazis, religious fanatics, Communists and criminals, among whom was Sirhan Sirhan, the assassin of presidential candidate Senator Robert Kennedy. In his own words, "The rights of all persons are wrapped in the same constitutional bundle as those of the most hated members of the community."

A. L. Wirin retired in 1972 after suffering a heart attack. He died of a stroke at the age of 77 at Kaiser Foundation Hospital in Hollywood, California.

For further reading, see Donald E. Collins. *Native American Aliens: Disloyalty and the Renunciation of Citizenship by Japanese Americans During World War II*. Westport, Conn.: Greenwood Press, 1985; Audrie Girdner, and Anne Loftis. *The Great Betrayal: The Evacuation of the Japanese-Americans during World War II*. Toronto: Macmillan, 1969; Peter Irons. *Justice at War: The Story of the Japanese American Internment Cases*. New York: Oxford University Press, 1983; and Samuel Walker. *In Defense of American Liberties: A History of the ACLU*. New York: Oxford University Press, 1990

DONALD E. COLLINS

[Also used to compile this entry: "Civil Rights Defender; A. L. Wirin Jeopardized Career in Backing Japanese Americans." *Pacific Citizen* 24 Jan. 1978 and obituaries in *Time* 20 Feb. 1978: 94 and the *New York Times* 6 Feb. 1978.]

World War I veterans   While much has been written about the Japanese Americans who served in World War II, little is known about the Japanese Americans who served in World War I. While most of those who served were NISEI, a good number were ISSEI who volunteered for the army despite their exemption from the draft.

While most *issei* undoubtedly signed up out of genuine feelings of patriotism for their adopted country, many others joined because they believed their service would entitle them to the citizenship they were prohibited from receiving any other way. A few claimed to have been tricked into joining the army by unscrupulous recruiters.

While some of the Japanese Americans who served in World War I came from the mainland, most came from Hawaii; a total of 838 Japanese Americans from Hawaii were drafted. At the time, it was customary to keep troops of various racial backgrounds in Hawaii in separate companies, and the enlistment of a sufficient number of Japanese soldiers led to the formation of the all-Japanese Company D of the First Regiment. Established in August 1917, this company was the only one in American history to receive its orders in Japanese and march to a Japanese cadence. Kinichi Sasaki, an *issei*, received a commission as a first lieutenant while SHI-GEFUSA KANDA, also an *issei*, became a hero for his actions in the Red Cross in France. *Issei* World War I veteran TOKUTARO SLOCUM and *nisei* veterans JOE KU-RIHARA and ERNEST KINZO WAKAYAMA would all go on to play significant—and dramatically different—roles of leadership in the Japanese American community in the years to come.

The *issei* veterans who had hoped for citizenship faced a rollercoaster ride in the years to come. Initially rejected for citizenship, Judge Horace Vaughn of the United States District Court in Hawaii granted citizenship to 400 *issei* veterans. However, the territorial government refused to recognize them as citizens, and their status and that of all other *issei* veterans was decided when the Supreme Court ruled that they could not be citizens in TOYOTA V. UNITED STATES in 1925. Then, in 1935, largely through the lobbying efforts of Slocum, a bill was passed in Congress which granted naturalization rights to some *issei* World War I veterans. For most, however, citizenship remained a distant dream that would become possible only with the passage of the MCCAR-RAN-WALTER IMMIGRATION AND NATURALIZATION ACT of 1952.

For further reading, see Harry Maxwell Naka. "The Naturalization of Japanese War Veterans of the World War Forces." Thesis, University of California, Berkeley, 1939; Franklin S. Odo and Kazuko Sinoto. *A Pictorial History of the Japanese in Hawaii, 1885–1924.* Honolulu: Bishop Museum Press, 1985; and United Japanese Society of Hawaii. *History of Japanese in Hawaii.* James H. Okahata, ed. Honolulu: United Japanese Society of Hawaii, 1971.

Y

yakudoshi   A Japanese term meaning "year of calamity or disaster," *yakudoshi* is a Buddhist and Shinto celebra-

tion marking particular years of one's life. According to Japanese folk belief, *yakudoshi* celebrations dispel bad luck associated with these particular years. At *yakudoshi* parties, guests are asked to shoulder the honoree's unfortunate burden together.

A man and woman celebrate *yakudoshi* during different years of their lives. For a man, *yakudoshi* is celebrated before his 25th and 42nd birthdays. It is believed that by age 25 a man should be prepared for marriage and the establishment of his social standing and career, and by age 42, he should be settled in his career and family life. For a woman, *yakudoshi* celebrations are held before her 19th and 33rd birthdays. A women is said to have her *yakudoshi* years earlier than a man because she matures more quickly and experiences greater change during her life. Consequently, according to Japanese culture, a woman enters adulthood at age 19, and at age 33 she concludes her childbearing years. A yakudoshi celebration for a woman reaching 33 is therefore said to assure the healthy birth of children she may have after that age.

It has been explained that the 33rd and 42nd years are designated as *yakudoshi* years because in ancient times they marked the onset of the declining physical condition of men and women. Another explanation is that the characters for 33 and 42 are phonetically unlucky in Japanese. The former can be read to mean an unfortunate state, while the latter can be read as death.

The years immediately preceding and following the *yakudoshi* years are also determined to be slightly unfavorable years that one must treat with caution. As a result, the *yakudoshi* years are also observed with visits to temples and shrines and prayers offered to Buddhist and Shinto deities for safeguarding and good fortune.

For further reading, see Patsy Y. Nakayama. "Culture and Tradition." *Hawaii Herald* 18 May 1990: 90–98.

STACEY HIROSE

Yamada, Mitsuye   Award-winning writer Mitsuye Yamada is best known for her poetry about the Japanese American CONCENTRATION CAMP experience, as well as for her human rights activism.

Yamada was born to Jack and Hide Yasutake in Kyushu, Japan, and was raised in Seattle, Washington. Her mother came to the United States at the age of 19 to join her husband, a former interpreter for the U.S. Immigration Service. Imprisoned in Justice Department–administered INTERNMENT CAMPS from 1941–1945, her father also wrote SENRYU, or Japanese satirical poems, under the pen name of Jakki. Yamada and her family were incarcerated at MINIDOKA in Idaho during World War II. After two years, she left with her brother to work and study at the University of Cincinnati. Their parents joined them there after her father's release from camp. In 1945, Yamada left Cincinnati to attend New

York University and then the University of Chicago, from which she received a master of arts degree. Her first book of poetry, *Camp Notes & Other Poems,* was published in 1976 and recounts her experience at Minidoka. Her second book of poetry, *Desert Run, Poems and Stories,* was published in 1988.

Yamada is emeritus professor of English at Cypress College, where she taught creative writing, children's literature and ethnic literature for 20 years. Her writings are widely anthologized in periodicals and books such as *The Forbidden Stitch: An Asian American Women's Anthology; California State Poetry Quarterly; Calyx; Bridge: An Asian American Perspective; Echoes from Gold Mountain: An Asian American Journal; Arrangements in Literature; 10 Contemporary Poets; Poetry from Violence* and *The Webs We Weave.* In 1982, she was the recipient of the Vesta Award from the Woman's Building of Los Angeles. She was awarded a writer's residency at Yaddo, in Saratoga Springs, New York, in 1984. Since 1988, she has served as a member of the national board of directors for Amnesty International USA. In 1981, PBS produced the film, *Mitsuye and Nellie: Asian American Poets,* based on Yamada and Nellie Wong's poetry.

The founder of Multicultural Women Writers of Orange County, Yamada's latest published book is entitled *Sowing Ti Leaves: Writings by Multi-Cultural Women,* co-edited with Sarie Sachie Hylkema. Yamada currently resides in Irvine, California, with her husband Yoshikazu, a research chemist.

For further reading, see Yamada's *Camp Notes.* San Lorenzo, Calif.: Shameless Hussy Press, 1976; *The Webs We Weave.* Literary Arts Press, 1986; and *Desert Run, Poems and Stories.* Latham, N.Y.: Kitchen Table: Women of Color Press, 1988. See also Mitsuye Yamada, and Sarie Sachie Hylkema, eds. *Sowing Ti Leaves: Writings by Multi-Cultural Women.* Irvine, Calif.: Multi-Cultural Women Writers of Orange County, 1990; Gloria Anzaldua, ed. *This Bridge Called My Back: Writings by Women of Color.* 1981; and Shirley Geok-lin Lim, Mayumi Tsutakawa and Margarita Donelly, eds. *The Forbidden Stitch: An Asian American Women's Anthology.* Corvallis, Or.: Calyx Books, 1989.   EMILY LAWSIN

Yamada, Waka (1879–1956)   Japanese social critic and author. Waka Yamada overcame her life as a PROSTITUTE in America to become a famous writer and critic on women's issues in Japan in the 1920s and 1930s.

Born Waka Asaba on December 1, 1879, in Kanagawa PREFECTURE in what is today the city of Yokosuka, she was the fifth of seven children in a farm family. Young Waka attended school until the fourth grade, at which point she was pulled out by her family so that she could contribute her labor to the farm. She was married off at age 16 to a man 10 years her senior. Her family's financial difficulties and her unhappy marriage may have made her susceptible to the inducements of procurers for pimps

in the United States who with promises of riches enticed her into boarding a ship bound for America. Waka ended up in a brothel in Seattle that serviced only white men, becoming known as "the Arabian Oyae." (Prostitutes typically served only white men or only Asian men.) Trapped as a prostitute for a five- or six-year period, Waka escaped with the help of an ISSEI journalist. The couple eluded thugs hired by Waka's pimp and fled to San Francisco. Here, her rescuer betrayed her, forcing her into prostitution once again. This time, she escaped to the famed Cameron House, a Presbyterian refuge for fleeing prostitutes located in San Francisco's Chinatown. At Cameron House Waka became a valued translator and hard-working student. While there, she met Kakichi Yamada (1865–1934) who taught English and several other languages. Having arrived in the United States nearly 20 years earlier as a DEKASEGI-SHOSEI, he had managed to learn several languages and the finer points of law and sociology while working at typical *issei* migrant labor occupations. Waka and Kakichi were married in late 1904 or early 1905. The couple returned to Japan after suffering material losses in the 1906 San Francisco earthquake.

The learned Kakichi sought to teach the virtually uneducated Waka all he knew. He tutored her in English and Japanese and introduced her to many fields of study. The couple's house in the Yotsuya district of Tokyo soon became a haven for intellectuals and feminists, drawn by Kakichi's teaching and Waka's budding interest in feminist issues. She became a member of the feminist group Seitosha and began publishing translations and her own writings in their journal, *Seito* ("Bluestocking," named after a British women's literary club), starting from 1914. She became part of a circle that included many prominent Japanese feminists. She wrote prolifically through the 1920s for many magazines, including her own *Women and the New Society.* Beginning in 1931, she wrote a "Dear Abby"–type advice column for the *Tokyo Asahi Shimbun,* becoming a famous and popular figure in the process. In the late 1930s, she became a champion of maternalism—the elevation and protection of the status of motherhood—starting the Motherhood Protection League (Bosei Hogo Remmei) in 1934 and helping to get a law passed in the Diet (Japanese parliament) that provided financial aid to poor mothers of small children. She also built a home for needy mothers and children in 1939. All the while, she kept her past as a prostitute a secret.

In 1937, the magazine *Shufunotomo* sponsored a lecture tour of the U.S. that included a visit with Eleanor Roosevelt in the White House. The tour also included a stop in Seattle where Waka faced down a jeering audience familiar with her past there, silencing them with her dignified demeanor and scholarly discourse.

During World War II, her Hatagaya House for Mothers and Children was leveled. She rebuilt it after the war as the Hatagaya Girls School on the model of the Cameron House that had helped her change her life. She remained there until her death in 1956.

For further reading, see Tomoko Yamazaki. *The Story of Yamada Waka: From Prostitute to Feminist Pioneer.* Translated by Ann Kostant and Wakako Hironaka. New York: Kodansha International, 1986 for a biography of Yamada; see Yuji Ichioka. "Ameyuki-san: Japanese Prostitutes in Nineteenth-Century America." *Amerasia Journal* 4.1 (1977): 1–21 for information on Japanese prostitutes in America.

Yamaguchi, Kristi (1971–)

Kristi Yamaguchi became a national hero when she won the gold medal in women's figure skating at the 1992 Winter Olympics in Albertville, France. Despite being born clubfooted, Yamaguchi, a YONSEI from Fremont, California, began skating at the age of six. Although she had won the U.S. national title for pairs with partner Rudy Galindo in 1989 and 1990, Yamaguchi decided to concentrate exclusively on her solo skating. She spent most of her time training for the Olympics in Edmonton, Canada, with her coach Christy Kjarsgaard-Ness. Yamaguchi's hard work and dedication were rewarded when she defeated Midori Ito of Japan and Nancy Kerrigan of the U.S. to become the first American to win a gold medal in women's figure skating since Dorothy Hamill in 1976. Although she fell while attempting a triple loop, Yamaguchi successfully landed the difficult triple Lutz. Her graceful performance sparked E. M. Swift of *Sports Illustrated* to comment, "She landed her jumps so softly it seemed as if she were skating in her slippers." In addition to the Olympic gold, Yamaguchi has also captured the United States national and the world championship figure skating titles.

For further reading, see Martha Duffy. "When Dreams Come True." *Time,* 2 Mar. 1992: 48–49; Michael Martinez. "Yamaguchi Has Her Sights Set at a Higher Level." *The New York Times,* 5 Jan. 1992: 8-1–2; Jana Monji. "Star Skater." *Rafu Shimpo,* 1 Aug. 1991: 1; and E. M. Swift. "Stirring." *Sports Illustrated,* 2 Mar. 1992: 16–21.   SCOTT KURASHIGE

Yamamoto, Hisaye (1921–)

Respected NISEI writer known for her witty and sensitive short stories and essays examining Japanese American life, especially the relationships between *nisei* and ISSEI. Yamamoto was one of the first Japanese American writers to receive national attention after World War II.

Yamamoto was born in Redondo Beach, California, in 1921 and spent her early years in various Southern California farming communities. As a teenager, she began contributing to the Los Angeles–based Japanese American newspaper *Kashu Mainichi* under the pseudonym Napoleon and later wrote a column entitled "Napoleon's Last Stand." She graduated from Compton Junior College with a degree in languages. During the war, Yamamoto was interned at POSTON, where she was a reporter and columnist for the *Poston Chronicle* newspaper. Leaving Poston as a part of the WAR RELOCATION AUTHORITY's effort to resettle *nisei,* she worked as a cook in Springfield, Massachusetts. The death of a younger brother, killed in Italy while a member of the 442ND REGIMENTAL COMBAT TEAM, called her back to Poston.

After the war, Yamamoto returned to Los Angeles and worked from 1945 to 1948 for the *Los Angeles Tribune,* a weekly newspaper serving the African American community. She left the *Tribune* with the idea of returning to school but also to care for an adopted son. With the 1949 publication in *Partisan Review* of an essay on sexual harassment entitled "The High-Heeled Shoes," Yamamoto first garnered national attention. In 1950 she was awarded a John Hay Whitney Foundation Opportunity Fellowship, and she spent the following year writing some of her best and most well-known stories in addition to translating René Boylesve's "L'Enfant à la Balustrade." "Yoneko's Earthquake," one of the stories written during this period, brought Yamamoto to the attention of the poet and critic Yvor Winters, who encouraged her to accept a Stanford writing fellowship. She chose instead to work as a volunteer with the Catholic Worker organization founded by Dorothy Day. Between 1953 and 1955, Yamamoto lived with her adopted son on the Catholic Worker's Staten Island farm. After marrying Anthony DeSoto, she left the farm and returned to Los Angeles to raise a family.

Although her early stories have been reprinted in numerous literary anthologies, her work since the early 1960s has been confined largely to the holiday issues of the various Japanese American newspapers. Three of her stories, "Seventeen Syllables" (1949), "The Brown House" (1951), and "Epithalamium" (1960), were selected by Martha Foley as "Distinctive Short Stories" of the years in which they were published. Her story "Yoneko's Earthquake" (1951) was chosen by Foley as one of the best American short stories of 1951. In 1986 Yamamoto won an American Book Award for Lifetime Achievement from the Before Columbus Foundation. Fifteen of her stories were collected in *"Seventeen Syllables" and Other Stories* and published in 1988. A television film entitled *Hot Summer Winds,* based on "Seventeen Syllables" and "Yoneko's Earthquake," was directed by Emiko Omori and broadcast nationally on PBS in 1991. Yamamoto currently lives in Eagle Rock, California.

In addition to her collection of short stories, *"Seventeen Syllables" and Other Stories* (Latham, N.Y.: Kitchen Table Women of Color Press, 1988), Yamamoto has written numerous pieces that have appeared in the Japanese American vernacular press. See King-kok Cheung and Stan Yogi. *Asian American Litera-*

ture: An Annotated Bibliography (New York: Modern Language Association of America, 1988) for a more or less complete listing of her work.

Secondary work on Yamamoto includes King-kok Cheung. *Articulate Silences: Hisaye Yamamoto, Maxine Hong Kingston, Joy Kogawa*. Ithaca, N.Y.: Cornell University Press, 1993 and "Double-Telling: Intertextual Silence in Hisaye Yamamoto's Fiction." *American Literary History* 3.2 (1991): 277–93; Charles L. Crow "Home and Transcendence in Los Angeles Fiction." In David Fine, ed. *Los Angeles Fiction*. Albuquerque: University of New Mexico, 1984. 189–203 and "A MELUS Interview: Hisaye Yamamoto." *MELUS* 14.1 (Spring 1987): 73–84; Dorothy Ritsuko McDonald and Katharine Newman. "Relocation and Dislocation: The Writings of Hisaye Yamamoto and Wakako Yamauchi." *MELUS* 7.3 (Fall 1980): 116–25; and Stanley Stuart Yogi. "Legacies Revealed: Uncovering Buried Plots in the Stories of Hisaye Yamamoto and Wakako Yamauchi." Thesis, University of California, Berkeley, 1988.

STAN YOGI

Yamasaki, Minoru (1912–1986)

Minoru Yamasaki was a world-renowned architect most famous for his work as chief architect of the World Trade Center, the world's tallest building at the time of its construction. Yamasaki was born in Seattle in 1912. His uncle was an architect and Yamasaki became inspired by his drawings. Yamasaki graduated from the University of Washington in 1933 and went on to earn a master's degree in architecture from New York University. Upon completion of his education, Yamasaki took a job with Shreve, Lamb and Harmon, the firm that designed the Empire State Building. After working at Shreve et al. from 1936 to 1943, Yamasaki moved to Detroit, where he served as chief designer for the firm of Smith, Hinchman and Grylls. Seeking greater autonomy, Yamasaki left the firm and formed his own partnership. During this time, he worked on the Consulate General's office in Kobe, Japan, for the State Department.

Yamasaki ended his partnership on good terms and struck out on his own. It was as head of his own architectural firm that he made his mark in the field. His business experienced dramatic growth in the early 1960s. Despite being plagued by medical problems, Yamasaki, with the aid of his carefully chosen staff, went on to design well over 250 residential, commercial and industrial buildings. Some of Yamasaki's notable structures include the St. Louis Airport Terminal (completed in 1956), the Federal Science Pavilion at the World's Fair in Seattle (1962), the Woodrow Wilson School of Public and International Affairs at Princeton University (1965), the Century Plaza Hotel (1966) and the Century Plaza Towers (1975), both in Los Angeles.

Yamasaki's most ambitious and defining work by far, however, is the World Trade Center in lower Manhattan. Commissioned in 1962, the World Trade Center consists of offices, a transportation center for railways and a shopping concourse. Yamasaki wrote of the complex in his autobiography: "the Trade Center, with its location facing the entry to New York Harbor, could symbolize the importance of world trade to this country and its major metropolis and become a physical expression of the universal effort of men to seek and achieve world peace." Yamasaki's 50-person firm was chosen to carry out the enormous project, carrying a $280,000,000 estimate, over more than 40 firms, some of which had over 1,000 staff members. Disturbed by the continued deterioration and cramped conditions of urban America, Yamasaki generously created open spaces "where people can spend a few moments to relieve the tensions and monotonies of the usual working day." In addition, the World Trade Center features an innovative cantilever structure that utilizes the exterior wall of the building to minimize movement under high wind conditions. A distinctive part of the Manhattan skyline, the World Trade Center consists of two 110-story buildings that were the tallest in the world until completion of the Sears Tower in Chicago. Yamasaki died on February 5, 1986, at the age of 73.

For further reading, see Minoru Yamasaki. *A Life in Architecture*. New York and Tokyo: Weatherhill, 1979.

SCOTT KURASHIGE

Yamashita v. Hinkle

Takuji Yamashita and Charles Hio Kono v. J. Grant Hinkle, secretary of state of the State of Washington, was one of several naturalization cases involving Japanese immigrants to reach the United States Supreme Court. In 1906, Yamashita had filed an application for naturalization in the Superior Court of the State of Washington that had been granted. Thinking himself a citizen, he tried to form a land company 16 years later. In May 1921, Yamashita attempted to file articles of incorporation for the Japanese Real Estate Holding Company, based on his citizenship. The secretary of state refused to accept these articles, citing laws in the state forbidding non-citizens from forming land corporations. This action was upheld in the state supreme court and appealed to the U.S. Supreme Court. On November 13, 1922, the Supreme Court upheld the decision at the same time that it ruled on the OZAWA V. UNITED STATES case. As a result of these decision, ISSEI citizenship status was cemented: on the basis of their ancestry, *issei* were ineligible for American citizenship.

For further reading, see Frank F. Chuman. *The Bamboo People: The Law and Japanese-Americans*. Del Mar, Calif.: Publisher's Inc., 1976. For the case transcript, see Consulate-General of Japan. *Documental History of Law Cases Affecting Japanese in the United States, 1916–1924. 2 Vols*. New York: Arno Press, 1978. 121–75.

Yamashita, Soen Journalist. Soen Yamashita was one of several Hawaii ISSEI who returned to Japan prior to World War II and who wrote in support of the Japanese war effort. He was born in 1898 in Hiroshima PREFECTURE and came to the U.S. in 1914 to learn English. After graduating from Iolani High School in Honolulu, he joined the staff of the NIPPU JIJI newspaper. He went to Japan as a correspondent for the paper in 1933 and remained there through World War II, working with Hawaii NISEI in Japan. He became the director of a Foreign Ministry–sponsored agency overseeing *nisei* organizations in Japan. In 1942, he published a book on Hawaii containing strong nationalistic sentiments. He saw America as having turned Hawaii from "Mark Twain's Pacific paradise" into a "Pacific Gibraltar." He also saw the imminent Japanese takeover of Hawaii as justified since (a) Japan really "discovered" Hawaii in the 13th century and (b) the Japanese population in Hawaii was so large that "[i]f one speaks of liberation of Hawaii's people, than it is more logical to refer to the Japanese than to the Hawaiians." Although he saw the Americanization of the *nisei* as problematic, he held to the hope that they would be able to "sweep away the temptations of the culture of freedom . . . and the ideal of individualism" in favor of Japanese values. Yamashita's fate after the war is unknown.

For further reading, see John Stephan. *Hawaii under the Rising Sun: Japan's Plans for Conquest after Pearl Harbor.* Honolulu: University of Hawaii Press, 1984.

Yamataya v. Fisher A U.S. Supreme Court case involving the Act of March 3, 1891, which provided that immigrants likely to become public charges could be excluded from entering the United States. Kaoru Yamataya landed in Seattle, Washington, on July 11, 1901, but an immigration inspector ordered her deportation on the grounds that she was a pauper and likely to become a public charge. Yamataya's petition for a writ of *habeas corpus* was denied by a lower court, and she appealed to the U.S. Supreme Court. The Supreme Court affirmed the judgment of the lower court, stating that her deportation was allowed by the Act of March 3, 1891. The Court did note, however, that newly arriving immigrants who faced the possibility of deportation were still entitled to a full hearing under the due process clause of the Fourteenth Amendment. Unfortunately for Yamataya, she did not know the English language well enough to understand the notice of a hearing that she received. However, the Court established that immigration officials could not arbitrarily deport aliens who entered the country without giving them hearings.

For further reading, see Frank F. Chuman. *The Bamboo People: The Law and Japanese-Americans.* Del Mar, Calif.: Publisher's Inc., 1976.   DENNIS YAMAMOTO

Yamato Colony (Calif.) The first of KYUTARO ABIKO's three Japanese Christian farming colonies. Located in Livingston, California, between Turlock and Merced in the San Joaquin Valley, the colony overcame an initially harsh environment, some tough economic times and occasional flare-ups of the ANTI-JAPANESE MOVEMENT to establish a stable community that continues to this day. Having made a good deal of money as a LABOR CONTRACTOR, Abiko formed the American Land and Produce Company, which purchased 3,200 acres in Livingston in 1907 in an attempt to form a Japanese Christian utopian colony. He was certainly not the only person to have this dream. As a way to insulate themselves from the racism pervading the United States, to establish economic self-sufficiency and to provide an environment where their unique culture might be encouraged and developed, many racial and ethnic minorities tried to form such utopian farming colonies. Though not the first, Abiko's colonies proved to be the most durable of all the Japanese attempts. After purchasing the land, he encouraged other Japanese to settle there, emphasizing the opportunity to be landowners rather than tenants or sharecroppers. He also extended generous credit terms as an added inducement. A core of Japanese did settle in Livingston, making a special effort to support the larger community by not establishing their own businesses and purposely patronizing white merchants. Even so, the colony was hardly a utopia at first. Problems with wind and with the water supply had to be solved before the land could produce salable crops. Additionally, the failure of Abiko's bank put the financial future of the colony in doubt.

The beginning of Yamato's success was the formation of the Livingston Cooperative Society in 1914. Working together, Yamato farmers more efficiently marketed their produce and purchased supplies. In 1927 the co-op divided into the Livingston Fruit Growers Association and the Livingston Fruit Exchange. During World War II, the three Abiko colonies—Yamato, Cressey, and CORTEZ—formed a corporation to run the farms administered by a Caucasian in anticipation of mass removal and were thus one of the few farm communities to survive the war intact. After the war, NISEI began to take over the farms and helped to unite the two co-ops into the Livingston Farmers Association in 1956. Although the remnants of the Yamato Colony remain to this day, things are a little different. By 1980, nearly a third of the co-op members were non-Japanese.

For further reading, see Kesa Noda. *The Yamato Colony: 1906–1960.* Livingston, Calif.: Livingston-Merced JACL Chapter, 1981. Early studies of Livingston/Yamato Colony include Manchester E. Boddy. *Japanese in America.* Los Angeles: Privately printed, 1921; Betty Francis Brown. "The Evacuation of the Japanese Population from a California Agricultural

Community." Thesis, Stanford University, 1944; Horace F. Chansler "Assimilation of the Japanese in and around Stockton." Thesis, College of the Pacific, 1932; and Winnifred Raushenbush. "Their Place in the Sun." *Survey Graphic* 56 (May 1926): 141–45, 203. See also Valerie J. Matsumoto. *Farming the Home Place: A Japanese American Community in California, 1919–1982.* Ithaca, N.Y. Cornell University Press, 1993 for more on the World War II corporation. Eugene Tashima. "Livingston Sansei: Rural Perspectives on Group Identity and Community." Thesis, University of California, Los Angeles, 1985 examines the contemporary Japanese American community in Livingston through the eyes of *sansei* males.

Yamato Colony (Fla.) Japanese agricultural community in Florida. There were at least three "Yamato Colonies" in the U.S. started by Japanese immigrants. Though short-lived, the legacy of the Yamato Colony in Florida endures to this day. In November 1903, an American-educated Japanese man named Jo Sakai arrived in Jacksonville with plans to establish a Japanese farming colony in Florida. Sakai was born on August 7, 1874, in Miyazu in Kyoto PREFECTURE. He graduated from Doshisha University in Kyoto and went on to New York University's School of Commerce, Accounting and Finance, graduating just before his arrival in Florida. His idea to start a colony received surprising support from Floridians and enthusiastic interest from the business community. The reason for this might have been the chronic shortage of labor that had plagued Florida since the 1860s and the reputation of the Japanese as expert farmers. Carrying a letter of introduction from the dean of his business school, Sakai met with Florida Governor William Jennings. Jennings was supportive of Sakai's proposal and would later become involved in a similar project with California Japanese on land near Middleburg, Florida. Sakai visited Leon County (in the Tallahassee area) and Lee and Manatee Counties; he was offered over 1,000 acres for his colony at each location.

James Ingraham, the president of the Model Land Company, had also been impressed by the skill shown by Japanese farmers in California and mentioned this to a friend at New York University. He was soon put in touch with Sakai and succeeded in selling him on a piece of property near Boca Raton. The deal was facilitated by the especially good terms granted by Ingraham, the fact that Model Land Co. was a subsidiary of the Florida East Coast Railway and the idea that Sakai could develop a self-sustaining, land-owning colony rather than one based on sharecropping. Sakai signed up with Ingraham in late December 1903.

The Yamato Colony was established in 1904. Sakai recruited colonists from Japan, especially from his own hometown. After a few difficult years, a big pineapple crop in 1906 seemed to secure the colony's future. It grew steadily—in 1907, a rail station and a post office were built and Yamato Colony was incorporated. But just as things were starting to look good, a blight struck the pineapple fields in 1908, severely crippling Yamato's economy. Competition from Cuba dealt the final blow. Additionally, a fledgling ANTI-JAPANESE MOVEMENT hit Florida by 1912 and Japanese migration slowed dramatically. The post office closed in 1919 and by the thirties, only about 30 Japanese settlers remained.

An interesting footnote to the story of the Yamato Colony is that of George Morikami. The last Yamato Colony survivor, he became wealthy in the postwar real estate boom and donated money to build a park and museum of Japanese culture named after him that remain to this day.

For further reading, see Thomas Gregerson. "Florida: Sunshine State Was Home of Yamato Japanese Colony in 1903." *Rafu Shimpo* 17 June 1985: 1–2 and George E. Pozzetta and Harry A. Kersey. "Yamato Colony: A Japanese Presence in South Florida." *Tequesta* 36 (1976): 66–77.

Yamato Colony (Tex.) Japanese farming colony in Texas. In addition to the relatively well-known Yamato colonies in California and Florida, there was another such venture undertaken in Texas. Begun by seven Japanese men in around 1917, this Yamato Colony was to be a sugar plantation. The men purchased 400 acres of land near Brownsville and tried to make a go of growing sugar cane there. Although the cane grew well, the venture turned out not to be very profitable, largely because of the postwar depression and its adverse effects on the sugar market. Although the colony was dissolved in 1921, many of the original colonists remained in the area.

For further reading, see Thomas K. Walls. *The Japanese Texans.* San Antonio: Institute of Texan Cultures, 1987.

Yamato damashii Phrase meaning "Japanese spirit." With the rise of Japanese militarism in the 1930s until the end of World War II, *Yamato damashii* implied Japanese militarism and nationalism and was equated with unquestioning loyalty to the Japanese emperor and Japan. The phrase was used by Japanese militarists and pro-Japan ISSEI and NISEI to also describe the spiritual characteristics supposedly unique to Japanese people. These characteristics included physical and moral fortitude, devotion, courage and sincerity. The term is seldom used today. STACEY HIROSE

Yamauchi, Wakako (1924–) Well-known playwright and accomplished short story writer and painter. Winner of numerous Rockefeller grants for playwriting and a 1977 Los Angeles Drama Critics nomination for Outstanding New Play (*And the Soul Shall Dance.*)

Yamauchi was born Wakako Nakamura in Westmoreland, California, in 1924. Her family farmed in nearby

Brawley. After a particularly bad crop failure, Yamauchi's family moved north to Oceanside, where Yamauchi first met the NISEI writer HISAYE YAMAMOTO, who would become a life-long friend. During the war, Yamauchi was interned at POSTON, where she was a staff artist for the *Poston Chronicle*. Toward the end of the war, she worked for a time in a Utah tomato canning factory before moving to Chicago to work in a candy factory. She returned to Poston, however, in the last days of the camp because of her father's death. Upon leaving Poston, she moved with her mother and sister to San Diego and then to Los Angeles, where she attended art school and lived for a time with Hisaye Yamamoto. She married Chester Yamauchi in 1948. Although the couple divorced, she continues to write under her married name.

Yamauchi had always wanted to paint and to write. Since drawing came easily to her, she pursued painting first and did not launch her literary career until the 1950s. After receiving numerous rejections for her story "And the Soul Shall Dance," Yamauchi took a correspondence course in short story writing and began to write stories and essays for the RAFU SHIMPO. "And the Soul Shall Dance" languished for years before the *Rafu Shimpo* asked Yamauchi for a contribution and she decided to submit it. Hisaye Yamamoto brought the story to the attention of the editors of *Aiiieeeee!: An Anthology of Asian American Writing,* who included the story in the collection, thus introducing Yamauchi to a larger audience. She continued to write short stories and essays regularly for the *Rafu Shimpo,* and several of these works have been anthologized or reprinted.

Yamauchi embarked on a career as a playwright in 1977 when "And the Soul Shall Dance" came to the attention of MAKO, artistic director of the East West Players, a Los Angeles ASIAN AMERICAN THEATER group. He asked her to turn the story into a play. Her effort was fruitful. East West Players as well as theaters across the country have produced the play. A PBS television version of the play has had several national showings. Yamauchi has since written several other plays, including *The Music Lesson* (based on her short story entitled "In Heaven and Earth" about a NIKKEI drifter's effect on a rural family), *The Memento* (a psychological drama about a *nisei* woman's desires and jealousies), *12-1-A* (a play about life in the Poston internment camp) and *The Chairman's Wife* (a play based on the life of Chiang Ching, Mao Tse-tung's widow). Yamauchi currently lives in Gardena, California.

For further reading: There is no published collection of Yamauchi's fiction or drama. The play of "And the Soul Shall Dance" appeared in *West Coast Plays* 11/12 (Winter/Spring 1982): 117–64. See King-kok Cheung, and Stan Yogi. *Asian American Literature: An Annotated Bibliography* (New York: Modern Language Association of America, 1988) for a more or less complete listing of her work.

Secondary sources include Dorothy Ritsuko McDonald, and Katharine Newman. "Relocation and Dislocation: The Writings of Hisaye Yamamoto and Wakako Yamauchi." *MELUS* 7.3 (Fall 1980): 116–25 and Stanley Stuart Yogi. "Legacies Revealed: Uncovering Buried Plots in the Stories of Hisaye Yamamoto and Wakako Yamauchi." Thesis, University of California, Berkeley, 1988.   STAN YOGI

Yankee samurai   Nickname given to the NISEI and KIBEI who served in the MILITARY INTELLIGENCE SERVICE. (See MILITARY INTELLIGENCE SERVICE and MILITARY INTELLIGENCE SERVICE LANGAUGE SCHOOL.)

Yano guardianship case   Important decision by the California state supreme court effectively invalidating the section of the 1920 (CALIFORNIA) ALIEN LAND LAW that prohibited ISSEI from serving as guardians over minor children in whose name agricultural land had been purchased. This decision allowed *issei* to circumvent the land law by purchasing land in the name of their citizen children.

Hayao Yano had purchased 15 acres of land in Butte County on December 6, 1919, in the name of his two-year-old daughter Tetsubumi. He filed a petition with the superior court in Sutter County to be named guardian of Tetsubumi on October 23, 1920, for the purpose of administering the land, a petition which was denied on November 6 under the provisions of the 1913 (CALIFORNIA) ALIEN LAND LAW. This decision was appealed to the state supreme court, with the support of the JAPANESE ASSOCIATION. In its decision of May 1, 1922, the supreme court overturned the lower court's ruling, allowing Yano to be appointed guardian of his daughter's estate. In so doing a key provision of the 1913 and 1920 Alien Land Laws had been ruled invalid. In the years to come, purchasing agricultural land in the name of NISEI children would become the most common means of getting around the provisions of the land laws. For further reading, see Frank F. Chuman. *The Bamboo People: The Law and Japanese-Americans.* Del Mar, Calif.: Publisher's Inc., 1976 and Yuji Ichioka. *The Issei: The World of the First Generation Japanese Immigrants, 1885–1924.* New York: The Free Press, 1988. The legal transcript can be found in Consulate-General of Japan. *Documental History of Law Cases Affecting Japanese in the United States, 1916–1924.* 2 Vols. New York: Arno Press, 1978. 500–50.

Yano, Rodney J.T. (1943–1969)   Recipient, Congressional Medal of Honor. Rodney J. T. Yano is one of four Japanese Americans to receive America's highest military honor.

Born in Kona, Hawaii, Yano entered military service in Honolulu, Hawaii, during the Vietnam War. Sergeant

Yano distinguished himself while serving with the Air Cavalry Troop aboard the troop's command-and-control helicopter during action against enemy forces entrenched in dense jungle. Under fire, Sergeant Yano was covered with burning phosphorous and severely wounded when a grenade exploded prematurely. Partially blinded and using only one arm, Yano in complete disregard to his welfare, continued to hurl blazing ammunition from the helicopter, afflicting further injuries upon himself. He later died of his wounds. His "indomitable courage and profound concern for his comrades" and "conspicuous gallantry at the cost of his life" were acknowledged with the Congressional Medal of Honor, awarded by the president in the name of the Congress.

For further reading, see *Congressional Medal of Honor; The Names the Deeds*. Chico, Calif.: Sharp & Dunnigan Publications, 1988.   TRACY ENDO

Yashima, Taro   See IWAMATSU, ATSUSHI.

Yasuda, Frank (1868–1958)   Cabin boy, trading post operator, founder of the Yukon River town of Beaver, Alaska. Born in Ishinomaki, Miyagi PREFECTURE, Yasuda arrived in San Francisco in 1884 and briefly worked there before serving as a cabin boy aboard the U.S. Revenue cutter *Bear,* which traveled up the Arctic coast in Alaska.

He became storekeeper of the Barrow government relief station until early in the new century, having married an Inupiat Eskimo wife, Nevalo. Fearing the epidemics afflicting the region, Yasuda, his family and a group of Inupiats left the Arctic coast and traveled through the Brooks Range to interior Alaska to mine placer gold. Several years of travel brought them through the Chandalar River mining region to the Yukon River, which provided major river boat transportation for miner's supplies. On the Yukon River the community of Beaver was founded. Yasuda ran a trading post there. The ethnic composition of Beaver was distinctive: Inupiat Eskimos and Japanese—in the middle of traditional Athabascan Indian country.

Yasuda and Beaver lent stability and focus to the region and a post office and school were established. Forcibly removed during World War II, Yasuda joined other Alaskan Japanese aliens and Japanese Alaskans in internment. Yasuda returned after the war and continued to live in Beaver until his death in 1958.

Yasuda's life has been fictionalized in a controversial and widely-read Japanese novel, *Arasuka Monogatari,* by Jiro Nitta that was recently translated into English under the title *An Alaskan Tale* (University Press of America, 1991).   RONALD K. INOUYE

Yasui, Masuo (1886–1957)   Shopkeeper, landowner. Masuo Yasui is credited with laying the foun-

Yasui Family, ca. 1927. *Yasui Family Collection, Japanese American National Museum Photographic & Moving Image Archive*

dation for a thriving Japanese American community in Oregon's Hood River Valley. After coming to the U.S. at the age of 16 to join his father, he and his brother Renichi Fujimoto worked with their father on the railroads of Montana. Masuo moved to Portland in 1903, working as a SCHOOLBOY while he learned English and studied law. His English speaking ability and legal expertise quickly made him a leader in the local Japanese community.

Taking a trip east to Hood River in 1905, Masuo was immediately attracted to the natural beauty of the area. He also recognized the need for a store that would serve the Japanese laborers in the sawmills, logging camps and orchards in the surrounding area. Calling Renichi over from Montana, the two opened such a store. Like similar endeavors in other Japanese American communities, the Yasui brothers' store served many functions besides being a place where dry goods could be purchased. The store served as information center, savings bank, gathering place and travel agency, among other things.

Masuo also played a major role in the development of the Japanese American community in Hood River. At the time, the Hood River Valley was in the process of being cleared of timber by the logging industry, and the leftover, stump-filled land could be purchased for as little as 25 cents an acre. Yasui purchased agricultural land in the vicinity and entered into joint agreements with Japanese laborers to farm the land, apparently also sharing in the ownership of the land. Though he grew asparagus and strawberries, apple and pear orchards became the main crops in the valley. Bill Hosokawa claims that Yasui had an interest in one out of every 10 boxes of apples and pears shipped out of Hood River by the eve of World War II.

In 1912, Yasui married Shidzuyo Miyake, a woman whom he had known in Japan and who was his age. The couple had nine children, seven of whom lived to adulthood. Much has been made of the fact that two of the children became doctors and one a lawyer. The most famous of the siblings was Minoru (1916–86), whose challenges to the World War II–era curfew and evacuation orders guarantee his place in history. (See YASUI VS. U.S.)

After the attack on Pearl Harbor, Yasui was taken away immediately by the FBI and spent the next four years in various Justice Department administered IN-TERNMENT CAMPS. His land sold off at bargain prices prior to the mass removal of all Japanese Americans, he and his wife never returned to Hood River, living out their remaining years in Portland. Yasui died in 1957, suffering from Alzheimer's disease.

Robert S. Yasui, one of Masuo's sons, wrote a book about the Yasui family entitled *The Yasui Family of Hood River, Oregon* (Hood River, Or.: Holly Yasui, 1987) that contains a chapter on Masuo (pp. 3–24). Masuo is also mentioned in *Nisei: The Quiet Americans* by Bill Hosokawa (New York: William Morrow & Co., 1969) and in two histories of Japanese Americans in Oregon: Wendy Lee Ng. "Collective Memory, Social Networks, and Generations: The Japanese-American Community in Hood River, Oregon." Diss. University of Oregon, 1989 and Barbara Yasui. "The Nikkei in Oregon, 1834–1940." *Oregon Historical Quarterly* 76.3 (Sept. 1975): 225–57. See also Akemi Kikumura. *Issei Pioneers: Hawaii and the Mainland, 1885–1924.* Los Angeles: Japanese American National Museum, 1992.

Yasui v. United States   One of four landmark World War II cases challenging the forced removal and/or detention of all West Coast Japanese Americans. Minoru "Min" Yasui, a NISEI attorney, worked for the Japanese consulate in Chicago up until the day Pearl Harbor was bombed. On the advice of his father, MASUO YASUI, Min quit the consulate and attempted to volunteer for the United States Army. He was rejected purely on racial grounds. In the meantime, his ISSEI father was arrested by the FBI for being suspected of helping Japan in the war effort. Masuo Yasui was sent to the Justice Department INTERNMENT CAMP in Missoula, Montana. He remained in detention until 1945.

Min Yasui was deeply affected by his father's arrest and his own rejection by the army. This, combined with his background as a lawyer, led to his decision to challenge the curfew order passed on March 24, 1942. This order required that all "enemy aliens" and persons of Japanese ancestry be indoors between 8 P.M. and 6 A.M. At 11 P.M. on the night of March 28, 1942, Yasui attempted to get himself arrested by breaking the curfew law. He ran into a policeman, declared himself to be of Japanese ancestry and demanded to be detained. The policeman told him to go home before he got into serious trouble. Unsuccessful, Yasui then went to the Second Avenue police station in Portland and again

requested to be detained. The sergeant working that night was more than happy to oblige him. Thus, Yasui became the first Japanese American to challenge General JOHN L. DEWITT's orders.

The trial of Min Yasui began on June 12, 1942, with Judge James Fee presiding. While the prosecution of Yasui was the responsibility of the Justice Department, it was the WAR RELOCATION AUTHORITY (WRA) that provided the strategy in the case. Although independent from the Justice Department, the WRA saw this test case as instrumental in defending the process that led to the detention of the Japanese American population. Victory in the Yasui case would set the stage for a successful defense of the CONCENTRATION CAMPS.

The government based its case against Yasui on racial grounds. "Racial characteristics," it was argued, were what made Japanese Americans a threat to society. Although no proof of fifth column activity could be found, this did not stop the government prosecutors from stating as fact that there was such organized work "of undisclosed and undetermined dimensions." To find proof of this, stated the government lawyers, "would place upon the State an intolerable burden of proof at a time when it is struggling for survival." While they conceded that "the great majority" of Japanese Americans were loyal to the United States, the government lawyers echoed DeWitt's claim that it was "impossible during this period of emergency to make a particular investigation of the loyalty of each person in the Japanese community."

On November 16, 1942, Judge Fee issued his opinion on Yasui's case. First, he ruled that the curfew order, as it applied to American citizens, was unconstitutional. However, he also found that Yasui's employment at the Japanese consulate constituted forfeiture of his U.S. citizenship—thus, he was legally classified as an "enemy alien." In his judgment, Fee wrote that Yasui worked as a "propaganda agent" at the Japanese consulate and only resigned when he could serve Japan better as an agent in the U.S. military. For this reason, Judge Fee ruled that Yasui was guilty of violating the curfew order. Two days later, Fee sentenced Yasui to one year in prison and a fine of $5,000. An appeal was immediately filed.

On February 19, 1943, Yasui stood with his fellow resistors Fred Korematsu and Gordon Hirabayashi at the court of appeals (see KOREMATSU V. U.S. and HIRABAYASHI V. U.S.). Earl Bernard, attorney for Yasui, argued from a very advantageous position: on one hand, he had Judge Fee's ruling that said that the curfew law as applied to citizens was unconstitutional. On the other hand, he had the government's agreement that Yasui had not renounced his citizenship by working at the Japanese consulate. Working against him, however, was the "military necessity" argument being pursued by the government lawyers. After everyone had their chance to present their case in the three appeals, both sides felt certain that the judges were sympathetic to the government's brief and prepared for the anticipated appeals to the Supreme Court.

In the meantime, Justice Department lawyers, confident of victory, became eager to rush the three cases to the Supreme Court. Motivating them was the fear that the Mitsuye Endo case (see ENDO, EX PARTE) could reach the Supreme Court at the same time. The strength of the Endo case, they feared, had the possibility of hampering almost sure victory in the other three cases. To speed up the process, the Justice Department lawyers asked the court of appeals to use a procedure called "certification," a somewhat obscure procedure whereby the Supreme Court would answer constitutional questions raised by the appellate. In Yasui's case, the Supreme Court was asked to rule on his citizenship status.

On June 21, 1943, the Supreme Court issued its opinion on Yasui's case. In referring to Hirabayashi's curfew conviction, which the Court upheld that same day, the justices reversed Judge Fee's ruling that the curfew order was unconstitutional in its application to citizens and also found that Fee had wrongly decided that Yasui forfeited his citizenship by working at the Japanese consulate. The case was returned to the trial court for resentencing with a strong hint that a one-year penalty was too harsh.

Yasui ended up serving nine months in prison. He became a prominent attorney and a leader of the Japanese American community in Denver, Colorado, after the war. In the 1980s, his case was reopened and his conviction was eventually vacated (see CORAM NOBIS CASES). For further reading, see Peter Irons. *Justice at War: The Story of the Japanese American Internment Cases.* New York: Oxford University Press, 1983. For a transcript of the case and an account of the reopening of the case in the 1980s, see Peter Irons, ed. *Justice Delayed: The Record of the Japanese American Internment Cases.* Middletown, Conn.: Wesleyan University Press, 1989. See Robert S. Yasui. *The Yasui Family of Hood River, Oregon.* Hood River, Or.: Holly Yasui, 1987 for biographical information on Min Yasui and the Yasui family.

GLEN KITAYAMA

Yatabe, Thomas T. (1897–?) Known as the "Grand Old Man of the JACL." Thomas Yatabe was one of the first Japanese Americans born on the mainland United States and figured prominently in the early activities of the NISEI. As a youngster, he was one of 93 Japanese American children ordered to attend a racially segregated school in the controversial SAN FRANCISCO SCHOOL BOARD SEGREGATION ORDER OF 1906. In 1918, Yatabe was one of the cofounders of the American Loyalty League, an organization formed to advance the interests of *nisei* in San Francisco. Though this organization proved to be short-lived, it is recognized as the basis for the

JAPANESE AMERICAN CITIZENS LEAGUE (JACL). In addition, Yatabe was the first *nisei* from California to be granted a license to practice dentistry in the state. When he set up his professional practice in Fresno in 1923, he also established a new branch of the American Loyalty League there. The Fresno American Loyalty League was one of the groups that combined to form the national JACL at its founding convention in 1930. In 1934, Yatabe became the JACL's first elected national president. During World War II, Yatabe was incarcerated at JEROME, where he continued to preach his belief that *nisei* must be loyal and faithful to the U.S. government. After resettling (see RESETTLEMENT) in 1943, Yatabe founded the Chicago chapter of the JACL.

For further reading, see Bill Hosokawa. *Nisei: The Quiet Americans.* New York: William Morrow and Company, Inc., 1969.

Yellow Brotherhood Formed in 1969 in Los Angeles, Yellow Brotherhood (YB) was a pioneering self-help group dedicated to addressing the growing drug abuse problem among Asian youth. From a core of seven people—all of them from a gang called the Ministers—YB came to include many other Asian gangs throughout the city. It received no government funding, but was able to establish tutorials, counseling and educational programs through community donations, car washes and other means. YB's teaching philosophy was radical in outlook. Borrowing from Malcolm X, it taught Asian youth that the white establishment loved it when they debilitated themselves through drugs and gang activity because those activities kept them from realizing their full potential. Eventually, YB was forced to disband in around 1975 as many of the members grew older and pursued careers.

For further reading, see Gary Asamura. "The Unsung Heroes of the Yellow Brotherhood." *Amerasia Journal* 15.1 (1990): 156–58 and Sherri Miyashiro. "Yellow Brotherhood." In *Gidra Twentieth Anniversary Edition* (1990): 122–23.

GLEN KITAYAMA

yellow peril Term prevalent among ANTI-JAPANESE MOVEMENT agitators in the early 1900s to describe the unique "threat" of Japanese immigration as a precursor to a Japanese invasion. The "yellow peril" idea was crucial in broadening the base of the anti-Japanese movement from its San Francisco labor origins to include westerners of all classes and draw support from around the country by the 1920s.

In the early stages of the anti-Japanese movement, Japanese immigrants were targeted mostly by the laboring classes as an economic threat. Japanese laborers were accused of lowering the standard of living of white workers, of being dirty and unhealthy, and of being "unassimilable." This type of rhetoric was aimed at the

Chinese before them and at immigrants from southern, central and eastern Europe arriving at about the same time on the East Coast. However, as more and more ISSEI shed their migrant labor orientation and began to regard America as their permanent home, the rhetoric changed. By the 1910s and '20s, the typical *issei* had moved up from being a laborer to being a small farmer or sharecropper or a small business operator. The *issei* no longer directly competed with other laborers, and the old arguments against them no longer held. The rhetoric against the *issei* now cited their supposed taking of the best farmland, thereby driving out white farmers, and the supposed high birthrate of the *issei* women who arrived after the GENTLEMEN'S AGREEMENT. These charges, in combination with Japan's growing military and economic strength as manifested in its stunning victory in the Russo-Japanese War of 1904–05, led to a fear that the *issei* were the first wave of a coming Japanese invasion of California. This fear of the "yellow peril", fueled as it was by capitalist economic interests, Japan's growing strength and pure racism, was a unique feature of the anti-Japanese movement. No such fear of invasion accompanied agitation against any other immigrant group.

Among the many groups and individuals who propagated the "yellow peril" myth were William Randolph Hearst's newspapers, which concocted "war scares" in 1907 and 1912–13 that had many Californians believing that war with Japan was imminent. Hearst also continued his attack on the Japanese through World War I—this despite the fact that Japan fought on the same side as the United States. There was Homer Lea's novel *The Valor of Ignorance,* published in 1909, which detailed a Japanese attack on the West Coast, aided and abetted by Japanese immigrants. There were the 1920–21 novels *Pride of Palomar* by Peter B. Kyne and *Seed of the Sun* by Wallace Irwin in which ruthless *issei* landowners under orders from Japan try to take over California land and white women until thwarted by the native Californian derring-do. There were even movies like *Patria,* produced in 1916, which depicted a Japanese attack (with the help of Mexico) on California land and women. The racist fears of miscegenation and economic dominance spurred by "yellow peril" rhetoric played a key role in the passage of ALIEN LAND LAWS that prevented *issei* from purchasing land and in the passage of the IMMIGRATION ACT OF 1924, which ended all Japanese immigration. Lingering "yellow peril" sentiment no doubt played a major role in the decision to remove and incarcerate all West Coast Japanese Americans during World War II as well. The term has been used in recent years to refer to such Japan-bashing works as the 1992 bestselling novel *Rising Sun* by Michael Crichton.

For further reading, see Roger Daniels. *The Politics of Prejudice: The Anti-Japanese Movement in California and the Struggle for Japanese Exclusion*. 2nd edition. Berkeley: University of California Press, 1977. Richard Austin Thompson. *The Yellow Peril, 1890–1924*. New York: Arno Press, 1979, is a reprinting of a 1957 doctoral dissertation that analyzes the "yellow peril" literature. Two of the "yellow peril" works cited above have been recently reissued: Wallace Irwin. *Seed of the Sun*. New York: Arno Press, 1978 and Peter B. Kyne. *The Pride of Palomar*. New York: Arno Press, 1978.

yobiyose   Japanese American term for pre-1924 Japanese immigrants who came to the U.S. as children to join their parents, older siblings or other relatives. Though they are ISSEI, *yobiyose* often have much in common with NISEI, representing a sub-generation between the *issei* and *nisei*. The *yobiyose* are the Japanese American analog to the "1.5 generation" Korean Americans of today.

Yoneda, Karl Goso (1906–   )   Labor organizer, journalist, historian, activist. Karl Yoneda has been a prominent figure in the Japanese American community as a labor organizer and journalist in the 1930s; a leader in MANZANAR and a volunteer for the MILITARY INTELLIGENCE SERVICE during World War II; and a historian, teacher and social activist in the 1960s and '70s. A KIBEI born in Southern California, Yoneda went to Japan with his family at the age of 11. Compelled by books as a young man he developed an interest in Marxism and left home at the age of 16 bound for China in search of a Russian writer whose works he admired. In order to avoid being drafted into the Japanese army, he returned to the United States and quickly became involved in the labor movement in California. He joined the Communist Party there, and spent the 1930s as editor of the Communist newspaper *Rodo Shimbun* and as an organizer of Japanese labor in California and Alaska. He married fellow Communist Elaine Black in 1933, a union which would last for over 55 years.

With the coming of World War II, Yoneda suffered a double blow when the American Communist Party booted out all members of Japanese ancestry and the United States government forcibly evicted all Japanese Americans from their West Coast homes. Ending up in Manzanar accompanied by his wife and young son (as a Caucasian, authorities had tried to prevent her from coming, but she was determined to join her son and husband who were required to go), Yoneda emerged as one of the leaders of the faction of the camp population that advocated working with the administration. He and others—many of them members of the JAPANESE AMERICAN CITIZENS LEAGUE—formed the Manzanar Citizens Federation to press for improved living conditions and to help in the war effort. Though disagreeing with the need for the incarceration of Japanese Americans, Yoneda believed that Japanese Americans should first work to defeat fascism in Japan and Germany and then to address the wrongs inflicted on them by the U.S. Government. As tensions flared in Manzanar between the pro- and anti-cooperation factions leading to the MANZANAR IN-CIDENT, Yoneda and the others perceived as being pro-administration began to fear for their lives and were removed from the camp for their own protection. He eventually volunteered to serve in an intelligence capacity for the United States Army in Asia and played a valuable role as a propagandist and translator in the Pacific.

Yoneda spent the postwar years as a chicken farmer and longshoreman, an earnest member of the Communist Party and the INTERNATIONAL LONGSHOREMEN'S AND WAREHOUSEMEN'S UNION, and as an activist. He was active in the campaign to repeal TITLE II of the Internal Security Act and in the REDRESS MOVEMENT. He also researched and wrote a well-received book in Japanese on Japanese American labor and has served as a teacher and advocate for labor issues in the Asian American studies world. His autobiography, *Ganbatte: Sixty-Year Struggle of a Kibei Worker,* was published in 1983.

For further reading, see Karl G. Yoneda. *Ganbatte: Sixty-Year Struggle of a Kibei Worker.* Los Angeles: Asian American Studies Center, University of California, Los Angeles, 1983.

yonsei Fourth-generation Japanese Americans. The *yonsei* are the children of the SANSEI, the grandchildren of the NISEI and the great-grandchildren of the ISSEI. As with the terms for the other generations, the word *yonsei* comes from the Japanese character for the generation number, in this case, "four." For the most part, the *yonsei* are still children or young adults and do not yet have a definable group identity. It seems probable that usage of generational terms such as *yonsei* will decline in the years to come in favor of more generic terms such as JAPANESE AMERICANS or NIKKEI since intergenerational mixing becomes more and more prevalent the further removed one gets from the immigrant generation. It is very likely that most *yonsei* have at least one parent who is not a *sansei.* (That parent might be *nisei, yonsei* or non-Japanese American, among other possibilities.)

Yoshiike, Hiroshi Hiroshi Yoshiike is recognized as the pioneer of the floriculture industry in Northern California. He was born in Nagano PREFECTURE in 1858 and came to the U.S. in 1882, initially working as a SCHOOLBOY. In 1885, he returned to Japan and came back to Oakland with a wife and a few chrysanthemum

plants that were different from locally known varieties. He began to grow these commercially in 1886 on a rented lot near downtown Oakland. The success of this part-time venture led to his opening a flower stand in the center of town. By 1890, he had moved to an acre parcel nearby and built five glass houses on it. Yoshiike retired following the 1906 earthquake and spent the remainder of his life in Japan.

For further reading, see Noritaka Yagasaki. "Ethnic Cooperativism and Immigrant Agriculture: A Study of Japanese Floriculture and Truck Farming in California." Diss., University of California, Berkeley, 1982.

Yoshimura, Wendy (1943–) Artist Wendy Yoshimura will best be remembered as the person arrested with the notorious Patty Hearst in 1975. She was born in MANZANAR and moved to Hiroshima with her NISEI parents after the Second World War. They moved back to California in 1956, settling in Fresno. Yoshimura attended Roosevelt High School there and went on to Fresno City College, Merritt College in Oakland and the California College of Arts and Crafts in Oakland. In 1972, police found an "arsenal of illegal weapons and explosives" in a Berkeley garage rented by her and arrested her boyfriend William Brandt and two others. Brandt pled guilty to illegal weapons charges and Yoshimura disappeared for three and a half years. She was arrested with Patricia Hearst in September 1975 in San Francisco; her trial for illegal possession of weapons began on October 18, 1976. After 44 hours of jury deliberation, she was convicted on January 20, 1977. Eleven of the 12 jurors were white; the lone black female juror was reportedly harassed by the others to render a unanimous verdict. Yoshimura was sentenced to one to 15 years in state prison. In the meantime, Hearst received five years' probation after pleading no contest to assault and robbery charges. The apparent discrepancy in the sentencing led to protests by the Asian American community. Yoshimura served her time at Frontera Prison in 1979–80 and was paroled after a year. In 1981, she received an $8,000 grant from the California Arts Council to work for the Japantown Center Art and Media Workshop.

[Entry compiled from the following newspaper articles: "Yoshimura Jurors Rehear Testimony." *Los Angeles Times* 18 Jan. 1977; Okamura, Ray. "Bias Charged Against Yoshimura Decision." *Rafu Shimpo* 26 Jan. 1977: 1; "Miss Yoshimura Gets 1–15 Years in Weapons Case." *Los Angeles Times* 18 Mar. 1977: I-3; "Hearst Sentence Hit by Yoshimura Attorney." *Rafu Shimpo* 10 May 1977: 1; Hager, Philip. "Ex-Fugitive Wendy Yoshimura Now Lost in Her Art." *Los Angeles Times* 1 June 1981: II-1.]

ONE HUNDRED TITLES: A BASIC LIBRARY ON JAPANESE AMERICANS

All things considered, there is an enormous amount of literature on the Japanese American experience. Unfortunately, much of it is dated or problematic in some way. Often, the most widely available works are the ones that are most problematic, while some of the best work remains relatively inaccessible, whether buried in obscure academic journals or consisting of unpublished master's theses or doctoral dissertations. For one who is trying to find good introductory works on Japanese Americans or who is trying to build a library of such titles, difficulties abound.

The following list is one attempt to sort through the enormous amount of literature on Japanese Americans to arrive at a core bibliography. In compiling this list, I have tried to identify the best work on Japanese Americans, whether academic or popular, historical or social scientific, fiction or nonfiction, obscure or well-known. I have tried to list works that cover the breadth of the Japanese American experience, including topics on which there has been relatively little research. Please note that there are many other worthwhile works which have not been included in this list for reasons of space. I hope that this list will serve to generate dialogue on the state of Japanese American studies and help to indicate the areas where research is lacking.

1. Ano, Masaharu. "Loyal Linguists: Nisei of World War II Learned Japanese in Minnesota." *Minnesota History* 45 (1977): 273–87. Focuses on NISEI in the MILITARY INTELLIGENCE SERVICE LANGUAGE SCHOOL at Camp Savage and Fort Snelling, Minnesota, during World War II.

2. Asian Women United of California. *Making Waves: An Anthology of Writings By and About Asian American Women*. Boston: Beacon Press, 1989. An anthology that includes both historical/social science and creative pieces; includes prose by Valerie Matsumoto, Kesaya E. Noda, R. A. Sasaki and WAKAKO YAMAUCHI; poetry by JANICE MIRIKITANI

and Sakae S. Roberson; and historical studies by Valerie Matsumoto and Gail M. Nomura dealing specifically with Japanese American women.

3. Befu, Harumi. "Contrastive Acculturation of California Japanese: Comparative Approach to the Study of Immigrants." *Human Organization* 24 (Fall 1965): 209–16. Looks at two California Japanese American communities and compares their strikingly different acculturation patterns.

4. Chan, Sucheng. *Asian Americans: An Interpretive History*. Boston: Twayne Publishers, 1991. Twayne's Immigrant Heritage of America Series. Thomas J. Archdeacon, general ed. One of two major recent histories of Asian Americans.

5. Chuman, Frank F. *The Bamboo People: The Law and Japanese-Americans*. Del Mar, Calif.: Publisher's Inc., 1976. A history of laws pertaining to Japanese Americans.

6. Commission on Wartime Relocation and Internment of Civilians. *Personal Justice Denied: Report of the Commission on Wartime Relocation and Internment of Civilians*. Washington, D.C.: Government Printing Office, 1982. Report of the COMMISSION ON WARTIME RELOCATION AND INTERNMENT OF CIVILIANS is a concise overview of the Japanese American experience during World War II.

7. Consulate-General of Japan. *Documental History of Law Cases Affecting Japanese in the United States, 1916–1924. 2 Vols.* San Francisco: Consulate-General of Japan, 1925. New York: Arno Press, 1978. The Asian Experience in North America: Chinese and Japanese. Roger Daniels, advisory ed. Two-volume compilation of legal cases involving Japanese Americans up to 1924. Volume one contains naturalization cases while volume two contains ALIEN LAND LAW cases.

8. Daniels, Roger. *The Politics of Prejudice: The Anti-Japanese Movement in California and the Struggle*

for Japanese Exclusion. 1962. 2nd edition. Berkeley: University of California Press, 1977. Definitive history of the ANTI-JAPANESE MOVEMENT in California between 1905 and 1924.

9. ———. *Asian America: Chinese and Japanese in the United States since 1850*. Seattle: University of Washington Press, 1988. General history of Chinese and Japanese Americans. Incorporates much of Daniels's earlier work on Japanese Americans.

10. ———, Sandra C. Taylor, and Harry H. L. Kitano., eds. *Japanese Americans: From Relocation to Redress*. Salt Lake City: University of Utah Press, 1986. Rev. ed. Seattle: University of Washington Press, 1991. Anthology of papers coming out of the International Conference on Relocation and Redress held in Salt Lake City in 1983 covering many different aspects of the Japanese American World War II experience.

11. Dower, John W. *War without Mercy: Race and Power in the Pacific War*. New York: Pantheon Books, 1986. Examines racial stereotyping on both the American and Japanese sides during World War II and how these stereotypes recur in different forms during times of peace.

12. Drinnon, Richard. *Keeper of Concentration Camps: Dillon S. Myer and American Racism*. Berkeley: University of California Press, 1987. Revisionist biography of WAR RELOCATION AUTHORITY (and later Bureau of Indian Affairs) director DILLON S. MYER.

13. Duus, Masayo. *Unlikely Liberators: The Men of the 100th and the 442nd*. Honolulu: University of Hawaii Press, 1987. A history of 100TH INFANTRY BATTALION and the 442ND REGIMENTAL COMBAT TEAM, the famed NISEI World War II U.S. Army units, derived mainly from interviews with *nisei* veterans.

14. Eaton, Allen Hendershott. *Beauty Behind Barbed Wire: The Arts of the Japanese in Our War Relocation Camps*. New York: Harper, 1952. Includes 92 photographs of art objects created in the 10 World War II CONCENTRATION CAMPS.

15. Endo, Russell. "Japanese of Colorado: A Sociohistorical Portrait." *Journal of Social and Behavioral Sciences* 31 (Fall 1985): 100–10. Provides an historical and contemporary overview of Japanese Americans in Colorado.

16. Ethnic Studies Oral History Project/United Okinawan Association of Hawaii. *Uchinanchu: A History of Okinawans in Hawaii*. Honolulu: Ethnic Studies Program, University of Hawaii at Manoa, 1981. Major anthology focusing on the Okinawan

community in Hawaii. Includes many historical pieces as well as a section of oral history transcripts of Okinawan ISSEI from Hawaii.

17. Fugita, Stephen S., and David J. O'Brien. *Japanese American Ethnicity: The Persistence of Community*. Seattle: University of Washington Press, 1991. Examines the persistence of Japanese American identity and community in the face of structural assimilation.

18. Gardiner, C. Harvey. *Pawns in a Triangle of Hate: The Peruvian Japanese and the United States*. Seattle: University of Washington Press, 1981. Definitive study of the World War II odyssey of JAPANESE PERUVIANS.

19. Girdner, Audrie, and Anne Loftis. *The Great Betrayal: The Evacuation of the Japanese-Americans during World War II*. Toronto: Macmillan, 1969. General journalistic overview of the Japanese American World War II experience.

20. Glenn, Evelyn Nakano. *Issei, Nisei, War Bride: Three Generations of Japanese American Women in Domestic Service*. Philadelphia: Temple University Press, 1986. Study of Japanese American women in domestic service, based largely on oral histories of former workers.

21. Grodzins, Morton. *Americans Betrayed: Politics and the Japanese Evacuation*. Chicago: University of Chicago Press, 1949. Examines the role of West Coast politicians and economic interest groups in the forced removal of all Japanese Americans during World War II. Research for this work was conducted by Grodzins as a staff member of the JAPANESE AMERICAN EVACUATION AND RESETTLEMENT STUDY project, but it was published separately.

22. Hane, Mikiso. *Peasants, Rebels and Outcastes: The Underside of Modern Japan*. New York: Pantheon Books, 1982. Looks at the effect of Japan's modernization on the peasantry—the group from which the vast majority of ISSEI came.

23. Hata, Donald Teruo. *'Undesirables': Early Immigrants and the Anti-Japanese Movement in San Francisco, 1892–1893: Prelude to Exclusion*. New York: Arno Press, 1978. The Asian Experience in North America: Chinese and Japanese. Roger Daniels, advisory ed. About the earliest Japanese migrants to the U.S. and the beginning of anti-Japanese agitation.

24. Hayashi, Brian Masaru. " 'For the Sake of Our Japanese Brethren': Assimilation, Nationalism, and Protestantism among the Japanese of Los Angeles, 1895–1942." Diss., University of California, Los Angeles, 1990. Examines the diversity

of the Japanese American Protestant community in pre–World War II Los Angeles by focusing on three very different Japanese American churches.

25. Hellig, David J. "Afro-American Reactions to the Japanese and the Anti-Japanese Movement, 1906–1924." *Phylon* 38.1 (Mar. 1977): 93–104. Analyzes the attitude towards Japanese Americans reflected in the African American press during the ANTI-JAPANESE MOVEMENT period.

26. Higgs, Robert. "Landless by Law—Japanese Immigrants in California Agriculture to 1941." *Journal of Economic History* 38.1 (Mar. 1978): 205–26. Economic study of the ISSEI in agriculture concludes that they had achieved middle class status by the eve of World War II.

27. Hirabayashi, Lane Ryo, and George Tanaka. "The Issei Community in Moneta and the Gardena Valley, 1900–1920." *Southern California Quarterly* 70.2 (Summer 1988): 127–58. Examines the strawberry farming origins of what would later become a major Japanese American residential community.

28. Hohri, William. *Repairing America: An Account of the Movement for Japanese American Redress.* Pullman: Washington State University Press, 1988. Autobiographical account by the leader of the NATIONAL COUNCIL FOR JAPANESE AMERICAN REDRESS, one of three major REDRESS MOVEMENT organizations.

29. Ichihashi, Yamato. *Japanese in the United States: A Critical Study of the Problems of the Japanese Immigrants and their Children.* Stanford: Stanford University Press, 1932. New York: Arno Press, 1969. Hugely influential study of the Japanese American community, written in part as a response defending the ISSEI from the wild claims of ANTI-JAPANESE MOVEMENT proponents.

30. Ichioka, Yuji. "A Study in Dualism: James Yoshinori Sakamoto and the Japanese American Courier, 1928–1942." *Amerasia Journal* 13.2 (1986–87): 49–81. Analyzes the life and writings of JAMES YOSHINORI SAKAMOTO, founder of the first exclusively English language Japanese American newspaper.

31. ———. *The Issei: The World of the First Generation Japanese Immigrants, 1885–1924.* New York: The Free Press, 1988. Historical study of the mainland ISSEI experience, focusing on the actions and thoughts of the *issei* themselves. Incorporates the numerous published articles on the *issei* by Ichioka that have appeared earlier.

32. ———, ed. "Views from Within: The Japanese American Evacuation and Resettlement Study." Los Angeles: UCLA Asian American Studies Center, 1989. Papers from a conference reassessing the JERS project held in 1987. Includes articles by Yuji Ichioka, S. FRANK MIYAMOTO, Lane Ryo Hirabayashi and James Hirabayashi, Peter T. Suzuki, Robert F. Spencer, CHARLES KIKUCHI, Dana Y. Takagi and James M. Sakoda.

33. ———. "Japanese Immigrant Nationalism: The Issei and the Sino-Japanese War, 1937–1941." *California History* 69.3 (Fall 1990): 260–75, 310–11. Examines ISSEI support of and identification with Japan in the period just prior to World War II.

34. Inada, Lawson F. *Before the War: Poems as They Happened.* New York: Morrow, 1971. Anthology of poems by influential SANSEI poet, writer and teacher.

35. Irons, Peter. *Justice at War: The Story of the Japanese American Internment Cases.* New York: Oxford University Press, 1983. An examination of the U.S. government response to the Hirabayashi, Korematsu and Yasui cases that exposes the government's cover-up of data that would have disproved its claims of "MILITARY NECESSITY."

36. ———, ed. *Justice Delayed: The Record of the Japanese American Internment Cases.* Middletown, Conn.: Wesleyan University Press, 1989. Compilation of the legal records of the Endo, Hirabayashi, Korematsu and Yasui cases, including the *coram nobis* efforts of the 1980s; includes an introduction that provides an overview of the CORAM NOBIS CASES.

37. Ito, Hiroshi [psued]. "Japan's Outcastes in the United States." In DeVos, George, and Hiroshi Wagatsuma, ed. *Japan's Invisible Race: Caste in Culture and Personality.* Berkeley: University of California Press, 1966. 200–21. 1950s-era study of the BURAKUMIN (outcast) population among Japanese Americans.

38. Ito, Kazuo. *Issei: A History of Japanese Immigrants in North America.* Shinichiro Nakamura, Jean S. Gerard, trans. Seattle: Executive Committee for the Publication of *Issei: A History of Japanese Immigrants in North America,* 1973. One thousand plus page volume based on oral history data obtained from ISSEI in the Pacific Northwest in the 1960s. Originally published in Japanese.

39. Iwata, Masakazu. *Planted in Good Soil: A History of the Issei in the United States Agriculture.* 2 vols. New York: P. Lang, 1990. American University Studies, Series 9, History, Vol. 57. Epic, region-by-region study of Japanese Americans in agriculture.

40. James, Thomas. *Exile Within: The Schooling of Japanese Americans, 1942–1945.* Cambridge: Harvard University Press, 1987. Study of various aspects of education in the CONCENTRATION CAMPS, including pre-WAR RELOCATION AUTHORITY educational programs largely implemented by Japanese Americans themselves, the philosophical underpinnings of the WRA educational philosophy, the RESETTLEMENT of NISEI college students, and schooling in TULE LAKE "SEGREGATION CENTER."

41. Kanazawa, Tooru J. *Sushi and Sourdough: A Novel.* Seattle: University of Washington Press, 1989. Novel about ISSEI prospectors in Alaska.

42. Kashima, Tetsuden. *Buddhism in America: The Social Organization of an Ethnic Religious Institution.* Westport, Conn.: Greenwood Press, 1977. Study of the Japanese American Buddhist church.

43. Kikumura, Akemi. *Through Harsh Winters: The Life of a Japanese Immigrant Woman.* Novato, Calif.: Chandler and Sharp Publishers, 1981. A life history of an ISSEI woman in rural central California.

44. Kimura, Yukiko. *Issei: Japanese Immigrants in Hawaii.* Honolulu: University of Hawaii Press, 1988. Social history of the ISSEI in Hawaii that incorporates many previous works on the subject by the author.

45. Kitano, Harry H. L. *Japanese Americans: The Evolution of a Subculture.* 1969. 2nd edition. Englewood Cliffs, N.J.: Prentice-Hall, Inc., 1976. Influential sociological and historical study of the Japanese American community.

46. ———, and Akemi Kikumura. "The Japanese American Family." In Mindel, Charles H., and Robert W. Habenstein, ed. *Ethnic Families in America: Patterns and Variations.* New York: Elsevier Scientific Publishing Co., Inc., 1976. 41–60. Also published in *Asian-Americans: Social and Psychological Perspectives, Vol. II.* Russell Endo, Stanley Sue and Nathaniel N. Wagner, eds. Palo Alto, Calif.: Science and Behavior Books, Inc., 1980. 3–16. An examination of Japanese American family dynamics.

47. Kotani, Roland. *The Japanese in Hawaii: A Century of Struggle.* Honolulu: Hochi, Ltd., 1985. Popular history of Japanese Americans in Hawaii commemorating the 100th anniversary of large-scale Japanese migration to Hawaii.

48. Lukes, Timothy J., and Gary Y. Okihiro. *Japanese Legacy: Farming and Community Life in California's Santa Clara Valley.* Cupertino, Calif.: California History Center, 1985. Local History Studies 31. Community history of Japanese Americans in the Santa Clara Valley in California.

49. Masumoto, David Mas. *Country Voices: The Oral History of a Japanese American Family Farm Community.* Del Rey, Calif.: Inaka Countryside Publications, 1987. The community is Del Rey, California; the work mixes oral history, fiction and memoir to provide a penetrating look at Japanese American farm life.

50. Matsumoto, Valerie. *Farming the Home Place: A Japanese American Community in California, 1919–1982.* Ithaca, N.Y.: Cornell University Press, forthcoming, 1993. Study of the Japanese American community in CORTEZ, a farming colony in central California.

51. Mirikitani, Janice, et al., eds. *Ayumi: A Japanese American Anthology.* San Francisco: Japanese American Anthology Committee, 1980. Anthology of literature by Japanese Americans including sections on ISSEI, NISEI, SANSEI/YONSEI and art. The pieces in the *issei* section are presented in both Japanese and English.

52. Miyamoto, Kazuo. *Hawaii: End of the Rainbow.* Tokyo: Charles E. Tuttle, 1964. Epic novel focusing on the fortunes of one Japanese American family in Hawaii; many real ISSEI and NISEI appear in these pages.

53. Miyamoto, S. Frank. *Social Solidarity among the Japanese in Seattle.* University of Washington Publications in the Social Sciences 11.2 (Dec. 1939): 57–130. Seattle: Asian American Studies Program, University of Washington, 1981. Occasional Monograph Series No. 2. Seattle: University of Washington Press, 1984. Classic study of the Japanese American community in Seattle on the eve of World War II.

54. Modell, John. *The Economics and Politics of Racial Accommodation: The Japanese of Los Angeles 1900–1942.* Chicago: University of Illinois Press, 1977. Economic study of the pre–World War II Japanese American community in the Los Angeles area.

55. Mori, Toshio. *Yokohama, California.* Introd. William Saroyan. Caldwell, Idaho: Caxton Printers, Ltd., 1949. Introd. Lawson Fusao Inada. Seattle: University of Washington Press, 1985. Collection of short stories set in a fictional Northern California Japanese American community.

56. Moriyama, Alan T. *Imingaisha: Japanese Emigration Companies and Hawaii, 1894–1908.* Honolulu: University of Hawaii Press, 1985. A study of Japanese American EMIGRATION COMPANIES and their role in fostering Japanese emigration to Hawaii.

57. Murayama, Milton. *All I Asking for Is My Body.* 1959. Afterword by Franklin Odo. Honolulu:

University of Hawaii Press, 1988. Novel set in the plantation camps of pre–World War II Hawaii.

58. Nakano, Mei. *Japanese American Women: Three Generations, 1890–1990*. Berkeley and Sebastopol, Calif.: National Japanese American Historical Society and Mina Press, 1990. Study of ISSEI, NISEI and SANSEI women on the mainland; accompanied a museum exhibit by the National Japanese American Historical Society.

59. Nelson, Douglas W. *Heart Mountain: The History of an American Concentration Camp*. Madison, Wis.: The State Historical Society of Wisconsin, 1976. Definitive study of one World War II American CONCENTRATION CAMP.

60. Nomura, Gail M. "The Debate Over the Role of Nisei in Prewar Hawaii: The New Americans Conference, 1927–1941." *Journal of Ethnic Studies* 15.1 (Spring 1987): 95–115. Study of the NEW AMERICANS CONFERENCES, annual forums in which the future role of the NISEI in Hawaii was debated.

61. ———. "*Tsugiki*, A Grafting: A History of a Japanese Pioneer Woman in Washington State." *Women's Studies* 14.1 (1987): 15–37. Reprinted in Blair, Karen J., ed. *Women in Pacific Northwest History: An Anthology*. Seattle: University of Washington Press, 1987. 207–29. On TEIKO TOMITA, TANKA poet and pioneering ISSEI woman.

62. ———. "Washington's Asian/Pacific American Communities." In White, Sid, and S. E. Solberg, eds. *Peoples of Washington: Perspectives on Cultural Diversity*. Pullman: Washington State University Press, 1989. 113–55. General history of Asian/Pacific Americans in Washington (state).

63. Odo, Franklin S., and Kazuko Sinoto. *A Pictorial History of the Japanese in Hawaii, 1885–1924*. Honolulu: Bishop Museum Press, 1985. Handsome collection of photographs, tables and text documenting the ISSEI experience in Hawaii.

64. Okada, John. *No-No Boy*. Rutland, Vt.: Charles E. Tuttle, 1957. San Francisco: Combined Asian American Resources Project, Inc., 1976. Seattle: University of Washington Press, 1979. Novel focusing on a "NO-NO BOY" protagonist and his identity dilemmas in post–World War II Seattle.

65. Okamura, Raymond Y. "The American Concentration Camps: A Cover-Up through Euphemistic Terminology." *Journal of Ethnic Studies* 10.3 (Fall 1982): 95–108. Analyzes the official terminology that is still often used to describe the Japanese American World War II internment experience.

66. Okihiro, Gary Y. "Japanese Resistance in America's Concentration Camps: A Re-evaluation." *Amerasia Journal* 2.1 (1973): 20–34. Reinterprets unrest in America's World War II CONCENTRATION CAMPS from a resistance perspective.

67. ———. *Cane Fires: The Anti-Japanese Movement in Hawaii, 1865–1945*. Philadelphia: Temple University Press, 1991. History of Japanese Americans in Hawaii that makes the case that there was an organized ANTI-JAPANESE MOVEMENT in Hawaii similar to that on the mainland.

68. Okinawa Club of America, comp. *History of the Okinawans in North America*. Ben Kobashigawa, trans. Los Angeles: UCLA Asian American Studies Center and The Okinawa Club of America, 1988. Compilation of various works documenting the history of OKINAWANS in the mainland United States.

69. Okubo, Mine. *Citizen 13660*. New York: Columbia University Press, 1946. New York: Arno Press, 1948. Seattle: University of Washington Press, 1983. Book of line drawings and text based on the author's experiences at Tanforan "ASSEMBLY CENTER" and TOPAZ.

70. Ota, Shelley Ayame Nishimura. *Upon Their Shoulders*. New York: Exposition Press, 1951. Epic novel centering on a Japanese American family in Hawaii.

71. Papanikolas, Helen Z., and Alice Kasai. "Japanese Life in Utah." In Papanikolas, Helen Z., ed. *The Peoples of Utah*. Salt Lake City: Utah State Historical Society, 1976. 333–62. General history of the Japanese American community in Utah.

72. Saiki, Patsy Sumie. *Ganbarre! An Example of Japanese Spirit*. Honolulu: Kisaku, Inc., 1982. About the small number of Japanese Americans in Hawaii who were forcibly removed and interned during World War II.

73. Sato, Susie. "Before Pearl Harbor: Early Japanese Settlers in Arizona." *Journal of Arizona History* 14.4 (Winter 1973): 317–34. Study of the pre–World War II community in Arizona.

74. Sawada, Mitziko. "Dreams of Change: The Japanese Immigrant to New York City, 1891–1924." Diss., New York University, 1985. Contrasts the pre-immigration conceptions of ISSEI in New York with the post-immigration reality.

75. ———. "After the Camps: Seabrook Farms, New Jersey, and the Resettlement of Japanese Americans, 1944–47." *Amerasia Journal* 13.2 (1986–87): 117–36. Study of SEABROOK FARMS, New Jersey, a community where many Japanese Americans who resettled from World War II CONCENTRATION CAMPS moved to; also discusses WAR RELOCATION AUTHORITY policy towards RESETTLEMENT.

76. Shibutani, Tamotsu. *The Derelicts of Company K: A Sociological Study of Demoralization*. Berkeley: University of California Press, 1978. Study of the effects of demoralization on an underachieving NISEI military unit during World War II.

77. Shinagawa, Larry Hajime, and Gin Yong Pang. "Marriage Patterns of Asian Americans in California, 1980." In Chan, Sucheng, ed. *Income and Status Differences between White and Minority Americans*. Lewiston, N.Y.: The Edwin Mellen Press, 1990. Mellen Studies in Sociology, Vol. 3. 225–82. Presents INTERRACIAL MARRIAGE statistics for Japanese Americans and other Asian Americans based on 1980 census data, utilizing a hypergamy framework.

78. Sone, Monica. *Nisei Daughter*. Boston: Little, Brown and Company, 1953. S. Frank Miyamoto, introd. Seattle: University of Washington Press, 1979. Autobiographical account of growing up NISEI that begins in Seattle, continues in MINIDOKA and ends with college.

79. Stephan, John. *Hawaii under the Rising Sun: Japan's Plans for Conquest after Pearl Harbor*. Honolulu: University of Hawaii Press, 1984. On Japan's plans for occupying Hawaii after a successful attack during World War II; several Hawaii ISSEI played roles in formulating the plans.

80. Suzuki, Bob H. "Education and Socialization of Asian Americans: A Revisionist Analysis of the 'Model Minority' Thesis." *Amerasia Journal* 4.2 (1977): 23–52. Reprinted in *Asian-Americans: Social and Psychological Perspectives, Vol. II*. Russell Endo, Stanley Sue, and Nathaniel N. Wagner, eds. Palo Alto, Calif.: Science and Behavior Books, Inc., 1980. 155–75. Detailed debunking of the basic tenets of the so-called "MODEL MINORITY" thesis as regards Asian Americans.

81. Suzuki, Peter T. "The University of California Japanese Evacuation and Resettlement Study: A Prolegomenon." *Dialectical Anthropology* 10 (1986): 189–213. Highly critical evaluation of the JAPANESE AMERICAN EVACUATION AND RESETTLEMENT STUDY.

82. Takahashi, Jerrold Haruo. "Changing Responses to Racial Subordination: An Exploratory Study of Japanese American Political Styles." Diss., University of California, Berkeley, 1980. Exploration of NISEI political thinking as that generation came of age in the 1930s.

83. Takaki, Ronald. *Pau Hana: Plantation Life and Labor in Hawaii, 1835–1920*. Honolulu: University of Hawaii Press, 1983. History of the multiracial sugar plantation labor work force in Hawaii of which Japanese Americans were a major part.

84. ———. *Strangers from a Different Shore: A History of Asian Americans*. Boston: Little, Brown and Company, 1989. One of two major recent histories of Asian Americans.

85. Tateishi, John. *And Justice For All: An Oral History of the Japanese American Detention Camps*. New York: Random House, 1984. Volume of edited oral history transcripts based on interviews with 30 former CONCENTRATION CAMP internees.

86. tenBroek, Jacobus, Edward N. Barnhart and Floyd Matson. *Prejudice, War, and the Constitution*. Berkeley: University of California Press, 1954. Studies the factors that brought about the mass removal and incarceration of West Coast Japanese Americans in World War II CONCENTRATION CAMPS; focuses on the role of the military and Washington bureaucrats while discounting that of West Coast officials and the press. The third published volume of the JAPANESE AMERICAN EVACUATION AND RESETTLEMENT STUDY.

87. Thomas, Dorothy S. *The Salvage*. Berkeley: University of California Press, 1952. Looks at the RESETTLEMENT of internees from out of the CONCENTRATION CAMPS in the East and Midwest; includes 15 life histories of such people. The second published volume of the JAPANESE AMERICAN EVACUATION AND RESETTLEMENT STUDY.

88. ———, and Richard Nishimoto. *The Spoilage*. Berkeley: University of California Press, 1946, 1969. Looks at the Japanese American community in the CONCENTRATION CAMPS, with special emphasis on segregation, the "disloyal" at TULE LAKE "SEGREGATION CENTER" and RENUNCIATION OF CITIZENSHIP. The first published volume of the JAPANESE AMERICAN EVACUATION AND RESETTLEMENT STUDY.

89. Tsuchida, Nobuya. "Japanese Gardeners in Southern California, 1900–1941." In Cheng, Lucie, and Edna Bonacich, eds. *Labor Immigration Under Capitalism: Asian Workers in the United States Before World War II*. Berkeley: University of California Press, 1984. 435–69. Examines the beginnings of Japanese gardeners' organizations in the Los Angeles area.

90. Tsurutani, Hisashi. *America Bound: The Japanese and Opening of the American West*. Betsey Scheiner, trans. Tokyo: Japan Times, Inc., 1989. Originally published in 1977 as *Amerika Seibu Kaitaku to Nihonjin*. On Japanese immigrants to the United States—primarily those who worked on the railroad and in mines—and their role in the development of the West.

91. Uchida, Yoshiko. *Picture Bride*. Flagstaff, Ariz.: Northland Press, 1987. Novel centering on an

ISSEI PICTURE BRIDE from her life in Japan to her incarceration in an American CONCENTRATION CAMP during World War II.

92. Walls, Thomas K. *The Japanese Texans*. San Antonio: Institute of Texan Cultures, 1987. Study of Japanese Americans in Texas; includes a chapter on the three Justice Department administered World War II INTERNMENT CAMPS in Texas.

93. Waugh, Isami Arifuku. "Hidden Crime and Deviance in the Japanese-American Community, 1920–1946." Diss., University of California, Berkeley, 1978. Study of crime among the ISSEI and NISEI in Los Angeles before and during World War II.

94. Weglyn, Michi. *Years of Infamy: The Untold Story of America's Concentration Camps*. New York: William Morrow & Co., 1976. Classic study of Japanese Americans and America's World War II CONCENTRATION CAMPS.

95. Yagasaki, Noritaka. "Ethnic Cooperativism and Immigrant Agriculture: A Study of Japanese Floriculture and Truck Farming in California." Diss., University of California, Berkeley, 1982. Sprawling study of pre–World War II floriculture and TRUCK FARMING in both San Francisco and Los Angeles; also includes a chapter on Japanese American immigrant banking.

96. Yamamoto [DeSoto], Hisaye. *Seventeen Syllables and Other Stories*. Latham, N.Y.: Kitchen Table Women of Color Press, 1988. Collection of short stories by a Southern California based NISEI writer.

97. Yanagisako, Sylvia Junko. *Transforming the Past: Tradition and Kinship among Japanese Americans*. Stanford: Stanford University Press, 1985. Study of Japanese American kinship, emphasizing the process of cultural change; focuses on marriage, filial relations and sibling relations.

98. Yasui, Barbara. "The Nikkei in Oregon, 1834–1940." *Oregon Historical Quarterly* 76.3 (Sept. 1975): 225–57. History of the pre–World War II Japanese American community in Oregon.

99. Yoneda, Karl G. *Ganbatte: Sixty-Year Struggle of a Kibei Worker*. Los Angeles: Asian American Studies Center, University of California, Los Angeles, 1983. Autobiography of a KIBEI labor organizer and Communist.

100. Yoshida, Ryo. "A Socio-Historical Study of Racial/Ethnic Identity in the Inculcated Religious Expression of Japanese Christianity in San Francisco, 1877–1924." Diss., Graduate Theological Union (Berkeley, Calif.), 1989. Examination of the Japanese American Christian church in San Francisco and the evolution of a uniquely Japanese American theology.

INDEX

Page numbers in **boldface** indicate main essay headings; page numbers with "c" indicate chronology entries; page numbers in *italic* indicate illustrations or tables. Only main essays and chronology entries are listed under general subjects (e.g., armed forces).

B